JEPPESEN.

A&P TECHNICIAN

POWERPLANT

TEXTBOOK

JEPPESEN
MAINTENANCE
Mastery Realized.

Support Materials

Look for these support materials to complement your A&P Technician Powerplant Textbook:

- **A&P Technician Powerplant Workbook**
- **A&P Technician Powerplant Test Guide**
- **Federal Aviation Regulations**
- **AC 43.13-1B/2A Acceptable Methods, Techniques and Practices/Aircraft Alterations**
- **Aircraft Technical Dictionary**
- **Standard Aviation Maintenance Handbook**

These items are among the wide variety of Jeppesen reference materials available through your authorized Jeppesen Dealer. If there is no Jeppesen Dealer in your area, you can contact us directly:

Jeppesen Sanderson
Sanderson Training Systems
55 Inverness Drive East
Englewood, CO 80112-5498

55 Inverness Drive East, Englewood, CO 80112-5498
ISBN 0-88487-207-6

JS312694-002

PREFACE

Congratulations on taking the first step toward learning to becoming a certified Powerplant Mechanic. The *A&P Technician Powerplant Textbook* contains the answers to many of the questions you may have as you begin your training program. It is based on the "study/review" concept of learning. This means detailed material is presented in an uncomplicated way, then important points are summarized through the use of bold type and illustrations. The textbook incorporates many design features that will help you get the most out of your study and review efforts. These include:

Illustrations — Illustrations are carefully planned to complement and expand upon concepts introduced in the text. The use of bold in the accompanying caption flag them as items that warrant your attention during both initial study and review.

Bold Type — Important new terms in the text are printed in bold type, then defined.

Federal Aviation Regulations — Appropriate FARs are presented in the textbook. Furthermore, the workbook offers several exercises designed to test your understanding of pertinent regulations.

This textbook is the key element in the training materials. Although it can be studied alone, there are several other components which we recommend to make your training as complete as possible. These include the *A&P Technician Powerplant Workbook* and *Study Guide*, as well as *AC 43.13-1B/2A* and *FAR Handbook for Aviation Maintenance Technicians*. When used together, these various elements provide an ideal framework for you and your instructor as you prepare for the FAA computerized and practical tests.

The A&P Technician Powerplant course is one of three segments of your training as an aviation maintenance technician. The Powerplant portion of your training introduces you to the concepts, terms, and common procedures used in the operation and maintenance of reciprocating and gas turbine engines.

TABLE OF CONTENTS

CHAPTER 1

RECIPROCATING ENGINES

INTRODUCTION

The lack of an efficient and practical propulsion system has been a limiting factor in aircraft development throughout history. For example, in 1483 Leonardo daVinci conceived a flying machine he called the aerial screw. However, since there were no means of propulsion at that time, the aerial screw was never developed. In fact, the first patent for a heat engine was not taken out until 1791 by John Barber. Unfortunately, Barber's engine was neither efficient nor practical. It was not until 1860 that a truly practical piston engine was built by Etienne Lenoir of France. Lenoir's engine, employing a battery ignition system and natural gas as fuel, was used to operate industrial machinery such as lathes. The next major breakthrough in piston engine development came in 1876 when Dr. August Otto developed the four-stroke, five-event cycle which is the operating cycle used by most modern reciprocating aircraft engines.

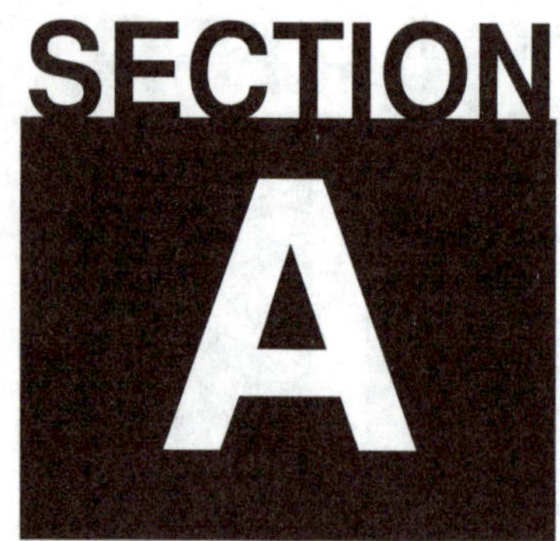

DESIGN AND CONSTRUCTION

All heat engines convert heat energy into mechanical energy by taking in a specific volume of air and heating it through the combustion of a fuel. The heated air expands, creating a force that is converted into mechanical energy to drive a propeller or other device. The most common type of heat engine is the reciprocating engine. Reciprocating engines derive their name from the back-and-forth, or reciprocating movement of their pistons. It is this reciprocating motion that produces the mechanical energy needed to accomplish work.

TYPES OF RECIPROCATING ENGINES

Many types of reciprocating engines have been designed for aircraft since the Wright Brothers first used a four-cylinder in-line engine to make aviation history. The two most common means of classifying reciprocating engines are by cylinder arrangment with respect to the crankshaft (radial, in-line, V-type, or opposed) and the method of cooling (liquid-cooled or air-cooled).

RADIAL ENGINES

A radial engine consists of a row, or rows of cylinders arranged radially about a central crankcase. The two basic types of radial engines include the rotary-type radial engine and the static-type radial engine. During World War I, **rotary-type radial engines** were used almost exclusively because they produced the greatest horsepower for their weight. The cylinders of a rotary-type radial engine are mounted radially around a small crankcase and rotate with the propeller, while the crankshaft remains stationary. Some of the more popular rotary engines were the Bently, the Gnome, and the LeRhone. [Figure 1-1]

Figure 1-1. On rotary-type radial engines, the propeller and cylinders are physically bolted to the crankcase and rotate around the stationary crankshaft.

Probably the biggest disadvantage rotary-type radial engines possessed was that the torque effect produced by the large rotating mass of the propeller and cylinders made aircraft somewhat difficult to control. This difficulty, coupled with carburetion, lubrication, and exhaust system problems, limited development of the rotary-type radial engine.

In the late 1920s, the Wright Aeronautical Corporation, in cooperation with the U.S. Navy, developed a series of five-, seven-, and nine-cylinder **static-type radial engines**. These engines demonstrated reliability far greater than any other previous designs. The radial engine enabled the long distance flights accomplished by Charles Lindbergh and other aviation pioneers to wake up the world to the realization that the airplane was a practical means of travel.

Static-type radial engines differ from rotary-type radial engines in that the crankcase is bolted to the airframe and remains stationary. This dictates that the crankshaft rotate to turn the propeller. Static-type radial engines have as few as three cylinders and as many as 28, but it was the higher horsepower

Figure 1-2. Radial engines helped revolutionize aviation with their high power and dependability.

applications that proved most useful. Outstanding reliability coupled with a high power-to-weight ratio made them ideal for powering early military and civilian transport aircraft. [Figure 1-2]

To increase their operational flexibility, static radial engines have been designed with a varying number of cylinder rows. One of the most common is the **single-row radial engine** which has an odd number of cylinders attached radially to a crankcase. A typical configuration consists of five to nine cylinders evenly spaced on the same circular plane with all pistons connected to a single crankshaft. To further increase a radial engine's power, while maintaining a reasonable engine frontal area, **multiple-row radial engines** were developed. One of the most common multiple-row radial engines consisted of two single row engines in line with each other connected to a single crankshaft. This type of engine is sometimes referred to as a **double-row radial engine** and typically has a total of 14 or 18 cylinders. To help cool a multiple-row radial engine, the rear rows of cylinders are staggered so they are behind the spaces between the front cylinders. This configuration increases the amount of airflow past each cylinder.

Figure 1-3. The Pratt and Whitney R-4360 engine was the largest practical radial engine used in aviation. However, the advent of both the turbojet and turboprop engines has all but eliminated the usefulness of large multiple-row radial engines on modern aircraft designs.

One of the largest multiple-row radial engines was the Pratt and Whitney R-4360, which consisted of 28 cylinders arranged in four staggered rows of seven cylinders each. The R-4360 developed a maximum 3,400 horsepower and represented the most powerful production radial engine ever used at that time. [Figure 1-3]

IN-LINE ENGINES

An in-line engine generally has an even number of cylinders that are aligned in a single row parallel with the crankshaft. This engine can be either liquid-cooled or air cooled and the pistons can be located either upright above the crankshaft or inverted below the crankshaft. [Figure 1-4]

An in-line engine has a comparatively small frontal area and, therefore, allows for better streamlining. Because of this, in-line engines were popular among early racing aircraft. Another advantage of the in-line engine is that, when mounted with the cylinders inverted, the crankshaft is higher off the ground. The higher crankshaft allowed greater propeller ground clearance which, in turn, permitted the use of shorter landing gear. Since in-line engines were used primarily on tail-wheel aircraft, the shorter main gear provided for increased forward visibility on the ground.

Although in-line engines offered some advantages over radial engines, they did have certain drawbacks that limited their usefulness. For example, in-line

Figure 1-4. A popular version of the in-line engine consisted of cylinders that were inverted. A typical in-line engine consists of four to six cylinders and develops anywhere from 90 to 200 horsepower.

engines have relatively low power-to-weight ratios. In addition, the rearmost cylinders of an air-cooled in-line engine receive relatively little cooling air, so in-line engines were typically limited to only four or six cylinders. With these limitations, most in-line engine designs were confined to low- and medium-horsepower engines used in light aircraft.

V-TYPE ENGINES

Further evolution of the reciprocating engine led to the development of the **V-type engine**. As the name implies, the cylinders of a V-type engine are arranged around a single crankshaft in two in-line banks that are 45, 60, or 90 degrees apart. Since V-type engines had two rows of cylinders, they were typically capable of producing more horsepower than an in-line engine. Furthermore, since only one crankcase and one crankshaft were used, most V-type engines had a reasonable power-to-weight ratio while retaining a small frontal area. The cylinders on a V-type engine could be above the crankshaft or below it, in which case the engine is referred to as an **inverted V-type engine**. Most V-type engines had 8 or 12 cylinders and were either liquid-cooled or air cooled. The V-12 engines developed during World War II achieved some of the highest horsepower ratings of any reciprocating engines, and today are typically found on restored military and racing aircraft. [Figure 1-5]

OPPOSED-TYPE ENGINES

Today, opposed-type engines are the most popular reciprocating engines used on light aircraft. A typical opposed engine can produce as little as 36 horsepower to as much as 400 horsepower. Opposed engines always have an even number of cylinders, and a cylinder on one side of a crankcase "opposes" a cylinder on the other side. While some opposed engines are liquid-cooled, the majority are air cooled. Opposed engines are typically mounted in a horizontal position when installed on fixed-wing aircraft, but can be mounted vertically to power helicopters.

Opposed-type engines have high power-to-weight ratios because they have a comparatively small, lightweight crankcase. In addition, an opposed engine's compact cylinder arrangement reduces the engine's frontal area and allows a streamlined installation that minimizes aerodynamic drag. Furthermore, opposed engines typically vibrate less than other engines because an opposed engine's power impulses tend to cancel each other. [Figure 1-6]

In the 1980s, Porsche Aviation Products developed an FAA certificated aircraft engine that was based on one of their automotive engines. The **Porsche Flugmotoren (PFM) 3200** is a direct descendant of the 214 horsepower engine used in the Porsche 911 sports car. The PFM 3200 is a geared, horizontally-opposed six cylinder engine that displaces 193 cubic inches and produces approximately 200 horsepower. The Porsche engine employs a dual electronic ignition system and dual electrical system consisting of two alternators, two batteries, and two electrical buses. In addition, the PFM 3200 utilizes a single engine control called a **power lever**. The power lever automatically governs the throttle, mixture, and propeller pitch settings. This reduces pilot workload and, at the same time, maintains the engine's peak performance for the given conditions.

Figure 1-5. V-type engines provide an excellent combination of weight, power, and small frontal area.

Figure 1-6. A horizontally opposed engine combines a good power-to-weight ratio with a relatively small frontal area. These engines power most light aircraft in use today.

ENGINE COMPONENTS

As an aviation maintenance technician, you must be familiar with an engine's components in order to understand its operating principles. Furthermore, having an understanding of an engine's basic construction greatly enhances your ability to perform routine maintenance operations.

The basic parts of a reciprocating engine include the crankcase, cylinders, pistons, connecting rods, valves, valve-operating mechanism, and crankshaft. The valves, pistons, and spark plugs are located in the cylinder while the valve operating mechanism, crankshaft, and connecting rods are located in the crankcase. [Figure 1-7]

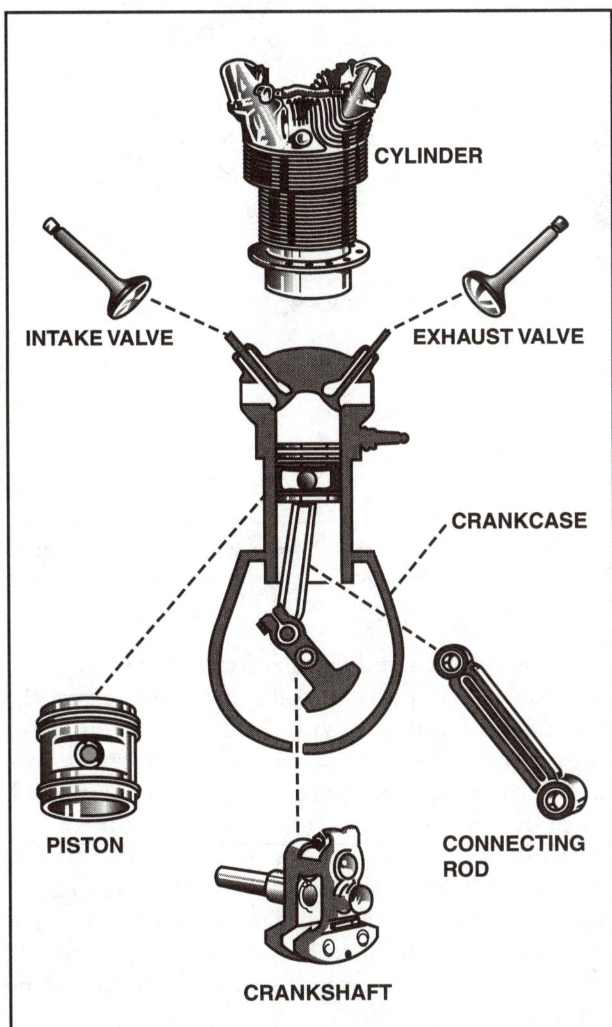

Figure 1-7. In a basic reciprocating engine, the cylinder forms a chamber where the fuel/air mixture is compressed and burned. The piston, on the other hand, compresses the fuel mixture and transmits the power produced by combustion to the crankshaft through the connecting rods. The intake valve allows the fuel/air mixture into the cylinder while the exhaust valve lets the exhaust gases out of the cylinder.

Although a number of engine configurations have had their place in aircraft development, the horizontally opposed and static-type radial designs represent the vast majority of reciprocating engines in service today. Because of this, the discussion on engine components centers on these types.

CRANKCASE

The crankcase is the foundation of a reciprocating engine. It contains the engine's internal parts and provides a mounting surface for the engine cylinders and external accessories. In addition, the crankcase provides a tight enclosure for the lubricating oil as well as a means of attaching a complete engine to an airframe. Given the requirements placed on a crankcase, as well as the internal and external forces they are subjected to, crankcases must be extremely rigid and strong. For example, due to the internal combustion forces exerted on the cylinders and the unbalanced centrifugal and inertial forces inflicted by a propeller, a crankcase is constantly subjected to bending moments which change continuously in direction and magnitude. Therefore, to remain functional, a crankcase must be capable of absorbing these forces and still maintain its integrity.

Today, most crankcases consist of at least two pieces; however, there are some one-piece and up to five-piece case assemblies. To provide the strength and rigidity required while maintaining a relatively light weight, most aircraft crankcases are made of cast aluminum alloys.

OPPOSED ENGINE CRANKCASES

A typical horizontally opposed engine crankcase consists of two halves of cast aluminum alloy that are manufactured either with sand castings or by using permanent molds. Crankcases manufactured through the permanent mold process, or permamold, as it is called by some manufacturers, are denser than those made by sand casting. This denser construction allows molded crankcases to have somewhat thinner walls than a sand cast crankcase and exhibit less tendency to crack due to fatigue. Most opposed crankcases are approximately cylindrical, with smooth areas machined to serve as cylinder pads. A **cylinder pad** is simply a surface where a cylinder is mounted to a crankcase.

To allow a crankcase to support a crankshaft, a series of transverse webs are cast directly into a crankcase parallel to the case's longitudinal axis.

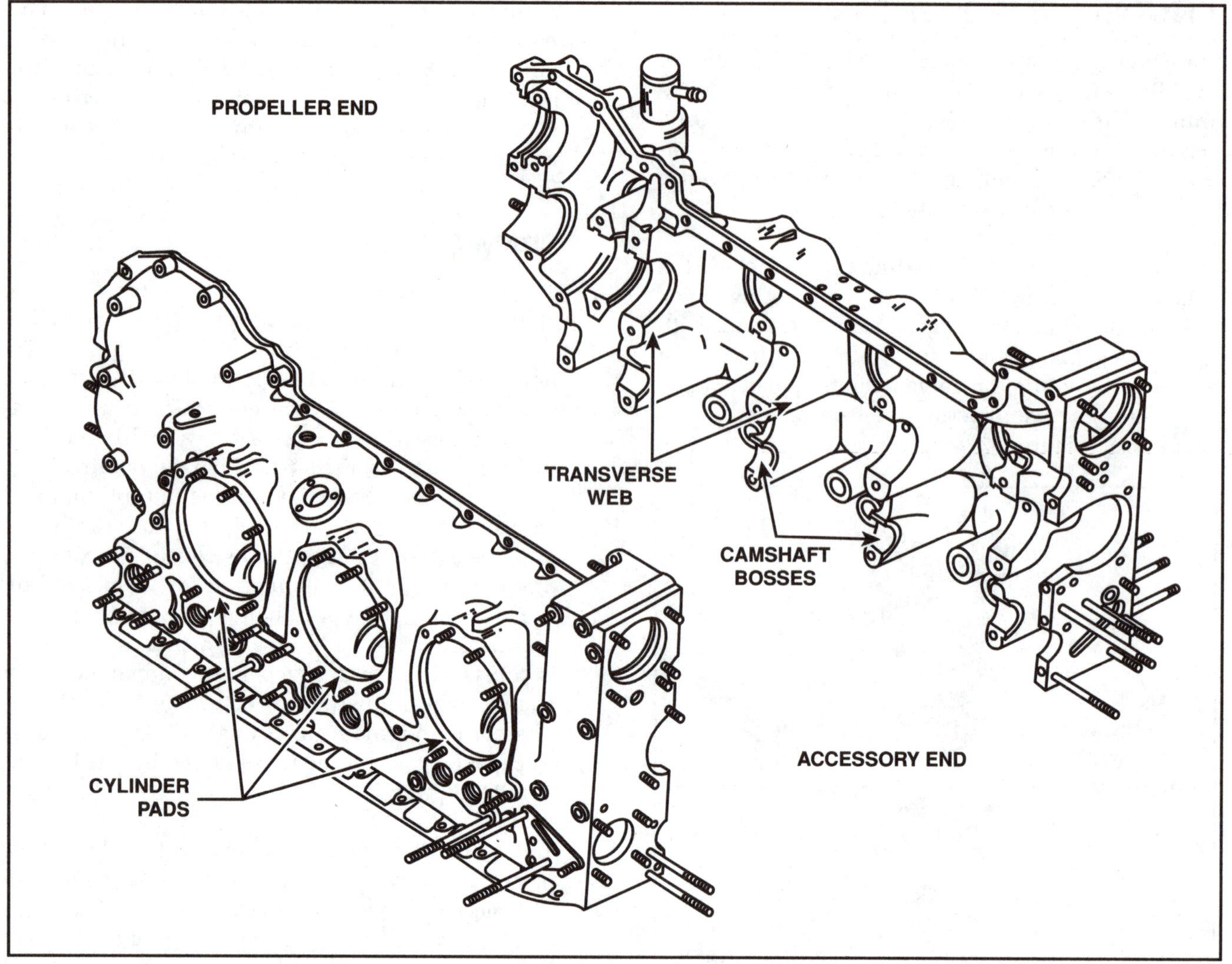

Figure 1-8. In addition to the transverse webs that support the main bearings, a set of camshaft bosses are typically cast into a crankcase. These bosses support the camshaft which is part of the valve operating mechanism.

These webs form an integral part of the structure and, in addition to housing the bearings that support the crankshaft, the webs add strength to the crankcase. [Figure 1-8]

The crankcase is also an integral part of the lubrication system. Oil passages are drilled throughout the case halves to allow lubricating oil to be delivered to the moving parts housed within the crankcase. In addition, **oil galleries** are machined into the case halves to scavenge, or collect, oil and return it to the main oil tank or sump.

Most crankcase halves split vertically and are aligned and held together with studs and bolts. Through bolts are typically used at the crankshaft bearings while smaller bolts and nuts are used around the case perimeter. Since the oil supply in most modern horizontally opposed engines is carried inside the crankcase, provisions are made to seal the case to prevent leakage. To ensure that the seal does not interfere with the tight fit for the bearings, most crankcase halves are sealed with a very thin coating of a non-hardening gasket compound. In addition, on some engines a fine silk thread extending around the entire case perimeter is imbedded in the compound. With this type of setup, when the crankcase halves are bolted together with the proper torque, the gasket material and silk thread form an effective oil seal without interfering with bearing fit.

RADIAL ENGINE CRANKCASES

Unlike opposed engine crankcases, radial engine crankcases are divided into distinct sections. The number of sections can be as few as three or as many as seven depending on the size and type of engine. In general, a typical radial engine crankcase separates into four main sections: the nose section, the power section, the supercharger section, and the accessory section. [Figure 1-9]

The **nose section** is mounted at the front of a radial engine crankcase and bolts directly to the power section. A typical nose section is made of an aluminum alloy that is cast as one piece with a domed or convex shape. The nose section usually houses and supports a propeller governor drive shaft, the propeller shaft, a cam ring, and a propeller reduction gear assembly if required. In addition, many nose sections have mounting points for magnetos and other engine accessories.

The second portion of a crankcase is referred to as the **power section** and represents the section of the crankcase where the reciprocating motion of the pistons is converted to the rotary motion of the crankshaft. Like an opposed engine crankcase, the power section absorbs intense stress from the crankshaft assembly and the cylinders. A power section can be either one, two, or three pieces. A one-piece power section usually consists of a solid piece of aluminum alloy. A split power section, on the other hand, is typically manufactured from aluminum or magnesium and then bolted together. As with an opposed engine crankcase, a radial engine power section contains machined bosses that rigidly support the crankshaft bearings and the crankshaft.

Cylinders are attached around the perimeter of the power section to machined **cylinder pads**. In general, studs are installed into threaded holes in the power section to provide a means of retaining the cylinders. The inner circumference of a cylinder pad is sometimes chamfered or tapered to permit the installation of a large rubber O-ring around the cylinder skirt. This O-ring effectively seals the joint between the cylinder and the cylinder pads.

The diffuser or **supercharger section** is located directly behind the power section and is generally made of cast aluminum alloy or magnesium. As its name implies, this section houses the supercharger and its related components. A supercharger is an engine accessory that is used to compress air and distribute it to the engine's cylinders. This compression increases the air density so the engine can operate at high altitudes and still produce the same amount of power as it would at sea level. The supercharger section also incorporates mounting lugs to secure the engine assembly to the engine mounts.

The **accessory section** is usually cast of either an aluminum alloy or magnesium. On some engines, it is cast in one piece and then machined to provide a means for mounting accessories such as magnetos, carburetors, pumps, starters, and generators. However, on other engines, the accessory section consists of an aluminum alloy casting and a separate

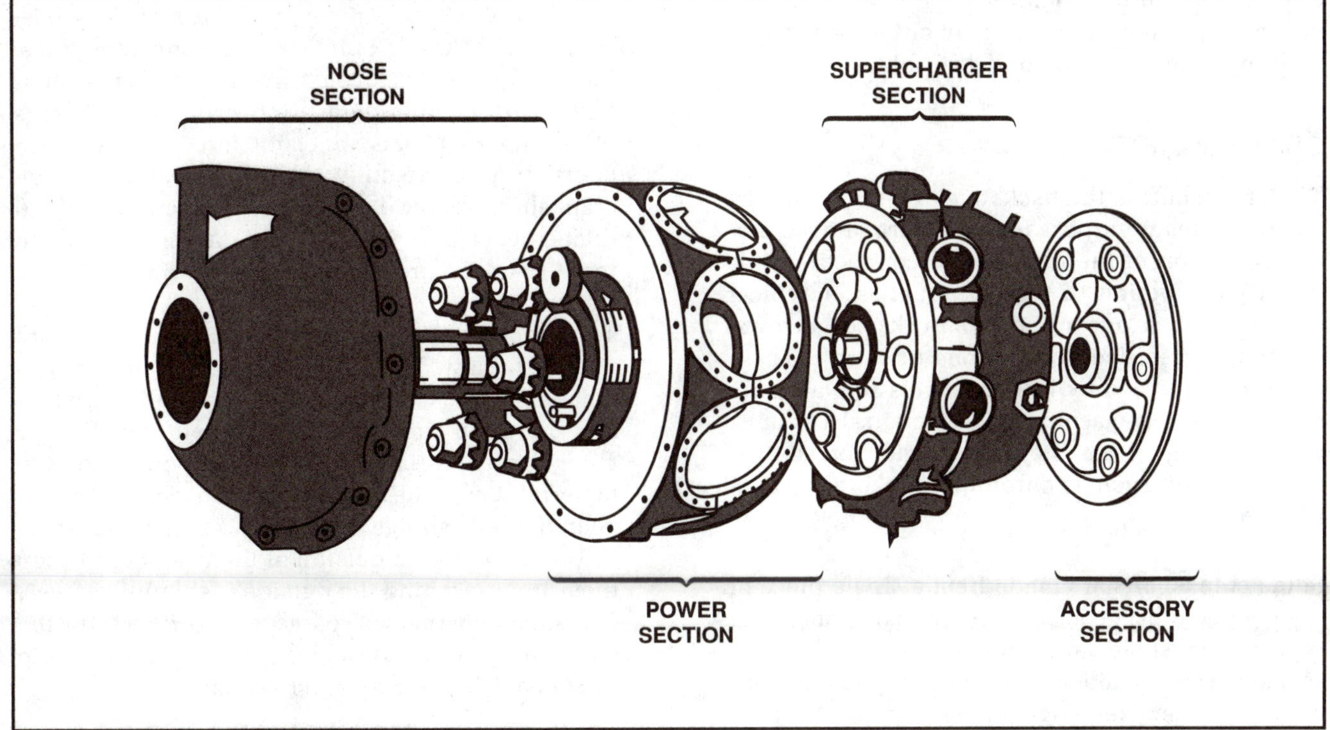

Figure 1-9. The four basic sections of a radial engine crankcase are the nose section, power section, supercharger section, and accessory section.

cast magnesium cover plate on which the accessories are mounted.

A typical accessory section houses gear trains containing both spur- and bevel-type gears that drive various engine components and accessories. Spur-type gears are generally used to drive more heavily loaded accessories or those requiring the least play or backlash in the gear train. On the other hand, bevel gears permit angular location of short stub shafts leading to the various accessory mounting pads.

ENGINE MOUNTING POINTS

For opposed engines, mounting points, sometimes called **mounting lugs**, are typically cast as part of the crankcase. However, some mounting lugs may be a bolt-on addition. As a general rule, lower-horsepower engines use mounting lugs that are cast into the crankcase, while higher-powered engines employ mounting lugs that are bolted to the crankcase. On all engines, the mounting arrangement supports the entire powerplant including the propeller and, therefore, must be designed to withstand various engine, centrifugal, and g-loading conditions.

As previously discussed, mounting lugs for radial engines are spaced about the periphery of the supercharger section to attach the engine to the engine mount. The mounting lugs may either be integral with the diffuser section or detachable.

CRANKSHAFTS

The crankshaft is the backbone of a reciprocating engine. Its main purpose is to transform the reciprocating motion of the pistons and connecting rods into rotary motion to turn a propeller. A typical crankshaft has one or more **cranks**, or **throws**, located at specified points along its length. These throws are formed by forging offsets into a crankshaft before it is machined. Since crankshafts must withstand high stress, they are generally forged from a strong alloy such as chromium-nickel molybdenum steel.

Some crankshafts are made from a single piece of steel, while others consist of several components. A typical crankshaft can have as few as one throw or as many as eight and varies depending on the number of cylinders and engine type. Regardless of the number of throws or the number of pieces used in construction, all crankshafts utilize the same basic

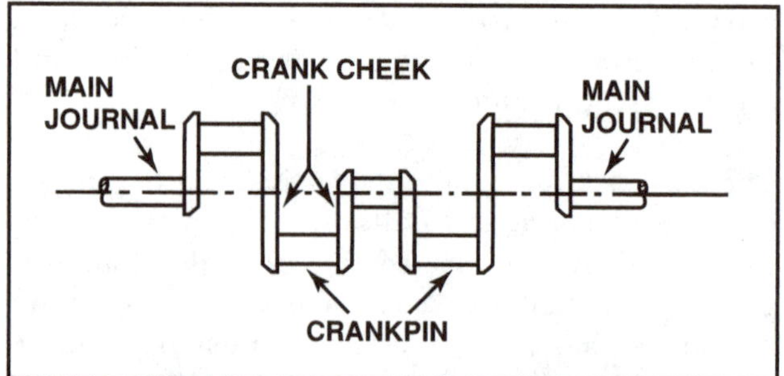

Figure 1-10. All crankshafts consist of a main bearing journal, one or more crankpins, and several crank cheeks.

parts. These parts include the main bearing journal, the crankpin, and the crank cheek. In addition, although they are not true parts of the crankshaft, counterweights and dampers are often installed on many crankshafts to reduce engine vibration. [Figure 1-10]

The **main bearing journals**, or **main journals**, represent the centerline of a crankshaft and support the crankshaft as it rotates in the main bearings. All crankshafts require at least two main journals to support the crankshaft, absorb the operational loads, and transmit stress from the crankshaft to the crankcase. To help minimize wear, most main bearing journals, or crank journals, as they are sometimes called, are hardened through nitriding to resist wear.

Crankpins, or connecting-rod bearing journals, serve as attachment points for the connecting rods. Most crankpins are forged directly into a crankshaft and are offset from the main bearing journal. This offset design means that any force applied to a crankpin in a direction other than parallel to the crankshaft center line causes the crankshaft to rotate. Like main journals, crankpins are nitrided to resist wear and provide a suitable bearing surface.

To reduce total crankshaft weight, crankpins are usually hollow. This hollow construction also provides a passage for lubricating oil. In addition, a hollow crankpin serves as a collection chamber for sludge, dirt, carbon deposits, and other foreign material. Once these substances reach a crankpin chamber, or **sludge chamber**, centrifugal force throws them to the outside of the chamber to keep them from reaching the outside crankpin surfaces. On some engines, a passage is drilled in the crankpin to allow oil from the hollow crankshaft to be sprayed onto the cylinder walls.

On opposed engines, the number of crankpins must correspond with an engine's cylinder arrangement.

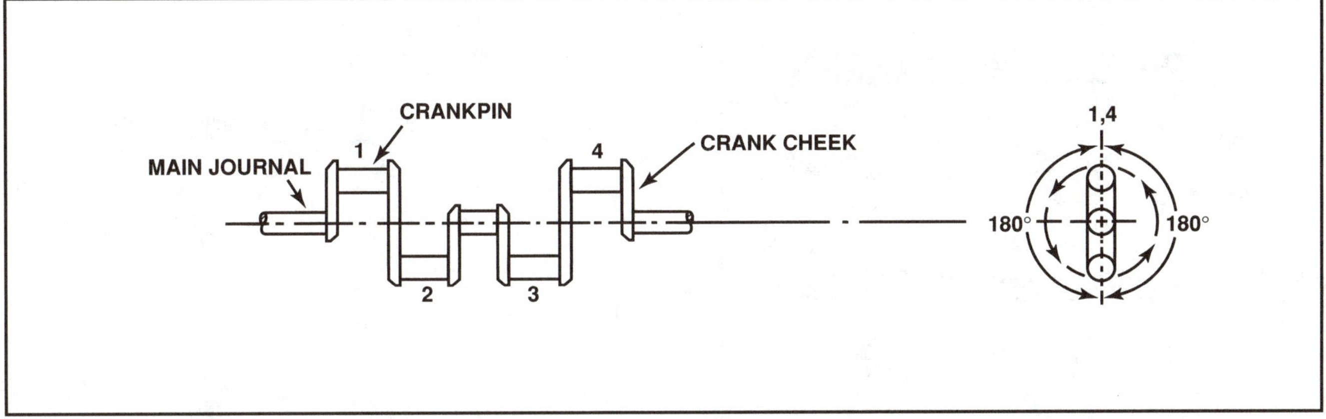

Figure 1-11. On a four cylinder engine, the number one and four throws are 180 degrees apart from the number two and three throws.

The arrangement of the crankpins varies with the type engine and allows each piston to be at a different position in the cranking cycle as the crankshaft rotates. The position of the crankpins on a crankshaft in relation to each other is expressed in degrees. [Figure 1-11]

Two **crank cheeks**, or **crank arms**, are required to connect the crankpin to the crankshaft. In some designs, the cheek extends beyond the journal to form a **counterweight** that helps balance the crankshaft. In addition, most crank cheeks have drilled passage ways that allow oil to flow from the main journal to the crankpin.

CRANKSHAFT BALANCE

Excessive engine vibration can cause metal structures to become fatigued and fail or wear excessively. In some instances, excessive vibration is caused by an unbalanced crankshaft. Therefore, to prevent unwanted vibration, most crankshafts are balanced both statically and dynamically.

A crankshaft is **statically balanced** when the weight of an entire crankshaft assembly is balanced around its axis of rotation. To test a crankshaft for static balance, the outside main journals are placed on two knife edge balancing blocks. If the shaft tends to rotate toward any one position during the test, it is out of static balance.

Once a crankshaft is statically balanced it must be dynamically balanced. **Dynamic balance** refers to balancing the centrifugal forces created by a rotating crankshaft and the impact forces created by an engine's power impulses. The most common means of dynamically balancing a crankshaft is through the use of dynamic dampers. A **dynamic damper** is a weight which is fastened to a crankshaft's crank cheek assembly in such a way that it is free to move back and forth in a small arc. Some crankshafts utilize two or more of these assemblies, each being attached to a different crank cheek. The construction of the dynamic damper used in one type of engine consists of a movable slotted-steel counterweight attached to a crank cheek by two spool-shaped steel pins that extend through oversized holes in the counterweight and crank cheek. The difference in diameter between the pins and the holes allows the dynamic damper to oscillate back and forth. [Figure 1-12]

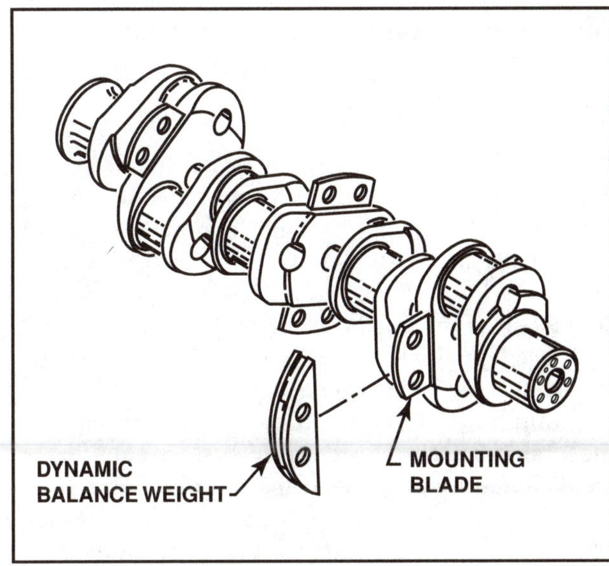

Figure 1-12. Movable counterweights serve as dynamic dampers to reduce the centrifugal and impact vibrations in an aircraft engine.

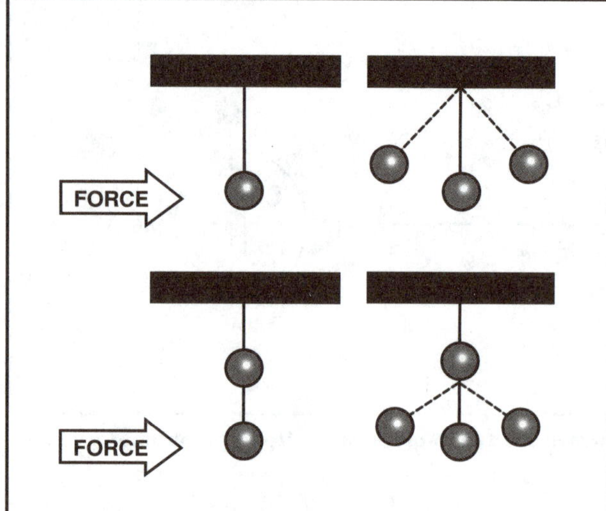

Figure 1-13. Think of the crankshaft as a pendulum that swings at its natural frequency once a force is applied. The greater the force, the greater the distance the pendulum swings. However, if a second pendulum is suspended from the first and a force is applied, the second pendulum begins to oscillate opposite the applied force. This opposite oscillation dampens the oscillation of the first pendulum leaving it nearly stationary. You can think of a dynamic damper as a short pendulum hung from a crankshaft that is tuned to the frequency of the power impulses.

Each time a cylinder fires, a pulse is transmitted into the crankshaft that causes it to flex. When the engine is running, the crankshaft receives hundreds of these pulses each minute and flexes, or vibrates, constantly. To help minimize these vibrations, the dynamic damper oscillates, or swings, each time the crankshaft receives a pulse from a firing cylinder. These oscillations are opposite the crankshaft vibrations and, therefore, absorb some of the force produced by the power impulse. [Figure 1-13]

CRANKSHAFT TYPES

The type of crankshaft used on a particular engine depends on the number and arrangement of an engine's cylinders. The most common types of crankshafts are the single-throw, two-throw, four-throw, and six-throw crankshafts. The simplest crankshaft is the **single-throw** or **360 degree** crankshaft used on single-row radial engines. As its name implies, a single-throw crankshaft consists of a single crankpin with two main journals that support the crankshaft in the crankcase. A single-throw crankshaft may be constructed out of either one or two pieces. One-piece crankshafts are used with a connecting rod that splits so it can be installed on the crankpin. However, with a two-piece, the crankpin separates, allowing the use of a one piece connecting rod. [Figure 1-14]

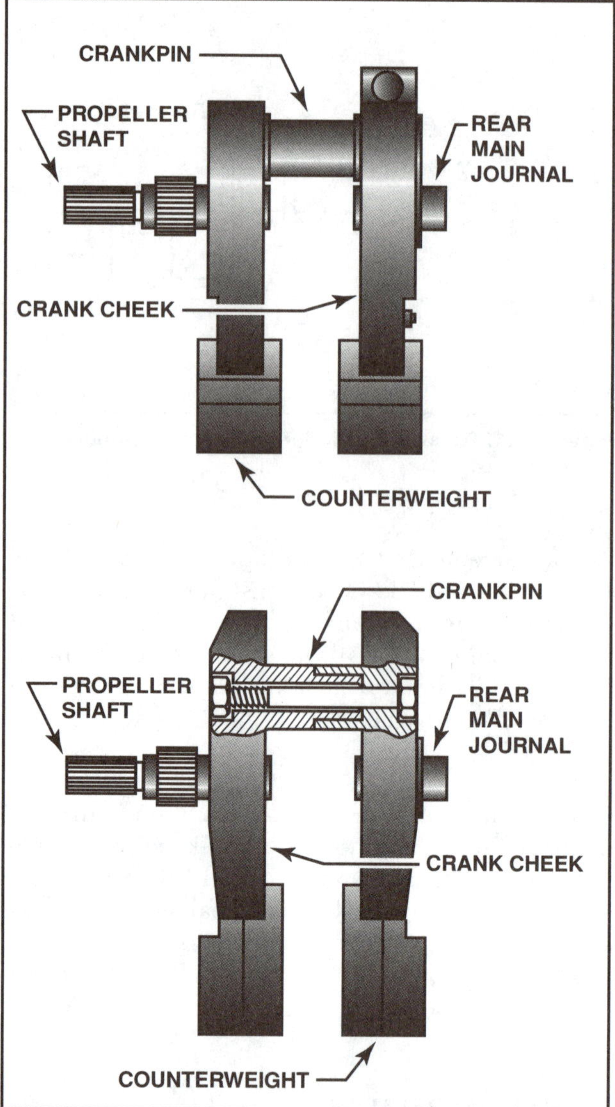

Figure 1-14. With a one-piece, single-throw crankshaft, the entire crankshaft is cast as one solid piece. However, with a clamp type two-piece crankshaft, the two pieces are held together by a bolt that passes through the crankpin.

Twin-row radial engines require a **two-throw crankshaft**, one throw for each bank of cylinders. The throws on a two-throw crankshaft are typically set 180 degrees from each other and may consist of either one or three pieces. Although they are not commonly encountered, two cylinder opposed engines also use two-throw crankshafts.

Four cylinder opposed engines and four cylinder in-line engines use **four-throw crankshafts.** On some four-throw crankshafts two throws are arranged 180 degrees apart from the other two throws. Furthermore, depending on the size of the crankshaft and power output of the engine, a four-throw crankshaft has either three or five main bearings. [Figure 1-15]

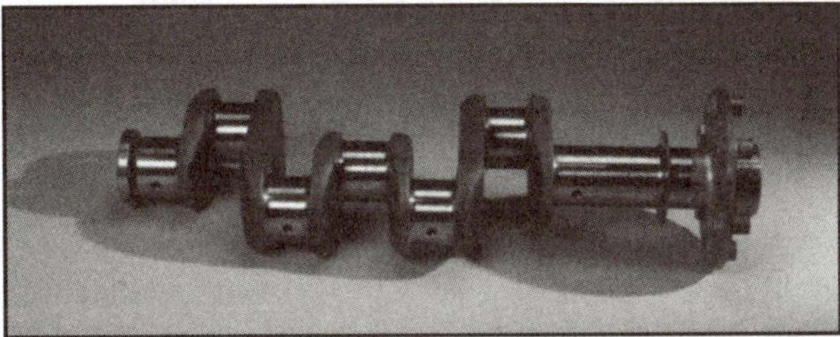

Figure 1-15. A typical four-throw crankshaft used in a horizontally opposed engine is machined as one piece with throws that are 180 degrees apart.

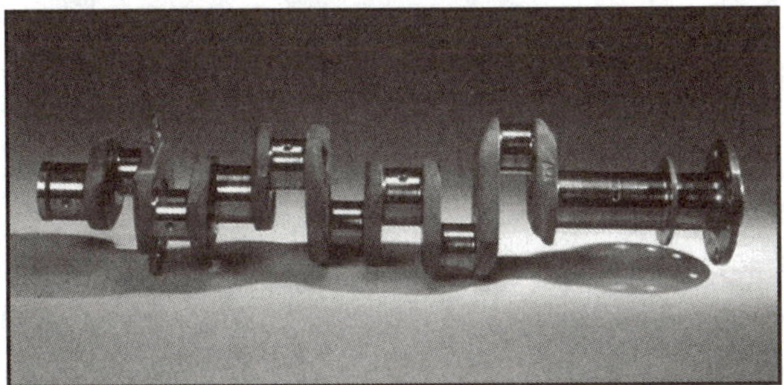

Figure 1-16. With a typical six-throw crankshaft, the throws are 60 degrees apart. On the six throw crankshaft pictured above, the crank journals are numbered from the flanged end. If you were to number each throw in 60° increments from the flanged end, the order would be 1, 4, 5, 2, 3, 6.

Six cylinder opposed and in-line engines and 12 cylinder V-type engines use **six-throw crankshafts.** A typical six-throw crankshaft is forged as one piece and consists of four main bearings and six throws that are 60 degrees apart. [Figure 1-16]

BEARINGS

A bearing is any surface which supports and reduces friction between two moving parts. Typical areas where bearings are used in an aircraft engine include the main journals, crankpins, connecting rod ends, and accessory drive shafts. A good bearing must be composed of material that is strong enough to withstand the pressure imposed on it, while allowing rotation or movement between two parts with a minimum of friction and wear. For a bearing to provide efficient and quiet operation, it must hold two parts in a nearly fixed position with very close tolerances. Furthermore, bearings must be able to withstand radial loads, thrust loads, or a combination of the two.

There are two ways in which bearing surfaces move in relation to each other. One is by the sliding movement of one metal against another, and the second is for one surface to roll over another. Reciprocating engines use bearings that rely on both types of movement. The three different types of bearings typically used in aircraft reciprocating engines include the plain bearing, the ball bearing, and the roller bearing. [Figure 1-17]

PLAIN BEARINGS

Plain bearings are generally used for crankshaft main bearings, cam ring and camshaft bearings, connecting rod end bearings, and accessory drive shaft bearings. These bearings are typically subject to

Figure 1-17. Of the three most common types of bearings used in reciprocating engines, the plain bearing relies on the sliding movement of one metal against another, while both roller and ball bearings have one surface roll over another.

radial loads only; however, flange-type plain bearings are often used as thrust bearings in opposed reciprocating engines.

Plain bearings are usually made of nonferrous metals such as silver, bronze, babbit, tin, or lead. One type of plain bearing consists of thin shells of silver-plated steel, with lead-tin plated over the silver on the inside surface only. Smaller bearings, such as those used to support various accessory drive shafts, are called **bushings**. One type of bushing that is used in aviation is the oil impregnated porous oilite bushing. With this type of bushing, the heat produced by friction draws the impregnated oil to the bearing surface to provide lubrication during engine operation.

BALL BEARINGS

A ball bearing assembly consists of grooved inner and outer races, one or more sets of polished steel balls, and a **bearing retainer**. The balls of a ball bearing are held in place and kept evenly spaced by the bearing retainer, while the inner and outer **bearing races** provide a smooth surface for the balls to roll over. However, some races have a deep groove that matches the curvature of the balls to provide more support and allow a bearing to carry high radial loads. Because the balls of a ball bearing offer such a small contact area, ball bearings have the least amount of rolling friction.

Because of their construction, ball bearings are well suited to withstand thrust loads and are, therefore, used as thrust bearings in large radial and gas turbine engines. In applications where thrust loads are heavier in one direction, a larger race is used on the side of the increased load.

Most of the ball bearings you will work with as a technician are used in accessories such as magnetos, alternators, turbochargers, and vacuum pumps. Many of these bearings are prelubricated and sealed to provide trouble-free operation between overhauls. However, if a sealed ball bearing must be removed or replaced, it is important that you use the proper tools to avoid damaging the bearing and its seals.

ROLLER BEARINGS

Roller bearings are similar in construction to ball bearings except that polished steel rollers are used instead of balls. The rollers provide a greater contact area and a corresponding increase in rolling friction over that of a ball bearing. Roller bearings are available in many styles and sizes, but most aircraft engine applications use either a straight roller or tapered roller bearing. **Straight roller bearings** are suitable when the bearing is subjected to radial loads only. For example, most high-power aircraft engines use straight roller bearings as crankshaft main bearings. **Tapered roller bearings**, on the other hand, have cone-shaped inner and outer races that allow the bearing to withstand both radial and thrust loads.

CONNECTING RODS

The connecting rod is the link which transmits the force exerted on a piston to a crankshaft. Most connecting rods are made of a durable steel alloy; however, aluminum can be used with low horsepower engines. The lighter a connecting rod is, the less inertia it produces when the rod and piston stop and then accelerate in the opposite direction at the end of each stroke. A typical connecting rod is forged and has a cross-sectional shape of either an "H" or an "I." However, there are a few connecting rods that are tubular. One end of a connecting rod connects to the crankshaft and is called the **crankpin end**, while the other end connects to the piston and is called the **piston end**. The three types of connecting rod assemblies you should be familiar with are the plain-type, the master-and-articulated-rod type, and the fork-and-blade type.

PLAIN CONNECTING ROD

Plain connecting rods are used in opposed and in-line engines. The piston end of a plain connecting rod is fitted with a bronze bushing to accommodate the piston pin. The bushing is typically pressed into the connecting rod and then reamed to the dimension required by the piston pin. The crankpin end, on the other hand, is usually fitted with a two-piece bearing and cap which is held on the end of the rod by bolts or studs. In this case, the main bearing insert is typically made of steel that is lined with a nonferrous alloy such as babbitt, lead, bronze, or copper.

To provide proper fit and balance, connecting rods are often matched with pistons and crankpins. Therefore, if a connecting rod is ever removed, it should always be replaced in the same cylinder and in the same relative position. To help do this, connecting rods and caps are sometimes stamped with numbers to identify the cylinder and piston assembly with which they should be paired. For example,

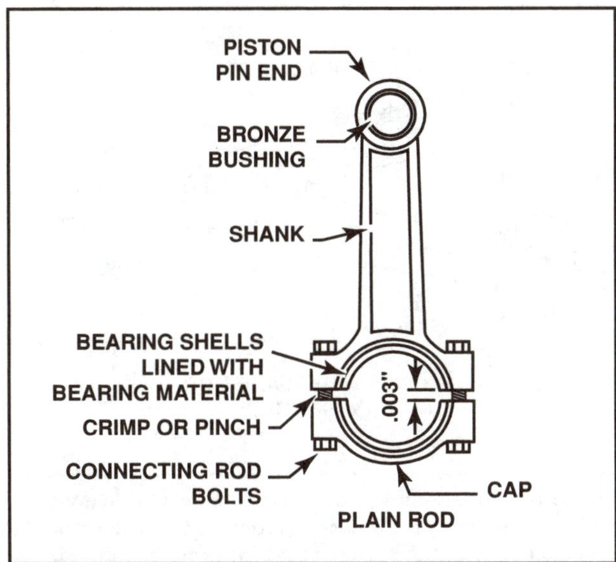

Figure 1-18. On a typical plain connecting rod, a two piece bearing shell fits tightly in the crankpin end of the connecting rod. The bearing is held in place by pins or tangs that fit into slots cut into the cap and connecting rod. The piston end of the connecting rod contains a bushing that is pressed into place.

a number "1" indicates the connecting rod or cap belong with the number 1 cylinder and piston assembly. [Figure 1-18]

MASTER-AND-ARTICULATED ROD ASSEMBLY

The master-and-articulated rod assembly is commonly used in radial engines. With this type of assembly, one piston in each row of cylinders is connected to the crankshaft by a **master rod**. The remaining pistons are connected to the master rod by **articulated rods**. Therefore, in a nine cylinder engine there is one master rod and eight articulating rods, while a double row 18 cylinder engine has two master rods and 16 articulating rods.

Master rods are typically manufactured from a steel alloy forging that is machined and heat-treated for maximum strength. Articulated rods are constructed of a forged steel alloy in either an I- or H- cross-sectional profile. Bronze bushings are pressed into the bores in each end of the articulated rod to serve as bearings.

The master rod serves as the only connecting link between all the pistons and the crankpin. The small end, or piston end of a master rod, contains a plain bearing called a **piston pin bearing** which receives the piston pin. The crankpin end of a master rod contains the **crankpin bearing**, sometimes called a **master rod bearing**. A typical crankpin bearing consists of a plain bearing that is able to withstand the radial loads placed on the rod assembly. A set of flange holes are machined around the crankpin end of a master rod to provide an attachment point for the articulated rods.

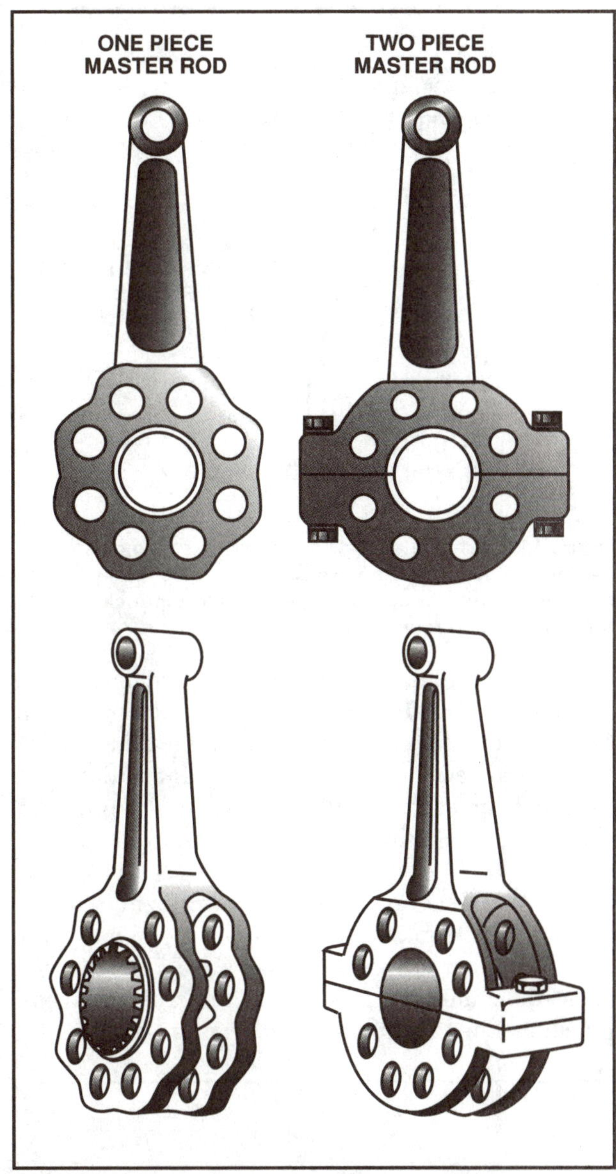

Figure 1-19. With a single piece master rod, the master-and-articulated rods are assembled and installed on the crankpin before the crankshaft sections are joined together. On the other hand, with a multiple piece master rod, the crankpin end of the master rod and its bearing are split and installed on the crankpin. The bearing cap is then set in place and bolted to the master rod.

A master rod may be one piece or multiple pieces. As a general rule, a one piece rod is used on multiple piece crankshafts while a multiple piece, or **split type** master rod is used with single piece crankshafts. [Figure 1-19]

Each articulated rod is hinged to the master rod by a **knuckle pin**. Some knuckle pins are pressed into the

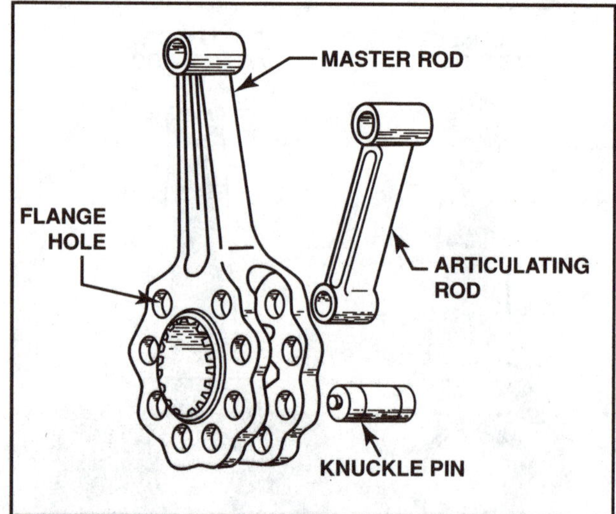

Figure 1-20. Articulated rods are attached to the master rod by knuckle pins, that are pressed into holes in the master rod flanges during assembly. A knuckle pin lock plate is then installed to retain the pins.

master rod so they do not rotate in the flange holes, while other **full floating knuckle pins** have a loose fit that allows them to rotate in both the flange holes and articulated rods. In either type of installation, a lock plate on each side retains the knuckle pins and prevents lateral movement. [Figure 1-20]

Since the flange holes on a master rod encircle the center of the crankpin, the crankpin is the only portion of a master rod assembly that travels in a true circle as the crankshaft rotates. The remaining knuckle pins travel in an elliptical path. [Figure 1-21]

Figure 1-21. You can see that each knuckle pin rotates in a different elliptical path. As a result, each articulated rod has a varying degree of angularity relative to the center of the crank throw.

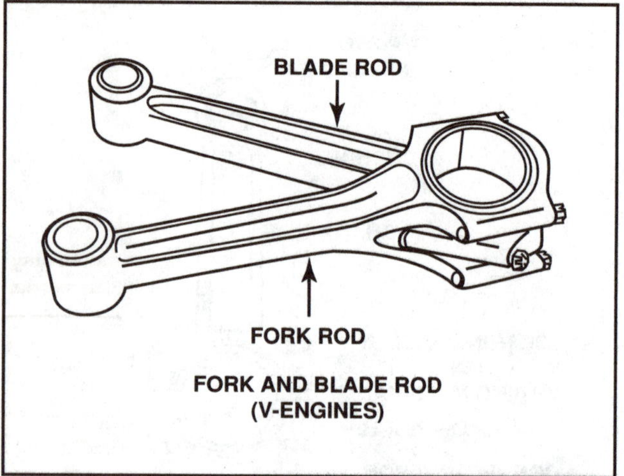

Figure 1-22. A fork-and-blade rod assembly used in a V-type engine consists of a blade connecting rod whose crankpin end fits between the prongs of the fork connecting rod.

Because of the varying angularity, all pistons do not move an equal amount in each cylinder for a given number of degrees of crankshaft rotation. To compensate for this, the knuckle pin holes in the master rod flange are positioned at varying distances from the center of the crankpin.

FORK-AND-BLADE ROD ASSEMBLY

The fork-and-blade rod assembly is used primarily in V-type engines and consists of a **fork connecting rod** and a **blade connecting rod**. The forked rod is split at the crankpin end to allow space for the blade rod to fit between the prongs. The fork-and-blade assembly is then fastened to a crankpin with a two-piece bearing. [Figure 1-22]

PISTONS

The piston in a reciprocating engine is a cylindrical plunger that moves up and down within a cylinder. Pistons perform two primary functions; first, they draw fuel and air into a cylinder, compress the gases, and purge burned exhaust gases from the cylinder; second, they transmit the force produced by combustion to the crankshaft.

Most aircraft engine pistons are machined from aluminum alloy forgings. **Ring grooves** are then cut into a piston's outside surface to hold a set of piston rings. As many as six ring grooves may be machined around a piston. The portion of the piston between the ring grooves is commonly referred to as a **ring land**. The piston's top surface is called the **piston head** and is directly exposed to the heat of combustion. The **piston pin boss** is an enlarged area inside the piston that provides additional bearing area for a

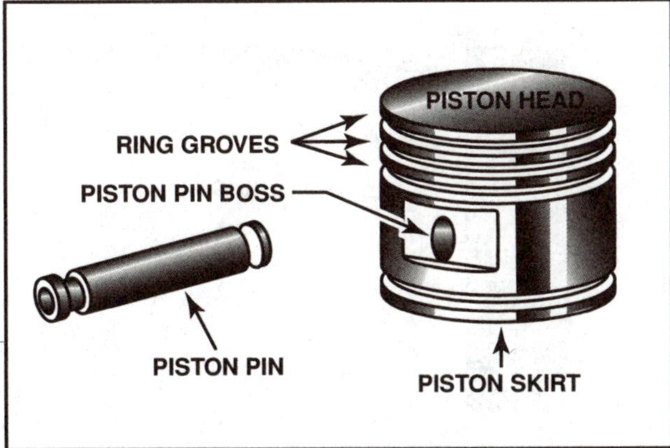

Figure 1-23. A typical piston has ring grooves cut into its outside surface to support piston rings. In addition, cooling fins are sometimes cast into the piston interior to help dissipate heat, while the piston pin boss provides support for the piston pin.

piston pin which passes through the piston pin boss to attach the piston to a connecting rod. To help align a piston in a cylinder, the piston base is extended to form the **piston skirt**. On some pistons, cooling fins are cast into the underside of the piston to provide for greater heat transfer to the engine oil. [Figure 1-23]

Pistons are often classified according to their head design. The most common types of head designs are the flat, recessed, cupped, and domed. In addition, piston skirts can be the simple trunk type, the trunk type that is relieved at the piston boss, and the slipper type which is relieved along the piston base to reduce friction. [Figure 1-24]

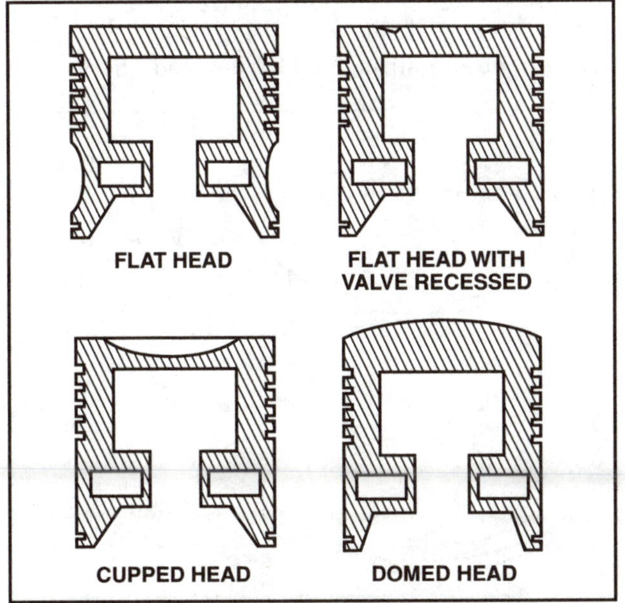

Figure 1-24. Most modern aircraft engines use flat-head pistons. However, as an aviation technician, you should be familiar with all piston head designs.

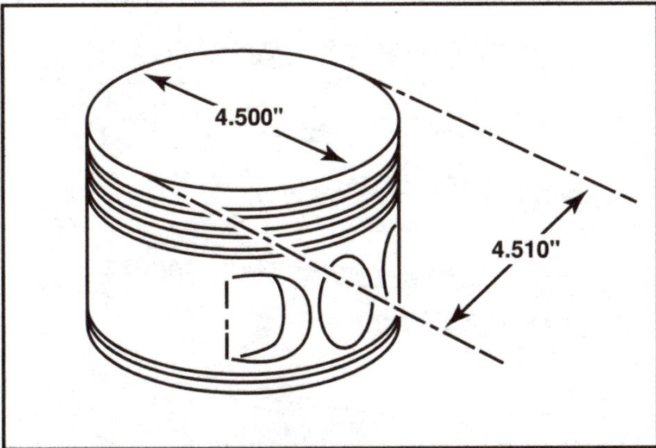

Figure 1-25. Several engines now use cam ground pistons to compensate for the greater expansion parallel to the piston boss during engine operation. The diameter of a cam ground piston measures several thousandths of an inch larger perpendicular to the piston boss than parallel to the piston boss.

All pistons expand as they heat up. However, due to the added mass at the piston boss, most pistons expand more along the piston boss than perpendicular to the piston boss. This uneven expansion can cause a piston to take on an oblong, or oval shape, at normal engine operating temperatures, resulting in uneven piston and cylinder wear. One way to compensate for this is with a **cam ground piston**. A cam ground piston is machined with a slightly oval shape. That is, the diameter of the piston parallel to the piston boss is slightly less than the diameter perpendicular to the piston boss. This oval shape compensates for any differential expansion and produces a round piston at normal operating temperatures. Furthermore, the oval shape holds the piston centered in the cylinder during engine warmup and helps prevent the piston from moving laterally within a cylinder. [Figure 1-25]

PISTON RINGS

Piston rings perform three functions in aircraft reciprocating engines. They prevent leakage of gas pressure from the combustion chamber, reduce oil seepage into the combustion chamber, and transfer heat from the piston to the cylinder walls. The rings fit into the piston grooves but spring out to press against the cylinder walls. When properly lubricated, piston rings form an effective seal.

Most piston rings are made of high-grade gray cast iron. However, in some engines, chrome-plated mild steel piston rings are used because of their ability to withstand high temperatures. After a ring is made, it is ground to the desired cross-section and then split so it can be slipped over a piston and into a ring

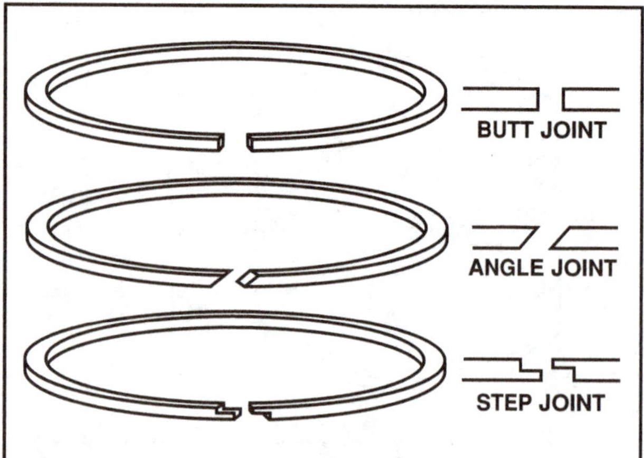

Figure 1-26. Of the three types of joints used in piston ring gaps, the butt joint is the most common in aircraft engines.

groove. The point where a piston ring is split is called the **piston ring gap**. The gap can be a simple butt joint with flat faces, an angle joint with angled faces, or a step joint. [Figure 1-26]

Since the piston rings expand when the engine reaches operating temperature, the ring must have a specified clearance between the ring gap faces. If the gap is too large, the two forces will not close up enough to provide an adequate seal. On the other hand, an insufficient gap will result in the ring faces binding against each other and the cylinder wall causing cylinder wall scoring.

When installing piston rings, the ring gaps must be staggered, or offset, to ensure that they do not align with each other. This helps prevent combustion chamber gases from flowing past the rings into the crankcase. This **blow-by**, as it is often called, results in a loss of power and increased oil consumption. If three piston rings are installed on one piston, it is common practice to stagger the ring gaps 120 degrees from each other.

In order for piston rings to seal against the cylinder wall, the rings must press against the cylinder wall snugly. Furthermore, the rings must exert equal pressure on the entire cylinder wall as well as provide a gas-tight fit against the sides of the ring grooves. The two broad types of piston rings used in reciprocating engines are compression rings or oil rings. [Figure 1-27]

Compression rings prevent gas from escaping past the piston during engine operation and are placed in the ring grooves immediately below the piston head. The number of compression rings used on each piston is determined by the type of engine and its design. However, most aircraft engines typically

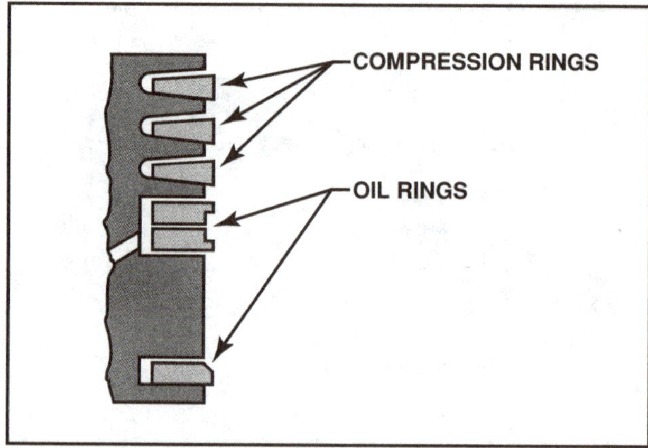

Figure 1-27. Compression rings are installed in the upper ring grooves and help prevent the combustion gases from escaping by a piston. Oil rings, on the other hand, are installed near the middle and bottom of a piston and control the amount of oil applied to the cylinder wall.

use two or three compression rings on each piston. The cross section of a compression ring can be rectangular, wedge shaped, or tapered. A rectangular compression ring fits flat against a cylinder wall with a large contact area to provide a tight seal. However, the large contact area also takes longer to **seat**, or wear enough so that the contour of the ring exactly matches the contour of the cylinder wall. On the other hand, tapered rings are beveled to reduce their contact area which help reduce friction and hasten ring seating. [Figure 1-28]

Wedge shaped rings also have a beveled face that promotes ring seating. In addition, wedge shaped rings are beveled and, therefore, require a beveled ring groove. However, less material is cut away in making a beveled ring groove so both the ring land and groove are stronger. The beveled shape also

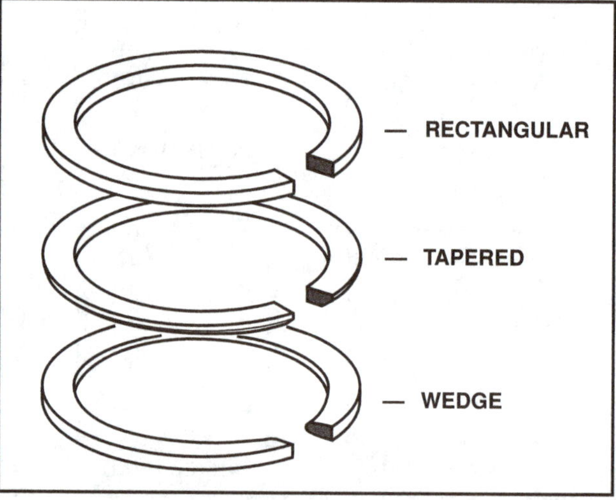

Figure 1-28. Of the three different ring cross sections, the tapered face presents the narrowest bearing edge to the cylinder wall to help reduce friction and hasten ring seating.

helps prevent the ring from sticking in the groove. Since compression rings receive the least amount of lubrication and are closest to the heat of combustion, they are more prone to sticking. Therefore, most compression rings are wedge shaped.

Oil rings control the amount of oil that is applied to the cylinder walls as well as prevent oil from entering the combustion chamber. The two types of oil rings that are found on most engines are oil control rings and oil scraper rings. **Oil control rings** are placed in the grooves immediately below the compression rings. Pistons may have one or more oil control rings and, depending on the type of piston, as many as two rings can be installed in a single ring groove. The primary purpose of oil control rings is to regulate the thickness of the oil film on the cylinder wall. To allow an oil control ring to remove excess oil and return it to the crankcase, small holes are drilled in the piston ring grooves, or ring lands. In addition, some pistons use **ventilated-type oil control rings** which typically consist of two or more pieces with small slots machined around the ring. These slots allow excess oil to drain into the ring groove so it can return to the crankcase.

If too much oil enters the combustion chamber, the oil will burn and leave a thick coating of carbon on the combustion chamber walls, the piston head, the spark plugs, and the valves. If this carbon should enter the ring grooves or valve guides it can cause the valves and piston rings to stick. Furthermore, carbon buildup can cause spark plug misfiring as well as detonation, preignition, or excessive oil consumption. To help prevent this, an **oil scraper ring** is used to regulate the amount of oil that passes between the piston skirt and the cylinder wall.

An oil scraper ring, sometimes called an **oil wiper ring**, usually has a beveled face and is installed in a ring groove at the bottom of the piston skirt. The ring can be installed with the beveled edge away from the piston head or in the reverse position, depending upon cylinder position and engine design. If the bevel is installed so that it faces the piston head, the ring pushes oil downward toward the crankcase. On the other hand, in the reverse position the scraper ring retains surplus oil above the ring on the upward piston stroke, and this oil is returned to the crankcase by the oil control rings on the downward stroke. It is very important that these rings be installed in accordance with the manufacturer's instructions. [Figure 1-29]

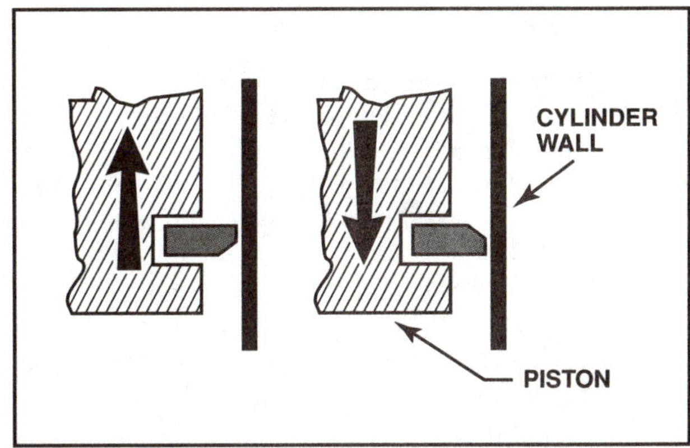

Figure 1-29. An oil scraper ring installed with its beveled edge away from the cylinder head forces oil upward along the cylinder wall when the piston moves upward. However, if the beveled edge is facing the cylinder head, the ring scrapes oil downward to the crankcase when the piston moves down.

PISTON PINS

A piston pin joins the piston to the connecting rod. A typical piston pin is machined in the form of a tube from a nickel-steel alloy forging that is case-hardened. Piston pins are sometimes called **wrist pins** because of the similarity between the relative motions of the piston and the connecting rod and that of the human arm.

Piston pins may be stationary, semifloating, or full-floating. As their name implies, **stationary piston pins** are held tightly in place by a setscrew that prevents movement. **Semifloating piston pins**, on the other hand, are retained stationary in the connecting rod by a set clamp that engages a slot in the pin. **Full-floating** piston pins are free to rotate in both the connecting rod and the piston, and are used in most modern aircraft engines.

A piston pin must be held in place laterally to prevent it from rubbing and scoring the cylinder walls. Three devices that are used to hold a piston pin in place are circlets, spring rings, and metal plugs. A **circlet** is similar to a snap ring that fits into a groove cut into each end of the piston boss. A **spring ring** also fits into grooves cut into the ends of a piston boss but consists of a single circular spring-steel coil. Both circlets and spring rings are used primarily on earlier piston engines. The more current practice is to install a plug of relatively soft aluminum called a **piston-pin plug**. These plugs are inserted into the open ends of the piston pins and provide a good bearing surface against the cylinder walls. However, due to the plug's soft aluminum construction and cylinder lubrication, the metal-to-metal contact causes no damage to the cylinder walls.

CYLINDERS

The cylinder provides a combustion chamber where the burning and expansion of gases takes place to produce power. Furthermore, a cylinder houses the piston and connecting rod assembly as well as the valves and spark plugs. When designing and constructing a cylinder, manufacturers must look at several factors. For example, a cylinder must be strong enough to withstand the internal pressures developed during engine operation yet be lightweight to minimize engine weight. In addition, the materials used in the construction of a cylinder must have good heat-conducting properties for efficient cooling. And finally, a cylinder assembly must be comparatively easy and inexpensive to manufacture, inspect, and maintain.

A typical air-cooled engine cylinder consists of a cylinder head, barrel, mounting flange, skirt, cooling fins, and valve assembly. On some of the earliest two- and four-cylinder horizontally opposed engines, the cylinder barrels were cast as part of the crankcase halves. This required the use of removable cylinder heads. However, on almost all modern engines, the individual cylinders are cast as a component, separate from the crankcase, and the heads are permanently attached during the manufacturing process. To do this, the cylinder head is expanded through heating and then screwed down onto a chilled cylinder barrel. A gas-tight joint results when the head cools and contracts and the barrel warms up and expands. [Figure 1-30]

Figure 1-30. The cylinder assembly along with the piston assembly, connecting rods, crankshaft, and crankcase constitute the power section of a reciprocating engine.

CYLINDER BARRELS

Generally speaking, the material used to construct a cylinder barrel must be as light as possible, yet have the proper characteristics for operating under high temperatures and pressures. Furthermore, a cylinder barrel must possess good bearing characteristics as well as high tensile strength. The most commonly used material that meets these requirements is a high-strength steel alloy such as chromium-molybdenum steel, or nickel chromium molybdenum steel.

Cylinder barrels are machined from a forged blank, with a **skirt** that projects into the crankcase and a **mounting flange** that is used to attach the cylinder to the crankcase. The lower cylinders on radial engines and all the cylinders on inverted engines typically employ cylinders with extended cylinder skirts. The longer skirt helps keep oil from draining into the combustion chamber and causing hydraulic lock after an engine has been shut down. The exterior of a cylinder barrel consists of several thin **cooling fins** that are machined into the exterior cylinder wall and a set of threads that are cut at the top of the barrel so that it can be screwed into the cylinder head.

The inside of a cylinder, or **cylinder bore**, is usually machined smooth to a uniform, initial dimension and then honed to a final dimension. However, some cylinder bores are machined with a slight taper. In other words, the diameter of the top portion of the barrel is slightly smaller than the diameter at the cylinder skirt. This is called a **choke bore cylinder** and is designed to compensate for the uneven expansion caused by the higher operating temperatures and larger mass near the cylinder head. With a choke bore cylinder, the greater expansion at the top of the cylinder is compensated for by the taper, resulting in a uniform cylinder diameter at normal operating temperatures. The amount of choke is usually between .003 and .005 inches. [Figure 1-31]

The inside wall of a cylinder barrel is continually subject to the reciprocating motion of the piston rings. Therefore, in an effort to minimize cylinder barrel wear and increase barrel life, most cylinder walls are hardened. The two most common methods used to provide a hard wearing surface are through nitriding and chrome plating. **Nitriding** is a form of case hardening that changes the surface strength of steel by infusing the metal with a hardening agent.

During the nitriding process, a cylinder barrel is first ground to the required size and smoothness and then placed in a special furnace filled with

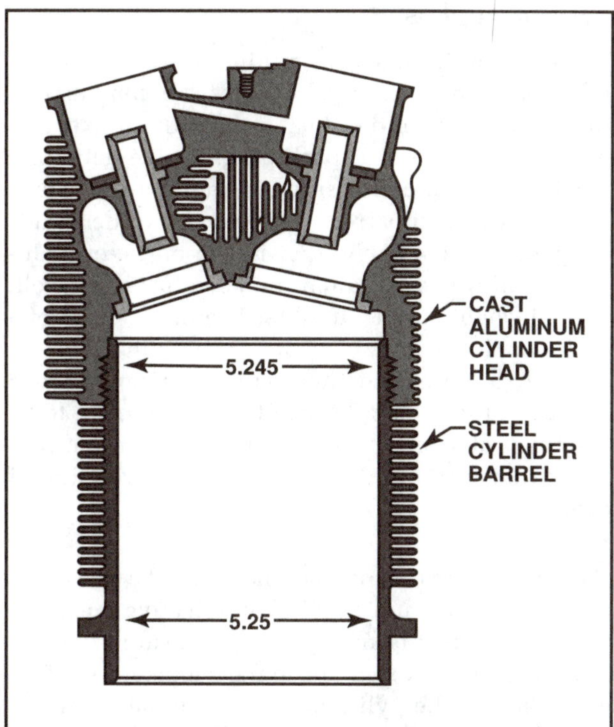

Figure 1-31. In most reciprocating engines, the greater mass of the cylinder head retains heat and expands thereby causing the upper portion of the cylinder to expand more than the lower portion. However, with a choke-bored cylinder, the diameter at the top of the cylinder is less than the diameter at the bottom of the cylinder which helps compensate for the uneven expansion.

ammonia gas. The furnace heats a cylinder barrel to approximately 1,000 degrees Fahrenheit and breaks down the ammonia gas into nitrogen and hydrogen. The steel in the cylinder barrel contains a small percentage of aluminum and the nitrogen combines with the aluminum to form a layer of hard, wear-resistant aluminum nitrides. The depth of a nitrided surface depends on the length of time it is exposed to the ammonia gas but a typical thickness is approximately 0.020 inch. However, the surface hardness gradually decreases with depth until the hardness is the same as the core metal.

Since nitriding is not a plating or coating, it changes a cylinder bore by only two to four ten thousandths of an inch. This dimensional change requires a cylinder to be honed to an accurate, micro-smooth finish after the nitriding process is complete. Most manufacturers identify a nitrided cylinder by applying a band of blue paint around the cylinder base, or to certain cooling fins.

One of the problems with nitrided cylinders is that they do not hold oil for extended periods of time. This problem increases a cylinder's susceptibility to corrosion and, for this reason, if an engine is left out of service for any extended period, the cylinder walls should be coated with a sticky preservative oil.

Chrome plating refers to a method of hardening a cylinder by applying a thin coating of chromium to the inside of aircraft cylinder barrels. Chromium is a hard, natural element which has a high melting point, high heat conductivity, and a very low coefficient of friction. The process used to chrome plate a cylinder is known as **electroplating**.

Chromed cylinders have many advantages over both plain steel and nitrided cylinders. For example, chromed cylinders are less susceptible to rust or corrosion because of chromium's natural corrosion resistance. Therefore, chromed cylinders tend to wear longer. Another benefit of chrome plating is that once a cylinder wears beyond its usable limits, it may be chrome plated back to its original size. To help you identify a cylinder that has been chrome plated, a band of orange paint may be applied around the cylinder base or to some of the cooling fins.

A problem associated with chrome plating cylinders is that, in its natural state, chromium is so smooth that it will not retain enough oil to provide adequate lubrication for the piston rings. To overcome this problem, a reverse current is sent through a cylinder for a controlled period of time after the chromium has been applied. The current causes microscopic surface cracks to open up and form a network of interconnecting cracks that help hold lubricating oil on the cylinder wall. This procedure is often referred to as **chrome channeling**. [Figure 1-32]

Figure 1-32. This figure illustrates a reproduction of a photomicrograph of the tiny cracks that form in chrome plating once a reverse current is applied. These cracks retain oil and thus aid in lubrication.

As a general rule, engines with chrome plated cylinders tend to consume slightly more oil than engines with nitrided or steel cylinders. The reason for this is that the plating channels retain more oil than the piston rings can effectively scavenge. Furthermore, chrome plated cylinders are typically more difficult to seal, or break-in, immediately after an engine is overhauled. This is caused by the oil film on the cylinder wall not allowing the necessary wear, or seating, of the piston rings during the break-in period.

In an effort to overcome the shortcomings of chrome plated and nitrided cylinders, some new plating processes have been developed. One of these processes involves mechanically impregnating silicon carbide particles onto a chromed cylinder wall, instead of channeling. The silicon carbide provides a somewhat rough finish so it retains lubricating oil, yet is still smooth enough to allow effective oil scavenging. Furthermore, the silicon carbide provides a surface finish that is more conducive to piston ring seating during the engine break-in period. This plating process is commonly referred to as either **CermiCrome** or **NuChrome** plating.

In another type of plating process called **CermiNil**, nickel with silicon carbide particles, is used for the plating material. The nickel, although not as durable as chromium, provides for an extremely hard finish while the silicon carbide particles increase the hardness of the material and aid in lubricating oil retention. A unique characteristic in this process is that the silicon carbide particles are infused throughout the plating instead of only to the surface. This tends to further increase the cylinders wearability while the surface finish is smooth enough to allow for effective oil scavenging.

CYLINDER FINISHES

In the past, engine manufacturers applied special paints to the exterior of cylinder barrels to protect the cylinder from corrosion. In addition, this special paint would change color when exposed to high temperatures, indicating a possible overheat condition that may have damaged the cylinders. Textron-Lycoming cylinders are typically painted with a gray enamel that appears burned when exposed to excessive heat. Similarly, Teledyne Continental cylinders are treated with a gold paint that turns pink when subjected to an overheat condition.

CYLINDER HEADS

The cylinder head acts as a lid on the cylinder barrel to provide an enclosed chamber for combustion. In addition, cylinder heads contain intake and exhaust valve ports, spark plugs, valve actuating mechanisms, and also serve to conduct heat away from the cylinder barrels. Air-cooled cylinder heads are generally made of either forged or die-cast aluminum alloy because aluminum conducts heat well, is lightweight, and is durable. The inner shape of a cylinder head may be flat, semi-spherical, or peaked, to resemble the shape of a house roof. However, the semi-spherical type has proved to be the most satisfactory because it is stronger and provides for more rapid and thorough scavenging of exhaust gases.

Cooling fins are cast or machined onto the outside of a cylinder head and provide an effective means of transferring heat from the cylinder head to the surrounding air. However, due to the temperature differences across the cylinder head, it is necessary to provide more cooling-fin area on various sections of a cylinder head. For example, since the exhaust valve region is typically the hottest part of the internal surface, more fin area is provided around the portion of the cylinder head that contains the exhaust valve. On the other hand, the intake portion of the cylinder head typically has few cooling fins because the fuel/air mixture cools this area sufficiently.

After a cylinder head is cast, spark plug bushings, or inserts, are installed. Typically, each cylinder head has two spark plugs for increased performance. On older engines, spark plug openings consisting of bronze or steel bushings were shrunk and screwed into the cylinder head. However, in most modern engines, stainless steel **Heli-Coil** spark plug inserts are used. The use of Heli-Coil inserts allows for the repair of damaged threads by replacing the insert.

To allow the fuel/air mixture to enter the cylinder as well as let the exhaust gases exit, intake and exhaust ports are machined into each cylinder head. The surfaces around each of these ports are also machined to permit the attachment of the intake and exhaust manifolds. To provide an adequate seal, a synthetic rubber seal is typically used between the cylinder head and intake manifold. However, because of the heat associated with the exhaust gases, a metal seal is generally used with the exhaust manifold. Each manifold is held in place by a mounting flange and a series of mounting studs that are threaded into the cylinder head. [Figure 1-33]

Figure 1-33. The threaded studs used to attach the intake and exhaust manifolds typically remain threaded into the cylinder head unless a stud needs to be replaced.

CYLINDER NUMBERING

It is sometimes necessary to refer to a specific area on an engine or a specific cylinder. Therefore, it is important that you be familiar with the established engine directions and the manufacturer's system of cylinder numbering. For example, regardless of how an engine is mounted in an aircraft, the propeller shaft end is always referred to as the front of an engine, and the accessory end is always the rear of an engine. Furthermore, when referring to either the right or left side of an engine, always assume you are viewing the engine from the rear, or accessory, end. By the same token, crankshaft rotation is also referenced from the rear of an engine and is specified as either clockwise or counterclockwise.

In order to identify a specific cylinder, all engine cylinders are numbered. However, the numbering system used on an opposed engine is not standard. For example, while both Teledyne Continental and Textron-Lycoming make four- and six-cylinder horizontally opposed engines, each manufacturer uses a different cylinder numbering system. As an example, Continental starts its cylinder numbering with the most rearward cylinder while Lycoming begins with the most forward. About the only similarity between the two systems is that the odd numbered cylinders are on the right while the even numbered cylinders are on the left. [Figure 1-34]

Unlike opposed engines, all radial engines are numbered in the same way. For example, single-row radial engine cylinders are numbered consecutively starting with the top cylinder and progressing clockwise as viewed from the rear of the engine. However, on double-row radial engines, all odd-numbered cylinders are in the rear row, and all even numbered cylinders are in the front row. For example, the top cylinder of the rear row is the number one cylinder, while the number two cylinder is the first cylinder in the front row clockwise from the number one cylinder. The number three cylinder is the next

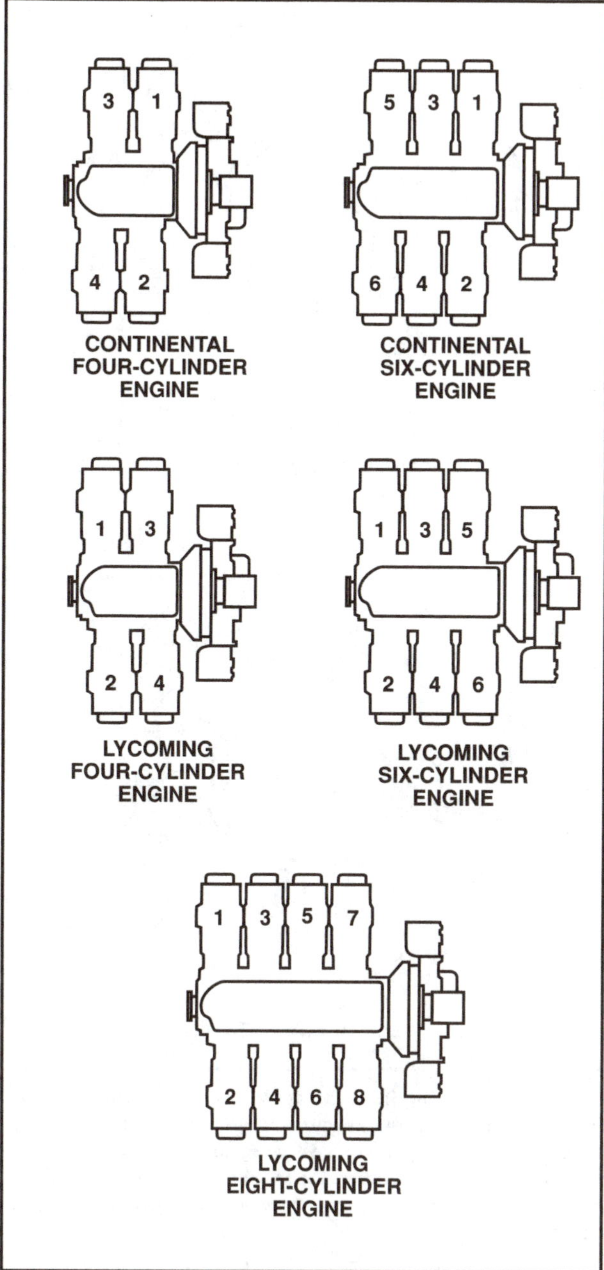

Figure 1-34. Since the cylinder numbering varies from manufacturer to manufacturer, you should always refer to the appropriate service information or the numbers indicated on each cylinder flange to determine how the cylinders on a specific engine are numbered.

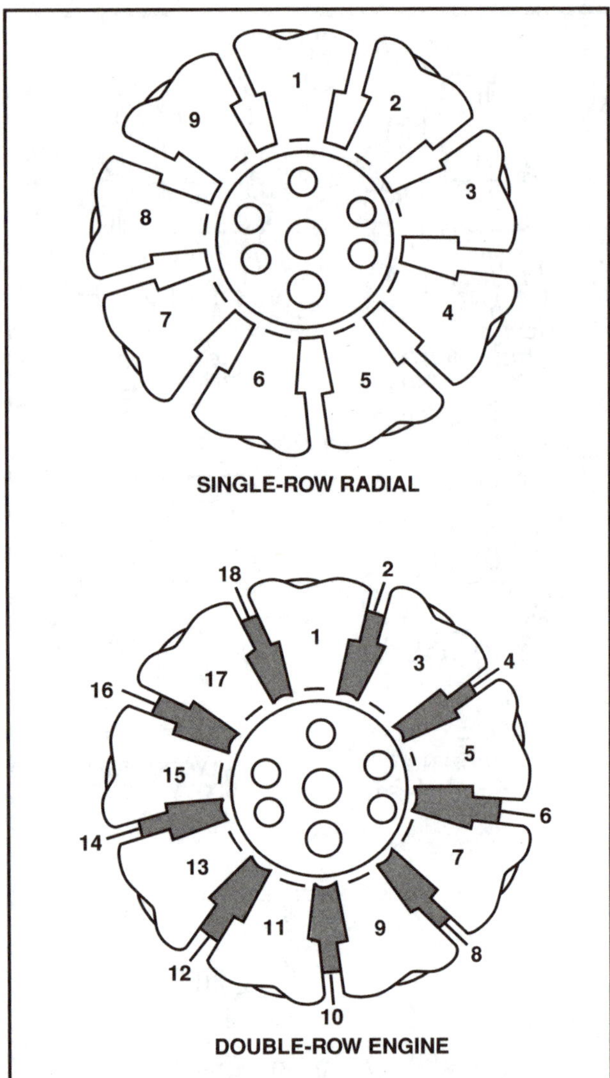

Figure 1-35. Looking from the accessory end forward, all single-row radial engines are numbered consecutively beginning at the top cylinder and progressing clockwise. On twin-row radials, however, the front row of cylinders are all even numbered while the rear row of cylinders are odd numbered.

cylinder clockwise from the number two cylinder but is in the rear row. [Figure 1-35]

VALVES

Engine valves regulate the flow of gases into and out of a cylinder by opening and closing at predetermined times in the combustion process. Each cylinder has at least one **intake valve** and one **exhaust valve**. The intake valve controls the amount of fuel/air mixture that enters a cylinder through the intake port, while the exhaust valve allows the exhaust gases to exit the cylinder through the exhaust port.

The valves used in aircraft engine cylinders are subject to high temperatures, corrosion, and extreme

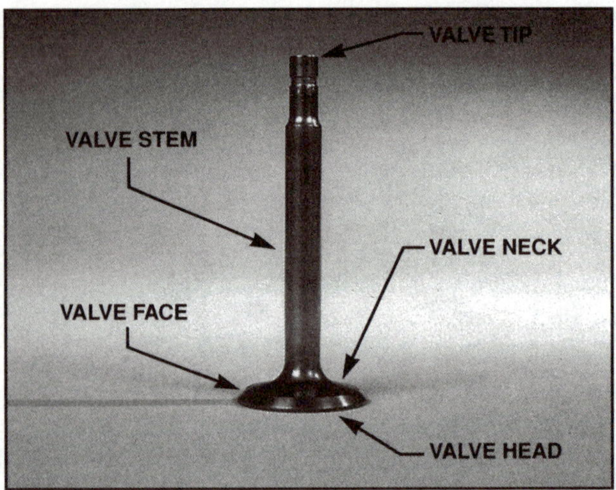

Figure 1-36. The basic components of a poppet valve include the valve head, valve face, valve neck, valve stem, and valve tip.

operating stresses. Therefore, valves must be constructed of metals that are able to resist these attritional factors. For example, intake valves operate at lower temperatures than exhaust valves and, therefore, are typically made of chrome, nickel, or tungsten steel. However, since exhaust valves must endure much higher temperatures they are usually made of more heat resistant metals such as inconel, silicon-chromium or cobalt-chromium alloys.

As mentioned, each cylinder must have at least one intake and one exhaust valve; however, on some high powered engines, two intake and two exhaust valves are provided for each cylinder. The most common type of valve used in aircraft engines is the **poppet valve** which gets its name from the popping action of the valve. [Figure 1-36]

Poppet valves are classified according to their head shape which may come in four basic designs: the flat-headed valve, the semi-tulip valve, the tulip valve, and the mushroom valve. As its name implies, the **flat-head valve** has a flat head and is typically used only as an intake valve in aircraft engines. The **semi-tulip** valve has a slightly concave area on its head while the **tulip** design has a deep, wide indented area on its head. On the other hand, **mushroom** valves have convex heads and are not commonly found on aircraft engines. [Figure 1-37]

The valve face is that portion of the valve that creates a seal at the intake and exhaust ports. A valve face is typically ground to an angle of between 30 and 60 degrees to form a seal against the **valve seat** when the valve is closed. In some engines, the intake valve face is ground to 30 degrees while the exhaust valve face is ground to 45 degrees. The

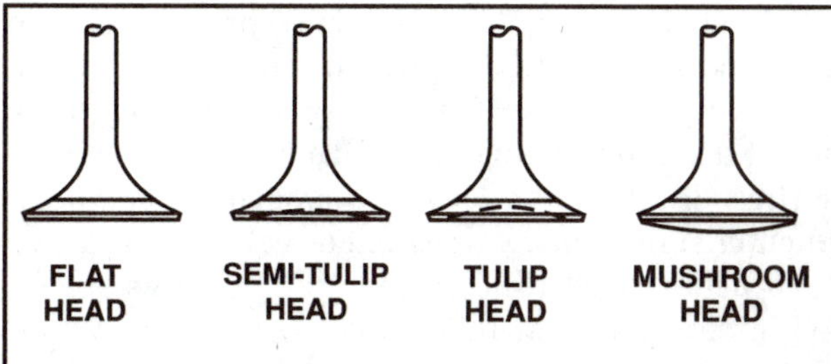

Figure 1-37. Aircraft engine valves are classified according to their head profile.

engine manufacturer specifies the exact angle which is based on airflow, efficiency, and sealing ability. Valve faces are often made more durable by welding **Stellite**, an alloy of cobalt and chromium, to the valve face. Once applied, the face is ground to the correct angle. Stellite resists high temperatures and corrosion and withstands the shock and wear associated with valve operation.

The **valve stem** acts as a pilot to keep the valve head properly aligned as it moves back and forth. Most valve stems are surface hardened to resist wear and are joined to the valve head at the **valve neck**. The **tip** of a valve stem is also hardened to withstand both wear and hammering. In some cases, a **rotator cap** is placed over a valve tip to increase service life. A groove is machined around the valve stem near the tip for a **split key** or **keeper key** which acts as a lock ring to keep the valve spring retaining washers in place and hold the valve in the cylinder head. [Figure 1-38]

On some radial engines, the valve stems have an additional groove below the split key groove. This second groove is used to hold a **safety circlet** or **spring ring**, which prevents the valve from falling into the cylinder in the event the valve tip breaks off.

To help dissipate heat better, some exhaust valve stems are hollowed out and then partially filled

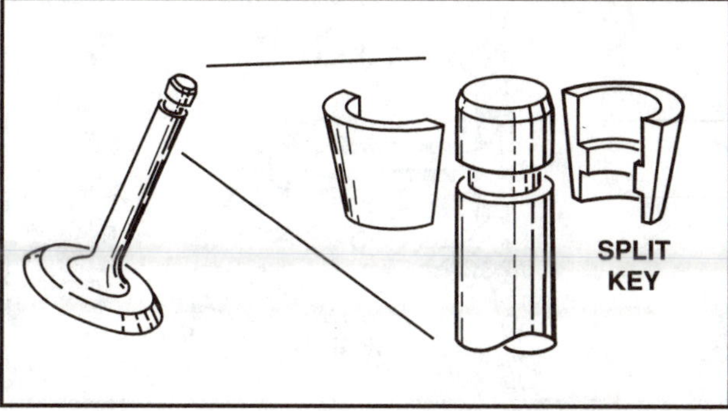

Figure 1-38. The groove near the tip of a valve stem allows a split retainer key to hold spring tension on a valve as well as keep the valve from falling into the cylinder.

with **metallic sodium**. When installed in an operating engine, the sodium melts when the valve stem reaches approximately 208 degrees Fahrenheit. The melted sodium circulates naturally due to the up and down motion of the valve and helps carry heat from the valve head into the stem where it is dissipated through the cylinder head. In some cases, sodium filled valves can reduce a valve's operating temperature by as much as 400 degrees Fahrenheit. [Figure 1-39]

When overhauling an aircraft engine, you must determine if the old valves are sodium filled or not. As a general rule, Teledyne Continental engines do not use sodium filled valves, while many Textron Lycoming engines use sodium filled exhaust valves. In all cases, determine which type of valve should be installed and follow the manufacturer's recommendations and instructions.

Sodium is a dangerous material that burns violently when exposed to air. Because of this, sodium filled valves should never be cut, broken, or handled in a manner that would allow the sodium to come in contact with air. In all cases, sodium valves must be disposed of in an appropriate manner.

VALVE SEATING COMPONENTS

As discussed earlier, a valve's face must seat firmly against the cylinder head. To accomplish this, several

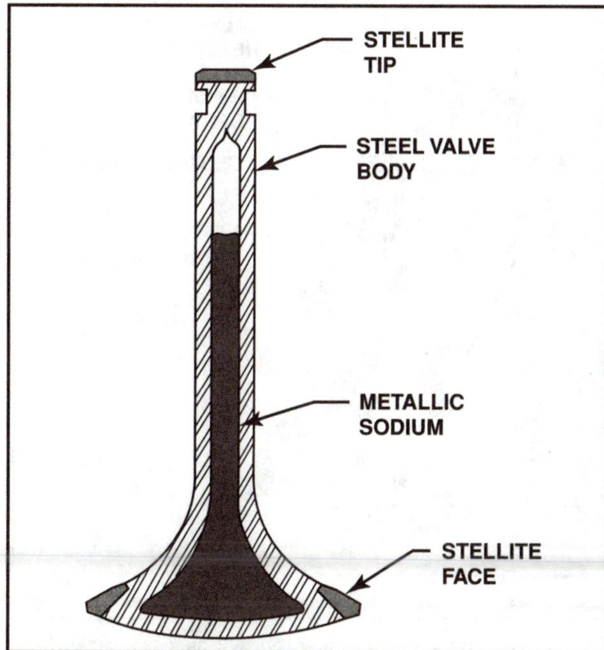

Figure 1-39. Some valves are filled with metallic sodium to reduce their operating temperatures. During operation, the sodium melts and transfers heat to the valve stem where the heat is conducted away by the cylinder head.

individual components are utilized, including valve seats, valve guides, valve springs, and valve spring retainers. [Figure 1-40]

A **valve seat** is a circular ring of hardened metal that provides a uniform sealing surface for the valve face. A typical valve seat is made of either bronze or steel and machined to an oversize fit. To install a valve seat, the cylinder head is heated and the valve seat is chilled and then pressed into the head with a special tool called a mandrel. When the assembly cools, the cylinder head shrinks and firmly retains the valve seat. Once installed, the valve seat is precisely ground to provide a sealing surface for the valve face. Typically, the valve seat is ground to the same angle as the valve face. However, there are some instances where a valve face may be ground to an angle that is one quarter to one degree shallower than the valve seat. The angular difference produces an interference fit that sometimes results in more positive seating.

A **valve guide** is a cylindrical sleeve that provides support to the valve stem and keeps the valve face aligned with the valve seat. A typical valve guide is made of steel, tin-bronze, or aluminum-bronze and is installed in a cylinder head with a shrink fit in the same manner as a valve seat.

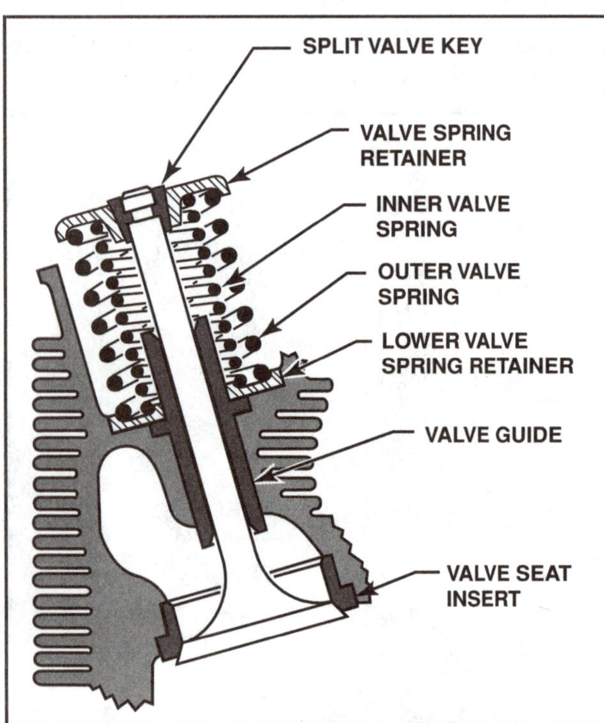

Figure 1-40. The valve seat insert provides a sealing surface for the valve face while the valve guide supports the valve and keeps it aligned with the seat. Valve springs close the valve and are held in place by a valve retainer and a split valve key.

Valve springs are helical-coiled springs that are installed in the cylinder head and provide the force that holds the valve face firmly against the valve seat. Most aircraft engines utilize two or more valve springs of different sizes and diameters to prevent a phenomenon called **valve float** or **valve surge**. Valve float occurs when the frequency of a valve spring begins to vibrate at its resonant frequency. When this occurs, the spring loses its ability to hold the valve closed. By installing two or more springs of different sizes, it is nearly impossible for both springs to vibrate at the same time, leaving one spring free to close the valve. Furthermore, two or more springs reduce the chance of failure due to breakage caused by heat or metal fatigue.

The valve springs are held in place by a **valve spring retainer** and a split valve key. A valve spring retainer seat is usually located between the cylinder head and the bottom of the valve spring, while a valve spring retainer is installed on the top of the valve spring. The retainer is fitted with a split valve key that locks the valve spring retainer to the valve stem.

VALVE OPERATING MECHANISMS

All reciprocating engines require a valve operating mechanism to open each valve at the correct time, hold it open for a certain period, and then close the valve. A typical valve-operating mechanism consists of an internally driven camshaft or cam ring that pushes against a valve lifter. The valve lifter, or tappet, transmits the force from the cam to a push rod, which in turn, actuates a rocker arm to depress and open the valve against the valve spring tension that holds the valve closed. [Figure 1-41]

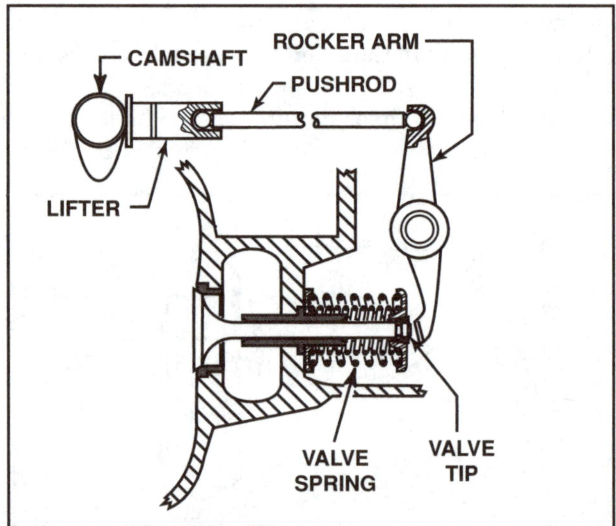

Figure 1-41. The components in a typical valve operating mechanism, include a camshaft or cam ring, a tappet or lifter, a push rod, and a rocker arm.

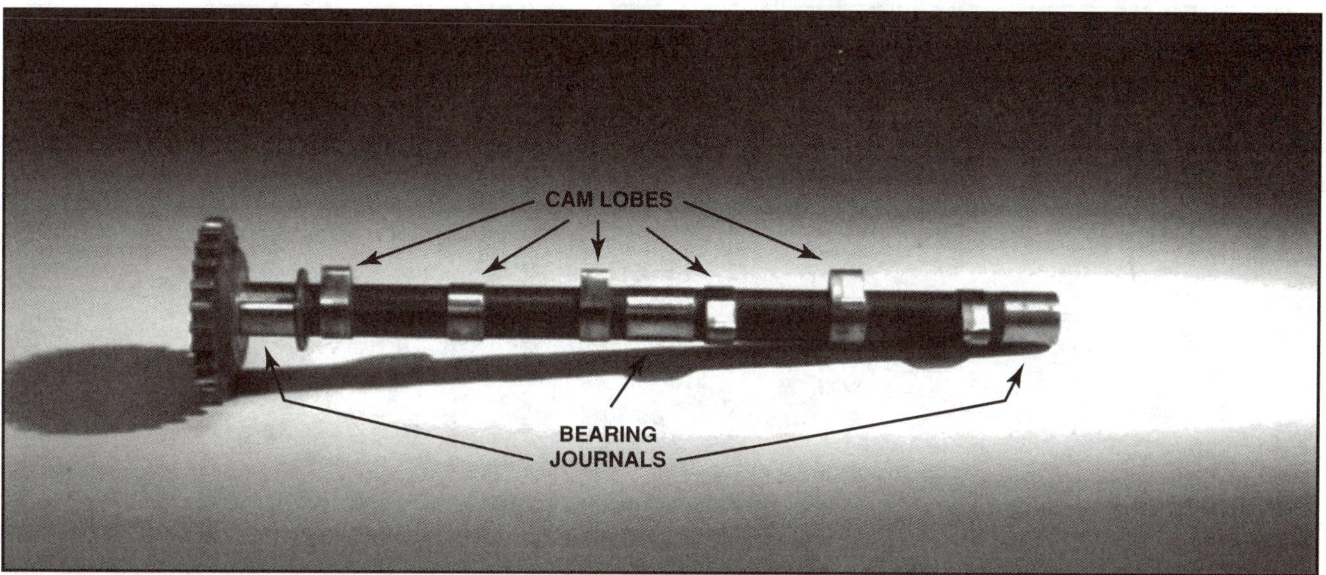

Figure 1-42. The raised lobe on a camshaft transforms the rotary motion of the camshaft to linear motion.

OPPOSED ENGINES

On an opposed engine, valve operation begins with a **camshaft**. A typical camshaft consists of a round shaft with a series of cams, or **lobes**, that transform the circular motion of the crankshaft to the linear motion needed to actuate a valve. The shape of a cam lobe determines valve lift, which is the distance a valve is lifted off its seat, and valve duration, the length of time a valve is held open. Since a cam lobe bears against another surface, all lobes are hardened to resist wear. [Figure 1-42]

The camshaft is supported by several bearing journals that ride in a set of camshaft bosses which are cast into the crankcase. The force used to rotate a camshaft is derived from the crankshaft through a set of gears. The speed of rotation is always one-half that of the crankshaft. The reason for this is that on a four-stroke engine, each cylinder fires once for every two crankshaft rotations. Therefore, each valve must open and close once for every two rotations of the crankshaft. [Figure 1-43]

As the camshaft rotates, the lobe raises the valve lifter. A **valve lifter**, or **tappet**, transmits the lifting force of the cam to the push rod. Valve lifters in opposed engines can be solid or hydraulic. As its name implies, a **solid lifter** consists of a solid metal cylinder that transmits the lifting force from the camshaft to the push rod. The camshaft end of a solid lifter is flat with a polished surface, while the push rod end contains a spherical cavity that houses the push rod. Holes drilled in the lifter allow oil to flow through the lifter to lubricate the push rod.

Most opposed engines use **hydraulic lifters**. Hydraulic lifters differ from solid lifters in that a hydraulic lifter uses oil pressure to cushion the impact of the cam lobe striking the lifter and removes any play within the valve operating mechanism. A typical hydraulic lifter consists of a movable cam follower face, a lifter body, a hydraulic plunger and plunger spring, a check valve, and a

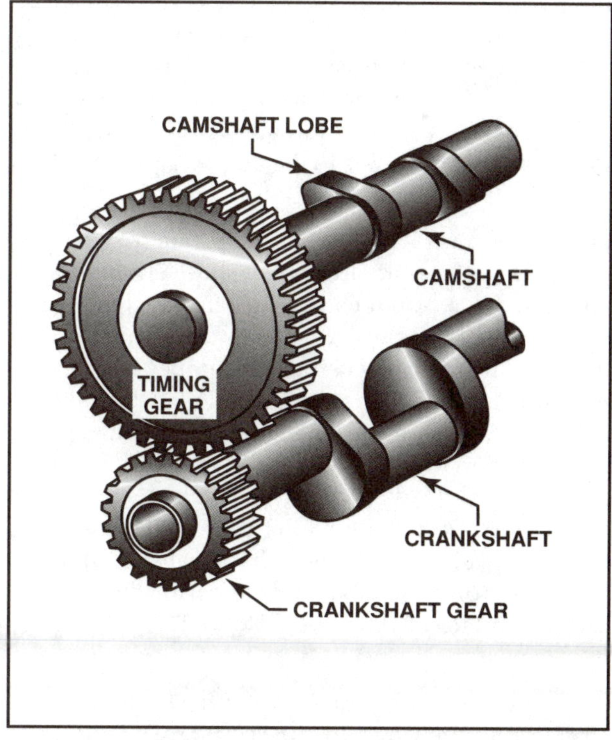

Figure 1-43. In a typical opposed engine, the camshaft timing gear has twice as many teeth as the gear on the crankshaft. In this configuration, the camshaft is driven at one-half the crankshaft's rotational speed.

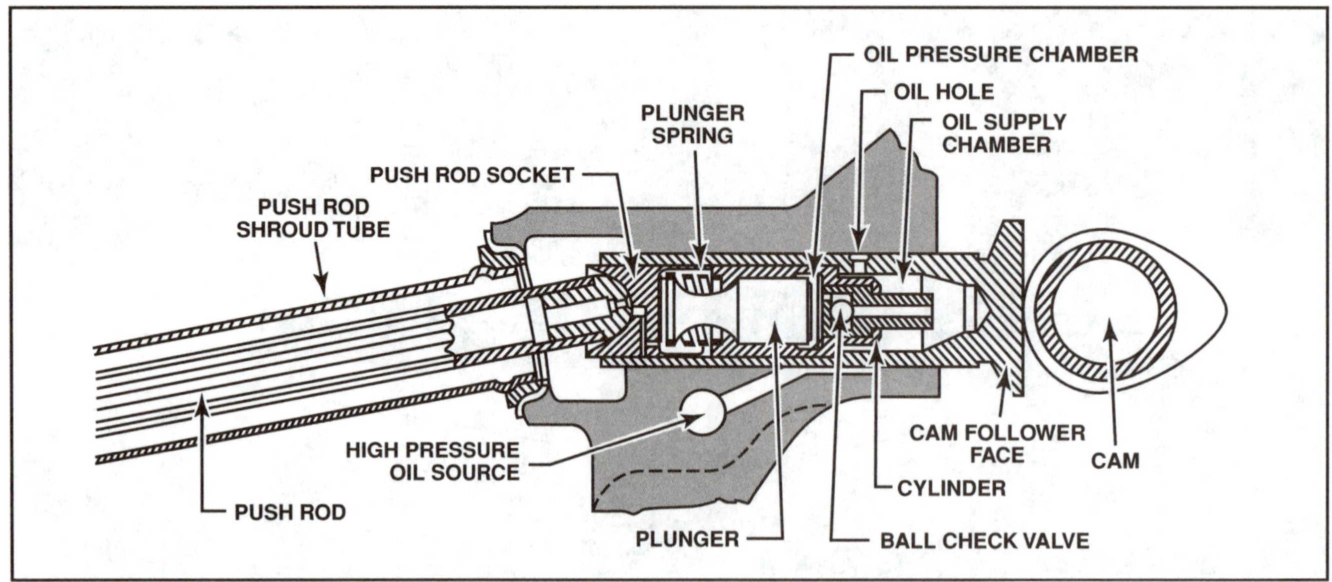

Figure 1-44. A typical hydraulic lifter consists of a push rod socket, a hydraulic plunger and plunger spring, a check valve, a lifter body, and a cam follower face.

push rod socket. The entire lifter assembly sits in a hole in the crankcase and rests on the camshaft. [Figure 1-44]

The **cam follower face** is the smooth hardened surface of the lifter that rides on the cam lobe. When the follower face is on the back side of a cam lobe, the hydraulic **plunger spring** forces the **hydraulic plunger** outward so that the **push rod socket** presses firmly against the push rod. As the hydraulic plunger moves outward, a **ball check valve** moves off its seat and allows oil to flow from the **oil supply chamber** to the **oil pressure chamber**.

Once the camshaft rotates and the cam lobe strikes the follower face, the lifter body and cylinder move outward. This action causes the check valve to seat and trap oil in the oil pressure chamber. This trapped oil acts as a cushion to dampen the abrupt pressure applied to the push rod. Once the valve is off its seat, some oil leaks between the plunger and the cylinder to compensate for any dimensional changes in the valve operating mechanism caused by heating. Immediately after the valve closes, the ball check valve moves back off its seat and oil flows from the supply chamber to the pressure chamber in preparation for another cycle.

A second type of hydraulic lifter is similar in construction to the lifter just discussed, except a disk-type check valve is used instead of a ball check valve. In either case, the hydraulic lifter eliminates all the clearances between the various components of a valve operating mechanism, thereby reducing the amount of hammering and wear. [Figure 1-45]

As mentioned earlier, the lifting force of the cam lobe is transmitted through a lifter and a **push rod**. A typical push rod consists of a hollow steel or aluminum alloy tube with polished ends. One end of the push rod rides in the valve lifter socket while the other end fits into a socket in the rocker arm. Push rods typically have holes drilled on each end to allow oil to flow from the valve lifter to the valve components in the cylinder head. On most aircraft reciprocating engines, the push rods are enclosed by a thin metal shroud, or tube, that runs from the

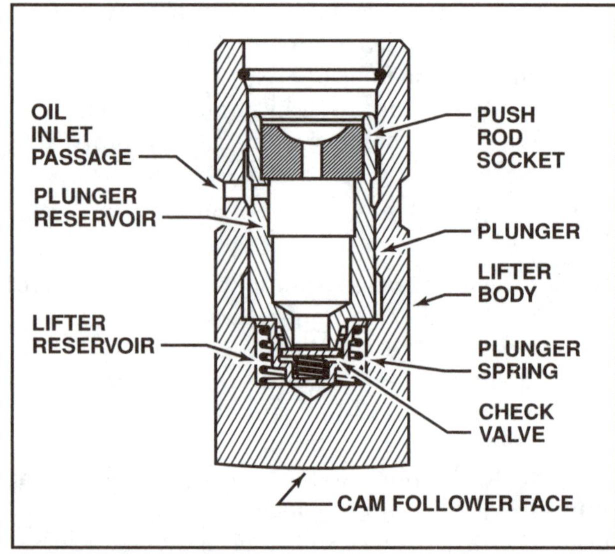

Figure 1-45. A second type of hydraulic lifter uses a disk-type check valve instead of a ball check valve.

cylinder head to the crankcase. In many cases, these tubes also provide a return path for the oil that is pumped up to the cylinder head.

A **rocker arm** is a pivoting lever located in the cylinder head that changes the lifting movement of the push rod into the downward motion needed to open a valve. A typical rocker arm is made of forged steel and has a cup-shaped socket to hold the push rod end and a flat surface that pushes against the valve tip. [Figure 1-46]

The entire rocker arm pivots on a shaft that is suspended between two **rocker arm bosses** that are cast into the cylinder head. Each rocker arm boss contains a bronze bushing that provides a bearing surface for the shaft. Each rocker shaft is machined with a press fit and held in place by the rocker-box cover or by covers inserted over the outside of each rocker arm boss. When the push rod pivots the rocker arm, the rocker arm exerts force against the valve springs to open the valve. The amount the valve opens and the length of time the valve remains open is based on the shape of the cam lobes. [Figure 1-47]

For many engines, the FAA has approved the use of a more modern style rocker arm. This newer style rocker arm is forged out of a single piece of stainless steel and rotates on a roller bearing that is pressed into the rocker arm. In addition, the valve end of the rocker arm is fitted with a roller. The use of a roller helps eliminate side loads when the valve is depressed which, in turn, helps minimize valve guide and valve stem wear.

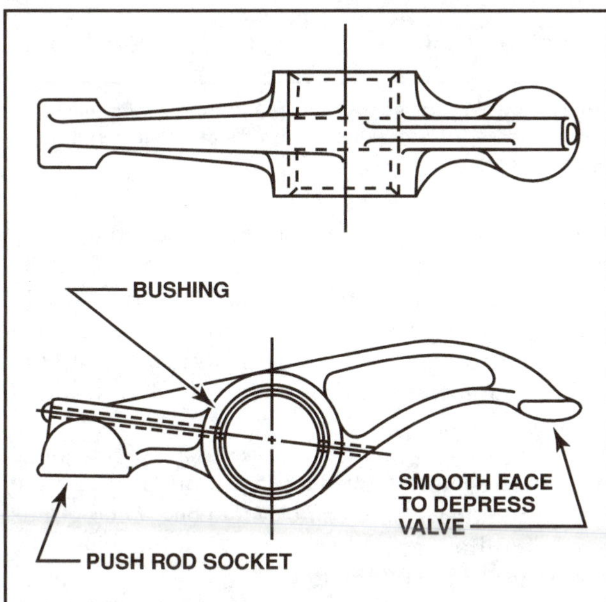

Figure 1-46. One end of this rocker arm is cup-shaped to hold a push rod, while the other end is machined smooth to push against the tip of a valve stem. When rotated by the push rod, the rocker arm pivots on its center bushing and depresses the valve.

Figure 1-47. A rocker arm is supported by a shaft that is suspended between a set of rocker arm bosses.

RADIAL ENGINES

Radial engines utilize some of the same components in their valve operating mechanisms as opposed engines, but there are some significant differences. For example, in place of a camshaft, a radial engine uses one or two **cam rings**, depending on the number of cylinder rows. A cam ring is a circular piece of steel with a series of raised cam lobes on its outer edge. A cam ring for a typical seven cylinder engine has three or four lobes while a cam ring in a nine cylinder engine has four or five lobes. The cam lobes in a radial engine differ from those in an opposed engine in that each lobe is constructed with a **cam ramp** on each side of a lobe. This ramp reduces the initial shock of an abruptly rising lobe. The smooth area between the lobes is called the **cam track**. On a single row radial engine a single cam ring with two cam tracks is used. One track operates the intake valve while the second track operates the exhaust valve.

In a single row radial engine, the cam ring is usually located between the propeller reduction gearing and the front end of the power section. In a twin row radial engine, a second cam for the valves in the rear row is installed between the rear end of the power section and the supercharger section.

The cam ring is mounted concentrically with the crankshaft and is driven by the crankshaft through a series of gears. However, unlike a camshaft, the

5 Cylinders		7 Cylinders		9 Cylinders		Direction of Rotation
Number of Lobes	Speed	Number of Lobes	Speed	Number of Lobes	Speed	
3	1/6	4	1/8	5	1/10	With Crankshaft
2	1/4	3	1/6	4	1/8	Opposite Crankshaft

Figure 1-48. Assume that you want to know how fast the cam turns on a certain nine cylinder engine. If the cam ring has four lobes and rotates opposite the crankshaft, the cam ring turns at 1/8 the crankshaft speed.

speed at which a cam ring rotates varies. To determine a given cam ring's rotation speed, you must know the number of lobes on the cam ring, the cam ring's direction of rotation relative to the crankshaft, and the number of cylinders on the engine. The direction of cam ring rotation varies on different engines and depends on whether the cam ring has internal or external drive teeth. Externally driven cam rings turn in the same direction as the crankshaft, while internally driven rings turn opposite from crankshaft rotation. [Figure 1-48]

If a table is not available, cam ring speed can be determined by using the formula:

$$\text{cam ring speed} = \frac{1}{\text{number of lobes} \times 2}$$

In place of a cam follower face, a radial engine uses **cam rollers**. A cam roller consists of a small wheel that rolls along the cam track. When the cam roller rides over a lobe on the cam ring, the roller pushes against a **tappet** that is enclosed in a **tappet guide**. The tappet, in turn, actuates a push rod that performs the same function as an opposed engine push rod. Radial engine rocker arms have adjusting screws and lock screws that allow adjustment of the push rod-to-rocker arm clearance. In addition, many radial engine rocker arms are equipped with **rollers** on their valve ends to reduce friction, eliminate side loading on the valve stem, and lessen tip deformation. [Figure 1-49]

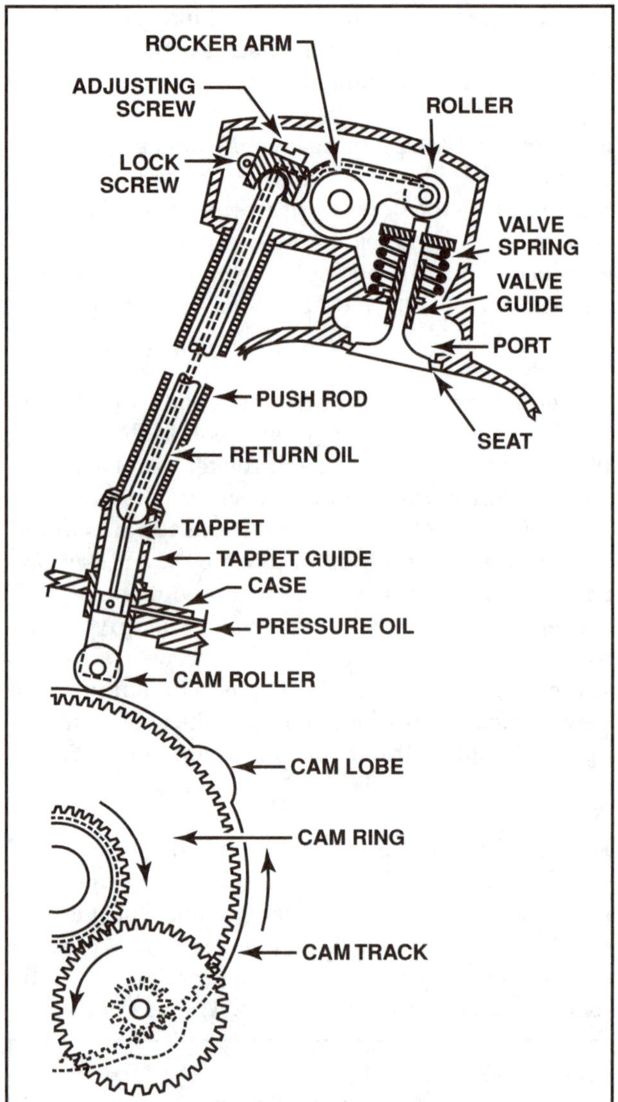

Figure 1-49. A radial engine valve operating mechanism performs the same functions as the mechanism used in an opposed engine.

VALVE CLEARANCE ADJUSTMENT

Valve clearance describes the clearance, or space, between the tip of the valve stem and the rocker arm face. For an engine to run properly, the correct valve clearance must be maintained. During normal engine operating temperatures, the cylinder assemblies expand and force the cylinder head, along with its valve operating components, further away from the crankcase. However, due to their relatively small mass, the push rods expand less. As a result, the clearance between the rocker arm and valve stem increases. If this valve clearance is not controlled, an engine will run poorly, and valve damage could result.

An engine manufacturer's maintenance manual specifies either a cold or hot valve clearance. As its name implies, a **cold clearance** is set when the engine is cold and, due to the expansion properties discussed earlier, is typically less than the **hot** or **running clearance**, which is set when the engine is hot. Engines that require valve adjustments have adjustment screws and locknuts mounted in their rocker arms at the push rod fitting. To set the valve clearance, the engine is turned until the piston in the cylinder being adjusted is at the beginning of the power stroke. With the piston in this position, there is no pressure applied to either of the push rods and the rocker arm is as far from the valve tip as possible. Once this is done a thickness gauge of the correct dimension is placed between the rocker arm and the valve stem. If you cannot insert the thickness gauge between the two surfaces, or if the thickness gauge moves too freely between the surfaces, the clearance must be adjusted. To do this, the locknut in the rocker arm is loosened and the adjustment screw is turned until the face of the rocker arm just touches the feeler gauge. The locknut is then tightened to hold the adjustment screw in place.

Engines utilizing hydraulic lifters do not require periodic valve adjustments since they automatically maintain a zero running valve clearance during normal operation. Because of this, hydraulic lifters are often called **zero clearance**, or **zero lash lifters**. However, the valve operating mechanism clearance is typically checked during engine overhaul. If the clearance is not within specifications, push rods of varying lengths are installed until the correct clearance is achieved. For example, if the valve clearance is too great, a longer push rod is installed whereas, if the valve clearance is too small, a shorter push rod is used.

Some large radial engines incorporate a **floating cam ring** that requires a special procedure when adjusting valve clearance. To obtain the correct adjustment, the cam ring must be seated to eliminate cam bearing clearance. This usually involves depressing two valves to seat the cam ring, allowing an accurate measurement on a third valve. This procedure is repeated for each cylinder.

PROPELLER REDUCTION GEARS

The amount of power produced by an aircraft reciprocating engine is determined by several factors, including the amount of pressure exerted on the pistons during each power stroke and the number of power strokes completed in a given time period. As a general rule, the faster an engine turns, the more power it produces; however, this same rule does not apply to propellers. For example, as a propeller blade tip approaches the speed of sound, the propeller can no longer efficiently convert the power produced by an engine into thrust. In other words, most propellers must be operated at a specific speed to achieve maximum efficiency. Therefore, to allow an engine to run at the speed required to produce its maximum rated power output while, at the same time, maintain a reasonable propeller speed, some high-powered engines must use a propeller reduction gear system. As its name implies, a propeller reduction gear system permits a propeller to turn slower than the engine. This allows an engine to turn at a relatively fast speed and a propeller to turn at a more efficient slower speed. Reduction gear systems currently used on aircraft engines utilize spur gears, planetary gears, or a combination of the two.

If you recall from your General textbook, **spur gears** have their teeth cut straight across their circumference and can be either external or internal. The simplest type of reduction gearing consists of two external tooth spur gears, one small gear on an engine crankshaft and one larger gear on the propeller shaft. When configured this way, the amount of reduction is based primarily on the size of the propeller shaft gear. The larger the gear, the slower the propeller turns. However, this reduction system does have some disadvantages. For example, when using two external tooth spur gears, the propeller turns opposite the crankshaft. Furthermore, since the propeller shaft is off-center from the engine crankshaft, the propeller acts like a gyroscope and places severe torsional loads on the engine case. This requires the use of a stronger and heavier crankcase. [Figure 1-50]

One way to overcome some of the drawbacks of a simple spur gear arrangement is to use an internal-tooth spur gear on the propeller shaft and an external-tooth spur gear on the crankshaft. In addition to

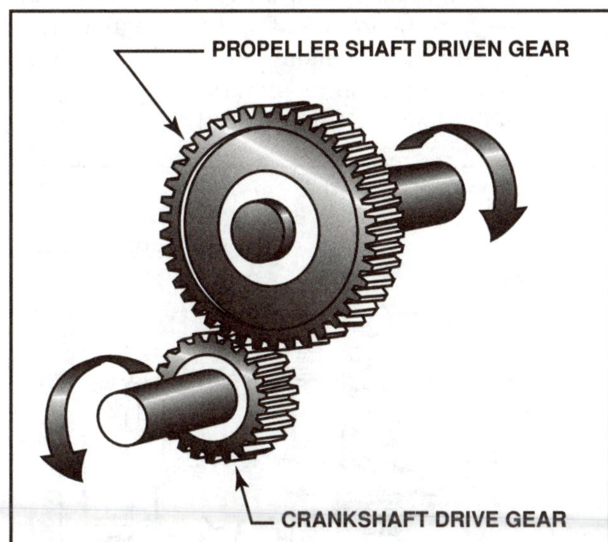

Figure 1-50. With a gear reduction system that uses two externally driven spur gears, the amount of reduction is determined by the ratio of the gear teeth. For example, if the drive gear has 25 teeth and the driven gear has 50 teeth, a ratio of 1:2 exists and the propeller turns at one half the crankshaft speed.

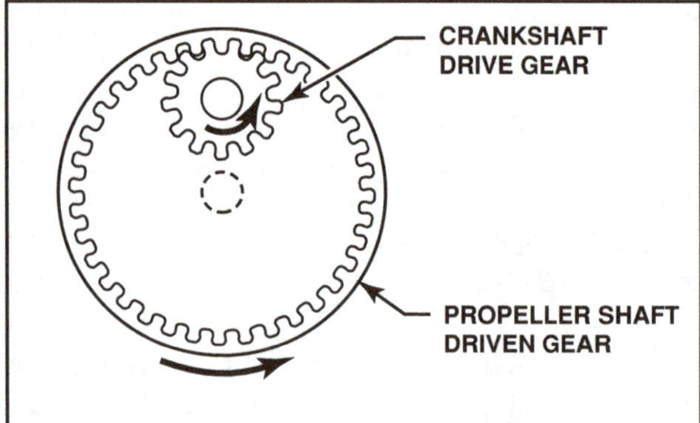

Figure 1-51. With a gear reduction system that uses one internal-tooth gear and one external-tooth gear the propeller and crankshaft turn in the same direction and are more closely aligned.

allowing the propeller to turn in the same direction as the engine, this arrangement keeps the propeller shaft more closely aligned with the crankshaft, thereby eliminating much of the stress placed on the crankcase. [Figure 1-51]

Whenever a reduction gear is used that does not keep the propeller shaft perfectly aligned with the crankshaft, additional vibration is induced into an engine. To help minimize this vibration, some engines use a quill shaft between the crankshaft and propeller shaft. A **quill shaft** is a hardened steel shaft that is splined on both ends and installed between two gears, or shafts, to absorb torsional vibration. One end of the quill shaft fits into the front end of the crankshaft, while the opposite end is inserted into the front end of the propeller drive shaft. With this arrangement, the quill shaft drives the propeller and absorbs vibration from the gear reduction mechanism. [Figure 1-52]

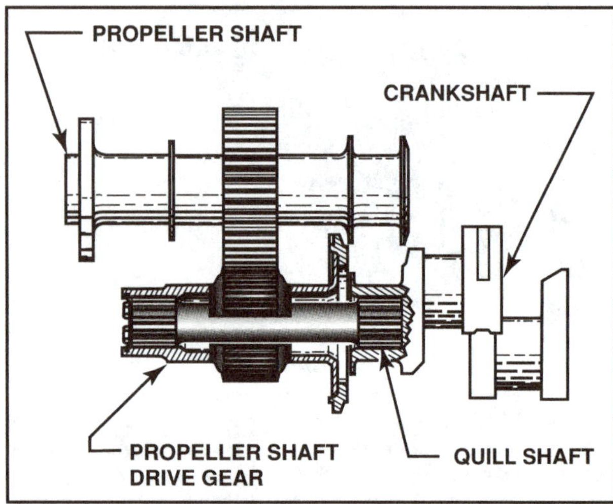

Figure 1-52. A quill shaft minimizes torsional vibration between the propeller shaft and the crankshaft.

One of the best ways to reduce vibration is to keep the propeller shaft and crankshaft perfectly aligned. A gear reduction system that does this is the **planetary reduction gear**. In a planetary gear system, the propeller shaft is attached to a housing which contains several small gears called **planetary gears**. The planetary gears rotate between a **sun gear** and a **ring** or **bell** gear. The crankshaft drives either the sun gear or ring gear, depending on the individual installation. The planetary gear reduction system keeps the propeller shaft aligned with the crankshaft, transmits power with a minimum of weight and space, and keeps the propeller's direction of rotation the same as the engine. Planetary gears are used on some horizontally opposed engines, as well as radial and turboprop engines. [Figure 1-53]

The reduction rate that a particular gearing arrangement achieves is found by the formula:

$$\text{Gear Ratio} = \frac{\text{Teeth On Ring Gear} + \text{Teeth On Sun Gear}}{\text{Teeth On Ring Gear}}$$

Notice that neither the number of teeth on the planetary gears nor the number of planetary gears attached to the spider enter into the computation for gear reduction. For example, if there are 72 teeth on the ring gear and 36 teeth on the sun gear, the propeller turns at a ratio of 1.5 to 1. However, reduction ratios are traditionally expressed in whole numbers, so this example is expressed as a 3-to-2 reduction. In other words, the crankshaft must

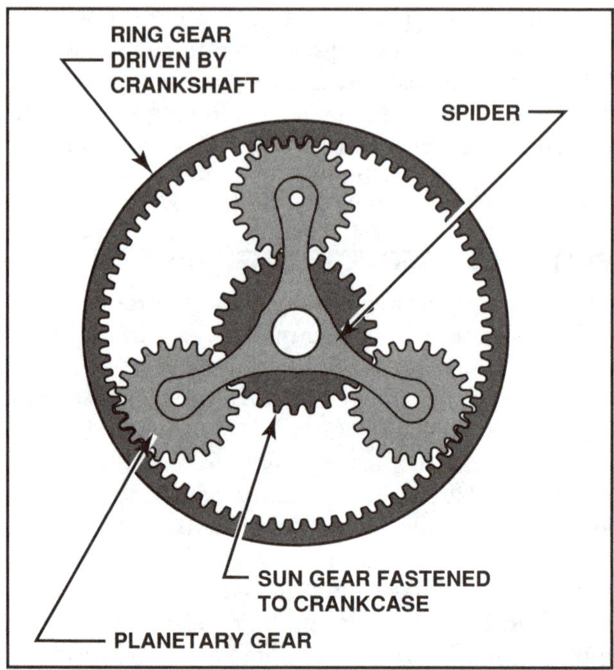

Figure 1-53. In a planetary gear reduction system, the propeller is attached to the planetary gear spider and the crankshaft turns either the sun gear or the ring gear.

turn three revolutions for every two revolutions of the propeller shaft.

PROPELLER SHAFTS

All aircraft reciprocating engines are equipped with a propeller shaft. As an aviation technician you must be familiar with the various types of propeller shafts including the tapered, splined, and flanged.

Tapered propeller shafts were used on most of the early, low-powered engines. On a tapered propeller shaft, the shaft tapers, or gets smaller in diameter, as you move out toward the end of the shaft. To prevent a propeller hub from rotating on a tapered shaft, one or more key slots are milled into the shaft. In addition, the end of the shaft is threaded to receive a propeller retaining nut. [Figure 1-54]

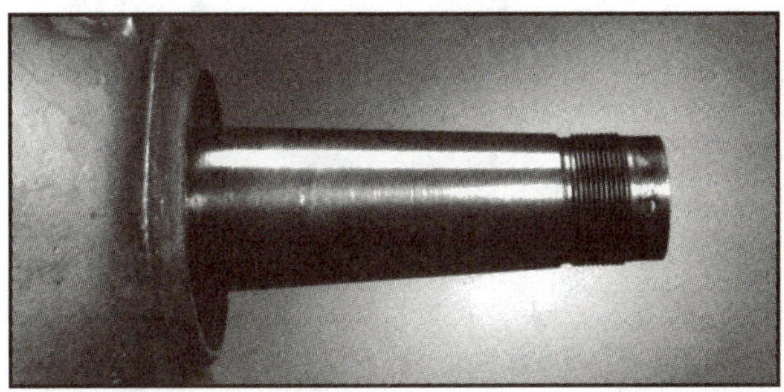

Figure 1-54. As you can see, a tapered propeller shaft changes in diameter along its length and utilizes a metal key to keep a propeller from rotating.

Increases in engine power demanded a stronger method of attaching propellers. Therefore, most high powered radial engines use **splined propeller shafts**. A spline is a rectangular groove that is machined into the propeller shaft. Most splined shafts have a master spline that is approximately twice the size of any other spline. This master spline assures that a propeller is attached to a propeller shaft a specific way so that vibration is kept to a minimum. [Figure 1-55]

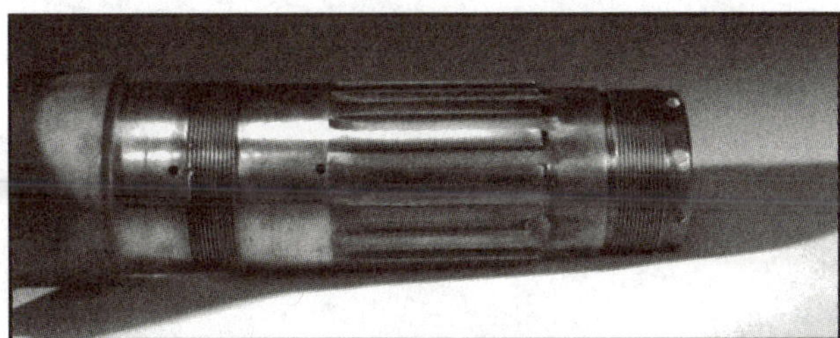

Figure 1-55. All splined propeller shafts are identified by an SAE number. For example, SAE 50 identifies a splined shaft that meets SAE design specifications for a 50 size shaft. The SAE number does not refer to the actual number of splines.

Figure 1-56. Before you remove a propeller from a flanged propeller shaft, it is a good practice to mark the propeller hub and flange. This makes reattaching the propeller easier since you can identify how the propeller should be positioned.

Most modern horizontally opposed aircraft engines use a **flanged propeller shaft**. With this type of propeller shaft, a flat flange is forged directly onto the end of a crankshaft and a propeller is bolted to the flange. To provide additional support for the propeller, most flanged propeller shafts incorporate a short shaft forward of the flange and a series of studs around the flange circumference. [Figure 1-56]

ENGINE IDENTIFICATION

Today, almost all reciprocating engines are identified by a series of letters and numbers that indicate the type and size of the engine. For simplicity, most manufacturers use the same identification system. In most cases, an engine identification code consists of a letter or series of letters followed by a number and model designation. The first letters indicate an engine's cylinder arrangement and basic configuration. A list of the letters used include:

- O - Horizontally opposed engine
- R - Radial engine
- I - In-line engine
- V - V-type engine
- T - Turbocharged
- I - Fuel injected
- S - Supercharged
- G - Geared nose section (propeller reduction gearing)
- L - Left-hand rotation (for multi-engine installations)
- H - Horizontal mounting (for helicopters)
- V - Vertical mounting (for helicopters)
- A - Modified for aerobatics

The numbers in an engine identification code indicate an engine's piston displacement in cubic inches. For example, an 0-320 indicates a horizontally opposed engine with a displacement of 320 cubic inches. Some engine identification codes include a letter designation after the displacement to indicate a model change or modification to a basic engine. You must check with the manufacturer's specification sheets to correctly interpret these letters, since their meaning differs among manufacturers.

Consider an LIO-360-C engine. This code designates an engine that has left hand rotation, is fuel injected and horizontally opposed, displaces 360 cubic inches, and is a C model. As a second example, a GTSIO-520-F engine is geared, turbo-supercharged, fuel injected, horizontally opposed, displaces 520 cubic inches, and is an F model.

OPERATING PRINCIPLES

ENERGY TRANSFORMATION

An aircraft engine is a form of **heat engine** that converts the chemical energy of fuel into heat energy. Once converted, the heat energy causes an increase in gas pressure within a cylinder. The increased gas pressure is then converted into mechanical energy when the expanding gases force the piston downward. Since the fuel used to produce heat is burned inside the engine, an aircraft engine is referred to as an **internal combustion** engine. When fuel is burned outside an engine to produce mechanical energy, the process is called **external combustion**.

A steam engine is an example of an external combustion engine. Fuel is burned in a boiler to heat water and produce steam. The steam is then channeled into an engine to force pistons to turn a crankshaft or spin a turbine. However, since external combustion engines do not effectively convert the heat provided by the fuel into work, they are relatively inefficient. This is offset somewhat by the low cost fuels required to operate an external combustion engine. As a result, external combustion engines remain a viable alternative for applications such as electrical powerplants.

Unlike external combustion engines, internal combustion engines require a specific type of fuel. For example, some automotive engines only burn liquified petroleum gases such as butane or propane, while others use diesel fuel, gasoline, or alcohol. Since aircraft reciprocating engines are internal combustion engines, they too require the use of a specific type of fuel. For example, most aircraft reciprocating engines require leaded fuel to provide upper cylinder lubrication and a specific octane rating to alleviate excessive operating temperatures. For a fuel to be used in a type certificated aircraft, the Federal Aviation Administration and engine manufacturer must approve its use.

Regardless of the type of internal combustion engine, the process of converting the chemical energy of fuel into mechanical energy is essentially the same. A fuel metering device, such as a carburetor or fuel manifold, first measures liquid fuel and then converts it into fuel vapor. Next, this vapor is mixed with the correct amount of air to produce a combustible mixture which is compressed and ignited within a cylinder. When the mixture burns, it releases energy and causes the noncombustible gases, such as nitrogen, to expand. Since air is composed of approximately 78% nitrogen, the expansion potential is substantial. The expanding gas exerts pressure on an engine's pistons, driving them downward to rotate the crankshaft and create mechanical energy. For simplicity, the process just described can be divided into a set sequence of timed events. This sequence is identical for all 4-stroke reciprocating engines. The individual events and the sequence in which they occur are listed here.

Intake — Fuel and air are drawn into a cylinder when the intake valve opens and the piston travels downward.

Compression — The fuel-air mixture is compressed in the cylinder by the upward motion of the piston.

Ignition — Once compressed, the fuel-air mixture is ignited by a spark.

Power — The burning gases expand and force the piston downward which, in turn, rotates the crankshaft to produce work.

Exhaust — The burned gases are scavenged and forced out of a cylinder through the exhaust port as the piston moves upward a second time. Once the piston reaches the top of the cylinder, the sequence is repeated.

ENERGY TRANSFORMATION CYCLES

All engines continually repeat a cycle when they operate. One **cycle** represents one complete series of events that an internal combustion engine goes through to produce mechanical energy. In other words, one cycle includes the intake, compression, ignition, power, and exhaust events.

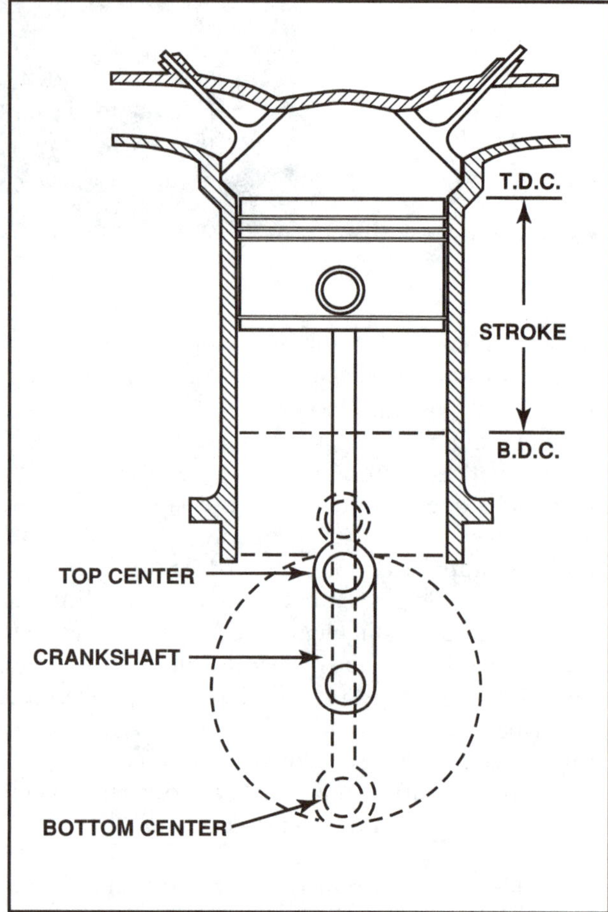

Figure 1-57. One stroke is equivalent to the distance a piston head travels between bottom dead center and top dead center. In all reciprocating engines, one complete stroke occurs with each 180 degrees of crankshaft rotation.

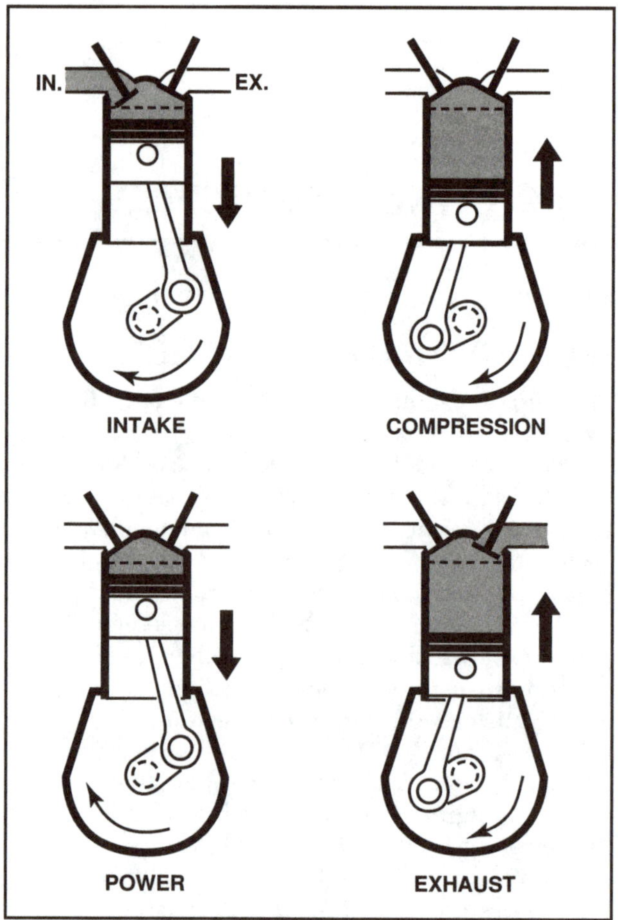

Figure 1-58. The four strokes that take place in a four-stroke, Otto cycle include the intake, compression, power, and exhaust.

The two operating cycles in general use today are the **four-stroke**, or **Otto cycle** developed by August Otto, and the **two-stroke cycle**. The majority of piston engines operate on the more efficient four-stroke cycle; however, there are several small, nonaviation powerplants that use the two-stroke cycle. A **stroke** is simply the total distance a piston travels between the outward and inward limits within a cylinder. In a cylinder, the most outward limit is referred to as **top dead center (TDC)** while the most inward limit is known as **bottom dead center (BDC)**. [Figure 1-57]

FOUR-STROKE CYCLE

As the name implies, the four-stroke cycle consists of four strokes, intake, compression, power, and exhaust. One complete four-stroke cycle requires two revolutions of the crankshaft. The four-stroke cycle is sometimes referred to as a constant volume cycle because the burning fuel inside the cylinder increases the gas pressure with almost no change in volume. [Figure 1-58]

In the four-stroke cycle, the exact timing of when the valves open and close and when ignition occurs varies considerably among engine types. However, timing is always determined by crankshaft position. In the following discussion, the timing of each event is specified in terms of crankshaft travel, and is measured in degrees of rotation, during the stroke that the event occurs. For example, the intake valve on a specific engine may open 15 degrees before top dead center while on the exhaust stroke. Since a certain amount of travel is required to fully open a valve, the specified timing represents the start of valve opening rather than the full-open valve position.

INTAKE STROKE

The intake stroke begins with the piston at top dead center and the intake valve open. During this stroke, crankshaft rotation pulls the piston downward thereby reducing the pressure within the cylinder. Lower pressure inside the cylinder allows air that is under atmospheric pressure to flow through the carburetor where it is mixed with the correct amount of fuel. The resulting fuel/air mixture then passes through an intake manifold pipe, down through an intake port, and past an intake valve into the cylinder. The quantity, or weight, of fuel and air that enters the cylinder is determined by the throttle position. For example, when the throttle is full open, the greatest amount of fuel and air enters a cylinder and the engine runs at its fastest speed.

COMPRESSION STROKE

Once a piston reaches bottom dead center on the intake stroke, the piston reverses direction and begins the compression stroke. Depending on the specific engine, the intake valve typically closes about 50 to 75 degrees past bottom dead center on the compression stroke. Delaying the closing of the intake valve until the piston is past bottom dead center allows the momentum of the incoming gases to charge the cylinder more completely. After the intake valve closes, the piston's continued upward travel compresses the fuel/air mixture to obtain the most favorable burning characteristics. As the piston approaches top dead center, the mixture is ignited by an electric spark provided by two spark plugs installed in each cylinder head. The exact time ignition occurs varies depending on the requirements of the specific engine, but is typically from 20 to 35 degrees before top dead center. By igniting the mixture before the piston reaches top dead center, complete combustion and maximum pressure are ensured when the piston begins the power stroke. Each manufacturer determines the optimum ignition point for each engine model.

POWER STROKE

As a piston moves through top dead center on the compression stroke, it reverses direction again to begin the power stroke. During the power stroke, the piston is pushed downward by the rapidly expanding gases within the cylinder. The temperature of these gases can exceed 3,000 degrees Fahrenheit while pushing down on the piston with a force in excess of 15 tons. However, as the burning gases expand, they cool considerably, exiting the cylinder at a reasonable temperature.

The linear motion produced by the back and forth movement of a piston is converted to rotary motion through the use of a connecting rod and crankshaft. The rotary motion is then used to drive a propeller or a gear case.

To aid in scavenging the exhaust gases out of a cylinder, the exhaust valve opens well before bottom dead center on the power stroke while there is still pressure in the cylinder. This positive pressure helps expel the exhaust gases out the exhaust port after the desired expansion of hot gases has been obtained. Proper exhaust gas scavenging is an important consideration in engine design since any exhaust products remaining in a cylinder will dilute the incoming fuel/air charge during the subsequent intake stroke. In addition, thorough exhaust gas scavenging helps control cylinder operating temperatures.

The rapid burning of a fuel/air charge in an engine produces a power impulse. If an engine is designed with uneven or widely spaced power impulses, excessive engine vibration may occur. For example, one and two cylinder engines have relatively few power impulses compared to four and six cylinder engines and, therefore, vibrate more. Consequently, more cylinders produce more power impulses and less vibration.

EXHAUST STROKE

As a piston travels through bottom dead center on the power stroke and starts upward on an exhaust stroke, it begins to expel the burned exhaust gases out the exhaust port. The speed at which exhaust gases leave a cylinder tends to cause the pressure within the cylinder to drop, leaving an area of low pressure. This low pressure speeds the flow of fuel and air into the cylinder as the intake valve begins to open. In order to maximize usage of the reduced cylinder pressure, the intake valve on a typical engine is timed to open anywhere from 8 to 55 degrees before top dead center, on the exhaust stroke.

VALVE TIMING

Proper valve timing is crucial for efficient engine performance. Valve timing is the term used to describe the point at which the intake and exhaust valves begin to open and close during the four-stroke cycle. For example, as previously discussed, the intake valve begins to open before the piston reaches top dead center on the exhaust stroke. This allows the piston to draw a greater quantity of fuel and air into the cylinder. The number of crankshaft degrees that the intake valve opens before the piston reaches top dead center is called **valve lead**. If the valve does not open at the proper time, the volume of fuel and air taken into the cylinder will be affected, causing the engine to run rough or not at all.

You may also recall that the exhaust valve remains open beyond top dead center and into the intake stroke. The number of degrees the exhaust valve remains open past top dead center is called **valve lag**. The combination of valve lead and lag is called **valve overlap** and represents the number of degrees that both the intake and exhaust valves are unseated. The primary purpose of valve overlap is to allow the fuel/air charge to enter the cylinder as early as possible to increase engine efficiency and aid in cylinder cooling. In addition, valve overlap takes advantage of the inertia in the outflowing exhaust gases to provide more complete exhaust gas scavenging.

As a piston passes bottom dead center on the intake stroke, valve lag is used again to keep the intake valve open into the compression stroke. This permits the maximum amount of fuel and air to enter the combustion chamber prior to compression. Valve lead, on the other hand, is incorporated a second time when the exhaust valve is opened prior to bottom dead center on the power stroke. If you recall, the exhaust valve is opened early to improve exhaust gas scavenging and to help remove heat from the cylinder. To help you better visualize valve movement through a complete engine cycle, some engine manufacturers provide a timing diagram in their maintenance manuals. [Figure 1-59]

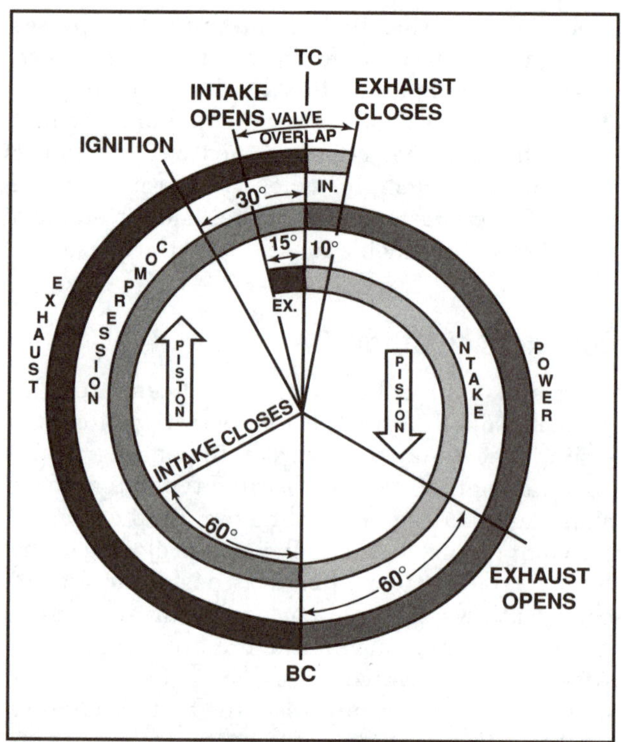

Figure 1-59. To read this diagram, begin at the inside of the spiral. Notice that the intake valve opens 15 degrees before top center on the exhaust stroke while the exhaust valve remains open 10 degrees into the intake stroke. As you follow the spiral into the compression stroke, notice that the intake valve closes 60 degrees past bottom center on the compression stroke. At this point, both valves are closed and ignition takes place at 30 degrees before top center on the compression stroke. As the cycle proceeds, the exhaust valve opens 60 degrees before bottom center on the power stroke and remains open throughout the exhaust stroke. The intake valve, on the other hand, opens 15 degrees prior to top center on the exhaust stroke.

In this example, notice that the valve lead and lag is greater near bottom center than it is near top center. The exhaust valve leads bottom center by 60 degrees and the intake valve lags by 60 degrees. On the other hand, when the piston is near top center, the intake valve leads top center by 15 degrees while the exhaust valve lags by 10 degrees. The reason for this is that the linear distance a piston travels for a given degree of crankshaft rotation varies from top center to bottom center. In other words, when the piston is at or near top center, it moves more per degree of crankshaft rotation than if the piston were at bottom center. [Figure 1-60]

As you can see, a piston moves further in the first 90 degrees of rotation than in the second 90 degrees. In addition, piston velocity is highest at the 90 degree point and lowest at top and bottom center positions. This reduction in speed at both top center and bottom center provides a smoother transition for the piston when it is changing its direction of travel.

Once you know the specific valve timing for an engine, you can calculate the amount of crankshaft rotation that each valve is open or closed. For example, given an intake valve that opens 15 degrees before top dead center and closes 45 degrees after bottom dead center, you can calculate the intake valve's **duration**, which is the amount of time the valve is open. In this example, once the intake valve opens, the piston travels 15 degrees to reach top center, 180 degrees to reach bottom center, and then 45 degrees past bottom center for a total of 240 degrees of rotation. By the same token, if an exhaust valve opens 70 degrees before bottom dead center and closes 10 degrees after top dead center, the piston travels 70 degrees to reach bottom center, 180 degrees to reach top center, and then an additional 10 degrees past top center for a total duration of 260 degrees. To determine how many degrees a crankshaft will rotate with both valves closed, or seated, you must determine the number of degrees between the point where the intake valve closes and the point where the exhaust valve opens. Given that the intake valve closes 45 degrees after bottom dead center on the compression stroke and the exhaust valve opens 70 degrees before bottom center on the

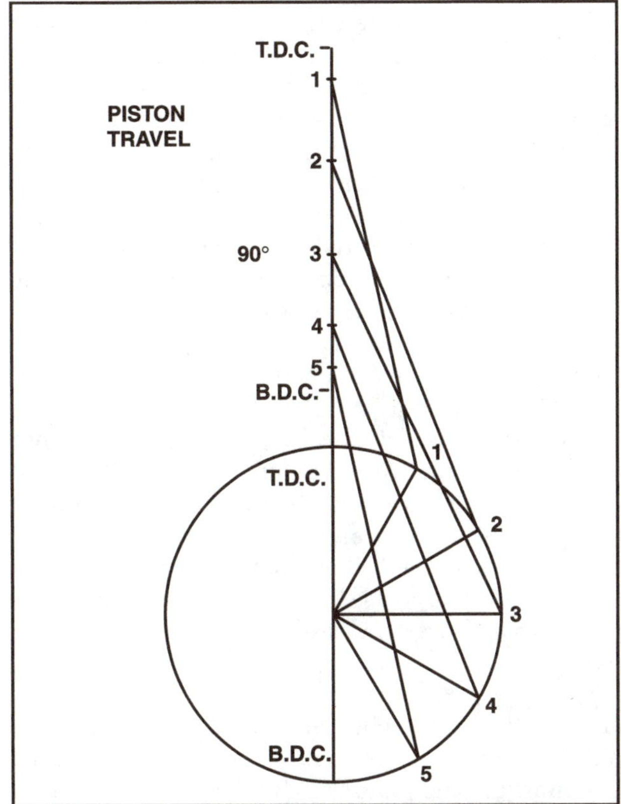

Figure 1-60. The circle divided into even segments represents the travel of a crankpin while the vertical line above the circle represents the path of a piston. To represent the connecting rod length, equal length lines are drawn from each segment line to the piston path. From the figure, you can see that a piston moves more per degree of travel when the piston is near top center than when it is near bottom center.

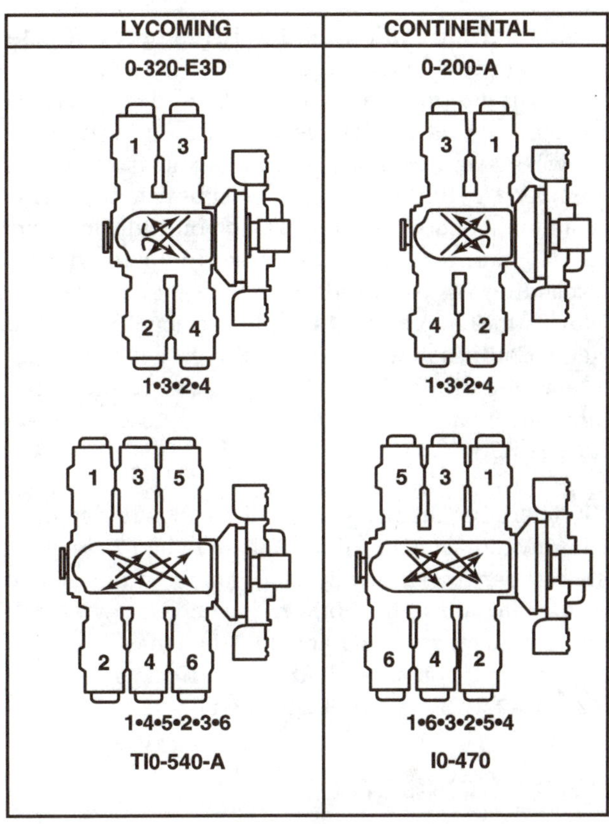

Figure 1-61. Notice that the firing pattern and cylinder numbering method varies between engine manufacturers and engine models.

intake stroke, the degree of travel with both valves seated is 245 degrees.

FIRING ORDER

An engine's firing order represents the sequence in which the ignition event occurs in different cylinders. Each engine is designed with a specific firing order to maintain balance and reduce vibration. For example, a four cylinder Continental model O-200-A has a firing order of 1-3-2-4. By the same token, a four cylinder Lycoming model O-320-E3D has the same firing order, but the cylinders are numbered differently. For this reason, caution should be exercised and manufacturer's maintenance instructions followed carefully. [Figure 1-61]

In radial engines, the firing order must follow a specific pattern that allows the power impulses to follow the motion of the crank throw during rotation. For example, on all single-row radial engines, the odd numbered cylinders fire in succession first, followed by the even cylinders. Therefore, the firing order on a seven cylinder radial engine is 1-3-5-7-2-4-6 while the firing order on a nine cylinder radial engine is 1-3-5-7-9-2-4-6-8.

A double-row radial engine is essentially two single-row radial engines that share a common crankshaft. Like the single-row radial, the power pulses must occur between alternate cylinders in each row, in sequence. In other words, two cylinders in the same row can never fire in succession. In addition, to balance the power pulses between the two rows, when a cylinder fires in one row, its opposite cylinder must fire in the second row. For example, consider a 14 cylinder double-row radial engine, consisting of two rows of seven cylinders each. If you recall from the discussion in the previous section, on a double-row radial engine, all the odd numbered cylinders are in the rear row while all the even numbered cylinders are in the front row. Therefore, if the number 1 cylinder fires in the back row, the cylinder opposite the number 1 cylinder in the front row must fire. In a 14 cylinder double-row engine, the number 10 cylinder is opposite the number 1 cylinder. The power pulses then go back and forth between rows in alternating cylinders to obtain a firing order of 1-10-5-14-9-4-13-8-3-12-7-2-11-6.

A method for computing the firing order of a 14 cylinder, double-row radial engine is to start with any cylinder number, 1 through 14 and either add 9 or subtract 5, whichever results in a number between 1 and 14. For example, if you start with the number **1** cylinder, 5 cannot be subtracted to arrive at a number between 1 and 14, so you add 9 to arrive at **10**. Then, since you cannot add 9 to 10 without exceeding 14, you need to subtract 5 to arrive at **5**. Now, add 9 to 5 to get **14**, and subtract 5 from 14 to get **9**. Continue this pattern until you have the complete 14 cylinder firing order. Once complete, the identical firing order of 1-10-5-14-9-4-13-8-3-12-7-2-11-6 results.

To determine the firing order of an 18 cylinder, double-row radial engine, the numbers 11 and 7 are used; that is, begin with any cylinder number from 1 to 18 and either add 11 or subtract 7, whichever will result in a number between 1 and 18. Once these numbers are applied, you should arrive at a firing order of 1-12-5-16-9-2-13-6-17-10-3-14-7-18-11-4-15-8.

TWO-STROKE CYCLE

The two-stroke cycle is similar to the four-stroke cycle in that the same five events occur in each operating cycle. However, the five events occur in two piston strokes rather than four strokes. This means that one cycle is completed in one crankshaft revolution. [Figure 1-62]

As a two-stroke cycle begins, the piston moves up and two events occur simultaneously. The piston compresses the fuel/air charge in the cylinder and creates an area of low pressure within the crankcase. This low pressure pulls fuel and air into the crankcase through a check valve. Once the piston is a few degrees before top dead center, ignition occurs and the fuel/air mixture begins to burn. As the piston passes top dead center the pressure from the expanding gases begin to force the piston downward on the power stroke. This downward stroke also compresses the fuel/air charge in the crankcase. As the piston approaches the bottom of the power stroke, the exhaust port is uncovered and spent gases are purged from the cylinder. A split second later, the piston uncovers the intake port and allows the pressurized fuel/air charge in the crankcase to enter the cylinder. The cycle then repeats itself as the piston compresses the fuel/air charge in the cylinder and draws a fresh fuel/air charge into the crankcase.

To help prevent the incoming fuel/air mixture from mixing with the exhaust gases, most two-stroke engines utilize pistons with baffled heads that deflect the fuel/air charge upward away from exiting exhaust gases. Baffled heads do not, however, completely eliminate the mixing problem. Since both the exhaust and intake events take place almost simultaneously, some of the fuel/air charge becomes diluted by the exhaust gases and some is

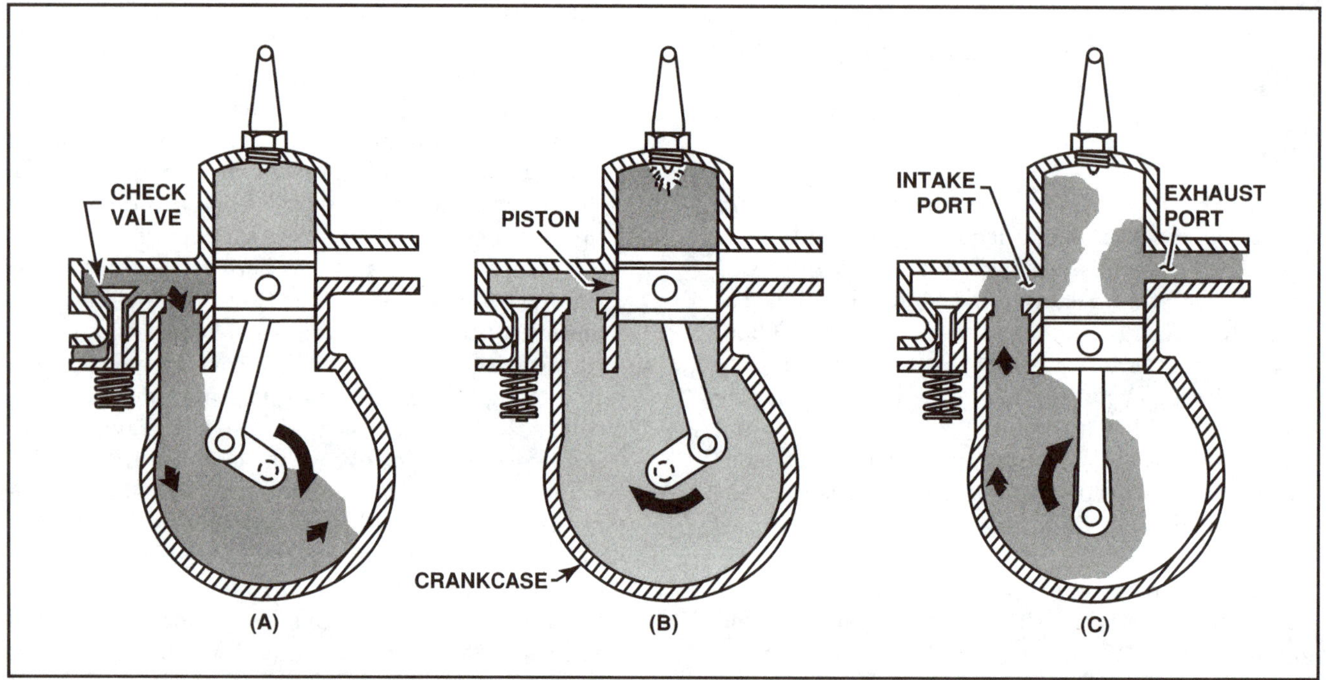

Figure 1-62. In a two-stroke engine, the piston controls the flow of gases into and out of the cylinder through the intake and exhaust ports. This eliminates the need for either an intake or exhaust valve and their associated operating mechanisms. This simplifies a two-stroke engine's construction and minimizes weight.

discharged out the exhaust port before being compressed and ignited. This reduces the engine's overall efficiency.

Lubrication for a two-stroke engine is typically provided by the fuel/air mixture as it circulates in the crankcase. However, the fuel alone does not provide the lubrication. Instead, oil is typically added to the fuel when the fuel tank is filled. This eliminates the need for an oil sump which greatly reduces a two-stroke engine's weight.

The extreme simplicity and light weight of a two-stroke cycle engine make it useful for such applications as chain saws, lawn mowers, and ultralight aircraft. However, the two-stroke engine's use is limited for aviation applications because it is less efficient and more difficult to cool than the four-cycle engine.

WORK-POWER CONSIDERATIONS

All aircraft engines are tested and rated according to their ability to do work and produce power. An engine's design and construction determines how effective it is in converting a fuel's chemical energy to work and power. The following discussion provides an explanation of work and power as well as a means of calculating both. In addition, several of the factors that affect an engine's power output are also discussed.

WORK

If a force is applied to an object and the object moves, work is done. The amount of work done is directly proportional to the force applied and the distance the object moves. In mathematical terms, work is defined as the product of force times distance.

$$\text{Work (W)} = \text{Force (F)} \times \text{Distance (D)}$$

Example:

If an engine weighing 400 pounds is lifted 10 feet, the work done is 4,000 foot-pounds.

$$\begin{aligned}\text{Work} &= 400 \text{ pounds} \times 10 \text{ feet} \\ &= 4{,}000 \text{ foot-pounds}\end{aligned}$$

If a force is applied to an object and the object does not move, no work is done. By the same token, no work is done if an object moves with no force applied to it.

In the English system, work is typically measured in **foot-pounds**. One foot-pound is equal to one pound of force applied to an object through the distance of one foot. In the metric system, the unit of work is the **joule**. One joule is the work done by a force of one **newton** acting through a distance of one meter. One pound is equal to 4.448 newtons.

The work produced by an engine is used to turn a propeller which, in turn, produces thrust to move an aircraft. In addition, an engine does work by turning electrical generators and hydraulic pumps. When an engine drives an alternator to produce the electricity that turns a motor or drives a hydraulic pump to cycle landing gear, the engine has performed work because the force supplied by the engine resulted in movement.

POWER

When determining the amount of work done, the time required to do the work is not considered. Power, on the other hand, does take time into consideration. For example, a low powered motor can be geared to lift a large weight if time is not a factor. However, if it is important to lift the weight quickly, more power is required. Power is calculated with the formula:

$$\text{Power} = \frac{\text{Force} \times \text{Distance}}{\text{Time}}$$

Power is defined as the time-rate of doing work. In the English system, power is expressed in foot-pounds per second, whereas the unit of power in the metric system is joules per second.

When rating engines, power is a primary consideration because it represents how quickly an engine-propeller combination can respond to power demands. Power is a critical factor when determining whether or not an engine can deliver the force needed to produce a specific amount of work in a given time. For example, a large airplane needs more power to take off in the same distance as a small airplane because more force is needed to accelerate a heavier object the same distance in the same amount of time.

HORSEPOWER

Another unit of measure for power is the horsepower. Horsepower was first used by James Watt to compare the performance of his steam engine with a typical English dray horse. One horsepower is the amount of power required to do 33,000 foot-pounds of work in one minute or 550 foot-pounds of work in one second. Therefore, the formula used to calculate horsepower is:

$$\text{Horsepower} = \frac{\text{Force} \times \text{Distance}}{33{,}000 \times \text{Time}}$$

INDICATED HORSEPOWER

Indicated horsepower (IHP) is the total power actually developed in an engine's cylinders without reference to friction losses within the engine. To calculate indicated horsepower, the average effective pressure within the cylinders must be known. One way to determine the effective pressure is to attach a mechanical indicating device to the engine cylinder that records the actual pressure existing in the cylinder during a complete operating cycle. From this data, an average pressure is computed. This average pressure is referred to as **indicated mean effective pressure** and is included in the indicated horsepower calculation with other engine specifications. The formula used to calculate an engine's indicated horsepower rating is:

$$\text{Indicated Horsepower} = \frac{\text{PLANK}}{33{,}000}$$

Where:

P = the **Indicated Mean Effective Pressure**, or **IMEP** inside the cylinder during a power stroke.
L = the length of the stroke in feet or fractions of a foot.
A = the area of the piston head in square inches.
N = the number of power strokes per minute for one cylinder. On a four-stroke engine, this is found by dividing the rpm by two.
K = the number of cylinders on the engine.

In the formula above, the area of the piston times the mean effective pressure provides the force acting on the piston in pounds. This force multiplied by the length of the stroke in feet results in the work performed in one power stroke, which, when multiplied by the number of power strokes per minute, gives the number of foot-pounds per minute of work produced by one cylinder. Multiplying this result by the number of cylinders in the engine gives the amount of work performed, in foot-pounds, by the engine. Since horsepower is defined as work done at the rate of 33,000 foot-pounds per minute, the total number of foot-pounds of work performed by the engine is divided by 33,000 to find the indicated horsepower.

To check your understanding of this formula, compute the indicated horsepower for a six-cylinder engine that has a bore of five inches, a stroke of five inches, and is turning at 2,750 rpm with a measured IMEP of 125 psi per cylinder.

Where:

P = 125 psi
L = .416 foot
A = π 2.5^2 = 19.63 square inches.
N = 2,750 ÷ 2 = 1,375
K = 6

$$\text{IHP} = \frac{\text{PLANK}}{33{,}000}$$

$$= \frac{125 \times .416 \times 19.63 \times 1{,}375 \times 6}{33{,}000}$$

$$= \frac{8{,}421{,}270}{33{,}000}$$

$$= 255.19$$

In this problem, the indicated horsepower is approximately 255 IHP.

FRICTION HORSEPOWER

The indicated horsepower calculation discussed in the preceeding paragraph is the theoretical power of a frictionless engine. However, there is no such thing as a frictionless engine. All engines require energy to draw a fuel/air charge into the combustion chamber, compress it, and expel exhaust gases. Furthermore, gears, pistons, and accessories create friction that must be overcome. Engine lubrication is crucial in limiting friction and wear, but friction cannot be completely eliminated. Therefore, not all of the horsepower developed in an engine goes to driving the propeller. The power required to overcome the friction and energy losses is known as **friction horsepower** and is measured by driving an engine with a calibrated motor and measuring power needed to turn the engine at a given speed.

BRAKE HORSEPOWER

The actual amount of power delivered to the propeller shaft is called brake horsepower. One way to determine brake horsepower is to subtract an engine's friction horsepower from its indicated horsepower. In practice, the measurement of an engine's brake horsepower involves the measurement of a quantity known as **torque**, or twisting moment. Torque is a measure of load and is properly expressed in pound-inches or pound-feet.

There are a number of devices that are capable of measuring torque, including the dynamometer and torquemeter. Early powerplant design engineers measured brake horsepower using a **Prony brake dynamometer**, which consists of a hinged collar, or brake, clamped to the propeller shaft. The collar acts as an adjustable friction brake. An arm of a known length is rigidly attached to the hinged collar and bears on a set of scales. As the propeller shaft rotates, it tries to spin the brake which, in turn, applies force to a scale. If the resulting force registered on the scale is multiplied by the length of the arm, the resulting product represents the torque exerted by the rotating shaft.

Once the torque is known, the work done per revolution of the propeller shaft is computed using the equation:

$$\text{Work per revolution} = 2\pi \times \text{Torque}$$

If the work per revolution is multiplied by the rpm, the result is work per minute, or power. Since work is expressed in foot-pounds per minute, this quantity is divided by 33,000 to arrive at an engine's brake horsepower. The resulting formula for calculating brake horsepower is:

$$\text{Brake Horsepower} = \frac{2\pi \times \text{Torque} \times \text{rpm}}{33{,}000}$$

Given:

Torque = 600 foot-pounds
rpm = 2,700

$$\text{Brake Horsepower} = \frac{6.28 \times 600 \times 2{,}700}{33{,}000}$$

$$= \frac{10{,}173{,}600}{33{,}000}$$

$$= 308.3$$

If the friction between the brake collar and propeller shaft imposes a load without stopping the engine, brake horsepower can be computed without knowing the amount of friction between the collar and drum. As long as the torque increase is proportional to the rpm decrease, the horsepower delivered at the shaft remains unchanged. [Figure 1-63]

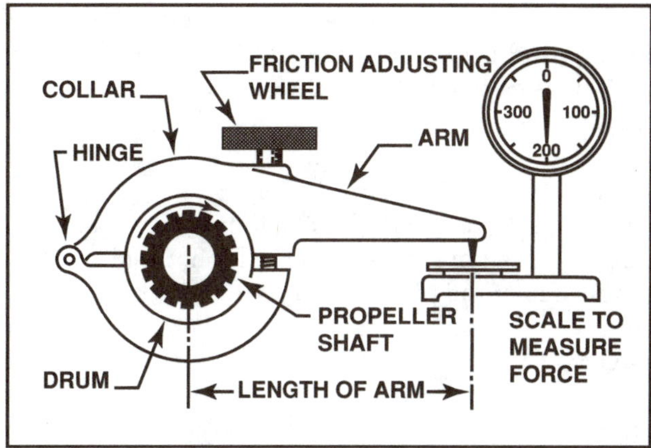

Figure 1-63. In the example above, the 3-foot arm of the prony brake is exerting a force of 200 pounds on the scale. This results in a torque of 600 foot-pounds.

Today, the brake horsepower on most modern engines is measured with an **electric or hydraulic dynamometer**. With an electric dynamometer, an engine drives an electrical generator. The output of the generator is used to do work, and the amount of work done in a given time is used to calculate the power the engine is producing. [Figure 1-64]

PISTON DISPLACEMENT

Piston displacement is defined as the volume of air displaced by a piston as it moves from bottom center to top center. To determine a piston's displacement, you must multiply the area of a piston head by the length of the piston stroke. If you recall from

Figure 1-64. With a dynamometer, the power produced by an engine is used to drive an electrical generator or fluid pump so the power output can be accurately measured.

your previous study of mathematics and the discussion on indicated horsepower (PLANK), the area of a circle is calculated with the formula:

$$A = \pi r^2$$

For example, one cylinder of a four-cylinder aircraft engine has a bore, or diameter, of four inches. What is the area of the piston head?

Given:

Bore = 4 inches

$$\begin{aligned} \text{Area} &= \pi r^2 \\ &= 3.14 \times 2^2 \\ &= 12.56 \text{ square inches} \end{aligned}$$

Once the area of one piston is known, total piston displacement is calculated with the formula:

$$\text{Total Piston Displacement} = A \times L \times N$$

Where:

A = area of piston head in square inches
L = length of the stroke in inches
N = number of cylinders

Using the example presented earlier, determine the total displacement if each of the four cylinders has a stroke of six inches.

Given:

Area = 12.56 square inches
Stroke = 6 inches
Number of cylinders = 4

$$\begin{aligned} \text{Piston Displacement} &= A \times L \times N \\ &= 12.56 \times 6 \times 4 \\ &= 301.44 \text{ cubic inches} \end{aligned}$$

The total engine displacement is 301.44 cubic inches. Since the amount of work done by the expanding gases is determined in part by the piston area and the piston stroke, it should be evident that increasing either the cylinder bore or the piston stroke increases piston displacement.

ENGINE EFFICIENCY

Energy is the capacity for doing work and cannot be created or destroyed. However, energy can be transformed from potential, or stored energy into kinetic energy. Aircraft reciprocating engines transform the potential, or chemical energy stored in fuel into heat energy during the combustion process. The heat energy is then converted to kinetic energy by mechanical means. Engine design and construction, fuel type, and environmental conditions all play a part in how efficiently an engine converts a fuel's potential energy. To determine how efficient an engine is, several factors must be examined, including an engine's thermal, volumetric, and mechanical efficiency.

THERMAL EFFICIENCY

An engine's thermal efficiency (TE) is a ratio of the amount of heat energy converted to useful work to the amount of heat energy contained in the fuel used to support combustion. In other words, thermal efficiency is a measure of the inefficiencies experienced when converting the heat energy in fuel to work. For example, consider two engines that produce the same amount of horsepower, but consume different amounts of fuel. The engine using less fuel converts a greater portion of the available energy into useful work and, therefore, has a higher thermal efficiency. Thermal efficiency is found by the formula:

$$\text{Thermal Efficiency} = \frac{\text{Horsepower} \times 33{,}000}{F \times \text{BTU} \times K}$$

Where:

Horsepower = An engine's brake or indicated horsepower
33,000 = Number of foot-pounds of work per minute in one horsepower
F = Weight of fuel burned per minute
BTU = Heat value of the fuel burned measured in BTU's
K = Constant representing the number of foot-pounds of work each BTU is capable of doing in one second.

Thermal efficiency can be calculated using either brake or indicated horsepower. If brake horsepower is used, the result is **brake thermal efficiency (BTE)**, and if indicated horsepower is used, you get **indicated thermal efficiency (ITE)**.

The constant, 33,000, is the number of foot-pounds of work per minute in one horsepower. Therefore, when horsepower is multiplied by 33,000, the output of an engine in foot-pounds per minute results.

Almost all engine performance data relating to fuel consumption is expressed in terms of gallons per hour. Therefore, you must be able to convert gallons per hour to pounds per minute. For example, the weight of 100LL aviation gasoline is six pounds per gallon. If a particular engine burns 10 gallons per hour, you must multiply the gallons consumed per hour by six pounds and divide the product by 60, the number of minutes per hour. The resulting fuel burn is one pound per minute ($10 \times 6 \div 60 = 1$).

In the English system of measurement, the relationship between heat and work is the **British Thermal Unit**, or **BTU**, of heat energy. Each pound of aviation gasoline contains 20,000 BTU's of heat energy, therefore, the number 20,000 is typically used in the formula for determining thermal efficiency.

By multiplying the pounds per minute of fuel an engine burns by 20,000, you get the total number of BTU's, or total heat energy that is produced in a given engine. One BTU is capable of doing 778 foot-pounds of work. Therefore, when you multiply the total number of BTU's by the constant 778, both the top and bottom of the formula produce a product that is in foot-pounds.

Based on the information just presented, the formula used to calculate thermal efficiency can be simplified to read:

$$\text{Thermal efficiency} = \frac{\text{Horsepower} \times 33{,}000}{\text{F} \times 20{,}000 \times 778}$$

or

$$\text{Thermal efficiency} = \frac{\text{Horsepower} \times 33{,}000}{\text{F} \times 15{,}560{,}000}$$

To check your understanding of this formula, determine the brake thermal efficiency of a piston engine that produces 150 brake horsepower while burning 8 gallons of aviation gasoline per hour.

$$\text{BTE} = \frac{150 \times 33{,}000}{(8 \times 6 \div 60) \times 20{,}000 \times 778}$$

$$= \frac{4{,}950{,}000}{.8 \times 20{,}000 \times 778}$$

$$= \frac{4{,}950{,}000}{12{,}448{,}000}$$

$$= .398$$

$$= 39.8 \text{ percent}$$

Most reciprocating engines are between 30 and 40 percent efficient. The remaining heat is lost through the exhaust gases, the cooling system, and the friction within the engine. In fact, of the total heat produced in a reciprocating engine, 30 to 40 percent is utilized for power output; 15 to 20 percent is lost in cooling; 5 to 10 percent is lost in overcoming friction of moving parts; and 40 to 45 percent is lost through the exhaust.

VOLUMETRIC EFFICIENCY

Volumetric efficiency (VE) is the ratio of the volume of fuel and air an engine takes into its cylinders to the total piston displacement. For example, if an engine draws in a volume of fuel and air that is exactly equal to the engine's total piston displacement, volumetric efficiency would be 100 percent. By the same token, if an engine draws in 288 cubic inches of fuel and air and has a total piston displacement of 320 cubic inches, the volumetric efficiency would be 90 percent.

Because the density of the air drawn into an engine varies with changes in atmospheric conditions, the only way to accurately calculate volumetric efficiency is to correct for nonstandard temperature and pressure. If you recall from your earlier studies, standard temperature and pressure at sea level is 59°F (15°C) and 29.92 inches of mercury (1013.2 millibars) respectively. Based on this, the formula for determining volumetric efficiency is:

$$\text{VE} = \frac{\text{Vol. of mixture corrected for nonstd. conditions}}{\text{Total piston displacement}}$$

The volumetric efficiency of most **normally aspirated engines** is less than 100 percent. The reason for this is because bends, surface roughness, and obstructions inside the induction system slow the flow of air which, in turn, reduces the air pressure within the manifold. On the other hand, **turbocharged engines** compress the air before it enters the cylinders, and often have volumetric efficiencies greater than 100 percent.

Anything that decreases the density, or volume of air entering a cylinder decreases volumetric efficiency. Some of the typical factors that affect volumetric efficiency of a non-turbocharged engine include:

1. **Part throttle operation** — This restricts the volume of air that flows into the cylinders.

2. **Long, small diameter, intake pipes** — As air flows through an induction system, friction slows the air flow, causing a decrease in air density. The amount of friction created is directly proportional to the length of the intake pipes and inversely proportional to their cross-sectional area. In other words, long, small diameter intake pipes create the most friction while short, large diameter intake pipes create less friction.

3. **Induction systems with sharp bends** — Each time intake air turns a corner in an induction system, air flow slows and less air enters the cylinders.

4. **High carburetor air temperatures** — As the temperature of the intake air increases, air density decreases. A lower air density means less air enters the cylinders.

5. **High cylinder head temperatures** — As the cylinder heads and corresponding combustion chambers heat up, air density in the cylinders decreases and volumetric efficiency decreases.

6. **Incomplete scavenging** — If the valve overlap in an engine is incorrect, exhaust gases will displace some of the incoming fuel/air mixture. When this happens, less fuel and air is drawn into the cylinders and a lower volumetric efficiency results.

7. **Improper valve timing** — If the intake valve does not remain open long enough to allow a complete charge of fuel and air to enter a cylinder, volumetric efficiency drops.

8. **Increases in altitude** — As an aircraft climbs, ambient air pressure drops and air density decreases. As an engine draws the "thin" air into its cylinders, its volumetric efficiency drops. This problem can be overcome, to a certain degree, by turbocharging an engine. Turbocharging increases the induction air pressure above atmospheric pressure which, in turn, increases the density of the fuel/air charge entering the cylinders.

MECHANICAL EFFICIENCY

Mechanical efficiency is the ratio of brake horsepower to indicated horsepower and represents the percentage of power developed in the cylinders that reaches the propeller shaft. For example, if an engine develops 160 brake horsepower and 180 indicated horsepower, the ratio of brake horsepower to indicated horsepower is 160:180, which represents a mechanical efficiency of 89 percent. Since aircraft engines are mechanically efficient, it is not unusual for ninety percent of the indicated horsepower to be converted into brake horsepower.

The factor that has the greatest effect on mechanical efficiency is the friction within the engine itself. The friction between moving parts in an engine remains relatively consistent throughout an engine's speed range. Therefore, the mechanical efficiency of an engine is highest when the engine is running at an rpm that maximum brake horsepower is developed.

FACTORS AFFECTING POWER

According to the general gas law which combines Boyle's Law and Charles' Law, a definite relationship between gas volume, temperature, and pressure exists. That relationship is the reason why the internal combustion process must be precisely controlled for an engine to produce power efficiently.

MANIFOLD PRESSURE

Changes in manifold air pressure affect the amount of power an engine can produce for a given rpm. Manifold air pressure, or manifold absolute pressure (MAP) readings are monitored by a gauge and provide a means of selecting power settings. Absolute pressure is the pressure above a complete vacuum indicated in inches of mercury (in. Hg.) or pounds per square inch absolute (psia). MAP gauges indicate absolute pressure of the fuel/air mixture at a point just outside a cylinder intake port.

Excessive pressures and temperatures shorten engine life by overstressing cylinders, pistons, connecting rods, bearings, crankshaft journals, and valves. Continued operation past upper manifold absolute pressure limits leads to worn engine parts, decreasing power output and lower efficiency, or worse, engine failure.

DETONATION AND PREIGNITION

A fuel/air mixture burns in a very controlled and predictable way when normal combustion takes place. Even though the process happens in a fraction of a second, the mixture starts burning at the point where it is ignited by the spark plugs, then burns away from the plugs until it is all consumed. The dual spark plug design common in most aircraft reciprocating engines promotes a complete even burn of the fuel/air charge by providing two ignition sparks at the same time. The plugs are arranged across from one another so that, as the flame advances from each spark plug, the mixture burns in a wavelike form toward the center of the cylinder. This type of combustion causes a smooth buildup of temperature and pressure so that maximum force is applied to the piston at exactly the right time in the power stroke. [Figure 1-65]

Detonation is the uncontrolled, explosive ignition of the fuel/air mixture in the cylinder. Detonation causes high cylinder temperatures and pressures which lead to a rough running engine, overheating, and power loss. If detonation occurs in an engine, damage or even failure of pistons, cylinders, or valves can happen. The high pressures and temperatures, combined with the high turbulence generated, cause a "hammering" or "scrubbing" action on a cylinder and piston that can burn a hole completely through either of them in seconds. You can detect detonation as a "knock" in the engine. [Figure 1-66]

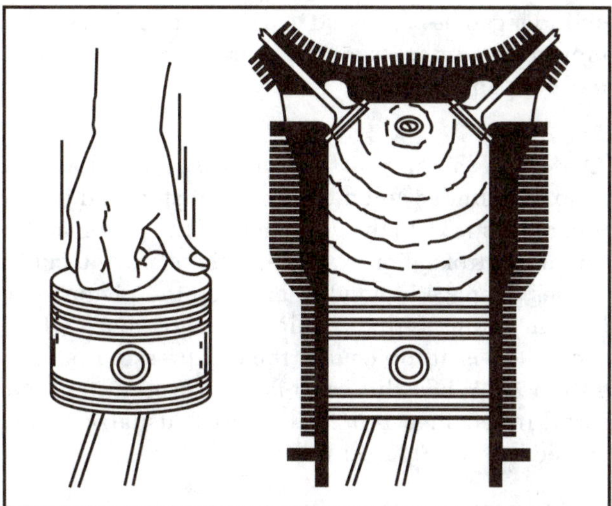

Figure 1-65. During normal combustion, the fuel/air mixture burns evenly, producing a steady force similar to the even pressure of someone pushing down on the piston.

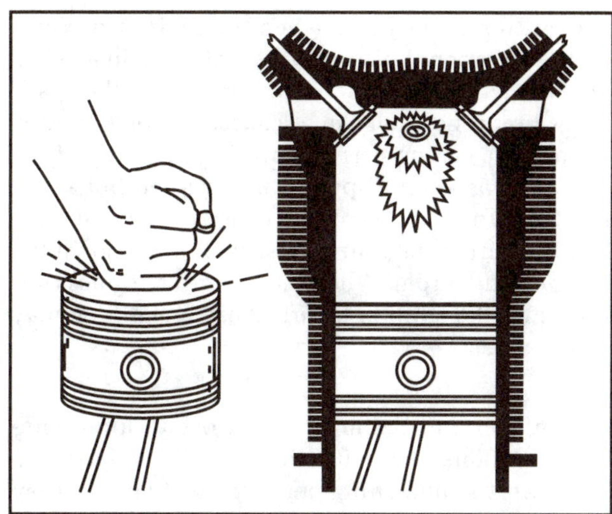

Figure 1-66. When detonation occurs, the fuel/air charge burns in an explosive fashion causing a rapid increase in pressure that produces a "hammering" action on the piston.

Detonation is caused by several conditions such as using a fuel grade lower than recommended and allowing the engine to overheat. Wrong ignition timing, heavy engine load at low rpm, fuel/air mixture too lean, and compression ratios of 12:1 or higher are also possible causes of detonation. [Figure 1-67]

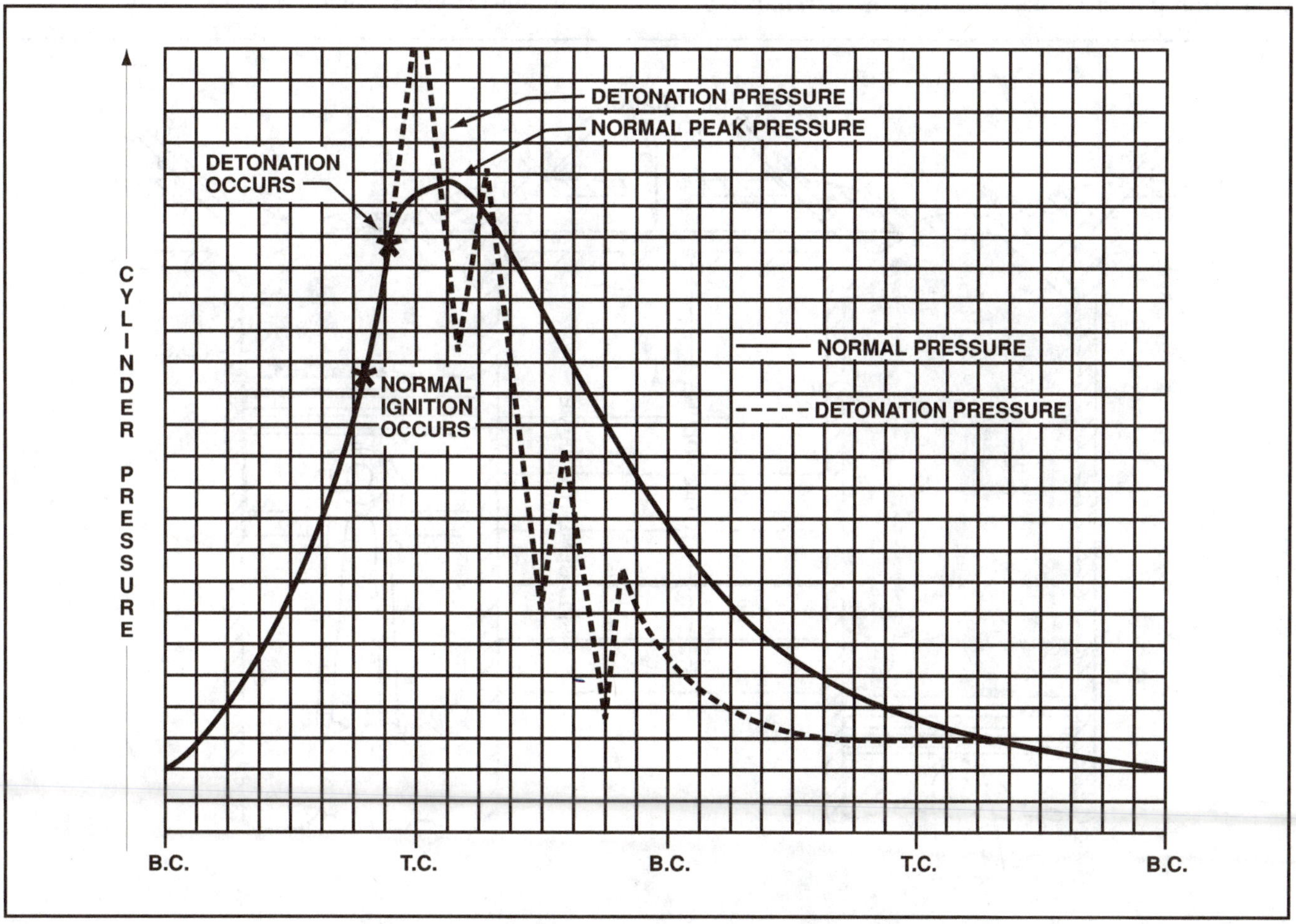

Figure 1-67. This chart illustrates the pressure created in a cylinder as it passes through its various strokes. As you can see, when normal combustion occurs, cylinder pressure builds and dissipates evenly. However, when detonation occurs, cylinder pressure fluctuates dramatically.

Preignition takes place when the fuel/air mixture ignites too soon. It is caused by hot spots in a cylinder that ignite the fuel/air mixture before the spark plugs fire. A hot spot can be caused by something as simple as a carbon particle, overheated valve edges, silica deposits on a spark plug, or a red-hot spark plug electrode. Hot spots are caused by poor engine cooling, dirty intake air filters, or shutting down the engine at high rpm. When the engine continues running after the ignition is turned off, preignition may be the cause.

Preignition and detonation can occur simultaneously, and one may cause the other. Sometimes it is difficult distinguishing between the two, but they both cause engine roughness and high operating temperatures.

COMPRESSION RATIO

All internal combustion engines must compress the fuel/mixture to receive a reasonable amount of work from each power stroke. The fuel/air charge in the cylinder can be compared to a coil spring, in that the more it is compressed, the more work it is potentially capable of doing.

An engine's compression ratio is defined as the ratio of cylinder volume with the piston at the bottom of its stroke to the volume with the piston at the top of its stroke. For example, if there are 140 cubic inches of space in a cylinder when the piston is at bottom center and 20 cubic inches of space when the piston is at top center, the compression ratio is 140 to 20. When this ratio is expressed in fraction form, it becomes 140/20, or 7 to 1, usually represented as 7:1. [Figure 1-68]

To a great extent, an engine's compression ratio determines the amount of heat energy that is converted into useful work. Specifically, high compression ratios allow the fuel/air mixture to release its energy rapidly and produce maximum pressure inside a cylinder just as the piston begins the power stroke. As a general rule, the higher the compression ratio, the greater an engine's power output.

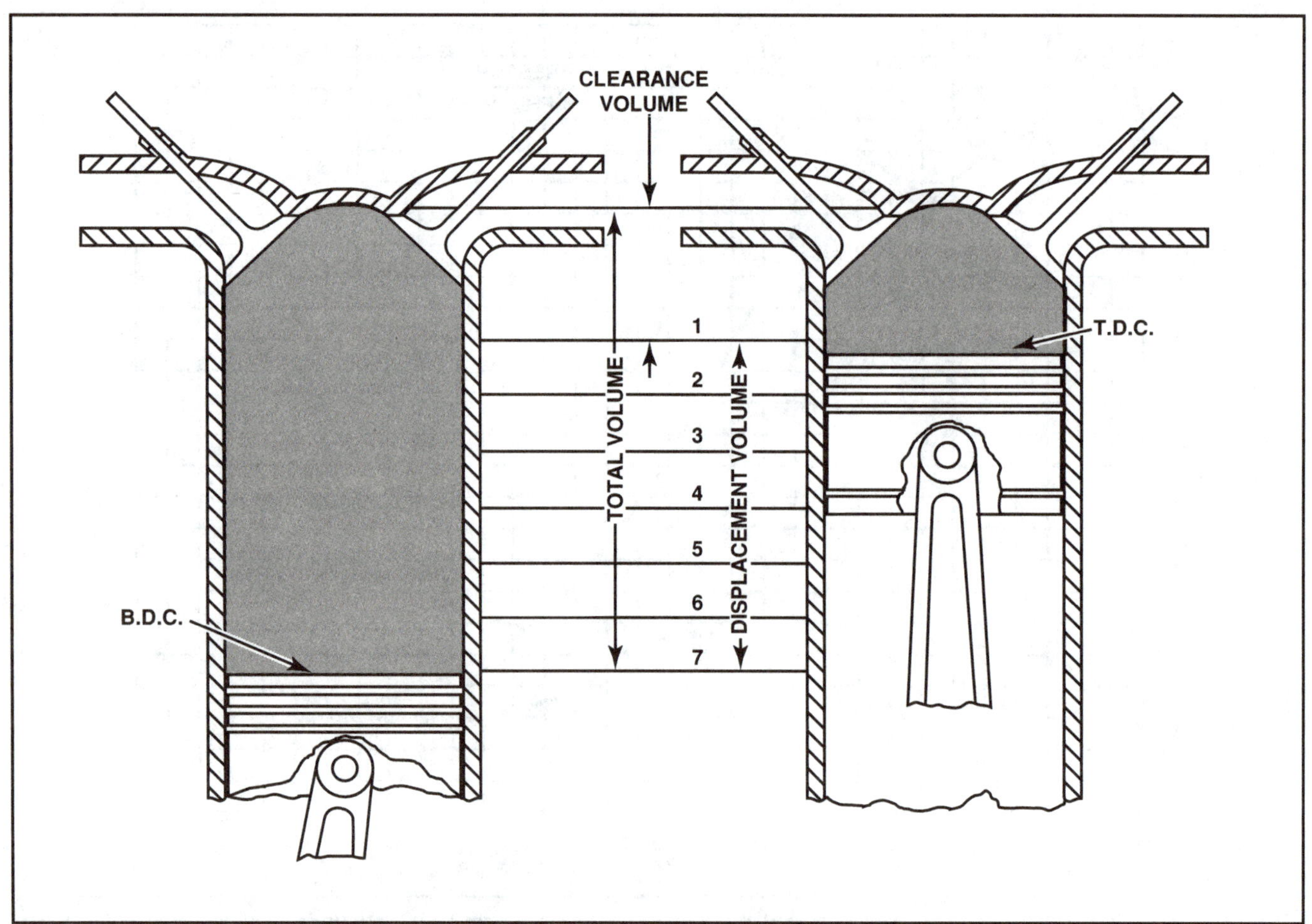

Figure 1-68. A cylinder's compression ratio compares cylinder volume with a piston at bottom dead center to the cylinder volume when the piston is at top dead center. In this example, the compression ratio is 7:1.

Compression ratios can be increased or decreased by altering an engine's design. For example, if the crankshaft "throw" is lengthened, a piston's stroke increases which, in turn, increases the compression ratio. By the same token, if you shave a cylinder head's mating surface, you effectively decrease the distance between the cylinder head and piston head which increases the compression ratio. Another way to increase compression ratios without changing the piston stroke length include installing domed pistons.

To some degree, the characteristics of available fuels determine the practical limits of compression ratios that can be used in engine design. For example, if the compression ratio of an engine is increased up to or beyond a fuel's critical pressure, detonation will occur. Because of this, engine manufacturers specify the correct grade of fuel to be used based, in part, on an engine's compression ratio. Use of fuel grades lower than recommended should be avoided.

If an engine is turbocharged, the degree of turbocharging limits the engine's compression ratio. Although turbocharging does not change an engine's compression ratio, it does increase manifold pressure as well as each cylinder's mean effective pressure. If you recall from your study of the gas laws, as the pressure of a gas increases, the temperature also increases. As a result, turbocharging raises the temperature of the fuel/air mixture in an engine's cylinders and increases the possibility of detonation. Therefore, compression ratios in turbocharged engines must be limited to allow for the increased operating temperatures.

IGNITION TIMING

When the ignition event is properly timed, complete combustion and maximum pressure occur just after the piston passes top dead center at the beginning of the power stroke. To accomplish this, ignition timing is typically set to ignite the fuel/air charge shortly before a piston reaches top center on the compression stroke. For example, some small Continental engines ignite the fuel/air charge between 25 and 32 degrees before top center on the compression stroke.

An automobile engine employs a variable timing device on the ignition distributor to change the ignition timing as engine operating conditions change. Aircraft engines, on the other hand, use fixed timing, which is a compromise between the timing required to give best performance for takeoff and best performance at cruise.

If the ignition event occurs too early, an engine loses power because maximum cylinder pressure builds too early. In other words, when the fuel/air charge is ignited early, the force of the expanding gases opposes the engine's rotational inertia because the piston is still moving upward. On the other hand, late ignition also causes a loss of power, since cylinder volume is increasing at the same time the gases are expanding. The result is that gas pressure on the piston head does not build to expected levels. Furthermore, late ignition does not allow enough time for complete combustion before the exhaust valve opens. Burning gases then engulf the valve, increase its temperature, and often lead to detonation or engine damage due to overheating.

ENGINE SPEED

The amount of power an aircraft engine produces is determined by cylinder pressure, piston area, the distance a piston moves on each stroke, and the number of times this movement occurs in one minute. Stated in simple terms, the faster an engine runs, the more power it produces. However, there are some limitations to how fast an engine can rotate. Some of these limitations include ignition timing, valve timing, and the inertia of rapidly moving pistons. For example, when intake and exhaust valves move too quickly, they can "float," or not seat properly. In addition, the inertia of pistons reversing their direction of travel thousands of times per minute can overstress crankshaft journals and bearings when engine rpm exceeds safe limits.

Another limitation on an engine's maximum rotational speed is propeller tip speed. In order to efficiently produce thrust, the tip speed of a propeller blade must not exceed the speed of sound. If you recall, the further from the propeller hub a point is, the faster that point moves through the air. Therefore, engines that operate at high rpm's must either be fitted with short propeller blades or some form of propeller reduction gearing. Reduction gears allow an engine to turn at higher speeds to produce

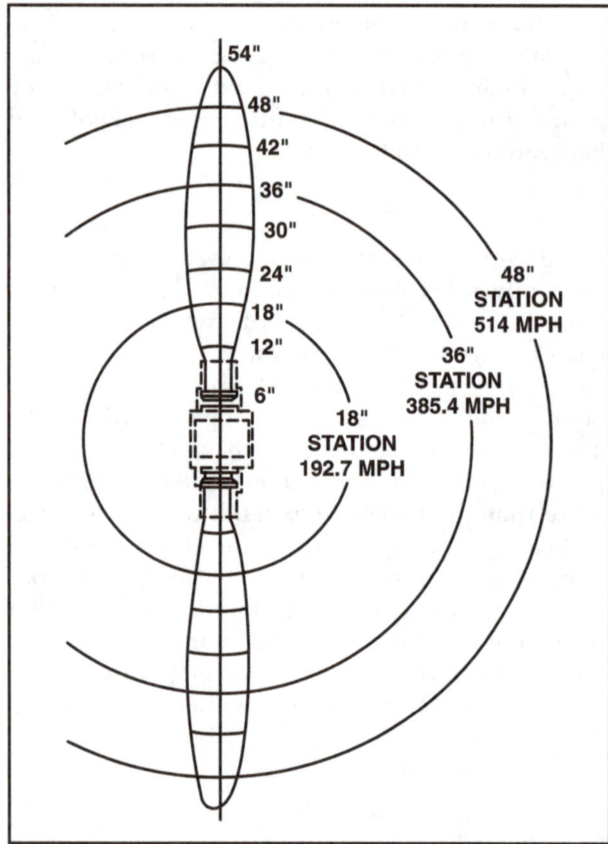

Figure 1-69. As this figure illustrates, a propellerís speed is highest at the blade tips. If you recall from Section A, when propeller tip speeds exceed the speed of sound, propeller efficiency drops.

more power while the propeller rotates at a slower, more efficient speed. [Figure 1-69]

SPECIFIC FUEL CONSUMPTION

An engine's specific fuel consumption is the number of pounds of fuel burned per hour to produce one horsepower. For example, if an engine burns 12 gallons per hour while producing 180 brake horsepower, the brake specific fuel consumption is .4 pounds per horsepower hour. Most modern aircraft reciprocating engines have a brake specific fuel consumption (BSFC) that is between .4 and .5 pounds per horsepower hour. While not actually a measure of power, specific fuel consumption is useful for comparing engine efficiencies.

An engine's specific fuel consumption varies with several factors including: engine speed, engine design, volumetric efficiency, and friction losses. The best specific fuel consumption for most engines occurs at a cruise power setting when producing approximately 75 percent power. The amount an engine's specific fuel consumption varies with engine rpm can be illustrated in a chart. [Figure 1-70]

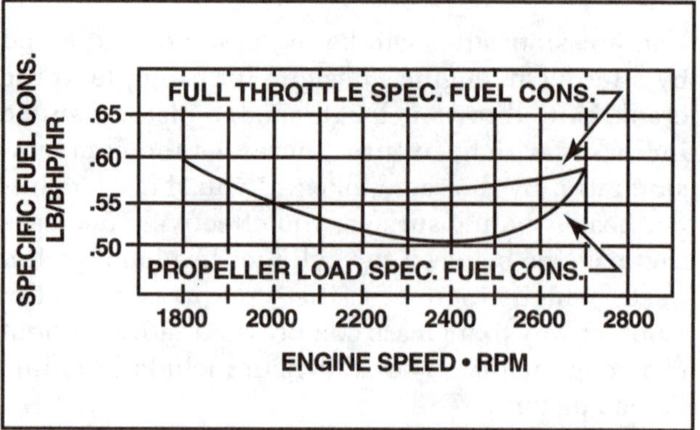

Figure 1-70. Aircraft engines operate most efficiently around 2,400 rpm. Below 2,400 rpm an engine is not developing as much power as it is capable of for the amount of fuel it is using. On the other hand, above 2,400 rpm, friction horsepower increases, causing an overall drop in brake horsepower. As shown by the lower curve, a typical engine requires about 0.51 pounds of fuel per hour for each horsepower it produces at 2,400 rpm.

ALTITUDE

As an aircraft climbs, ambient air pressure drops and air density decreases. **Density altitude** is a term that describes the density of the air at a given altitude corrected for nonstandard pressure and temperature. Any time an aircraft engine operates at a density altitude that is higher than sea level, less air is drawn into the engine for combustion. Whenever less air is available for combustion, engine power output decreases.

Even though the actual, or true altitude at a location does not change, density altitude can change constantly. For example, on a hot day as the air heats and pressure drops, air becomes less dense, causing the density altitude to increase. One way to overcome the problems associated with high density altitudes is by turbocharging an engine. Turbocharging increases the induction air pressure above atmospheric pressure which, in turn, increases the density of the fuel/air charge entering the cylinders.

FUEL/AIR RATIO

Gasoline and other liquid fuels must be converted from their liquid state to a vapor before they will burn. In addition, the ratio of fuel vapor to oxygen in the air must be chemically correct for complete combustion. A **stoichiometric mixture** is a perfectly balanced fuel/air mixture of 15 parts of air to 1 part of fuel, by weight. A fuel/air mixture that is leaner than 15:1 has less fuel in the fuel/air mixture, while a rich mixture has more fuel. Combustible fuel/air ratios range from 8:1 to 18:1.

Mixture controls allow adjustment of the fuel/air ratio from idle cut-off to full rich conditions. Leaning raises engine operating temperatures while enriching provides a cooling effect. Leaning becomes necessary as altitude increases, because air density drops, causing the fuel/air ratio to gradually become richer. **Best power mixture** develops maximum power at a particular rpm and is typically used during takeoff. **Best economy mixture** provides the best specific fuel consumption which results in an aircraft's maximum range and optimum fuel economy.

DISTRIBUTION OF POWER

When considering the amount of power that is available in aviation gasoline compared to the amount of power that is actually delivered to the propeller shaft, you can easily see that an aircraft engine is a fairly inefficient machine. For example, a typical six cylinder engine develops 200 brake horsepower when burning 14 gallons of fuel per hour. However, the burning fuel releases enough heat energy to produce 667 horsepower. When you examine the distribution of power you will see that 200 of the 667 horsepower is delivered to the propeller while approximately 33 horsepower is used to turn the engine and compress the air in the cylinders. In addition, an equivalent of about 434 horsepower is lost to the air through the cooling and exhaust systems. The power loss continues when power is delivered to the propeller, because in order to propel an aircraft through the air, the torque produced by an engine must be converted into thrust. Since a propeller converts only about 90% of the torque it receives into thrust, the actual **thrust horsepower** delivered by the propeller is 180 horsepower. Thrust horsepower represents the actual horsepower developed by the thrust of the propeller. [Figure 1-71]

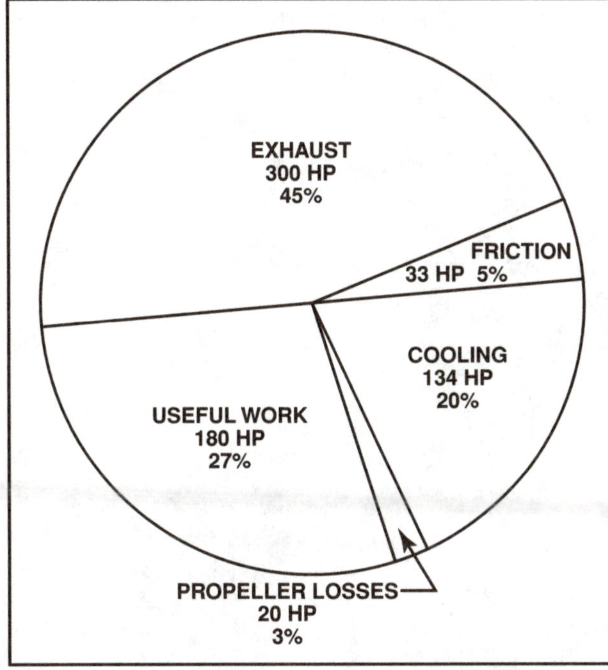

Figure 1-71. The distribution of power in 14 gallons of aviation gasoline when consumed by a typical 200 bhp engine.

POWER CURVES

Most engine manufacturers produce a set of power curves for each engine they build. These charts show the power developed for each rpm as well as indicate the specific fuel consumption at each power setting. [Figure 1-72]

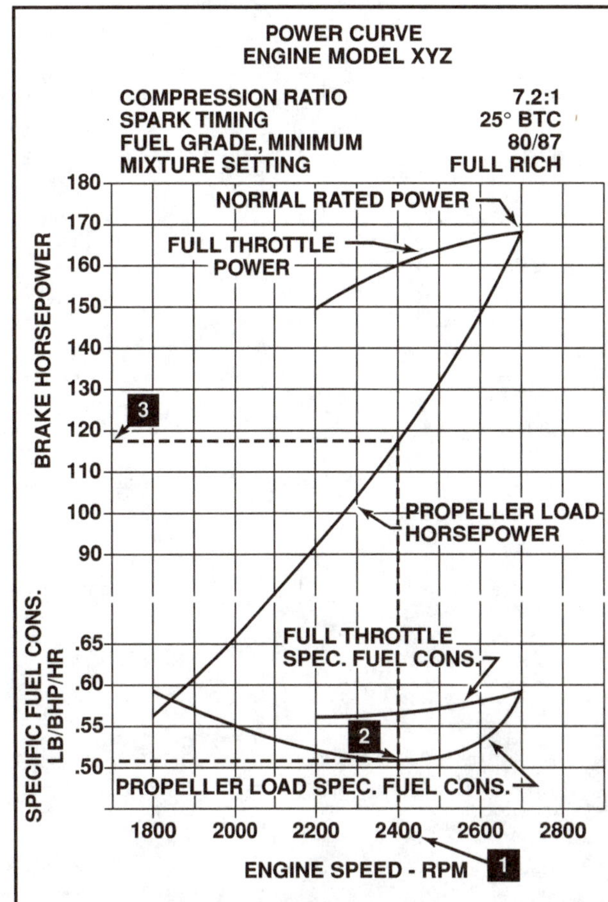

Figure 1-72. This figure illustrates a typical power curve for a four-cylinder aircraft engine. The upper curve shows the maximum amount of power produced at full throttle on a dynamometer. The diagonal power curve represents the amount of horsepower produced with less than full throttle. The two bottom curves represent the specific fuel consumptions for full throttle operations and propeller load conditions. To use this chart, let's assume you have an engine operating at a cruise power setting of 2,400 rpm (item 1). At this power setting, the specific fuel consumption is 0.51 LB/BHP/HR (item 2), and the engine produces 118 brake horsepower (item 3). By multiplying the specific fuel consumption by the brake horsepower, you can determine the engine's fuel consumption of 60.18 pounds per hour (.51 × 118 = 60.18).

RECIPROCATING ENGINE OPERATION, MAINTENANCE, INSPECTION, AND OVERHAUL

INTRODUCTION

As a powerplant technician, you must be able to operate, maintain, inspect, and overhaul aircraft engines. Performing those tasks requires you to develop the ability to determine when an engine is running normally and when engine performance is deteriorating. In addition, you must acquire the knowledge to effectively troubleshoot engine problems, then perform the necessary repair work. Furthermore, you are required to be proficient in special skills and processes that are commonly used during an engine overhaul. Therefore, the following information is provided as a foundation to your future experiences in the operation, maintenance, inspection, and overhaul of reciprocating engines.

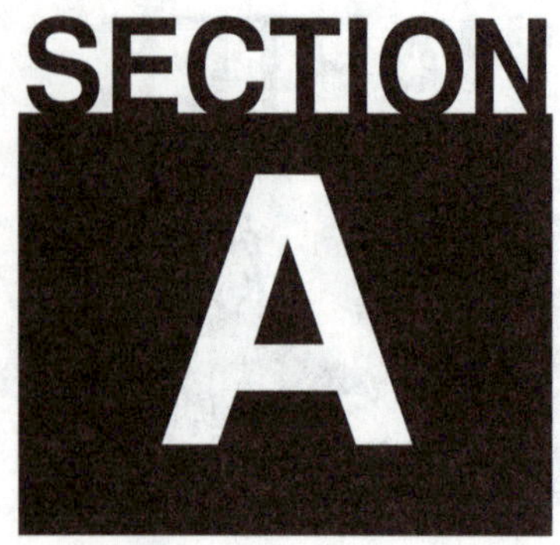

SECTION A ENGINE OPERATION, MAINTENANCE, AND INSPECTION

OPERATION

As an aviation maintenance technician, you must be thoroughly familiar with the procedures for operating a reciprocating engine from the cockpit. This includes understanding the engine instrumentation, ground run procedures, and safety items associated with starting and running an aircraft engine. A good place to begin is with the location and movement of the engine controls. To aid in this process, all modern aircraft are equipped with standardized engine controls. [Figure 2-1]

Once you are familiar with the engine controls, you should locate each of the engine instruments. In addition, you should locate and read all placards and other markings on or near the instruments. Important engine operating information is displayed by the engine instruments and must be monitored continuously during an engine run. Therefore, you, as an engine operator, must be skilled in the interpretation of instrument readings to prevent engine damage.

ENGINE INSTRUMENTATION

A basic understanding of how engine instruments work is an important part of the knowledge you must have as an engine operator and troubleshooter. Part of this knowledge includes knowing how to interpret the instrument markings so you can comprehend how an engine is performing. Instrument markings establish operational ranges as well as minimum and maximum limits. In addition, the markings allow you to distinguish between normal operation, time limited operation, and unauthorized operating conditions. Engine instrument range markings are based on limits found in the engine's Type Certificate Data Sheet. Traditionally, instrument markings consist of green, blue, yellow, and red lines or arcs and intermediate blank spaces.

Green arcs are the most widely used of all the instrument markings and usually indicate a safe, or normal range of operation. Usually, the upper end of a green arc indicates the maximum limit for continuous operation while the low end indicates the min-

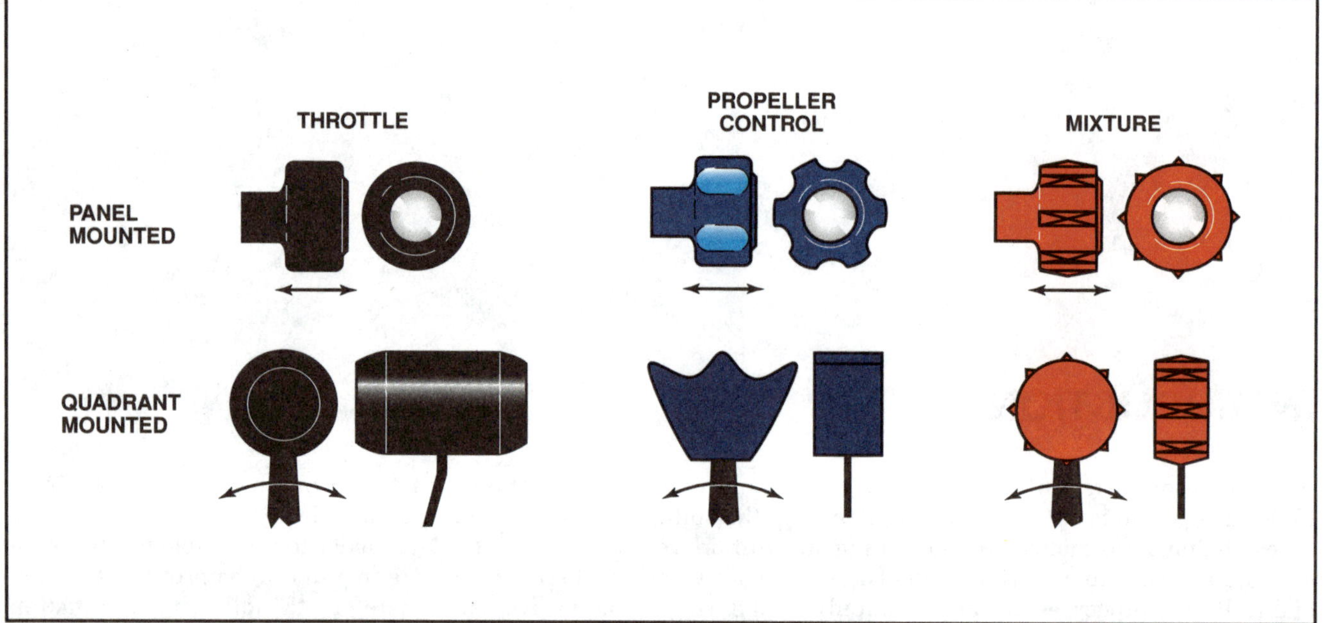

Figure 2-1. For standardization purposes, the primary engine controls are arranged from left to right beginning with the throttle, propeller control, and mixture. In addition, each lever is color coded and uniquely shaped.

imum limit for continuous operation. Operation within a green arc is typically not time restricted.

Blue arcs are used to indicate an allowable range of operations under a unique set of circumstances. For example, a blue arc may indicate an acceptable fuel flow when flying above a specific altitude. Blue arcs are rarely used and may only be seen on certain engine instruments, such as the tachometer, fuel flow, manifold pressure, cylinder head temperature, or torque meter.

A **yellow arc** indicates a precautionary range of time limited operation permitted by the manufacturer. However, in some cases, a yellow arc may be omitted on instruments if it is too small to be clearly visible. When this is the case, the manufacturer's instructions will specify a caution range. Engine operation in the yellow arc is typically an indication of an impending problem or a warning to change an operational setting.

A **red line** indicates a maximum or minimum safe operating limit. Operation beyond a red line typically results in a dangerous operating condition. In addition, other limits of a transient or momentary nature may be indicated by a red triangle, dot, or diamond mark. A red arc, on the other hand, indicates a restricted operating range where excessive vibration or other stresses could endanger the engine or airframe.

The colored arcs and lines on engine instruments are typically painted directly on the instrument face. However, some older aircraft instrument markings may be painted on the instrument glass. If this is the case, a white line is used as an **index mark** between the instrument glass and case. Any discontinuity in the white radial line indicates the instrument glass has moved. Since misalignment between the glass and case renders the instrument range and limit markings inaccurate and unreliable, the glass must be repositioned and secured.

Now that you understand how to interpret the markings on engine instruments, the following discussion looks at some of the typical instruments found on reciprocating engine powered aircraft. As each instrument is discussed, it is important to keep in mind that the performance limits of individual engine models vary considerably. Therefore, the procedures and operational ranges that are used in this section do not necessarily correspond to any specific engine.

CARBURETOR AIR TEMPERATURE

Carburetor air temperature (CAT) is measured at the carburetor entrance by a temperature sensing bulb in the ram air intake duct. The sensing bulb senses the air temperature in the carburetor and then sends a signal to a cockpit instrument that is calibrated in degrees Centigrade. The primary purpose of a CAT gauge is to inform a pilot when the temperature at the carburetor can support the formation of ice. [Figure 2-2]

In addition to identifying the conditions necessary for the formation of ice, excessively high carburetor air temperatures can indicate the onset of detonation. For example, if a CAT gauge has a red line identifying a maximum operating temperature, engine operation above that temperature increases the chance of detonation occurring.

Observation of the CAT before engine startup and just after shutdown provides an indication of fuel temperature in the carburetor body. During startup, this information can be used to determine if the fuel is warm enough to support vaporization. On the other hand, a high CAT after engine shutdown is a warning that fuel trapped in a pressure-type carburetor could expand and produce potentially damaging fuel pressures. High CAT temperatures after shutdown can also indicate the onset of **vapor lock**, which is the formation of vaporized fuel bubbles in a fuel line that interfere with the flow of fuel to the engine. Any time high CAT readings are observed after shutdown, the fuel selector valve and throttle

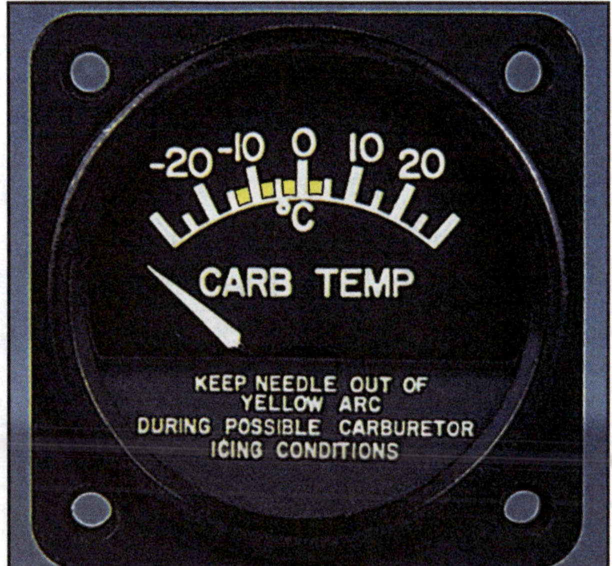

Figure 2-2. The carburetor air temperature gauge depicted above indicates that the danger of induction system icing exists when the temperature is between – 15°C to + 5°C.

should be left open until the engine cools. This helps relieve fuel pressure by allowing expanding fuel to return to the tank.

Information provided by CAT gauges can also be useful in troubleshooting. For example, if severe enough, backfiring may cause a momentary rise in CAT. On the other hand, an induction fire would be indicated by a steady increase in CAT readings.

FUEL PRESSURE

Some engines have a fuel pressure gauge that displays the pressure of fuel supplied to the carburetor or fuel control unit. Most fuel pressure instruments display fuel pressure in pounds per square inch (psi), and provide indications to the pilot that the engine is receiving the fuel needed for a given power setting. A pilot also uses fuel pressure gauges to verify the operation of an auxiliary fuel pump. [Figure 2-3]

One type of fuel pressure gauge uses a **Bourdon tube** which is a metal tube that is formed in a circular shape with a flattened cross section. One end of the tube is open, while the other end is sealed. The open end of the Bourdon tube is connected to a capillary tube containing pressurized fuel. As the pressurized fuel enters the Bourdon tube, the tube tends to straighten. Through a series of gears, this movement

Figure 2-3. The top fuel pressure gauge is typical for an engine equipped with a float type carburetor. Notice the minimum fuel pressure of approximately 0.5 psi and the maximum of approximately 8 psi. However, the bottom fuel pressure is more typical for engines equipped with a fuel injection system.

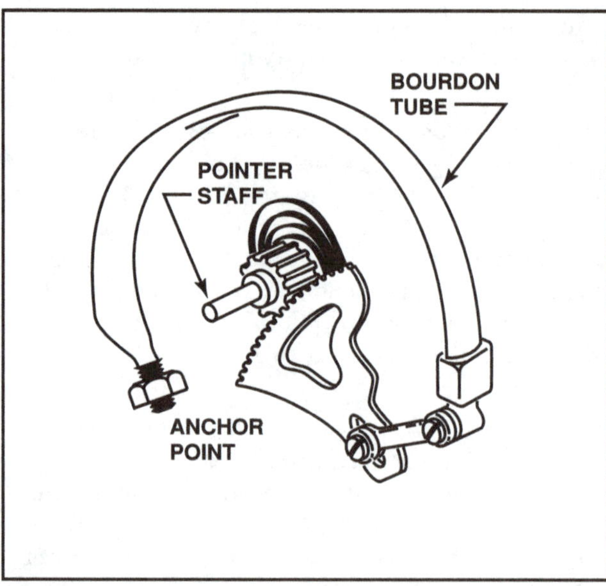

Figure 2-4. As pressurized fuel enters a Bourdon tube, the tube straightens and causes an indicator needle to move. Since the amount a Bourdon tube straightens is proportional to the pressure applied, they are often used to indicate pressure.

is used to move an indicating needle on the instrument face. [Figure 2-4]

Another type of fuel pressure indicator utilizes a **pressure capsule**, or **diaphragm**. Like the Bourdon tube, a diaphragm type pressure indicator is attached to a capillary tube, which attaches to the fuel system and carries pressurized fuel to the diaphragm. As the diaphragm becomes pressurized, it expands, causing an indicator needle to rotate. [Figure 2-5]

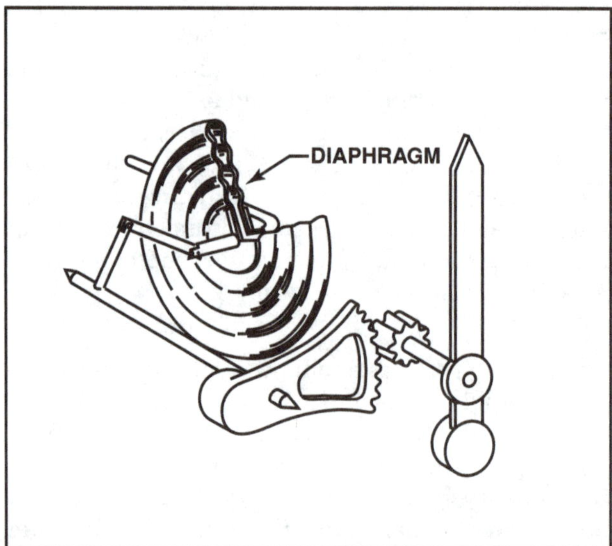

Figure 2-5. Pressure applied internally to a diaphragm causes it to expand, thereby causing rotation of a sector gear. The sector gear, in turn, rotates a pinion gear which is attached to a pointer on a common shaft.

A third type of fuel pressure indicator uses a **bellows** that is attached to a capillary tube. The advantage of bellows over a Bourdon tube or diaphragm is its ability to provide a greater range of motion. The bellows inside the instrument case expands and moves an indicator needle as the fuel pressure increases. [Figure 2-6]

Electric fuel pressure indicating systems are used when the distances between the engine and cockpit become prohibitive for the use of capillary tubing. Another reason for using electric fuel pressure indicators is to avoid bringing fuel into the cockpit. Aircraft with electric fuel pressure indicating systems typically use pressure sensors, or **transducers**, that transmit electrical signals proportional to the fuel pressure to the cockpit. An electric fuel pressure gauge in the cockpit receives the signals and displays fuel pressure information.

On aircraft with direct fuel injection or continuous-flow fuel injection systems, fuel pressure is measured as a pressure drop across the injection nozzles. The pressure drop at the nozzles is proportional to the amount of fuel being supplied to the engine as well as engine power output. Therefore, the gauges in this type of fuel pressure indication system may also be calibrated in percentages of power as well as psi.

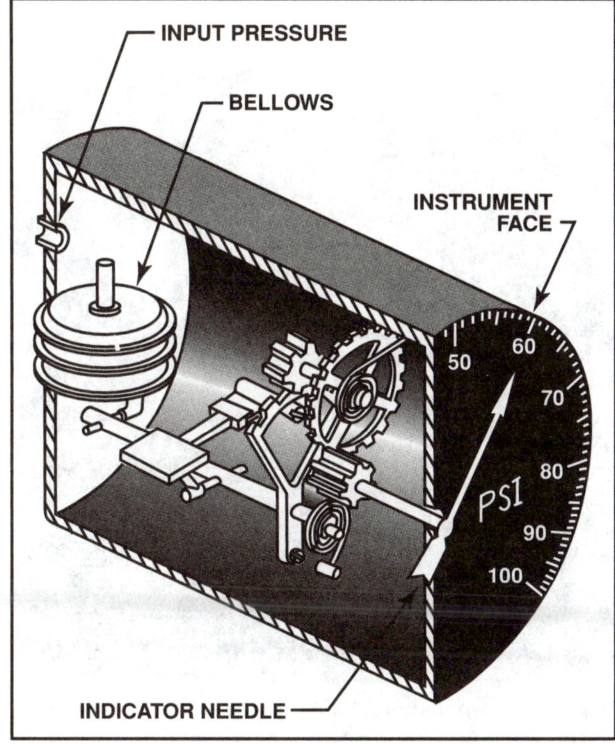

Figure 2-6. A bellows offers the advantage of a greater range of motion than a Bourdon tube or diaphragm and, therefore, is sometimes used with aircraft.

FUEL FLOW INDICATOR

A fuel flow indicator measures the rate of fuel an engine burns in gallons per hour or pounds per hour. This provides the most accurate indication of an engine's fuel consumption. In addition, when combined with other instrument indications, the amount of fuel an engine burns can be used to determine the power settings necessary to obtain maximum power, speed, range, or economy. [Figure 2-7]

On aircraft with a continuous-flow fuel injection system, the fuel flow indicator measures the pressure drop across the fuel injection nozzles to determine fuel flow. This can be done because, as you recall, fuel pressure in a direct fuel injection system is proportional to fuel flow. With this type of system, a higher fuel flow produces a greater pressure differential across the injectors, and a corresponding increase in fuel flow is indicated in the cockpit. However, if an injector nozzle becomes clogged, the pressure differential across that nozzle increases, producing a false, or high fuel flow reading.

Another type of fuel flow measurement system measures the volume of fuel flowing to an engine. This type of system is commonly referred to as an **autosyn** system and incorporates a movable vane that is in the fuel line leading to the engine. As fuel flows through the fuel line, the vane is displaced an amount proportional to the fuel flow. A spring force opposes the fuel flow and returns the vane to neutral when no fuel is flowing. The vane movement is

Figure 2-7. A typical fuel flow indicator displays the number of gallons or pounds per hour an engine consumes. In the fuel flow gauge above, normal fuel flow is from 4.5 to 11.5 gallons per hour.

electrically transmitted to the flow indicator in the cockpit where an indicator needle indicates the fuel flow.

The movement of the vane must be linear to get an accurate flow measurement. To do this, the restriction created by the vane must get larger as the vane increases its rotation. This increase is calibrated into the design of the flowmeter sender unit.

Because the volume of jet fuel changes dramatically with temperature, the fuel flow on several turbine engines is measured in terms of mass rather than volume. A typical mass flow system works on the **magnesyn** principle. The system consists of two cylinders, an impeller, and a turbine which are mounted in the main fuel line leading to the engine. The impeller is driven at a constant speed by a three-phase motor which is powered by the aircraft electrical system. The impeller imparts an angular swirling motion to the fuel as it proceeds to the turbine. As the fuel impacts the turbine, the turbine rotates until a calibrated restraining spring force balances the rotational force. The deflection of the turbine positions a permanent magnet in a transmitter to a position corresponding to the fuel flow in the line. The position of the permanent magnet is then transmitted electrically to a permanent magnet in a receiver which positions the indicator needle in the cockpit. This system is by far the most accurate means of monitoring fuel flow because it accounts for changes in fuel viscosity and volume caused by changes in temperature.

In addition to a fuel flow gauge, some aircraft are equipped with fuel totalizers. A computerized fuel system (CFS) with a **fuel totalizer** is used in both reciprocating and turbine engine aircraft and provides a pilot with a digital readout on the amount of fuel used, fuel remaining, current rate of fuel consumption, and the time remaining for flight at the current power setting. Early totalizers were mechanical counters that responded to electric pulses, however, new systems utilize electronic counters with digital readouts. Totalizer indicators are usually mounted on the instrument panel and are electrically connected to a flowmeter installed in the fuel line to the engine. When the aircraft is serviced with fuel, the counter is set to the total amount of fuel in all tanks. As the fuel passes through the metering element of the flowmeter, it sends a signal to the microprocessor that automatically calculates the amount of fuel remaining.

MANIFOLD PRESSURE

A manifold absolute pressure (MAP) gauge measures the absolute pressure of the fuel/air mixture within the intake manifold. A MAP gauge is used on all aircraft that have a constant-speed propeller to indicate engine power output. Since MAP directly affects a cylinder's mean effective pressure (mep), a pilot uses MAP gauge indications to set the engine power at a pressure level that will not damage the engine. This is especially true for aircraft with turbocharged engines because it helps the pilot to avoid excessive manifold pressure. [Figure 2-8]

Before an engine is started, the manifold pressure gauge displays the local ambient, or atmosphere pressure. However, once the engine is started, the manifold pressure drops significantly, sometimes to half the existing ambient air pressure. At full power, the manifold pressure in normally aspirated engines will not exceed ambient pressure, however, in turbocharged engines the manifold pressure can exceed ambient pressure.

A manifold pressure gauge consists of a sealed diaphragm constructed from two discs of concentrically corrugated thin metal which are soldered together at the edges to form a chamber. The chamber is evacuated, creating a partial vacuum which can be used as a reference point to measure absolute pressure. Depending on the type of gauge, the

Figure 2-8. A manifold absolute pressure gauge displays absolute air pressure in the engine's intake manifold in inches of mercury. The green arc indicates the normal operating range and the red line shows the maximum allowable manifold pressure.

engine manifold pressure is either applied to the inside of the diaphragm or to the outside of the diaphragm. If the engine manifold pressure is applied to the outside of the diaphragm, the instrument case must be completely sealed. In either case, when pressure is applied to the diaphragm, the diaphragm movement is transmitted to an indicator pointer through mechanical linkage.

Another manifold pressure gauge uses a series of stacked diaphragms or bellows which are particularly useful for measuring low or negative pressures. In a MAP gauge, one of the bellows measures ambient atmospheric pressure while the other measures pressure in the intake manifold. Differential pressure between the two bellows causes motion, which is transmitted to the gauge pointer through a mechanical linkage. Regardless of which type of sealed chamber exists in the instrument, the pressure line from the manifold to the instrument case must contain a restriction to prevent pressure surges from damaging the instrument. In addition, the restriction causes a slight delay in gauge response to changes in manifold pressure, preventing jumpy or erratic instrument pointer motion. [Figure 2-9]

Some aircraft instrument installations provide a **purge valve** that allows you to purge moisture that collects in the pressure line near the MAP gauge. With the engine running at idle, the purge valve is opened for 30 seconds or more, then closed. When this is done, the engine's vacuum creates a strong suction through the purge valve which effectively removes the moisture from the pressure line.

Whenever you run an engine with a manifold pressure gauge, you should check the gauge for proper operation. For example, before the engine is started, the MAP gauge should indicate the local atmospheric pressure. However, once the engine is started, the MAP should drop. If this does not happen, and the gauge continues to indicate atmospheric pressure, the sense line between the instrument and induction manifold may be disconnected, broken, or collapsed. When engine power is increased, the manifold pressure should increase evenly and in proportion to the engine power output. If this does not occur, the restriction in the sense line is probably too large.

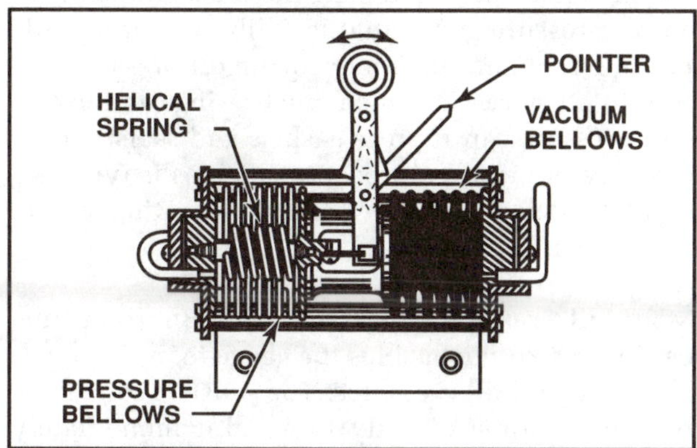

Figure 2-9. The differential pressure bellows of a manifold pressure gauge measures the difference between intake manifold pressure and a partial vacuum.

Figure 2-10. The green arc between 75°F and 245°F on this oil temperature instrument shows the desired oil temperature range for continuous operation. The red line is located at 245°F and indicates the maximum permissible oil temperature.

OIL TEMPERATURE

The oil temperature gauge allows a pilot to monitor the temperature of the oil entering the engine. This is important because oil circulation cools the engine as it lubricates the moving parts. Most oil temperature gauges are calibrated in degrees Fahrenheit and sense oil temperature at the engine's oil inlet. [Figure 2-10]

Most modern oil temperature systems are electrically operated and use either a Wheatstone bridge circuit or a ratiometer circuit. A **Wheatstone bridge** circuit consists of three fixed resistors and one variable resistor whose resistance varies with temperature. [Figure 2-11]

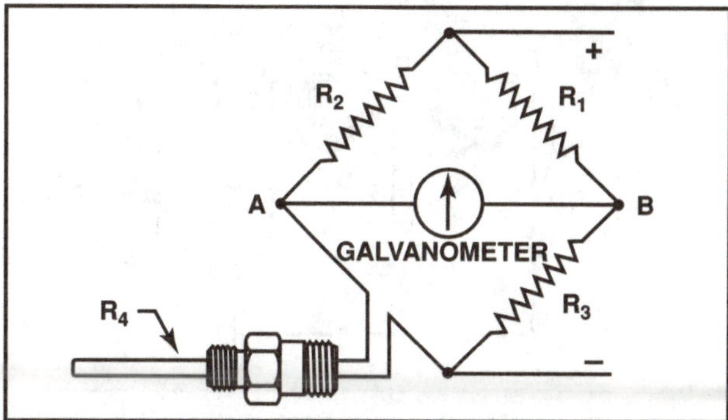

Figure 2-11. A typical Wheatstone bridge has three fixed resistors and one variable resistor. The temperature probe contains the variable resistor, whose resistance varies with the temperature of the oil flowing past the probe. The bridge in the circuit consists of a galvanometer that is calibrated in degrees to indicate temperature.

When power is applied to a Wheatstone bridge circuit and all four resistances are equal, no difference in potential exists between the bridge junctions. However, when the variable resistor is exposed to heat, its resistance increases, causing more current to flow through the fixed resistor R3 than the variable resistor. The disproportionate current flow produces a voltage differential between the bridge junctions, causing current to flow through the galvanometer indicator. The greater the voltage differential, the greater the current flow through the indicator and the greater the needle deflection. Since indicator current flow is directly proportional to the oil temperature, an indicator calibrated in degrees provides an accurate means of registering oil temperature.

A **ratiometer** circuit measures current ratios and is more reliable than a Wheatstone bridge, especially when the supply voltage varies. Typically, a simple ratiometer circuit consists of two parallel branches powered by the aircraft electrical system. One branch consists of a fixed resistor and coil, and the other branch consists of a variable resistor and coil. The two coils are wound on a rotor that pivots between the poles of a permanent magnet, forming a meter movement in the gauge. [Figure 2-12]

The shape of the permanent magnet provides a larger air gap between the magnet and coils at the bottom than at the top. Therefore, the flux density, or magnetic field, is progressively stronger from the bottom of the air gap to the top. Current flow through each coil creates an electromagnet that reacts with the polarity of the permanent magnet, creating torque that repositions the rotor until the magnetic forces are balanced. If the resistances of the temperature probe and fixed resistor are equal, current flow through each coil is the same and the indicator pointer remains in the center position. However, if the probe temperature increases, its resistance also increases, causing a decrease in current through the temperature sensing branch. Consequently, the electromagnetic force on the temperature sensing branch decreases, creating an imbalance that allows the rotor to rotate until each coil reaches a null, or balance. The pointer attached to the rotor then indicates the oil temperature.

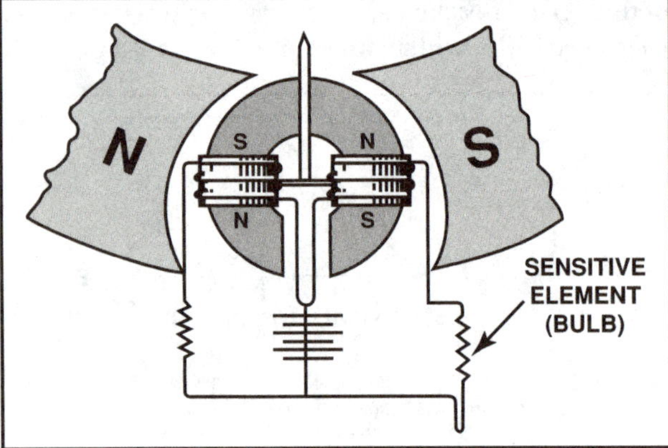

Figure 2-12. A ratiometer temperature measuring system operates with two circuit branches that balance electromagnetic forces. One branch contains a coil and fixed resistor while the other contains a coil and variable resistor, located in the temperature sensing probe. The coils are wound on a rotor which pivots in the center of a permanent magnet air gap.

Ratiometer temperature measuring systems are especially useful in applications where accuracy is critical or large variations of supply voltages are encountered. Therefore, a ratiometer circuit type oil temperature sensing system is generally preferred over Wheatstone bridge circuits by aircraft and engine manufacturers.

Some older oil temperature gauges used a **vapor pressure**, or Bourdon tube type instrument. With this type of instrument, a Bourdon tube is connected by a capillary tube to a liquid filled temperature sensing bulb. The bulb is installed in the engine's oil inlet line where the volatile liquid in the bulb is heated by the oil. As the liquid in the sensing bulb heats up, the capillary and Bourdon tubes also heat up. This causes the vapor pressure within the capillary and Bourdon tubes to increase, which, in turn, causes the Bourdon tube to straighten. The motion of the Bourdon tube is then transmitted to an indicator through a mechanical linkage.

OIL PRESSURE

The engine lubrication system supplies oil under pressure to the moving parts of the engine. To allow a pilot to monitor the effectiveness of a given lubrication system, all aircraft engines are equipped with an oil pressure gauge that is calibrated in pounds per square inch. Since inadequate oil pressure can lead to oil starvation in engine bearings and excessive pressure can rupture gaskets and seals, the oil pressure in most reciprocating engines is typically regulated over a fairly narrow operating range. [Figure 2-13]

Many oil pressure gauges utilize a Bourdon tube because its design enables the gauge to measure relatively high fluid pressures. The gauge is connected by a metal tube directly to a point immediately downstream from the engine oil pump. Therefore, an oil pressure gauge measures the oil pressure being delivered to the engine. To protect the gauge

Figure 2-13. The oil pressure limits of 25 psi minimum and 90 psi maximum on this gauge are representative of a typical small aircraft engine. The normal operating range of 60 to 90 psi ensures enough oil pressure to protect bearing surfaces without rupturing engine seals and gaskets.

Figure 2-14. A typical cylinder head temperature gauge consists of a relatively large green arc and a single red line. The instrument above has a normal operating range that begins at 200°F and peaks at a red line of 475°F.

from occasional pressure surges, most gauges have a small restriction at their inlet. In addition, most fittings that attach the oil line to the engine also have a small restriction to limit oil loss in the event the oil line breaks.

One disadvantage of this type of oil pressure indicating system is that it does not work well in cold weather because the oil in the line between the engine and cockpit gauge tends to congeal. The congealed oil then causes false readings of either low or no oil pressure. This error can be minimized by filling the oil line with a very light oil.

The trend in larger more modern aircraft is to replace Bourdon tube pressure instruments with electrical transmitters. This allows long oil filled lines between engines and instruments to be replaced with lightweight wire. In addition to saving weight, electrical transmitters also provide greater accuracy.

Oil pressure instrument readings are a critical indicator of engine operation and should be monitored frequently, especially during engine starts. For example, some aircraft manuals caution you to shut down an engine after 30 seconds in warm weather or one minute in extremely cold weather if no sign of oil pressure is present. Engine shutdown in this case is a precaution taken to prevent possible damage to an engine until the reason for lack of oil pressure can be determined. On the other hand, excessive pointer oscillation typically indicates that air is trapped in the oil line leading to the instrument or that some unit in the oil system is functioning improperly. In addition, low oil pressure or fluctuations from zero to normal are often signs of low oil quantity.

CYLINDER HEAD TEMPERATURE

The engine temperature can have a dramatic impact on engine performance. Therefore, most reciprocating engine powered aircraft are equipped with a cylinder head temperature (CHT) gauge that allows a pilot to monitor engine temperatures. [Figure 2-14]

Most cylinder head temperature gauges are galvanometer-type meters that display temperatures in degrees Fahrenheit. If you recall from your study of electricity, a galvanometer measures the amount of electrical current produced by a thermocouple. A **thermocouple** is a circuit consisting of two dissimilar metal wires connected together at two junctions to form a loop. Anytime a temperature difference exists between the two junctions, a small electrical current is generated that is proportional to the temperature difference and measurable by the galvanometer. Typical dissimilar metal combinations used are iron and constantan, or chromel and alumel. Since a thermocouple generates its own electrical current, it is capable of operating independent of aircraft power.

The two junctions of a thermocouple circuit are commonly referred to as a hot junction and a cold junction. The **hot junction** is installed in the cylinder head in one of two ways; the two dissimilar wires may be joined inside a bayonet probe which is then inserted into a special well in the top or rear of the hottest cylinder, or the wires may be imbedded in a special copper spark plug gasket. The **cold junction**, or **reference junction**, on the other hand, is typically located in the instrument case.

Thermocouple instrument systems are polarized and extremely sensitive to resistance changes within their electrical circuits. Therefore, several precautions must be observed when replacing or repairing them. First, be sure to observe all color-coding and polarity markings because accidentally reversing the wires causes the meter to move off-scale on the zero side. In addition, ensure that all electrical connections are clean and torqued to the correct value.

Thermocouple wiring leads are typically supplied in matched pairs and secured together by a common braid. Furthermore, the leads are a specified length, matched to the system to provide accurate temperature indications. The length of the leads cannot be altered because doing so changes their resistance. In some cases, the wiring leads are permanently attached to a thermocouple, necessitating the replacement of the entire wiring harness and thermocouple if a wire breaks or becomes damaged.

Simple CHT systems use a single indicator that monitors the hottest cylinder. With this type of system, overall engine temperature must be interpreted in a general way. There are, however, more complex systems which monitor each cylinder and can be set to warn you when a cylinder approaches its maximum temperature limit.

EXHAUST GAS TEMPERATURE

Another performance monitoring instrument often used in reciprocating engine installations is the exhaust gas temperature (EGT) gauge. An EGT gauge measures the temperature of the exhaust at some point past the exhaust port. Since the fuel/air mixture setting has a direct effect on the combustion temperature, a pilot can use an EGT gauge to obtain the best mixture setting for fuel efficiency. A typical EGT gauge is calibrated in degrees Fahrenheit with 25°F divisions. [Figure 2-15]

Figure 2-15. The fuel/air mixture can be set for best fuel efficiency by using an EGT gauge and following the aircraft checklist instructions.

Like the cylinder head temperature gauge, EGT gauges also use thermocouples to sense temperature. However, the thermocouple wiring for an EGT is usually made from alumel and chromel. Alumel is typically used as the negative lead, and is enclosed in green insulation, while chromel is the positive lead and is normally enclosed in white insulation. The hot junction of an EGT thermocouple is usually mounted somewhere on the exhaust manifold and is directly exposed to the exhaust gas stream. The cold junction, on the other hand, is located in the instrument case.

EGT readings are commonly used to set the fuel/air mixture for best economy and best power settings. For example, leaning the fuel/air mixture to obtain a peak EGT value indicates a mixture that results in best economy and maximum endurance. However, most engine manufacturers caution against continuous operation at peak EGT with high power settings. Depending on the engine manufacturer's instructions, a common method of setting best power is to adjust the mixture to peak EGT, then enrichen it to approximately 25°F cooler than peak EGT.

ENGINE ANALYZERS

Many reciprocating engine-powered aircraft utilize some form of analyzer to monitor engine performance. Cylinder head temperature gauges and exhaust gas temperature gauges are used as simple engine analyzers. A more complex form of engine analyzer is known as an **exhaust gas analyzer (EGA).** An exhaust gas analyzer operates like automotive tailpipe emissions testers in that it samples an engine's exhaust gas and analyzes its chemical composition. From the information provided by an analyzer, a pilot can adjust the mixture for the most efficient operation.

It is often difficult to detect small changes on engine instrument indications, yet it is critical for a pilot to know if a system is operating abnormally. Therefore, in addition to an engine analyzer, many larger aircraft may be equipped with a system of **annunciator lights** to attract the operator's attention when a gauge indication leaves its normal range.

TACHOMETER

An engine's crankshaft rpm is displayed by a tachometer that is calibrated in hundreds of rpm. The tachometer is a primary engine instrument used extensively by a pilot to monitor engine condition

Figure 2-16. The tachometer is a primary engine instrument which provides engine rpm indications. A typical tachometer instrument face is calibrated in hundreds of rpm and has both a green arc and red line.

and verify that the engine is developing the appropriate rpm and power output for a given throttle setting. Most tachometers are divided into 100 rpm increments and have a red line that indicates a maximum rpm setting. [Figure 2-16]

There are four common types of tachometers; mechanical, magnetic, electric, and electronic. **Mechanical tachometers** were used on early aircraft and consisted of a set of flyweights driven by a flexible drive shaft through a set of gears. The flexible shaft extends from the instrument to the engine where it attaches to a drive gear in the engine. As the drive shaft rotates the flyweights in the instrument, centrifugal force pulls the flyweights outward. This outward movement is transferred to a pointer through a gear mechanism. [Figure 2-17]

Magnetic tachometers also utilize a flexible drive shaft, however, a cylindrical magnet inside a **drag cup** takes the place of flyweights. As the drive shaft rotates the magnet inside the drag cup, electromagnetic forces are produced which cause the drag cup to rotate in the same direction as the magnet. However, the drag cup is attached to a spring which opposes the magnetic force of the rotating magnet and allows the cup to rotate an amount proportional to the rotational speed of the magnet. [Figure 2-18]

When a flexible drive shaft is used to operate a tachometer, the distance between the engine and cockpit is a limiting factor. For this reason, electric

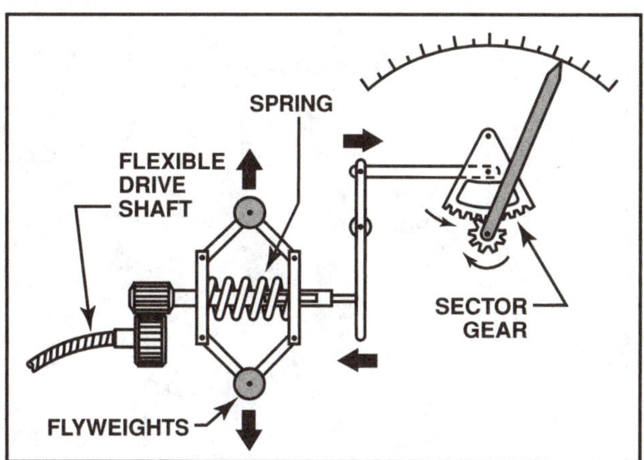

Figure 2-17. A mechanical tachometer consists of a set of flyweights driven by a flexible shaft attached to the engine. The outward movement of the flyweights is transferred to the pointer and is proportional to the engine's speed.

tachometers were developed so instrument wiring could be used in place of a drive shaft. A typical three phase AC electric tachometer system consists of a two or four-pole generator, sometimes referred to as a tachometer generator, or **tach generator**, mounted on the engine accessory case and a synchronous motor inside the indicator. As the engine runs, the tach generator produces an AC voltage with a frequency that is directly proportional to engine rpm. The AC voltage produced drives the synchronous motor in the indicator, causing it to turn at the same speed as the generator. The synchronous motor spins a magnet and drag cup

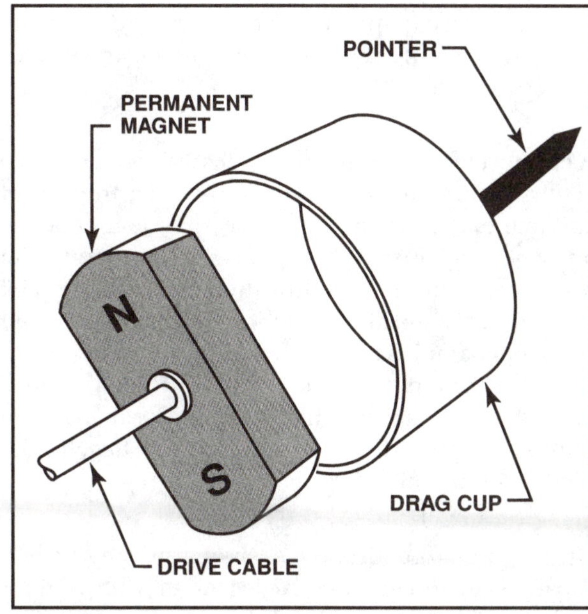

Figure 2-18. Magnetic tachometers utilize a rotating permanent magnet and drag cup to provide rpm indications. Electromagnetic forces generated by the spinning magnet are balanced by a spring attached to the drag cup.

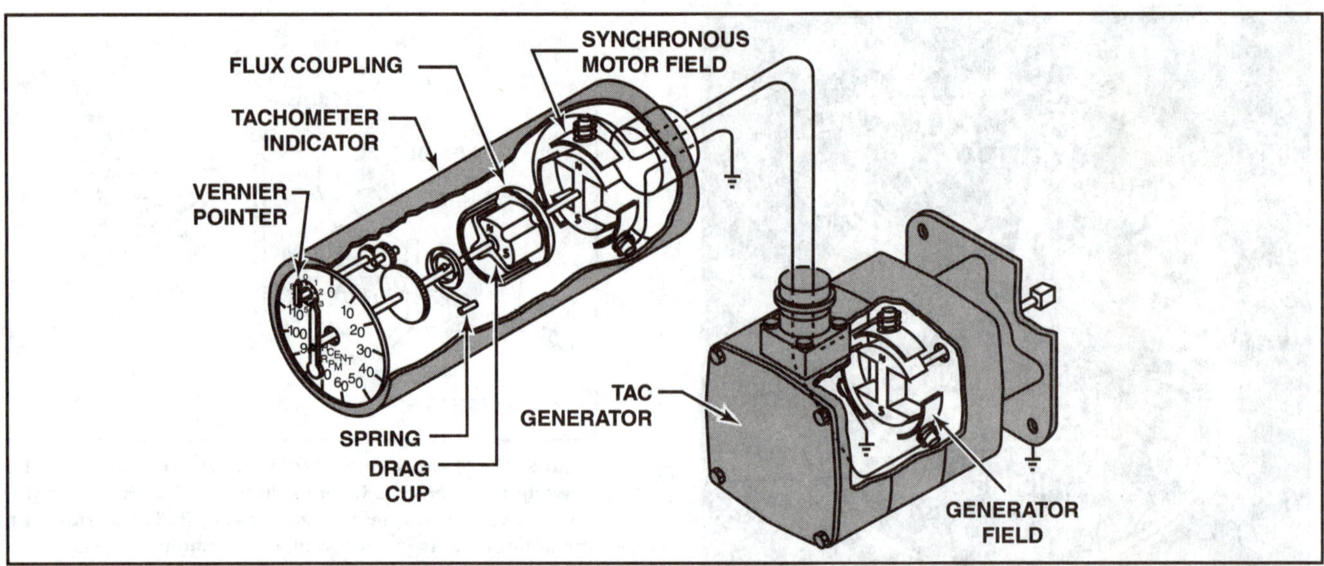

Figure 2-19. A typical electric tachometer consists of a three phase AC generator mounted on the engine accessory case and a synchronous motor in the indicator. The tach generator is driven by the accessory gearing in a running engine and produces an AC voltage at a frequency directly proportional to engine rpm. The synchronous motor in the indicator is, in turn, driven by the AC voltage from the tach generator at the same speed, or frequency. The motor spins a drag cup assembly to move the instrument pointer.

assembly similar to that of the magnetic tachometer to provide rpm indications. [Figure 2-19]

Electronic tachometers, on the other hand, produce engine rpm indications by counting electric pulses from the magneto ignition system. A special pair of breaker points in one of the engine magnetos sends pulses to a module which uses digital circuitry to convert the pulses to a voltage for powering the tachometer instrument in the cockpit. As engine rpm increases, pulse frequency and voltage increase, causing the meter movement to register increasing rpm.

A simple electronic tachometer is installed with two electrical connections; one connection to ground and one to a magneto. This type of system depends on magneto pulses strong enough to operate the instrument without amplification. A more complex version of the electronic tachometer has an internal solid state amplifier which requires a third connection for 12 volt power from the aircraft electrical system. The internal amplifier amplifies weak magneto pulses and provides a uniform pulse voltage to the digital counter circuitry.

On multi-engine aircraft, each engine may have a separate tachometer or a single tach may be used for both engines. If a single tach is used, the indicating needle for the right engine is identified by an "R" while the indicating needle for the left engine is identified by an "L." [Figure 2-20].

FAR Part 27 Airworthiness standards, on the other hand, require that all helicopters have at least two tachometer systems. One tachometer indicates engine rpm, while the second tachometer provides main rotor rpm.

SUCTION GAUGE

The suction gauge is not officially classified as an engine instrument since it does not indicate any engine performance information. However, as an aviation maintenance technician, you will refer to the suction gauge to adjust the suction regulator and to verify the operation of the vacuum pump. Most suction gauges are calibrated in inches of mercury and represent a reductionin pressure below atmospheric pressure. The normal operating range on a typical suction gauge is between 3 and 6 inches of mercury.

INSTRUMENT MAINTENANCE PRACTICES

As an aviation maintenance technician, there is little you can do in terms of making repairs to engine instruments. However, you can do some basic preventative maintenance that does not require you to disassemble an instrument. For example, tachometers that are mechanically driven with flexible drive shafts require periodic maintenance to prevent erratic indications. The drive shaft must be lubricated with an approved lubricant such as graphite. In addition, the hardware that attaches the drive shaft to the instrument, airframe, and engine should be secure. The drive shaft should be installed away from excessive heat or fluids without sharp bends or

Figure 2-20. Multi-engine aircraft are sometimes equipped with a single tachometer that provides rpm indications for both engines. The needle with an "R" represents the right engine while the needle with an "L" represents the left engine.

kinks, and should not impose any strain on the instrument. In addition, the drive shaft should be secured at frequent intervals to prevent whipping, which causes pointer oscillation.

Electric and electronic tachometer installations must be checked periodically to be sure the tach generators and instruments are securely mounted and do not vibrate when the engine is running. Furthermore, the tachometer electrical wiring should be properly laced and clamped to prevent chafing caused by vibration and looseness. In addition, verify that the wiring bundle is not under tension from being clamped too tightly and is protected from corrosive fluids and excessive heat.

During a 100-hour or annual inspection, FAR Part 43 Appendix D requires you to check the instruments for poor condition, mounting, marking, and improper operation. As an A&P technician, you can correct minor discrepancies on instruments such as tightening mount screws and B nuts, repairing chipped paint on the instrument case, or replacing range markings on a glass instrument face. Chipped paint on the case is a cosmetic flaw that has no bearing on the proper operation of the instrument, therefore the instrument is serviceable and does not require immediate correction. However, any discrepancy that requires opening the instrument case such as a cracked or fogged glass, loose pointer, or pointer that will not zero out must be corrected by an approved repair station. In this case, all you can do as a technician is remove and replace the defective instrument.

GROUND OPERATIONS

Conducting an engine runup is a ground operation that can present a safety hazard to personnel and can damage an aircraft and surrounding equipment. Therefore, certain precautions must be taken. For example, all engine runups should be conducted in an area specifically designated for that purpose. Furthermore, the aircraft should be positioned on a clean level surface and aimed so the blast from the propeller does not blow dirt into any hangar or onto another aircraft. Rather than relying solely on the aircraft's brakes, chock the wheels securely, or tie the aircraft down to prevent movement during engine power checks.

Ground service equipment such as auxiliary power carts or hydraulic service units should be positioned well away from the propeller arc with their wheels chocked and brakes set. In addition, adequate fire protection should be stationed nearby, being certain that personnel and fire extinguishers are well clear of the propeller area. Furthermore, a reliable means of communication between the engine operator and ground personnel should be established.

HYDRAULIC LOCK

Hydraulic lock is a condition that can develop in a radial engine after shutdown, where oil or liquid fuel accumulates and pools in the lower cylinders, or lower intake pipes. Since fluids are not compressible, any attempt to start an engine with hydraulic lock can cause severe damage to the piston, connecting rod, valves, or cylinder. Therefore, before attempting to start any radial engine that has been shut down for more than 30 minutes, you should check for hydraulic lock. To do this, make sure the ignition switches are "off," then pull the propeller through in the direction of rotation a minimum of two complete revolutions. Any liquid present in a cylinder will be indicated by an abnormal amount of effort required to rotate the propeller.

To eliminate a hydraulic lock, remove either the front or rear spark plug and pull the propeller through in the direction of rotation, allowing the piston to expel any liquid that is present. Never attempt to clear the hydraulic lock by pulling the propeller through in the opposite direction of

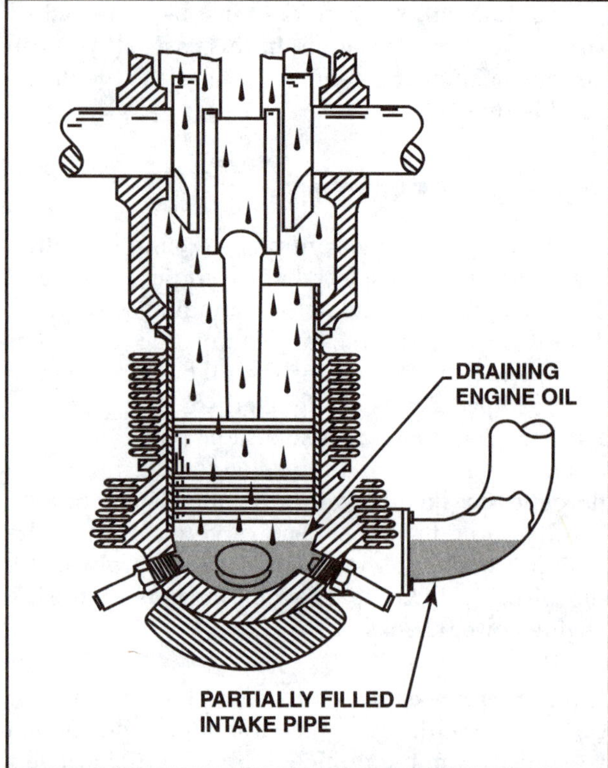

Figure 2-21. Oil or fuel can seep past the piston rings on the lower cylinders of a radial engine, causing hydraulic lock. The presence of hydraulic lock is identified by an abnormal amount of effort required to rotate the propeller. If a start is attempted under these conditions, severe engine damage can result.

rotation, since that could inject the liquid from the cylinder into the intake pipe, increasing the possibility of a complete or partial lock on a subsequent start. [Figure 2-21]

ENGINE STARTING

Starting an aircraft engine is a specialized procedure and varies with an individual engine and aircraft. Therefore, before starting any aircraft engine, be sure to study the procedures in the appropriate airplane flight manual and get instruction from an experienced operator. However, certain general guidelines apply to all reciprocating engine powered aircraft. Before attempting an engine start, check engine fluids and verify that all cockpit engine controls are intact and fully operational. In addition, station extra personnel with fire extinguishing equipment nearby in safe areas.

There is always a possibility of fire when starting an engine. Because of this, you should always have a carbon dioxide fire extinguisher of adequate capacity available. For starting large aircraft where it is not possible to see the engine when it is being started, a fire guard should be stationed near the engine.

Induction system fires are the most common type of fire and occur most frequently in reciprocating engines. The reason for this is if an engine is overprimed and then fires back through the carburetor, the gasoline in the induction system can ignite. If an induction fire occurs, continue cranking the engine to draw the fire back into the cylinders. If this fails, signal the fire guard to extinguish the fire.

To start an engine with a typical float-type carburetor, place the mixture control in the full rich position. Almost all reciprocating engines are equipped with either a carburetor-heat or an alternate-air position on the carburetor air inlet system. For starting and ground operation these controls should be in the cold or closed position. Prime the engine as required, and open the throttle about one-half inch. Turn the master switch on, and turn the engine over with the starter switch. When the engine starts, check for positive oil pressure and adjust the throttle to produce about 1,000 rpm.

If an engine becomes flooded during a start attempt, place the mixture control in the idle cutoff position. This shuts off all fuel flow to the cylinders. With the mixture in the cutoff position, place the ignition switch in the off position, open the throttle all the way, and crank the engine with the starter until the fuel charge in the cylinders has been cleared. Once this is done, repeat the normal start procedure.

Fuel-injected engines have several different starting requirements. For example, once the mixture is placed in the full rich position and the throttle is opened about one-half inch, both the master switch and the fuel pump are turned on until adequate fuel flow is observed. This procedure is required to prime the engine. Once primed, the fuel pump is turned off, the magneto switches are turned on, and the starter is engaged. When the engine starts, check for positive oil pressure.

ENGINE WARM-UP

Proper engine warm-up is important, particularly when the condition of the engine is unknown. An improperly adjusted idle mixture, intermittently firing spark plugs, or improperly adjusted engine valves all have an overlapping effect on engine stability. Therefore, the warm-up should be made at a speed that results in maximum engine stability. This typically results when the engine speed is between 800 and 1,000 rpm.

During warm-up, monitor the engine instruments to ensure normal operation. For example, the oil pressure gauge should indicate pressure within 30 seconds after a start. If that does not happen, the engine should be shut down immediately.

At warm-up rpm, the mixture control's effectiveness in changing the fuel/air ratio is minimal between the rich and lean positions. Control of the fuel/air ratio in this rpm range is predominantly governed by throttle position. Therefore, you should set the mixture control at the recommended position and refrain from attempts to try and hasten the warm-up by leaning the mixture.

Carburetor heat can be used as required when icing conditions are present. For engines equipped with a float-type carburetor, it may be desirable to raise the carburetor air temperature during warm-up to prevent ice formation and to ensure smooth operation. However, the warm air provided by the carburetor heat system is not filtered and, therefore, should not be used if dust and dirt may be ingested.

A **magneto safety check** can be performed during warm-up. The purpose of this check is to ensure that all ignition connections are secure and that the ignition system will permit operation at the higher power settings used during later phases of the ground check. This test is accomplished at idle rpm with the propeller in the high rpm, low pitch position. To conduct the check, move the ignition switch from the "both" position to "right" then return to "both," from "both" to "left" and return to "both," from "both" to "off" momentarily, and return to "both." While switching from the "both" position to a single magneto, a slight but noticeable drop in rpm should occur. This indicates that the opposite magneto is properly grounded out. Complete cutting out of the engine when switching from "both" to "off" indicates that both magnetos are properly grounded. Failure to obtain any drop in rpm while in a single magneto position, or failure of the engine to cut out while switching to "off" indicates that one or both ground connections are incomplete.

GROUND CHECK

After engine warm-up, a ground check is performed to verify the operation of the powerplant and accessory equipment. This check typically requires you to properly interpret instrument readings based on established performance criteria. Generally, the ground check items are included in the preflight runup checklist.

During the ground check, head the aircraft into the wind, if possible, to take advantage of the cooling airflow. A ground check may be performed as follows:

1. Open the cowl flaps.
2. Set the mixture in the full rich position.
3. Verify that the propeller control is in the low pitch, high rpm position.
4. Place the carburetor heat control in the cold position.
5. Open the throttle to the specified rpm and lean the mixture as required.
6. If the engine is carbureted, apply carburetor heat and observe a slight drop in rpm. Once rpm stabilizes, return the carburetor heat to the cold position.
7. Move the magneto switch from "both" to "right" and back to "both." Then, switch from "both" to "left" and back to "both." You should observe a slight rpm drop while operating on the right and left magnetos. The drop on either magneto should be approximately the same, and the maximum drop should not exceed that specified by the engine manufacturer.
8. If the aircraft is equipped with a constant-speed propeller, check the propeller operation according to propeller manufacturer's instructions.
9. Check the fuel pressure and oil pressure. They must be within the established tolerances.
10. Check the ammeter and suction gauge for proper system operation.
11. Retard the throttle to the idle position.

In addition to the operations outlined above, check the aircraft generator and hydraulic systems. The test procedures for these systems are generally detailed on the aircraft checklist for runup.

IGNITION OPERATION

By comparing the rpm drop encountered when checking the magnetos to a known standard, you can determine if a magneto is properly timed and if all the ignition leads are properly grounded. For example, a rapid rpm drop which occurs when you switch to one magneto may indicate that the spark plugs or ignition harness is faulty because these defects take effect immediately. Faulty spark plugs or a defective ignition harness is often manifested by dead cylinders or intermittent firing at the instant the magneto switch is moved. On the other hand, a slow rpm drop is usually caused by incorrect ignition timing or faulty valve adjustment. These conditions result in a loss of power, but do not occur as rapidly as a dead spark plug.

An engine that quits firing completely when switched to one magneto is definite evidence that the selected magneto ignition system is malfunctioning. On the other hand, an absence of an rpm drop could indicate a defective ground connection on one side of the ignition system. Another indication of a defective ignition system is an excessive rpm difference between the left and right switch positions which may indicate a difference in timing between the left and right magnetos.

POWER CHECK

When conducting a ground check, most aircraft manufacturers also require a power check. The purpose of a power check is to measure an engine's performance against an established standard. The standard is determined by the manufacturer and represents the amount of power an engine can develop at a given rpm and manifold pressure. With a constant air density, a given propeller and blade angle always requires the same rpm to absorb the same horsepower from the engine.

To conduct a power check, place the propeller in the low pitch, high rpm position and advance the throttle to obtain the target rpm established by the manufacturer. Under these conditions, the manifold pressure gauge should indicate the pressure specified by the manufacturer if all of the cylinders are operating properly. However, if the engine is weak, or if one or more cylinders are dead or intermittently firing, the operating cylinders must provide more power for a given rpm. Consequently, the throttle must be opened further, resulting in higher manifold pressure. Therefore, a higher than normal manifold pressure for a given rpm usually indicates a dead cylinder or late ignition timing. On the other hand, an excessively low manifold pressure indicates that the ignition timing is early. In addition to causing a low manifold pressure, early ignition timing can cause detonation and loss of power at high power settings.

IDLE SPEED AND MIXTURE

When an engine is operated at idle for long periods of time, many pilots tend to use an excessively rich fuel/air mixture to aid in cylinder cooling. However, after prolonged operation, the excess fuel has a tendency to build up and foul out the spark plugs. With a properly adjusted idle mixture setting, it is possible to run the engine at idle rpm for long periods. Such a setting results in minimal plug fouling and exhaust smoking.

In addition to properly adjusting the mixture control in the cockpit, you should conduct a mixture check during the ground check to verify that the carburetor mixture screw is properly adjusted. To perform a mixture check, close the throttle and move the mixture control to the "idle cutoff" position. Observe the change in rpm just before it drops off dramatically and return the mixture control to the "rich" position.

If the mixture is adjusted properly, engine rpm should increase by an amount recommended by the manufacturer (usually 20 rpm). If the increase in rpm is less than that recommended or if no increase occurs, the idle mixture is too lean. However, if the rpm increases above the recommended value, the mixture is too rich.

ACCELERATION AND DECELERATION

Aircraft engines must be capable of accelerating and decelerating rapidly. Therefore, when conducting a ground check, you should conduct an acceleration and deceleration check. To perform an acceleration test, move the throttle from idle to full power smoothly and rapidly. The engine should accelerate without hesitation and with no evidence of engine backfiring. The deceleration check is made by retarding the throttle from full power back to idle. The rpm should decrease smoothly and evenly, with little or no tendency for the engine to afterfire.

An acceleration and deceleration check often reveals borderline conditions that are not apparent during other checks. This is true because the high cylinder pressures developed during this check put added strain on both the ignition system and the fuel metering system. This added strain is typically sufficient to point out certain defects that otherwise would go unnoticed.

ENGINE STOPPING

The procedure used to shut down an engine varies from engine to engine based on the type of carburetor or fuel injection system installed. Therefore, the shutdown instructions provided by the manufacturer should be followed exactly. As a rule, most engines are shut down by placing the mixture control in the "idle cut off" position. This procedure helps ensure that all of the fuel in the cylinders and induction system is burned. If all the fuel is burned, the chances of an accidental start caused by propeller movement is minimized. Once the engine quits, the ignition switch is turned off and the key is taken out of the ignition.

If an engine becomes excessively warm during taxi,

you should allow the engine to idle for a short time before you shut it down. This allows both the cylinder head temperature and oil temperature to cool to reasonable levels prior to engine shutdown.

ENGINE PERFORMANCE

A reciprocating engine consists of many parts that must work properly if the engine is to operate efficiently. If a component or system fails or operates improperly, engine performance suffers. Therefore, it is important that you understand the interrelationships that exist among various engine systems, and know that a given malfunction can have an underlying cause that is seemingly unrelated.

COMPRESSION

In order for an engine to produce power, all cylinder openings must close and seal completely on the compression strokes. Based on this, there are three items that must occur to obtain maximum efficiency. First, the piston rings must be in good condition so that there is no leakage between the piston and the cylinder walls. Second, the intake and exhaust valves must close tightly to eliminate compression loss through the valve ports. Third, valve timing must be correct when the engine is operating at its normal rated rpm. If any one of these items is not correct, the cylinder will not seal and poor compression will result. Anytime cylinder compression is low, engine performance suffers.

FUEL MIXTURE

For best operation, each cylinder must be provided with the proper fuel/air mixture. If the fuel/air mixture is too rich or too lean, the amount of brake horsepower an engine produces decreases. [Figure 2-22]

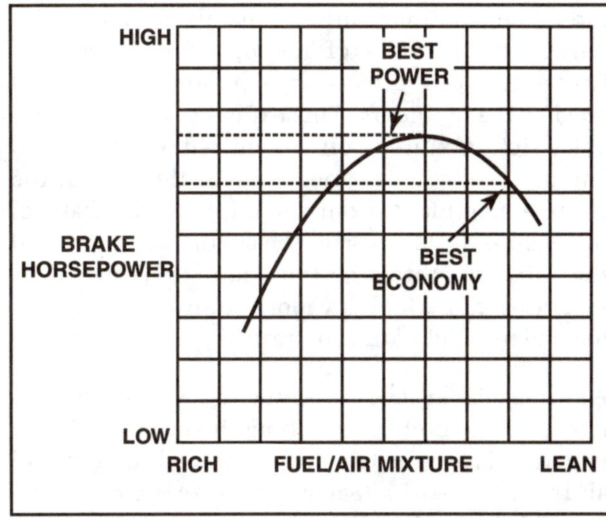

Figure 2-22. The power an engine develops is determined in part by the fuel/air mixture. As you can see in the graph above, an engine's power output increases to a maximum point as the fuel mixture is leaned. However, beyond this point, the power output falls off as the mixture is further leaned.

When an engine is first started, the mixture is typically placed in the full rich position to promote engine starting. However, once started, a full rich mixture does not allow the engine to produce its rated power for any given throttle setting. Therefore, before an aircraft takes off, the mixture is leaned so the engine can produce its maximum, or best, power. Once in cruise, though, the mixture is further leaned to achieve the engine's best economy. Specific leaning procedures should be in accordance with the respective Pilot/Owner's Handbook.

The temperature of combustion in a cylinder varies directly with the ratio of the fuel/air mixture. For example, excessively rich mixtures burn cool because excess fuel enters the cylinders and provides a cooling effect. As the mixture is leaned, the amount of excess fuel available decreases and cylinder temperatures increase. However, if the fuel/air mixture becomes too lean, combustion can not occur and cylinder temperatures drop off. [Figure 2-23]

INDUCTION MANIFOLD

An engine's induction manifold is responsible for distributing the fuel/air mixture to the cylinders. When a carburetor introduces liquid fuel into the airstream, air must vaporize the fuel in the

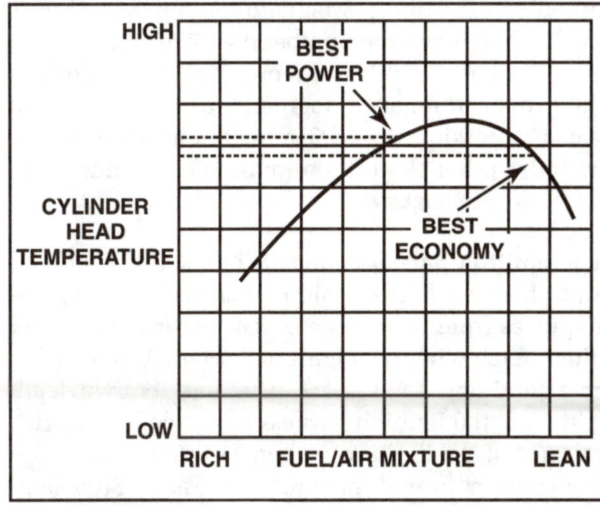

Figure 2-23. Cylinder head temperature varies with the fuel/air ratio. Notice that excessively rich and excessively lean mixtures produce lower cylinder temperatures.

induction manifold. Any fuel that does not vaporize clings to the walls of the induction manifold. Obviously, this affects the amount of fuel that reaches the cylinders. This explains why an apparently rich mixture is often required to start a cold engine. In a cold engine, some of the fuel in the airstream condenses out and clings to the walls of the manifold. However, as the engine warms up and the airflow through the induction manifold increases, more fuel is vaporized, leaving less fuel to condense out of the airstream.

Any leak in an engine induction system has an effect on the mixture reaching the cylinders. This is particularly true of a leak at the cylinder end of an intake pipe. If a leak exists, excess air is introduced into the fuel/air mixture, causing the mixture to become excessively lean to the point that normal combustion can not occur. This is especially true at low rpm settings since the total volume of airflow is relatively low and the additional air coming in through a leak leans the fuel/air mixture appreciably.

IGNITION TIMING

An ignition system consists of two magnetos, an ignition harness, and a set of spark plugs. The **magneto** is a high voltage generating device that generates the electrical energy necessary to ignite the fuel/air mixture. A magneto generates a series of peak voltages which are released by the opening of a set of breaker points. A distributor then routes these high voltage impulses to the cylinders in proper order. In order for a magneto to operate correctly, it must be timed internally so the points open at the correct time. In addition, a magneto must also be timed to the engine. Magneto-to-engine timing is established when the number one firing position on the distributor is set to fire cylinder number one at the proper number of degrees before top center of the compression stroke. Timing the magneto to any cylinder other than the number one cylinder produces severe backfiring.

The **ignition harness** consists of a set of insulated and shielded high tension lines which carry the impulses from the magneto distributor to the spark plugs. Each wire in an ignition harness is referred to as a **lead** and each spark plug has its own lead. Although the ignition harness is simple, it is a critical part of the ignition system. A number of things can cause failure of the ignition harness. For example, insulation may break down on a wire inside the harness and allow some or all of the high voltage energy to leak through the shielding to ground. In addition, open circuits may result from broken wires or poor connections. In some cases, a bare wire could be exposed through chafed insulation and contact the shielding, or two wires could become shorted together.

Any serious defect in an individual lead prevents the high voltage impulse from reaching the spark plug. As a result, only one spark plug in the cylinder fires. This can lead to a substantial power loss and a corresponding loss in aircraft performance. Two bad leads to the same cylinder cause the cylinder to go completely dead.

Among the most common ignition harness defects, and the most difficult to detect, are high voltage leaks. However, a complete harness check typically reveals these and other defects.

Although the spark plug is simple both in construction and in operation, it is, nevertheless, the direct or indirect cause of many malfunctions in aircraft engines. Therefore, you must make sure you install the plug specified for a particular engine. One of the reasons a particular plug is specified is its heat range. The **heat range** of a spark plug determines the temperature at which the nose of the plug operates.

MAINTENANCE

As an aviation maintenance technician performing engine maintenance, you should bear in mind that engine reliability is paramount in aircraft operations. The only way to maintain this reliability is to perform the appropriate engine maintenance on a regularly scheduled basis. Airworthiness standards relating to the design, construction, maintenance, and overhaul of aircraft engines are listed in FAR Part 33, Airworthiness Standards: Aircraft Engines. Appendix A of Part 33 requires engine manufacturers to provide a set of instructions for continued airworthiness with each engine they produce. Instructions for continued airworthiness include maintenance manuals, operating instructions, inspection items and intervals, overhaul procedures, and Airworthiness Limitations. Therefore, engine maintenance tasks and overhaul operations are established by engine manufacturers to ensure reliable operation and are scheduled at specified intervals based on accumulated hours of operation.

ENGINE TROUBLESHOOTING

The need for troubleshooting is dictated by unsatisfactory powerplant performance. Efficient troubleshooting is based on a systematic analysis of what is happening so you will be able to determine the cause of a malfunction. There is no magic in successful troubleshooting, but rather an application of logic and a thorough knowledge of the basics of engine operation. For example, if you are faced with a problem of deteriorating engine performance, the first thing you should do is get all of the facts. Take nothing for granted, and ask the pilot questions. For example, find out if the trouble comes about suddenly or was it a gradual decrease in performance? Under what conditions of altitude, humidity, temperature, or power setting does this performance loss show up? Does temporarily switching to one magneto cause any change in performance? What effect did leaning the mixture or applying carburetor heat have on the problem? Did switching from one fuel tank to another, or turning on the fuel boost pump have any effect on the problem?

After getting all of the facts, perform a ground check to see if the problem can be duplicated. The next step is to eliminate all of the areas that are not likely to cause the trouble. For example, if the magneto drop is normal, but there is a loss of power, the ignition system more than likely is not the problem. To assist in the troubleshooting process, some manufacturers provide troubleshooting flow charts or trouble-cause-remedy charts. [Figure 2-24]

BACKFIRING

When an excessively lean fuel/air mixture passes into a cylinder, the mixture may not burn at all or will burn so slowly that combustion continues through the power and exhaust strokes. If this occurs, the flame can linger in the cylinder and ignite the contents of the intake manifold and the induction system when the intake valve opens. This causes an explosion known as backfiring, which can damage the carburetor and other parts of the induction system.

Backfiring is seldom the fault of the carburetor and, in most cases, is limited to one or two cylinders. Usually, backfiring is the result of incorrect valve clearance, defective fuel injector nozzles, or other conditions which result in a leaner mixture entering the cylinder. In some instances, an engine backfires in the idle range, but operates satisfactorily at medium and high power settings. The most likely cause, in this case, is an extremely lean idle fuel/air mixture. Enriching the mixture usually corrects this difficulty. Because backfiring cylinders fire intermittently, they typically run cooler than cylinders that are operating normally. Therefore, a backfiring cylinder can sometimes be detected by a **cold cylinder check**.

AFTERFIRING

Afterfiring, sometimes called afterburning, often results when the fuel/air mixture is too rich. Overly rich mixtures, like excessively lean mixtures, also burn slowly. However, the slow burn rate of a rich mixture is due to the lack of sufficient oxygen. If an overly rich mixture burns past the power stroke and into the exhaust stroke, unburned fuel can be forced out of a cylinder into the exhausted gases. If this occurs, air from outside the exhaust stacks will mix with the unburned fuel, causing it to ignite and explode in the exhaust system. Afterfiring is perhaps more common with engines that have long exhaust ducting that can retain greater amounts of unburned fuel. Typical causes of afterfiring include an improperly adjusted carburetor or an unseated exhaust valve.

Afterfiring can also be caused by cylinders which are not firing because of faulty spark plugs, defective fuel injection nozzles, or incorrect valve clearances. The unburned mixture from these dead cylinders passes into the exhaust system, where it ignites and burns. Unfortunately, the resulting afterburn can easily be mistaken for evidence of a rich carburetor. Cylinders which are afterfiring intermittently can cause a similar effect. Again, the malfunction can be remedied by finding the cause and correcting the defect.

COLD CYLINDER CHECK

A cold cylinder check can help determine the operating characteristics of each cylinder on an engine. The tendency of any cylinder or cylinders to be cold or only slightly warm indicates lack of combustion within the cylinder. A cold cylinder check is made with a cold cylinder indicator which is simply an accurate pyrometer with a probe that is touched to a cylinder. Engine difficulties which can be analyzed by use of the cold cylinder indicator are:

1. Rough engine operation.
2. Excessive rpm drop or intermittent misfiring dur ing the ignition system check.
3. High manifold pressure for a given engine rpm during the ground check when the propeller is in the full low pitch position.
4. Improper valve clearances.

To conduct a cold cylinder check, you must run the engine until the cylinders are warm. When doing this, it is imperative that you head the aircraft into the wind to minimize irregular cooling and to ensure even propeller loading. Once the engine is running, duplicate the conditions that produce the

TROUBLE	PROBABLE CAUSE	REMEDY
Engine fails to start	Lack of fuel.	Check fuel system for leaks. Fill fuel tank. Clean dirty lines, strainers, or fuel valves.
	Underpriming.	Use correct primimg procedure.
	Overpriming.	Open throttle and "unload" engine by rotating the propeller.
	Incorrect throttle setting.	Open throttle to one-tenth of its range.
	Defective spark plug wires.	Clean and regap or replace spark plugs.
	Defective ignition wire.	Test and replace any defective wires.
	Defective or weak battery.	Replace with charged battery.
	Improper operation of magneto or breaker points.	Check internal timing of magnetos.
	Water in carburetor.	Drain carburetor and fuel lines.
	Internal failure.	Check oil sump strainer for metal particles.
	Dirty air filter.	Clean or replace.
Low power or engine running unevenly.	Mixture too rich; indicated by sluggish engine operation, red exhaust flame, and black smoke.	Check primer. Readjust carburetor mixture.
	Mixture too lean; indicated by overheating or backfiring.	Check fuel lines for dirt or other restrictions. Check fuel supply.
	Leaks in induction system.	Tighten all connections. Replace defective parts.
	Defective spark plugs.	Clean or replace spark plugs.
	Improper grade of fuel.	Fill tank with recommended grade.
	Magneto breaker points not working properly.	Clean points. Check internal timing of magneto.
	Defective ingition wire.	Test and replace any defective wires.
	Defective spark plug leads.	Replace connectors on spark plug wire.
	Incorrect valve clearance.	Adjust valve clearance.
	Restriction in exhaust system.	Remove restriction.
	Improper ignition timing.	Check magnetos for timing and synchronization.
	Improperly adjusted carburator heat valve.	Adjust carburator heat control linkage.
Engine fails to develop full power.	Throttle lever out of adjustment.	Adjust throttle lever.
	Leak in induction system.	Tighten all connections and replace defective parts.
	Restriction in carburetor airscoop.	Examine airscoop and remove restriction.
	Improper fuel.	Fill tank with recommend fuel.
	Propeller governor out of adjustment.	Adjust governor.
	Faulty ingition.	Tighten all connections. Check system. Check ignition timing.
Rough running engine.	Cracked engine mount(s).	Repair or replace engine mount(s).
	Unbalanced propeller.	Remove propeller and have it checked for balance.
	Defective mounting bushings.	Install new mounting bushings.
	Lead deposit on spark plugs.	Clean or replace spark plugs.
	Primer unlocked.	Lock primer.

Figure 2-24. This trouble-cause-remedy chart lists some general conditions or troubles which may be encountered with reciprocating engines, such as "engine fails to start." The chart then goes on to give probable causes contributing to the condition. Corrective actions are indicated in the "remedy" column.

difficulties you want to analyze. Operate the engine at its roughest speed until cylinder head temperatures reach approximately 300°F, or until temperatures stabilize at a lower reading. Once this occurs, shut down the engine by moving the mixture to idle cut off. When the engine ceases firing, turn off the ignition and master switches.

As soon as the engine is secured, check the temperature of each cylinder using the cold cylinder tester. Start with the number one cylinder and proceed in numerical order around the engine as rapidly as possible. Recheck any low readings.

In interpreting the results of a cold cylinder check, remember that the temperatures are relative and cylinder temperature taken alone means little. However, when the temperature of one cylinder can be compared with the temperatures of other cylinders, cylinder problems can be identified.

COMPRESSION TESTING

A cylinder compression test determines if the valves, piston rings, and pistons are adequately sealing the combustion chamber. Cylinders with good compression provide the most power while cylinders with low compression provide minimal power. Low compression for the most part can be traced to valves that leak because of incorrect valve clearances or because the valve timing is too early or too late. Several other conditions can cause leaking valves such as carbon particles between the valve face and seat or valves that have been burned or warped. In addition, low compression can result from excessive wear of piston rings and cylinder walls or pistons that have become worn, scuffed, or damaged in some way.

Before performing a compression test, you should run an engine so the piston rings, cylinder walls, and other parts are freshly lubricated. However, it is not necessary to operate an engine prior to accomplishing a compression check during engine buildup or on individually replaced cylinders. In these cases, spray a small quantity of lubricating oil into the cylinder or cylinders before conducting the test and turn the engine over several times to seal the piston and rings in the cylinder barrel.

The two basic types of compression testers are the differential compression tester and the direct compression tester. A **differential pressure tester** checks the compression of an aircraft engine by measuring air leakage in a cylinder. Tester operation is based, in part, on Bernoulli's principle. In other words, for a given airflow through a fixed opening, a constant pressure drop across the opening results. Any change in the speed of airflow past the opening causes a corresponding change in pressure. Therefore, if pressurized air is supplied to a cylinder through a pressure gauge with both intake and exhaust valves closed, the amount of air that leaks by the valves or piston rings will create a corresponding pressure drop at the indicator. A perfect cylinder, of course, would have no leakage and no pressure drop would occur. [Figure 2-25]

When performing a differential compression test, you must follow the aircraft manufacturer's instructions. However, there are some general guidelines that apply to most tests. The following is a list of common steps taken when performing a differential compression test:

1. Remove the most accessible spark plug from the cylinder and install the compression tester adapter in the spark plug hole.
2. By hand, rotate the engine in the direction of normal operation until the piston in the cylinder you are testing is at top dead center on the compression stroke. If you pass top center, back the propeller up at least 180 degrees prior to turning the propeller again in the direction of rotation. This is necessary to eliminate the effect of backlash in the valve operating mechanism and to keep the piston rings seated on the lower ring lands.
3. Connect the compression tester to a 100 to 150-psi air supply. With the shutoff valve on the compression tester closed, adjust the regulator of the compression tester to obtain 80 psi on the regulated pressure gauge.

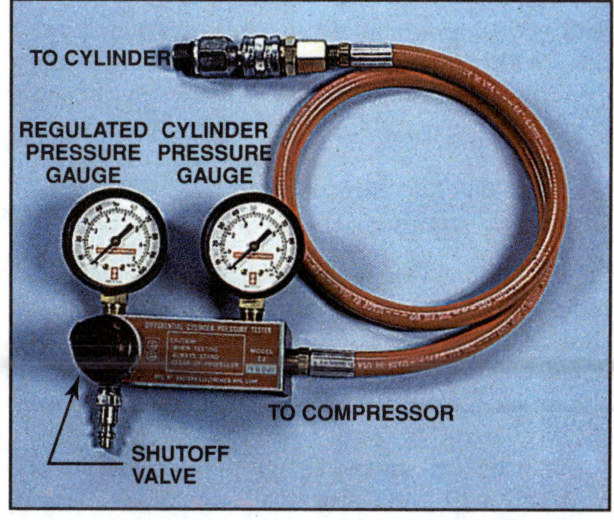

Figure 2-25. A differential compression tester measures leakage in a cylinder and is a valuable diagnostic tool.

4. Recheck the compression tester to verify that the shutoff valve on the tester is closed and connect the tester to the spark plug adapter. Verify that the propeller path is clear of all objects and personnel, then open the shutoff valve on the compression tester. If the piston is past top dead center when pressure is applied, the propeller will rotate in the direction of engine rotation.
5. With the regulated pressure at 80 psi, read the cylinder pressure gauge. If the cylinder pressure gauge reading is below the minimum specified for the engine being tested, move the propeller in the direction of rotation to seat the piston rings in their grooves. However, if you move the propeller while air pressure is applied to the cylinder, make sure you have a tight grip on the propeller to prevent its rotation. Check all the cylinders and record the readings.

If low compression is indicated on any cylinder, turn the engine through with the starter or restart and run the engine to takeoff power and recheck the low cylinder. When checking the compression, listen carefully to see if you can determine the source of the leakage. Air can leak from the cylinder in three places: past the intake valve, past the exhaust valve, and past the piston rings. Leakage, or **blow-by** past the exhaust valve is typically identified by a hissing or whistling heard at the exhaust stack. On the other hand, air leaking past the intake valve can usually be heard through the carburetor. A hissing sound in the crankcase breather indicates air leaking past the piston rings.

If the piston ring gaps on a piston happen to be aligned when a compression test is done, a worn or defective ring indication will result. If this happens, you should run the engine for a period of time so the ring gaps have a chance to shift.

A **direct compression test** indicates the actual pressures within the cylinder. This method is less effective than the differential pressure method in discerning a particular defective component within the cylinder. However, the consistency of the readings provided by a direct compression test indicate an engine's condition as a whole.

In general, most engine maintenance manuals contain instructions on performing a direct compression test. However, some general guidelines apply to most tests and are presented here:

1. Remove the most accessible spark plug from each cylinder.
2. Clear the area around the prop arc and rotate the engine with the starter to eject excess oil accumulations and loose carbon particles from the cylinders.
3. Install a tester in each cylinder and tighten the recommended amount. If only one tester is available, check each cylinder individually.
4. With the throttle open, rotate the engine at least three complete revolutions by engaging the starter and record the compression readings. It is advisable to use external power when cranking the engine because a weak aircraft battery may result in a slow engine-turning rate and lower than expected compression readings.
5. Re-check any cylinder that registers a compression value significantly lower than the other cylinders to verify accuracy. A reading approximately 15 psi lower than the others indicates a cylinder leak that must be repaired. To be sure the low reading is not the result of a faulty tester, repeat the compression check with a tester known to be accurate.

VALVE ADJUSTMENT

As you know, for an engine to produce its maximum rated power, the valves must open and close properly and seal tightly against their seats. One important aspect of making sure the valves operate properly is valve clearance. For example, when valve clearance is excessive, the valves do not open as wide or remain open as long as they should. This reduces valve duration and the valve overlap period. On the other hand, when valve clearance is less than it should be, the valve overlap period is lengthened.

When valve clearances are wrong, it is unlikely that all clearances are wrong in the same direction. Instead, there is typically too much clearance on some cylinders and too little on others. Naturally, this results in a variation in valve overlap between cylinders. When this happens, it is impossible to set the idle adjustment to give correct mixtures on all cylinders, and all cylinders produce differing amounts of power. Variations in valve clearance of as little as 0.005 inch have a definite effect on mixture distribution between cylinders.

Another aspect of valve clearance is its effect on volumetric efficiency. For example, excessive intake valve clearance results in the valve opening late and closing early. This produces a throttling effect on the cylinder because the valve is not open long enough to admit a full charge of fuel and air. This cuts down on power output, particularly at high power settings. Insufficient intake valve clearance has the opposite effect. In other words, the intake valve opens early, closes late, and stays open longer than it should. At low power, early opening of the intake valve can cause backfiring.

Improper exhaust valve clearance also affects engine performance, For example, excessive exhaust valve clearance shortens the exhaust event and causes poor scavenging. The late opening may also lead to cylinder overheating because the hot exhaust gases are held in the cylinder beyond the time specified for their release. On the other hand, when exhaust valve clearance is insufficient, the early opening causes a power loss by shortening the power event. In other words, the pressure in the cylinder is released before all the useful expansion has worked on the piston. In addition, the late valve closing causes the exhaust valve to remain open for a larger portion of the intake stroke. This may result in a portion of the fuel/air mixture being lost through the exhaust port.

In order for a valve to seat, the valve must be in good condition, with no significant pressure being exerted against the end of the valve by the rocker arm. If the expansion of all parts of the engine were the same, the problem of ensuring valve seating would be very easy to solve. Practically no free space would be necessary in the valve system. However, since there is a great difference in the amount of expansion of various parts of the engine, there is no way of providing a constant operating clearance in the valve train on engines equipped with solid lifters.

The clearance in the valve actuating system is very small when the engine is cold but increases when the engine is operating at normal temperature. The disparity is caused by differences in the expansion characteristics of the various metals and by the differences in temperatures of the various parts.

Valve clearances decrease with a drop in temperature; therefore, insufficient clearance could result in a valve being held open when extremely cold temperatures are encountered. This would make cold weather starting difficult, if not impossible, because of the inability of the cylinders to pull a charge into the combustion chamber. Furthermore, if an engine with insufficient valve clearance were started, unseated valves would allow some of the fuel/air mixture to leak by the valves on the compression stroke.

Accurate valve adjustment also establishes the intended valve seating velocity. If valve clearances are excessive, the valve seating velocity will be too high. The result is valve pounding and stem stretching, either of which is conducive to valve failure.

The engine manufacturer specifies the valve inspection period for each engine. In addition to the regular inspection periods, inspect and adjust the valve mechanism any time there is rough engine operation, backfiring, loss of compression, or hard starting. Because of variations in engine designs, various methods are required for setting valves to obtain correct and consistent clearance. In all cases, follow the exact procedure described by the engine manufacturer, since obscure factors may be involved.

INSPECTIONS

As an aviation maintenance technician, you will probably spend the majority of your time inspecting various aircraft components. In fact, the Federal Aviation Regulations require specific inspections at set intervals in order for an aircraft to remain airworthy. When these inspections are done, impending problems are typically found before they become major. Some of the more common types of inspections you will be involved in include the preflight inspection, 50-hour inspection, 100-hour inspection, and annual inspection.

PREFLIGHT INSPECTION

As an aviation maintenance technician, there may be times when you are asked to do a preflight inspection. Although a typical preflight inspection involves checking the entire aircraft, the following discussion is concerned with only the part of the inspection that applies to the powerplant.

The first step in any inspection is to verify that the ignition switch is OFF and the mixture is in the idle cutoff position. The best way to conduct a thorough inspection on an engine is to open the cowling. With the engine exposed, start at the rear of the accessory section near the firewall and inspect all of the fluid lines. Verify that no lines are loose, chafing against something, or showing signs of excessive wear or deterioration. [Figure 2-26]

If all the fluid lines are in good condition, check the oil level to be sure that it is at the specified operat-

Figure 2-26. The best way to conduct a thorough inspection on an engine is to open the cowling. On some aircraft, the access door on the cowl is large enough to conduct an inspection. However, other aircraft may require the removal of the top cowl.

ing level. Many engines have a tendency to throw oil out the crankcase breather if the sump is completely full; therefore, many aircraft are operated with less than full oil.

Check all of the wire connections to the magneto to be sure there are no loose connections or chafed wires. Check the general condition of the spark plug leads and for any indication of looseness where they attach to the spark plugs. In addition, be sure that all of the leads are secured so they cannot be burned by the exhaust. Check all of the wiring to the generator or alternator and to the voltage regulator. If the battery and master relay are ahead of the firewall, check them as well.

Check below the engine for any indication of fuel or oil leaks. If blue fuel stains or accumulations of oil are visible on the lower cowl or the nose strut, a leak exists somewhere on the engine. Examine the engine baffling paying particular attention to those around the cylinders. If a piece of the baffling is cracked or broken, or if it does not seal, localized hot spots could develop. Check the paint on the cylinders for any indication of discoloration which could indicate the maximum temperature limits were exceeded. Check the primer lines as they enter the cylinders or, if the engine is fuel injected, the injector lines where they attach to the nozzles.

Carefully examine the area where the exhaust risers join the cylinders to be sure that there are no blown gaskets and that all of the nuts are in place. In addition, you should check all of the exhaust system for security and any indication of leaks.

Drain the main fuel strainer and take a fuel sample. There must be no indication of water in the fuel sample and the correct type of fuel must be used.

Inspect the carburetor air filter for both security and cleanness. In addition, check as much of the induction system as possible for visible traces of fuel dye stains. If fuel stains are present, there is probably a leak in the induction system.

Check the propeller for nicks or scratches and, if possible, all of the attaching bolts or nuts for security and for proper safety. If a constant-speed propeller is installed, check for excessive oil leakage at the propeller base and verify that the linkage on the propeller governor is secure.

At times, a customer may request that you runup an engine as part of a preflight check. If this is the case, you should start the engine using the appropriate checklist. Once started, the oil and fuel pressure should raise to the proper operating range. During the runup, the engine should develop the required static rpm and manifold pressure, and the magneto drop should be within the specified limits with equal drops on both magnetos. In addition, a magneto safety check should be performed to be sure that the switch is operating properly. If the aircraft is equipped with a constant-speed propeller, the propeller should cycle smoothly between low and high pitch. In addition, on a carbureted engine, when the carburetor heat control is pulled a slight drop in rpm should occur.

50-HOUR INSPECTION

Although a 50-hour inspection is not required by the Federal Aviation Regulations, it is recommended by almost all engine manufacturers. A typical 50-hour inspection requires you to conduct a runup and check all of the engine's subsystems including the ignition, fuel, lubrication, exhaust, cooling, and turbocharging systems. In addition, most manufacturers provide a checklist for conducting a 50-hour inspection.

IGNITION SYSTEM

The spark plug leads should be checked for security and for any indication of corrosion. All of the leads should be securely fastened to both the spark plug and to the magneto distributor block. In addition, there should be no evidence of chafing or wear to any part of an ignition lead. The spark plugs should be examined where they screw into the cylinder heads for any indication of leakage from the cylinder.

FUEL AND INDUCTION SYSTEM

Check the primer lines for indication of leaks and for security. Remove and clean the fuel inlet strainers and check the mixture control and throttle linkage for proper travel, freedom of movement, and security. Lubricate the controls if it is necessary. Check the air intake and air box for leaks and for any indication of filter damage. In addition, look for evidence of dust or other solid contaminants that may have leaked past the filter. Check the fuel pump vent lines to see if there is evidence of fuel or oil seepage which could indicate that either a fuel or oil seal is leaking.

LUBRICATION SYSTEM

Most engine manufacturers recommend that you drain and replace the engine oil during a 50-hour inspection. If the engine is equipped with an oil screen, it should be removed and inspected for metal particles. However, if the engine is equipped with an oil filter, the filter is removed and cut open so you can inspect it for any traces of metal particles. Check all of the oil lines for any indication of leakage or signs of chafing.

EXHAUST SYSTEM

Check all of the flanges on the exhaust pipes where they attach to the cylinder head for evidence of leakage. If they are loose or show any signs of warpage, they must be removed and machined flat before they are reassembled. In addition, check the general condition of the entire exhaust manifold and muffler assembly, paying particular attention for evidence of leaks.

COOLING SYSTEM

Check all of the cowling and baffles for any indication of damage or missing parts. If a small crack is found, you can usually stop drill it to prevent further growth. However, if substantial cracking exists, additional structural repair may be necessary.

CYLINDERS

Check the rocker box covers for indication of leaks. If a leak is found replace the rocker box gasket. Carefully check the entire cylinder for signs of overheating. Typical indications of a cylinder that has overheated include burned or discolored paint on one or more cylinders. If a cylinder has overheated, further inspection by borescope or by removing the cylinder may be required.

TURBOCHARGER

If an engine is equipped with a turbocharger, the oil feed and return lines should be checked for leaks or chafing. In addition, you should check all of the brackets and heat shielding for security and for any indication of damage or cracks. Check the waste gate for freedom of action and the alternate air door for operation and sealing.

100-HOUR OR ANNUAL INSPECTION

FAR Part 91 states that all general aviation aircraft must go through an annual inspection to remain airworthy. All annual inspections are based on calendar months and, therefore, are due on the last day of the 12th month after the last annual was completed. For example, if a previous annual was completed on June 11, 1995, the next annual inspection is due on June 30, 1996.

Annual inspections must be performed regardless of the number of hours flown in the previous year. Furthermore, they may be performed by airframe and powerplant mechanics holding an **inspection authorization** (IA). The IA cannot delegate the inspection duties to an airframe and powerplant mechanic, nor may an IA merely supervise an annual inspection.

If the person performing the annual inspection finds a discrepancy that renders the aircraft unairworthy, they must provide the aircraft owner with a written notice of the defect. Furthermore, the aircraft may not be operated until the defect is corrected. However, if the owner wants to fly the aircraft to a different location to have the repairs performed, a special flight permit may be obtained to ferry the aircraft to the place where repairs are to be made.

In addition to an annual inspection, all general aviation aircraft that are operated for hire must be inspected every 100 flight hours. This inspection covers the same items as the annual inspection. The major difference is that an A&P technician may perform a 100-hour inspection. As in the case of an annual inspection, the person conducting a 100-hour inspection cannot delegate inspection duties.

The operating hours are the primary consideration for determining when the next 100-hour inspection is due. As the name implies, a 100-hour inspection is due 100 hours after the last 100-hour inspection was completed, regardless of the date. However, there is a provision for extending the 100-hour interval, up to a maximum of 10 hours, to permit the aircraft to fly to a place where the inspection can be accomplished. When this is done, the number of hours in excess of the 100-hour interval are deducted from the next inspection interval. For example, if a flight to a place where a 100-hour inspection can be conducted takes the aircraft six hours beyond the 100-hour inspection interval, the next 100-hour inspection would be due in 94 hours. In other words, the next inspection interval is shortened by the same amount of time the previous inspection was extended.

The following paragraphs examine the basic steps required to complete a 100-hour or annual inspection. However, like any other inspection, the manufacturer's instructions must be followed at all times.

INSPECTION CHECKLISTS

FAR 43.15 lists the performance criteria for performing inspections. In addition, FAR 43.15 specifically states that a checklist which meets the minimum requirements listed in FAR 43 Appendix D must be used for all annual and 100-hour inspections. This, however, does not preclude you from developing a more extensive checklist or using one prepared by a repair station or manufacturer. As long as the checklist covers the items listed in Appendix D it may be used. Most major aircraft manufacturers provide inspection checklists for their aircraft by type and model number. These forms are readily available through the manufacturer's representatives and are highly recommended. They meet the minimum requirements of Appendix D and contain many details covering specific items of equipment installed on a particular aircraft. In addition, they often include references to service bulletins and letters which could otherwise be overlooked. [Figure 2-27]

PRELIMINARY PAPERWORK

One important aspect of conducting a 100-hour or annual inspection is the paperwork involved. Before starting the actual inspection, you should review all of the aircraft records including the Type Certificate Data Sheets. In addition, you should check and list all of the Airworthiness Directives that apply to the engine and all of its components including the carburetor, magnetos, alternator or generator, propeller, and ignition switches. Check the General Aviation Airworthiness Alerts to become familiar with the types of problems other mechanics have found with similar engines. And, finally, go through the manufacturer's service bulletins and service letters to see if there is any additional maintenance recommended or required by the manufacturer.

Once you have reviewed the aircraft paperwork, perform a **conformity inspection** to verify that all of the accessories and equipment on the engine are approved. If an accessory does not appear in an equipment list or Type Certificate Data Sheet, check to see if the item was installed according to a supplemental type certificate. Check the total time on the engine and propeller and compare it with the list of life-limited parts to see if any items are nearing their retirement time. See if there are any Major Repair and Alteration Forms (FAA 337) on the engine or propeller. If there are, check the work to be sure that it was done as described on the form.

CLEANING

Once the paperwork is done you can move on to the actual inspection. According to FAR Part 43 the first step in performing a 100-hour or annual inspection is to open all necessary inspection plates, access doors, fairings, and cowling and clean the aircraft and engine. The cleaning is done to remove any oil, grease, or dirt that could hide cracks or other defects during the inspection. As you open a cowl, look for accumulations of oil or other fluids that may indicate the presence of a leak. If no abnormal amounts of fluid are present, clean the engine and engine compartment using stoddard solvent or a commercial degreaser. To prevent damage to electrical components, you should tape over all vent holes on the magnetos and alternator. In addition, avoid spilling solvent or water directly onto any electrical component, vacuum pump, or starter.

PRE-INSPECTION RUNUP

Once the engine is clean, perform a pre-inspection runup to determine if the engine runs properly and to heat the oil and coat the cylinder walls. During the runup, verify that the temperatures and pressures are within the correct operating range. In addition, verify that the engine develops its proper static rpm and that the magneto drop is within an acceptable range. The drop must be the same or nearly so on both magnetos. Check for any abnormal noises in the engine and for any vibrations that are not characteristic of that engine.

If the engine is equipped with a constant-speed propeller, cycle it several times to check for proper operation. When a prop is cycled, it should respond smoothly and the recovery should be within the time limit allowed.

INSPECTION REPORT

This form meets requirements of FAR Part 43 **Work Order No. ______**

Make	Model	Serial No.	Registration No.
Owner		Date	
Type of Inspection		Tach Time	

A. PROPELLER GROUP

	L	R	100	500	insp.
1. Inspection spinner and back plate					
2. Inspect blades for nicks and cracks					
3. Inspect hub for cracks and corrosion					
4. Check for grease and oil leaks					
5. Check mounting bolts and safety					
6. Constant speed — check blades for tightness in hub					
7. Constant speed — remove prop, remove sludge					
8. Lubricate as per manual					
9. Inspect complete assembly					
10. Replace spinner					

B. ENGINE GROUP

	L	R	100	500	insp.
1. Remove engine cowls					
2. Clean cowling, check for cracks missing fasteners, etc.					
3. Compression check: /80 L. #1 #2 #3 #4 #5 #6 R. #1 #2 #3 #4 #5 #6					
4. Drain oil					
5. Check oil screens and clean					
6. Replace oil filter element					
7. Check oil temp sender unit for leaks and security					
8. Clean and check oil radiator fins					
9. Remove and flush oil radiator					
10. Check and clean fuel screens					
11. Drain carburetor					
12. Service fuel injector nozzles					
13. Check fuel system for leaks					
14. Check oil lines for leaks and security					
15. Check fuel lines for leaks and security					
16. Service air cleaner					
17. Check induction air and heat ducts					
18. Check condition of carb heat box					
19. Check mag points for proper clearance					
20. Check mags for oil seal leakage					
21. Check breaker felts for lubrication					
22. Check distributor block for cracks, burned areas, corrosion, height of contact springs					
23. Check ignition harness and insulators					

Figure 2-27. FAR Part 43 requires the use of a checklist when conducting either a 100-hour or annual inspection. The checklist must include at least those items contained in FAR Part 43, Appendix D.

Figure 2-28. When changing oil during an inspection, the oil filter should be cut open so you can check for metal particles or other contamination.

After you have checked each of the engine's systems, shut down the engine and bring the aircraft into the hangar. While the engine is still warm, drain the oil and remove the top spark plug from each cylinder so you can perform a compression test.

LUBRICATION SYSTEM

Once you have done a compression test on each cylinder and the engine has cooled, remove the oil filter or screen. If a filter is installed cut the element apart so you can check for metal particles. If a screen is installed, inspect both the screen and screen housing for metal. The presence of some metal particles in the oil is normal; however, an excessive amount is an indication of impending engine failure and their source must be found. [Figure 2-28]

Install and torque a new filter element or the original screen in place. Reinstall and safety the drain plug and fill the oil sump with new oil. Check all of the oil lines, the oil cooler, and the entire engine for any indication of oil leakage that might indicate a leaking gasket or defective component.

IGNITION SYSTEM

Remove the remaining spark plugs and examine all of them. Once way of determining combustion chamber problems is by examining the condition of the spark plugs. For example, normal operation is indicated by a spark plug having a relatively small amount of light brown or tan deposit on the nose of the center electrode insulator. However, if heavy deposits are found, it is a good indication that the rings or valve seals are worn allowing oil to seep into the cylinder. If there is an excess of gray, clinker-like deposits in a spark plug, lead fouling is occurring. One cause of lead fouling is using a fuel with a higher than recommended tetraethyl lead content. Replacing the spark plug with one having a hotter heat range may reduce the fouling, but be sure the hotter plug is approved for the engine.

A dry, black, soot-like deposit on a spark plug indicates that the engine is operating with an excessively rich mixture. If this is the case, check the induction system for obstructions in the filter or for a malfunctioning carburetor heat valve. A brown, shiny glaze on a spark plug could indicate silicon contamination. If this is the case, you should perform a careful inspection of the carburetor air filter for air leaks around the filter element or for holes in the element itself. Any unfiltered air leaking into the induction system allows sand or dust to enter the engine. Once in a cylinder, the intense heat inside the combustion chamber turns the silicon in the sand into a glass-like contaminant that becomes conductive at high temperature and causes the spark plug to fail.

In addition to checking for deposits and lead fouling, any spark plug whose electrodes are worn to one-half their original dimensions should be replaced. If the electrodes are not worn, the plugs may be reconditioned. To recondition a spark plug begin by removing any lead deposits with a vibrator-type cleaner, then lightly blast the electrodes with an approved abrasive. The ground electrode is then carefully moved over with a spark plug gaping tool to set the proper gap between the ground and the center electrodes.

Once a plug has been reconditioned, it must be tested. If the plug fires consistently under pressure in a tester, it may be reinstalled in the engine. Anytime a spark plug is installed a new gasket should be used along with a small amount of the thread lubricant recommended by the engine manufacturer.

When a spark occurs between the electrodes of a spark plug, metal is taken from one electrode and deposited onto another. Therefore, when a spark plug fires positively, the ground electrodes wear more than the center electrode and when a spark plug fires negatively, the center electrode wears more than the ground electrode. Furthermore, lead and other impurities produced during the combustion process tend to precipitate to the lower spark plugs, causing them to wear. To help equalize spark plug wear, each time spark plugs are removed they should be replaced in the cylinder next in the firing order to the one from which they were removed and switched from top to bottom.

The threads in the spark plug bushing in a cylinder should be clean enough so a spark plug can be screwed down against its gasket with finger pressure only. Once finger tight, a spark plug must be torqued to the manufacturer's recommended torque value using a torque wrench of known accuracy.

Before installing a lead on each spark plug, wipe the lead terminal with a rag dampened with trichlorethylene. Once clean, insert the lead straight into the spark plug and tighten the lead nut to the torque recommended by the manufacturer.

With all the plugs and leads installed, check the magneto to engine timing using a timing light. In addition, inspect the condition of the breaker points and the inside of the breaker compartment for any indication of moisture or oil. As a final check, make sure the magneto grounding or **P-leads** are secure and show no signs of wear or chafing.

FUEL SYSTEM

Clean the main fuel strainer and screen along with the screen in the carburetor or fuel injection unit. Replace the cleaned screens using a new gasket and, after testing them under pressure for leaks, safety the screens in place. Check all of the controls and lubricate them as specified by the airframe manufacturer, being sure to use an approved lubricant.

If the engine is fuel injected, check the manufacturer's recommendations for cleaning the injector nozzles. In addition, check all of the injection lines for security and chafing.

INDUCTION SYSTEM

Remove and clean or replace the induction air filter and check the entire system for leaks or deformation. Check the operation of the carburetor heat or alternate air valve. Be sure the alternate air doors open fully so the induction airflow into the engine will not be restricted.

All flexible induction tubing should be carefully inspected to be sure that there are no kinks and that the tubing is in good condition. Furthermore, you should verify that the wire support within the tubing is intact so the tubing cannot collapse.

EXHAUST SYSTEM

Remove the shroud from the muffler and check it for any indication of leakage. In some cases, there is an AD or manufacturer's service bulletin requiring the muffler or exhaust system to be pressure tested. Remember, even a pinhole leak can fill the cabin with deadly carbon monoxide gas. Be sure the cabin heat valve operates freely and has no obstructions in either the valve or the hose carrying heated air into the cabin. Check all of the cylinder heads at the exhaust port for indication of blown gaskets and for any indication of cracks or other leakage. Carefully check where the exhaust gas temperature probes enter the exhaust pipes, as this is a possible source of leakage.

TURBOCHARGER

If the engine is equipped with a turbocharger, be sure to follow the inspection procedure specified by the manufacturer. As a minimum, the exhaust portion of the turbocharger and waste gate should be checked. In addition, the induction air section, including all relief valves, intercoolers, and manifold pressure sensors should be checked and tested. The lubrication system and mounting should also be carefully checked for leaks and security.

COOLING SYSTEM

Check all of the cooling fins and baffling for cracks or damage. In addition, inspect all of the baffles and seals for general condition and security. If a cooling fin is cracked, check the manufacturer's specifications for allowable limits. To repair a cracked fin, you should remove the damaged area of the fin then contour file the affected area. The cowl flaps should be checked for security and for full travel, both in their open and closed position.

ELECTRICAL SYSTEM

As you know, electrical systems vary between aircraft models and the manufacturer's recommendations must be followed in detail. The alternator and its mounting should be checked for security and for any indication of vibration-induced cracks. The voltage regulator and any relays or solenoids in the system should be checked for security. In addition, all wires attached to electrical components should be checked for security, proper support, and chafing.

ACCESSORIES AND CONTROLS

Check all of the air, fuel, and hydraulic pumps for indications of leakage, and for the condition of their seals. Check the vent and breather lines for security and for proper positioning. Check the instrument air system to be sure that all filters are changed according to the manufacturer's recommendations and the oil separator shows no sign of malfunctioning.

Check all controls for freedom and for proper travel. The stops on the engine component should be reached just before the stop in the cockpit. Check the condition of the firewall to be sure that all controls, lines, and wires passing through are properly sealed and there is no corrosion or other indication of damage. Be sure that all of the engine shock mounts are in good condition and the mounting bolts are properly torqued. It is important that the electrical grounding strap between the engine and the airframe be in good condition since the rubber shock mounts will not allow starter current to return through the airframe.

PROPELLER

The extreme stress a propeller encounters dictates the need for a thorough inspection. Any nicks, cracks, or scratches in the blade must be carefully dressed and any questionable area must be checked using an approved non-destructive test method. Be sure the blades are secure in the hubs and that there is no oil leakage. Check the spinner and spinner bulkhead for any indication of cracks or damage, and check the governor for security and for full travel of its control.

POST-INSPECTION RUNUP AND RECORDS

After an inspection is complete, recowl the engine and conduct a post-inspection runup. If the engine checks out satisfactorily, complete the engine maintenance records and fill out all of the shop records.

Federal Aviation Regulations require you to make an engine log entry whenever maintenance or an inspection is performed. For example, when maintenance is performed, you must make a log entry that includes at least the following information.

1. The date the work was completed.
2. A description or reference to data acceptable to the FAA of the work perfomed.
3. The name of the person performing the work if you did not actually do it yourself.
4. Your signature.
5. Your certificate number
6. The rating or ratings you hold.

It is important to note that, when a log entry is made after maintenance is completed, the signature consitutes the approval for return to service for the work performed.

The log entry for an inspection is somewhat different from an entry for perfoming maintenance. The following is a list of items that must be included in an inspection log entry.

1. The date the inspection is completed.
2. The total time in service.
3. The type of inspection performed.
4. A certification statement that is worded similarly to "I certify that this aircraft has been inspected in accordance with a(n) (insert type) inspection and was determined to be in an airworthy condition."
5. Your signature.
6. Your certificate number.
7. The rating or ratings you hold.

If an aircraft is not approved for return to service because of needed maintenance, noncompliance with applicable specifications, airworthiness directives, or other approved data, the certification statement should be worded to say; "I certify that this aircraft has been inspected in accordance with a(n) (insert type) inspection and a list of discrepancies dated (insert date) has been provided for the aircraft owner."

If either a major repair or major alteration is performed to an aircraft, you must make an appropriate log entry and complete an FAA 337 form. Once complete, the original 337 form is given to the aircraft owner while a duplicate is sent to the local FAA office within 48 hours of completing the work.

To help reduce paperwork, certified repair stations are permitted to substitute a work order for a 337 form. In this case, the original work order is given to the aircraft owner and a duplicate is retained by the repair station for at least two years.

ENGINE REMOVAL AND OVERHAUL

ENGINE REMOVAL

Engine removal is a major task and must be accomplished in an orderly fashion to prevent personal injury or damage to the aircraft. Although the exact steps involved in removing a reciprocating engine vary from one make of aircraft model to another, there are some general guidelines you can use. However, these guidelines are no substitute for the manufacturer's instructions.

REASONS FOR REMOVAL

There are several reasons why an engine may have to be removed from an aircraft. For example, the accumulation of the number of hours recommended between overhauls or degradation in performance are reasons for removal. Also, a sudden engine stoppage or excessive metal particles found in the oil are certainly valid reasons for engine removal. In addition, some routine maintenance and repairs may require an engine to be removed from an aircraft. However, before you remove or replace an engine, you should always consult the applicable manufacturer's instructions to determine if engine removal is required.

ENGINE LIFE SPAN

Engine life is affected by environmental, operational, and design factors. In addition, the level of quality a manufacturer builds into the engine and the degree to which preventive maintenance is accomplished have a direct bearing on the useful life of an engine. As a result, it can be difficult to establish definite engine replacement times. However, by tracking the service life of several different engines, it is possible for manufacturers to establish a recommended **time between overhauls (TBO)**.

Aircraft owners who operate under FAR Part 91 are not obligated to comply with a manufacturer's recommended TBO. However, if an aircraft is operated for hire in an air taxi operation, FAA airworthiness regulations require the operator to adhere to TBO or the maximum time in service established in their operating manuals.

When a manufacturer delivers a new engine, a permanent record of the engine's operating time is established in the powerplant logbook. Anytime maintenance is done on that engine, a logbook entry is made referencing the **total time (TT)** the engine has accumulated since it was new. After an engine reaches its TBO, an overhaul should be accomplished and total time records should be continued without interruption. In addition, accumulated engine operation time should be referenced as the amount of time **since major overhaul (SMOH)**. Engine maintenance requirements are based on either time since new or time since the most recent major overhaul.

ATTRITION FACTORS

Whether an engine has reached its recommended TBO or not, signs or symptoms of severe performance deterioration could require removal and overhaul. As engine components wear, symptoms signaling a drop in performance become apparent. Increased oil consumption, higher engine operating temperatures, and a general loss of power all point to a possible need for replacement parts. Careful monitoring of these conditions may result in the decision to remove an engine for maintenance prior to the recommended time before overhaul. Normal engine life can be shortened due to several environmental and operational reasons. For example, operating at maximum power settings for prolonged periods of time, frequent starts in extremely cold temperatures, and lack of preventative maintenance can all shorten the useful life of an engine.

SUDDEN STOPPAGE

A sudden stoppage is defined as a very rapid and complete arrest of the engine. With a typical sudden engine stoppage, engine rpm drops to zero in less than one complete propeller revolution. Common causes of a sudden stoppage include engine seizure or a propeller blade striking an object. Whenever an engine is stopped suddenly, the inertia of the moving parts creates high torque forces that can result in cracked or broken flywheel gear teeth, timing gear damage, a bent or broken crankshaft, or damaged crankshaft bearings. When a sudden stoppage occurs, an engine manufacturer's instructions usually require a complete engine teardown and inspection.

SUDDEN SPEED REDUCTION

A sudden reduction in engine speed occurs when one or more propeller blades strike a movable object such as a runway light, tool box, hangar, or another aircraft. When this occurs, engine rpm drops rapidly until the object struck is cleared. However, the engine continues to run and the rpm typically returns to its previous value. Whenever a sudden reduction in engine speed occurs, the engine should be shut down as quickly as possible to prevent further damage. Inspections of engines that experience a sudden speed reduction reveal varying amounts of damage. For example, if the speed reduction occurs at a low rpm, very little internal damage typically results. The reason for this is that at low rpm, engine power output is also low and the propeller absorbs most of the shock. However, when a sudden speed reduction occurs at a high engine rpm, the potential for severe internal engine damage is much greater.

When an engine is subjected to a sudden reduction in speed, you must comply with the manufacturer's inspection procedures for that engine. As a minimum, you must make a thorough external inspection of the engine mounts, crankcase, and, if applicable, the nose section. In addition, you should remove the engine oil screens or filters and inspect them for the presence of metal particles. Once this is done, drain the oil, straining it through a clean cloth, and check both the cloth and strained oil for metal particles. Presence of heavy metal particles indicates a definite engine failure requiring engine removal. However, if the metal particles have the appearance of fine filings, continue the inspection to determine serviceability.

Remove the propeller and check for misalignment of the crankshaft, or propeller drive shaft on engines using a propeller gear reduction. This task is performed by attaching a dial indicator to the front of the engine case and letting the indicator arm ride on the crankshaft as it is turned. Engines with flange-type propeller shafts must be checked at the outside edge of the flange while spline-type propeller shafts should be checked at both the front and rear cone seats. The amount a shaft is misaligned is referred to as its **runout**. The runout tolerance must fall within the limits specified in the manufacturer's maintenance manual. If the runout is excessive, the crankshaft must be removed and replaced. However, if the crankshaft runout does not exceed the manufacturer's established limits, you should install a serviceable propeller and check the propeller tracking. If propeller tracking measurements are good, start the engine to see if it operates smoothly with normal power output. If operation is normal during the ground check, shut the engine down and repeat the inspection for metal particles in the oil system. The presence of metal indicates internal engine damage requiring further inspection. However, if there are no heavy metal particles in the engine oil, the engine should be scheduled for a flight test. If engine operation is within normal parameters during the flight test, look again for metal in the oil system. If no metal is found, continue the engine in service, but recheck the oil screens for the presence of metal after 10 hours of operation, and again after 20 hours. If no indication of internal failure is found after 20 hours of operation, the engine probably requires no further special inspections.

METAL PARTICLES IN OIL

The presence of an excessive number of metal particles in an engine oil filter or screen or in the oil itself generally indicates an internal failure. However, due to the construction of aircraft oil systems, it is possible for metal particles to collect in the oil system sludge at the time of a previous engine failure. Furthermore, carbon buildup can break loose from an engine's interior and may be mistaken for metal particles. In any case, the source of any foreign particles in an engine's oil must be identified and corrected before the aircraft is released for flight.

One way to determine if a particle is metal or carbon is to place the material on a flat metal object and strike it with a hammer. If the particle is carbon, it will disintegrate, however, if it is metal, it will remain intact or change shape, depending upon its malleability. If you find some particles that are metal, use a magnet to determine whether the particles are ferrous or nonferrous. Ferrous particles are typically produced by wearing piston rings, whereas nonferrous particles are typically produced by main bearings.

Another way to correctly identify the type and quantity of foreign particles in an engine's oil is through regular participation in a **spectrometric oil analysis**

program or **S.O.A.P.**, which requires an oil sample to be sent to a laboratory for analysis. When this is done, you are provided with a list of the type of particles found along with possible sources of the particles. In addition, if a laboratory observes a sudden increase in the amounts of metal that the test is designed to detect, they immediately contact the operator by telephone. When using spectrometric oil analysis, testing must occur on a regular basis to provide a baseline for comparison so accurate information can be obtained. A closely followed oil analysis program can detect problems before they become serious and prevent catastrophic engine failure. [Figure 2-29]

UNSTABLE ENGINE OPERATION

Engines must be removed for closer examination when unstable engine operation persists for a period of time. Excessive engine vibration, back firing, afterfiring, cutting out while in flight, and low power output are all symptoms of one or more problems that require removal of an engine. This is especially true with intermittent malfunctions if previous troubleshooting attempts have not been successful. Duplication of an intermittent malfunction is sometimes easier if the engine is mounted on a test stand with specialized test equipment.

Many operators now utilize manual or computerized engine condition monitoring that provides a base line to which unstable engine operations can be compared. The baseline information, coupled with trend analysis techniques, can help predict an engine failure before it occurs or pinpoint a problem requiring maintenance.

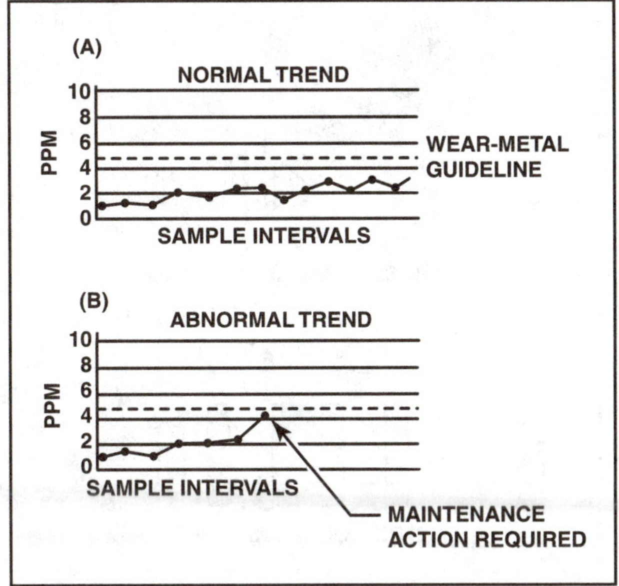

Figure 2-29. (A) (Over time, a normal engine experiences a gradual increase in the amount of metal suspended in its oil. (B) (Once a baseline is established, a sudden increase in the amount of metal usually indicates an internal engine problem.

PREPARATION FOR REMOVAL

When an engine is removed from an aircraft, flammable fluids often leak from the engine and create a fire hazard. Therefore, an engine removal should be done in a well ventilated area with a least one fire extinguisher nearby. Once the aircraft is parked, chock the main gear wheels to keep the aircraft from rolling during the removal operation. If the aircraft has tricycle-type landing gear, the tail must be supported to prevent the aircraft from tipping back when the engine is removed. In addition, the landing gear shock struts may need to be deflated to prevent damage from over-extension once the engine weight is removed from the aircraft.

MAGNETO, FUEL, AND BATTERY DISARMING

Before starting the engine removal process, make sure that the magneto switch is in the OFF position. In addition, once the engine cowl is removed, it is a good idea to remove at least one spark plug from each cylinder. When these steps are taken, you eliminate the chance of the engine suddenly kicking back or starting when the propeller is turned. To help prevent fuel from spilling, make sure that all fuel shutoff valves are closed. Fuel selector valves are either manually or electrically operated. If an electric solenoid-operated shutoff valve is installed, it may be necessary to apply battery power to close the valve. After ensuring that all fuel is shut off, disconnect the battery to reduce the possibility of electrical sparks. If the aircraft will be out of service for more than a few days, the battery is normally removed and taken to a battery shop where it can be cleaned, serviced, and charged.

Once the cowling is removed, clean and check the cowling for cracks and elongated fastener holes so repairs can be made while the engine is removed. If the cowling is not in need of repair, move it to a safe place where it will not be damaged.

DRAINING ENGINE OIL

You should begin draining the oil once the magnetos and battery are disarmed. When doing this, drain the oil into a clean container and place a large metal drip pan under the engine to catch any spills. Begin by removing the drain plug or opening the drain

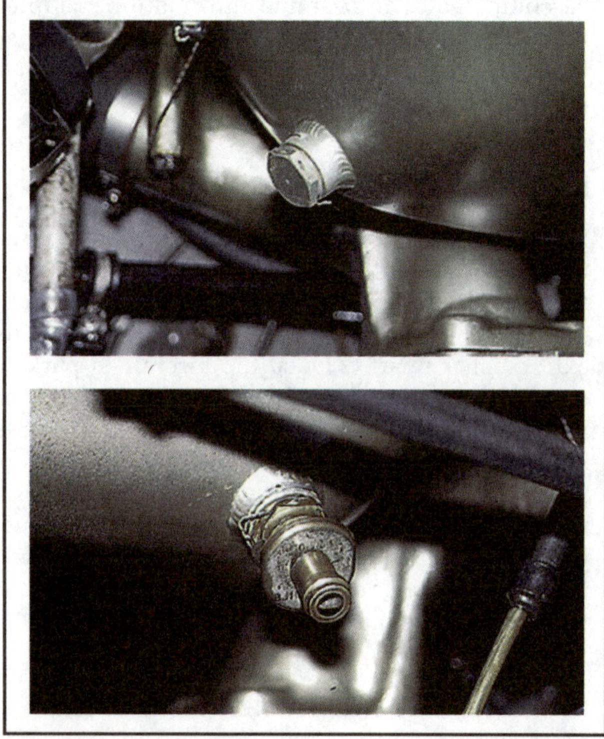

Figure 2-30. Most of the engine oil in a typical horizontally opposed engine is drained by removing one or more oil drain plugs or opening a drain valve.

valve. Additional points that should be drained of oil include the oil cooler, oil return line, and oil filter. Leave all valves and drains open until the oil system is completely drained. After draining the oil, reinstall the drain plugs, close all drain valves, and wipe any excess oil from around the drain points. [Figure 2-30]

PROPELLER REMOVAL

With the spark plugs removed, the propeller can be easily turned and removed for inspection and necessary repairs. When removing a fixed pitch propeller from a light aircraft, one person can typically conduct the operation safely with no additional equipment. However, when removing a large constant speed propeller, the use of a propeller sling with a frame and hoist is imperative. In addition, it is best to have one or two additional people assist you to prevent damaging the propeller or surrounding equipment. In either case, you should follow the manufacturer's instructions for propeller removal.

FLUID LINE DISCONNECTION

Once the oil is drained and the propeller is removed, you can begin disconnecting and draining the remaining fuel and hydraulic lines. These fluid lines typically include flexible rubber hoses, aluminum-alloy tubing, and stainless steel tubing. For example, most fuel lines are constructed of flexible rubber hose that must be drained once removed. In addition, on carbureted engines, once the fuel line is removed, the carburetor must also be drained. Most rigid tubing is secured to a threaded fitting at the firewall by a standard B-nut. Hoses may also be secured in this manner or they may be threaded into a receptacle, or secured by hose clamps. Some firewall attach points have a quick-disconnect fitting containing a check valve that prevents fluid loss when the line is disconnected. [Figure 2-31]

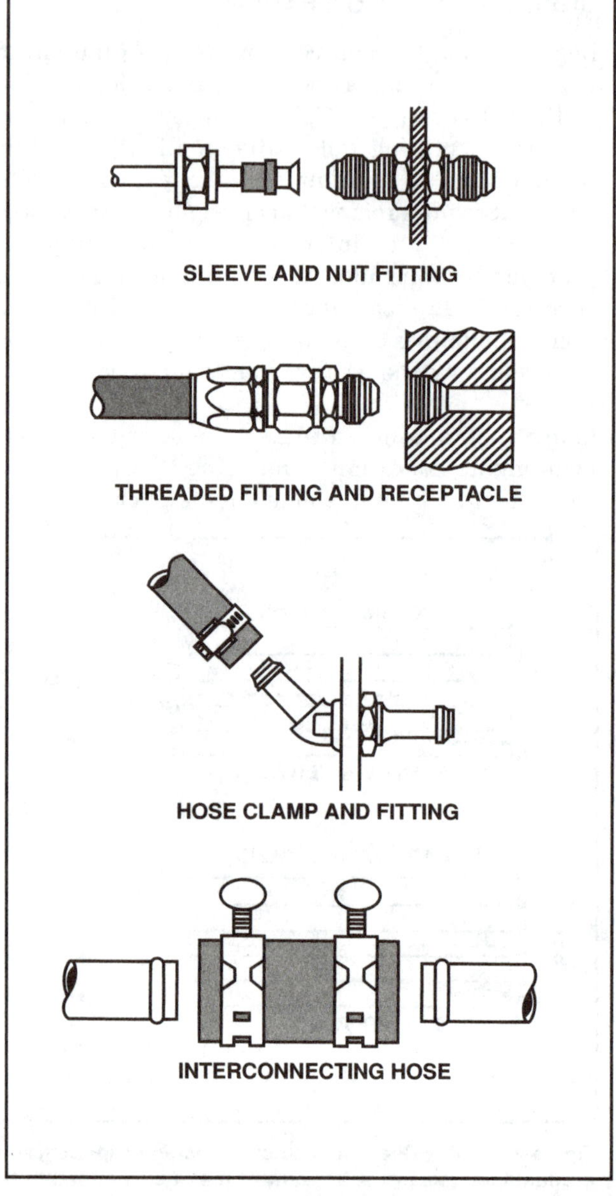

Figure 2-31. Fluid lines are typically connected to the firewall or accessory by either a B-nut, a threaded fitting that threads into a receptacle, or by hose clamps.

After a fuel line has drained, it should be plugged or covered with moisture-proof tape. This helps prevent insects, dirt, or other foreign matter from entering the line and keeps any residual fluids from dripping out. Once plugged, all lines and fittings should be labeled to help prevent possible confusion when reinstalling them on a new engine.

ELECTRICAL DISCONNECTION

Depending on the type of engine and equipment installed, electrical leads may be disconnected at the accessory or at the engine firewall. When disconnected at the firewall, AN and MS connectors are often used to simplify disconnections. A typical AN or MS electrical connector consists of a plug and receptacle assembly for one or more wires. To help prevent accidental disconnection during aircraft operation, the plug assembly screws to the receptacle assembly and is secured with safety wire.

Another type of wiring connection you may see consists of a junction box that serves as a disconnect point. With this type of setup, a single lead or group of individual leads run from terminal strip screw posts in a junction box to the engine or accessory. The wire leads used with this type of system are typically terminated with a ring connector that fits on a screw post and is secured with a nut and washer. Disconnection is accomplished by removal of the nut, allowing the ring terminal to be lifted off the terminal post. [Figure 2-32]

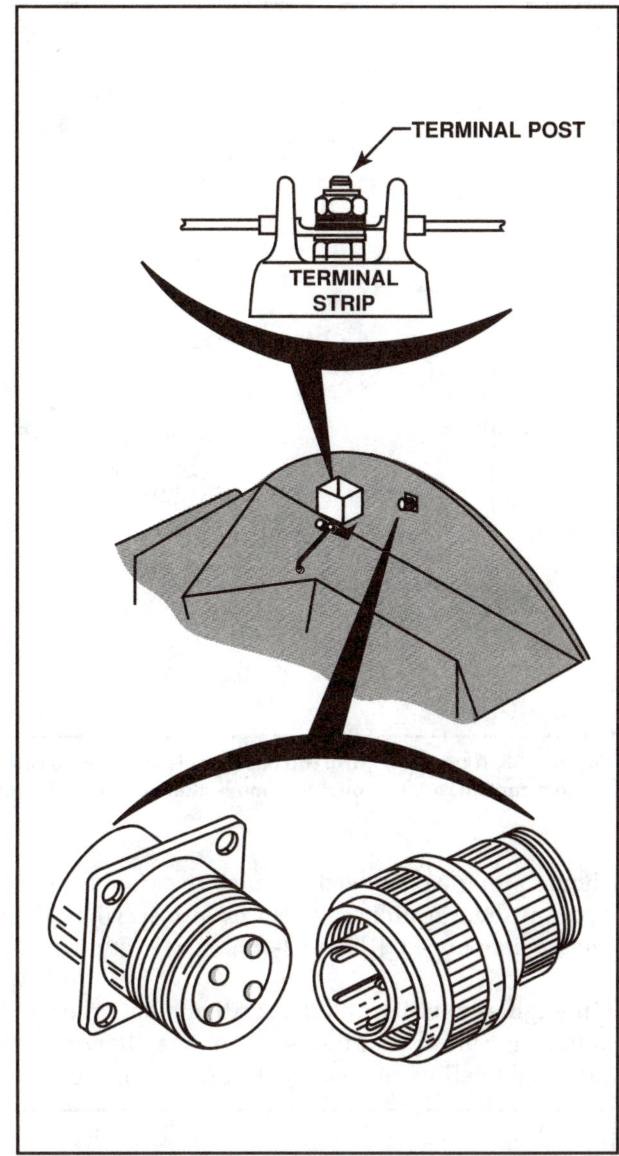

Figure 2-32. On aircraft that utilize firewall electrical disconnect points, there are generally two kinds of electrical disconnects used. One type consists of a junction box containing terminal strips with terminal posts while a second type consists of a plug-type connector such as a Cannon plug or Amphenol connector.

Small aircraft with simple electrical systems often utilize knife-type or wrist-lock connectors that are sealed in some type of protective sheathing. To disconnect this type of connector, remove the sheathing and separate the connector.

To protect the exposed ends of connectors from dirt and moisture you should wrap them with moisture-proof tape whenever they are disconnected. Also, coil loose cables and secure conduits out of the way to prevent entanglement and damage when the engine is removed. If the wires lack legible identification, label them to eliminate confusion when reinstalling the engine.

ENGINE CONTROL DISCONNECTION

The engine control rods and cables allow operation of the throttle and mixture from within the cockpit. A typical control rod is threaded at both ends with a clevis attached at one end and a rod end bearing attached to the other end. On most aircraft, the rod end bearing is connected to the carburetor or fuel control by a bolt secured with a castle nut and cotter pin. To remove a control rod, begin by removing the cotter pin and castle nut. Once this is done, remove the bolt passing through the control assembly.

After the engine control linkages have been disconnected, the nuts and bolts should be inspected for wear. Cotter pins get replaced, but if the nuts and bolts do not need replacement, place them back in the control rod ends so they do not get lost. All control rods

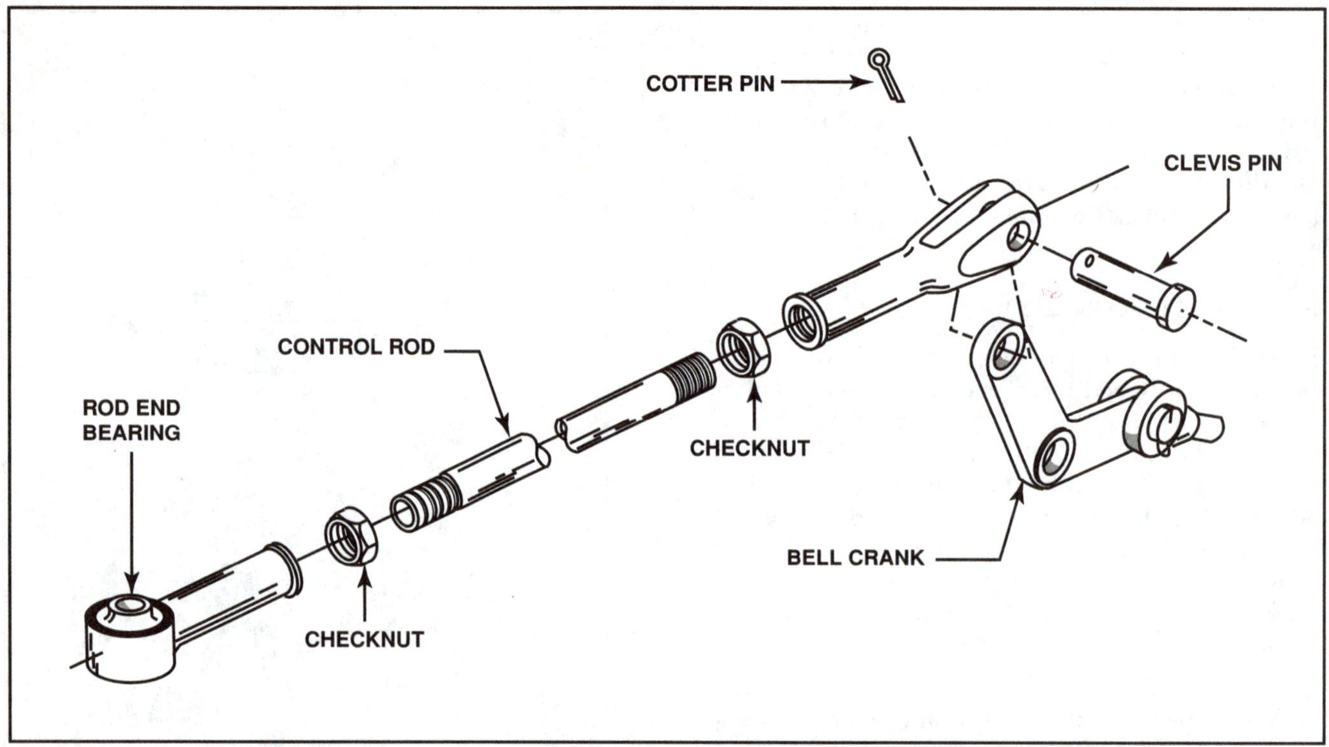

Figure 2-33. A typical control rod has a clevis attached to one end and a rod end bearing attached to the other end. To prevent damaging a control rod, it is best to remove them completely from the aircraft before the engine is removed.

should either be removed completely or tied back to prevent them from being bent or broken when the engine is removed. [Figure 2-33]

On engine installations that utilize a bellcrank to actuate a control rod, the bellcrank may have to be removed to allow removal of a control rod. If this is the case, a turnbuckle which joins the bellcrank actuating cable must be removed. However, before you remove the turnbuckle, it is a good idea to mark the position of the control cable end threads at the turnbuckle. The marks will assist you during reinstallation to roughly obtain the original position before trimming the controls. [Figure 2-34]

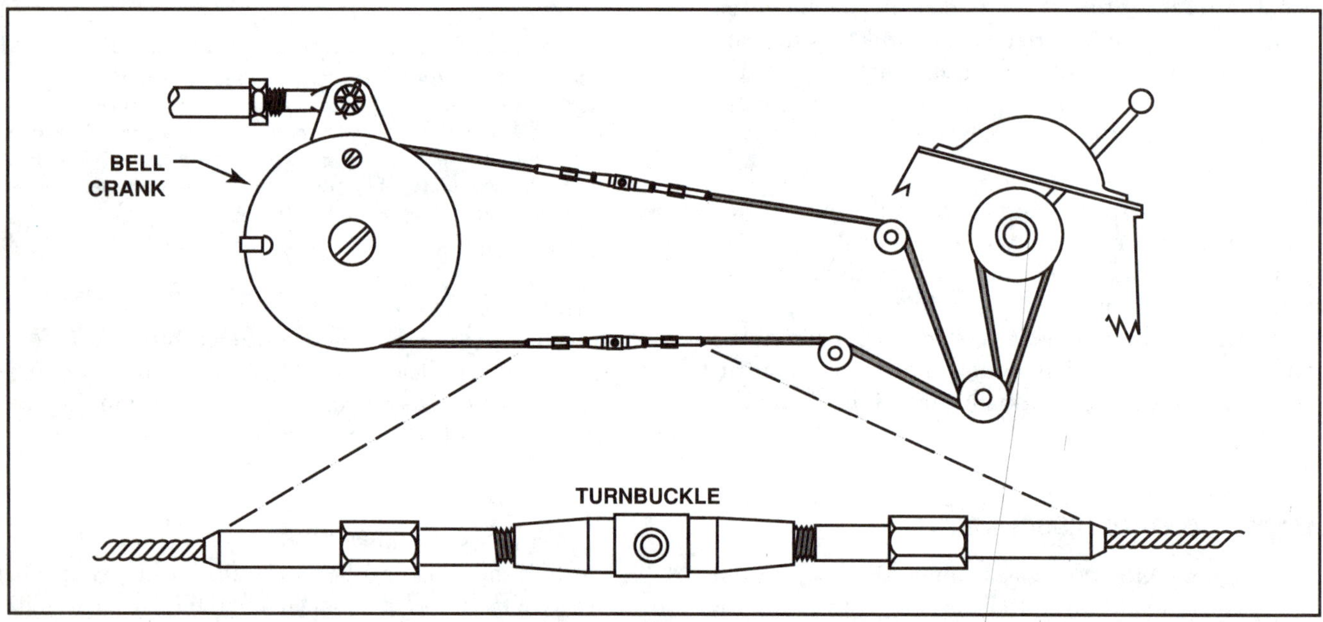

Figure 2-34. Some control systems in use today consist of a cable and pulley arrangement to actuate engine controls. If this is the case, the cable assembly may have to be separated at a turnbuckle in order to remove the control rod.

OTHER DISCONNECTIONS

Air intake and exhaust system components must also be disconnected to facilitate engine removal. However, because the installation of these components vary among different engines and aircraft, it is best to refer to the manufacturer's instructions for specific removal instructions.

ENGINE HOISTING

After all engine connections are free and clear, the engine is ready for hoisting. If an engine has been thoroughly prepared for removal, the actual removal process is typically a simple task. One decision that must be made is whether to remove only the engine, or both the engine and engine mount. With a typical overhaul the engine is removed without the engine mount. However, if the engine is being replaced with a **quick engine change assembly (QECA)**, the separation point is usually the firewall; therefore, the mount must be removed with the engine. A QECA is essentially a powerplant with the necessary accessories already installed on the engine mounting assembly. In addition, some radial engine QECA's are supplied with nacelles, so removal in this case would include the engine nacelle.

Before the engine can be freed from its attach points, a sling must be installed so the engine's weight can be supported with a hoist. Aircraft engines have selected points for attaching a hoisting sling. The location of these points and the type of sling arrangement used vary according to the engine's size and weight. Therefore, engine manufacturers typically provide information on where to support an engine as well as the type of hoist apparatus to use. As a matter of safety, the sling and hoist should be carefully inspected and deemed safe for use before installing it on an engine. In addition, make sure that the hoist has sufficient capacity to lift the engine safely, observing the change in capacity as the hoist arm is extended. In most cases, when the hoist arm is fully extended, lifting capacity is greatly reduced. [Figure 2-35]

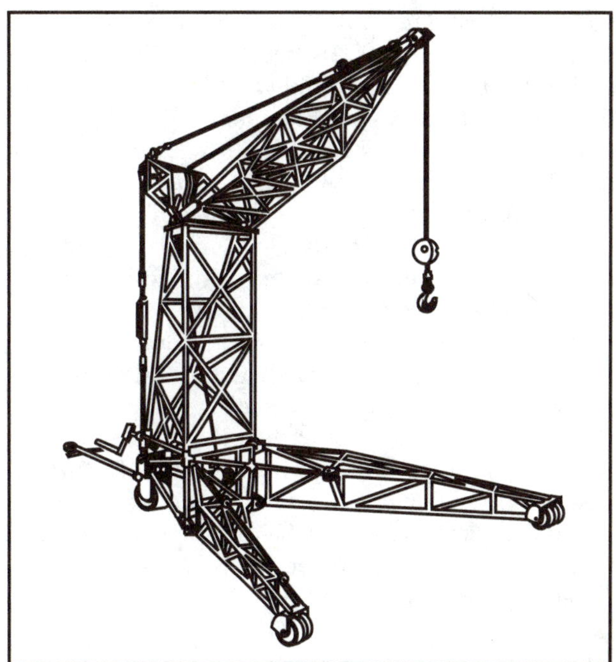

Figure 2-35. When choosing a hoist and frame assembly, make sure the hoist can reach the engine with adequate clearance and is rated for the weight of the engine being lifted.

Some engine hoisting frames are fitted with power operated hoists. Power hoists should be used with caution, since considerable damage can be done by an inexperienced operator.

Before you actually begin lifting an engine, recheck the aircraft tail supports and wheel chocks. If everything is set, raise the engine enough to remove the engine weight from the engine mount. Next, remove the nuts from the engine mount attachments in the order specified in the manufacturer's instructions. Before the last nuts are removed, be sure that the engine is steadied and secure with no lateral loading. If everything is secure, remove the remaining engine mount hardware and gently move the engine free of the mount attachments. If the engine binds at any point, investigate the reason and maneuver the engine as necessary until it slips free. Once the engine is moved clear of the airframe, carefully lower the engine onto an engine stand and secure it with the appropriate hardware.

ENGINE COMPARTMENT

Anytime an engine is removed from an aircraft the opportunity exists to thoroughly inspect the engine compartment and make repairs as necessary. To begin, you should inspect the entire engine nacelle for corrosion, cracks, missing rivets, or any other visible defects. Cracks in the cowling or ducts can be stop-drilled or patched if they do not exceed limits specified in the manufacturer's structural repair manual.

Engine controls should be checked for integrity and freedom of movement. In addition, cables should be inspected for broken wire strands while cable pulleys are checked for binding, flat spots, and chipped edges. Furthermore, pulley bearings can be checked for excessive play. The anti-friction bearings in the control rods should move freely and the rods should be free of deformities. Inspect areas where cables and rods pass through bulkheads or panels for evidence of chafing and misalignment.

Check the outer surface of all exposed electrical wiring for breaks, chafing, deteriorated insulation, or other damage. In addition, inspect crimped and soldered terminals for security and cleanliness. Connector plugs must also be checked for damage, corrosion, and overall condition. Check bonding straps for fraying, loose attachments, and corrosion at terminal ends. The electrical resistance of the complete bond must not exceed the resistance values specified in the applicable manufacturer's instructions. Any damage found must be repaired and defective parts should be replaced as specified in the manufacturer's specifications and Federal Aviation Regulations.

Hydraulic and pneumatic tubing should be free from dents, nicks, and kinks, and all connectors should be checked for the correct tightness. Check all air ducts for dents and the condition of the fabric or rubber anti-chafing strips at their joints. Dents should be worked out, and anti-chafing strips should be replaced if they have pulled loose or no longer form a tight seal.

Thoroughly inspect all hoses and replace those hoses that have been damaged by weather checking or cold flow. **Weather checking** is a cracking of the outside covering of hoses that sometimes penetrates to the reinforcement webbing. **Cold flow**, on the other hand, refers to deep and permanent impressions or cracks caused by hose clamps. Both types of damage weaken hoses and could eventually cause leaks to develop. In addition to the hoses, you should inspect the exhaust assembly for security, cracks, and excessive corrosion.

If the engine installation employs a dry sump oil system, the oil tank is generally removed to permit thorough cleaning. Furthermore, the oil cooler and temperature regulator are usually removed and sent to a repair facility for overhaul, or are included as an exchange unit and returned with the run-out engine.

ENGINE MOUNTS

Before a new or overhauled engine can be installed on an aircraft, an inspection of the engine mount structure must be accomplished. The engine mount should be checked for bends, dents, flat spots, or elongated bolt holes. Typically, dye penetrants are used to help reveal cracks, porous areas, or other defects. Ferrous parts, such as the engine mounting bolts, are usually checked by magnetic particle inspection.

Many types of engine mount structures are in use, however, most are typically constructed from formed and riveted sheet metal rails, forged alloy fittings, welded alloy steel tubing, or a combination of all three. Engine mount structures consisting of riveted aluminum usually provide two mounting rails to which the engine is mounted. These aluminum mount structures are typically used for mounting large horizontally opposed engines, especially on multi-engine aircraft. Steel tube mount structures, on the other hand, are used on both large and small, horizontally opposed, and radial engines. Steel tube engine mounting structures bolt to the engine firewall and their shape provides some separation between an engine and firewall.

Most modern reciprocating engine aircraft utilize **dynafocal** engine mounts. With a dynafocal engine mount, the engine mounting points are turned inward so they point toward the engine's center of gravity. This design helps prevent the transmission of engine vibration to the airframe. [Figure 2-36]

A typical engine mounting structure incorporates vibration isolating **shock mounts** that help dampen engine vibrations and permit restricted engine

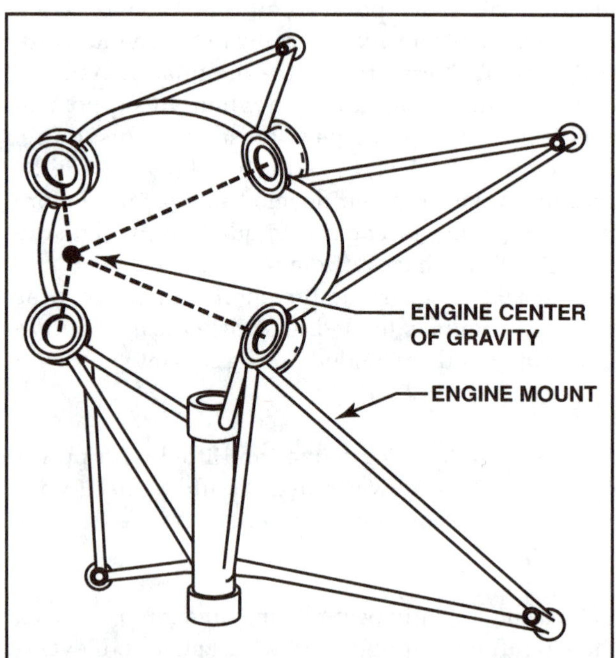

Figure 2-36. With a dynafocal engine mount, the mounting points are turned inward so they point toward the engine's center of gravity.

movement. Shock mounts contain rubber components that are arranged so the engine weight rests on the rubber. The rubber absorbs much of the engine vibration thereby reducing the amount of vibration that is transmitted to the airframe.

OVERHAUL

Aircraft operators run the risk of premature engine or component failure if scheduled maintenance is delayed or neglected. On the other hand, a well-maintained engine can provide many hours of reliable operation without failure up to the recommended TBO. After reaching TBO, however, the engine should be overhauled for continued airworthiness so that worn or damaged parts can be detected and replaced. The best way to identify parts that are defective or worn beyond airworthy limits is to disassemble the engine and perform a complete and thorough inspection.

Engine manufacturers provide overhaul instructions that contain specific tolerances and general instructions to aid in determining the airworthiness of each part. Parts that do not meet the manufacturer's specifications must be replaced, while parts that do meet tolerances are reinstalled in the engine. However, if a part is near its airworthiness limits, you may want to replace it since that part could eventually fail or exceed the acceptable limits before the next scheduled overhaul.

TOP OVERHAUL

A top overhaul is defined as an overhaul of those parts associated with the engine cylinders. During a typical top overhaul, the cylinders, pistons, and valve operating mechanisms are reconditioned while the piston rings are replaced. In addition, the valve guides and seats are inspected and replaced if necessary. When performing a top overhaul, you should remove as few parts as necessary to gain access to the cylinders. However, in most cases, you must remove the intake manifold, ignition harness, and exhaust collectors. Engine accessories such as magnetos, starters, and alternators typically receive normally scheduled maintenance during a top overhaul.

Top overhauls are not performed as frequently in modern aircraft engines as in earlier models because more durable materials are now available. Furthermore, a top overhaul is not universally recommended because some engine manufacturers believe that if you are going to remove all of an engine's cylinders, it is relatively inexpensive to overhaul the rest of the engine. An alternative view, however, is that since most crankcase assemblies are relatively more durable than cylinders and valve trains, a top overhaul is often the most economical way to bring an engine back to original performance levels in the short term. In many cases, the final decision on whether to perform a top overhaul or major overhaul is up to the owner or operator.

MAJOR OVERHAUL

A major overhaul entails a complete engine reconditioning at periodic intervals. The exact interval is based on manufacturer recommendations or an FAA approved number of accumulated hours since new or last major overhaul.

During a major overhaul, an engine is completely dismantled, cleaned, inspected, repaired as needed, reassembled, and tested. Any engine part failing to meet specified tolerances is rejected and either scrapped or repaired. Parts such as gaskets, seals, and some hardware are used only once, and, therefore, are normally replaced regardless of their condition. Instructions provided by the manufacturer specify the parts that must be replaced. Furthermore, all accessories are removed for overhaul or replacement.

Engine manufacturers establish types of fits, tolerances, and limits on production drawings when designing and building their engines. This set of measurements is the authoritative source of allowable tolerances for new engine parts. Additionally, the manufacturer establishes serviceable limits which show the maximum amount of wear a part can have and still be considered serviceable. When performing an overhaul, the serviceable part tolerance limits are typically used for parts that are being reinstalled while the new part tolerances are used on any new parts being installed.

It is important to note that the total time on an engine must be continued when it is overhauled. In addition, the amount of hours indicating the time since major overhaul should be added to the engine log. Only new engines and **rebuilt engines** are granted a **zero time** status. FAR Part 43 describes a rebuilt engine as an engine that has been disassembled, cleaned, inspected, repaired as necessary, reassembled, and tested to the same tolerances and limits as a new engine. A rebuilt engine can contain either new or used parts that conform to new part tolerances and limits or to approved oversized or undersized dimensions. In other words, the term rebuilt means that the repaired engine conforms to new parts specifications, which is a higher level of quality than that provided by the serviceable limits in an overhauled engine. An engine can only be rebuilt and carry a zero time status if the engine manufacturer or an agency approved by the manufacturer performs the work. Zero time status allows the owner or operator to start a new maintenance record with no reference to previous operating history. Each manufacturer or agency that rebuilds an engine must make several entries in the new engine log. Among those entries are the date the engine was rebuilt, each change made as required by airworthiness directives, and each change made in compliance with manufacturer's service bulletins, if that bulletin requires an entry.

Advertisements for engine overhauls or exchange programs sometimes use the term **remanufactured engine**. It is important to note that this term is not defined by the FAR's and, therefore, the vendor should be questioned about what is meant by "remanufactured."

OVERHAUL PROCEDURES

Specific overhaul procedures for any given engine are listed in the maintenance and overhaul manuals written for that engine; therefore, the overhaul practices and procedures discussed here are general in nature. This discussion takes you through all the steps in a major overhaul on a typical horizontally opposed engine.

Throughout the overhaul process, the engine manufacturer's manuals, service bulletins, and other service information must be available. Therefore, the first task you must complete in the overhaul process is to research the airworthiness directives and manufacturer's service bulletins that apply. In addition, you should gather all the necessary inspection forms and tooling needed to complete the overhaul.

When an engine is brought to you for an overhaul, you should do an inventory of all accessories sent with the engine. If the engine is still installed on the aircraft, all of the engine accessories such as the alternator, vacuum pump, hydraulic pump, propeller and its governor are usually still on the engine. If this is the case, these accessories will have to be removed and sent to specialty shops or an appropriate repair station for overhaul. Additional items such as intercylinder baffles, carburetor or fuel injection systems, magnetos, ignition leads, and the induction system components are considered to be engine parts and are kept with the engine.

DISASSEMBLY

Before beginning engine disassembly, you should mount the engine on a stand and inspect its general condition. Any signs of oil leakage, overheating, or impact damage should be noted for further inspection during the disassembly. Next, spray wash the engine exterior. To remove some of the more stubborn, baked on dirt and oil, use a petroleum solvent or degreaser. However, be sure you thoroughly rinse any residual solvent from the engine.

Once the engine is clean, remove the fuel metering system, magnetos, pumps, and other accessories, and send them to the various specialty shops for overhaul. The remaining parts, such as the exhaust system, intercylinder baffles, ignition leads, spark plugs, and induction system components should also be removed and set aside. Whenever you are disassembling an engine or any of its components, you should mark all parts. This is usually done by attaching a tag to each part as it is removed. Remember to place nuts, bolts, and other small parts in suitable containers during disassembly to prevent loss and damage. Safety wire, cotter pins, and some other safety devices are not used more than once, so they should be discarded and replaced with new safety devices. As with any other work you do, you should always use the proper tools for the job to avoid damaging engine parts or hardware. If special tools are required, you should obtain and use them rather than improvising. [Figure 2-37]

Figure 2-37. After being mounted on an engine stand, an engine is disassembled for a thorough visual inspection and cleaning.

Crankshaft bearings, oil seals, gaskets, and stressed bolts and nuts are normally replaced during an overhaul and should be discarded unless directed otherwise by manufacturer instructions. In all cases, consult the applicable manufacturer's maintenance and overhaul manuals or service bulletins for a complete listing of replacement items. Loose or damaged studs and other fittings should be tagged or marked for a closer examination during inspection because they could be evidence of more serious wear and damage.

At this point, the engine can be completely disassembled and laid out on a clean workbench for a preliminary inspection. A preliminary visual inspection must be done before cleaning the internal engine parts because indications of an impending failure are often detected from residual deposits of metallic particles in oil residue and sludge. Cleaning before inspection could flush the particles from parts and recesses in the engine, possibly preventing the detection of an engine problem. [Figure 2-38]

CLEANING

After an engine is torn down and a preliminary visual inspection has been done, the disassembled parts must be cleaned by soaking or spraying each component with a degreaser or cleaning solvent. Use a commercial safety solvent approved by the engine manufacturer rather than water-soluble degreasing solutions that contain soap or caustic compounds. The reason for this is that water-soluble solutions could be corrosive to aluminum or magnesium. In addition, soap residues can become trapped in relatively porous engine components such as case halves, causing oil contamination and oil foaming when the engine is returned to service. [Figure 2-39]

Figure 2-38. Engine parts are laid out in an orderly fashion on a clean workbench after the cleaning process to facilitate inspection procedures. Keeping parts arranged in an orderly manner minimizes loss and accidental damage.

While degreasing removes dirt, grease, and soft carbon, it is often inadequate for removing hard carbon deposits that sometimes build up on interior engine surfaces. To remove hard carbon deposits, you can use an approved decarbonizing solution; however, you must exercise caution and follow the manufacturer's recommendations. Decarbonizing solutions are available in a water-soluble base or hydrocarbon base. Of the two, the hydrocarbon base is preferable because water-soluble decarbonizing solutions carry the same corrosion dangers as water-soluble degreasers. Decarbonizer solution is usually quite active, so you must adhere to several precautions. For example, you should always wear protective clothing and eye protection when using a decarbonizer. In addition, take care to avoid leaving engine parts in a decarbonizing solution longer than the prescribed time periods. Furthermore, be sure the solution is safe for magnesium parts before immersing them, and avoid placing steel parts and magnesium parts in the same container. The reason for this is the cleaning solution could cause a chemical reaction between the dissimilar metals that could corrode the magnesium. Be especially careful with accessory housings that often have a high magnesium content.

Figure 2-39. Several manufacturers produce cleaning fixtures that circulate an approved safety solvent for cleaning engine parts. These fixtures make cleaning much easier by containing solvent splashes and by providing a contained area for small parts that could otherwise be misplaced or lost.

After the parts have soaked in a decarbonizing solution for the appropriate time, they must be removed and thoroughly cleaned to remove any traces of the decarbonizing solution. Any one of several cleaning methods may be used, such as blasting a part with steam, or brushing the part with mineral spirits. With the exception of bearings or polished surfaces, any remaining carbon deposits are usually removed by scraping, wire brushing, or grit-blasting with plastic pellets or organic materials such as rice, baked wheat, or crushed walnut shells. However, before beginning any grit-blasting process, you must insert rubber plugs in all drilled oil passages and be sure that all machined surfaces are masked with a recommended material. Furthermore, old hardware can be screwed into threaded holes to prevent grit from getting into the screw threads. Since valve seats are typically hardened, they can usually be left unprotected during grit-blasting. In fact, grit blasting can often be used to remove the glaze that forms on valve seats, as well as the enamel from cylinder cooling fins that does not come off in a decarbonizing solution. The key to avoiding damage when using a grit blast is to use the lowest air pressure that is practical and only blast the part long enough to remove the carbon.

It is important to note that any mechanical means of cleaning hard carbon deposits can cause unintentional damage if applied too vigorously. Therefore, you should pay extra attention when cleaning any part with abrasive tools.

To clean machined and polished bearing surfaces such as journals and crankpins, use crocus cloth moistened with mineral spirits. Once all the carbon is removed, polish the surfaces with a piece of dry crocus cloth.

When cleaning a crankshaft with hollow crankpins that serve as sludge chambers, you must remove the plugs from the crankpin ends to facilitate a cleaning and visual inspection. If the sludge chamber is not thoroughly cleaned, accumulated sludge loosened during cleaning may clog the crankshaft oil passages and cause subsequent bearing failures.

After all of the parts have been thoroughly cleaned, steel parts must be coated with a film of protective oil. Applying the protective oil coating is important because if steel parts are left exposed to the air, they will quickly rust. If the oil coating must be removed to perform additional inspections later on, it is imperative that you reapply an oil coating to prevent corrosion.

VISUAL INSPECTION

Once an engine part is clean, it must be inspected closely for damage. The first type of inspection that is usually done is a thorough visual inspection aided by a magnifying glass, flashlight, and, if necessary, a borescope. Visual inspections are done to detect many different visible surface defects in parts. As a maintenance technician, you must have an understanding of the terms used to describe the nature of a particular defect. Some of the more common types of damage you will look for include:

Abrasion — An area of roughened scratches or marks usually caused by foreign matter between moving parts.

Brinelling — One or more indentations on bearing races usually caused by high static loads or application of force during installation or removal. Indentations are rounded or spherical due to the impression left by the bearing's balls or rollers.

Burning — Surface damage caused by excessive heat as a result of improper fit, insufficient lubrication, or over-temperature operation.

Burnishing — Polishing of one surface by sliding contact with a smooth, harder surface. Usually no displacement or removal of metal occurs.

Burr — A sharp or roughened projection of metal usually resulting from machine processing, drilling, or cutting.

Chafing — Describes the wear caused by a rubbing action between two parts under light pressure.

Chipping — The breaking away of pieces of material, caused by excessive stress concentrations or careless handling.

Corrosion — Loss of metal by a chemical or electrochemical action. The corrosion products are generally removed by mechanical means.

Crack — A partial separation of material usually caused by vibration, overloading, internal stresses, defective assembly, or fatigue.

Cut — Loss of metal, usually to an appreciable depth caused by a sharp object, such as a saw blade, chisel, or screwdriver.

Dent — A small, rounded surface depression usually found in sheet metal. Most dents are the result of impact with another object.

Erosion — Loss of surface metal caused by the mechanical action of foreign objects, such as grit or fine sand. The eroded area will be rough and may be lined in the direction the foreign material moved relative to the surface.

Flaking — The breaking loose of small pieces of metal or coated surfaces caused by defective plating or excessive loading.

Fretting — A form of surface corrosion caused by minute movement between two parts clamped

together under considerable pressure. Found sometimes between crankcase halves.
Galling — A severe condition of chafing or fretting in which a transfer of metal from one part to another occurs. Galling is usually caused by slight movement between mated parts under high loads.
Gouging — A furrowing condition in which a displacement of metal occurrs. Gouging is usually caused by a piece of metal or foreign material becoming trapped between moving parts.
Grooving — A recess or channel with rounded and smooth edges that usually results from improperly aligned parts.
Inclusion — Presence of foreign or extraneous material that is wholly confined within a portion of metal. The included material is often introduced during the manufacture of rod, bar, or tubing by rolling or forging.
Nick — A sharp sided gouge or depression with a "V" shaped bottom. Nicks are generally the result of careless handling of tools and parts.
Peening — A series of blunt surface depressions.
Scuffing or **Pick Up** — A buildup or rolling of metal from one area to another which is usually caused by insufficient lubrication, clearance, or foreign matter.
Pitting — Small hollows of irregular shape in the surface, usually caused by corrosion or minute mechanical chipping of surfaces.
Scoring — A series of deep scratches caused by foreign particles between moving parts, or careless assembly or disassembly techniques.
Scratches — Shallow, thin lines or marks, varying in degree of depth and width, caused by improper handling or the presence of fine foreign particles during operation.
Spalling — A bearing defect in which chips of the hardened bearing surface are broken out.
Stain — A localized change in color that is noticeably different in appearance from the surrounding area.
Upsetting — A displacement of material beyond the normal surface contour commonly referred to as a bulge or bump. When a part is upset, there is usually no metal loss.

CRANKCASE

Forces working in a crankcase produce highly stressed areas which can eventually develop cracks, especially around mating and bearing surfaces, mounting bosses, threaded holes and studs, openings, and structural fillet areas. Although more elaborate methods for crack detection are available, a thorough visual inspection can save wasted time and effort by quickly detecting serious damage requiring replacement.

In addition to checking for cracks, it is important to closely inspect all lubrication channels and oil ports. Furthermore, you must check for loose or bent studs and examine hole threads with a flashlight. If stripped threads are encountered, mark the hole for repairs later after completing the visual inspection.

GEARS

The primary purpose of a gear is the transmission of force through motion; therefore, stress and wear occur continually. For that reason, it is important to visually examine all gears for cracked or chipped teeth and the presence of pitting or excessive wear. Deep pit marks or excessive wear on gear teeth are reasons for rejecting and replacing a gear. Minor scratches and abrasions on a gear's bearing surfaces can normally be dressed out with a fine abrasive cloth, however, deep scratches or scoring is unacceptable.

BEARINGS

Ball bearings and roller bearings should be closely examined for smoothness and freedom of movement. As you visually inspect a bearing, feel the bearing parts carefully to detect any roughness, flat spots on balls or rollers, and dents or corrosion on the races. In addition, check for pitting, scoring, and galling on the outside surfaces of races. Pitting on a thrust bearing race that cannot be removed by polishing with crocus cloth or other mild abrasive usually requires part replacement. You must also check journal bearings for damage such as galling, burning, scoring, spalling, misalignment, or an out-of-round condition.

Bearing inserts such as bushings and plain bearings are usually replaced, however, looking at them could help you detect wear on their mating surfaces or mounting bosses. Scratching and light scoring of aluminum bearing surfaces in the engine is usually acceptable if the damage is within the limits stated in the engine manufacturer's overhaul manual. However, the presence of other defects could require rejection of the part even if it falls within specific tolerance limits.

CRANKSHAFT

A crankshaft is usually the heaviest and most highly stressed part of an aircraft engine. Since very few repairs are approved for a crankshaft, a visual inspection is done mainly to determine if the crankshaft falls within wear tolerance limits. Inspect the main and crankpin journal bearing surfaces for burning, pitting, scoring, or spalling, giving extra attention to the fillets at the edges of journal surfaces. If pitting exists in an amount that cannot be removed by polishing with crocus cloth or other mild abrasives, the crankshaft may have to be replaced. When a crankshaft is equipped with oil transfer tubes, check them for tightness.

CONNECTING RODS

Connecting rods must be checked for small cracks, corrosion, pitting, nicks, or other damage. In addition, if an engine has been subjected to an overspeed or excessively high manifold pressure, slight amounts of movement between the bearing insert and the rod can cause galling. If galling does exist or if a connecting rod is twisted or bent, the rod must be replaced.

PISTONS AND PISTON PINS

Check pistons carefully after cleaning to be sure all carbon is removed from the ring grooves and oil relief holes. Once this is done, use a magnifying glass to inspect for cracks, scores, and scratches on the outside and inside of all pistons. Another method of visually detecting cracks is to carefully heat the piston, which expands any existing cracks and forces out residual oil. Pistons with deep scoring, cracked or broken ring lands, cracked skirts, and badly scored piston pin holes should be rejected. [Figure 2-40]

Examine piston pins for scoring, cracks, and pitting. In addition, you must remove all piston pin plugs and check the interior surfaces of piston pins for pitting and corrosion. Since pins are often case hardened, cracks will show up inside the pin more often than on the outside. If pitting is found and cannot be removed by polishing with crocus cloth or other mild abrasives, reject the pin and replace it.

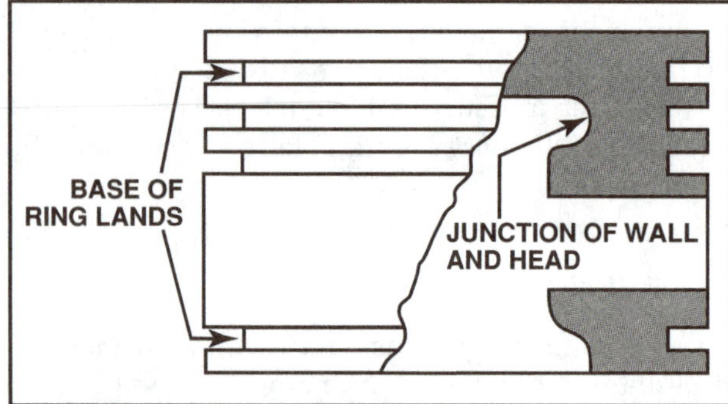

Figure 2-40. When visually inspecting a piston, be alert for cracks that form at the base of ring lands and at the junction of the piston head and wall.

CYLINDERS

In order to perform an effective visual inspection of a cylinder for external and internal cracks, the cylinder must be free of carbon deposits and paint. Cracks near the edge of fins are repairable, however, cracks at the base of a fin are reasons for rejection and replacement. The amount of fin damage permitted on a given cylinder is based on a percentage of the total fin area and is established by the manufacturer. If dented or bent fins are found, it is best to leave them as they are because straightening a fin typically results in the fin breaking.

When inspecting a cylinder's interior, light amounts of pitting, rust, and scoring are typically not a cause for concern. The reason for this is because the damage is usually removed when lapping in a new set of rings. If large amounts of pitting, rust, and scoring exist, it must be removed by regrinding or honing.

Inspect valve seat inserts for pitting, burning, scoring, and assymetry. If any of these exist, the valve seat must be refaced. In addition to inspecting the valve seats, the spark plug thread inserts should be checked for condition of the threads and looseness by running a tap of the proper size through the insert. Any missing or damaged threads requires replacement of the insert.

Look closely at valve guides to be certain that all carbon was removed during the cleaning process. This is important because carbon deposits tend to cover or fill pitting damage inside the guide, making detection difficult. If a guide with pitting is left in the engine, carbon deposits may again collect in the pits and cause valve sticking when the engine is returned to service.

Rocker shaft bosses need to be checked for scoring, cracks, rocker shaft to shaft boss clearance and out-of-round conditions. Scoring is usually caused by the rocker shaft turning in the bosses because either the shaft is too loose in the bosses or the rocker arm is too tight on the shaft. Sticking valves, on the other hand, cause the rocker shaft to work up and down, causing uneven wear on the rocker shaft bosses.

CAMSHAFT

The condition of the lobes on a camshaft directly influence an engine's performance; therefore, you must examine the surfaces of all camshaft lobes for irregularities such as feathered edges, abrasions, nicks, or upsets. Lobe surface damage that, in turn, damages a lifter, is a reason to reject and replace the camshaft. Additional defects that are cause for rejection include spalling, pitting, and surface cracks.

VALVES AND VALVE MECHANISMS

Most horizontally opposed engines operate with hydraulic valve lifters that must be disassembled, cleaned, and visually inspected during an overhaul. The plunger and cylinder in a hydraulic lifter are matched units, therefore, take care to avoid interchanging parts of one lifter with parts from another lifter. Lifter parts should be free from nicks, scratches, and chipped shoulders. To verify that a check valve is seating properly, quickly press the plunger into the cylinder. The plunger should bounce back, indicating satisfactory operation. If the plunger does not bounce back satisfactorily, a leakage test can be done using specially designed test equipment before discarding the lifter as defective.

In addition to inspecting hydraulic lifters, you must also verify that all push rods are clean, especially the oil passage through each rod. Ball ends should be smooth and free from nicks and scratches, and must fit tightly in the rod ends. To check for straightness, push rods are rolled across a flat, clean surface.

Inspect valve rockers for cracks and worn, pitted, or scored tips. In addition, visually verify that all oil passages are free from obstructions. If a rocker shaft turns excessively in a cylinder head, scoring typically results. Another problem often seen is burnishing and galling on a rocker shaft caused by the bronze rocker bushing and the heat of friction.

Some engine overhaul manuals require valve replacement, however, in cases where valves can be reused, a detailed inspection is required. Overheating, as well as nicks and scratches in the valve stem near the spring retainer groove renders a valve unserviceable.

Valve springs are also subjected to a great deal of wear and tear, and, therefore, must be checked visually for cracks, rust, and broken ends. If any corrosion exists or if a valve spring shows signs of wear, it must be discarded and replaced.

THREADED FASTENERS

Depending on the particular component, replacement of threaded fasteners such as bolts, nuts, studs, and screws may be required by the overhaul manual. However, in cases where it is allowable to reuse threaded fasteners, the parts should be carefully examined for evidence of cracks or mutilated threads. Cross-threading caused by improper installation, torn threads caused by trapped foreign matter, and flattened threads caused by improper fit are all typical examples of thread damage. Small defects such as slight nicks or burrs can be dressed out with a small file, fine abrasive cloth, or stone. However, if the fastener shows damage caused by overtightening or the use of improper tools, replace it with a new one.

STRUCTURAL INSPECTION

Once all engine parts have been visually inspected, key components must be structurally inspected to verify their integrity. If a structural inspection reveals a faulty part, the part is immediately removed from the overhaul process and replaced with a new part. Some of the more common structural inspections that are used include magnetic particle, liquid penetrant, eddy current, ultrasonic, and radiography inspection.

MAGNETIC PARTICLE INSPECTION

The nondestructive inspection method most often used for parts made of iron or iron alloys is magnetic particle inspection. Magnetic particle inspection is useful for detecting cracks, splits, seams, and voids that form when a metal ruptures. It is also useful for detecting cold shuts and inclusions of foreign matter that occured when the metal was cast or rolled.

With magnetic particle inspection, a part is magnetized and an oxide containing magnetic particles is poured or sprayed over the part's surface. If you recall from your general studies, when a material containing large amounts of iron is subjected to a strong magnetic field, the magnetic domains within the material align themselves and the part becomes magnetized. When this happens, the part develops a north and south pole and lines of flux flow in a continuous stream from the north pole to the south pole. If a break occurs within the part, another set of magnetic poles appears, one on either side of the break. Therefore, when conducting magnetic particle inspection, the poles produced by a fault attract the magnetic particles in the oxide, thereby giving you an indication of the break.

In order to detect a crack with magnetic particle inspection, the part must be magnetized so the lines of flux are perpendicular to the fault. This is because a flaw that is parallel to the lines of flux causes a

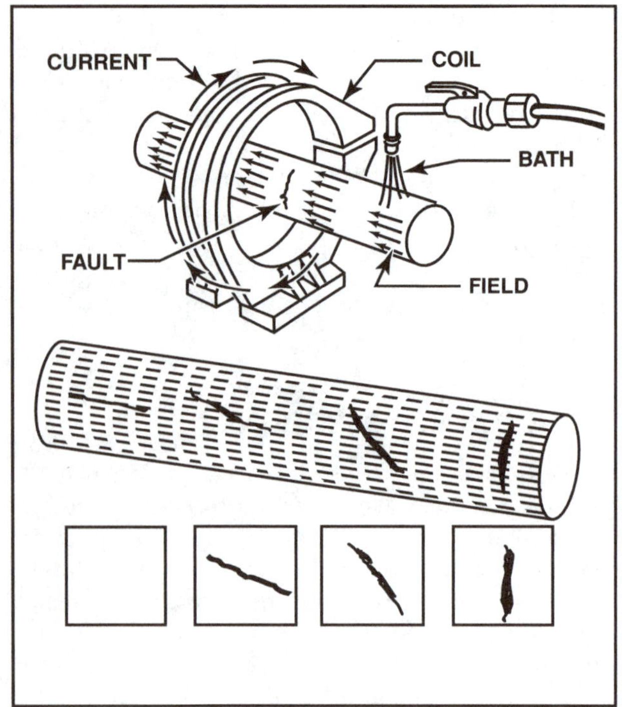

Figure 2-41. When a part is magnetized in a coil, or solenoid, the lines of flux pass through the material longitudinally. As the flux lines pass through the part, faults that run across the part or at an angle are detected.

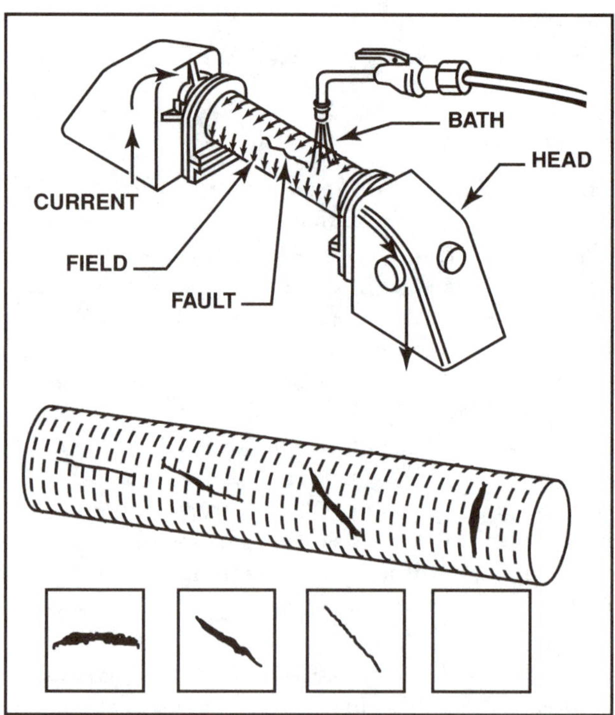

Figure 2-42. When current passes through a part, lines of flux encircle the part, making it circularly magnetized. This circular magnetization allows for the detection of faults extending lengthwise and at an angle along the part.

minimal disruption in the magnetic field. On the other hand, a defect that is perpendicular to the field creates a large disruption and is relatively easy to detect. To ensure that the flux lines are nearly perpendicular to a flaw, a part should be magnetized both longitudinally and circularly.

In longitudinal magnetization, the magnetizing current flows either through a coil that encircles the part being tested, or through a coil around a soft iron yoke. In either method, the magnetic field is oriented along the material so that magnetic fields form on either side of faults located across a material. [Figure 2-41]

With circular magnetization, current flows through the part being inspected, creating lines of magnetic flux that encircle the part. When this occurs, flaws or faults located along the material are magnetized and, therefore, attract magnetic particles. Current is sent through the part by placing it between the heads of the magnetizing equipment. However, if the part is tubular, it is slipped over a conductive rod that is then placed between the heads of a magnetizing machine. [Figure 2-42]

Large flat objects are circularly magnetized by using test probes that are held firmly against the surface with current passed through them. The magnetic field is oriented perpendicular to current that flows between the probes. [Figure 2-43]

The medium used to indicate the presence of a fault by magnetic particle inspection is ferromagnetic. In other words, the material is finely divided, has a high permeability, and a low retentivity. Furthermore, for operator safety it is nontoxic. There is no one medium that is best for all applications. However, in general, a testing medium consists of extremely fine iron oxides that are dyed gray, black, red, or treated with a dye that causes them to fluoresce when illuminated with an ultraviolet lamp.

The iron oxides may be used dry, or they can be mixed with kerosene or some other light oil and sprayed over a surface. Dry particles require no special preparation, making them well suited for field applications where portable equipment is used. Dry particles are typically applied with hand shakers, spray bulbs, or powder guns.

Wet particles are flowed over a part as a bath. The wet method is typically used with stationary equipment that continuously agitates the bath to keep the particles in suspension. Particles are either mixed

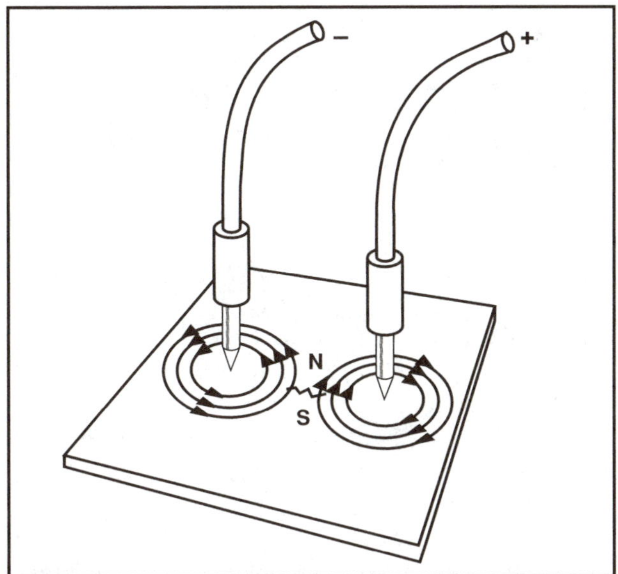

Figure 2-43. Current flowing through a flat object from high-current probes magnetizes the part circularly and detects cracks or faults that are in line with the probes.

in the vehicle with proportions recommended by the manufacturer or they come pre-mixed. The particle concentration of the bath requires close monitoring with adjustments made as necessary each time the system is used. Measuring particle concentration is accomplished by collecting a sample of the agitated bath in a centrifuge tube. A volume of particles settles to the bottom of the tube allowing measurement and comparison to be made against the manufacturer's standardization guide.

Since the bath is continuously recycled, it often becomes contaminated and discolored. When this happens, you must drain and clean the equipment, then refill with a fresh bath.

Different types of magnetizing procedures must be used for different applications. The two methods you must be familiar with are the residual magnetism method and the continuous magnetism method. When a part is magnetized and the magnetizing force is removed before the testing medium is applied, the part is tested by the residual method. This procedure relies on a part's residual or permanent magnetism. The residual procedure is only used with steels that have been heat-treated for stressed applications. Continuous magnetization requires a part to be subjected to a magnetizing force when the testing medium is applied. The continuous process of magnetization is most often used to locate invisible defects since it provides a greater sensitivity in locating subsurface discontinuities than does residual magnetism. When performing an engine overhaul, most overhaul manuals specify the type of magnetization to be used on various parts. [Figure 2-44]

PART	METHOD OF MAGNETIZATION	D.C. AMPERES	CRITICAL AREAS	POSSIBLE DEFECTS
CRANKSHAFT	CIRCULAR AND LONGITUDINAL	2500	JOURNALS, FILLETS, OIL HOLES, THRUST FLANGES, PROP FLANGE	FATIGUE CRACKS, HEAT CRACKS
CONNECTING ROD	CIRCULAR AND LONGITUDINAL	1800	ALL AREAS	FATIGUE CRACKS
CAMSHAFT	CIRCULAR AND LONGITUDINAL	1500	LOBES, JOURNALS	HEAT CRACKS
PISTON PIN	CIRCULAR AND LONGITUDINAL	1000	SHEAR PLANES, ENDS, CENTER	FATIGUE CRACKS
ROCKER ARMS	CIRCULAR AND LONGITUDINAL	800	PAD, SOCKET UNDER SIDE ARMS AND BOSS	FATIGUE CRACKS
GEARS TO 6 INCH DIAMETER	CIRCULAR OR ON CENTER CONDUCTOR	1000 TO 1500	TEETH, SPLINES, KEYWAYS	FATIGUE CRACKS
GEARS OVER 6 INCH DIAMETER	SHAFT CIRCULAR TEETH BETWEEN HEADS TWO TIMES 90°	1000 TO 1500	TEETH, SPLINES	FATIGUE CRACKS
SHAFTS	CIRCULAR AND LONGITUDINAL	1000 TO 1500	SPLINES, KEYWAYS, CHANGE OF SECTION	FATIGUE CRACKS, HEAT CRACKS
THRU BOLTS ROD BOLTS	CIRCULAR AND LONGITUDINAL	500	THREADS UNDER HEAD	FATIGUE CRACKS

Figure 2-44. A typical magnetic particle inspection schedule for aircraft engine parts provides details on method of magnetization, current required, critical areas, and a list of possible defects. In this case, the fluorescent method is preferred and a wet continuous procedure is required.

Magnetization of a part after it is inspected is often detrimental to its operation in an aircraft. Therefore, before a part is returned to service, it must be thoroughly demagnetized. In order to demagnetize a part, the magnetic domains must be disorganized. To accomplish this, the part is subjected to a magnetizing force opposite that of the force used to magnetize it. For example, if the magnetizing force was AC, the domains alternate in polarity, and if the part is slowly removed from the field while current is still flowing, the reversing action progressively becomes weaker. Thus, the domains are left with random orientation and the part is demagnetized.

AC current does not penetrate a surface very deeply. For this reason, complete demagnetization of some parts require DC demagnetization. To accomplish this, a part is placed in a coil and subjected to more current than initially used to magnetize the part. Current is flowed through the coil and then the direction of current flow is reversed while decreasing the amount. The direction of current flow continues to be reversed in direction and decreased until the lowest value of current is reached.

The presence of any residual magnetism is checked with a magnet strength indicator. Parts must be demagnetized to within the limits specified in the appropriate overhaul manual before they are returned to service. Although in many cases overhaul manual instructions specify the magnetic particle method of inspection for a certain component, the best advice is to consult the overhaul manual for warnings or restrictions before proceeding. For example, magnetizing the plunger assembly of a hydraulic valve lifter interferes with the steel check valve's ability to seat properly and it is difficult to demagnetize the assembly sufficiently to prevent further problems.

LIQUID PENETRANT INSPECTION

Liquid penetrant inspection is a method of nondestructive inspection suitable for locating cracks, porosity, or other types of faults open to the surface. Penetrant inspection is usable on ferrous and nonferrous metals, as well as nonporous plastic material. The primary limitation of dye penetrant inspection is that a defect must be open to the surface.

Dye penetrant inspection is based on the principle of **capillary attraction**. The area being inspected is covered with a penetrating liquid that has a very low viscosity and low surface tension. This penetrant is allowed to remain on the surface long enough to allow the capillary action to draw the penetrant into any fault that extends to the surface. After sufficient time, the excess penetrant is washed off and the surface is covered with a developer. The developer, by the process of reverse capillary action, blots the penetrant out of cracks or other faults, forming a visible line in the developer. If an indication is fuzzy instead of sharp and clear, the probable cause is that the part was not thoroughly washed before the developer was applied. [Figure 2-45]

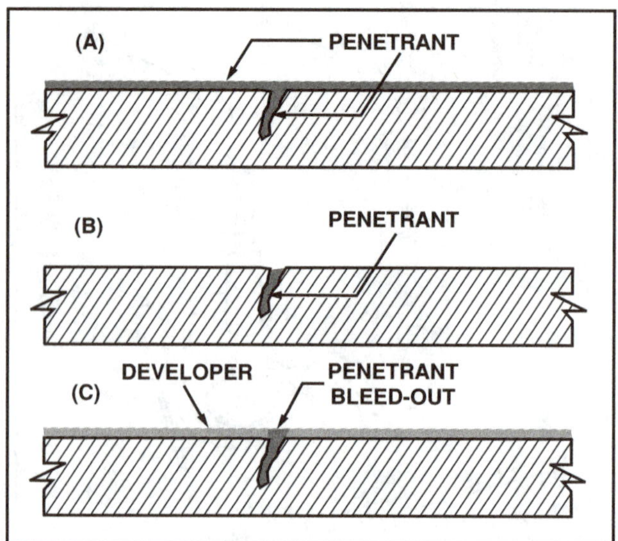

Figure 2-45. (A) — When performing a liquid penetrant inspection, the penetrant is spread over the surface of the material being examined, and allowed sufficient time for capillary action to take place. (B) — The excess penetrant is then washed from the surface, leaving any cracks and surface flaws filled. (C) — An absorbent developer is sprayed over the surface where it blots out any penetrant. The crack then shows up as a bright line against the white developer.

There are two types of dyes used in liquid penetrant inspection: fluorescent and colored. An ultraviolet light is used with a fluorescent penetrant and any flaw shows up as a green line. With the colored dye method, faults show up as red lines against the white developer.

When using liquid penetrant it is important that the surface be free of grease, dirt, and oil. Only when the surface is perfectly clean can the penetrant be ensured of getting into cracks or faults. The best method of cleaning a surface is with a volatile petroleum-based solvent, which effectively removes all traces of oil and grease. However, some materials are damaged by these solvents, so care must be taken to ensure the proper cleaner is used. If vapor degreasing is not practical, the part is cleaned by scrubbing with a solvent or a strong detergent solution. Parts to be inspected with liquid penetrant should not be cleaned by abrasive blasting, scraping, or heavy brushing. These methods tend to close any discontinuities on the surface and hide defects that could otherwise be detected. After the part is clean, rinse and dry it thoroughly.

Once clean, penetrant is typically applied to a surface by immersing the part in the liquid or by swabbing or brushing a penetrant solution onto a part's surface. However, some manufacturer's do offer dye penetrant in spray cans to allow application in small areas for localized inspection. Whichever system is used, the area inspected is completely covered with the penetrating liquid which is then allowed to remain on the surface for the manufacturer's recommended length of time.

The amount of time required for a penetrant to cure is called its **dwell time** and is determined by the size and shape of the discontinuities for which you are looking. For example, small, thin cracks require a longer dwell time than large and more open cracks. Dwell time is decreased if a part is heated; however, if the part gets too hot the penetrant evaporates.

Once the appropriate dwell time passes, liquid penetrants are removed using either water, an emulsifying agent, or a solvent. **Water-soluble penetrants** are the easiest to remove. Typically, this type of penetrant is flushed away with water that is sprayed at a pressure of 30 to 40 psi. The spray nozzle is held at a 45 degree angle to the surface to avoid washing the penetrant out of cracks or faults.

Post-emulsifying penetrants are not water soluble. They must be treated with an emulsifying agent before they can be washed from a part's surface. This allows you to control the amount of penetrant that is removed prior to cleaning. By varying the emulsifier dwell time, surface penetrant can be emulsified while the penetrant absorbed into cracks or other defects is left untouched. As a result, the surface penetrant is rinsed off but the absorbed penetrant remains to expose the defect.

Some penetrants are neither water soluble nor emulsifiable, but instead are **solvent-removeable**. When using this type of penetrant, excess penetrant is removed with an absorbent towel, and the part's surface is then wiped with clean towels dampened with solvent. The solvent should not be sprayed onto the surface nor should the part be immersed in solvent, since this will wash the penetrant out of faults or dilute it enough to prevent proper indication in the developer.

Once the excess penetrant is removed, a developer is applied. There are three kinds of developers used to draw penetrants from faults. While all three types do the same job, the method of application differs. One thing to keep in mind is that penetrant begins to bleed out of any fault as soon as the surface penetrant is removed. Because of this, covering the surface to be inspected with developer as soon as possible helps to pinpoint the location of any fault.

A dry developer consists of a loose powder material such as talcum that adheres to the part and acts as a blotter to draw the penetrant out of any surface faults. When using a dry developer, the part is typically placed in a bin of loose developer. For larger components, dry powder is applied with a soft brush, or blown over the surface with a powder gun. After the powder remains on the surface for the recommended time, the excess is removed with low-pressure air flow.

The penetrant used with a dry developer is often treated with a fluorescent or colored dye. These parts are typically examined under black light so faults appear as a green indication as the light causes the dye to fluoresce, or glow. Colored dye penetrants are usually red and any faults appear as red marks, clearly visible on the surface.

A wet developer is similar to a dry developer in that it is applied as soon as the surface penetrant is rinsed off the part. However, a wet developer typically consists of a white powder mixed with water that is either flowed over the surface or a part is immersed in it. The part is then air-dried and inspected in the same way as a part on which dry developer was used. Wet developers are typically used with penetrants that are treated with either fluorescent or colored dyes.

The most commonly used developer for field maintenance is the nonaqueous type. Nonaqueous developer consists of a white, chalk-like powder suspended in a solvent that is normally applied from a pressure spray can, or sprayed onto a surface with a paint gun. The part being inspected must be thoroughly dry before a thin, moist coat of developer is applied. The developer dries rapidly and pulls out any penetrant that exists within a fault. The penetrant stains the developer and is easily seen with a black light when a fluorescent penetrant is used. If a white light is desired, use a colored dye.

EDDY CURRENT INSPECTION

Eddy current inspection is a testing method that requires little or no part preparation and can detect surface and subsurface flaws in most metals.

Furthermore, it can differentiate among metals and alloys, as well as a metal's heat treat condition. Eddy current inspection is based on the principle of current acceptance. In other words, it determines the ease with which a material accepts induced current. As AC is induced into a material being tested, the AC is measured to determine the material's characteristics.

Eddy currents are electrical currents that flow through electrically conductive material under the influence of an induced electromagnetic field. The ease with which a material accepts the induced eddy currents is determined by four properties: its conductivity, permeability, mass, and by the presence of any voids or faults.

ULTRASONIC INSPECTION

Ultrasonic testing equipment is based on an electronic oscillator that produces AC of the proper frequency, which is amplified to the proper strength and sent to a transducer that is touching the material being tested. The transducer causes the test material to vibrate at the oscillator's frequency. When the vibrations reach the other side of the material and bounce back, they create an electrical impulse at the transducer that is seen on the CRT display.

RADIOGRAPHIC INSPECTION

One of the most important methods of nondestructive inspection available is radiographic inspection. Radiographic inspection allows a photographic view inside a structure. In other words, this method uses certain sections of the electromagnetic spectrum to photograph an object's interior.

X-ray and gamma ray radiation are forms of high energy, short wavelength electromagnetic waves. The amount of energy these rays contain is related inversely to their wavelength. In other words, the shorter the wavelength, the greater the energy. They have no electrical charge or mass, travel in straight lines at the speed of light, and are able to penetrate matter. The depth of penetration is dependent upon the ray's energy.

There are certain characteristics that make x-rays and gamma rays especially useful in nondestructive inspection. For example, both types of rays are absorbed by the matter through which they pass. The amount of absorption is proportional to the density of the material. Furthermore, x-rays and gamma rays ionize certain materials, making it possible for them to expose photographic film and cause certain materials to fluoresce, or glow.

DIMENSIONAL INSPECTION

Once an engine part is found to be structurally sound, it must be measured to verify that it is within the manufacturer's tolerances. This check is referred to as a dimensional inspection and requires the use of several precision measuring instruments such as micrometer calipers, telescoping gauges, and dial indicators. Once a part has been measured, its dimensions must be compared to the serviceable dimension limits required by the manufacturer. A list of both new parts limits and serviceable limits are provided in a typical overhaul manual. [Figure 2-46]

In most cases, the values given in a manufacturer's table of limits are clearance dimensions, not actual part sizes. The limits are specified as the fit of one part in another. For example, the tolerances given for "piston pin in piston" represent the clearance between the piston pin boss and the piston pin. To determine this clearance, you must measure the piston pin's outside diameter and then measure the inside diameter of the piston pin boss in the piston. The difference between these two values represents the "piston pin in piston" clearance. The capital "L" in the 0.013L "piston pin in piston" serviceable limit denotes a loose fit, meaning that the inside diameter of the piston pin boss is greater than the outside diameter of the piston pin.

Some fits, such as a bushing in the small end of a connecting rod, call for an **interference**, or **tight fit** and are indicated by a capital "T" following the dimension numerals. All interference fits require special procedures or equipment to assemble the parts because there is no clearance between the two dimensions. For example, dimension 0.0025T to 0.0050T means that the bushing must be from two and a half to five thousandths of an inch larger than the hole into which it fits.

All the parts listed in the table of limits must be inspected to ascertain if their dimensions comply with the part specifications listed. If a part does not fall within the tolerances listed, it must be replaced or repaired. The exception to this requirement are dimensions given for interference fits, such as the bushing in connecting rod example just mentioned. If the bushings do not have damage requiring replacement, you would not remove them simply to measure their fit.

CRANKCASE

In order to perform a dimensional inspection on a crankcase you must temporarily assemble the case

DESCRIPTION	SERVICEABLE LIMITS	NEW PARTS	
		MINIMUM	MAXIMUM
First piston ring in cylinder (P/N 635814)..........................Gap:	0.059	0.033	0.049
First piston ring in cylinder (P/N 639273)..........................Gap:	0.074	0.048	0.064
Second piston ring in cylinder (P/N 635814)......................Gap:	0.050	0.024	0.040
Second piston ring in cylinder (P/N 639273)......................Gap:	0.069	0.043	0.059
Third piston ring in cylinder...Gap:	0.059	0.033	0.049
Fourth piston ring in cylinder...Gap:	0.050	0.024	0.040
Fifth piston ring in cylinder..Gap:	0.059	0.033	0.049
Piston pin in piston (standard or 0.005" oversize)....Diameter:	0.013L	0.0001L	0.0007L
Piston pin in cylinder.......................................End Clearance:	0.090	0.031	0.048
Piston pin in connecting rod busing..........................Diameter:	0.0040L	0.0022L	0.0026L
Bushing in connecting rod..Diameter:		0.0025T	0.0050T
Connecting rod bearing on crankpin.........................Diameter:	0.006 L	0.0009L	0.0034L
Connecting rod on crankpin............................Side Clearance:	0.016	0.006	0.010
Bolt in connecting rod..Diameter:		0.0000	0.0018L
Connecting bearing and bushing twist or convergence per inch of length..:	0.001	0.0000	0.0005
CRANKSHAFT			
Crankshaft in main bearing....................................... Diameter:	0.005L	0.0012L	0.0032L
Propeller reduction gear shaft in bearing................ Diameter:		0.0012L	0.0032L
Propeller drive shaft in shaft.................................... Diameter:		0.0012L	0.0032L
Crankpins...Out-of-Round:	0.0015	0.0000	0.0032L
Main journals...Out-of-Round:	0.0015	0.0000	0.0005
Propeller drive shaft... Out-of-Round:	0.002	0.0000	0.002
Propeller drive shaft in thrust bearing............End Clearance:	0.020	0.006	0.0152
Crankshaft run-out at center main journals (shaft supported at thrust rear journals) full indicator reading..:	0.015	0.000	0.015
Propeller shaft run-out at propeller flange (when supported at front and rear journals) full indicator reading..:	0.003	0.000	0.002
Damper pin bushing in crankcheek extension..........Diameter:		0.0015T	0.003 T
Damper pin busing in counterweight.........................Diameter:		0.0015T	0.003 T
Damper pin in counterweight...........................End Clearance:	0.040	0.001	0.023
Alternator drive gear on reduction gear....................Diameter:		0.001T	0.004 T
Crankshaft gear on crankshaft.................................Diameter:		0.000	0.002 T
CAMSHAFT			
Camshaft journals in crankcase................................Diameter:	0.005L	0.001L	0.003 L
Camshaft in crankcase.....................................End Clearance:	0.014	0.005	0.009
Camshaft run-out at center (shaft supported at end journals) full indicator reading:..:	0.003	0.000	0.001
Camshaft gear on camshaft flange...........................Diameter:		0.005T	0.0015L
Governor gear on crankshaft....................................Diameter:	0.006L	0.002L	0.002 L
CRANKCASE AND ATTACHED PARTS			
Thru bolts in crankcase...Diameter:		0.005T	0.0013L
Hydraulic lifter in crankcase......................................Diameter:	0.0035L	0.001 L	0.0025L
Governor drive shaft in crankcase............................Diameter:		0.0014L	0.0034L

Figure 2-46. When doing a dimensional inspection on engine components, you must measure each component and compare the dimensions to the limits in the overhaul manual.

halves. For example, to check main bearing clearances, the main bearing inserts must be installed in the crankcase halves and the case halves must be reassembled and torqued. A telescoping gauge is then adjusted to the inside diameter of each bearing and measured with a micrometer caliper. The crankshaft journals are then carefully measured with the same micrometer. Once both dimensions are known, the journal dimensions are subtracted from the main bearing insert dimensions to obtain the clearance between the inserts and the crankshaft journal.

With the crankcase halves assembled, the camshaft bearing clearances must also be checked. Since the camshaft bearings on many engines are machined into the crankcase there is no need for camshaft bearing inserts. To check the camshaft bearing clearances, use the same procedures discussed earlier for checking crankshaft bearing clearances. [Figure 2-47]

CRANKSHAFT

A crankshaft has a number of critical bearing surfaces that require dimensional inspection. For example, the dimensions of main bearing journals are normally measured with a micrometer caliper to determine crankshaft journal to main bearing clearances in the crankcase. In addition, rod bearing journals are checked with a micrometer caliper to determine rod bearing to rod bearing journal clearances.

Another crankshaft dimensional inspection requires you to check a crankshaft's runout. To check for runout, a crankshaft is supported on vee-blocks at locations specified in the overhaul manual. A dial indicator is then placed at points along the crankshaft and the crankshaft is rotated. The total runout is the sum of the over and under indications on the dial indicator. If the total indicator reading exceeds the dimensions given in the manufacturer's table of limits, the crankshaft must be replaced. No attempt should be made to straighten a bent crankshaft because this will probably rupture the nitrated surface of the bearing journals, leading to eventual crankshaft failure.

Figure 2-47. A dimensional inspection of the main journal bearing inserts and camshaft bearings requires assembly of the crankcase halves. Once assembled, a telescoping gauge and micrometer are used to determine the appropriate clearances.

CONNECTING RODS

Connecting rods must be checked for twist and convergence. To check for twist, arbors are inserted into each end of a connecting rod. The arbors are then laid across parallel blocks. Using a set of thickness gauges, measure to see if there is any space between the arbors and the parallel blocks. The amount of twist is determined by the thickness of the gauge that can be inserted. [Figure 2-48]

To check a connecting rod for convergence, you must check the distance between the large and small arbors on both sides of the connecting rod. To do this, attach a **parallelism gauge** to one end of the large arbor. Adjust the gauge until it just touches the small arbor. Next, move the parallelism gauge to the other end of the large arbor. If the gauge does not touch the small arbor, determine the clearance between the gauge and arbor with a thickness gauge. The difference in distance between the two arbors is the amount of convergence, or bend present in the rod. [Figure 2-49]

Any rods that are twisted or bent beyond serviceable limits must be replaced. When replacement is necessary, the weight of the new rod should be matched

Figure 2-48. To check a connecting rod for twist, place parallel blocks under the ends of the arbors and attempt to pass a thickness gauge between each arbor end and the block. If a gap is present, the connecting rod is twisted. The amount of twist permitted is specified in the engine overhaul manual.

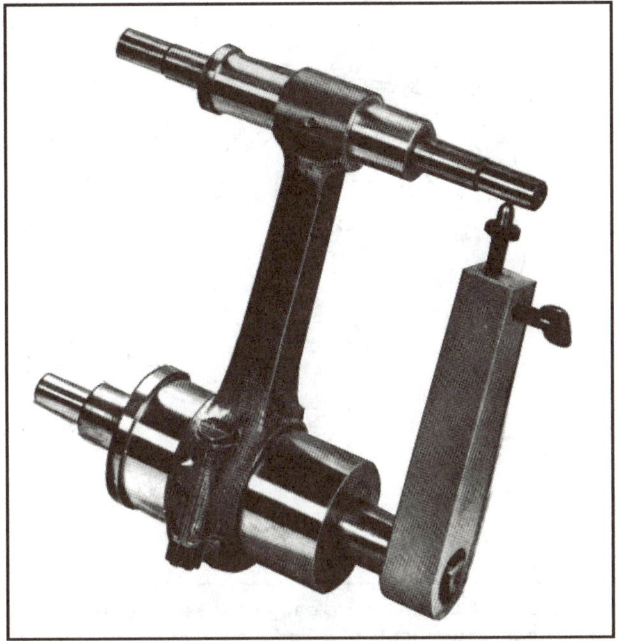

Figure 2-49. To check a connecting rod for convergence, mount a parallelism gauge to one end of the large arbor and measure the distance between the arbors on both sides. The difference in the measurements is the amount of bend in the rod.

within one-half ounce to the opposite rod to minimize vibrations.

PISTONS, RINGS, AND PISTON PINS

Piston heads should be dimensionally checked for flatness using a straightedge and a thickness gauge. If you detect the presence of a depression in the top of a piston, the piston was most likely subjected to detonation. In such cases, the piston must be discarded due to an increased possibility of stress cracking around the pin bosses and at the junction of the piston head and walls. If the piston head is flat, measure the outside diameter of a piston with a micrometer at the piston skirt and each ring land. The measurements are used later after checking cylinder bore dimensions to determine acceptable piston to cylinder clearances. [Figure 2-50]

In addition to the pistons, the piston rings must be dimensionally checked. The two things you must measure on each piston ring are end gap clearance and side clearance. **End gap** is the space between the two ends of a piston ring once it is installed in a cylinder. **Side clearance**, on the other hand, is the space between a piston ring and ring land.

The end gap of piston rings is measured by placing a ring into a cylinder barrel and squaring the ring with a piston. Once the ring is positioned, a thickness gauge is used to measure the gap between the ends of the ring. If the gap is correct, the ring is suitable for use in that cylinder. However, if the end gap is too small the ring could bind once it reaches its operating temperature and expands. On the other hand, if the gap is excessive, the ring will allow excessive blow-by.

Figure 2-50. A straightedge and thickness gauge are used to check the flatness of a piston head. The presence of a depression in the top of a piston head may indicate damage from detonation and is often cause for rejection.

To check a piston ring's side clearance, install the ring in its proper ring groove and measure the clearance between each ring and ring land with a thickness gauge. To obtain an accurate measurement, the ring being measured must be held into the ring groove. If tapered rings are installed, hold a straightedge against the side of the piston. [Figure 2-51]

Piston pins are checked dimensionally in several ways. First, the clearance between a piston pin and

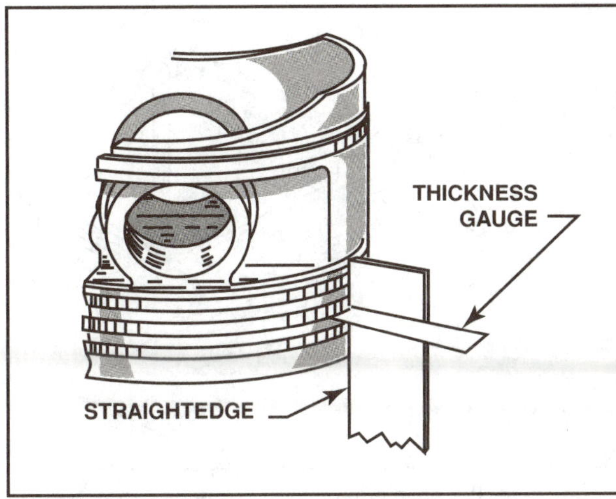

Figure 2-51. To check side clearance, use a straightedge to hold the piston rings squarely in their grooves and insert a thickness gauge between each ring and ring land.

bore of the piston pin boss must be measured. This is done by obtaining both the piston pin bore dimension and piston pin outside diameter. The bore dimension is taken with a telescoping gauge and micrometer while the piston pin outside diameter is measured with a micrometer. By subtracting the piston pin diameter from the bore dimension, a piston pin to piston pin bore clearance is obtained.

Some overhaul manuals require you to check the end clearance between the piston pin and cylinder wall. To do this, a piston pin's length must be checked with a micrometer caliper or vernier caliper and compared with the cylinder bore dimensions. Finally, you must check a piston pin for straightness. To do this, place a piston pin on vee-blocks and measure the runout with a dial indicator. [Figure 2-52]

CYLINDERS

Cylinder barrels are checked for wear using a cylinder bore gauge, a telescoping gauge and a micrometer, or an inside micrometer. Dimensional inspection of a cylinder barrel is done to obtain cylinder taper, out-of-roundness, bore diameter wear, and fit between piston skirt and cylinder. All cylinder barrel measurements must be taken at a minimum of two positions 90 degrees apart.

Cylinder taper is the difference between the diameter of the cylinder at the bottom and the diameter at the top. The natural wear pattern of a cylinder usually results in a larger diameter at the top of a cylinder because the heat, pressure, and erosive conditions are more intense. On the other hand, some cylinders are designed with an intentional taper, or choke. In such a case, you must be able to distinguish wear from intentional taper. When a step is present in the taper, you must exercise care while making measurements to avoid inaccurate readings. [Figure 2-53]

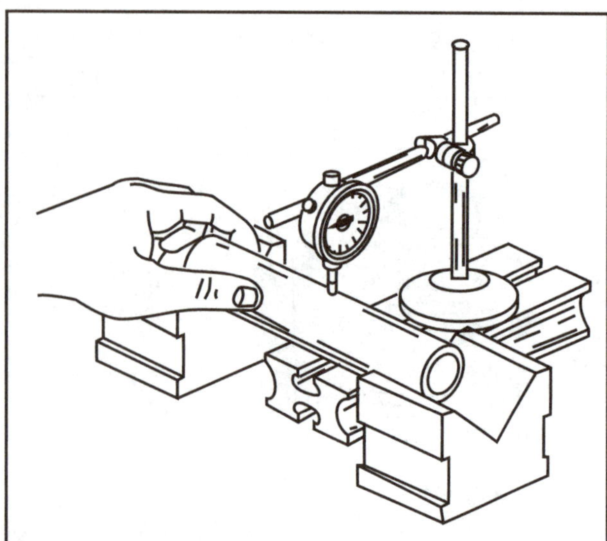

Figure 2-52. Piston pins are dimensionally inspected for straightness with vee-blocks and a dial indicator. As a pin is rotated on the vee-blocks, runout is recorded on the dial indicator.

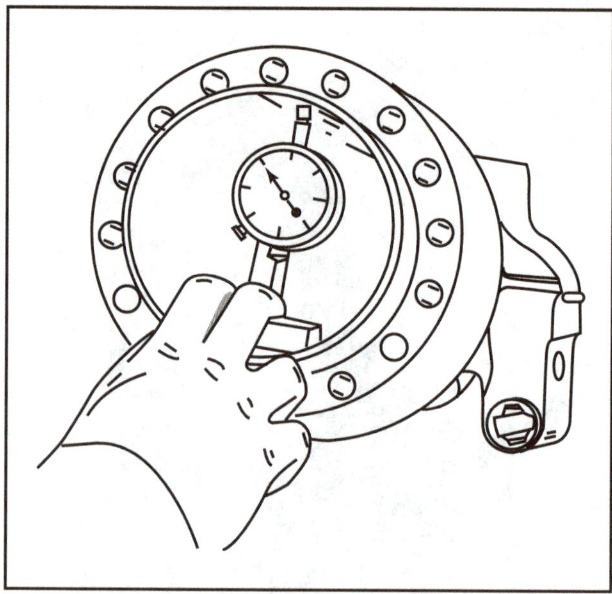

Figure 2-53. A cylinder bore gauge can be used to provide accurate measurements of cylinder bore, taper, and an out-of-round condition.

When inspecting for an out-of-round condition, measurements are usually taken at the top of the cylinder. However, a measurement should also be taken at the cylinder skirt to detect dents and bends caused by careless handling. In addition, a cylinder's flange should be checked for warpage. To do this, place the cylinder on a suitable jig and check for any gaps between the flange and jig with a thickness gauge. [Figure 2-54]

Another dimensional inspection that should be made on a cylinder is to check the valve guides for wear and excessive clearance. This inspection is sometimes accomplished with a maximum wear gauge provided by the engine manufacturer. When using a wear gauge, a valve guide is worn beyond serviceable limits if you are able to insert the gauge into either end of the valve guide. If a wear gauge is not provided, the inside diameter of a valve guide is checked with a small hole gauge and micrometer. To do this, a small hole gauge is placed inside the valve guide and expanded until it fits snugly. The hole gauge is then removed and measured with a micrometer.

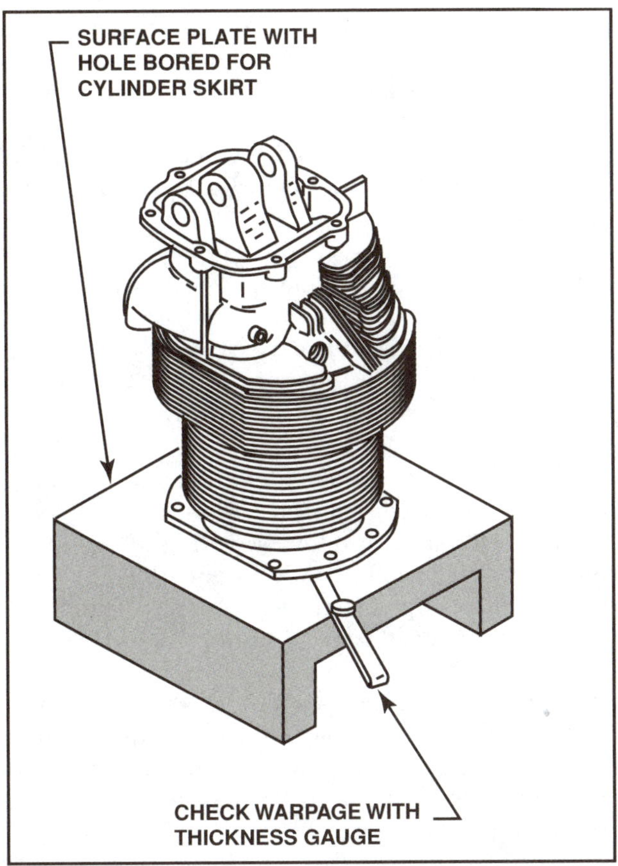

Figure 2-54. To inspect a cylinder flange for warpage, place the cylinder on a jig and attempt to pass a thickness gauge between the flange and jig at several points around the flange.

CAMSHAFT

The dimensions of camshaft bearing journals are measured with a micrometer caliper. This is usually done when checking clearances between the camshaft and camshaft bearings in the crankcase. In addition, if the overhaul manual specifies the taper on the lobes, a dimensional check must be made to determine if taper is within limits.

Like a crankshaft, a camshaft should be checked for straightness by placing it on vee-blocks and measuring the runout with a dial indicator. If the readings exceed serviceable limits, the camshaft is rejected and replaced.

VALVES AND VALVE MECHANISMS

Valves, valve springs, rocker arms, and rocker shafts must be dimensionally inspected to detect parts that are worn beyond serviceable limits. Since valves are subjected to a great deal of heat and tension, a thorough dimensional inspection of each valve is essential. One item you must check for is **valve stretch**, which is a lengthening of the valve stem. To check a

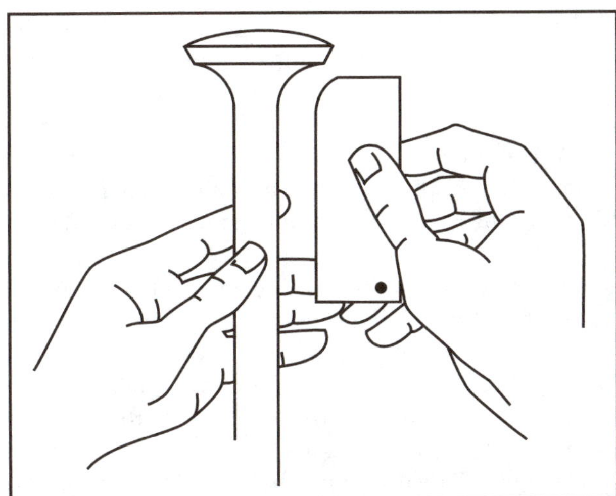

Figure 2-55. One method for detecting stretched valves is to hold a contour gauge along the underside of each valve head.

valve for stretch, a contour gauge or radius gauge can be placed along the underside of the valve head. [Figure 2-55]

Another method of checking for stretch is to measure the valve stem diameter at several places using a micrometer caliper. The three most common places to measure are at the end of the stem near the spring retainer groove, at the middle of the stem, and at the stem neck. If the stem's diameter is smaller at the center or neck than at the end, the valve is stretched.

In addition to inspecting valves for stretch, you must also check the runout of the valve face. To accomplish this, chuck each valve in a valve grinder and measure the runout with a dial indicator. If the runout is within limits, measure the valve head thickness, or valve margin. [Figure 2-56]

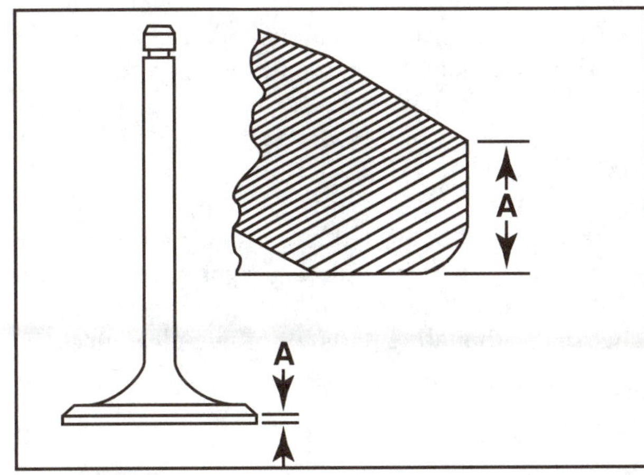

Figure 2-56. In order to reuse a valve, the valve stem must run true with the valve face and the valve margin must be within the manufacturer's specifications.

Valve springs are checked for compression and wire diameter. To check for compression, a valve spring tester is used to compress each spring to a height specified in the overhaul manual. The number of pounds required to compress the spring is then read from a dial on the tester. To measure a spring's wire diameter use a small caliper or micrometer.

Each rocker arm shaft bushing and rocker arm shaft must be measured to determine the clearance between the two. The inside diameter of each rocker arm shaft bushing is measured with a small T-gauge or hole gauge and micrometer. Next, the outside diameter of the rocker arm shaft is measured with a micrometer. The difference between the dimensions represents the shaft-to-bushing clearance.

OIL PUMP HOUSING

To help ensure proper oil pump operation, the distance between an oil pump's mating surface and the pump gears must fall within limits. To measure the distance between the two, a depth gauge is used. To use a depth gauge, retract the spindle until it is flush with the gauge's fixed bar. Then, lay the bar across the oil pump housing and extend the spindle until it contacts the oil pump gear. Now, read the micrometer head to obtain the distance between the housing and gear.

REPAIR

Once you have completed the visual, structural, and dimensional inspections, you may begin making repairs. Damage such as burrs, nicks, scratches, scoring, or galling can be removed with a fine oil stone, crocus cloth, or similar abrasive substance. Swiss pattern files or small edged stones work well for removing small nicks. Flanged surfaces that are bent, warped, or nicked can be repaired by lapping on a surface plate. Defective threads can sometimes be repaired with a suitable die or tap; however, avoid tapping a hole too deep and creating an oversized tapped hole. If galling or scratches are removed from the bearing surface of a journal, the surface should be buffed to a high finish with fine crocus cloth. After completing repairs, parts should be thoroughly cleaned to remove all abrasives, then checked with mating parts for proper clearances.

CRANKCASE

Cracks, damaged studs or threads, and excessive bearing clearances are examples of repairable crankcase defects. Cracks can only be repaired by the engine manufacturer or a certified repair station. To repair a crack, a form of inert gas welding is used. Once a crack is welded, the bead is peened to relieve stress and then machined to match the rest of the surface. Bearing cavity damage may also be repaired by welding, then machining to the proper dimension.

Camshafts normally rotate in bearings cut into a crankcase with no bearing inserts. Therefore, camshaft bearings with excessive clearances can only be repaired by line-boring the bearings and installing an oversized camshaft.

If bent or loose studs were identified during inspection, they must be removed and replaced. If standard size studs will no longer work, oversize studs may be used. Oversize studs are identified by color coding and stamped identification marks to indicate the amount of oversizing. [Figure 2-57]

If internal case threads cannot be repaired using a tap, Heli-Coil inserts may be used. Heli-Coils provide new threads that allow standard studs to be installed. There is no decrease in strength when this type of repair is made.

CRANKSHAFT

If slight roughness exists on any of a crankshaft's main journals or crankpins, polish the surfaces with fine crocus cloth. To do this, place the crankshaft in a lathe and hold the crocus cloth against the surface to be polished while it rotates. If sludge chambers were removed for cleaning, reinstall them at this time.

All major repairs made on a crankshaft must be done by the manufacturer or certified repair station. For example, crankshaft main journals or crankpins that are out-of-round may be ground to an acceptable undersize. However, once a crankshaft is ground, it must be re-nitrided and undersized bearing inserts must be installed in the crankcase.

CONNECTING RODS

The only repairs you may do on connecting rods is to replace the bushings and bearing inserts. However, because of the interference fit between the rod and bushing, rebushing a connecting rod requires an arbor press and a special bushing installation drift. After pressing the new bushing into place it must be reamed to the dimensions specified in the overhaul manual. Because of the extremely

TYPICAL PART NO.	OVERSIZE ON PITCH DIA. OF COARSE THREAD (INCHES)	OPTIONAL IDENTIFICATION MARKS ON COARSE THREAD END		IDENTIFICATION COLOR CODE
		STAMPED	MACHINED	
XXXXXX	STANDARD	NONE		NONE
XXXXXXXP003	.003			RED
XXXXXXP006	.006			BLUE
XXXXXXP009	.009			GREEN
XXXXXXP007	.007			BLUE
XXXXXXP012	.012			GREEN

Figure 2-57. Oversize studs have color codes and stamped identification marks to show the degree of oversize.

close tolerances required, special equipment is generally required to ream connecting rod bushings.

PISTONS

Most pistons are replaced during an overhaul; however, if a piston was installed shortly before an overhaul and it is within limits, it may be reused. Repairs to pistons are limited to the removal of light scoring. For example, scoring on a piston skirt is repairable only if very light because removal of deep scores could inadvertently alter the piston's contour and exceed clearance limits. When removing scoring on a piston skirt, use nothing more abrasive than crocus cloth. Scoring above a piston's top ring groove may be machined or sanded out as long as the piston diameter is not reduced below its specified minimum.

Whether reusing pistons or installing a new set, piston weights should be as close as possible to one another. The maximum allowable weight difference is listed in the manufacturer's table of limits. New pistons can often be purchased in matched sets whose weight differences are considerably below the manufacturer's maximum.

VALVES AND VALVE MECHANISMS

If there is sufficient valve margin, a valve can be refaced by grinding to the proper angle. Various types of valve grinding machines are used for refacing valves. However, a wet valve grinder is preferred because a mixture of soluble oil and water is used to keep the valve cool and carry away the grinding chips.

Like many machining tasks, it is important that you be familiar with the machine you are operating. Valve grinding machines do vary depending on the manufacturer. Therefore, you should take time to familiarize yourself with the grinding machine you intend to use before you grind a valve. The following discussion will look at some of the steps that are common to most grinding machines.

Before you grind a valve, the stone must be trued. This is usually done by drawing a diamond dresser across the stone, cutting just deep enough to true and clean the stone. Using the overhaul manual specifications, set the machine's movable head to the correct valve face angle. Valves are usually ground to a standard angle of 30° or 45°. However, in some instances an interference fit from 0.5° to 1.5° less than the standard angle may be required. An interference fit is used to obtain a more positive seal by producing an extremely narrow contact surface. Theoretically, an interference fit provides a fine line contact between the valve and seat. With this line contact, all the load that the valve exerts

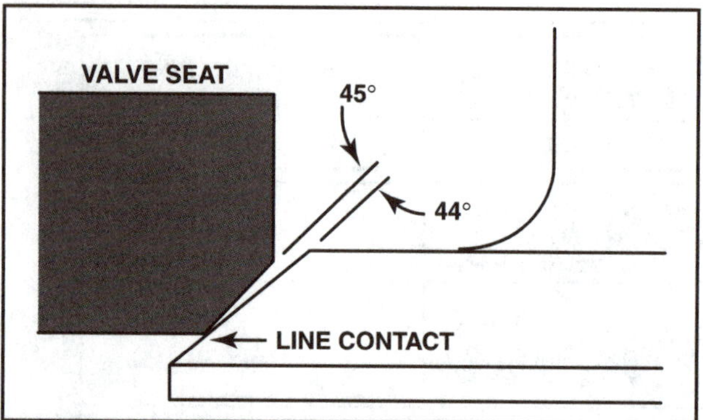

Figure 2-58. An interference fit provides a positive seal along a fine contact area.

against the seat is concentrated in a very small area. [Figure 2-58]

To prepare a valve for grinding, insert the valve into the chuck, leaving approximately two inches distance between the valve face and the chuck. If the valve is chucked any further out, excessive wobbling may occur. Prior to grinding, check the travel of the valve face across the stone. Adjust both the "in" and "out" travel stops so that the valve completely passes the stone on both sides but does not travel so far that the stem is accidentally ground. [Figure 2-59]

With the valvFe set correctly in place, switch on the grinder and direct the flow of the grinding fluid onto the valve face. Next, back the valve fixture, or workhead table, all the way out and adjust the workhead table laterally to place the valve directly in front of the stone. Advance the valve inward and bring the valve up to the stone slowly until you begin to hear a light grinding sound. The intensity of the grinding sound provides an indication of the amount of cut being made by the stone as it grinds the valve. Slowly draw the valve back and forth across the full width of the stone without increasing the cut. When the grinding sound diminishes or ceases, the cut is complete. Next, move the workhead table to the outer travel stop, stopping rotation of the valve, and inspect the valve to determine if further grinding is necessary. If another cut is needed, slowly bring the valve inward to contact the stone before increasing the cut. Listening for the intensity of the grinding sound, slowly increase the cut. When grinding valves, make light cuts and avoid trying to hurry the process by making heavy cuts. Heavy cuts cause chattering which produces a rough valve surface. Remove only enough material to clean up any wear marks or pits on the valve face.

After grinding, check the valve margin to be sure that the valve edge has not been ground too thin. A thin edge is called a **feather edge** and can overheat, causing preignition. Furthermore, a feather edge has a tendency to burn away in a short period of time, requiring another overhaul much earlier than planned. [Figure 2-60]

Valve tips can also be resurfaced on a valve grinder to remove cupping or wear. To resurface a valve tip, position the valve in a clamp to allow grinding of

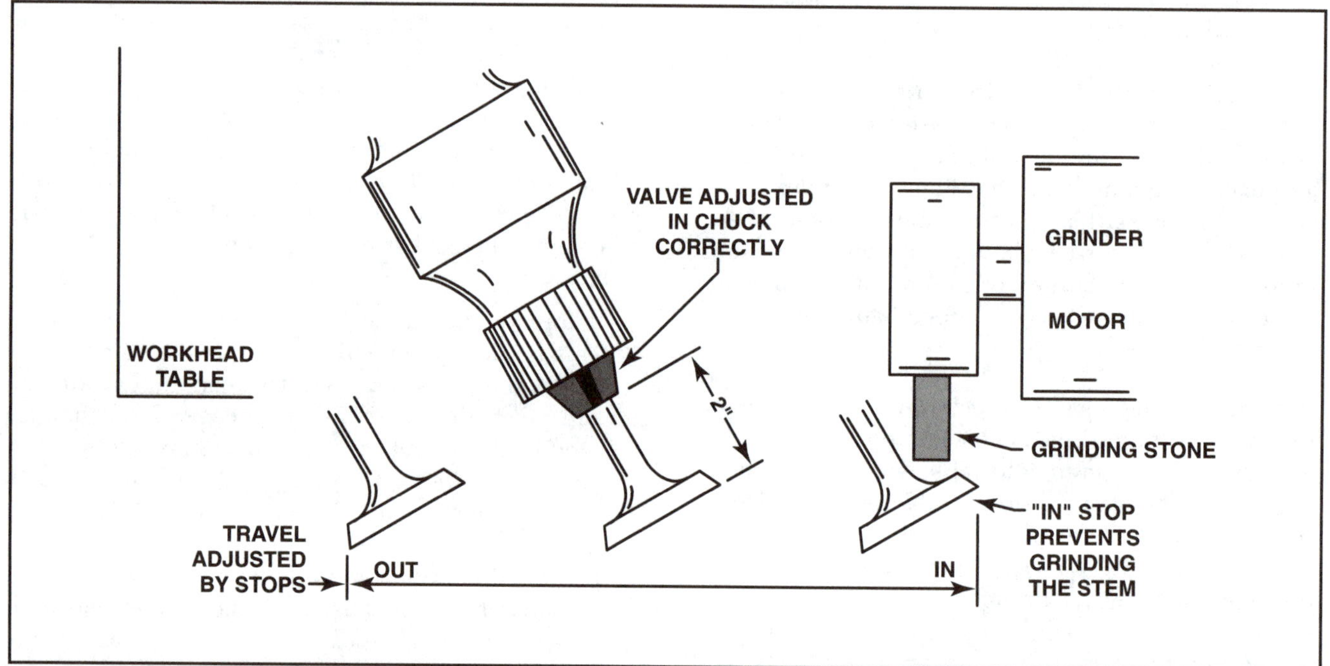

Figure 2-59. Once a valve is locked into a chuck correctly, adjust the ìinî and ìoutî stops so the valve passes the stone completely on both sides.

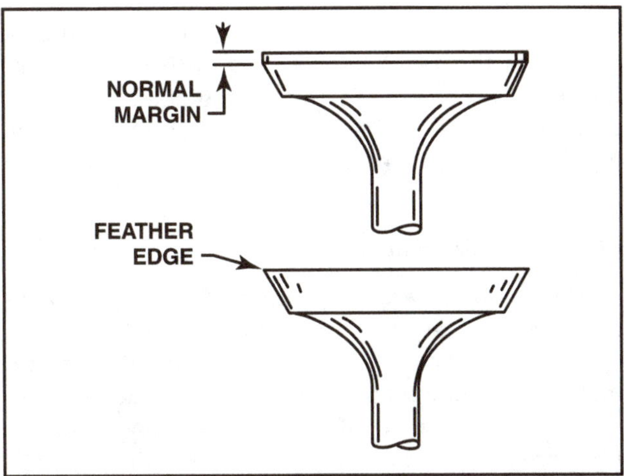

Figure 2-60. After grinding, a valve should still have an acceptable margin. A feather edge is caused by grinding a valve too much.

the valve tip on the side of the stone. Switch on the grinder and press the valve lightly against the stone, moving the tip across the side of the stone without going off the stone's edge. Take care to keep the valve tip cool by covering it with plenty of grinding fluid. [Figure 2-61]

The bevel on the edge of the valve tip will be partially removed when the valve tip is ground. To restore this bevel, mount a vee-way positioned at a 45° angle to the stone. Place the valve in the vee-way and hold the valve in the vee-way with one hand while grasping the valve head with the other hand. Twist the valve tip edge onto the stone and, with a light touch, grind all the way around the tip. This bevel prevents scratching of the valve guide when the valve is installed.

CYLINDERS

Many different types of repairs are approved for cylinders. Some of the more common repairs include removing fin damage, welding cracks, and replacing rocker shaft bushings, valve guides, spark plug thread inserts, and studs. Other approved repairs include honing or grinding cylinder barrels, and replacing or refacing valve seats.

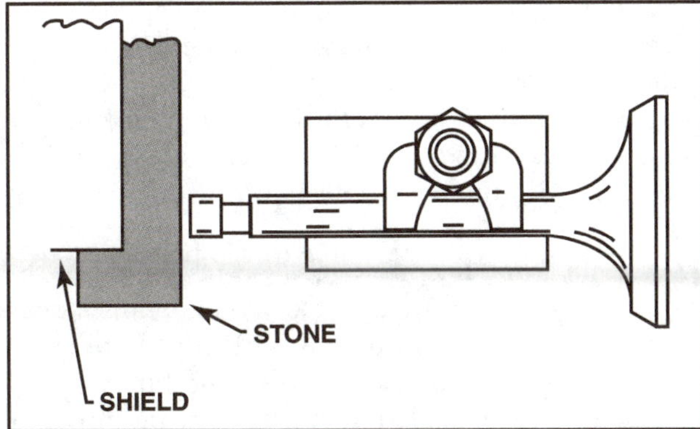

Figure 2-61. To accurately grind a valve tip, the valve must be held securely in place and be aligned perpendicular to the side of the grinding stone.

Exterior cracks and other damage on the edges of cylinder fins can be repaired by removing the damaged portion of the fin with a die grinder and rotary file. After removing the damage, finish file the sharp edges to a smooth contour. The percentage of total fin area that is removed must not exceed the limits established by the manufacturer. If too much material or too many fins are removed, localized hot spots can develop within the cylinder. [Figure 2-62]

Another method of repairing cracks on the edges of cylinder fins involves grinding out the crack and filling the cracked area by welding. The weld material is then ground or machined to the original contour. Repairs to cylinders that require welding can only be done by the manufacturer or a certified repair station.

Some cylinders have rocker shaft bosses equipped with bushings which may be replaced when worn beyond serviceable limits. However, it is advisable to use special rebushing tools for removing and inserting a bushing. If the proper tools are not used, the rocker shaft bosses could be broken off.

Replacement of valve guides also requires special tooling and must be done in accordance with an engine manufacturer's instructions. Extracting worn valve guides usually requires you to drive the guide out with a special piloted drift or pull the guide out with a valve guide puller. Most valve guides are flared on their outside end, and, therefore, must be driven or pulled toward the outside of the cylinder. Because of the interference fit between the guides and cylinder, you must heat the cylinder and chill the extraction tool to allow removal and installation of valve guides. Heating the cylinder expands the

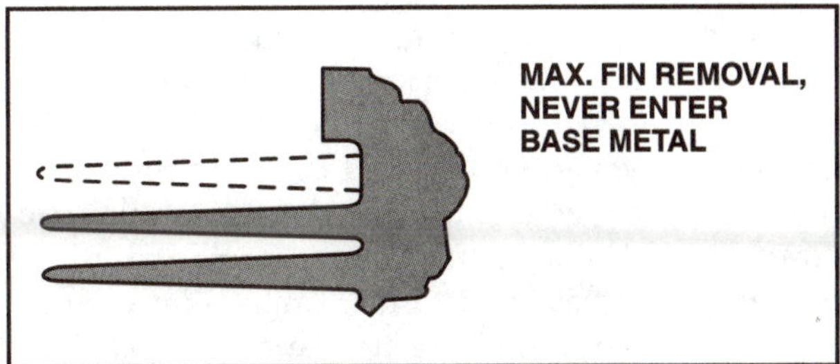

Figure 2-62. When repairing a damaged fin on a cylinder, you must not remove any of the primary cylinder casting. In addition, fin loss near spark plug openings or exhaust ports can cause dangerous local hot spots.

valve guide hole and the chilled extraction tool causes the guide to contract. The combination of these two factors typically reduces the interference fit enough to allow removal.

Similar to valve guide replacement procedures, valve seat inserts are removed and replaced by heating a cylinder and chilling the valve seat inserts. Some engine manufacturers supply special tools that simplify valve seat extraction and installation.

Spark plug thread inserts having missing or damaged threads are usually replaced with Heli-Coil inserts as specified by an engine manufacturer. You should use special Heli-Coil tools and follow the overhaul manual instructions carefully to prevent damaging the cylinder beyond repair.

The studs which secure the exhaust pipe to a cylinder are subjected to extreme heat and highly corrosive exhaust gases and, therefore, must be replaced occasionally. If a stud is still intact, a special stud removing tool is used to remove the stud. However, if a stud is broken, it must be drilled and removed with a screw extractor. Once an old stud is removed, install a new stud as per the manufacturer's instructions.

Typical repairs to a cylinder barrel include honing, grinding, oversizing, and chroming. A cylinder barrel that is structurally sound and within serviceable limits may only need to be **deglazed**. Cylinder walls become glazed, or very smooth after several hours of operation. The smooth walls prevent new rings from wearing or seating against the cylinder. Therefore, in order to allow the rings to seat, you must remove the glaze from a cylinder wall with a deglazing hone. Most deglazing hones mount in a drill and are turned at a relatively slow speed as they are moved in and out of the cylinder. The combination of a circular and reciprocating motion produces a cross-hatched pattern that promotes ring seating.

If a cylinder barrel is scored, scratched, or pitted to an extent that deglazing is not enough to remove the damage, the cylinder will probably have to be ground. However, you should compare the barrel dimensions to the manufacturer's table of limits to verify that there is enough material to permit grinding. In some cases, an engine manufacturer permits a cylinder to be ground to a standard oversize. Since aircraft cylinders are relatively thin, standard oversizes are typically 0.010, 0.015, or 0.020 inch. Furthermore, cylinders often have nitrided surfaces which must not be ground away. Another option is to grind a cylinder and then apply chrome plating to build up the cylinder to its original diameter. Because the process of grinding and chrome plating requires specialized equipment, these repairs are usually performed by certified repair stations.

REFACING VALVE SEATS

Modern reciprocating engines are equipped with either bronze or steel valve seats. Steel seats are made of hard, heat resistant steel alloy and are commonly used as exhaust seats. Bronze seats, on the other hand, are made of aluminum bronze or phosphor bronze alloys and are used for both intake and exhaust seats.

Valve seat inserts normally need to be refaced during each overhaul. In addition, valve seats must be ground anytime a corresponding valve or valve guide is replaced. Grinding equipment is used for refacing steel valve seats while cutters or reamers are preferred for refacing bronze seats. However, bronze seats may be ground if cutters or reamers are not available. The disadvantage of using a stone on bronze is that bronze, a fairly soft metal, loads the grinding stone quickly. Therefore, much time is consumed in redressing the stone to keep it clean.

Steel valve seats can be ground with either wet or dry valve seat grinding equipment. However, a wet grinder is preferred because the continuous flow of oil and water washes away the chips and keeps the stone and seat cool. This produces a smoother, more accurate surface than a dry grinder. The stones used to grind a steel seat may be either silicon carbide or aluminum oxide.

The three grades of stones used to resurface valve seats are rough, finishing, and polishing stones. A rough stone is used to make an initial rough cut and to remove all pits, scores, and burn marks as well as align the valve seat with the valve guide. Once cut, a finishing stone is used to remove any grinding marks and produce a smooth finish. If the manufacturer requires a highly polished valve seat, a polishing stone will produce the desired finish.

Anytime a stone becomes grooved or loaded with metal, it must be cleaned. To clean and dress a stone prior to grinding operations, install the stone on a special stone holder and use a diamond dresser. A diamond dresser is also useful in cutting down a stone's diameter, when necessary. However, dressing of a stone should be kept to a minimum when possible.

To begin the valve seat refacing process, mount the cylinder firmly in a hold down fixture. Next, insert an expanding pilot in the valve guide from the inside of the cylinder and place an expander screw in the pilot from the top of the guide. The pilot must be tight in the guide since any movement decreases the quality of the completed grind. Once the pilot and expander screw are in place, insert the fluid hose through one of the spark plug holes. [Figure 2-63]

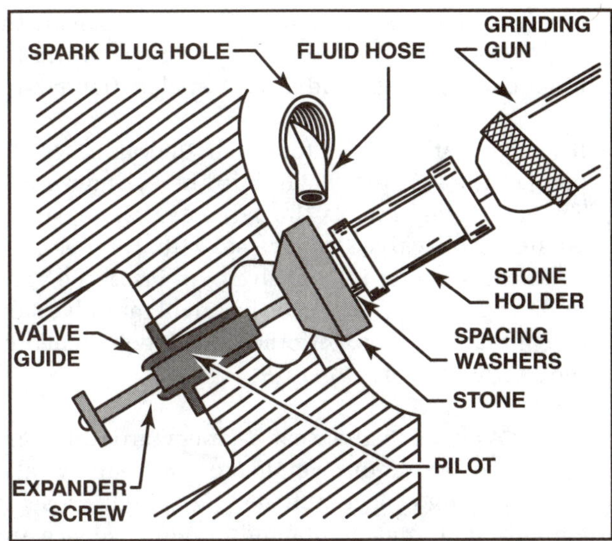

Figure 2-63. This illustration shows a typical setup for grinding valve seats in an aircraft engine cylinder.

While grinding, a steady hand and considerable skill is required. Center the gun accurately on the stone holder. If the gun is tilted off center during the grinding process, chattering and a rough grind will result. The stone should be rotated at a speed of 8,000 to 10,000 rpm to grind properly. The maximum pressure used on the stone at any time should be no more than that exerted by the weight of the gun. In addition, you should ease pressure off the stone every second or so to allow the coolant to wash away any chips and allow the stone to maintain its correct rotational speed. Grind off only the material necessary to achieve the desired finish by inspecting the valve seat frequently during the grinding procedure.

Once a valve seat is ground, you must verify that the seat is even and true. To do this, a special dial indicator is used to measure the seat's runout. An acceptable runout is normally between 0 and 2 thousandths of an inch. If the seat is even and true, the amount of contact area between the valve face and seat must be checked. To do this, a blue dye known as Prussian blue is spread evenly on the valve seat and the valve is pressed against the seat. To determine the contact area, remove the valve and observe the amount of Prussian blue that transfers to the valve. The contact surface area should be one-third to two-thirds the width of the valve face unless the valves were ground with an interference fit. In addition, the contact area should occur as close to the center of the valve face as possible.

If the valve seat contacts the upper third of the valve face, the top corner of the valve seat is reground to a lesser angle. This is known as "narrowing the seat." On the other hand, indications that the seat is contacting the bottom third of the valve face requires grinding the inner corner of the valve seat to a greater angle. [Figure 2-64]

The angle of a valve seat determines which stones should be used when narrowing a valve seat. For example, with a 30° seat, it is common practice to use a 15° cutting stone on the seat's upper corner and a 45° stone on the inner corner. On the other

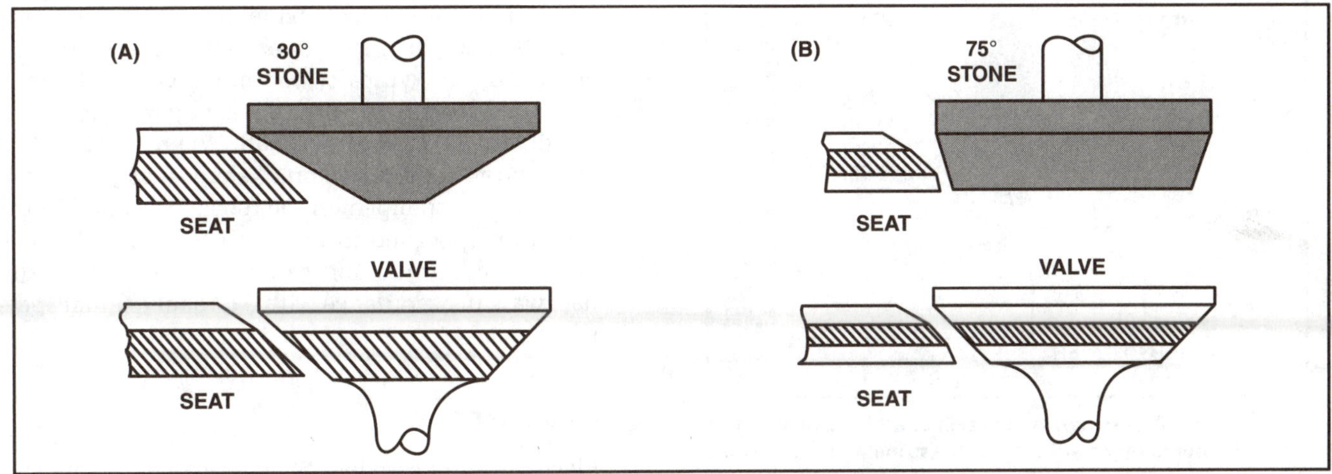

Figure 2-64. — If a valve seat contacts the upper third of the valve face, the seat can be regrouped to a lesser angle. (B) — Contact with the bottom third of the valve face requires regrinding a valve seat's inner corner to a greater angle.

hand, to narrow the seat of a 45° valve seat, the upper corner is reground to a 30° angle while the inner corner is reground to a 75° angle. [Figure 2-65]

If a valve seat is ground too much, the valve face will contact the seat too far up into the cylinder head. This adversely affects the valve clearance, spring tension, and valve to valve seat fit. To check if a valve seats too far into a valve seat, insert the valve into the guide and check the height of the valve stem above the rocker box or other location specified by the overhaul manual.

After a valve or valve seat has been ground, some manufacturers require you to lap a valve to its valve seat. **Lapping** is accomplished by applying a small amount of lapping compound to the valve face and then rotating the valve in the valve seat with a lapping tool. Once a smooth, gray finish appears at the contact area, remove all lapping compound from the valve face, seat, and adjacent areas. [Figure 2-66]

Once a valve and valve seat combination have been lapped, you must check the mating surfaces for leaks. This is done by installing the valve in the cylinder, and pouring kerosene or solvent into the valve port. While holding finger pressure on the valve stem, check to see if the kerosene leaks past the valve into the combustion chamber. If no leaking occurs, the valve reseating operation is finished. However, if kerosene leaks past the valve, continue lapping until the leakage stops.

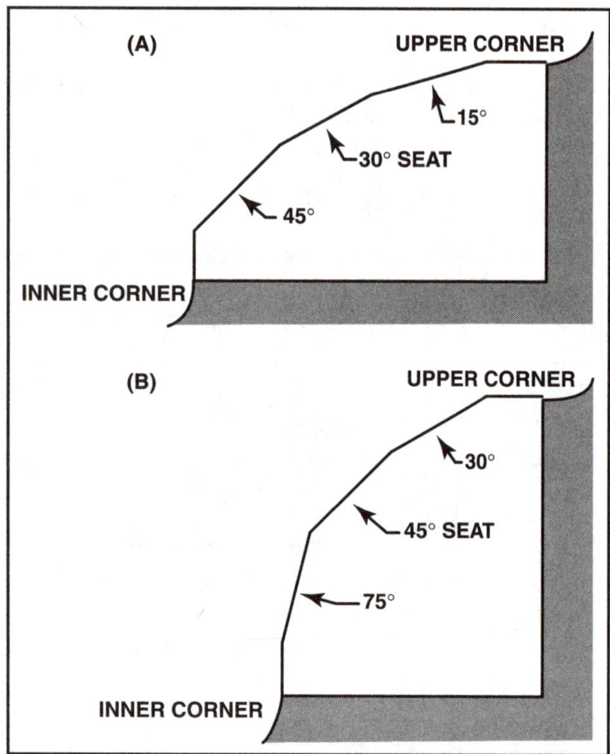

Figure 2-65. (A) — To narrow the seat of a 30° valve seat, the upper corner is reground with a 15° stone and the bottom corner with a 45° stone. (B) — For a 45° valve seat, use a 30°stone to grind the top corner and a 75° stone to grind the bottom corner.

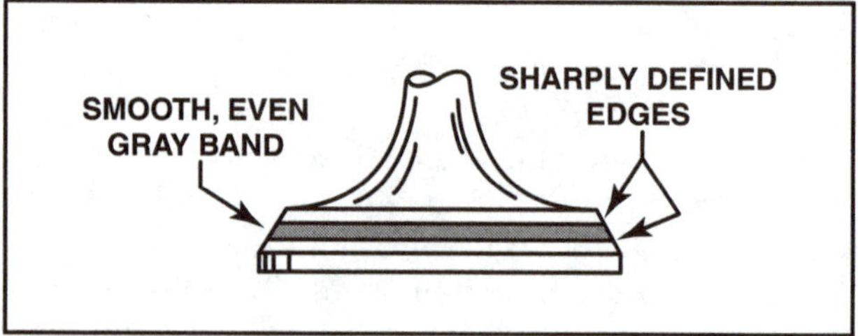

Figure 2-66. Proper valve lapping produces an extremely smooth surface and a sell defined contact area.

REASSEMBLY

After all of the parts have been inspected and repaired as necessary, the engine is ready to be reassembled. Whenever you are assembling an aircraft component, it is vital that you follow the manufacturer's instructions. However, there are some general assembly procedures that pertain to most reciprocating engines. The following discussion looks at some of these general procedures as well as how they are completed in a typical reassembly process.

CRANKSHAFT

Generally, a reconditioned crankshaft is supplied fully assembled, however, if that is not the case, reinstall all sludge chamber components and counterweights. If the crankshaft has hollow crankpins, reinstall the sludge chamber tubes carefully, making certain they are positioned correctly in the crankshaft to avoid covering the ends of oil passages. In addition, install all expansion plugs and secure any gears that attach to the crankshaft as necessary. The crankshaft is typically mounted vertically in a buildup fixture while the connecting rods are lubricated and attached to the shaft. When attaching the connecting rods to the crankshaft, make sure that the numbers stamped on the rods are pointed in the direction specified in the overhaul manual. Once assembled, torque and safety the connecting rod hardware in accordance with overhaul manual specifications.

CRANKCASE

Place the crankcase halves on a clean, flat work surface and install the main bearing inserts, ensuring that the tangs or dowels are properly placed. Next, lubricate and install the hydraulic lifter bodies in one of the crankcase halves and lay the camshaft in place after lubricating its bearing journal surfaces. Once this is done, lubricate the main bearings and install the crankshaft. Install the front oil seal around the propeller shaft and apply a thin layer of non-hardening gasket compound to the outside mating surface of each half of the crankcase. If the manufacturer recommends, a length of fine silk thread is embedded in the gasket compound on one of the crankcase halves.

Install the remaining hydraulic lifter bodies in the other crankcase half, then while holding them in place with rubber bands or other suitable devices, carefully lower the crankcase half onto the second half. Be very careful to properly seat the front oil seal and observe any special instructions regarding the seating of the main bearings. Install new nuts on all of the studs and through bolts and, using hold-down plates over the cylinder pads, torque all of the fasteners in the sequence recommended by the manufacturer.

The crankcase may now be mounted in a vertical position and the gears and accessory case installed. When installing the camshaft drive gear, it is vital that you align the timing marks properly. If this is not done, the valves will not open at the correct time in the combustion cycle and the engine will not run.

CYLINDERS

When installing a set of valves in a cylinder, lubricate the valve stems with a lubricant specified by the manufacturer and insert the valves in the valve guides. Place the cylinder over a post-type fixture to hold the valves in place while you slip the valve springs and retainers over each valve stem. Using a spring compressor, compress the valve springs and install the valve keeper keys. Once both valves are installed, slip a cylinder base seal around each cylinder skirt and install any intercylinder baffles or fin stabilizers that can be attached without getting in the way of further assembly.

PISTONS AND RINGS

When installing a new set of rings on a piston, it is important to observe several precautions. For example, chrome-plated rings may be used in plain steel or nitrided cylinders only. On the other hand, if a cylinder has been chrome-plated, cast iron rings must be used. In each case, you must use a ring expander to install rings on a piston. Use of a ring expander will help you avoid accidentally scratching a piston or breaking a piston ring. In addition, always install new rings with the part number on the ring toward the top of the piston.

Once the rings are installed, lubricate the pistons, rings, and piston pins with a manufacturer approved lubricant. Stagger the ring gaps as specified in the overhaul manual and attach the pistons to their corresponding connecting rods with a piston pin. Compress the piston rings with an appropriate ring compressor tool, then slip the piston into the cylinder up to the piston pin. Now, reposition the ring compressor on the lowest oil ring and slide the piston completely into the cylinder. At this point, verify that all push rods, push rod housings, and oil seals are in place and then ease each cylinder onto its cylinder pad. With each cylinder attached to the crankcase, lubricate and install the rocker arm assemblies.

FINAL ASSEMBLY

Install the oil sump on the crankcase with a new gasket and tighten the attaching hardware. Next, follow the overhaul manual instructions carefully to properly time and install the magnetos on their mount pads. Using new seals and gaskets, install the carburetor or fuel injection system components and the induction system. Other accessories such as the engine-driven pumps, the alternator, and baffling are now installed and safetied.

BLOCK TESTING

The final step in the overhaul process is to test the engine. A block test accomplishes piston ring seating, bearing burnishing, and provides valuable information that is used to evaluate engine performance. Piston ring seating is accomplished chiefly by controlled engine operation in the high speed range. On the other hand, **bearing burnishing** creates a highly polished surface on new bearings and bushings and is completed at low engine speeds.

Engine performance is evaluated in a test cell during block testing by specialized test equipment and standard engine instruments. Operational test procedures vary with individual engines, however, the failure of any internal part during an engine run-in requires return of the engine for teardown and repair. If failure of an engine accessory occurs, a new accessory is installed and the block test continues. Following successful completion of block test

Figure 2-67. Block testing of an overhauled engine is conducted in a test cell with specialized test equipment and standard engine instruments.

requirements, engines not slated for immediate installation and operation on an aircraft should receive a corrosion prevention treatment and be placed in storage. [Figure 2-67]

LOG ENTRIES

Once an overhaul is complete, you must make the appropriate log entries. In addition to the information required by the Federal Aviation Regulations, you should include a list of the items you replaced. Furthermore, the details of all dimensional and structural inspections as well as service bulletins and airworthiness directives complied with should be listed. If any major repairs were done, a 337 form must be completed and kept in the engine logbook.

ENGINE INSTALLATION

After an engine has been repaired, overhauled, or replaced, it must be prepared for installation. With a repaired or overhauled engine, preparation typically entails returning the engine to the configuration it was in immediately after it was removed. However, if the engine being installed is shipped new from the factory, additional assembly is typically required. For example, most engines used on light aircraft include only ignition and carburetor components when shipped from the factory. Therefore, all of the accessories such as the alternator, starter, vacuum pump, and baffling must be installed. In addition, if an engine was preserved in storage, de-preservation procedures are usually outlined in the overhaul manual provided by the engine manufacturer.

If an aircraft owner wishes to substitute a different model engine for the original model, a **Supplemental Type Certificate**, or **STC** is required for the change. Without an STC, engine replacement is limited to a new or overhauled engine of the original model with which the aircraft was certificated.

HOISTING FOR INSTALLATION

When a new or overhauled engine is ready to be hoisted for installation, move the engine stand as close as possible to the aircraft. Attach the sling to the engine, hook the hoist to the sling, and raise the hoist until it is supporting most of the engine weight. Next, remove the bolts attaching the engine to the stand and hoist the engine to the desired height.

MOUNTING THE ENGINE

Before you mount an engine on an aircraft, make sure you have the appropriate hardware nearby and inspect the engine mount structure and shock mounts for integrity. With the engine suspended from the hoist, utilize as many people as necessary to safely maneuver the engine into position on the aircraft. To help prevent injuring personnel or damaging the aircraft or engine, ease the engine into position slowly, checking to be certain the engine clears all obstacles. Position the engine so that the engine mounting lugs line up with the mounting points on the engine mount and exhaust tailpipe. Because engines are so heavy, they possess a great deal of inertia when swinging from the hoist. Therefore, exercise caution to avoid damaging the nacelle framework, ducts, or firewall connections.

Once the engine is correctly aligned, insert the mounting bolts and secure them with the appropriate nuts. Once secure, torque the engine mounting nuts to the manufacturer's recommended value. The applicable manufacturer's instructions outline the sequence for tightening the mounting bolts to ensure security. While the nuts are being tightened, the hoist should support the engine weight sufficiently to allow proper mounting bolt alignment. If this is not done, the weight of the engine on the mounting bolts could make it impossible to tighten the nuts to the proper torque. In other words, improper alignment could result in false torque readings as the nuts pull the engine into the proper position.

Once the nuts are properly torqued, they can be safetied and the engine hoist can be removed. Next, connect bonding straps across each engine mount to provide an electrical path from the mount to the airframe. Failure to provide adequate bonding could result in the starter electrical current seeking a return path through engine controls or metal fuel lines. If this should happen, resulting sparks or heat could start a fire or cause extensive damage to engine connections.

CONNECTIONS AND ADJUSTMENTS

After an engine is mounted, the electrical leads and fluid lines necessary for operation should be connected to the engine and accessories. Typically, there are no rules that govern the order in which the accessories should be connected. However, you should always follow the manufacturer's instructions to ensure an efficient installation.

As you know, engine induction systems vary with aircraft/engine combinations. However, all induction systems must be leak-free. You must install the induction system components carefully using the proper clamps and hardware and, in some cases, the induction system must be pressure checked for leaks. Pressure checks usually require blocking the system at one end, and supplying compressed air at a specified pressure at the other end. The leakage rate is then measured to verify that it falls within acceptable limits.

In addition to ensuring a leak-free system, air induction filters must be cleaned to ensure an unrestricted flow of clean air. Since the materials used in air filters varies, you must follow the manufacturer's cleaning and replacement instructions.

The exhaust system must also be carefully connected to prevent exhaust gas leakage. When assembling the exhaust system, carefully examine the entire system and repair or replace any damaged components as necessary. During assembly, all clamps and nuts should be gradually and progressively tightened to the correct torque. In addition, all clamps should be tapped with a rawhide mallet as they are tightened to reduce the chance of binding. On some systems, a ball joint connects a stationary portion of the exhaust system to another portion that is attached to the engine. This ball joint compensates for slight misalignments, normal engine movement, and vibration caused by engine operation. Ball joints must be installed with the specified clearance to prevent binding when the hot exhaust gases cause the system to expand.

Hoses used with low pressure systems, such as vacuum and instrument air, are generally attached and held in place with clamps. However, before installing these clamps, examine them carefully and replace any that are badly distorted or defective. After a hose is installed, it must be adequately supported and routed away from engine or airframe parts that could cause damage. Usually, rubber lined supporting clamps called **Adel clamps** are installed at specified intervals to provide the protection and support needed.

Before installing metal tubing with threaded fittings, make sure that the threads are clean and in good condition. If specified in the instructions, apply a thread sealing compound to the fitting before installation. Exercise care to prevent cross-threading any fittings and to ensure correct torque. Remember, over torquing a fitting increases the likelihood of leaks and failures.

When connecting electrical leads to the starter, generator, or other electrical units, make sure that all connections are clean and secure. When leads are secured on a threaded terminal post with a nut, a lock washer is usually inserted under the nut to prevent the nut from backing off. When required, knurled connector plugs are secured with steel safety wire to prevent accidental disconnection. To help prevent electrical leads within the engine nacelle from chafing, all wiring must be anchored as necessary to provide a secure installation.

Each aircraft model has an engine control system specifically designed for a particular airframe/engine combination. Typical engine controls consist of rigid push-pull rods, flexible push-pull wire encased in a coiled wire sheath, cables and pulleys, or any combination of the three. Regardless of type, all engine controls must be accurately adjusted to ensure instantaneous response to a control input. Therefore, all adjustments must be made in accordance with the procedures outlined in the manufacturer's instructions.

Most light aircraft utilize flexible push-pull controls for the engine throttle, mixture, and carburetor heat or alternate air. When installing flexible controls, there are a few general rules that should be followed. For example, in order for a flexible control line to operate properly, it must be adequately supported. Support is typically provided by a terminal mounting clamp at the cockpit end and another terminal mounting clamp at the engine end. Sections of the control line between the cockpit and engine are supported by intermediate clamps spaced every three to four feet along straight sections and on both sides of bends. All bends should have a minimum

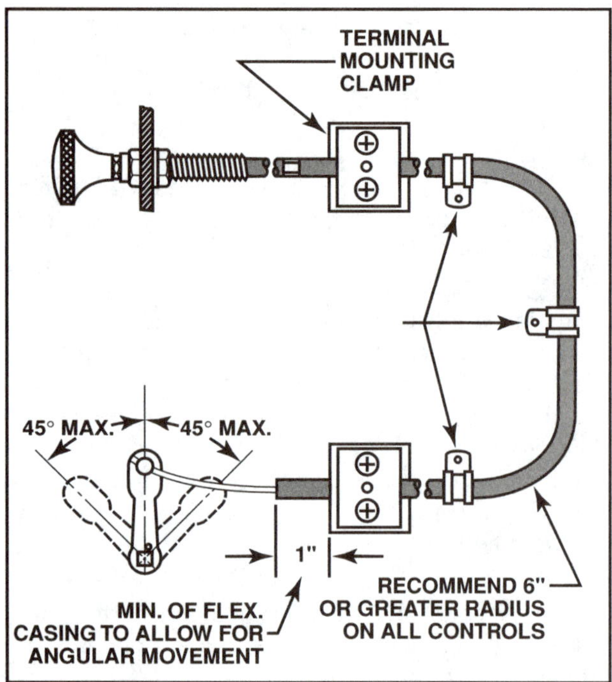

Figure 2-68. Many small single-engine airplanes utilize a push-pull wire type throttle control which is encased in a protective sheath.

six inch radius and large bends should be supported with clamps along their length as necessary. The control line must be positioned with the flex casing extending a minimum of one inch past the terminal mounting clamp at the engine. This extension of flex casing allows angular movement and smooth motion of the control line as the engine control is positioned. The engine component being controlled by a flexible control is generally limited to 45 degrees of angular motion to either side of center. [Figure 2-68]

A typical throttle control system of cables, pulleys, and a drum requires several adjustment steps. A drum is basically a pulley with at least one complete loop of cable around it to prevent slippage. To assist the adjustment process and ensure a reliable reference point, the drum has an alignment hole for a locking pin. To adjust a control system, begin by loosening the serrated throttle control arm at the carburetor. Next, back off the throttle stop until the throttle valve is in the fully closed position and insert a locking pin in the drum. Adjust the control rod to the length specified and re-tighten the serrated throttle control arm. Next, loosen the cable turnbuckles enough to allow positioning of the throttle control lever so the quadrant locking pin can be inserted. Once this is done, re-tighten the turnbuckles and adjust the cable tension to the manufacturer's specifications using a tensiometer. When the correct cable tension is achieved, safety the turnbuckles and remove the lockpins from the drum and quadrant. [Figure 2-69]

A properly adjusted engine control must have a degree of **cushion**, or **springback**, at its fully open and fully closed positions. In other words, the stops for the throttle and mixture on a carburetor or fuel control must be reached before the throttle or mixture controls reach their stop in the cockpit. The presence of a cushion ensures that the throttle and mixture valves are opening and closing fully. Without the cushion, it would be difficult to determine whether a throttle or mixture valve is fully opened or closed from inside the cockpit. On multiengine aircraft, throttle and mixture controls must have equal amounts of cushion so the control levers align in any selected power setting. This reduces the likelihood of having to set each control individually to synchronize engine operations.

After completing the engine installation and adjustments, the propeller can be installed. If the propeller being installed is a fixed pitch propeller, it can typically be lifted into position and attached to the propeller shaft. However, if a constant-speed propeller is being installed, you must obtain the proper gaskets or O-rings prior to installation. Large propellers require the use of an appropriate sling and hoist arrangement due to their size and weight. Never attempt to lift a propeller into place with inadequate personnel or equipment. In addition, you should always follow the manufacturer's recommended installation procedure.

GROUND TEST PREPARATION

Once an engine is completely installed on an aircraft or test stand, you can prepare the engine for a test run. Install properly gapped spark plugs and torque to manufacturer specifications, then attach ignition wiring, being careful to connect the wiring properly. Fill the engine with an oil approved by the manufacturer and check all oil and fuel line connections for security.

PRE-OILING

To prevent engine bearing failure during the initial start, you should pre-oil the engine. When an engine sits idle for an extended period of time, engine oil drains away from the internal bearing surfaces. If the engine is started and there is little or no oil on the bearings, the friction created during engine start can destroy the bearings before lubricating oil can reach

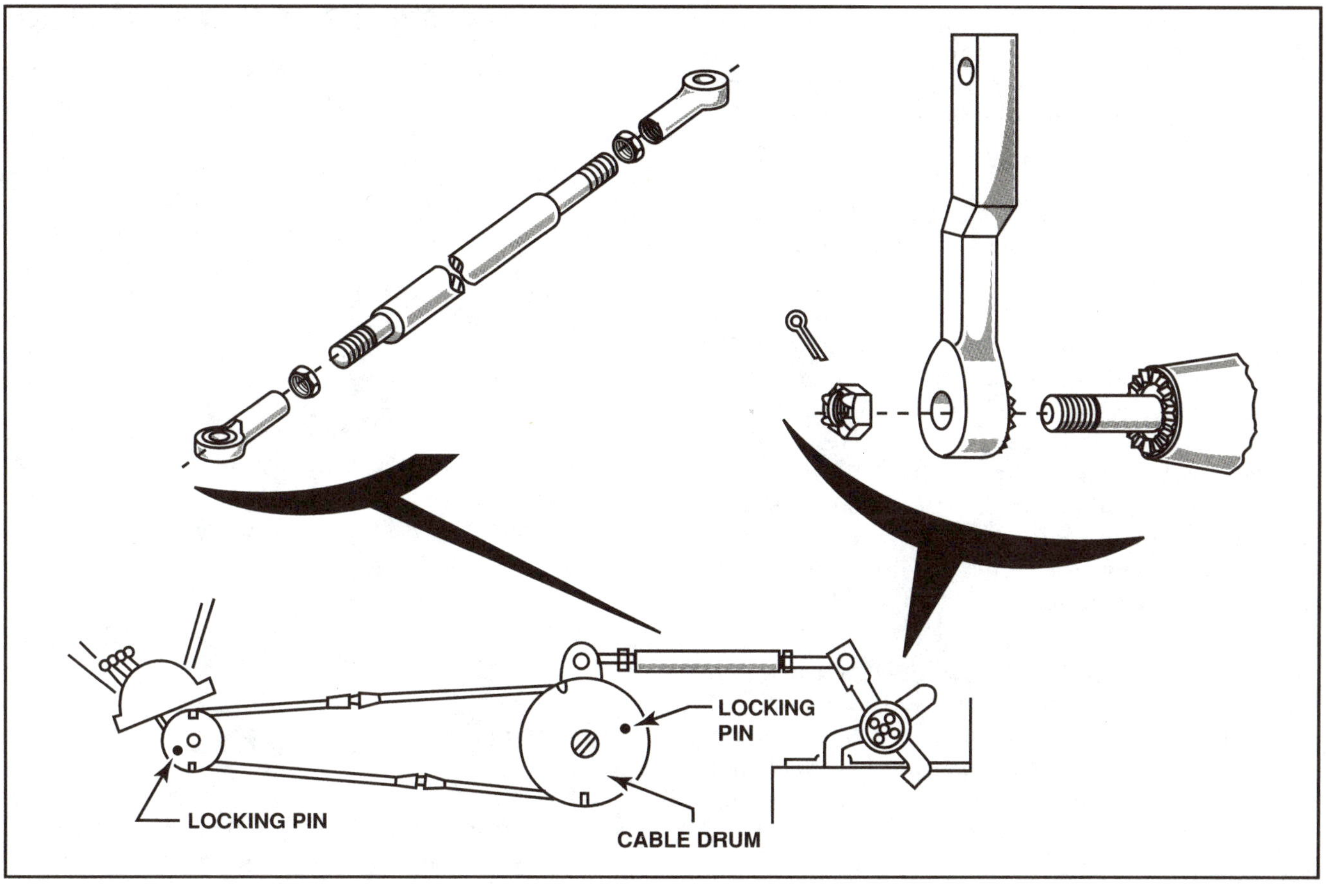

Figure 2-69. When adjusting a throttle control system that utilizes cables, pulleys, and a drum, it is important that you follow the manufacturer's instructions.

them. Pre-oiling is the process of forcing oil throughout the engine prior to starting.

One method of pre-oiling requires one spark plug to be removed from each cylinder. This allows the engine to be easily turned over with the starter. Once this is done, a pressure oiler is attached to the engine. On a typical dry-sump engine, the oil line on the inlet side of the engine-driven oil pump is disconnected to allow connection of the pre-oiler tank. In addition, the oil return line is disconnected, or an opening is made in the oil system at the nose of the engine to allow oil to flow out of the engine. [Figure 2-70]

To force oil from the pre-oiler tank through the engine, the tank is pressurized while the engine is turned over with the starter. Generally, shop air is used to pressurize the pre-oiler, however, it is best to consult manufacturer's instructions for the correct pressure limits. Once all the oil galleries are full, oil will flow out the oil return line. When this happens, stop cranking the engine and disconnect the pre-oiler tank.

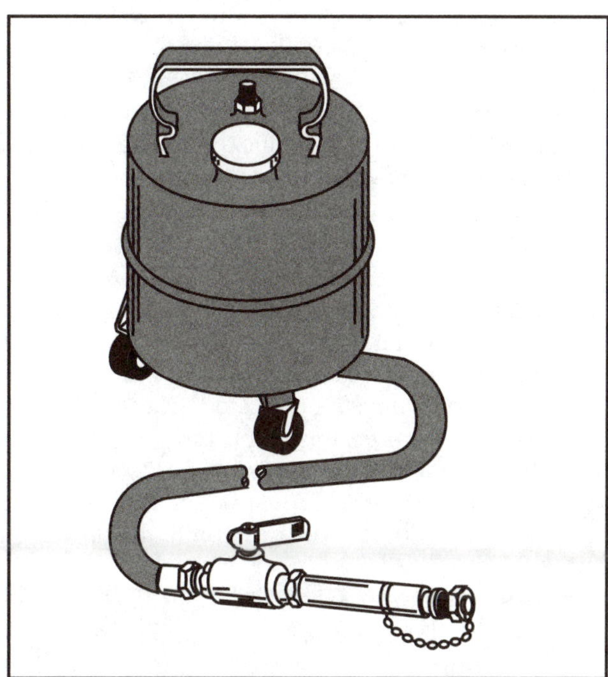

Figure 2-70. Pre-oiling an engine with a special tank such as this helps prevent bearing failure when an engine is first started after an overhaul or after being idle for long periods of time.

Pre-oiling engines equipped with a wet sump is similar except the pre-oiler is connected at the oil temperature fitting. With the pre-oiler connected and pumping oil, the engine is turned over with the starter until an indication of oil pressure appears on the oil pressure gauge. Once this occurs, discontinue cranking the engine, disconnect the pre-oiler tank, and check the oil level to make sure the engine was not inadvertently overfilled.

Another way you can pre-oil an engine is with the engine driven oil pump. To do this, remove one spark plug from each cylinder and fill the engine oil sump to the proper level. Once this is done, place the mixture in the idle-cutoff position, the fuel shutoff valve and ignition switch in the off position, and the throttle in the idle position. Now, crank the engine with the starter until the oil pressure gauge indicates oil pressure.

After the engine has been pre-oiled, replace the spark plugs and reconnect the oil system lines. Generally, the engine should be operated within four hours after it has been pre-oiled. If this is not possible, it may be necessary to repeat the pre-oiling procedure.

FUEL SYSTEM BLEEDING

Before you attempt to start a newly installed engine, the fuel system should be bled to purge any air bubbles from the fuel lines and pumps and to help flush any preservative oil from the fuel system. The procedure used to bleed a fuel system varies with the type of carburetor or fuel injection unit installed, so you must consult the manufacturer's maintenance instructions for specific directions.

COWL FLAP RIGGING

If an aircraft has cowl flaps, they must be rigged to accurately regulate the passage of cooling air through the engine compartment. When cowl flap adjustments have been completed, operate the system and recheck the adjustments to be sure the cowl flaps open and close to the specified limits. Also verify that the cowl flap position indicators, if installed, indicate the true position of the flaps.

Once all ground test preparations are complete and you are satisfied that the engine can be safely run, verify that the aircraft battery is reinstalled and, if necessary, have a ground power cart plugged into the aircraft. Consult the aircraft checklist to start and runup the engine as necessary.

POST-RUN CHECKS AND ADJUSTMENTS

After the initial ground run and flight test, an engine must receive final adjustments and a thorough visual inspection. Exercise caution to avoid burns from the hot engine as you examine various items. Fuel pressure and oil pressure adjustments could be needed, as well as rechecks of ignition timing, valve clearances, and idle speed and mixture. Remove the oil sump plugs and screens so they can be examined for the presence of any metal particles, then clean and reinstall them.

Visually inspect all lines for leakage and tight connections, correcting any discrepancies found. Check hose clamps to see if any of them need to be re-tightened, especially if the hoses are new. Scrutinize oil system connections for oil leakage and inspect cylinder hold down nuts or cap screws for security. Press gently on safety-wired items checking for looseness and broken safety wire.

ENGINE PRESERVATION

Engines that are going to be put in storage or transported to an overhaul facility must be preserved and protected to prevent corrosion and other forms of damage. Regardless of whether an engine is waiting to be overhauled or is newly overhauled, damaging rust and other forms of corrosion will occur unless the engine is protected. Preservation is also recommended when an engine remains on the aircraft if engine operation is limited or suspended for an extended period of time. The following discussion centers on engines that have been removed from an aircraft, however, the preservation materials and methods discussed are used for all types of engine storage.

CORROSION PREVENTATIVE COMPOUNDS

The primary purpose of engine and engine accessory preservation procedures is to prevent corrosion. If you recall from your earlier studies, corrosion occurs whenever a base metal such as steel, iron, or aluminum combines with oxygen to form an oxide. Therefore, if a base metal is properly sealed, corrosion will not occur. Most corrosion preventive compounds are petroleum based products that form a wax-like film over the metal surfaces to prevent air from reaching the metal's surface. Several of these corrosion preventive compounds are manufactured to different specifications to meet specific aviation needs. For example, light corrosion preventive compounds are typically mixed with engine oil to form a protective barrier for short term preservation. Light compounds can also be sprayed into a cylinder or other components. Short term corrosion preventive compounds are intended for use in engines that remain inactive for less than 30 days. Light compounds typically meet MIL-C-6529 Type I, Type II, or Type III specifications. A Type I compound is a concentrate that must be blended with three parts of MIL-L-22851 or MIL-L-6082 grade 1100 oil to one part concentrate. On the other hand, a Type II compound is ready-mixed with MIL-L-22851 oil and needs no dilution. A Type III compound is used only in turbine engines and consists of a preservative material ready-mixed with 1010 grade oil. An important point to bear in mind is that the correct proportions of lubricating oil and corrosion preventive compounds must be mixed externally, then added to the engine. Adding the preservative mixture to the oil already in the engine is not good maintenance practice and must be avoided.

A heavy corrosion preventive compound is used for long term preservation and forms a heavy wax-like barrier over a metal surface. Before you can apply a heavy compound, it must be heated to a liquid state for application. Once the compound cools, the only way to remove it is with a commercial solvent or kerosene spray.

Although corrosion preventive compounds act as moisture barriers, they eventually break down over a period of time in the presence of excessive moisture. Furthermore, the compounds can eventually dry out as their oil base gradually evaporates. If this should happen, moisture can come in contact with the metal allowing corrosion to begin.

DEHYDRATING AGENTS

Dehydrating agents, often referred to as **desiccants**, are often used during engine preservation because they absorb moisture from the atmosphere. **Silica gel** is a common desiccant and is an ideal dehydrating agent since it does not dissolve when saturated. As a corrosion preventive measure, bags of silica gel are placed around and inside the accessible parts of a stored engine. Silica gel is also used in clear plastic plugs called **dehydrator plugs** which are screwed into an engine's spark plug holes. The silica gel in the dehydrator plugs is typically treated with **Cobalt chloride** to provide a visual indication of the moisture content in the air inside an engine. For example, cobalt chloride treated silica gel remains a bright blue color with a low relative humidity. However, as humidity increases, the shade of blue grows progressively lighter, becoming lavender at 30 percent relative humidity. If the relative humidity exceeds 30 percent, the color changes from lavender to various shades of pink, becoming completely white at 60 percent relative humidity. When the relative humidity is less than 30 percent, corrosion does not normally take place. Therefore, if the dehydrator plugs are bright blue, the air in the engine has a relatively low moisture content and internal corrosion is kept to a minimum.

Cobalt chloride-treated silica gel is also used in humidity indicator envelopes. These envelopes can be fastened to a stored engine in a manner that allows inspection through a small window in the sealed engine container. Desiccants in storage should be sealed in containers to keep them from becoming saturated with moisture before they are used. Avoid leaving the container open or inadequately sealed.

ENGINE PRESERVATION PROCESS

Before an engine is removed from an aircraft for preservation, a corrosion preventive compound should be added to the oil. Once this is done, the engine must be run for 15 minutes to coat the engine's internal parts.

Any engine taken out of service and prepared for storage must receive a thorough corrosion preventive treatment around the exhaust ports. This is necessary because exhaust gas residue is potentially corrosive. A corrosion preventive compound should be sprayed into each exhaust port to coat the exhaust port interior and exhaust valve. Next, a moisture-proof and oil-proof gasket should be placed over each exhaust port, held in place by a metal or wooden plate. These covers form a seal that helps keep moisture from entering the engine through the exhaust ports.

Once the engine is removed, each cylinder interior should be sprayed with a corrosion preventive compound. This is done to prevent moisture and oxygen from reacting with the deposits left by combustion. To do this, each cylinder should be sprayed with the piston at bottom dead center, allowing the entire cylinder interior to be coated. Rotate the engine until one piston is at bottom dead center and then apply the compound by inserting a spray nozzle into the spark plug opening. Once that cylinder is sprayed, rotate the engine again until the next piston is at bottom dead center and spray the cylinder. After spraying each cylinder with its piston at bottom dead center, respray each cylinder without rotating the crankshaft. Once this is done, the crankshaft must not be moved, or the corrosion preventive seal will be broken. Immediately after the corrosion preventive compound dries, a dehydrator plug should be inserted in each spark plug opening. In addition, each ignition harness lead should be attached to a dehydrator plug with lead supports. [Figure 2-71]

The intake manifold must also be sealed when placing an engine in storage. If the carburetor is going to remain on the engine during storage, the throttle valve should be wired open and a seal installed over the air inlet. On the other hand, if the carburetor is removed, install the seal at the carburetor mounting pad. In either case, the seal should be an oil-proof and moisture-proof gasket backed by a wooden or metal plate securely bolted into place. To help remove excess moisture, silica gel should be placed in the intake manifold. Normally, the silica gel bags are suspended from the cover plate to reduce the possibility of overlooking their removal when the engine is removed from storage.

Just before an engine is boxed up, the engine exterior should be sprayed with a heavy corrosion preventive coating. If this cannot be done, you should at least apply a corrosion preventive compound to the propeller shaft. Follow up by securing a plastic sleeve, or moisture-proof paper around the shaft. A final inspection should be performed to be certain

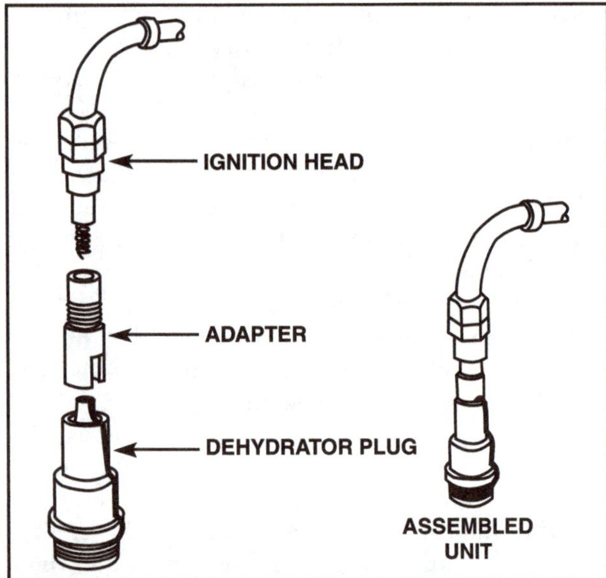

Figure 2-71. Securing the ignition harness leads to the dehydrator plugs protects them from being damaged as the engine is moved.

that all openings are sealed, and that only the proper accessories have been included for storage or shipping.

STORAGE

Once preserved, engines sent out for overhaul or newly overhauled engines put into storage should be protected by a shipping container. Metal or wooden containers are constructed with mounts for holding and protecting an engine.

When storing an engine horizontally in a metal shipping container, special ventilatory plugs are normally installed. If stored vertically, only the upper spark plug holes in each cylinder receive a ventilatory plug while the lower spark plug holes are fitted with non-ventilatory plugs. Dehydrator plugs with the dessicant removed work well as non-ventilatory plugs.

ENGINE SHIPPING CONTAINERS

Engines that are being shipped out for maintenance or overhaul must be protected from damage. Therefore, most engines are packed in wooden crates or metal shipping containers. Some overhauled engines are sealed in pressurized containers with an inert gas such as nitrogen.

After an engine is carefully lowered into a shipping container, it is secured with the same type of hardware and mounting fixtures used to mount the engine to the aircraft. Some containers provide a special mounting area for accessories that have been detached from the engine but are also being sent back for overhaul. Wooden crates and metal containers are available for horizontal mounting or vertical mounting of the engine.

In addition to the shipping container, most engines are wrapped in plastic or foil envelopes. However, before the protective envelope is sealed, silica gel packets should be placed around the engine to dehydrate the air sealed into the envelope. The amount of silica gel used is determined by the size of the engine. The protective envelope is then gathered around the engine and partially sealed, leaving an opening from which as much air as possible is exhausted. The envelope is then completely sealed.

While lowering the shipping container cover into position, be careful that it does not twist and tear the protective envelope. Secure the cover, then mark the case with the appropriate removal or preservation dates and indicate whether the engine is repairable or serviceable. [Figure 2-72]

INSPECTION OF STORED ENGINES

Most maintenance shops provide a scheduled inspection system for engines in storage. The humidity indicators on engines stored in shipping cases are normally inspected every 30 days. When the protective envelope must be opened to inspect the humidity indicator, the inspection period may be extended to once every 90 days, if local conditions permit. The humidity indicator of a metal container is inspected every 180 days under normal conditions.

Humidity indicator colors in wooden shipping crates showing the presence of more than 30 percent relative humidity require the replacement of all dessicants. When more than half the dehydrator plugs in spark plug openings indicate the presence of excessive moisture, the cylinder interiors should be re-sprayed with corrosion preventive compound. A metal container with a humidity indicator showing a safe blue color and air pressure below 1 p.s.i. needs only to be repressurized. An indicator with a pink condition, on the other hand, indicates that the engine should be re-preserved if it is to remain in storage.

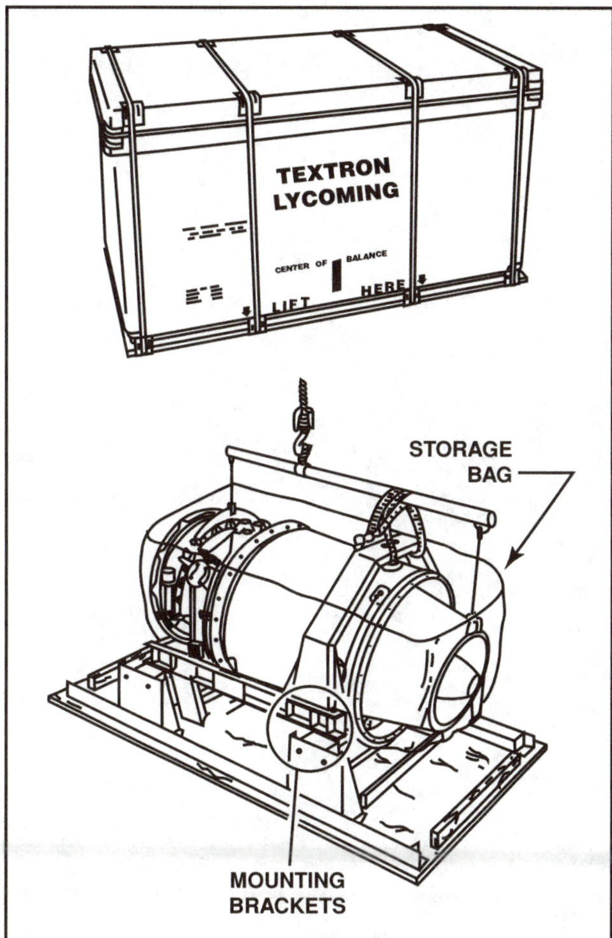

Figure 2-72. Engines needing repairs or overhaul are nevertheless costly, and must be protected during storage and shipment. For this reason, shipping crates or containers tailored to a specific engine model must always be used when the engine is being transported.

ENGINE DEPRESERVATION

Engines that have been preserved for storage must undergo depreservation before they are put into service. Depreservation procedures are typically included in the engine manufacturer's overhaul manual or provided by the overhauler who preserved the engine. The information presented here provides a general overview of these procedures since they vary with the type of engine and the degree of preservation.

When engines are supplied in pressurized containers, the first task is to bleed off the gas pressure through the container's pressure valve. The container cover can then be lifted off and placed aside. After hoisting the engine and removing any separate accessories, secure the engine to a stand or mount it on the aircraft. Next, remove all covers and dessicant bags from the engine. Typical locations of cover plates include engine breather tubes, intake and exhaust outlets, and accessory mounting pads. As each cover is removed, inspect the uncovered area for corrosion and foreign objects. Furthermore, if the dehydrator plugs indicate water contamination when they are removed, thoroughly inspect the cylinder walls for corrosion. Any cylinder showing signs of corrosion or other damage should be removed and inspected further.

Remove the oil screens from the engine and thoroughly wash them in kerosene or an approved solvent to remove preservative accumulations that could restrict oil circulation and cause engine failure. After cleaning, immerse the screens in clean oil, then reinstall them in the engine.

On radial engines, carefully check the interior of the lower cylinders and intake pipes for the presence of excessive corrosion preventive compound. Excess compound can drain through the engine interior and settle at low points, creating a liquid, or hydraulic lock. Any liquid preservative compounds remaining in a cylinder, intake, or exhaust port that cannot be drained should be removed with a hand pump.

Once you are done with the engine interior, remove the protective covering from the propeller shaft. Lightly coat the propeller shaft with engine oil or whatever lubricant the engine manufacturer recommends. To complete the de-preservation procedure verify that the engine exterior is clean. Often a quantity of compound runs out of the engine when the dehydrator plugs and oil screens are removed. Spray engine areas in need of cleaning with a recommended solvent that does not leave any residue or interfere with the proper functioning of the accessories.

ACCESSORY DEPRESERVATION

Good engine performance depends, in part, on the condition of the engine accessories. Although an engine is in a condition to give top performance after being completely overhauled, any oversight or error in reinstalling the accessories can result in an engine malfunction or possibly irreparable damage. Therefore, follow recommended procedures in the overhaul manual or the instructions that come with overhauled or new accessories regarding depreservation and preparation for operation.

Before depreserving any of the accessories enclosed with the engine, refer to the accessory records to determine how long the engine and accessories have been in storage. Some accessories are life-limited and are considered unsafe for use if their storage time exceeds the manufacturer's time limits. Before installing any replacement accessory, check it visually for signs of corrosion and for freedom of operation. Remove any plastic plugs and movement restraints placed on the accessory for shipment. In addition, lubricate the accessory drive shaft and clean the mounting pad and flange prior to installation. Always install an accessory with new O-rings or gaskets between the mounting pad and the accessory.

CHAPTER 3

TURBINE ENGINES

INTRODUCTION

Efforts to design a working gas turbine engine had been under way for years prior to World War II. Engineers eventually succeeded in placing a few engines in combat aircraft briefly during the closing stages of the war. The war effort had brought about many advances in gas turbine technology which could now be used for commercial aircraft design. Turbine engines offered many advantages over reciprocating engines and airlines were interested. Increased reliability, longer mean times between overhaul, higher airspeeds, ease of operation at high altitudes, and a high power to engine weight ratio made turbine power very desirable. Aircraft such as Lockheed's Super Constellation represented the practical limits of piston power technology and required frequent engine maintenance; therefore, air carriers turned to gas turbine engines for solutions. During the decade of the 50's, a gradual transfer from piston power to gas turbine jets and turboprops started taking place. Old workhorses such as the Douglas DC-3 and DC-7 gave way to the Boeing 707 and Douglas DC-8.

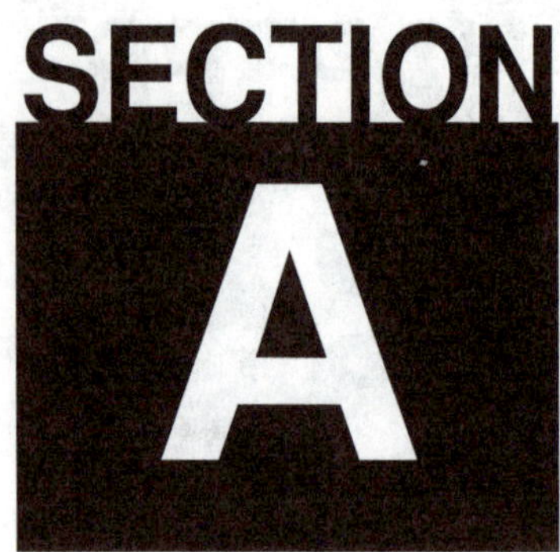

DESIGN AND CONSTRUCTION

Newton's third law of motion states that for every action, there is an equal and opposite reaction. Jet propulsion applies this law by taking in a quantity of air and accelerating it through an orifice or nozzle. The acceleration of the air is the action and forward movement is the reaction. In nature, a squid propels itself through the water using a form of jet propulsion. A squid takes sea water into its body and uses its muscles to add energy to the water, then expels the water in the form of a jet. This action produces a reaction that propels the squid forward. [Figure 3-1]

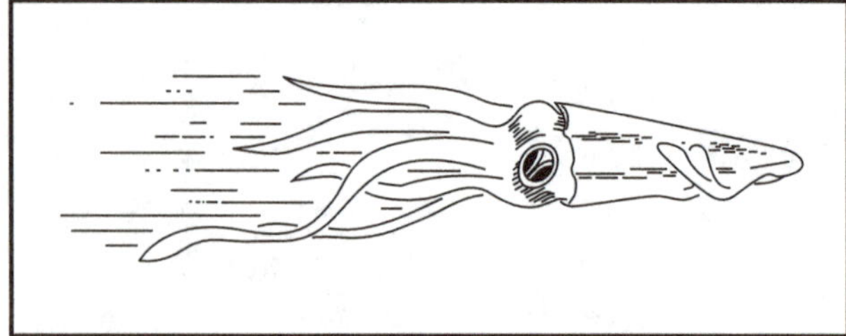

Figure 3-1. Many technological developments were made by observing nature in action. A squid propels itself through the water by jet reaction in much the same way a turbojet engine propels an aircraft.

As early as 250 B.C., a writer and mathematician named Hero devised a toy that used the reaction principle. The toy, called the **aeolipile**, consisted of a covered kettle of water that was heated to produce steam. The steam was then routed through two vertical tubes and into a spherical container. Attached to the spherical container were several discharge tubes arranged radially around the container. As steam filled the container, it would escape through the discharge tubes and cause the sphere to rotate. [Figure 3-2]

A more modern example of Newton's reaction principle is observed when the end of an inflated balloon is released. As the air in the balloon rushes out the opening, the balloon flies wildly around a room. In spite of the everyday examples, scientists' efforts to apply Newton's reaction principle to mechanical designs met with little success until this century.

Figure 3-2. Hero's aeolipile, conceived long before the acceptance of Newton's Laws of Motion, proved that power by reaction was possible.

HISTORY OF JET PROPULSION

The history of mechanical jet propulsion began in 1900, when Dr. Sanford Moss submitted his masters thesis on gas turbines. Later, Dr. Moss became an engineer for the General Electric Company in England. While there, Dr. Moss had the opportunity to apply some of his concepts in the development of the turbo-supercharger. This unique supercharger consisted of a small turbine wheel that was driven by exhaust gases. The turbine was then used to drive a supercharger.

Research done by Dr. Moss influenced Frank Whittle of England in the development of what became the first successful turbojet engine. Dr. Whittle was granted his first patent for the jet engine

Figure 3-3. Dr. Frank Whittle of England patented the first turbojet engine, the Whittle W1, in 1930. Its first flight occurred in a Gloster E28/39 aircraft in 1941.

in 1930 and eleven years later, his engine completed its first flight in a Gloster model E28/39 aircraft. The engine produced about one thousand pounds of thrust and propelled the aircraft at speeds over 400 miles per hour. [Figure 3-3]

While Whittle was developing the gas turbine engine in England, Hans Von Ohain, a German engineer, designed and built a jet engine that produced 1,100 pounds of thrust. This engine was installed in the Heinkel He-178 aircraft and made a successful flight on August 27, 1939. As a result, it became recognized as the first practical flight by a jet propelled aircraft. [Figure 3-4]

In the United States, research in the field of jet propulsion was lagging. Most of the country's

Figure 3-4. German engineer Hans Von Ohain designed and built the turbojet engine that powered the Heinkel He-178 to the world's first jet-powered flight in 1939.

Figure 3-5. First flown in 1942, the Bell XP-59 was the first American jet-powered aircraft.

efforts were being directed toward the development and production of high powered reciprocating engines. However, in 1941 the General Electric Company received a contract to research and develop a gas turbine engine. General Electric was chosen for this important project because of its extensive experience in building electrical generating turbines and turbo-superchargers. The result was the GE-1A engine, a centrifugal-compressor type engine that produced approximately 1,650 pounds of thrust. Two of these engines were used to power the Bell XP-59 "Airacomet" which flew for the first time in October 1942. The Airacomet proved the concept of jet powered flight, but was never used in combat due to its limited flight time of 30 minutes. [Figure 3-5]

JET PROPULSION TODAY

Today, the majority of commercial aircraft utilize some form of jet propulsion. In addition, there are currently several manufacturers that produce entire lines of jet powered aircraft that cruise in excess of 600 miles per hour and carry more than four hundred passengers or several tons of cargo.

Another step in the progression of commercial and military aviation was the ability to produce an engine that would propel an aircraft faster than the speed of sound. Today, there are several military aircraft that travel at speeds in excess of Mach one. One such aircraft is the SR-71 Blackbird which flys in excess of Mach five. In commercial aviation however, there is currently only one aircraft that flies faster than Mach one. This aircraft, the Concorde, was built by the British and French and placed into service in the mid seventies. Currently, there are more than ten Concordes in service that are capable of flying at 2.2 times the speed of sound.

In addition to military and commercial aviation, jet propulsion has become extremely popular for use on business jets. These two and three engine aircraft have become extremely popular in recent years due in part to the efficiency and reliability of jet engines.

TYPES OF JET PROPULSION

Newton's reaction principle has been applied to several propulsive devices used in aviation. All produce thrust in the same manner, they accelerate a mass of gases within the engine. The most common types of propulsive engines are the rocket, the ramjet, the pulsejet, and the gas turbine.

ROCKET

A rocket is a nonairbreathing engine that carries its own fuel as well as the oxygen needed for the fuel to burn. There are two types of rockets in use: solid-propellant rockets and liquid-propellant rockets. **Solid-propellant rockets** use a solid fuel that is mixed with an oxidizer and formed into a specific shape that promotes an optimum burning rate. Once ignited, the fuel produces an extremely high velocity discharge of gas through a nozzle at the rear of the rocket body. The reaction to the rapid discharge is forward motion of the rocket body. Solid fuel rockets are used primarily to propel some military weapons and, at times, provide additional thrust for takeoff of heavily loaded aircraft. These booster rockets attach to an aircraft structure and provide the additional thrust needed for special-condition takeoffs. [Figure 3-6]

The second type of rocket is the **liquid-fuel rocket**, which uses fuel and an oxidizing agent such as liquid oxygen. The two liquids are carried in tanks aboard the rocket. When the liquids are mixed, the reaction is so violent that a tremendous amount of heat is generated. The resulting high velocity gas jet behind the rocket provides enough thrust to propel an object.

RAMJET

A ramjet engine is an **athodyd**, or **aero-thermodynamic-duct**. Ramjets are air-breathing engines with

Figure 3-6. RATO, or rocket assisted takeoff devices are small, solid propellant rocket motors that are attached to an airplane to provide additional thrust for high altitude or overweight takeoff conditions.

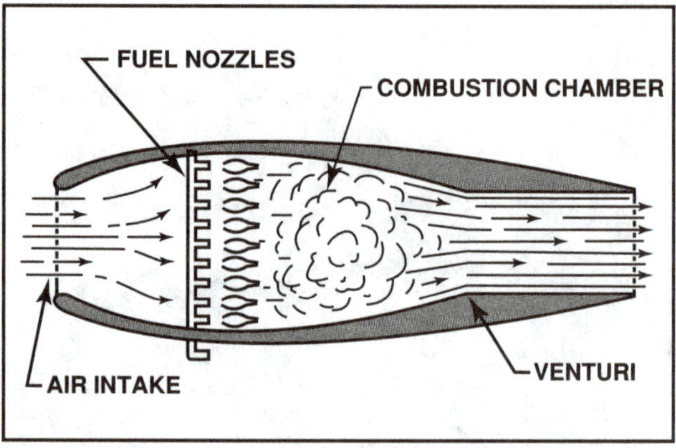

Figure 3-7. As a ramjet moves forward, air enters the intake and proceeds to a combustion chamber where fuel is added. Once ignited, the heat from the burning fuel accelerates the flow of air through a venturi to produce thrust.

no moving parts. However, since a ramjet has no rotating compressor to draw air into the engine, a ramjet must be moving forward at a high velocity before it can produce thrust. Once air enters the engine, fuel is injected and ignited to provide the heat needed to accelerate the air and produce thrust. Because ramjets must be moving forward to produce thrust, they are limited in their use. At present, ramjets are used in some military weapons delivery systems where the vehicle is accelerated to a high initial velocity so the ramjet can take over for sustained flight. [Figure 3-7]

PULSEJET

Pulsejet engines are similar to ramjets except that the air intake duct is equipped with a series of shutter valves that are spring loaded to the open position. Air drawn through the open valves enters a combustion chamber where it is heated by burning fuel. As the air within the combustion chamber expands, the air pressure increases to the point that the shutter valves are forced closed. Once closed, the expanding air within the chamber is forced rearward to produce thrust. A pulsejet is typically considered more useful than a ramjet because pulsejets will produce thrust prior to being accelerated to a high forward speed. [Figure 3-8]

GAS TURBINE ENGINE

The gas turbine engine is by far the most practical form of jet engine in use today. In fact, the turbine engine has become the standard on nearly all transport category, business, and military aircraft. Because of this, the discussion presented in this section will focus on the gas turbine engine. The four most common types of gas turbine engines are the turbojet, turbo-propeller, turboshaft, and turbofan.

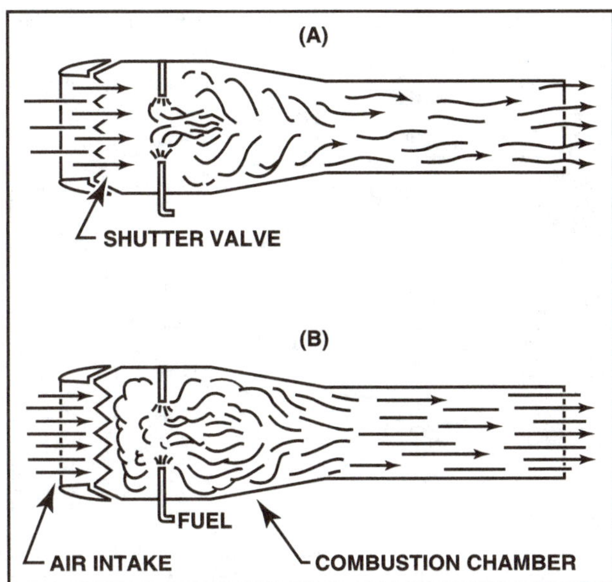

Figure 3-8. (A) — In the pulsejet engine, air is drawn into the combustion chamber and mixed with fuel when the shutter valves open. (B) — As the fuel burns, the air pressure within the chamber increases and forces the shutter valves to close. Once closed, the expanding air within the engine accelerates rearward through the exhaust nozzle to produce thrust.

TURBOJET ENGINES

The basic operating principles of a turbojet engine are relatively straight forward; air enters through an inlet duct and proceeds to the compressor where it is compressed. Once compressed, the air flows to the combuster section where fuel is added and ignited. The heat generated by the burning fuel causes the compressed air to expand and flow toward the rear of the engine. As the air moves rearward, it passes through a set of turbine wheels that are attached to the same shaft as the compressor blades. The expanding air spins the turbines which, in turn, drives the compressor. Once past the turbines, the air proceeds to exit the engine at a much higher velocity than the incoming air. It is this difference in velocity between the entering and exiting air that produces thrust.

When discussing a turbojet engine you must be familiar with the term **engine pressure ratio**, or **EPR**. An engine's EPR is the ratio of the turbine discharge pressure to the engine inlet air pressure. EPR gauge readings are an indication of the amount of thrust being produced for a given power lever setting. Total pressure pickups, or EPR probes, measure the air pressure at two points in the engine; one EPR probe is located at the compressor inlet and a second EPR probe is located just aft of the last stage turbine in the exhaust section. EPR readings are often used as verification of power settings for take-off, climb, and cruise. EPR readings are affected by and are dependent on pressure altitude and outside air temperature (OAT).

TURBOPROP ENGINES

A gas turbine engine that delivers power to a propeller is referred to as a turboprop engine. Turboprop engines are similar in design to turbojet engines except that the power produced by a turboprop engine is delivered to a reduction gear system that spins a propeller. Reduction gearing is necessary in turboprop engines because optimum propeller performance is achieved at much slower speeds than the engine's operating rpm. Turboprop engines are used extensively in business and commuter type aircraft because the combination of jet power and propeller efficiency provides good performance characteristics at speeds between 300 and 400 miles per hour. In addition, most turboprop engines provide the best specific fuel consumption of any gas turbine engine. [Figure 3-9]

TURBOSHAFT ENGINES

A gas turbine engine that delivers power to a shaft that can drive something else is referred to as a turboshaft engine. The biggest difference between a turbojet and turboshaft engine is that on a turboshaft engine, most of the energy produced by the expanding gases is used to drive a turbine rather than produce thrust. Many helicopters use a turboshaft type of gas turbine engine. In addition, turboshaft engines are widely used as auxiliary power units and in industrial applications to drive electrical generators and surface transportation systems. Output of a turboprop or turboshaft engine is measured by **shaft horsepower** rather than thrust.

TURBOFAN ENGINES

A turbofan engine consists of a multi-bladed ducted propeller driven by a gas turbine engine. Turbofans were developed to provide a compromise between

Figure 3-9. Turboprop powerplants have become a popular choice on corporate twin-engine aircraft.

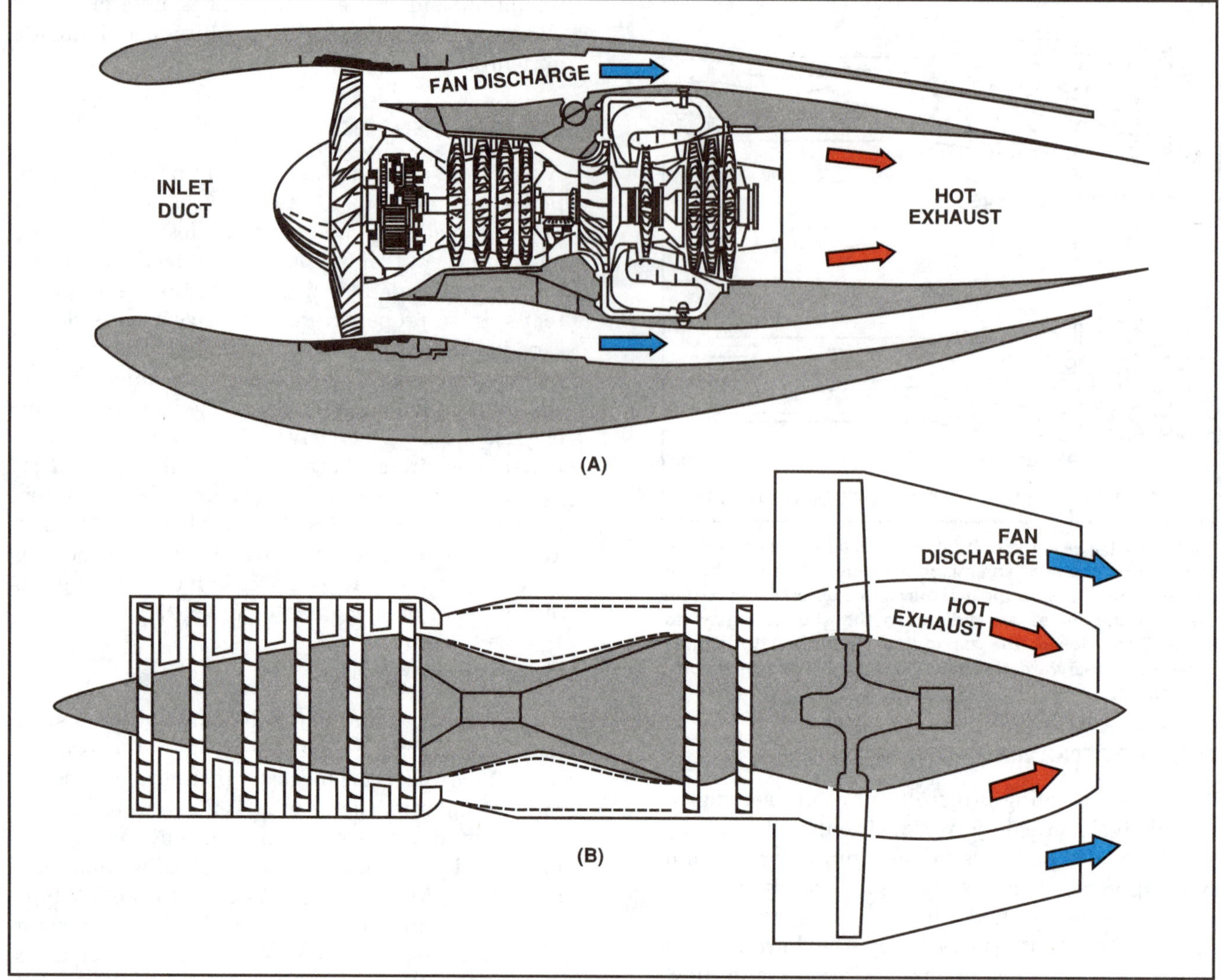

Figure 3-10. (A) — A forward-fan turbofan engine uses a relatively large diameter ducted fan that produces thrust and provides intake air to the compressor. (B) — An aft-fan turbofan engine has a fan mounted on the aft turbine. This arrangement is rarely used, since an aft fan cannot contribute to air compression at the inlet.

the best features of the turbojet and the turboprop. Turbofan engines have turbojet-type cruise speed capability, yet retain some of the short-field takeoff capability of a turboprop. Nearly all present day airliners are powered by turbofan engines for the reasons just mentioned as well as the fact that turbofans are very fuel efficient.

A turbofan engine may have the fan mounted to either the front or back of the engine. Engines that have the fan mounted in front of the compressor are called **forward-fan engines**, while turbofan engines that have the fan mounted to the turbine section are called **aft-fan engines**. [Figure 3-10]

The inlet air that passes through a turbofan engine is usually divided into two separate streams of air. One stream passes through the engine core while a second stream coaxially bypasses the engine core. It is this bypass stream of air that is responsible for the term bypass engine. When discussing bypass engines there are three terms you must be familiar with; they are thrust ratio, bypass ratio, and fan pressure ratio. A turbofan engine's **thrust ratio** is a comparison of the thrust produced by the fan to the thrust produced by the engine core exhaust. On the other hand, a turbofan's **bypass ratio** refers to the ratio of incoming air that bypasses the core to the amount of air that passes through the engine core. Turbofans in civil aircraft are generally divided into three classifications based on bypass ratio:

1. Low bypass (1:1)
2. Medium bypass (2:1 or 3:1)
3. High bypass (4:1 or greater)

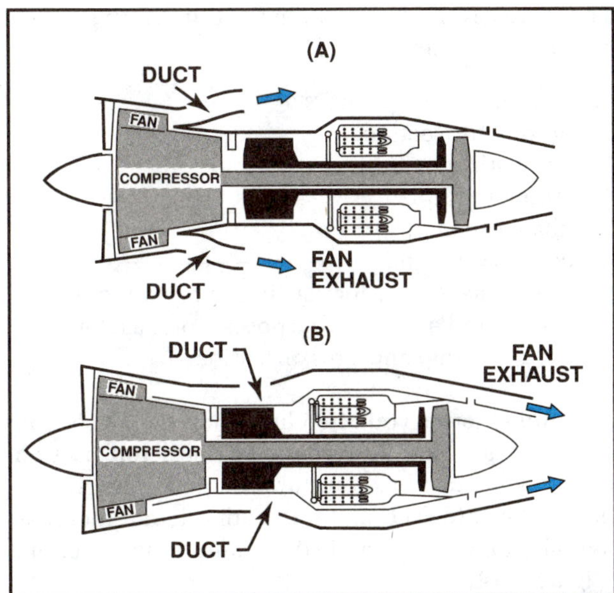

Figure 3-11. (A) — Bypass air is ejected directly overboard in forward-fan engines with a short fan duct. (B) — However, in a ducted fan, bypass air is ducted along the engine's entire length.

Generally, airflow mass in the fan section of a low bypass engine is the same as airflow mass in the compressor. The fan discharge could be slightly higher or lower depending on the engine model, but bypass ratios are approximately 1:1. In some engines the bypass air is ducted directly overboard through a short fan duct. However, in a **ducted fan engine**, the bypass air is ducted along the entire length of the engine. Full fan ducts reduce aerodynamic drag and noise emissions. In either case, the end of the duct usually has a converging discharge nozzle that increases velocity and produces reactive thrust. [Figure 3-11]

Medium or intermediate bypass engines have airflow bypass ratios ranging from 2:1 to 3:1. These engines have thrust ratios similar to their bypass ratios. The fans used on these engines have a larger diameter than the fans used on low bypass engines of comparable power. Fan diameter determines a fan's bypass ratio and thrust ratio.

High bypass turbofan engines have bypass ratios of 4:1 or greater and use the largest diameter fan of any of the bypass engines. High bypass turbines offer higher propulsive efficiencies and better fuel economy than low or medium bypass turbines. Consequently, they are the engines of choice on large airliners used for long flights. Some common high bypass turbofan engines include Pratt and Whitney's JT9D and PW4000, the Rolls-Royce RB-211, and the General Electric CF6. One version of

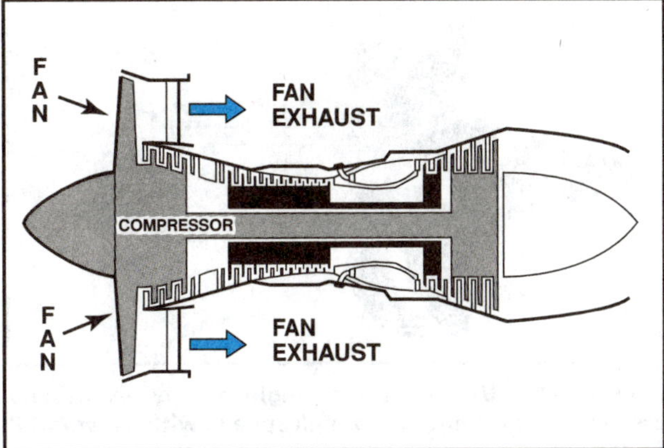

Figure 3-12. All high bypass turbofan engines use large diameter fans that produce bypass ratios of 4:1 or greater.

the JT9D has a bypass ratio of 5:1 with 80 percent of the thrust provided by the fan, and only 20 percent by the core engine. [Figure 3-12]

Another term you must be familiar with is **fan pressure ratio** which is the ratio of air pressure leaving the fan to the air pressure entering the fan. The fan pressure ratio on a typical low bypass fan is approximately 1.5:1, whereas for some high bypass fans the fan pressure ratio may be as high as 7:1. To obtain high fan pressure ratios, most high bypass engines are designed with high aspect ratio blades. **Aspect ratio** is the ratio of a blade's length to its width, or chord. Therefore, a long blade with a narrow chord has a higher aspect ratio than a short blade with a wide chord. Although high aspect ratio fan blades are used most often, low aspect ratio blades are coming into wider use today. Technological advances in blade construction have overcome the weight problems associated with low aspect ratio blades in the past. Weight savings in low aspect ratio blades have been achieved with hollow titanium blades having composite inner reinforcement materials. Additionally, low aspect ratio blades are desirable because of their resistance to foreign object damage, especially bird strikes.

UNDUCTED FAN ENGINES

Recent developments have produced new engine designs with higher efficiencies than anything currently in use. The new engines are designated **ultra high bypass (UHB) propfan** and **unducted fan engine (UDF)**. These new designs utilize titanium, lightweight stainless steel, and composite materials to surpass the fuel economy of several high bypass turbofan engines by more than 15 percent. Engine designers have achieved 30:1 bypass ratios by incorporating single or dual propellers with composite

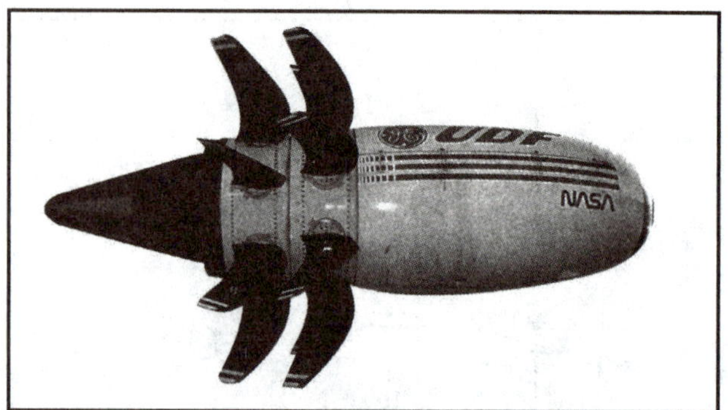

Figure 3-13. Unducted fan engines may eventually power transport aircraft at high speeds with substantial fuel savings.

blades that are 12 to 15 feet in diameter. The use of composite blades reduces weight and allows safe operation at tip speeds higher than conventional blades. [Figure 3-13]

Current research and development could produce 10,000 to 15,000 horsepower engines for an aircraft that carries 150 to 200 passengers at speeds near 0.8 Mach. Another design encases the propfan in a conventional cowl-type inlet which can achieve Mach 0.9. These engines are known as **ducted ultra high bypass** engines.

ENGINE COMPONENTS

All gas turbine engines consist of the same basic components. However, the nomenclature used to describe each component does vary among manufacturers. Nomenclature differences are reflected in applicable maintenance manuals. The following discussion uses the terminology that is most commonly used in industry.

There are seven basic sections within every gas turbine engine. They are the

1. air inlet.
2. compressor section.
3. combustion section.
4. turbine section.
5. exhaust section.
6. accessory section.
7. systems necessary for starting, lubrication, fuel supply, and auxiliary purposes, such as anti-icing, cooling, and pressurization.

Additional terms you often hear include hot section and cold section. A turbine engine's **hot section** includes the combustion, turbine, and exhaust sections. The **cold section**, on the other hand, includes the air inlet duct and the compressor section. [Figure 3-14]

AIR INLET DUCTS

The air inlet duct on a turbojet engine is normally considered to be a part of the airframe rather than the engine. However, understanding the function of an air inlet duct and its importance to engine performance make it a necessary part of any discussion on gas turbine engine design and construction.

The air inlet to a turbine engine has several functions, one of which is to recover as much of the total pressure of the free airstream as possible and deliver this pressure to the compressor. This is known as **ram recovery** or **pressure recovery**. In addition to recovering and maintaining the pressure of the free airstream, many inlets are shaped to raise the air

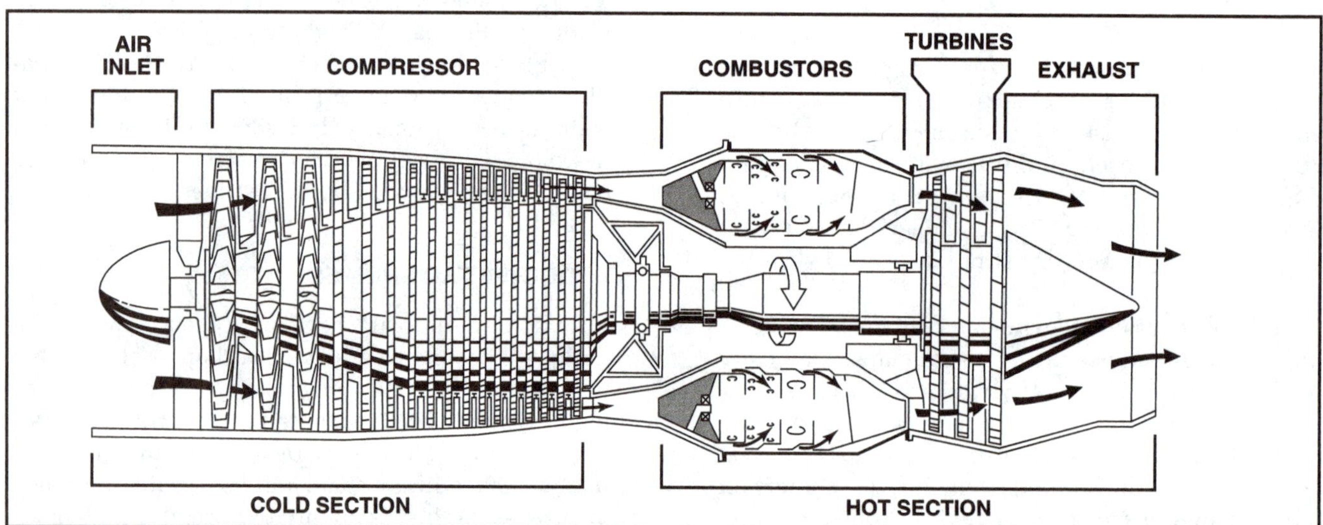

Figure 3-14. The basic components of a gas turbine engine include the air inlet, compressor, combustors, turbines, and exhaust. The air inlet and compressor section is sometimes referred to as an engine's cold section, while the combustors, turbines, and exhaust are sometimes referred to as an engine's hot section.

Figure 3-15. To ensure the operating efficiency of an inlet duct, periodic inspection for foreign object damage and corrosion is required.

pressure above atmospheric pressure. This **ram effect** results from forward movement which causes air to "pile up" in the inlet. The faster the aircraft flys, the more air piles up, and the higher the inlet air pressure rises above ambient.

Another function of the air inlet is to provide a uniform supply of air to the compressor so the compressor can operate efficiently. Furthermore, the inlet duct must cause as little drag as possible. It takes only a small obstruction to the airflow inside a duct to cause a severe loss of efficiency. If an inlet duct is to deliver its full volume of air with a minimum of turbulence, it must be maintained as close to its original condition as possible. Therefore, any repairs to an inlet duct must retain the duct's smooth aerodynamic shape. To help prevent damage or corrosion to an inlet duct, an inlet cover should be installed any time the engine is not operating. [Figure 3-15]

Many air inlet ducts have been designed to accomodate new airframe-engine combinations and variations in engine mounting locations. In addition, air inlets are designed to meet certain criteria for operation at different airspeeds. Some of the most common locations where engine inlets are mounted are on the engine, in the wing, and on the fuselage.

Figure 3-16. A McDonnell-Douglas DC-10 is designed with wing mounted engines and an engine in the vertical stabilizer. The air inlet ducts on all of these engines are mounted to the engine and positioned directly in front of the compressor.

ENGINE-MOUNTED INLETS

Several large commercial aircraft and large military aircraft use wing mounted engines. In a few cases, such as the DC-10 and L-1011, a combination of wing mounted and vertical stabilizer mounted engines are used. In both cases, the air inlet duct is located directly in front of the compressor and is mounted to the engine. Integral mounting of the inlet with an engine reduces air inlet length which helps to increase inlet efficiency. [Figure 3-16]

In addition to the wing and vertical stabilizer mounted engines, some commercial aircraft and the majority of small business jets are fitted with aft fuselage mounted engines. The air inlet ducts on engines mounted in this fashion are identical to air inlet ducts on wing mounted engines in that the duct is relatively short and is mounted directly to the engine. [Figure 3-17]

Figure 3-17. Engines mounted on the aft fuselage allow for short air inlet ducts that attach to the front of each engine. In this configuration, inlet efficiency is maintained.

Figure 3-18. The Hawker-Siddeley 801 "Nimrod" was developed from the de Havilland Comet airframe and utilizes wing mounted air inlets that are aerodynamically shaped to reduce drag.

WING-MOUNTED INLETS

Some aircraft with engines mounted inside the wings feature air inlet ducts in the wing's leading edge. Aircraft such as the Aerospatiale Caravelle, de Havilland Comet, and de Havilland Vampire all utilize wing-mounted inlets. Typically, wing-mounted inlets are positioned near the wing root area. [Figure 3-18]

FUSELAGE-MOUNTED INLETS

Engines mounted inside a fuselage typically use air inlet ducts located near the front of the fuselage. For example, many early military aircraft were designed with an air inlet duct in the nose of the fuselage. In addition, some modern supersonic military aircraft have inlet ducts located just under the aircraft nose. Although using an air inlet of this type allows the aircraft manufacturer to build a more aerodynamic aircraft, the increased length of the inlet does introduce some inefficiencies. [Figure 3-19]

Some military aircraft use air inlet ducts mounted on the sides of the fuselage. This arrangement works well for both single and twin engine aircraft. By mounting an intake on each side of an aircraft, the duct length can be shortened without adding a significant amount of drag to the aircraft. However, a disadvantage to this arrangement is that some sudden flight maneuvers can cause an imbalance in ram air pressure between the two intakes. The air pressure imbalance felt on the compressor face results in a slight loss of power. [Figure 3-20]

Figure 3-19. The single-entrance inlet duct takes full advantage of ram effect much like engine-mounted air inlets. Although the aircraft is aerodynamically clean, the length of the duct makes it slightly less efficient than engine-mounted types.

Figure 3-20. The divided-entrance duct with side-mounted intakes has a shorter length, providing improved inlet efficiency.

SUBSONIC INLETS

A typical subsonic air inlet consists of a fixed geometry duct whose diameter progressively increases from front to back. This **divergent** shape works like a venturi in that as the intake air spreads out, the velocity of the air decreases and the pressure increases. This added pressure contributes significantly to engine efficiency once the aircraft reaches its design cruising speed. At this speed, the compressor reaches its optimum aerodynamic efficiency and produces the most compression for the best fuel economy. It is at this design cruise speed that the inlet, compressor, combustor, turbine, and exhaust duct are designed to match each other as a unit. If any section mismatches any other because of damage, contamination, or ambient conditions, engine performance suffers. For additional information on subsonic air inlets, refer to the discussion on turbine engine induction systems in Section B of Chapter 5.

SUPERSONIC INLETS

On supersonic aircraft a typical air inlet duct has either a fixed or variable geometry whose diameter progressively decreases, then increases from front to back. This **convergent-divergent** shape is used to slow the incoming airflow to subsonic speed before it reaches the compressor.

In addition to the convergent-divergent shape, many supersonic inlets employ a movable plug or throat that changes the duct's geometry. The variable geometry is necessary so the duct can be adjusted as needed to accomodate a wide range of flight speeds. For additional information on supersonic air inlets, refer to the discussion on turbine engine induction systems in Section B of Chapter 5.

BELLMOUTH INLETS

Bellmouth inlets have a convergent profile that is designed specifically for obtaining very high aerodynamic efficiency when stationary or in slow flight. Therefore, bellmouth inlets are typically used on helicopters, some slow moving aircraft, and on engines being run in ground test stands. A typical bellmouth inlet is short in length and has rounded shoulders offering very little air resistance. However, because their shape produces a great deal of drag in forward flight, bellmouth inlets are typically not used on high speed aircraft. Since a bellmouth duct is so efficient when stationary, engine manufacturers typically collect engine performance data from engines fitted with a bellmouth inlet.

FOREIGN OBJECT DAMAGE

Prevention of foreign object damage (FOD) is a top priority among turbine engine operators and manufacturers. One of the easiest ways to help prevent foreign object damage is to install an inlet screen over an engine's inlet duct. The use of inlet screens is common on many rotorcraft and turboprop engines as well as on engines installed in test stands. However, inlet screens are seldom used on high mass airflow engines because icing and screen failures can cause serious engine damage. [Figure 3-21]

Figure 3-21. Several helicopters and turboprop aircraft utilize inlet screens to help prevent foreign object damage.

Additional devices that help prevent foreign object damage include sand or ice separators. The basic design of a sand or ice separator consists of an air intake with at least one venturi and a series of sharp bends. The venturi is used to accelerate the flow of incoming air and debris so the debris has enough inertia that it cannot follow the bends in the intake. This allows sand particles and other small debris to be channeled away from the compressor and into a sediment trap. [Figure 3-22]

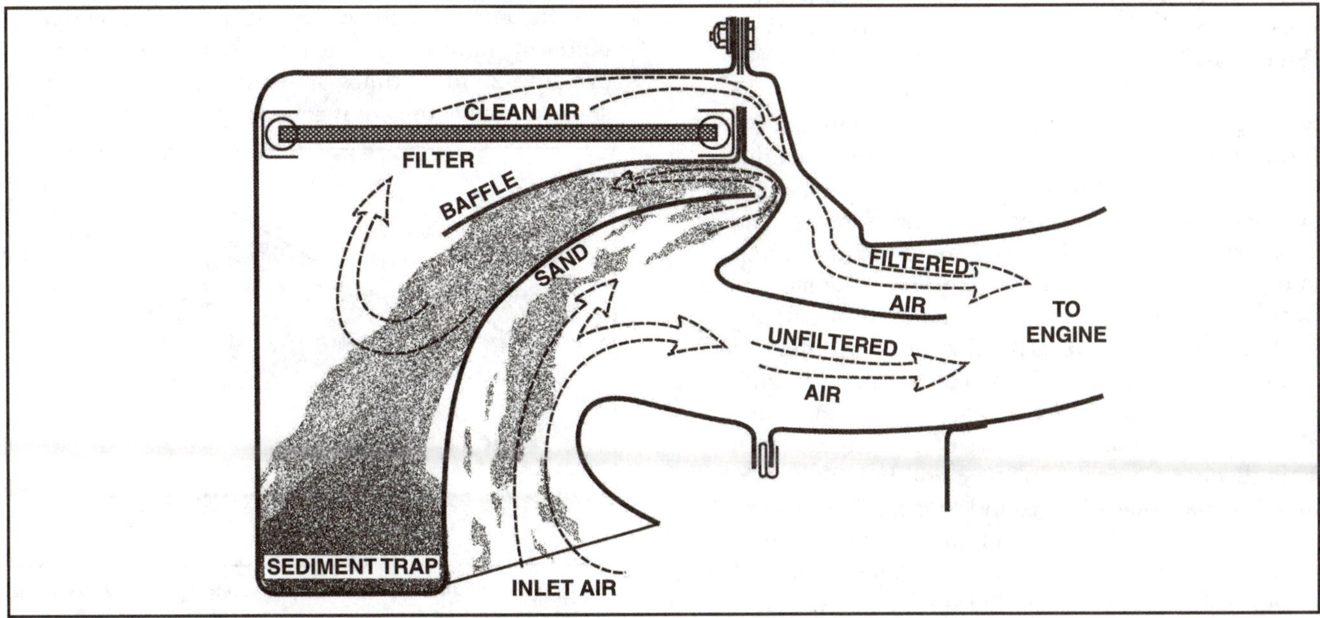

Figure 3-22. The sand and dust separator pictured is typical for the turbine powered helicopter. The venturi in the air inlet accelerates the air and sand so the sand has too much inertia to make the turn leading to the engine.

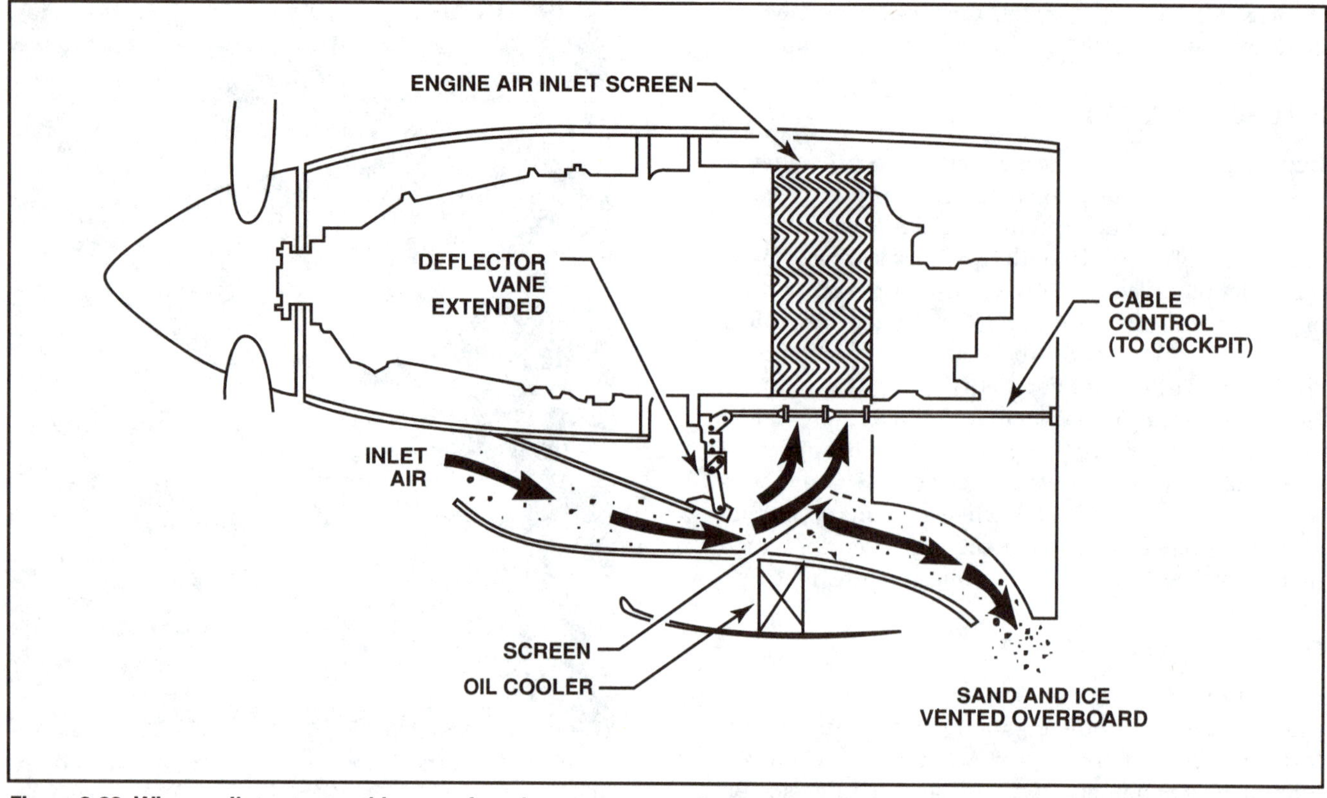

Figure 3-23. When a pilot actuates this type of sand separator, a small vane extends into the airstream. The inertia of the sand and ice particles after they pass through the venturi carries them past the air intake and discharges them overboard.

Another type of separator used on some turboprop aircraft incorporates a movable vane which extends into the inlet airstream. Once extended, the vane creates a more prominent venturi and a sudden turn in the engine inlet. Combustion air can follow the sharp curve but sand or ice particles cannot because of their inertia. The movable vane is operated by a pilot through a control handle in the cockpit. [Figure 3-23]

Some gas turbine engine inlets have a tendency to form a vortex between the ground and the inlet during ground operations. This vortex can become strong enough to lift water and debris such as sand, small stones, or small hardware from the ground and direct it into the engine. To help alleviate this problem, a **vortex dissipater**, sometimes called a **vortex destroyer** or **blow-away jet** is installed on some gas turbine engines. A typical vortex dissipater routes high pressure bleed air to a discharge nozzle located in the lower part of the engine cowl. This discharge nozzle directs a continuous blast of bleed air between the ground and air inlet to prevent a vortex from developing. Most aircraft equipped with a vortex dissipater also have a landing gear switch that arms the dissipater whenever the engine is operating and weight is on the main gear. [Figure 3-24]

COMPRESSOR SECTION

As discussed earlier, a gas turbine engine takes in a quantity of air, adds energy to it, then discharges the air to produce thrust. Based on this, the more air that is forced into an engine, the more thrust the engine can produce. The component that forces air into the engine is the compressor. To be effective, a modern compressor must increase the intake air pressure 20 to 30 times above the ambient air pressure and move the air at a velocity of 400 to 500 feet

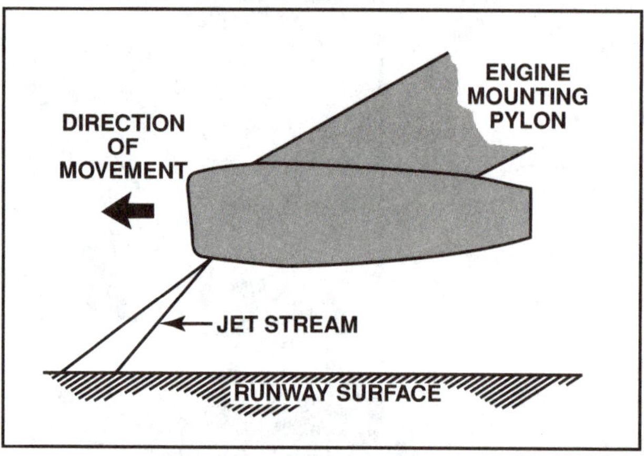

Figure 3-24. Engines that utilize a vortex dissipater use high pressure bleed air from the compressor to prevent the formation of a low pressure vortex that can suck debris into the engine.

per second. One way of measuring a compressor's effectiveness is to compare the static pressure of the compressor discharge with the static air pressure at the inlet. If the discharge air pressure is 30 times greater than the inlet air pressure, that compressor has a **compressor pressure ratio** of 30:1.

In addition to supporting combustion and providing the air necessary to produce thrust, the compressor section has several secondary functions. For example, a compressor supplies bleed air to cool the hot section and heated air for anti-icing. In addition, compressor bleed air is used for cabin pressurization, air conditioning, fuel system deicing, and pneumatic engine starting. There are two basic types of compressors used today; the centrifugal flow compressor and the axial flow compressor. Each is named according to the direction the air flows through the compressor, and one or both may be used in the same engine.

CENTRIFUGAL FLOW COMPRESSORS

The centrifugal compressor, sometimes called a **radial outflow compressor**, is one of the earliest compressor designs and is still used today in some smaller engines and auxiliary power units (APU's). Centrifugal compressors consist of an impeller, a diffuser, and a manifold. [Figure 3-25]

The **impeller**, or **rotor,** consists of a forged disk with integral blades, fastened by a splined coupling to a common power shaft. The impeller's function is to take air in and accelerate it outward by centrifugal force. Centrifugal compressors can have one or two impellers. Compressors having only one impeller are referred to as **single-stage compressors** while compressors having two impellers are referred to as **double-stage compressors**. Although a two-stage impeller compresses the air more than a single-stage impeller, the use of more than two stages in a compressor is typically considered impractical. The benefits of additional stages are negated by the energy lost when the airflow slows down as it passes from one impeller to the next. In addition, the added weight from each additional impeller requires more energy from the engine to drive the compressor. [Figure 3-26]

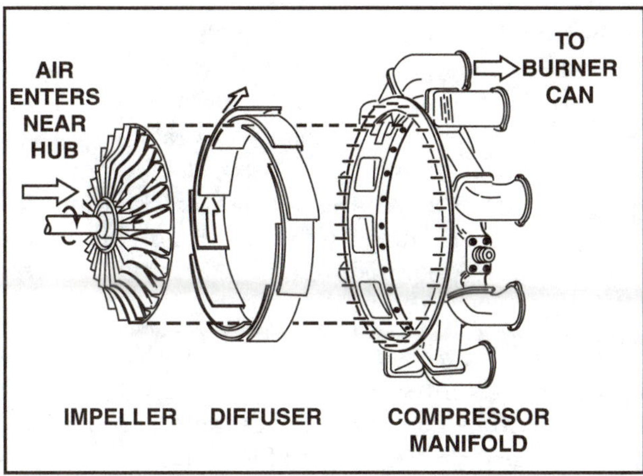

Figure 3-25. A single-stage centrifugal compressor consists of an impeller, a diffuser, and a compressor manifold.

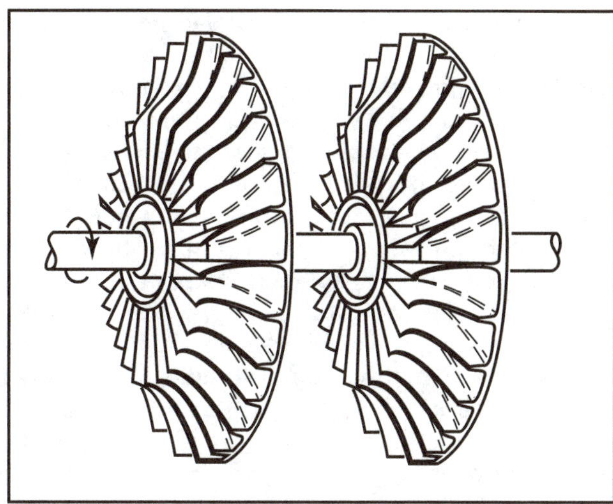

Figure 3-26. A two-stage impeller is sometimes used to obtain higher compressor pressure ratios. However, due to efficiency losses, centrifugal compressors typically do not exceed two stages.

When two impellers are mounted back-to-back a **double-sided** or **double-entry impeller** is created. A single-stage, double-sided impeller allows a higher mass airflow than that of a similar sized single-stage, single-sided impeller. Therefore, engines with double-sided impellers typically have a smaller overall diameter. [Figure 3-27]

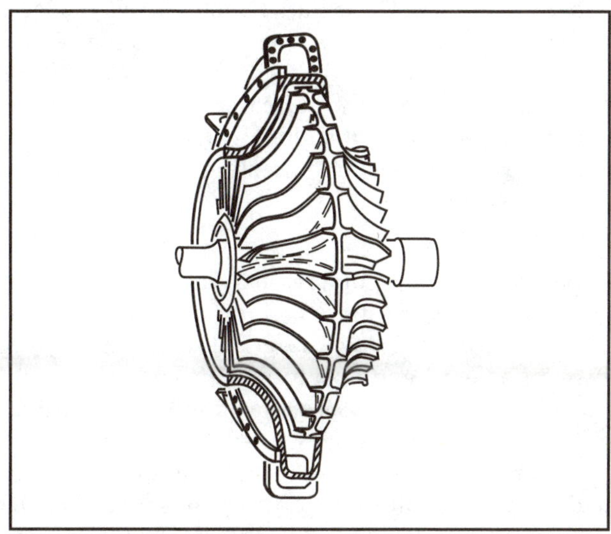

Figure 3-27. A single-stage, dual-sided impeller enables a small diameter engine to produce a high mass airflow.

One drawback of the double-sided impeller is that the ducting required to get the intake air from one side of the impeller to the other is complicated. For example, included in the ducting for double-entry compressor engines is a **plenum chamber**. This chamber is necessary because the air must enter the engine at almost right angles to the engine axis. Therefore, in order to give a positive flow, the air must surround the engine compressor at a positive pressure before entering the compressor. In addition to the plenum chamber, some double-entry compressors utilize **auxiliary air-intake doors (blow-in doors)**. These blow-in doors admit air into the engine compartment during ground operation when air requirements for the engine exceed that of the incoming airflow. The doors are held closed by spring action when the engine is not operating. During operation, however, the doors open whenever engine compartment pressure drops below atmospheric pressure. During takeoff and flight, ram air pressure in the engine compartment aids the springs in holding the doors closed.

Once through the impeller, the air is expelled into a divergent duct called a **diffuser**, where it loses velocity and increases in pressure. The diffuser acts as a divergent duct where the air spreads out, slows down, and increases in static pressure.

The **compressor manifold** distributes the air in a smooth flow to the combustion section. The manifold has one outlet port for each combustion chamber so that the air is evenly divided. A compressor outlet elbow is bolted to each of the outlet ports. The elbows act as air ducts and are often referred to as **outlet ducts**, **outlet elbows**, or **combustion chamber inlet ducts**. These outlet ducts change the radial direction of the airflow to an axial direction. To help the elbows perform this function in an efficient manner, **turning vanes** or **cascade vanes** are sometimes fitted inside the elbows. These vanes reduce air pressure losses by presenting a smooth, turning surface. [Figure 3-28]

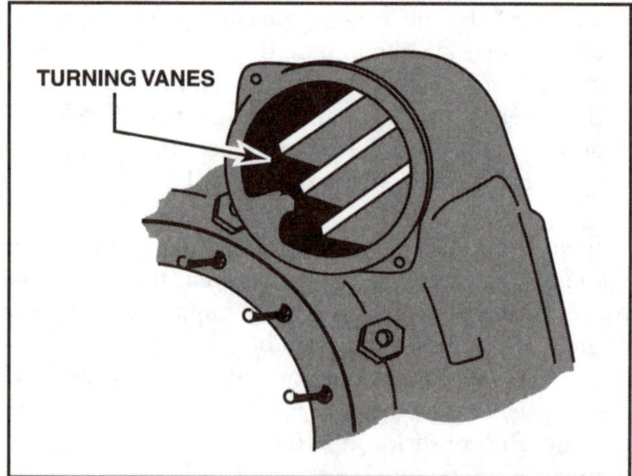

Figure 3-28. The turning vanes in a compressor manifold help direct the compressor outlet air to the combustion section.

Centrifugal flow compressors offer several advantages including simplicity of manufacture, relatively low cost, low weight, low starting power requirements, and operating efficiency over a wide range of rotational speeds. In addition, a centrifugal flow compressor's short length and spoke-like design allow it to accelerate air rapidly and immediately deliver it to the diffuser in a short distance. Tip speeds of centrifugal compressors may reach Mach 1.3, but the pressure within the compressor casing prevents airflow separation and provides a high transfer of energy into the airflow. Although most centrifugal compressors are limited to two stages, the high pressure rise per stage allows modern centrifugal compressors to obtain compressor pressure ratios of 15:1.

A typical centrifugal compressor has a few disadvantages that make it unsuitable for use in some engines. For example, the large frontal area required for a given airflow increases aerodynamic drag. Also, practical limits on the number of stages restrict its usefulness when designing larger and more powerful engines.

AXIAL FLOW COMPRESSORS

An axial flow compressor has two main elements, a rotor and a stator. The **rotor** consists of rows of blades fixed on a rotating spindle. The angle and airfoil contour of the blades forces air rearward in the same manner as a propeller. The **stator** vanes, on the other hand, are arranged in fixed rows between the rows of rotor blades and act as diffusers at each stage, decreasing air velocity and raising pressure. Each consecutive row of rotor blades and stator vanes constitutes a **pressure stage**. The number of stages is determined by the amount of air and total pressure rise required.

Unlike a centrifugal compressor, which is capable of compressor pressure ratios of 15:1, a single stage in an axial flow compressor is capable of producing a compressor pressure ratio of only 1.25:1. Therefore, high compressor pressure ratios are obtained by adding more compressor stages.

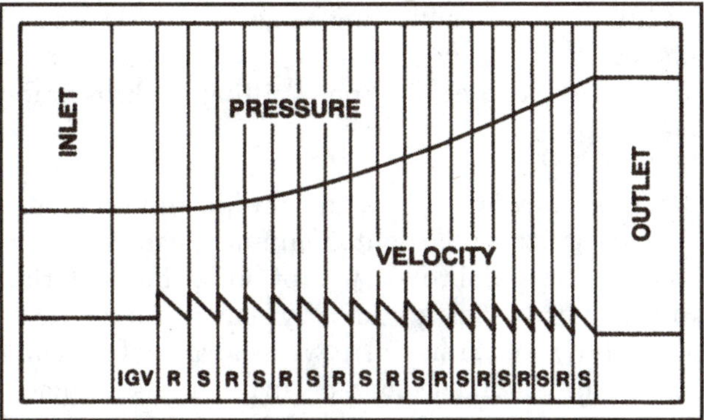

Figure 3-29. In an axial compressor, airflow velocity is maintained nearly constant while air pressure increases as the airflow proceeds through each stage of compression.

The task of an axial compressor is to raise air pressure rather than air velocity. Therefore, each compressor stage raises the pressure of the incoming air while the air's velocity is alternately increased then decreased as airflow proceeds through the compressor. The rotor blades slightly accelerate the airflow, then the stator vanes diffuse the air, slowing it and increasing the pressure. The overall result is increased air pressure and relatively constant air velocity from compressor inlet to outlet. [Figure 3-29]

As air passes from the front of an axial flow compressor to the rear, the space between the rotor shaft and the stator casing gradually decreases. This shape is necessary to maintain a constant air velocity as air density increases with each stage of compression. To accomplish the convergent shape, each stage of blades and vanes is smaller than the one preceding it. [Figure 3-30]

The case on most axial flow compressors is horizontally divided into two halves, allowing the

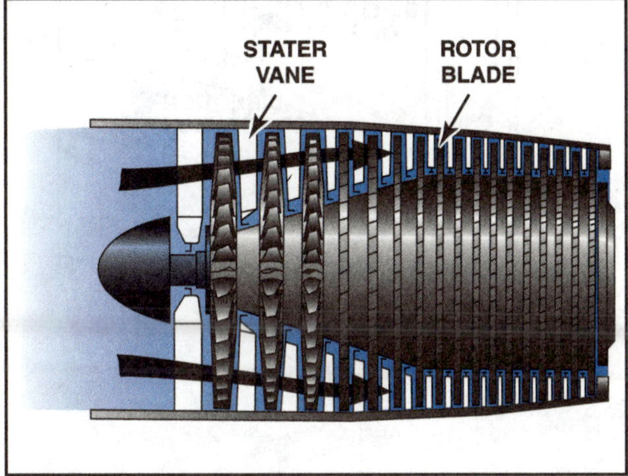

Figure 3-30. In an axial flow compressor, the divergent shape allows the air velocity to remain nearly constant, while pressure gradually increases.

removal of one of the halves for inspection or maintenance of both rotor blades and stator vanes. The compressor case also provides a means of extracting bleed air for ancillary functions.

Some disadvantages of axial flow compressors are relatively high weight and high starting power requirements. Also, the low pressure rise per stage of 1.25:1 requires many stages to achieve high compressor pressure ratios. Furthermore, axial flow compressors are expensive and difficult to manufacture.

In spite of the disadvantages just mentioned, axial flow compressors outperform centrifugal flow compressors in several areas. High ram efficiency is obtained because of their straight-through design, which takes full advantage of any ram effect. Another advantage of axial flow compressors is their ability to obtain higher compressor pressure ratios by adding additional stages. In addition, the small frontal area of an axial flow compressor helps to reduce aerodynamic drag.

Compressor Rotor Blades

The rotor blades used in an axial flow compressor have an airfoil cross-section with a varying angle of incidence, or twist. This twist compensates for the blade velocity variation caused by its radius. In other words, the further from the axis of rotation a blade section is, the faster it travels. [Figure 3-31]

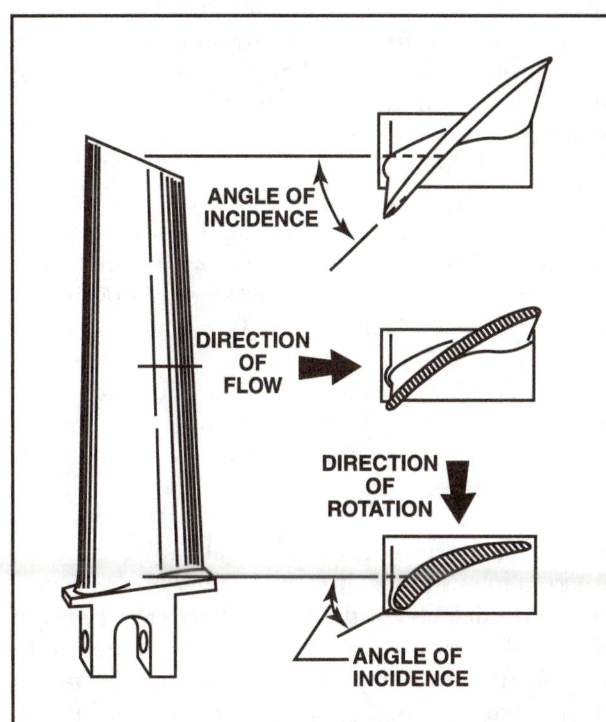

Figure 3-31. Compressor rotor blades are twisted to compensate for blade velocity variations along the length of the blade.

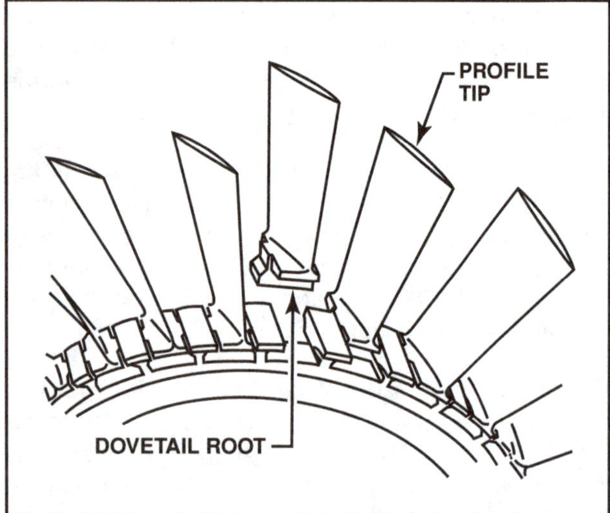

Figure 3-32. A dovetail on the base of this compressor blade fits loosely into a dovetail slot in the compressor wheel. A small locking device such as a pin, key, or plate prevents the blade from backing out.

Axial flow compressors typically have 10 to 18 compression stages, and in the turbofan engine, the fan is considered to be the first stage rotor. The base, or **root** of a rotor blade often fits loosely into the rotor disk. This loose fit allows for easy assembly and vibration damping. As the compressor rotor rotates, centrifugal force keeps the blades in their correct position, and the airstream over each blade provides a shock absorbing or cushioning effect. Rotor blade roots are designed with a number of different shapes such as a **bulb**, **fir tree**, or **dovetail**. To prevent a blade from backing out of its slot, most methods of blade attachment use a pin and a lock tab or locker to secure the coupling. [Figure 3-32]

Some long fan blades have a mid-span **shroud** that helps support the blades, making them more resistant to the bending forces created by the airstream. The shrouds, however, do block some of the airflow and create additional aerodynamic drag that reduces fan efficiency. In addition, when the mating surfaces on a mid-span shroud become excessively worn, the shrouds can overlap. This is known as **shingling** and can cause fan vibration and engine damage.

Some blades are cut off square at the tip and are referred to as **flat machine tips**. Other blades have a reduced thickness at the tips and are called **profile tips**. All rotating machinery has a tendency to vibrate, and profiling a compressor blade increases its natural vibration frequency. By increasing the blade's natural frequency above the frequency of rotation, a blades's vibration tendency is reduced. In addition, the thin trailing edge of profile tipped blades causes a vortex which increases air velocity and helps prevent air from spilling back over the blade tips.

On some newer engines the profile tipped blades are designed with tight running clearances and rotate within a shroud strip of abradable material. Since rotor blades are usually made of a stainless steel alloy, the shroud strip wears away with no loss of blade length if contact loading takes place. Sometimes after engine shutdown, a high pitched noise can be heard as the rotor coasts to a stop. The noise is caused by contact between the blade tip and shroud strip and is the reason why profile tip blades are sometimes referred to as squealer tips.

Another blade design that increases compressor efficiency utilizes a localized increase in blade camber, both at the blade tip and blade root. The purpose of this design is to compensate for the friction caused by the boundary layer of air near the compressor case. The increased blade camber helps overcome the friction and makes the blade extremities appear as if they were bent over at each corner, hence the term **end bend**. [Figure 3-33]

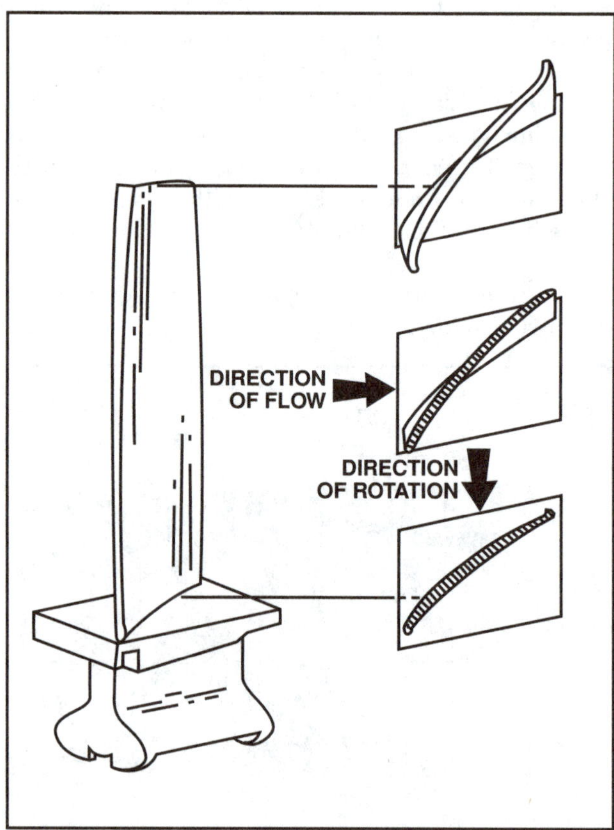

Figure 3-33. End bend refers to the increased blade camber on some compressor blades. The increased camber helps prevent airflow stagnation near the blade tips.

Compressor Stator Vanes

Stator vanes are the stationary blades located between each row of rotating blades in an axial flow compressor. As discussed earlier, the stator vanes act as diffusers for the air coming off the rotor, decreasing its velocity and raising its pressure. In addition, the stators help prevent swirling and direct the flow of air coming off each stage to the next stage at the appropriate angle. Like rotor blades, stator vanes have an airfoil shape. In addition, the angle of attack of stator vanes can be fixed or variable. Stator vanes are normally constructed out of steel or nickel because those metals have high fatigue strength. However, titanium may also be used for stator vanes in the low pressure and temperature stages.

Stator vanes may be secured directly to the compressor casing or to a stator vane retaining ring, which is secured to the compressor case. Most stator vanes are attached in rows with a dovetail arrangement and project radially toward the rotor axis. Stator vanes are often shrouded at their tips to minimize vibration tendencies. [Figure 3-34]

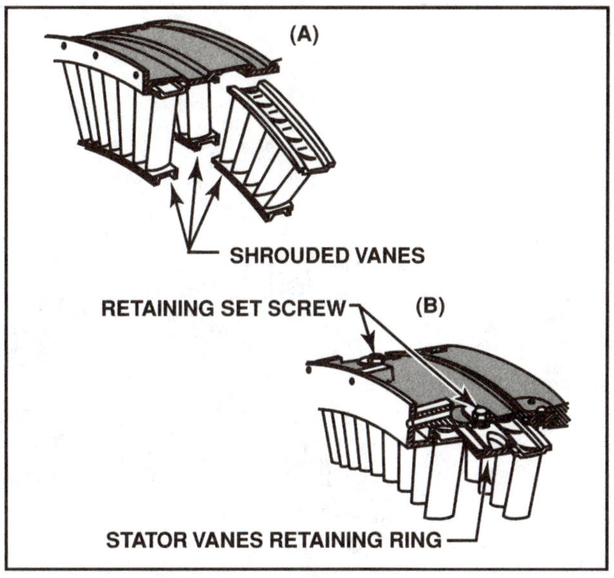

Figure 3-34. Compressor stator vanes may be attached directly to the compressor case — (A) or to a retaining ring that is attached to the case by a retaining screw — (B). In addition, stator vanes are sometimes equipped with shrouds to minimize the effects of vibration.

The set of stator vanes immediately in front of the first stage rotor blades are called **inlet guide vanes**. These vanes direct the airflow into the first stage rotor blades at the best angle while imparting a swirling motion in the direction of engine rotation. This action improves the aerodynamics of the compressor by reducing the drag on the first stage rotor blades. Some axial compressors with high compressor pressure ratios utilize variable inlet guide vanes plus several stages of variable stator vanes. These variable inlet guide vanes and stators automatically reposition themselves to maintain proper airflow through the engine under varying operating conditions.

The last set of vanes the compressor air passes through is the **outlet vane assembly**. These vanes straighten the airflow and eliminate any swirling motion or turbulence. The straightened airflow then proceeds to the diffuser to prepare the air mass for combustion.

MULTIPLE-SPOOL COMPRESSORS

In a basic axial flow compressor, the compressor and turbine are connected by a single shaft and rotate as a single unit. Since there is only one compressor unit, the compressor is commonly referred to as a **single-spool compressor**. While single-spool compressors are relatively simple and inexpensive to manufacture, they do have a few drawbacks. For example, in a long axial compressor the rear stages operate at a fraction of their capacity, while the forward stages are typically overloaded. Furthermore, the large mass of a single-spool compressor does not respond quickly to abrupt control input changes. [Figure 3-35]

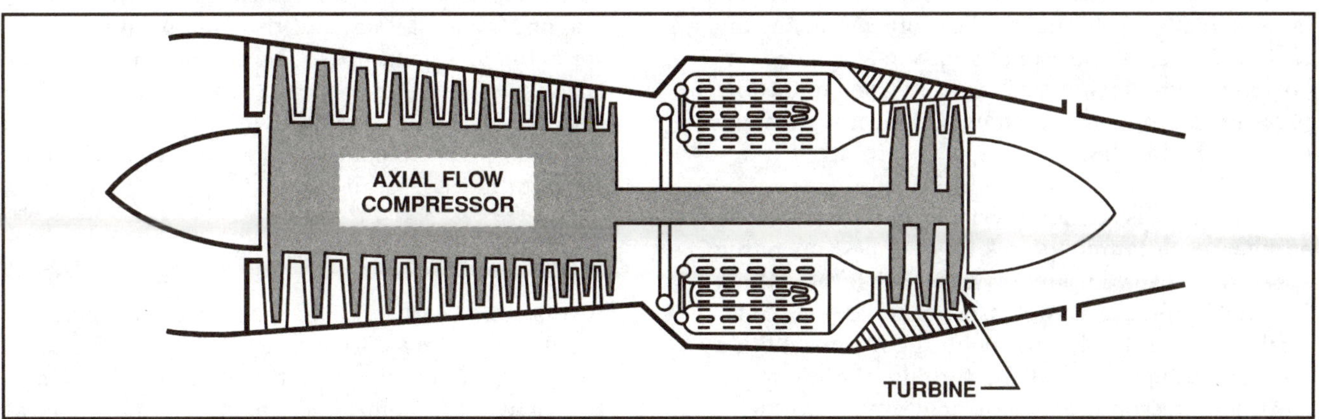

Figure 3-35. In a single-spool compressor, there is only one compressor unit that is connected by a shaft to the turbine section.

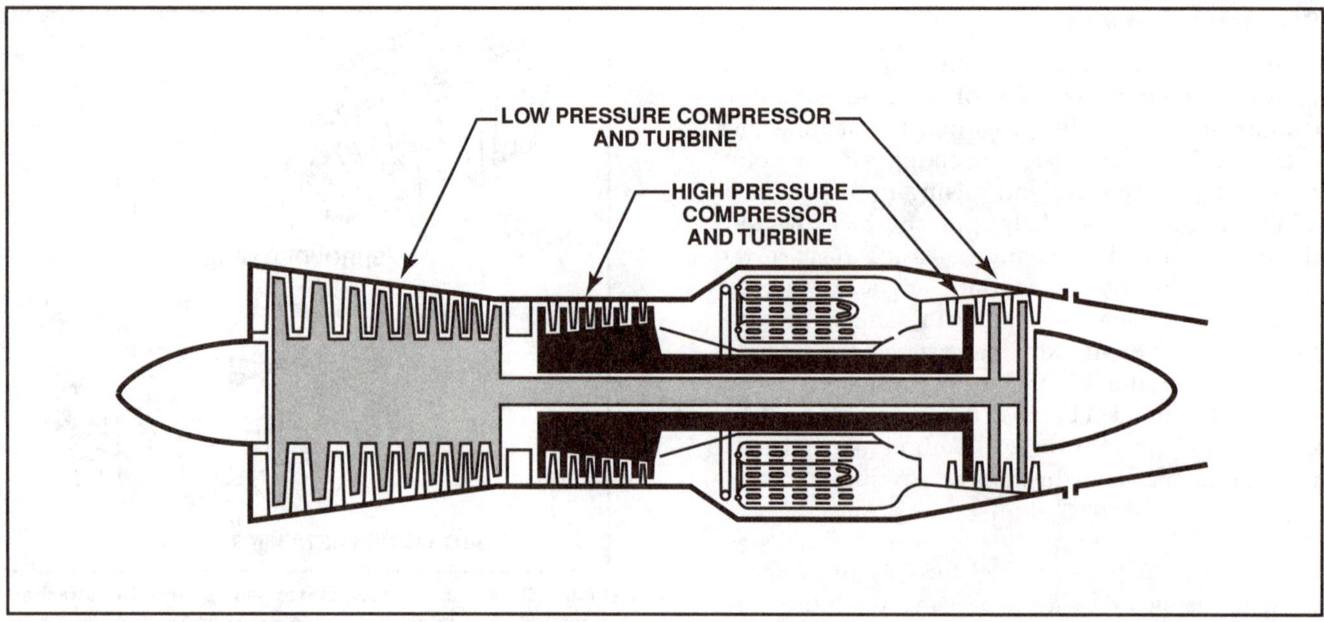

Figure 3-36. In a dual-spool axial flow engine, the low pressure compressor is driven by the low pressure turbine while the high pressure turbine drives the high pressure compressor. Splitting the compressor creates two rotating groups, each with considerably less mass than a single-spool compressor. The smaller mass allows the compressors to respond more quickly to power lever inputs and perform better at high altitudes. In addition, a smaller starter can be used since it turns less mass.

Engine designers devised a way to overcome the limitations of single-spool compressors by splitting the compressor into two or three sections. Each section is connected to a portion of the turbine section by shafts that run coaxially, one within the other. For example, split-compressor engines with two compressor sections are identified as **dual-spool** or **twin-spool** compressors. The front section of a dual-spool compressor is called the **low pressure**, **low speed**, or **N_1 compressor**. This low pressure compressor is typically driven by a two-stage turbine at the rear of the turbine section. The second compressor section of a twin-spool compressor is called the **high pressure**, **high speed**, or **N_2 compressor** and is typically driven by a single stage high-pressure turbine at the front of the turbine section. The shaft connecting the low pressure compressor and turbine typically rotates inside the shaft connecting the high pressure compressor and turbine. On some turbofan engines, the forward fan is attached to the low pressure compressor, and they both turn at the same speed. [Figure 3-36]

Since the spools are not physically connected to one another, each is free to seek its own best operating speed. However, for any given power lever setting, the high pressure compressor speed is held relatively constant by the fuel control governor. With a constant energy level at the turbine, the low pressure compressor speeds up or slows down with changes in the inlet air flow caused by atmospheric pressure fluctuations or flight maneuvering. For example, low pressure compressors speed up as the aircraft gains altitude, since the atmosphere is less dense and more rotational speed is needed to force the required amount of air through the engine. Conversely, as the aircraft descends, the air becomes more dense and easier to compress so the low pressure compressor slows down. This way, the low pressure compressor supplies the high pressure compressor with a fairly constant air pressure and mass airflow for each power setting.

On many turbofan engines, the compressor section is divided into three sections and is referred to as a **triple-spool compressor**. In this arrangement the fan is referred to as the low speed, or N_1 compressor. The compressor next in line is called the **intermediate**, or N_2 compressor, and the innermost compressor is the high pressure, or **N_3 compressor**. The low speed compressor is typically driven by a multiple stage low pressure turbine, while the intermediate and high pressure compressors are driven by single stage turbines. [Figure 3-37]

COMPRESSOR STALL

As discussed earlier, compressor blades are actually small airfoils and therefore, are subject to the same aerodynamic principles that apply to aircraft wings. Like a wing, a compressor blade has an angle of attack, which is the acute angle between the chord

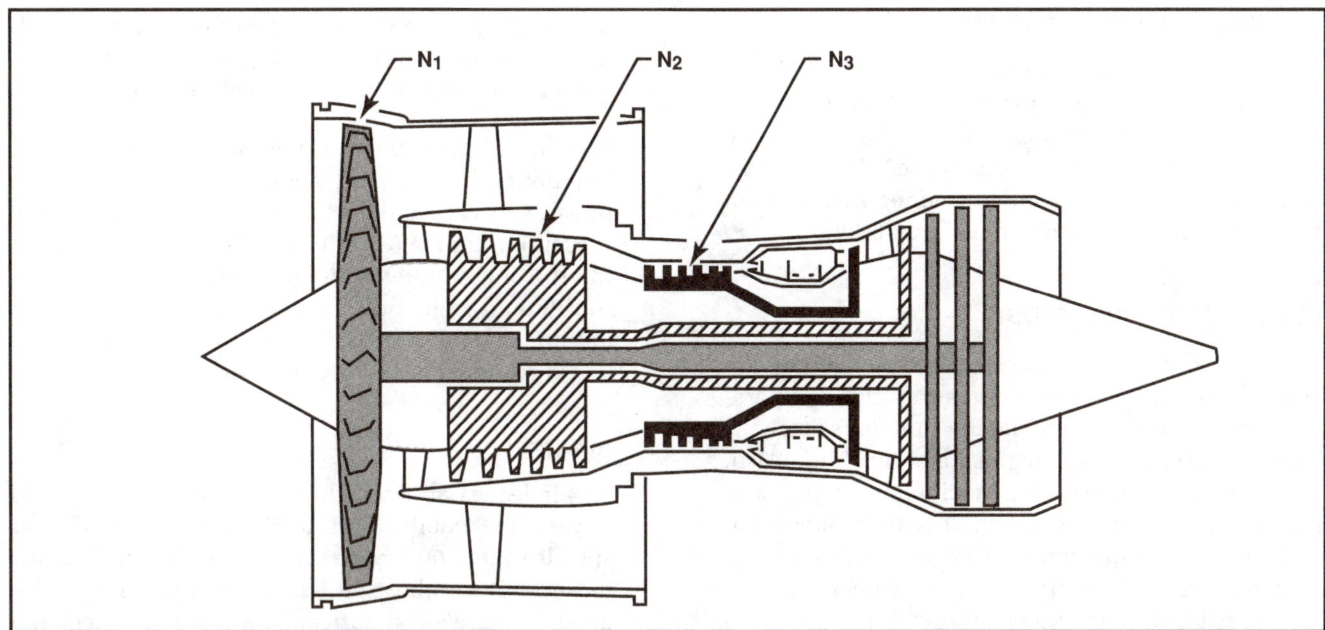

Figure 3-37. The triple-spool compressors used on many turbofan engines allow each compressor section to reach its optimum speed for varying power requirements and flight conditions.

of the blade and the relative wind. The angle of attack of a compressor blade is the result of inlet air velocity and the compressor's rotational velocity. These two forces combine to form a vector, which defines the airfoil's actual angle of attack to the approaching inlet air. As with an aircraft wing, a compressor blade's angle of attack can be changed.

A **compressor stall** can be described as an imbalance between the two vector quantities, inlet velocity, and compressor rotational speed. Compressor stalls occur when the compressor blades' angle of attack exceeds the critical angle of attack. At this point, smooth airflow is interrupted and turbulence is created with pressure fluctuations. Compressor stalls cause air flowing in the compressor to slow down and stagnate, sometimes reversing direction. A compressor stall can usually be heard as a pulsating or fluttering sound in its mildest form to a loud explosion in its most developed state. Quite often the cockpit gauges will not show a mild or **transient stall** but will indicate a developed stall. Typical instrument indications include fluctuations in rpm and an increase in exhaust gas temperature. Most transient stalls are not harmful to the engine and often correct themselves after one or two pulsations. However, severe stalls, or **hung stalls**, can significantly impair engine performance, cause loss of power, and can damage the engine.

The only way to overcome a stalled condition is to reduce the angle of attack on the rotor blades. One way this can be done is through the use of **variable inlet guide vanes** and variable stator vanes which direct the incoming air into the rotor blades at an appropriate angle. For example, as a compressor's rotational speed decreases, the stator vanes are progressively closed to maintain the appropriate airflow angle to the proceeding rotor blades. The position of the stator vanes is controlled automatically by the fuel control unit. To do this, the fuel control unit monitors compressor inlet temperature and engine speed.

Another way the angle of attack can be changed is by bleeding off some of the air pressure within the compressor. To do this, some engines incorporate automatic air-bleed valves which operate during low rpm conditions or during engine startup. The automatic valves open to relieve pressure caused by air piling up at the compressor's high pressure end. This regulation of air pressure helps prevent the compressor from stalling and allows for easier engine starting.

Compressor stalls typically occur when the engine inlet air becomes turbulent or disrupted when an aircraft flys in severe turbulence or performs abrupt flight maneuvers. Another cause is excessive fuel flow produced by a sudden engine acceleration, accompanied by incompatible engine rpm and airflow combinations. In addition, contamination or damage to compressor blades, stator vanes, or turbine components can also cause a compressor stall.

COMBINATION COMPRESSORS

Hybrid axial flow-centrifugal flow compressors were developed to combine the best features of centrifugal and axial compressors and eliminate some of their disadvantages. This design is currently being used in some smaller engines installed on business jets and helicopters. [Figure 3-38]

COMPRESSOR AIR BLEEDS

In addition to supplying air for combustion, the compressor supplies high pressure, high temperature air for various secondary functions such as cabin pressurization, heating, and cooling. Also, compressor air is used for deicing, anti-icing, and for pneumatic engine starting. This air is referred to as **bleed air**, or **customer bleed air** and is tapped from the compressor through bleed ports at various stages. A **bleed port** is a small opening adjacent to the compressor stage selected for bleed air supply. The choice of which compressor stage to bleed air from depends on the air pressure or temperature required for a particular function. Air bled from the final or highest pressure stage often requires cooling, since compression can heat the air to temperatures in excess of 650 degrees Fahrenheit.

Bleeding air from the compressor does cause a small but noticeable drop in engine power. Sometimes power loss can be detected by observing the engine pressure ratio (EPR) indicator. For example, selecting the engine inlet anti-ice function causes a drop in EPR and engine rpm if the engine power lever is left in a fixed position. Exhaust gas temperature (EGT) readings may shift noticeably as well.

DIFFUSER

As air leaves an axial flow compressor and moves toward the combustion section, it is traveling at speeds up to 500 feet per second. This is far too fast to support combustion, therefore the air velocity must be slowed significantly before it enters the combustion section. The divergent shape of a diffuser slows compressor discharge while, at the same time, increasing air pressure to its highest value in the engine. The diffuser is usually a separate section

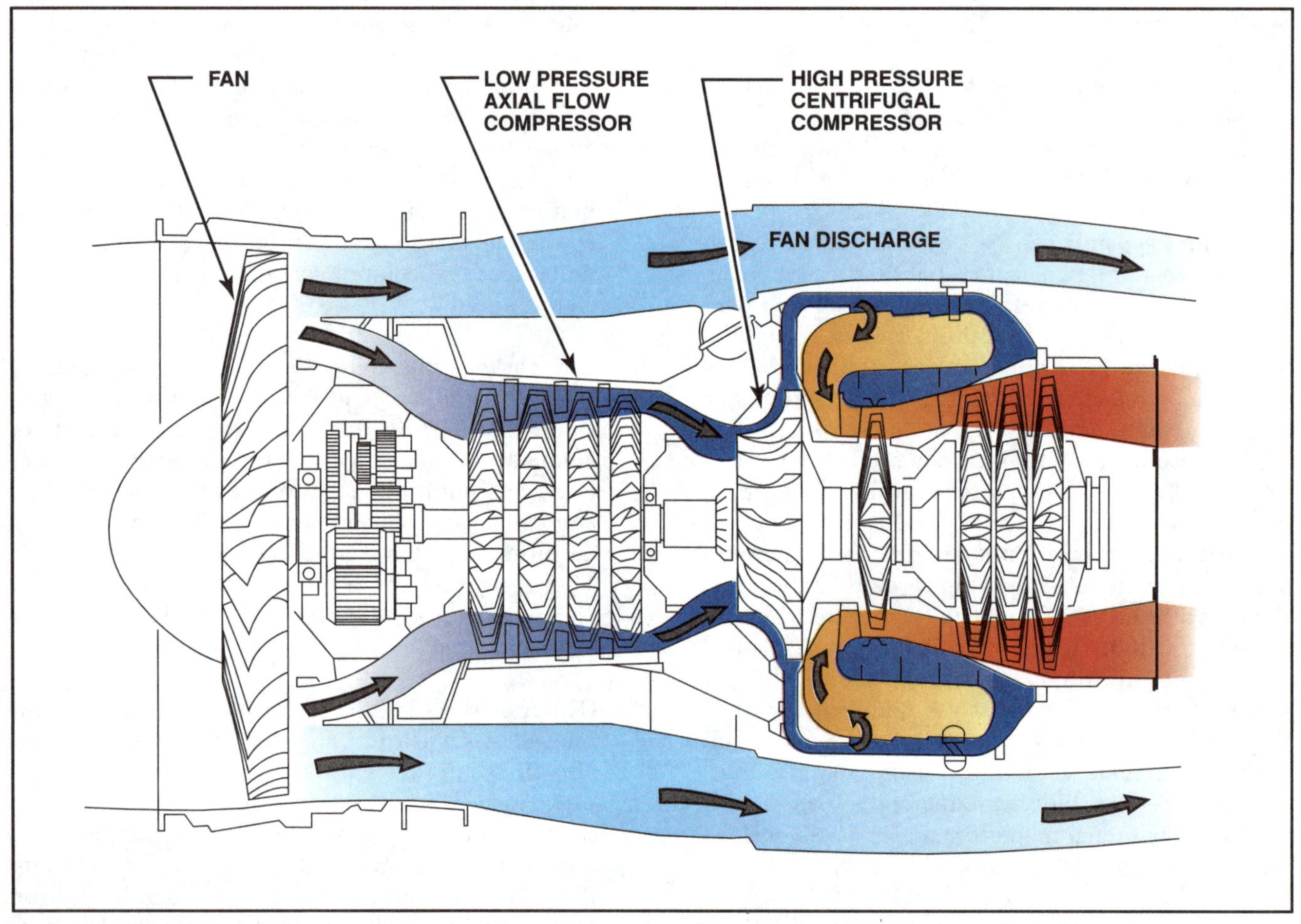

Figure 3-38. The Garrett TFE731 engine has a two-stage compressor that uses an axial flow compressor for the low pressure stage and a single stage centrifugal compressor for the high pressure stage.

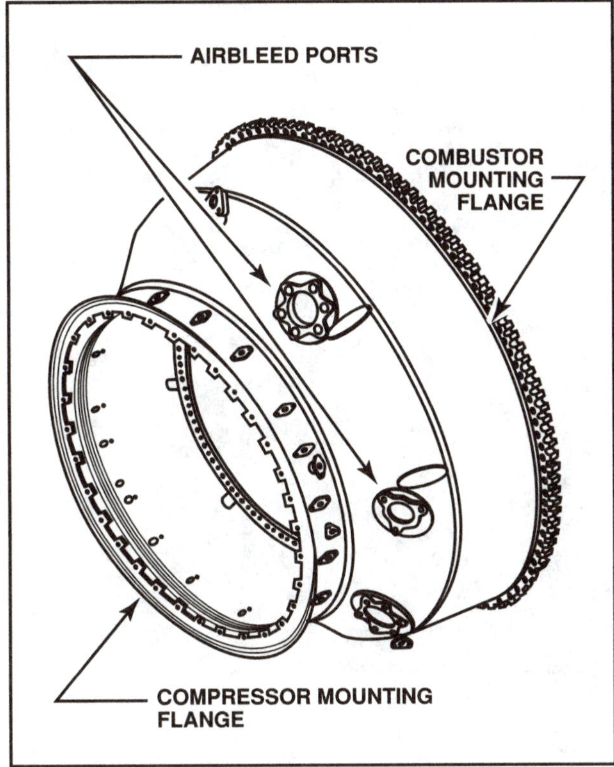

Figure 3-39. High-velocity air from the compressor section enters the diffuser where air velocity decreases and air pressure increases to a maximum.

bolted to the rear of the compressor case and ahead of the combustion section. [Figure 3-39]

COMBUSTION SECTION

A combustion section is typically located directly between the compressor diffuser and turbine section. All combustion sections contain the same basic elements: one or more combustion chambers (combustors), a fuel injection system, an ignition source, and a fuel drainage system.

The **combustion chamber** or **combustor** in a turbine engine is where the fuel and air are mixed and burned. A typical combustor consists of an outer casing with a perforated inner liner. The perforations are various sizes and shapes, all having a specific effect on the flame propagation within the liner.

The fuel injection system meters the appropriate amount of fuel through the fuel nozzles into the combustors. Fuel nozzles are located in the combustion chamber case or in the compressor outlet elbows. Fuel is delivered through the nozzles into the liners in a finely atomized spray to ensure thorough mixing with the incoming air. The finer the spray, the more rapid and efficient the combustion process.

A typical ignition source for gas turbine engines is the **high-energy capacitor discharge system**, consisting of an exciter unit, two high-tension cables, and two spark igniters. This ignition system produces 60 to 100 sparks per minute, resulting in a ball of fire at the igniter electrodes. Some of these systems produce enough energy to shoot sparks several inches, so care must be taken to avoid a lethal shock during maintenance tests.

A fuel drainage system accomplishes the important task of draining the unburned fuel after engine shutdown. Draining accumulated fuel reduces the possibility of exceeding tailpipe or turbine inlet temperature limits due to an engine fire after shutdown. In addition, draining the unburned fuel helps to prevent gum deposits in the fuel manifold, nozzles, and combustion chambers which are caused by fuel residue.

To accomplish the task of efficiently burning the fuel/air mixture a combustion chamber must

1. mix fuel and air effectively in the best ratio for good combustion.
2. burn the mixture as efficiently as possible.
3. cool the hot combustion gases to a temperature the turbine blades can tolerate.
4. distribute hot gases evenly to the turbine section.

In order to allow the combustion section to mix the incoming fuel and air, ignite the mixture, and cool the combustion gases, airflow through a combustor is divided into primary and secondary paths. Approximately 25 to 35 percent of the incoming air is designated as primary while 65 to 75 percent becomes secondary. Primary, or **combustion air**, is directed inside the liner in the front end of a combustor. As this air enters the combustor, it passes through a set of **swirl vanes**, which gives the air a radial motion and slows down its axial velocity to about five or six feet per second. The reduction in airflow velocity is very important because kerosene-type fuels have a slow flame propagation rate. Therefore, an excessively high velocity airflow could literally blow the flame out of the engine. This malfunction is known as a **flameout**. A vortex created in the flame area provides the turbulence required to properly mix the fuel and air. Once mixed, the combustion process is complete in the first third of a combustor.

The secondary airflow in the combustion section flows at a velocity of several hundred feet per second around the combustor's periphery. This flow of

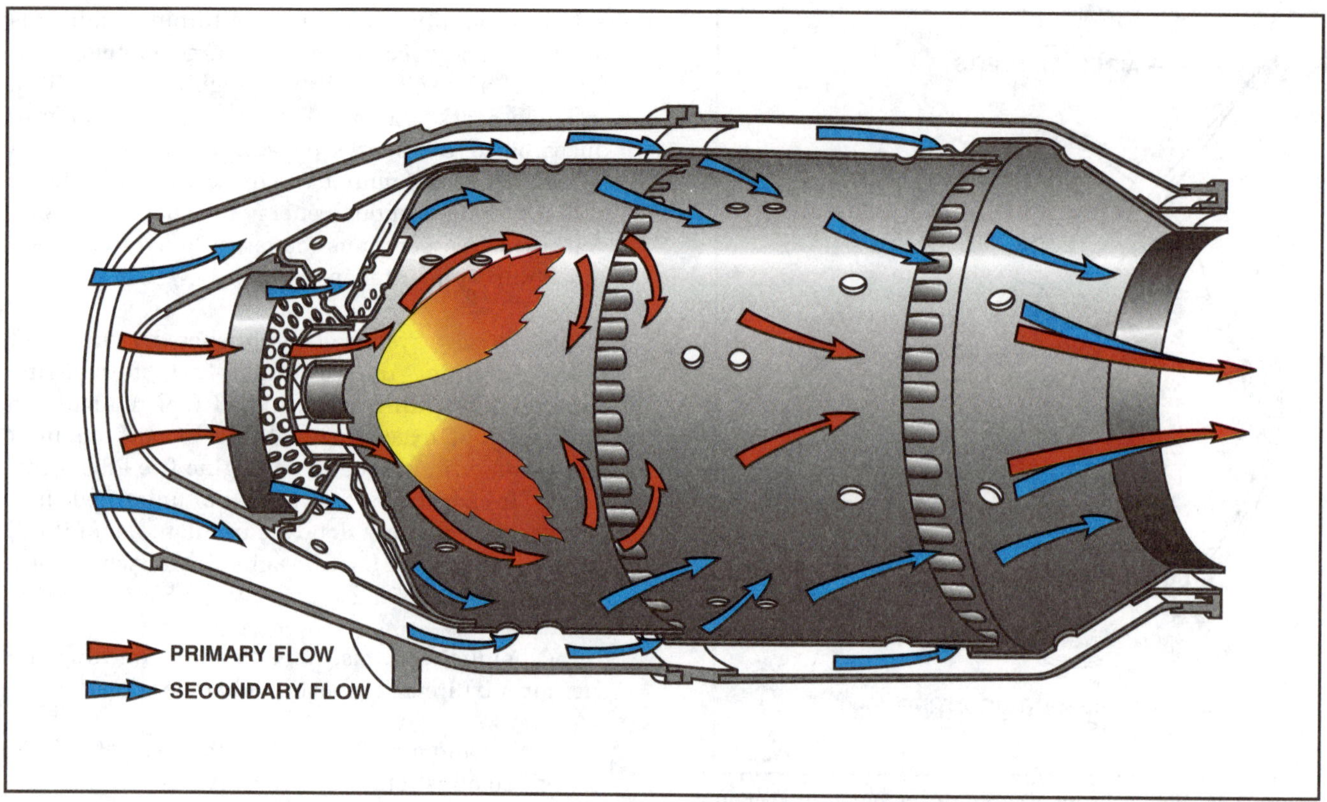

Figure 3-40. As air flows into the combustion section it separates into primary and secondary flows. The primary flow is used to support combustion while the secondary flow cools the hot gases before they enter the turbine section.

air forms a cooling air blanket on both sides of the liner and centers the combustion flames so they do not contact the liner. Some secondary air is slowed and metered into the combustor through the perforations in the liner where it ensures combustion of any remaining unburned fuel. Finally, secondary air mixes with the burned gases and cool air to provide an even distribution of energy to the turbine nozzle at a temperature that the turbine section can withstand. [Figure 3-40]

There are currently three basic types of combustion chambers, the multiple-can type, the annular or basket type, and the can-annular type. Functionally, they are the same but their design and construction is different.

MULTIPLE-CAN TYPE

The multiple-can type combustion chamber consists of a series of individual combustor cans which act as individual burner units. This type of combustion chamber is well suited to centrifugal compressor engines because of the way compressor discharge air is equally divided at the diffuser. Each can is constructed with a perforated stainless steel liner inside the outer case. The inner liner is highly heat resistant and is easily removed for inspection once the combustion can is removed from the engine. Each combustion can has a large degree of curvature which provides a high resistance to warpage. However, the shape is inefficient in terms of the amount of space required and the added weight.

The individual combustors in a typical multiple-can combustion chamber are interconnected with small **flame propagation tubes.** The combustion starts in the two cans equipped with igniter plugs, then the flame travels through the tubes and ignites the fuel/air mixture in the other cans. Each flame propagation tube is actually a small tube surrounded by a larger tube or jacket. The small inner tube carrys the flame between the cans and the outer tube carries airflow between the cans that cools and insulates. There are 8 or 10 cans in a typical multiple-can combustion section. The cans are numbered clockwise when facing the rear of the engine on most American-built engines, with the number one can being on the top. All the combustor cans discharge exhaust gases into an open area at the turbine nozzle inlet. [Figure 3-41]

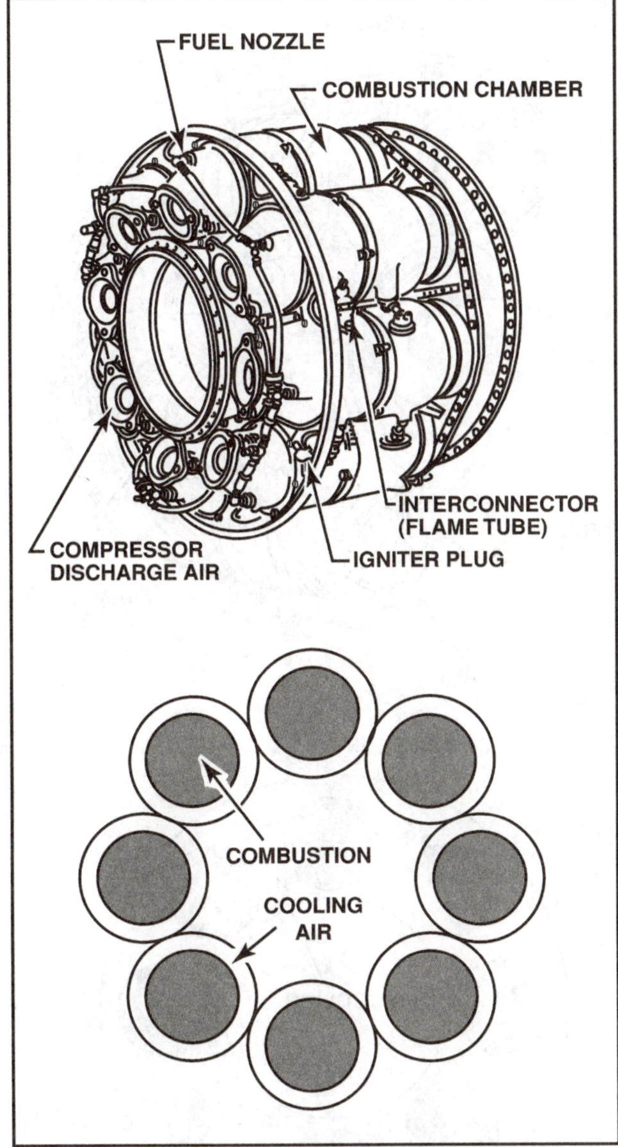

Figure 3-41. Used primarily in early turbine engine designs, multiple-can combustors consisted of a series of individual burner cans arranged radially around an engine. The multiple-can design has the advantage of easy removal of any combustor for maintenance or replacement.

ANNULAR TYPE

Today, annular combustors are commonly used in both small and large engines. The reason for this is that, from a standpoint of thermal efficiency, weight, and physical size, the annular combustor is the most efficient. An annular combustion chamber consists of a housing and perforated inner liner, or basket. The liner is a single unit that encircles the outside of the turbine shaft housing. The shroud can be shaped to contain one or more concentric baskets. An annular combustor with two baskets is known as a double-annular combustion chamber. Normally, the ignition source consists of two spark igniters similar to the type found in multiple-can combustors.

In a conventional annular combustor, airflow enters at the front and is discharged at the rear with primary and secondary airflow much the same as in the multiple-can design. However, unlike the can type combustors, an annular combuster must be removed as a single unit for repair or replacement. This usually involves complete separation of the engine at a major flange. [Figure 3-42]

Some annular combustors are designed so the airflow can reverse direction. These **reverse-flow** combustors serve the same function as the conventional flow type, except the air flows around the chamber and enters from the rear. This results in the combustion gases flowing in the opposite direction of the normal airflow through the engine. This idea was first employed by Whittle in his early designs.

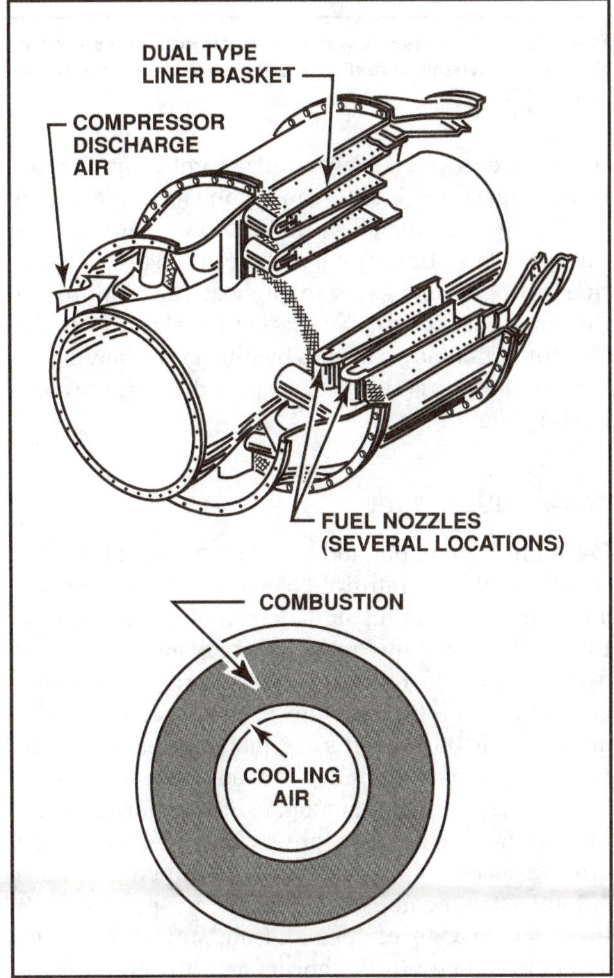

Figure 3-42. An annular combustor has the highest efficiency for its weight of any combustor design. However, the engine must be disassembled to repair or replace an annular combustor. Also, the shallow curvature makes this combustor more susceptible to warping.

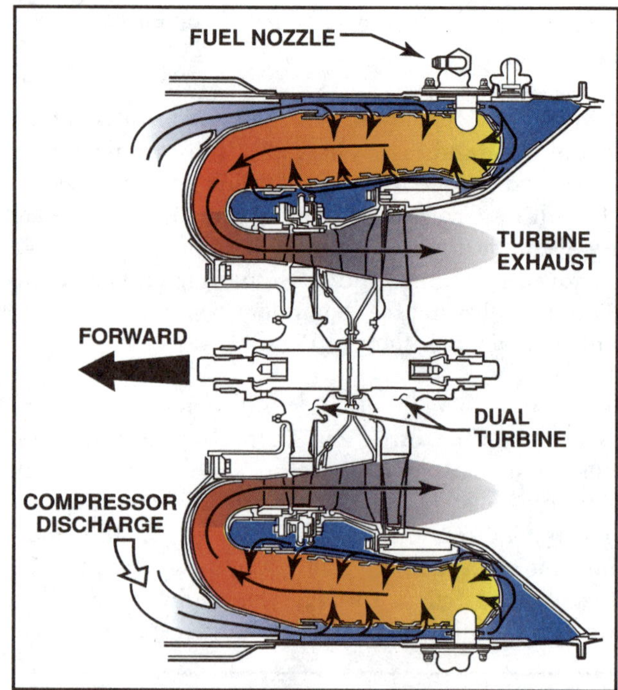

Figure 3-43. A reverse-flow combustor is light and compact. The turbine wheels actually lie within the combustor, rather than behind it.

In a typical reverse-flow annular combustor, the turbine wheels are inside the combustor area rather than downstream, as with the conventional flow designs. This allows for a shorter and lighter engine that uses the hot gases to preheat the compressor discharge air. These factors help make up for the loss of efficiency caused by the gases having to reverse their direction as they pass through the combustor. [Figure 3-43]

CAN-ANNULAR TYPE

Can-annular combustion sections represent a combination of the multiple-can combustor and the annular type combustor. The can-annular combustor was invented by Pratt & Whitney and consists of a removable steel shroud that encircles the entire combustion section. Inside the shroud, or casing, are multiple burner cans assembled radially around the engine axis with bullet-shaped perforated liners. A fuel nozzle cluster is attached to the forward end of each burner can and pre-swirl vanes are placed around each fuel nozzle. The pre-swirl vanes enhance the combustion process by promoting a thorough mixing of fuel and air and slowing the axial air velocity in the burner can. Flame propagation tubes connect the individual liners and two igniter plugs are used for initiating combustion. An individual can and liner is removed and installed as one unit for maintenance. This design combines the ease of overhaul and testing of the multiple-can arrangement with the compactness of the annular combustor. [Figure 3-44]

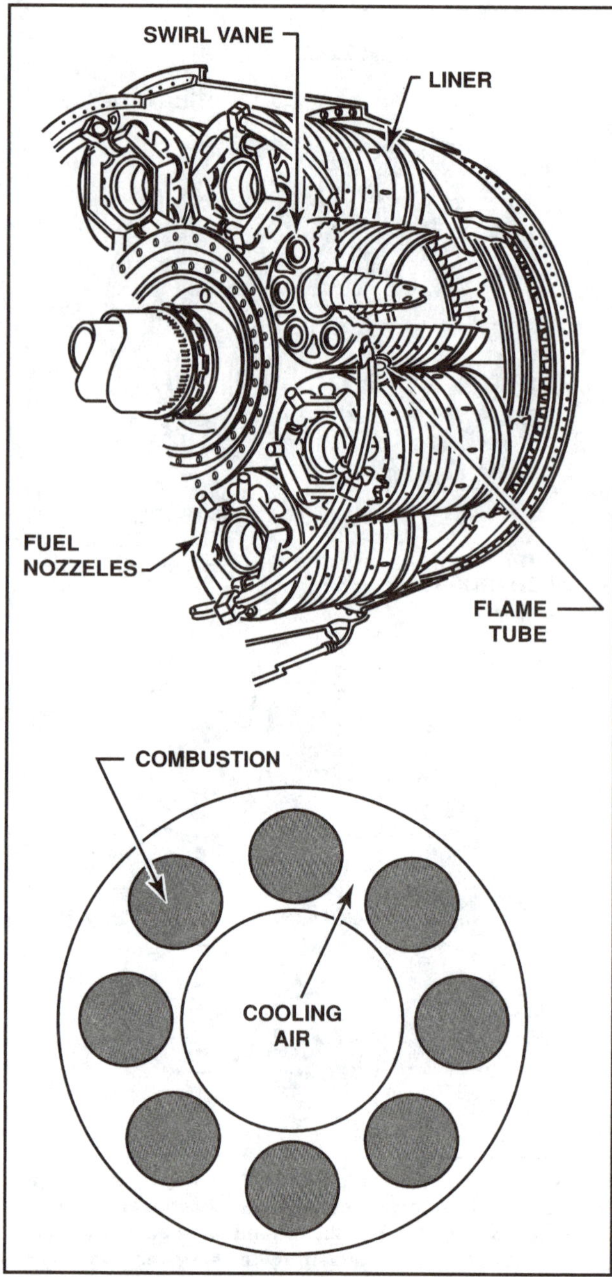

Figure 3-44. A can-annular combustor contains individual burner cans in an annular liner. The short burner cans combine the compact efficiency of the annular type combustor with the ease of the multiple-can combustor maintenance.

FLAMEOUT

As mentioned earlier, a combustion flame can be extinguished by high airflow rates. However, excessively slow airflow rates can also contribute to this problem. Although flameout is uncommon in modern engines, combustion instability can still occur and occasionally causes a complete flameout. Given the correct set of circumstances, turbulent weather, high altitude, slow acceleration, and high-speed maneuvers can induce combustion instability and cause a flameout. There are two types of flameouts, a **lean die-out** and a **rich blow-out**. A lean die-out usually occurs at high altitude where low engine speeds and low fuel pressure form a weak flame that can die out in a normal airflow. On the other hand, a rich blow-out typically occurs during rapid engine acceleration when an overly-rich mixture causes the fuel temperature to drop below the combustion temperature or when there is insufficient airflow to support combustion.

TURBINE SECTION

After the fuel/air mixture is burned in the combustor, its energy must be extracted. A **turbine** transforms a portion of the kinetic energy in the hot exhaust gases into mechanical energy to drive the compressor and accessories. In a turbojet engine, the turbine absorbs approximately 60 to 80% of the total pressure energy from the exhaust gases. The turbine section of a turbojet engine is located downstream of the combustion section and consists of four basic elements; a case, a stator, a shroud, and a rotor. [Figure 3-45]

CASE

The turbine casing encloses the turbine rotor and stator assembly, giving either direct or indirect support to the stator elements. A typical case has flanges on both ends that provide a means of attaching the turbine section to the combustion section and the exhaust assembly.

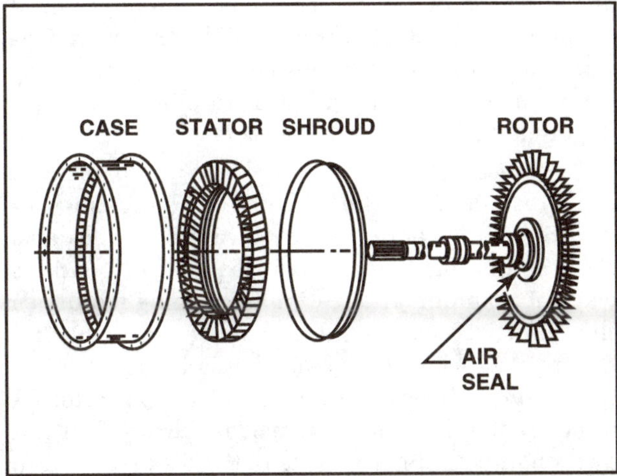

Figure 3-45. The four basic elements of a turbine assembly in a gas turbine engine are the case, stator, shroud, and rotor.

TURBINE STATOR

A stator element is most commonly referred to as the **turbine nozzle**; however, you may also hear the stator elements referred to as the **turbine guide vanes**, or the **nozzle diaphragm**. The turbine nozzle is located directly aft of the combustion section and immediately forward of the turbine wheel. Because of its location, the turbine nozzle is typically exposed to the highest temperatures in a gas turbine engine.

The purpose of the turbine nozzle is to collect the high energy airflow from the combustors and direct the flow to strike the turbine rotor at the appropriate angle. The vanes of a turbine nozzle are contoured and set at such an angle that they form a number of converging nozzles that convert some of the exhaust gases' pressure energy to velocity energy. In addition, the angle of the stator vanes is set in the direction of turbine wheel rotation. Since the gas flow from the nozzle must enter the turbine blade passageway while it is still rotating, it is essential to aim the gas in the general direction of turbine rotation. As a result, the velocity energy of the exhaust gases is more efficiently converted to mechanical energy by the rotor blades.

SHROUD

The turbine nozzle assembly consists of an inner and outer shroud that retains and surrounds the nozzle vanes. The number of vanes employed varies with different types and sizes of engines. The vanes of a turbine nozzle are assembled between the outer and inner shrouds, or rings, in a variety of ways. Although the actual elements may vary slightly in their configuration and construction, there is one similarity among all turbine nozzles: the nozzle vanes must be constructed to allow for thermal expansion. If this is not done, the rapid temperature changes imposed by the engine would cause severe distortion or warping of the nozzle assembly.

The thermal expansion of turbine nozzles is dealt with in several ways. One way requires the vanes to be assembled loosely in the inner and outer shrouds. With this method, the shrouds are built with a series of contoured slots conforming to the shape of an individual vane. The slots are slightly larger than the vanes, and therefore, provide a loose fit. In order to provide the strength and rigidity required, the inner and outer shrouds are encased in an inner and outer support ring. These

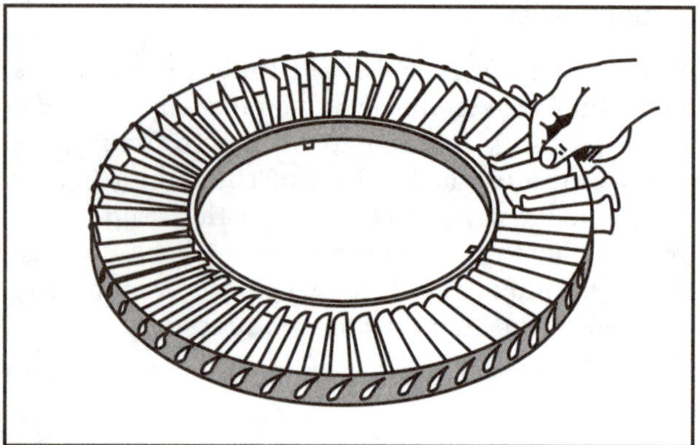

Figure 3-46. A loose fit between the vanes and shrouds allows thermal expansion to occur without warping the turbine nozzle assembly.

support rings also facilitate removal of the nozzle vanes as a unit. Without the support rings, the vanes could fall out as the shrouds were removed. [Figure 3-46]

A second method of attaching the nozzle vanes is to rigidly weld or rivet the vanes into the inner and outer shrouds. To allow for expansion, the inner or outer shroud ring is cut into segments. As thermal expansion takes place, the shrouds expand and close the gaps between the shroud segments, allowing sufficient expansion to prevent stress and warping. [Figure 3-47]

TURBINE ROTOR

The rotating elements of a turbine section consist of a shaft and a turbine rotor, or wheel. The **turbine wheel** is a dynamically balanced unit consisting of blades attached to a rotating disk. The **turbine disk** is the anchoring component for the turbine blades and is bolted or welded to the main shaft. The shaft rotates in bearings that are lubricated by oil between the outer race and the bearing housing. This reduces vibration and allows for a slight misalignment in the shaft.

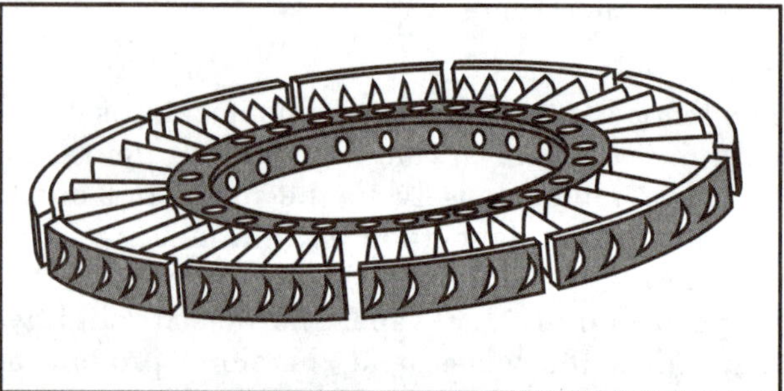

Figure 3-47. When vanes are riveted or welded into segmented shrouds, the gaps between shroud segments allow for thermal expansion.

As the high velocity gases pass through the turbine nozzle and impact the turbine blades, the turbine wheel rotates. In some engines, a single turbine wheel cannot absorb sufficient energy from the exhaust gas to drive the compressor and accessories. Therefore, many engines use multiple turbine stages, each stage consisting of a turbine nozzle and wheel.

The severe centrifugal loads imposed by the high rotational speeds, as well as the elevated operating temperatures exert extreme stress on the turbine blades. At times, these stresses can cause turbine blades to grow in length. If left unchecked, this **growth** or **creep** can result in the turbine blades rubbing against the engine's outer casing.

TURBINE BLADES

Turbine blades are airfoil shaped components designed to extract the maximum amount of energy from the flow of hot gases. Blades are either forged or cast, depending on their alloy composition. Early blades were manufactured from steel forgings; however, today most turbine blades consist of cast nickel-based alloys. In either case, once a blade is forged or cast, it must be finish-ground to the desired shape. As an alternative to metal turbine blades, the development of a blade manufactured from reinforced ceramic material holds promise. Because of ceramic's ability to withstand high temperatures, greater engine efficiencies may be possible. Their initial application is likely to be in small, high speed turbines that operate at very high temperatures.

Turbine blades fit loosely into a turbine disk when an engine is cold, but expand to fit tightly at normal operating temperatures. The most commonly used method for attaching turbine blades is by **fir tree slots** cut into the turbine disk rim and matching bases cast or machined into the turbine blade base. [Figure 3-48]

Once installed, a turbine blade may be retained in its groove by peening, welding, rivets, or locktabs. The peening method is used frequently in various ways. A common application of peening requires a small notch to be ground in the edge of the blade's fir tree root prior to the blade being installed. After the blade is inserted into the disk, the notch is filled by the disk metal, which is "flowed" into it by a small punch mark made in the disk adjacent to the notch. The tool used for this job is similar to a center punch.

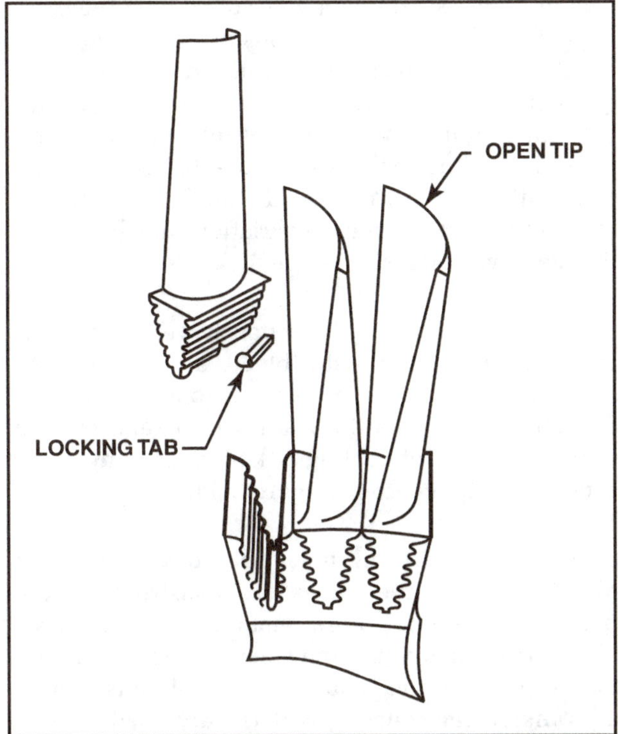

Figure 3-48. The loose fit of a fir tree base allows the base of a turbine blade to expand as it heats to operating temperature.

Turbine blades are generally classified as impulse, reaction, or a combination impulse-reaction type. In a turbine that uses **impulse blades**, the blades merely change the direction of airflow coming from the turbine nozzle and cause relatively no change in gas pressure or velocity. The turbine wheel simply absorbs the force required to change the direction of airflow and converts it to rotary motion. [Figure 3-49]

Reaction turbine blades, on the other hand, produce a turning force based on an aerodynamic action. To do this, the turbine blades form a series of converging ducts that increase gas velocity and reduce pressure. The result is similar to what happens to an airfoil in that the reduced pressure produces a lifting force.

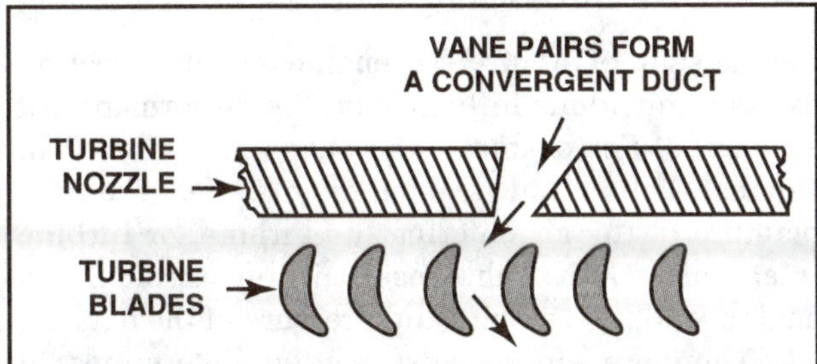

Figure 3-49. In an impulse turbine system, the turbine nozzle vanes form a series of converging ducts that increase the velocity of the exhaust gases. The impulse turbine blades then extract energy from the gases as the blades redirect the flow of high velocity gases.

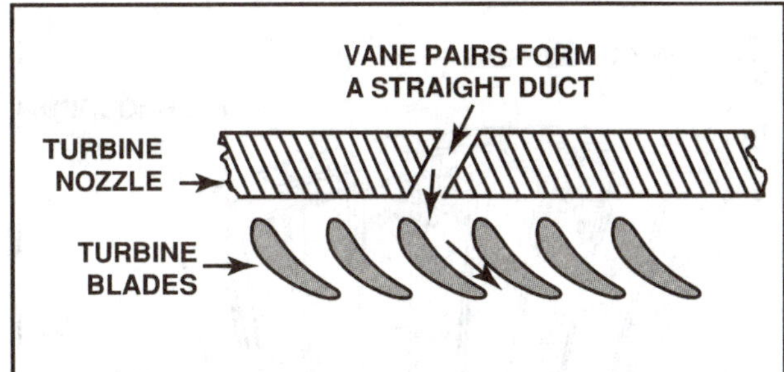

Figure 3-50. The nozzle guide vanes in a reaction turbine direct the exhaust gas flow to strike the turbine blades at a positive angle of attack. The convergent shape between the turbine blades then increases gas velocity and decreases its pressure to create a component of lift that rotates the turbine wheel.

However, in a turbine, the force is exerted in the direction of rotation. [Figure 3-50]

To more evenly distribute the workload along the length of the blade, most modern turbine engines incorporate **impulse-reaction turbine blades**. With this type of blade, the blade base is impulse shaped while the blade tip is reaction shaped. This design creates a uniform velocity and pressure drop across the entire blade length. [Figure 3-51]

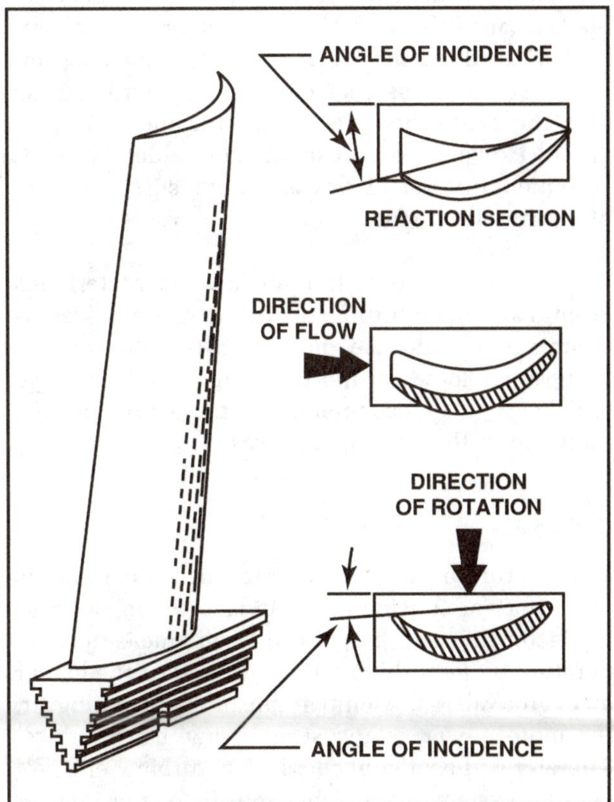

Figure 3-51. To help account for the different rotational speeds along the length of a turbine blade, most turbine engines use impulse-reaction type turbine blades. This type of blade is constructed with an impulse section at its base and a reaction section at its tip.

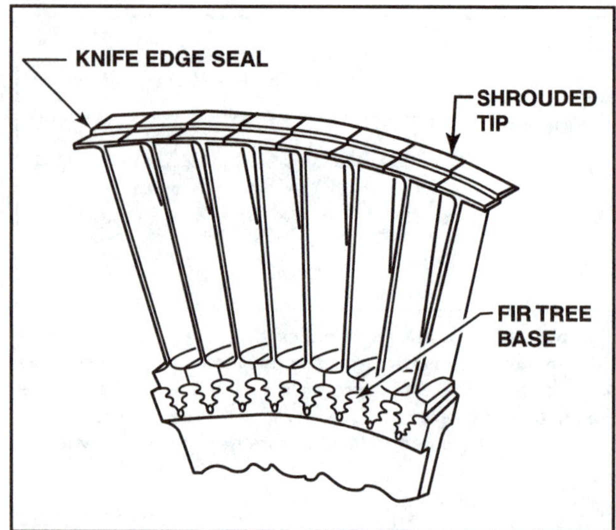

Figure 3-52. Shrouded blades form a band around the turbine wheel perimeter which helps reduce blade vibration and increase efficiency.

Turbine blades can be open or shrouded at their ends. Open ended blades are used on high speed turbines, while shrouded blades are commonly used on turbines having slower rotational speeds. With shrouded blades, a shroud is attached to the tip of each blade. Once installed, the shrouds of the blades contact each other, thereby providing support. This added support reduces vibration substantially. The shrouds also prevent air from escaping over the blade tips, making the turbine more efficient. However, because of the added weight, shrouded turbine blades are more susceptible to blade growth. [Figure 3-52]

To further improve the airflow characteristics around shrouded turbine blades, a knife-edge seal is machined around the outside of the shroud that reduces air losses at the blade tip. The knife-edge seal fits with a close tolerance into a shrouded ring mounted in the outer turbine case.

COOLING

When a turbine section is designed, temperature is an important consideration. In fact, the most limiting factor in running a gas turbine engine is the temperature of the turbine section. However, the higher an engine raises the temperature of the incoming air, the more power, or thrust an engine can produce. Therefore, the effectiveness of a turbine engine's cooling system plays a big role in engine performance. In fact, many cooling systems allow the turbine vane and blade components to operate in a thermal environment 600 to 800 degrees Fahrenheit above the temperature limits of their metal alloys.

One of the most common ways of cooling the components in the turbine section is to use engine bleed air. For example, turbine disks absorb heat from hot gases passing near their rim and from the blades through conduction. Because of this, disk rim temperatures are normally well above the temperature of the disk portion nearest the shaft. To limit the effect of these temperature variations, cooling air is directed over each side of the disk.

To sufficiently cool turbine nozzle vanes and turbine blades, compressor bleed air is typically directed in through the hollow blades and out through holes in the tip, leading edge, and trailing edge. This type of cooling is known as **convection cooling** or **film cooling**. [Figure 3-53]

In addition to drilling holes in a turbine vane or blade, some nozzle vanes are constructed of a porous, high-temperature material. In this case, bleed air is ducted into the vanes and exits through the porous material. This type of cooling is known as **transpiration cooling** and is only used on stationary nozzle vanes.

Modern engine designs incorporate many combinations of air cooling methods that use low and high pressure air for both internal and surface cooling of turbine vanes and blades. However, to provide additional cooling, the turbine vane shrouds may also be perforated with cooling holes.

COUNTER-ROTATING TURBINES

While not common in large engines, some small turboshaft engines feature counter-rotating turbine wheels. Counter-rotating turbines are chosen by engine designers for their effectiveness in dampening gyroscopic effects and reducing engine vibration, not for aerodynamic reasons.

EXHAUST SECTION

The design of a turbojet engine exhaust section exerts tremendous influence on the performance of an engine. For example, the shape and size of an exhaust section and its components affect the temperature of the air entering the turbine, or **turbine inlet temperature**, the mass airflow through the engine, and the velocity and pressure of the exhaust jet. Therefore, an exhaust section determines to some extent the amount of thrust developed.

A typical exhaust section extends from the rear of the turbine section to the point where the exhaust

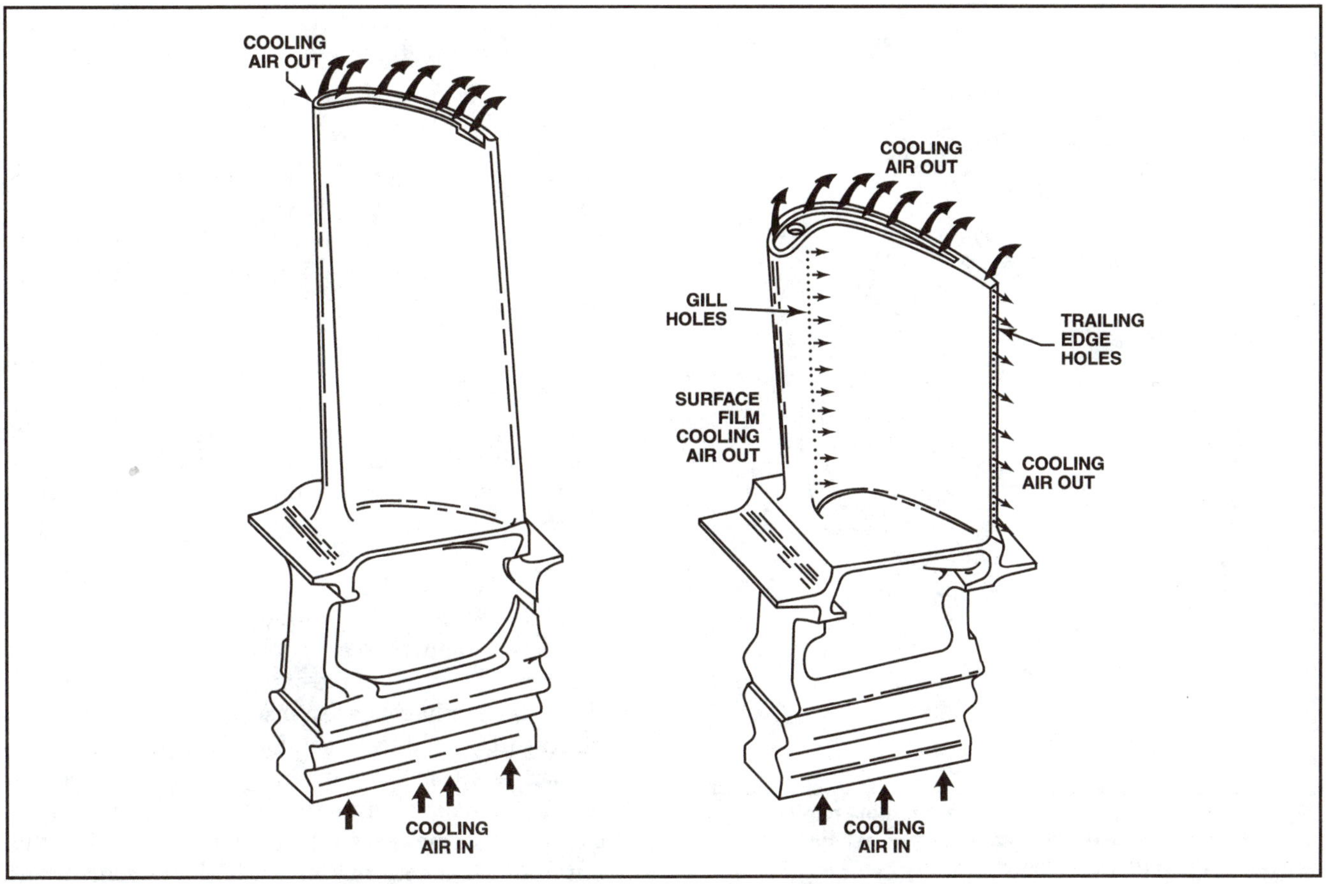

Figure 3-53. An internally cooled blade receives cooling air at the root and expels the air at the tip or through holes in the leading and trailing edges.

gases leave the engine. An exhaust section is comprised of several components including the exhaust cone, exhaust duct or tailpipe, and exhaust nozzle. [Figure 3-54]

EXHAUST CONE

A typical exhaust cone assembly consists of an **outer duct**, or **shell**, an **inner cone**, or **tail cone**, three or more radial hollow **struts**, and a group of **tie**

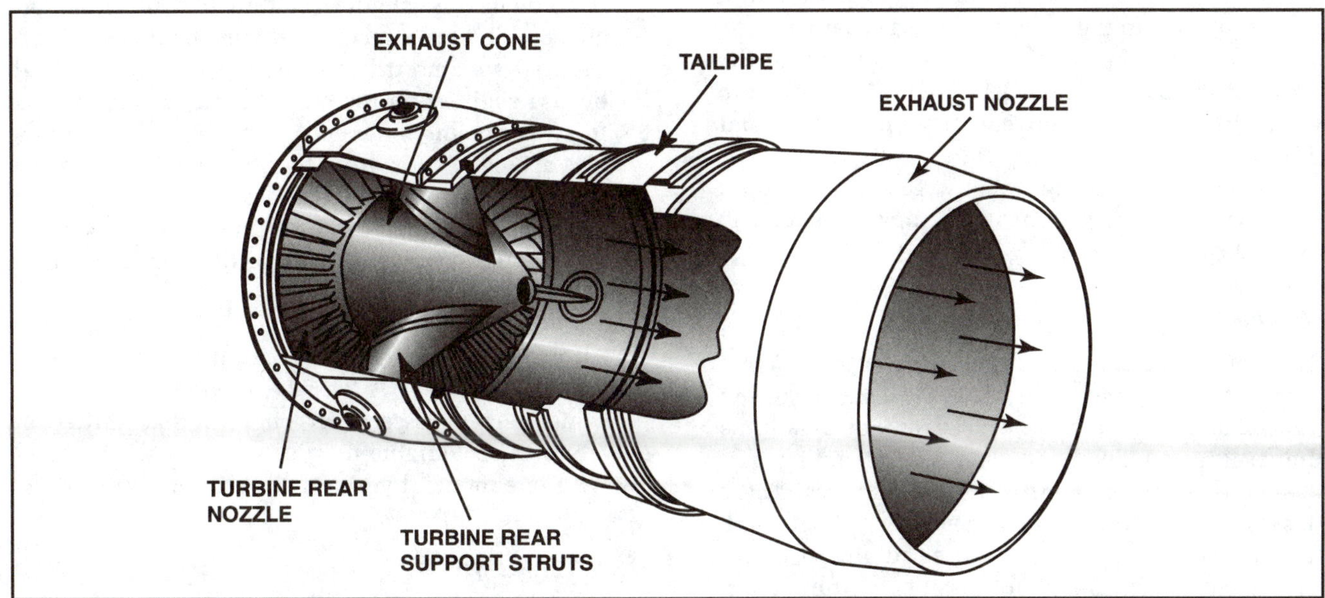

Figure 3-54. A typical exhaust section has an exhaust cone, tailpipe, and exhaust nozzle. The exhaust cone is considered the rearmost component of a typical gas turbine engine. The tailpipe and exhaust nozzle are usually classified as airframe components.

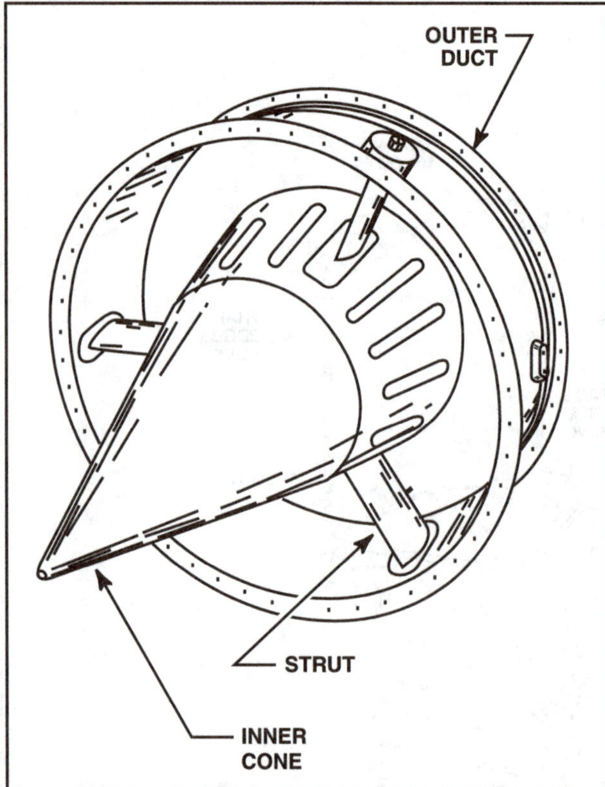

Figure 3-55. The exhaust cone is the rearmost engine component. It straightens and smooths the exhaust gas to extract the greatest possible thrust.

rods that assist the struts in centering the inner cone within the outer duct. The outer duct is usually made of stainless steel and attaches to the rear flange of the turbine case. [Figure 3-55]

The purpose of an exhaust cone assembly is to channel and collect turbine discharge gases into a single jet. Due to the diverging passage between the outer duct and inner cone, gas velocity within the exhaust cone decreases slightly while gas pressure rises. Radial struts between the outer shell and inner cone support the inner cone, and help straighten the swirling exhaust gases that would otherwise exit the turbine at an approximate angle of 45 degrees.

TAILPIPE

A tailpipe is an extension of the exhaust section that directs exhaust gases safely from the exhaust cone to the exhaust, or jet nozzle. The use of a tailpipe imposes a penalty on an engine's operating efficiency due to heat and duct friction losses. These losses cause a drop in the exhaust gas velocity and, hence, the thrust. Tailpipes are used almost exclusively with engines that are installed within an aircraft's fuselage to protect the surrounding airframe. Engines installed in a nacelle or pod, however, often require no tailpipe, in which case the exhaust nozzle is mounted directly to the exhaust cone assembly.

EXHAUST NOZZLE

An exhaust, or jet nozzle, provides the exhaust gases with a final boost in velocity. An exhaust nozzle mounts to the rear of a tailpipe, if a tailpipe is required, or to the rear flange of the exhaust duct if no tailpipe is necessary.

Two types of exhaust nozzle designs used on aircraft are the converging design, and the converging-diverging design. On a converging exhaust nozzle, the nozzle diameter decreases from front to back. This convergent shape produces a venturi that accelerates the exhaust gases and increases engine thrust.

The diameter of a converging-diverging duct decreases, then increases from front to back. The converging portion of the exhaust nozzle accelerates the turbine exhaust gases to supersonic speed at the narrowest part of the duct. Once the gases are moving at the speed of sound they are accelerated further in the nozzle's divergent portion, so the exhaust gases exit the nozzle well above the speed of sound. For additional information on both convergent and convergent-divergent exhaust nozzles, refer to Chapter 6, Section B.

On fan or bypass type engines, there are two gas streams venting to the atmosphere. High temperature gases are discharged by the turbine, while a cool airmass is moved rearward by the fan section. In a low by-pass engine, the flow of cool and hot air are combined in a **mixer unit** that ensures mixing of the two streams prior to exiting the engine. High bypass engines, on the other hand, usually exhaust the two streams separately through two sets of nozzles arranged coaxially around the exhaust nozzle. However, on some high bypass engines, a common or integrated nozzle is sometimes used to partially mix the hot and cold gases prior to their ejection. [Figure 3-56]

An exhaust nozzle opening can have either a fixed or variable area. A variable geometry nozzle is sometimes necessary on engines that utilize an afterburner. Variable nozzles are typically operated with pneumatic, hydraulic, or electric controls.

AFTERBURNERS

Afterburners are used to accelerate the exhaust gases, which in turn, increases thrust. An afterburner is

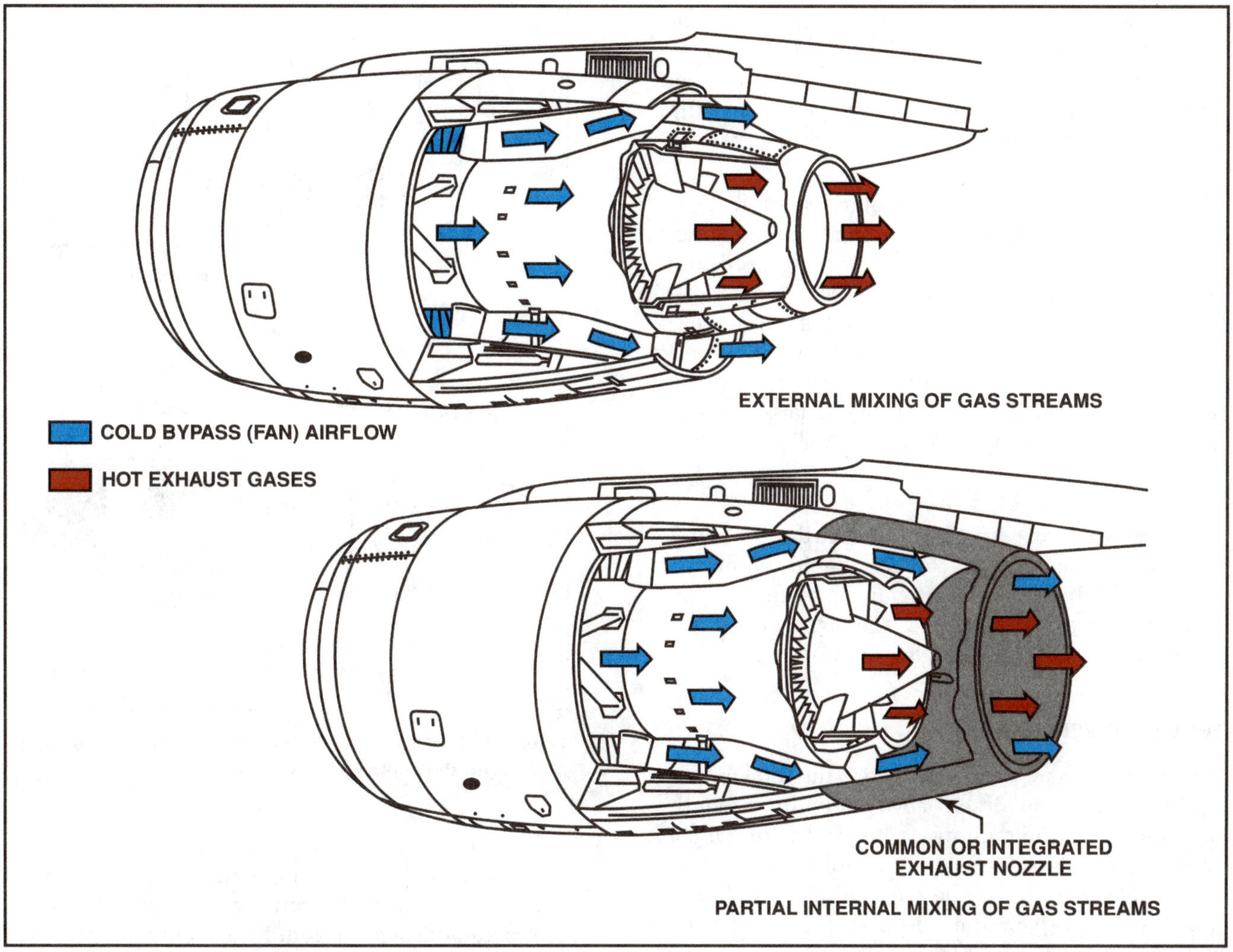

Figure 3-56. On some high bypass engines, cold bypass air mixes with hot exhaust gases after the gases exit the engine. Other high bypass engines use a common or integrated exhaust nozzle that partially mixes the gas streams internally.

typically installed immediately aft of the last stage turbine and forward of the exhaust nozzle. The components that make up an afterburner include the fuel manifold, an ignition source, and a flame holder. [Figure 3-57]

The addition of an afterburner to a gas turbine engine is made possible by the fact that the gases in the tailpipe still contain a large quantity of oxygen. If you recall, approximately 25 percent of a compressor's discharge air is used to support combustion, while the remaining 75 percent is used for cooling. Once the cooling air passes through an engine, a portion of it is mixed with the exhaust gases at the rear of the turbine section. The tailpipe entrance is fitted with a **fuel manifold**, consisting of a set of afterburner fuel nozzles, or **spray-bars**, that inject fuel into the tailpipe. The fuel and air mix, then ignite and burn in the afterburner. The additional heat generated by combustion accelerates the exhaust gases and creates additional thrust.

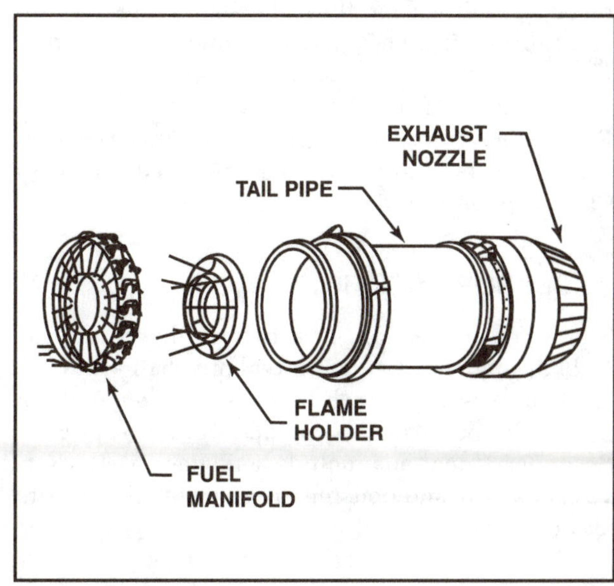

Figure 3-57. An afterburner is used to increase thrust and consists of a fuel manifold, an ignition source, and a flame holder.

To ensure thorough fuel-air mixing, a tubular grid or spoke-shaped obstruction, called a **flame holder**, is placed downstream of the fuel nozzles. The presence of the flame holder creates turbulence, causing the approaching gases to swirl and thoroughly mix.

The use of an afterburner dramatically increases the temperature and thrust produced by an engine. Therefore, when an afterburner is being used, the area of the exhaust nozzle must be increased. If this is not done, an area of back pressure at the rear of the turbine would be created which could increase the turbine temperature beyond its safe level. By increasing the size of the exhaust nozzle, the exhaust gas temperature can be reduced to tolerable limits.

Afterburning is used primarily on military aircraft to assist in takeoff or produce rapid climb-out speeds. Afterburners can provide as much as a 100 percent increase in thrust at the expense of fuel flows three to five times higher than normal.

THRUST REVERSERS

On most turbine engine aircraft, the brakes are unable to slow the aircraft adequately during landing rollout. The amount of kinetic energy that must be dissipated is so great that, if only brakes were used, brake wear would be prohibitive. In addition, the heat buildup in the wheel area generated by braking could lead to a brake fire. Therefore, most turbojet and turbofan powered aircraft are fitted with thrust reversers to assist in braking. Thrust reversers redirect the flow of exhaust gases to provide thrust in the opposite direction. In other words, thrust reversers provide a force in the opposite direction of travel that slows forward motion. For further information on the various types of thrust reverser systems that are used, refer to Chapter 5, Section B.

ACCESSORY SECTION

The accessory section, or **accessory drive**, of a gas turbine engine is used to power both engine and aircraft accessories such as electric generators, hydraulic pumps, fuel pumps, and oil pumps. Secondary functions include acting as an oil reservoir, or sump, and housing the accessory drive gears and reduction gears.

The accessory drive location is selected to keep the engine profile to a minimum for streamlining. Typical places where an accessory drive is located include the engine's midsection, or the front or rear of the engine. However, inlet and exhaust locations usually determine if front or rear-mounted gearboxes are a design option. Rear-mounted gearboxes typically allow the narrowest engine diameter and lowest drag configuration. In a few rare instances, the engine design dictates that the accessory drive be located at the top of the engine near the compressor. [Figure 3-58]

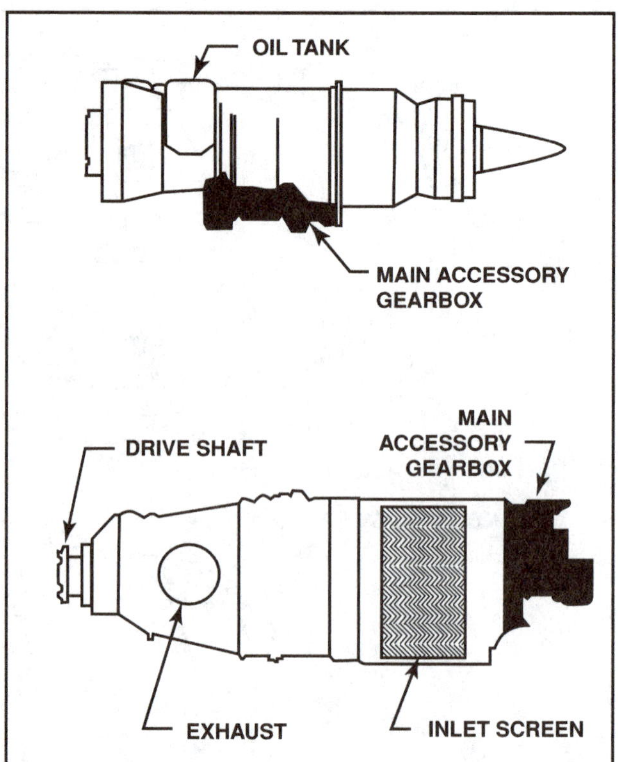

Figure 3-58. Accessory drives are typically designed to blend with the engine profile to minimize drag.

The power needed to drive the accessories is typically taken from the engine's main power shaft. A set of beveled gears is used to drive an accessory shaft which, in turn, drives an accessory gearbox. The accessory gearbox then distributes power to each accessory drive pad. Since turbine engines operate at a relatively high rpm, reduction gearing is necessary in the accessory drive system to provide appropriate drive speeds for the accessories. In some installations, an **intermediate** or **transfer gearbox** is necessary to obtain the appropriate reduction gearing necessary for the accessories. [Figure 3-59]

The more accessories an engine has, the greater the power needed to drive the accessory gearbox. In fact, the accessory drive system on a large high bypass engine can require as much as 500 horsepower from the engine.

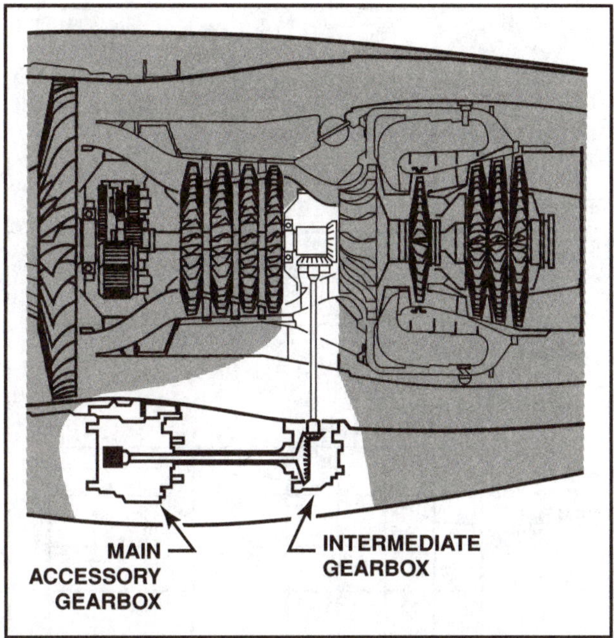

Figure 3-59. With a typical waist mounted accessory section, a radial shaft geared to the main engine shaft transfers power to the drive pads through an intermediate gearbox.

ENGINE STATION NUMBERING

Engine manufacturers usually assign station numbers to several points along a turbine engine's gas path. These numbered locations are similar to fuselage stations, and provide a technician with a means of rapidly locating certain engine areas during maintenance. Station numbers also establish locations for taking pressure and temperature readings. For example, engine pressure ratio, or EPR, compares air pressure at the engine inlet with air pressure at the exhaust to determine engine thrust. Standard labels are used to identify the locations EPR readings are taken because different engines have different types of inlet and exhaust ducts. The engine inlet is station P_{t2}, which means pressure total at station 2. By the same token, turbine discharge pressure is taken at station P_{t7}. Engine pressure ratio is therefore expressed by the ratio $P_{t7} : P_{t2}$. Engine stations are also designated by the label T_t, meaning temperature total for engine instruments that require temperature information. For example, engine inlet temperature is taken at station T_{t2}. [Figure 3-60]

NOISE SUPPRESSION

Some of the energy released from the burning fuel in a jet engine is unintentionally converted to noise. With increasing air traffic around densely populated areas, noise control has become a big issue that impacts both engine designers and operators. Much of the noise produced by a turbine engine results when hot, high-velocity gases mix with cold, low-velocity air surrounding the engine. This high-intensity noise includes both low- and high-frequency vibrations, with low frequencies being predominant.

Increasing use of turbofan engines has probably done more to reduce noise levels both inside the aircraft cabin and on the ground than any other factor. Turbofan engines seldom require noise suppressors because their exhaust sections are designed to mix the hot and cold gas streams prior to their release into the atmosphere, which greatly reduces exhaust noise.

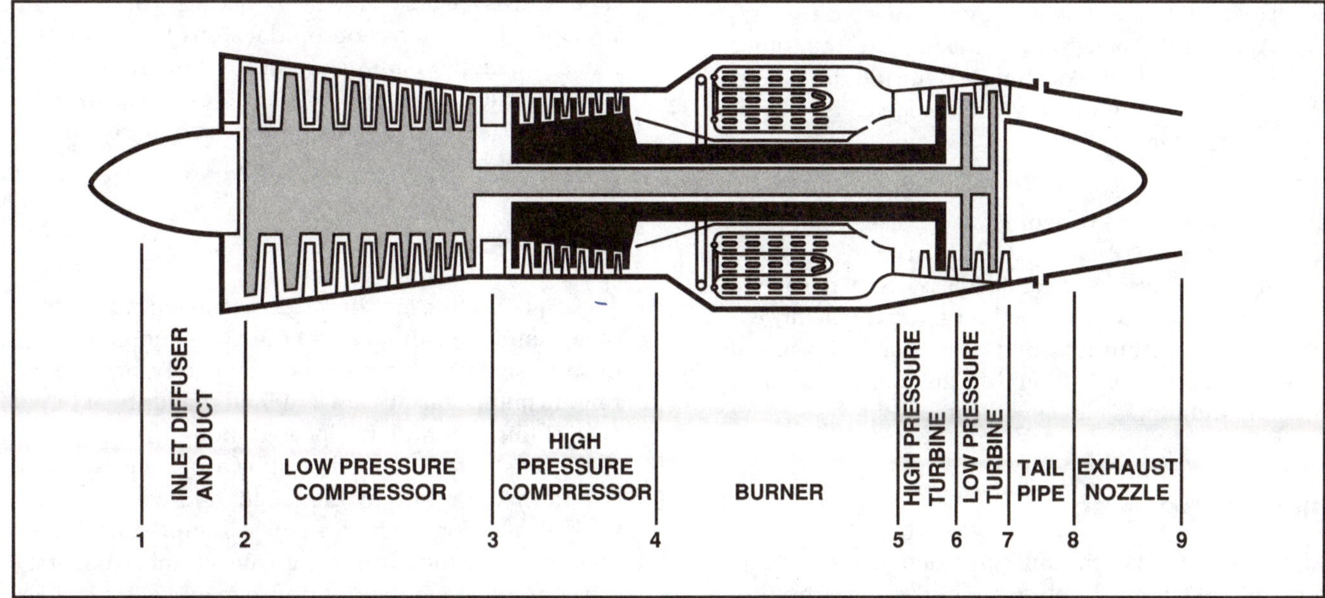

Figure 3-60. Engine station numbers provide a standard means of identifying points along an engine's gas path.

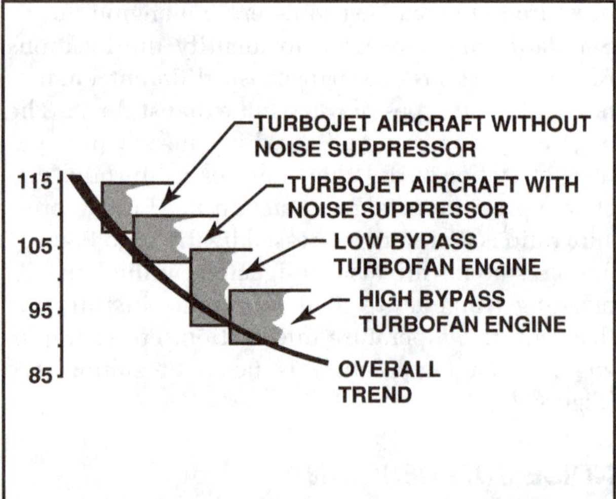

Figure 3-61. By referring to the graph above, you can see that the decibel level of early turbojet aircraft without noise suppression equipment typically exceeded 110 decibels. In comparison, modern high bypass turbofan engines produce less than 100 decibels of sound.

Turbojet engines, especially older designs, frequently require additional noise suppression equipment. The additional equipment typically includes a device that breaks up airflow behind the tail cone, and some new forms of sound insulating material. In addition, some airframe components are being redesigned and installed as noise reduction kits to meet new Federal standards.

The sound intensity of engine noise levels is measured in **decibels** (db). A decibel is the ratio of one sound to another. One db is the smallest change in sound intensity that the human ear can detect. Approximately 60 db is a comfortable level for conversation and background music. On the other hand, loud music peaks at more than 100 db. Sound that reaches approximately 130 db can cause physical pain. [Figure 3-61]

To help answer the concerns over noise around airports, the Federal Aviation Administration has established guidelines for aircraft operators that specify maximum noise limits based on aircraft weight. All older aircraft that utilize louder turbojet engines were given a grace period to modify the engines to meet the maximum noise levels. [Figure 3-62]

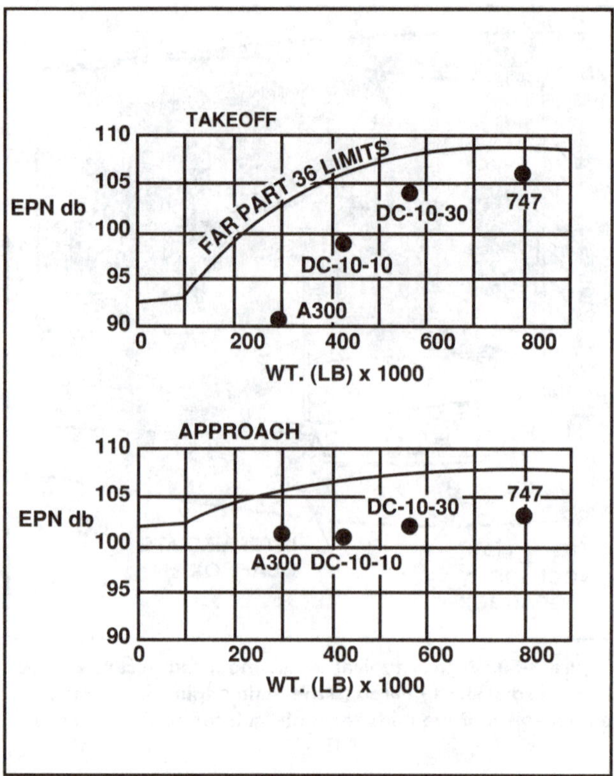

Figure 3-62. The curves on the two graphs shown here represent the maximum decibel levels aircraft are allowed to produce during the takeoff and approach phases of flight. Below each curve are the decibel levels produced by different aircraft.

ENGINE MOUNTS

Engine mount design and construction for gas turbine engines is relatively simple. Since gas turbine engines produce little torque, they do not need heavily constructed mounts. The mounts do, however, support the engine weight and allow for transfer of stresses created by the engine to the aircraft structure. On a typical wing mounted turbofan engine, the engine is attached to the aircraft by two to four mounting brackets. However, because of induced propeller loads, a turboprop develops higher torque loads, so engine mounts are proportionally heavier. By the same token, turboshaft engines used in helicopters are equipped with stronger and more numerous mount locations. [Figure 3-63]

BEARINGS

The combination of compressor and turbine rotors on a common shaft make up the main engine power, or rotor shaft, which must be adequately supported. Engine main bearings are assigned that critical function of support and are located along the length of the rotor shaft. The number of bearings necessary is determined, in part, by the length and weight of the rotor shaft. For example, since a split-spool axial compressor typically has a greater number of rotating components it requires more main bearings than a centrifugal compressor.

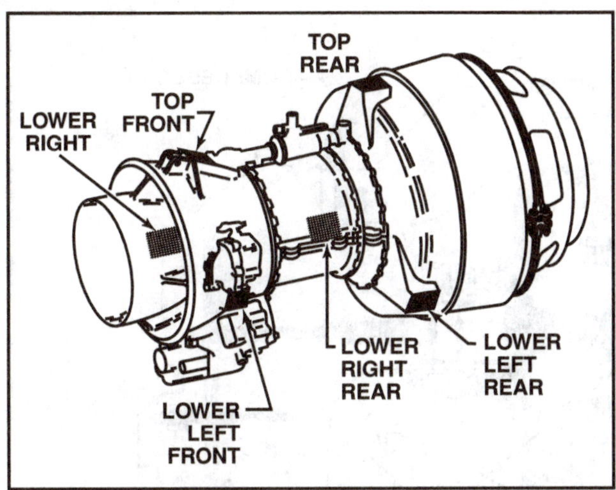

Figure 3-63. Turboshaft engines experience higher torque loads and thus require stronger engine mounts.

Generally, ball and roller bearings are used to support an engine's main rotor shaft. Both ball and roller bearing assemblies are encased in strong housings with inner and outer races that provide support, and hold lubricating oil. These type bearings are preferable because they

1. offer little rotational resistance.
2. enable precision alignment of rotating elements.
3. tolerate high momentary overloads.
4. are easily replaced.
5. are relatively inexpensive.
6. are simple to cool, lubricate, and maintain.
7. accommodate both radial and axial loads.
8. are relatively resistant to elevated temperatures.

A special type of roller bearing that is sometimes used in turbine engines is the **oil-dampened bearing.** With this type of bearing, oil is routed into a cavity formed by the bearing housing and bearing race. Once the oil within this cavity is pressurized by the engine's lubrication system, an oil film is produced. The oil film effectively dampens rotor vibrations and compensates for slight misalignments in rotor segments.

Disadvantages of both ball and roller bearings include their vulnerability to damage caused by foreign matter and tendency to fail without appreciable warning. Therefore, proper lubrication and sealing against entry of foreign matter is essential. Commonly used types of oil seals are labyrinth, helical thread, and carbon.

A **labyrinth seal** differs from most seals in that the seal does not press or rub against an outer surface to

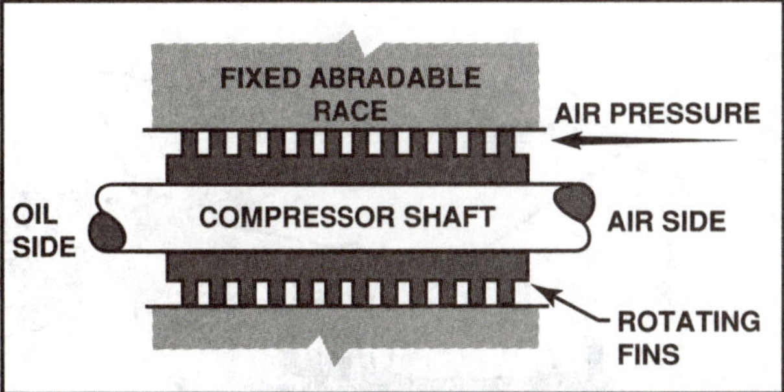

Figure 3-64. The rotating fins of a labyrinth seal do not touch their outer fixed race to create a seal. Instead, air pressure is used to prevent oil from leaking past the seal.

create a seal. Instead, each seal consists of a series of rotating fins that come very close, but do not touch a fixed abradable race. With this type of seal, air pressure on one side of the seal leaks past each fin, decreasing the air pressure at each fin. By the time the air reaches the opposite side of the seal, its pressure is near zero. Therefore, the positive pressure prevents oil from leaking past the seal. [Figure 3-64]

Helical seals are similar to labyrinth seals except the helical seals depend on reverse threading to stop oil leakage. **Carbon seals** are completely different in that they are spring-loaded to hold the carbon ring against the rotating shaft, much like carbon brushes in an electric motor.

TURBOPROP ENGINES

A turboprop engine is a gas turbine engine that drives a propeller to produce thrust. Turboprops, like all gas turbine engines, have a compressor section, combustion section, turbine section, and exhaust section. These sections carry out the same functions as if they were installed in a turbojet engine. However, a turboprop engine is designed with a few differences. For example, the turbine of a turboprop engine extracts up to 85 percent of the engine's total power output to drive the propeller. To do this, most turboprop engines utilize multiple stage turbines. In addition, the turbine blades in a turboprop engine are designed to extract more energy from the exhaust gases than the blades found in a turbojet engine.

In addition to the turbine used to drive the compressor and accessories, most turboprop engines use a free turbine to drive a propeller. The **free turbine** is an independent turbine that is not mechanically connected to the main turbine. This free turbine, or **power turbine,** is placed in the exhaust stream

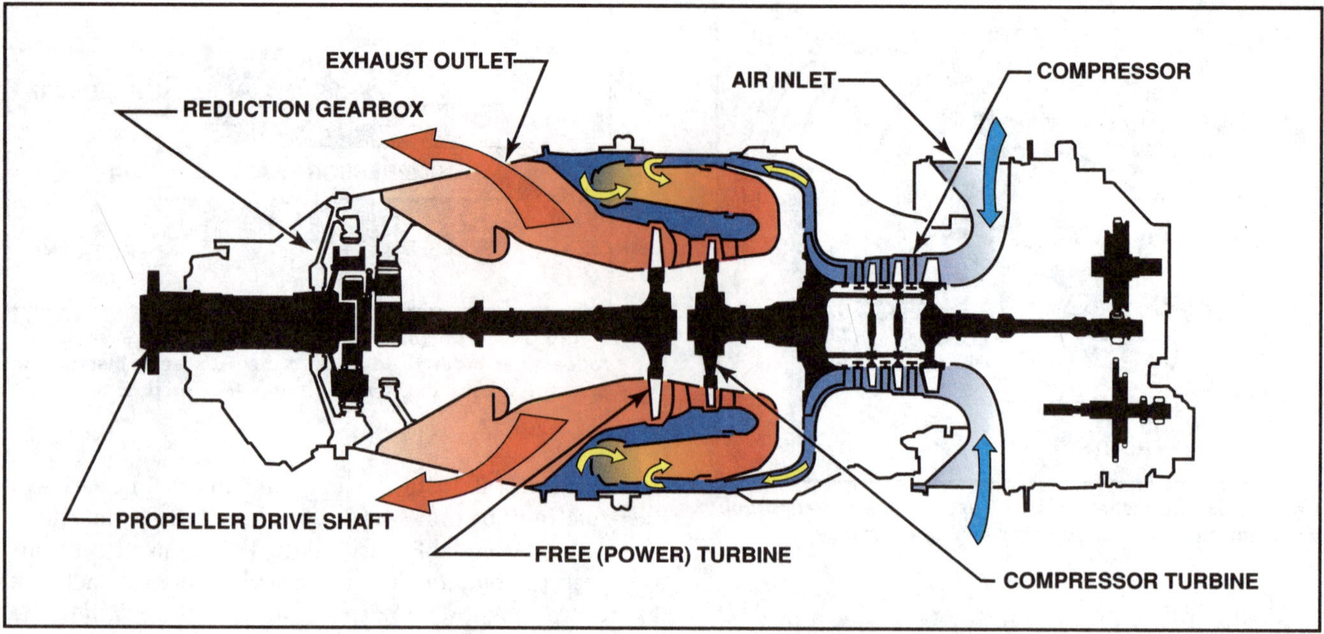

Figure 3-65. Propellers driven by a free turbine rotate independently of the compressor turbine.

downstream from the main turbine and is dedicated to driving only the propeller. [Figure 3-65]

A second method of transferring the exhaust gas energy to the propeller is through a fixed shaft. In this case, the main turbine typically has an additional turbine wheel that extracts the energy needed to drive a propeller. With these **fixed shaft engines**, the main power shaft goes directly into a reduction gearbox to convert the high-speed low torque turbine output into low-speed high torque energy to drive a propeller.

To prevent the propeller on a turboprop engine from driving the turbine, a sophisticated propeller control system must be used to adjust propeller pitch as necessary to match the engine's output. For example, in normal cruise flight, both the propeller and engine rpm remain constant. Therefore, in order to maintain a constant-speed condition, the propeller's blade angle and fuel flow must be adjusted simultaneously. In other words, when fuel flow is increased, the propeller's pitch must also increase.

TURBOSHAFT ENGINES

Turboshaft engines are gas turbine engines that operate something other than a propeller by delivering power to a shaft. Turboshaft engines are similar to turboprop engines, and in some instances, both use the same design. Like turboprops, turboshaft engines use almost all the energy in the exhaust gases to drive an output shaft. The power may be taken directly from the engine turbine, or the shaft may be driven by its own free turbine. Like free turbines in turboprop engines, a free turbine in a turboshaft engine is not mechanically coupled to the engine's main rotor shaft, so it may operate at its own speed. Free turbine designs are used extensively in current production model engines. Turboshaft engines are frequently used to power helicopters and auxiliary power units aboard large commercial aircraft.

AUXILIARY POWER UNITS

Turbine powered transport aircraft require large amounts of power for starting and operation. For example, large amounts of electrical power are sometimes needed for passenger amenities such as lighting, entertainment, and food preparation. In addition, engine starting and ground air conditioning require a high-pressure, high-volume pneumatic air source that frequently is not available at remote airports. To meet these demands for ground power when the aircraft engines are not running, most large turbine aircraft are equipped with **auxiliary power units**, or **APUs**.

A typical APU consists of a small turbine powerplant driving an electric generator identical to those mounted on the aircraft's engines. In addition, an APU's compressor supplies bleed air to a load compressor for heating, cooling, anti-ice, and engine starting. As with any other gas turbine engine, bleed air loads generally place the greatest demand on an APU.

An APU is typically started using its own electric starter motor and aircraft battery power. With fuel supplied from one of the aircraft's main fuel tanks, an APU can start, provide electric power, heat or cool the cabin, and start the main engines without the aid of any ground or portable power source.

After an APU is started, it runs at its rated speed regardless of the electrical and pneumatic loads imposed. To do this, however, an APU's fuel control unit must automatically adjust the fuel flow. For example, if APU bleed air is used to start one of the aircraft's engines, the APU's fuel control unit automatically meters enough extra fuel to satisfy the load increase, keeping the APU on-speed. A heavily loaded APU running near its maximum exhaust gas temperature is protected by a load control valve that modulates the pneumatic load to maintain a safe operating temperature. Therefore, if the APU temperature approaches a critical level, the pneumatic load is automatically reduced to prevent overheating.

To keep from damaging an APU, most manufacturers specify a cool-down period before the APU may be shut down. This cool-down period typically requires that the bleed valve be closed and the exhaust gas temperature (EGT) stabilized. A typical cool-down period is three minutes. This minimizes the possibility of thermal shock that can occur when a heavily loaded, hot APU engine is abruptly shut down. [Figure 3-66]

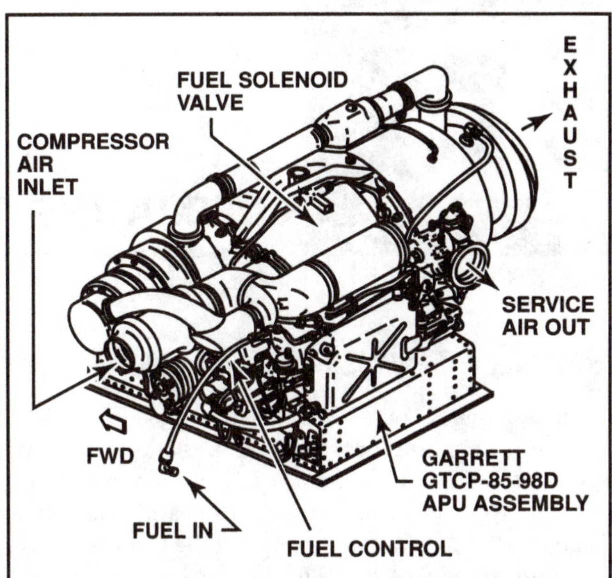

Figure 3-66. The Garrett GTCP-85-98D APU assembly provides on-board aircraft electrical and pneumatic power for ground operations.

OPERATING PRINCIPLES

ENERGY TRANSFORMATION

Like the piston engine, a gas turbine engine is a form of **heat engine** that converts the chemical energy of fuel into heat energy. Once converted, the heat energy causes an increase in gas pressure that is converted into kinetic energy in the form of a high velocity stream of air. The kinetic energy is then converted into mechanical energy when the expanding gases rotate a series of turbine wheels that drive a compressor and accessories. In the case of turboprop or turboshaft engines, the expanding gases may also drive a second power turbine which drives a propeller or gearbox.

ENERGY TRANSFORMATION CYCLE

The energy transformation cycle in a gas turbine engine is known as the **Brayton cycle** or **constant pressure cycle**. The Brayton cycle is similar to the four-stroke cycle in that an intake, compression, combustion, and exhaust event occur in both cycles. However, unlike a piston engine, all four events happen simultaneously and continuously in a gas turbine engine. This gives the gas turbine engine the unique ability to produce power continuously. There is a downside, however, in that a gas turbine engine must burn a great deal of fuel to support the continuous production of power. [Figure 3-67]

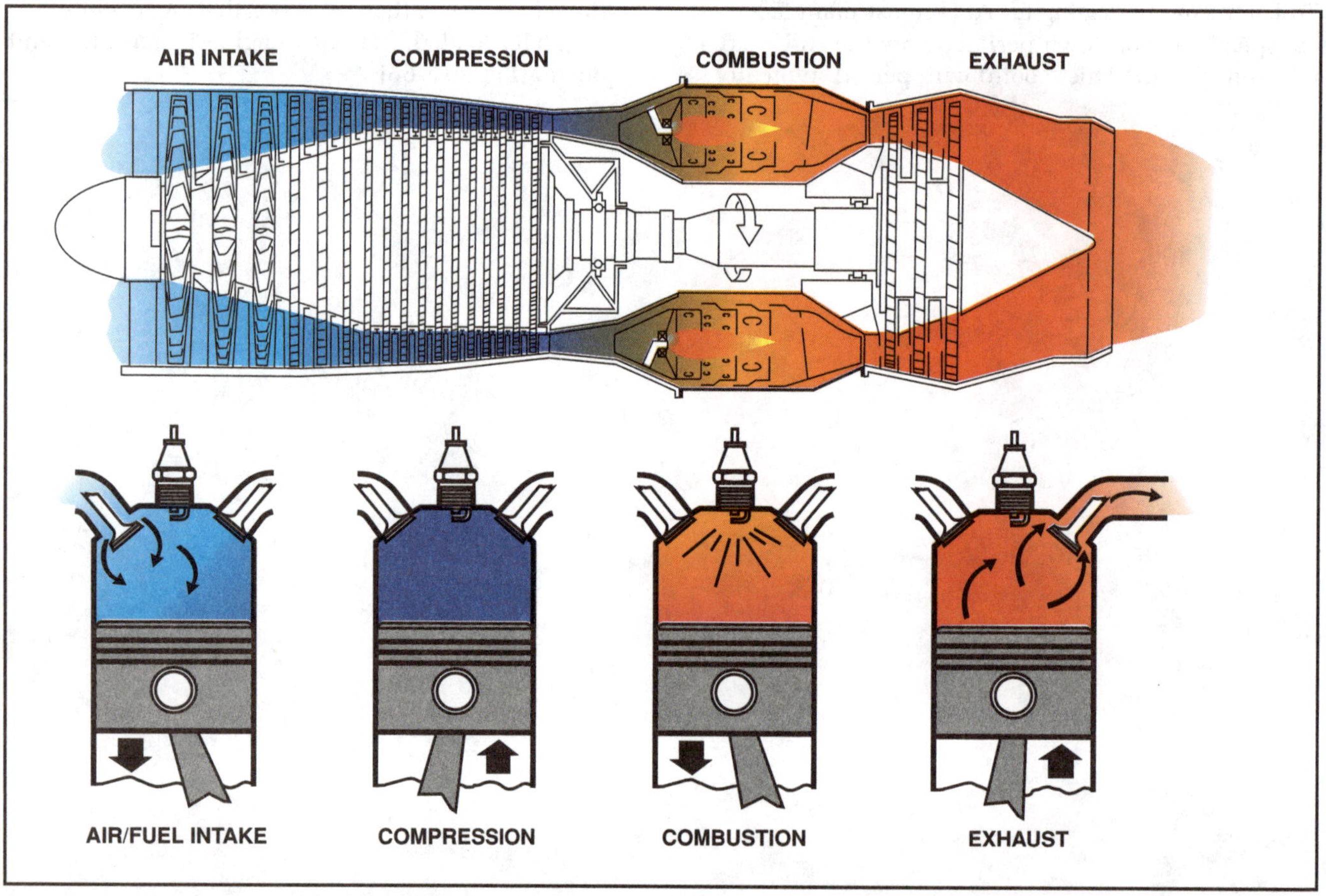

Figure 3-67. In a gas turbine engine, air is taken in through an air inlet, compressed in the compressor, mixed with fuel and ignited in the combustors, then exhausted through the turbines and exhaust nozzle. This allows a gas turbine engine to perform the same functions as a cylinder and piston in a reciprocating engine except that, in a turbine engine, the events happen continuously.

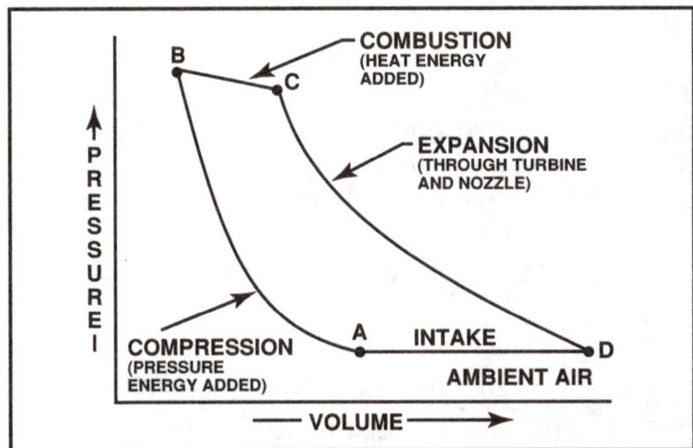

Figure 3-68. This chart illustrates the changes in pressure and volume during turbine engine operation. Point (A) represents the condition of the air just before it enters the compressor. Once in the compressor, air pressure increases and volume decreases. Point (B) represents the pressure and volume of the air as it leaves the compressor. In the combustion section (point C) heat energy is added to the air mass causing the air to expand in volume with little or no change in pressure. Once heated, the air expands and loses pressure as it flows through the turbine section (point D).

The continuous intake event in a gas turbine engine draws ambient air into the engine through an inlet duct to the first compressor stage. Each compressor stage then compresses the air to increase static air pressure. In the combustor, fuel is sprayed into the incoming airflow and ignited, resulting in continuous combustion. The resulting release of heat energy increases the air's volume while maintaining a relatively constant pressure. When the exhaust air leaves the combustion chamber, it passes through the turbine where static air pressure drops and air volume continues to increase. In addition, since there is little resistance to the flow of expanding gases, gas velocity increases dramatically. [Figure 3-68]

PRODUCING THRUST

If you recall from Section A, a gas turbine engine produces thrust based on Newton's third law of motion which states that for every action, there is an equal and opposite reaction. In a turbojet engine, the acceleration of a mass of air by the engine is the action while forward movement is the reaction.

VELOCITY AND PRESSURE

As air passes through a gas turbine engine its velocity and pressure must change in order to produce thrust. For example, in the compressor section, static air pressure must be increased while velocity remains relatively constant. In addition, after combustion, gas velocity must be increased dramatically to rotate the turbine. The most common way of inducing a velocity or pressure change is through the application of **Bernoulli's principle.** If you recall from your earlier studies, Bernoulli's principle states that when a fluid or gas is supplied at a constant flow rate through a duct, the sum of the potential, or pressure energy, and kinetic, or velocity energy, is constant. In other words, as air velocity increases, air pressure decreases and as air velocity decreases, air pressure increases.

To clarify Bernoulli's principle, consider a quantity of air flowing through a converging duct. As the duct decreases in diameter, the air must accelerate to allow the same quantity of air to flow through the smaller opening. This increases the air's kinetic energy. Since energy cannot be created or destroyed, the air's potential, or pressure energy must decrease. By the same token, if a quantity of air passes through a divergent duct, the air's potential, or pressure energy must increase because its kinetic, or velocity energy decreases.

Another thing to keep in mind is that, whenever one form of energy in an airmass is converted to another, the temperature of the airmass changes. If you recall from your study of the gas laws, whenever air pressure decreases, air temperature also decreases. [Figure 3-69]

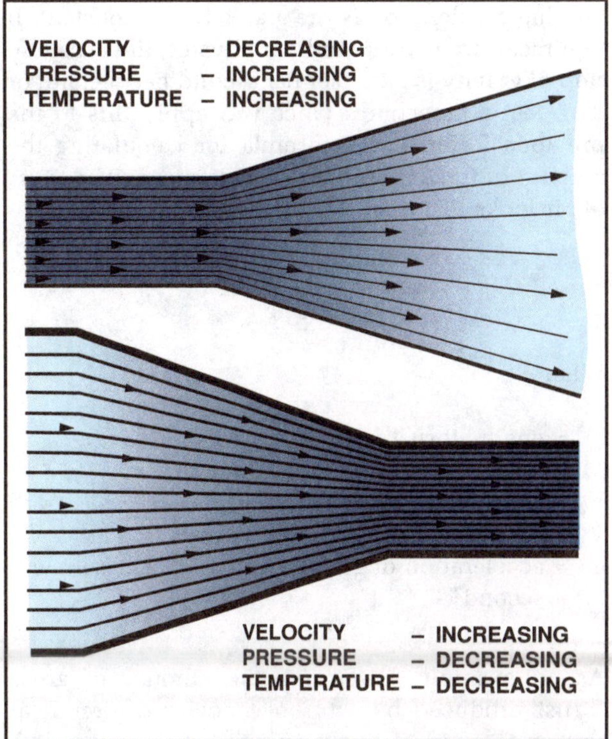

Figure 3-69. When air passes through a diverging duct, air velocity decreases while air pressure and temperature increase. By the same token, when a quantity of air passes through a converging duct, air velocity increases while air pressure and temperature decrease.

THRUST CALCULATIONS

As stated earlier, a jet engine produces thrust by accelerating an airmass to a velocity higher than that of the incoming air. The thrust, in turn, becomes the propelling force which moves an aircraft. Newton's second law of motion states that force is proportional to the product of mass and acceleration. Furthermore, the acceleration produced when a given force acts on a mass is directly proportional to the force and is inversely proportional to the mass. This relationship is expressed by the formula:

$$F = M \times A$$

Where:

F = force
M = mass
A = acceleration

To calculate the acceleration of a given air mass through a gas turbine engine, you must know the difference between the speed of the exiting jet exhaust and the intake air. In addition, once the acceleration is known, it must be compared to a constant. The most widely used constant when discussing acceleration is the gravitational constant. If you recall from your study of physics, the acceleration of gravity is 32.2 feet per second per second, or 32.2 feet per second^2. Once you apply this to the previous formula, the formula for calculating the amount of force required to accelerate a given mass of air looks like this:

$$F = \frac{M_s (V_2 - V_1)}{g}$$

Where:

F = engine thrust in pounds
M_s = mass airflow through the engine
V_2 = air velocity at the exhaust
V_1 = forward velocity of the engine
g = acceleration of gravity which is 32.2 feet per second^2

As an example, determine the amount of **gross thrust** produced by a turbojet powered aircraft at rest on the end of a runway with the engines producing takeoff thrust. The takeoff power setting moves 50 pounds of air through one of the engines every second and produces an exhaust velocity, V_2, of 1,300 feet per second.

Given:

M_s = 50 pounds per second
V_1 = 0 feet per second
V_2 = 1,300 feet per second
g = 32.2 feet per second, per second

$$F_{gross} = \frac{M_s \times (V_2 - V_1)}{g}$$

$$= \frac{50 \text{ lbs./sec.} \times (1{,}300 \text{ ft./sec.} - 0)}{32.2 \text{ ft./sec.}^2}$$

$$= \frac{65{,}000 \text{ lb.-ft./sec.}^2}{32.2 \text{ ft./sec.}^2}$$

$$= 2{,}018.6 \text{ pounds}$$

In this example, one engine produces 2,018.6 pounds of gross thrust. However, during flight, the engine will be moving forward, greatly reducing the velocity change across the engine. Consider the same aircraft in the previous example flying at 500 miles per hour (734 feet per second). Its net thrust can be calculated using the basic formula, as follows:

Given:

M_s = 50 pounds per second
V_2 = 1,300 feet per second
V_1 = 734 feet per second

$$F_{net} = \frac{M_s \times (V_2 - V_1)}{g}$$

$$= \frac{50 \times (1{,}300 - 734)}{32.2}$$

$$= \frac{50 \times 566}{32.2}$$

$$= 878.9 \text{ pounds net thrust}$$

It should be easy to see from this formula that the net thrust produced by a gas turbine engine can be increased by two methods: first, by increasing the mass flow of air through the engine, and second, by increasing the exhaust velocity.

If the velocity of a turbojet engine remains constant with respect to the aircraft, exhaust thrust decreases if the speed of the aircraft is increased. This is because V_1 increases in value as the speed of the aircraft increases. This does not present a serious problem, however, because as aircraft speed increases, more air enters the engine resulting in an increase in exhaust velocity. The resultant net thrust is almost constant with increases in airspeed.

THERMAL EFFICIENCY

A turbine engine's thermal efficiency is the ratio of the actual power an engine produces divided by the thermal energy in the fuel consumed. At cruise, a large gas turbine engine with a 30:1 compression ratio can operate with a thermal efficiency as high as 50 percent. In comparison, if you recall from Chapter 1, the thermal efficiency of a typical reciprocating engine is between 30 and 40 percent.

There are three primary factors which determine the thermal efficiency of a gas turbine engine. They are the turbine inlet temperature, the compression ratio, and the component efficiencies of the compressor and turbine.

As discussed earlier, the higher a gas turbine engine raises the temperature of the incoming air, the more thrust the engine can produce. The primary limiting factor to increasing the temperature of the air is the amount of heat the turbine section can withstand. Therefore, if the turbine inlet temperature (TIT) limits on a given engine can be increased, higher thermal efficiencies will result. [Figure 3-70]

You should also recall that the more a gas turbine engine compresses the incoming air, the more thrust the engine can produce. The reason for this is that engines with high compression ratios force more air into the engine, allowing more heat energy from the burning fuel to be transferred to the internal airflow. Anytime there is an increase in the amount of heat energy transferred from the fuel to the air, an engine's thermal efficiency also increases.

As you would expect, high compressor and turbine efficiencies in a gas turbine engine promote a higher thermal efficiency. The reason for this is that compressor and turbine efficiency directly impact the compression ratio of a given engine, which, in turn, has a direct impact on thermal efficiency. [Figure 3-71]

FACTORS AFFECTING THRUST

The amount of thrust a given engine is capable of producing is affected by a number of environmental, design, and operational factors. For example, temperature, altitude, and airspeed directly affect inlet air density and consequently, thrust. The combination of these three variables is sometimes represented by a single variable, called **stagnation density**. Operating rpm and the efficiency of a given fan design are additional parameters that directly determine the amount of thrust an engine produces.

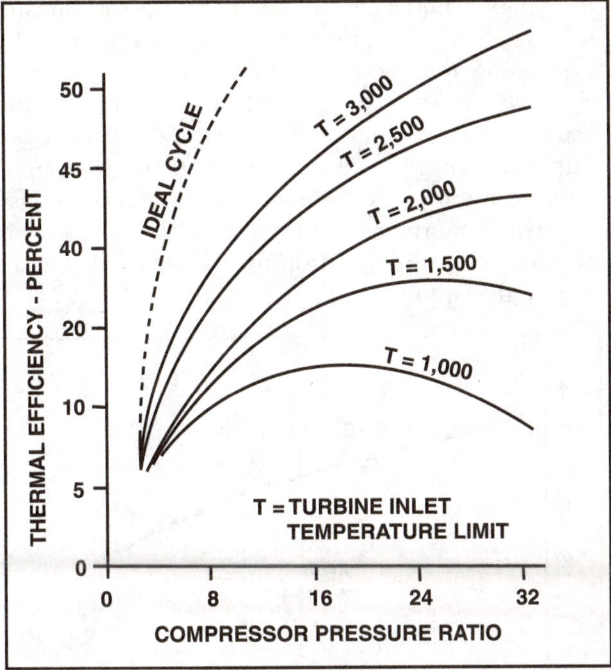

Figure 3-70. Turbine inlet temperature (TIT) readings between 2,500 and 3,000 degrees Fahrenheit with compression ratios near 32:1 give 50 percent or better thermal efficiencies.

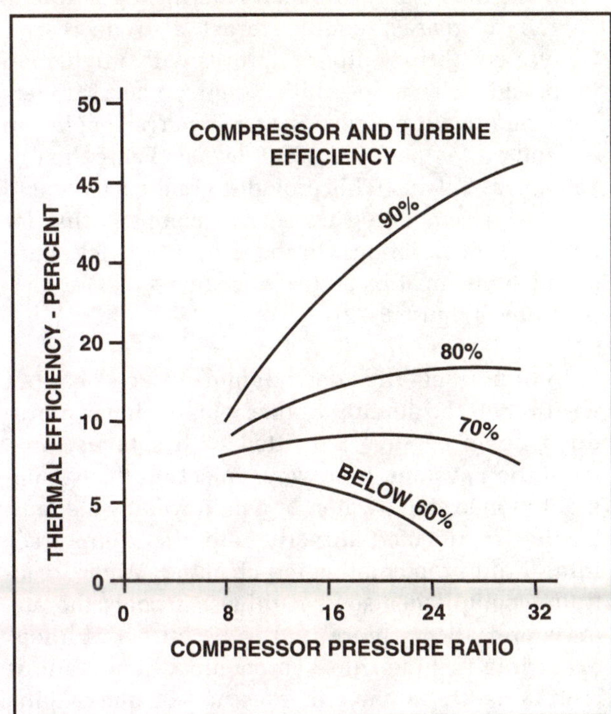

Figure 3-71. Compressor and turbine efficiency near 90 percent is necessary to reach thermal efficiencies above 20 percent.

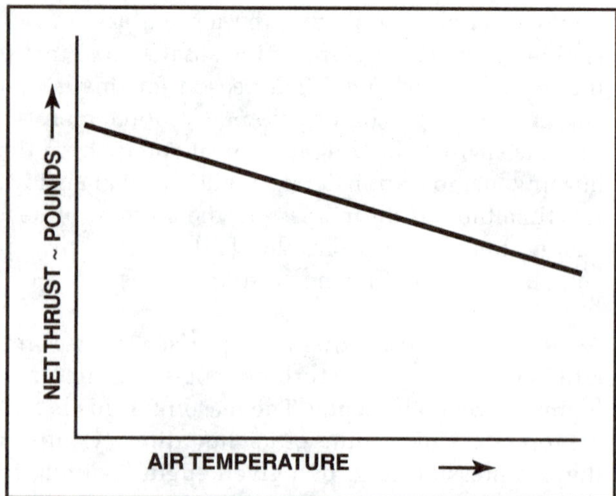

Figure 3-72. Air density decreases as temperature rises, and the lower the density of the air, the less thrust an engine can produce.

TEMPERATURE

As previously discussed, the air mass flowing through a turbine engine is the working fluid that the engine uses to produce thrust. Furthermore, the more dense the air passing through an engine is, the more thrust the engine can produce. If you recall from your study of aerodynamics, air density is inversely related to temperature. In other words, as outside air temperature (OAT) increases, air density decreases. Anytime the density of the air entering a gas turbine engine decreases, engine thrust also decreases. Conversely, thrust output improves with a reduction in outside air temperature. Engine manufacturers base their thrust calculations for any given engine on a standard temperature of 59 degrees Fahrenheit or 15 degrees Celsius. This provides a reference point to use when calculating thrust and compensating for temperature variations. In the field, all performance calculations must be adjusted for non-standard temperatures. [Figure 3-72]

To counteract the detrimental effects of hot weather on the amount of thrust an engine can produce, some engines are fitted with a **thrust augmentation** system. In a **water injection** thrust augmentation system, water, or a mixture of water and alcohol is injected directly into the compressor inlet or into the combustion chamber. Water injection accomplishes several things; it cools the airmass and allows more fuel to be burned without exceeding turbine inlet temperature limits, and it maintains the same air pressure in the engine because water molecules are added to the airmass. More information is given on water injection systems in Chapter 6.

ALTITUDE

As altitude increases, air pressure drops. Air at standard temperature at sea level exerts a pressure of 14.69 pounds per square inch. However, this pressure decreases as the altitude increases. Approximately one-half of the air in the atmosphere is below 18,000 feet. Therefore, the pressure at 18,000 feet is about 7.34 psi, or half that at sea level. Above 18,000 feet, air pressure continues to drop, but at a higher rate. At 20,000 feet, standard air pressure drops to 6.75 pounds per square inch, and at 30,000 feet it is only 4.36 pounds per square inch.

Temperature, like ambient air pressure, also decreases as altitude increases. Normally, decreasing temperatures result in an increase in air density, leading some to think that increases in altitude result in higher air density. The opposite, however, is true because the pressure losses experienced when climbing has a greater effect on air density than decreasing temperatures. In other words, the temperature lapse rate is less than the pressure lapse rate. Therefore, as an aircraft climbs, engine performance is impacted by decreasing air density.

At approximately 36,000 feet, the air temperature stabilizes at –69.7 degrees Fahrenheit and remains at that temperature up to approximately 80,000 feet. This layer in the atmosphere divides the troposphere from the stratosphere and is called the tropopause. Between these altitudes, the air density no longer increases due to the effects produced by decreasing temperatures. As a result, the rate of decrease in air density with increasing altitude becomes more rapid above 36,000 feet. Because of this, long-range jet aircraft find 36,000 feet an optimum altitude to fly. Below this altitude, the dense air creates more aerodynamic drag, and above this altitude the rapidly dropping density decreases engine thrust output. [Figure 3-73]

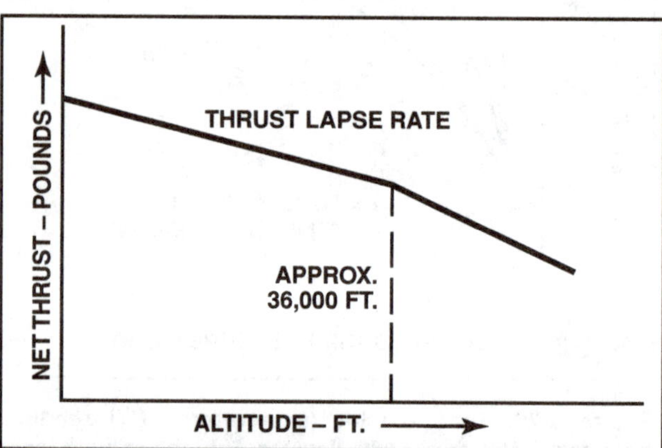

Figure 3-73. Air density decreases with altitude, and, therefore, as an aircraft climbs, engine thrust decreases.

AIRSPEED

If you recall from the earlier discussion on thrust, as forward airspeed increases, the airmass acceleration in the engine decreases, so less thrust is produced. However, as the aircraft speeds up, more air is forced into the engine. This is known as **ram effect** and results in an increase in air pressure within an engine which, in turn, produces more thrust. Therefore, increasing aircraft speed causes two opposing trends to occur; a decrease in thrust due to the reduction in airmass acceleration and an increase in thrust due to ram effect. The net effect on thrust is found by subtracting the lost thrust due to the reduction in airmass acceleration from the increase in thrust realized from ram effect. The result is referred to as ram recovery. [Figure 3-74]

ENGINE RPM

Early turbojet engines had somewhat of a linear relationship between compressor rpm and engine thrust. In other words, the faster the compressor rpm, the more thrust produced. Because of this, engine power output on these engines could be set using an rpm gauge. However, modern turbofan engines with dual spool compressors have a non-linear relationship between compressor rpm and thrust produced. In fact, at low engine speeds, large increases in rpm produce relatively small increases in thrust and at high engine speeds, a small increase in rpm produces a large increase in thrust. Therefore, power in most modern gas turbine engines is set using an engine pressure ratio (EPR) indicating system since thrust and EPR have a more proportional relationship than thrust and rpm.

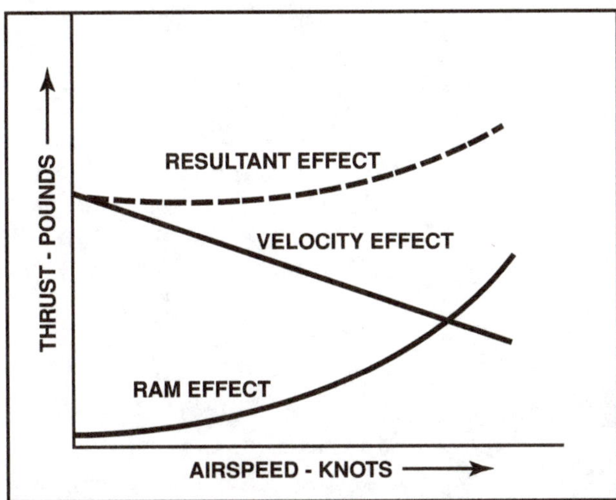

Figure 3-74. As airspeed increases, the amount an engine can accelerate a given airmass decreases. However, ram effect becomes more pronounced with increases in airspeed. The resultant effect, or ram recovery, produces a slight increase in engine thrust.

Compressor aerodynamics limit engine rpm because compressor efficiency begins to drop when the blade tips reach the speed of sound. Therefore, efficient compressor design requires engine operation at a speed that does not subject the compressor blades to the severe shock waves produced by supersonic blade speeds. As you know, the longer a compressor blade is, the higher the tip rotational speed for a given rpm. This explains why most large diameter compressors turn at a relatively slow rotational speed. In contrast, small diameter turbine engines may be capable of compressor speeds in excess of 50,000 rpm.

FAN EFFICIENCY

Turbofan engines have replaced turbojet engines on most transport and business jet aircraft. The turbofan engine design is quieter and much more fuel efficient. As an example, if a turbojet and a turbofan engine have the same rated thrust, the turbofan engine will burn less fuel because of the greater propulsive efficiency of the fan. Therefore, the more efficient the fan is, the more thrust the engine can produce.

TURBINE ENGINE OPERATION, INSPECTION, MAINTENANCE, AND OVERHAUL

INTRODUCTION

As a powerplant technician, you are expected to have the knowledge and skill to operate, maintain, and overhaul turbine engines. In order to perform those tasks adequately, you must develop the ability to distinguish normal engine performance from deteriorating engine performance. In addition, you must accumulate the working knowledge and experience necessary to effectively troubleshoot and repair a turbine engine. In other words, you are expected to be proficient in special skills and processes that are commonly used to accomplish turbine engine repairs and overhauls. Therefore, the following discussion provides information to help you achieve a basic understanding of turbine engine operation, maintenance, and overhaul procedures.

OPERATION, INSPECTION, AND MAINTENANCE

OPERATION

As an aviation maintenance technician, you must be thoroughly familiar with the procedures for operating a gas turbine engine from the cockpit. This includes understanding the engine instrumentation, ground run procedures, and safety items associated with starting and running an aircraft engine. A good place to begin in obtaining an understanding of these items is to familiarize yourself with the location and movement of the engine controls. [Figure 4-1]

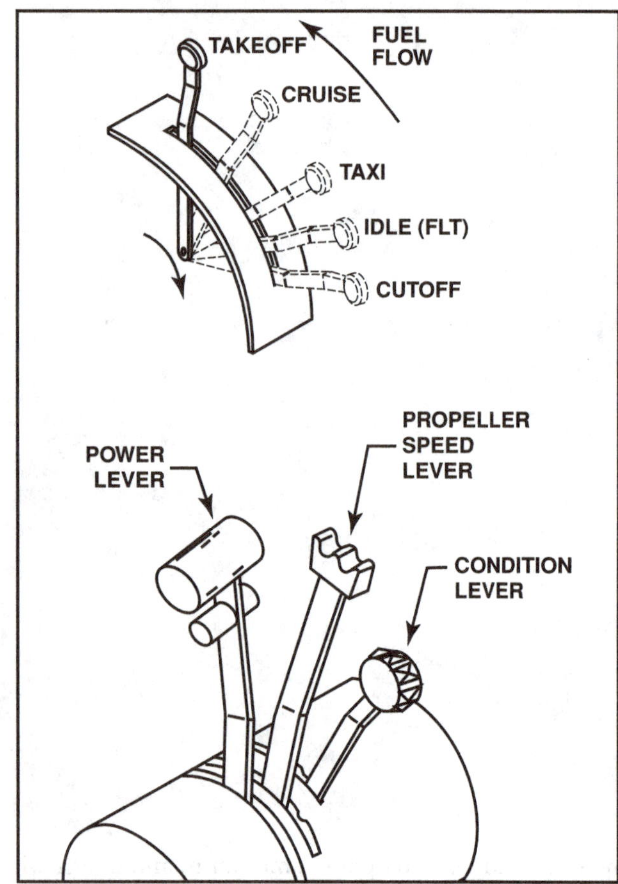

Figure 4-1. Most turbojet and turbofan engines have a single power lever that provides fuel control as well as engine speed control. On the other hand, most turboprop engines employ a power lever for engine speed control, a condition lever for fuel cutoff, and a propeller control to change propeller blade pitch.

Once you are familiar with the engine controls, you should locate each of the engine instruments. In addition, you should locate and read all placards and other markings on or near the instruments. Important engine operating information is displayed by the engine instruments and must be monitored continuously during an engine run. Therefore, you, as an engine operator, must be skilled in the interpretation of instrument readings to prevent engine damage.

ENGINE INSTRUMENTATION

Engine instruments that indicate oil pressure, oil temperature, engine speed, exhaust gas temperature, and fuel flow are common to both turbine and reciprocating engines. However, there are some instruments that are unique to gas turbine engines. These instruments provide indications of engine pressure ratio, turbine discharge pressure, and torque. In addition, most gas turbine engines have multiple temperature sensing instruments that provide pilots with temperature readings in and around the turbine section. Some of the common temperature indications that may be provided include turbine inlet temperature (TIT), turbine gas temperature (TGT), interstage turbine temperature (ITT), and turbine outlet temperature (TOT). As a turbine engine operator and troubleshooter, you must understand how all of a turbine engine's instruments operate in order to determine an engine's level of performance.

COMPRESSOR SPEED

Turbine engine fan and compressor speed is displayed on a tachometer that is calibrated in percent rpm. In addition, a separate tachometer is used for each compressor section in an engine. For example, an engine with a twin-spool compressor will have an N_1 tachometer for the low-pressure compressor and an N_2 tachometer for the high-pressure compressor. [Figure 4-2]

Compressor rpm is a direct indication of the thrust being produced by engines using a centrifugal type

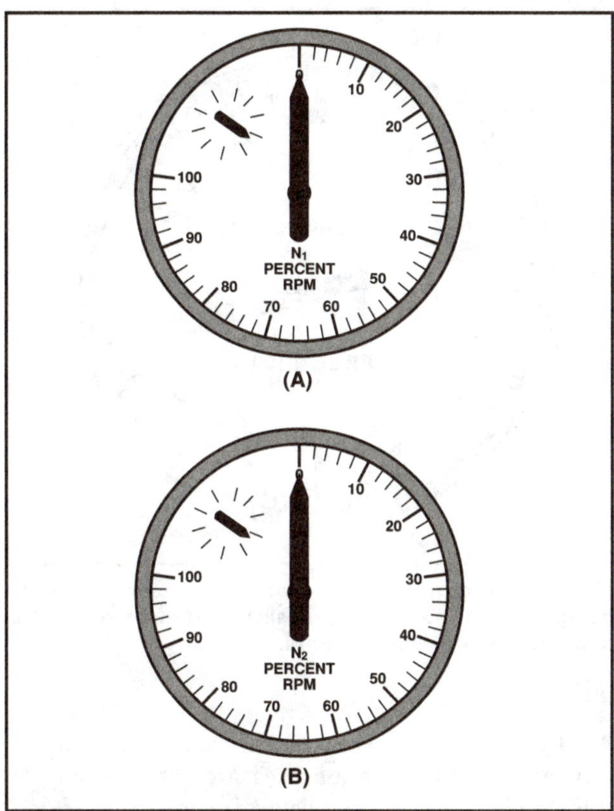

Figure 4-2. (A) — An N_1 tachometer indicates fan or low-pressure compressor rpm. (B) — An N_2 tachometer indicates high-pressure compressor rpm.

compressor. However, for engines that utilize an axial-flow compressor, compressor rpm is used primarily to monitor engine speed during engine start and help the pilot identify an overspeed condition.

With turboprop engines that incorporate a free-turbine, engine rpm is indicated on an N_g tachometer. On the other hand, propeller, or free-turbine rpm is indicated on an N_p tachometer.

Two slightly different kinds of electronic tachometers are found on turbine engines. The first type is often used as a fan speed sensor to measure the rpm of the fan and low-pressure compressor. It uses a sensor which contains a coil of wire that generates a magnetic field. The sensor is mounted in the shroud around the fan so, when each fan blade passes the sensor, the magnetic field is interrupted. The frequency at which the fan blades cut across the field is measured by an electronic circuit and then transmitted to an rpm gauge in the cockpit.

Another type of electronic tachometer used on turbine engines consists of a gear driven shaft which turns a rotor with a permanent magnet and a stationary pickup coil. Each time the field of the rotating permanent magnet cuts across the coil, voltage is induced. The frequency of the induced voltage is measured by an electronic circuit and used to position a pointer to indicate correct rpm.

ENGINE PRESSURE RATIO

An engine pressure ratio (EPR) gauge is used to indicate the amount of thrust produced in many turbofan powered aircraft. An engine's EPR is the ratio of turbine discharge pressure to compressor inlet pressure. Pressure measurements are recorded by total pressure pickups, or EPR probes, installed in the engine inlet Pt_2 and at the exhaust Pt_7. Once collected, the data is sent to a differential pressure transducer which drives a cockpit EPR gauge. [Figure 4-3]

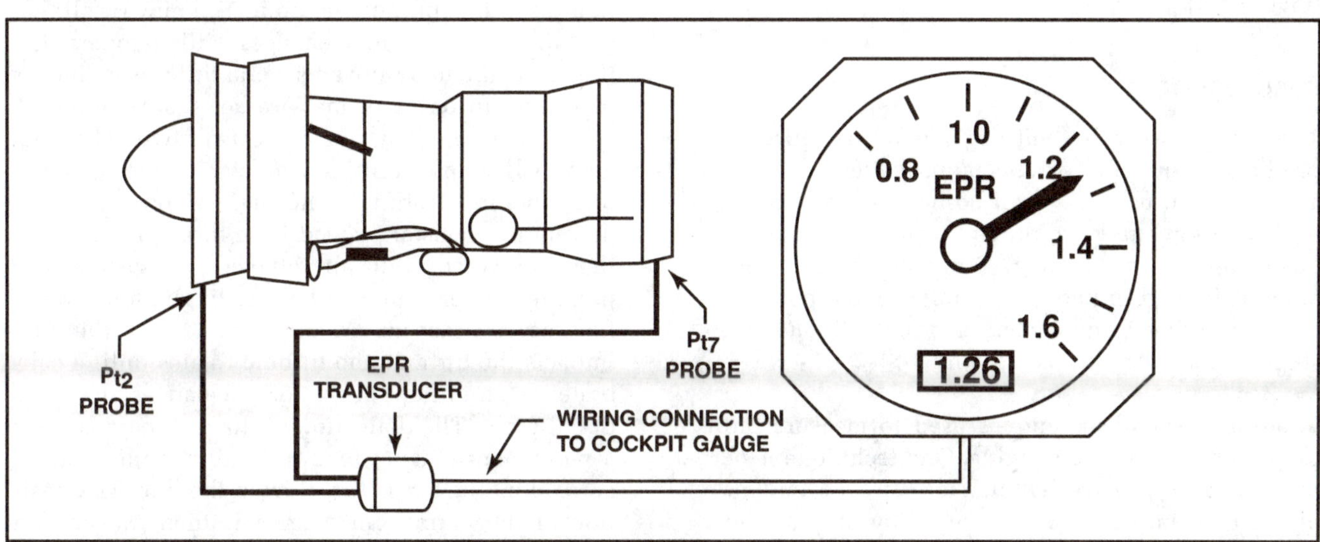

Figure 4-3. An engine pressure ratio (EPR) gauge provides a reliable indication of the thrust being produced by calculating the ratio of turbine discharge pressure Pt_2 to compressor inlet pressure Pt_7.

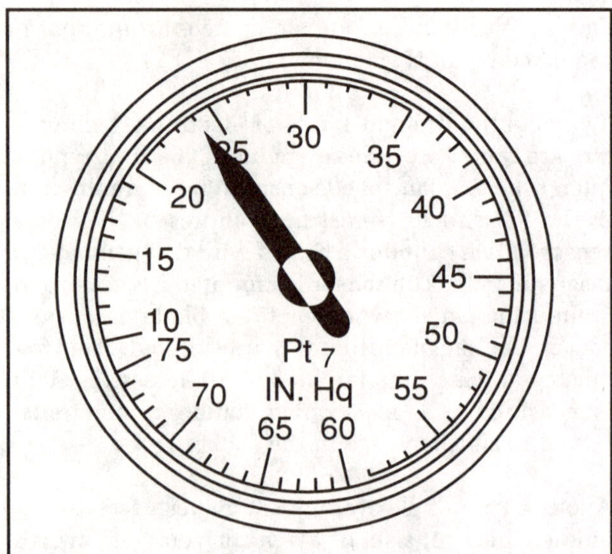

Figure 4-4. Thrust indications in some aircraft may be provided by a Pt_7 turbine discharge pressure gauge.

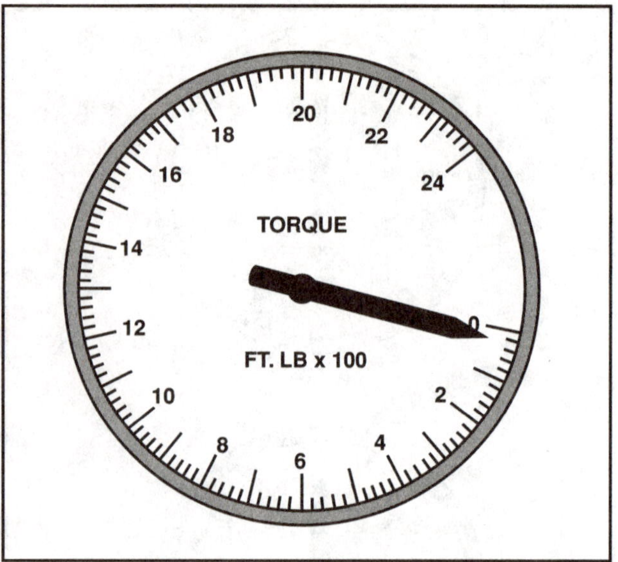

Figure 4-5. A torquemeter indicates the amount of torque being produced to drive a propeller on turboprop engines or a rotor on turboshaft engines.

EPR system design automatically compensates for the effects of airspeed and altitude. However, changes in ambient temperature do require a correction to be applied to EPR indications to provide accurate engine power settings.

TURBINE DISCHARGE PRESSURE

In some aircraft, turbine discharge pressure is indicated on an individual Pt_7 gauge. This instrument displays the total engine internal pressure immediately aft of the last turbine stage. When corrected for variations in inlet pressure caused by airspeed, altitude, and ambient air temperature, turbine discharge pressure provides an indication of thrust. [Figure 4-4]

TORQUEMETER

Turboprop and turboshaft engines are designed to produce torque for driving a propeller or rotor. Therefore, turboprop or turboshaft engines often utilize a torquemeter to provide a pilot with engine power output information. Torquemeters are most often calibrated in percentage units or foot-pounds; however, other torquemeters may be calibrated in shaft horsepower and psi. [Figure 4-5]

There are several techniques used to measure the torque produced by an engine. One technique is to put sensors on a driveshaft that measure the amount of twist in the shaft that is caused by torque. The electrical signals from the sensors are processed and used to position the cockpit indicator.

Another technique used to measure torque relies on a measurement of torque pressure. The sensor for this type of system consists of a small oil filled cylinder and piston. The sensor is installed in the reduction gearbox in a manner that allows the torque reaction force to be applied to the piston. Pressure on the piston increases in proportion to the applied torque reaction force. The pressure is measured, causing the instrument pointer to indicate the torque produced.

FUEL FLOW INDICATOR

Fuel flow for gas turbine engines is indicated in pounds of fuel burned per hour. You may recall that the volume of jet fuel changes with temperature, therefore, the fuel flow on several turbine engines is measured in terms of mass rather than volume. A typical mass flow system consists of two cylinders, an impeller, and a turbine which are mounted in the main fuel line leading to the engine. The impeller is driven at a constant speed by a three-phase motor that is powered by the aircraft electrical system. The impeller imparts an angular swirling motion to the fuel as it proceeds to the turbine. As the fuel impacts the turbine, the turbine rotates until a calibrated restraining spring force balances the rotational force. The deflection of the turbine positions a permanent magnet in a transmitter to a position corresponding to the fuel flow in the line. The position of the permanent magnet is then transmitted electrically to a permanent magnet in a receiver which positions the indicator needle in the cockpit.

This system is by far the most accurate means of monitoring fuel flow because it accounts for changes in fuel viscosity and volume caused by changes in temperature. For example, as fuel density increases, more spin energy is imparted to the turbine. The degree of turbine rotation increases correspondingly to accurately measure mass fuel flow.

In addition to fuel flow indications, some turbine aircraft are equipped with fuel totalizers. A computerized fuel system (CFS) with a **fuel totalizer** provides a pilot with a digital readout on several fuel parameters. The parameters are: the amount of fuel used, fuel remaining, current rate of fuel consumption, and the time remaining for flight at the current power setting. When linked to distance measuring equipment, a totalizer can show the range of an aircraft at the present power setting. Often, a single instrument mounted in the forward instrument panel indicates both fuel flow and totalizer data. When an aircraft is serviced with fuel, the counter is set to the total amount of fuel in all tanks. As the fuel passes through the metering element of the flowmeter, it sends a signal to the microprocessor that automatically calculates the amount of fuel remaining.

EXHAUST GAS TEMPERATURE

The most limiting factor in running a gas turbine engine is the temperature of the turbine section. The temperature of a turbine section must be monitored closely to prevent overheating the turbine blades and other exhaust section components. One common way of monitoring the temperature of a turbine section is with an exhaust gas temperature (EGT) gauge. In other words, EGT is an engine operating limit that is used to monitor the mechanical integrity of a turbine and overall engine operating conditions. [Figure 4-6]

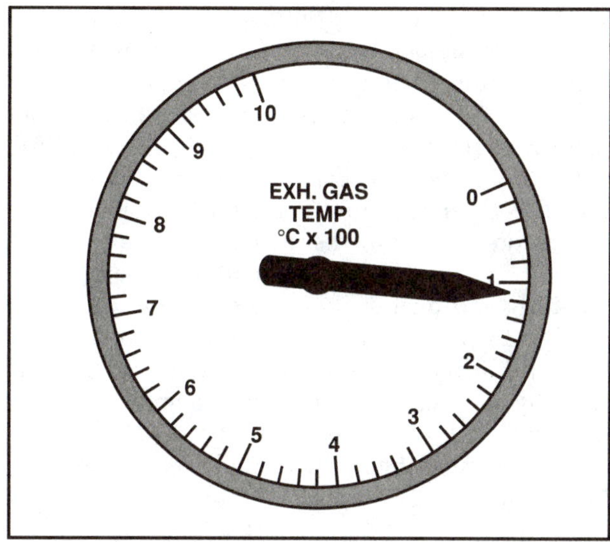

Figure 4-6. An exhaust gas temperature gauge for a gas turbine engine is essential for monitoring the temperature of the turbine section.

Variations of EGT systems bear different names based on the location of the temperature sensors. Common turbine temperature sensing gauges include the turbine inlet temperature (TIT) gauge, turbine outlet temperature (TOT) gauge, interstage turbine temperature (ITT) gauge, and turbine gas temperature (TGT) gauge.

The **turbine inlet temperature (TIT)** gauge senses temperature at the inlet to the power turbine and is the most critical of all the engine variables. However, it is not always practical to measure turbine inlet temperature in some large engines. Therefore, in these engines, the temperature thermocouples are generally inserted at the turbine discharge. The result is a measurement of **turbine outlet temperature (TOT)**. For all practical purposes, turbine outlet temperature is the same as a turbine's exhaust gas temperature and both provide a relative indication of turbine inlet temperature. Even though the temperature of the gases exiting a turbine is lower than at the inlet, it provides some surveillance over the engine's internal operating conditions. On other engines, the temperature sensing probes are placed at some point within the turbine section. For example, if the probes are placed between two turbine stages, the indicator in the cockpit will display the **interstage turbine temperature (ITT)**. In this type of system, the interstage turbine temperature is directly proportional to the turbine inlet temperature.

Each type of EGT system consists of several thermocouples spaced at intervals around the circumference of the engine exhaust section casing. Due to the high pressures and temperatures involved, chromel-alumel thermocouples typically are used. An EGT indicator in the cockpit shows the average temperature measured by the individual thermocouples.

ENGINE INDICATING AND CREW ALERTING SYSTEM

Engine parameters on most modern business jets and transport aircraft are displayed electronically on a cathode ray tube (CRT) or liquid crystal display (LCD). The most common electronic system is the **engine indicating and crew alerting system**, or

EICAS. A typical EICAS utilizes two CRT or LCD displays mounted in the middle of an instrument panel. As the name implies, the engine indication function displays all primary and secondary powerplant instruments. The primary instrument indications of EPR, N_1, and EGT are presented with both digital and analog movements on the top display. The secondary engine instrument indications of N_2, N_3, fuel flow, engine vibration and oil pressure, temperature, and quantity are presented on the lower display. In addition, a crew alerting function monitors and displays system faults and aircraft system warning messages to the crew. Common systems that an EICAS computer monitors include the aircraft's electrical, hydraulic, bleed air, and pressurization systems. [Figure 4-7]

During routine cruise operations with no system faults or abnormal readings, the lower screen is often blank. However, if a fault is detected, the upper screen displays a warning and the instrument representation for the faulty system moves to the lower screen. On aircraft that have EICAS installed, crew workload is reduced during normal operations because secondary information is not displayed. In the event that one CRT fails, all needed information is displayed on the operable CRT. In this case, information is displayed digitally and the system is automatically converted to a compact mode. In the event the second CRT fails, the flight crew can still find critical engine information on a backup display.

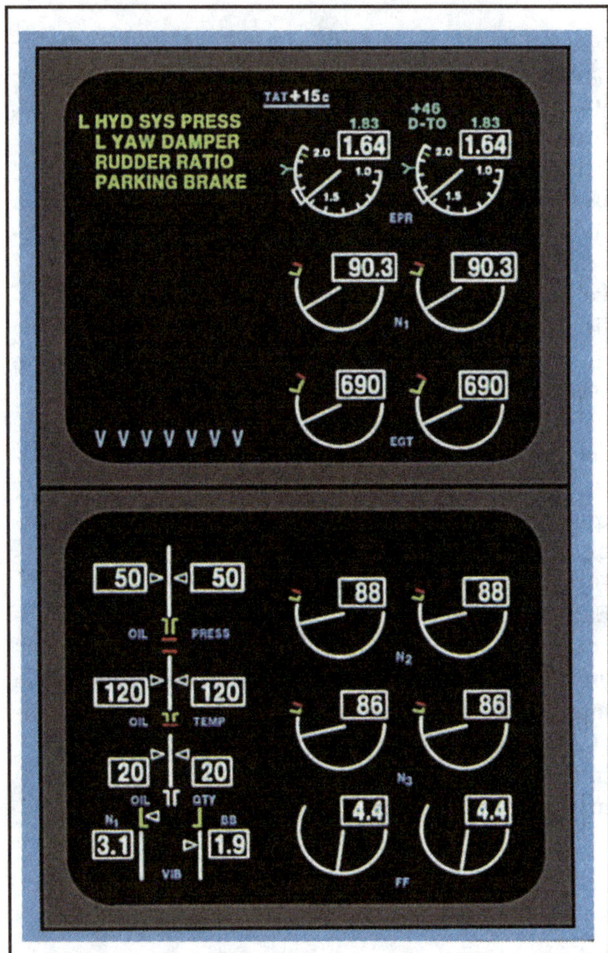

Figure 4-7. EICAS displays both engine monitoring instrumentation and alert messages in a dual CRT or LCD format. The upper screen displays primary engine instrumentation and alerting functions while the lower screen displays all secondary engine instrumentation.

GROUND OPERATIONS

As a maintenance technician, there are many instances where you may be required to operate a gas turbine engine. For example, troubleshooting a discrepancy reported by a flight crew often involves engine operation to duplicate and analyze the discrepancy. Additional reasons for conducting an engine run is to check the performance of an engine system following maintenance or to taxi an aircraft from one maintenance area to another. Therefore, you must be familiar with the procedures for starting and running a gas turbine engine.

The intent of the following discussion is to provide you with a basic explanation of turbine engine starting and runup operations. For specific information regarding a particular engine, you must consult the checklist and instructions provided by the aircraft manufacturer.

Turbine engine operation must be conducted in an area specifically designated for that purpose to reduce hazards to personnel, hangars, and other equipment. If possible, always run a gas turbine engine in front of a blast shield so the jet blast is deflected upward. In addition, if the aircraft does not need to be moved during the ground run, chock the wheels and set the brakes.

Prepare for an engine run by removing the engine inlet and exhaust covers, then check for proper oil levels, adequate fuel, and fluid leaks that could be a fire hazard. To prevent foreign object damage, remove loose objects from the ramp around the engine and remove any tools or other loose objects from the turbine inlet prior to start. In addition, all ground support equipment such as auxiliary power carts, hydraulic service units, and fire extinguishers must be positioned a safe distance from the aircraft. Always observe the warnings to remain safely outside the turbine intake and exhaust danger arcs when the engine is running. [Figure 4-8]

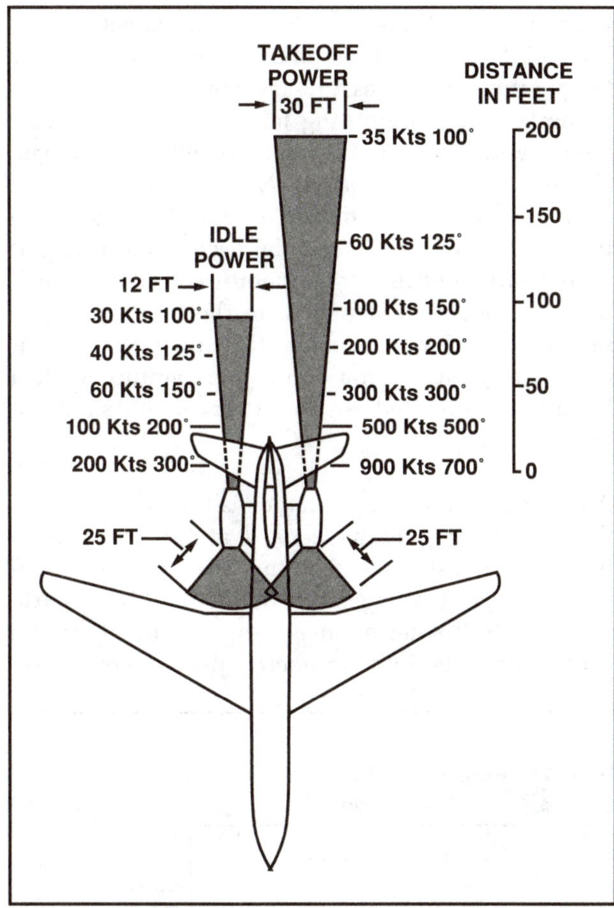

Figure 4-8. Ground personnel must be cautious when near operating turbojet and turbofan engines. Intake safety arcs are established to prevent injury to personnel and engine damage due to ingestion. Likewise, exhaust safety arcs are designed to prevent damage to surrounding equipment and personnel from jet blast.

Check the condition of the compressor and turbine visually, verifying freedom of motion. In addition, check the communications equipment between the cockpit and ground safety personnel for proper operation.

ENGINE STARTING

Upon entering the cockpit, verify that the master switch is "off," the landing gear handle is in the "down" position, and the generator switches are "off." In addition, check to make sure the power levers are in the "cutoff" or "fuel shutoff" position, and the starter and ignition switches are "off." If using a ground power unit for starting, verify that the voltage being supplied to the aircraft is correct. When ground personnel indicate that conditions are safe for engine start, flip the master switch and battery or external power switches "on," and switch on the fuel boost pumps.

Operation of the starter, ignition, and fuel control is usually based on N_1 or N_2 indications and time. Therefore, you must observe the engine instruments and elapsed time during engine start. A typical start sequence requires you to engage the starter and then switch on the ignition. Once the engine accelerates to the specified rpm, open the fuel valve. Immediately check the fuel flow indicator to confirm fuel flow, and then watch the EGT indicator to confirm a light-off. A sharp rise in EGT indicates a start has begun. Continue to observe the EGT indicator to verify that temperature does not exceed its limits and lead to a hot start.

A **hot start** is one in which ignition occurs when there is an excessively rich fuel/air mixture. If a hot start is allowed to proceed, the exhaust gas temperature will exceed the allowable limit and the engine will be damaged. To minimize the possibility of a hot start, the exhaust gas temperature, turbine inlet temperature, or interstage turbine temperature gauge must be monitored during a start. If any temperature indication exceeds its allowable limit, fuel to the engine should be shut off immediately. Consult the engine manufacturer's maintenance manual for inspection or overhaul requirements following a hot start.

If a **hung start** occurs, engine start is normal and exhaust gas temperature is within limits, but the engine fails to accelerate or reach idle rpm. Hung starts occur when the starter cuts out too soon, or when the starting power source fails to provide enough energy to rotate the engine to a sufficient speed. If a hung start occurs, the engine must be shut down and the cause for insufficient starting speed corrected before another attempt is made.

Once an engine starts and becomes self-accelerating, release the start switch and monitor the engine instruments for proper indications. Following a successful engine start, the engine should idle between 40 and 70 percent, depending on the engine model. In addition, the EGT, fuel flow, oil and fuel temperatures, oil pressure, and tachometer readings should be compared to the allowable range for each. Be aware, however, that fuel flow indications may be unreliable at idling rpm because of the inaccuracies that are frequently inherent in fuel flowmeters at their lower ranges.

ENGINE FIRE

In the event that an engine fire starts or the fire warning light illuminates during the start cycle, cut off the fuel flow to the engine and continue motoring the engine with the starter. If the fire persists, small amounts of CO_2 can be discharged into the inlet duct while the engine is being motored. However, be careful to avoid discharging excessive amounts of CO_2 directly into a hot engine. The cooling effect produced by large amounts of CO_2 can shrink the turbine housing around the turbine blades causing engine disintegration.

POWER CHECK

If an engine idles properly and engine parameters appear to be normal, verify that the engine is capable of producing takeoff thrust. However, before you can do this, you must calculate an EPR or discharge pressure value which represents takeoff thrust for the prevailing atmospheric conditions. In most cases, a takeoff thrust setting curve is provided by the engine manufacturer to make these calculations. [Figure 4-9]

Ambient conditions have a dramatic effect on turbine performance; therefore, compressor inlet air temperature and pressure measurements must be accurate when computing takeoff thrust. Air temperature measurements should be made a few feet above the runway surface where air is drawn into an engine's compressor inlet. The free air temperature indicator in an aircraft may be used at airports that do not provide runway temperature measurements, however, accuracy depends on the location of the sensing bulb. For an accurate thrust computation, it is best to measure the actual temperature with a handheld calibrated thermometer in the shade of the airplane.

A turbine engine's performance is based, in part, on the actual air pressure sensed at the compressor inlet. Air pressure at the compressor inlet of a stationary aircraft is referred to as the field barometric pressure. Altimeter settings provided by air traffic control provide field barometric pressure corrected

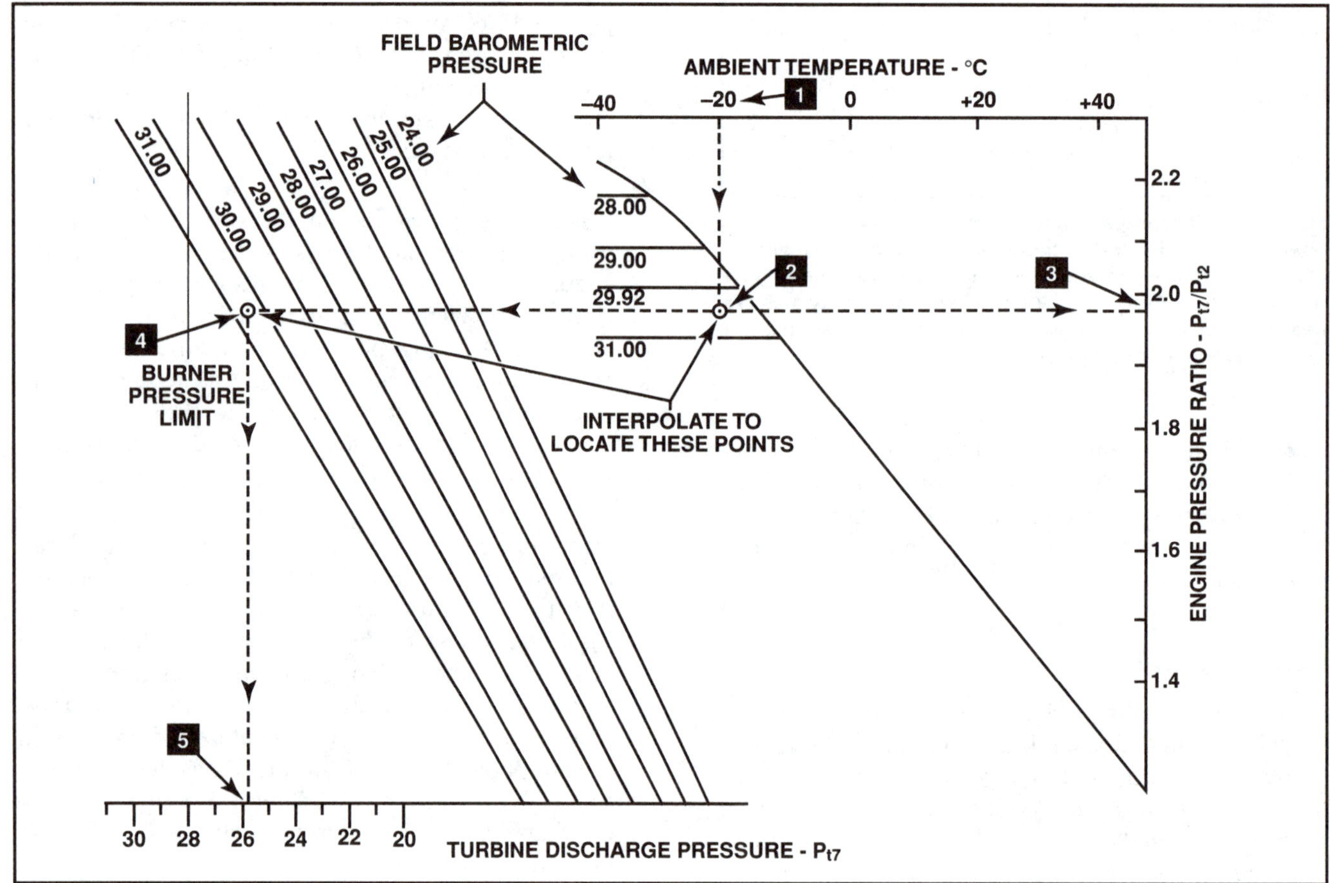

Figure 4-9. Given an ambient temperature of –20°C and a field barometric pressure of 30.50 in. Hg., you can determine the takeoff EPR and turbine discharge pressure using the chart above. To determine the takeoff EPR, locate –20°C on the ambient temperature line (item 1) and move downward to intercept the barometric pressure scale at 30.50 in. Hg. (item 2). From this point, project a horizontal line to the right that intercepts the engine pressure ratio axis at 1.975 (item 3). To determine turbine discharge pressure, go back to the intersection of the ambient temperature and barometric pressure (item 2) and project a line left to the second barometric pressure scale (item 4). From here, drop straight down to the turbine discharge pressure line to arrive at a value of approximately 25.75 in. Hg. (item 5).

to sea level and, therefore, are unusable for computing engine performance. Field barometric pressure is easily obtained by setting the aircraft altimeter to zero and reading the altimeter setting on the face of the instrument.

Variations in relative humidity have a negligible effect on turbojet engine thrust. Therefore, relative humidity measurements are not a concern when checking gas turbine engine performance.

Once the takeoff EPR is known, adjust the throttle to obtain takeoff power. While advancing the power lever to the computed EPR, carefully observe the EGT, tachometer, fuel flow, and oil pressure readings to avoid exceeding maximum limits. To make precise thrust measurements using a takeoff thrust setting curve, an aircraft must be stationary and engine operation must be stabilized. If the predetermined EPR reading can be achieved and all other engine instruments are reading within their proper ranges, takeoff thrust is being produced.

ENGINE SHUTDOWN

Once an engine run is complete, you must follow the appropriate shutdown procedures. Typically, before a gas turbine engine is shut down, the engine is run at idle for 30 seconds or more. This permits component temperatures to stabilize and oil system scavenging to occur. After the recommended time period, move the power lever to the "cutoff" or "fuel shutoff" position. Once the engine quits, move the fuel boost, fuel valve, generator, battery, external power, and master switches to their "off" position. If the appropriate shutdown procedures are not followed, uneven engine cooling could result. In addition, a rapid shutdown can lead to incorrect oil quantity indications that result from poor scavenging.

COLD WEATHER OPERATIONS

Starting a gas turbine engine that is cold-soaked from sitting idle in cold weather poses special challenges and requires you to follow special procedures. For example, when starting a cold-soaked engine, it is best to use a ground power supply so an adequate rotational speed can be obtained. A typical turbojet requires an N_2 speed of at least 10 percent for a successful light. In addition, if there is no indication of fan rotation on the N_1 tachometer, ice buildup could be interfering with fan rotation.

When you do get a successful engine start in cold weather, EGT indications may be much lower than during warm weather starts. Furthermore, since oil viscosity increases as temperature decreases, oil pressure indications may run full scale until the oil warms. It is also possible that the lubrication oil system's "filter blocked" warning light could illuminate until oil temperature rises.

ENGINE PERFORMANCE

Turbine engine performance is based on standards established by the Society of Automotive Engineers (SAE). These standards are known as engine power ratings and are listed on an engine's Type Certificate Data Sheet. In most cases, engine power ratings are expressed in values of EPR, percent N_1, or torque. Since aircraft and engine maintenance manuals often define engine performance using engine power rating terminology, you must be familiar with each of the ratings.

Power ratings common to most modern commercial gas turbine engines include takeoff power, maximum continuous power, maximum cruise power, cruise power, maximum climb power, ground idle, and flight idle. A **takeoff** power rating represents the amount of power an aircraft engine is allowed to produce for takeoff. In most cases, a takeoff power setting is time-limited; therefore, you must exercise caution during engine runs to make sure you comply with ground operation time limits. If takeoff power time limits are exceeded, the turbine section could overheat.

Maximum continuous power is a power level used at the discretion of the pilot for unusual or emergency situations. Depending on the engine model, maximum continuous power may be synonymous with **maximum cruise** power. As the name implies, a maximum continuous power setting is not subject to any time limitations. However, both max continuous and max cruise power settings result in increased fuel burns which shorten an aircraft's range capability.

A **cruise** power rating is used to extend an aircraft's range by providing the best fuel economy during flight. There is no time limit on this power setting.

An engine's **maximum climb** power rating is used for normal climb to cruise altitude. This power rating is higher than a cruise power rating and is not subject to time limitations. As with any maximum rating, when an engine is run at its maximum climb rating, a great deal of fuel is consumed.

Ground idle is the lowest allowable engine speed for ground operation. A typical ground idle rating is between 50 percent and 70 percent. The ground idle speed on a single-spool engine is indicated on the N_1 tachometer. However, if the engine has a dual or triple-spool compressor, ground idle speed is indicated on the N_2 and N_3 tachometers respectively.

Flight idle is the lowest allowable engine speed in flight and is used primarily for descent, approach, and landing. On many engines, flight idle is approximately 10 percent rpm higher than ground idle speed. The reason for this is that the slightly higher idle speed provides greater stall protection and quicker response to power needs. Some aircraft are equipped with power controls that automatically reset flight idle speed for increased idle rpm at higher altitudes.

DERATED ENGINE

When the power output of an engine is intentionally limited to less than the maximum power the engine can produce, the engine is said to be derated. An engine may be derated if it is installed in an aircraft that does not require the engine's maximum rated power. Another reason for derating an engine is to accommodate a component limitation such as a rotorcraft transmission. Derating an engine also provides a benefit of increased engine life.

PART-THROTTLE ENGINE

Part-throttle, or **flat-rated** engines are configured to produce takeoff thrust under standard sea level conditions before the power lever is advanced to the full-throttle position. When a part-throttle engine is operated in atmospheric conditions above standard, takeoff thrust is obtained by advancing the power lever further forward than when operating at sea level conditions. However, you must be careful when conducting a ground run on a part-throttle engine to avoid advancing the throttle too far and exceeding the takeoff thrust setting. This is especially true on cold days when the amount of thrust an engine can produce increases. Most commercial turbine engines are configured as part-throttle engines.

FULL-THROTTLE ENGINE

Most military aircraft use engines that are configured as full-throttle engines. With a full-throttle engine, takeoff power is obtained when the power lever is advanced to the full throttle position on a standard sea level day. However, with this type of engine, total thrust output decreases as temperatures increase and increases as temperatures decrease. A typical full-throttle engine is equipped with automatic limiting devices in the fuel control system to prevent engine damage caused by overspeed or overtemperature conditions. Therefore, when operating a full-throttle engine, the power lever is advanced to the full forward stop for each takeoff regardless of ambient conditions.

INSPECTIONS

As an aviation maintenance technician, you will probably spend the majority of your time inspecting various aircraft components. In fact, the Federal Aviation Regulations require specific inspections at set intervals in order for an aircraft to remain airworthy. When these inspections are done, impending problems are typically found before they become major.

Inspection intervals and requirements vary among aircraft depending on the specific operating conditions, the FAR part the aircraft operates under, and the components that are installed. On a typical transport category aircraft, inspections are scheduled in accordance with the number of flight cycles an aircraft experiences as well as the number of hours of operation. A **flight cycle** is typically defined as one takeoff and subsequent landing. The reason a flight cycle is used is because a high number of flight cycles in a given number of operational hours typically results in more wear and tear. For example, the operating conditions of a regional service airline or corporate flight department typically involve short flights with many takeoffs and landings. This type of operation tends to produce more wear than if the same aircraft were used on long-haul flights. Because of these differences, inspection programs must be tailored to the type of operation an aircraft experiences.

The following discussion addresses the typical inspection requirements associated with a transport category or business type aircraft. As a general rule, the two broad classifications of inspections conducted on gas turbine engines include routine and nonroutine inspections. The intent of the following discussion is to provide you with some of the items found on a typical inspection checklist. For a more detailed breakout of the inspections required on a particular aircraft, each aircraft operator has an FAA approved inspection schedule. A typical inspection schedule lists intervals, details, procedures, and special equipment needed to accomplish each inspection.

To aid the inspection process, many gas turbine engines are equipped with openings, or ports, that allow you to inspect the inside of the engine without disassembly. Some of the common tools used to inspect the inside of a gas turbine engine are the borescope, fiberscope, and electronic imaging.

A **borescope** is an internal viewing device which allows you to visually inspect areas inside a turbine engine without disassembling the engine. A borescope may be compared to a small periscope with an eyepiece at one end and a strong light, mirror, and lens at the other end. A conducting cord connects the probe to a control panel for adjusting light intensity and magnification. [Figure 4-10]

A **fiberoptic borescope**, or **fiberscope** is similar to a standard borescope, but has a flexible, articulated probe that can bend around corners. This allows you to view areas deep inside an assembly that previously required disassembly to inspect. In a typical fiberscope, a bundle of optical glass fibers transmit light from a light source to the scope's end, or probe. The probe is then inserted into the structure being inspected. The maximum length available for fiberoptic borescopes is four feet.

Special attachments allow mounting of a camera to the borescope to photographically record what is seen through the scope. The pictures taken aid in describing a situation to an inspector for airworthiness determination.

Electronic imaging is a relatively new technique which provides sharp, color images on a video monitor. Since the image is in color and can be magnified, it is much easier for inspectors to differentiate between an actual defect and an unclear image.

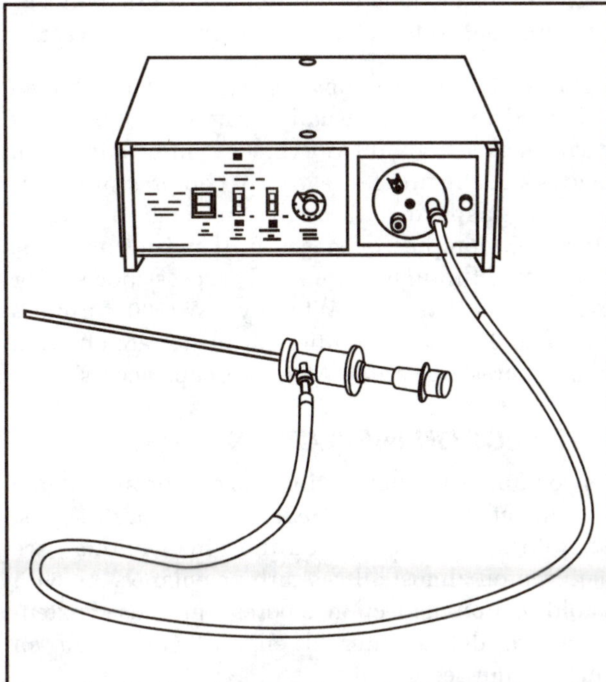

Figure 4-10. A typical borescope consists of a control panel, conducting cable, and rigid probe. The tip of the probe contains a light and lens that allow you to examine internal engine components.

Fiber-optic technology and light emitting diodes (LEDs) are utilized in many video imaging systems. Computer enhancement provided by this type of inspection equipment is particularly useful when videotaped because it allows several inspectors in different locations to consult on a given image.

ROUTINE INSPECTIONS

Routine inspections are those inspections that are mandated by an approved inspection schedule or Federal Aviation Regulations. All routine inspections are performed periodically at intervals specified by FAA approved company or airline operations manuals. Examples of routine inspections include the preflight inspection, continuous or progressive inspection, cold section inspection, and hot section inspection.

PREFLIGHT INSPECTION

A preflight inspection is a visual inspection of all external parts that can be seen from the ground. Most preflight inspections are accomplished by a flight crew prior to each flight; however, there may be occasions when you are asked to complete or assist with a preflight inspection. Engine-related items contained in a typical preflight inspection include opening access panels to check for fluid leaks, checking fluid levels, and visually examining the engine inlet, fan, tailpipe, and turbine.

PROGRESSIVE/CONTINUOUS INSPECTION

As mentioned earlier, most transport category and business type aircraft are on progressive or continuous inspection programs. The progressive inspection is designed for aircraft operators who do not wish to have their aircraft grounded for several days while an annual or 100 hour inspection is being accomplished. Instead, the inspection may be performed in segments each 90 days, or at each 25 hour interval. Like a continuous inspection program, a progressive inspection program must be approved by the FAA and an approved inspection procedures manual must be used. According to FAR 91.409, some of the items that must be included in an inspection procedures manual include:

1. An explanation of the progressive inspection, including the continuity of inspection responsibility, the making of reports, and the keeping of records and technical reference material.
2. An inspection schedule, specifying the intervals in hours or days when routine and detailed inspections will be performed and including instructions for exceeding an inspection interval by not more than 10 hours while en route and for

changing an inspection interval because of service experience.
3. Sample routine and detailed inspection forms and instructions for their use.
4. Sample reports and records, as well as instructions for their use.

The frequency and detail of the progressive inspection must provide a complete inspection of the aircraft within each 12 calendar months and be consistent with the manufacturer's recommendations, field service experience, and the kind of operation in which the aircraft is engaged. The progressive inspection schedule must ensure that the aircraft, at all times, will be airworthy and will conform to all applicable FAA aircraft specifications, type certificate data sheets, airworthiness directives, and other approved data.

A continuous airworthiness program also requires special approval from the FAA as well as an approved maintenance manual describing the procedures that must be followed to maintain the airworthiness of an aircraft. Additional information that must be included in an approved maintenance manual include:

1. The method of performing routine and nonroutine maintenance (other than required inspections), preventive maintenance, and alterations.
2. A designation of the items of maintenance and alteration that must be inspected (required inspections), including at least those that could result in a failure, malfunction, or defect if not performed properly or if improper parts or materials are used.
3. The method of performing required inspections and a designation by occupational title of personnel authorized to perform each required inspection.
4. Procedures for the reinspection of work performed pursuant to previous required inspection findings.
5. Procedures, standards, and limits necessary for required inspections and the acceptance or rejection of the items required to be inspected and for periodic inspection and calibration of precision tools, measuring devices, and test equipment.
6. Procedures to ensure that all required inspections are performed.
7. Instructions to prevent any person who performs any item of work from performing any required inspection of that work.
8. Instructions and procedures to prevent any decision of an inspector, regarding any required inspection from being countermanded by persons other than supervisory personnel of the inspection unit, or a person at that level of administrative control that has overall responsibility for the management of both the required inspection functions and the other maintenance, preventive maintenance, and alterations functions.
9. Procedures to ensure that required inspections, other maintenance, preventive maintenance, and alterations that are not completed as a result of shift changes or similar work interruptions are properly completed before the aircraft is released to service.

The routine inspections that are a part of a continuous inspection program are often given a specific name. Some examples of terms used by airlines to define routine inspections include "number 1 service," "number 2 service," "A" check and "B" check. The content and inspections required for each of these checks is defined in the approved maintenance manual.

COLD SECTION INSPECTION

Any routine or non-routine inspection performed on components of a turbine engine's inlet, compressor, or diffuser is known as a **cold section** inspection. Compressor blades are vulnerable to damage and erosion caused by ingestion of sand, ice, and other foreign objects. In addition, the accumulations of dirt and oxides which form on blades and vanes deteriorate engine performance. Therefore, routine periodic inspections to a turbine engine's cold section are needed to detect signs of change or wear.

Cold section inspections are typically conducted using a borescope to visually verify the condition of each stage of compressor blades and vanes. Fan blades and the first few stages of compressor blades can be inspected through the engine intake. However, compressor stages further back must be inspected through numbered access ports. For example, a Pratt and Whitney PW2000 turbine's 16th and 17th stage compressor blades are checked with a borescope at the AP8 borescope access port.

HOT SECTION INSPECTION

As you know, the hot section of a gas turbine engine is subject to a great deal of heat and stress. Therefore, periodic, routine inspections are required on almost all gas turbine engines. As with a cold section inspection, a borescope is used extensively to detect internal engine damage in an engine's hot section.

If you recall from Chapter 3, combustion liners are often constructed of thin stainless steel which expands when heated to operational temperatures, then shrinks as the engine cools after shutdown. This frequent expansion and shrinkage can cause stress cracks and warping. In addition, the corrosive gases produced by combustion often causes combustion liners to slowly erode. The presence of burned areas or hot spots in a combustion liner or on an exhaust tail cone indicate a malfunctioning fuel nozzle or other fuel system problem.

Another defect found during hot section inspections is misalignment of combustion liners known as **burner can shift**. This defect seriously affects combustor efficiency and engine performance.

A turbine section is subjected to a great deal of heat and stress in a highly corrosive environment. Therefore, an inspection of the turbine section is vital to detecting defects before they become serious. Easily accessed areas are inspected with a flashlight and magnifying glass or a dye penetrant. However, internal turbine sections are inspected with a borescope through access ports. In the example of a PW2000 engine, first stage turbine blades are viewed through the AP10 borescope access port. On the other hand, inspection of the high pressure nozzle guide vanes is sometimes accomplished using a borescope and looking out the end of the combustors. [Figure 4-11]

One thing you must be alert for when inspecting turbine blades is the presence of stress rupture cracks. **Stress rupture cracks** are hairline cracks that appear on the leading and trailing edges of turbine blades at a right angle to a blade's length. The presence of stress rupture cracks or rippling on the trailing edges of turbine blades typically indicates that an engine encountered a serious overtemperature incident.

In addition to inspecting the turbine blades, the turbine disk must also be examined carefully. Since the integrity of a turbine disk is critical to flight safety, any cracking on a turbine disk requires disk replacement.

NON-ROUTINE INSPECTIONS

A non-routine inspection is any inspection that must be done as a result of a component failure or incident that could potentially damage an engine. Some examples of incidents requiring a non-routine inspection include ingestion of birds, ice, or other foreign objects, and temperature or rpm overlimit incidents. Although damage to compressor or turbine blades may not be immediately noticed with respect to engine performance after an incident, the need for an inspection still exists. For example, if an engine experiences an overtemperature incident, the initial damage may not be noticed immediately.

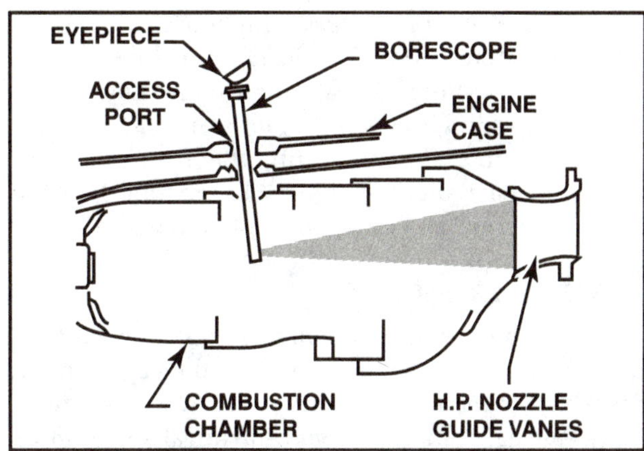

Figure 4-11. On some engines, the high pressure nozzle guide vanes are inspected with a borescope that is inserted into one of the engine's combustors.

However, if gone unchecked, the damage could result in blade disintegration later.

FOREIGN OBJECT DAMAGE

Foreign object damage (FOD) can occur anytime something is drawn into a gas turbine engine. Typical FOD consists of small nicks, dents, and scratches. However, FOD damage caused by bird strikes or ice can cause total destruction of an engine.

In addition to the physical damage caused by FOD, engine performance can also be effected. For example, typical performance deterioration that can result from FOD includes an increase in EGT readings with a corresponding decrease in EPR indications. Other possible indications would be a change in the relationship between N_1 and N_2 rotational speeds and excessive vibration.

Whenever a FOD incident occurs, the engine involved must be inspected. The level of inspection depends on the severity of the damage. For example, if an external inspection reveals little damage, a borescope inspection may be the only thing that has to be completed. If no damage exists within an engine and the damage on the fan blades, vanes, or compressor is minor, repairs can be made while the engine remains on the aircraft and the aircraft returned to service. However, if substantial damage is clearly visible, the engine will probably have to be removed and sent to an overhaul facility to be repaired.

A specific type of damage that may be caused by FOD is fan blade shingling. **Shingling** is the term used to describe the overlapping of midspan shrouds on fan blades. Anytime rotating fan blades enounter a force that pushes a blade sideways, shingling can occur. Common causes of shingling include FOD, compressor overspeed, or a compressor stall.

Whenever shingling occurs, you must inspect the top and bottom surfaces of the shrouds involved for scoring or galling. In addition, any blade that encounters shingling typically must be removed and inspected in accordance with the manufacturer's maintenance manual. If any cracks are found during the inspection, the fan blade must be replaced.

ENGINE OVERSPEED

If a gas turbine engine encounters an overspeed condition, most manufacturers require the engine to be inspected. Since damage from an overspeed typically results from excessive centrifugal force, most overspeed inspections are primarily concerned with the engine's rotating elements. The extent of an overspeed inspection varies depending on the speed the engine was operated. For example, the inspection required on some engines that experience an overspeed between 101 and 105 percent can be done while the engine remains on the aircraft. However, if the overspeed exceeds 105 percent, the inspection requires the engine to be removed and disassembled.

ENGINE OVERTEMPERATURE

Although the electronic controls on modern gas turbine engines have greatly reduced the possibility of experiencing an overtemperature condition, they do still happen. Most overheat incidents occur during an engine start; however, they can also occur in flight. Many overtemperature inspections can be accomplished with the engine installed on the aircraft. However, if significant damage is discovered during the inspection, the engine typically has to be removed to be repaired. Since the procedures involved with performing an overtemperature inspection vary from engine to engine, you must refer to the manufacturer's maintenance manual for specific inspection details.

MAINTENANCE

As you know, there are literally hundreds of different gas turbine engines used in aviation today. Therefore, it would be impractical to list and explain the various maintenance procedures for all turbine engines. Instead, you must rely on the information provided in the appropriate maintenance manuals for the specific engine requiring maintenance. For the purpose of this textbook, the material covered will look at some general maintenance practices that are common to most turbine engines.

Engine manufacturers are responsible for providing maintenance and overhaul information in the **Instructions for Continued Airworthiness** section in each set of maintenance manuals they produce. In addition, Federal Aviation Regulations require that each set of maintenance manuals provide detailed servicing information, troubleshooting guides, and schedules for cleaning, inspecting, adjusting, testing, and lubricating engine parts. Furthermore, an FAA approved set of maintenance manuals must include a section entitled **Airworthiness Limitations** which sets forth mandatory replacement times, inspection intervals, and component cycle limits.

There are two general classifications of maintenance performed on gas turbine engines: line maintenance and shop maintenance. **Line maintenance** is any type of maintenance that can be done while the engine is installed on an aircraft. On the other hand, **shop maintenance** refers to maintenance that requires an engine to be taken off an airplane. Since shop maintenance includes a great deal of the maintenance done during a overhaul, it will be covered in detail in Section B of this chapter.

LINE MAINTENANCE

Tasks that fall under the classification of line maintenance include performing inspections, troubleshooting, cleaning, trimming, verifying instrumentation readings, checking fluid levels, and replacing accessories. The following paragraphs will look at some of these tasks and provide you with procedures that are common to several turbine engines.

TROUBLESHOOTING

A typical turbine engine maintenance manual provides one or more troubleshooting tables to aid in pinpointing the cause of common malfunctions. However, it is not possible for these tables to list all malfunctions. Instead, troubleshooting tables provide you with a starting point in the troubleshooting process. This, combined with a thorough knowledge of the engine systems, logical reasoning, and experience will provide you with the information necessary to diagnose and correct complicated or intermittent malfunctions. [Figure 4-12]

Standard engine instrument readings are used with troubleshooting guides to provide clues as to the cause of a given engine malfunction. In addition, some aircraft are equipped with built-in test equipment, or **BITE** test systems. BITE systems consist of sensors, transducers, and computer monitoring devices which detect and record engine data such as vibration levels, temperatures, and pressures. A typical BITE test requires you to make entries on a keypad in the cockpit or at a remote terminal in order

INDICATED MALFUNCTION	POSSIBLE CAUSE	SUGGESTED ACTION
Engine has low RPM, exhaust gas temperature, and fuel flow when set to expected engine pressure ratio.	Engine pressure ratio indication has high reading error.	Check inlet pressure line from probe to transmitter for leaks. Check engine pressure ratio transmitter and indicator for accuracy.
Engine has high RPM, exhaust gas temperature, and fuel flow when set to expected engine pressure ratio.	Engine pressure ratio indication has low reading error due to: Misaligned or cracked turbine discharge probe. Leak in turbine discharge pressure line from probe to transmitter. Inaccurate engine pressure ratio transmitter or indicator.	Check probe condition. Pressure test turbine discharge pressure line for leaks. Check engine pressure ratio transmitter and indicator for accuracy.
NOTE: Engines with damage in turbine section may have tendency to hang up during starting.	If only exhaust gas temperature is high, other parameters normal, the problem may be thermocouple leads or instrument.	Recalibrate exhaust gas temperature instrumentation.
Engine vibrates throughout RPM range, but indicated amplitude reduces as RPM reduced.	Turbine damage.	Check turbine as outlined in preceeding item.
Engine vibrates at high RPM and fuel flow when compared to constant engine pressure ratio.	Damage to compressor section.	Check compressor section for damage.
Engine vibrates throughout RPM range, but is more pronounced in cruise or idle RPM range.	Engine-mounted accessory such as constant-speed drive, generator, hydraulic pump, etc.	Check each component in turn.
No change in power setting parameters, but oil temperature high.	Engine main bearings.	Check scavenge oil filters and magnetic plugs.
Engine has higher than normal exhaust gas temperature during take-off, climb, and cruise. RPM and fuel flow higher than normal.	Engine bleed air valve malfunction. Turbine discharge pressure probe or line to transmitter leaking.	Check operation of bleed valve. Check condition of probe and pressure line to transmitter.
Engine has high exhaust gas temperature at target engine pressure ratio for takeoff.	Engine out of trim.	Check engine with Jetcal. Retrim as desired.
Engine rumbles during starting and at low power cruise conditions.	Pressurizing and drain valve malfunction. Cracked air duct. Fuel control malfunction.	Replace pressurizing and drain valves. Repair or replace duct. Replace fuel control.
Engine RPM hangs up during starting.	Subzero ambient temperatures. Compressor section damage. Turbine section damage.	If hang up is due to low ambient temperature, engine usually can be started by turning on fuel booster pump or by positioning start lever to run earlier in the starting cycle. Check compressor for damage. Inspect turbine for damage.
High oil temperature.	Scavenge pump failure. Fuel heater malfunction.	Check lubricating system and scavenge pumps. Replace fuel heater.
High oil consumption.	Scavenge pump failure. High sump pressure. Gearbox seal leakage.	Check scavenge pumps. Check sump pressure as outlined in manufacturer's maintenance manual. Check gearbox seal by pressurizing overboard vent
Overboard oil loss.	Can be caused by high airflow through the tank, foaming oil, or unusual amounts of oil returned to the tank through the vent system.	Check oil for foaming; vacuum-check sumps; check scavenge pumps.

Figure 4-12. Troubleshooting guides provide suggestions to assist you in determining the cause of a malfunction and possible remedies.

to retrieve engine data. However, even this sophisticated equipment can only provide you with the symptoms a problem, leaving you to determine the actual problem.

FIELD CLEANING

Like any other aircraft component, the interior of a gas turbine engine must be periodically cleaned. If this is not done, the aerodynamic efficiency of the compressor blades will decrease as dirt, oil, and soot accumulate. The decrease in efficiency often leads to poor acceleration, reduced EPR, and excessive exhaust gas temperatures. Aircraft operated near salt water also require frequent cleaning to help prevent corrosion caused by salt deposits.

The two most common methods of removing dirt and salt deposits from inside a turbine engine are a fluid wash and an abrasive grit blast. With a **fluid wash**, either clean, demineralized water or an emulsion type cleaner are sprayed into an engine's intake. The use of water alone is typically used to remove salt deposits and, therefore, is often referred to as a **desalinization wash.** On the other hand, a fluid wash using an emulsion cleaner followed by a water rinse is typically used to remove baked on dirt and soot deposits. This type of wash is known as a **performance recovery wash.** To help you determine how often an engine must be cleaned, several manufacturers provide a recommended wash schedule. [Figure 4-13]

When performing a fluid wash, it is imperative that you follow the manufacturer's instructions. On turboprop engines, a fluid wash is usually accomplished by spraying, or pouring the washing liquid into the compressor inlet while the engine is motored with the starter. This is know as a **motoring wash** and is typically done at speeds that range from 10 to 25 percent. On the other hand, a fluid wash conducted on a large turbojet or turbo fan aircraft is accomplished by spraying the washing liquid into the engine's inlet while the engine idles at approximately 60 percent. [Figure 4-14]

When compressor contamination is too heavy to be effectively removed by an internal engine wash, a more vigorous **abrasive grit blast** cleaning is available. This heavy cleaning procedure involves injecting an abrasive grit such as Carboblast into the engine intake at selected power settings. Carboblast typically contains ground walnut shells or apricot pits. In all cases, follow the engine manufacturer's recommended procedure, using only the type and amount of material specified for a particular engine. The greater cleaning capability of this procedure provides a longer time interval between cleanings when compared to the solvent and water methods. However, an abrasive grit cleaning typically does little to clean turbine blades and vanes because most of the cleaning grit burns up before it reaches the turbines. [Figure 4-15]

ENGINE TRIMMING

Engine trimming refers to a process whereby an engine's fuel control unit is adjusted to allow an engine to produce its maximum rated thrust. Trimming is normally performed after an engine or fuel control unit is changed or whenever an engine does not produce its maximum thrust.

Manual trimming procedures vary widely between engine models; therefore, before you attempt to trim an engine, you should take time to review the spe-

OPERATING ENVIRONMENT	NATURE OF WASH	RECOMMENDED FREQUENCY	RECOMMENDED METHOD	REMARKS
Continuously salt laden	Desalination	Daily	Motoring	Strongly recommended after last flight of day.
Occasionally salt laden	Desalination	Weekly	Motoring	Strongly recommended. Adjust washing frequency to suit condition.
All	Performance Recovery	100 to 200 hours	Motoring or Running.	Strongly recommended. Performance recovery required less frequently. Adjust washing frequency to suit engine operating conditions as indicated by engine condition monitoring system. Motoring wash for light soil and multiple motoring or running washes for heavy soil is recommended.

Figure 4-13. As you can see in the wash schedule above, engines that are operated in a salt laden environment should be washed frequently. On the other hand, the need for a performance recovery wash is much less frequent.

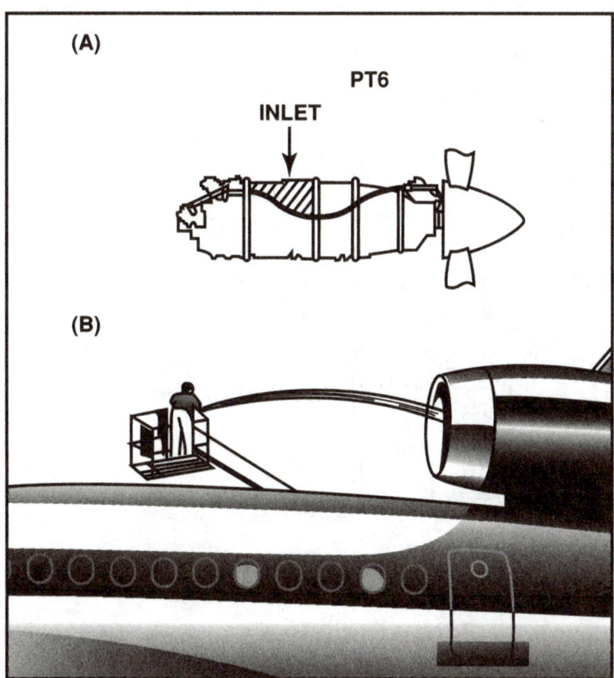

Figure 4-14. (A) — A fluid wash conducted on a typical turboprop engine is accomplished by pouring or spraying a cleaning fluid into the compressor inlet. (B) — A fluid wash done on a large turbojet or turbo fan engine is accomplished by spraying large quantities of wash fluid into an engine as it idles.

Figure 4-15. Abrasive grit blast cleaning is used to remove heavy engine contamination. To perform an abrasive grit blast, an engine is run while a specific quantity of abrasive grit is fed into the engine.

cific procedures in the engine's maintenance manual. A typical trimming procedure requires you to install calibrated instruments for reading turbine discharge pressure or EPR. In addition, a calibrated tachometer must be installed to read N_2 rpm. Once the instrumentation is installed, the aircraft should be pointed into the wind. However, if the velocity of the wind blowing into the intake is too great, elevated compression and turbine discharge pressures will result which, ultimately, will produce a low trim setting. Another step in the trimming procedure is to measure the barometric pressure at the engine inlet and the ambient temperature. This is required to correct performance readings to standard sea-level conditions. To obtain a temperature reading, it is common practice to hang a thermometer in the shade of the nose wheel well. The ideal conditions for trimming a turbine engine are no wind, low humidity, and standard temperature and pressure.

Once you have calculated the maximum power output for the engine you are trimming, start the engine and let it idle as specified in the maintenance manual. This is necessary so the engine has time to stabilize. To ensure an accurate trim setting, all engine bleed air must be turned off. Bleeding air off the compressor has the same effect as decreasing the compressor's efficiency. Therefore, if a trim adjustment is made with the bleeds on, an inaccurate, or overtrimmed condition will result.

With the engine running at idle and maximum power, observe the turbine discharge or EPR readings to determine how much trimming is necessary. If trimming of either the idle or maximum settings are necessary, it is typically accomplished by turning a screw type adjustment on the fuel control unit.

EGT AND TACHOMETER CHECKS

As you know, two of the most important factors affecting turbine engine life are EGT and engine rpm. If the cockpit indications of these two variables are incorrect, serious engine damage can result. For example, excessively high exhaust gas temperatures can reduce turbine blade life by as much as 50 percent, while low exhaust gas temperatures significantly reduce turbine engine efficiency and thrust. In addition, inaccurate rpm indications can lead to unintentional overspeed conditions resulting in premature engine failures. To help protect against EGT and rpm inaccuracies, these instrument systems are required to be periodically checked.

One way to check the accuracy of an engine's EGT and rpm indicating systems is with a **jet calibration**

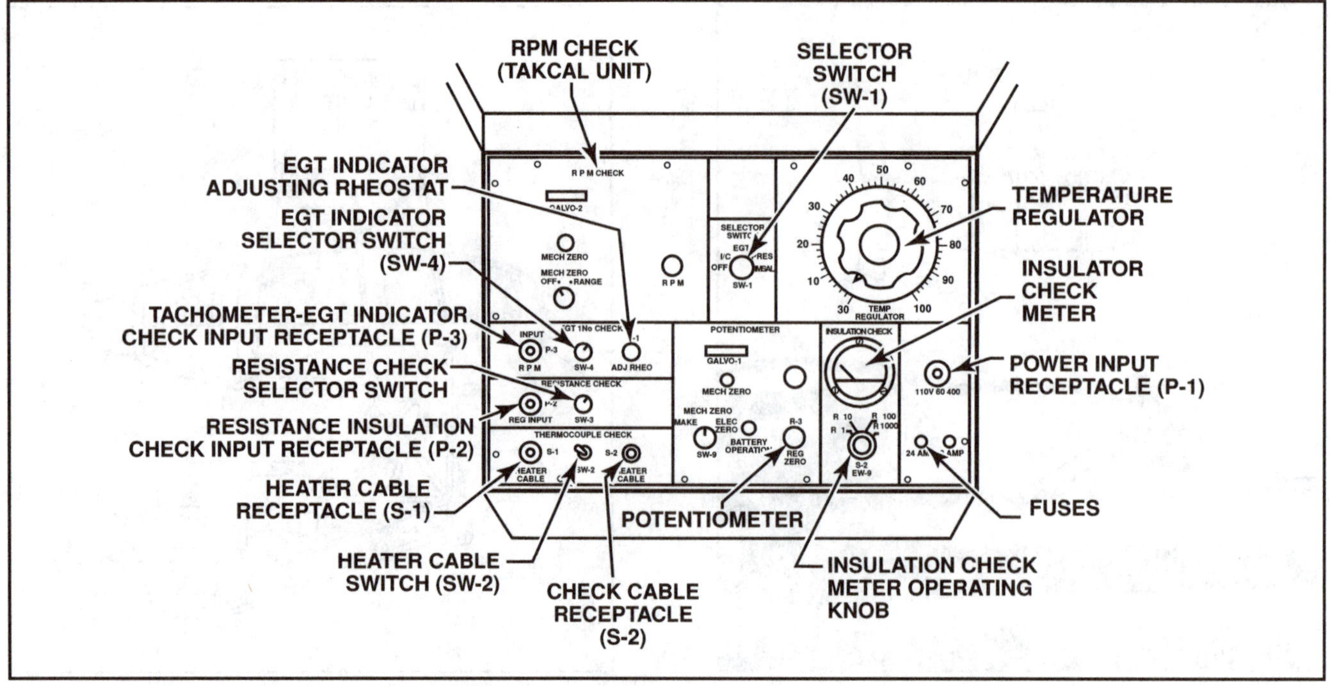

Figure 4-16. The instrument compartment on a Jetcal analyzer is conveniently marked off so you can easily identify the controls used for checking rpm, EGT, wire resistance, and insulation breaks.

(Jetcal) test unit. Jetcal is the trade name for several models of a widely used jet calibration test units manufactured by Howell Instruments, Inc. One model of Jetcal Analyzer consists of a portable EGT and rpm test unit. [Figure 4-16]

Specifically, a portable Jetcal analyzer allows you to:

1. Functionally check the aircraft EGT system for error without running the engine or disconnecting the wiring.
2. Detect inoperative or inaccurate thermocouples either in or out of the wiring harness.
3. Check the wiring harness for continuity, resistance, and accuracy, as well as identify breaks in harness wiring and poor or dirty electrical connections.
4. Check the insulation on the circuit wiring for short circuits to ground or short circuits between leads.
5. Check EGT indicators either in the instrument panel or disconnected from the aircraft EGT system for error.
6. Determine engine RPM with a accuracy of ±0.1 percent during engine run-up as well as check and troubleshoot the aircraft tachometer system.
7. Verify a proper relationship between the EGT and engine RPM on engine run-up.
8. Check aircraft fire detector, overheat detector, and wing anti-icing systems by using tempcal probes.

Usually, operating procedures are listed on an instruction plate attached to the Jetcal analyzer instrument case. However, there are some safety precautions you must be aware of before operating a Jetcal unit.

1. Do not use a standard volt-ohmmeter to check the potentiometer for continuity or you may damage the meter and battery cells.
2. Finish the thermocouple harness continuity and accuracy checks before engine run-up to be certain the EGT gauge is providing accurate readings.
3. Be sure the Jetcal is electrically grounded when using an AC power supply.
4. Use the appropriate heater probes on the engine thermocouples you intend to test. The temperature gradients vary with the design of the heater probes. Therefore, be certain you never attempt to modify a heater probe for testing other types of thermocouples.
5. Do not leave heater probe assemblies in the tailpipe during engine run-up.
6. To prevent damage to the Jetcal analyzer and heater probe assemblies, do not allow the heater probes to exceed 900°C.

EGT Circuit Checks

Continuity checks of the EGT circuit are designed to detect errors caused by one or more inoperative aircraft thermocouples. A continuity check is made by raising the temperature of a heater probe to between 500 and 700°C, and then placing the hot probe over each of the aircraft thermocouples. As each thermocouple heats up, the EGT gauge for that engine registers a temperature rise for each functionally correct thermocouple. Detecting a rise on the aircraft EGT gauge may be difficult with EGT systems having eight or more thermocouples in a single harness. This is due to the electrical characteristics of the parallel circuit in which the thermocouples operate. In this case, the Jetcal provides instructions for alternative testing of the aircraft thermocouples.

If the continuity of an EGT circuit checks out, the next step is to do a functional check of the EGT circuit. The time required to test an EGT system depends on several factors including: the number of engines, the number of thermocouples in a harness, the position of the harness in an engine, the number of errors found, and the time required to correct any errors. A normal functional test on a single engine can typically be performed in 10 to 20 minutes.

During an EGT circuit functional check and a thermocouple harness check, the Jetcal analyzer is guaranteed to be accurate within ±4°C. A functional check is made by heating the engine thermocouples in the tail pipe to the engine test temperature. The heat is supplied by the heater probes through the necessary cables. When the engine thermocouples are hot, their temperatures will register on the aircraft EGT indicator. At the same time, a set of thermocouples embedded in the heater probes are also sensing and registering the temperature put out by the probes. If the temperature indicated on the aircraft's EGT gauge is within the specified tolerance of the temperature reading on the Jetcal unit, the EGT circuit is operating properly. However, if the temperature difference exceeds the allowable tolerance, you must troubleshoot the aircraft system to determine which parts are malfunctioning.

EGT thermocouple electrical resistance and insulation are also checked with a Jetcal during a functional test. The resistance and insulation check circuits make it possible to analyze and isolate any error in the aircraft's EGT system. Since variations in resistance effect the amount of current flow in a thermocouple circuit, the resistance of a thermocouple harness must conform to a narrow tolerance. Erroneous temperature readings caused by incorrect harness resistance can result in overtemperature damage to the turbine and tailpipe.

To check an EGT indicator, remove it from the instrument panel and disconnect the thermocouple circuit leads. Attach the instrument cable and EGT indicator adapter leads to the indicator terminals and place the indicator in its Normal operating position. Once the Jetcal analyzer switches are set to the proper position, the indicator reading should correspond with the potentiometer readings on the Jetcal panel. [Figure 4-17]

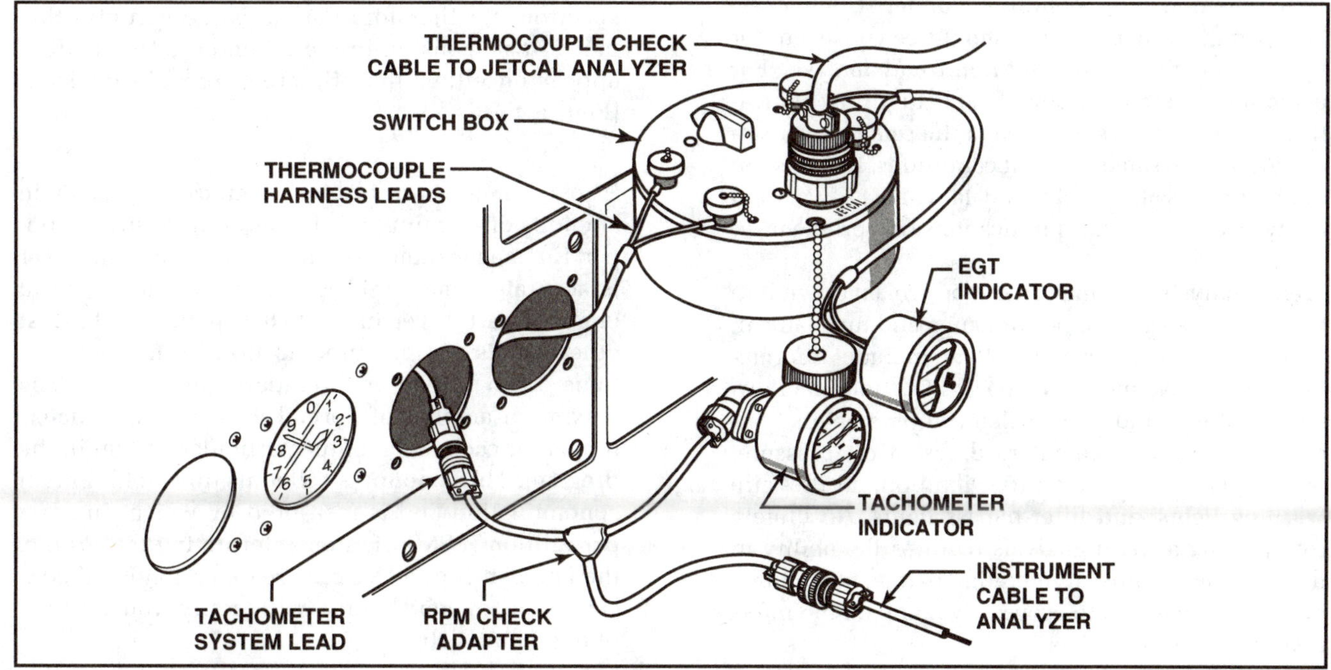

Figure 4-17. To test an EGT indicator, remove the indicator from the aircraft instrument panel and attach the Jetcal adapter cable. Next, attach the aircraft thermocouple harness leads and Jetcal analyzer cable to the Jetcal switch box.

Tachometer Check

Tachometer indications can be verified to within ±0.1 percent during engine run by measuring the frequency produced by the tachometer generator with the rpm check, or takcal, circuit in a Jetcal analyzer. To do this, the aircraft tachometer and the rpm check circuit are connected in parallel so as to provide simultaneous indications when the engine is run. To simplify the comparison between the aircraft's tachometer and the check circuit, the scale of the rpm check circuit is also calibrated in percent rpm.

TREND ANALYSIS

Performance monitoring of engines is a technique used by aviation maintenance organizations and engine manufacturers to improve engine service life and reduce operating costs. The monitoring of an engine's performance and condition over a period of time provides a database for trend analysis. Trend analysis alerts an operator to deteriorating performance, providing an opportunity to take corrective action before an engine failure occurs. After establishing a normal relationship between performance parameters during initial monitoring, recorded engine operating data is reviewed at regular intervals. Significant changes in the relationships between performance parameters may signal impending failures.

Data collection methods range from onboard computers to manual entries on paper forms. Regardless of the method used, conditions under which a certain parameter is measured should be consistent for the measurement to be useful in trend analysis. For example, EGT measurements and fuel flow indications should always be taken at the same power setting under the same ambient conditions. If this is not done, it is possible to obtain data which skews trend analysis and gives false indications of a problem.

Trend analysis information can be broken down into two broad categories; performance and mechanical. Typical performance parameters include information on EPR, N_1 speed, N_2 speed, EGT, and fuel flow. On the other hand, the mechanical parameters typically include instrument readings of oil pressure, oil temperature, oil quantity, vibration, oil pressure warning lights, and filter bypass lights. Accurately interpreting a trend analysis requires the ability to discern small shifts in operating parameters on one or more gauges and to accurately compare the information to base line data.

SPECTROMETRIC OIL ANALYSIS PROGRAM

A spectrometric oil analysis program, or **SOAP**, is another tool available to aircraft operators to help detect developing problems in an engine. Spectrometric analysis for metal particles suspended in oil is possible because metallic ions emit characteristic light spectra when vaporized by an electric arc. Each metal produces a unique spectrum, allowing easy identification of the metals present in the oil samples. The wavelength of spectral lines identifies each metal and the intensity of a line is used to measure the quantity of that metal in a sample.

When participating in a spectrometric oil analysis program, periodic samples of used oil are taken from an engine after shutdown or prior to servicing. Samples are taken from a sediment free location in the main oil tank and sent to an oil analysis laboratory. In the lab, a film of the used oil sample is picked up on the rim of a rotating, high purity, graphite disc electrode. A precisely controlled, high voltage, AC spark is discharged from a vertical electrode to the rotating disc. When this occurs, the film of oil on the disc begins to burn. Light emitted by the burning oil passes through a series of slits, precisely positioned to detect the wave lengths of various metals. As light passes through the slit, photo multiplier tubes electronically convert the light waves into energy which automatically prints the analytical results on the laboratory record sheets. The wear metals present are so small that they flow freely through system filters. The spectrometer therefore measures the particles that move in suspension in the oil and are too small to appear on either the oil screen or chip detector. [Figure 4-18]

Alloyed metals in turbine engines may contain amounts of aluminum, iron, chromium, silver, copper, tin, magnesium, lead, nickel, or titanium. Silver is accurately measured in concentrations down to one-half part silver in 1,000,000 parts of oil. Most other metals are measured accurately in concentrations down to two or three parts per million. The maximum amount of normal wear has been determined for each metal of the particular system in the program. This amount is called its threshold limit of contamination and is measured by weight in parts per million (PPM). If, after interpreting the results, the lab identifies a sharp increase or abnormal concentration of metal, they will notify you by telephone immediately.

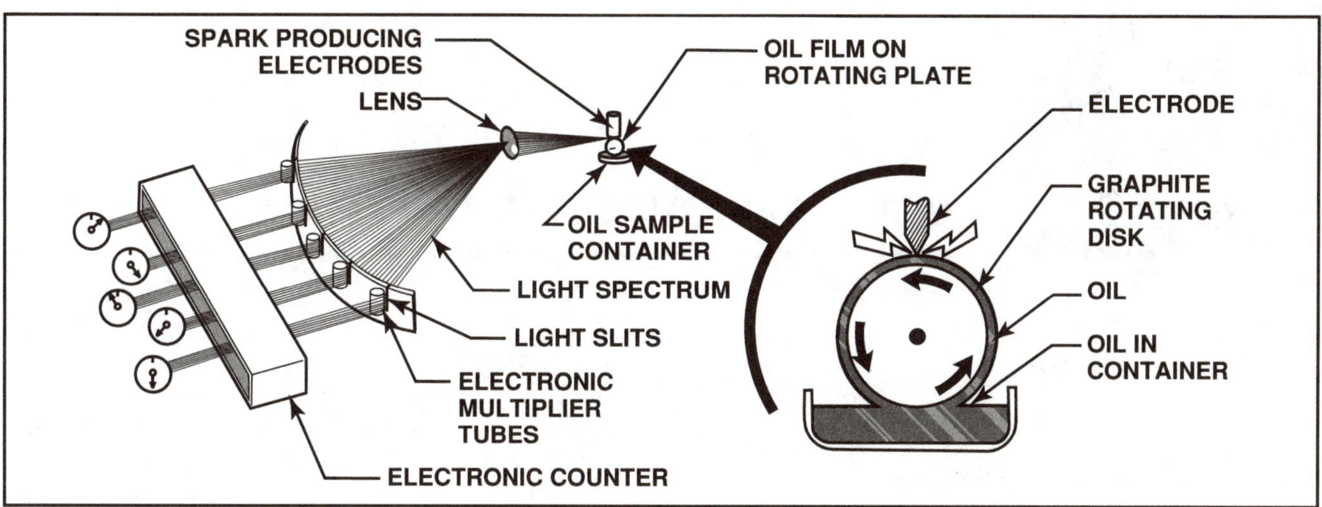

Figure 4-18. In spectrometric oil testing, a sample of used oil is sent to a lab where the oil is applied to a rotating, graphite disk and ignited by a high voltage, AC spark. As the oil burns, it emits light that passes a series of slits that are positioned to detect the wave lengths of different metals. The light energy passing through the slits is then converted into energy that is measured by an electronic counter.

ENGINE REMOVAL AND OVERHAUL

ENGINE REMOVAL

When engine removal becomes necessary for heavy maintenance or overhaul, many gas turbine powerplants are removed as a quick engine change assembly, or QECA. A QECA is essentially a powerplant with the necessary accessories already installed on the engine mounting assembly. Although the exact steps involved in removing a gas turbine engine vary from one make of aircraft model to another, there are some general guidelines you can use. However, these guidelines are no substitute for the manufacturer's instructions.

REASONS FOR REMOVAL

There are several reasons why an engine may have to be removed from an aircraft. For example, the accumulation of the number of hours or cycles recommended between overhaul or degradation in performance are reasons for removal. Additional reasons include serious foreign object or hot start damage as well as excessive metal particles found in the oil. Some routine maintenance and repairs may also require an engine to be removed from an aircraft. However, before you remove or replace an engine, you should always consult the applicable manufacturer's instructions to determine if engine removal is required.

ENGINE LIFE SPAN

Turbine engines have evolved into highly reliable powerplants with long service lives. Therefore, a given model may or may not have a specified TBO in the same way a reciprocating engine does. For example, instead of establishing a TBO for the entire engine, most manufacturers establish a recommended operating time between overhauls for each component or section of a turbine engine. However, some aircraft operators may obtain permission from the FAA to operate a turbine engine beyond TBO limits. Obtaining permission to go beyond a manufacturer's limitations depends on the part of the Federal Aviation Regulations an aircraft operates under as well as the approved inspection program requirements. In addition, the submission of trend analysis data and engine manufacturer data is usually required.

FOREIGN OBJECT DAMAGE

As discussed earlier, foreign object damage (FOD) can occur anytime something is drawn into a gas turbine engine. Whenever a FOD incident occurs, the engine involved must be inspected. The level of inspection depends on the severity of the damage. For example, if an external inspection reveals little damage, a borescope inspection may be the only thing that has to be completed. If no damage exists within an engine and the damage on the fan blades, vanes, or compressor is minor, repairs can be made while the engine remains on the aircraft. However, if substantial damage is clearly visible, the engine will probably have to be removed and sent to an overhaul facility to be repaired.

HOT START

If you recall, a hot start is one in which ignition occurs when there is an excessively rich fuel/air mixture. If a hot start is allowed to proceed, the exhaust gas temperature will exceed its allowable limit and the engine will be damaged. Whenever a hot start occurs, the affected engine typically must be inspected. Many overtemperature inspections can be accomplished with the engine installed on the aircraft. However, if significant damage is discovered during the inspection, the engine typically has to be removed to be repaired.

PREPARATION FOR REMOVAL

Turbine engine removal procedures have some similarities to reciprocating engine removal procedures.

For example, when removing a turbine engine, flammable fluids often leak from the engine and create a fire hazard. Therefore, an engine removal should be done in a well ventilated area with at least one fire extinguisher nearby. Once the aircraft is parked, chock the main gear wheels to keep the aircraft from rolling during the removal operation. If the aircraft has tricycle-type landing gear, check the maintenance manual to see if the tail must be supported to prevent the aircraft from tipping back when the engine is removed. In addition, the landing gear shock struts may need to be deflated to prevent damage from over-extension once the engine weight is removed from the aircraft.

IGNITION, FUEL, AND BATTERY DISARMING

Before starting the engine removal process, make sure the ignition system has been disconnected. On engines using high voltage ignition units, the voltage supply to the ignition unit must be disconnected and the unit allowed to sit for the time prescribed by the manufacturer. If this is not done, a lethal shock could result.

To help prevent fuel from spilling, make sure that all fuel shutoff valves are closed. Fuel selector valves are either manually or electrically operated. If an electric solenoid-operated shutoff valve is installed, it may be necessary to apply battery power to close the valve. After ensuring that all fuel is shut off, disconnect the battery to reduce the possibility of electrical sparks.

PROPELLER REMOVAL

Before removing a turboprop engine, the propeller must be taken off the engine. When removing a large constant speed propeller, the use of a propeller sling with a frame and hoist is imperative. In addition, it is best to have one or two additional people assist you to prevent damaging the propeller or surrounding equipment. In either case, you should follow the manufacturer's instructions for propeller removal.

FLUID LINE DISCONNECTION

The fluid lines that are used with gas turbine engines include flexible hoses, aluminum alloy tubing, and stainless steel tubing. Due to the temperatures radiated by a turbine engine as well as the fluid pressures required for operation, rigid tubing is used more on turbine engines than flexible tubing. For example, most fuel lines are constructed of rigid tubing that must be drained once it is removed. To simplify the removal process, most main fuel lines are readily accessible through an access panel. [Figure 4-19]

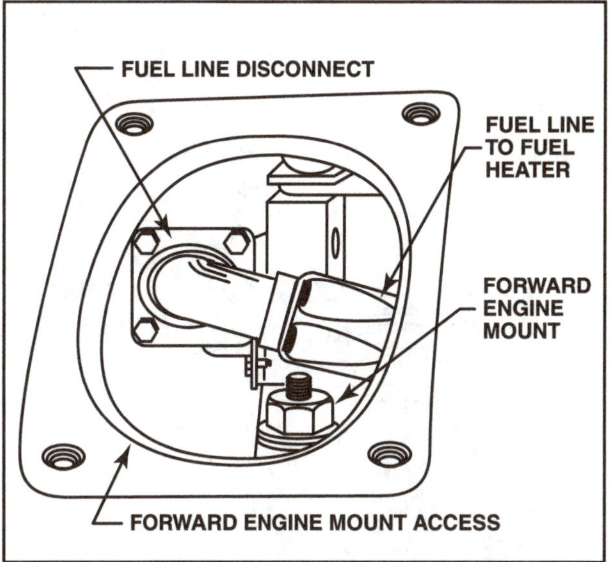

Figure 4-19. To disconnect the main fuel line on many turbine engines, remove the bolts from the hose flange. On other aircraft, the fuel line may have a quick disconnect that is connected at the firewall.

After a fuel line has drained, it should be plugged or covered with moisture-proof tape. This helps prevent insects, dirt, or other foreign matter from entering the line and keeps any residual fluids from dripping out. Once plugged, all lines and fittings should be labeled to help prevent possible confusion when reinstalling them on a new engine.

ELECTRICAL DISCONNECTION

Depending on the type of engine and equipment installed, electrical leads may be disconnected at the accessory or at the engine firewall. When disconnected at the firewall, AN and MS connectors are often used to simplify disconnections. A typical AN or MS electrical connector consists of a plug and receptacle assembly for multiple wires. To help prevent accidental disconnection during aircraft operation, the plug assembly screws to the

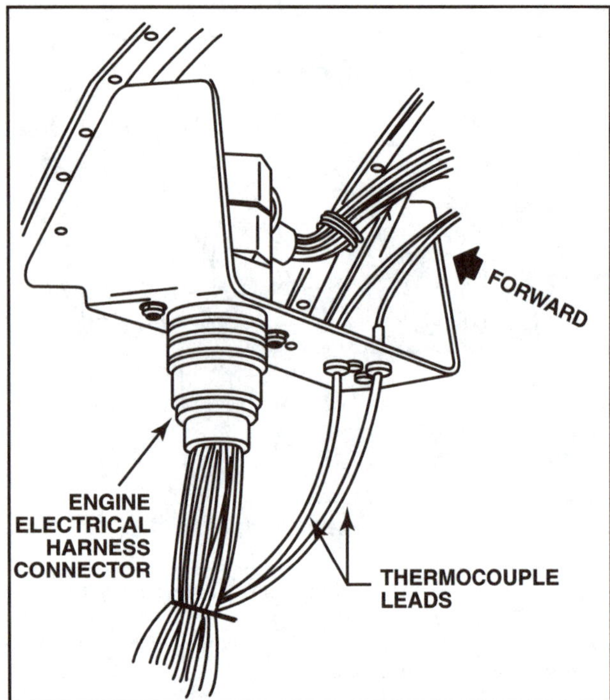

Figure 4-20. Most electrical connections are grouped in bundles and are disconnected at the firewall or junction by separating an AN or MS electrical connector.

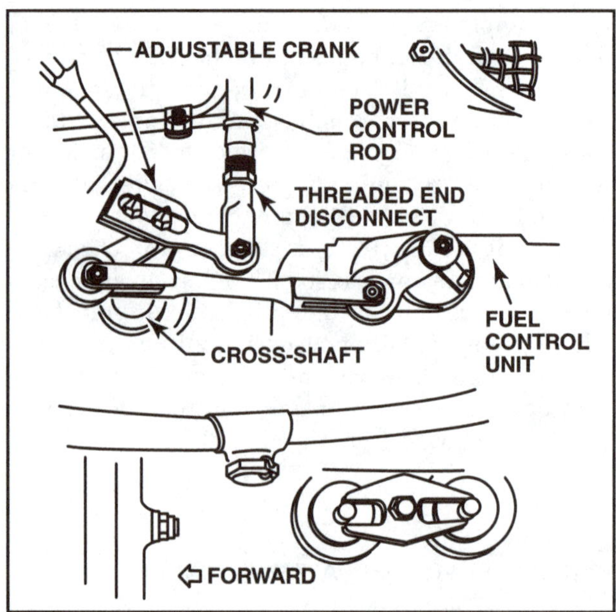

Figure 4-21. On engines that are controlled by a single power lever only one control rod and end must be removed to remove the engine. However, when removing a turboprop engine, you will have to remove the connections for the power lever, condition lever, and propeller control.

receptacle assembly and is secured with safety wire. [Figure 4-20]

To protect the exposed ends of connectors from dirt and moisture you should wrap them with moisture-proof tape whenever they are disconnected. Also, coil loose cables and secure conduits out of the way to prevent entanglement and damage when the engine is removed. If the wires lack legible identification, label them to eliminate confusion when reinstalling the engine.

ENGINE CONTROL DISCONNECTION

The engine control rods and cables allow operation of the throttle and mixture from within the cockpit. On a typical control rod, one or both ends are threaded with a clevis or rod end bearing attached. On most aircraft, a rod end bearing is connected to the fuel control unit by a bolt secured with a lock nut. To remove a control rod, begin by removing the lock nut. Once this is done, remove the bolt passing through the control assembly. [Figure 4-21]

After the engine control linkages have been disconnected, the nuts and bolts should be inspected for wear. Cotter pins must be replaced, but if the nuts and bolts do not need replacement, place them back in the control rod ends so they do not get lost. All control rods should either be removed completely or tied back to prevent them from being bent or broken when the engine is removed.

OTHER DISCONNECTIONS

Air intake, exhaust system components, and bleed air ducts must also be disconnected to facilitate engine removal. However, because the installation of these components varies among different engines and aircraft, it is best to refer to the manufacturer's instructions for specific removal procedures.

ENGINE HOISTING

After all engine connections are free and clear, the engine is ready for removal. If an engine has been thoroughly prepared, the actual removal process is typically a simple task. When removing an engine that is part of a QECA, the separation point is usually the firewall and the mount is removed with the engine.

Turbofan and turbojet engines are usually removed from an aircraft using one of several methods. One method requires an engine dolly which consists of an engine buildup stand mounted on a hydraulic

Figure 4-22. On an Airbus A320, an engine dolly is positioned under the engine and raised with a hydraulic lift to support the engine.

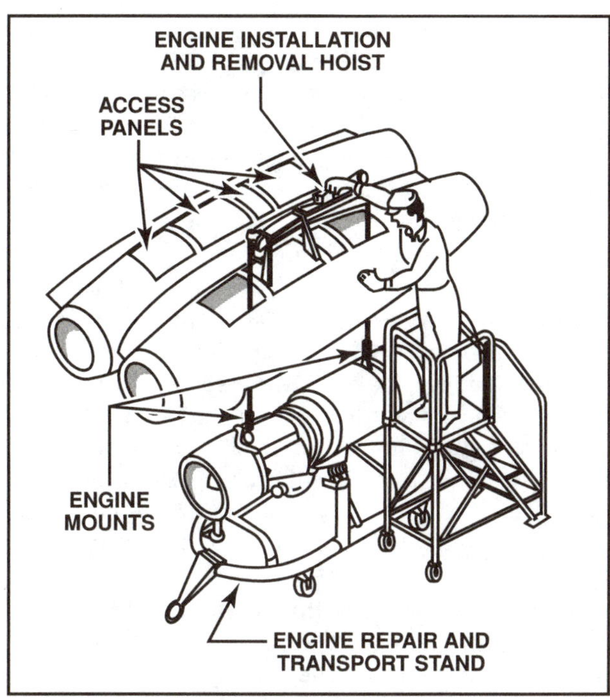

Figure 4-23. Pod-mounted engines such as those on a Lockheed Jetstar may be removed and lowered onto a transport truck by a two-cable hoist. The hoist attaches to the engine mount structure.

lift. The dolly is positioned under the engine while the hydraulic lift is used to raise the dolly into position for attachment to the engine. Once the engine is securely bolted onto the dolly, the dolly is slowly raised until all the engine weight is supported by the dolly. At this point, the nuts are removed from the engine mount attachments in the order specified in the manufacturer's instructions. Before the last nuts are removed, be sure that the engine is steadied and secure with no lateral loading. If everything is secure, remove the remaining engine mount hardware and gently move the engine free of the mount attachments. If the engine binds at any point, investigate the reason and maneuver the engine as necessary until it slips free. Once the engine is moved clear of the airframe, carefully lower the engine onto an engine stand and secure it with the appropriate hardware. [Figure 4-22]

Another method used to remove an engine requires mounting a hoist and a special sling on the top of the engine nacelle or pylon. Once mounted, the hoist is connected to the designated points on the engine mounts through the access ports in the pylon. When the engine is secured to the hoist, slowly remove all slack in the cables until all the engine weight is supported by the cables. With the engine weight supported, remove the fastening hardware, verify that all engine disconnections have been made, and lower the engine onto an engine buildup stand and transport truck. Operate the hoist in a manner that keeps the cables properly tensioned. [Figure 4-23]

When removing a turboprop engine, a conventional hoist that lifts the engine from the aircraft is typically used. When using this type of hoist, a sling is usually attached to the engine at prescribed points and the hoist is then attached to the sling. As a matter of safety, the sling and hoist should be carefully inspected and deemed safe for use before installing them on an engine. In addition, make sure that the hoist has sufficient capacity to lift the engine safely.

Some engine hoisting frames are fitted with power operated hoists. Power hoists should be used with caution, since considerable damage can be done by an inexperienced operator.

ENGINE COMPARTMENT

Anytime an engine is removed from an aircraft the opportunity exists to thoroughly inspect the engine compartment and make repairs as necessary. To begin, you should inspect the engine nacelle for corrosion, cracks, missing rivets, or any other visible defects. Cracks in the cowling or ducts can be stop-drilled or patched if they do not exceed limits specified in the manufacturer's structural repair manual.

Engine controls should be checked for integrity and freedom of movement. In addition, cables should be inspected for broken wire strands while cable pulleys are checked for binding, flat spots, and chipped edges. Furthermore, pulley bearings can be checked for excessive play. The anti-friction bearings in the control rods should move freely and the rods should be free of deformities. Inspect areas where cables and rods pass through bulkheads or panels for evidence of chafing and misalignment.

Check the outer surface of all exposed electrical wiring for breaks, chafing, deteriorated insulation, or other damage. In addition, inspect crimped and soldered terminals for security and cleanliness. Connector plugs must also be checked for damage, corrosion, and overall condition. Check bonding straps for fraying, loose attachments, and corrosion at terminal ends.

Hydraulic and pneumatic tubing should be free from dents, nicks, and kinks, and all connectors should be checked for the correct tightness. Check all air ducts for dents and the condition of the fabric or rubber anti-chafing strips at their joints. Dents should be worked out, and anti-chafing strips should be replaced if they have pulled loose or no longer form a tight seal.

Thoroughly inspect all hoses and replace those hoses that have been damaged by weather checking or cold flow. **Weather checking** is a cracking of the outside covering of hoses that sometimes penetrates to the reinforcement webbing. **Cold flow**, on the other hand, refers to deep and permanent impressions or cracks caused by hose clamps. Both types of damage weaken hoses and could eventually cause leaks to develop.

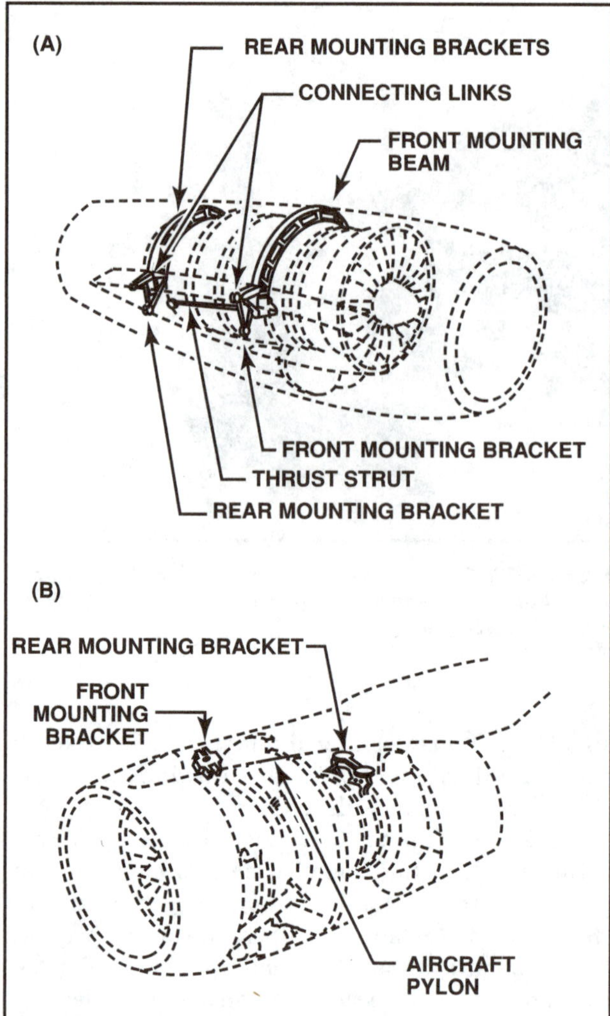

Figure 4-24. (A) — Many business jet aircraft have engines mounted on short thrust struts extending from the sides of the aft fuselage. The thrust struts support mounting brackets and beams with attachment points for an engine. (B) — Large transport category aircraft with engines mounted on wing pylons are typically equipped with mounting fixtures that support the engine at the front and rear.

ENGINE MOUNTS

Before a new or overhauled engine can be installed on an aircraft, an inspection of the engine mount structure must be accomplished. The engine mounts used for turboprop engines should be checked for bends, dents, flat spots, or elongated bolt holes. Typically, dye penetrants are used to help reveal cracks, porous areas, or other defects. Ferrous parts, such as the engine mounting bolts, are usually checked by magnetic particle inspection.

The strength and integrity of a turbine engine mount is as vitally important as a reciprocating engine mount. The construction of a typical turbofan or turbojet engine mount is much different from those used with turboprop engines. For example, most turbine engine mounts are made of stainless steel and support the engine from the front and back. However, because there are several different engine-airframe combinations and engine mounting locations, the type and location of engine mount fixtures varies significantly.

For example, wing mounted engines are typically suspended on pylons whereas aft-fuselage mounted engines are attached to the aircraft on thrust struts. On aircraft such as the Boeing 727, Lockheed L1011, and the McDonnell-Douglas DC-10 or MD-11 that have engines mounted in the vertical stabilizer, the engine mounts are fastened directly to the internal airframe structure. [Figure 4-24]

REMOVAL OF ACCESSORIES

In the event that you must remove a turbine engine that is not part of a QECA, the engine's accessories must be removed from the engine. Take care to note the location and attachments of accessories before removal to expedite buildup of the replacement powerplant. Hold the accessories aside for re-installation on the replacement engine or for overhaul, as required. If accessories are to be sent out to be overhauled or placed in storage, preserve them in accordance with the manufacturer's instructions. In addition, attach all the required accessory identification and record cards to each removed component.

After you have removed the accessories, all exposed drives and ports should be covered. If this is not done, dirt or other foreign objects could get into the engine and cause serious damage.

ENGINE OVERHAUL

Most turbine engines are maintained and overhauled on what is referred to as an **on-condition** basis. This means that each part or assembly on the engine is overhauled on the basis of its own life-limit. The life limit of a hot section, for example, is different from the life-limit of an accessory drive gearbox. In other words, a single life-limit, or TBO, is seldom established for the engine. The on-condition method replaces the TBO concept of overhauling an engine after a specified number of operational hours. The on-condition method of maintenance and overhaul is made possible by the reliability and modular construction of turbine engines. **Modular construction** is a concept that treats an engine as a set of separate modules assembled together. The inspection, line maintenance, and overhaul requirements of each module can be addressed separately. The modular concept reduces down time and expense for operators because maintenance and overhaul activities are spread over a longer period of time. In most cases, replacement of a module is considered to be a minor repair, requiring no FAA Form 337. On the other hand, a form 337 is required for the overhaul of an engine module since it is considered a major repair. [Figure 4-25]

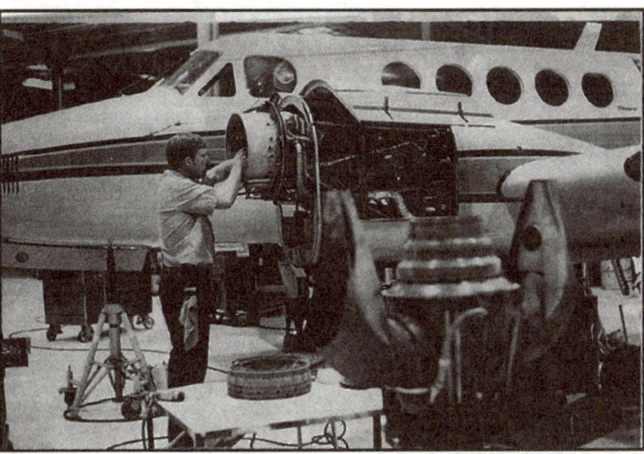

Figure 4-25. The modular design of some turboprop engines makes it possible to perform many maintenance tasks while the engine remains on the aircraft.

OVERHAUL PROCEDURES

Turbine engines are overhauled by the manufacturer or an approved overhaul facility. One reason for this is that there are several specialized tools required during the disassembly, inspection, and reassembly of turbine engines. Since you, as an aircraft maintenance technician, are not permitted to perform an overhaul on a turbine engine, the information presented here is provided to give you an overview of the steps involved in overhauling a typical turbine engine.

As with any engine overhaul, the specific overhaul procedures for any given engine are listed in the maintenance and overhaul manuals written for that engine. Therefore, the overhaul practices and procedures discussed here are general in nature.

DISASSEMBLY

Turbine engines are disassembled either vertically or horizontally. When the vertical method is used, the forward part of the engine is usually mounted in a fixture facing downward. A small engine may be mounted on a fixture with castors so it can be rolled from one work area to another. On the other hand, large engines are often mounted vertically on a stationary fixture which is surrounded by scaffolding. Another vertical mounting method for large engines involves securing the engine to an elevator which can be lowered into the shop floor. Scaffolds or elevators permit access to any point along the engine's length. When disassembled horizontally, an engine is typically mounted in a stand designed to allow the engine to be turned over for access to all external engine areas.

Once mounted on a disassembly stand, the engine is dismantled into modules, or main subassemblies. Each module is then mounted on a separate stand and moved to an area where it is further disassembled for cleaning, inspection, and overhaul. Large or heavy modules such as the compressor section and turbine section are lifted from the mounted engine by cranes or hoists.

CLEANING

Once disassembled, each engine component is cleaned so flaws and defects can be more easily detected. In addition, cleaning is required so that oxide deposits and dirt can be removed from a serviceable part to prepare it for special applications such as plating, anodizing, or painting before it is placed back in service.

All engine components are cleaned using approved cleaning methods and agents to prevent unintentional damage. For example, some cleaning solutions may strip plating from a part or cause a reaction with a base metal. As another example, you should refrain from cleaning titanium components with trichlorethylene. The reason for this is that entrapped traces of trichlorethylene can cause corrosion. Some commonly used cleaning methods include washing with organic solvents, vapor degreasing, steam cleaning, and tumbling in a grit solution. An effective cleaning method for hot section components consists of a series of controlled acid or alkali baths and water rinses. Grit blasting may also be useful on either cold or hot section components.

BEARINGS

Turbine engine bearings receive special handling during the cleaning process. This is necessary to prevent the onset of surface corrosion once a bearing has been removed from an engine. Most turbine engine overhaul instructions specify that bearings should be cleaned in an environmentally controlled room. Because of the close tolerances, even the slightest damage from corrosion and other sources is critical. For this reason, turbine engine bearings should never be left unprotected.

To properly handle bearings, lint-free cotton or synthetic rubber gloves are used to keep the acids, oils, and moisture on your hands from contaminating any bearing surface. In addition, each bearing must be cleaned in a separate container filled with fresh cleaning solvent. Shop cleaning vats and vapor degreasing should not be used because of possible contaminants left from cleaning other parts.

Once clean, shop air should never be used to blow a bearing dry since moisture in the air supply can corrode the bearing. It is better to use a lint-free cloth or let the bearing air dry. Once dry, immediately lubricate a bearing using the specified lubricant.

VISUAL INSPECTION

Heavy maintenance inspections performed during overhaul start with a thorough visual examination after the engine parts have been cleaned. Typically, an inspection light and magnifying glass are used for close visual inspections.

Before conducting an actual inspection, it is advisable to review an engine's operation logs for entries made since the last inspection. Entries of hot starts, hung starts, oil and fuel pressure fluctuations, and overspeed or overtemperature incidents provide clues to what type of defects may be found.

The terms used to describe the types of defects and damage found in turbine engines are similar to the terms used to describe damage found in reciprocating engines. However, additional terms are needed to describe defects and repairs unique to turbine engines. These additional terms include:

Blending — A method of filing compressor or turbine blades and vanes to remove damage and recontour them back to an aerodynamic shape.

Blistering — Raised areas indicating a separation of a surface layer from a base metal. Blistering is often evident as peeling or flaking of a metal plating.

Bow — A stress-induced bend or curve in a blade's contour.

Bulge — An outward bending or swelling caused by excessive pressure or weakening due to excessive heat.

Compression — A squeezing force which is produced by two opposing forces acting on a part.

Creep — A condition of permanent elongation in rotating airfoils caused by thermal stress and centrifugal loading.

Dynamic Balancing — A procedure which balances the main rotating assembly of a turbine engine both in the rotational plane and along the rotor axis.

Electrolytic Action — Breakdown of surfaces caused by electrical activity between dissimilar metals. Electrolytic action is also known as galvanic corrosion.

Flowing — The spreading out of a plated or painted surface caused by poor adhesion to the base or excessive loading on the part's surface.

Glazing — The development of a hard, glossy surface on bearing surfaces in the presence of oil, heat, and pressure.

Growth — A term used interchangeably with creep to indicate elongation of a compressor or turbine blade.

Guttering — Deep, concentrated erosion resulting from enlargement of cracks or repeated exposure to a concentrated flame.

Profile — The contour or aerodynamic shape of a blade or surface.

Shear — A tearing force produced by two opposing parallel forces acting on a part.

Static Balancing — A procedure which balances the main rotating assembly of a turbine engine to help reduce vibration.

Tension — A force which tends to pull an object apart.

Untwist — A straightening and loss of blade curvature resulting from gas loads, thermal stress, and centrifugal loading.

COMPRESSOR SECTION

A turbine engine's fan blades or first stage compressor blades are vulnerable to damage caused by ingestion of foreign objects and erosion. Therefore, compressor blades and vanes must be visually examined to detect cracks, dents, gouges, and other defects caused by FOD. It is very important that you be able to detect and correct critical blade defects because a single blade failure can lead to total engine failure. [Figure 4-26]

Light or minor foreign object damage can typically be repaired by blending the affected area away and then contouring to a final shape. On the other hand, severe damage or any damage in a blade's root requires blade replacement.

Blade and vane erosion results from ingestion of sand, dirt, dust, and other fine airborne contaminants. The abrasive effect of repeated ingestion can wear through a blade's surface coating and into the base metal. Slipstreams around the engine core of modern high bypass engines reduce blade erosion by directing some of the contaminants around, rather than through a compressor. However, wing mounted turbofan engines often have little ground

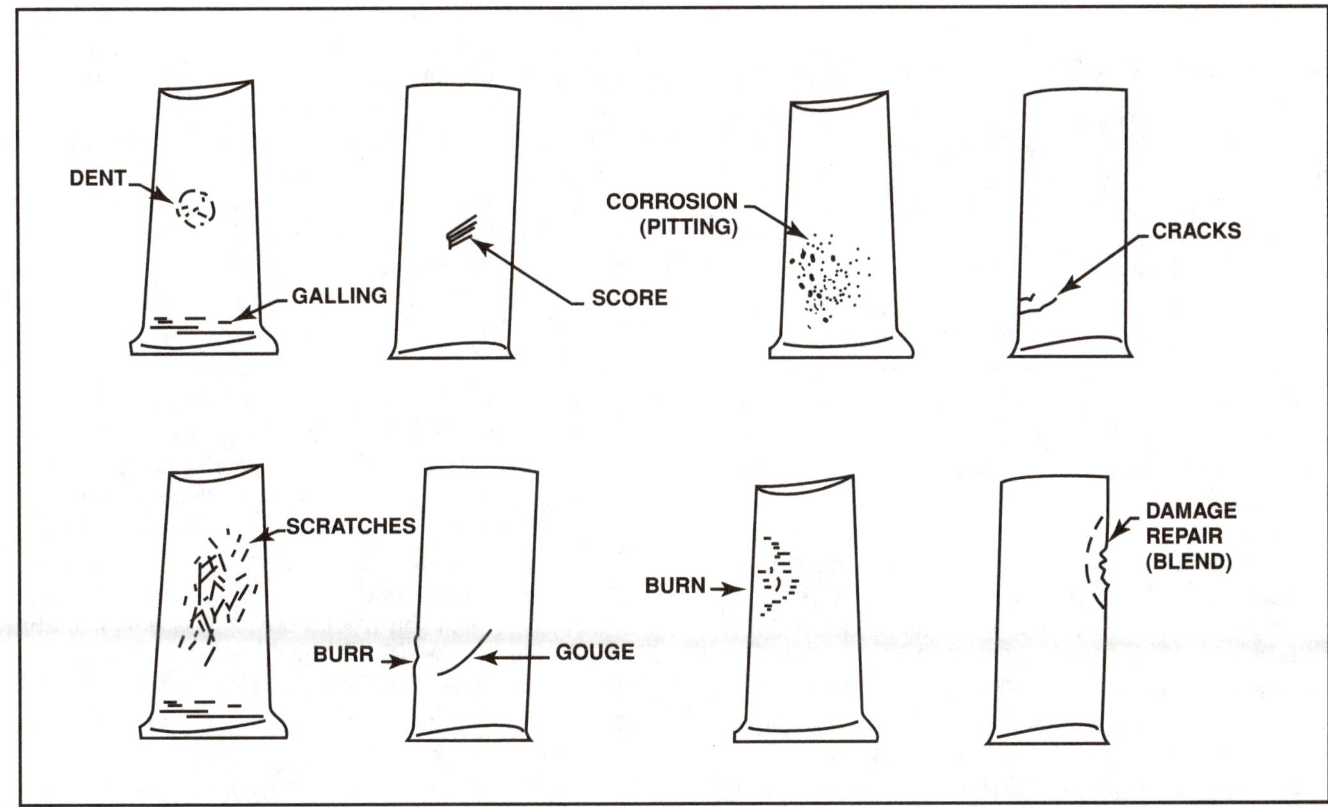

Figure 4-26. Compressor blades are subject to stress, metal fatigue, and FOD related defects ranging from light scratches and small dents to dangerous defects such as cracks and deep gouges.

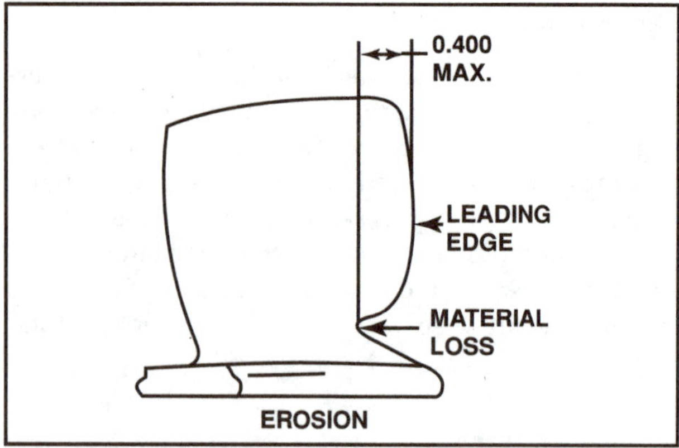

Figure 4-27. Blade erosion is accumulative and occurs over many hours of operation. Erosion shows up as a loss of material on a blade's leading edge and near a blade's root.

clearance, making them vulnerable to blade erosion during ground operations. [Figure 4-27]

For a compressor to perform efficiently, the clearance between a compressor blade and the compressor case liner must be as small as possible. However, accumulative compressor blade creep, or growth eventually causes the blade tips to rub on the lining. Severe rubbing can cause galling on compressor blade tips which reduces blade efficiency and strength.

COMBUSTION SECTION

The types of defects that are acceptable for a given combustion section vary among engine models. Therefore, when inspecting a combustion chamber, you must follow the manufacturer's instructions. Typically, a combustion section is examined for the same types of damage in both line maintenance and heavy maintenance inspections. However, the method of inspection often differs. For example, when inspecting a combustion chamber during line maintenance, a borescope is required. However, during an overhaul, the entire combustion section is disassembled allowing a detailed inspection without a borescope.

Some of the more common defects found during an inspection include cracks, burner can shift, hot spots or scorched areas, warpage, and erosion. Combustion liners should also be checked for excess weld material or slag around all welded seams. If the welded material is not thoroughly fused into the base metal, the weld should be removed and reapplied. If this is not done, pieces of excess weld could break loose and damage turbine components downstream. By the same token, a liner having two or more converging cracks that are progressing from a free edge must be repaired or replaced to prevent a piece of metal from breaking free and causing damage elsewhere. Minor cracks in the baffling around a fuel nozzle support seat should be repaired if a single crack connects more than two air holes. In addition, minor cracks in a liner and around igniter boss pads should also be repaired. However, cracks in a cone or swirl vane are cause for rejection of the combustion liner.

A malfunctioning fuel nozzle can seriously damage a combustion liner. Typically, hot spots or scorched areas on a combustion liner result from flame contact due to a malfunctioning or misaligned fuel nozzle. For example, a partially clogged fuel nozzle often causes damage known as **hot streaking** in a combustion section. Hot streaking typically consists of burn marks along the length of a combustion section that result from unatomized fuel contacting the combustion liner and then burning. Severe hot streaking can result in a flame passing through the entire turbine section to the tailpipe.

TURBINE SECTION

As you know, the turbine section of an engine is subjected to a great deal of heat and stress. Therefore, it is common to find damage in the form of cracking, warping, erosion, and burning. Cracking is probably the most common type of damage found in a turbine engine, followed by erosion which is caused by the flow of gases and the impingement of impurities in the gases on internal components. To aid in the inspection of a complete turbine section, it is best to inspect the turbine nozzle vanes, turbine disk, and turbine blades separately.

Turbine Nozzle Vanes

If you recall from Chapter 2, the hottest gases in a turbine engine pass through the first set of turbine nozzle vanes. Because of this, small cracks are frequently found. Depending on the size and orientation of the cracks, a small amount of cracking may be acceptable. Since stress is initially relieved by the development of small cracks, the small amount of crack progression in non-moving parts is usually negligible. However, anytime a set of cracks appear to be converging, the cracked component must be replaced to prevent major engine damage from occurring.

In addition to cracking, many operational hours of intense thermal stress and high-speed gases impacting

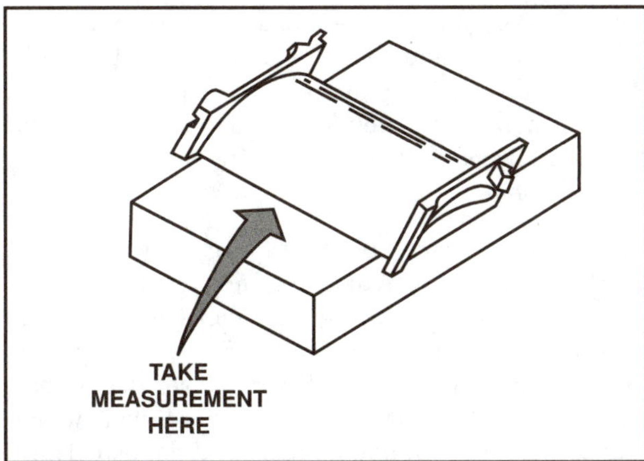

Figure 4-28. Checking a vane for bowing is accomplished by placing the vane on a flat plate fixture and inserting a thickness gauge under the leading and trailing edge.

a set of vanes can cause bowing and warping. The amount a given vane is bowed is measured on the trailing edge of each vane using a flat plate fixture and thickness gauge. Vanes which are bowed more than the allowable limits are either replaced or repaired in accordance with overhaul instructions. Typically, bowing is greater on the trailing edge than the leading edge. Therefore, if the trailing edge is within serviceable limits, the leading edge will more than likely be within limits as well. [Figure 4-28]

Turbine Disk

A turbine disk is typically inspected visually using a strong inspection light and magnifying glass. Because of the centrifugal forces a turbine wheel is subjected to, any cracks found on a turbine disk are cause for rejection and replacement. However, some manufacturers do allow continued use of a turbine disk if slight pitting exists as long as the pitting can be blended by stoning and polishing.

Turbine Blades

Turbine blades routinely incur damage because of the extreme environment in which they operate. Because of the potential for catastrophic engine failure should a turbine blade fail, cracking is not permitted in a turbine blade. Of particular concern during visual inspections are **stress rupture cracks** on turbine blade leading and trailing edges. Stress rupture cracks are perceptible as fine hairline cracks that appear at right angles to the blade length. Typical causes of stress rupture cracks include excessive temperatures or centrifugal loading.

Turbine blades are more prone to blade creep than compressor blades due to the high temperatures and centrifugal loads imposed during each engine cycle. A turbine **engine cycle** consists of engine start, operation for a period of time, and shutdown. Each engine cycle subjects turbine blades to high heat and high rotational speeds. As a result, every turbine blade becomes slightly longer with each engine cycle. Although the additional length may be only millionths of an inch, the accumulative effect produced by numerous engine cycles can eventually eliminate blade-to-case clearances.

Blade creep is divided into three stages, or classifications — primary, secondary, and tertiary. **Primary creep** occurs during an engine's first run when new blades experience operational stresses for the first time. **Secondary creep** occurs slowly during many hours of operation. Engine manufacturers take secondary creep into consideration when establishing a turbine's service life. **Tertiary creep** is a third stage which occurs at an accelerated rate after a period of secondary creep. The onset of tertiary creep is attributed to hot starts, overtemperature events, extended operation at high power settings, and blade erosion.

Loads imposed by the flow of gases across turbine blades and vanes can cause them to untwist. When turbine blades and vanes begin untwisting, the efficiency of the turbine system decreases resulting in the deterioration of total engine performance. In order to check blades and vanes for untwist, they must be removed during engine tear down. Once removed, they can be measured in special shop fixtures. When a blade is removed for inspection, it must be reinstalled in the exact slot from which it came. This is necessary to maintain turbine wheel balance.

Curling of blade tips is usually acceptable if no sharp bends exist and the curling is within prescribed limits. Leading edge limits are typically a one-half square inch area at the tip while trailing edge limits are much less. Cracking or breaking of a blade tip commonly results from sharp bends at the tip and are cause for blade replacement.

EXHAUST SECTION

The exhaust section of a turbine engine is subjected to the same high stresses and corrosive environment as the turbine section. Therefore, warping, buckling, and cracking are common defects found during inspections. A malfunctioning fuel nozzle or combustion chamber can produce hot spots, or hot streaking, on the exhaust cone and tailpipe. If you recall, a fuel nozzle spraying a solid stream of fuel can produce a flame long enough to burn the exhaust cone. By the same token, if secondary airflow does not properly control the flame zone, the combustion flame may be allowed to contact the exhaust cone or tailpipe. Warping in an exhaust duct liner generally indicates the occurrence of a severe overtemperature event.

BEARINGS

Bearing inspections should be completed in the same environmentally controlled room in which the bearings were cleaned. Handle bearings with lint-free cotton or synthetic rubber gloves during the inspection process. To properly inspect a bearing, an inspection must be conducted with the proper lighting and magnification to detect flaws. Bearings tend to become work-hardened with many hours of operation and, as a result, become brittle and susceptible to chipping. In some cases, the only way a bearing may be reused is if there are no detectable flaws on any part of the bearing. In other cases, some very minor surface defects may be accepted. To determine the exact type and number of defects that are permissible, refer to the manufacturers specifications.

Once an inspection is complete and a bearing is deemed to be serviceable, a magnetism check must be accomplished. Studies show that a bearing can become magnetized from the effects of rotation at high speeds, lightening strikes absorbed by an aircraft, and arc welding on the engine if the welding equipment is improperly grounded. To determine if a bearing has been magnetized, a magnetic field detector apparatus is utilized. Any bearing that is found to be magnetized must be degaussed, or demagnetized. Degaussing is a procedure which destroys the magnetic field in a magnetized part. To degauss a part, the part is placed near or passed through an electromagnetic coil which uses alternating current to create an alternating magnetic field. When a part is brought into close proximity to a degausser, the magnetic domains in the part are forced out of alignment so there is no longer a magnetic field in the part. Once a bearing has been degaussed and passes the magnetism check, it should be stored in vapor proof paper until it is needed for engine reassembly.

MARKING PARTS

A method of identifying areas to be repaired on cold and hot section components is needed during the inspection process. This saves time during repair procedures because a technician can clearly see the area that needs repair. Approved marking materials for both cold and hot sections include chalk, special layout dye, and some commercial felt-tip applicators and marking pencils. The use of either wax or grease marking pencils is also acceptable for marking parts that are not directly exposed to extreme heat.

You must be very careful to use only approved marking materials when marking parts that are directly exposed to an engine's hot gas path. This includes turbine blades and disks, turbine vanes, and combustion chamber liners. Never use a common graphite-lead pencil or any marker which leaves a carbon, copper, zinc, or lead deposit. These deposits can be drawn into the metal when heated, causing intergranular stress. In addition, layout dye, or dychem, can be potentially dangerous to hot section components if not completely removed. For these reasons, specific marking procedures and materials specified by an engine manufacturer take precedence over general marking practices.

STRUCTURAL INSPECTION

Structural inspections are conducted using nondestructive testing methods such as magnetic particle, fluorescent or dye penetrant, radiography, eddy current, and ultrasonic. The purpose of a structural inspection is to detect hidden flaws that are undetectable through visual inspection. For example, a hairline crack in a hot section component may only be visible with a fluorescent or dye penetrant. As another example any defects that exist below the surface of a component are detectable only through magnetic particle, radiography, eddy current, or ultrasonic testing.

As you know, magnetic particle testing can only be used on ferrous materials. The particles may be applied in either a dry form or wet in a solvent solution. The dry form works best on cast or forged parts with rough surfaces. A wet solution with fluorescent particles and an ultraviolet lamp best detects fine cracks in smooth surfaces.

Dye penetrant test kits are available with red dye or green dye. Red dye is convenient for daylight use because the developer may be sprayed from a can on the tested part. The developer causes penetrant trapped in a surface defect to turn red. The red mark or line on the part's surface is then clearly visible. Green dye kits work best on parts which can be removed and placed in a drip tray. After cleaning, a green fluorescent penetrating fluid is sprayed on the part and allowed to dry. An ultraviolet lamp is then used in a darkened room to illuminate defects, which show up as bright yellow-green lines.

Radiography is a testing method which uses X-rays or Gamma rays to penetrate a part and reveal hidden flaws. This testing method requires special training and licensing because it presents a hazard to personnel and requires certain safety precautions. Defects missed by visual and dye-penetrant methods are typically detected by radiography. This method may occasionally be utilized to verify suspected defects in an area which is not easily accessible. However, several inherent limitations of this method limit its usefulness in engine overhaul applications.

Eddy current inspection locates both surface and subsurface discontinuities in metal parts. The specialized test equipment supplies alternating current at a specified frequency to a test coil which is held on the part to be tested. The magnetic field produced by the test coil induces a secondary magnetic field in the part being tested. The secondary magnetic field causes eddy current flow in the part which is measured and analyzed electronically. Discontinuities in a component disrupt the induced magnetic field and produce an anomaly which is detected by the test equipment and analyzed.

Ultrasonic testing introduces high frequency sound waves through a part to detect discontinuities. There are two types of ultrasonic test equipment available; the immersion type and the contact type. Immersion equipment is heavy and stationary while contact equipment is small and portable. Both types beam sound waves through a part and display the response on a CRT for analysis. Examination of the variations found in a standard response pattern provides indications of discontinuities and flaws in a part.

DIMENSIONAL INSPECTION

Close tolerances and fits make dimensional inspections of turbine engine parts very important in determining their serviceability. For example, correct clearances between compressor and turbine blades and the engine housing is crucial to engine efficiency. Blade tip clearances are usually measured with a thickness gauge. Additional components that must be dimensionally checked during an overhaul are listed by manufacturers for each engine model in the overhaul manual. When specified, special tools provided by the engine manufacturer must be used to obtain accurate readings. [Figure 4-29]

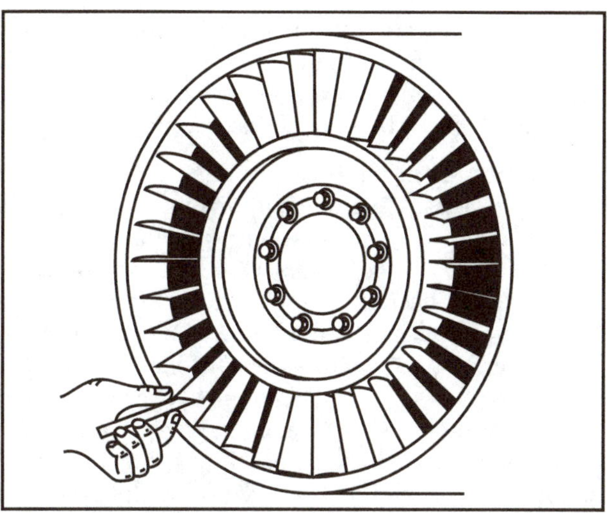

Figure 4-29. A thickness gauge is typically used to check clearances between turbine blades and the shroud unless a special tool is required by the manufacturer.

REPAIRS

The decision to repair or replace a turbine engine component is based on many factors. For example, mandatory replacement may be specified for certain parts in the overhaul manual instructions. On the other hand, some parts may be inspected for serviceability and repaired or replaced as necessary. If repairs can restore serviceability to a defective part, the remaining service life projections must be considered. Furthermore, repairs that must be built up or welded to serviceable limits typically require specialized equipment and facilities.

One popular technique used to build up a component and restore it to its original dimensions is **plasma coating**. The plasma coating process has proven to be a valuable means of extending the service life of blades and vanes and reducing overhaul costs. Plasma coating involves spraying an atomized metallic material onto the base metal of a part at a high velocity and at a high heat. For example, to build up a compressor blade, the blade is sprayed with ionized argon gas heated to 50,000°F traveling at speeds over 2,200 feet per second. Metallic powder is then introduced into the gas stream, causing a coat of molten metallic particles to bond to the airfoil. The process is controlled to produce multiple coatings as thin as 0.00025 inch each. Each coating becomes thoroughly fused to the base metal to provide excellent adhesion characteristics. Once the coating process is complete, the blade or vane airfoil can be ground to new part dimensions.

Another application of this process is referred to as **ceramic coating** and is used to coat compressor parts for corrosion protection. In addition, the ceramic coating produces a smooth surface that reduces air friction and surface drag, improving a compressor's performance. Some experimental processes are now used to apply ceramic materials on many of an engine's hot section components including combustors, turbine nozzle diaphragms, turbine disks, turbine blades, and vanes.

In addition to the various types of coating processes used to build up engine components to serviceable limits, there are several welding methods that are used to make engine repairs. One such type of welding is called electron beam welding. Electron beam welding is a relatively new technique that is used to make repairs to compressor airfoils constructed from titanium alloys. When done properly, electron beam welding is as strong or stronger than a new blade or vane, making it possible to rework some compressor airfoils that would otherwise be rejected.

The primary difference between electron beam welding and other conventional welding techniques is that electron beam welding produces a narrower bead. This is possible because the welding process is done in a vacuum chamber which allows better control over the oxygen level. Heat is concentrated in a smaller area using this method, which subsequently reduces the stress on the base metal at the weld. As a result, this method of repair can often be used when damage to an airfoil exceeds blending or contouring repair limits. An insert of new material can be welded into place and then ground to the airfoil's original shape. As with most welding procedures, heat-treatment procedures are normally used to relieve stress in the area of the weld.

COMPRESSOR SECTION

One of the most common repairs made to a compressor section is the removal of foreign object damage from blades and vanes by blending. Blending, as you recall, is a method of repairing damaged blades and vanes by removing metal with hand tools to smooth out all rough edges and restore an aerodynamic shape. Blending should be performed parallel to the length of a blade using smooth contours to minimize stress points. Common files, emery or crocus cloth, and Carborundum stones are commonly used in blend repairs. Use of power tools is not permitted when blending because of the increased possibility of creating a heat stress buildup or inflicting accidental damage to adjacent areas.

A typical blend repair has a length to depth ratio of approximately 4 to 1 and is completed in several steps. First, the damaged area is scalloped by filing enough material away to create a saddle or dished out shape. Next, a stone or finish file is used to smooth out score marks and radius the edges of the repair. Last, the repair is polished with emery or crocus cloth to restore the original finish. Usually, repaired blades must be inspected by magnetic particle or dye penetrant methods to verify that all damage has been removed. Repaired areas are often marked with a felt tip dye marker to help maintenance personnel identify reworked areas during future inspections.

The amount of damage that is permissible on engine fan blades, inlet guide vanes, and compressor blades typically varies from engine to engine. Therefore, it is important that the manufacturer's repair instructions be referred to before any repair is made. As a general rule, nicks, dents, erosion, and scoring on the face of a fan blade require no repair as long as the damage does not exceed 0.030 inch. The area where the deepest damage is permitted is on a fan blade's leading edge above a mid-span shroud. Damage in this area can typically extend into a blade up to 0.060 inch. The areas where no damage is permitted include the fillet areas at a blade's base and where a shroud meets the blade face. [Figure 4-30]

The amount of damage that is permissible on hollow inlet guide vanes is typically much less than the damage allowed on compressor fan blades. The reason for this is that inlet guide vanes are typically hollow and the vane walls are constructed of thin material. Based on this, blending out damage may result in inadvertently penetrating a vane wall if too much material is removed. Furthermore, attempting to repair an inlet guide vane by straightening, brazing, welding, or soldering is usually not permitted.

As a general rule, any sharp, V-shaped dent or any cracking and tearing of a guide vane requires vane replacement. However, small, shallow dents can typically be left unrepaired if they are rounded, have a gradual contour, and fall within the manufacturer's specifications. In addition, trailing edge damage of an inlet guide vane may be blended if one-third of the weld seam remains after a repair is made. Guide vanes that are rubber filled can -usually be reused if some cracking exists as long as the cracks extend inward from the outer airfoil and do not appear to be converging. In addition, there can be no indication of pieces breaking away. [Figure 4-31]

Typically, minor damage on the outer half of an axial-flow compressor blade is repairable if the repaired area can be kept within the manufacturer's limits. However, some manufacturers may allow damage to be left unrepaired if the damage meets certain criteria. For example, if light damage to the

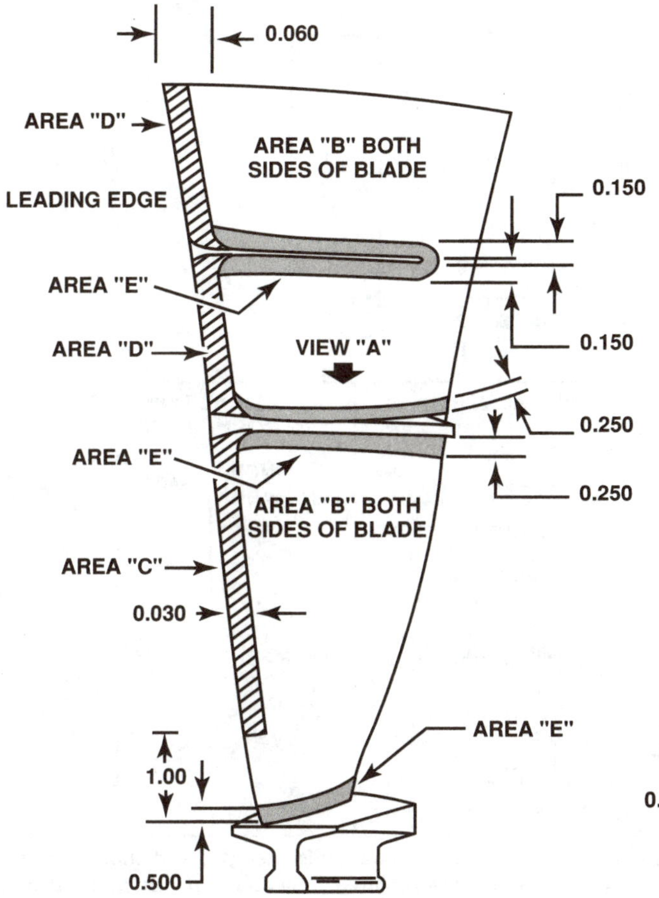

0.060
AREA "D"
AREA "B" BOTH SIDES OF BLADE
LEADING EDGE
0.150
AREA "E"
VIEW "A"
AREA "D"
0.150
0.250
AREA "E"
0.250
AREA "B" BOTH SIDES OF BLADE
AREA "C"
0.030
AREA "E"
1.00
0.500

BLADE AREA	PERMISSIBLE DAMAGE (NO REPAIR REQUIRED)
Area B	Erosion, nicks, scoring, or dents, maximum allowable depth 0.015".
Area C	Nicks or dents maximum allowable depth 0.030".
Area D	Nicks or dents, maximum allowable depth 0.060".
Area E	No damage permissible in fillet areas.

NOTES:

(1) Blend-rework of damaged areas is required only in the instance of sharp bottomed damage. Damaged area must be removed and blended to a minimum radius 0.125"

(2) In area "C" and "D", only one blend repair is permitted. Repaired areas are to be inspected with portable fluorescent penetrant or dye-check.

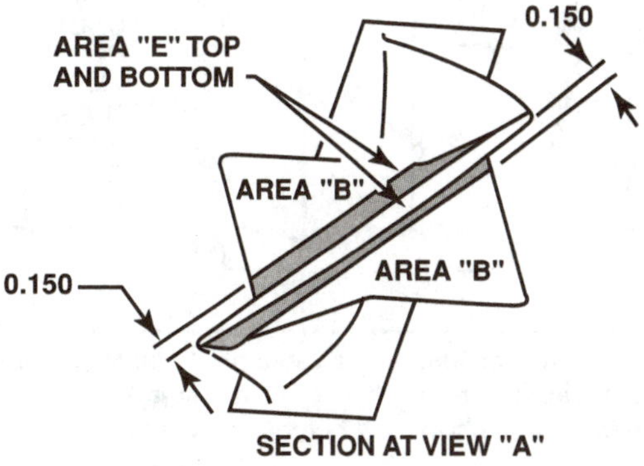

AREA "E" TOP AND BOTTOM
0.150
AREA "B"
AREA "B"
0.150
SECTION AT VIEW "A"

Figure 4-30. Light damage on a fan blade which falls within permissible damage limits can be left unrepaired. On the other hand, no damage is permitted in fillet areas and cracks require replacement of a fan blade.

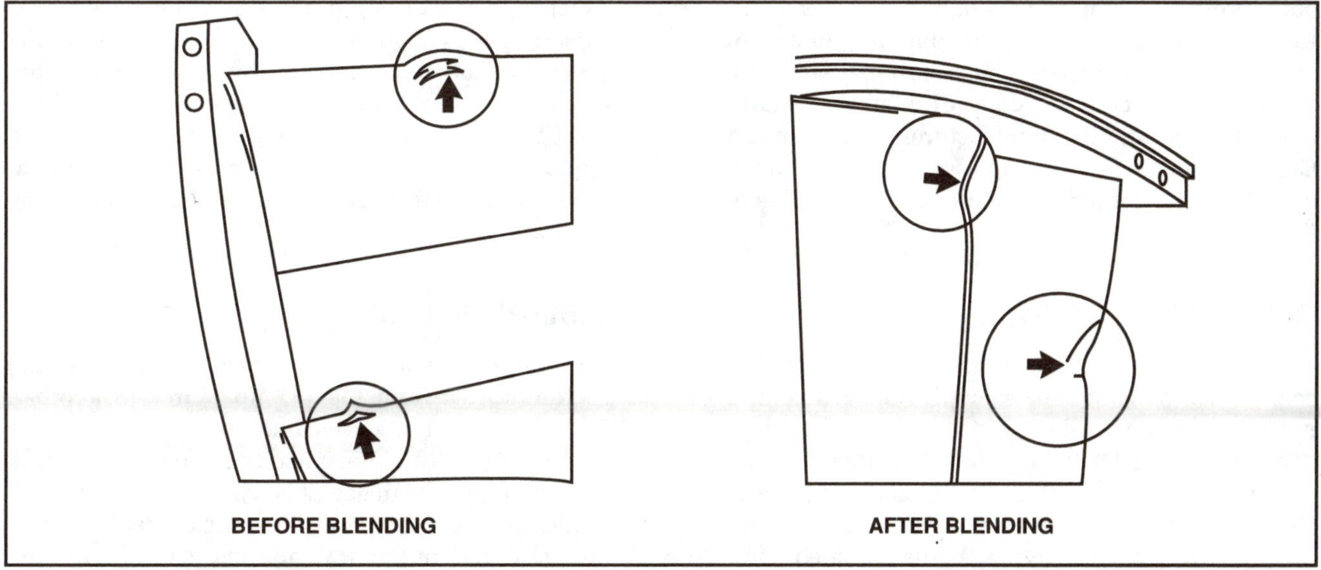

Figure 4-31. If an inlet guide vane becomes damaged and the damage does not penetrate the outer shell of the vane, the damage can be blended and contoured.

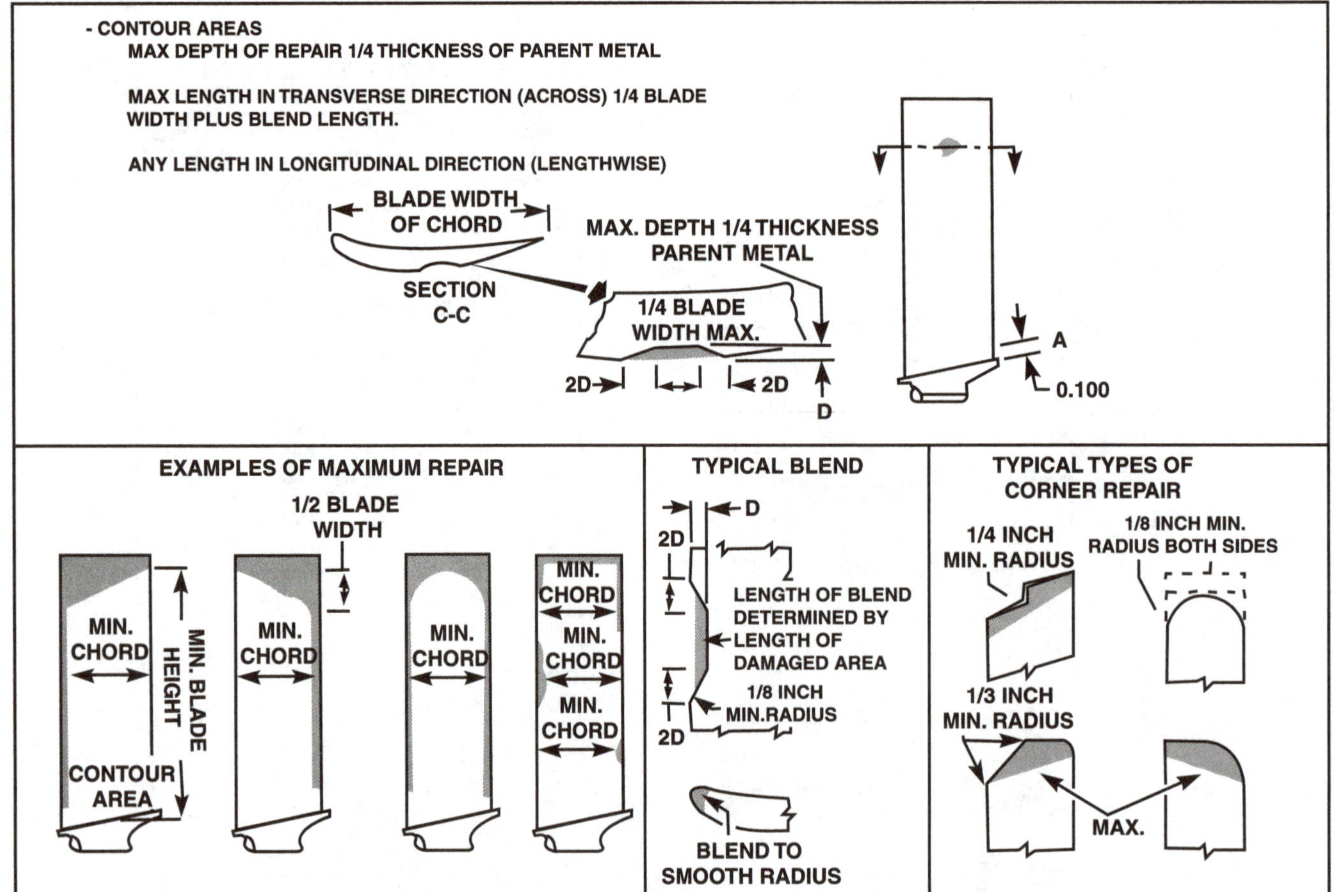

Figure 4-32. Compressor blade repairable limits and blended repairs are based on blade width, length, and chord dimensions. Typically, most leading and trailing edge damage as well as tip damage may be repaired provided that , after the damage is removed, the minimum chord and height are maintained.

leading or trailing edge of a compressor blade is visible from either side of a blade, confined to the outer half of the blade, well-rounded, and within acceptable limits, the damage may be left unrepaired. On the other hand, damage on the inner half of a blade is critical. Minor damage must be repaired or the blade must be replaced, depending on the severity of the damage and the manufacturer's requirements. Cracks of any size on compressor blades are unacceptable and require replacement of the blade. [Figure 4-32]

COMBUSTION SECTION

Various methods are used to restore combustion section components. For example, cracked components can typically be welded while some worn components can be restored using a ceramic coating process that builds up component thickness. However, most of the repair processes used on combustion components require the use of specialized equipment that is generally found only at certified repair stations.

Welding is the most widely used method for repairing cracks in combustion liners that are outside of acceptable limits but within repairable limits. The exact type of welding process used on a particular liner depends on the material used to build the liner. Typically, combustion liners are constructed of stainless steel and can be repaired using either inert gas or electron beam welding. However, once a component has been welded, it must be heat-treated to relieve any stress buildup caused by the welding process.

TURBINE SECTION

The amount of damage that is permitted in a turbine section varies from one manufacturer to another. Therefore, it is imperative that you refer to the manufacturer's instructions when tying to determine if a specific type of damage is acceptable. As a general guideline, a maximum of three nicks, dents, or pits are permitted on the front and rear face of a turbine blade. However, only one nick, dent, or pit is permitted within a quarter inch of a fillet. Other areas

INSPECTION	MAXIMUM SERVICEABLE	MAXIMUM REPAIRABLE	CORRECTION ACTION
BLADE SHIFT	Protrusion of any blade root must be equal within 0.015"' either side of disk.	Not repairable	Return blade disk assembly to an overhaul facility.
AREA A Nicks (3 maximum)	0.015" long by 0.005" deep	.015 long by 0.010" deep	Blend out damage
Dents and pits (3 maximum)	0.010" deep	.015 long by 0.010" deep	Blend out damaged
AREA B Nicks, dents, and pits	One 0.020" deep	Not repairable	Replace blade
LEADING AND TRAILING EDGES Nicks, dents, and pits	One 0.020" deep	Two 1/8" deep	Blend out damaged area/ Replace blade

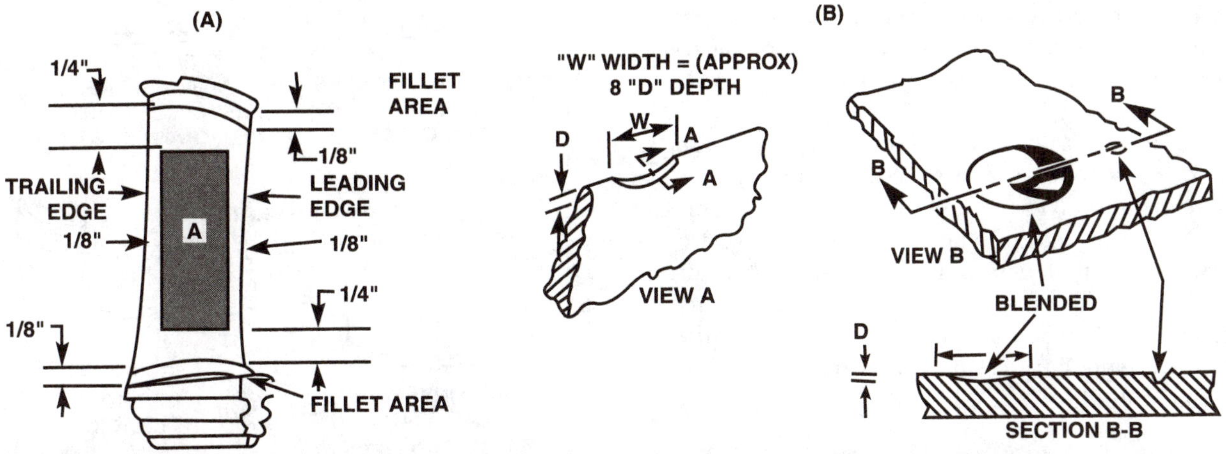

Figure 4-33. A— Both the chart and the first figure indicate the location and type of damage that is generally repairable on a turbine blade. However, if any crack or rippling on a trailing edge exists, blade replacement is required. B— As a general rule, anytime you make a repair to a turbine blade, the width of the repair should be approximately eight times the depth.

where some minor damage may be permissible include the leading and trailing edges. However, the amount of damage that is serviceable is typically limited. [Figure 4-33]

Another type of damage that is common to turbine blades is erosion. One method used to repair erosion is to weld a new piece of blade into place using electron beam welding techniques. Once a new piece is welded, the blade is ground to the appropriate shape and heat treated to relieve any stress concentrations produced during the welding process. Another technique used to repair erosion is plasma coating. With this process, atomized metallic material is sprayed onto the eroded section of a turbine blade in multiple coats. Once the coating process is complete, a blade is ground to its original shape.

Additional turbine components that often require repair during an overhaul are the turbine nozzle vanes. Typical damage that can be repaired on turbine nozzle vanes include nicks, dents, scratches, bowing, and cracking. Most nicks, dents, and scratches are repaired using simple blending and contouring techniques that help relieve stress concentrations and maintain a smooth airflow. If a turbine nozzle vane is bowed, it can usually be repaired by straightening. However, the material used to build some nozzle vanes cannot withstand the straightening process. In situations where straightening is not a permissible repair, the bowed

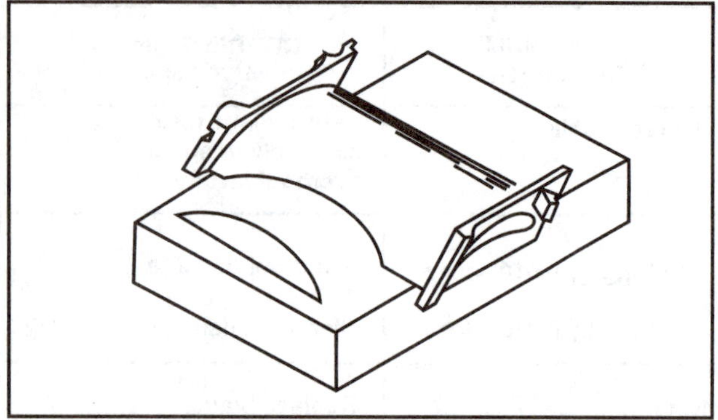

Figure 4-34. To repair a badly damaged turbine nozzle vane, the damaged area is removed and a new piece of material is welded in its place.

area can be cut away and a new piece of blade material can be welded in place. Once welded in place, the vane is ground to the proper shape and heat-treated for stress relief. [Figure 4-34]

Since turbine nozzle vanes do not rotate, they are not subject to the extreme stresses turbine blades must withstand. Therefore, minor cracking is permissible in most nozzle vanes. However, there are several factors that determine whether a crack or multiple cracks are permissible. To determine the exact criteria for permissible cracking, you must refer to the specific manufacturers overhaul manual. [Figure 4-35]

EXHAUST SECTION

Damage in an exhaust section that can typically be repaired includes minor warping, buckling, and cracking. Warping and buckling are generally repaired by straightening whereas cracks are typically welded. Additional repairs that can be accomplished by welding include filling small holes with weld metal and replacing larger areas of damage by welding a new piece of metal in position. Typically gas or electron beam welding techniques are used to repair engine exhaust sections constructed of stainless steel.

BALANCING

Approved repair procedures to a turbine engine are designed to maintain the strength and balance with which an engine was originally engineered. This is crucial because of the high rotational speeds at which turbine engines operate. If the main rotating assembly of a turbine engine is not balanced, severe vibration can occur. To help ensure that proper balance is maintained, both compressor and turbine

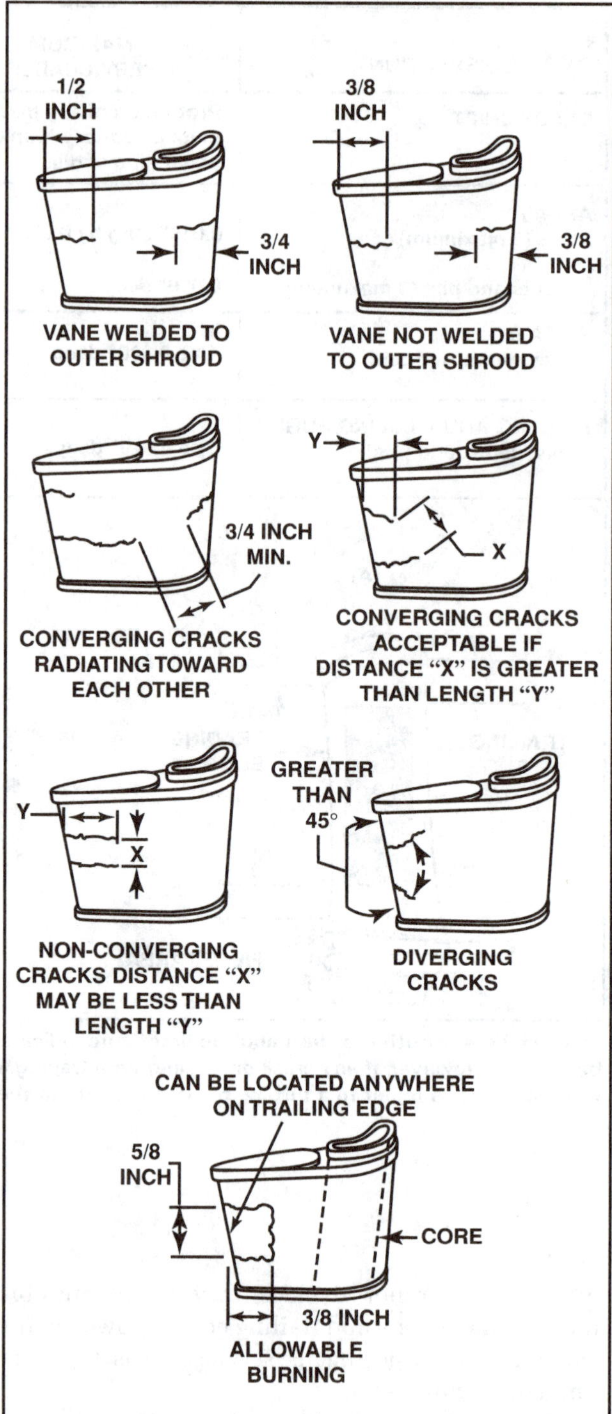

Figure 4-35. This figure illustrates some basic criteria for determining whether a crack or multiple cracks are acceptable in a turbine nozzle vane. However, to determine the exact criteria you must refer to the manufacturer's maintenance manuals.

blade replacement must be done in a specific way. For example, typically an engine manufacturer places restrictions on the number of blades that can be replaced in a given stage and on a single rotor before the rotor must be re-balanced.

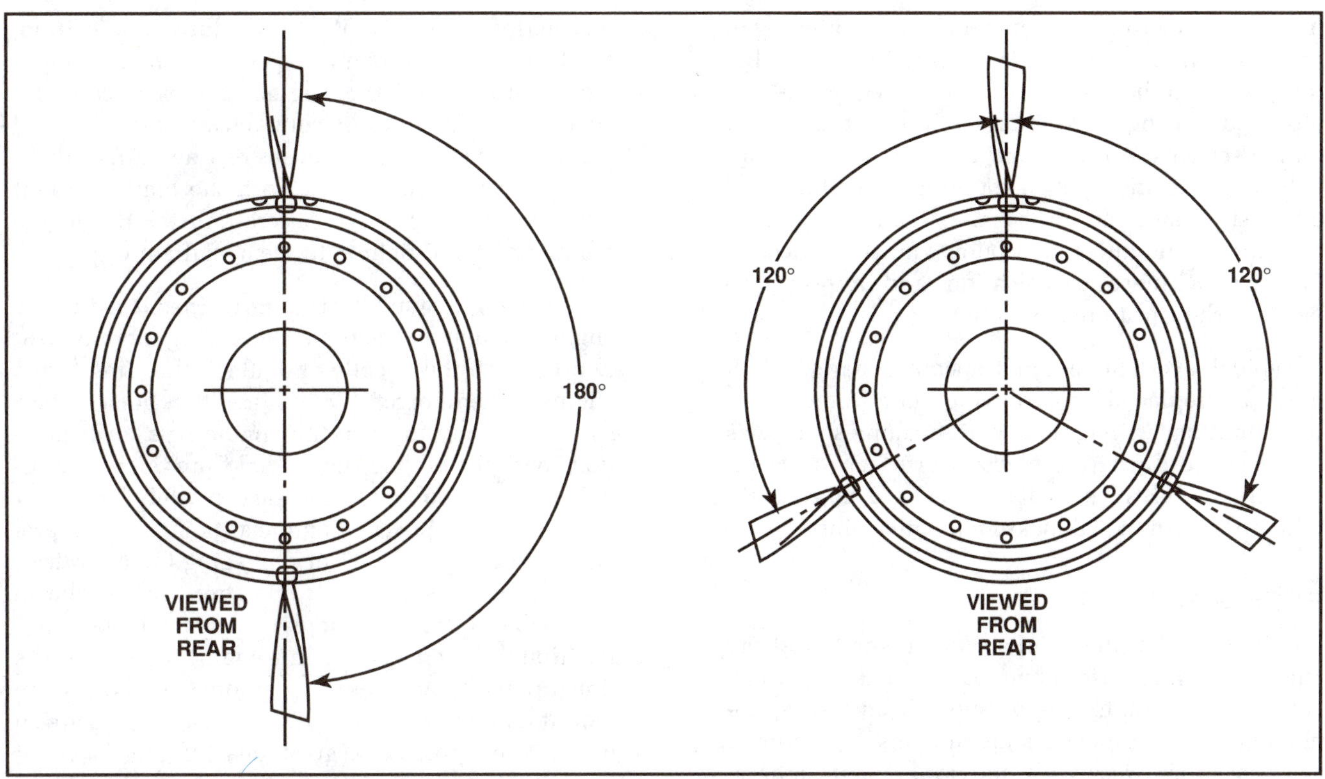

Figure 4-36. If a blade having the exact same moment-weight is not available to replace a damaged blade, blade replacement on a compressor or turbine wheel having an even number of blades is accomplished by replacing two blades with equal moment-weight. However, if the compressor or turbine wheel has an odd number of blades, replacement is done by replacing the damaged blade and each blade 120 degrees to the left and right of the damaged blade.

A single blade replacement is generally accomplished by installing a new blade with an equal moment-weight. To determine the moment-weight of a single blade, each compressor or turbine blade is marked with a code indicating the blade's moment-weight in inch-ounces or inch-grams. If a new blade with the same moment-weight as the damaged blade is not available, multiple blades must be replaced. For example, on a compressor or turbine wheel with an even number of blades, the damaged blade and the blade opposite, or 180 degrees away, are replaced with blades having an equal moment-weight. If a damaged blade exists on a compressor or turbine wheel with an odd number of blades, three blades with equal moment-weights must be replaced; the damaged blade and the blades 120 degrees to the right and left. [Figure 4-36]

Most engines are limited to a maximum rpm that is less than the lowest rpm at which a rotating assembly begins to vibrate. However, if repairs are not done properly, the rpm at which vibration begins can be lowered into an engine's operational rpm range. Furthermore, if vibrations occur in one assembly they can induce vibrations in other assemblies having the same natural frequency. If allowed to continue, severe vibrations can eventually lead to complete engine destruction. Because of this, a turbine engine is normally checked for both static and dynamic balance during the repair process. As you recall, static balancing procedures ensure that an engine's main rotating assembly is balanced in the rotational plane. On the other hand, dynamic balancing ensures that the main rotating assembly is balanced both in the rotational plane and along the rotor's axis.

REASSEMBLY

As a general rule, the same fixtures and tooling used to disassemble a gas turbine engine are used to reassemble an engine after heavy maintenance or overhaul. In addition, torque wrenches and other torque measuring tools are needed to ensure components are properly torqued to manufacturer specifications. Closely machined mating surfaces and tight clearances typical of turbine engine construction demand the utmost care during reassembly.

Turbine engines may be reassembled vertically or horizontally. Reassembly procedures are basically the reverse process of disassembly, however, more time is needed to ensure proper fit and tightening of hardware. In addition, it is absolutely crucial that the specified hardware tightening sequences are observed during reassembly to prevent incorrect torque settings. A turbine engine has many circular bolt-ring sets and special torquing procedures are often stipulated by the engine manufacturer. In addition, all modules, or sections, must be checked for airworthiness certification and appropriate paperwork prior to reassembly.

A typical overhaul manual specifies parts which must be replaced regardless of condition when reassembling an engine. Some examples of parts which are ordinarily replaced during an overhaul include all bearings, seals, gaskets, O-rings, lockwire, lockwashers, tablocks, and cotter pins.

ENGINE TESTING

The final step in the overhaul process is to test the engine. Engine performance is evaluated in a test cell during block testing by specialized test equipment and standard engine instruments. Operational test procedures vary with individual engines, however, the failure of any internal part during an engine run-in requires return of the engine for teardown and repair. If failure of an engine accessory occurs, a new accessory is installed and the block test continues. Following successful completion of block test requirements, engines not slated for immediate installation and operation on an aircraft should receive a corrosion prevention treatment and be placed in storage.

ENGINE INSTALLATION

After an engine has been repaired, overhauled, or replaced, it must be prepared for installation. With a repaired or overhauled engine, preparation typically entails returning the engine to the configuration it was in immediately after it was removed. However, if the engine being installed is shipped new from the factory, additional assembly is typically required. For example, if an engine was preserved in storage, de-preservation procedures are usually outlined in the overhaul manual provided by the engine manufacturer.

MOUNTING THE ENGINE

Before you mount an engine on an aircraft, make sure you have the appropriate hardware nearby and inspect the engine mount structure and shock mounts for integrity. When using an engine dolly to install an engine, observe the precautions and instructions listed on the dolly's ground handling instruction placards. With the dolly in position, carefully raise the engine up to the engine mount attach fittings. As the engine is raised, carefully check all engine to nacelle clearances to avoid pinching or kinking any hoses or lines. After aligning the rear engine mount with the mating mount attachment fittings on the aircraft, install the engine mount bolts and tighten to the specified torque.

When using a hoist and sling to install a turbine engine, maneuver the replacement engine into position beneath the nacelle and attach the sling to the engine. Then, carefully operate the hoist cables simultaneously to raise the engine in a level position. With the engine suspended from the hoist, utilize as many people as necessary to safely maneuver the engine into position on the aircraft. To help prevent injuring personnel or damaging the aircraft or engine, ease the engine into position slowly, checking to be certain the engine clears all obstacles. Position the engine so that the engine mounting lugs line up with the mounting points on the engine mount and exhaust tailpipe. Because engines are so heavy, they possess a great deal of inertia when swinging from the hoist. Therefore, exercise caution to avoid damaging the nacelle framework, ducts, or firewall connections.

Once the engine is correctly aligned, insert the mounting bolts and secure them with the appropriate nuts. Once secure, torque the engine mounting nuts to the manufacturer's recommended value. The applicable manufacturer's instructions outline the sequence for tightening the mounting bolts to ensure security. While the nuts are being tightened, the hoist should support the engine weight sufficiently to allow proper mounting bolt alignment. If this is not done, the weight of the engine on the mounting bolts could make it impossible to tighten the nuts to the proper torque. In other words, improper alignment could result in false torque readings as the nuts pull the engine into the proper position. Once the nuts are properly torqued, they should be safetied according to the manufacturer's specifications.

CONNECTIONS AND ADJUSTMENTS

After an engine is mounted, the air conditioning duct can be connected between the pylon and engine bleed air duct. Tighten the duct connections to the proper torque and remove the dolly or hoist and sling from the engine. With the engine hoist removed, the electrical leads and fluid lines necessary for operation should be connected to the engine and accessories. Typically, there are no rules that govern the order in which the accessories should be connected. However, you should always follow the manufacturer's instructions to ensure an efficient installation.

Hoses used with low pressure systems are generally attached and held in place with clamps. However, before installing these clamps, examine them carefully and replace any that are badly distorted or defective. After a hose is installed, it must be adequately supported and routed away from engine or airframe parts that could cause damage. Usually, rubber lined supporting clamps called Adel clamps are installed at specified intervals to provide the protection and support needed.

Before installing metal tubing with threaded fittings, make sure that the threads are clean and in good condition. If specified in the instructions, apply a thread sealing compound to the fitting before installation. Exercise care to prevent crossthreading any fittings and to ensure correct torque. Remember, over torquing a fitting increases the likelihood of leaks and failures.

When connecting electrical leads to an accessory, make sure that all connections are clean and secure. When leads are secured on a threaded terminal post with a nut, a lock washer is usually inserted under the nut to prevent the nut from backing off. When required, knurled connector plugs are secured with steel safety wire to prevent accidental disconnection. To help prevent electrical leads within the engine nacelle from chafing, all wiring must be anchored as necessary to provide a secure installation

Each aircraft model has an engine control system specifically designed for a particular airframe/engine combination. Typical engine controls consist of rigid push-pull rods, flexible push-pull wire encased in a coiled wire sheath, cables and pulleys, or any combination of the three. Regardless of type, all engine controls must be accurately adjusted to ensure instantaneous response to a control input. Therefore, all adjustments must be made in accordance with the procedures outlined in the manufacturer's instructions.

Before you actually rig an engine's fuel and power controls, you should inspect all bellcranks for looseness, cracks, or corrosion and examine rod ends for damaged threads. Once a control is rigged, check for the correct number of visible threads after final adjustment. In addition, examine cable drums for wear and cable guards for proper position and tension.

The power lever control cables and push-pull rods in the airframe between the cockpit and engine pylon are not usually disturbed during an engine change, so they sometimes require no rigging. However, the portion of the engine control system from the pylon to the engine must be re-rigged after each engine or fuel control change. [Figure 4-37]

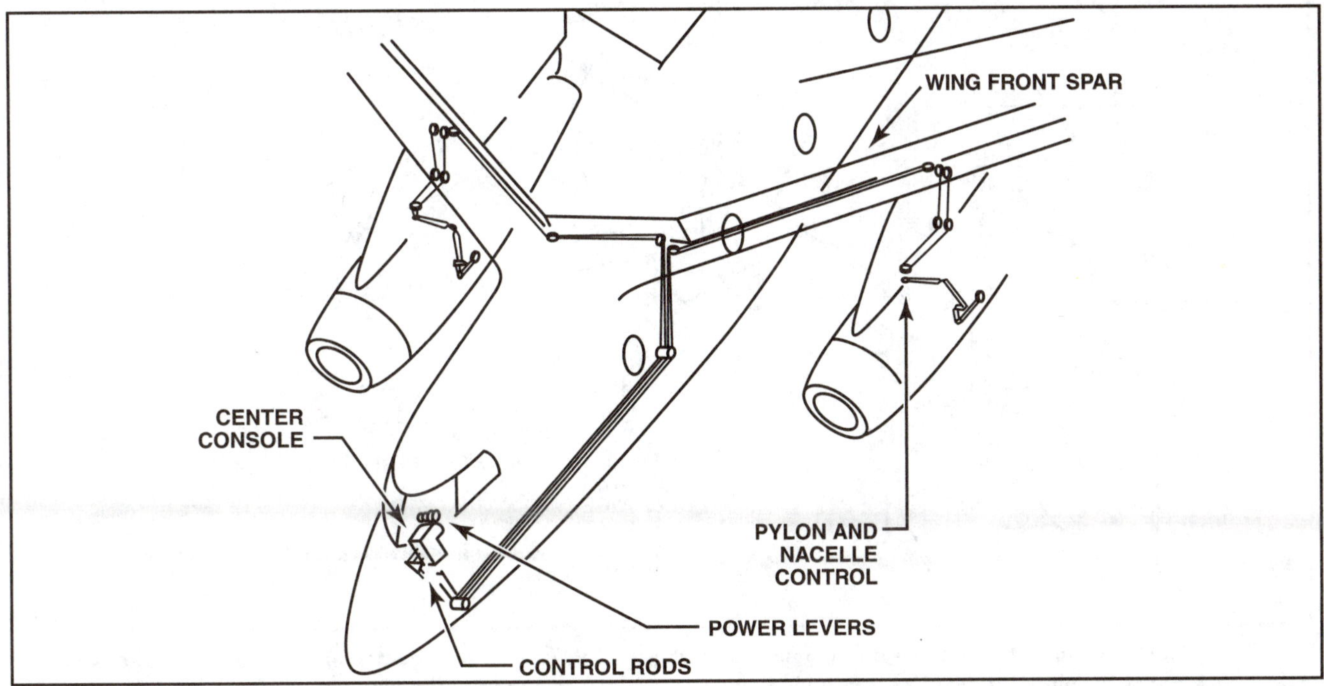

Figure 4-37. The control system components in the airframe generally remain undisturbed during an engine change. However, the controls in the engine pylon must always be re-rigged.

Before adjusting the power controls at the engine, be sure that the power lever is free from binding and the controls have full-throw at the console. If they do not have full-throw or are binding, their path through the airframe should be checked and discrepancies repaired. A properly adjusted engine control must have a degree of **cushion**, or **spring-back**, at its fully open and fully closed positions. In other words, the stops for the power and condition levers on a fuel control must be reached before the power or condition controls reach their stop in the cockpit. The presence of a cushion ensures that the power and fuel valves are opening and closing fully. Without the cushion, it would be difficult to determine whether a power or condition valve is fully opened or closed from inside the cockpit. On multi-engine aircraft, power controls must have equal amounts of cushion so the control levers align in any selected power setting. This reduces the likelihood of having to set each control individually to synchronize engine operations.

After completing the engine installation and adjustments on a turboprop engine, the propeller can be installed. When installing a constant-speed propeller, you must obtain the proper gaskets or O-rings prior to installation. Large propellers require the use of an appropriate sling and hoist arrangement due to their size and weight. Never attempt to lift a propeller into place with inadequate personnel or equipment. In addition, you should always follow the manufacturer's recommended installation procedure.

ENGINE ALIGNMENT

After a new or replacement turbine engine is installed in a helicopter, it is very important to check the alignment of the engine to the transmission. This must be done to avoid placing excessive stress on the main input shaft couplings. Alignment is normally accomplished by shimming the mount legs between the fuselage and the engine mount. This procedure may not be required if the engine mounts are not disturbed during an engine change. However, if the engine mounts are changed, or the drive shaft shows excessive wear, alignment checks should be accomplished. Some maintenance shop operators check the alignment at every engine installation for an added margin of safety. [Figure 4-38]

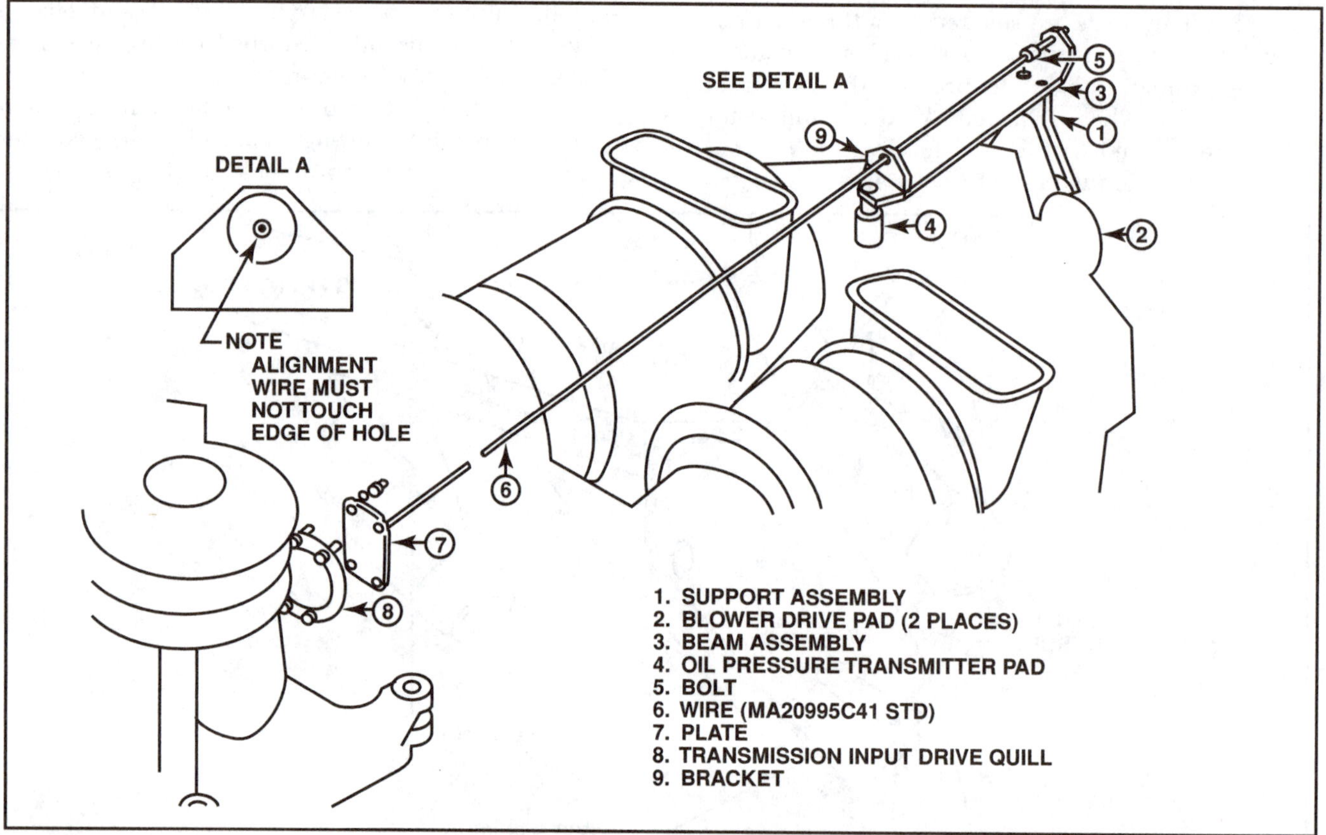

Figure 4-38. To check engine-to-transmission alignment, a beam assembly is typically mounted to an engine drive pad. A piece of safety wire is then strung from the beam assembly to a plate on the transmission. The wire passes through a target hole in a bracket attached to the beam assembly. When the wire is taut, it should pass through the target hole without touching the side of the hole. If it touches, the mounts should be shimmed until the correct alignment is obtained.

ENGINE TRIMMING

Engine trimming refers to a process whereby an engine's fuel control unit is adjusted to allow an engine to produce its maximum rated thrust. Trimming is normally performed after an engine or fuel control unit is changed or whenever an engine does not produce its maximum thrust.

Manual trimming procedures vary widely between engine models; therefore, before you attempt to trim an engine, you should take time to review the specific procedures in the engine's maintenance manual. A typical trimming procedure requires you to install calibrated instruments for reading turbine discharge pressure or EPR. In addition, a calibrated tachometer must be installed to read N_2 rpm. Once the instrumentation is installed, the aircraft should be pointed into the wind. However, if the velocity of the wind blowing into the intake is too great, elevated compression and turbine discharge pressures will result which, ultimately, will produce a low trim setting. Another step in the trimming procedure is to measure the barometric pressure at the engine inlet and the ambient temperature. This is required to correct performance readings to standard sea-level conditions. To obtain a temperature reading, it is common practice to hang a thermometer in the shade of the nose wheel well. The ideal conditions for trimming a turbine engine are no wind, low humidity, and standard temperature and pressure.

Once you have calculated the maximum power output for the engine you are trimming, start the engine and let it idle as specified in the maintenance manual. This is necessary so the engine has time to stabilize. To ensure an accurate trim setting, all engine bleed air must be turned off. Bleeding air off the compressor has the same effect as decreasing the compressor's efficiency. Therefore, if a trim adjustment is made with the bleeds on, an inaccurate, or overtrimmed condition will result.

With the engine running at idle and maximum power, observe the turbine discharge or EPR readings to determine how much trimming is necessary. If trimming of either the idle or maximum settings are necessary, it is typically accomplished by turning a screw type adjustment on the fuel control unit. [Figure 4-39]

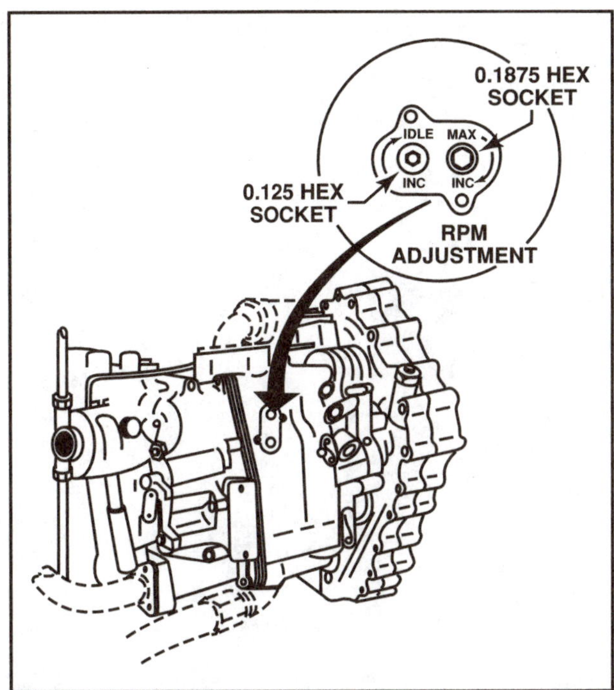

Figure 4-39. A typical turbine engine fuel control unit is equipped with adjustment screws for trimming the engine. Trimming procedures allow you to adjust both idle rpm and maximum rated thrust.

ENGINE PRESERVATION

Engines that are going to be put in storage or transported to an overhaul facility must be preserved and protected to prevent corrosion and other forms of damage. Regardless of whether an engine is waiting to be overhauled or is newly overhauled, damaging rust and other forms of corrosion will occur unless the engine is protected. Preservation is also recommended when an engine remains on the aircraft if engine operation is limited or suspended for an extended period of time. For example, to protect an engine's fuel system, fuel lines are typically filled with a corrosion preventative oil and all openings are sealed. To protect an engine as a whole, most are sealed in a bag or container with quantities of a desiccant. The desiccant absorbs the moisture within the sealed enclosure thereby preventing the onset of corrosion.

CHAPTER 5

INDUCTION SYSTEMS

INTRODUCTION

The induction system is designed to supply air to the engine so that, when fuel is added, combustion can take place. On reciprocating engines, outside air passes through an air intake and is then routed to a carburetor or other fuel metering device. Once fuel is added, the fuel/air mixture is delivered into an intake manifold where it is ducted to the cylinders for combustion. In a turbine engine induction system, large quantities of air are ducted through an inlet into a compressor. Once through the compressor, the resulting high pressure airmass is diffused, mixed with fuel, and ignited in a combustion chamber to produce thrust. Due to the large quantities of air consumed by a turbine engine, the induction system plays a very large role in the level of efficiency that the engine is able to attain.

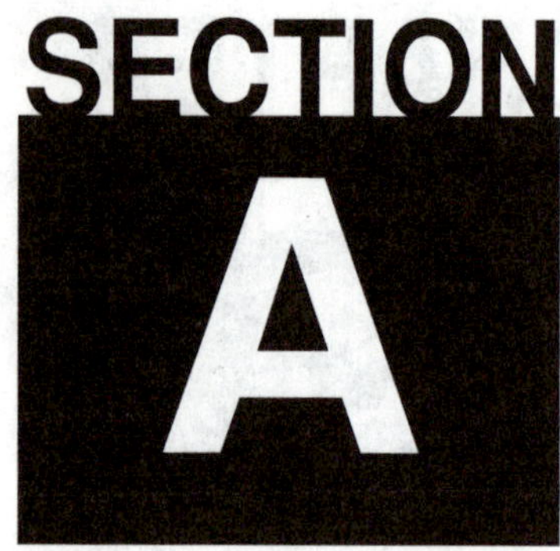

SECTION A

RECIPROCATING ENGINES

The primary purpose of an induction system in a reciprocating engine is to provide air in sufficient quantity to support normal combustion. Reciprocating engine induction systems can be broadly classified as normally aspirated, supercharged, and turbocharged.

NORMALLY ASPIRATED SYSTEMS

A typical induction system on a normally aspirated engine consists of four major components, or sections: an air intake, an induction air filter, a fuel delivery system, and an induction manifold. Additional subsystems such as an alternate air source, an ice removal or prevention system, and a temperature indicating system are typically included to support the operation of the four primary components.

AIR INTAKES

An air intake, sometimes referred to as an **air scoop**, is designed to direct outside air into a carburetor or other fuel metering device. The intake is generally located to take advantage of ram air pressure as much as possible. Therefore, the intake opening is usually found in the propeller slipstream because of the extra velocity the propeller imparts to the airstream. By taking advantage of ram air pressure, the pressure within the intake is typically higher than any other point in a normally aspirated induction system. Because of this pressure rise, a well designed intake scoop can have a substantial effect on an engine's power output.

AIR FILTERING

For an engine to provide reliable operation and a long service life, the induction air must be free of foreign material. To accomplish this, filters are typically installed in air intake ducts to prevent dust, sand, abrasive materials, or other contaminants from entering the engine.

While dust may only be a minor irritant to the human body, it is a serious source of trouble for an aircraft engine. Dust consists of small particles of hard, abrasive material that can be carried into the engine cylinders by the induction air. Dust particles can cause accelerated wear on cylinder walls and piston rings, silicon fouling of spark plugs, and contaminate the oil. Once in the oil, the particles are carried throughout the engine, causing further wear on bearings and gears. In extreme cases, dust accumulation can clog an oil passage and cause oil starvation. Dust may also collect in a fuel metering device and upset its ability to provide the proper mixture ratio at all power settings.

Filter Maintenance

The efficiency of any filtration system depends upon proper maintenance and service. Periodic removal, cleaning, or replacement of filter elements is essential to ensure proper engine performance. Many early air filters were constructed from screen wire that was filled with a reusable fiber material known as **flock**. To maintain such a filter, clean and service it by washing it in safety solvent. Once clean, soak the filter element in a mixture of engine oil and preservative oil. After all the fibers are thoroughly saturated, suspend the filter and allow to excess oil to drain.

Newer types of air filters include paper filters similar to the ones used in automobiles. As air passes through the porous paper filter element, dust and sand particles become trapped on the filter surface. Some manufacturers approve a method of cleaning paper filters by blowing the dust out in the opposite direction to the normal airflow. Some paper filters may be washed in a mild soap and water solution and allowed to dry. However, when servicing this type of filter be sure to follow the manufacturer's recommendations or restrictions.

The most effective filter available today is a polyurethane foam filter impregnated with a glycol solution. The glycol solution makes the filter sticky so dust and dirt stick to the element. To service this type of filter, the foam element is removed and discarded and a new one is installed. It is not recommended that these filters be cleaned.

FUEL DELIVERY SYSTEM

The fuel delivery system on a normally aspirated engine can be either a carburetor or a fuel injection system. The purpose of a fuel delivery system is to meter the amount of fuel and air that is delivered to the cylinders. A complete discussion as to how the fuel and air are metered is covered in Section B of Chapter 7.

INTAKE MANIFOLD

An intake manifold typically consists of ducting that goes from the fuel metering device to the individual cylinders. On a typical horizontally opposed engine, the intake manifold is the connecting point of all the individual pipes which deliver air or fuel/air mixture to the cylinders. One end of each cylinder's intake pipe is typically bolted to the cylinder intake port on each cylinder while the other end is attached to the manifold with a short section of synthetic rubber hose or rubber packing and packing nut. Both of these methods permit some movement between the intake pipes and manifold as the cylinders expand and contract. In some installations, the intake manifold goes through the oil sump before it branches out to go to each cylinder. This increases the temperature of the fuel/air mixture which, in turn, promotes better fuel vaporization.

In large radial engines, even distribution of the fuel/air mixture is difficult to achieve. Therefore, to help ensure equal distribution, some radial engines utilize a **distribution impeller** which is attached directly to the rear of the crankshaft. As the fuel/air mixture goes into the center of the distribution impeller, centrifugal force distributes the mixture to the cylinders. Since the impeller is attached directly to the crankshaft, it operates at the same speed and does not boost the pressure within the manifold.

One very important characteristic of an intake manifold is that it must maintain a gastight seal. If a seal is not maintained, air will leak into the intake manifold and lean out the mixture. This, in turn, will cause an engine to run rough. Small induction leaks are most noticeable at idle because the pressure differential between the manifold and atmosphere is greatest at low rpm.

INDUCTION SYSTEM ICING

Induction system icing occurs when water freezes in an induction system and restricts airflow to the engine. When this happens, an engine may run rough, lose power, or even quit in flight. Complaints of poor engine performance in flight that cannot be verified on a post-flight ground check could indicate that induction system icing occurred while in flight. When ice accumulation causes poor engine performance, the problem and the cause disappear once the ice melts. That is why it is very important to understand how induction icing forms, what the indications of it are, and the ways in which it can be prevented or removed.

Induction ice can form when an aircraft is flying through clouds, fog, rain, sleet, snow, or even in clear air when the relative humidity is high. Induction icing is generally classified as one of three types: fuel evaporation, throttle, and impact.

FUEL EVAPORATION ICE

Fuel evaporation ice, sometimes referred to as **carburetor ice**, is a result of the temperature drop that occurs when fuel is vaporized. In a carburetor, as fuel is released into the airstream, it turns into a vapor and absorbs heat from the surrounding air. This can cause a drop in air temperature of 30°F or more. In some cases, this loss of heat is enough to cause the moisture in the air to condense and freeze. Because of this phenomenon, a carburetor typically accumulates ice before any other part of an aircraft in flight. In fact, carburetor ice can occur at ambient air temperatures up to 70°F and when relative humidity is as low as 50 percent. Optimum conditions for carburetor ice exist when the outside air temperature is between 30°F and 40°F and the relative humidity is above 60 percent.

In a fuel injection system, fuel is injected and vaporized at or near the intake port of each cylinder. In this case, the heat of combustion offsets the temperature drop caused by fuel vaporization. Therefore, fuel evaporation icing is typically not a concern in fuel injected engines.

THROTTLE ICE

Throttle ice is formed on the rear side of the throttle, or **butterfly valve** when it is in a partially closed position. The reason for this is that, as air flows across and around the throttle valve, a low pressure area is created on the downstream side. This has a cooling effect on the fuel/air mixture which can cause moisture to accumulate and freeze on the backside of the butterfly valve. Since throttle icing typically occurs when the butterfly valve is partially closed, a small amount of ice can cause a relatively large reduction in airflow and a corresponding loss of engine power. In severe cases, a large accumulation of ice can jam the throttle and render it immovable. Since the temperature drop created by the low pressure area is not that great, throttle ice seldom occurs at temperatures above 38°F.

IMPACT ICE

Impact ice is caused by visible moisture striking an aircraft and then freezing. Therefore, the air intake and air filter are the areas of an induction system that are most susceptible to impact icing. However, impact ice can also collect at points in an induction system where the airflow changes direction, or where dents and protrusions exist. Whenever an induction system encounters impact icing, air flow to the remaining system is restricted. Severe cases of impact icing can cause a total blockage to airflow and complete engine failure.

ICE DETECTION AND REMOVAL

Since the accumulation of ice in an induction system restricts the amount of air that can enter an engine, the first indication of icing is a decrease in engine power output. On an aircraft equipped with a fixed-pitch propeller, the decrease in engine power is indicated by a drop in rpm followed by engine roughness. However, if an aircraft has a constant-speed propeller, the first indication of induction ice is a decrease in manifold pressure with no change in engine rpm.

To prevent degradation of engine performance or engine failure brought about by induction icing, a means of preventing or removing ice is necessary. The most commonly used method of preventing and eliminating carburetor ice is to duct warm air into the carburetor. This type of ice removal system is known as a **carburetor heat** system. With this type of system, unfiltered air is drawn from within the engine cowling through a sheet metal shroud that surrounds an exhaust pipe. The shroud is commonly called a **heater muff** and functions as an air-to-air heat exchanger that warms the intake air and then directs it to a **carburetor air box**. [Figure 5-1]

With a carburetor heat system, carburetor heat is applied at the first sign of carburetor icing. Once applied, and if ice did exist, engine output will increase. On engines with a fixed-pitch propeller, an increase in power output is indicated by an increase in rpm shortly after carburetor heat is applied. However, engines equipped with a constant-speed propeller, increased power output is indicated by an increase in manifold pressure.

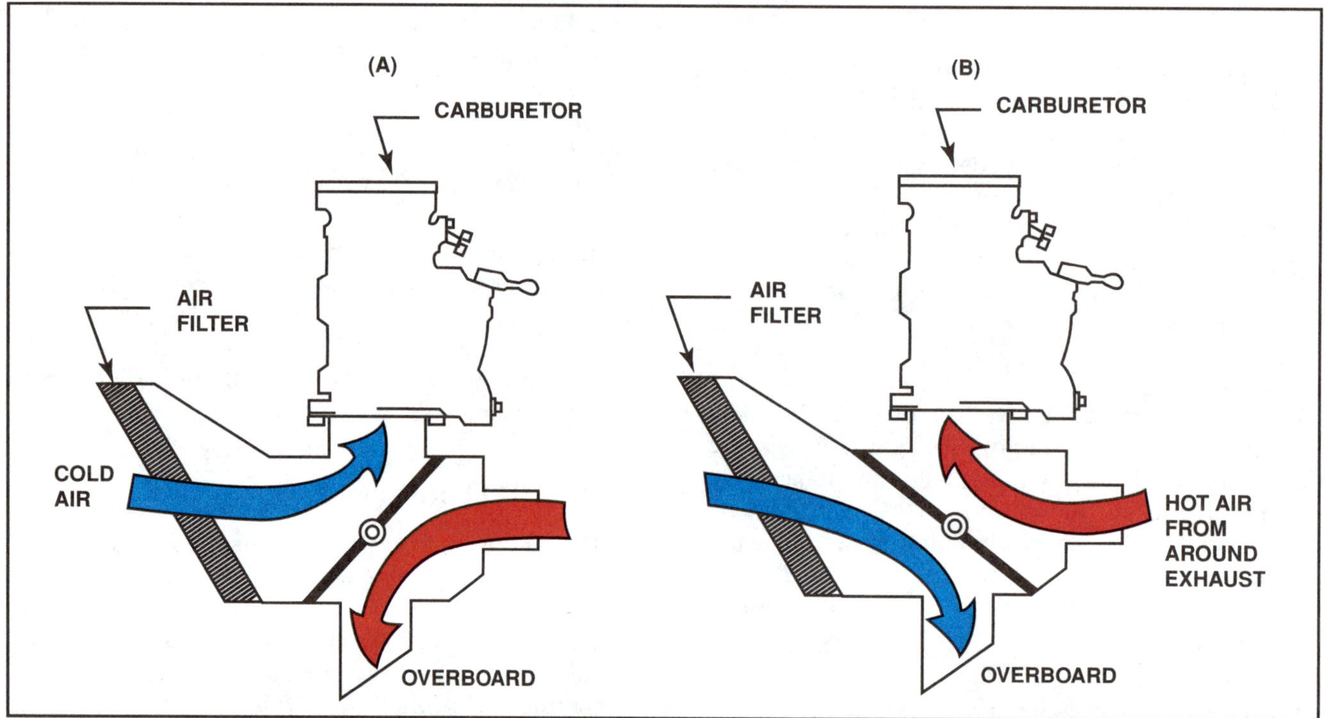

Figure 5-1. (A) — When the carburetor heat control is placed in the cold position, filtered ram air entering the main air scoop is ducted to the carburetor while heated air is ducted overboard. (B) — In the hot position, the air door is repositioned to route hot, unfiltered air into the carburetor.

Although carburetor heat is extremely effective at eliminating carburetor ice, improper or careless use can cause damage to an engine. For example, since carburetor heat air is unfiltered, excessive use increases the chance of dirt and foreign material entering the engine. Because of this, the carburetor heat should always be in the "cold" position when the aircraft is on the ground. This is especially true when operating in sandy or dusty locations. As another precaution, the carburetor heat control should be left in the "cold" position when starting an engine. If placed in the "hot" position, damage to the carburetor heat air box could result if the engine backfires.

Another thing you need to be aware of is that warm air is less dense than cold air. Therefore, when carburetor heat is applied, the fuel/air mixture becomes richer. In addition, the weight of the fuel/air charge is reduced which, in turn, causes a noticeable loss in power due to decreased volumetric efficiency. And finally, high intake air temperatures resulting from the use of carburetor heat can lead to detonation, especially during takeoff and high power operations.

Based on the information just presented, anytime an engine fails to develop full power, a possible factor is inadvertent application of carburetor heat or a carburetor heat control that is misrigged. Therefore, when troubleshooting an engine that is not developing full power, you should verify the position of the carburetor heat control and rigging before you assume some other component is at fault.

Another type of system that is used to eliminate induction ice sprays a deicing fluid into the air stream ahead of the carburetor. With this type of system, alcohol is commonly used as a deicing fluid. A typical system includes an alcohol reservoir, an electric pump, a spray nozzle, and cockpit controls.

Although the use of heated air and deicing fluid is effective at removing both carburetor and throttle ice, there is little that can be done to remove impact ice when it blocks an air intake. In this case, an **alternate air supply** must be provided. On carbureted engines, an alternate air supply is provided by a carburetor air box which can draw air from the main intake or from inside the cowling. However, since fuel injected engines do not use a carburetor air box, an **alternate air door** must be installed. When opened, an alternate air door allows warm, unfiltered air flow into the induction system. The operation of an alternate air door may be controlled automatically or manually from the cockpit. [Figure 5-2]

TEMPERATURE INDICATING SYSTEM

To help inform a pilot when the temperature at the carburetor can support the formation of ice, some aircraft are fitted with a carburetor air temperature gauge, or **CAT** gauge. With this type of system, carburetor air temperature is measured at the carburetor entrance by a temperature sensing bulb in the ram air intake duct. The sensing bulb senses the air temperature in the carburetor and then sends a sig-

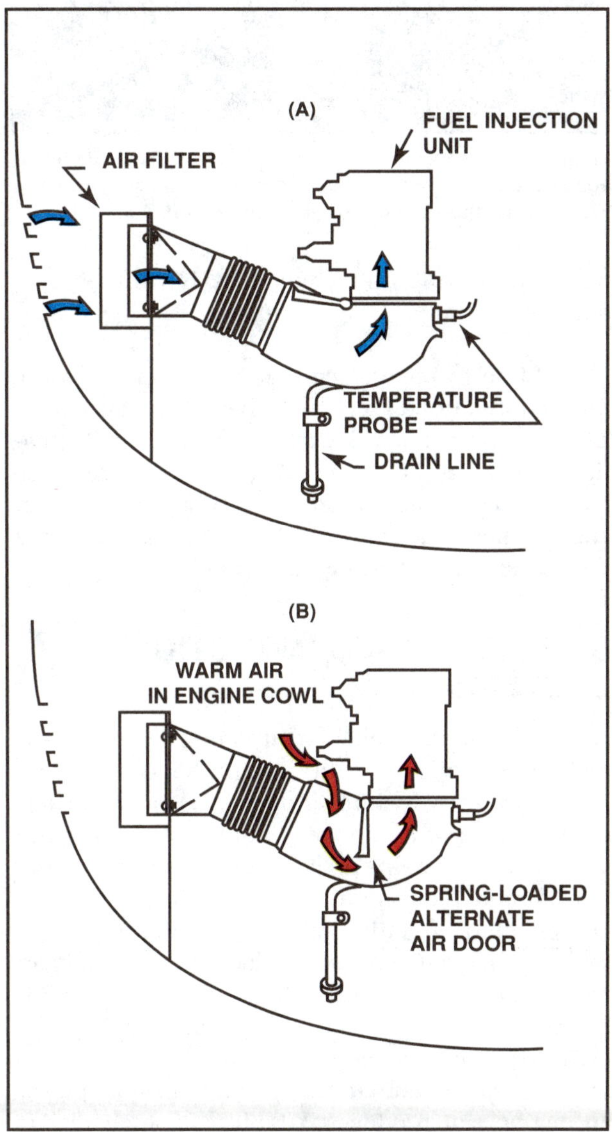

Figure 5-2. (A) — Under normal conditions, the induction system installed on a fuel injected engine ducts filtered air into the fuel injection unit. (B) — However, if the filter or intake should become clogged with ice or other debris, a spring-loaded alternate air door will open and allow unfiltered air from inside the cowling to enter the induction system.

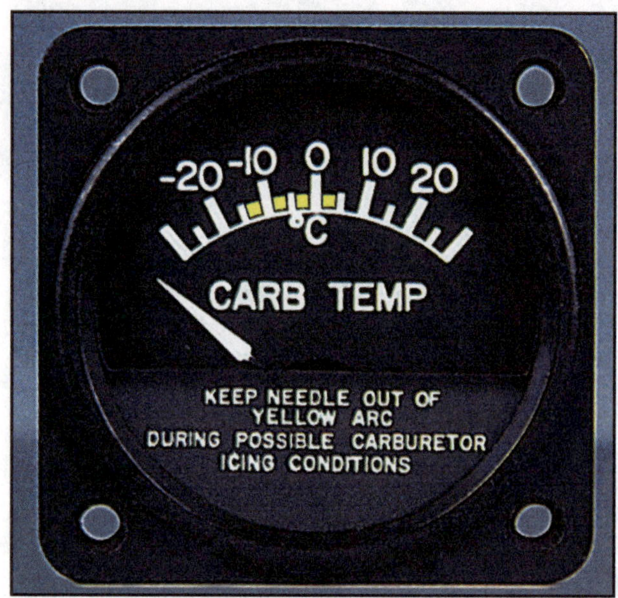

Figure 5-3. The carburetor air temperature gauge depicted above indicates that the danger of induction system icing exists when the temperature is between –15°C to + 5°C.

nal to a cockpit instrument that is calibrated in degrees Centigrade. [Figure 5-3]

In addition to identifying the conditions necessary for the formation of ice, excessively high carburetor air temperatures can indicate the onset of detonation. For example, if a CAT gauge has a red line identifying a maximum operating temperature, engine operation above that temperature increases the chance of detonation occurring.

SUPERCHARGED INDUCTION SYSTEMS

As you know, the higher an airplane climbs, the less oxygen is available to the engine for combustion. Therefore, as a reciprocating engine powered aircraft climbs, the power output of the engine decreases. To help prevent this loss of engine power, more oxygen must be forced into an engine. One method of getting more air into an engine is with a supercharger. A **supercharger** is basically an engine driven air pump that increases manifold pressure and forces the fuel/air mixture into the cylinders. The higher the manifold pressure, the more dense the fuel/air mixture and the more power an engine can produce. A typical supercharger is capable of boosting manifold pressure above 30 inches while producing a volumetric efficiency in excess of 100 percent.

The components in a supercharged induction system are similar to those in a normally aspirated system with the addition of a supercharger between the fuel metering device and intake manifold. A supercharger is typically driven by an engine's crankshaft through a gear train at one speed, two speeds, or variable speeds. In addition, superchargers can have one or more stages. One **stage** represents an increase in pressure. Superchargers are generally classified as either single stage, two stage, and multi stage depending on the number of times compression occurs.

SINGLE STAGE, SINGLE SPEED SUPERCHARGER

An early version of a single stage, single speed supercharger is known as a sea level supercharger, or **ground boost blower**. With this type of supercharger, a single gear-driven impeller is used to increase the power produced by an engine at all altitudes. The drawback, however, is that with this type of supercharger, engine power output still decreases with an increase in altitude in the same way that it does with a normally aspirated engine. [Figure 5-4]

Single stage, single speed superchargers are found on many radial engines and use an air intake that faces forward so the induction system can take full advantage of the ram air. Intake air passes through ducts to a carburetor where fuel is metered in proportion to the airflow. The fuel/air charge is then

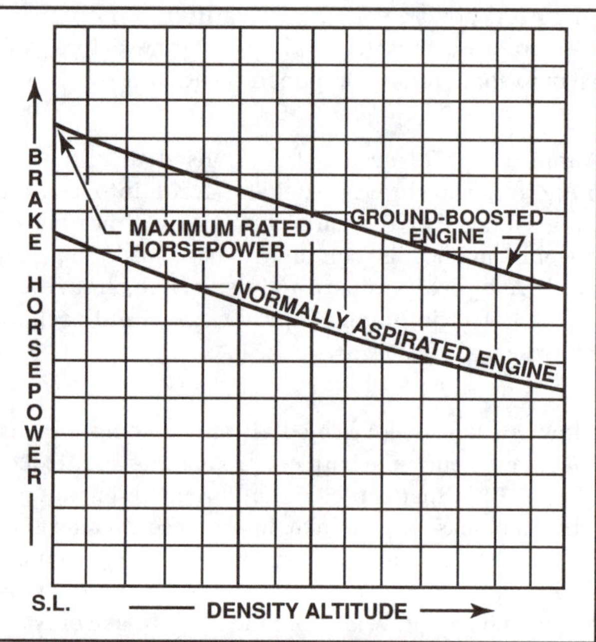

Figure 5-4. The lower curve illustrates how the power output of a normally aspirated engine declines as altitude increases. The upper curve illustrates how a ground-boosted engine has a higher power output at all altitudes but still decreases as altitude increases.

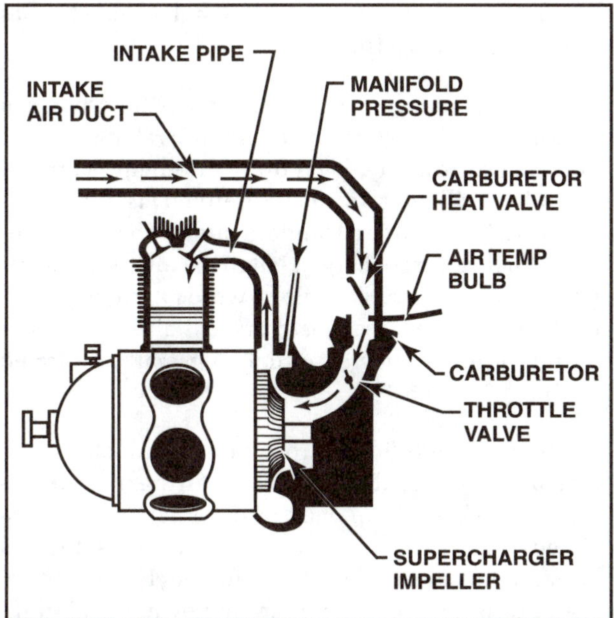

Figure 5-5. This simplified figure traces the path of induction air from the intake to the cylinders in a single stage, single speed supercharger induction system.

ducted to the supercharger, or **blower** impeller which accelerates the fuel/air mixture outward in the same manner as a centrifugal compressor used on a turbine engine. Once accelerated, the fuel/air mixture passes through a diffuser, where air velocity is traded for pressure energy. Once compressed, the resulting high pressure fuel/air charge is directed to the cylinders. [Figure 5-5]

The gear ratio of a typical single stage impeller gear train varies from approximately 6:1 to 12:1. Based on this, the impeller speed on an engine equipped with a 10:1 impeller gear ratio operating at 2,600 rpm would be 26,000 rpm. This high speed rotation requires that an impeller be forged out of a high grade aluminum alloy.

On all supercharged engines, the manifold pressure gauge sense line is installed after the supercharger so the pressure of the fuel/air mixture is known before it enters the cylinders. By knowing the pressure of the mixture before it enters the cylinders, a more accurate indication of engine performance is provided.

SINGLE STAGE, TWO SPEED SUPERCHARGER

Some of the large radial engines used through World War II used a single stage, two speed supercharger. With this type of supercharger, a single impeller may be operated at two speeds. At the low speed, the impeller gear ratio is approximately 8:1; however, at the high speed, the impeller gear ratio is stepped up to 11:1. The low impeller speed is often referred to as the **low blower** setting while the high impeller speed is called the **high blower** setting. On engines equipped with a low speed supercharger, the activation of a lever or switch in the cockpit activates an oil operated clutch that switches from one speed to the other.

Under normal operations, takeoff is made with the supercharger in the low blower position. In this mode, the engine performs as a ground boosted engine and the power output decreases as the aircraft gains altitude. However, once the aircraft reaches a specified altitude, a power reduction is made, and the supercharger control is switched to the high blower position. The throttle is then reset to the desired manifold pressure. An engine equipped with this type of supercharger is called an **altitude engine**. [Figure 5-6]

TURBOCHARGER SYSTEMS

A drawback of gear driven superchargers is that they use a large amount of the engine's power output for the amount of power increase they produce.

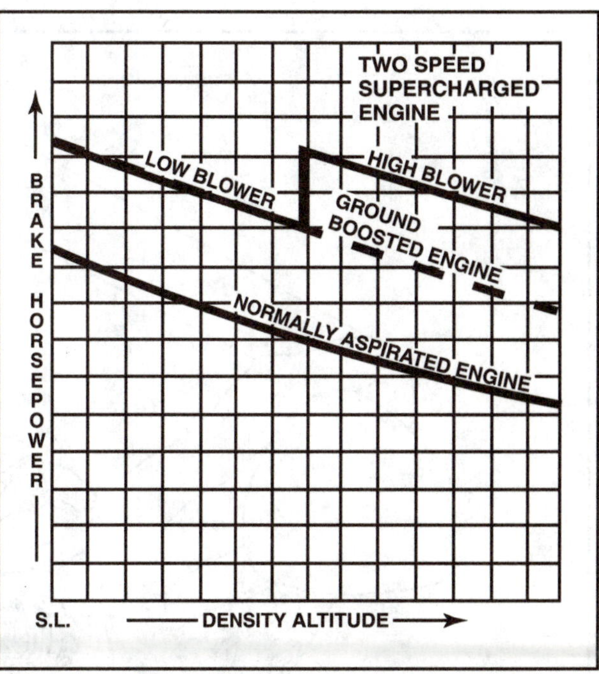

Figure 5-6. On engines equipped with a two speed supercharger, when the low blower speed is selected, the engine's brake horsepower is boosted above that of a normally aspirated engine. However, power output still decreases as the aircraft climbs. To help compensate for this, the high blower setting can be selected once the aircraft reaches a higher altitude.

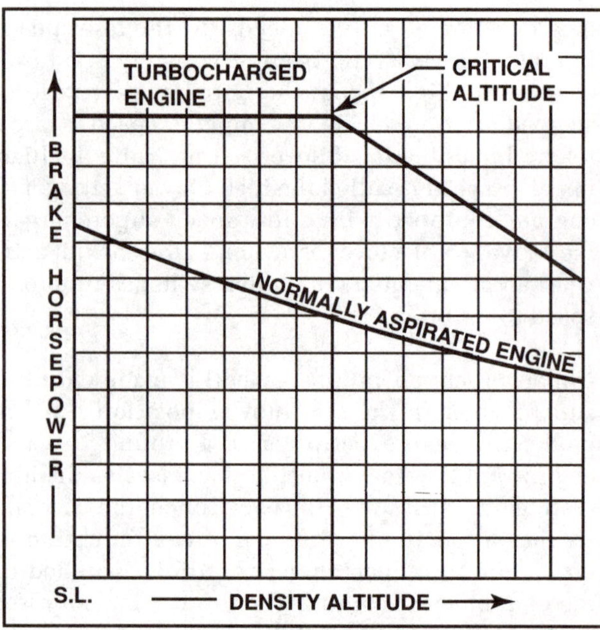

Figure 5-7. With a turbocharged engine, the turbocharger allows an engine to produce its rated sea-level horsepower up to the engine's critical altitude. Once above the critical altitude, the engine's power output decreases similar to that of a normally aspirated engine.

This problem is avoided with a **turbosupercharger**, or **turbocharger**, because turbochargers are powered by an engine's exhaust gases. In other words, a turbocharger recovers energy from hot exhaust gases that would otherwise be lost.

Another advantage of turbochargers is that they can be controlled to maintain an engine's rated sea-level horsepower from sea-level up to the engine's critical altitude. **Critical altitude** is defined as the maximum altitude under standard atmospheric conditions that a turbocharged engine can produce its rated horsepower. In other words, when a turbocharged engine reaches it critical altitude, power output begins to decrease like a normally aspirated engine. [Figure 5-7]

The components in a turbocharged induction system are similar to those in a normally aspirated system with the addition of a turbocharger and its associated controls. The turbocharger itself is located between the air intake and the fuel metering device. As an example, on a popular single-engine aircraft, air enters a filtered air intake located on the nose of the aircraft, below the propeller. From here, the air is ducted to the turbocharger at the rear of the engine. The turbocharger compresses the intake air and then sends the air to the air metering section of the fuel metering device. Once metered, the air is routed through the intake manifold to the cylinder intake ports where it is mixed with a metered amount of fuel. [Figure 5-8]

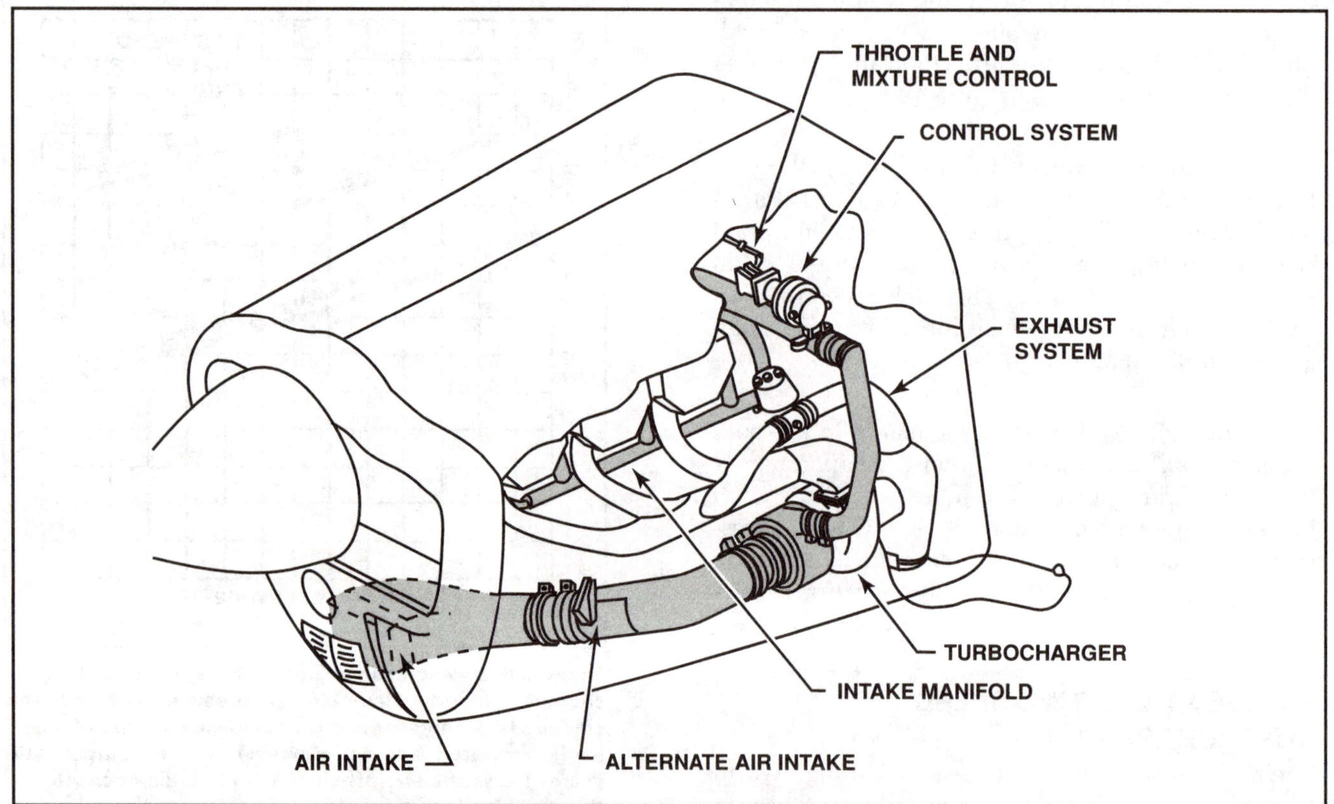

Figure 5-8. Pictured above is what a typical turbocharger induction system looks like installed in a light aircraft.

A typical turbocharger consists of a single rotating shaft with a centrifugal **compressor impeller** mounted on one end and a small radial **turbine** mounted on the other end. Both the impeller and turbine are surrounded by individual housings that are joined by a common bearing housing. The bearing housing contains two aluminum bearings that support the center shaft. In this configuration, as exhaust gases spin the turbine, the impeller draws in air and compresses it. [Figure 5-9]

In addition to the friction caused by high rotation speeds, turbochargers are heated by the exhaust gases flowing through the turbine, and the compression of intake air. Therefore, a continuous flow of engine oil must be pumped through the bearing housing to cool and lubricate the bearings. Approximately four to five gallons of oil per minute are pumped through a typical turbocharger bearing housing to lubricate the bearings and take away heat. The turbine inlet temperature may get as high as 1,600°F, and the large flow of oil is needed to keep the bearings within a safe operating temperature.

Once the engine oil passes through the bearings, it flows out a large opening in the bottom of the bearing housing and back to the engine oil sump. Some turbochargers may utilize an additional oil scavenge pump to ensure reliable oil flow from the turbocharger back to the engine oil sump.

Since the temperature of a gas rises when it is compressed, turbocharging causes the temperature of the induction air to increase. To reduce this temperature and lower the risk of detonation, many turbocharged engines use an intercooler. An **intercooler** is a small heat exchanger that uses outside air to cool the hot compressed air before it enters the fuel metering device.

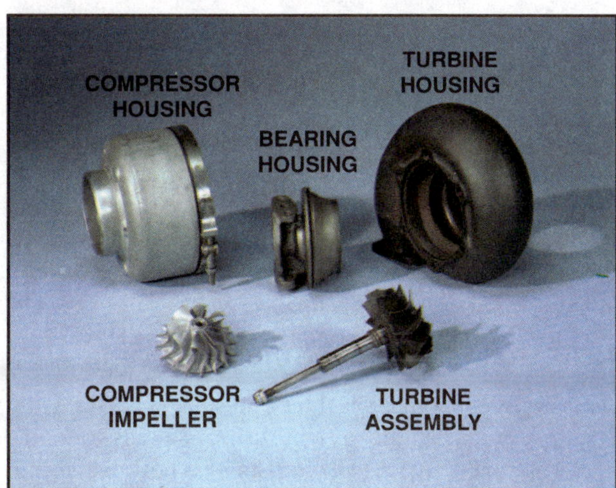

Figure 5-9. A turbocharger consists of a compressor impeller and turbine mounted on a single rotating shaft. Both the impeller and turbine are surrounded by separate housings that are joined by a common bearing housing.

TURBOCHARGER CONTROL SYSTEMS

If all the exhaust gases were allowed to pass through the turbine of a turbocharger, excessive manifold pressures, or **overboosting** would result. On the other hand, if the amount of exhaust gases allowed to flow to a turbocharger were limited, the turbocharger would be excessively limited at higher altitudes. Therefore, turbochargers are designed to allow control over the amount of exhaust gases which pass through the turbocharger's turbine.

To control the amount of exhaust gases that flow past a turbocharger turbine, a valve known as a **waste gate** is used. When a waste gate is fully open, all of the exhaust gases bypass the turbocharger and pass out the exhaust stack. However, when a waste gate is fully closed, all of the exhaust gases are routed through the turbine before they exit through the exhaust. The position of a waste gate can be adjusted either manually or automatically. [Figure 5-10]

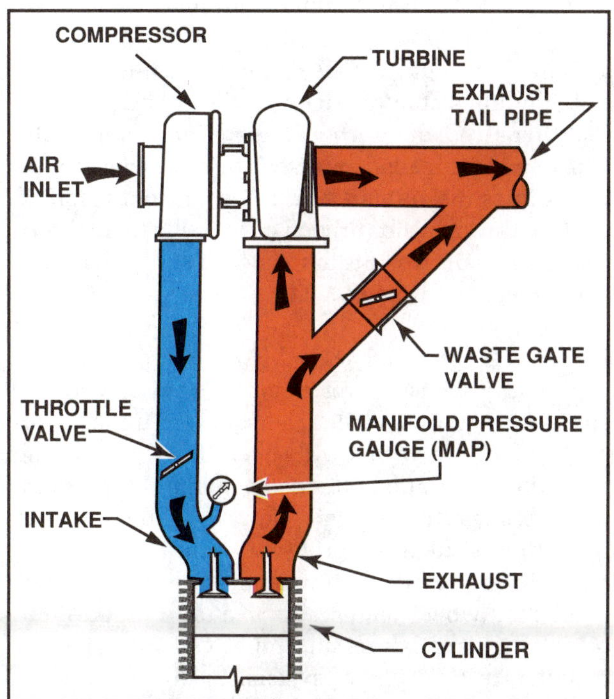

Figure 5-10. A waste gate is used to direct the exhaust gases to a turbocharger. When the waste gate is fully open, all the exhaust gases bypass the turbocharger. However, when the waste gate is fully closed, all the exhaust gases are routed through the turbocharger.

MANUAL CONTROL SYSTEMS

One of the simplest forms of turbocharger control uses a manual linkage between the engine throttle valve and the waste gate valve. For takeoff at low density altitudes, the throttle is advanced until the engine develops full takeoff power as indicated on the manifold pressure gauge. At this point, the waste gate will be fully or nearly fully open. As the aircraft gains altitude, engine power decreases requiring the pilot to advance the throttle forward a little to partially close the waste gate. As the waste gate is gradually closed, the manifold pressure increases proportionally and the engine produces its rated horsepower. This process is continued as the aircraft climbs to its critical altitude. Once at its critical altitude, the throttle will be advanced all the way forward and the waste gate will be fully closed.

A second type of manual control system allows you to set the position of the waste gate using a control in the cockpit. With this type of system, the engine is started with the waste gate in the fully open position. Then, just prior to takeoff, the throttle is advanced full forward and the waste gate is slowly closed using the cockpit control until full engine power is developed. Once the aircraft takes off and begins climbing, the pilot must monitor the engine performance and close the waste gate as necessary to maintain the desired power output.

The final type of manual waste gate controller utilizes an adjustable restrictor in the exhaust section that bypasses the turbocharger. The amount the restrictor is threaded in or out of the exhaust pipe determines the amount of exhaust gas that is forced to flow through the turbocharger. With this type of system, no adjustments to the restrictor can be made from the cabin. [Figure 5-11]

On aircraft equipped with this type of control system, the waste gate restrictor is adjusted so the engine develops its rated horsepower under standard conditions with a wide open throttle. By doing this, the maximum obtainable manifold pressure decreases as the aircraft gains altitude and the induction system is protected from being overboosted. To provide additional protection against an overboost when temperatures and pressures are below standard, a pressure relief valve is typically installed in this type of system. In this case, when manifold pressure rises to within approximately one inch of its rated pressure, the relief valve begins to off-seat. This way, by the time maximum manifold pressure is reached, the pressure relief valve is open enough to bleed off excess pressure.

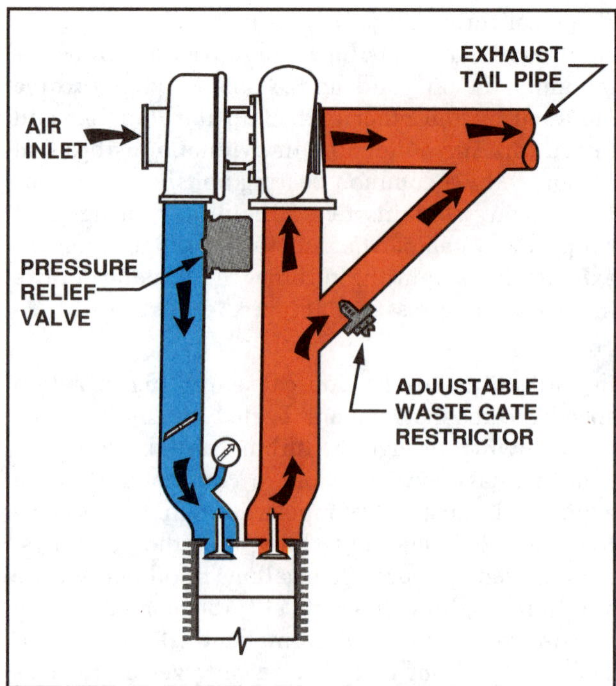

Figure 5-11. On turbocharging systems equipped with an adjustable waste gate restrictor, the amount the restrictor is threaded in or out determines how much of the exhaust bypasses the turbocharger.

AUTOMATIC CONTROL SYSTEMS

As the name implies, an automatic turbocharger control system automatically positions the waste gate so the engine maintains the power output level selected. To do this, these systems use a combination of several components including a waste gate actuator, an absolute pressure controller, a pressure-ratio controller, and a rate-of-change controller.

WASTE GATE ACTUATOR

The waste gate in an automatic control system is positioned by a waste gate actuator. With a waste gate actuator, the waste gate is held open by spring pressure and is closed by oil pressure acting on a piston. Oil pressure is supplied to the actuator from the engine's oil system.

ABSOLUTE PRESSURE CONTROLLER

On Teledyne-Continental engines, the waste gate actuator is controlled by an absolute pressure controller, or **APC**. An APC consists of a bellows and a variable restrictor valve. The bellows senses the absolute pressure of the air before it enters the fuel metering device. This pressure is commonly referred to as **upper deck pressure**. As the bellows

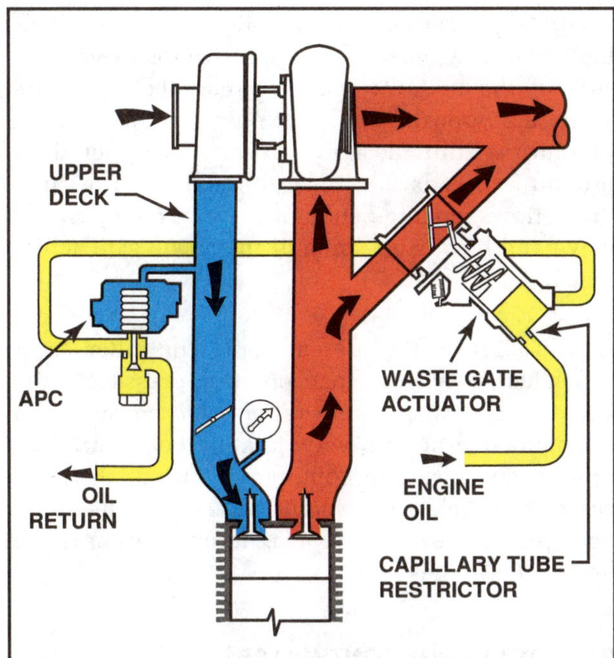

Figure 5-12. The automatic control system used with several turbocharged Teledyne-Continental engines uses a waste gate actuator that is controlled by an absolute pressure controller.

expands and contracts, it moves the **variable restrictor valve** to control the amount of oil that flows out of the waste gate actuator. [Figure 5-12]

With this automatic control system, oil flows into the waste gate actuator through a **capillary tube restrictor**. Once the actuator chamber fills, the oil flows out of the actuator to the absolute pressure controller and then back to the engine. The rate at which the oil flows through the APC and back to the engine is determined by the position of the variable restrictor valve.

When the engine is not running, no oil pressure exists and the spring pressure inside the waste gate actuator holds the waste gate in the fully open, or bypass position. In addition, the upper deck pressure is low so the bellows holds the variable restrictor valve closed. Once the engine is started, engine oil flows into the waste gate actuator cylinder and the APC. Since the restrictor valve in the APC is closed, oil pressure will build in the system until it can partially overcome the spring pressure in the waste gate actuator. As oil pressure builds, the waste gate begins to close and direct some of the exhaust to the turbocharger. This process continues until the upper deck pressure builds enough to compress the APC bellows and open the restrictor valve. Once the restrictor valve opens, oil is allowed to flow back to the engine. Since oil is supplied to the waste gate actuator through a restricted opening, oil flows out of the actuator faster than it flows in. This permits the oil pressure within the actuator to decrease rapidly and allow spring force to open the waste gate until the two forces balance.

In this type of system, when the throttle is advanced to obtain takeoff power, the increased flow of exhaust gases through the turbocharger causes an increase in upper deck and manifold pressure. When the upper deck pressure increases to approximately one inch above the desired manifold pressure, the APC bellows contracts and causes the restrictor to open partially and drain oil back into the engine sump. The reason the APC is set to open approximately one inch above the maximum manifold pressure is to account for the pressure drop across the throttle body. As some of the exhaust gases bypass the turbocharger, the turbine speed decreases enough to hold the desired manifold pressure.

As the aircraft climbs, the air becomes less dense and the upper deck pressure starts to decrease. The APC senses the decrease and closes the variable restrictor valve enough to slow the oil flow from the waste gate actuator. This increases the oil pressure within the actuator which repositions the waste gate to direct more exhaust gases through the turbocharger.

As the aircraft continues to ascend, the waste gate valve continues to close in response to decreases in upper deck pressure. Once the engine's critical altitude is reached, the waste gate will be fully closed and all the exhaust gases will flow through the turbocharger. If the aircraft climbs above this altitude, manifold pressure will decrease.

A variation of the absolute pressure controller is the **variable absolute pressure controller**, or **VAPC**. A VAPC functions similarly to an APC with a bellows controlling the position of a restrictor valve. However, with a VAPC, the position of the restrictor valve seat is controlled by a cam that is actuated by the throttle control.

PRESSURE-RATIO CONTROLLER

Some engines are restricted to a maximum altitude at which they are allowed to maintain their maximum rated manifold pressure. On engines that are limited in this way, a secondary control device known as a pressure-ratio controller is installed in parallel with the absolute pressure controller. The purpose of a pressure-ratio controller is to monitor both the ambient and upper deck pressures and prevent the turbocharger from boosting the upper deck pressure higher than 2.2 times the ambient pressure. [Figure 5-13]

To explain how a pressure-ratio controller works, assume an aircraft is equipped with a turbocharging system that has a manifold pressure limit of 36 inches of mercury at 16,000 feet. As the airplane takes off and begins climbing, the absolute pressure controller slowly closes the waste gate so the manifold pressure remains at 36 inches. As the aircraft approaches 16,000 feet, the waste gate will be fully or nearly fully closed to maintain the 36 inches of manifold pressure. The atmospheric pressure at 16,000 feet is approximately 16.22 inches of mercury; therefore, at 16,000 feet, the pressure-ratio controller begins to unseat because the upper deck pressure (37 inches) will exceed 2.2 times the ambient pressure ($16.22 \times 2.2 = 35.68$ inches). If the aircraft continues to climb to 18,000 feet where the ambient pressure is approximately 14.95 in. Hg., the pressure-ratio controller will unseat as necessary to maintain an upper deck pressure of 32.89 inches ($14.95 \times 2.2 = 32.89$).

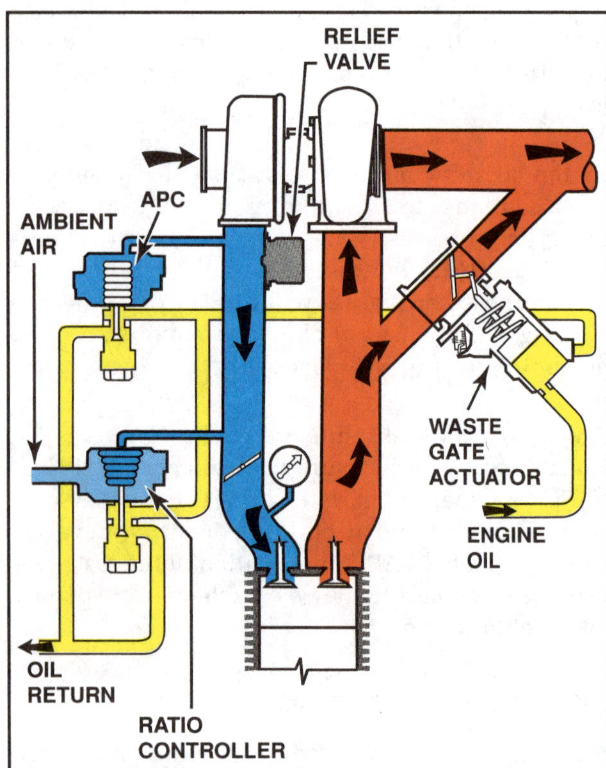

Figure 5-13. On turbocharging systems that are restricted to a maximum differential between manifold and ambient pressures, a pressure ratio controller is installed in parallel with the absolute pressure controller in the oil line between the waste gate actuator and the engine sump.

A typical pressure-ratio controller consists of a bellows that positions a variable restrictor valve. One side of the bellows senses upper deck pressure while the opposite side is exposed to the ambient pressure within the cowl. When the upper deck pressure exceeds 2.2 times the ambient pressure, the bellows expands enough to open the restrictor valve and bleeds off some of the waste gate actuator oil.

As a backup to the pressure-ratio controller, most turbocharger systems incorporate a **pressure relief valve**. A typical pressure relief valve consists of a spring loaded pop-up valve that is mounted to the upper deck near the compressor output. In most cases, the relief valve remains seated until the upper deck pressure exceeds its maximum rated pressure by 1 to 1.5 inches.

RATE-OF-CHANGE CONTROLLER

In addition to an absolute pressure controller, a pressure ratio controller, and a pressure relief valve, many automatic turbocharger control systems utilize a rate-of-change controller. A rate-of-change controller is installed in parallel with the absolute pressure controller and pressure-ratio controller, and prevents the upper deck pressure from increasing too rapidly. Under normal conditions, the rate-of-change controller remains seated; however, if the throttle is advanced too abruptly and the upper deck pressure rises too rapidly, the rate-of-change controller unseats and allows waste gate actuator oil to flow back to the engine. In most cases, a rate-of-change controller is set between 2.0 and 6.5 inches per second.

SEA LEVEL BOOSTED ENGINES

Some turbocharger systems are designed to maintain sea level engine performance from sea level up to their critical altitude. In other words, the turbocharger maintains sea level manifold pressure and does not boost manifold pressure above that level. Engines that are equipped with this type of turbocharger system are referred to as sea level boosted engines.

The turbocharger system in all sea level boosted engines is controlled automatically. However, the components used in this type of system differ from those used in other automatic control systems. The three units that permit automatic control include an exhaust bypass valve assembly, a density controller, and a differential pressure controller.

The **exhaust bypass valve assembly** functions in a manner similar to the waste gate actuator previously discussed. Engine oil pressure acts on a piston which is connected to the waste gate valve through a mechanical linkage. Increased oil pressure on the piston moves the waste gate valve toward the closed position to direct exhaust gases through the turbocharger. Conversely, when the oil pressure is decreased, spring tension moves the waste gate valve toward the open position to allow the exhaust gases to bypass the turbocharger. The amount of oil pressure acting on the exhaust bypass valve assembly is controlled by the density controller and differential pressure controller. [Figure 5-14]

The **density controller** regulates the bleed oil flow from the exhaust bypass valve assembly only during full throttle operation. To do this, a density controller utilizes a nitrogen filled bellows that senses the density of the upper deck air. The bellows is contained in a rigid housing that extends into the upper deck airstream. This way, if the density of the air is not equal to that needed to produce full engine power, the density controller can adjust the oil pressure acting on the exhaust bypass valve assembly so more exhaust is directed to the turbocharger.

To regulate the oil pressure within the exhaust bypass valve assembly, the bellows in a density controller positions a metering valve to bleed off the appropriate amount of oil. Therefore, if the density of the upper deck air is too low to produce full power, the bellows in the density controller will expand and position the metering valve to stop the flow of oil back to the engine. On the other hand, if upper deck air density is too high, the bellows will contract and position the metering valve to permit oil flow back to the engine.

When a sea level boosted engine is operated at less than full throttle, the **differential pressure controller** regulates turbocharger output. A differential pressure controller consists of a diaphragm that controls the position of an oil metering valve. One side of the diaphragm is exposed to upper deck pressure while the other side is exposed to manifold pressure. In this configuration, the differential pressure controller monitors the pressure differential, or drop, across the throttle body. A typical differential pressure controller is set to allow between a 2 to 4 inch pressure drop across the throttle body. If this differential is exceeded, the diaphragm positions the metering valve to allow oil to bleed from the exhaust bypass valve assembly thereby reducing the degree of turbocharging. On the other hand, if the pressure differential decreases below the preset valve, the diaphragm will position the metering valve to stop the flow of oil out of the exhaust bypass valve assembly. This will force the waste gate closed and increase the degree of turbocharging.

In addition to controlling the degree of turbocharging during part throttle operations, the differential pressure controller reduces the duration of a condi-

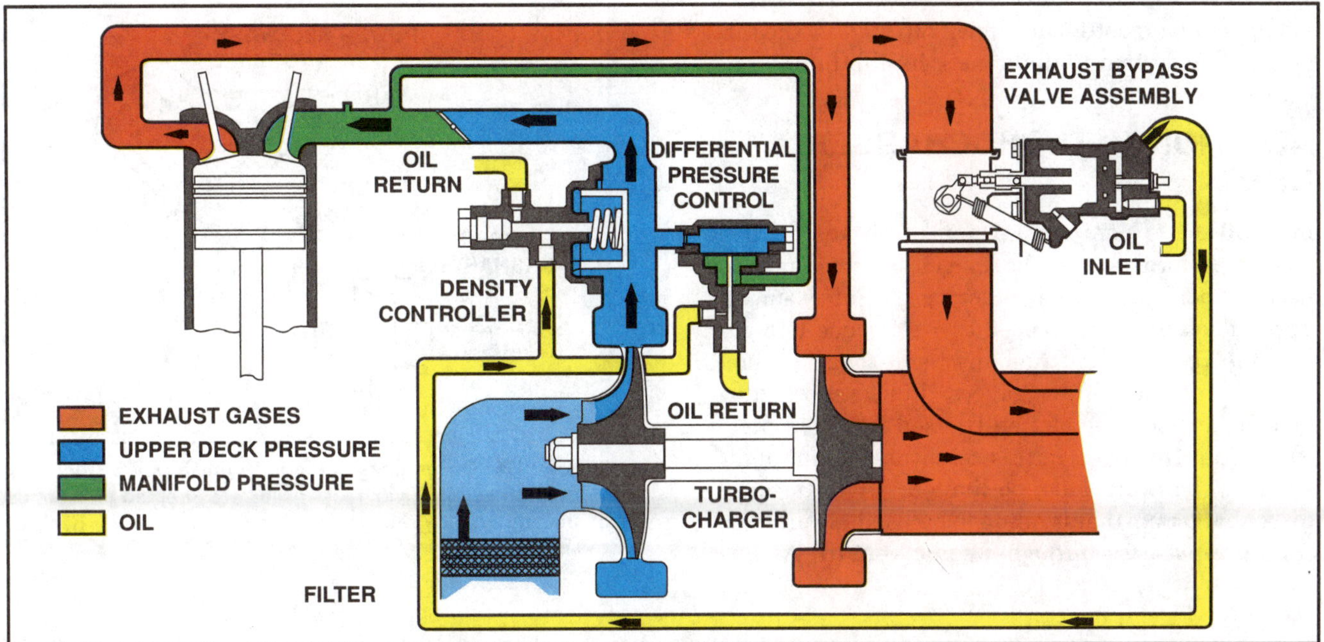

Figure 5-14. A sea level boosted turbocharger system maintains an engine's sea level performance up to the engine's critical altitude. To do this, the turbocharging system utilizes an exhaust bypass valve assembly, a density controller, and a differential pressure controller.

tion known as bootstrapping. **Bootstrapping** describes a condition that occurs when a turbocharger system senses small changes in temperature or rpm and continually changes the turbocharger output in an attempt to establish equilibrium. Bootstrapping typically occurs during part-throttle operation and is characterized by a continual drift or transient increase in manifold pressure.

OPERATIONAL CONSIDERATIONS

When operating a turbocharged engine, there are some additional considerations you should be aware of. For example, as a general rule, turbocharged engines are more sensitive to throttle movements then normally aspirated engines. therefore, when operating a turbocharged engine, you should avoid rapid throttle movements. If throttle movements are not controlled, engine or turbocharger damage could result. For example, advancing the throttle too rapidly could cause the turbocharger to **overboost** the induction system. If severe enough, an overboost could damage the intake manifold or even the pistons and cylinders.

Rapid throttle movements can also cause what is know as an **overshoot**. In this case, the turbocharger controllers can not keep up with the throttle movement and the manifold pressure overshoots the desired value requiring the operator to retard the throttle as appropriate. Although not as serious as an overboost, an overshoot can increase the operator's workload. To avoid an overshoot, it is best to make gradual throttle movements that allow the turbocharging system to find a new equilibrium.

ADDITIONAL TURBOCHARGER USES

In addition to compressing intake air to improve engine performance, turbocharger systems are also used to perform several other tasks. For example, upper deck pressure is used as a reference to regulate the operation of fuel discharge nozzles, fuel pumps, and fuel flow gauges. Furthermore, turbocharger discharge air can be used for cabin pressurization. However, in this case, the amount of air entering the cabin must be limited. To do this, the turbocharger air that is going to be used for pressurization must pass through a **sonic venturi**. As turbocharger air passes through a sonic venturi, it is accelerated to transonic speed to produce a shock wave. Once formed, the shock wave slows the remaining airflow in the venturi thereby limiting the amount of air entering the cabin. [Figure 5-15]

TURBOCOMPOUND SYSTEMS

A turbocompound engine is a reciprocating engine in which exhaust driven turbines are coupled to the engine crankshaft. This system of obtaining additional power is sometimes called a **power recovery turbine system**, or **PRT**. It is not a supercharging system, and it is not connected in any manner to the air induction system of the aircraft. Instead, a PRT system enables an engine to recover energy from the velocity of the exhaust gases that would otherwise be lost as the gases are ducted overboard. Depending on the type of engine, the amount of horsepower recovered varies with the amount of input horsepower. A typical PRT in a large radial engine has three turbines that can recover up to 390 horsepower from the exhaust gases.

On engines that have a power recovery turbine, an exhaust collector nozzle directs the exhaust gases onto a turbine wheel. As the turbine spins, a turbine wheel shaft transmits the recovered power to the engine crankshaft through gears and a fluid coupling. The fluid coupling is necessary to prevent torsional vibration from being transmitted to the crankshaft. [Figure 5-16]

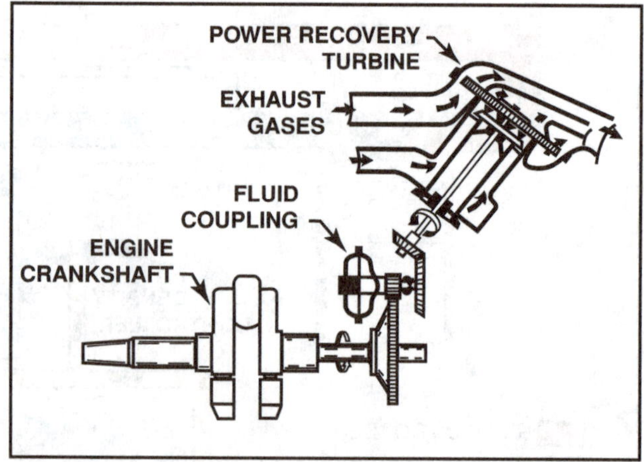

Figure 5-16. On engines equipped with a power recovery turbine, the engine's exhaust gases are directed by a series of turbine wheels that transmit rotational energy back to the crankshaft.

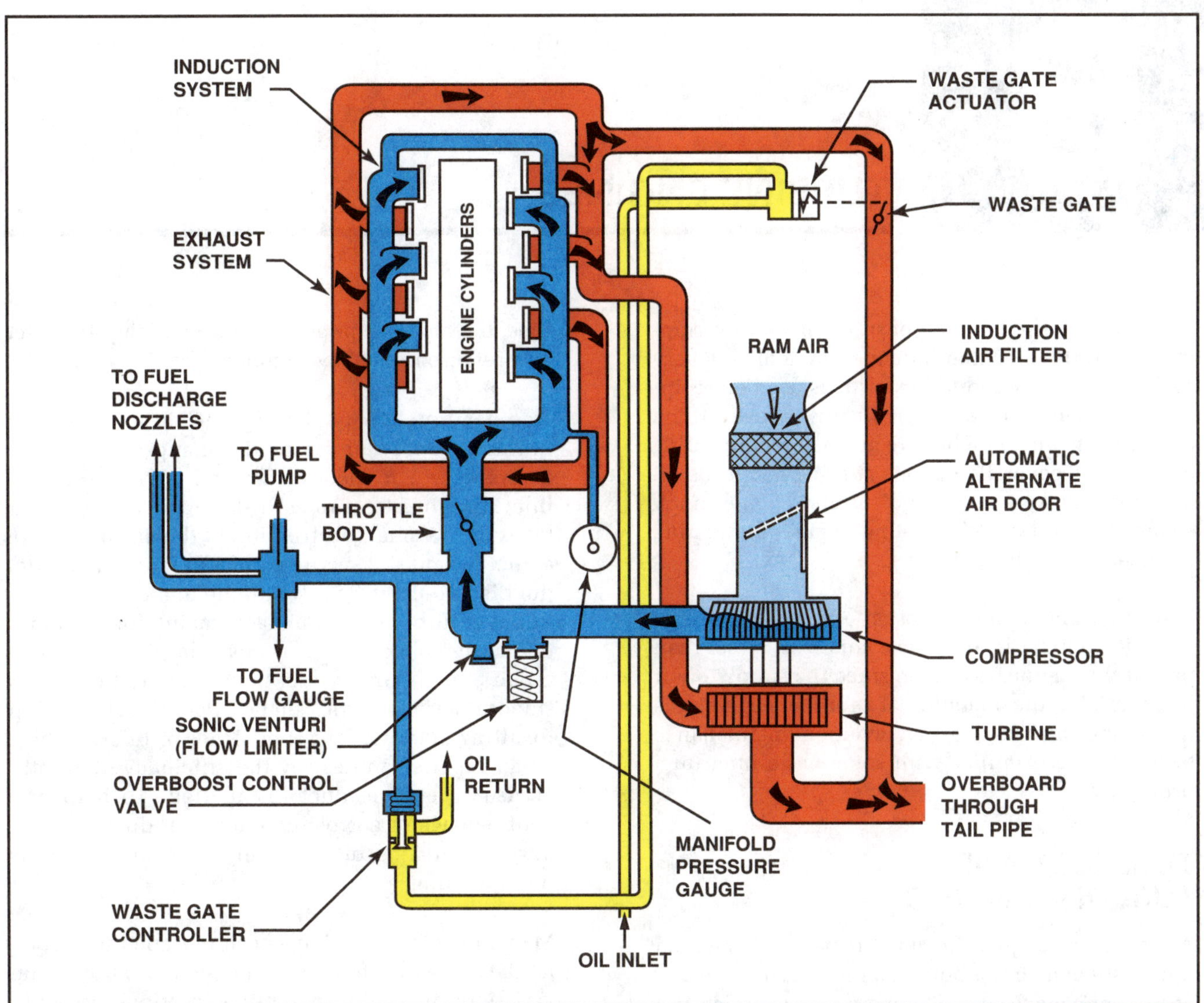

Figure 5-15. The turbocharger system utilized in many general aviation aircraft supplies not only induction air, but also serves as a reference pressure. The fuel discharge nozzles, fuel pump, and fuel flow gauge all use upper deck pressure as a reference pressure to perform fuel metering functions properly. In addition, on many aircraft, the turbocharger provides air for cabin pressurization.

TURBINE ENGINES

Beyond the basic function of supplying air for combustion, turbine engine induction systems are very different from the induction systems used on reciprocating engines. One reason for this is that turbine engines consume much more air than reciprocating engines and generally operate at faster airspeeds. In addition, intake air enters a turbine engine much sooner than on a reciprocating engine eliminating the need for intricate ducting.

Typically, the air inlet duct on a turbine engine is considered to be an airframe component rather than part of the engine. However, since the supply of air is essential to the operation of a turbine engine, it is important that you, as an aviation maintenance technician, be familiar with some basic inlet duct principles.

TURBOJET AND TURBOFAN INLETS

A gas turbine engine consumes between six and ten times as much air per hour as a reciprocating engine of the equivalent size. Therefore, the air inlet of a turbine engine must be correspondingly larger. In addition, to help ensure optimum performance, the air inlet duct on a turbojet or turbofan engine must furnish a relatively distortion free, high energy supply of air to the compressor. If this is not done, improper combustion, excessive turbine temperatures, or a compressor stall can occur. In fact, given the speeds at which turbine aircraft travel, even a small inefficiency in an air inlet duct will result in a large decrease in engine performance.

The air inlet to a turbine engine has several functions, one of which is to recover as much of the total pressure of the free airstream as possible and deliver this pressure to the compressor. This is known as **ram recovery** or **pressure recovery**. In addition to recovering and maintaining the pressure of the free airstream, many inlets are shaped to raise the air pressure above atmospheric pressure. This **ram effect** results from forward movement which causes air to "pile up" in the inlet. The faster the aircraft flies, the more air piles up, and the higher the inlet air pressure rises above ambient.

Another function of the air inlet is to provide a uniform supply of air to the compressor so the compressor can operate efficiently. To do this, the inlet duct must cause as little drag as possible. It takes only a small obstruction to the airflow inside a duct to cause a severe loss of efficiency. If an inlet duct is to deliver its full volume of air with a minimum of turbulence, it must be maintained as close to its original condition as possible. Therefore, any repairs to an inlet duct must retain the duct's smooth aerodynamic shape. Poor workmanship resulting in protruding rivet heads or inferior sheet metal repairs can destroy the efficiency of an otherwise acceptable duct installation. To help prevent damage or corrosion to an inlet duct, an inlet cover should be installed any time the engine is not operating.

Many air inlet ducts have been designed to accommodate new airframe/engine combinations and variations in engine mounting locations. In addition, air inlets are designed to meet certain criteria for operation at different airspeeds. However, in order to maintain an even airflow and minimize pressure losses caused by friction, all inlet ducts must be designed with a sufficiently straight section. Some of the most common locations where engine inlets are mounted are on the engine, in the wing, and on the fuselage.

The inlet ducts used on modern turbojet and turbofan aircraft are typically mounted in one of several locations, depending on engine location. For example, engines mounted on wing or fuselage pylons utilize an air inlet duct that is directly in front of the compressor and is mounted to the engine. This allows for the shortest possible inlet duct with a minimum of pressure loss. [Figure 5-17]

Some aircraft with engines mounted inside the wings feature air inlet ducts in the wing's leading edge. Aircraft such as the Aerospatiale Caravelle,

Figure 5-17. A Boeing 757 is designed with wing mounted engines that utilize engine mounted inlet ducts that are directly in front of the compressor.

de Havilland Comet, and de Havilland Vampire all utilize wing-mounted inlets. Typically, wing-mounted inlets are positioned near the wing root area. [Figure 5-18]

Engines mounted inside a fuselage typically use air inlet ducts located near the front of the fuselage. For example, many early military aircraft were designed with an air inlet duct in the nose of the fuselage. In addition, some modern supersonic military aircraft have inlet ducts located just under the aircraft nose. Although using an air inlet of this type allows the aircraft manufacturer to build a more aerodynamic aircraft, the increased length of the inlet does introduce some inefficiencies. [Figure 5-19]

Some military aircraft use air inlet ducts mounted on the sides of the fuselage. This arrangement works well for both single and twin engine aircraft. By mounting an intake on each side of an aircraft, the duct length can be shortened without adding a significant amount of drag to the aircraft. However, a disadvantage to this arrangement is that some sudden flight maneuvers can cause an imbalance in ram air pressure between the two intakes. The air pressure imbalance felt on the compressor face results in a slight loss of power.

Figure 5-18. The Hawker-Siddeley 801 "Nimrod" was developed from the de Havilland Comet airframe and utilizes wing mounted air inlets that are aerodynamically shaped to reduce drag.

Figure 5-19. The single-entrance inlet duct takes full advantage of ram effect much like engine-mounted air inlets. Although the aircraft is aerodynamically clean, the length of the duct makes it slightly less efficient than engine-mounted types.

SUBSONIC INLETS

A typical subsonic air inlet consists of a fixed geometry duct whose diameter progressively increases from front to back. This **divergent** shape works like a **diffuser** in that as the intake air passes through the duct it spreads out. As the air spreads out, its velocity decreases and its pressure increases. In most cases, subsonic inlets are designed to diffuse the air in the front portion of the duct. This allows the air to progress at a fairly constant pressure before it enters the engine. [Figure 5-20]

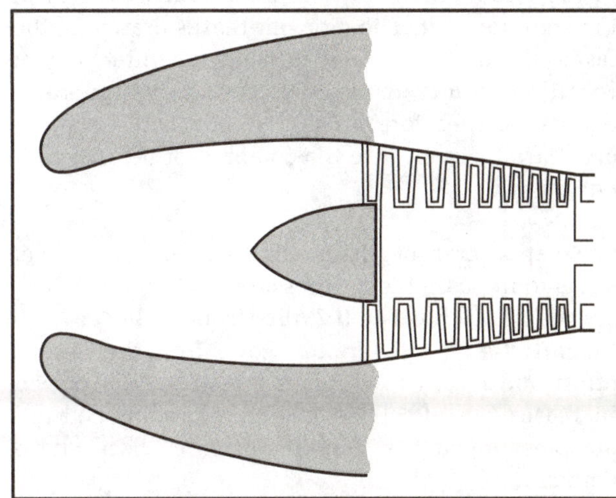

Figure 5-20. Subsonic turbine engine inlets use a divergent profile that diffuses incoming air. At cruise airspeeds, the divergent shape causes air velocity to decrease and static air pressure to increase.

A turbofan inlet is similar in design to a turbojet inlet except that the inlet discharges only a portion of its air into the engine. The remainder of inlet air passing through the fan flows around, or bypasses, the engine core to create thrust much in the same way a propeller does. In addition, the bypass air helps cool the engine and reduce noise.

A turbofan engine utilizes one of two types of inlet duct designs. One type is the short duct design that allows a large percentage of fan air to bypass the engine core and produce thrust. This type of duct is typically used on high bypass engines. The other duct design forms a shroud around the engine core and is used on low and medium bypass engines. Full fan ducts reduce aerodynamic drag and noise emissions. In addition, a full duct generally has a converging discharge nozzle that produces reactive thrust. Full ducts are not used on high bypass engines because the weight penalty caused by such a large diameter duct would offset the benefits. [Figure 5-21]

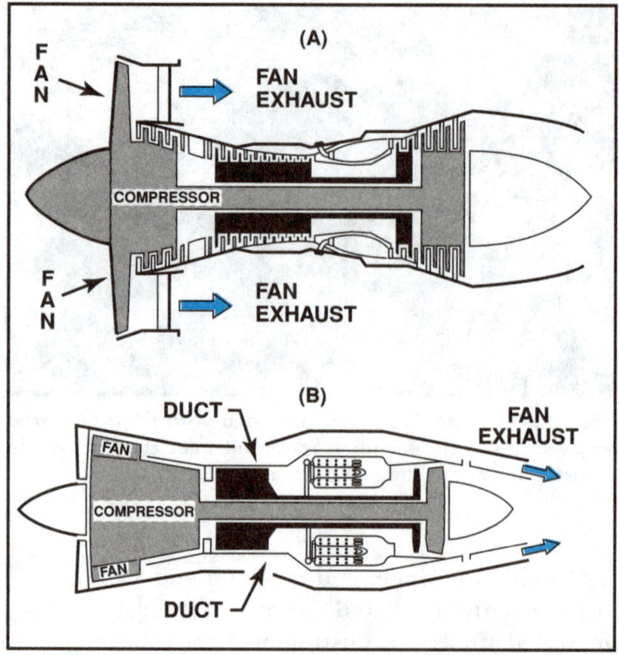

Figure 5-21. (A) — A high-bypass turbofan engine uses a short duct that allows a large portion of the incoming air to bypass the engine. (B) — On the other hand, some low and medium bypass engines use long inlet ducts that reduce surface drag of the fan discharge air and enhance thrust.

RAM EFFECT

In addition to the pressure rise created by the divergent shape of an inlet duct, turbine engines realize an additional pressure rise from ram effect. Ram effect results from forward movement which causes air to "pile up," or compress in an inlet. The faster an aircraft flies, the more the air compresses, and the higher the inlet air pressure rises above ambient. The resulting pressure rise causes an increase in mass airflow and jet velocity which, in turn, increase engine thrust.

Without ram effect, the compressor must pull air in through the inlet. The more air that is drawn in, the faster the air must flow through the inlet. If you recall, anytime air is accelerated, its pressure decreases. Therefore, an aircraft inlet, while stationary, introduces air into the compressor below ambient pressure.

Once an aircraft begins moving forward, ram effect starts to increase the air pressure in the inlet. At airspeeds of Mach 0.1 to 0.2, the airmass piles up sufficiently for air pressure to recover from the venturi effect and return to ambient pressure. As airspeed increases, ram effect becomes more pronounced and air pressure at the compressor inlet rises above ambient.

The increase in air pressure produced by an inlet duct and ram effect contributes significantly to engine efficiency once the aircraft reaches its design cruising speed. At this speed, the compressor reaches its optimum aerodynamic efficiency and produces the most compression for the best fuel economy. It is at this design cruise speed that the inlet, compressor, combustor, turbine, and exhaust duct are designed to match each other as a unit. If any section mismatches any other because of damage, contamination, or ambient conditions, engine performance suffers.

SUPERSONIC INLETS

Air entering the compressor on a turbine engine must flow slower than the speed of sound. Therefore, the inlet duct on a supersonic aircraft must decrease the speed of the inlet air before it reaches the compressor. To understand how a supersonic inlet does this, you must first understand how supersonic airflow reacts to converging and diverging openings.

AIRFLOW PRINCIPLES

Air flowing at subsonic speeds is considered to be incompressible while air flowing at supersonic speeds is compressible. Because of this, air flowing at supersonic speeds reacts differently when forced to flow through either a convergent or divergent

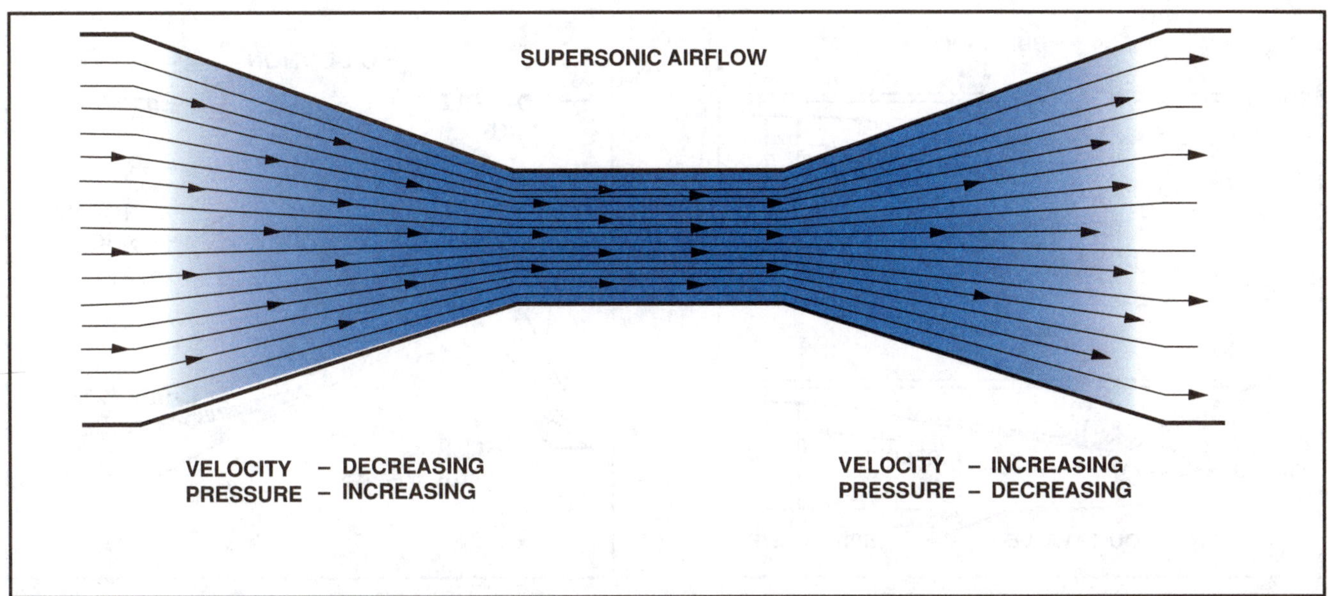

Figure 5-22. When air traveling at supersonic speeds flows through a convergent duct, its velocity decreases while its pressure increases. On the other hand, when air traveling at supersonic speeds flows through a divergent duct, its velocity increases and its pressure decreases.

opening. For example, when supersonic airflow is forced through a convergent duct, it compresses, or piles up, and its density increases. This causes a decrease in air velocity and a corresponding increase in pressure. On the other hand, when supersonic airflow passes through a divergent duct, it expands and its density decreases. As it expands, its velocity increases and its pressure decreases. [Figure 5-22]

In addition to understanding the velocity and pressure changes that occur with supersonic airflow, you should recall from your earlier studies that, whenever something travels through the air at the speed of sound, a shock wave forms. Once formed, any air flowing through the shock wave slows to a subsonic speed and increases in pressure.

INLET DESIGN

To slow the inlet air to a subsonic velocity, all supersonic aircraft utilize **convergent-divergent**, or **CD** inlet ducts. With a CD duct, the diameter of the duct progressively decreases, then increases from front to back. When supersonic air enters the convergent portion of the duct, its velocity decreases until the narrowest part of the inlet is reached. At this point, the air has slowed to the speed of sound and a shock wave forms. As the air passes through the shock wave it enters the divergent portion of the inlet where velocity continues to decrease and pressure increases. Once the air reaches the compressor, its velocity is well below sonic speed and its pressure has increased. [Figure 5-23]

An engine inlet duct on a supersonic aircraft must perform efficiently at subsonic, transonic, and supersonic speeds. Since the optimum inlet shape changes for each range of airspeeds, a typical supersonic aircraft utilizes an inlet duct with variable geometric construction. Several methods are used to vary the geometry, or shape of an inlet duct. One method uses a movable wedge that is retracted during slow speed flight. However, as the aircraft accelerates to supersonic speeds, the wedge is extended

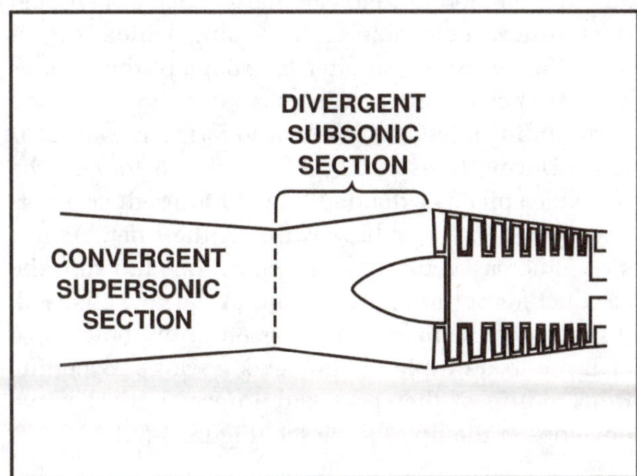

Figure 5-23. With a convergent-divergent inlet duct, the convergent section slows the incoming air velocity to Mach 1.0 at its narrowest point and forms a shock wave. The divergent section then reduces the air velocity further while increasing air pressure.

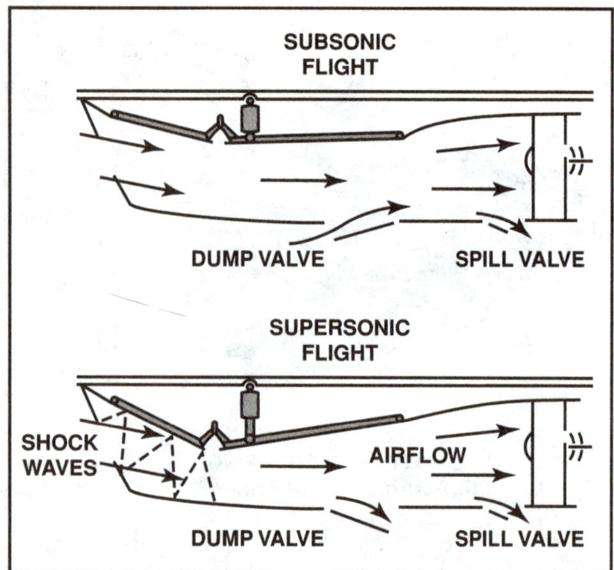

Figure 5-24. Some supersonic aircraft utilize a variable geometry inlet that maintains efficient airflow at subsonic, transonic, and supersonic speeds. At subsonic speeds, the wedge is retracted to take full advantage of ram effect. Once the aircraft reaches supersonic speeds, the wedge is extended to produce a convergent-divergent shape.

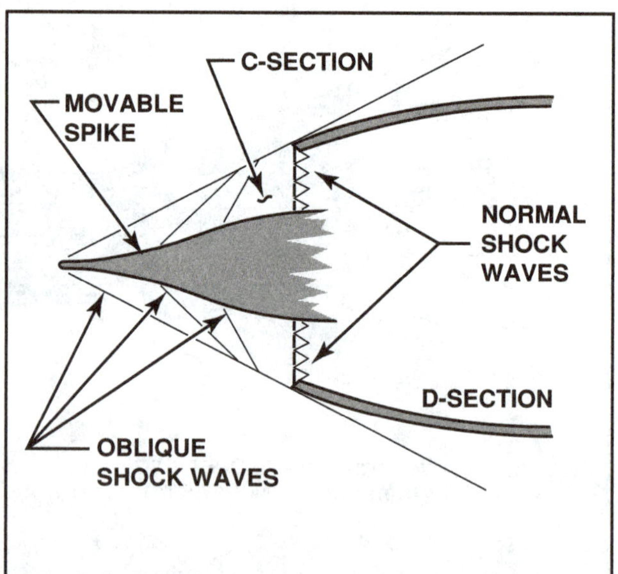

Figure 5-25. One method of varying the geometry of an inlet duct uses a movable spike. The spike can be repositioned in flight to alter the inlet shape for maximum inlet efficiency.

into the inlet airstream to produce a convergent-divergent shape. [Figure 5-24]

In addition to the movable wedge, this type of inlet duct incorporates a dump valve and spill valve. During subsonic flight, the dump valve is opened into the airstream to allow more air into the diverging portion of the inlet. At the same time, the spill valve is open to help prevent turbulence. During supersonic flight, both the dump and spill valve are opened to allow excess airflow to vent to the atmosphere.

Another method used to vary the geometry of an inlet duct utilizes a movable spike, or plug, which is positioned as necessary to alter the shape of the inlet as aircraft speed changes. The shape of the spike and surrounding inlet duct combine to form a movable CD inlet. During transonic flight (Mach .75 to 1.2), the movable spike is extended forward to produce a normal shock wave, or bow wave, at the inlet. As airspeed increases, the spike is repositioned to shift the CD duct for optimum inlet shape at the new airspeed. As airspeed increases to supersonic, the bow wave changes to multiple oblique shock waves extending from the tip of the spike and a normal shock wave develops at the lip of the inlet. [Figure 5-25]

BELLMOUTH INLET DUCT

Bellmouth inlets have a convergent profile that is designed specifically for obtaining very high aerodynamic efficiency when stationary or in slow flight. Therefore, bellmouth inlets are typically used on helicopters, some slow moving aircraft, and on engines being run in ground test stands. A typical bellmouth inlet is short in length and has rounded shoulders offering very little air resistance. However, because their shape produces a great deal of drag in forward flight, bellmouth inlets are typically not used on high speed aircraft. Since a bellmouth duct is so efficient when stationary, engine manufacturers typically collect engine performance data from engines fitted with a bellmouth inlet. [Figure 5-26]

TURBOPROP INLETS

Turboprop engines develop the majority of their thrust with propeller rather than jet propulsion. Therefore, the air inlet duct on a turboprop engine is typically smaller than those used on turbojet or turbofan engines. For example, on a reverse-flow turboprop engine, such as a PT-6, the air entrance to the compressor is located toward the rear of the engine. Depending on the aircraft installation, an air scoop located at the front of the nacelle below the propeller is generally used to duct air back to the engine inlet. In such installations, ducting similar to that used on reciprocating engines is utilized to route intake air to the engine.

On turboprop engines that have an intake at the front of the engine, a **ducted spinner** is generally considered to be the best inlet design to use.

Figure 5-26. Engine calibration on a test stand is usually accomplished with a bellmouth inlet that is fitted with an anti-ingestion screen. Duct losses are considered to be zero because of the smooth rounded edges if this type inlet.

However, ducted spinners are heavier, more difficult to maintain, and harder to de-ice than a conventional streamlined spinner. Another option is to use a **conical spinner** which is a modified version of the streamline spinner. [Figure 5-27]

TURBOPROP FILTER/SEPARATOR

Prevention of foreign object damage (FOD) is a top priority among turbine engine operators and manufacturers. One of the easiest ways to help prevent foreign object damage is to install an inlet screen over an engine's inlet duct. The use of inlet screens is common on many rotorcraft and turboprop engines as well as on engines installed in test

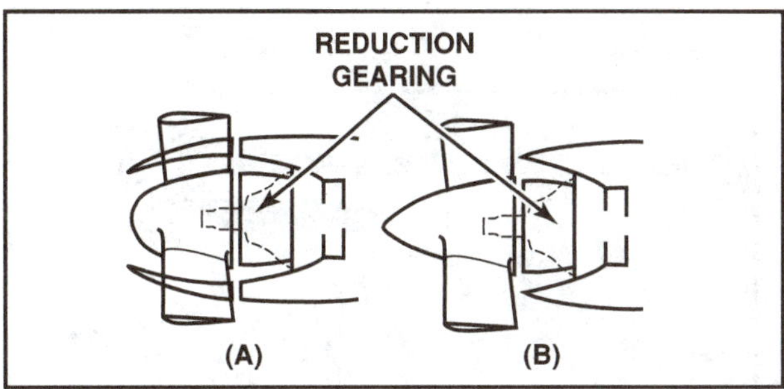

Figure 5-27. (A) — A ducted spinner inlet is the most efficient design for turboprop engines. (B) — Although less efficient, conical spinner inlets present fewer design problems than ducted spinners.

stands. However, inlet screens are seldom used on high mass airflow engines because icing and screen failures can cause serious engine damage.

Additional devices that help prevent foreign object damage include sand or ice separators. The basic design of a sand or ice separator consists of an air intake with at least one venturi and a series of sharp bends. The venturi is used to accelerate the flow of incoming air and debris so the debris has enough inertia that it cannot follow the bends in the intake. This allows sand particles and other small debris to be channeled away from the compressor.

One type of separator used on some turboprop aircraft incorporates a movable vane which extends into the inlet airstream. Once extended, the vane creates a prominent venturi and a sudden turn in the engine inlet. Combustion air can follow the sharp curve but sand and ice particles cannot because of their inertia. The movable vane is operated by the operator through a control handle in the cockpit. [Figure 5-28]

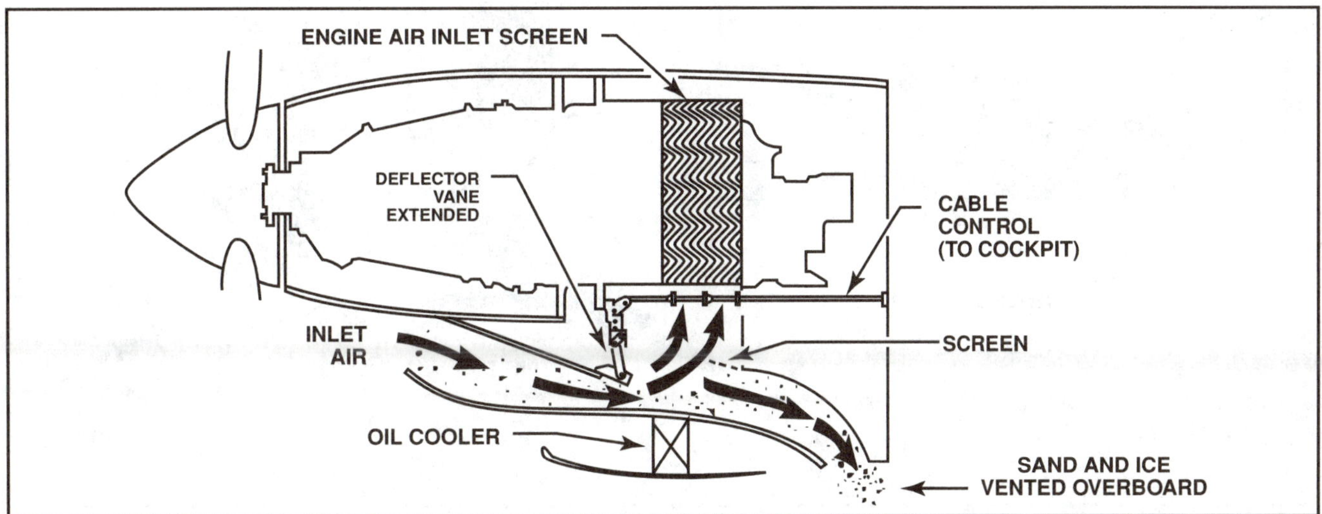

Figure 5-28. A typical induction system filter/separator utilizes a deflector vane to produce a venturi. The venturi accelerates sand, ice, and other debris and carries it overboard.

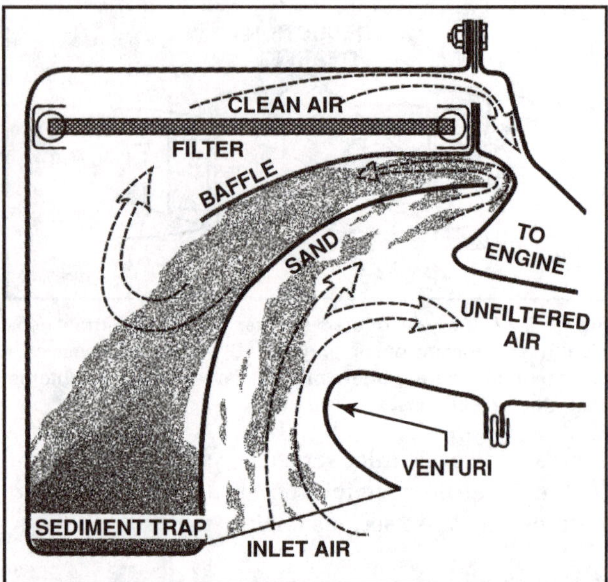

Figure 5-29. This particle separator is typical of the type found on turbine powered helicopters. The venturi in the air inlet accelerates the air and sand so the sand has too much inertia to make the turn leading to the engine.

TURBOSHAFT FILTER/SEPARATOR

One of the most critical aspects of air inlet system design for a turboshaft engine is the prevention of foreign object damage to the compressor. This is especially difficult in helicopter operations where landings are often conducted in unimproved areas. Therefore, many helicopters are fitted with a **particle separator** on the engine inlet.

One type of particle separator relies on a venturi and sharp directional changes in airflow to filter sand and ice particles out of the induction air. The venturi accelerates the flow of incoming air and debris so the debris has enough inertia that it cannot follow the bends in the intake. This allows sand particles and other small debris to be channeled away from the compressor and into a sediment trap. [Figure 5-29]

Another type of particle separator uses several individual filter elements that act as a **swirl chamber**. With this type of system, as incoming air passes through each element, a swirling motion is imparted by helical vanes. The swirling motion creates enough centrifugal force to throw the dirt particles to the outside of the chamber. The particles then drop to the bottom of the separator where they are blown overboard by compressor bleed air through holes on each side of the filter unit. As the foreign particles are swirled out of the intake air, clean air then passes through the filter into the engine inlet. [Figure 5-30]

INLET ANTI-ICE SYSTEMS

When a turbine powered aircraft flies through icing conditions, ice can build up in the engine's inlet duct and on its inlet guide vanes. This disrupts the airflow into the compressor and reduces the engine's efficiency. Furthermore, large pieces of ice could break off and enter the engine causing serious

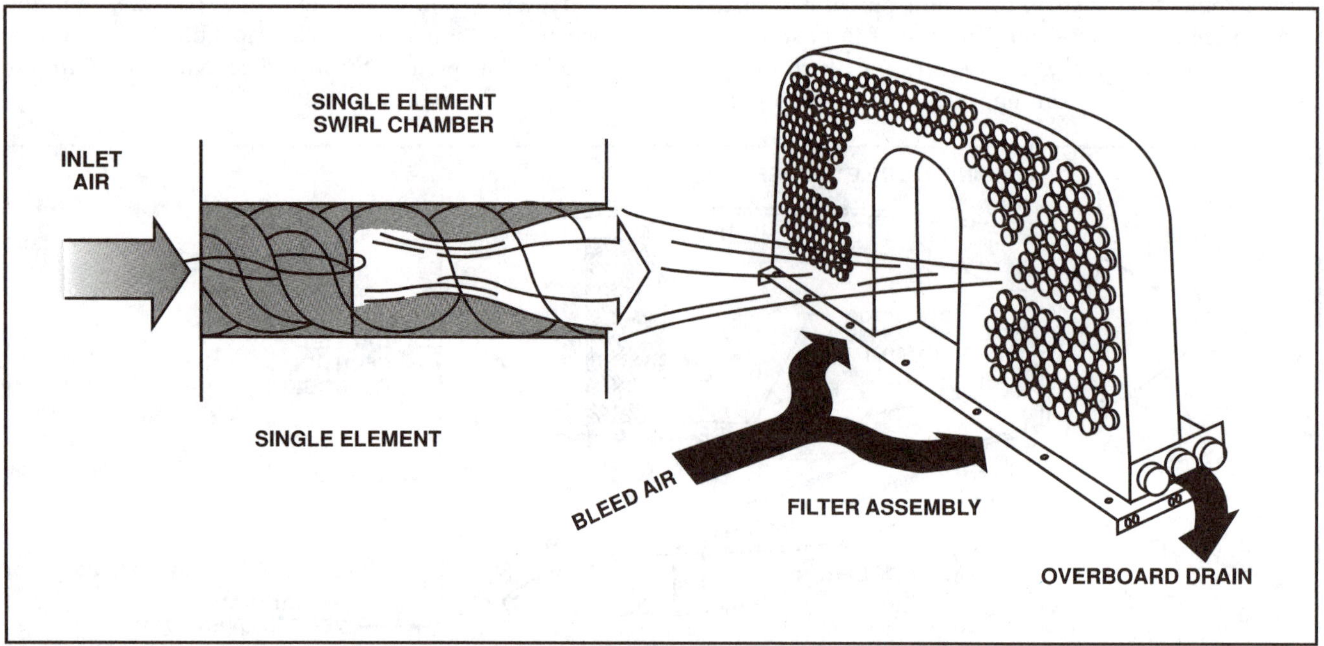

Figure 5-30. A swirl chamber particle separator is used on the Bell 206 helicopter. The swirling motion forces foreign particles to the outside of each filter element and then deposits the particles at the bottom of the filter for removal.

damage to compressor blades. To prevent ice formation and ingestion, turbine engine inlet ducts are typically equipped with some form of anti-ice system to prevent ice formation.

A typical turbine engine inlet anti-ice system ducts high temperature bleed air from the compressor to the air inlet. When the anti-icing system is switched on, a bleed valve directs hot air to the inlet duct leading edge, nose dome, and inlet guide vanes to prevent ice from building. In addition, an indicator light illuminates in the cockpit to indicate that the anti-icing system is on. A disadvantage of this type of system is that, whenever bleed air is taken from a turbine engine, engine power output decreases. The power decrease is generally indicated by a slight rise in EGT and a shift in both EPR and fuel flow.

One way manufacturers avoid the power loss associated with a bleed air anti-ice system is to install an electric system. With an electric anti-ice system, electric heating elements are embedded in a rubber boot or placed behind a metal leading edge surrounding the intake.

CHAPTER 6

EXHAUST SYSTEMS

INTRODUCTION

In both a reciprocating and turbine engine, the purpose of the exhaust system is to remove the spent gases of combustion and safely route them overboard. For an engine to operate at its maximum efficiency, these systems must function properly. In addition, because a failure of this system could have disastrous results, such as fires or introducing toxic gases into the cabin, it is imperative that the system be inspected and maintained according to the manufacturer's recommendations.

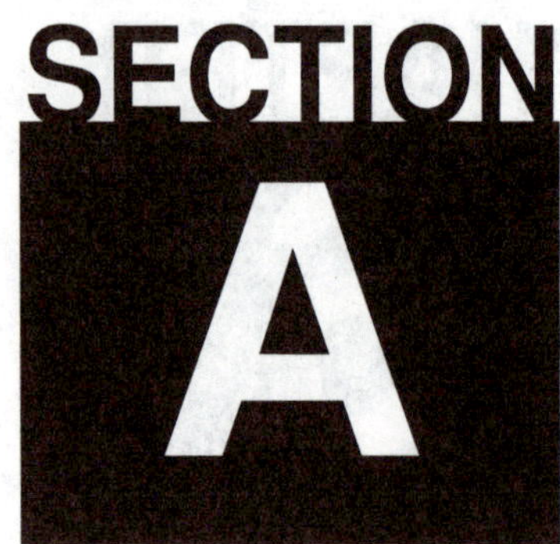

SECTION A

RECIPROCATING ENGINE

A reciprocating engine produces high temperature and noxious gases as combustion takes place within the engine. Since these exhaust gases are corrosive and the exhaust system is subjected to a wide range of temperatures, many modern exhaust systems are made up of components using nickel-chromium steel or other corrosive and heat resistant alloys. These metals not only resist corrosion and heat but possess low expansion coefficients and low weight, and provide long, trouble-free operation with a minimum of maintenance.

TYPES OF EXHAUST SYSTEMS

There are two general types of exhaust systems in use on reciprocating aircraft engines: the short stack or open system and the collector system. The short stack system is generally used on nonsupercharged engines and low powered engines where noise level is not a factor. The collector system is used on most large nonsupercharged engines and on installations where it would improve nacelle streamlining or provide easier maintenance in the nacelle area. It is also found on all turbosupercharged engines where the exhaust gases must be collected and routed to the turbine. The disadvantage of the collector system is that it increases the back pressure of the exhaust system, which in turn reduces horsepower. However, the increased horsepower achieved by turbosupercharging more than offsets the loss created by the back pressure.

SHORT STACKS

Early in-line and V-engines often used straight stacks which were simply short sections of steel tubing welded to a flange and bolted to the cylinder exhaust port. These short stacks were effective at getting the exhaust out of the engine compartment, but they had no silencing capability, and when the aircraft was side-slipped, cold air could flow into these stacks and warp the exhaust valves.

The short stack system is relatively simple, and its removal and installation consists essentially of removing and installing the hold-down nuts and clamps.

COLLECTOR SYSTEMS

The collector systems you might encounter on an airplane include the opposed type engine exhaust manifold and the radial engine collector rings.

OPPOSED ENGINE EXHAUST MANIFOLD

There are many types of collector systems used on horizontally opposed engines. A typical system consists of risers from each cylinder and an exhaust collector on each side of the engine. The risers are attached to each cylinder with brass or special locknuts which are heat resistant. [Figure 6-1]

On some systems, a crossover tube connects the exhaust stacks on the left side of the engine with the stacks on the right side. Sections of the exhaust system are usually joined together with spring-loaded ball joints. When properly installed, the ball joints are loose enough to allow movement but tight enough to prevent leakage. Ball joints also compensate for slight misalignment of the parts. The exhaust collector tube may be routed to a turbocharger, a muffler, an exhaust augmentor, or simply overboard, depending upon the installation. [Figure 6-2]

RADIAL ENGINE EXHAUST COLLECTOR RINGS

Radial engines use an exhaust manifold made up of pieces of tubing that are fitted together with loose slip joints. In addition to aiding in aligning exhaust components, slip joints compensate for expansion when an engine is running, expanding or contracting to fit together tightly and eliminate leakage.

Figure 6-1. Risers and collectors can be constructed as one unit, or the risers can be connected to the collector with ring clamps, or each riser can be a separate part of the collector system.

Each section of the collector is bolted to a bracket on the blower section of the engine, and is partly supported by a sleeve connection between the collector ring ports and the short stack on the engine exhaust ports. The exhaust tailpipe is joined to the collector ring by a telescoping expansion joint, which allows

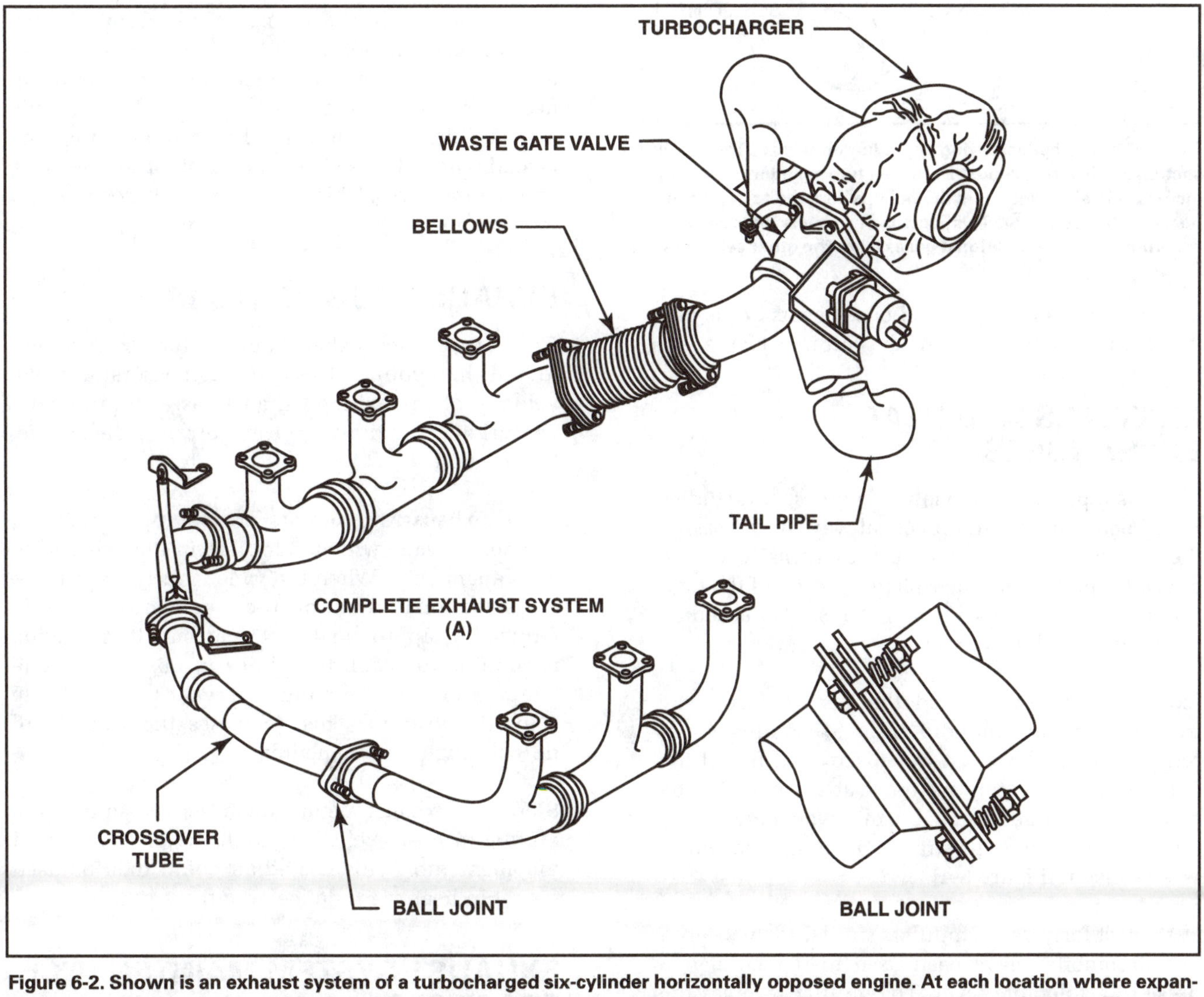

TURBOCHARGER
WASTE GATE VALVE
BELLOWS
TAIL PIPE
COMPLETE EXHAUST SYSTEM
(A)
CROSSOVER
TUBE
BALL JOINT
BALL JOINT

Figure 6-2. Shown is an exhaust system of a turbocharged six-cylinder horizontally opposed engine. At each location where expansion and contraction occurs, bellows are installed to allow for the change in physical dimensions without any leakage. The waste gate valve is hydraulically opened to allow exhaust gases to pass directly out the tail pipe, or closed to force these gases out through the turbocharger turbine section. The turbocharger in this installation is wrapped in a heat blanket to improve efficiency and decrease air temperatures inside the cowling.

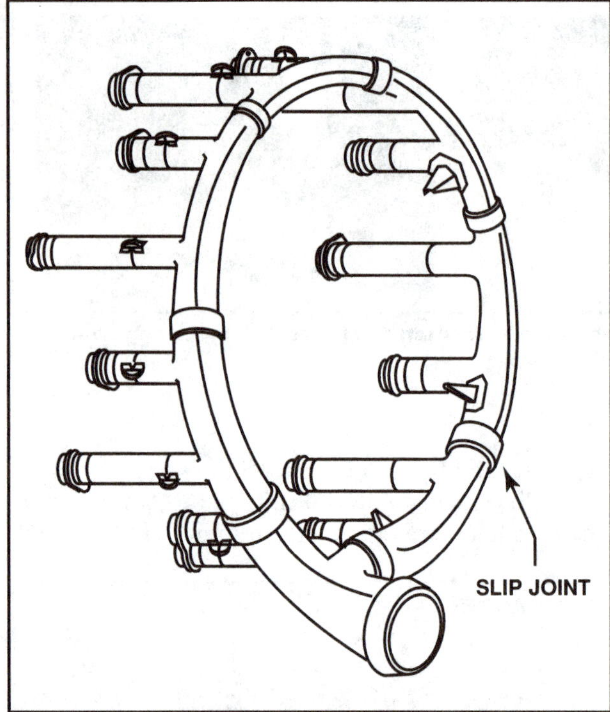

Figure 6-3. The collector ring is graduated in size. The small section carries the exhaust from only two cylinders. The ring increases in size as it nears the point where the tailpipe connects to the collector. This increase in size is necessary to accommodate the additional gases from the other cylinders.

enough slack for the removal of segments of the collector ring without removing the tailpipe. [Figure 6-3]

MUFFLERS AND HEAT EXCHANGERS

Noise is a problem in aviation engines, and studies have been made to find practical ways of increasing the frequency and reducing the intensity of the noise. Propellers produce a large portion of the total noise, but the energy in the exhaust also accounts for an appreciable amount.

Exhaust collectors carried the gases safely away from the engine, but did little to nothing about reducing noise levels. It was discovered that if the ends of the collectors were cut at a taper and the exhaust discharged through a relatively narrow slot rather than through the straight open pipe, the noise was reduced. [Figure 6-4]

In the last forty years, mufflers similar to those used on automobiles have been used to reduce engine noise to a tolerable level. The muffler receives the exhaust from the cylinders and passes it through a series of baffles to break up the sound energy. The exhaust is then passed out through a tailpipe.

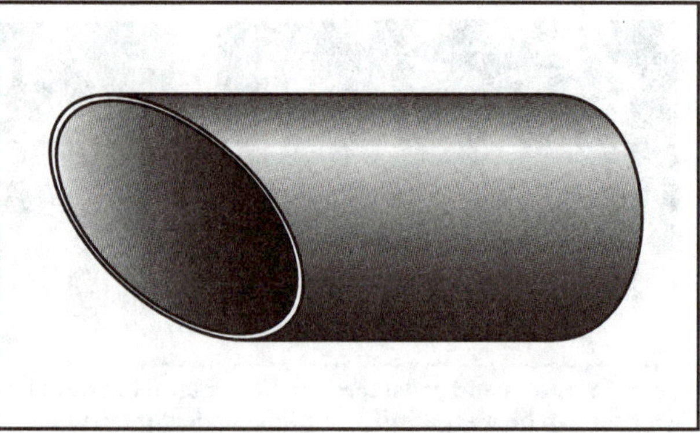

Figure 6-4. The discharged exhaust leaving the tapered opening, called a bayonet, created a slightly low pressure. This helped reduce exhaust back pressure and noise.

In addition, a stainless steel shroud or shell can be placed around the muffler. This type of setup is referred to as a heat exchanger. This shroud brings in unheated outside air into a space between the muffler and the shroud. Since the muffler is being heated by the exhaust gases, the air in this space is heated. Then through heater hoses and ducting, the heated air can be used as cabin heat, or for de-ice or anti-ice purposes. This shroud is easily removed so the muffler can be inspected. [Figure 6-5]

EXHAUST AUGMENTORS

On some engines, exhaust augmentors are installed to aid in cooling. Exhaust augmentors use the velocity of the exiting exhaust gases to produce a venturi effect to draw more airflow over the engine. [Figure 6-6]

Some exhaust augmentors are equipped with an augmentor vane which is located in the exit end of each augmentor. When the vane is fully closed, the cross-sectional area of the augmentor tube is reduced by approximately 45 percent. If the engine is running too cool, the pilot can raise the engine temperature, by moving the vanes toward the "closed" position. This decreases the velocity of flow through the augmentor.

Since the exhaust augmentor heats up similar to a muffler, a heat exchanger could be placed around the augmentor. This heated air could then be used for cabin heat or for de-ice or anti-ice purposes.

EXHAUST SYSTEM MAINTENANCE PRACTICES

The corrosion resistant steel of which exhaust systems are made is thin, and the systems operate at

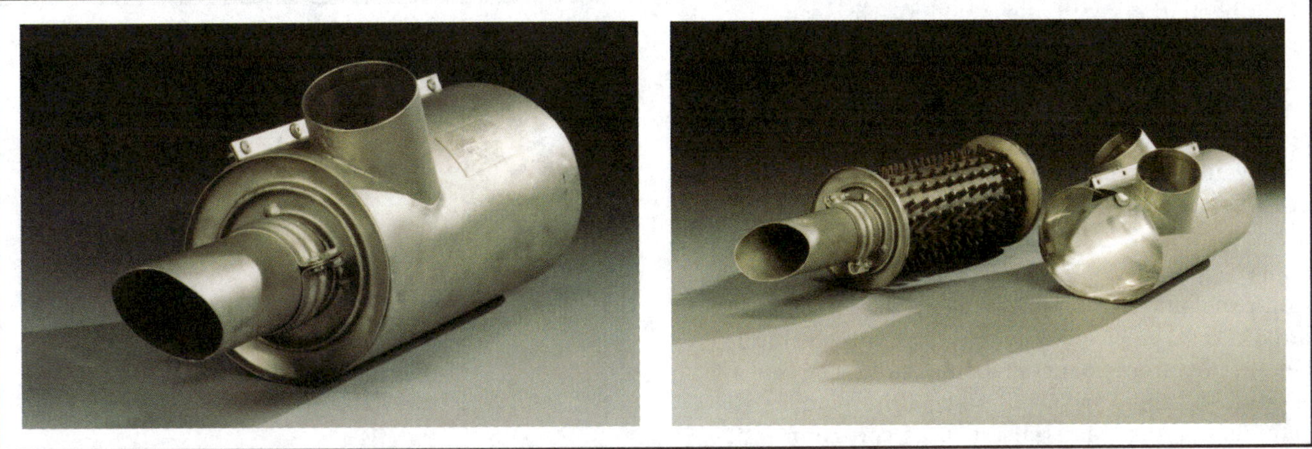

Figure 6-5. On the left is the muffler with the shroud in place. The shroud is typically held on the muffler with stainless steel screws. On the right the shroud has been removed for clarity. The knobs on the muffler help transfer heat from the muffler to the air space inside the shroud.

high temperatures. These difficult conditions, coupled with the fact that an exhaust system failure can result in carbon monoxide poisoning of crew and passengers, partial or complete loss of engine power, and/or an aircraft fire, make inspection of the exhaust system extremely important. Carbon monoxide is a colorless, odorless gas that is a by-product of internal combustion processes. It displaces oxygen in the human body, producing incapacitation and death at higher levels of exposure.

Before discussing inspection and maintenance procedures for exhaust system components, a precaution to be observed must be mentioned. Galvanized or zinc plated tools should never be used on the exhaust system, and exhaust system parts should

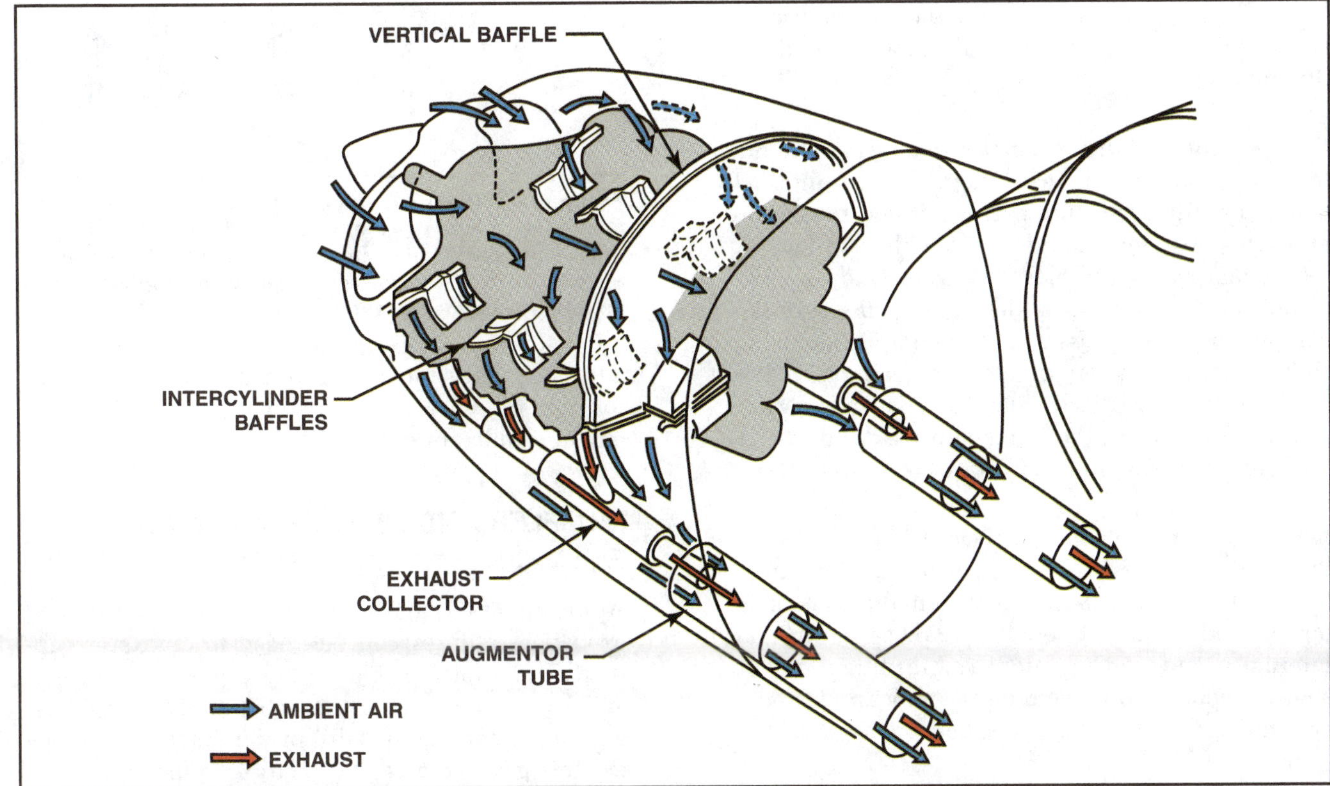

Figure 6-6. The exhaust from the cylinders on each side flow through a collector and discharge into the inlet of a stainless steel augmentor tube. This flow of high velocity gas creates a low pressure and draws air from above the engine through the cylinder fins.

never be marked with a lead pencil. The lead, zinc, or galvanized mark is absorbed by the metal of the exhaust system when heated, creating a distinct change in its molecular structure. This change softens the metal in the area of the mark, causing cracks and eventual failure. Use felt-tip markers, India ink, or Prussian blue to mark exhaust components.

Some exhaust system components receive a corrosion-resistant coating of ceramic material. These units should be cleaned using a degreasing solution. Under no circumstances should sand blasting or alkaline cleaners be used, since this removes the ceramic coating. Materials such as corrosion-resistance steel can be blast cleaned using sand that has not been previously used to clean iron or steel materials. Used sand contains metal particles that can become embedded in the metal and allow corrosion to form.

EXHAUST SYSTEM INSPECTION

During an inspection of the exhaust system, be especially alert for any cracks, dents, or missing parts. An ice pick or similar pointed instrument is useful in probing suspected areas. Cracks are probably the most common problem with an exhaust system. A crack usually allows exhaust gas to escape. Escaping gas often shows up as a flat gray or a sooty black streak on the outside of the stack or muffler. [Figure 6-7]

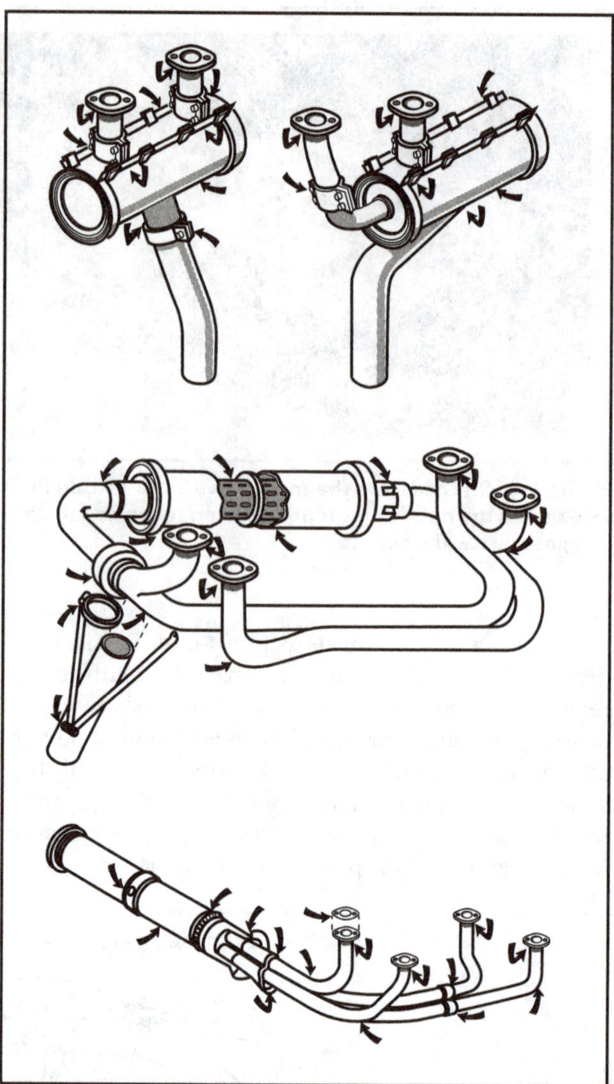

Figure 6-7. The arrows point out the primary inspection points for various types of exhaust systems. The top diagram represents a separate system, the middle diagram is a crossover-type system, and the bottom diagram shows an exhaust/augmentor system.

If a component of the exhaust system is inaccessible for a thorough visual inspection, such as internal baffles or diffusers, or a part is hidden by nonremovable parts, you should disassemble it and check for contamination and possible leaks. One way you can check for leaks, is to close the openings of the component, then pressurize the component using compressed air (approximately 2 p.s.i). With the component pressurized, apply a soap and water solution over all of the joints and welds. If cracks are present, the escaping air causes bubbles to form.

Weld areas are especially subject to cracks due to the stress produced by the expansion and contraction of the thin material of which the system is made. In addition, poor quality weld beads protrude internally and concentrate heat, resulting in hot spots. A good quality weld tapers smoothly into the base metal and thus dissipates heat evenly.

When inspecting the exhaust system, it is very important to carefully examine the areas used to heat air for carburetor deicing and cabin heat. In addition, you should periodically check the cabin for the presence of carbon monoxide while the engine is operating.

MUFFLER AND HEAT EXCHANGER FAILURES

Approximately half of all muffler and heat exchanger failures can be traced to cracks or ruptures in the heat exchanger surfaces used for cabin and carburetor heat sources. Failures in the heat exchanger surface, usually in the outer wall, allow exhaust gases to escape directly into the cabin heat system. If exhausted gases are drawn into the engine induction system, engine overheating and loss of power can occur. Failures in the exhaust system, in most cases, are caused by the high temperatures at which an exhaust system operates. This in turn leads to thermal and vibration fatigue cracking in areas of stress concentration. On aircraft using an exhaust heat exchanger as a source of cabin heat, the heater air shroud should be removed to facilitate inspection of the system.

EXHAUST MANIFOLD AND STACK FAILURES

Exhaust manifold and stack failures are usually fatigue failures at clamped points or at welds. Although these failures are primarily fire hazards, they also present carbon monoxide problems. Exhaust gases can enter the cabin via defective or inadequate seals at firewall openings, wing strut fittings, doors, and wing root openings.

INTERNAL MUFFLER FAILURES

Internal failures, such as baffles and diffusers, can cause partial or complete engine power loss by restricting the flow of the exhaust gases and increasing the back pressure. As opposed to other failures, erosion and carburization caused by extreme thermal conditions are the primary causes of internal failures. Many systems employ exhaust outlet guards to keep dislodged muffler baffles from obstructing the muffler outlet.

Engine backfiring and combustion of unburned fuel within the exhaust system are probable contributing factors. In addition, local hot spot areas caused by uneven exhaust gas flow can result in burning, bulging, or rupture of the outer muffler wall.

TURBOCHARGER EXHAUST SYSTEMS

When a turbocharger is included, the engine exhaust system operates under greatly increased pressure and temperature conditions. Extra precautions should be taken in exhaust system care and maintenance. During high altitude operation, the exhaust system pressure is maintained at or near sea level values. Due to the pressure differential, any leaks in the system will allow the exhaust gases to escape with torch-like intensity that can severely damage adjacent structures.

A common cause of malfunction is coke deposits, or carbon buildup, in the waste gate unit causing erratic system operation. Excessive deposit buildup may cause the waste gate to stick in the "closed" position, causing an over-boost condition. Coke deposit buildup in the turbo itself will cause a gradual loss of power in flight and a low manifold pressure reading prior to takeoff. Clean, repair, overhaul, and adjust the system components and controls in accordance with the applicable manufacturer's instructions.

AUGMENTOR EXHAUST SYSTEM

On exhaust systems equipped with augmentor tubes, the augmentor tubes should be inspected at regular intervals for proper alignment, security of attachment, and general overall condition. Even when augmentor tubes do not contain heat exchanger surfaces, they should be inspected for cracks along with the remainder of the exhaust system.

EXHAUST SYSTEM REPAIRS

It is generally recommended that exhaust stacks, mufflers, tailpipes, etc. be replaced with new or reconditioned components rather than repaired in the field. Welded repairs to exhaust systems are complicated by the difficulty of accurately identifying the base metal so that the proper repair materials can be selected.

Steel or low temperature, self-locking nuts should not be substituted for brass or high temperature locknuts used by the manufacturer. Old gaskets should never be reused. When disassembly is necessary, gaskets should be replaced with new ones of the same type provided by the manufacturer.

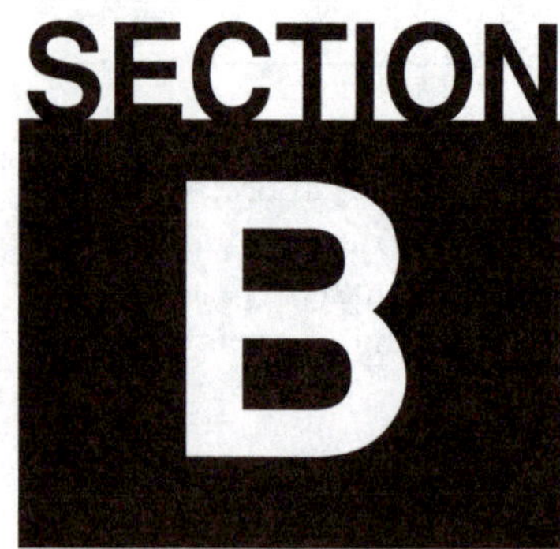

SECTION B TURBINE ENGINE

The turbine engine exhaust system must be capable of withstanding very high temperatures and is usually manufactured from nickel or titanium. In addition, the heat produced must not be allowed to transfer to nearby airframe components or structures. This can be accomplished by routing ventilating air around the exhaust pipe, and by covering the exhaust pipe with an insulating blanket. These insulating blankets use an inner layer of insulating material and an outer skin of stainless steel, which is dimpled to increase its strength.

TURBOJET EXHAUST SYSTEM

The exhaust section of the turbojet engine is located directly behind the turbine section. The exhaust section is composed of several items, whose main purpose is to direct the flow of gases rearward in such a manner as to prevent turbulence and at the same time impart a high final or exit velocity to the gases. [Figure 6-8]

CONE ASSEMBLY

The exhaust cone collects the gases discharged from the turbine and gradually converts them into a single jet. The collected gases are delivered either directly, or via the tailpipe, to the jet nozzle.

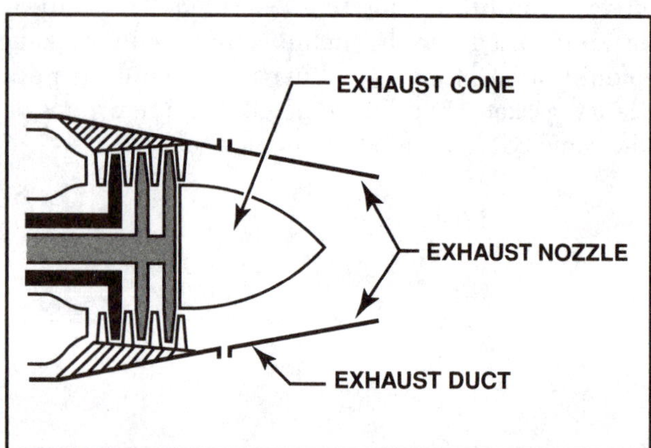

Figure 6-8. The components of the exhaust section include the exhaust cone assembly, the exhaust duct or tailpipe, if required, and the exhaust or jet nozzle.

TAILPIPE OR EXHAUST DUCT

The term "exhaust duct" is applied to the engine exhaust pipe, or tail pipe, which connects the turbine outlet to the jet nozzle of a nonafterburning engine. If the engine exhaust gases could be discharged directly into the outside air in an exact axial direction at the turbine exit, an exhaust duct might not be necessary. However, this is not practical. A larger thrust can be obtained from the engine if the gases are discharged from the aircraft at a higher velocity than is permissible at the turbine outlet. An exhaust duct is therefore added, both to collect and straighten the gas flow as it comes from the turbine, and to increase the velocity of the gases before they are discharged from the exhaust nozzle. Increasing the velocity of the gases, increases their momentum and increases the thrust produced.

The exhaust duct is essentially a simple, stainless steel, conical or cylindrical pipe. The assembly also includes an engine tailcone and the struts inside the duct. The tailcone and the struts add strength to the duct, impart an axial direction, and smooths the gas flow.

Immediately aft of the turbine outlet, and usually just forward of the flange to which the exhaust duct is attached, one or more sensors are usually attached to monitor the turbine discharge pressure. In addition, since it may be impractical to measure the inlet turbine temperature on large engines, exhaust gas temperature thermocouple probes may be attached at the turbine outlet.

EXHAUST NOZZLES

The rear opening of a turbine engine exhaust duct is called the exhaust nozzle. The nozzle acts as an orifice, the size of which determines the density and velocity of the gases as they emerge from the engine. Basically the nozzles come in two shapes, the convergent exhaust nozzle and the convergent-divergent exhaust nozzle

CONVERGENT EXHAUST NOZZLE

On most aircraft where the velocity of the exhaust gas remains subsonic, a convergent exhaust nozzle is used. A convergent type nozzle increases the velocity and decreases the pressure of the gas.

Adjusting the area of the exhaust nozzle changes both the engine performance and the exhaust gas temperature. Some engines are "trimmed" to their correct exhaust gas temperature by altering the exhaust nozzle area. To do this, you can bend small tabs to change the area, or you can fasten small adjustable pieces, called "mice" around the perimeter of the nozzle. This too changes the area.

CONVERGENT-DIVERGENT EXHAUST NOZZLE

Whenever the engine pressure ratio is high enough to produce exhaust gas velocities which might exceed Mach 1 at the engine exhaust nozzle, more thrust can be gained by using a convergent-divergent type of nozzle. The advantage of a convergent-divergent nozzle is greatest at high Mach numbers because of the resulting higher pressure ratio across the engine exhaust nozzle. [Figure 6-9]

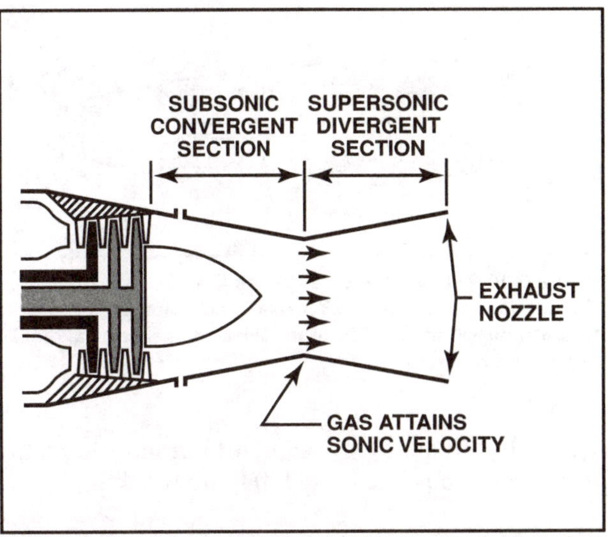

Figure 6-9. In a convergent-divergent nozzle, the convergent section is designed to handle the gases while they remain subsonic, and to deliver the gases to the throat of the nozzle just as they attain sonic velocity. The divergent section reduces the pressure of the Mach 1 gas and further increases its velocity to supersonic.

To ensure that a constant weight or volume of a gas flows past any given point after sonic velocity is reached, the rear part of a supersonic exhaust duct is enlarged to accommodate the additional weight or volume of a gas that flows at supersonic rates. If this is not done, the nozzle does not operate efficiently.

TURBOFAN EXHAUST

The bypass engine has two gas streams to eject to the atmosphere, the cool fan air, and the hot gases being discharged from the turbine. In a low bypass engine these two flows may be combined in a mixer unit, and discharged through the same nozzle. In a high bypass engine the fan air is usually discharged separately from the hot gases.

TURBOPROP EXHAUST

In a typical turboprop exhaust system, the exhaust gases are directed through a tail pipe assembly from the turbine section of the engine to the atmosphere. The exhaust arrangement used depends on the type of engine. Turboprop engines utilizing a through-flow burner typically expel the gases straight out the back of the engine and out the nacelle. This extracts the maximum amount of thrust from the velocity of the hot gases. Engines using a reverse flow combustor may exhaust the hot gases near the front of the engine. This design collects the exhaust gases and vents them overboard through exhaust stacks. There is very little additional thrust provided by this type of exhaust.

THRUST REVERSERS

Airliners powered by turbojets and turbofans, most commuter aircraft, and an increasing number of business jets are equipped with thrust reversers to:

1. aid in braking and directional control during normal landing, and reduce brake maintenance.
2. provide braking and directional control during emergency landings and balked takeoffs.
3. back an aircraft out of a parking spot in a "power back" operation.

While some thrust reversers are electrically powered, most large transport-category aircraft use hydraulically actuated reversers powered by main system hydraulic power, or by pneumatic actuators powered by engine bleed air. Thrust reversers are controlled by a cockpit lever at the command of the pilot. In a typical system, the power levers are retarded to ground idle, then reverse thrust is selected. The pilot then advances the power levers to takeoff power as required to slow the aircraft. The

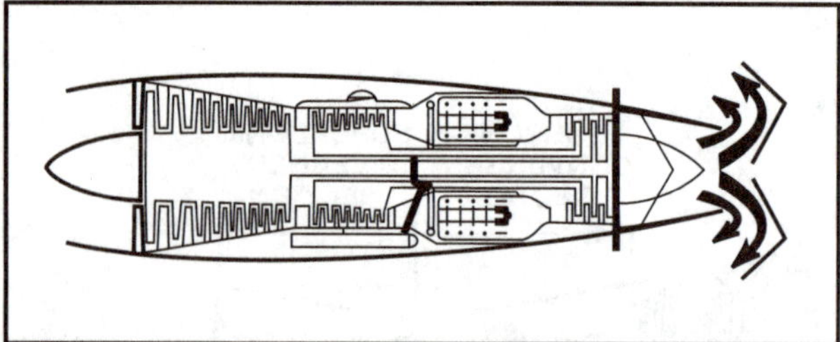

Figure 6-10. Thrust reversers change the direction of flow of the exhaust gases from a rearward direction to more of a forward direction. This diagram shows a mechanical blockage thrust reverser.

power levers are then retarded to ground idle and thrust reverse is deselected. [Figure 6-10]

Thrust reversers provide approximately 20 percent of the breaking force under normal conditions. Reversers must be capable of producing 50 percent of rated thrust in the reverse direction. However, exhaust gas exits a typical reverser at an angle to the engine's thrust axis. Because of this, maximum reverse thrust capability is always less than forward thrust capability. Operating in reverse at low ground speeds can cause re-ingestion of hot gases and compressor stalls. It can also cause ingestion of fine sand and other runway debris. The most frequently encountered thrust reversers can be divided into two categories, the mechanical-blockage type and the aerodynamic-blockage type.

MECHANICAL-BLOCKAGE TYPE

Mechanical blockage is accomplished by placing a movable obstruction in the exhaust gas stream either before or after the exhaust exits the duct. The engine exhaust gases are mechanically blocked and diverted to a forward direction by an inverted cone, half-sphere, or other device. The mechanical blockage system is also known as the "clamshell" thrust reverser because of its shape.

AERODYNAMIC-BLOCKAGE TYPE

The aerodynamic-blockage type of thrust reverser uses thin airfoils or obstructions placed in the gas stream. These vanes are often referred to as "cascades" and turn the escaping exhaust gases to a forward direction, which in turn causes a rearward thrust. Some aircraft may use a combination of the aerodynamic-blockage and the mechanical-blockage type reversers.

Mixed exhaust turbofans are configured with one reverser, while unmixed or bypass exhaust turbofans often have both cold stream and hot stream reversers. Some high bypass turbofans will have only cold stream reversing because most of the thrust is present in the fan discharge and a hot stream reverser would be of minimum value and become a weight penalty. [Figure 6-11]

NOISE SUPPRESSORS

Noise is best defined as unwanted sound that is both irritating and harmful. Since most major airports are located near large cities, the need to minimize turbine exhaust noise is apparent. The aircraft industry has reacted to the need for less offensive operations by continually improving noise reduction techniques on every new generation of engine and aircraft.

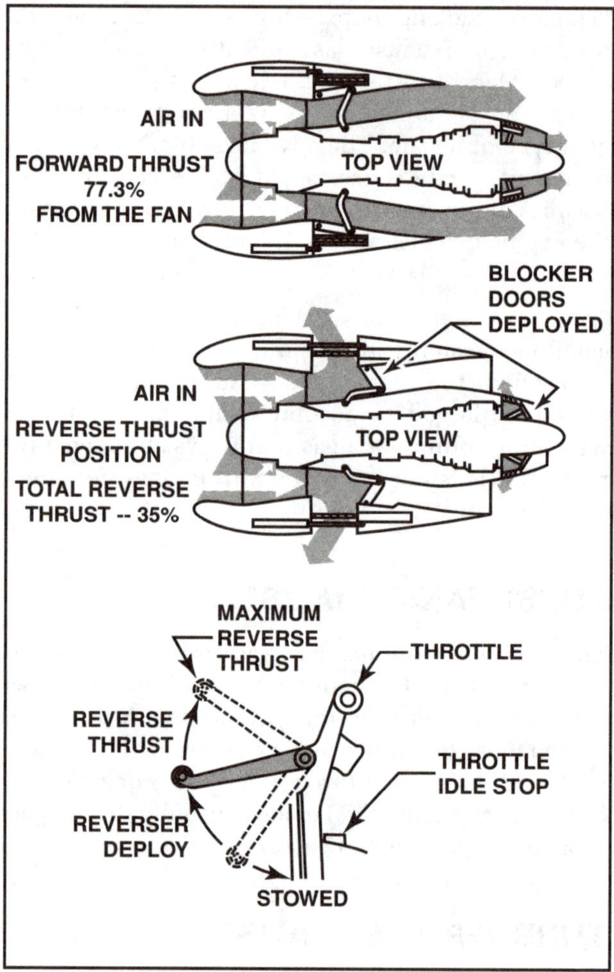

Figure 6-11. On this aerodynamic-blockage reverser diagram for a DC-10, the reverser doors are stowed when the engine is producing forward thrust. When deployed, the reverser doors divert both cold and hot stream air. To deploy the thrust reversers, the power lever is retarded to the idle stop, the reverser lever is raised from its stowed position, and the power lever is advanced to decelerate the aircraft as necessary.

Figure 6-12. Older turbojet engines used corrugated-perimeter noise suppressors attached to the exhaust duct. The corrugations divide the exhaust stream and reduce noise levels.

Noise suppressors used on the ground include portable devices which can be positioned near the rear of an engine whenever prolonged ground operation is anticipated. Furthermore, blast fences and designated run-up areas are provided on most large airports and aircraft operations are restricted to certain times of the day.

Older turbojet engines produce a combination of noise frequencies at very high levels. Although a turbojet compressor produces a great deal of high frequency sound, this noise decreases rapidly as the distance from the source increases. On the other hand, turbojet exhaust produces noise at a wide range of frequencies and at very high energy levels. This noise is audible over great distances and is more damaging to human hearing. One solution to turbojet exhaust noise is the use of a corrugated perimeter noise suppressor that helps break up the exhaust flow and raise its noise frequency. Furthermore, some older engines can be fitted with "hush kits" that reduce their noise emissions. [Figure 6-12]

Newer engines employ a variety of techniques to reduce harmful noise. For example, some turbofan engines blend fan discharge air with the exhaust gases to reduce sound emission. On these engines, the sound from the inlet is likely to be louder than from the tail pipe. In addition, the inlet and exhaust ducts on turbofan engines are lined with sound attenuating materials that greatly reduce noise levels. [Figure 6-13]

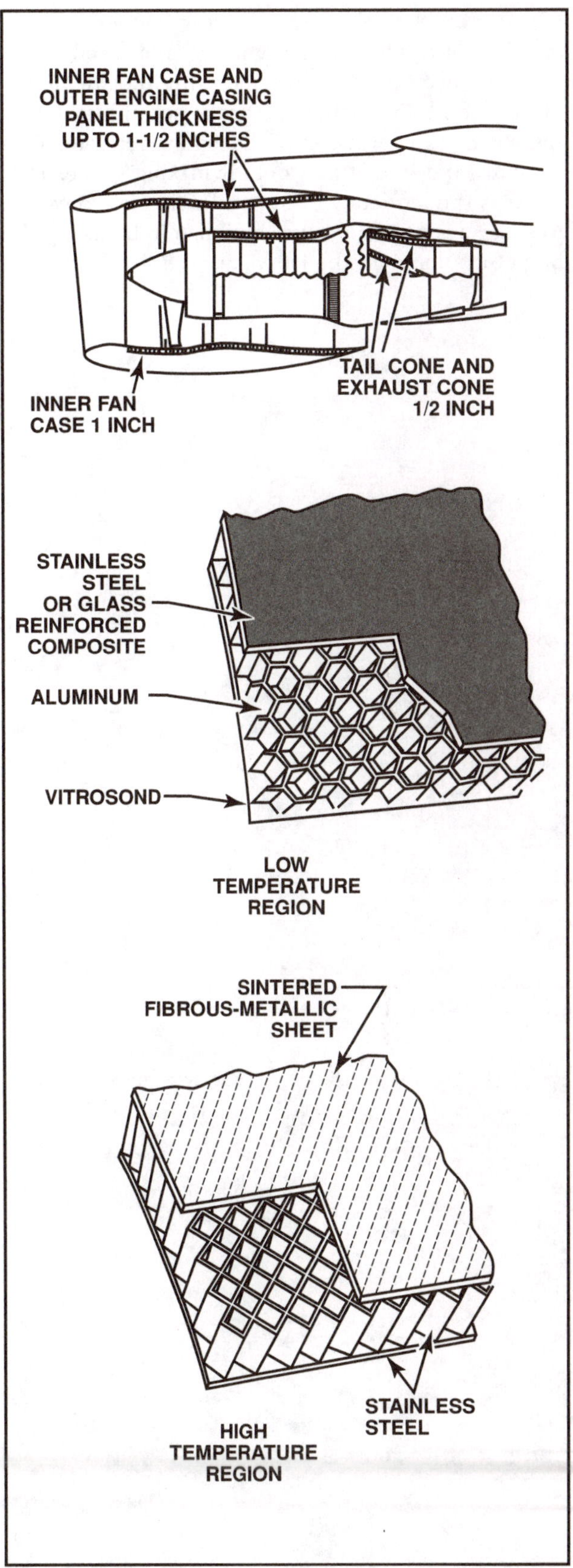

Figure 6-13. High bypass turbofan engines employ sound absorbing materials at specific locations to minimize noise emissions. Various materials and patterns are used depending on the temperature ranges at these locations.

Because of the characteristic of low frequency noise to linger at a relative high volume, noise reduction is often accomplished by increasing the frequency of the sound. Frequency change is accomplished by increasing the perimeter of the exhaust stream. This provides more cold and hot air mixing space. This reduces the tendency of hot and cold air molecules to shear against each other and also to break up the large turbulence in the jet wake.

ENGINE FUEL AND FUEL METERING

INTRODUCTION

An aircraft's fuel delivery system must supply fuel to a fuel metering device in the proper quantity while maintaining the quality of the fuel. On the other hand, the primary purpose of a fuel metering device is to blend the fuel and air needed for combustion. In early aircraft, the fuel system was simple, consisting of a fuel tank, fuel lines, a selector valve, and a carburetor. However, as aircraft engines increased in power and complexity, the quantity of fuel required increased dramatically. In addition, modern fuel systems have a greater number of components and design considerations to increase safety and efficiency. Due to the complexities and importance of an aircraft's fuel system, an aviation maintenance technician must be thoroughly familiar with the design, operation, and maintenance of the aircraft's fuel delivery system.

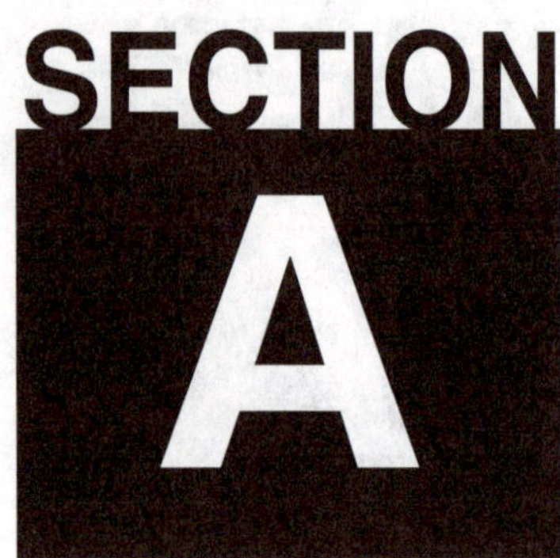

SECTION A FUEL SYSTEMS

Aircraft fuel systems are divided into two basic sections; an airframe section and a powerplant section. The airframe section consists of all fuel system components from the fuel tanks to the engine-driven fuel pump. The engine section, on the other hand, consists of an engine-driven fuel pump, if installed, a fuel metering device, and any other fuel delivery components on the engine. Although several components in an aircraft fuel system are airframe components, the purpose of the entire fuel system is to provide fuel to the engines. Therefore, the following section primarily discusses the components included in the airframe section to the extent that you must know to maintain and operate the aircraft engine. The engine section components, on the other hand, are discussed in the next section on fuel metering.

RECIPROCATING ENGINE FUELS

The dynamics of the internal combustion cycle demand certain properties from gasolines. Aircraft engines compound these demands because of the wide range of atmospheric conditions in which they must operate. One of the most critical characteristics of aviation gasoline is its **volatility**, which is a measure of a fuel's ability to change from a liquid into a vapor. Volatility is usually expressed in terms of **Reid vapor pressure** which represents the air pressure above a liquid required to prevent vapors from escaping from the liquid at a given temperature. The vapor pressure of 100LL aviation gasoline is approximately seven pounds per square inch at 100 degrees F.

For obvious reasons, a fuel's volatility is critical to its performance in an aircraft engine. For example, in a piston engine, the fuel must vaporize readily in the carburetor to burn evenly in the cylinder. Fuel that is only partially atomized leads to hard starting and rough running. On the other hand, fuel which vaporizes too readily can evaporate in the fuel lines and lead to **vapor lock**. Furthermore, in an aircraft carburetor, an excessively volatile fuel causes extreme cooling within the carburetor body when the fuel evaporates. This increases the chances for the formation of carburetor ice. Therefore, the ideal aviation fuel has a high volatility that is not excessive to the point of causing vapor lock or carburetor ice.

Aviation gasoline is formulated to burn smoothly without detonating or knocking, and fuels are numerically graded according to their ability to resist detonation. The higher the number, the more resistant a fuel is to knocking. The most common grading system used for this purpose is the **octane** rating system. The octane number assigned to a fuel compares the anti-knock properties of that fuel to a mixture of iso-octane and normal heptane. For example, grade 80 fuel has the same anti-knock properties as a mixture of 80 percent iso-octane and 20 percent heptane.

Some fuels have two performance numbers, such as 100/130. The first number is the lean mixture rating while the second number represents the fuel's rich mixture rating. To avoid confusion and to minimize errors in handling different grades of aviation gasolines, it has become common practice to designate different grades of fuel by their lean mixture performance number only. Therefore, aviation gasolines are identified as Avgas 80, 100, and 100LL. Although 100LL performs the same as grade 100 fuel, the "LL" indicates it has a lower lead content than the original 100/130 fuel.

One method petroleum companies use to help prevent engine detonation is to mix **tetraethyl lead** into aviation fuels. However, it has the drawback of forming corrosive components in the combustion chamber. For this reason, additional additives such as ethylene bromides are added to the fuel. These bromides actively combine with lead oxides produced by the tetraethyl lead allowing the oxides to be discharged from a cylinder during engine operation.

To aid in identifying the different grades of aviation fuel, each fuel grade is color-coded with dye for easy visual identification. The color code for the aviation gasolines currently available is as follows:

80 — Red
100 — Green
100LL — Blue

In addition to coloring fuels, a marking and coding system has been adopted to identify various airport fuel handling facilities and equipment, according to the kind and grade of fuel they contain. For example, all aviation gasolines are identified by name using white letters on a red background. In addition, valves, loading and unloading connections, switches, and other control equipment are color-coded according to the grade, or type of fuel they dispense. The fuel in piping is identified by name and by colored bands painted or decaled around the pipe at intervals along its length. [Figure 7-1]

Fuel trucks and hydrant carts are marked with large fuel identification decals on each side of the tank, or body, and have a small decal on the dashboard in the cab. These decals utilize the same color code. In addition, the fixed ring around fueller dome covers and hydrant box lids are also painted in accordance with the color code. In short, all parts of the fueling facility and equipment are identified and keyed into the same marking and color code.

FUEL SYSTEM REQUIREMENTS

All aircraft fuel systems must be designed to meet the specific operating requirements outlined in Part 23 of the Federal Aviation Regulations. Some of the requirements listed in the FARs include:

1. Each fuel system must be constructed and arranged to ensure fuel flow at a rate and pressure established for proper engine and auxiliary power unit functioning under all likely operating conditions. (FAR 23.951)
2. Each fuel system must be arranged so that no pump can draw fuel from more than one tank at a time, or provisions must be made to prevent air from being drawn into the fuel supply line. (FAR 23.951)
3. Turbine-powered aircraft must be capable of sustained operation when there is at least 0.75 cubic centimeters of free water per gallon of fuel at 80°F. In addition, an engine must be capable of sustained operation when the fuel is cooled to its most critical condition for icing. (FAR 23.951)
4. Each fuel system of a multi-engine aircraft must be arranged so that the failure of any one component (except a fuel tank) will not result in the loss of power of more than one engine or require immediate action by the pilot to prevent the loss of power. (FAR 23.953)
5. If a single tank or assembly of interconnected tanks is used on a multi-engine airplane, each engine must have an independent tank outlet with a fuel shutoff valve at the tank. (FAR 23.953)
6. A means of rapidly shutting off fuel in flight to each engine of a normal category aircraft must be provided to appropriate flight crewmembers. The engine fuel shutoff valve cannot be located on the engine side of any firewall. (FAR 23.995)

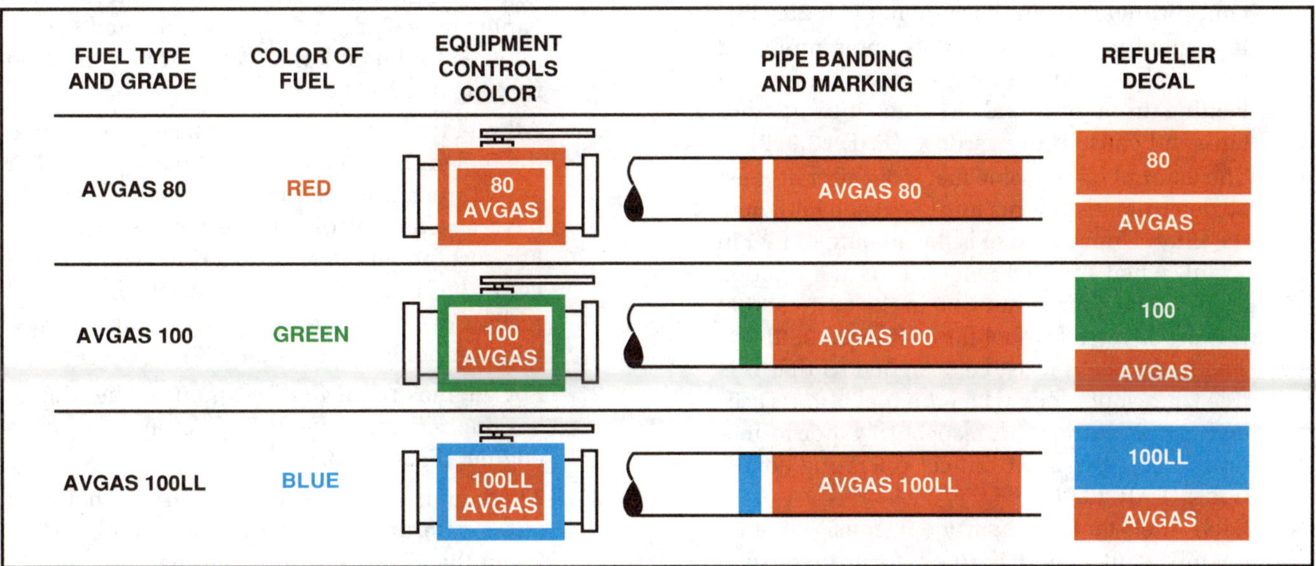

Figure 7-1. This illustration depicts the colors and types of markings used on fuel conduits and controls.

7. On multi-engine aircraft, the closing of an individual fuel shutoff valve for any engine shall not affect the fuel supply to the other engines. (FAR 23.1189)
8. Tanks used in multi-engine fuel systems must have two vents arranged so that they are not likely to both become plugged at the same time. (FAR 23.953)
9. All filler caps must be designed so that they are not likely to be installed incorrectly or lost in flight. (FAR 23.953)
10. The fuel systems must be designed to prevent the ignition of fuel vapors by lightning. (FAR 23.954)
11. The fuel flow rate of a gravity-feed system must be 150 percent of the takeoff fuel flow when the tank contains the minimum fuel allowable. The same requirement exists when the airplane is positioned in the attitude that is most critical for fuel flow. (FAR 23.955)
12. The fuel flow rate of a pump feed fuel system for each reciprocating engine must be 125 percent of the takeoff fuel flow required. (FAR 23.955)
13. If an aircraft is equipped with a selector valve that allows the engine to operate from more than one fuel tank, the system must not cause a loss of power for more than ten seconds for a single-engine or twenty seconds for a multi-engine airplane, between the time one tank is allowed to run dry and the time at which the required power is supplied by the other tank. (FAR 23.955)
14. Turbine-powered aircraft must have a fuel system that will supply 100 percent of the fuel required for operation in all flight attitudes, and the flow must not be interrupted as the fuel system automatically cycles through all of the tanks or fuel cells in the system. (FAR 23.955)
15. If a gravity feed system has interconnected tank outlets, it should not be possible for fuel feeding from one tank to flow into another tank and cause it to overflow. (FAR 23.957)
16. The amount of unusable fuel in an aircraft must be determined and this must be made known to the pilot. **Unusable fuel** is the amount of fuel in a tank when the first evidence of malfunction occurs. The aircraft must be in the attitude that is most adverse for fuel flow. (FAR 23.959)
17. The fuel system must be designed so that it is free from vapor lock when the fuel is at its critical temperature, with respect to vapor formation, under the most critical operating conditions. (FAR 23.961)
18. Each fuel tank compartment must be adequately vented and drained so no explosive vapors or liquid can accumulate. (FAR 23.967)
19. No fuel tank can be on the engine side of the firewall, and it must be at least one-half inch away from the firewall. (FAR 23.967)
20. Each fuel tank must have at least a 2 percent expansion space that cannot be filled with fuel. However, if the tank vent discharges clear of the airplane, no expansion space is required. (FAR 23.969)
21. Each fuel tank must have a drainable sump where water and contaminants will normally accumulate when the aircraft is in its normal ground attitude. In addition, each reciprocating engine fuel system must have a sediment bowl that is accessible for drainage and has a capacity of one ounce for every 20 gallons of fuel. (FAR 23.971)
22. Provisions must be made to prevent fuel that is spilled during refueling from entering the aircraft structure. (FAR 23.973)
23. The filler opening of an aircraft fuel tank must be marked at or near the filler opening with the word "Avgas" and, for aircraft with reciprocating engines, with the minimum grade of fuel. For turbine-powered aircraft, the tank must be marked with the permissible fuel designation. If the filler opening is for pressure fueling, the maximum permissible fueling and defueling pressure must be specified. (FAR 23.1557)
24. Each fuel tank must be vented from the top part of its expansion space. In addition, if more than one fuel tank has interconnected outlets, the airspace above the fuel must also be interconnected. (FAR 23.975)
25. If a carburetor or fuel injection system has a vapor elimination system that returns fuel vapors to one of the tanks, the returned vapors must go to the tank that is required to be used first. (FAR 23.975)
26. All fuel tanks are required to have a strainer at the fuel tank outlet or at the booster pump. For a reciprocating engine, the strainer should have an element of 8 to 16 meshes per inch. For turbine engines, the strainer should prevent the passage of any object that could restrict the flow or damage any of the fuel system components. (FAR 23.977)
27. For engines requiring fuel pumps, there must be one engine-driven fuel pump for each engine. (FAR 23.991)
28. There must be at least one drain that will allow safe drainage of the entire fuel system when the airplane is in its normal ground attitude. (FAR 23.999)

29. If the design landing weight of the aircraft is less than that permitted for takeoff, there must be provisions in the fuel system for jettisoning fuel to bring the maximum weight down to the design landing weight. (FAR 23.1001)

30. The fuel jettisoning valve must be designed to allow personnel to close the valve during any part of the jettisoning operation. (FAR 23.1001)

RECIPROCATING ENGINE FUEL SYSTEMS

A reciprocating engine fuel system must supply the proper amount of fuel to an engine at the right pressure and during all ground and flight operations. To do this, all fuel systems must contain some basic components including one or more fuel tanks, lines, valves, filtering devices, quantity gauges, and a primer. In addition, many fuel systems also include at least one fuel pump as well as fuel flow, pressure, and temperature gauges. Two examples of light aircraft reciprocating engine fuel systems are the gravity-feed system and the pressure-feed system.

GRAVITY-FEED SYSTEMS

The simplest form of aircraft fuel systems is the gravity-feed system used on many high-wing, single-engine aircraft. A typical gravity-feed system normally has two fuel tanks, a fuel selector valve, a fuel strainer, a primer, and a carburetor. [Figure 7-2]

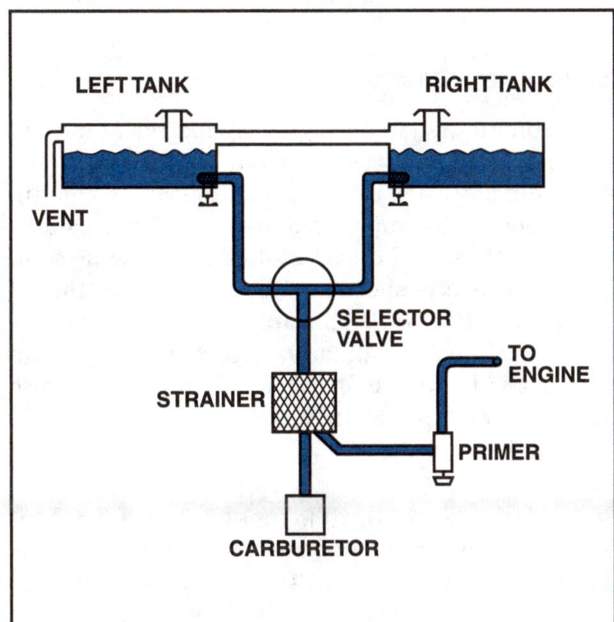

Figure 7-2. A typical gravity-feed fuel system consists of two fuel tanks, a selector valve, a strainer, a primer, and a carburetor.

PRESSURE-FEED SYSTEMS

On low-wing aircraft, the fuel metering device is above the fuel tanks. Therefore, a fuel pump must be used to pressure-feed fuel to the fuel metering device. High wing aircraft equipped with fuel-injection or pressure carburetors also require a fuel pump. In addition, a backup, or auxiliary pump is installed in case the engine-driven pump should fail. [Figure 7-3]

FUEL SYSTEM COMPONENTS

A typical fuel system includes multiple fuel tanks, lines, filtering units, pumps, gauges, and a priming system. In addition, some systems will include central refueling provisions, fuel dump valves, and a means of transferring fuel. Although most of the components just listed are considered to be airframe components, failure of any one component can lead to engine problems. Therefore, you must have a thorough understanding of how certain component failures impact engine operation.

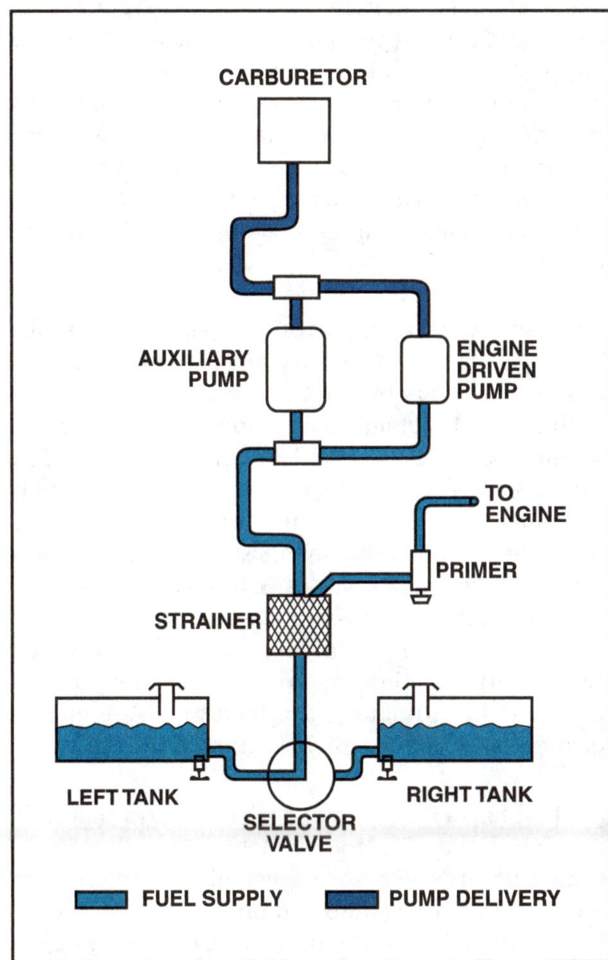

Figure 7-3. Pressure-feed fuel systems are used in aircraft where the fuel supply is located below the fuel metering device.

FUEL TANKS

The condition of an aircraft's fuel tank can have a tremendous effect on engine operations. Although fuel tanks are originally constructed to meet FAR certification requirements, they must be properly maintained to continue meeting their original design standards. For example, neglected or improperly maintained fuel tanks can lead to contaminated fuel being delivered to the engine or fuel flow restrictions. Therefore, to increase your ability to identify engine problems caused by an improperly maintained fuel tank, you must have a basic knowledge of fuel tank design and maintenance requirements.

Fuel tank construction varies depending on the type and intended use of the aircraft. In the early years of aircraft construction, fuel was retained in welded or riveted tanks that were positioned in a wing or fuselage cavity. Although the location of fuel tanks has not changed much, the materials used and methods of construction have changed. Some of the new materials used include 3003 and 5052 aluminum alloys and several composite type materials. These materials may include neoprene impregnated fabric used to form bladders, or fiberglass and honeycomb materials that are formed into rigid tanks. In some applications, a special corrosion resistant material composed of steel coated with an alloy of lead and tin is used. This material is commonly referred to as **terneplate**.

Even with the use of corrosion resistant materials, fuel cells are not corrosion proof. For example, any time water enters the fuel cell, corrosion can occur within a fuel system. In addition, fuel cell age can dramatically effect a fuel system's integrity. For example, as a fuel cell's gasket and sealant materials age, they become brittle and can dislodge into the fuel. Therefore, contaminants such as water, corrosion, and sealer materials can cause engine malfunctions by restricting or completely blocking fuel flow. As an example, a partial blockage of fuel flow can cause a dramatic leaning effect on the fuel/air mixture which, ultimately, can lead to severe engine damage or even a complete engine failure.

All fuel tanks incorporate design features that help alleviate fuel system contamination and other operational hazards. For example, all fuel tanks are required to have a sump and drain installed at their lowest point. The sump provides a convenient location for water and sediment to settle, allowing it to be drained from the system. Additional tank design requirements call for expansion space and venting. The expansion space provides room for the fuel to expand when exposed to warm temperatures while the venting prevents tank pressurization and allows air to take the place of the fuel as it is burned. Based on this, if a fuel vent becomes partially or completely blocked, a low pressure will form in the tank as the fuel is consumed. Eventually, this low pressure will slow or completely stop fuel flow from the tank. Therefore, if an engine is not receiving an adequate amount of fuel, especially at high power settings, you should check the fuel venting for blockage.

Another thing to keep in mind is that, if an aircraft's fuel system returns unused fuel from the fuel metering system, the unused fuel must be returned to the fuel tank that is required to be used first. In this case, if you, as the aircraft operator, have not used enough fuel from the first tank, it's possible for the tank to overflow. Therefore, it is important that you be familiar with a particular aircraft's fuel system before you operate the engine.

To prevent fuel from entering the fuselage or other structures during refueling, a **scupper** and drain are sometimes installed near the filler neck of the tank. A scupper collects overflowing fuel and directs it to an overboard drain. However, if the drain system for the scupper becomes obstructed, water and other contaminants can collect in the scupper and possibly enter the fuel tank when the filler cap is removed. Therefore, an improperly maintained scupper drain may present a source of fuel system contamination leading to possible engine troubles.

LINES AND FITTINGS

Fuel lines routed in an engine compartment present special maintenance considerations. Heat, vibration, and corrosive elements are typically greater in an engine compartment than in most other locations and, therefore, fuel lines installed in an engine compartment require special attention. Consider that, if a fuel line fails in flight, not only is the engine's operation affected, but an in-flight fire or explosion may occur. In order to maintain the integrity of these lines, special procedures must be used in their installation and care.

In modern aircraft, flexible fuel lines are often constructed from synthetic materials such as neoprene or Teflon™, with the line's diameter being dependent upon the engine's fuel flow requirements. Although these materials are designed to be both abrasive and chemical resistant, there are additional steps that can be taken to extend their life span. For example, to increase a fuel line's fire resistance and to help prevent deterioration, a fire sleeve may be installed over the line. A **fire sleeve** is a hollow silicone coated fiberglass tube that is slipped over a length of the hose during fabrication. The sleeve is held onto the hose by a stainless steel band that is wrapped around the sleeve at each end. Additionally, to prevent chemicals from entering the fire sleeve, the sleeve's ends are typically dipped in a silicone type sealer before final assembly. Although fire sleeves are invaluable in helping to protect flexible lines, they present a hazard by preventing the underlying line from being easily inspected. Therefore, the safest method for verifying the integrity of a shielded fuel line is to replace it at the aircraft manufacturer's recommended intervals.

In addition to using a fire sleeve, some fuel lines may require the use of stainless steel heat shields. These shields are strategically placed in the engine compartment to help radiate heat away from flammable fluid lines. Therefore, it is important to verify that these shields are installed where appropriate and maintained in their original condition. If they are not, the fuel within the fuel line could become warm enough to vaporize and cause vapor lock.

When working with Teflon fuel lines, keep in mind that, although Teflon offers a high degree of heat and chemical resistance, certain precautions must be followed to maintain their serviceability. For example, Teflon hoses tend to assume a permanent set when exposed to high temperatures. Therefore, to prevent a Teflon hose from cracking or splitting when being removed, a support wire should be tied between the end fittings of the hose to maintain its shape.

Another consideration when working with flexible hose is that, if a hose is allowed to remain twisted after installation, it is possible for the resulting torque on the hose to loosen the end fittings. Additionally, twisting a hose tends to weaken it which could lead to premature hose failure. To help you identify when a hose is twisted, many manufacturers incorporate a lay line. When a flexible hose is properly installed, the lay line should be straight, with no signs of spiraling. [Figure 7-4]

On aircraft equipped with rigid fuel lines, the rigid lines may be constructed from a number of materials including copper, aluminum, or stainless steel. Copper lines, although slightly weaker than aluminum, have the advantage of being able to transfer heat more readily than other types of materials. To further increase the cooling ability of a copper line, the line may be coiled to increase the tube's surface area. Coiling the tubing also allows the line to expand and contract under adverse temperature conditions. One disadvantage of using copper tubing however, is its tendency to work harden. Therefore, stress fractures may occur due to the vibration and subsequent work hardening of the line. Operational problems associated with a fractured primer line include leaking fuel and, in the case of a primer line, excess air being drawn into a cylinder causing a leaning of the fuel/air mixture. To help prevent fractures, some manufacturers require periodic annealing of the tubing to restore its ductility.

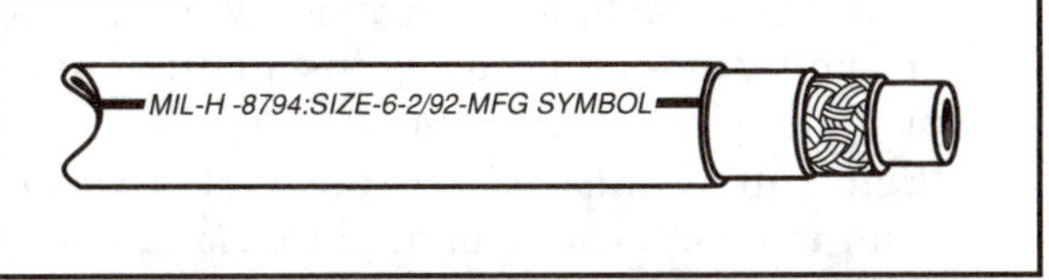

Figure 7-4. A lay line provides a method for visually identifying whether a hose is twisted after it is installed. It should be noted that, instead of using a solid lay line, some manufacturers use the identification markings as a lay line or an alternating pattern of lines and identification markings.

Aluminum fuel lines are typically constructed from 5052-O aluminum alloy. This material has good corrosion resistance, is reasonably easy to fabricate, and weighs less than comparable strength materials. For these reasons, aluminum tubing is used to fabricate aircraft fuel lines. However, since aluminum tubing does not transfer heat well and corrodes when exposed to high concentrations of corrosive elements, it is rarely used in an engine compartment.

For fuel tubing applications where high temperatures and corrosive conditions exist or where high strength is required, stainless steel tubing is used. Reciprocating engine aircraft typically use a limited amount of stainless tubing, however, turbine engine aircraft use it rather extensively.

Another critical aspect of fuel lines is how they are routed through the airframe and engine compartment. Several guidelines for the installation and routing of fuel lines include:

1. Whenever possible, fuel lines should be routed in separate sections of an aircraft. However, if this is not possible, a fuel line should be installed below electrical wiring and clamped to the airframe. Under no circumstances should an electrical wire bundle ever be clamped to a fuel line.

2. Support all fuel lines in a manner to avoid strain on the fittings and, during installation, never pull a line into place by the fitting.
3. Rigid tubing must always have at least one bend to compensate for slight misalignments and vibration. In addition, a bend relieves tension caused by expansion and contraction of a fuel line due to temperature and pressure changes.
4. All metal fuel lines should be electrically bonded at each structural attachment point with bonded cushion clamps.
5. Fuel lines should be installed in a way that protects them from being used as a handhold while performing other maintenance.
6. Where possible, fuel lines should be routed along the top or along the sides near the top in compartments so they cannot be stepped on or be damaged by cargo.
7. Sharp curves, steep rises, and steep falls should be avoided in fuel line installations to help prevent vapor lock.

FUEL STRAINERS

FAR Part 23 requires a main strainer or fuel filter to be installed in the fuel system to remove contaminants and to provide a method for draining the contaminants from the system. The strainer represents the lowest point in a fuel system and must be located between the fuel tank and either the fuel metering device or engine-driven fuel pump. A fuel strainer removes contaminants from the fuel by providing a low point in the system where water and solid contaminants can collect. These contaminants collect in the strainer's sediment bowl and are then drained through a strainer drain. Additional filtering is provided by a fine mesh screen or filter element within the strainer. [Figure 7-5]

Figure 7-5. A fuel strainer represents the lowest point in an aircraft's fuel system and should be checked periodically for contaminants that could restrict fuel flow to the engine.

ENGINE-DRIVEN FUEL PUMPS

Engine-driven fuel pumps are the primary fuel pressure pumps in a pressure-feed fuel system. The purpose of an engine-driven fuel pump is to deliver a continuous supply of fuel at the proper pressure during engine operation. To provide this continuous fuel supply, a positive-displacement pump must be used. A **positive-displacement pump** is a pump that delivers a specific quantity per revolution. One type of positive-displacement pump that is widely used is the vane-type fuel pump.

A typical vane-type fuel pump is mounted on an engine's accessory drive section and driven by a splined shear-shaft. A vane-type pump consists of a housing that contains a steel sleeve with an off-center bore, four vanes, a hollow steel rotor, and a coupling that turns the rotor. In this type of pump, the rotor turns on its center axis while the vanes are free to slide in and out of the rotor. As each pair of vanes passes the pump inlet, the volume between the vanes increases and fuel floods between the vanes at the pump inlet. As the vanes rotate toward the outlet, the volume between the vanes decreases. This pressurizes the fuel so that when the vanes reach the pump outlet, the fuel is forced out of the pump. [Figure 7-6]

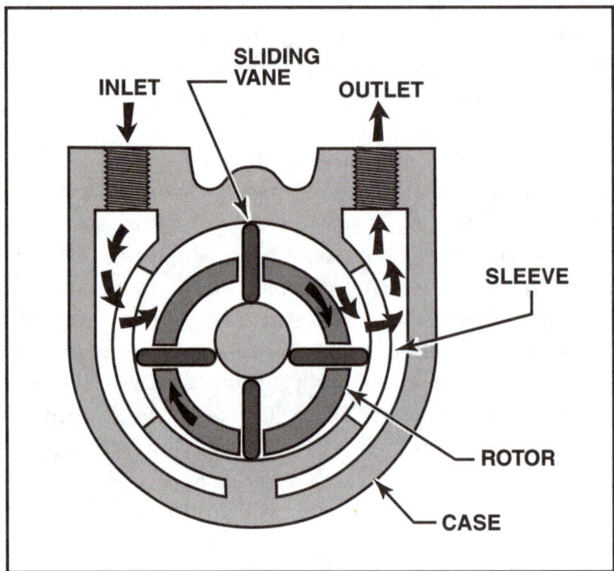

Figure 7-6. In a vane-type pump, a set of vanes slide in and out of a rotor as it rotates in a pump housing. Since the rotor is offset in the pump housing, the volume between each set of vanes alternately increases and decreases allowing the pump to pull fluid in on one side and force it out the other.

With vane-type fuel pumps, more fuel is delivered to the fuel metering device than is needed. Therefore, to prevent excessive fuel from overpressurizing the fuel metering unit, most engine-driven fuel pumps incorporate a spring loaded relief valve that returns excess fuel back to the inlet side of the fuel pump. To calibrate a fuel pump to a fuel metering unit, most relief valves have an adjusting screw which allows you to vary the spring tension of the relief valve. When the relief valve is functioning properly, it dampens fuel pressure fluctuations during throttle movements and maintains the fuel pressure within safe limits.

In a vane-type fuel pump with a **balanced relief valve**, the fuel pressure delivered to the fuel metering unit varies with changes in altitude and atmospheric pressure. To vary the fuel pressure, a diaphragm is installed on the back side of the relief valve. Fuel pressure acts on one side of the diaphragm while either atmospheric or carburetor inlet air is routed to the back side of the diaphragm. This way, the combined force of spring pressure and air pressure act on the relief valve to control the amount of fuel that flows to the fuel metering unit. As the pressure acting on the diaphragm varies, the pressure at which the relief valve bypasses fuel back to the pump's inlet also varies. [Figure 7-7]

AUXILIARY FUEL PUMPS

The primary purpose of an auxiliary fuel pump, or **boost pump** is to maintain a positive fuel pressure on the inlet side of the engine-driven fuel pump. This helps prevent pump cavitation and vapor lock by pressurizing the fuel in the lines. Additional uses for boost pumps include providing the required fuel pressure for starting and transferring fuel between tanks which enables a pilot to redistribute fuel weight in flight and maintain aircraft stability. In addition, a boost pump may serve as a backup source for fuel pressure to the engine if the engine-driven fuel pump becomes clogged or fails.

When operating boost or auxiliary fuel pumps, it is important to follow the aircraft and engine manufacturer's operating procedures closely. Depending on the design of the fuel system, some boost pumps are used only intermittently while others are required to be in operation continuously. In addition, some electric boost pumps utilize different switch positions to vary the fuel flow delivery rate.

Hand-Operated Pumps

Two hand-operated fuel pumps used in aircraft include the **wobble pump** and **manual primer**. A typical wobble pump consists of a vane and drilled shaft assembly that is rotated by a pump handle. The vane and shaft assembly are mounted inside a pump housing that is divided into four chambers, each with its own flapper valve. [Figure 7-8]

As the pump handle is pumped back and forth, the two vanes alternately draw fuel into two chambers

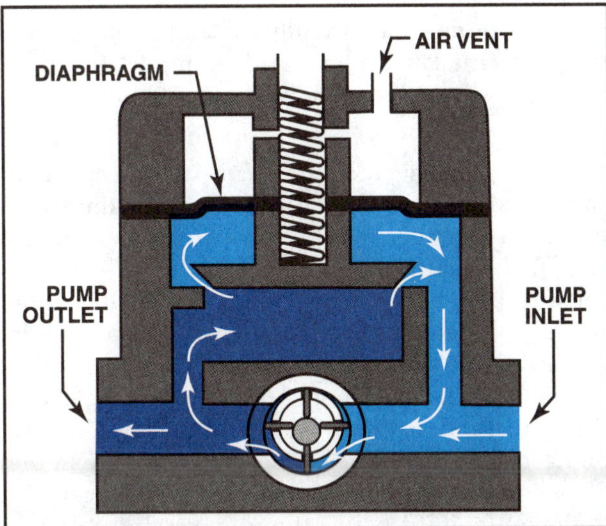

Figure 7-7. A vane-type fuel pump with a balanced-type relief valve has a diaphragm that allows either atmospheric or carburetor inlet pressure to act on the relief valve in combination with spring pressure. This way, as the amount of fuel needed by the engine decreases with altitude, the fuel pressure required to open the relief valve also decreases.

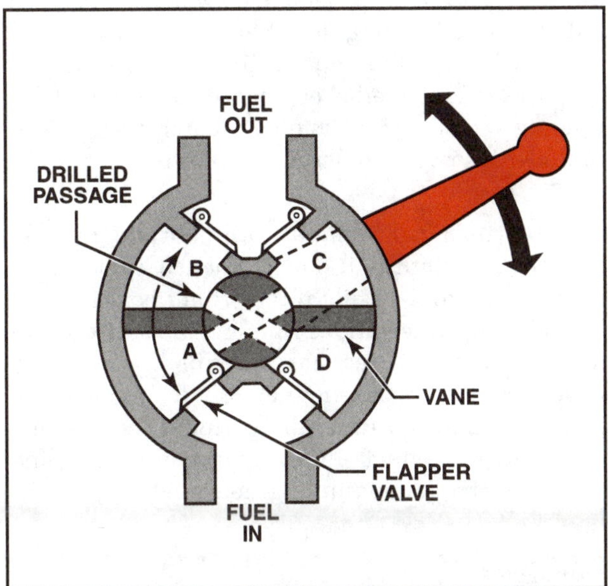

Figure 7-8. A typical wobble pump consists of two vanes that are attached to a rotating shaft with two drilled passages. When installed in a pump housing, the two vanes create four chambers that fuel is alternately drawn into and pumped out of.

while simultaneously pumping fuel out of the other two chambers. For example, when the pump handle is pulled upward, the volume of chambers A and C are reduced and fuel is forced out of the pump through the flapper valve in chamber C. At the same time, chambers D and B fill with fuel through the flapper valve in chamber D. When the pump handle is pushed downward, the volume of chambers B and D are reduced and fuel is forced out of the pump through the flapper valve in chamber B. At the same time, chambers A and C fill with fuel through the flapper valve in chamber A.

The design and capacity of a typical wobble pump allows the pump to be used as a backup to an engine-driven pump and for transferring fuel from one tank to another. In addition, on some aircraft, a wobble pump is used to pressurize the fuel system for starting as well as provide fuel for priming the engine.

A more basic type of hand-operated pump is the manual primer. In most cases, a manual primer is installed in a secondary fuel line that parallels the main fuel line coming off the fuel strainer. A basic manual primer consists of a small cylindrical tube inside the cockpit that, when pulled, draws fuel through a check valve and into a small chamber. Once the chamber is filled, the primer is pushed inward to force fuel through a second check valve and into the engine cylinders.

Since fluids tend to seep into the lower cylinders of a radial engine (causing liquid lock), priming is usually restricted to the upper cylinders. For example, on a nine-cylinder radial engine with a mutiple-point priming system, cylinders one, two, three, eight, and nine are the only cylinders that are primed.

For the most part, manual primers are reliable pumps that require little maintenance. However, it is important to note that if the primer is not in and locked when an engine is running, the suction produced in the cylinders can draw fuel through the primer and into the engine. This can cause the fuel/air mixture within the cylinders to become extremely rich which, in turn, can cause the engine to run rough, or stop running altogether.

Centrifugal Pump

The most commonly used type of boost pump is the centrifugal pump. Centrifugal pumps may be either submerged in a fuel tank or attached to the outside of the tank. A centrifugal pump is driven by an electric motor and uses a small impeller to build fuel pressure. Once fuel pressure builds to a predetermined level, fuel is no longer moved from the tank to the engine. Therefore, centrifugal pumps do not continually displace fuel and are not positive displacement pumps. [Figure 7-9]

As fuel is drawn into a centrifugal pump, the high-speed impeller throws the fuel outward at a high velocity. As the fuel is thrown outward, it is channeled to a discharge line that is routed to the engine. The high rotational speed produced by a centrifugal pump swirls the fuel and produces a centrifuge action that separates air from the fuel before it enters the fuel line. This, along with the increased pressure, greatly decreases the possibility of vapor lock.

Seals between the impeller and power section of a centrifugal pump prevent fuel from leaking into the motor. In addition, the motor chamber of submerged type pumps is vented to outside air. This way, any fumes or liquid fuel that seeps into the motor section is vented overboard.

Most centrifugal boost pumps have two operating speeds: high and low. The high speed setting is typically used during takeoff, high engine power settings, and at high altitudes, while the low speed is used for engine starting.

Pulsating Electric Pumps

Pulsating electric pumps are another type of auxiliary fuel pump that is widely used in small, low-wing aircraft. The design of this pump is similar to fuel pumps used in automotive fuel systems.

A typical pulsating fuel pump consists of a solenoid coil installed around a brass tube that connects a fuel inlet chamber with a fuel outlet chamber. To force fuel from the inlet chamber to the outlet chamber, a steel plunger is installed in the center of the coil. A calibrated spring forces the plunger to slide upward while the electromagnetic forces produced by the coil pull the plunger downward. One check valve at the brass tube's inlet admits fuel as the plunger slides up while a second check valve in the plunger allows fuel to pass through the plunger and to the outlet chamber as the plunger slides down. [Figure 7-10]

When no current flows through the coil, the calibrated spring forces the plunger up, opening the check valve and drawing fuel into the inlet cham-

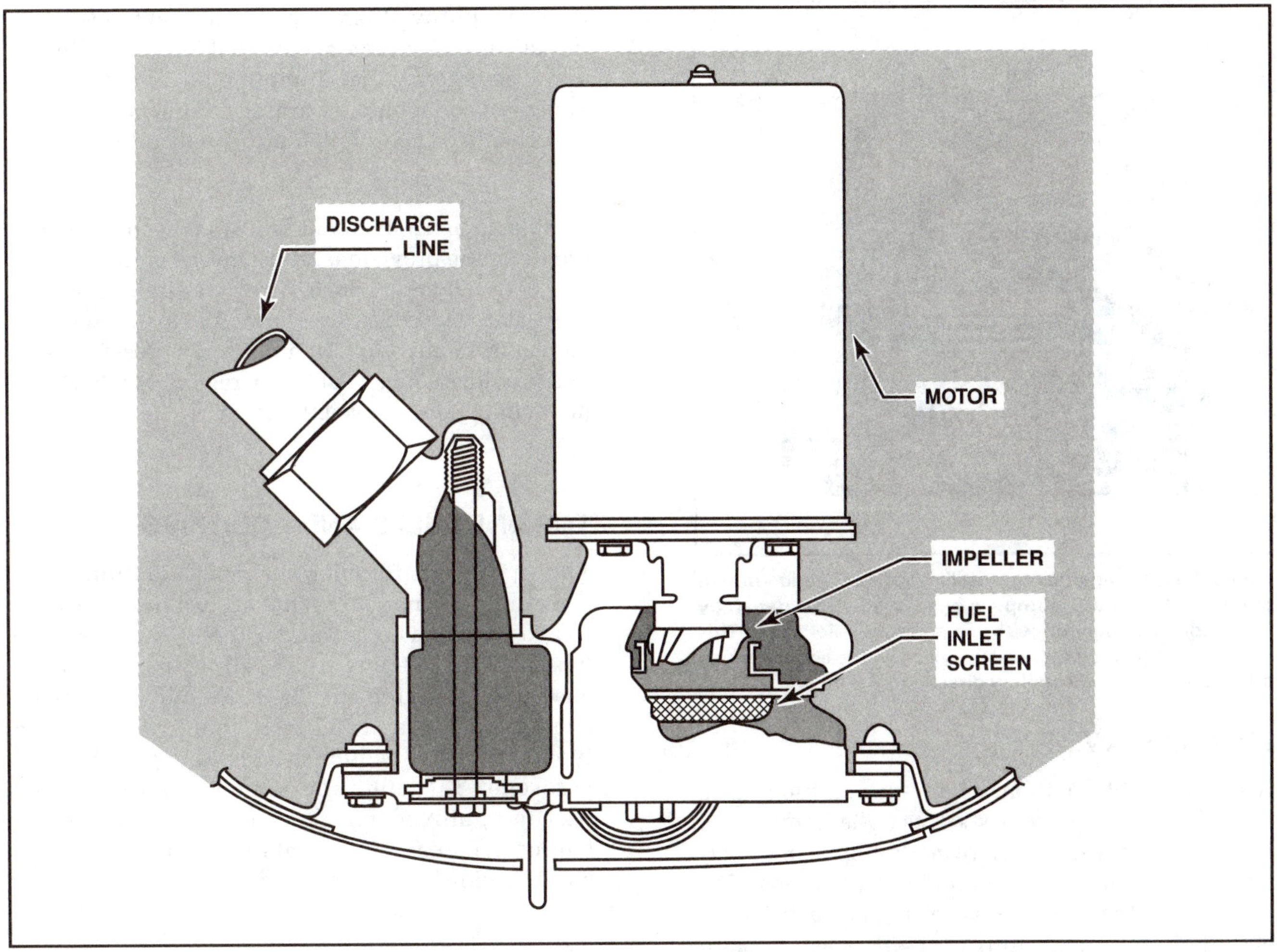

Figure 7-9. A centrifugal boost pump consists of an impeller that is driven by an electric motor.

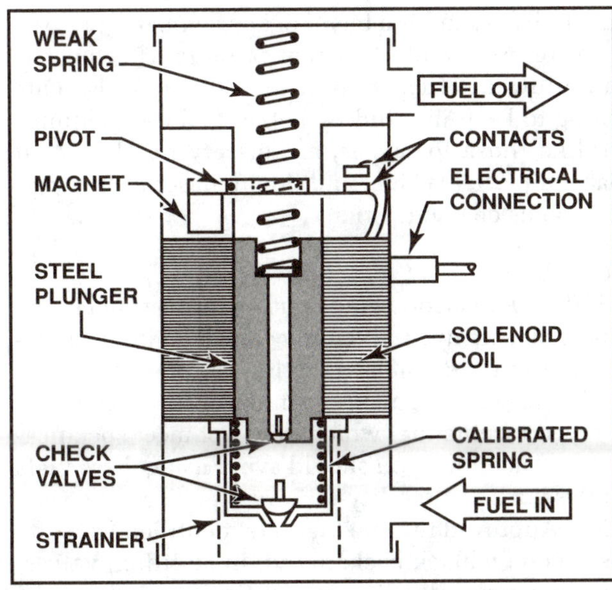

Figure 7-10. This pulsating-type boost pump uses a calibrated spring and an electromagnet to force a plunger up and down to pump fuel.

ber. In this position, the plunger attracts a magnet which pulls a set of electrical contacts closed allowing current to flow through the coil. The resulting electromagnetic forces pull the plunger downward which closes the inlet chamber check valve, opens the plunger check valve, and forces fuel to the outlet chamber. When the plunger is centered in the coil, the magnet is no longer attracted to the plunger and the contacts open allowing the calibrated spring to force the plunger back up. This repeated cycling of the plunger causes the pump to pulsate rapidly until fuel pressure builds up in the fuel line. Once the fuel metering device begins to control the fuel usage, the pump begins to pulsate at a slower rate to maintain a steady fuel pressure.

Pulsating electric pumps are normally installed in parallel with an engine-driven fuel pump. This arrangement allows either pump to provide fuel pressure to the engine regardless of the other pump's operation.

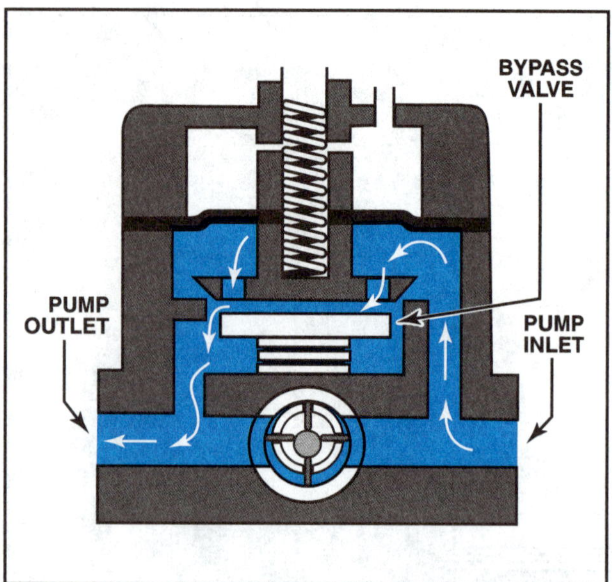

Figure 7-11. On engines that utilize both an engine-driven pump and a boost pump, a bypass valve is generally installed in conjunction with the pressure relief valve. This way, when boost pump pressure exceeds the engine-driven pump pressure, fuel can flow directly to the engine.

BYPASS VALVE

If an engine has both an engine-driven fuel pump and a boost pump, bypass valves (when pumps are in series) or check valves (when pumps are in parall) must be incorporated into the fuel system. The purpose of these valves is to let fuel bypass the engine-driven pump during engine starting or in case the pump fails. In most cases, a bypass valve consists of a spring loaded valve that is installed in conjunction with a pressure-relief valve. The spring tension acting on a bypass valve is calibrated so that whenever the boost pump pressure exceeds the engine-driven pump pressure, the valve opens and allows fuel to flow directly to the engine. [Figure 7-11]

TURBINE FUEL SYSTEMS

The purpose of a turbine engine fuel system is basically the same as a reciprocating engine fuel system. A turbine fuel system must store, transfer, and meter fuel to a turbine engine in the proper amount and at the right pressure. However, because of the type of fuel used, turbine fuel systems require a few additional components.

A turbine fuel system consists of tanks, lines, valves, pumps, filter devices, gauges, a fuel control unit, and fuel nozzles. In addition, a fuel heater is required to eliminate fuel metering problems caused by ice crystals in the fuel. In aircraft that have an approved landing weight that is less than the takeoff weight, a special valve is installed to allow emergency fuel dumping. Most turbine fuel systems also include a warning annunciator for low fuel quantity and low fuel pressure conditions.

Most large turbine aircraft fuel systems include central refueling provisions, and a means of transferring fuel between tanks. Such a fuel system is known as a crossfeed system and it allows fuel to be fed to any engine from any tank. In addition, a crossfeed system provides a means of balancing the fuel load and maintaining aircraft stability.

TURBINE FUELS AND ADDITIVES

The primary difference between aviation gasolines and turbine fuel is that all turbine fuels contain kerosene. The reason for this is that kerosene has more heat energy per gallon than standard gasolines. Aviation turbine fuels currently being used are JET A and JET A-1, which are kerosene types, and JET B, which is a blend of gasoline and kerosene. To determine which type of turbine fuel is approved for a given engine, check the engine type certificate data sheet or the aircraft specifications.

The difference between JET A and JET A-1 is that JET A-1 has a freeze point of –47°C (–52.6°F) whereas JET A has a freeze point of – 40°C (–40°F). JET B, which is similar to JP-4, is normally used by the military, and is a blend of approximately 30 percent kerosene and 70 percent gasoline. This fuel has an allowable freeze point of –50°C (–58°F). One thing to keep in mind is that jet fuel designations, unlike those for avgas, are merely numbers that label a particular fuel and do not describe any performance characteristics.

Unlike the various grades of reciprocating engine fuels that are dyed different colors to aid in recognition, all turbine fuels are either colorless or have a light straw color. An off-color may indicate an unapproved turbine fuel which does not meet specifications. Therefore, you should avoid using these fuels unless their suitability for aircraft use can be verified. Approved turbine fuels are identified by white letters on a black background. In addition, valves, loading and unloading connections, switches, and other control equipment are color-coded according to the type of fuel they dispense. The fuel in piping

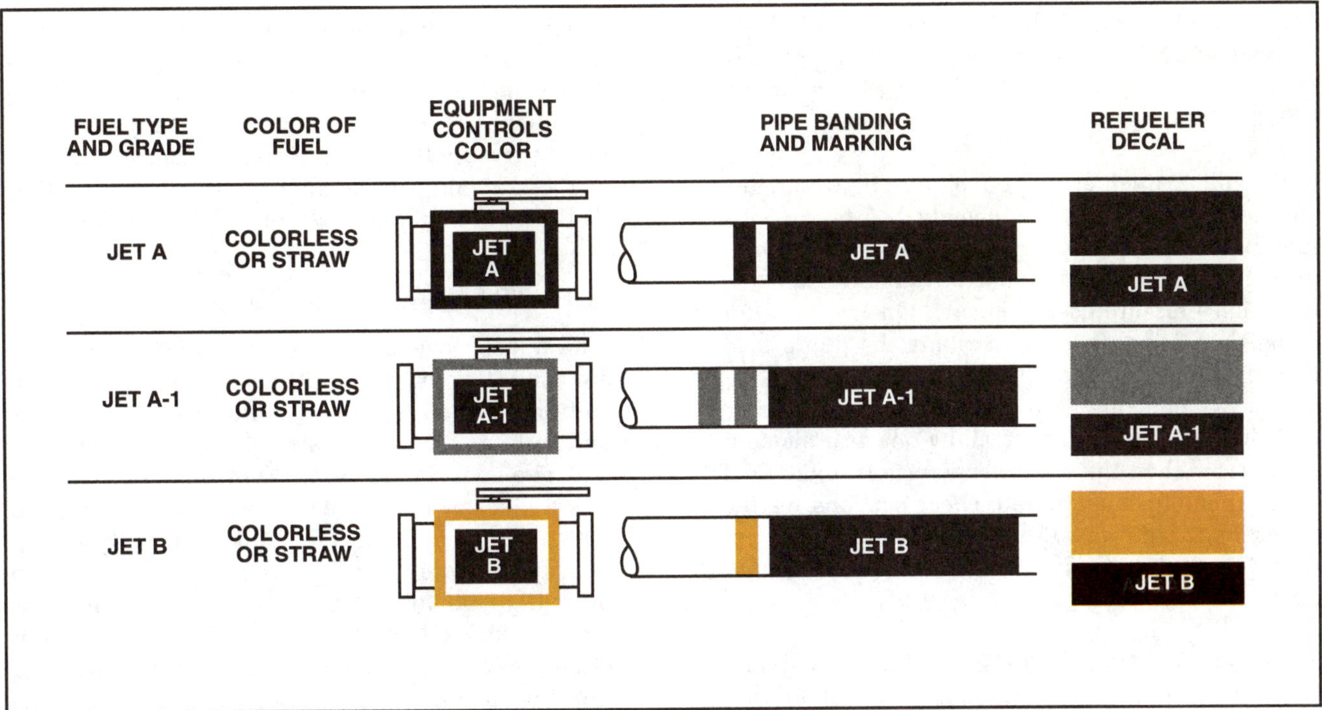

Figure 7-12. Fuel conduits and controls are marked and coded to identify each type of turbine fuel.

is identified by name and by colored bands painted or decaled around the pipe at intervals along its length. [Figure 7-12]

As a general rule, turbine fuels are much more viscous than reciprocating fuels. This allows the fuel to act as a lubricant in pumps and fuel control units. However, the high viscosity also allows turbine fuels to hold water and solid material that does not easily settle out. Any time water is present in fuel, the potential for fuel icing or microbial growth exists. Because of this, many aircraft and engine manufacturers recommend the use of anti-icing and anti-microbial fuel additives. Except for very low temperatures, anti-icing additives help prevent water that is entrained in fuel from freezing. On the other hand, anti-microbial agents kill the microbes, fungi, and bacteria which tend to form slime or matted waste inside fuel tanks. These micro-organisms can accumulate and clog filters and fuel lines as well as create corrosive compounds that corrode fuel cells.

Quite often, fuel additives are premixed in the fuel by the distributor. However, when fuels are supplied without additives, the appropriate quality of additives is metered into the fuel while refueling the aircraft. If metering is not available, the additives are poured into the fuel tanks just before refueling. This way, the turbulence created by the refueling process sufficiently mixes the additive with the fuel. The type and amount of additive used must be approved by the aircraft manufacturer in order to maintain the fuel system's airworthiness. Approved fuel and fuel additives for each turbine engine are found in the aircraft operator's manual or Type Certificate Data Sheet. PRIST™ is a commonly used additive which contains both anti-icing and anti-microbial agents.

ENGINE-DRIVEN PUMPS

The main fuel pump on all turbine engines is a constant displacement pump that is driven by the engine as an accessory. Subsequently, the amount of fuel delivered by the pump varies with engine speed. A typical engine-driven pump is designed to deliver a continuous supply of fuel to a fuel control unit in quantities that exceed the needs of the engine. Therefore, after the appropriate amount of fuel is metered, the fuel control returns surplus fuel to the fuel pump inlet.

Main engine-driven fuel pumps used on turbine engines are typically gear type pumps with one or two gear elements. In addition, some engine-driven fuel pumps also contain a centrifugal boost element that increases the fuel pressure before the fuel reaches the primary gear element. [Figure 7-13]

In a typical dual element fuel pump, when fuel enters the pump, a boost element boosts the inlet fuel pressure to between 30 and 60 psig. Once through the impeller, the fuel passes through one of two high pressure gear elements. One purpose for using two elements is to distribute the pump load thereby increasing pump life. Another reason for using two elements is to provide a backup in case one element should fail. To allow one gear element to operate when the other element fails, most dual element pumps incorporate shear sections on the drive shaft. This way, if one gear element locks up, its drive shaft will shear and the second element continues operating.

To prevent fuel from draining out of the fuel system when the engine is shutdown and to keep fuel from recirculating within a failed gear element, a check valve is installed at the outlet of each gear element. In addition, a pressure relief valve is built into the pump housing to limit pump fuel pressure and provide protection to the fuel system.

A typical large dual element gear pump can produce fuel pressures up to 1,500 psi with a volume of 30,000 pounds per hour. However, to help reduce the chance of pump cavitation, many of these pumps require the full time use of a boost pump. In fact, these pumps typically have very strict life limits if they are operated without a boost pump.

FUEL TRANSFER EJECTORS

Fuel transfer ejectors, sometimes called **jet pumps**, are used in some fuel systems to help the primary and/or boost pump scavenge fuel from a fuel tank and to facilitate the transfer of fuel from the main tank to a boost pump sump. Typically, transfer ejectors are located at the lowest point in a fuel tank and remain submerged until the tank is virtually empty. Transfer ejectors have no moving parts and consist primarily of a tube with a constriction. This way, when a fuel pump draws fuel through a transfer ejector, a low pressure area forms at the restriction. The low pressure area draws more fuel from the tank into the line and enables the pump to transfer virtually all the fuel from the tank. This lowers the amount of unusable fuel that would otherwise occupy a fuel tank and provides more flexibility when balancing a fuel load.

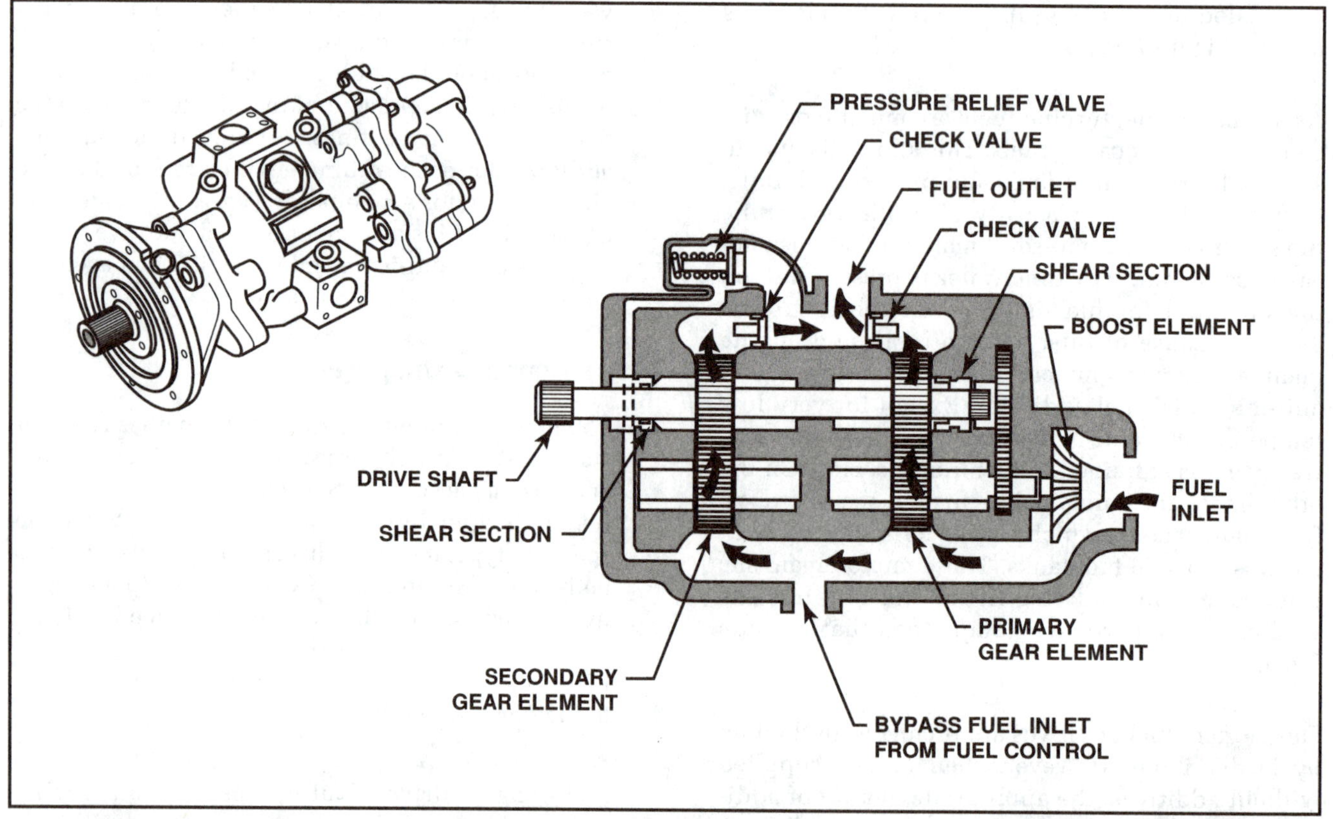

Figure 7-13. A typical engine-driven fuel pump housing for a turbine engine contains a centrifugal boost pump impeller, dual gear pump elements, check valves, and a relief valve.

FUEL HEATER

Water that is entrained in the fuel supply can present a hazard to fuel system operation if the water freezes. For example, if entrained water freezes, the resulting ice crystals can clog fuel filters or other fuel system components. In addition, when a fuel filter becomes clogged with ice crystals fuel begins to pass through a filter bypass valve. If this happens, unfiltered fuel containing sediment and ice crystals flows downstream to other fuel system components possibly resulting in component malfunction or fuel flow interruption.

To prevent such disastrous occurrences, most turbine engine fuel systems incorporate a fuel heater to eliminate and prevent the formation of ice crystals in the fuel supply. A typical fuel heater consists of a heat exchanger that utilizes either engine oil or bleed air to warm the fuel. [Figure 7-14]

In a typical fuel heater, fuel continuously flows through the heat exchanger while the flow of engine oil is regulated by a shutoff valve. Fuel heat is normally used when the fuel temperature approaches 32°F or when a fuel filter bypass warning light illuminates in the cockpit. Fuel heat is activated either manually or automatically. Manual activation consists of selecting fuel heat with a toggle switch in the cockpit. Switch closure energizes a solenoid which opens the shutoff valve and allows engine oil to pass through the fuel heater and warm the fuel.

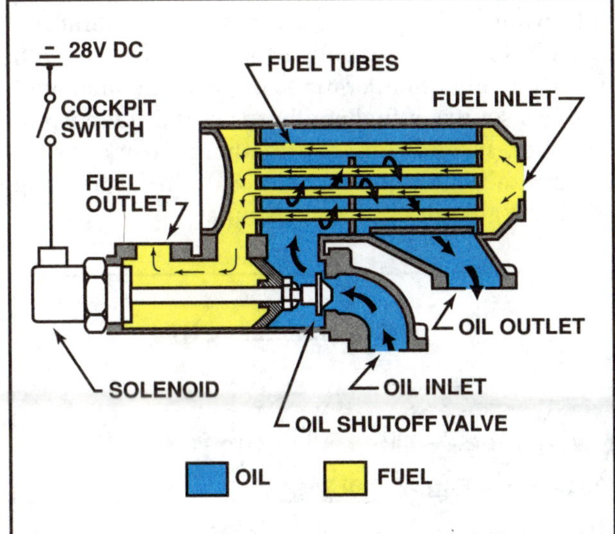

Figure 7-14. One type of fuel heater utilizes engine oil to heat turbine fuel and melt any ice crystals that are suspended in the fuel.

Excessive use of fuel heat can cause vapor lock or heat damage to the fuel control unit. Therefore, operating restrictions are typically placed on manually operated fuel heating systems. For example, fuel heat is generally operated for one minute prior to takeoff, and then for one minute during each 30 minutes of flight. It is important that fuel heat not be operated during takeoff, approach, or go-around. The dangers of using the fuel heater during these critical flight regimes include engine surging and flameout.

Fuel systems with automatic activation of the fuel heater are usually set for fuel temperatures between 35°F and 37°F. The cycle time is automatically controlled by an electric time and gate valve. To verify that the system is operating properly, you can observe gauge indications and the fuel filter light. In addition, as the system cycles on and off, oil temperature or EPR gauges will fluctuate. For example, with a fuel heater that uses engine oil to heat the fuel, oil temperatures should drop when fuel heat is activated. On the other hand, in systems that utilize bleed air as a source of heat, EPR readings usually decrease slightly when fuel heat is used.

FUEL FILTERS

Most turbine engine fuel systems utilize both coarse and fine filter elements. A coarse mesh filter is typically installed between the supply tank and the fuel pump while a fine mesh filter is placed between the fuel pump and the fuel control unit. The effectiveness of a fuel filter is measured in microns. One **micron** represents a size or distance equal to one millionth of a meter, or approximately .000039 inch. To put micron measurements in perspective, consider that objects must be approximately 40 microns or larger to be distinguishable by the human eye.

Since the passages in fuel control units are so small and can become plugged easily, most turbine engines must use micron filters to ensure a clean supply of fuel. One type of micron filter uses a cellulose fiber filter element that is capable of removing particles that are between 10 and 25 microns.

Another type of filter element is the screen disk element. A typical screen disk element consists of several wafer-type disks that are made out of a bronze, brass, or stainless steel wire mesh. In addition to

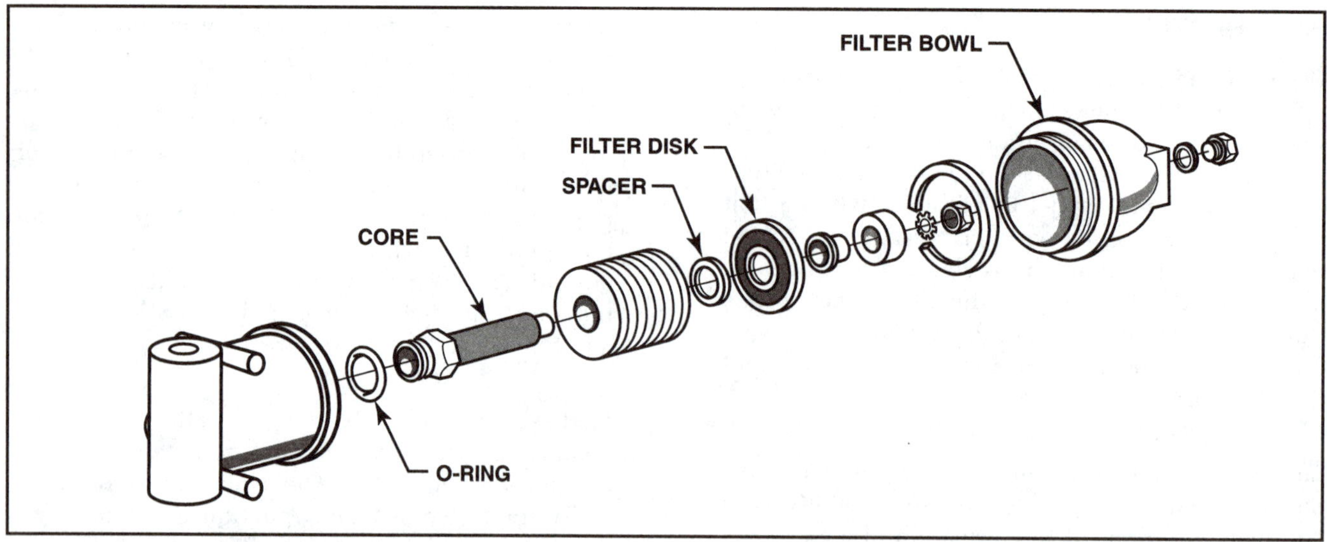

Figure 7-15. A typical screen disk filter element consists of several thin wafer disks. Each disk is constructed of a fine wire mesh that is capable of filtering extremely small particles.

being reusable, this type of filter element is well suited to withstand fairly high operating pressures. [Figure 7-15]

Two-stage filters fulfill the requirements for both coarse and fine filtration into one unit. A typical two-stage filter consists of a pleated mesh element that filters the main system fuel on its way to the combustor and has a filtration rating of 40 microns. On the other hand, a cylindrical mesh element rated at 10 microns provides the fine filtration needed for reliable servo mechanism operation in the fuel control unit. [Figure 7-16]

WATER INJECTION

Water injection is a means of augmenting engine thrust in a gas turbine engine. The maximum thrust produced by a turbine engine depends, in part, on the density, or weight of the airflow through the engine. In other words, the less dense the airflow passing through an engine, the less thrust produced. Decreases in ambient air pressure or increases in air temperature reduce air density. Therefore, either of these conditions will reduce the maximum thrust of the engine. However, in some cases, water injection may be used to cool the airflow and increase air density. In addition, the vaporization of water in the combustion chamber inlet increases the mass flow through the turbine relative to the compressor. As a result, the pressure and temperature drop across the turbine is less when water injection is used. This provides an increased tail pipe pressure which, in turn, results in additional thrust. Furthermore, the lower turbine inlet temperature resulting from water injection allows the fuel control to increase the fuel flow to the engine. With the advent of high bypass gas turbine engines and emphasis on noise reduction, water injection is seldom found on current production aircraft.

A typical water injection system uses a mixture of water and methanol. This is done because injecting only water reduces the turbine inlet temperature. The addition of methanol partially restores the drop in turbine inlet temperatures because the methanol acts as a source of fuel and burns in the combustion chamber. In addition, the methanol works as an antifreeze to help prevent the water from freezing when the aircraft climbs to altitude.

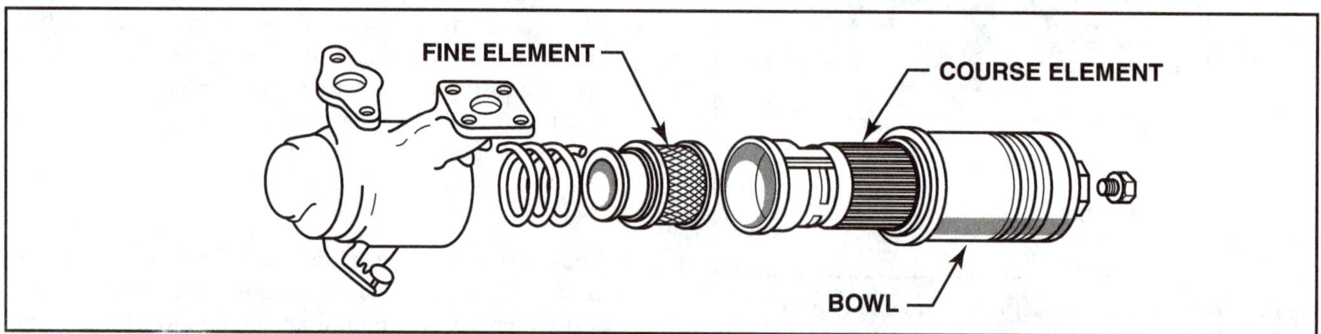

Figure 7-16. This two-stage filtration unit combines the requirements for coarse filtration and fine filtration into one unit.

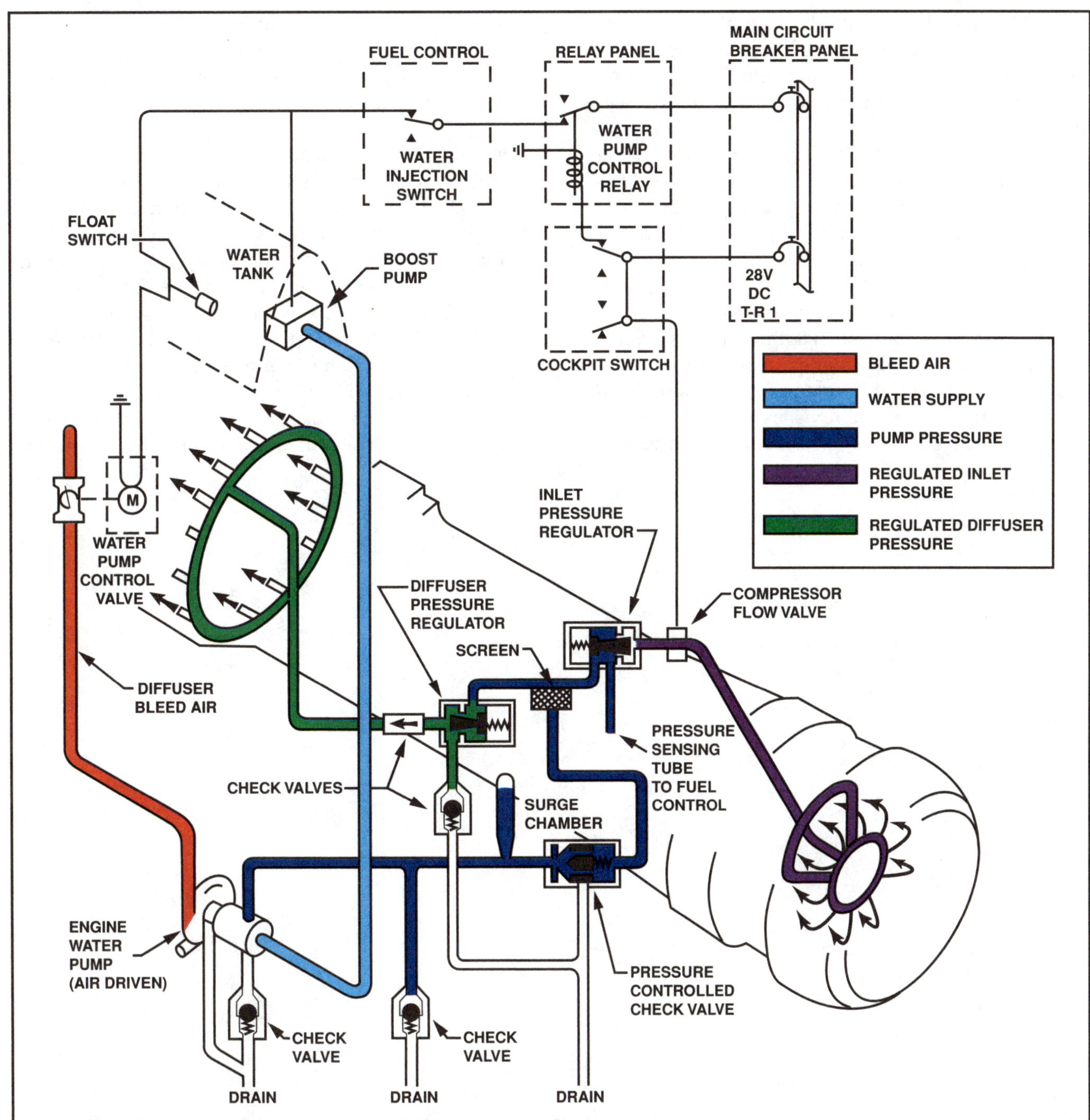

Figure 7-17. This represents the components included in a typical water injection system that injects water into both the compressor inlet and the diffuser.

Water may be injected directly into the compressor inlet, the diffuser just ahead of the combustion chamber, or both the inlet and diffuser. Although injecting water at the engine inlet is done, it does pose a disadvantage in that it can produce ice at the compressor inlet at takeoff rpm when ambient temperatures are below 40°F. Injecting water into the diffuser section is usually more suitable for engines using an axial flow compressor and provides a more even distribution. In addition, injection at the diffuser allows a greater quantity of water to be injected. On systems which utilize water injection at the compressor inlet and at the diffuser, full thrust augmentation is achieved by activating both injection nozzles. However, there is a limit to the amount of fluid injection any compressor or combustor can efficiently utilize. [Figure 7-17]

The water injection system shown in the figure 7-17 is controlled by a cockpit switch which arms the circuit and allows water to flow into both injection manifolds. Closure of the cockpit switch energizes the water pump control relay and provides power to the fuel control microswitch. Advancing the power lever to its take off position actuates the microswitch allowing power to flow to the water pump control valve. This also opens a compressor bleed air valve which allows bleed air to drive the water pump. The air-driven water pump supplies water at 200 to 300 psig to the dual manifold. If water injection is not needed at the compressor, it is deactivated by a cockpit switch. A pressure sensing tube alerts the fuel control unit to schedule fuel flow of a higher rate when water injection is being used. The pressure sensing tube may be absent in some systems when a water-alcohol mixture is used exclusively. In such a system, combustion of the alcohol keeps the turbine inlet temperature at its required value.

A tank float level switch causes the water pump control valve to close when the tank is empty. This switch also prevents system operation if the circuit is activated with an empty water tank. When the water injection system is not in use, a check valve at the diffuser prevents high temperature compressor air from flowing into the water system. Drains and check valves allow the water supply lines to empty when the system is not in use, preventing freeze-ups. Some water injection systems are designed so that crewmembers may use compressor bleed air to purge the system of water after a water injection operation.

RECIPROCATING ENGINE FUEL METERING

In this section, we will discuss the operation and maintenance of reciprocating engine fuel metering devices. As discussed earlier, an engine's fuel metering device is typically considered to be a powerplant subsystem. Therefore, as a powerplant technician, you must be familiar with the various types of fuel metering devices used on aircraft engines.

The fuel metering portion of an aircraft's fuel system controls the amount of fuel being delivered to the engine. To obtain the best engine performance and fuel economy, the fuel metering device must be able to properly mix fuel and air over a wide range of operating and environmental conditions. In addition, a fuel metering device must be able to atomize and distribute fuel in a manner that promotes complete and even burning in the cylinders. Without proper atomization, the fuel will not completely vaporize. In this situation, the unvaporized fuel will not ignite and the engine will run lean even though the correct amount of fuel is present. If this condition is not corrected, the lean mixture could eventually cause severe engine damage.

TYPES OF METERING DEVICES

There are a number of fuel metering devices used on modern aircraft. Each varies in design to accommodate different engine types as well as an aircraft's designed purpose. Today, modern reciprocating engines use either a carburetor or fuel injection unit to meter fuel to the engine. The two types of carburetors used include the float-type carburetor, and pressure-injection carburetor. On the other hand, the two types of fuel injection systems available are the continuous or direct fuel injection systems.

METERING PRINCIPLES

In order to understand how a fuel metering device works, you must be familiar with some basic fuel metering principles. For example, the operation of all fuel metering devices is based on some basic laws of physics and fluid mechanics. One physical principle that is widely used in fuel metering devices is Bernoulli's principle. If you recall, Bernoulli's principle states that when air flows through a venturi it is forced to speed up as it moves through the restricted portion of the venturi. You should also recall that as the air speeds up in a venturi, its pressure drops below the air ahead of, and behind, the restriction. For a fuel metering device, the pressure differential produced by a venturi is used to meter the fuel delivery rate. [Figure 7-18]

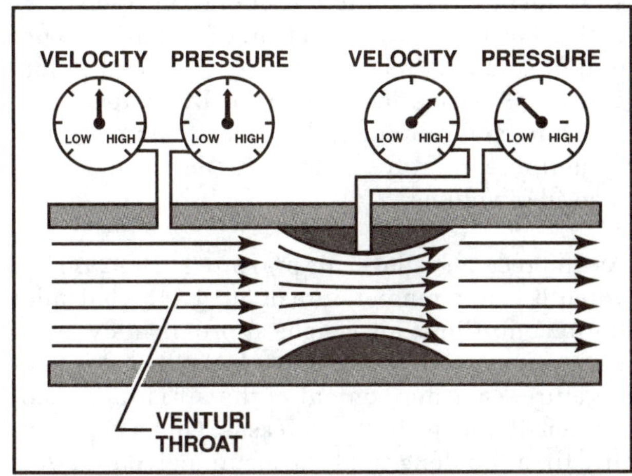

Figure 7-18. As air flows through the narrow portion, or throat, of a venturi its speed increases while its pressure decreases. This creates a pressure differential that can be used to meter the amount of fuel needed to produce a combustible mixture.

FUEL/AIR CHEMISTRY

In order for gasoline and other liquid fuels to burn, they must be mixed with air. Furthermore, for the mixture to burn properly, the ratio of fuel to air must be kept within a certain range. The acceptable range is governed by the chemical composition of the atmosphere and the fuel.

ATMOSPHERE CONTENT

Approximately seventy-eight percent of the atmosphere is nitrogen, while only twenty-one percent is oxygen. The remaining one percent of the atmosphere's content is a combination of other gases, primarily argon and carbon dioxide. Since nitrogen is an inert gas, it does not support combustion. Oxygen, on the other hand, is required to support combustion and even slight deviations from the atmosphere's normal twenty-one percent oxygen content can have a dramatic effect on the combustion process.

To achieve any specific fuel/air ratio, the air density must be taken into consideration. Density is defined as the mass, or weight, of a substance per unit of volume. Since the density of vaporized fuel and air is dramatically affected by temperature, pressure, and humidity, the only accurate method to define a mixture ratio is in terms of weight instead of volume.

As you recall, sea level air pressure is 29.92 in. Hg. when it is at a temperature of 59° F (15°C). Under these conditions, air weighs approximately .0765 pounds per cubic foot. However, if either the temperature, or water content of the air is increased, its density, or weight, decreases. Given this fact, any time the density of the air in a given fuel/air ratio decreases, an enrichening effect occurs that can cause the engine performance to decrease. On the other hand, if either the water content or temperature of the air is decreased, air density increases. Based on this, any time the air density is high, more air and more fuel can be drawn into an engine. Any time the mass of fuel and air entering an engine increases, engine performance also increases. As an additional consideration, when the water content of the air increases, a large quantity of oxygen molecules are displaced from the volume of air. In addition, since the water vapor is non-combustible, it causes the engine's volumetric efficiency to decrease. Therefore, the result of a fuel/air mixture with a high water content is a decrease in engine power output regardless of the aircraft's altitude.

FUEL/AIR RATIOS

The proportion of fuel and air that enters an engine is referred to as an air/fuel ratio or **mixture ratio**. For example, a mixture containing 12 pounds of air and 1 pound of fuel is referred to as a ratio of 12 to 1 (12:1). A mixture ratio can also be expressed as a decimal. For example, a ratio of 12:1 is equivalent to a .083 fuel/air mixture. As a general rule, an air/fuel ratio between 8:1 and 16:1 will burn in an engine cylinder. However, mixture ratios consisting of less than 8 parts air or more than 16 parts air typically result in incomplete combustion.

Theoretically, the perfect mixture for combustion of air and fuel is 1 pound of air for .067 pounds of fuel, or a 15:1 ratio. This chemically ideal ratio is known as a **stoichiometric mixture**. With a stoichiometric mixture, all the available fuel and oxygen are used for combustion. In addition, a stoichiometric mixture produces the highest combustion temperatures because the greatest amount of heat is released from the mass of air/fuel charge. However, a stoichiometric mixture is not necessarily an ideal mixture for proper engine operation. The reason for this is that, a reciprocating engine is not 100 percent efficient at burning fuel. Therefore, a richer mixture is required to provide adequate engine performance. For example, a typical reciprocating engine develops maximum power with a air/fuel mixture of approximately 12:1. On the other hand, an engine operates at maximum economy with an air/fuel mixture ratio of close to stoichometric, or 15:1.

MIXTURE RATIO TERMINOLOGY

Two common terms that are often used to describe a fuel/air mixture are **lean** and **rich**. In actuality, both terms are relative and describe variations in mixture ratios. Lean indicates that air has been added or fuel has been removed from a given mixture. As an example, a mixture ratio of 10:1 is leaner than a mixture of 8:1. On the other hand, rich indicates that air has been removed or fuel has been added to a given mixture. In other words, a mixture ratio of 8:1 is richer than a mixture ratio of 10:1.

In many cases, the position of the mixture control in the cockpit used to obtain a desired performance characteristic is expressed using a variety of terms. For example, full rich, idle-cutoff, lean best power, rich best power, and best economy are all terms that describe a specific fuel consumption rate that is determined by the position of the mixture control. For example, **full rich** describes the position of the mixture control which provides the maximum fuel flow from the fuel metering unit. This condition is achieved by placing the mixture control in the full forward position and is normally used while operating an aircraft on the ground. However, if the aircraft is operated at a high elevation airport, the mixture should be leaned slightly to compensate for the less dense air. Leaning is accomplished by pulling the mixture control back and helps prevent an overly rich mixture from entering the engine and fouling the spark plugs.

Idle-cutoff describes the position of the mixture control which completely cuts off the flow of fuel to the engine. This condition is achieved by placing the mixture control in the full out, or aft, position. The idle-cutoff position is always used to shut down an engine because it stops the flow of fuel and allows the engine to burn off all the fuel in the intake manifold and cylinders. This way, the engine is less likely to inadvertently start if the propeller is moved by hand.

Lean best power and **rich best power** describe the range of mixture ratios that provide the maximum rpm or manifold pressure for a given throttle position. Although both mixtures produce the same engine performance, a lean best power setting uses slightly less fuel than a rich best power setting.

The final term, **best economy**, describes the mixture ratio that will develop the greatest amount of engine power for the least amount of fuel flow. This condition is usually obtained by leaning the mixture control until the highest exhaust gas temperature and rpm are achieved while throttle is in a set position. Although this mixture ratio provides the best fuel economy, it can cause an engine to exceed its rated temperature limits if it is used for extended periods of time. Therefore, most engine manufacturers recommend using the best power mixture ratio for extended operations rather than the best economy ratio.

LEANING TECHNIQUES

To achieve a desired mixture ratio, the mixture control must be adjusted to compensate for varying conditions. For example, as an aircraft climbs, the amount of air entering an engine decreases as air density decreases. Any time less air enters an engine, the mixture ratio becomes excessively rich. Therefore, to maintain adequate engine performance as an aircraft climbs, the mixture must be leaned. On some aircraft, this is accomplished automatically; however, most reciprocating engines require the operator to manually lean the mixture.

When leaning the fuel/air mixture, different techniques may be used depending on the engine instruments installed in the aircraft. Engine instruments typically used to determine when the proper mixture ratio has been obtained include the tachometer, manifold pressure gauge, or an exhaust gas temperature gauge, if available.

When leaning is accomplished using a tachometer, gradually pull the mixture control aft toward the idle-cutoff position. While accomplishing this, monitor the tachometer to determine when the rpm reaches a maximum value. The position of the mixture control where the rpm is at its highest value is considered to be the engine's best economy ratio. To obtain the engine's best power ratio, enrichen the mixture by pushing the mixture control slightly forward. This technique may be used with all engines equipped with a fixed-pitch propeller aircraft.

Leaning the fuel/air mixture in an engine equipped with a constant speed propeller operating in its governing range is accomplished in a different manner than an engine with a fixed-pitch propeller. Simply stated, a governing range is where the propeller automatically changes pitch to maintain a constant engine rpm. Based on this, it becomes obvious that, if the rpm remains constant, the engine tachometer does not reflect changes in engine power. In this situation, the manifold pressure gauge is used in the same manner as the tachometer when leaning.

The most accurate method of leaning the mixture requires the use of an exhaust gas temperature gauge. An exhaust gas temperature, or EGT, gauge uses a temperature sensing thermocouple in the exhaust gas stream to measure the temperature of the exhaust gases. If you recall from your earlier studies, as the mixture is leaned, the temperature within the cylinders increases. Therefore, by monitoring the exhaust temperature you can set the fuel/air mixture for best economy or best power. For example, leaning the fuel/air mixture to obtain a peak EGT value indicates a mixture that results in best economy and maximum endurance. On the other hand, depending on the engine manufacturer's instructions, a common method of setting best power is to adjust the mixture to peak EGT then enrichen it to approximately 25°F cooler than peak EGT.

SPECIFIC FUEL CONSUMPTION

An engine's specific fuel consumption is the number of pounds of fuel burned per hour to produce one horsepower. For example, if an engine burns 12 gallons per hour while producing 180 brake horsepower, specific fuel consumption (SFC) is .4 pounds per horsepower hour. Most modern aircraft reciprocating engines have a brake specific fuel consumption that is between .4 and .5 pounds per horsepower hour. While not actually a measure of power, specific fuel consumption is used to determine the efficiency of an engine.

A properly functioning engine should have the specific fuel consumption values specified by the manufacturer. To verify specific fuel consumption

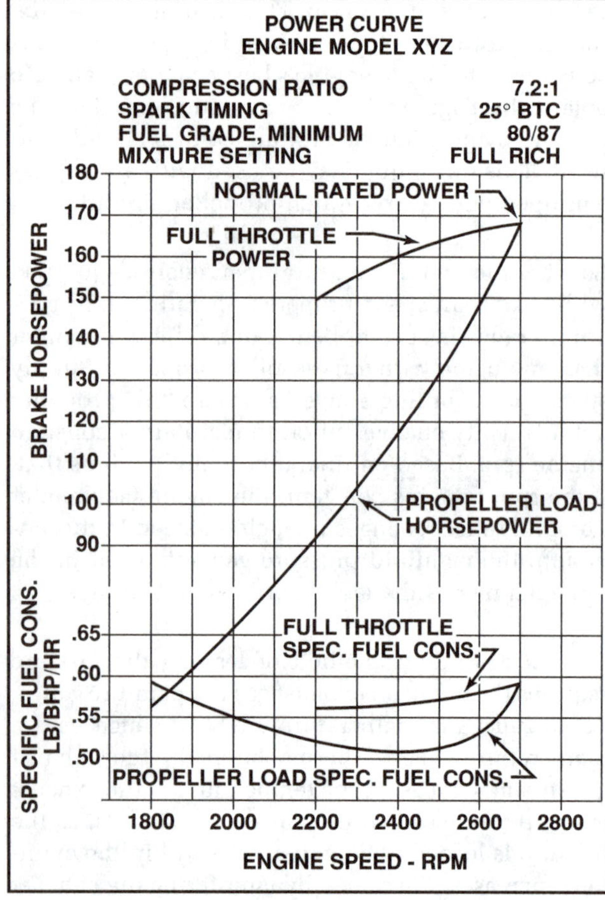

Figure 7-19. By operating an engine at a specific rpm for a given time period while monitoring the fuel flow rate from the metering unit during that time, you can determine the overall performance of the engine and confirm the proper operation of a fuel metering device.

values and the proper operation of a fuel metering device, you must perform an engine runup. Since it is not easy to measure an engine's brake horsepower, you can use other performance data to check the performance of the engine. For example, by running an engine at a given rpm for a specific period, while closely monitoring fuel flow, you can determine the engine's SFC. In order to simplify the presentation of data, several manufacturers provide an engine's specific fuel consumption on a chart. [Figure 7-19]

DETONATION AND PREIGNITION

A fuel/air mixture burns in a very controlled and predictable way when normal combustion takes place. Even though the process happens in a fraction of a second, the mixture starts burning at the point where it is ignited by the spark plugs, then burns away from the plugs until it is all consumed. The dual spark plug design common in most aircraft reciprocating engines promotes a complete even burn of the fuel/air charge by providing two ignition sparks at the same time. The plugs are located across from one another so that as the flame advances from each spark plug, the mixture burns in a wavelike pattern toward the center of the cylinder. This type of combustion causes a smooth buildup of temperature and pressure so that maximum force is applied to the piston at exactly the right time in the power stroke.

Detonation is the uncontrolled, explosive ignition of the fuel/air mixture in a cylinder. Detonation causes high cylinder temperatures and pressures which lead to a rough running engine, overheating, and power loss. If detonation is allowed to occur, damage or failure of pistons, cylinders, or valves can happen. The high pressures and temperatures, combined with the high turbulence generated, cause a "hammering" or "scrubbing" action on a cylinder and piston that can burn a hole completely through either of them in seconds. If it weren't for the noise created by the propeller, detonation could be identified by an audible "knocking" from within the engine.

Detonation is caused by several factors including the use of a lower-than-specified octane fuel or an excessively lean fuel/air mixture. In either case, the engine's operating temperature increases which, in turn, increases the chance of detonation.

Preignition takes place when the fuel/air mixture ignites too soon. It is caused by hot spots in a cylinder that ignite the fuel/air mixture before the spark plugs fire. A hot spot can be caused by something as simple as a carbon particle, overheated valve edges, silica deposits on a spark plug, or a red-hot spark plug electrode. Hot spots are caused by poor engine cooling, dirty intake air filters, or shutting down the engine at high rpm. When the engine continues running after the ignition is turned off, preignition may be the cause.

Preignition and detonation can occur simultaneously, and one may cause the other. Sometimes it is difficult to distinguish between the two, but either condition can cause an engine to run rough and have high operating temperatures.

BACKFIRE AND AFTERFIRE

While a lean fuel/air mixture can result in detonation, there is a point where the fuel/air mixture can become so lean that it burns at an extremely slow rate. This occurs because the fuel content is so low that it can barely support combustion. With a slow burning fuel/air mixture, it is possible for the fuel/air charge to still be burning when the intake valve opens on the next cycle. In this case, when the fresh fuel/air charge enters the cylinder, it is ignited before the intake valve closes and the engine backfires through the induction manifold, fuel metering unit, and out the induction air filter.

Therefore, backfiring always occurs in the induction system. This is completely different from **afterfiring** which occurs in the exhaust system. In most cases, afterfiring results from an excessively rich fuel/air mixture. For example, when an excessively rich fuel/air mixture is ignited, the lack of oxygen causes the mixture to burn slowly. If the fuel/air mixture is not completely burned before the exhaust valve opens, it mixes with the air in the exhaust system and continues to burn. This typically causes flames to appear as the unburned mixture exits the exhaust stacks.

CARBURETORS

Carburetors are classified as either **updraft** or **downdraft** depending on the direction of airflow through the carburetor. As you would guess, in an updraft carburetor the air flows upward through the carburetor barrel. On the other hand, in a downdraft carburetor, the air flows downward through the carburetor barrel. Most aircraft utilize an updraft carburetor that is mounted under the engine. Regardless of the type, all carburetors mix fuel and air to establish an optimum fuel/air ratio. In addition, all carburetors atomize fuel and produce a fuel/air mixture which is then distributed as evenly as possible to each of the engine's cylinders. Ideally, the fuel/air charge reaching each cylinder has exactly the same volume and fuel/air ratio. However, in reality, both the volume and ratio of the fuel/air charge that reaches the cylinders varies because of the different distances it has to travel through an induction manifold.

CARBURETOR VENTURI PRINCIPLES

All carburetors depend on the differential pressure created at the venturi throat to measure the amount of air delivered to an engine and meter the proper amount of fuel. If you recall, when air flows through a venturi, the speed of the air flowing through the venturi throat increases. At the same time, the pressure and temperature of the air in the venturi throat decreases. This inverse relationship can be explained by analyzing the airflow in terms of volume. For example, when a specific volume of air enters a venturi, the exact same volume of air leaves the venturi. The only way this can happen is if the air speeds up as it passes through the venturi throat. Based on this, the greater the volume of air passing through a venturi, the greater the speed increase required at the venturi throat. By the same token, the greater the speed increase, the greater the pressure drop.

To control the volume of air that passes through a venturi, all carburetors are equipped with a **throttle valve**. The throttle valve, sometimes referred to as a **butterfly valve**, consists of a flat, circular piece of metal that is always installed between the venturi and the engine. When the throttle valve is positioned parallel with the airflow, the maximum volume of air and fuel enter the engine and the engine develops its maximum power. In this case, the only thing that limits the volume of air entering the engine is the venturi. However, as the throttle valve is moved so that it is perpendicular to the airflow, less air is admitted into the engine and engine power output decreases. [Figure 7-20]

The position of a throttle valve is controlled by a mechanical linkage that is connected to the throttle lever in the cockpit. As the throttle lever is pushed forward, the throttle valve opens and engine power output increases. However, as the throttle lever is pulled backward, the throttle valve closes and engine power decreases.

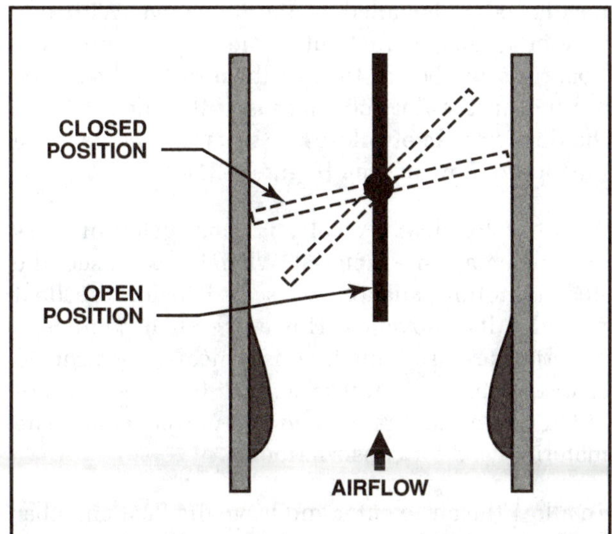

Figure 7-20. When the throttle valve is positioned parallel with the airflow, the maximum volume of air and fuel enter the engine. However, as the throttle valve is moved so it is perpendicular with the airflow, less air and fuel is admitted into the engine.

The size and shape of the venturi in a carburetor varies with the size and requirements of the engine for which the carburetor is designed. Therefore, although the carburetor installed on similar engines may appear to be identical, the size of the venturi is usually different.

CARBURETOR SYSTEMS

To provide for proper engine operation under various engine loads, speeds, and air densities, most carburetors include at least the following five systems:

1. Main metering
2. Idling
3. Mixture control
4. Accelerating
5. Power enrichment or economizer

Although most carburetors utilize each of these systems, the construction and principle of operation of these systems varies among carburetor types. Therefore, each system will be described in detail as it relates to the type of carburetor it is installed on. The two types of carburetors that are discussed here are the float-type carburetor and the pressure-injection carburetor.

FLOAT-TYPE CARBURETORS

The float-type carburetor is so named because it uses a float to regulate the amount of fuel that enters a carburetor. In a float-type carburetor, fuel is stored in a **float chamber**. The amount of fuel allowed to flow into a float chamber is controlled by a float-operated **needle valve** installed in the fuel inlet. With this type of system, as fuel enters the float chamber, the float rises and begins to close the needle valve. Once the fuel in the float chamber is at the correct level, the float completely closes, or seats the needle valve to stop the flow of fuel. [Figure 7-21]

A carburetor float typically is constructed of brass or some composite material. When brass is used, the float is hollow and the air sealed inside the float provides its buoyancy. However, when composite materials are used, the float is typically constructed as a solid piece. In this case, float buoyancy is provided by the air trapped in the porous composite material used for construction.

To allow the air to enter and leave the float chamber as the fuel level rises and falls, all float chambers are vented. A typical vent passage opens directly to the atmosphere or into the air intake. This way, the air pressure within the float chamber is always the same as atmospheric.

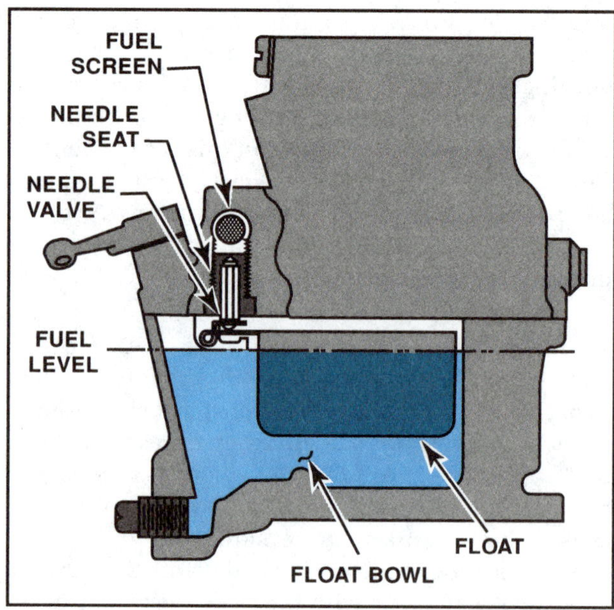

Figure 7-21. All float-type carburetors store a quantity of fuel in a float chamber. The amount of fuel allowed into a float chamber is controlled by a float actuated needle valve.

MAIN METERING

The purpose of the main metering system is to supply the correct amount of fuel to the engine at all speeds above idle. The main metering system is comprised of one or more venturi tubes, a main metering jet and discharge nozzle, and a throttle valve. [Figure 7-22]

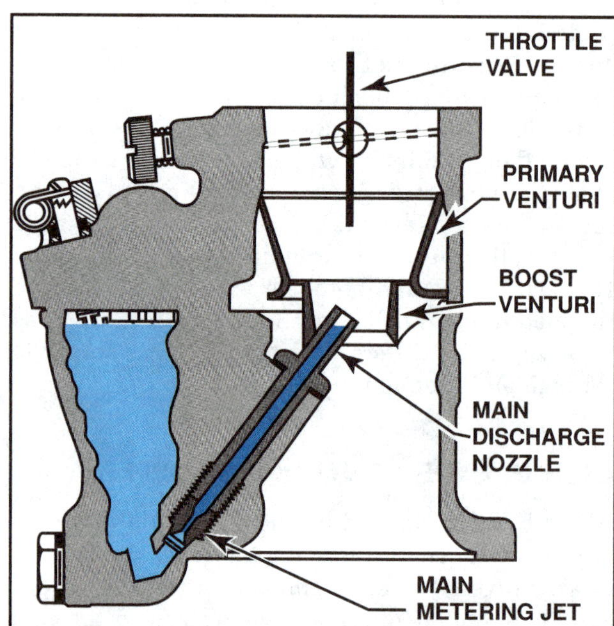

Figure 7-22. The primary components of a float-type carburetor's main metering system include one or more venturi tubes, a metering jet and discharge nozzle, and a throttle valve.

Fuel metering begins with the venturi. If you recall, as air flows through the venturi, its pressure decreases. It is this drop in pressure that the metering system relies on to meter the appropriate amount of fuel. In some carburetors, a single venturi is unable to create the pressure drop necessary to meter fuel. In this case, a second **boost venturi** is installed inside, or just prior to, the **primary venturi**.

The discharge nozzle delivers fuel to the intake air and is installed between the float chamber and the venturi. When an engine is at rest, the fuel level in the discharge nozzle matches that in the float chamber. In most cases, the float maintains a fuel level that is approximately 1/8 inch below the opening in the discharge nozzle. This distance is referred to as the **fuel metering head**. The purpose of the fuel metering head is to prevent fuel from leaking out of the nozzle when the engine is shut down.

The operation of the discharge nozzle is based on the difference in pressure between the venturi and the float chamber. For example, when no air flows through the venturi, the pressure in the float chamber and venturi are the same. However, once air starts flowing through the venturi, the air pressure in the venturi decreases below the air pressure in the float chamber. This pressure differential, or metering force, forces fuel to flow through the main metering jet and out the discharge nozzle into the airstream. Based on this, the greater the pressure differential between the float chamber and discharge nozzle, the more fuel is discharged. However, the maximum amount of fuel that can flow through the discharge nozzle is ultimately limited by the size of the main metering jet. [Figure 7-23]

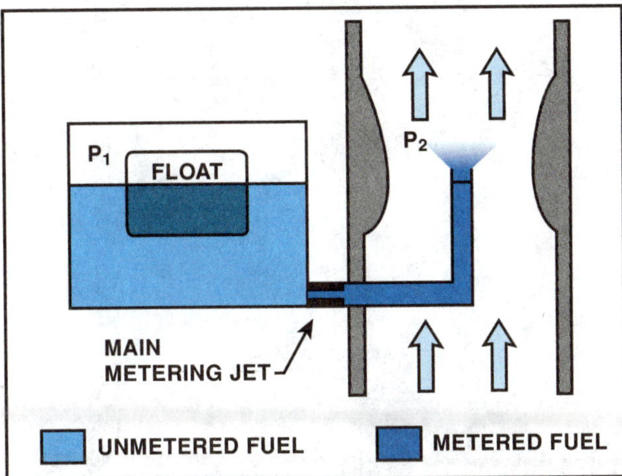

Figure 7-23. When intake air passes through the venturi, the pressure within the venturi (P_2) decreases below the pressure in the float chamber (P_1). This pressure differential forces fuel to flow from the discharge nozzle and into the airstream. The greater the pressure differential between P_1 and P_2, the greater the amount of fuel that is discharged.

Figure 7-24. A liquid's surface tension results from the cohesiveness of its molecules and tends to prevent the liquid from readily breaking apart. This can be seen when a container is slightly overfilled.

In most cases, a pressure differential of at least 0.5 in. Hg. is required to raise the fuel past the fuel metering head. At high power settings, the pressure differential is more than high enough to ensure a continuous flow of fuel. However, at low engine speeds, when the pressure differential is low, fuel delivery from the discharge nozzle is hampered by the fuel's surface tension. **Surface tension** is a physical property of fluids that is created by the cohesive forces of molecules. Because of this cohesiveness, liquids tend to hold together instead of spread out or break up. An example of a liquid's cohesive force is seen when a container is slightly overfilled. [Figure 7-24]

Air Bleed

When fuel enters a discharge nozzle, its surface tension tends to cause the fuel to adhere to itself and the walls of the nozzle. This can cause the fuel to intermittently discharge from the nozzle in large droplets instead of a fine, continuous spray. To decrease the surface tension of the fuel, an air bleed system is typically incorporated into the metering system.

An air bleed consists of a passage with a small calibrated orifice. One end of the passage opens into the discharge nozzle slightly below the fuel level while the other end opens into an area behind the venturi where the air is relatively motionless and the pressure is near atmospheric. To explain how the bleed air system works, consider a liquid filled container with a drinking straw. If you were to suck on the straw, a solid stream of liquid would smoothly rise up in the straw. However, if a small hole is pierced in the side of the straw above the liquid, air, in the form of bubbles, would be introduced into the liquid as it

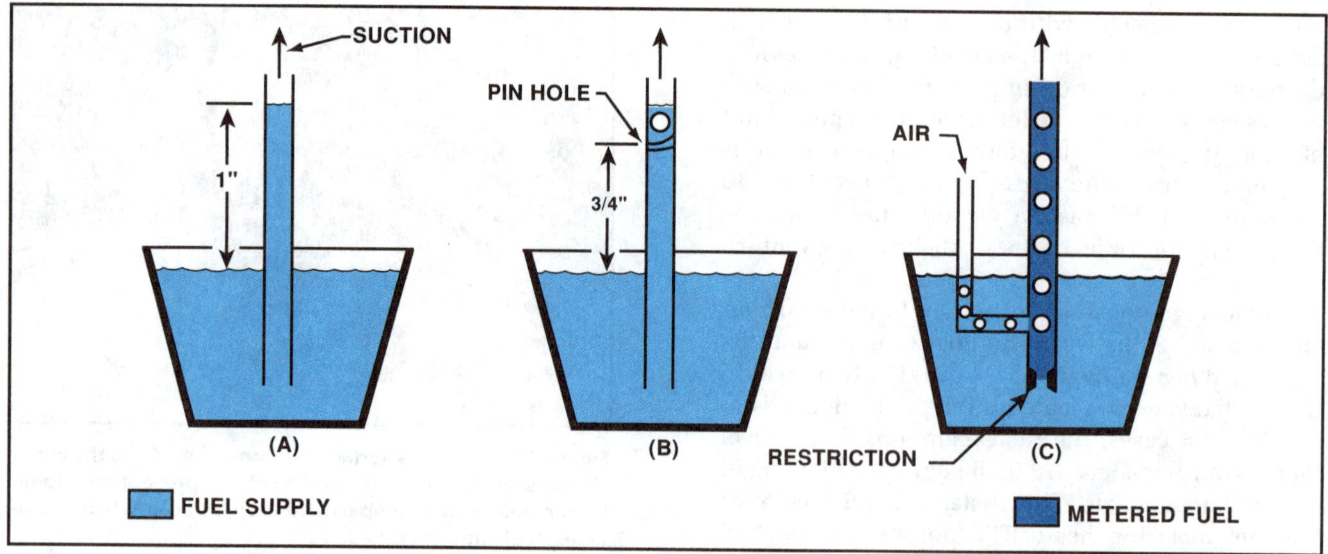

Figure 7-25. (A) — Air pressure, pushing down on a fluid in an open container, moves a solid stream of fluid up a straw when a vacuum is applied to the straw. (B) — A pin hole in the side of the straw introduces a small amount of air into the liquid stream, disrupting the solid stream and greatly reducing the amount of fluid that can be drawn through the straw. (C) — When air is introduced below the liquid level and a metering orifice is added, the fluid and the air emulsify better, resulting in a finely broken fluid/air charge that can rise in the straw.

is drawn up through the straw. The amount of air drawn through the pin hole is limited by the size of the pin hole and the opening in the bottom of the straw. For example, if the size of the pin hole is increased without increasing the amount of vacuum, the amount of liquid that can be drawn through the straw is dramatically reduced. However, if a metering orifice is placed at the bottom of the straw and air is introduced through a siphon tube below the level of the liquid, a larger amount of air can be drawn into the liquid stream. The greater amount of air bleed produces an even emulsion of air and liquid that can still be drawn up into the straw. [Figure 7-25]

When an air bleed is installed in a carburetor, the low pressure at the discharge nozzle draws fuel out of the float chamber and bleed air from behind the venturi. Ultimately, the bleed air and fuel mix in the discharge nozzle, creating an emulsion, or mixture, which lowers the fuel's density and helps to break up its surface tension. By disrupting this surface tension, the fuel discharges from the nozzle in a fine, uniform spray which promotes vaporization. [Figure 7-26]

An air bleed passage is equipped with an orifice that is matched to the discharge nozzle to provide the proper airflow. Therefore, if an air bleed passage should become either partially or completely blocked, the mixture will become excessively rich at higher power settings.

IDLING SYSTEM

When an engine is idling, the throttle valve is nearly closed. As a result, the air velocity through the venturi is greatly reduced which, in turn, dramatically reduces the pressure differential between the venturi and float chamber. In fact, in some cases, the pressure differential may be so low that a sufficient

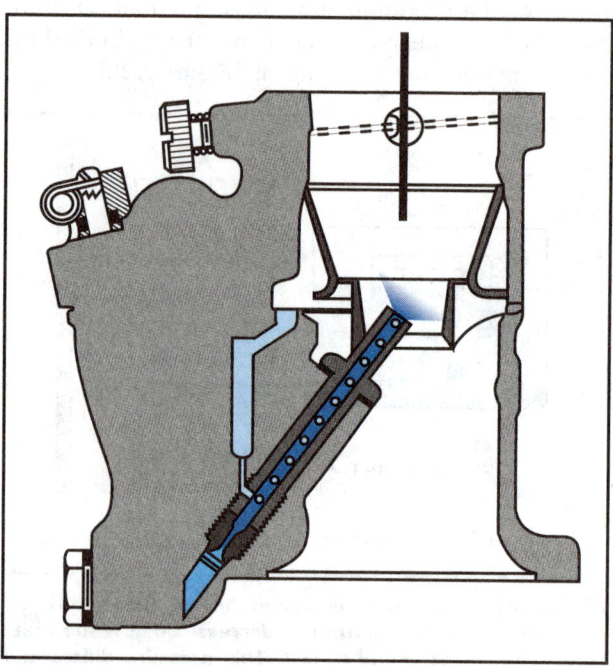

Figure 7-26. The incorporation of an air bleed in the main metering system decreases the fuel's surface tension which improves fuel atomization.

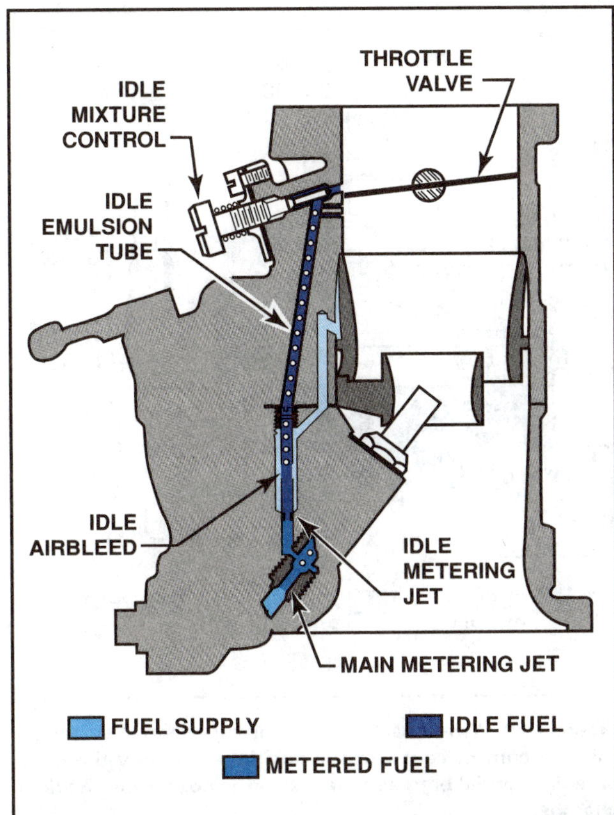

Figure 7-27. A typical idling system consists of multiple discharge ports in the carburetor barrel near the edge of the throttle valve.

amount of fuel cannot be drawn from the main discharge nozzle. To correct this condition, a series of two or three small passages are provided in the carburetor barrel near the edge of the throttle valve where a small amount of air can still flow. These passages, commonly referred to as **idle discharge ports**, or **idle jets**, are connected by an idle emulsion tube to an **annulus**, or ring, that draws fuel from the outlet of the main metering jet. The emulsion tube contains an idle metering jet that regulates the amount of fuel that can be drawn from the main discharge system and an idle air bleed that aids in emulsifying the fuel. [Figure 7-27]

When the throttle is closed, a venturi is established near the discharge ports. The resulting low pressure area created by the venturi draws fuel from the discharge ports and allows fuel to be discharged into the airstream.

To control the amount of fuel being discharged into the airstream, an adjustable needle valve is positioned in the upper idle discharge port. When the needle valve is screwed in, the amount of fuel discharged is reduced, and the idle mixture becomes leaner. Conversely, by unscrewing the valve, the amount of fuel discharged increases to enrichen the idle mixture. Adjustments to this valve are easily accomplished by way of a thumb screw, that is accessible from the outside of the carburetor. As a general rule, the mixture provided by the idling system is rich when compared to the main metering system. This is necessary for engine cooling since airflow around the cylinders of an idling engine is typically inadequate for effective cooling.

In a multiple port idle discharge system, as the throttle is opened, the edge of the throttle valve moves past each idle discharge port. As more of these ports become exposed, more fuel is allowed into the throat of the carburetor. By doing this, a smooth transition is provided between idle power settings and higher power settings where the main discharge nozzle becomes effective.

The relative position of the throttle to the idle discharge ports is an important consideration during engine starting. For example, if the throttle opening is less than that called for, an excessively rich mixture may be provided to the engine. This is because a smaller opening between the butterfly and throttle body creates a high vacuum near the idle discharge ports which draws more fuel.

MIXTURE CONTROL

A carburetor's mixture control system regulates the ratio of fuel and air supplied to the engine. If you recall, control of the fuel/air mixture is required in aircraft to allow the engine to operate efficiently at various altitudes and in a variety of conditions. The two most common methods used to control the mixture include the use of either a variable orifice or back suction.

Variable Orifice

With a variable orifice mixture control, the float chamber is vented to the atmosphere and a valve is installed in the float chamber that controls the size of the passage between the float chamber to the main metering jet. Some carburetors use a needle valve to control fuel flow while other carburetors

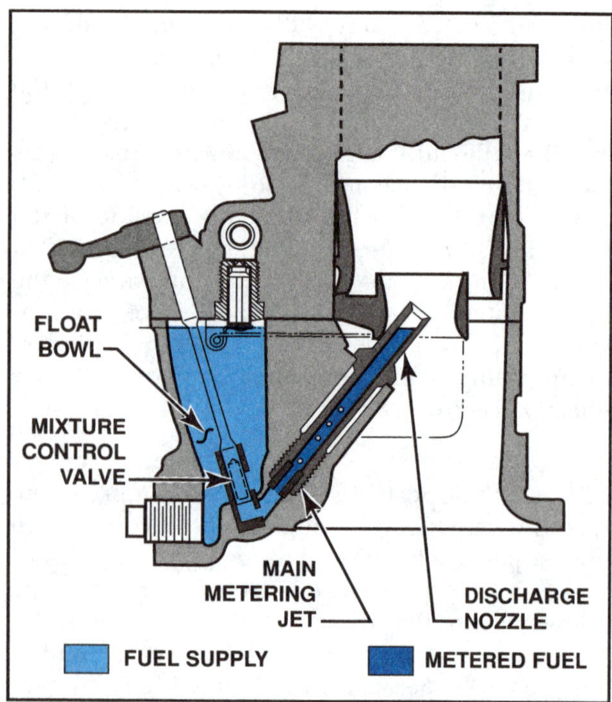

Figure 7-28. In a carburetor with a variable orifice mixture control, the mixture ratio is adjusted by changing the size of the passage between the float chamber and metering jet.

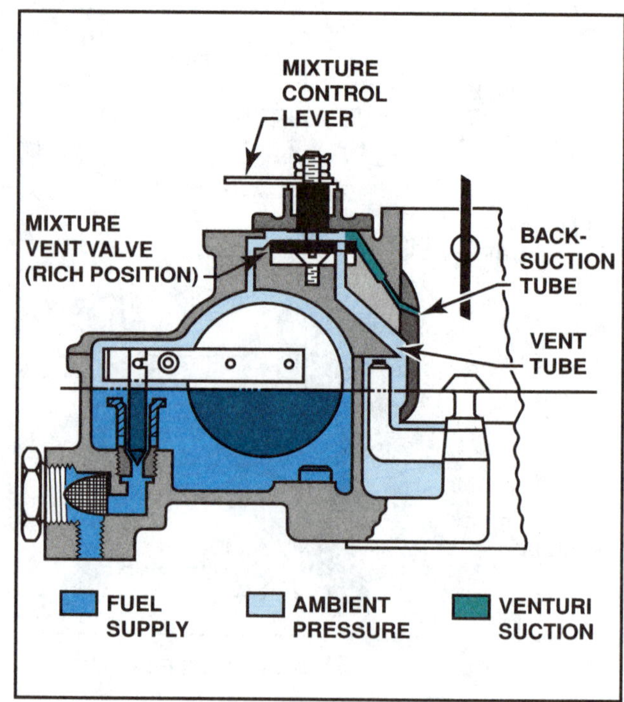

Figure 7-29. With a back suction mixture control system, a mixture control vent valve is positioned to vary the pressure differential between the discharge nozzle and the float chamber.

use a step-cut rotary valve. In either case, the valve is installed in series with the main fuel metering jet. [Figure 7-28]

When the mixture valve is in the idle-cutoff position, no fuel flows to the main metering jet. On the other hand, when the valve is fully open, the amount of fuel allowed to flow to the discharge nozzle is restricted only by the main metering jet. When placed in an intermediate position, the amount of fuel permitted to flow to the discharge nozzle is determined by the size of the opening in the mixture valve.

Back Suction Mixture Control

With a back suction mixture control system, low pressure is used to control the pressure differential between the venturi and the float chamber. With this type of system, low pressure air is taken from the venturi and routed through a mixture control vent valve into the float chamber. [Figure 7-29]

On carburetors that use a back suction mixture control, the float chamber is vented to the atmosphere and to a low pressure area near the venturi. With this type of system, when the mixture control is in the rich position, the vent valve is full open and the float chamber is vented to the atmosphere. This creates the largest pressure differential between the float chamber and discharge nozzle and, therefore, allows the greatest amount of fuel to flow to the discharge nozzle. On the other hand, when the mixture control is placed in the idle-cutoff position, the vent valve vents the float chamber to the low pressure air in the venturi. This eliminates the pressure differential between the float chamber and the discharge nozzle, thereby stopping the flow of fuel. Based on this, when the vent valve is placed in an intermediate position, the float chamber is vented to a combination of atmospheric air and venturi air. The combined air pressure of the two dictates the pressure differential between the float chamber and discharge nozzle which, in turn, controls the amount of fuel that is discharged.

Automatic Mixture Control

A few float-type carburetors utilize a mixture control system that automatically maintains the proper fuel/air mixture during flight. With this type of system, as an aircraft ascends, the mixture is automatically leaned to provide the optimum fuel/air ratio.

Likewise, as the aircraft descends, the automatic mixture control enrichens the mixture.

The simplest type of automatic mixture control (AMC) utilizes a sealed bellows that positions either a back suction or variable orifice type mixture control through an actuator. With this type of system, as the aircraft climbs, the bellows expands and reduces the amount of fuel permitted to flow to the discharge nozzle. This leans the fuel/air mixture allowing the engine to produce its maximum power output. On the other hand, as the aircraft descends, the bellows contracts and enrichens the mixture.

In aircraft that utilize an automatic mixture control you must be familiar with engine operational problems that indicate a malfunction with the mixture control system. For example, if an aircraft experiences rising cylinder head temperatures during a descent, this may indicate that the mixture is becoming progressively leaner. On aircraft equipped with an automatic mixture control system, this could be caused by the control actuator sticking in the extended position. On the other hand, if the engine does not produce full power at altitude, the control actuator could be stuck in the retracted position or the bellows may be punctured. In either case, an excessively rich mixture is provided to the engine.

ACCELERATION SYSTEM

When the throttle of a carburetor is rapidly opened, the airflow through the carburetor increases before the discharge nozzle has an opportunity to increase the amount of fuel flow. This delayed response creates a momentary leaning of the fuel/air mixture that can cause an engine to initially stagger before accelerating. To prevent this, many carburetors are equipped with an acceleration system. An acceleration system provides an immediate, but brief, increase in fuel flow in the throat of the carburetor to enrichen the mixture. By providing this extra fuel, the engine can accelerate smoothly and quickly, until the discharge nozzle can deliver fuel at a rate that is proportional to the airflow rate. The two most commonly used acceleration systems are the acceleration well and accelerator pump systems.

Acceleration Well

The simplest type of acceleration system uses an acceleration well in the main discharge nozzle. An

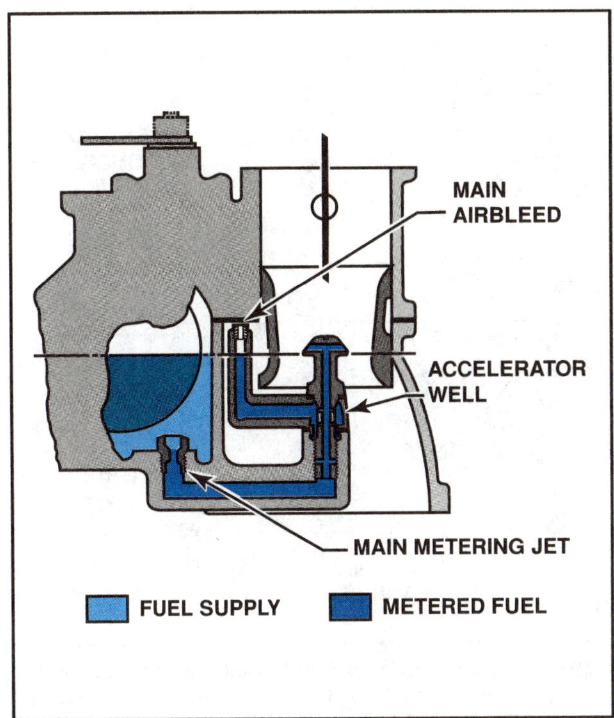

Figure 7-30. An acceleration well consists of an annular chamber that stores a charge of fuel around the main discharge nozzle. With this type of acceleration system, when the throttle is rapidly advanced, the fuel in the acceleration well discharges into the airstream to temporarily enrichen the mixture.

acceleration well is basically an enlarged annular chamber that surrounds the main discharge nozzle at the main air bleed junction. When the engine is running at a set speed, a charge of fuel is stored in the acceleration well. This way, when the throttle is rapidly advanced, the excess fuel in the acceleration well is drawn out through the discharge nozzle so ample fuel is available to produce a rich mixture. [Figure 7-30]

Accelerator Pump

A second type of acceleration system uses an accelerator pump to provide a momentary rich mixture when the throttle is advanced rapidly. A typical accelerator pump consists of a leather packing that is held against the walls of a pump chamber by a coiled spring. The pump is connected to the throttle valve shaft and, therefore, is actuated by the throttle linkage. This way, when the throttle valve is closed, the accelerator pump piston moves upward in the pump chamber. This action causes the pump chamber to fill with fuel from the float bowl through a pump inlet check valve. However, when the throttle valve is opened quickly, the piston moves down and

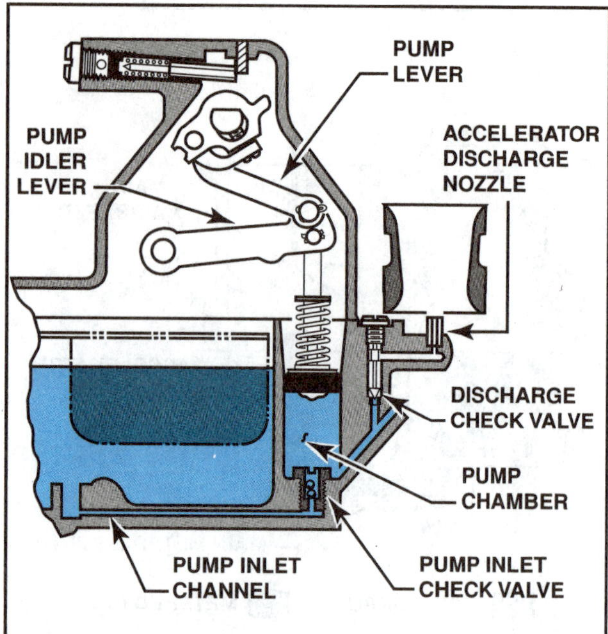

Figure 7-31. On carburetors equipped with an accelerator pump, advancing the throttle rapidly causes an accelerator pump piston to force stored fuel through a separate discharge nozzle into the airstream.

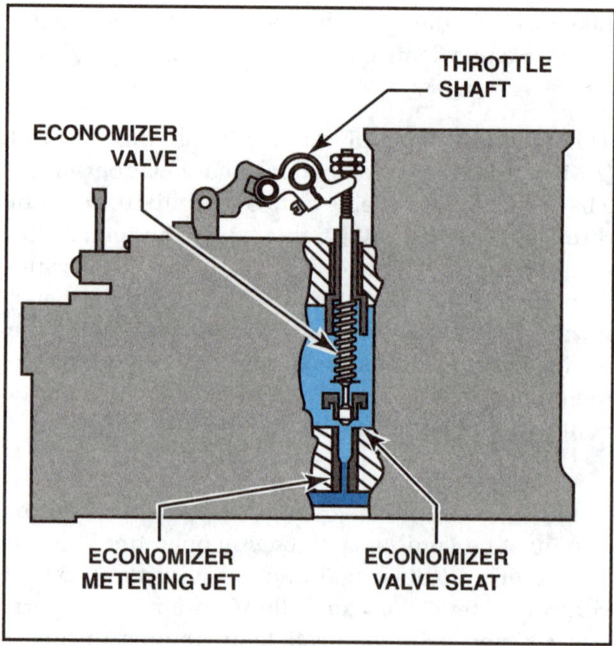

Figure 7-32. A needle-type economizer allows enrichment fuel flow through an economizer metering jet when the needle valve is pulled off its seat at full throttle settings.

forces the stored fuel past a discharge check valve and through a separate discharge nozzle into the airstream. [Figure 7-31]

Since the discharge check valve and nozzle are much smaller than the accelerator pump piston, the speed at which the piston pumps fuel must be limited. This is accomplished by installing the piston on a spring-loaded telescoping shaft. This way, when the throttle valve is opened rapidly, the telescoping shaft contracts so the throttle valve can be fully opened. At the same time, the spring on the telescoping shaft continues to force the piston downward to pump fuel at a rate the discharge nozzle can handle.

POWER ENRICHMENT/ECONOMIZER SYSTEM

Aircraft engines are designed to produce a maximum amount of power consistent with their weight. However, the heat generated while operating at maximum power is typically more than most engines are capable of dissipating without help. Therefore, provisions must be made to facilitate the dissipation of heat. One way of dissipating excess heat is to incorporate a power enrichment system that provides a rich fuel/air mixture at high power settings. This way, the excess fuel in the mixture helps cool the cylinders.

A typical power enrichment system functions at throttle settings above cruise power settings. In addition, although a power enrichment system increases the fuel flow at high power settings it does permit an operator to use a leaner mixture during normal cruise operations. For this reason, a power enrichment system is sometimes referred to as an **economizer system**.

Needle Type

The needle-type economizer system uses an enrichment metering jet that operates in parallel with the main metering jet. With this type of system, a needle valve is installed upstream of the enrichment jet and is operated by the throttle shaft. When the engine is operating below full throttle, a spring holds the needle valve on its seat. This action prevents fuel from flowing through the economizer jet. However, when the throttle is wide open, a linkage lifts the economizer needle valve off its seat to allow fuel to flow through the economizer jet and out to the discharge nozzle. [Figure 7-32]

Air Bleed Type

As you know, when the air velocity through the main venturi increases, the resulting decrease in pressure draws more fuel out of the discharge noz-

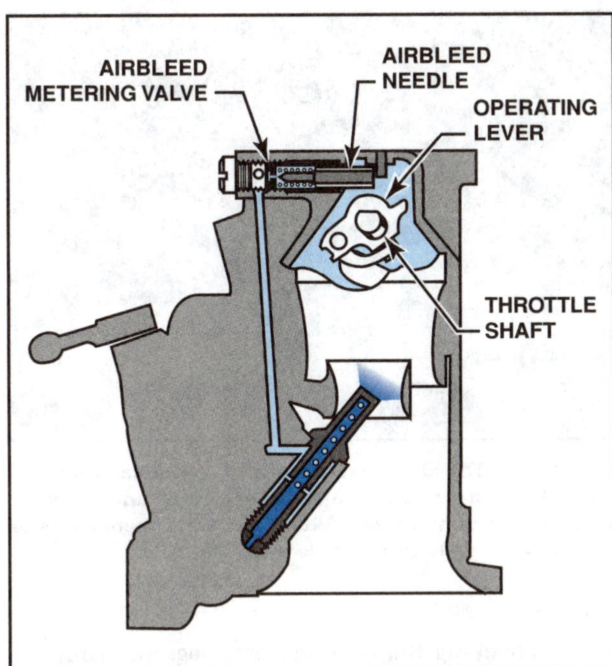

Figure 7-33. An air bleed economizer enrichens the fuel/air mixture at high power settings by controlling the size of the air bleed opening.

zle. In addition, to aid in fuel vaporization, a precisely sized air bleed is installed between the float chamber and the discharge nozzle. If you recall, the larger the air bleed, the leaner the fuel/air mixture. By the same token, if the size of the air bleed is decreased, the fuel/air mixture becomes richer. Based on this, if you can control the size of the air bleed, you can control the mixture ratio.

In an air bleed type economizer system, a needle valve and seat are installed at the air bleed entrance. When the engine is operating at cruising speeds, a spring holds the needle valve off its seat and the full effect of the air bleed is realized at the discharge nozzle. However, when the throttle valve is fully opened, an operating lever attached to the throttle shaft presses against the needle valve thereby restricting the air bleed. By restricting the air bleed, additional fuel is supplied to the discharge nozzle. [Figure 7-33]

CARBURETOR LIMITATIONS

Float-type carburetors are reliable and relatively easy to maintain; however, they do have several distinct disadvantages. For example, float-type carburetors utilize relatively low operating pressures which can result in incomplete vaporization and inadequate fuel flow from the discharge nozzle. In addition, the float design does not respond well to sudden aircraft maneuvers and unusual aircraft attitudes. Another disadvantage of float-type carburetors is their tendency to accumulate ice. **Carburetor icing** occurs when water freezes in a carburetor venturi and restricts airflow to the engine. When this happens, an engine may run rough, lose power, or even quit in flight. Two categories of carburetor icing include fuel evaporation ice and throttle ice.

Fuel evaporation ice results from the temperature drop that occurs when fuel is vaporized in the venturi. As fuel is discharged into the carburetor venturi, it turns into a vapor and absorbs heat from the surrounding air. This evaporation causes air temperature in the venturi to drop 30°F or more. In some cases, this loss of heat is enough to cause the moisture in the air to condense and freeze. Because of this phenomenon, a carburetor is typically one of the first areas in an aircraft to accumulate ice during a flight. In fact, carburetor ice can occur at ambient air temperatures up to 70°F with relative humidity as low as 50 percent. Optimum conditions for carburetor ice exist when the outside air temperature is between 30°F and 40°F and the relative humidity is above 60 percent.

Throttle ice is the term used to describe ice which forms on the rear side of the throttle valve when it is partially closed. As air flows across and around the throttle valve, a low pressure area is created on the downstream side. This has a cooling effect on the fuel/air mixture which can cause moisture to accumulate and freeze on the backside of the valve. Since throttle icing typically occurs with the throttle valve partially closed, a small amount of ice can cause a relatively large reduction in airflow and a corresponding loss of engine power. In severe cases, a large accumulation of ice can jam the throttle and render it immovable. Since the temperature drop created by the low pressure area is small, throttle ice seldom occurs at temperatures above 38°F.

FLOAT-TYPE CARBURETOR MAINTENANCE

As an aviation maintenance technician, you will be expected to perform basic maintenance on float-type carburetors. However, the exact type of maintenance you are allowed to perform depends on your proficiency level, the availability of replacement parts, and the availability of the required service equipment.

The most basic type of carburetor maintenance include those things that can be done while the carburetor is installed on the engine. Examples of this type of maintenance include periodically checking all control linkages for freedom of movement through their full range of motion. In addition, you should examine the fuel lines and air hoses for kinks, distortion, or indications of leakage.

While checking the linkages, lines, and hoses, verify the security of the carburetor mounting on the engine. Give special attention to the mounting flange and inspect it carefully for signs of cracks or leaks. This inspection item is important because a leak between the carburetor body and engine mounting flange allows additional air to be introduced into the fuel/air mixture. Such a defect can lean the fuel/air mixture enough to cause the engine to idle rough and produce less than full power. If severe enough, a leak can lean the mixture enough to cause detonation and engine damage.

Additional carburetor maintenance tasks include checking the main fuel filter and carburetor strainer on a regular basis. Also, you should verify that all safety wire and cotter pins are in place and secure. On carburetors equipped with an automatic mixture control, accelerator pump, or economizer, you should periodically clean all linkages and moving components. After cleaning, many manufacturers recommend applying a small amount of oil to the moving parts.

Although not part of a carburetor, the air filter should also be checked for security, cleanliness, and possible air leaks around the filter. In addition, the carburetor heat valve should be checked for proper travel and for air leaks. If you recall, application of carburetor heat decreases the density of the air entering the carburetor which decreases engine power output.

Idle Mixture Adjustments

For an engine to operate normally at idle rpm, the idle mixture must be adjusted correctly. When the idle mixture is correct, an engine will idle smoothly and spark plug fouling will be kept to a minimum. Based on this, if an engine does not idle properly or will not run at low rpm settings, the idle mixture may be set improperly.

The idle mixture on most carburetors is controlled by a needle valve that is constructed with a screw head or knurled knob to facilitate adjustments. In addition, most idle mixture valves are spring-loaded to maintain a setting. [Figure 7-34]

Figure 7-34. The idle mixture valve of a float carburetor is typically constructed with a screw head or knurled knob to facilitate adjustments. In addition, the adjustment screw is generally spring-loaded to hold a setting.

When checking the idle mixture, begin by running the engine until the cylinder head temperature rises to a normal value. Once the engine is warm, slowly retard the mixture toward the idle-cutoff position while simultaneously observing the tachometer. If the mixture is adjusted properly, the engine rpm will increase slightly before it drops off rapidly. A typical rpm increase is between 25 and 50 rpm, depending on the engine. An immediate rpm decrease with no momentary increase indicates an idle mixture that is too lean. On the other hand, a momentary increase of more than 25 rpm indicates a rich idle mixture. If the aircraft is equipped with a manifold pressure gauge, an optimum idle mixture will result in the manifold pressure decreasing just before it increases when the engine ceases to fire. The amount of manifold pressure drop varies from engine to engine but a typical pressure drop is about 1/4 inch.

If the idle mixture check reveals a setting that is too lean or too rich, increase or decrease the idle fuel flow as required. Continue checking and adjusting the idle mixture until the proper mixture is obtained. After each adjustment, clear the engine by briefly running it at a higher rpm to prevent spark plug fouling. In addition, once the correct rpm indications are obtained, repeat the idle mixture check with the cockpit mixture control several times to ensure a consistent response.

Idle Speed Adjustment

After adjusting the idle mixture, you may need to reset the idle rpm. In most cases, the aircraft manufacturer specifies the appropriate idle speed.

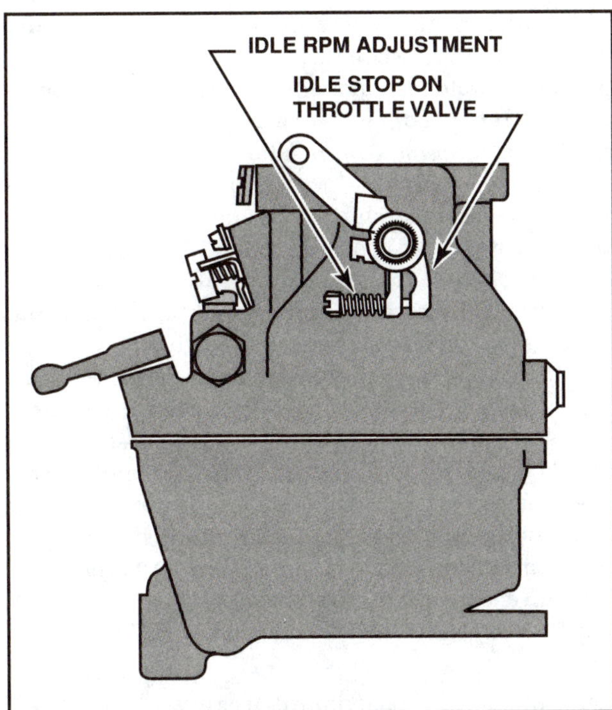

Figure 7-35. To adjust the idle speed on most carburetors, a spring-loaded screw is rotated to provide a contact for the idle stop on the throttle valve linkage.

Typical idle speeds range from 600 to 800 rpm. To allow you to adjust the idle speed, most carburetors are equipped with a spring-loaded adjustment screw. [Figure 7-35]

When checking the idle speed, it is important that the engine be warm before any adjustments are made. In addition, you should check the ignition system for proper operation. If everything is operating properly, open the throttle to clear the engine, then close the throttle and allow the rpm to stabilize. If the engine does not idle at the appropriate rpm, adjust the idle speed screw as needed and recheck the idle speed. To help ensure an accurate idle speed check, open the throttle to clear the engine after each adjustment.

CARBURETOR OVERHAUL

Typically, carburetor overhaul intervals are not specified by the manufacturer. However, it is common practice to overhaul the carburetor at the time of engine overhaul. Overhaul procedures require a complete teardown of the carburetor and a visual inspection of all internal components. In addition, dimensional checks are made to determine serviceability of each reusable component.

Disassembly

Carburetor disassembly should be done on a clean work bench where all carburetor parts can be laid out systematically. Carefully disassemble the carburetor using the sequence recommended in the overhaul manual to prevent accidental damage to delicate parts. In addition, as each assembly is dismantled, try to keep all the parts of that assembly together.

As a professional, you should always use the proper tools for each task to avoid damaging the carburetor parts. Whenever special tools are required, always obtain and utilize them rather than improvising. For example, all carburetors contain several small bronze parts that must be removed and installed with special tools to prevent damage.

Cleaning

Once a carburetor is completely disassembled and a preliminary visual inspection has been accomplished, you must clean all the components that will be reused. Recommended cleaning procedures and solvents are normally specified in the overhaul manual; however, some general procedures apply to most carburetors. For example, all metal parts are first placed in an approved carburetor cleaner, such as Stoddard Solvent, to remove grease and oil. After rinsing in fresh solvent, all parts should be air-dried. Do not use wiping cloths or shop rags for drying because lint and threads which are deposited on the parts can obstruct metering jets and cause close-fitting parts to bind.

Removal of carbon and gum deposits typically requires the use of a decarbonizing solution. However, be aware that certain decarbonizers attack some of the metals used in carburetor components. For that reason, always select decarbonizers approved by the manufacturer and check the instructions before use. In addition, decarbonizing fluids pose a potential health hazard and, therefore, you should always wear vision and hand protection when working with decarbonizer solutions.

After the parts have been decarbonized for the appropriate time, remove them from the decarbonizer bath. Rinse the clean parts with hot water, then dry them with clean, dry, compressed air. Give special attention to the internal passages, bleeds, and recesses when rinsing and drying. Carbon deposits which remain on aluminum parts may be removed with No. 600 wet sandpaper and water. In addition, corrosion on aluminum parts may be removed by immersion in an alkaline cleaner or an equivalent agent recommended by the manufacturer.

Inspection

Once all parts are thoroughly clean, complete a visual inspection to determine the serviceability of each component. In particular, look for corrosion, cracks, bent parts, and crossed threads. Also, parts which are subject to wear should either be dimensionally checked and compared against a table of limits or replaced.

When inspecting the float bowl and venturi castings, pay particular attention to the numerous fuel and air passages. To adequately inspect these passages requires the use of a magnifying glass and light. You should never insert a piece of wire in a passage because a piece of the wire could become lodged in the passage rendering the component useless.

The float assembly must be checked for freedom of motion, proper fit, and proper clearance. In particular, the fulcrum pin and bushing on which a float assembly is hinged should be inspected for binding. Additional inspections that should be made to a float assembly depend on what the float is constructed of. However, all float assemblies should be checked for leaks and buoyancy. This is important because if a float loses its buoyancy, it will sink in the float bowl and allow the fuel level to rise. If this happens, the carburetor may supply an excessively rich mixture. On carburetors that use a hollow brass float, the float should be immersed in hot water to check for possible leaks. Immersing the float in hot water causes the air and any fuel vapor present in the float to expand and bubble through any existing holes or cracks. If bubbles appear during the inspection, mark their location with a pencil. In most cases, a leaky float must be replaced; however, some manufacturers do permit minor leaks to be repaired. A typical repair begins with drilling a very small hole in the float to allow trapped fuel to drain. Next, immerse the float in boiling water to ensure that all fuel has evaporated. Once this is done, the leaks are filled with solder.

On carburetors that use a solid composite float, the float's buoyancy is derived from the air trapped inside the porous material. Because of this, any defects or loss of buoyancy is typically not repairable and requires float replacement.

In addition to inspecting the float, the float needle valve and seat must be inspected for excessive wear, grooves, scratches, and pits. If any sign of wear is visible, the needle valve may not seat properly. Typical symptoms of a needle valve that does not seat properly include a leaking discharge nozzle when the engine is shut down and carburetor flooding. Since a typical needle valve is constructed of hardened steel and the needle valve seat is made from bronze, the seat usually wears faster than the needle. In some cases, the needle valve may have a synthetic rubber tip to provide a more effective sealing surface and reduce wear between the valve tip and seat. If a rubber tip is installed, it should be checked for deterioration and tearing. In most cases, if either the needle valve or its seat show signs of wear, both must be replaced. In rare instances, you may encounter some older models of carburetors that have a needle valve and seat that can be lapped together to re-establish a tight seal.

Once the float and needle valve assembly have been inspected and repaired or replaced as necessary, the components may be reassembled to check the float level. As mentioned earlier, the fuel level in a float-type carburetor is between 3/16 and 1/8 inch from the top of the discharge nozzle. This is important because if the fuel level is too low, a greater pressure differential between the float chamber and venturi is required to draw fuel into the engine. On the other hand, if the fuel level is too high, an excessive amount of fuel could be drawn into the engine. As you recall, the fuel level in a carburetor is determined by the position of the float; therefore, an important thing that should be checked when overhauling a carburetor is the float level.

The method used to check float level depends on the carburetor model. For example, on carburetors where the float is suspended from the throttle body, the float level is measured with a ruler or by slipping the shank of the proper size twist drill between the gasket and float with the throttle body inverted. When the correct clearance exists, the drill should just touch the float without causing it to rise. [Figure 7-36]

When checking the float level in this way, it is important that you verify the clearance on both sides of the float. If the float clearance is incorrect, an adjustment tab is generally provided so you can correct the clearance as necessary.

In other carburetors, the float and needle valve assembly are mounted in the float bowl and fuel must be used to check the float level. To do this,

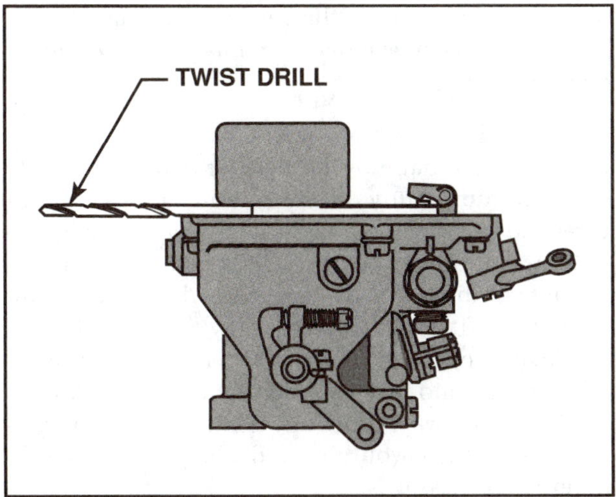

Figure 7-36. The float clearance on some carburetors is measured with a ruler or by slipping the shank of the proper size twist drill between the gasket and float with the throttle body inverted.

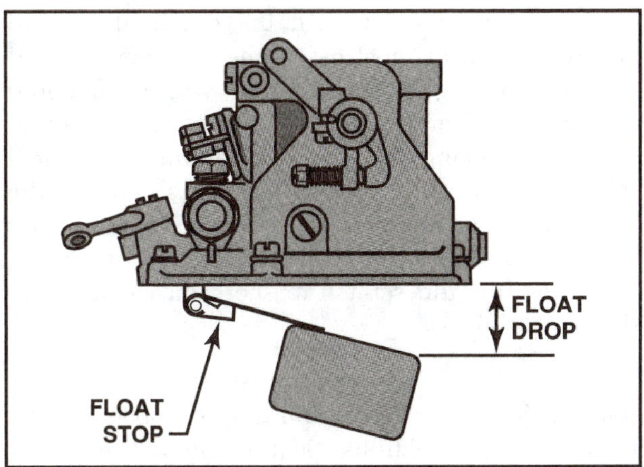

Figure 7-37. To determine the float drop, hold the throttle body in an upright position and measure the distance between the throttle body mounting flange and the top of the float. Once the float drop is known, you can calculate the total float travel by subtracting the float clearance from the float drop.

level the carburetor body on a flow bench and attach a fuel supply of the correct pressure to the fuel inlet. As the float bowl fills, the float will close the needle valve. Once the needle valve completely closes, a depth gauge is used to measure the distance between the surface of the fuel and the carburetor's parting surface. To help ensure an accurate measurement, the fuel level should be measured away from the edge of the float chamber. Measurements taken at the edge of the float bowl tend to be inaccurate because surface tension causes fuel to rise near the float bowl wall. If the fuel level is incorrect, it can be adjusted by inserting or removing shims from underneath the needle valve seat.

Once the proper fuel level is established, some manufacturers require you to check the total float travel. To do this, hold the throttle body in its upright position and let the float rest in its lowest position. The distance from the throttle body mounting flange to the top of the float is referred to as the float drop. To determine the total float travel, subtract the float level from the float drop. [Figure 7-37]

If either the float drop or float travel are insufficient, the float mechanism must be adjusted. Depending on the type of carburetor, adjustments are made by either bending an adjustment tab or filing the float stop.

After establishing the correct float travel, some manufacturers require you to check the side clearance of the float in the float chamber. This may be done with a special cutaway float bowl fixture that mounts to the bottom of the throttle body. After placing the test fixture on the throttle body, the distance between the float and test fixture is measured with a drill rod gauge of specified size. The gauge must pass completely around the float without binding. [Figure 7-38]

In addition to checking the float and needle valve assembly, you must visually inspect and dimensionally check the main metering system components. For example, verify the size of a metering jet

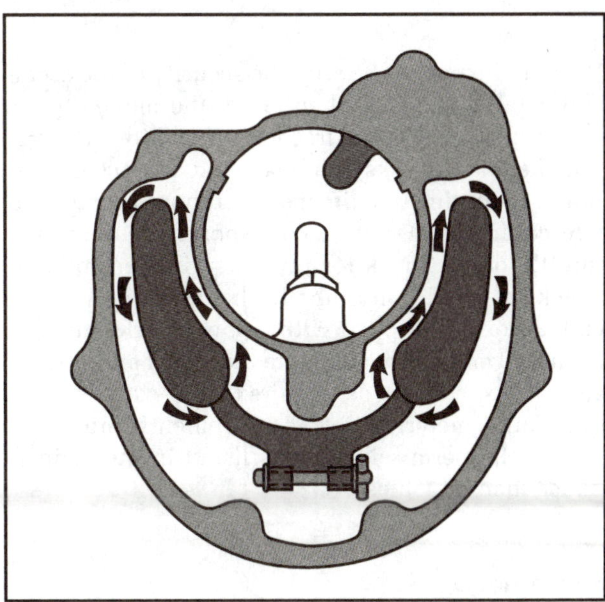

Figure 7-38. To check the side clearance between the float and float bowl, a special test fixture must be used so you can pass a drill rod of a specified size completely around the float.

by comparing the jet with the overhaul manual specifications. In most cases, the number stamped on the metering jet corresponds with a numbered drill size. Therefore, you may verify the correct jet size by inserting the shank of a numbered drill through the orifice. The drill shank should fit the metering jet orifice without excessive play. Do not insert the fluted portion of the drill into the metering jet as it could scratch or score the orifice, rendering it useless.

Inspect the main discharge nozzle for obstructions, kinks, and bent sections. Next, verify that the throttle valve moves freely through its full range of normal travel. In addition, perform a dimensional inspection on the throttle valve shaft and bushings to check for excessive wear and play. Visually check the bleed passages for obstructions and thoroughly examine the venturi area for corrosion, deep scratches, and scoring. When a boost venturi is installed inside the primary venturi, check for broken or bent support arms.

Closely examine the idle discharge jet and the idle system bleeds for obstructions, nicks, dents, and upsets which could narrow the openings. In addition, check to be sure that the mixture control shaft moves freely in the sleeve at the base of the float bowl. After completing the visual inspection, perform a dimensional check to verify that all portions of the mixture control fall within permissible limits as listed in the overhaul manual.

Visually inspect and verify the security of the accelerator pump linkage, then check the moving parts for proper travel and freedom of motion. Several dimensional checks are made on an accelerator pump including the dimension of the spring-loaded telescoping shaft and its corresponding hole in the throttle body. Check for proper spring tension and check the condition of the leather packing. When a carburetor is equipped with a power enrichment or economizer system, complete the visual and dimensional inspections as required. The valve, valve seat, and metering jet measurements must fall within the permissible limits listed in the maintenance manual tables.

REASSEMBLY

With the cleaning and inspection phases of the overhaul complete, reassemble the carburetor in the sequence outlined in the overhaul manual. Any special tools required for the reassembly must be utilized to prevent accidental damage to individual components.

Bear in mind that most carburetor bodies are made of aluminum alloy castings and, therefore, all threaded openings can be damaged fairly easily. To help prevent thread damage, it is common practice to put a drop or two of thread lubricant on threaded fittings before they are installed. However, you should insert at least one thread of the fitting into the casting before lubricant is applied. This way, lubricant is prevented from getting inside the carburetor and plugging the jets or other small passages.

When installing moving components such as the accelerator pump telescoping shaft, you should apply a small amount of lubricating oil to ease reassembly. When installing threaded components, make sure you tighten them to the recommended torque settings. In addition, after all components are assembled and torqued, safety them as required with safety wire or other specified safety devices.

After carburetor reassembly, a final check of the fuel level in the float bowl and proper operation of the float and needle valve assembly should be made. This check ensures that the carburetor has been reassembled properly and torquing of the threaded components has produced no binding of the float and needle valve assembly. To perform this check, level the carburetor body on a flow bench and attach a sight glass tube to the carburetor fuel drain port with a piece of flexible rubber hose. Align the glass tube vertically with a holding clamp and, using a ruler, mark a line on the glass tube level with the carburetor's parting surface. Next, attach a fuel supply of the correct pressure to the fuel inlet. After the float bowl fills to the correct level, the float should seat the needle valve and stop fuel flow. Measure the distance from the fuel surface in the center of the glass tube to the parting surface mark and compare the result with specified limits. [Figure 7-39]

Installation

Before you install a carburetor on an engine, you should consult the appropriate installation instructions. The first step in most installations requires the carburetor to be mounted onto the engine. Once the carburetor is secured and safetied, the fuel lines

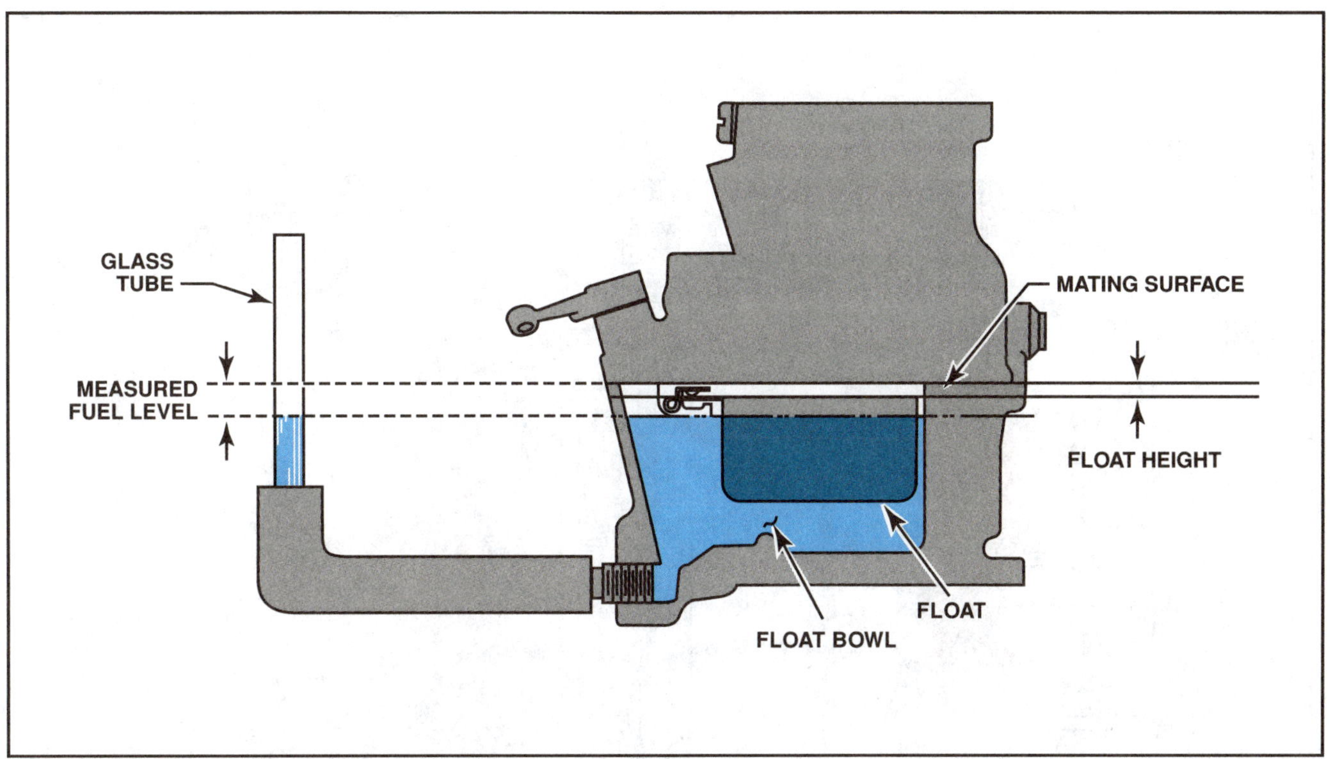

Figure 7-39. Once a line level with the carburetor's parting surface is marked on the sight glass, the distance between the fuel level and parting surface can be measured. This check verifies a correct fuel level and the proper functioning of the float and needle valve assembly.

and controls may be connected. When tightening the fittings, comply with specified torque values to avoid damaging the lines or fittings. To prevent excessive play and imprecise control movement, replace worn hardware as you connect the control linkages and rods.

With the controls attached and safetied, check the throttle and mixture for freedom of movement through their full range of motion. In a typical installation, the stops on the carburetor must be reached before the cockpit controls reach their stops. The amount of control travel that is possible between the carburetor stop and the cockpit stop is known as **springback**. A typical installation requires an equal amount of springback at both the full open and full closed positions.

Once the installation and rigging are complete, an engine runup is performed to verify proper operation. Items that should be checked during a runup include the idle mixture and idle rpm. If any adjustments are required, accomplish them using the procedures described earlier. Once the idle mixture and speed are set, apply full throttle briefly to confirm the engine's ability to develop its full rated power. Once the engine runup is complete, move the mixture control to idle-cutoff to verify proper operation and prompt engine shutdown.

PRESSURE-INJECTION CARBURETORS

Although pressure-injection carburetors are not used on modern reciprocating engines, you may run across them at some time in the field. Therefore, you should have at least a basic understanding of how a typical pressure-injection carburetor functions. Aircraft that may still use a pressure-injection carburetor include many of the aircraft that were used during WWII.

Pressure-injection carburetors differ from float-type carburetors in many ways. For example, pressure-injection carburetors do not utilize a float chamber to store fuel. Instead, fuel is delivered under pressure by a fuel pump through the carburetor and out the discharge nozzle. Since fuel pressure is responsible for forcing fuel out of the discharge nozzle, there is no need to place the discharge nozzle directly in a venturi. This greatly reduces carburetor icing incidents and aids in fuel vaporization.

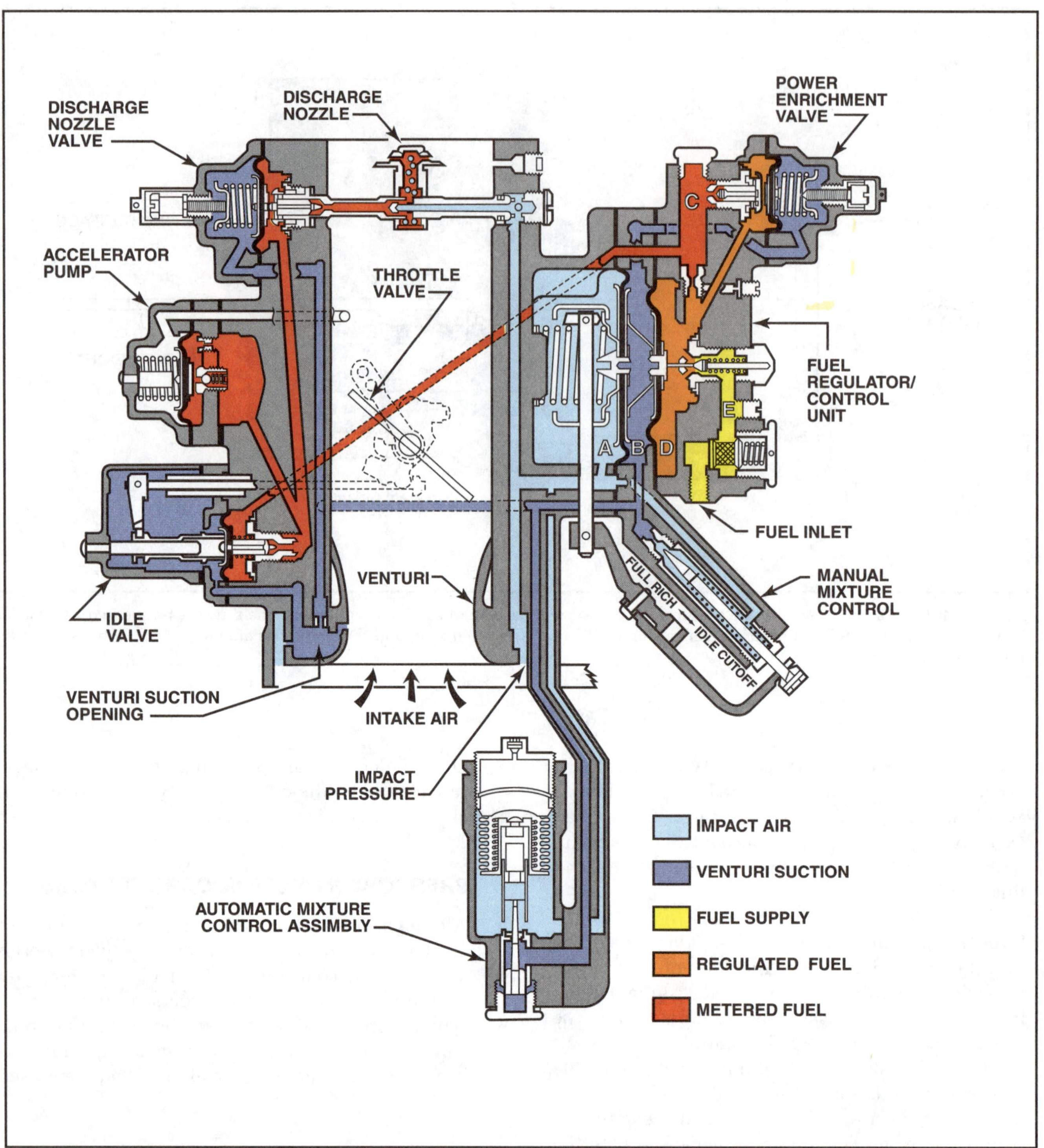

Figure 7-40. The Bendix PS7BD pressure carburetor is pictured above to provide an overview of a typical pressure carburetor. Notice that, although the operating principles of each system differ, a pressure carburetor utilizes the same basic systems that a float-type carburetor does.

Although the operation and design of pressure-injection carburetors differs as compared to float-type carburetors, individual systems for fuel metering, mixture control, idling, acceleration, and power enrichment are still required. However, the operating principles of these systems are different and, therefore, each system will be described in detail. [Figure 7-40]

MAIN METERING

The purpose of the main metering system is to supply the correct amount of fuel to the engine. The main metering system in a pressure carburetor is comprised of a fuel regulator, or fuel control unit, a main metering jet, and a throttle valve.

The **fuel regulator**, or **fuel control unit** is the device responsible for metering the appropriate amount of fuel for engine operation. A typical fuel regulator unit consists of five distinct chambers, an inner and outer diaphragm, a poppet valve assembly, and a main metering jet. [Figure 7-41]

To understand how a fuel regulator unit works, refer to the previous diagram. As filtered air enters the carburetor body, some of it flows into an **impact pressure annulus** around the venturi. As impact air enters the annulus, its velocity decreases while its pressure increases.

From the annulus, the impact air is directed into chamber A of the regulator unit where it presses against one side of the inner diaphragm. At the same time, low pressure air from within the venturi is vented to chamber B where it acts on the opposite side of the inner diaphragm. The difference between the impact pressure in chamber A and the suction, or low pressure in chamber B causes the inner diaphragm to move an amount that is proportional to the volume of air entering the engine. The force produced by the pressure differential between chambers A and B is often referred to as the **air metering force** and is proportional to the amount of air that flows through the venturi.

As the air metering force builds, it overcomes spring tension and opens a poppet valve. As the poppet valve opens, a regulated amount of pressurized fuel is allowed into chamber D. As regulated fuel fills chamber D, it pushes against the outer regulator diaphragm in an attempt to close the poppet valve. This fuel metering force balances the air meteing force to hold the poppet valve off its seat an amount that is proportional to the volume of air entering the engine.

When the engine is idling, an insufficient amount of airflow exists to produce a steady air metering force to open the poppet valve. Therefore, a coil spring is provided in chamber A to supplement the air metering force. At idle speeds, spring tension forces the diaphragm over and opens the poppet valve to provide the fuel pressure required to allow the engine to idle.

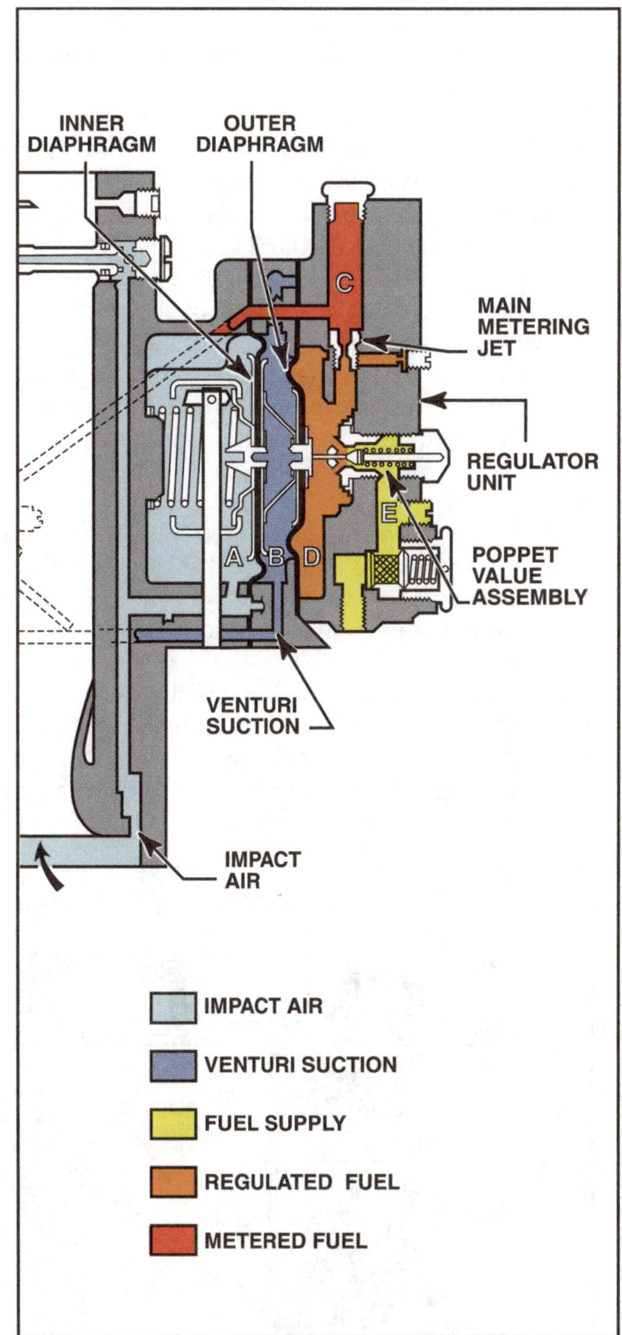

Figure 7-41. A fuel regulator unit consists of five separate chambers that are typically labeled A through E. Additional components include an inner and outer diaphragm, a poppet valve assembly, and a main metering jet.

Once regulated fuel fills chamber D, it passes through a metering jet into chamber C. At this point, the fuel is considered to be metered and its pressure remains constant during all engine operations. From chamber C, the metered fuel is routed through an idle needle valve and on to the discharge nozzle. [Figure 7-42]

At all power settings above idle, a combination of spring pressure and low pressure on the back side of a diaphragm hold the idle valve open far enough that it does not impede the flow of fuel. Therefore, above idle speeds, fuel metering is provided by the main metering jet only. Once through the idle needle valve, fuel flows up to a diaphragm type discharge nozzle valve. The discharge nozzle valve is spring loaded to the closed position and is opened by a combination of fuel pressure and low pressure on the back side of a diaphragm. The primary purpose of the discharge valve is to maintain a constant fuel pressure after the main metering jet. In addition, the spring force within the discharge valve provides a positive fuel cutoff when the mixture control is placed in the idle-cutoff position.

As mentioned earlier, fuel pressure forces fuel out of the discharge nozzle on pressure carburetors. Because of this, the discharge nozzle may be placed after the venturi and throttle valve so the icing problems associated with the venturi are avoided. Once the fuel

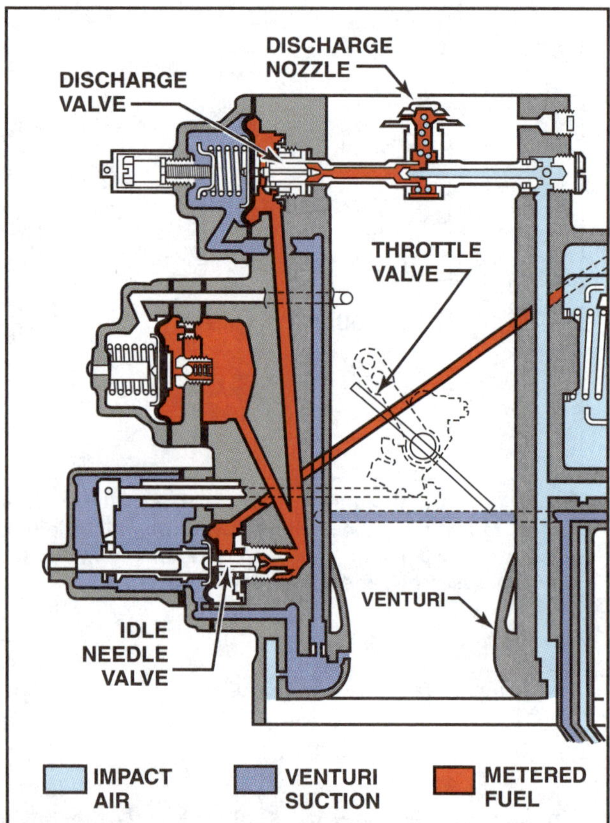

Figure 7-42. Once metered fuel flows out of chamber C it flows through the idle valve and the discharge nozzle valve before it is discharged into the airstream.

reaches the discharge nozzle, air from the impact annulus is mixed with the fuel in the discharge nozzle. This acts as an air bleed to help destroy the surface tension of the fuel to aid in vaporization.

As discussed earlier, the pressure differential between chambers A and B when the engine is idling is insufficient to hold the poppet valve off its seat. Because of this, a spring is installed in chamber A to hold the poppet valve open enough to let idling fuel into the carburetor. However, this spring pressure cannot precisely meter the fuel to the discharge nozzle. Therefore, to control the amount of fuel that actually flows to the discharge nozzle, the idle needle valve is used. The exact amount the needle valve is held open is determined by the idle speed adjustment which is attached to the throttle shaft.

MIXTURE CONTROL

As discussed earlier, a mixture control system regulates the ratio of fuel and air supplied to the engine. This allows the engine operator to control the fuel/air mixture so the engine can operate efficiently at various altitudes and in a variety of conditions. If a mixture control were not provided, the fuel/air mixture would become progressively richer as an aircraft climbs. In pressure carburetors, the amount of fuel that flows to the discharge nozzle is determined by the pressure differential between the A and B chambers. Therefore, by varying the pressure differential between these two chambers, the amount of fuel in the fuel/air mixture can be controlled.

The most common way of controlling the pressure differential is to provide an air bleed between chambers A and B that can be varied either manually or automatically. With a manual mixture control, the size of the air bleed is determined by the position of a needle valve that is controlled from the cockpit. With this type of system, when the mixture control in the cockpit is placed in the full rich position, the needle valve is seated and the maximum pressure differential exists between chambers A and B. On the other hand, as the mixture control is pulled out, the needle valve begins to off seat and the pressure differential decreases. [Figure 7-43]

In addition to leaning, a mixture control also provides an idle-cutoff so fuel flow can be completely stopped. If you recall, a spring is provided in chamber A to hold the poppet valve off its seat when an insufficient pressure differential exists between chambers A and B. Therefore, the only way to seat the poppet valve and completely stop the flow of fuel is to remove the spring pressure

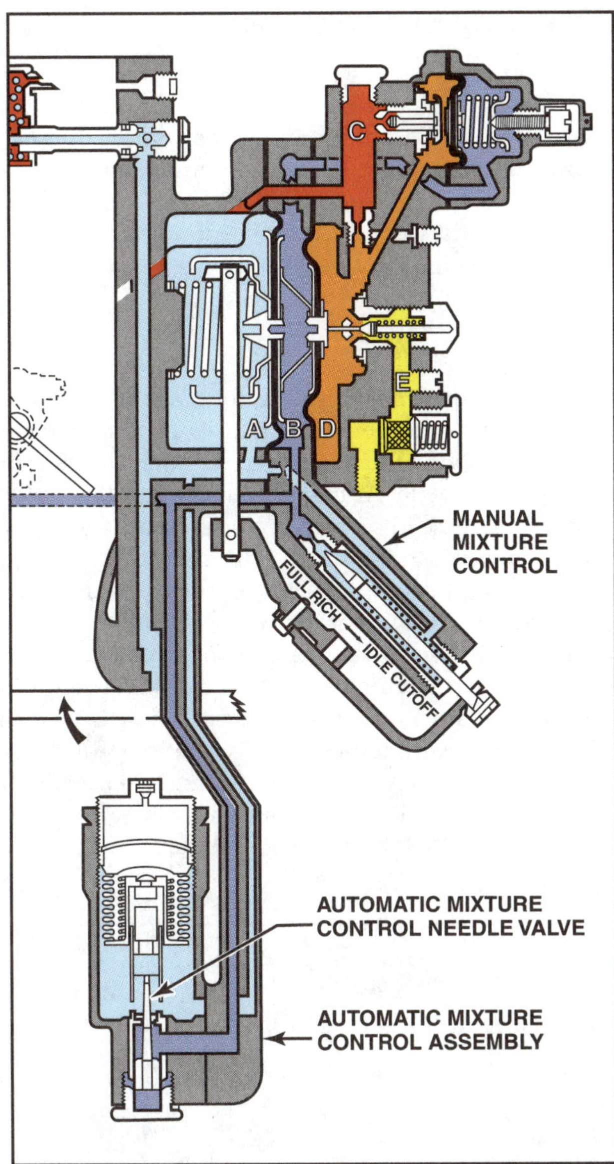

Figure 7-43. To provide a way of controlling the fuel/air mixture, an air bleed is provided between chambers A and B. By controlling the size of the air bleed, the pressure differential between chambers A and B is regulated and the amount of fuel allowed into the carburetor is controlled.

from the inner diaphragm. To do this, a release contact lever is installed in the regulator unit that extends from chamber A out to the mixture control. When the mixture control is placed in the idle-cutoff position, the release contact lever compresses the idle spring and removes all pressure from the diaphragm. With no pressure on the diaphragm, the poppet valve closes and cuts off the fuel flow to the carburetor.

Some pressure carburetors utilize an **automatic mixture control**, or **AMC**. On carburetors with an automatic mixture control, the fuel/air ratio is automatically adjusted to compensate for changes in air density caused by changes in altitude and temperature. A typical AMC consists of a brass bellows that is filled with helium and attached to a reverse tapered needle. Like a manual mixture control, an AMC maintains the appropriate pressure differential across the inner regulator diaphragm by varying the size of the air bleed between chambers A and B. For example, when the pressure is high, the bellows contracts causing the needle valve to move to it's maximum thickness, which in turn narrows the orifice. This decreases the size of the air bleed opening and allows the maximum pressure differential to exist between chambers A and B. On the other hand, as an aircraft climbs and the air density decreases, the bellows expands and allows more air to bleed between the two chambers. This reduces the pressure differential across the inner regulator diaphragm which closes the poppet valve slightly and reduces the fuel flow to the discharge nozzle.

On carburetors that use an automatic mixture control, you must be familiar with engine operational problems that indicate a malfunction with the control system. For example, if an engine begins running rough while cruising at a high altitude, but the problem clears up if you manually lean the mixture, the needle valve in the AMC could be sticking closed or the bellows may have ruptured. On the other hand, if an aircraft experiences rising cylinder head temperatures during a descent, this could indicate that the AMC needle valve is sticking in the open position and the mixture is becoming leaner.

ACCELERATION SYSTEM

If you recall, when the throttle is rapidly opened, the airflow through the carburetor increases faster than the fuel flow. This delayed response creates a momentary leaning of the fuel/air mixture that can cause an engine to initially stagger before accelerating. To prevent this, many carburetors are equipped with an acceleration system. An acceleration system provides an immediate, but brief, increase in fuel flow in the throat of the carburetor to enrichen the mixture. By providing this extra fuel, the engine can accelerate smoothly and quickly until the carburetor can deliver fuel at a rate that is proportional to the air flow.

A typical acceleration system on a pressure carburetor consists of a single diaphragm pump consisting of three chambers: an air chamber and a primary and secondary fuel chamber. The air chamber and primary fuel chamber are separated by a diaphragm while the primary and secondary fuel chambers are separated by a rigid divider with a combination check/relief valve and a single fuel bleed. [Figure 7-44]

When the engine is started, the manifold pressure decreases and partially compresses the spring in the accelerator pump's air chamber. At the same time, fuel fills the two fuel chambers. When the throttle is opened rapidly, manifold pressure increases and forces the pump diaphragm over. This forces fuel from the primary fuel chamber into the secondary fuel chamber and on to the discharge nozzle. The combination check/relief valve allows a rapid discharge of fuel when the throttle is first opened. However, the valve soon seats after the initial surge and the remaining fuel discharges through the fuel bleed to provide a sustained stream of fuel to the discharge nozzle.

When the throttle is retarded rapidly, the corresponding decrease in manifold pressure causes the pump spring to collapse rapidly and draw fuel into the primary fuel chamber. To prevent the rapid diaphragm movement from starving the discharge nozzle of fuel as the pump fills, the combination check/relief valve remains seated and permits fuel to fill the primary fuel chamber through the fuel bleed only.

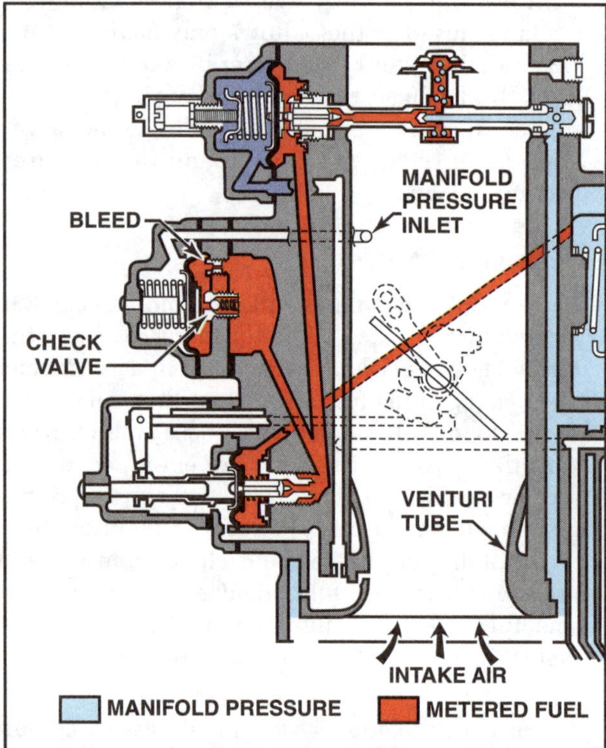

Figure 7-44. A typical accelerator pump on a pressure injection carburetor consists of a single diaphragm pump with an air chamber that is vented to manifold pressure and two fuel chambers.

POWER ENRICHMENT SYSTEM

The power enrichment system provides extra fuel for operations above cruise power settings. The extra fuel is used to aid in engine cooling and help prevent detonation. Power enrichment on pressure carburetors may be accomplished with either a double step idle valve or by incorporating an airflow power enrichment valve.

Double Step Idle Valve

In carburetors that utilize a double step idle valve for power enrichment, the idle needle valve is stepped to vary the amount of fuel that flows to the discharge nozzle. At low power settings, the first, or idle step of the idle needle valve off seats and allows only idle fuel to flow to the discharge nozzle. Once the engine is accelerated above idle to cruise power, venturi suction increases and the needle valve off seats further so that the second, or cruise step of the needle valve regulates the fuel flow. Above cruise power, venturi suction increases enough to completely off seat the needle valve so that additional fuel can flow to the discharge nozzle to enrichen the fuel/air mixture. At these high power settings, the only thing that limits the fuel flow is the main metering jet. [Figure 7-45]

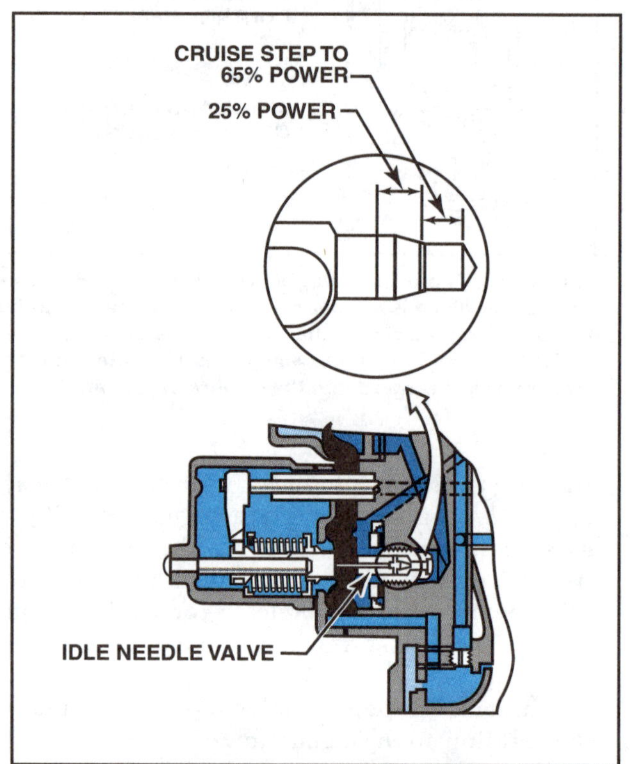

Figure 7-45. In carburetors that use a double step idle valve for power enrichment, the needle valve is cut in steps to regulate the amount of fuel that flows to the discharge nozzle for idle and cruise power settings.

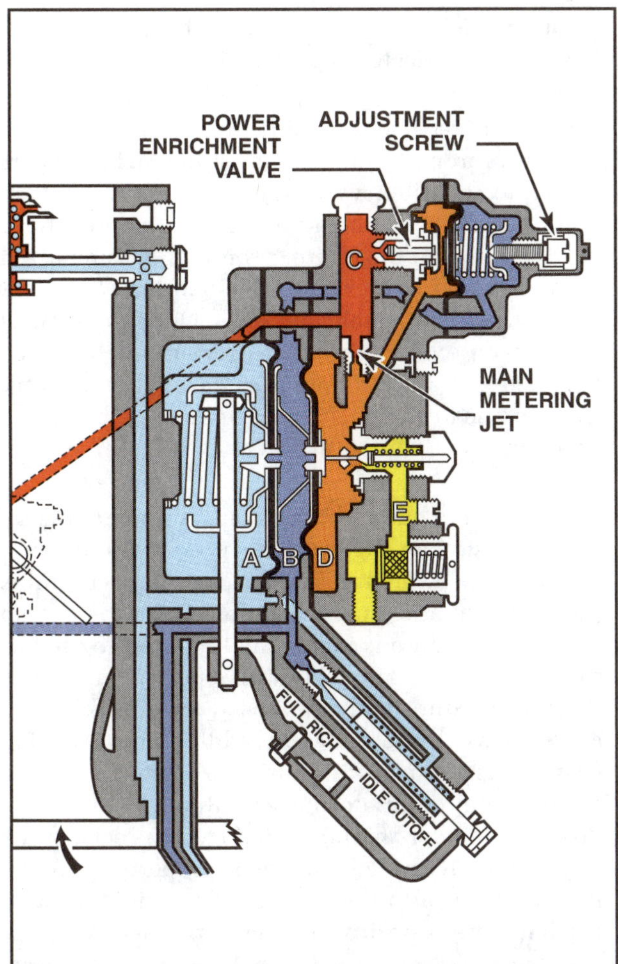

Figure 7-46. The power enrichment system pictured above utilizes a combination of venturi suction and fuel pressure to overcome spring tension and allow additional fuel to bypass the metering jet. This increases the fuel flow to the discharge nozzle which enrichens the fuel/air mixture.

Airflow Enrichment Valve

In carburetors that use an airflow enrichment valve for power enrichment, the enrichment valve is located in a fuel passage that is parallel with the main metering jet. A typical airflow power enrichment valve consists of a needle valve assembly that senses the pressure drop in the venturi to determine when the engine is operating at high power levels. [Figure 7-46]

When an engine equipped with an airflow enrichment valve is operated at cruise power settings, spring pressure holds the enrichment valve closed. As long as the enrichment valve is closed, the main metering jet limits the fuel flow to the discharge nozzle. However, when engine power is increased above cruise, the amount of air flowing through the venturi increases. The increased airflow ultimately causes the air pressure within the enrichment valve housing to decrease enough to off seat the enrichment needle valve. Once the enrichment valve opens, fuel is allowed to bypass the metering jet. This increases the amount of fuel that flows to the discharge nozzle which, in turn, enriches the fuel/air mixture.

WATER INJECTION

Water injection systems were once used on some large reciprocating engines to allow the engine to produce its maximum power without suffering from detonation or preignition. Because of this, water injection systems are also commonly referred to as **anti-detonation injection**, or **ADI systems**. With a typical ADI system, a mixture of water and alcohol are injected into the carburetor to create a fuel/air mixture that helps prevent detonation.

On most large reciprocating engines, the carburetor is adjusted to provide a somewhat rich mixture during high power operations. If you recall, the reason for supplying a rich mixture is that the extra fuel helps cool the engine and reduce the chance of detonation. However, a disadvantage of the richer mixture is that it does not allow the engine to produce its maximum power output. Based on this, if an anti-detonation system is installed to prevent detonation, the fuel/air mixture can be leaned to allow the engine to produce its maximum power.

PRESSURE CARBURETOR MAINTENANCE

A pressure carburetor is a precision piece of equipment that requires the use of a flow bench and other specialized tools to perform any internal maintenance. Therefore, typical maintenance performed on pressure carburetors is generally limited to inspection, installation, removal, and field adjustments.

When inspecting a pressure carburetor installed on an engine, you should check the same things that you do on a float-type carburetor. For example, check the carburetor for security and for possible leaks around the mating flange. Remember, if a leak exists, additional air will be drawn into the carburetor and the fuel/air mixture will become leaner. Depending on the size of the leak, this could result in rough idling or, in severe cases, detonation and engine damage.

Additional things to look at include security of all the control linkages as well as freedom of movement and proper contact with the stops. If all the controls

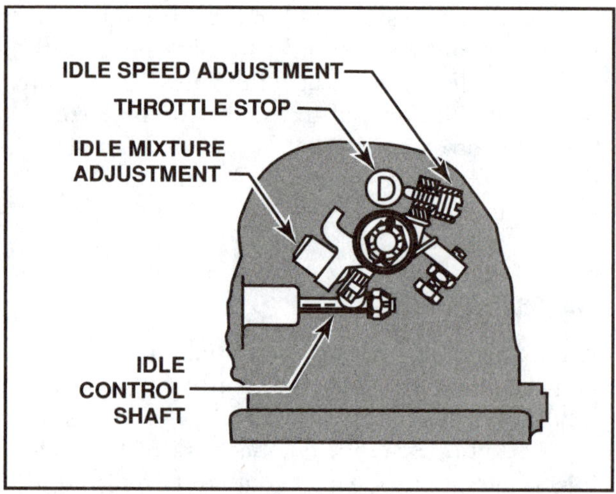

Figure 7-47. The adjustment screws used to vary both the idle mixture and the idle speed are typically collocated on the throttle valve shaft.

are rigged properly, you can also check both the idle mixture adjustment and the idle speed. Both the idle mixture and idle speed are manually adjusted by varying the length of one or more adjustment screws on the side of the carburetor. [Figure 7-47]

When checking the idle mixture adjustment, the procedures used with float-type carburetors are also used on pressure carburetors. In other words, when the engine is running and at operating temperature, slowly move the mixture control toward the idle-cutoff position while simultaneously observing the tachometer. If the mixture is adjusted properly, the engine rpm will increase slightly before it drops off rapidly. If the aircraft is equipped with a manifold pressure gauge, an optimum idle mixture will result in the manifold pressure decreasing just before the engine ceases to fire.

Once the idle mixture is adjusted, you may adjust the idle speed. To do this, begin by verifying the ignition system is operating properly and the mixture in the cockpit is set. If everything is operating properly, open the throttle to clear the engine and then close the throttle and allow the rpm to stabilize. If the engine does not idle at the appropriate rpm, adjust the idle speed screw as needed and recheck the idle speed.

CARBURETOR OVERHAUL

As mentioned earlier, the maintenance you can perform on pressure-injection carburetors is limited. In fact, because of the requirement for precision equipment and a flow bench, the overhaul of a pressure carburetor is typically conducted by the manufacturer or a certificated repair facility.

When you receive a freshly overhauled pressure carburetor from the manufacturer, the fuel chambers are typically filled with a preservative oil which must be removed. In addition, the manufacturer may require that the entire carburetor be submerged in, or filled with, fuel for a specified time to limber up all the diaphragms and seals. Once these steps have been completed, the carburetor may be installed on the aircraft. Since installations vary from engine to engine, it is best to refer to the appropriate installation instructions.

Once installed, the carburetor must be operationally tested. To start an engine with a pressure carburetor, the engine is primed and then the mixture control is placed in the idle-cutoff position. Once the engine starts, the mixture is immediately moved to the full rich position. During a typical operational check, the idle mixture and idle speed are checked and adjusted as appropriate. In addition, the engine should be run up to full power for a few minutes to verify the appropriate power output. Once this is done, the power should be reduced to recheck the idle speed. If the engine idles properly, pull the mixture control to the idle-cutoff position and verify that there is positive fuel cutoff.

FUEL INJECTION SYSTEMS

Although carburetors provide an extremely reliable means of metering the amount of fuel that flows into an engine, they do have two major limitations. First, because intake manifolds differ in length and shape, the fuel/air mixture is not distributed evenly in carbureted engines. This is critical in modern aircraft engines with high compression ratios since the introduction of a lean mixture in any one cylinder can result in detonation and possible engine damage. The second disadvantage shared by all carbureted engines is their susceptibility to carburetor icing.

To overcome these limitations, fuel injection systems have been incorporated into many aircraft designs. A fuel injection system differs from a carburetor in that, with fuel injection, fuel is injected either directly into each cylinder or into the intake port just behind the intake valve. When fuel is injected directly into the engine cylinders, the injection system is referred to as a **direct fuel injection system**. This type of fuel injection system was used on some early radial engines and offered the benefit of even fuel distribution and reduced chance of

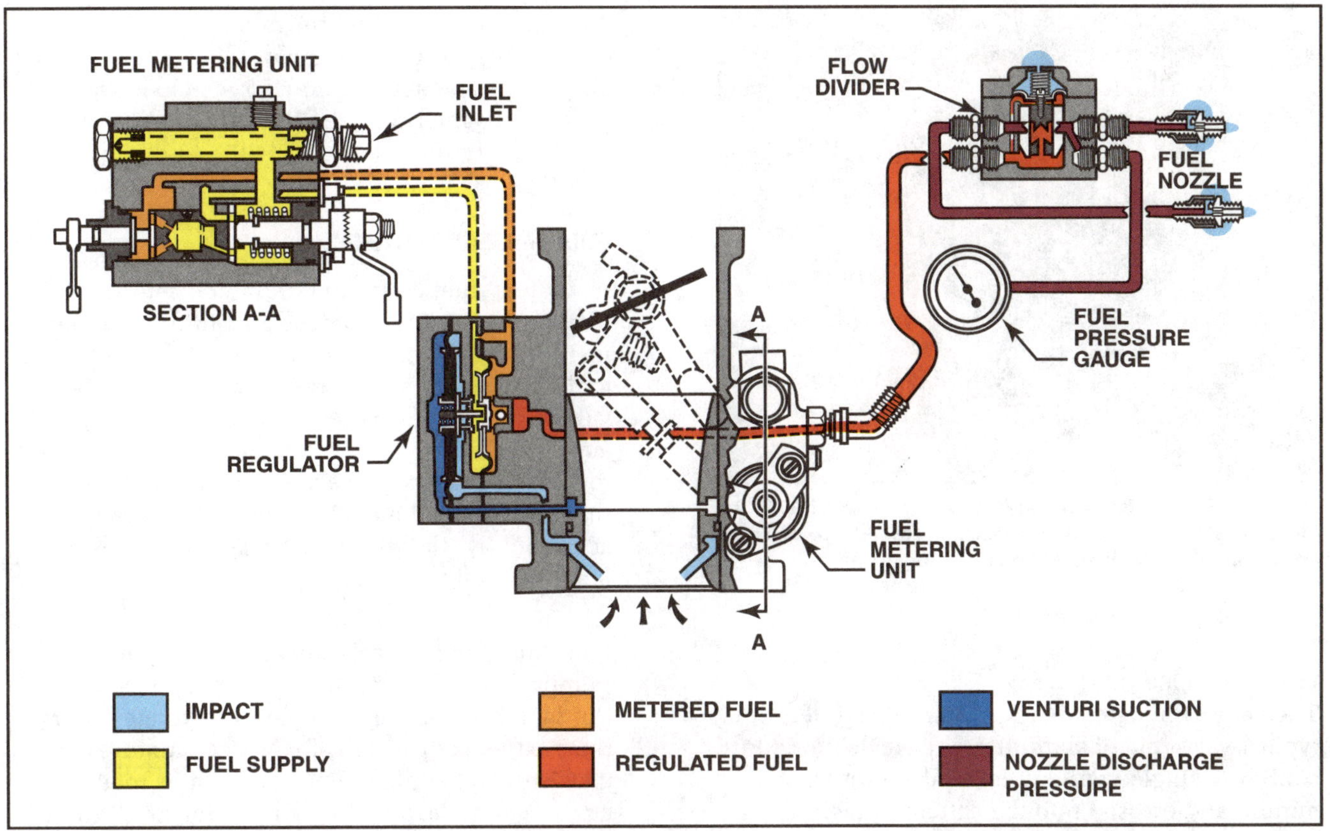

Figure 7-48. The primary components of an RSA fuel injection system include a venturi housing, a fuel metering unit, a fuel regulator, a flow divider, and several fuel nozzles.

backfiring. A typical direct fuel injection system is similar to a large pressure carburetor that meters the correct amount of fuel into two multi-cylindered piston pumps. These pumps then forced the metered fuel directly into the combustion chambers of the individual cylinders as timed, high pressure spurts. Although a direct fuel injection system worked well, the close manufacturing tolerances and complex components required by this type system made it impractical and too expensive for aircraft use.

The most common type of fuel injection system used in aircraft is the continuous-flow system. A **continuous-flow fuel injection system** differs from a direct fuel injection system in that fuel is injected and mixed with air in each intake port just behind the intake valve. In addition, fuel is continuously injected throughout the entire combustion cycle instead of only during the intake stroke. This allows the fuel plenty of time to vaporize and mix with the air before it is drawn into the cylinder when the intake valve opens.

Today, there are two types of continuous-flow fuel injection systems used on modern reciprocating engines. The first is the Precision Airmotive RSA system and the second is the Teledyne-Continental system. Because of the differences between the two systems, they are both discussed in detail.

RSA SYSTEM

Precision Airmotive produces two widely used fuel metering systems known as the **RS system** and the **RSA system**. Of the two, the RSA system is the most modern and, therefore, is the system discussed in this section. A typical RSA fuel injection system consists of five primary components: a venturi housing, a fuel metering unit, a fuel regulator, a flow divider, and several fuel nozzles. With this type of fuel injection system, fuel flows into the fuel metering unit where the position of the idle lever and mixture control determine how much fuel is metered to the fuel regulator. Once in the fuel regulator, a combination of air and fuel metering forces regulate how much fuel is sent to the flow divider for distribution to each of the fuel nozzles. In most cases, the venturi housing, fuel metering unit, and fuel regulator are generally cast as a single unit. However, for ease of understanding, the fuel metering unit is illustrated as a separate unit. [Figure 7-48]

Figure 7-49. A typical venturi housing consists of a single piece of cast aluminum with a venturi pressed into one end and a throttle valve installed on the opposite end.

VENTURI HOUSING

The venturi housing of a RSA fuel injection unit is typically cast out of aluminum as a single unit. Most contain a single venturi that is also cast from aluminum and pressed into the bottom of the housing. To control the airflow through the venturi, a throttle valve is installed at the top of the venturi housing. To provide adequate airflow for engine idling, three holes are sometimes drilled through the throttle valve near its edge. [Figure 7-49]

FUEL METERING UNIT

A typical fuel metering unit consists of a fuel strainer, a mixture control and idle valve, and a main and enrichment metering jet. Both the mixture and idle valves are spring-loaded, flat plate-type valves that are mechanically actuated to control the amount of fuel that flows into and out of the metering jets. The mixture valve is actuated by the mixture control in the cockpit while the idle valve is actuated by the throttle valve shaft through a mechanical linkage. [Figure 7-50]

Fuel metering begins when unmetered fuel is pumped into the fuel metering unit. Once through the fuel strainer, the fuel passes through a port in the mixture control valve. A typical mixture control consists of a flat plate-type valve that is rotated over a passageway leading to the metering jets. With this

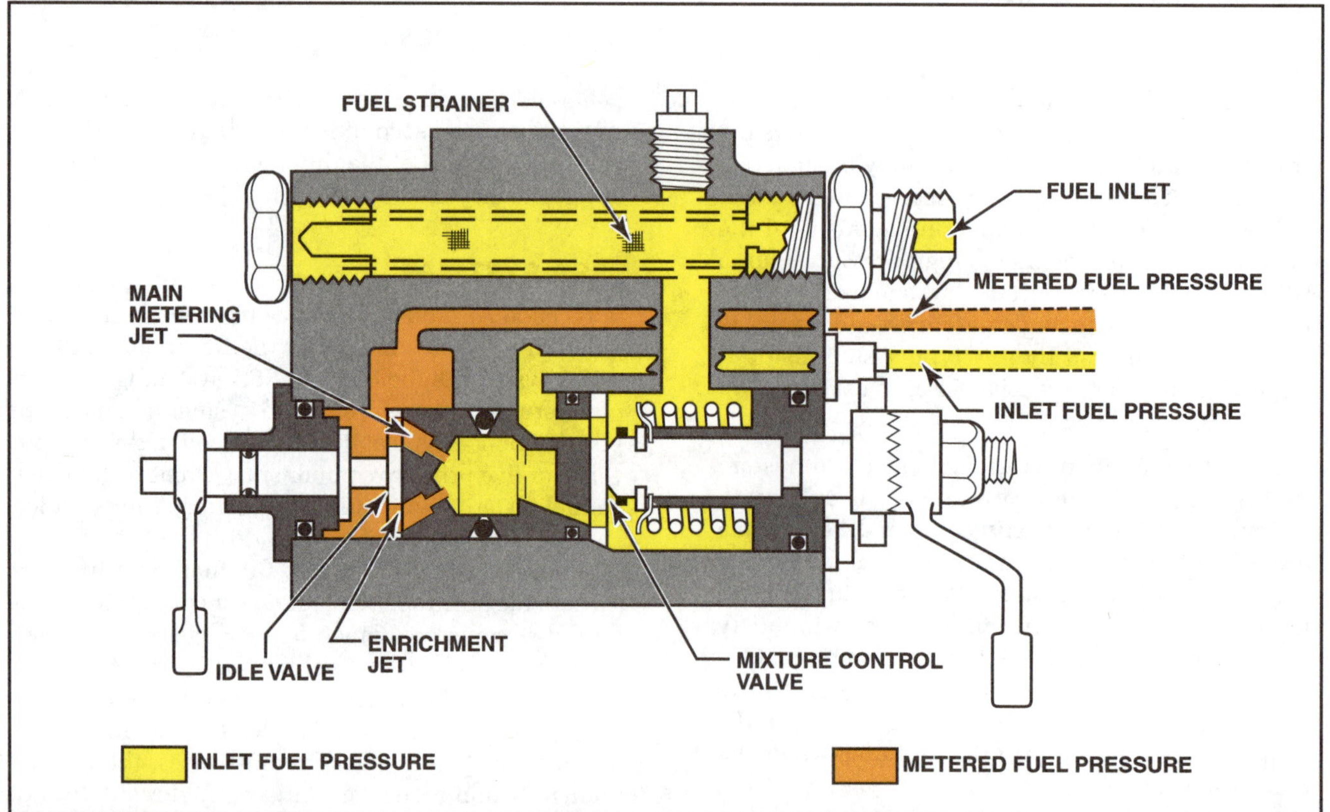

Figure 7-50. In a typical RSA fuel metering unit, after fuel flows through a wire strainer, it must pass through the mixture control valve to get to the metering jets. By the same token, the amount of fuel that is allowed to flow out of the metering jets is determined by the position of the idle valve.

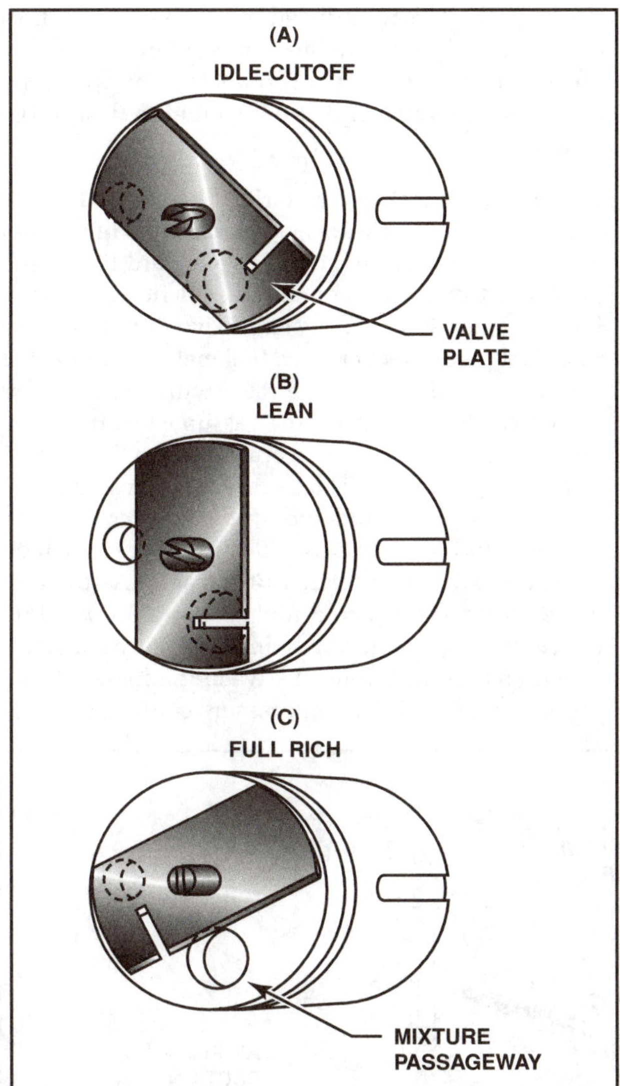

Figure 7-51. (A) — When the mixture control is set in the idle-cutoff position, the entire passageway leading to the metering jets is blocked. (B) — As the mixture is advanced to a lean setting, the valve plate begins to uncover the passageway leading to the metering jets and fuel begins to flow. (C) — In the full rich position, the valve plate completely exposes the passageway to the metering jets allowing maximum fuel flow.

type of valve, the passageway leading to the metering jet is uncovered as the mixture control in the cockpit is advanced. [Figure 7-51]

In the rich position, the opening afforded by the mixture control is larger than the metering jet, and the jet limits the flow. However, in any intermediate position, the opening is smaller than the main jet, and the mixture control becomes the flow limiting device.

A second passageway in the mixture control base allows unmetered, or inlet fuel pressure, to flow to the fuel regulator. This unmetered fuel pressure is used as a reference pressure for regulating the amount of fuel that flows to the engine. This will be discussed in more detail later in this section.

Once past the mixture valve, fuel can flow through the metering jets. However, the amount of fuel that can flow out of either the main or enrichment jet is determined by the position of the idle valve. A typical valve plate used with an idle valve proportionately uncovers both the main and enrichment jets as the throttle is advanced. For example, at low power settings, only a small portion of the main metering jet is uncovered. However, as the throttle is advanced, more of the main metering jet is uncovered to provide additional fuel. When the throttle is wide open, both the main and enrichment jet are uncovered to provide the fuel required for high power settings. [Figure 7-52]

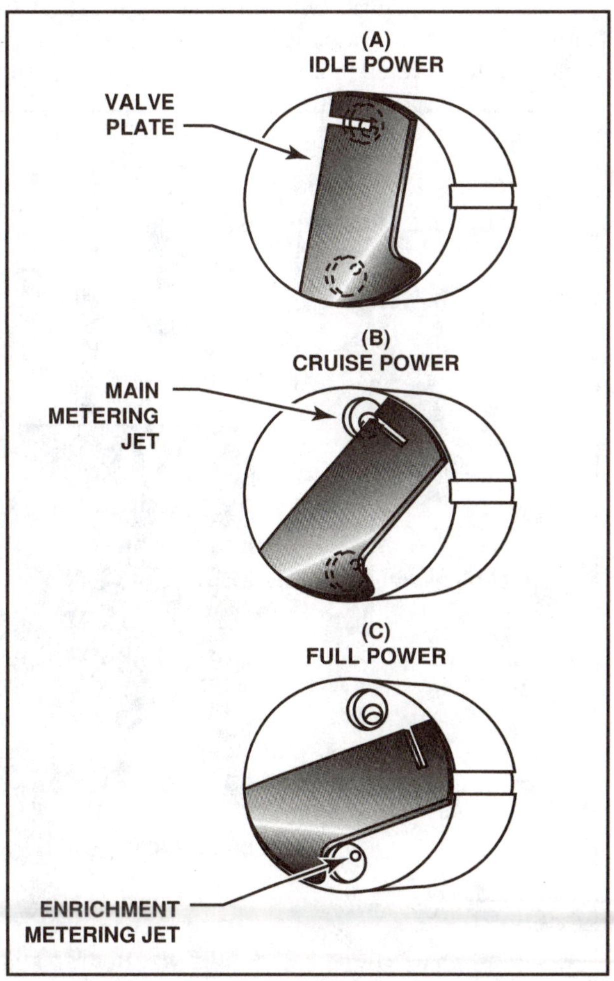

Figure 7-52. (A) — When the throttle is set at idle, a small portion of the main metering jet is uncovered. (B) — As the throttle is advanced to a cruise setting, nearly all the main metering jet is exposed. (C) — When the throttle is full forward, both the main and enrichment metering jets are exposed to provide maximum fuel flow.

FUEL REGULATOR

The purpose of the fuel regulator is to supply the correct amount of fuel to the engine. To do this, the fuel regulator receives metered fuel from the fuel metering unit and regulates it to the engine based on the amount of air being taken in through the venturi. A typical fuel regulator unit consists of four distinct chambers, an air and fuel diaphragm, and a ball valve. [Figure 7-53]

The fuel regulator uses the same operating principles as the regulator unit on pressure carburetors. In other words, as air enters the venturi housing, some of it flows into a series of impact tubes that project out of the base of the venturi. Once in the impact tubes, the air is directed into a sealed chamber where it acts on one side of the air diaphragm. At the same time, the chamber on the opposite side of the air diaphragm is vented to the low pressure air in the venturi. These two forces work together to move the air diaphragm an amount that is proportional to the volume of air that is drawn through the venturi. The force produced by the pressure differential across the air diaphragm is referred to as the **air metering force** and is responsible for opening a ball, or **servo valve** and allowing fuel to flow to the flow divider.

At the same time the air metering force opens the ball valve, inlet fuel pressure acts on one side of the fuel diaphragm to move the ball valve toward the closed position. However, as metered fuel flows into the fuel chamber and past the ball valve, it opposes the inlet fuel pressure to create a **fuel metering force** that balances the air metering force. To understand how these two forces work together, assume that the throttle is advanced from idle to cruise. When the throttle is advanced, the impact air pressure increases while the venturi pressure decreases. This increases the pressure differential across the air diaphragm which pulls the ball valve further off its seat. As the ball valve opens, the metered fuel pressure drops while the inlet fuel pressure remains relatively constant. The increased difference between the metered fuel pressure and the inlet fuel pressure causes more fuel

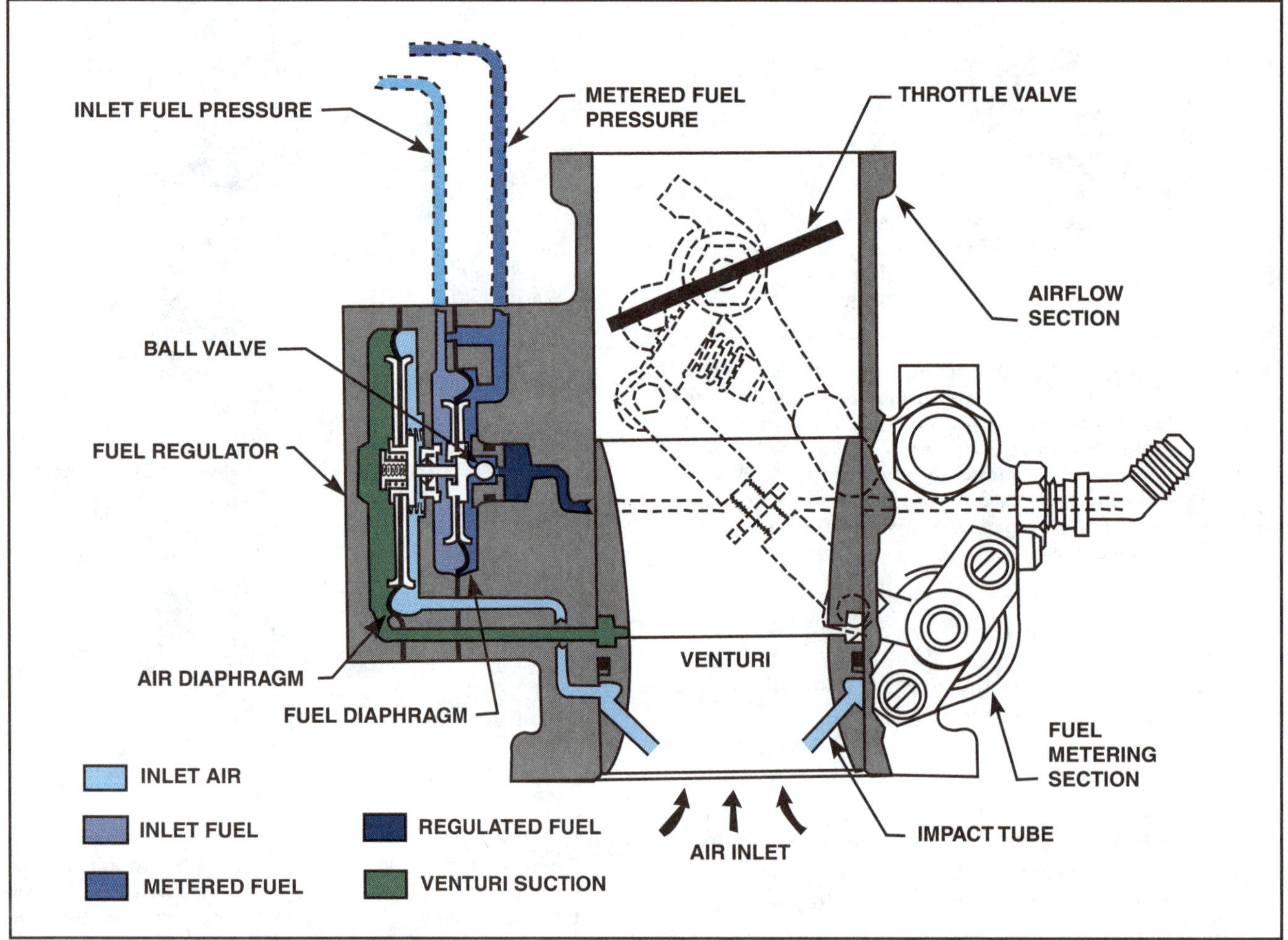

Figure 7-53. The fuel regulator in an RSA fuel injection system consists of four separate chambers, an air and fuel diaphragm, and a ball valve.

to flow through the main metering jet in the metering unit which, in turn, sends more fuel past the ball valve and on to the engine. Therefore, the function of the ball valve is to create a pressure differential across the metering jet that is proportional to the airflow being drawn into the engine.

IDLE SYSTEM

At idle, the airflow through the engine is low and the air metering force is unable to open the ball valve to maintain a pressure differential across the metering jet. Therefore, a method of holding the ball valve off its seat at idle speeds is required. In the RSA system, the force required to hold the ball valve off its seat is provided by a **constant head idle spring**. [Figure 7-54]

When a small amount of air is flowing through the venturi, the constant head spring holds the ball valve off its seat. Once the intake airflow increases, the air diaphragm moves outward to compress the constant head spring until the diaphragm bushing contacts the stop on the end of the ball valve shaft and takes over fuel regulation. To provide a smooth transition between idle and cruise power settings, the constant effort spring pre-loads the air diaphragm to approximately a neutral position.

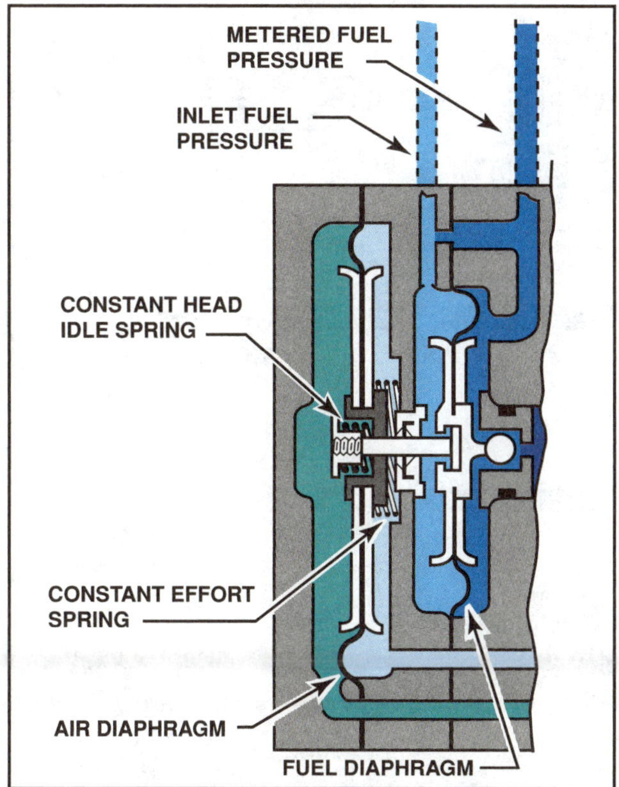

Figure 7-54. The idling system consists of a constant head idle spring that opposes a constant effort spring to pull the ball valve off its seat.

AUTOMATIC MIXTURE CONTROL

To help alleviate some of the work load on a pilot, some RSA fuel injection systems are equipped with an automatic mixture control. When this is the case, the automatic mixture control is installed in parallel with the manual mixture control. A typical automatic mixture control utilizes a sealed bellows that moves a reverse tapered needle to vary the size of an air bleed between the impact and venturi air chambers. The bellows is filled with helium and expands and contracts with changes in air density. For example, as an aircraft climbs, air density decreases and the bellows expands. Since the bellows is connected to the reverse tapered valve, the expansion movement pushes the needle valve off its seat to open the bleed air port. This reduces the pressure differential across the air diaphragm which partially closes the ball valve. [Figure 7-55]

FLOW DIVIDER

Metered fuel flows from the regulator through a flexible hose to the flow divider. Most flow dividers are located on top of the engine in a central location. A typical divider consists of a diaphragm operated valve and a spring. When there is no fuel pressure, a combination of atmospheric and spring pressure

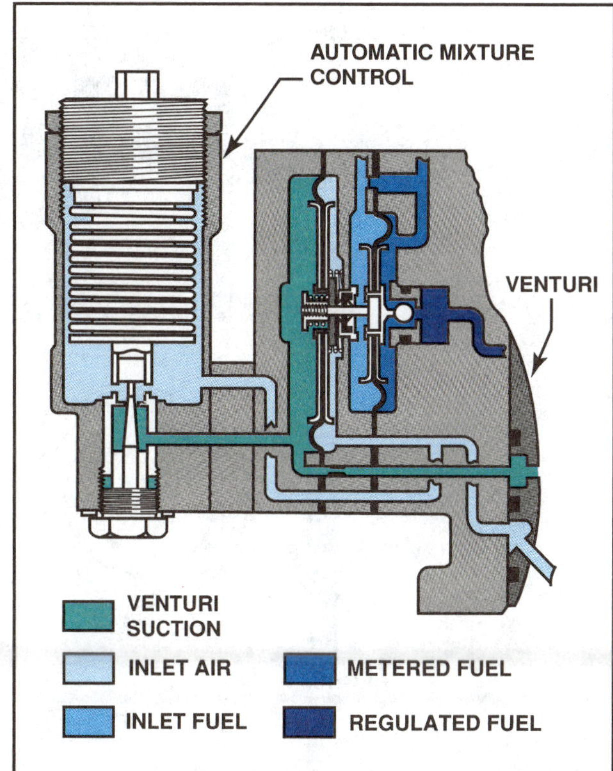

Figure 7-55. An Automatic mixture control installed in an RSA fuel injection system utilizes a helium filled bellows that controls a reverse tapered needle valve.

holds the valve in the closed position. However, once fuel pressure builds enough to overcome these two forces, the valve opens and allows fuel into the flow divider. From the flow divider, fuel flows through 1/8 inch stainless steel tubing out to each injector nozzle. In addition, an outlet is also provided for a pressure gauge in the cockpit. A typical pressure gauge is calibrated in pounds per square inch, gallons per hour, or pounds per hour.

By taking pressure readings at the flow divider, the pressure indications obtained reflect the collective pressure drop across all fuel injector nozzles. The gauge pressure is directly proportional to the pressure drop caused by the fuel flow through the nozzles.

At all speeds above idle, the small opening in the nozzles restrict the amount of fuel that can flow into each cylinder. This causes a back pressure to build up in the metered fuel lines which, in turn, influences the fuel metering force. Based on this, the nozzles control fuel pressure when engine rpm is above idle. [Figure 7-56]

During idle, fuel flow through the nozzles is insufficient to create the back pressure required for fuel metering. To remedy this, the coil spring on the air side of the diaphragm holds the flow divider valve closed until metered fuel pressure becomes sufficient to offseat the valve. Once metered fuel pressure rises enough to overcome spring tension, the flow divider opens and evenly distributes fuel to the cylinders during this low fuel flow condition. As an added benefit, when the mixture control is placed in the idle-cutoff position, the spring forces the divider valve down and provides a positive fuel cutoff to the nozzles. This action reduces the chance of vapor lock by trapping fuel in the injector lines.

INJECTION NOZZLES

The RSA system uses air bleed-type nozzles which are threaded into the cylinder heads near the intake ports. Each nozzle consists of a brass body constructed with a metering orifice, an air bleed hole, and an emulsion chamber. In addition, to help ensure that no contaminants are drawn into the air

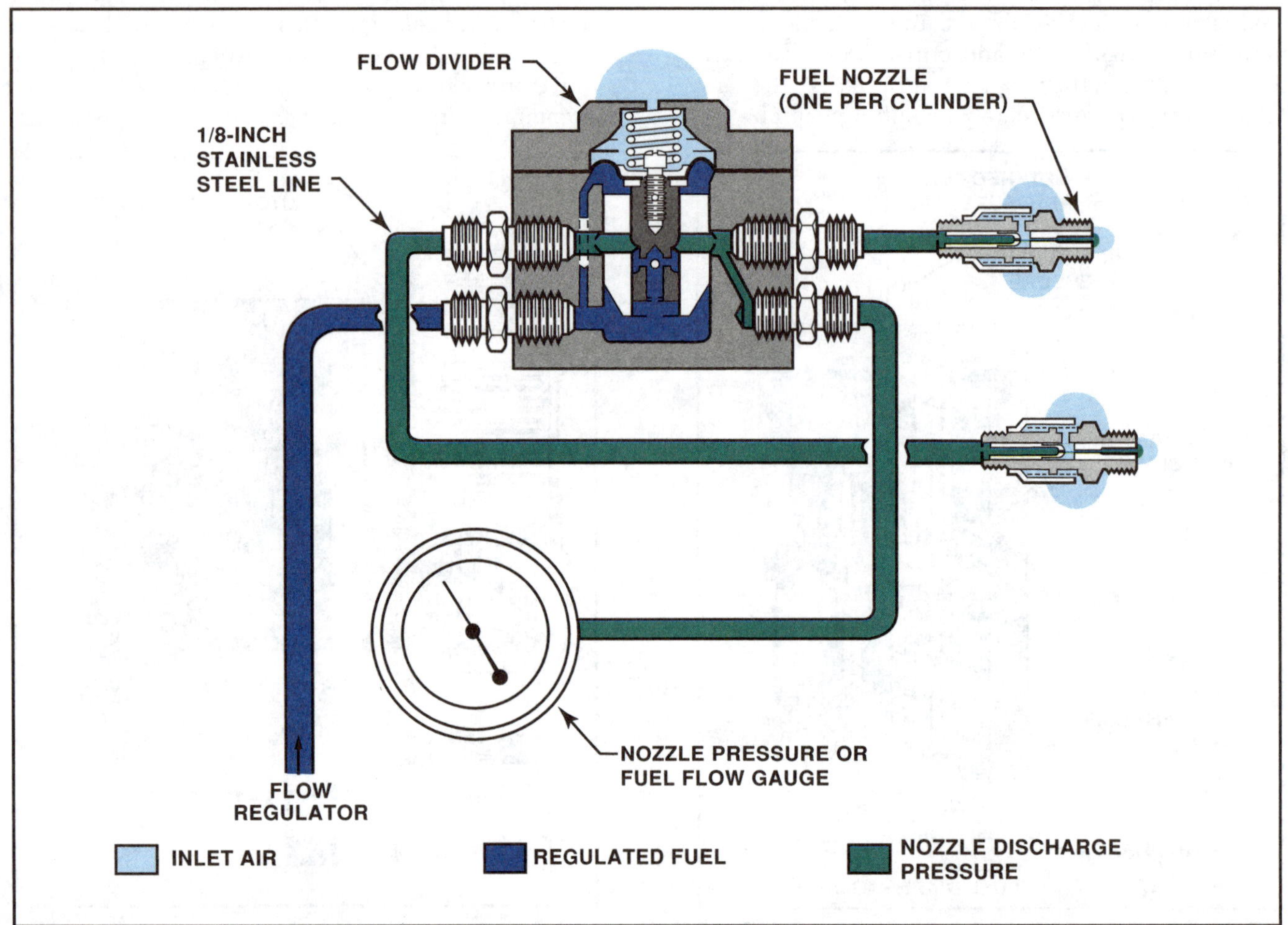

Figure 7-56. A flow divider ensures equal fuel flow at a regulated pressure to each nozzle. In addition, it provides a convenient location to take a system pressure reading.

bleed hole, a fine mesh metal screen and pressed steel shroud surround the brass body. To provide the air pressure needed to emulsify the fuel, the fuel nozzles used on some turbocharged engines include an extension that allows the nozzle to receive upper deck air pressure. [Figure 7-57]

Each nozzle incorporates a calibrated metering orifice, or jet, that is manufactured to provide a specific flow rate plus or minus two percent. The jet size is determined by the available fuel inlet pressure and the maximum fuel flow required by the engine. In addition, nozzles of the same type are interchangeable between engines, and between cylinders. To allow you to identify the size of the jet in any given nozzle, an identification mark is usually stamped on the hex flat of the nozzle opposite the air bleed hole. The identification mark generally consists of a single letter.

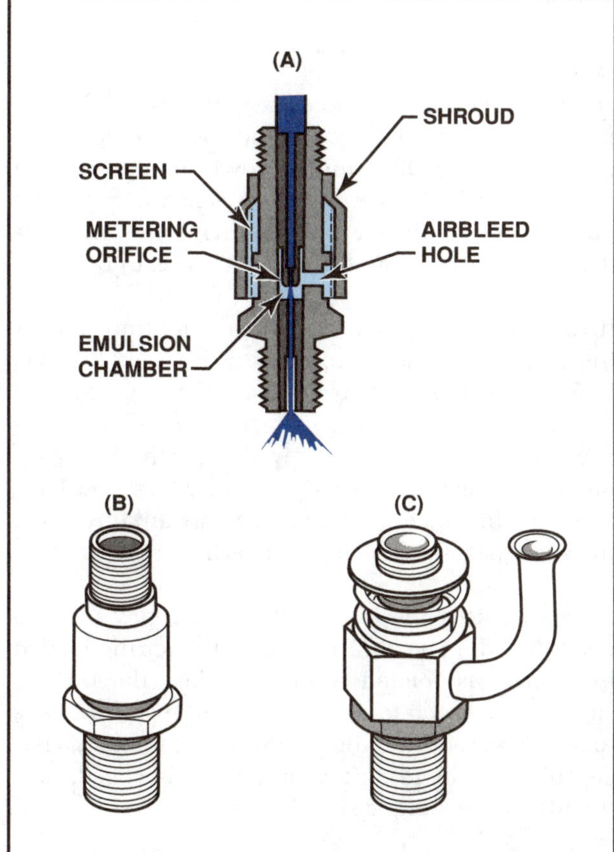

Figure 7-57. (A) — A typical RSA fuel injector consists of a shrouded brass body that houses a metering orifice, an air bleed hole, and an emulsion chamber. (B) — The nozzles used on normally aspirated engines are vented to ambient air that is drawn into the nozzle from under a shroud. (C) — Since the manifold pressure in a turbocharged engine often exceeds atmospheric pressure, the nozzles used on turbocharged engines have an extension that allows the nozzle to receive upper deck air pressure.

As fuel flows into a fuel nozzle, it passes through the metering jet and into an emulsion chamber where it is mixed with air. Since the end of the nozzle is exposed to manifold pressure which, on normally aspirated engines, is less than atmospheric pressure air is pulled into the nozzle through the air bleed. As the air and fuel mix in the emulsion chamber, the fuel is atomized. Since the manifold pressure in a turbocharged engine often exceeds atmospheric pressure, a higher pressure air source must be used for the air bleed. In most cases, the high pressure air is taken off the upper deck.

When installing a fuel nozzle, you should always attempt to position the bleed air hole so that it is pointing upward. This way, when the engine is shut down, fuel will be less likely to drain out of the nozzle and onto the engine. Another thing to watch out for is a clogged air bleed. If an air bleed should become plugged, the outlet side of the metering jet will be exposed to manifold pressure instead of atmospheric pressure. This increases the differential pressure across the nozzle metering jet which, in turn, causes more fuel to flow through the nozzle. Since the regulator unit delivers a set amount of fuel to the flow divider at a given power setting, the nozzle with the clogged air bleed will essentially take more fuel from the other nozzles. Based on this, the nozzle with the clogged air bleed will provide a rich mixture while the remaining nozzles will provide a lean mixture. Furthermore, since the fuel pressure gauge is also connected to the flow divider, a clogged air bleed causes a low fuel flow indication.

RSA SYSTEM INSPECTION AND MAINTENANCE

When inspecting an RSA fuel injection system on an airplane, you should begin by checking the security of all the components. For example, verify the security of the venturi housing, flow divider, and fuel lines. As with carburetors, give special attention to the mounting flange for evidence of cracks or leaks. This is important because a leak between the housing and the engine mounting pad will allow excess air to be introduced into the fuel/air mixture.

In addition to checking for security, you should periodically check all control linkages for freedom of movement and range of movement. Furthermore, you should examine the fuel lines for kinks, distortion, or indications of leakage. At the same time, verify that all fittings are properly tightened.

When inspecting the flow divider, verify that the vent hole that allows atmospheric air into the divider is free of obstructions. If the vent hole should become plugged, the pressure acting on one side of the diaphragm will not vary with changes in altitude and the divider valve will not open the correct amount, causing an excessively lean mixture.

As part of a regular maintenance program, the fuel nozzles should be cleaned periodically to remove any varnish or other contaminants. After the nozzles have been cleaned, visually inspect the metering jet for obstructions. If a nozzle is plugged, soak the nozzle in an approved cleaner and blow it out with compressed air until the obstruction is removed.

Once all the nozzles are clean, it is a good idea to make a flow comparison. To do this, install each nozzle on its respective fuel line and position equal sized containers under each nozzle outlet. Once in place, turn on the aircraft's electric boost pump, place the mixture in the full rich position, and advance the throttle. With the controls in this position, let the containers fill until all of them are at least half full. Once this occurs, place the mixture in the idle-cutoff position and turn off the boost pump. When fuel quits dripping from the nozzles, gather the containers and place them side-by-side on a level surface. The amount of fuel in each container should be approximately the same. If the level in any one container is substantially lower then the others, a restriction may exist in the nozzle, supply line, or flow divider.

FIELD ADJUSTMENTS

The two types of field adjustments that are made on a fuel injection system include the idle mixture and idle speed. The idle mixture on an RSA system is controlled by adjusting the position of the idle fuel valve in the fuel metering unit. If you recall, the idle valve is connected to the throttle valve by an adjustable mechanical linkage. Based on this, the idle mixture is adjusted by varying the length of the linkage between the two valves. On the other hand, the idle speed is adjusted by turning a spring loaded adjustment screw. [Figure 7-58]

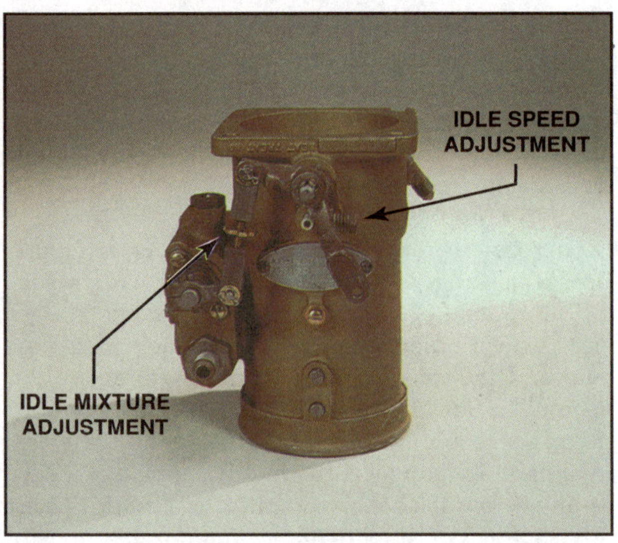

Figure 7-58. To adjust the idle speed on an RSA fuel injection unit, a spring-loaded adjustment screw is typically provided. On the other hand, the idle mixture is adjusted by changing the length of the connecting rod between the idle and throttle valves

To make an idle mixture adjustment, begin by starting the engine using the manufacturers starting checklist. Once the engine is warm, adjust the mixture as necessary and retard the throttle to idle. When engine speed has stabilized, slowly move the mixture control toward the idle-cutoff position while simultaneously observing the tachometer or manifold pressure gauge. On aircraft that are equipped with a tachometer, the mixture is adjusted properly if the engine rpm increases slightly just before it drops off rapidly. However, if equipped with a manifold pressure gauge, an optimum idle mixture is indicated by the manifold pressure decreasing just before the engine ceases to fire.

If the idle mixture check reveals a mixture that is too lean or too rich, increase or decrease the idle fuel flow as required. To increase the fuel flow, the length of the connecting linkage is increased; however, to decrease the fuel flow, the length of the connecting linkage must be decreased. Once you have adjusted the idle mixture, recheck the mixture using the same procedure discussed earlier.

After adjusting the idle mixture, you may need to reset the idle speed. To do this, the spring-loaded idle screw is rotated to adjust when the throttle shaft contacts the idle stop. If the idle speed needs to be increased, the idle screw is turned clockwise. On the other hand, to decrease the idle speed, turn the idle screw counter-clockwise.

TELEDYNE CONTINENTAL SYSTEM

A second type of continuous-flow fuel injection system is the Teledyne Continental fuel injection system. Unlike the RSA system which utilizes both fuel and air forces to meter fuel, the Teledyne Continental system only uses a fuel metering force to meter fuel. The basic components of a Teledyne

Continental system include an engine-driven injector pump, a fuel/air control unit, a fuel manifold valve, and injector nozzles.

INJECTOR PUMP

The injector pump used in a Teledyne Continental system consists of a vane-type pump that is driven by a splined shaft. Additional components that are included in a typical injector pump include a vapor-separator chamber, an adjustable orifice and relief valve, a vapor ejector, and a bypass valve. [Figure 7-59]

As fuel enters an injector pump, it passes through a vapor-separator chamber where it is swirled to remove any remaining fuel vapor. From here, the fuel passes through a vane-type pump. If you recall from Section A, all vane-type pumps are positive displacement pumps. This means that the pump delivers a specific quantity per revolution. Because of this, the output of an injector pump varies with engine speed. Furthermore, with vane-type pumps, more fuel is delivered to the fuel/air control unit than is needed. Therefore, all injector pumps incorporate a return passage that routes excess fuel back to the pump inlet. By incorporating a variable orifice in the return line, a fuel pressure that is proportional to the engine's speed is provided. For example, when the size of the orifice is increased, the pump's output pressure decreases. On the other hand, when the size of the orifice is decreased the output pressure increases.

The use of an adjustable orifice works well to control fuel flow when the engine is operating at or above cruise power settings. However, below cruise power settings the orifice does not restrict fuel flow enough to maintain a constant output pressure. To remedy this condition, a spring-loaded pressure relief valve is installed downstream from the orifice. This way, when an engine is operated at low power settings, the resistance offered by the spring-loaded relief valve permits the injector pump to maintain a constant output pressure.

To aid in removing excess fuel vapor from the vapor chamber, some of the excess output fuel is routed through a **vapor ejector** at the top of the vapor chamber. A vapor ejector is nothing more than a restriction in the fuel passageway that is open to the vapor chamber. As fuel flows through the ejector restriction, a low pressure area is created that draws fuel vapor out of the vapor chamber and returns it to the fuel tanks.

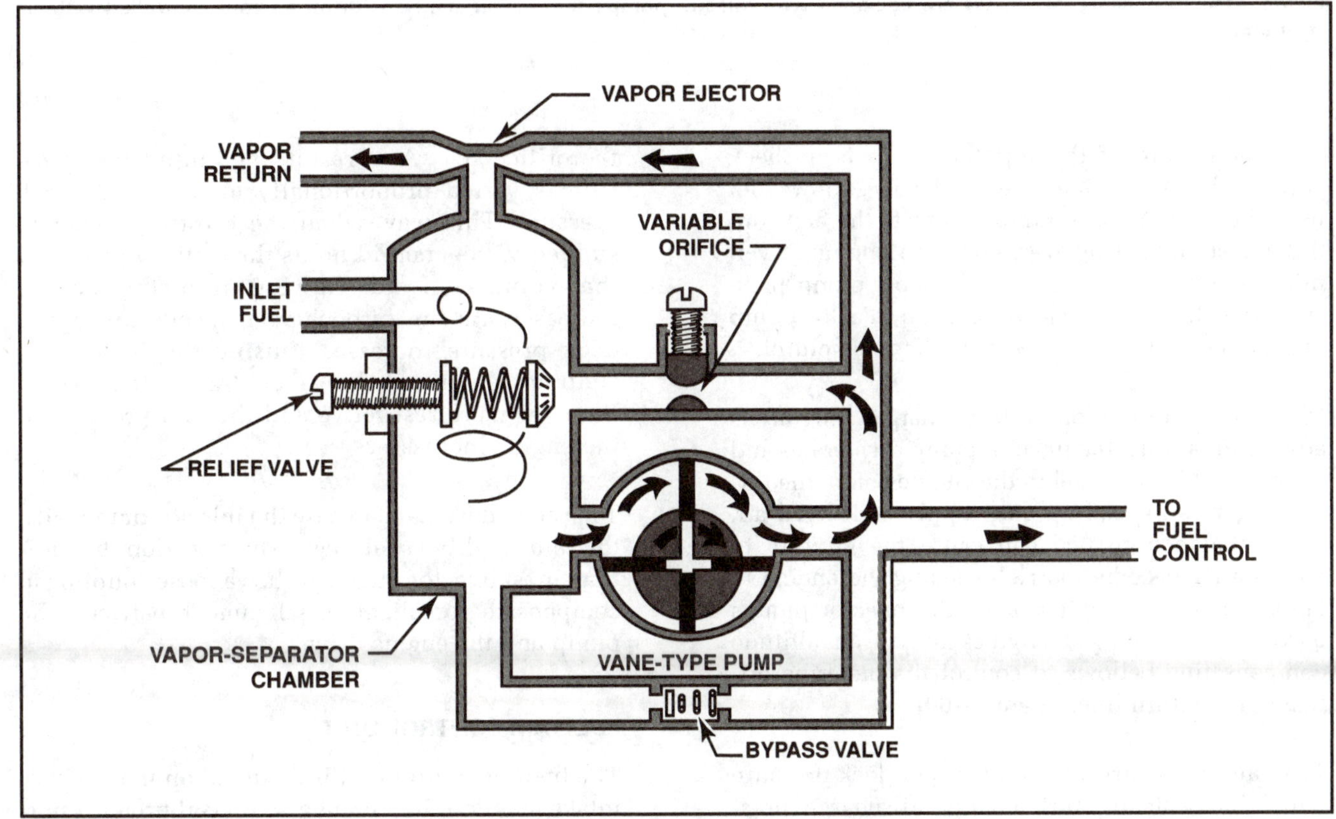

Figure 7-59. A typical injector pump in a Teledyne Continental fuel injection system consists of a vane-type pump that is housed with a vapor separator, an adjustable orifice and relief valve, a vapor ejector, and a bypass valve.

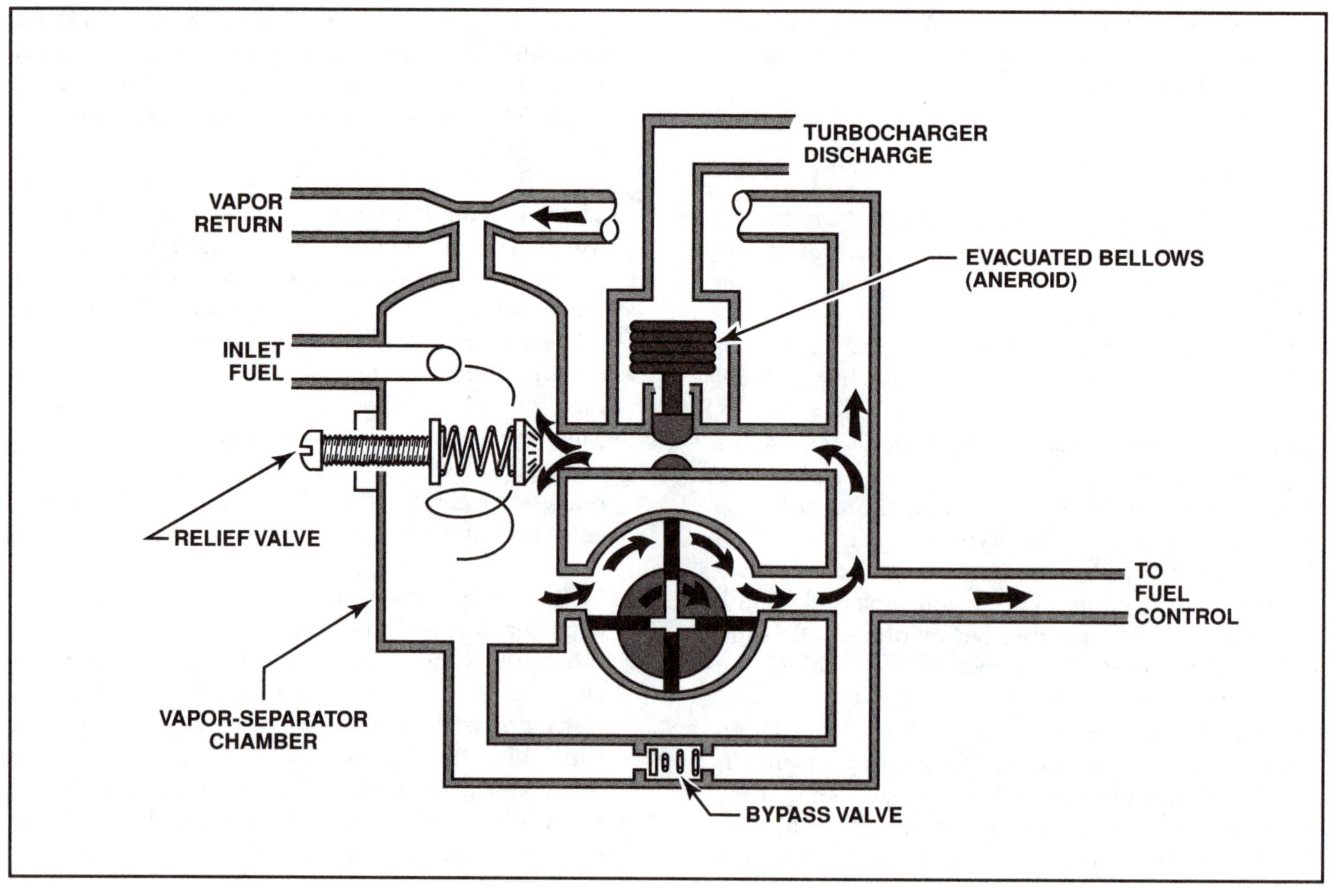

Figure 7-60. Turbocharged engines are equipped with injector pumps that are equipped with an aneroid controlled variable restrictor.

Another feature of the injector pump is a check valve in the bypass line. The check valve allows fuel from the aircraft boost pump to flow to the fuel control for starting. However, once the engine-driven injector pump pressure exceeds boost pump pressure, the check valve closes and the injector pump begins to supply fuel pressure to the fuel control.

When the throttle on a turbocharged engine is advanced rapidly, the injector pump accelerates and supplies additional fuel to the engine before the turbocharger can speed up and supply additional air. The imbalance created can cause the mixture to temporarily become too rich causing the engine to falter. To correct this problem, the injector pumps used on turbocharged engines utilize an altitude compensating bellows to control the metering orifice in the return line. [Figure 7-60]

The aneroid is surrounded by upper deck pressure which is basically turbocharger discharge pressure. As the upper deck pressure fluctuates, the aneroid moves the variable restrictor, controlling the orifice size. As a result, the output fuel pressure is varied proportionally to the upper deck pressure. This way, when the throttle is opened suddenly, the aneroid holds the orifice open until the volume of air flowing into the engine increases. As the turbocharger speeds up, upper deck pressure increases causing the bellows to contract. As the bellows contracts, the orifice becomes more restrictive and the fuel pressure to the engine increases.

To protect the engine in case the injector pump fails, the pump's drive shaft has a shear section. In addition, most injector pumps utilize a loose coupling to compensate for slight misalignment between the pump and the engine drive.

FUEL/AIR CONTROL UNIT

The fuel/air control unit is mounted on the engine's intake manifold in the same way a carburetor is normally mounted. The section of the fuel/air control unit which contains the throttle valve is known as

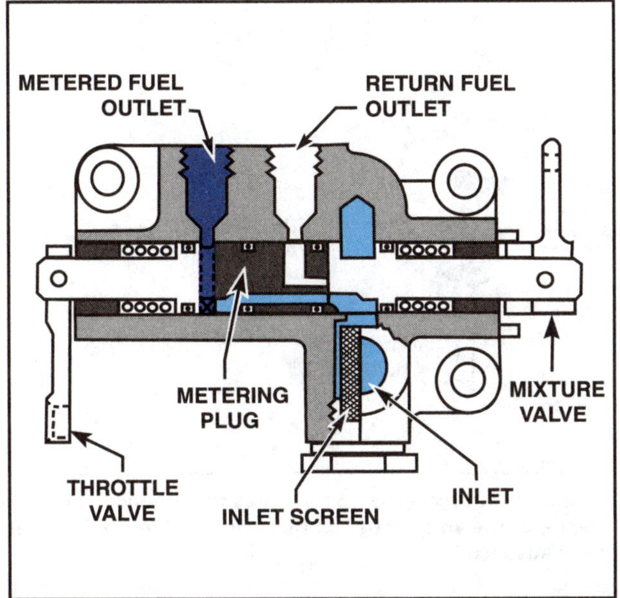

Figure 7-61. The fuel control assembly contains the manual mixture control valve and fuel metering valve. Both valves are rotary-type valves which are connected to cockpit control levers.

the **air throttle assembly**. The air throttle assembly of a Teledyne Continental fuel injection system differs from others in that it has no venturi. Attached to the side of the air throttle assembly is the **fuel control assembly**. In most cases, the fuel control unit body is made of bronze and houses both a mixture valve and a fuel metering valve. Both valves are rotary-type valves that are constructed of stainless steel and rotate in oil-impregnated bushings. [Figure 7-61]

The end of each valve rotates against a fixed metering plug in the center of the fuel control unit. The metering plug is also made of bronze and contains a fuel metering jet that meters the fuel flow to the engine. In addition, the metering plug contains one passage that connects the fuel inlet with the fuel return outlet and a second passage that connects the mixture control valve chamber with the fuel metering valve chamber. The mixture valve in a Teledyne Continental fuel control unit acts as a variable selector valve that directs fuel to either the metering jet or back to the fuel pump. [Figure 7-62]

Once past the mixture valve, fuel can flow through the metering jet. However, the amount of fuel that can flow out of the main metering jet is determined by the position of the fuel metering valve. A typical valve plate used with a fuel metering valve proportionately uncovers the outlet of the main jet as the throttle is advanced. For example, at low power settings, only a small portion of the main metering jet is completely uncovered. However, as the throttle is advanced, more of the main metering jet is uncovered to provide additional fuel. When the throttle is wide open, the main jet is completely uncovered to provide the fuel required for high power settings. The fuel metering valve is operated with a control arm that is connected to the cockpit throttle lever.

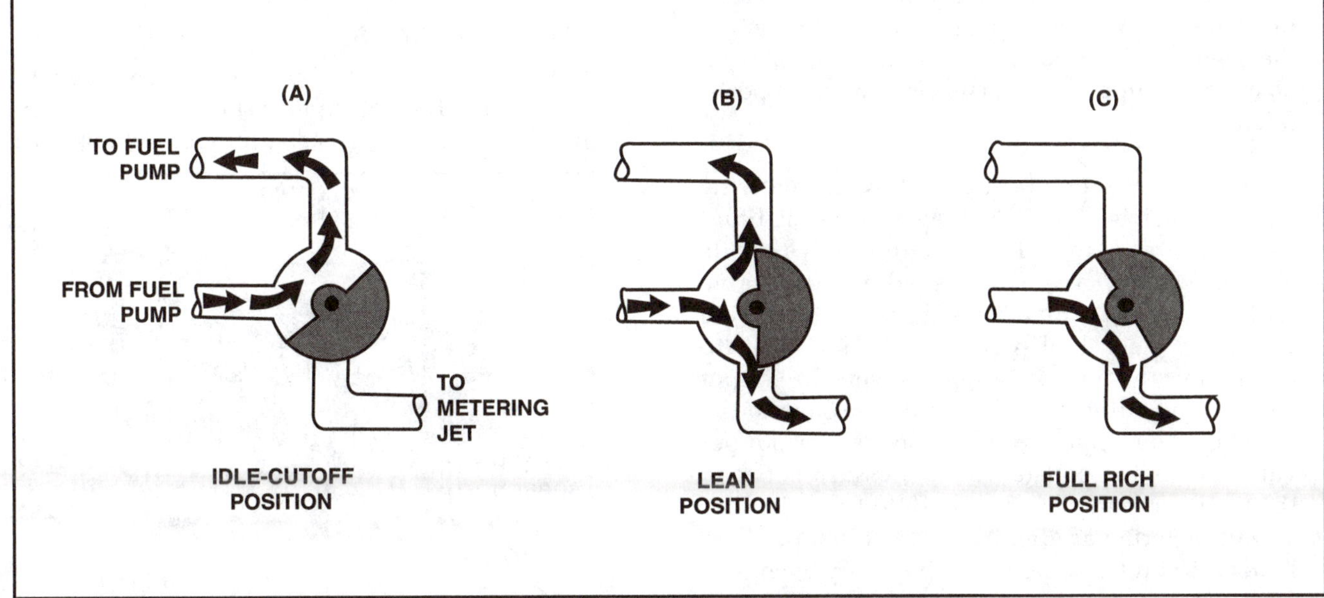

Figure 7-62. (A) — When the mixture valve is placed in the idle-cutoff position, fuel is routed from the pump outlet back to the pump inlet. (B) — As the mixture control is advanced to a lean setting, the mixture valve begins to uncover a portion of the passageway leading to the metering jet. (C) — When the mixture control is advanced to the full-rich position, all of the fuel from the injector pump is directed to the fuel manifold valve.

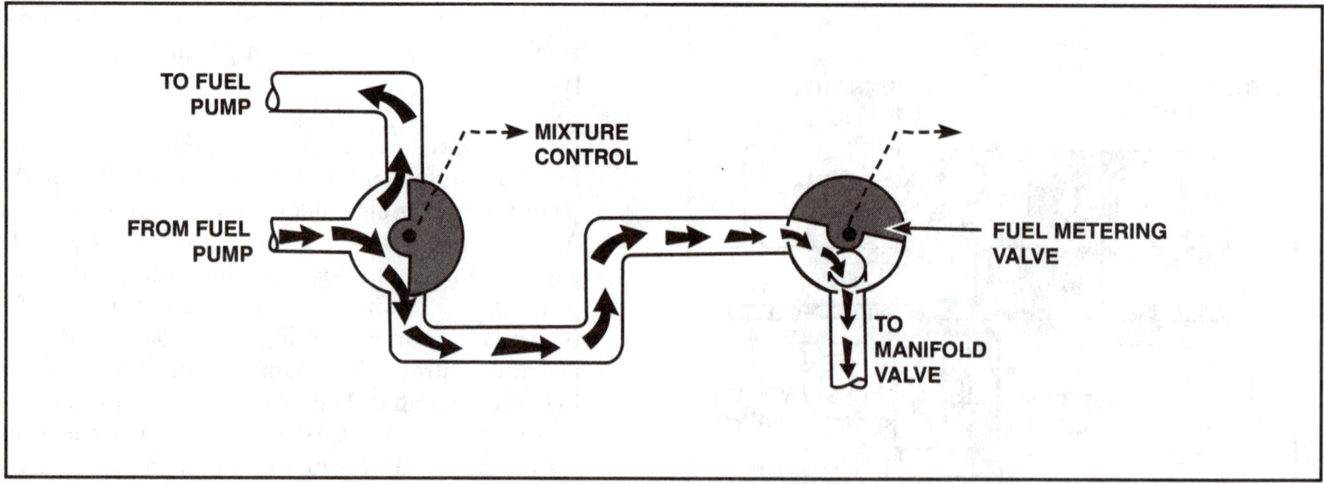

Figure 7-63. Once fuel flows past the mixture valve and metering jet, the fuel metering valve regulates the amount of fuel that flows to the manifold valve for distribution. The fuel metering valve regulates the amount of fuel that flows to the manifold valve by proportionately uncovering the outlet of the main jet as the throttle is advanced.

Therefore, the cockpit throttle lever controls both the throttle air valve and the fuel metering valve. [Figure 7-63]

FUEL MANIFOLD VALVE

Fuel flows from the fuel metering valve through a flexible fuel line to the fuel manifold valve. The purpose of a fuel manifold valve, or **distribution valve** is to evenly distribute fuel to all cylinders. In addition, the fuel manifold valve provides a positive fuel shutoff to the nozzles when the mixture control is placed in the idle-cutoff position. In most installations, the fuel manifold valve is mounted on top of the engine and consists of a fuel inlet, a diaphragm chamber, a poppet valve, and several outlet ports. [Figure 7-64]

When the fuel pressure supplied by the metering valve is sufficient, the diaphragm in the manifold valve is forced up to lift the cutoff valve off its seat. However, a spring-loaded poppet valve within the cutoff valve stays on its seat, blocking fuel flow. Once fuel pressure builds enough to completely offseat the cutoff valve, the poppet valve is forced open, allowing fuel to flow to the nozzles. The opposition caused by the poppet valve ensures a constant fuel pressure between the main metering jet and manifold valve for consistent metering at idle. Above idle, fuel pressure holds the cutoff and poppet valves fully open, and fuel pressure is maintained due to the restriction in each injector nozzle. When the mixture control is placed in the idle-cutoff position, fuel pressure to the fuel manifold valve drops and spring tension closes the cutoff valve. This provides a positive shutoff of fuel and traps fuel in the supply lines leading to the injector nozzles.

The chamber above the diaphragm is vented to ambient air pressure for unrestricted valve movement. To prevent air pressure fluctuations in the chamber above the diaphragm, the fuel manifold valve must be positioned to prevent ram air from entering the chamber vent. Therefore, most fuel manifold valves are positioned with the vent opening to the side or the rear.

INJECTOR NOZZLES

The injector nozzles used with the Teledyne Continental fuel injection system are air bleed type nozzles which are threaded into the cylinder heads

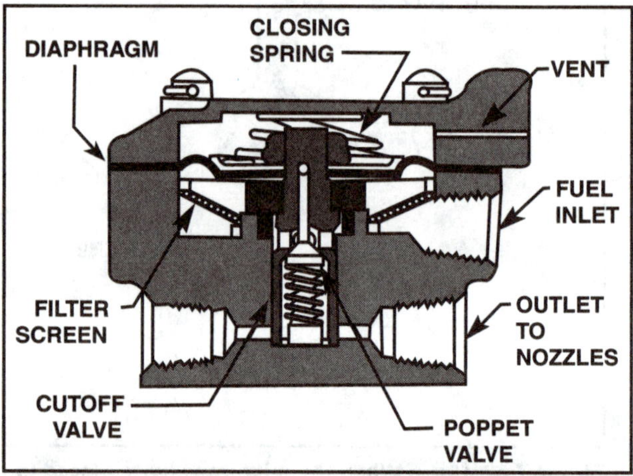

Figure 7-64. The fuel manifold valve distributes fuel evenly to all the cylinders and provides a positive fuel shutoff when the mixture is placed in the idle-cutoff position.

near the intake ports. Each nozzle consists of a brass body constructed with a metering orifice, multiple air bleed holes, and an emulsion chamber. In addition, to help ensure that no contaminants are drawn into the air bleed holes, a fine mesh screen and pressed steel shroud surround the brass body. [Figure 7-65]

Each nozzle incorporates a calibrated metering orifice, or jet, that is manufactured to provide a specific flow rate. Currently, there are three different sizes of metering jets used in Teledyne Continental injector nozzles. The jet size used is determined by the available fuel inlet pressure and the maximum fuel flow required by the engine. To allow you to identify the size of the jet in any given nozzle, a single letter identification mark is usually stamped on the hex flat of the nozzle. For example, an A-size nozzle will provide a specific amount of fuel for a given pressure. On the other hand, B-size nozzles provide one-half gallon more fuel per hour than an A-size nozzle with the same pressure. C-size nozzles provide the largest metering jet and a full gallon per hour more fuel than an A-size nozzle with the same pressure. When an engine is calibrated during its factory runup, the proper size nozzles are installed and this nozzle size should not be arbitrarily changed.

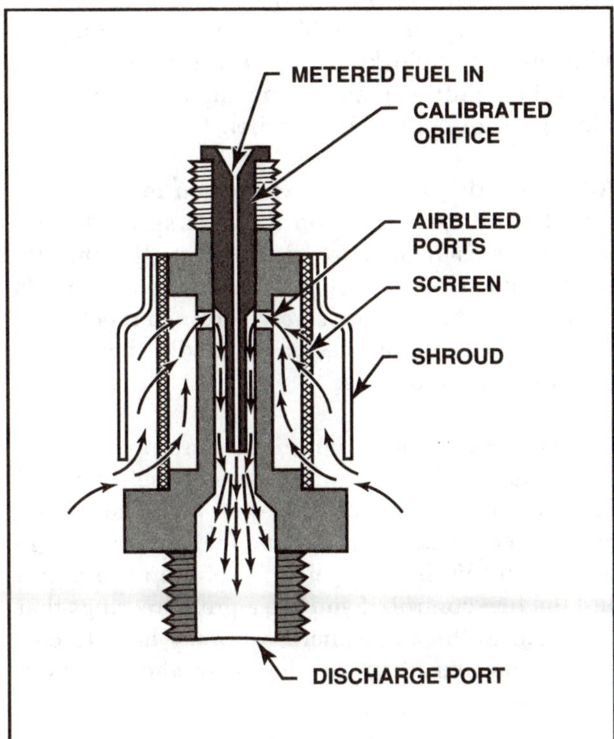

Figure 7-65. A typical Teledyne Continental fuel injector consists of a shrouded brass body that houses a metering orifice, multiple air bleed holes, and an emulsion chamber.

Once the fuel flows through the metering jet it enters an emulsion chamber where it is mixed with air. Since the end of the nozzle is exposed to manifold pressure which, on normally aspirated engines, is less than atmospheric pressure, air is pulled into the nozzle through the air bleed. As the air and fuel mix in the emulsion chamber, the fuel is atomized. Since the manifold pressure in a turbocharged engine often exceeds atmospheric pressure, a high pressure air source must be used for the air bleed. In most cases, the high pressure air is taken from the turbocharger side of the throttle valve, or upper deck. By doing this, high pressure turbocharger outlet air is directed into each injector nozzle as a source of bleed air.

To meet the requirements of different engine models, Teledyne Continental injector nozzles are manufactured in several different styles. For example, some engines require long nozzles so fuel is injected farther into the intake chamber while other engine designs function best with short nozzles. While nozzle styles differ in appearance, their purpose and method of injecting metered fuel is the same.

INSPECTION AND MAINTENANCE

All fuel injection system components should be checked for security and integrity of mounting at least once every one hundred hours. In addition, all lines should be inspected for indications of chafing or leaking as evidenced by the presence of fuel stains. An important thing to note is that all the injector nozzle supply lines on a given system are manufactured to the same length. This helps ensure that the same fuel pressure and quantity are delivered to each cylinder. Therefore, when installing or maintaining these fuel lines, they cannot be shortened. Instead, if an excess length of fuel line exists, it should be coiled midway between the nozzle and manifold.

Once you have inspected the fuel lines, you should check all moving parts for wear, and lubricate the ends of the throttle linkage rods with a drop of engine oil. In addition, the strainer in the fuel control unit and the fuel manifold valve must be checked and cleaned.

Normally, injector nozzles do not require much service, therefore, manufacturers commonly establish service intervals between 100 and 300 hours of operation. Nozzle maintenance typically consists of removal from the engine, soaking in acetone or lacquer thinner, and clearing out cleaning fluids with clean, dry, air. One way to identify a clogged nozzle is by the presence of fuel stains on a cylinder head around the nozzle. When a nozzle becomes clogged, fuel pressure forces fuel through the air bleed ports and onto the engine.

When cleaning nozzles, do not use wires, drills, or other cleaning tools to clear out orifice obstructions. Doing so can damage the precision passages, rendering the nozzle unserviceable. Manufacturers typically require nozzle replacement if an obstruction cannot be cleared by soaking the nozzle in an approved cleaner or by blowing it out with compressed air. Once the nozzles are clean, reinstall them and secure all other fuel system components.

In addition to inspecting and cleaning the injector nozzles, you should also inspect the fuel manifold. When inspecting the fuel manifold, verify that the vent hole is free of obstructions. If the vent hole should become plugged, the pressure acting on one side of the diaphragm will not vary with changes in altitude and the divider valve will not open the correct amount.

FIELD ADJUSTMENTS

The two types of field adjustments that are made on a fuel injection system include the idle mixture and idle speed. The idle mixture on a Teledyne Continental system is controlled by adjusting the position of the fuel metering valve in the fuel control unit. If you recall, the fuel metering valve is connected to the throttle valve by an adjustable linkage. Based on this, the idle mixture is changed by varying the length of the linkage between the two valves. On the other hand, the idle speed is adjusted by turning a spring loaded adjustment screw. [Figure 7-66]

To make an idle mixture adjustment, begin by starting the engine using the manufacturers starting checklist. Once the engine is warm, adjust the mixture as necessary and retard the throttle to idle. When engine speed has stabilized, slowly move the mixture control toward the idle-cutoff position while simultaneously observing the tachometer or manifold pressure gauge. On aircraft that are equipped with a tachometer, the mixture is adjusted properly if engine rpm increases slightly just before it drops off rapidly. However, if equipped with a manifold pressure gauge, an optimum idle mixture is indicated by the manifold pressure decreasing just before the engine ceases to fire.

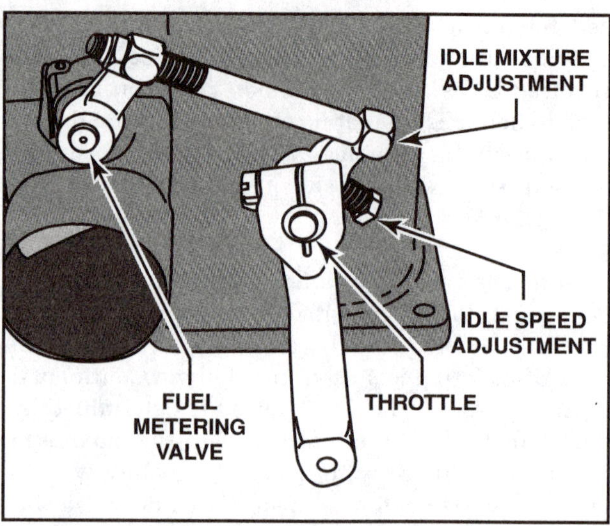

Figure 7-66. To adjust the idle speed on a Teledyne Continental fuel injection unit, a spring-loaded adjustment screw is typically provided. On the other hand, the idle mixture is adjusted by changing the length of the connecting rod between the fuel metering valve and the throttle valve.

If the idle mixture check reveals a mixture that is too lean or too rich, increase or decrease the idle fuel flow as required. To increase the fuel flow, the length of the connecting linkage is decreased by turning the adjustment nut counter-clockwise; however, to decrease the fuel flow, the length of the connecting linkage must be increased by turning the adjustment nut clockwise. Once you have adjusted the idle mixture, recheck the mixture using the same procedure discussed earlier.

After adjusting the idle mixture, you may need to reset the idle speed. To do this, the spring-loaded idle screw is rotated to adjust when the throttle shaft contacts the idle stop. If the idle speed needs to be increased, the idle screw is turned clockwise. On the other hand, to decrease the idle speed, turn the idle screw clockwise.

Once idle speed and idle mixture are properly set you should check both the low and high metered fuel pressures. Metered fuel pressure checks are made by connecting a calibrated fuel pressure gauge into a T-fitting in the fuel line between the pump and the fuel control. If you use a pressure gauge that is vented to the atmosphere, you may have to correct the gauge readings depending on the local field elevation.

To obtain an accurate low metered fuel pressure indication, the engine must be warmed up and idling at the proper rpm. If the indicated pressure does not correspond with the manufacturer's specifications, adjust the relief valve to obtain the correct pressure. To check the high metered fuel pressure, operate the engine at full throttle and observe the pressure gauge reading. Pressure readings not within the manufacturer's specifications can be corrected by adjusting the orifice in the fuel pump return line. When making this check and adjustment, try to limit high rpm engine operation to avoid overheating the engine.

Once all metered fuel pressure checks have been made, it may be necessary to recheck the idle speed and idle mixture adjustments. The reason for this is that all the adjustments effect one another.

Once all the adjustments are satisfactory and within specifications, remove the test gauge and prepare the aircraft for a test flight to verify the high metered fuel pressure. Since high metered fuel pressure is observed on the aircraft's own fuel flow gauge, a test flight is typically the best way to make this check. High metered fuel pressure should be checked at full throttle and maximum permissible rpm after ten to fifteen minutes at a cruise power setting.

TROUBLESHOOTING

Effective fuel injection system troubleshooting requires several skills. For example, you should not instantly assume that the fuel injection system is the cause of a rough running engine. Although the fuel injection system may be at fault, you must also check for proper ignition and consider the possibility of induction system problems before dismantling fuel injection components. Taking these preliminary steps may save time and effort. Typically, Teledyne Continental furnishes troubleshooting charts to help you diagnose fuel injection problems. In addition, the individual aircraft maintenance manuals may contain troubleshooting flowcharts to help you determine the cause of a rough running engine.

OVERHAUL

Fuel injection systems, like carbureted systems, are normally overhauled simultaneously with an engine overhaul. Overhaul of most fuel injection systems requires specialized tools, flow benches, and specialized training. Therefore, unless you are employed by a certified repair station which is equipped for fuel injection system overhauls, you are ordinarily limited to basic inspections and field adjustments.

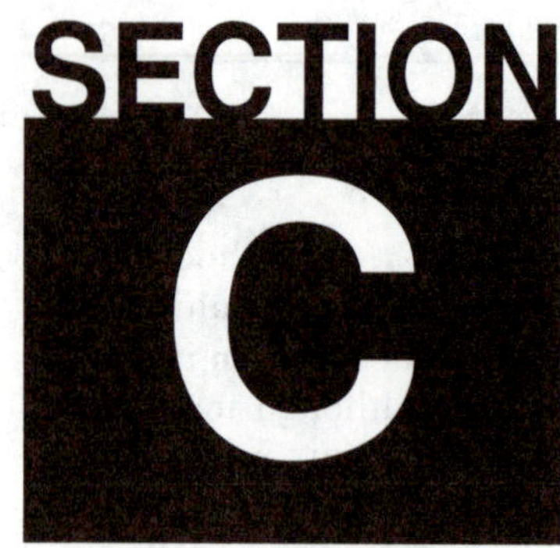

TURBINE ENGINE FUEL METERING

Turbine engine fuel metering devices have the same purpose as their reciprocating engine counterparts. In other words, they must meter fuel to a turbine engine for reliable ground and air operations. If you recall from your earlier studies on turbine engines, the power output of a turbine engine varies with the amount of air that is drawn into the compressor and the amount of heat that is generated in the combustion section. You should also recall that the amount of heat produced in the combustors is determined by the amount of fuel that is scheduled into the engine. Based on this, a turbine engine fuel metering device must schedule the proper amount of fuel to the engine to obtain a given power output. Due to the inertia of the main turbine and the large changes in airflow associated with power changes, turbine engines do not respond rapidly to abrupt power lever movements. For example, when an engine is decelerated and the fuel flow is decreased more rapidly than the airflow through the engine, an incombustible fuel/air mixture could result and cause what is known is a lean die-out. On the other hand, if an engine is accelerated too rapidly, and an excessive amount of fuel is scheduled into the combustors before the main turbine has time to accelerate, a rich blowout can occur. For these reasons, a turbine engine fuel metering device must control fuel flow and engine acceleration and deceleration rates. The main components of a typical turbine engine fuel metering system include a fuel control unit and fuel nozzles.

FUEL CONTROL UNITS

When the engine operator makes a power setting with the cockpit controls, the **fuel control unit**, or **FCU**, responds by adjusting fuel flow to the engine. The FCU meters fuel in accordance with the power lever position to provide the precise amount of fuel necessary for the desired thrust.

In order to perform its fuel metering functions, a fuel control unit monitors several engine operating parameters including power lever position, engine rpm, compressor inlet air temperature and pressure, and burner or compressor discharge pressure. Based on the detected parameter information, a fuel control provides the precise fuel flow needed. In addition, many fuel control units incorporate several automatic functions to help prevent flameouts, over-temperature occurrences, and over-speed conditions.

Turbine engine fuel controls are designed to meter fuel by weight rather than by volume. The reason for this is that the heat energy per pound of fuel is a constant value regardless of fuel temperature, while the heat energy per unit volume of fuel varies. If you may recall, as the temperature of turbine fuel increases, its volume also increases. By the same token, as the temperature of turbine fuel decreases, its volume decreases.

Fuel control units meter the correct amount of fuel into the combustion section to obtain an optimum air-to-fuel mixture ratio of 15:1 by weight. This ratio represents 15 pounds of combustor primary air to one pound of fuel. If you recall from Section B, a mixture ratio of 15:1 is the theoretically perfect mixture for combustion.

A typical fuel control unit is an engine-driven accessory that meters fuel using hydromechanical, hydro-pneumatic, or electronic forces. Today, hydromechanical and electronic fuel control units are used on most turbojet and turbofan engines. On the other hand, hydro-pneumatic units are used on several turboprop engines.

HYDROMECHANICAL

A typical hydromechanical fuel control unit is divided into a fuel metering section and a computing section. The fuel metering section consists of a fuel pump, a pressure regulating valve, a single metering valve, and a fuel shutoff valve. On the other hand, the computing section consists of a speed sensitive control, or governor, that responds to the position of the power lever and the speed of the engine. Additional components include a servo valve that controls the rate of engine acceleration and deceleration, and two bellows that adjust fuel flow based on burner and inlet air pressure. [Figure 7-67]

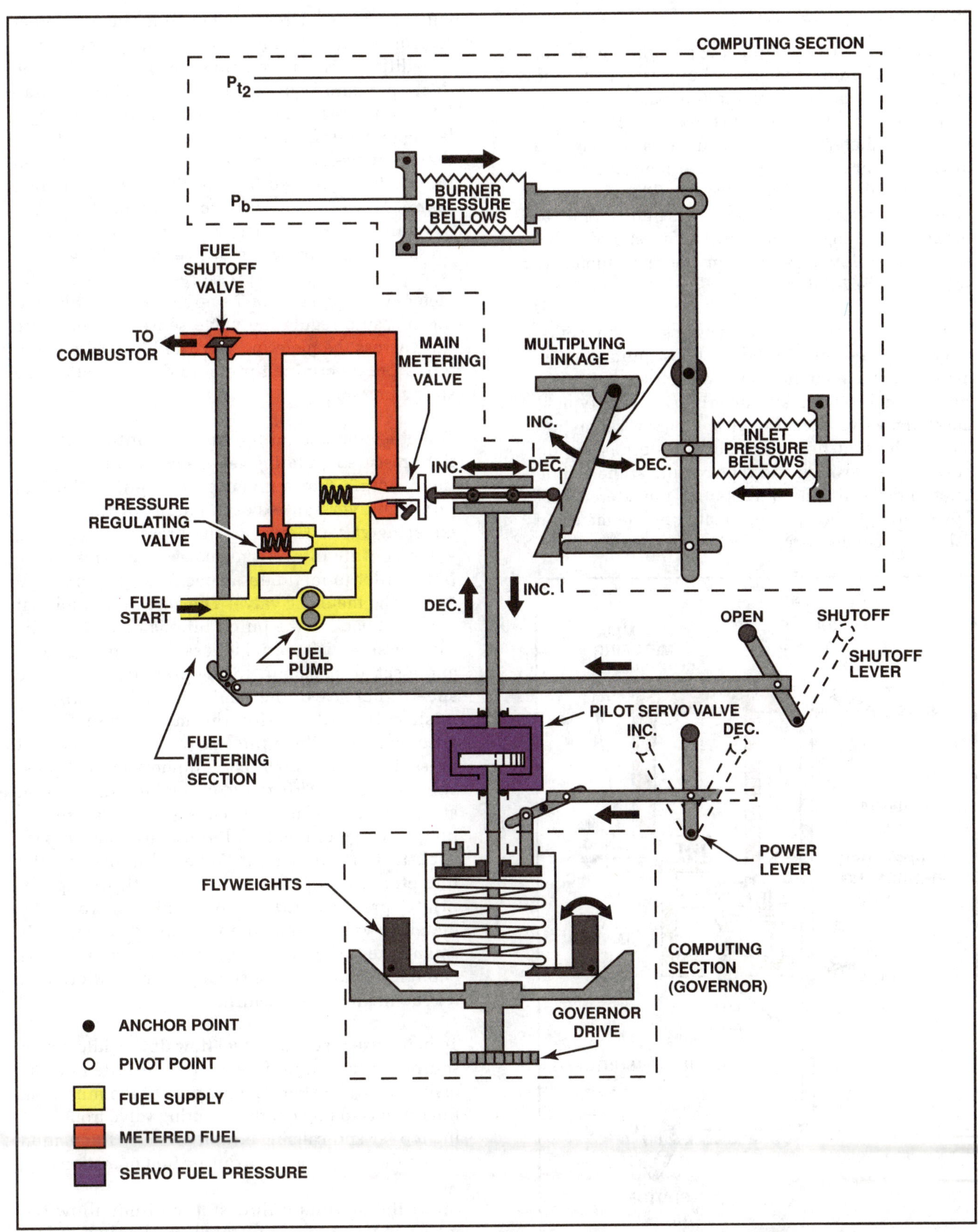

Figure 7-67. The simplified hydromechanical fuel control unit pictured here is provided as an overview of a typical system. The fuel metering portion of the fuel control unit utilizes a fuel pump to send pressurized fuel to a main metering valve and on to the combustion section. On the other hand, the computing section monitors power lever position, engine speed, burner pressure, and engine inlet pressure to control the amount of fuel that is allowed through the metering jet and in to the engine.

FUEL METERING SECTION

The primary purpose of the fuel metering section of a hydromechanical fuel control unit is to meter the appropriate amount of fuel to the combustion section at the correct pressure. In order to do this, a typical fuel metering section utilizes a positive displacement fuel pump, a main metering valve, and a pressure regulating valve. In addition, to provide a positive means of stopping the flow of fuel to the engine for engine shut down, a fuel shutoff valve is provided downstream from the main metering valve. [Figure 7-68]

To understand how the fuel metering section works, refer to figure 7-68. To begin, boost pump fuel is directed to the main fuel pump which sends unpressurized fuel to the main metering valve. A typical metering valve consists of a tapered valve that meters the fuel flow to the combustors based on power lever position and the pressure at the engine inlet and within the burners. As unmetered fuel flows through the opening created by the metering valve, it becomes metered fuel and a pressure differential is created across the metering valve. In order to properly meter fuel by weight, a constant pressure differential, or drop, must be maintained. To do this, a pressure regulating valve is installed in parallel with the main metering valve. A pressure regulating valve is similar to a pressure relief valve in that a spring-loaded valve controls the amount of fuel that is bypassed back to the inlet of the fuel pump. However, in order to maintain a constant pressure differential across the metering valve, a pressure regulating valve utilizes a diaphragm that is exposed to pump pressure on one side and metered fuel pressure on its opposite side. This way, the pressure regulating valve senses the pressure drop across the metering valve and is able to maintain a pre-determined pressure drop based on the spring pressure.

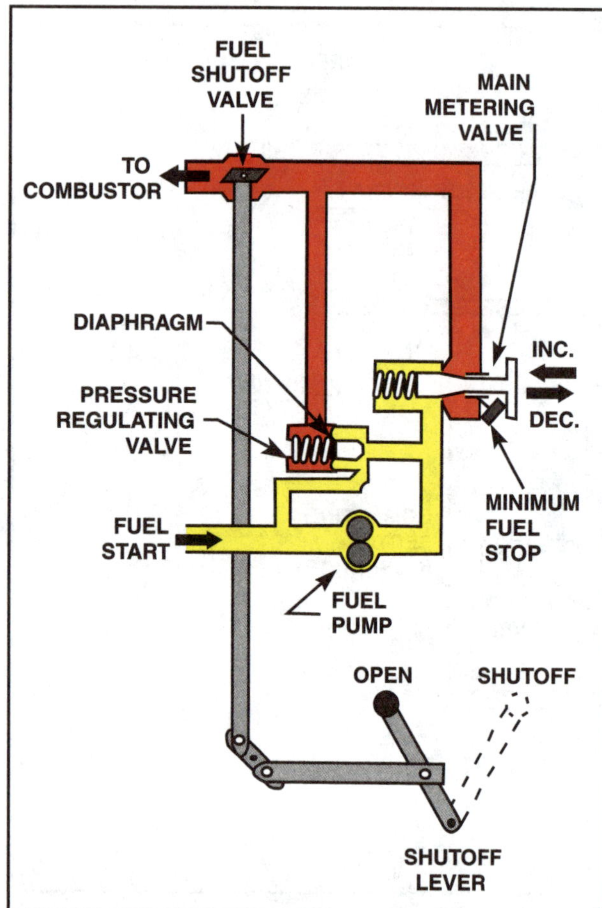

Figure 7-68. The components that make up the fuel metering section include a fuel pump, a main metering valve, a pressure regulating valve, and a fuel shutoff valve.

To better understand the function of the differential pressure regulating valve, consider the following example. For a given power setting the fuel pump delivers an excess amount of fuel to the metering valve. However, the pressure regulating valve continually returns excess fuel back to the pump inlet to maintain a specified pressure drop across the metering valve. The amount of fuel that is routed back to the pump inlet is determined by the pressure differential across the metering valve and a set, or constant, spring pressure. As engine speed increases, the main metering valve is pushed inward causing the metering orifice to become larger. When this occurs, the metered fuel pressure increases while the unmetered fuel pressure decreases. This reduced pressure differential across the metering valve causes the pressure regulating valve to close and allow less fuel to pass back to the pump inlet. When this occurs, the unmetered fuel pressure builds until the appropriate pressure differential exists across the metering valve. Once the pressure differential is established, the pressure regulating valve opens enough to maintain the same pressure differential for the higher power setting.

To help ensure adequate fuel flow during idle power settings, a minimum flow stop is installed on the main metering valve. The purpose of the minimum flow stop is to prevent the metering valve from closing too far and causing erratic pressure fluctuation across the metering valve during idle operations.

Since the minimum flow stop will not allow the metering valve to completely stop the flow of fuel to the combustors, a fuel shutoff valve must be installed to provide a positive means of stopping the flow of fuel for engine shutdown. In addition, the shutoff valve also ensures that the correct fuel pressure builds within the fuel control unit during an engine start cycle. Control of the fuel shutoff valve is provided by a mechanical, electric, or pneumatic linkage that is activated by a fuel shutoff lever in the cockpit.

COMPUTING SECTION

The computing section of the fuel control is responsible for positioning the metering valve to obtain the appropriate power output and control the rate of acceleration and deceleration. To do this, a typical computing section utilizes a speed sensitive governor, a servo valve, and two pressure sensitive bellows. [Figure 7-69]

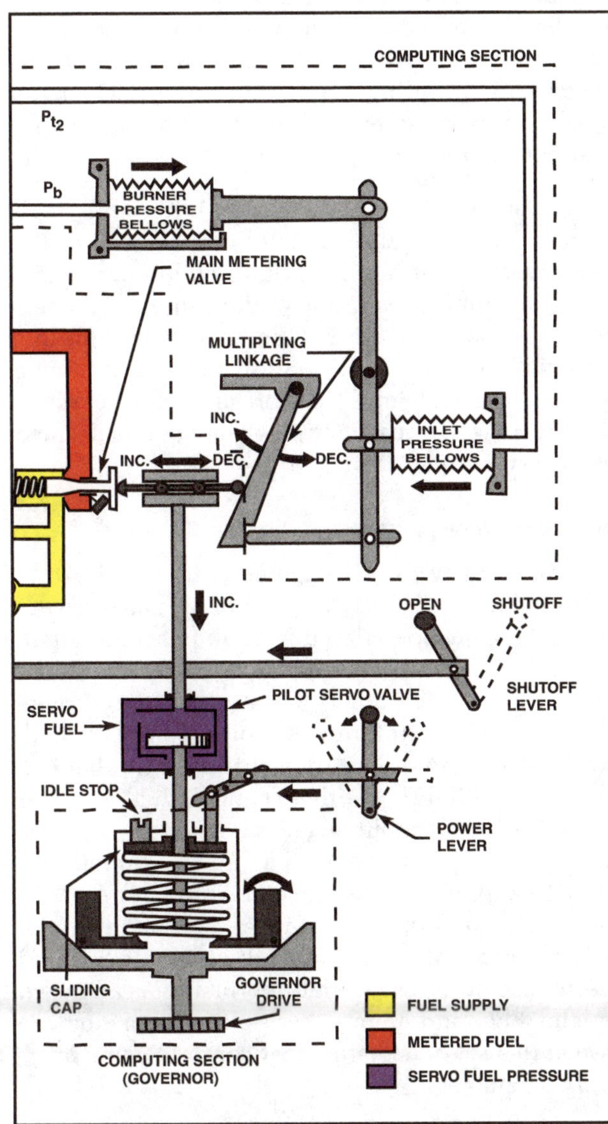

Figure 7-69. The computing section in a typical hydromechanical fuel control unit consists of a pilot servo valve that controls acceleration and deceleration rates, a governor that senses engine speed, and two pressure sensitive bellows.

During engine operation, forward movement of the power lever causes the spring cap to slide down the pilot servo valve rod and compress the flyweight speeder spring. This action forces the tops of the flyweights inward, creating an under-speed condition. When this occurs, the fuel in the pilot servo valve is displaced from top to bottom causing the slider to move down. The pilot servo valve is a hydraulic dampener which transforms sudden throttle movements into slow, smooth commands to reposition the main metering valve. As the slider moves down the inclined plane of the multiplying linkage, it moves to the left and forces the metering valve to open. Any time the metering valve is opened further, more fuel flows to the engine to increase the power output. As power output increases, engine speed also increases causing the governor drive to rotate faster. The increased rotational speed increases the centrifugal force acting on the flyweights causing them to return to an upright position.

On many engines, the static pressure within the combustors is a useful measure of mass airflow. For example, if mass airflow is known, the fuel/air ratio can be more carefully controlled. For this reason, a bellows that is vented to the combustion section is installed in many fuel control units. As burner pressure (P_b) increases, the burner pressure bellows expands to the right. If the pilot servo valve rod remains stationary, the multiplying linkage will force the slider to the left and open the metering valve to match fuel flow to the increased mass airflow.

Another factor that is important in determining the proper fuel/air ratio is the density and/or pressure of the air entering the engine. To permit a fuel control unit to sense the pressure of the air entering an engine, a second bellows that is vented to the engine inlet is installed. This way, when the inlet air pressure increases, the bellows expands and forces the multiplying linkage and slider to the left to increase fuel flow.

HYDRO-PNEUMATIC

As mentioned earlier, hydro-pneumatic fuel controls are often used on turboprop engines. A hydro-pneumatic fuel control differs from a hydromechanical fuel control in that a hydro-pneumatic fuel control utilizes a pneumatic computing section that determines fuel flow rates based on the position of the power lever, N_1 rpm, compressor discharge air (P_3), and outside air pressure (P_0).

Two governors, an N_1 governor, and an N_2 governor are also used in this type of fuel control unit. The N_1 governor controls compressor turbine speed while the N_2 governor controls the power turbine speed. The propeller of a free-turbine type of turboprop engine is driven by N_2 and, therefore, propeller rpm is controlled by the N_2 governor. Both governors sense compressor discharge air and are connected to the pneumatic computing section. Therefore, functions of the governors and pneumatic computing section are interdependent.

A starting flow control unit also is utilized in this type of fuel control and is installed between the main metering valve and fuel nozzles. A **starting flow control unit** consists of a casing which contains a ported plunger that slides in a ported sleeve. A rack and pinion assembly converts rotational movement of the input lever into linear motion for moving the plunger. The starting flow control unit ensures the correct fuel pressure to the nozzles and provides a means of draining residual fuel from the fuel manifolds when the engine is shutdown. This helps to prevent fuel from boiling and fouling the system with carbon due to heat absorption after engine shutdown.

ELECTRONIC

As turbine engines advanced in technology, scheduling the proper amount of fuel to the engine became more important. In fact, the only way a modern turbofan engine can realize its optimum designed efficiency is if the fuel is precisely scheduled to the engine while several engine parameters are monitored. To obtain the monitoring and control needed, most modern turbofan engines utilize an **electronic engine control**, or **EEC**, to schedule fuel.

In addition to its ability to monitor and precisely meter fuel, an EEC offers the benefit of saving fuel, increasing reliability, reducing operator workload, and reducing maintenance costs. Furthermore, a properly functioning EEC can prolong engine life by preventing over-temperature and over-speed occurrences. Today, there are two types of electronic engine controls used; the supervisory engine control system and the full-authority control system.

SUPERVISORY EEC

A supervisory EEC consists of an electronic control and a conventional hydromechanical fuel control unit. With this type of system, the hydromechanical fuel control unit controls most engine operations including starting, idle, acceleration, deceleration, and shutdown. On the other hand, the electronic control monitors several engine operating parameters and adjusts the fuel control unit to obtain the most effective engine operation based on the position of the power lever. With this type of system, once the operator sets the power lever to obtain a specific engine pressure ratio (EPR), the electronic engine control adjusts the fuel control unit as necessary to maintain the selected EPR as the aircraft climbs or as atmospheric conditions change. In addition, most EECs also limit an engine's operating speed and temperature to prevent over-speed and over-temperature occurrences. In fact, some supervisory EECs may be used primarily as an engine speed and temperature limiting control. For example, the supervisory EEC used on a Rolls Royce RB-211 works on a hydromechanical schedule until the engine is accelerated to near full engine power. However, once the engine nears its maximum rotational speed and operating temperature, the EEC begins operating as a limiter to limit the amount of fuel that goes to the engine. [Figure 7-70]

As a safety feature, if a supervisory EEC should malfunction, control automatically reverts back to the hydromechanical fuel control. In addition, a warning light illuminates in the cockpit to warn the aircraft operator that the EEC is no longer inputting information to the fuel control unit. By the same token, an aircraft operator can manually revert to the hydromechanical control whenever it is deemed necessary.

FULL-AUTHORITY EEC

A full-authority digital engine control, or **FADEC**, performs virtually all the functions necessary to support engine operation during all phases of flight. In addition, all FADEC systems are fully redundant and, therefore, eliminate the need for a hydromechanical fuel control unit. A typical FADEC system consists of a redundant, two-channel EEC that can pull information from either channel. In most cases, the EEC receives input on engine speed (N_1 and N_2), throttle lever position, bleed-air status, aircraft altitude, total inlet air pressure and temperature, stator vane angle, fuel flow rate, fuel and oil temperature, turbine exhaust pressure and temperature, and burner pressure. This input information is analyzed by the EEC and then a series of commands are issued to a set of actuators that control engine operating parameters.

On aircraft equipped with a FADEC system, the aircraft operator simply places the power lever in a specific position to obtain a given EPR, or power output, and the EEC automatically accelerates or

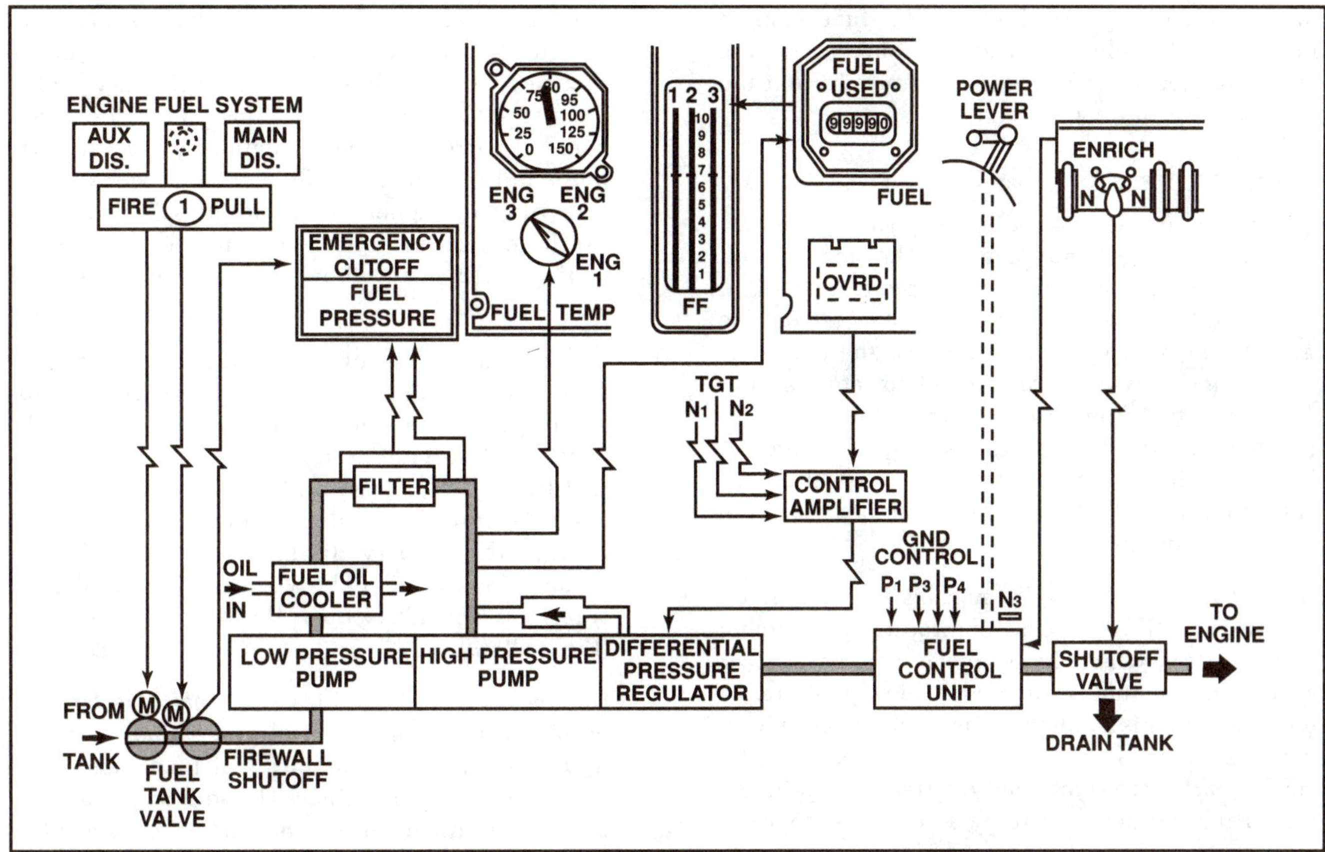

Figure 7-70. In the figure above, the control amplifier acts as the electronic control and receives input on N_1, N_2, and turbine gas temperature (TGT). With this type of system, the control operates on a hydromechanical schedule until the engine output approaches its maximum speed. At that point, the electronic circuit begins to function as a fuel limiter. To do this, the control amplifier sends a signal to the differential pressure regulator to divert more fuel back to the inlet side of the high pressure pump.

decelerates the engine to the EPR desired. In addition, the EEC maintains the selected EPR as the aircraft changes altitude or ambient conditions change. This greatly reduces pilot workload as well as overspeed and over-speed occurrences. In addition, since an EEC closely monitors and controls the engine operating parameters so that maximum thrust is obtained for a given amount of fuel, engines that are equipped with an EEC are usually more fuel efficient.

To provide a high degree of reliability, FADEC systems are designed with several redundant and dedicated subsystems. For example, as mentioned earlier, an EEC consists of two redundant channels that send and receive data. Each channel consists of its own processor, power supply, memory, sensors, and actuators. In addition, any one channel can take information from the other channel. This way, the EEC can still operate even if several faults exist. As a second backup should both channels fail, the actuators are spring loaded to a fail safe position so the fuel flow will go to minimum.

FUEL NOZZLES

Fuel nozzles, sometimes referred to as fuel distributors, are the last component in a turbine engine fuel metering system. Fuel nozzles are typically located in the diffuser or inlet of the combustion chamber where they deliver fuel in a specified quantity. In addition, since liquid fuel does not burn efficiently, the fuel nozzles must mix the fuel with air and vaporize it as it enters the combustion chamber. Most fuel nozzles can be classified as either an atomizing nozzle or a vaporizing nozzle.

ATOMIZING NOZZLES

Atomizing fuel nozzles receive fuel from a manifold, mix the fuel with air, and then deliver it to the combustor in an atomized spray pattern. In most cases, the spray pattern is cone shaped to provide a large fuel surface area of very fine fuel droplets. This spray pattern is designed to provide optimum fuel/air mixing as well as prevent the combustion flame from contacting the combustor lining. The most common types of atomizing fuel nozzles include the Simplex nozzle, the Duplex nozzle, the spill-type nozzle, the variable-port nozzle, and the air-spray type nozzle.

SIMPLEX NOZZLE

A Simplex nozzle is used on early jet engines and provides a single spray pattern. The nozzle itself incorporates an internally fluted spin chamber that imparts a swirling motion to the fuel as it exits the nozzle. The swirling motion reduces the fuel's forward velocity which promotes better atomization. To prevent fuel from dribbling out of the fuel manifold and into the combustor after engine shutdown, Simplex nozzles incorporate an internal check valve that shuts off the flow of fuel at the base of the nozzle. [Figure 7-71]

A disadvantage of Simplex nozzles is that they do not atomize the fuel well or produce a desirable flame pattern when the engine is turning at slow speeds and the fuel is supplied at a low pressure. To help remedy this problem, some fuel systems incorporate a second set of smaller Simplex nozzles. The small nozzles are sometimes referred to as primers, or starting nozzles, and spray a very fine atomized mist for improved engine starting.

DUPLEX NOZZLE

A Duplex nozzle differs from a Simplex nozzle in that a Duplex nozzle has two independent discharge orifices; one small and the other large. The use of two orifices provides several benefits including better fuel vaporization and a more uniform spray pattern. The small orifice is located in the center of the nozzle and discharges pilot, or primary, fuel at a wide angle during engine start and acceleration to idle. The second orifice encircles the center orifice and discharges main, or secondary, fuel when fuel flow increases above that needed for idle. Since the secondary fuel is discharged at higher flow rates and higher pressures, it narrows the spray pattern which, in turn, helps hold the flame in the center of the combustion liner at higher power settings. In addition, the high pressure secondary flow helps prevent orifice fouling caused by entrained contaminants. [Figure 7-72]

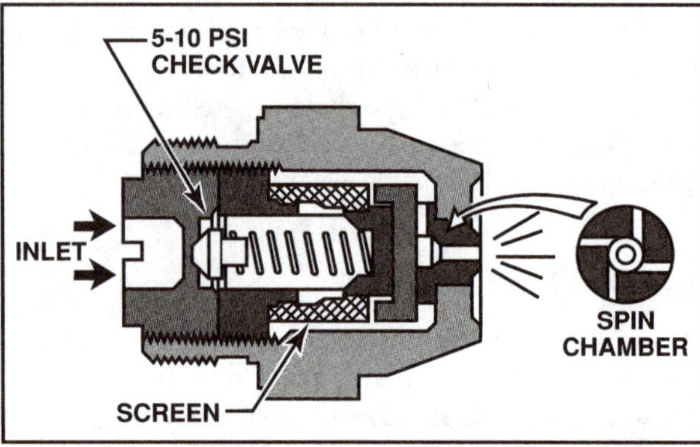

Figure 7-71. A Simplex nozzle provides a single spray pattern and incorporates an internally fluted spin chamber and a check valve. A typical Simplex nozzle is mounted internally in an engine and is accessible only when a combustor is removed.

Two common types of Duplex fuel nozzles are the single-line and dual-line. A single-line Duplex nozzle receives fuel at one port. Once the fuel enters the nozzle body, it enters a flow divider that distributes fuel through a primary and a secondary spray orifice. The flow divider always allows primary fuel to flow to the primary discharge orifice while secondary flow begins only when the inlet fuel pressure rises enough to open the flow divider valve. [Figure 7-73]

Duplex nozzles also utilize spin chambers for each orifice. In addition, the head of a Duplex nozzle is designed with air bleed holes which cool and clean the head and spray orifices. In addition, some primary air is provided for combustion by the holes. During engine start with only primary fuel flow, the cooling airflow helps prevent primary fuel from backflowing into the secondary orifice and carbonizing.

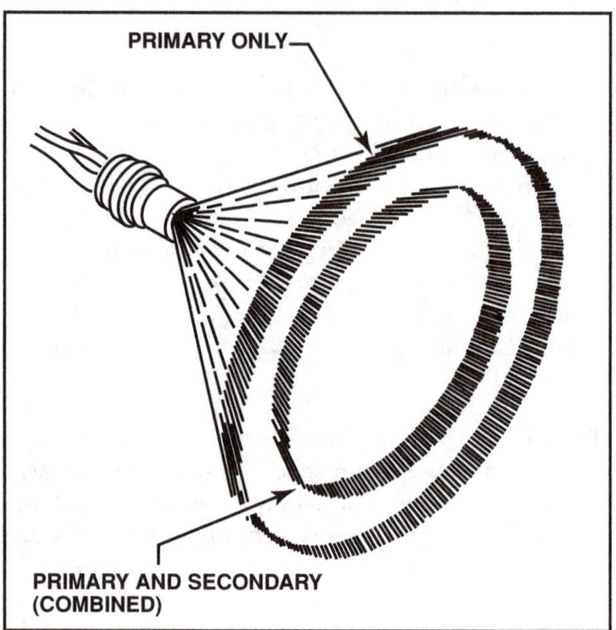

Figure 7-72. With a Duplex nozzle, primary fuel is ejected out of a small center orifice during engine starting and acceleration to idle. However, above idle, higher pressure, secondary fuel is ejected out of a larger orifice and combines with the primary fuel flow to create a narrower spray pattern.

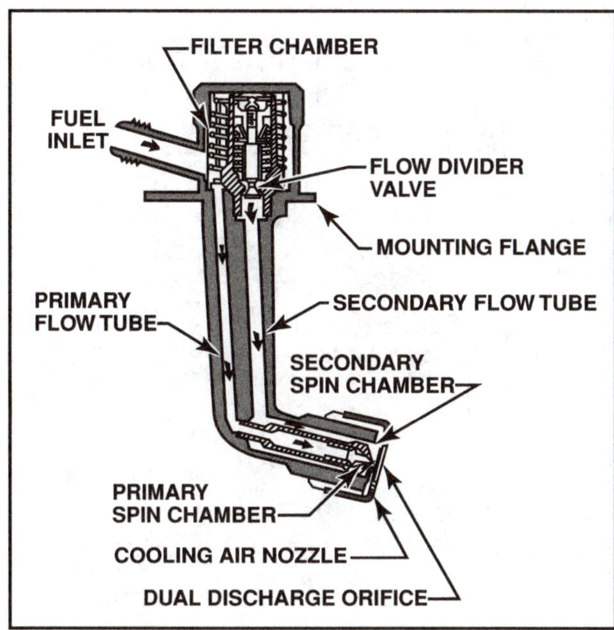

Figure 7-73. With a single line Duplex nozzle, fuel enters the nozzle body where it passes through a filter screen and a flow divider. Primary fuel always flows through the flow divider while secondary fuel only flows when inlet fuel pressure rises enough to open the flow divider valve.

SPILL-TYPE NOZZLE

On some turbine engines that supply high pressure fuel to the fuel nozzles at all times, spill-type nozzles may be used. A spill-type nozzle is basically a Simplex nozzle with a passage leading away from the spin chamber. This passage is referred to as a **spill passage** and is required to return the excess fuel supplied during low power output operations back to the nozzle inlet. The advantage of supplying fuel at high pressure to the nozzle at all times is improved atomization at all engine speeds. One disadvantage of this type of nozzle is the extra heat generated by recirculating large amounts of fuel at low engine speeds.

VARIABLE-PORT NOZZLE

A variable-port nozzle, or **Lubbock nozzle**, was developed to properly atomize fuel over a wide range of fuel flow rates. To do this, an internal spring-loaded piston regulates the swirl chamber inlet port size according to the fuel flow rate. For example, at low flow rates, the inlet ports are partially covered; however, at high flow rates, they are fully uncovered. One disadvantage of this type of nozzle is the tendency for the sliding piston to stick because of dirt particles in the fuel.

AIR-SPRAY NOZZLE

The final type of atomizing nozzle discussed here is the air-spray type nozzle used in some Rolls Royce engines. This type of atomizing nozzle differs from other nozzles in that there are openings in back of the nozzle that allow primary combustion airflow to aerate the fuel spray. Once the air enters the nozzle, it passes through a set of inner swirl vanes just prior to entering a swirl chamber. In the swirl chamber, the fuel and air are mixed and ejected through an orifice in the center of a set of outer swirl vanes. The turbulence created by the passage of the primary combustion air through the vanes helps to evenly distribute the fuel spray with combustion air.

VAPORIZING NOZZLES

Vaporizing nozzles differ from atomizing nozzles in that instead of delivering the fuel directly to the primary air in the combustor, a vaporizing nozzle premixes the primary air and fuel in a vaporizing tube. In most cases, the vaporizing tube extends into the combustion chamber so that when the fuel/air mixture is in the vaporizing tube, the heated air surrounding the tube causes the mixture to vaporize before exiting into the combustor flame zone. Some vaporizing type nozzles have only one outlet and are referred to as cane-shaped vaporizers. However, another type of vaporizing nozzle is T-shaped and provides two outlets. [Figure 7-74]

One shortcoming of vaporizing nozzles is that they do not provide an effective spray pattern for starting. To help alleviate this problem, an additional set

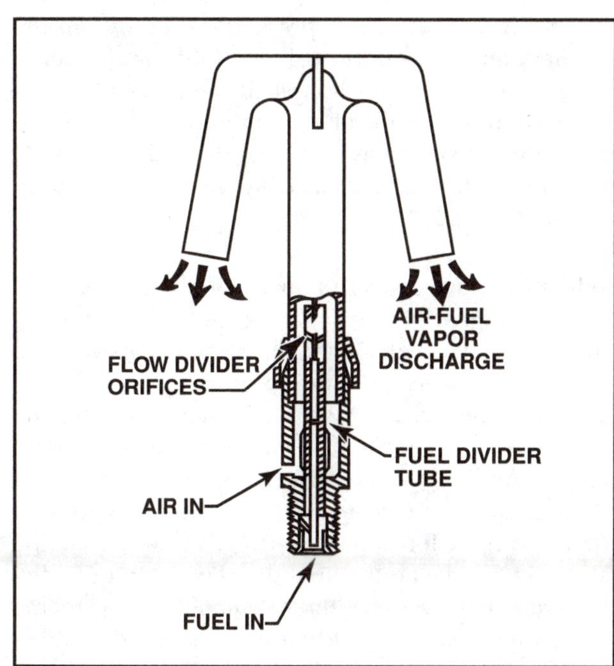

Figure 7-74. With a T-shaped vaporizing nozzle, fuel and air enter the nozzle body and are mixed and vaporized in two vaporizing tubes before being ejected into the combustion chamber.

of small atomizing-type spray nozzles may be installed to aid in engine starting. This system is generally referred to as a primer, or starting, fuel system. The Olympus engine in the Concord SST utilizes vaporizing fuel nozzles with separate primer fuel nozzles.

NOZZLE MALFUNCTIONS

A normally functioning fuel nozzle produces a spray pattern that holds the flame in the center of the liner. However, anytime an internal passage or air bleed hole becomes plugged a distorted spray pattern or incomplete atomization can result. In cases where spray pattern distortion occurs, the combustion flame can come in contact with the combustion liner. On the other hand, if the fuel doesn't atomize properly, an unatomized stream of burning fuel may extend beyond the combustion chamber and strike turbine components. When this occurs, the burning fuel leaves visible streaks on the components it contacts. This is often referred to as **hot streaking** and must be corrected immediately.

PRESSURIZATION AND DUMP VALVE

A pressurization and dump valve, commonly referred to as a P&D valve, is frequently incorporated into fuel metering systems which utilize dual line duplex nozzles. The operation of a P&D valve is two fold; first, the valve pressurizes the fuel in the primary and secondary fuel manifolds, and second, the valve empties, or dumps all the fuel in the two fuel manifolds upon engine shutdown. To accomplish these two things, a typical P&D valve consists of a spring-loaded pressurizing valve and a dump valve. [Figure 7-75]

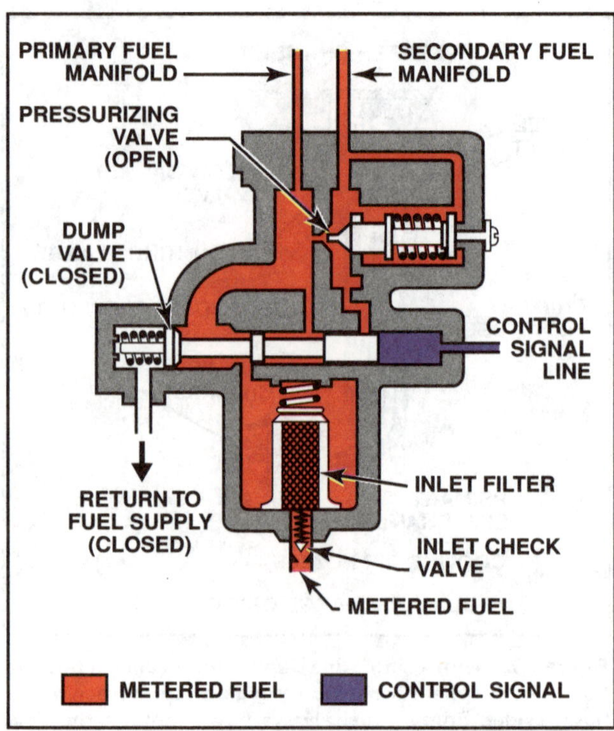

Figure 7-75. A typical pressurization and dump valve consists of a spring-loaded pressurizing valve and a dump valve that is positioned based on a control signal that corresponds to the power lever position.

When the power lever is opened for engine start, a pressure signal is sent from the fuel control unit to the P&D valve. The signal shifts the dump valve to the left, closing the dump port. Once closed, metered fuel pressure builds enough to open the inlet check valve so fuel can flow into the P&D valve. As fuel enters the P&D valve, it passes through an inlet screen and pressurizes the primary fuel manifold for engine starting. Once the engine starts and accelerates slightly above ground idle, metered fuel pressure builds enough to overcome the spring pressure holding the pressurizing valve closed and fuel begins flowing into the secondary manifold. At this point, both fuel manifolds are pressurized and fuel flows out both orifices in the Duplex fuel nozzle.

When the cockpit fuel cutoff lever is moved to the cutoff position, the fuel control pressure signal is removed. This allows spring pressure to open the dump valve and the dump port. At the same time, the dump valve blocks the flow of fuel to both fuel manifolds. With the fuel inlet blocked, the remaining fuel in the fuel manifold has a path to drain out of the dump port and back into the fuel supply. Since fuel flow through the P&D valve is stopped, spring pressure closes the inlet check valve, leaving metered fuel in the inlet line for the next engine start. [Figure 7-76]

Since the dump valve opens the dump port and stops the flow of fuel almost simultaneously, engine shutdown occurs almost instantly after the valve exposes the dump port. The purpose of dumping all manifold fuel at engine shutdown is to prevent the residual engine heat from vaporizing the fuel in the fuel lines. This is important because, if the fuel were allowed to vaporize, carbon deposits would form within the lines and manifolds and possibly clog the finely calibrated passageways.

DRAIN VALVES

Current EPA regulations prohibit the dumping of fuel onto the ground or siphoning of fuel in flight.

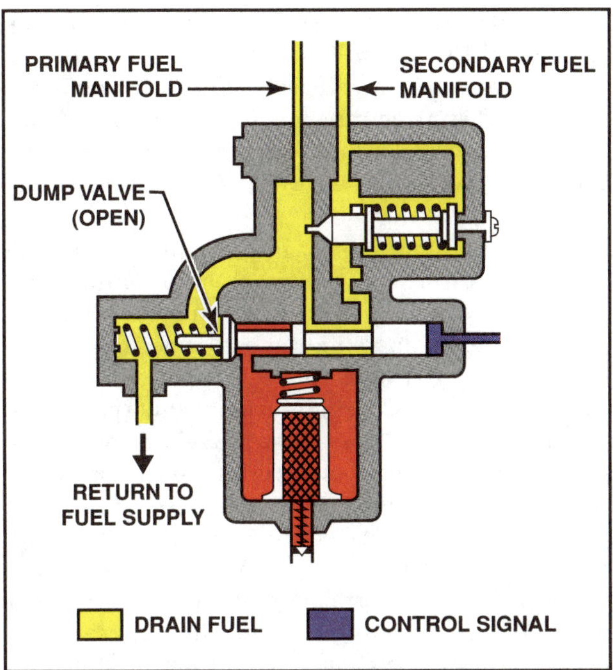

Figure 7-76. Upon engine shutdown, spring pressure forces the dump valve to the right, blocking the flow of fuel and opening the dump port so both fuel manifolds can drain.

Therefore, fuel that is dumped during engine shutdown must be either dumped into a separate storage tank or sent through a recovery system. If dumped to a storage tank, the tank must be drained manually into a container; however, if a recovery system is used, manual draining is eliminated. For example, one type of recovery system returns dumped fuel to the supply tank when the fuel cutoff lever is actuated. Another type of system uses bleed air to force fuel out of the fuel nozzles and into the combustion chamber. This system prolongs combustion slightly until fuel starvation occurs.

A system which neither recovers or burns dump fuel allows fuel to drain out of the lower nozzles and into the combustion chamber on shutdown. Once drained, the fuel evaporates in the combustor. This system is used only in engines that have no tendency to develop carbon buildups in the fuel nozzles from residual heat.

TURBINE FUEL CONTROL MAINTENANCE

Turbine engine fuel control repairs in the field consist of control replacement or occasional field adjustments. Furthermore, adjustments are limited to idle and maximum speed adjustments. If you recall, the process of adjusting a turbine engine fuel control is commonly referred to as trimming the engine. The primary purpose for trimming a fuel control unit is to ensure the availability of maximum thrust output when needed.

Trim checks are completed whenever engine thrust is suspect, and after such maintenance tasks as prescribed by the manufacturer. An engine change, fuel control change, or throttle linkage adjustments for proper control cushion and springback are all examples which require trimming procedures. A fuel control may also need to be retrimmed when deterioration of engine efficiencies occur as service time takes its toll. Another example is when wear and tear on engine control linkages cause misalignment between the cockpit and engine.

Manual trimming procedures vary widely between engine models; therefore, before you attempt to trim an engine, you should take time to review the specific procedures in the engine's maintenance manual. A typical trimming procedure requires you to install calibrated instruments for reading turbine discharge pressure or EPR. In addition, a calibrated tachometer must be installed to read N_2 rpm. Once the instrumentation is installed, the aircraft should be pointed into the wind. However, if the velocity of the wind blowing into the intake is too great, elevated compression and turbine discharge pressures will result which, ultimately, will produce a low trim setting. Another step in the trimming procedure is to measure the barometric pressure at the engine inlet and the ambient temperature. This is required to correct performance readings to standard sea-level conditions. To obtain a temperature reading it is common practice to hang a thermometer in the shade of the nose wheel well. The ideal conditions for trimming a turbine engine are no wind, low humidity, and standard temperature and pressure.

Once you have calculated the maximum power output for the engine you are trimming, start the engine and let it idle as specified in the maintenance manual. This is necessary so the engine has time to stabilize. To ensure an accurate trim setting, all engine bleed air must be turned off. Bleeding air off the compressor has the same effect as decreasing the compressor's efficiency. Therefore, if a trim adjustment is made with the bleeds on, an inaccurate, or over trimmed condition will result.

With the engine running at idle and maximum power, observe the turbine discharge or EPR readings to determine how much trimming is necessary. If trimming of either the idle or maximum settings is necessary, it is typically accomplished by turning a screw type adjustment on the fuel control unit. However, most manufacturers recommend that in order to stabilize cams, springs, and linkages within the fuel control, all final adjustments must be made in the increase direction. If an over adjustment is made, the trim should be decreased below target values, then increased back to the desired values. [Figure 7-77]

Typical trim adjustments only require simple hand tools such as an Allen wrench, screwdriver, or wrench. Adjustment components are usually equipped with some sort of friction lock that does not require the use of lockplates, locknuts, or lockwire. Some engines are designed to accommodate remote adjusting equipment. A remote control unit allows you to make the trim adjustments from the cockpit during ground test with the cowls closed.

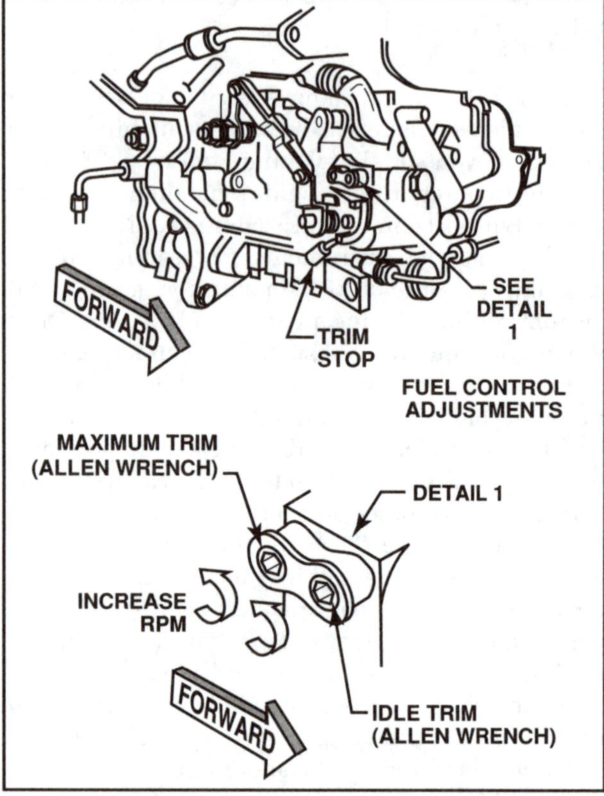

Figure 7-77. A typical turbine engine fuel control unit is equipped with adjustment screws for trimming the engine. Trimming procedures allow you to adjust both idle rpm and maximum rated thrust.

Another important part of the trim procedure is to check for power lever cushion, or springback. You should move the power lever full forward and release it before and after the trim run. The amount of lever springback is then measured against prescribed tolerances. If the cushion and springback are out of limits, you must make the necessary adjustments in accordance with the manufacturer's rigging instructions. Correct power lever springback ensures a pilot that takeoff power will be obtained and that additional power lever travel is available for emergencies. Correct springback is indicated when the fuel control reaches its internal stop before the cockpit power lever reaches its stop.

A trim check is normally followed by an acceleration check. After completing the trim check, place a mark on the cockpit power lever quadrant at the takeoff trim position. Then, advance the power lever from the idle position to takeoff thrust position and measure the time against a published tolerance. A typical acceleration time from idle to takeoff thrust for a large gas turbine engine ranges from 5 to 10 seconds.

Once the fuel control unit has been trimmed and control springback is correct, the engine should produce its rated thrust in standard conditions. In nonstandard conditions with high ambient temperatures, the rated thrust is degraded. While low humidity is desirable for purposes of accuracy during trimming procedures, high atmospheric humidity actually degrades rated thrust very little. The reason for this is that only 25 percent of the air passing through a turbine engine is used for combustion.

CHAPTER 8

ELECTRICAL, STARTING, AND IGNITION SYSTEMS

INTRODUCTION

As an aviation maintenance technician, you must be familiar with modern aircraft electrical systems, including the ways in which electricity is generated and routed to the various aircraft components. Although a great deal of the work done on these systems is often accomplished by certified repair stations, it is essential that you, as an aviation maintenance technician, have a thorough understanding of basic aircraft electrical systems.

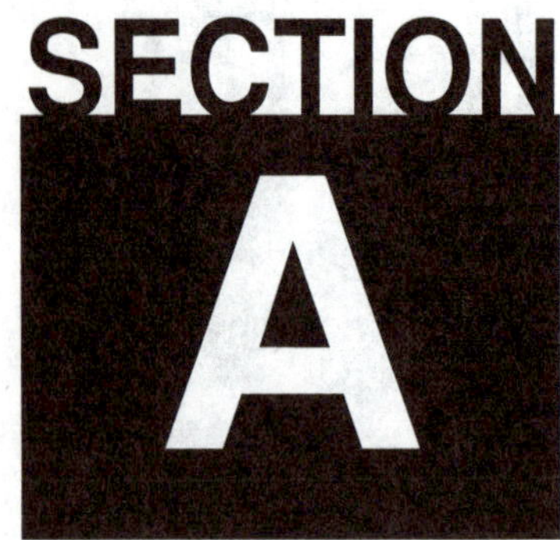

GENERATORS

Energy for the operation of most electrical equipment on large aircraft and some small aircraft is supplied by a generator. A **generator** is any piece of equipment which converts mechanical energy into electrical energy by electromagnetic induction. Generators designed to produce direct current are called **DC generators** whereas generators that produce alternating current are called **AC generators**.

On many older aircraft, the DC generator is the source of electrical energy. With this type of system, one or more DC generators are driven by the engine(s) to supply power for all electrical equipment as well as for charging the battery. In most cases only one generator is driven by each engine; however, some large aircraft have two generators that are driven by a single engine.

THEORY OF OPERATION

After it was discovered that electric current flowing through a conductor creates a magnetic field around the conductor, there was considerable scientific speculation about whether a magnetic field could create current flow. The English scientist, Michael Faraday, demonstrated in 1831 that this, in fact, could be accomplished. This discovery is the basis for the operation of the generator.

To show how an electric current is created by a magnetic field, several turns of wire are wrapped around a cardboard tube, and the ends of the conductor are connected to a galvanometer. A bar magnet is then moved through the tube. As the magnet's lines of flux are cut by the turns of wire, the galvanometer deflects from its zero position. However, when the magnet is at rest inside the tube, the galvanometer shows a reading of zero, indicating no current flow. When the magnet is moved through the tube in the opposite direction, the galvanometer indicates a deflection in the opposite direction. [Figure 8-1]

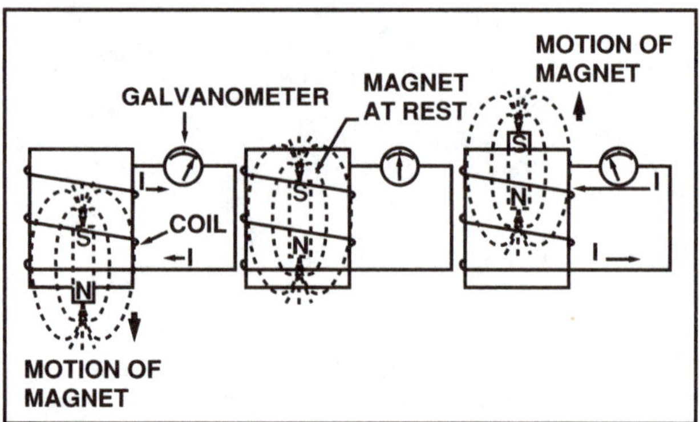

Figure 8-1. Current flow induced into a coil by magnetic flux lines is seen on a galvanometer. The direction of current flow is dependent upon how the magnetic fields cross the conductor.

The same results are obtained by holding the magnet stationary and moving the coil of wire. This indicates that current flows as long as there is relative motion between the wire coil and the magnetic field. The strength of the induced current depends on both the strength of the magnetic field and the speed at which the lines of flux are cut.

When a conductor is moved through a magnetic field, an electromotive force (EMF) is induced into the conductor. The direction, or polarity, of the induced EMF is determined by the direction the conductor is moved in relation to the magnetic flux lines.

The **left-hand rule for generators** is one way to determine the direction of the induced EMF. For example, if you point your left index finger in the direction of the magnetic lines of flux (north to south), and your thumb in the direction the conductor is moved through the magnetic field, your second finger indicates the direction of the induced EMF when extended perpendicular to your index finger. [Figure 8-2]

When a conductor in the shape of a single loop is rotated in a magnetic field, a voltage is induced in each side of the loop. Although the two sides of the loop cut the magnetic field in opposite directions, the induced current flows in one continuous direction within the loop. This increases the value of the induced EMF. [Figure 8-3]

When the loop is rotated half a turn so that the sides of the conductor have exchanged positions, the induced EMF in each wire reverses its direction. This is because the wire formerly cutting the lines of

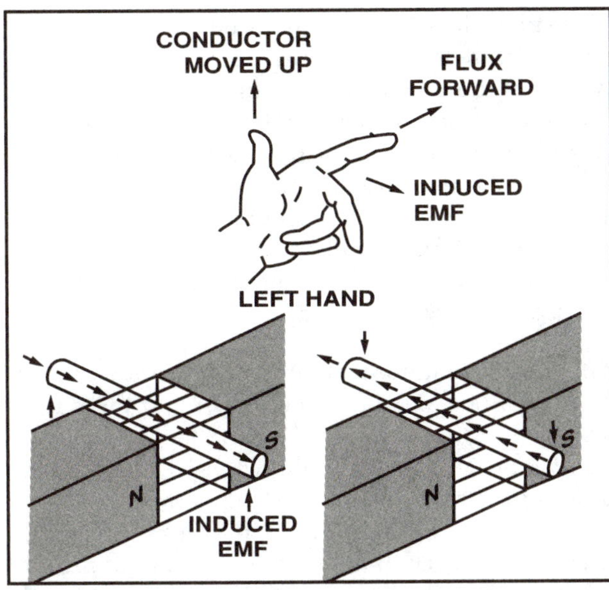

Figure 8-2. When applying the generator left-hand rule, your index finger points in the direction the lines of magnetic flux travel, your thumb indicates the conductor's direction of movement, and your second finger indicates the direction of induced EMF.

flux in an upward direction is now moving downward and the wire formerly cutting the lines of flux in a downward direction is now moving upward. In other words, the sides of the loop cut the magnetic field in opposite directions.

In a simple generator, two sides of a wire loop are arranged to rotate in a magnetic field. When the sides of the loop are parallel to the magnetic lines of flux, the induced voltage causes current to flow in one direction. Maximum voltage is induced at this position because the wires are cutting the lines of flux at right angles. This means that more lines of flux per second are cut than in any other position relative to the magnetic field.

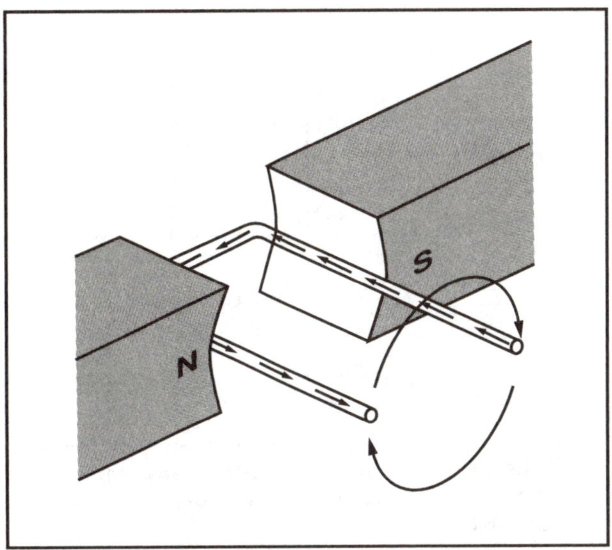

Figure 8-3. When a loop of wire is rotated in a magnetic field, the current induced in the wire flows in one continuous direction.

As the loop approaches the vertical position, the induced voltage decreases. This is because both sides of the loop become perpendicular to the lines of flux; therefore, fewer flux lines are cut. When the loop is vertical, the wires momentarily travel perpendicular to the magnetic lines of flux and there is no induced voltage.

As the loop continues to rotate, the number of flux lines being cut increases until the 90 degree point is reached. At this point, the number of flux lines cut is maximum again. However, each side of the loop is cutting the lines of flux in the opposite direction. Therefore, the direction, or polarity, of the induced voltage is reversed. Rotation beyond the 90 degree point again decreases the number of flux lines being cut until the induced voltage becomes zero at the vertical position. [Figure 8-4]

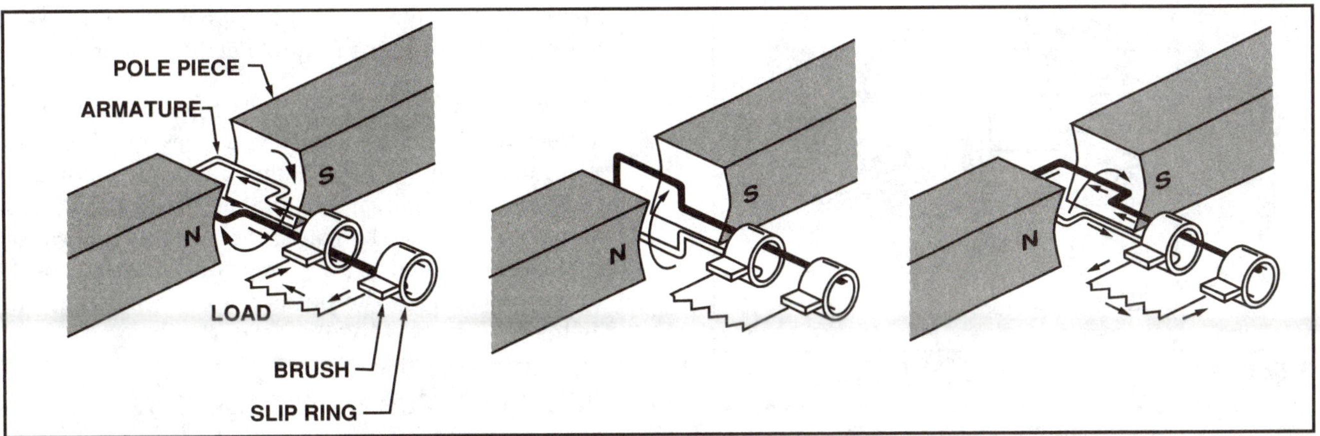

Figure 8-4. In a simple generator, the magnets are called pole pieces and the loop of wire is called the armature. Attached to each end of the loop is a slip ring on which a set of brushes ride to complete a circuit through a load. Maximum voltage is induced into the armature when it is parallel with the flux lines. Once the armature is perpendicular with the flux lines, no lines of flux are cut and no voltage is induced. As the armature rotates to the 90 degree point, the maximum number of flux lines are being cut, but in the opposite direction.

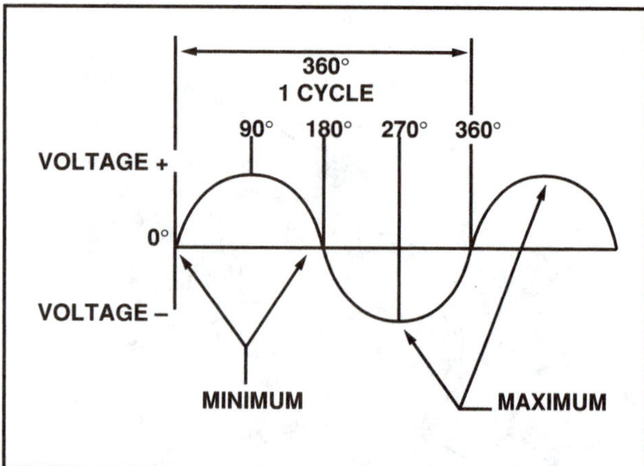

Figure 8-5. The output of an elementary generator is represented by the sine curve as a loop rotates 360 degrees through the lines of magnetic flux.

When the voltage induced throughout the entire 360 degrees of rotation is shown on an oscilloscope, the curve increases from a zero value at zero degrees, to a maximum positive voltage at 90 degrees. Once beyond 90 degrees the curve decreases until it reaches 180 degrees where the output is again zero. As the curve continues beyond 180 degrees the amount of negative voltage produced increases up to the 270 degree point where it is maximum. The amount of negative voltage then decreases to the zero point at 360 degrees. [Figure 8-5]

As you can see in the illustration, the output produced by a single loop rotating in a magnetic field is alternating current. By replacing the slip rings of the basic AC generator with two half-cylinders, commonly referred to as a single **commutator**, a basic DC generator is obtained. [Figure 8-6]

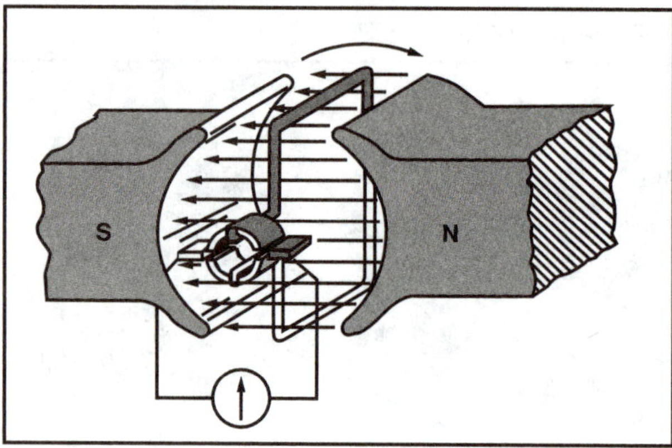

Figure 8-6. In this illustration the black side of the coil is connected to the black segment and the white side of the coil to the white segment. The segments are insulated from each other and two stationary brushes are placed on opposite sides of the commutator. The brushes are mounted so that each brush contacts each segment of the commutator as it revolves with the loop.

To explain how DC current is obtained, start with the armature at zero degrees where no lines of flux are cut and therefore, no output voltage is obtained. Once the armature begins rotating, the black brush comes in contact with the black segment of the commutator and the white brush comes in contact with the white segment of the commutator. Furthermore, the lines of flux are cut at an increasing rate until the armature is parallel to the lines of flux and the induced EMF is maximum.

Once the armature completes 180 degrees of rotation, no lines of flux are being cut and the output voltage is again zero. At this point, both brushes are contacting both the black and white segments on the sides of the commutator. After the armature rotates past the 180 degree point, the brushes contact only one side of the commutator and the lines of flux are again cut at an increasing rate.

The switching of the commutator allows one brush to always be in contact with that portion of the loop that travels downward through the lines of flux and the other brush to always be in contact with the half of the loop that travels upward. Although the current reverses its direction in the loop of a DC generator, the commutator action causes current to flow in the same direction. [Figure 8-7]

The variation in DC voltage is called **ripple**, and is reduced by adding more loops. As the number of loops increases, the variation between the maximum and minimum values of voltage is reduced. In fact, the more loops that are used, the closer the output voltage resembles pure DC. [Figure 8-8]

As the number of armature loops increases, the number of commutator segments must also increase. For example, one loop requires two commutator segments, two loops requires four segments, and four loops requires eight segments.

The voltage induced in a single-turn loop is small. Increasing the number of loops does not increase the maximum value of the generated voltage. However, increasing the number of turns in each loop does increase the voltage value. This is because voltage is obtained as an average only from the peak values. The closer the peaks are to each other, the higher the generated voltage value.

DC GENERATOR CONSTRUCTION

Generators used on aircraft differ somewhat in design because they are made by various manufacturers. However, all are of the same general construction and operate similarly. The major parts, or

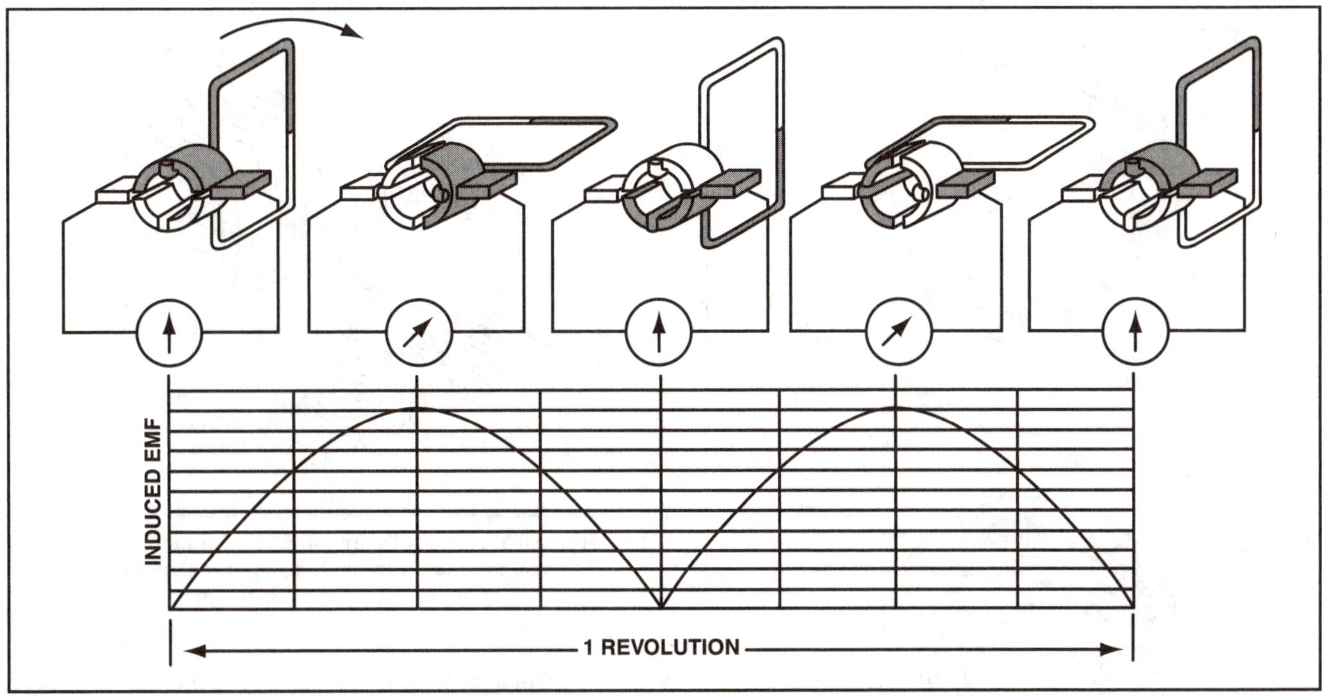

Figure 8-7. As the armature rotates in a DC generator, the commutator allows one brush to remain in contact with that portion of the loop that moves downward through the flux lines and the other brush to remain in contact with the portion of the loop that moves upward. This commutator action produces pulsating DC voltage that varies from zero to a maximum twice in one revolution.

assemblies, of a DC generator include the field frame, rotating armature, and brush assembly. [Figure 8-9]

FIELD FRAME

The field frame, or yoke, constitutes the foundation for the generator. The frame has two primary functions; 1) it completes the magnetic circuit between the poles and 2) it acts as a mechanical support for the other parts. In small generators, the frame is made of one piece of iron; however, in larger generators, it is usually made up of two parts bolted together. The frame is highly permeable and, together with the pole pieces, forms the majority of the magnetic circuit.

The magnetizing force inside a generator is produced by an electromagnet consisting of a wire coil

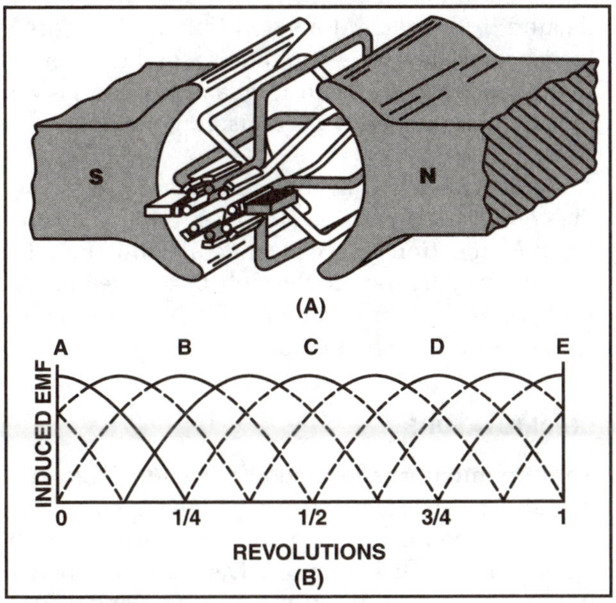

Figure 8-8. Increasing the number of loops in an armature reduces the ripple in DC voltage.

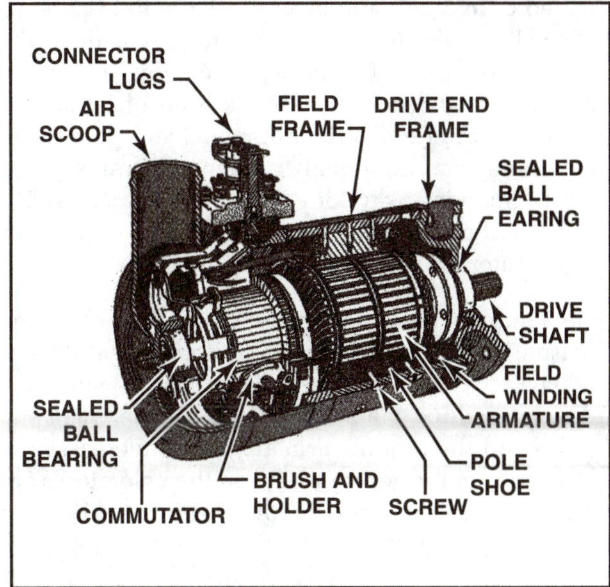

Figure 8-9. Cross section of a typical 24-volt generator with major parts labeled.

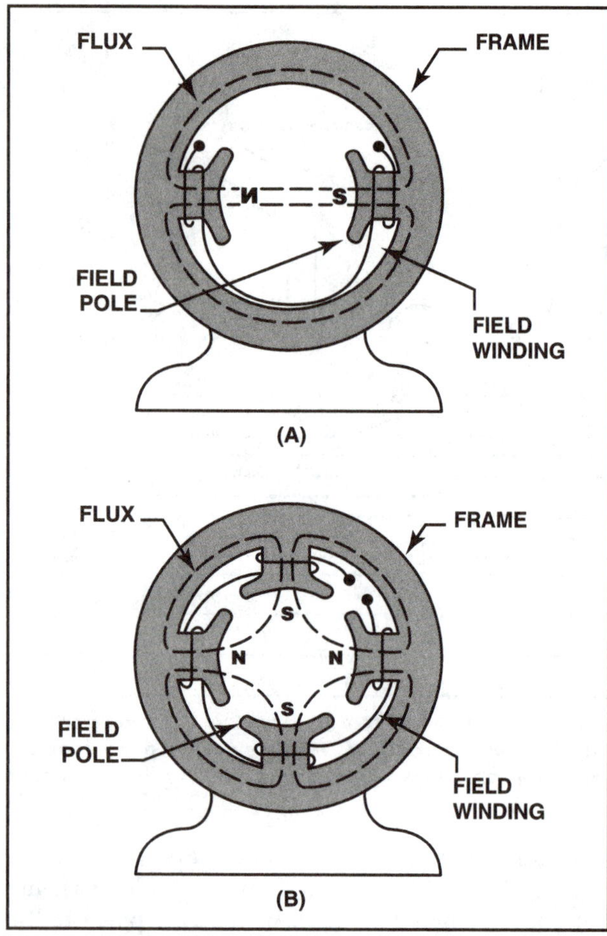

Figure 8-10. Generator field frames typically house either two or four pole shoes. These shoes are not permanent magnets, and rely on the field windings to produce a magnetic field. To try and produce the magnetic field necessary with only permanent magnets would greatly increase the physical size of the generator.

called a **field coil** and a core called a **field pole**, or **shoe**. The pole shoes are bolted to the inside of the frame and are usually laminated to reduce eddy current losses and concentrate the lines of force produced by the field coils. The frame and pole shoes are made from high quality magnetic iron or sheet steel. There is always one north pole for each south pole, so there is always an even number of poles in a generator. [Figure 8-10]

Note that the pole shoes project from the frame. The reason for this is that since air offers a great deal of resistance to a magnetic field, most generator designs reduce the length of air gap between the poles and the rotating armature. This increases the efficiency of the generator. When the pole pieces are made to project inward from the frame, they are called **salient poles**.

The field coils are made up of many turns of insulated wire. The coils are wound on a form that is

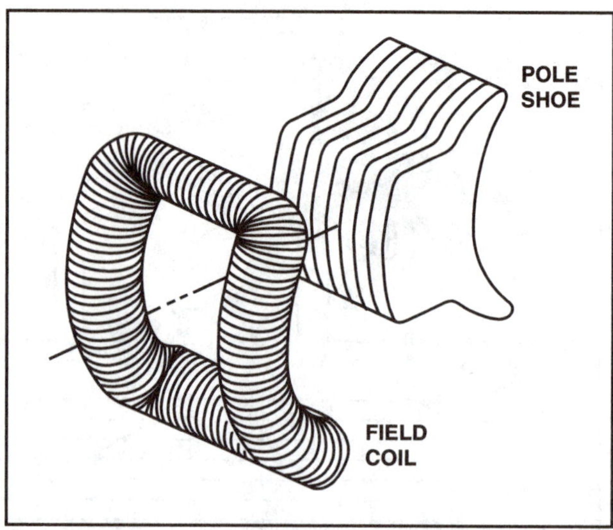

Figure 8-11. Field coils are form fitted around the pole shoes and are connected in such a manner that the north and south poles are in alternate polarity order.

securely fastened over the iron core of the pole shoes. The current used to produce the magnetic field around the shoes is obtained from an external source or from the current generated by the unit itself. Remember that the magnetic field created flows through the field coils and there is no electrical connection between the windings of the field coils and the pole shoes. [Figure 8-11]

ARMATURE

As mentioned earlier, the armature assembly consists of the armature coils, the commutator, and other associated mechanical parts. The armature is mounted on a shaft which rotates in bearings located in the generator's end frames. The core of the armature acts as a conductor when it is rotated in the magnetic field and it is laminated to prevent the circulation of eddy currents. [Figure 8-12]

A **drum-type armature** has coils placed in slots in the core of the armature. However, there is no electrical connection between the coils and core. The coils are usually held in the slots by wooden or fiber wedges. The coil ends are brought out to individual segments of the commutator.

COMMUTATORS

The commutator is located at one end of the armature and consists of wedge-shaped segments of hard-drawn copper. Each segment is insulated from the other by a thin sheet of mica. The segments are held in place by steel V-rings or clamping flanges fitted with bolts. Rings of mica also insulate the segments

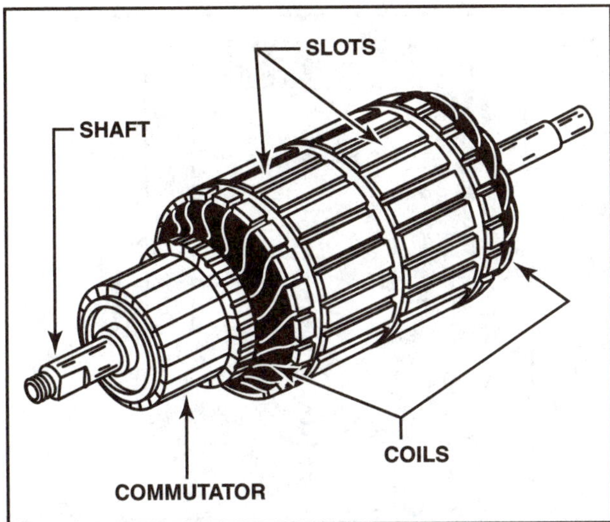

Figure 8-12. The armature rotates within the frame assembly and current is induced into it by the electromagnetic field created by the field coils and pole shoes.

from the flanges. The raised portion of each segment is called the **riser**, and the leads from the armature coils are soldered to each riser. In some generators, the segments have no risers. In this situation the leads are soldered to short slits in the ends of the segments. [Figure 8-13]

One end of a single armature coil attaches to one commutator segment while the other end is soldered to the adjacent segment. In this configuration, each coil laps over the preceding one. This is known as **lap winding**. When an armature rotates at operational speed, the magnetic fields that it produces lags behind the speed of rotation. Lap winding is a method for stabilizing these armature magnetic fields. [Figure 8-14]

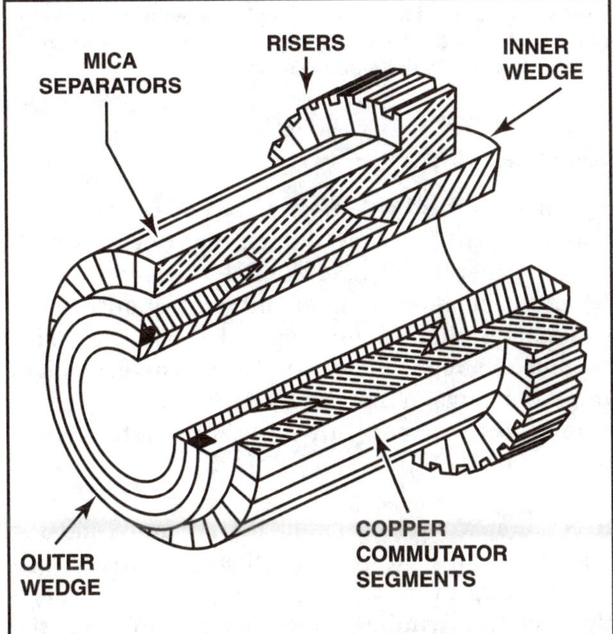

Figure 8-13. Each segment of a commutator is mounted to an inner wedge and separated by thin pieces of insulating mica. The risers on each segment hold the leads coming from the armature coils.

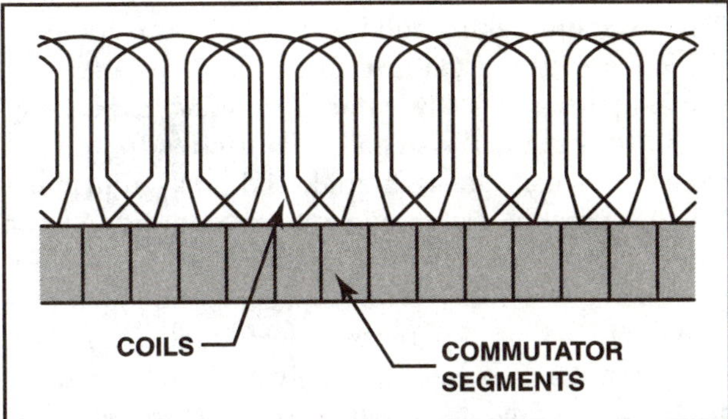

Figure 8-14. Lap winding connects one end of two coils to each commutator segment and the ends of each coil to adjacent segments.

BRUSHES

Brushes ride on the surface of the commutator and act as the electrical contact between armature coils and an external circuit. A flexible braided-copper conductor, called a pig-tail, connects each brush to the external circuit. The brushes are made of high-grade carbon and held in place by spring-loaded brush holders that are insulated from the frame. The brushes are free to slide up and down in their holders so they can follow any irregularities in the commutator's surface and allow for wear. A brushes' position is typically adjustable so that the pressure on the commutator can be varied, and so the brush position with respect to the risers can be changed as necessary. [Figure 8-15]

Figure 8-15. Carbon brushes connect to an external circuit through pig tails. The brushes are typically adjustable to allow varied pressure on the commutator and position on the segments.

The constant making and breaking of connections to the coils of the armature necessitates the use of a brush material that has a definite contact resistance. This material must also have low friction to prevent excessive wear. The high-grade carbon used to make brushes must be soft enough to prevent undue wear to the commutator and yet hard enough to provide reasonable brush life. The contact resistance of carbon is fairly high due to its molecular structure and the commutator surface is highly polished to reduce friction as much as possible. Oil or grease must never be used on a commutator and extreme care must be used when cleaning a commutator to avoid marring or scratching its surface.

TYPES OF DC GENERATORS

There are three types of DC generators. They are the series-wound, shunt-wound, and shunt-series or compound-wound. The difference between each depends on how the field winding is connected to the external circuit.

SERIES-WOUND

The field winding of a series-wound generator is connected in series with the external load circuit. In this type of generator, the field coils are composed of a few turns of large wire because magnetic field strength depends more on current flow than the number of turns in the coil.

Because of the way series-wound generators are constructed, they possess poor voltage regulation capabilities. For example, as the load voltage increases, the current through the field coils also increases. This induces a greater EMF which, in turn, increases the generator's output voltage. Therefore, when the load increases, voltage increases; likewise, when the load decreases, voltage decreases.

One way to control the output voltage of a series-wound generator is to install a rheostat in parallel with the field windings. This limits the amount of current that flows through the field coils thereby limiting the voltage output. [Figure 8-16]

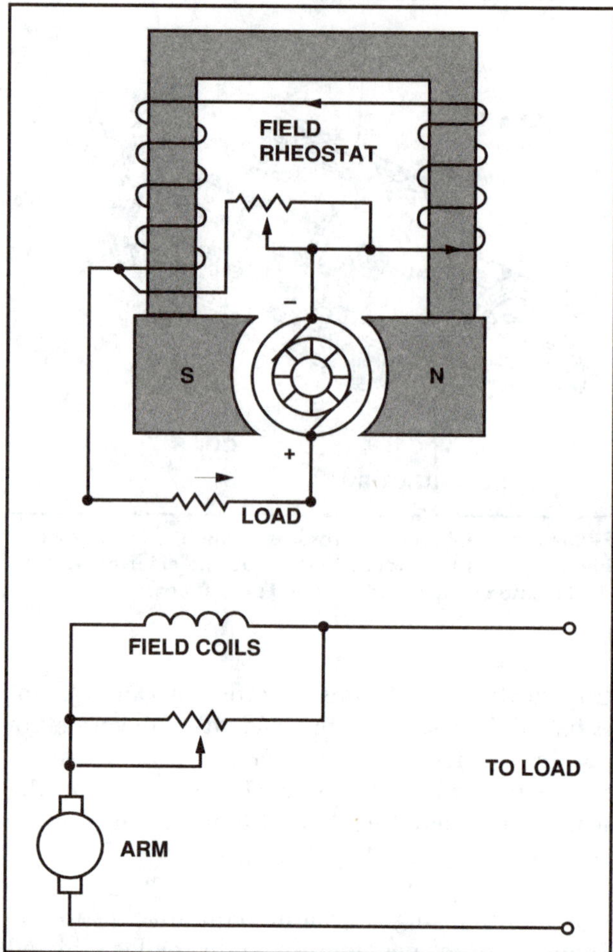

Figure 8-16. The diagram and schematic of a series-wound generator show that the field windings are connected in series with the external load. A field rheostat is connected in parallel with the field windings to control the amount of current flowing in the field coils.

Since series-wound generators have such poor voltage regulation capabilities, they are not suitable for use in aircraft. However, they are suitable for situations where a constant RPM and constant load are applied to the generator.

SHUNT-WOUND

A generator having a field winding connected in parallel with the external circuit is called a shunt-wound generator. Unlike the field coils in a series-wound generator, the field coils in a shunt-wound generator contain many turns of small wire. This permits the field coil to derive its magnetic strength from the large number of turns rather than the amount of current flowing through the coils. [Figure 8-17]

In a shunt-wound generator the armature and the load are connected in series; therefore, all the current flowing in the external circuit passes through the armature winding. However, due to the resistance in the armature winding some voltage is lost. The formula used to calculate this voltage drop is:

$$\text{IR drop} = \text{current} \times \text{armature resistance}$$

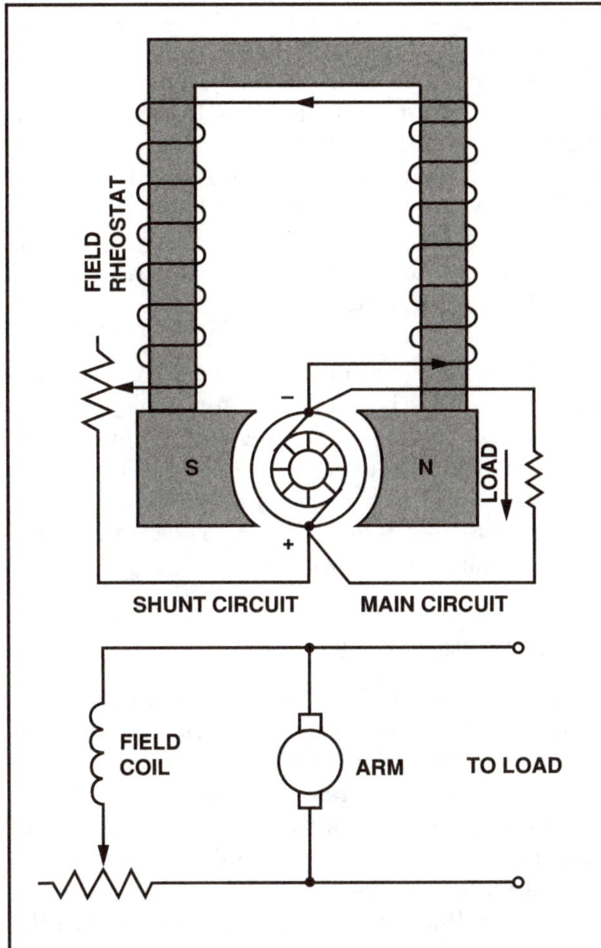

Figure 8-17. In a shunt-wound generator the field windings are connected in parallel with the external load.

From this formula you can see that as the load, or current, increases the IR drop in the armature also increases. Since the output voltage is the difference between induced voltage and voltage drop, there is a decrease in output voltage with an increased load. This decrease in output voltage causes a corresponding decrease in field strength because the current in the field coils decreases with a decrease in output voltage. By the same token, when the load decreases, the output voltage increases accordingly, and a larger current flows in the windings. This action is cumulative and, if allowed, the output voltage would rise to a point called **field saturation**. At this point there is no further increase in output voltage. Because of this, a shunt-wound generator is not desired for rapidly fluctuating loads.

To control the output voltage of a shunt generator, a rheostat is inserted in series with the field winding. In this configuration, as armature resistance increases, the rheostat reduces the field current which decreases the output voltage. For a given setting on the field rheostat, the terminal voltage at the armature brushes is approximately equal to the generated voltage minus the IR drop produced by the armature resistance. However, this also means that the output voltage at the terminals drops when a larger load is applied. Certain voltage-sensitive devices are available which automatically adjust the field rheostat to compensate for variations in load. When these devices are used, the terminal voltage remains essentially constant.

The output and voltage-regulation capabilities of shunt-type generators make them suitable for light to medium duty use on aircraft. However, most of these units have generally been replaced by DC alternators.

COMPOUND-WOUND

A compound-wound generator combines a series winding and a shunt winding so that the characteristics of each are used. The series field coils consist of a relatively small number of turns made of large copper conductor, either circular or rectangular in cross section. As discussed earlier, series field coils are connected in series with the armature circuit. These coils are mounted on the same poles as the shunt field coils and, therefore, contribute to the magnetizing force, or **magnetomotive force**, which influences the generator's main field flux. [Figure 8-18]

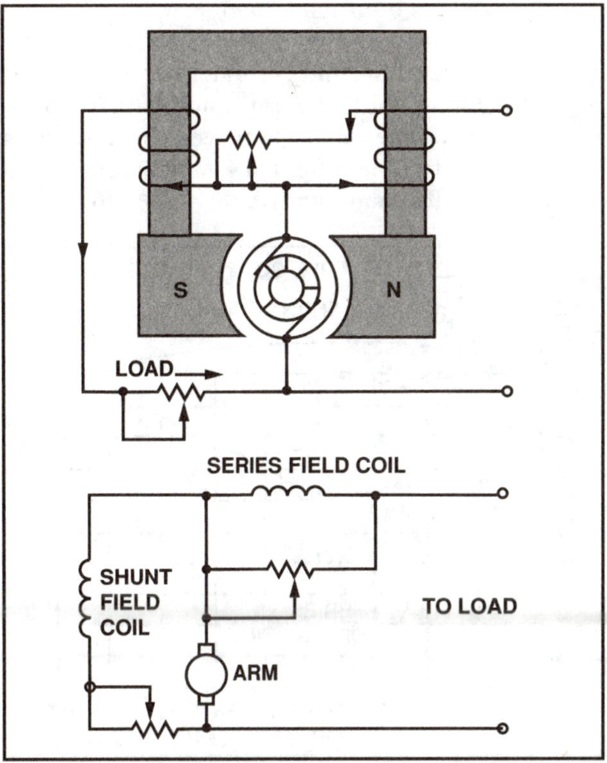

Figure 8-18. Compound-wound generators utilize both series and shunt windings. In this type of generator, voltage regulation is controlled by a diverter.

If the ampere-turns of the series field act in the same direction as those of the shunt field, the combined magnetomotive force is equal to the sum of the series and shunt field components. Load is added to a compound-wound generator in the same manner as a shunt-wound generator; by increasing the number of parallel paths across the generator. When this is done, the total load resistance decreases causing an increase in armature-circuit and series-field circuit current. Therefore, by adding a series field, the field flux increases with an increased load. Thus, the output voltage of the generator increases or decreases with load, depending on the influence of the series field coils. This influence is referred to as the **degree of compounding**.

The amount of output voltage produced by a compound-wound generator depends on the degree of compounding. For example, a **flat-compound** generator is one in which the no-load and full-load voltages have the same value. However, an **under-compound** generator has a full-load voltage less than the no-load voltage, and an **over-compound** generator has a full-load voltage that is higher than the no-load voltage.

Generators are typically designed to be over-compounded. This feature permits varied degrees of compounding by connecting a variable shunt across the series field. Such a shunt is sometimes called a **diverter**. Compound generators are used where voltage regulation is of prime importance.

If, in a compound-wound generator, the series field aids the shunt field, the generator is said to be **cumulative-compounded**. However, if the series field opposes the shunt field, the generator is said to be **differentially compounded**. [Figure 8-19]

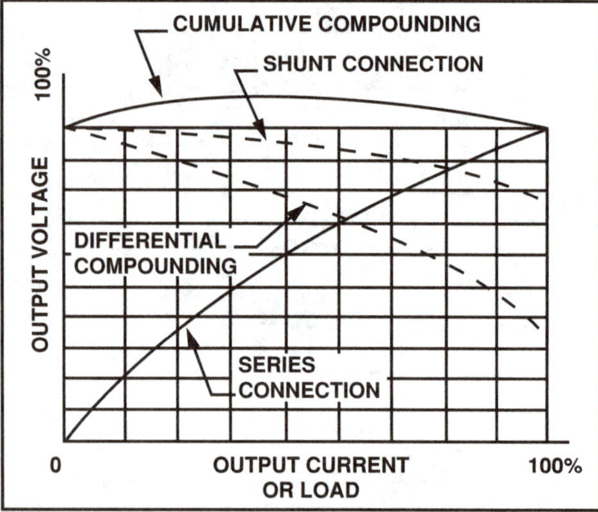

Figure 8-19. The generator characteristics chart above illustrates a summary of characteristics involving various types of generators.

Differentially compounded generators have somewhat the same characteristics as series generators in that they are essentially **constant-current generators**. In other words, they produce the same amount of current regardless of the load size. However, they do generate voltage when no load is applied and the voltage drops as the load current increases. Constant-current generators are ideally suited as power sources for electric arc welders and are used extensively for this task.

If the shunt field of a compound-wound generator is connected across both the armature and the series field, it is known as a **long-shunt connection**. However, if the shunt field is connected across the armature alone, it is called a **short-shunt connection**. These connections produce essentially the same generator characteristics.

STARTER-GENERATORS

Many small turbine engines are equipped with starter generators rather than separate starters and generators. This saves appreciably in weight, as both starters and generators are very heavy. A typical starter generator consists of at least two sets of windings and one armature winding. When acting as a starter, a high current flows through both sets of field windings and the armature to produce the torque required to start the engine. However, in the generator mode, only the high resistance shunt-winding receives current while the series-winding receives no current. The current flowing through the shunt-winding is necessary to produce the magnetic field that induces voltage into the armature. Once power is produced, it flows to the primary bus.

ARMATURE REACTION

As you know, anytime current flows through a conductor, a magnetic field is produced. Therefore, it stands to reason that when current flows through an armature, electromagnetic fields are produced in the windings. These fields tend to distort or bend the lines of magnetic flux between the poles of the generator. This distortion is called **armature reaction**. Since the current flowing through the armature increases as the load increases, the distortion becomes greater with larger loads. [Figure 8-20]

Armature windings of a generator are spaced so that during rotation there are certain positions when the brushes contact two adjacent segments on the commutator, thereby shorting the armature windings. When the magnetic field is not distorted, there is no voltage induced in the shorted windings and no harmful results occur. However, when the field is distorted by armature reaction, a voltage is induced in the shorted windings and sparking takes place between the brushes and the commutator segments. Consequently, the commutator becomes pitted, the wear on the brushes becomes excessive, and the output of the generator is reduced.

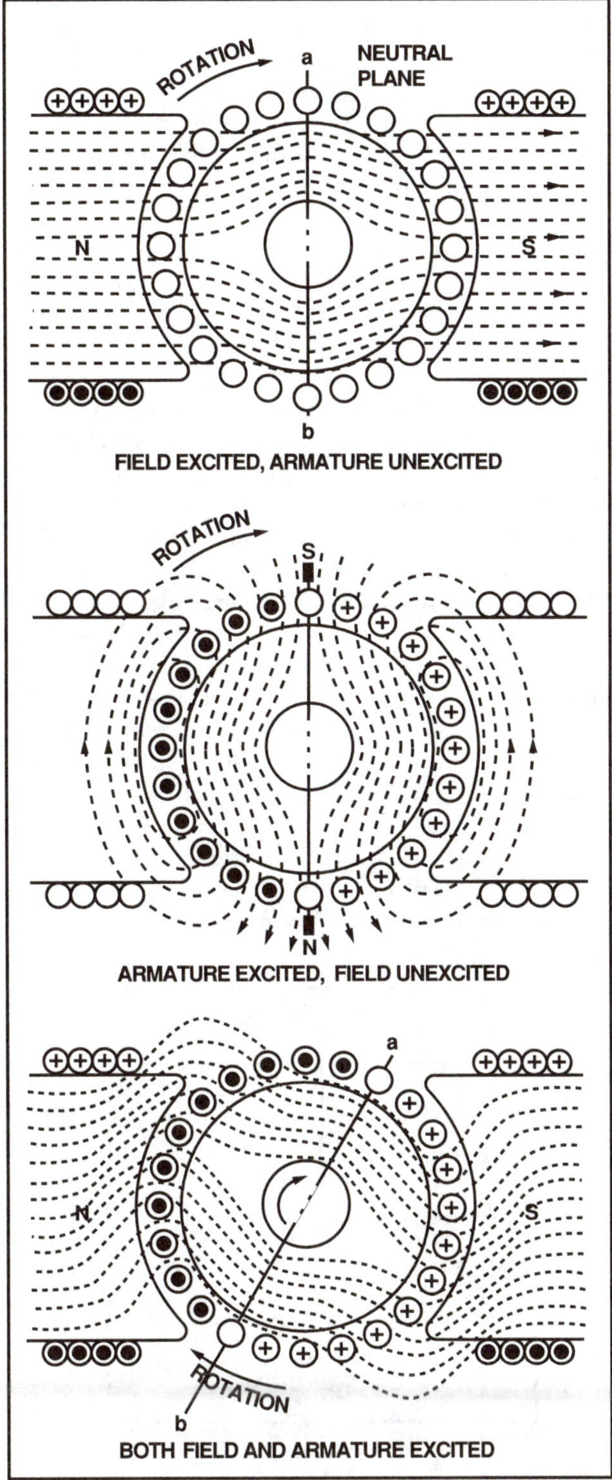

Figure 8-20. The lines of flux in the field coil flow in a horizontal path from north to south and induce voltage into the armature. However, as this is done, magnetic fields are produced in the armature that tend to distort or bend the lines of flux produced by the field coil.

To correct this condition, the brushes are set so that the plane of the coils being shorted is perpendicular to the distorted magnetic field. This is accomplished by moving the brushes forward in the direction of rotation. This operation is called **shifting the brushes** to the neutral plane, or **plane of commutation**. The neutral plane is the position where the plane of the two opposite coils is perpendicular to the magnetic field in the generator. On a few generators, the brushes are shifted manually ahead of the normal neutral plane to the neutral plane caused by field distortion. On nonadjustable brush generators, the manufacturer sets the brushes for minimum sparking.

In some generators, special field poles called **interpoles** are used to counteract some of the effects of field distortion when the speed and load of the generator are changing constantly. An interpole is another field pole that is placed between the main poles. [Figure 8-21]

An interpole has the same polarity as the next main pole in the direction of rotation. The magnetic flux produced by an interpole causes the current in the armature to change direction as the armature winding rotates under the interpole's field. This cancels

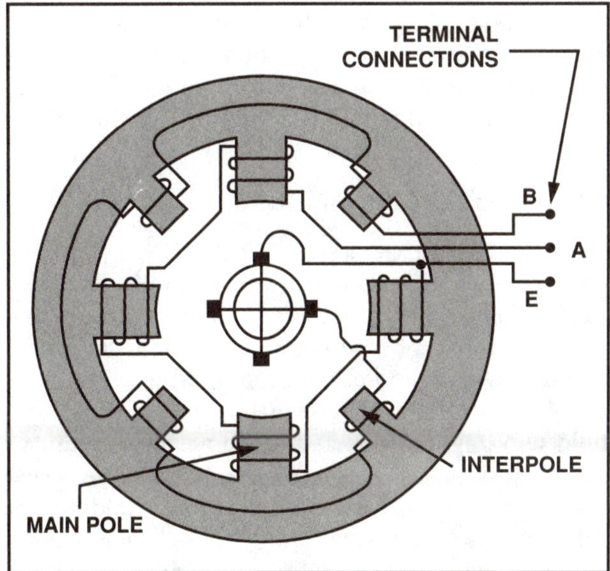

Figure 8-21. This generator has four poles and four interpoles. The interpoles are used to counter the effect of armature reaction.

the electromagnetic fields produced by the armature windings. The interpoles are connected in series with the load and, therefore, the magnetic strength of the interpoles varies with the generator load. Since the field distortion also varies with the load, the magnetic field of the interpoles counteract the effects of the field around the armature windings and minimize distortion. In other words, the interpoles keep the neutral plane in the same position for all loads.

GENERATOR RATINGS

A generator is rated according to its power output. Since a generator is designed to operate at a specified voltage, the rating is usually given as the number of amperes the generator can safely supply at its rated voltage. For example, a typical generator rating is 300 amps at 28.5 volts. A generator's rating and performance data are stamped on the name plate attached to the generator. When replacing a generator make sure it is the proper rating.

The rotation of generators is termed as either clockwise or counterclockwise, as viewed from the driven end. If no direction is stamped on the data plate, the rotation is marked by an arrow on the cover plate of the brush housing. To maintain the correct polarity, it is important to use a generator with the correct direction of rotation.

The speed of an aircraft engine varies from idle rpm to takeoff rpm; however, the majority of flight, is conducted at a constant cruising speed. The generator drive is usually geared between 1-1/8 and 1-1/2 times the engine crankshaft speed. Most aircraft generators have a speed at which they begin to produce their normal voltage. This is termed the **coming-in speed**, and is typically around 1,500 rpm.

GENERATOR TERMINALS

On large 24-volt generators, electrical connections are made to terminals marked B, A, and E. The positive armature lead connects to the B terminal, the negative armature lead connects to the E terminal, and the positive end of the shunt field winding connects to terminal A. The negative end of the shunt field winding is connected to the negative terminal brush. Terminal A receives current from the negative generator brush through the shunt field winding. This current passes through the voltage regulator and back to the armature through the positive brush. Load current, which leaves the armature through the negative brush, comes out of the E lead and passes through the load before returning through the positive brush.

GENERATOR VOLTAGE REGULATION

Efficient operation of electrical equipment in an aircraft depends on a voltage supply that varies with a system's load requirements. Among the factors which determine the voltage output of a generator, the strength of the field current is the only one that is conveniently controlled.

One way to control the field current is to install a rheostat in the field coil circuit. When the rheostat is set to increase the resistance in the field circuit, less current flows through the field coils and the strength of the magnetic field decreases. Consequently, less voltage is induced into the armature and generator output decreases. When the resistance in the field circuit is decreased with the rheostat, more current flows through the field coils, and the magnetic field becomes stronger. This allows more voltage to be induced into the armature which produces a greater output voltage. [Figure 8-22]

One thing to keep in mind is that, the weaker the magnetic field is, the easier it is to turn the armature. On the other hand, if the strength of the magnetic field is increased, more force is required to turn the armature. This means that, when the load on a generator increases, additional field current must be supplied to increase the voltage output as well as overcome the additional force required to turn the armature.

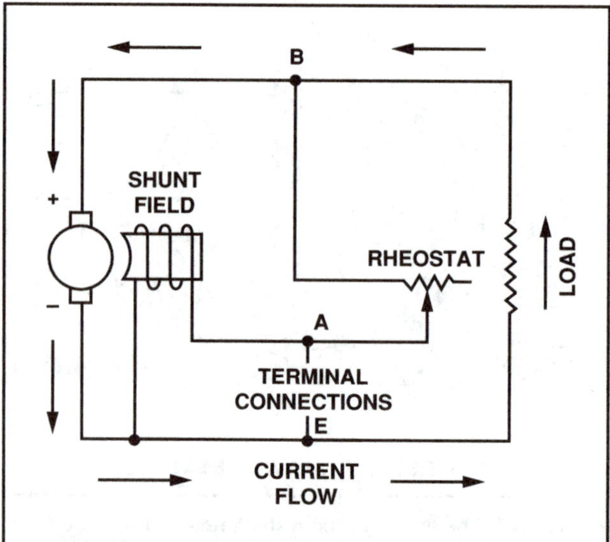

Figure 8-22. When generator voltage is regulated by field rheostat, more resistance results in less output voltage while less resistance results in more output voltage.

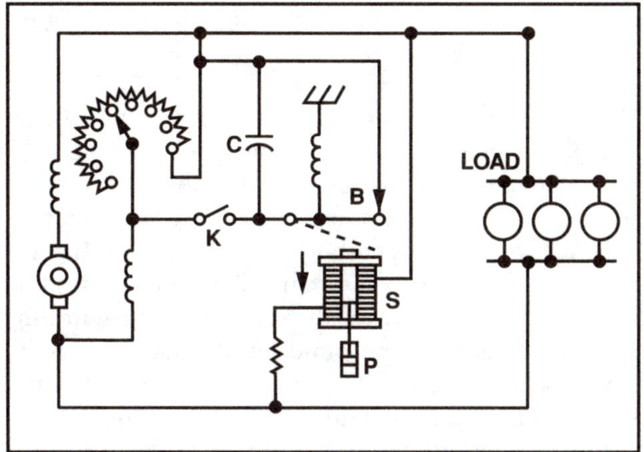

Figure 8-23. With the generator running at normal speed and switch K open, the field rheostat is adjusted so that the output voltage is about 60 percent of normal. At this level, solenoid S is weak and contact B is held closed by the spring. However, when K is closed, a short circuit is placed across the field rheostat. This action causes the field current to increase and the output voltage to rise.

This principle is further developed by the addition of a solenoid which electrically connects or removes the field rheostat from the circuit as the voltage varies. This type of setup is found in a **vibrating-type voltage regulator**. [Figure 8-23]

When the output voltage rises above a specified critical value, the downward pull of the solenoid's coil exceeds the spring tension and contact B opens. This reinserts the field rheostat in the field circuit. The additional resistance reduces the field current and lowers output voltage. When the output voltage falls below a certain value, contact B closes, shorting the field rheostat and the terminal voltage starts to rise. Thus, an average voltage is maintained with or without load changes. The dashpot P provides smoother operation by acting as a dampener to prevent hunting, and capacitor C across contact B helps eliminate sparking.

With a vibrating-type voltage regulator, contact B opens and closes several times per second to maintain the correct generator output. Based on this, if the solenoid should malfunction or the contacts stick closed, excess current would flow to the field and generator output would increase.

Certain light aircraft employ a **three-unit regulator** for their generator systems. This type of regulator includes a current limiter, a reverse current cutout, and a voltage regulator. [Figure 8-24]

The action of the voltage regulator unit is similar to the vibrating-type regulator described earlier. The **current limiter** is the second of three units, and it limits the generator's output current. The third unit is a **reverse-current cutout** which disconnects the

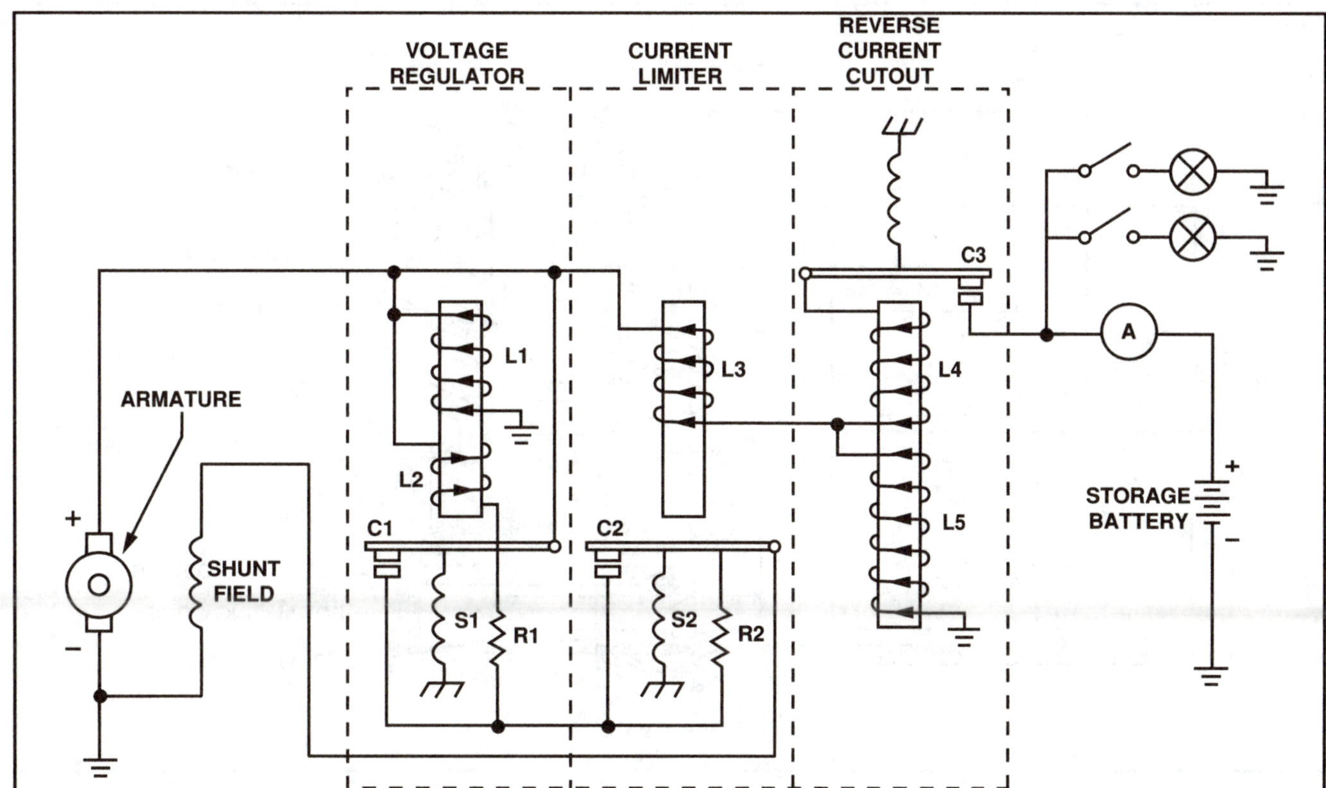

Figure 8-24. A voltage regulator contains three coils: a voltage regulator coil, a current limiter coil, and a reverse current cutout coil.

battery from the generator when the generator output is lower than the battery output. If the battery were not disconnected, it would discharge through the generator armature when the generator voltage falls below that of the battery. When this occurs the battery attempts to drive the generator as a motor. This action is called **motoring** the generator and, unless prevented, the battery discharges in a short time.

Since contacts have a tendency to pit or burn when large amounts of current flow through them, vibrating-type regulators and three-unit regulators cannot be used with generators that require a high field current. Therefore, heavy-duty generator systems require a different type of regulator, such as the **carbon-pile** voltage regulator. The carbon-pile voltage regulator relies on the resistance of carbon disks arranged in a pile or stack. The resistance of the carbon stack varies inversely with the pressure applied. For example, when the stack is compressed, less air exists between the carbon disks and the resistance decreases. However, when the pressure is reduced, more air is allowed between the disks causing the resistance to increase.

Pressure on the carbon pile is created by two opposing forces: a spring and an electromagnet. The spring compresses the carbon pile, and the electromagnet exerts a pull on the spring which decreases the pressure. [Figure 8-25].

Whenever the generator voltage varies, the pull of the electromagnet varies. If the generator voltage rises above a specific amount, the pull of the electromagnet increases, thereby decreasing the pressure exerted on the carbon pile and increasing its resistance. Since this resistance is in series with the field, less current flows through the field winding and there is a corresponding decrease in field strength. This results in a drop in generator output. On the other hand, if the generator output drops below a specified value, the pull of the electromagnet decreases and the carbon pile places less resistance in the field winding circuit. This results in an increase in field strength and a corresponding increase in generator output. A small rheostat provides a means of adjusting the current flow through the electromagnet coil.

DC GENERATOR SERVICE AND MAINTENANCE

Because of their relative simplicity and durable construction, generators operate many hours without trouble. The routine inspection and service done at each 100-hour or annual inspection interval is generally all that is required to keep a generator in good

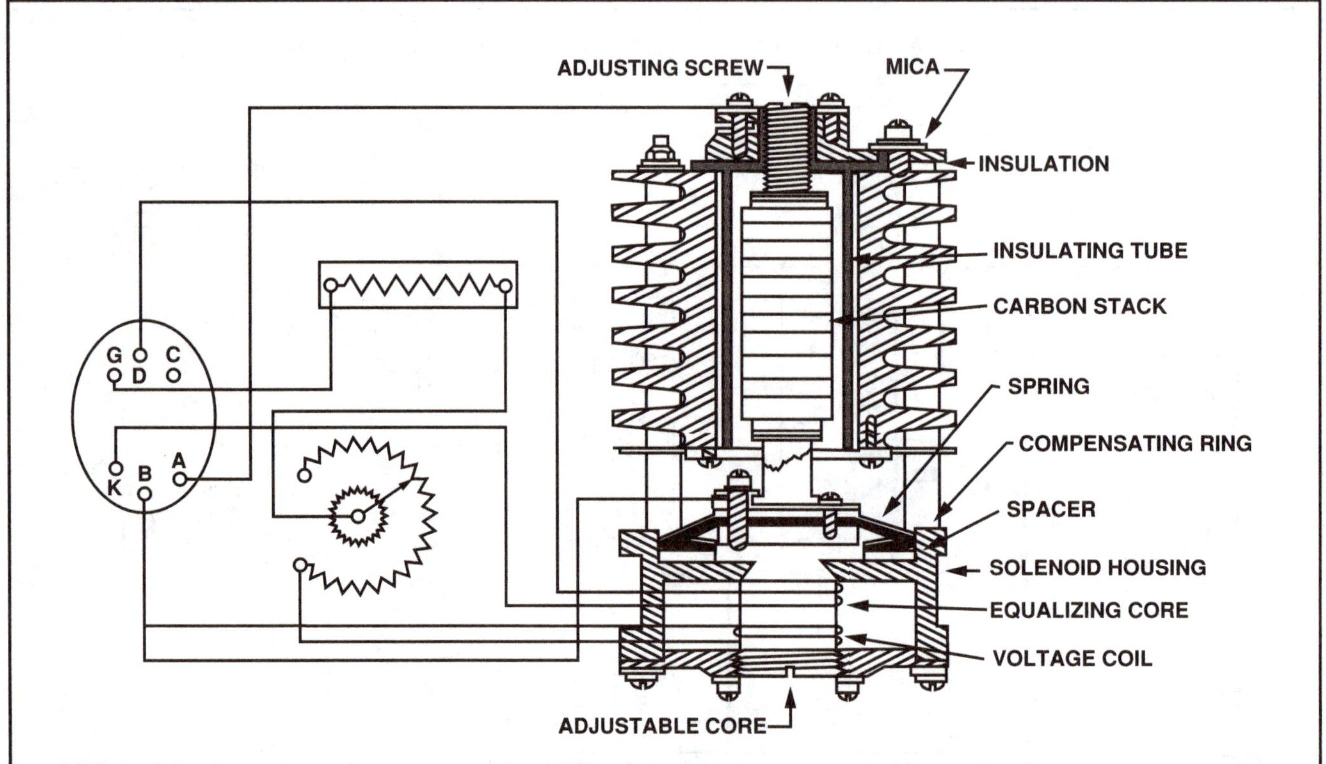

Figure 8-25. A carbon pile voltage regulator relies on the amount of air space within a stack of carbon disks to control generator voltage. Pressure is maintained on the disks by a spring while an electromagnet controls spring tension

working order. Generator overhaul is often accomplished at the same time as engine overhaul. This minimizes aircraft down time and increases the likelihood of trouble free operation when the aircraft is placed back in service.

ROUTINE INSPECTION AND SERVICING

The 100-hour and annual inspection of a generator should include the following items:

1. Inspect generator for security of mounting, check the mounting flange for cracks and loose mounting bolts.
2. Inspect mounting flange area for oil leaks.
3. Inspect generator' electrical connections for cleanliness and security of attachment.
4. Remove band covering the brushes and commutator. Use compressed air to blow out accumulated dust. Inspect brushes for wear, and freedom of movement. Check tension of the brush springs, using a spring scale.
5. Inspect commutator for cleanliness, wear, and pitting.
6. Inspect area around the commutator and brush assemblies for any solder particles. The presence of solder indicates that the generator has overheated and melted the solder attaching the armature coils to the risers. When this happens, an open is created in the armature.

If a DC generator is unable to keep an aircraft battery charged, and if the ammeter does not show the proper rate of charge, you should first check the aircraft electrical system associated with the battery and generator. Physically check every connection in the generator and battery circuit and electrically check the condition of all fuses and circuit breakers. Check the condition of all ground connections for the battery, battery contacts, and the generator control units. When you have determined that there is no obvious external problem and the generator armature turns when the engine is cranked, check the generator and the voltage regulator.

One of the easiest ways to determine which unit is not operating is to connect a voltmeter between the G terminal of the voltage regulator and ground. This checks the generator's output voltage. However, because this check requires the generator to be turning it must be accomplished with the engine running, or on an appropriate test stand. In either case, observe proper safety precautions. Even when the field winding is open, or the voltage regulator is malfunctioning, the generator should produce residual voltage. In other words, the voltage produced by the armature cutting across the residual magnetic field in the generator frame produces voltage. This should be around one or two volts.

If there is no residual voltage, it is possible that the generator only needs the residual magnetism restored. Residual magnetism is restored by an operation known as **flashing the field**. This is accomplished by momentarily passing current through the field coils in the same way that it normally flows. The methods vary with the internal connections of the generator, and with the type of voltage regulator used. For example, in an "A" circuit generator the field is grounded externally, and you must touch the positive terminal of the battery to the armature. You also may have to insulate one of the brushes by inserting a piece of insulating material between the brush and commutator. To flash the field in an internally grounded "B" circuit generator, the positive battery terminal is touched to the field. Whatever the case, be certain to follow the specific manufacturer instructions. Failure to do so could result in damage to the generator and/or voltage regulator.

If the generator produces residual voltage and no output voltage, the trouble could be with the generator or the regulator. To determine which, operate the engine at a speed high enough for the generator to produce an output, and bypass the voltage regulator with a jumper wire. This method varies with the type of generator and regulator being used, and should be performed in accordance with the manufacturer's recommendations. If the generator produces voltage with the regulator shorted, the problem is with the voltage regulator. If this is the case, be sure that the regulator is properly grounded, because a faulty ground connection prevents a regulator from functioning properly. It is possible to service and adjust some vibrator-type generator controls. However, due to expense, time involved, and test equipment needed to do the job properly, most servicing is done by replacing a faulty unit with a new one.

If the generator does not produce an output voltage when the regulator is bypassed, remove the generator from the engine and overhaul or replace it with an overhauled unit.

GENERATOR OVERHAUL

Generator overhaul is accomplished any time a generator is determined to be inoperative, or at the same time the aircraft engine is overhauled. Although an overhaul can be done in some aircraft repair facilities, it is more often the job of an FAA Certified Repair Station licensed for that operation.

The steps involved in the overhaul of a generator are the same for the overhaul of any unit: (1) disassembly, (2) cleaning, (3) inspection and repair, (4) reassembly, and (5) testing.

DISASSEMBLY

Disassembly instructions for specific units are covered in the manufacturer's overhaul manual and must be followed exactly. Specialized tools are sometimes required for removing pole shoes since the screws holding these in place are usually staked to prevent them from accidentally backing out. Special instructions must also be followed when removing bearings. If the incorrect procedures or tools are used, damage to the bearings or their seating area could result.

CLEANING

Care must be taken when cleaning electrical parts. The proper solvents must be used, and generally parts are not submerged in solvent tanks. Using the wrong solvent could remove the lacquer-type insulation used on field coils and armatures resulting in short circuits after the generator is reassembled.

INSPECTION AND REPAIR

Inspect components for physical damage, corrosion, or wear, and repair or replace as required. Testing for proper operation of electrical components is accomplished using a growler and an electrical multimeter. A **growler** is a specially designed test unit for DC generators and motors and a variety of tests on the armature and field coils are performed using this equipment. Growlers consist of a laminated core wound with many turns of wire that are connected to 110 volts AC. The top of the core forms a vee into which the armature of a DC generator fits. The coil and laminated core of the growler form the primary of a transformer, while the generator armature becomes the secondary. Also included on most growlers is a 110 volt test lamp. This is a simple series circuit with a light bulb that illuminates when the circuit is complete. [Figure 8-26]

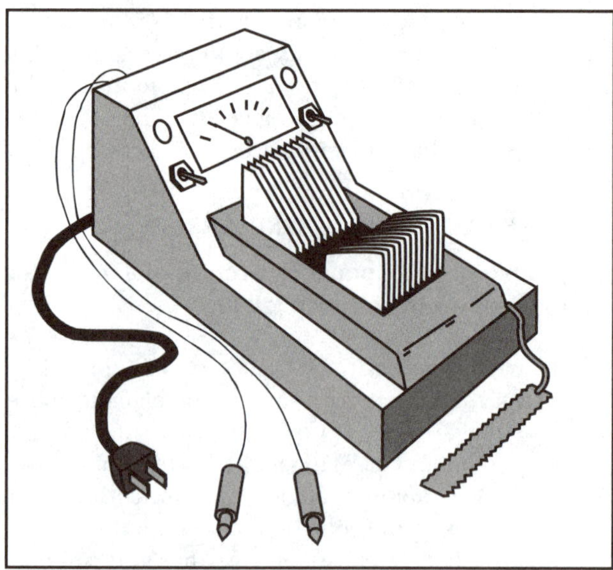

Figure 8-26. A growler is used to test the armature of a DC generator for open circuits.

To test an armature for an open, place it on an energized growler. Using the probes attached to the test lamp, test each armature coil by placing the probes on adjacent segments. The lamp should light with each set of commutator bars. Failure of the test lamp to illuminate indicates an open in that coil, and replacement of the armature is called for.

Armatures are also tested for shorts by placing them on a growler, energizing the unit and holding a thin steel strip, typically a hacksaw blade, slightly above the armature. Slowly rotate the armature on the growler, if there are any shorts in the armature windings, the blade vibrates vigorously. [Figure 8-27]

A third test for armature shorts is accomplished using a 110 volt test lamp to check for grounds. To use a test lamp, one lead is touched to the armature shaft while the second lead is touched to each commutator segment. If a ground exists between any of the windings and the core of the armature, the test lamp illuminates. [Figure 8-28]

Figure 8-27. When a short exists in the armature windings the hacksaw blade vibrates vigorously.

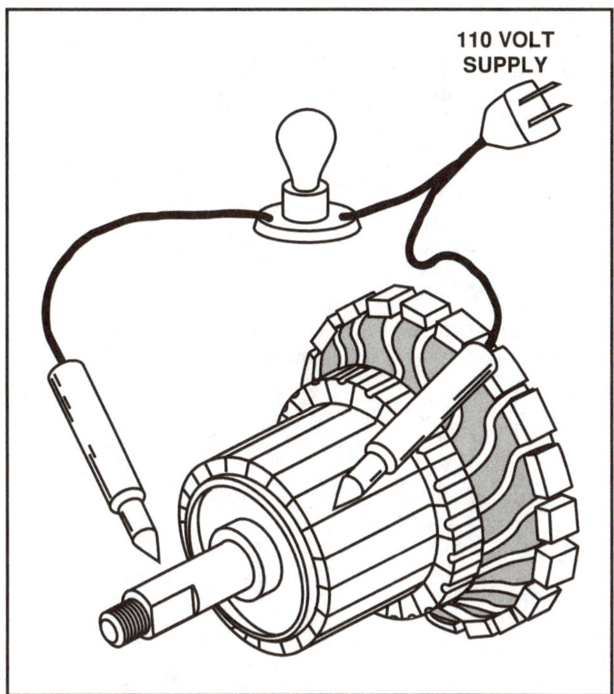

Figure 8-28. When a ground exists between the windings and the armature core, the test light illuminates. This test is also accomplished using an ohmmeter.

You can also test a generator's field coil for shorts by using a test lamp. To do this, one probe is placed at the field winding and the other probe at the generator frame. If the light illuminates, a short exists. [Figure 8-29]

You can also test the field coil for continuity using an ohmmeter set to the low-ohms scale. A shunt field coil should indicate between 2 and 30 ohms, depending on the specific coil. A series type field coil shows almost no resistance. In some cases a current draw test is specified by the manufacturer. This test is accomplished by connecting a battery of proper voltage across the field coils and measuring the current flow. This value must be within the limits specified in the manufacturer's test specifications. [Figure 8-30]

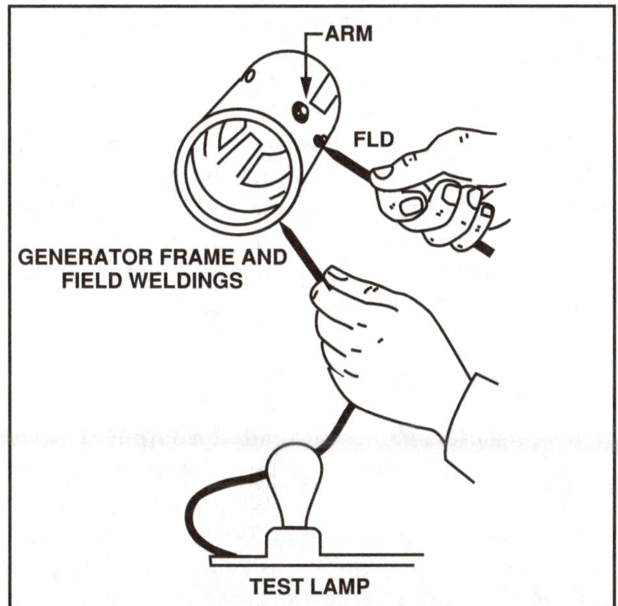

Figure 8-29. In order for the frame and field windings to be considered good, the light should not illuminate.

To resurface or to remove irregularities and pitting from a commutator, an armature is turned in a special armature lathe, or an engine lathe equipped with a special holding fixture. When doing this, remove only enough metal to smooth the commutator's surface. If too much material is removed, the security of the coil ends are jeopardized. If the commutator is only slightly roughened, it is smoothed using No. 000 sandpaper. Never use emery cloth or other conductive material since shorting between commutator segments could result.

With some commutators, the mica insulation between the commutator bars may need to be **undercut**. However, when doing this, you must follow the most recent instructions provided by the manufacturer. This operation is accomplished using a special attachment for the armature lathe, or a hack-saw blade. When specified, the mica is undercut about the same depth as the mica's thickness, or approximately 0.020 inch.

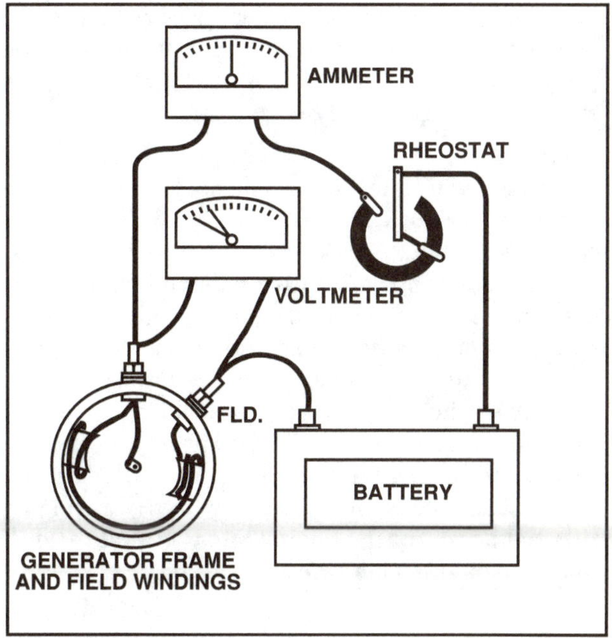

Figure 8-30. To test for shorted turns in a field coil, measure the current drawn by the field at a specific voltage. The current drawn by the field must be within the manufacturer's prescribed range in order for the field windings to be good.

REASSEMBLY

Prior to reassembly, the painted finish on the exterior of the frame is restored. In certain cases the special insulated coatings on the interior surfaces are renewed. Furthermore, all defective parts are replaced according to the reassembly order specified by the manufacturer.

When reassembling a generator, make certain that all internal electrical connections are properly made and secured, and that the brushes are free to move in their holders. Check the pigtails on the brushes for freedom, and make sure they do not alter or restrict the brushes' free motion. The purpose of the pigtail is to conduct current and help eliminate any current in the brush springs that could alter its spring action. The pigtails also eliminate possible sparking caused by movement of the brush within the holder, thus minimizing brush side wear.

Generator brushes are normally replaced at overhaul, or when half worn. When new brushes are installed they must be seated, or contoured, to maximize the contact area between the face of the brush and the commutator. Seating is accomplished by lifting the brush slightly to permit the insertion of No. 000, or finer sandpaper, rough side out. With the sandpaper in place, pull the sandpaper in the direction of armature rotation, being careful to keep the ends of the sandpaper as close to the commutator as possible to avoid rounding the edges of the brush. When pulling the sandpaper back to the starting point, the brush is raised so it does not ride on the sandpaper. [Figure 8-31]

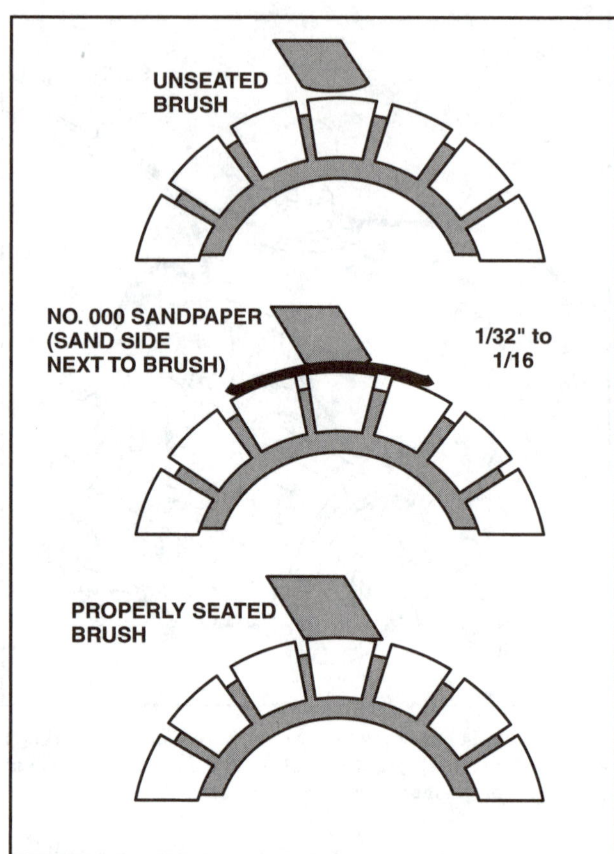

Figure 8-31. When a new brush is installed in a generator, the brush must be contoured to fit the commutator. To do this, insert a piece of No. 000 sandpaper between the brush and the commutator and sand the brush in the direction of rotation.

The brush spring tension is checked using a spring scale. A carbon, graphite, or light metal brush should only exert a pressure of 1-1/2 to 2-1/2 psi on the commutator. If the spring tension is not within the limits set by the manufacturer, the springs must be replaced. When a spring scale is used, the pressure measurement exerted by a brush is read directly on the spring scale. The scale is attached at the point of contact between the spring arm and the top of the brush, with the brush installed in the guide. The scale is then pulled up until the arm just lifts the brush off the commutator. At that instant, the force on the scale is read.

After the generator has run for a short period, the brushes should be reinspected to ensure that no pieces of sand are embedded in the brush. Under no circumstance should emery cloth or similar abrasive be used for seating brushes or smoothing commutators, since they contain conductive materials.

TESTING

Operational testing of generators is accomplished on test benches built for that purpose. Bench testing allows the technician the opportunity to flash the field, and ensure proper operation of the unit before installation. Generator manufacturers supply test specifications in their overhaul instructions that should be followed exactly.

GENERATOR SYSTEMS

When installed on most aircraft, the output of a generator typically flows to the aircraft's bus bar where it is distributed to the various electrical components. In this type of system, the allowable voltage drop in the main power wires coming off the generator to the bus bar is two percent of the regulated voltage when the generator is producing its rated current. As added insurance to make sure that a given electrical load does not exceed a generator's output capability, the total continuous electrical load permitted in a given system is limited to 80 percent of the total rated generator output. For example, if an aircraft has a 60 amp generator installed, the maximum continuous load that can be placed on the electrical system is 48 amps.

In the event a generator quits producing current or produces too much current, most aircraft systems have a generator master switch that allows you to disconnect the generator from the electrical system. This feature helps prevent damage to the generator or to the rest of the electrical system. On aircraft that utilize more than one generator connected to a common electrical system, the Federal Aviation Regulations require individual generator switches that can be operated from the cockpit. This allows you to isolate a malfunctioning generator and protect the remaining electrical system.

ALTERNATORS

There are two types of alternators used in today's aircraft. They are the DC alternator and the AC alternator. DC alternators produce relatively small amounts of current and, therefore, are typically found on light aircraft. AC alternators, on the other hand, are capable of producing a great deal of power and, therefore, are typically found on larger aircraft and military aircraft. Furthermore, since AC electricity can be carried through smaller conductors, AC alternators allow an appreciable weight savings.

DC ALTERNATORS

DC alternators do the same thing as DC generators. They produce AC that is then converted to DC before it enters an aircraft's electrical system. The difference, however, is that in an alternator the magnetic poles rotate and induce voltage into a fixed, or stationary winding. Furthermore, the AC current produced is rectified by six solid-state diodes instead of a commutator. [Figure 8-32]

All alternators are constructed in basically the same way. The primary components of an alternator include the rotor, the stator, the rectifier, and the brush assembly.

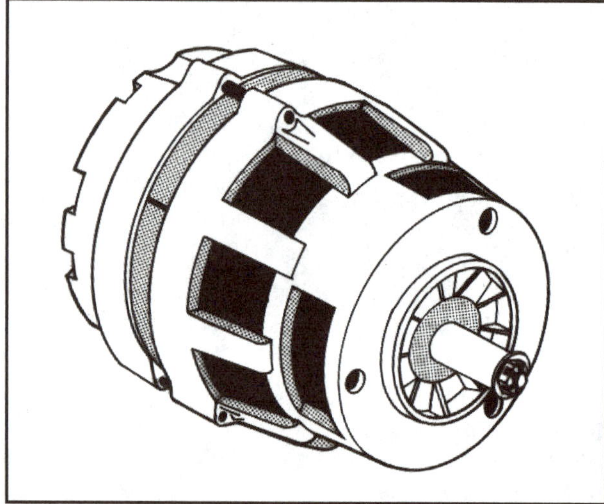

Figure 8-32. DC alternators are used in aircraft that require a low or medium amount of electrical power.

ROTOR

An alternator **rotor** consists of a wire coil wound on an iron spool between two heavy iron segments with interlacing fingers. Some rotors have four fingers while others have as many as seven. Each finger forms one pole of the rotating magnetic field. [Figure 8-33]

The two coil leads pass through one segment and each lead attaches to an insulated **slip ring**. The slip rings, segments, and coil spool are all pressed onto a hardened steel rotor shaft which is either splined or has a key slot. In an assembled alternator, this shaft is driven by an engine accessory pad, or fitted with a pulley and driven by an accessory belt. The slip-ring end of the shaft is supported in the housing with a needle bearing and the drive end with a ball bearing. Two carbon brushes ride on the smooth slip rings to bring a varying direct current into the field and carry it out to the regulator.

STATOR

As the rotor turns, the load current is induced into stationary stator coils. The coils making up the stator are wound in slots around the inside periphery of the stator frame, which is made of thin laminations of soft iron. Most alternators are three-phase

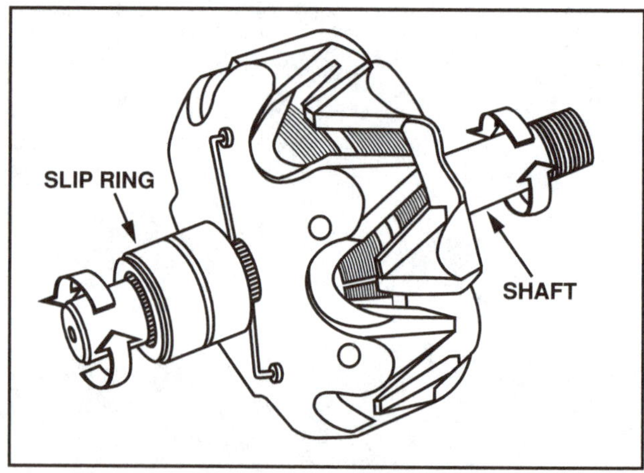

Figure 8-33. Rotors consist of interlacing fingers that form the poles of the rotating magnetic field.

alternators. This means that the stator has three separate coils that are 120 degrees apart. To do this, one end of each coil is brought together to form a common junction of a Y-connection. [Figure 8-34]

With the stator wound in a three-phase configuration, the output current peaks in each set of windings every 120 degrees of rotation. However, after the output is rectified, the DC output becomes much smoother. [Figure 8-35]

Because an alternator has several field poles and the large number of stator windings, most alternators produce their rated output at a relatively low rpm. This differs from a generator which must rotate at a fairly high speed to produce its rated output.

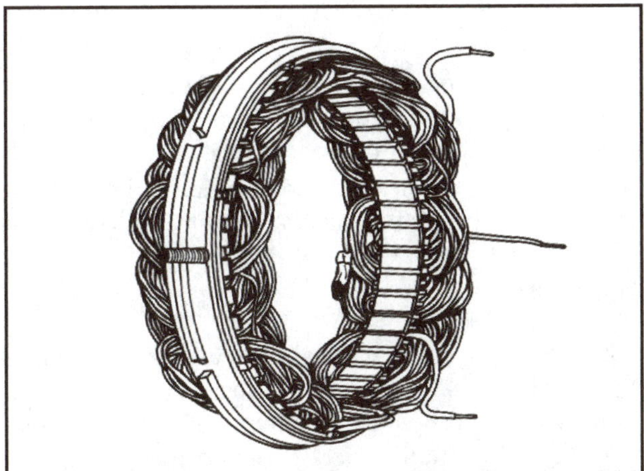

Figure 8-34. Three sets of coils in a stator are typically brought together to form a Y-connection.

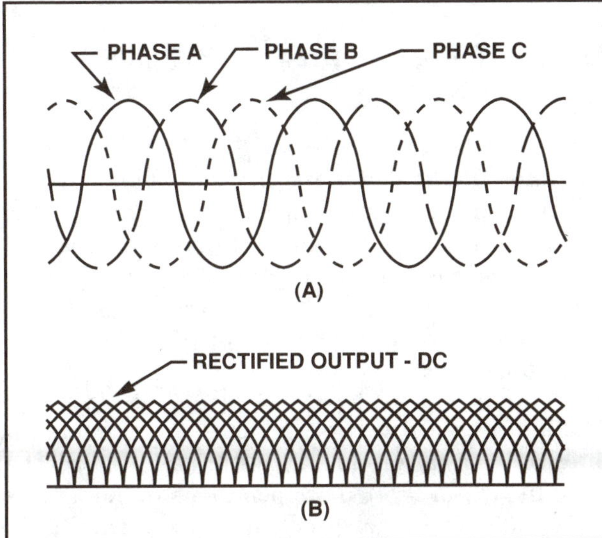

Figure 8-35. (A)—The waveform produced by a three-phase stator winding results in a peak every 120 degrees of rotation. (B)—Once rectified, the output produces a relatively smooth direct current, with a low-amplitude, high-frequency ripple.

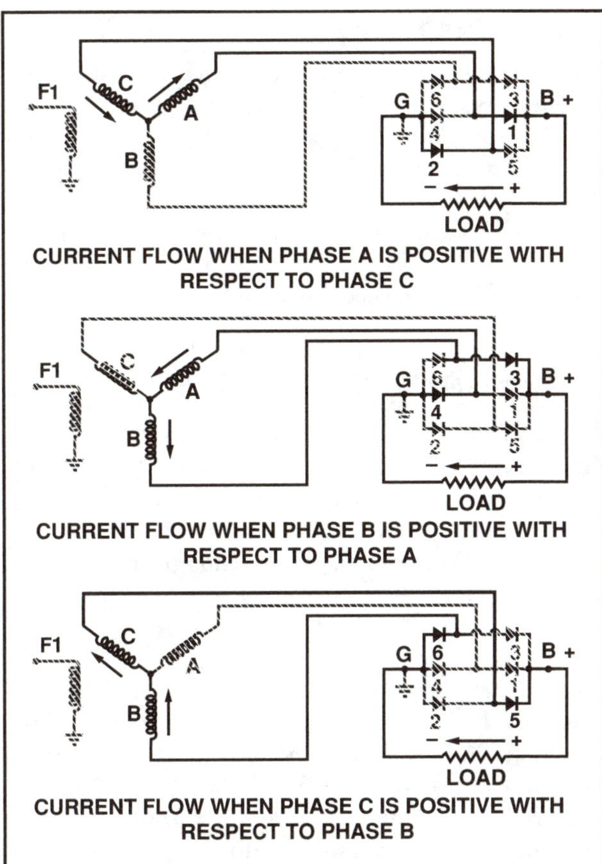

Figure 8-36. This circuit diagram illustrates how the AC produced in each winding is rectified into DC.

RECTIFIERS

The three-phase, full-wave rectifier in an alternator is made up of six heavy-duty silicon diodes. Three of the diodes are pressed into the slip-ring end frame, and the other three are pressed into a heat sink that is electrically insulated from the end frame. [Figure 8-36]

By referring to figure 8-36, you can see that at the instant the output terminal of winding "A" is positive with respect to the output end of winding "C," current flows through diode 1 to the load, and back through diode 2 which is pressed into the alternator end frame. From this diode, it flows back through winding "C."

As the rotor continues to turn, winding "B" becomes positive with respect to winding "A" and the current flows through diode 3 to the load, and then back through diode 4 and winding "A."

When the rotor completes 240 degrees of rotation, "C" becomes positive with respect to "B." When this occurs, current flows through diode 5 to the load, and back through diode 6. After 360 degrees of rotation, the process begins again.

BRUSH ASSEMBLY

The brush assembly in an alternator consists of two brushes, two brush springs, and brush holders. Unlike a generator which uses brushes to supply a path for current to flow from the armature to the load, the brushes in an alternator supply current to the field coils. Since these brushes ride on the smooth surface of the slip rings, the efficiency and service life of alternator brushes is typically better.

ALTERNATOR CONTROLS

The voltage produced by an alternator is controlled in the same way as in a generator, by varying the DC field current. Therefore, when the output voltage rises above the desired value, the field current is decreased. By the same token, when the output voltage drops below the desired value, the field current is increased.

The process of increasing and decreasing the field current could be accomplished in low-output alternators with vibrator-type controls that interrupt the field current by opening a set of contacts. However, a more efficient means of voltage control has been devised that uses a transistor to control the flow of field current.

The transistorized voltage regulator utilizes both vibrating points and transistors for voltage control. The vibrating points operate the same as they do in vibrator-type voltage regulators. However, instead of the field current flowing through the contacts, the transistor base current flows through them. Since this current is small compared to the field current that flows through the emitter-collector there is no arcing at the contacts. [Figure 8-37]

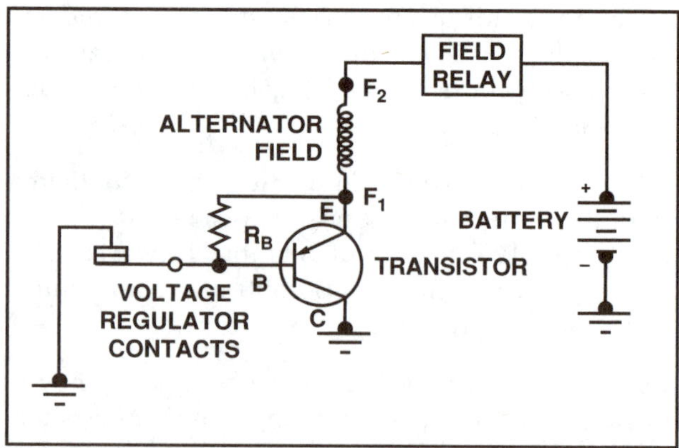

Figure 8-37. Alternator field current flows from the emitter to the collector only when the voltage regulator contacts are closed and current flows to the base.

In a completely solid-state voltage regulator, semiconductor devices replace all of the moving parts. These units are very efficient, reliable, and generally have no serviceable components. Therefore, if a completely solid-state unit becomes defective, it is typically removed from service and replaced.

Alternator control requirements are different from those of a generator for several reasons. For example, since an alternator uses solid-state diodes for rectification, current cannot flow from the battery into the alternator. Therefore, there is no need for a reverse-current cutout relay. Furthermore, since the alternator field is excited by the system bus whose voltage is limited, there is no way an alternator can put out enough current to burn itself out. Because of this, there is no need for a current limiter.

With an alternator there must be some means of shutting off the flow of field current when the alternator is not producing power. To do this, most systems utilize either a field switch or a field relay that is controlled by the master switch. Either setup allows you to isolate the field current and shut it off if necessary.

Another control that most aircraft alternator circuits employ is some form of overvoltage protection. This allows the alternator to be removed from the bus should a malfunction occur that increases the output voltage to a dangerous level. This function is often handled by an **alternator control unit** or **ACU**. Basically, the ACU drops the alternator from the circuit when an overvoltage condition exists.

DC ALTERNATOR SERVICE AND MAINTENANCE

When an alternator fails to keep the battery charged, you should first determine that the alternator and battery circuits are properly connected. This includes checking for open fuses or circuit breakers. If everything is connected properly, check for battery voltage at the alternator's battery, or "B" terminal and at the "Batt" or "+" terminal of the voltage regulator.

There are basically two problems that prevent an alternator from producing electrical power. The most likely is a shorted or open diode in the rectifying circuit. The other problem is the possibility of an open circuit in the field.

To check for a shorted circuit, measure the resistance between the alternator's "B" terminal and ground. To accomplish this, set the ohmmeter on

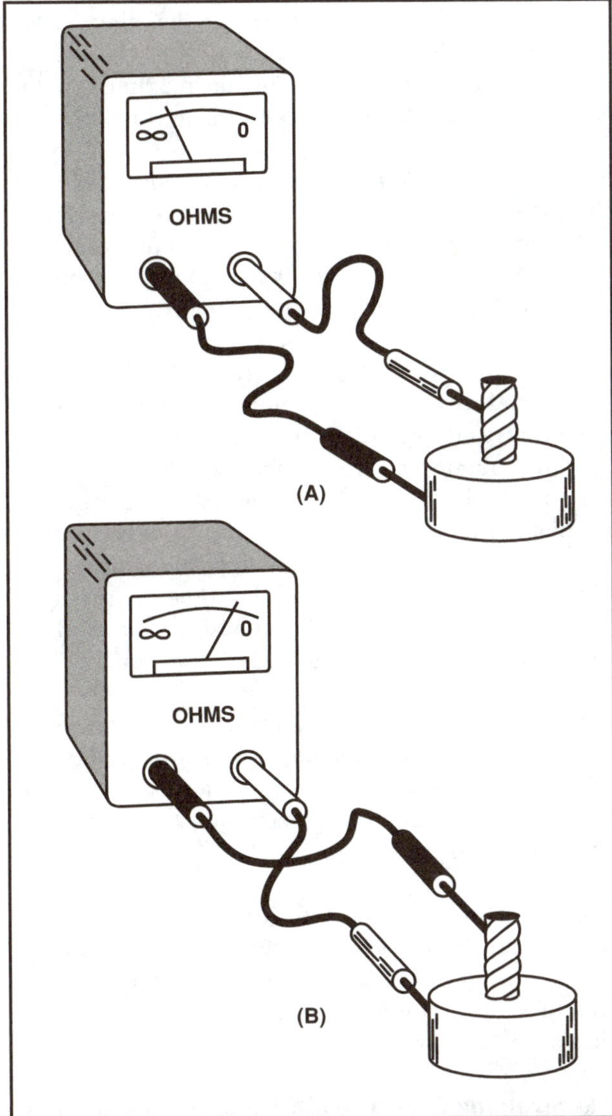

Figure 8-38. (A) — A good diode produces a high resistance reading when reverse biased. (B) — On the other hand, resistance should be low when forward biased. A shorted diode typically causes a low resistance reading when checked in the forward and reverse biased direction while an open diode produces high resistance readings in either direction.

the R × 1 scale and measure resistance. Then, reverse the ohmmeter leads and measure the resistance again. If the diodes are good, you get a relatively low resistance reading when the diodes are forward biased, and an infinite or very high reading when the diodes are reverse biased. If an infinite or very high reading is not obtained, one or more of the diodes are shorted. [Figure 8-38]

Since the diodes in an alternator are connected in parallel, an open diode cannot be detected with an ohmmeter. However, if the diodes are checked individually, an ohmmeter will identify an open diode.

Solid-state diodes are quite rugged and have a long life when properly used. However, they can be damaged by excessive voltage or reverse current flow. For this reason you should never operate an alternator that is not connected to an electrical load.

Since alternators receive their field current from the aircraft bus and do not rely on residual magnetism to be started, you must never flash the field or polarize an alternator.

To aid in systematic alternator troubleshooting, some manufacturers have specialized test equipment. This test equipment is usually plugged into the aircraft electrical system between the voltage regulator and the aircraft bus. Through the use of indicator lights, the test equipment tells you whether a problem exists in the voltage regulator, the overvoltage sensing circuit, or the alternator field/output circuit. By using this type of test equipment, you can save time and avoid the unnecessary replacement of good components.

To avoid burning out the rectifying diodes during installation, it is extremely important that the battery be connected with the proper polarity. In addition, anytime an external power source is connected to the aircraft, ensure correct polarity is applied.

AC ALTERNATORS

Direct current is used as the main electrical power for small aircraft because it is storable and aircraft engines are started through the use of battery power. However, large aircraft require elaborate ground service facilities and external power sources for starting. Therefore, they can take advantage of the appreciable weight savings provided by using alternating current as their primary power source.

In addition to saving weight, alternating current has the advantage over direct current in that its voltage is easily stepped up or down. Therefore, when needed, AC carries current a long distance by passing it through a step-up transformer. This promotes additional weight savings since high voltage AC is conducted through a relatively small conductor. Once the voltage arrives at its destination it passes through a step-down transformer where voltage is lowered and current is stepped up to the value needed.

In some situations, such as charging batteries or operating variable speed motors, direct current is required. However, by passing AC through a series of semiconductor diodes it is easily changed into DC with relatively little loss. This is another advantage of AC as compared to DC.

TYPES OF AC ALTERNATORS

AC alternators are classified in order to distinguish differences. One means of classification is by the output voltage phase numbers. Alternating current alternators can be single-phase, two-phase, three-phase, and sometimes even six-phase or more. However, almost all aircraft electrical systems use a three-phase alternator.

In a **single-phase alternator**, the stator is made up of several windings connected in series to form a single circuit. The windings are also connected so the AC voltages induced into each winding are in phase. This means that, to determine a single-phase alternator's total output, the voltage induced into each winding must be added. Therefore, the total voltage produced by a stator with four windings is four times the single voltage in any one winding. However, since the power delivered by a single-phase circuit is pulsating, this type of circuit is impractical for many applications. [Figure 8-39]

Two-phase alternators have two or more single-phase windings spaced symmetrically around the stator so that the AC voltage induced in one is 90 degrees out of phase with the voltage induced in the other. These windings are electrically separate from each other so that when one winding is cutting the maximum number of flux-lines, the other is cutting no flux lines.

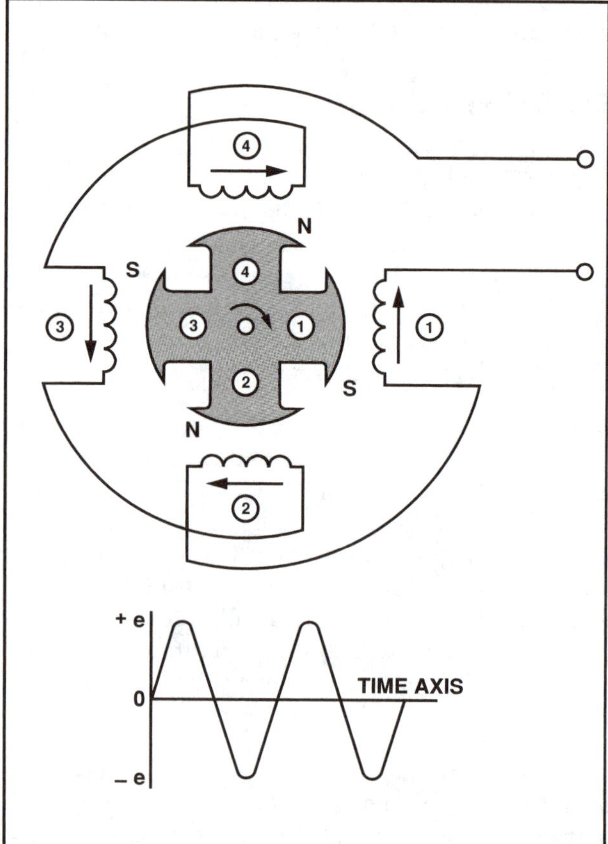

Figure 8-39. In this single-phase alternator the rotating field induces voltage into the stationary stator. The number of stator windings determines the output voltage.

A **three-phase** or **polyphase** circuit is used in most aircraft alternators. The three-phase alternator has three single-phase windings spaced so that the voltage induced in each winding is 120 degrees out of phase with the voltage in the other two windings. [Figure 8-40]

The three individual phase voltages produced by a three-phase alternator are similar to those generated by three single-phase alternators, whose voltages are out of phase by 120 degrees. In a three-phase alternator, one lead from each winding is connected to form a common junction. When this is done, the stator is Y- or star-connected. A three-phase stator can also be connected so that the phases are end-to-end. This arrangement is called a delta connection.

Still another means of classifying alternators is to distinguish between the type of stator and rotor used. When done this way, there are two types of alternators, the revolving-armature type and the revolving-field type.

The **revolving-armature type** alternator is similar in construction to the DC generator, in that the armature rotates within a stationary magnetic field. This type of setup is typically found only in alternators with a low power rating and generally is not used.

The **revolving-field type** alternator has a stationary armature winding (stator) and a rotating-field winding (rotor). The advantage of this configuration is that the armature is connected directly to the load without sliding contacts in the load circuit. Direct connection to the armature circuit makes it possible

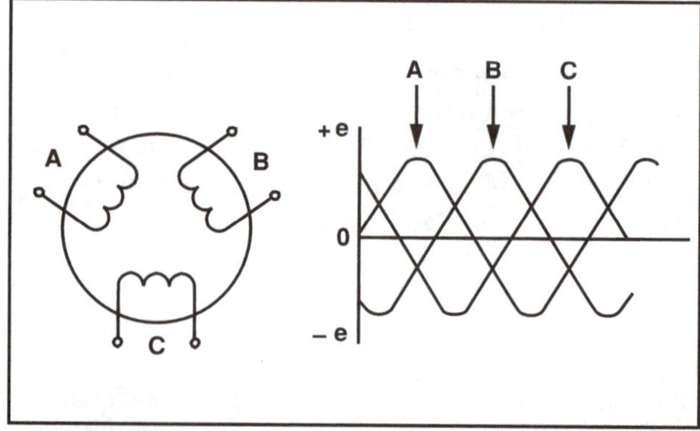

Figure 8-40. Sinewave "A" is 120 degrees out of phase with sinewave "B," and sinewave "B" is 120 degrees out of phase with sinewave "C."

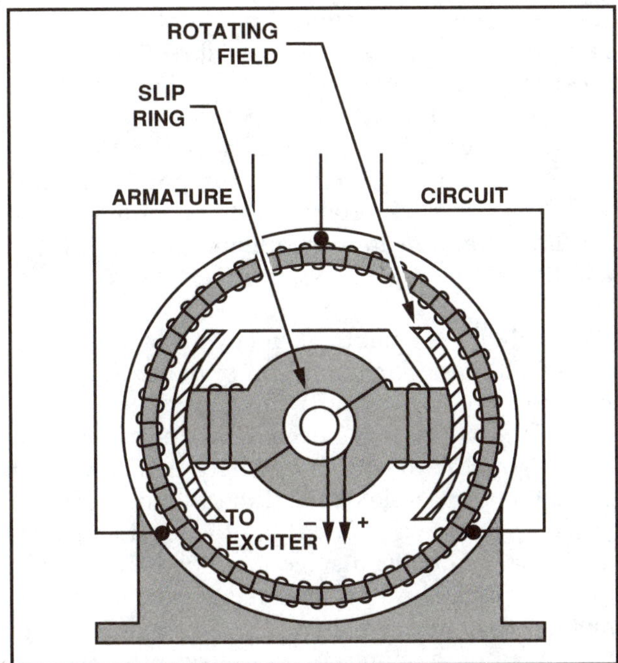

Figure 8-41. In a revolving-field type alternator, the armature is directly connected to the load without the use of sliding contacts. The rotating-field alternator is used almost universally in aircraft systems.

to use large cross-section conductors that are adequately insulated for high voltage. [Figure 8-41]

BRUSHLESS ALTERNATORS

The AC alternators used in large jet-powered aircraft are of the brushless type and are usually air cooled. Since the brushless alternators have no current flow between brushes or slip rings they are very efficient at high altitudes where brush arcing is often a problem.

As discussed earlier, alternator brushes are used to carry current to the rotating electromagnet. However, in a brushless alternator, current is induced into the field coil through an exciter. A brushless alternator consists of three separate fields, a permanent magnetic field, an exciter field, and a main output field. The permanent magnets furnish the magnetic flux to start the generator producing an output before field current flows. The magnetism produced by these magnets induces voltage into an armature that carries the current to a generator control unit, or GCU. Here, the AC is rectified and sent to the exciter field winding. The exciter field then induces voltage into the exciter output winding. The output from the exciter is rectified by six silicon diodes, and the resulting DC flows through the output field winding. From here, voltage is induced into the main output coils. The permanent magnet, exciter output winding, six diodes, and output field winding are all mounted on the generator shaft and rotate as a unit. The three-phase output stator windings are wound in slots that are in the laminated frame of the alternator housing. [Figure 8-42]

The main output stator winding ends of a brushless alternator are connected in the form of a Y, and in the case of the previous figure, the neutral winding is brought to the outside of the housing along with

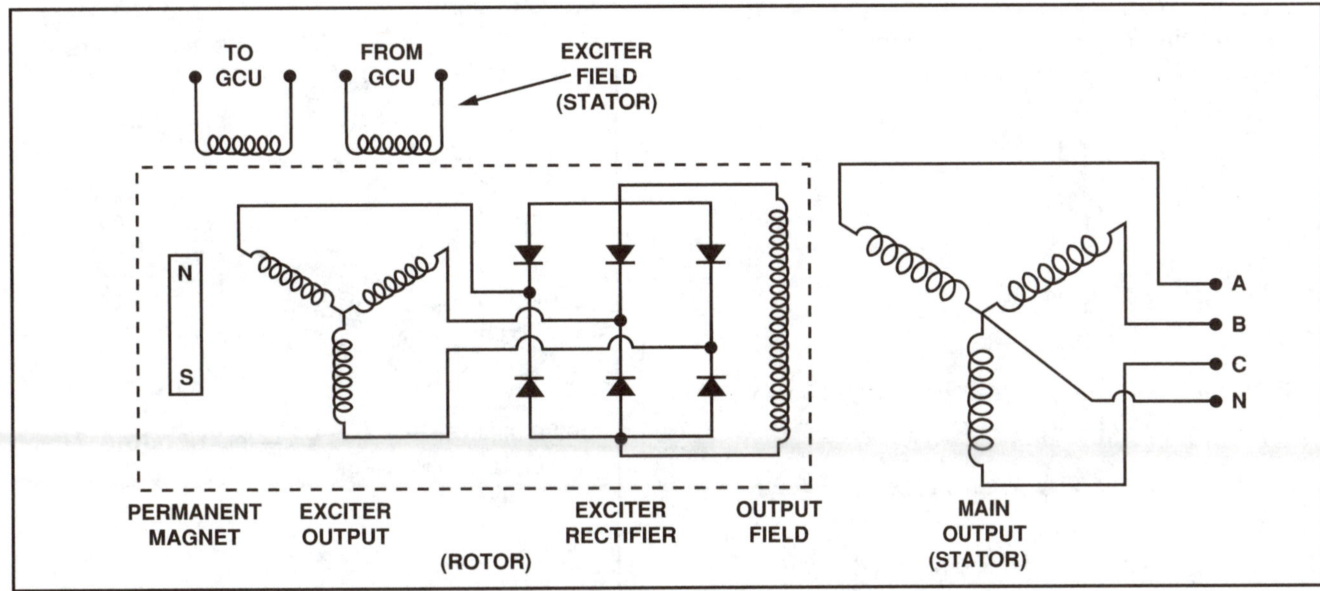

Figure 8-42. In a brushless alternator there are actually three generators. The permanent magnet generator, the exciter generator, and the main generator. The permanent magnet generator induces voltage into the exciter generator which in turn supplies the field current for the main generator.

the three-phase windings. These alternators are usually designed to produce 120 volts across a single phase and 208 volts across two phases.

The GCU actually monitors and regulates the main generator's output by controlling the amount of current that flows into the exciter field. For example, if additional output is needed, the GCU increases the amount of current flowing to the exciter field winding which, in turn, increases the exciter output. A higher exciter output increases the current flowing through the main generator field winding thereby increasing alternator output.

Since brushless alternators utilize a permanent magnet, there is no need to flash the field. In addition, the use of a permanent magnet eliminates the need to carry current to a rotating assembly through brushes.

ALTERNATOR RATINGS

AC alternators are rated in volt-amps which is a measure of the apparent power being produced by the generator. Because most AC alternators produce a great deal of power, their ratings are generally expressed in kilo-volt amperes or KVA. A typical Boeing 727 AC alternator is rated at 45 KVA.

FREQUENCY

The AC frequency produced by an AC generator is determined by the number of poles and the speed of the rotor. The faster the rotor, the higher the frequency. By the same token the more poles on a rotor, the higher the frequency for any given speed. The frequency of AC generated by an alternator is determined using the equation:

$$F = \frac{P}{2} \times \frac{N}{60} = PN$$

Where:
F = Frequency
P = the number of poles
N = the speed in rpm

With this formula you can determine that a two-pole, 3,600 rpm alternator has a frequency of 60 hertz.

$$F = \frac{2 \times 3{,}600}{120} = 60 \text{ Hz}$$

Since AC constantly changes rate and direction, it always produces a back voltage that opposes current flow. If you recall from your general studies, this opposition is called inductive reactance. The higher the AC frequency produced by an alternator, the more times the current switches direction and the greater the back voltage, or inductive reactance. Because aircraft systems use 400-hertz AC, inductive reactance is high and current is low. However, because of this higher frequency, motors wound with smaller wire produce a high torque value. Furthermore, transformers are made much smaller and lighter.

To provide a constant frequency as engine speed varies and maintain a uniform frequency between multiple generators, most AC generators are connected to a **constant speed drive** unit, or **CSD**. Although CSDs come in a variety of shapes and sizes, their principle of operation is essentially the same. The drive units consist of an engine-driven axial-piston variable-displacement hydraulic pump that supplies fluid to an axial-piston hydraulic motor. The motor then drives the generator. The displacement of the pump is controlled by a governor which senses the rotational speed of the AC generator. The governor action holds the output speed of the generator constant and maintains an AC frequency at 400-hertz, plus or minus established tolerances. [Figure 8-43]

Some modern jet aircraft produce AC with a generator called an **Integrated Drive Generator** or **IDG**. An

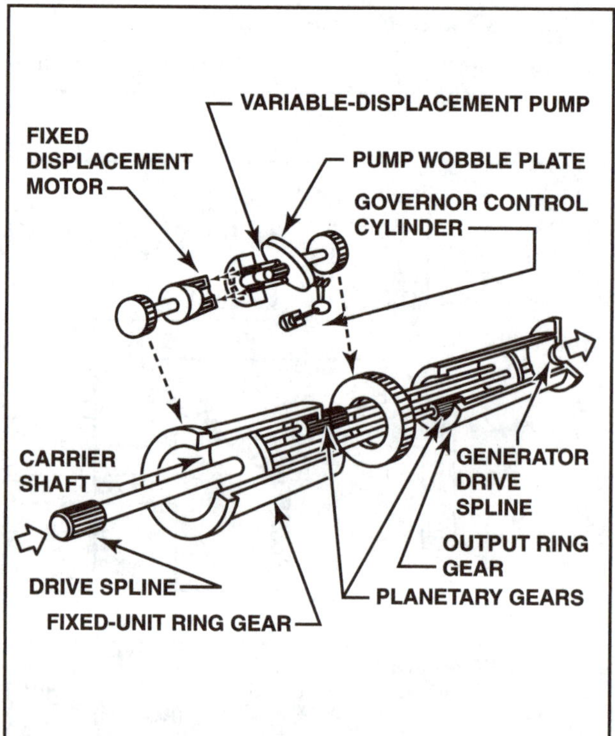

Figure 8-43. A constant-speed drive axial-gear differential, like the one above, is used in the Sunstrand Integrated Drive Generator.

IDG differs from a CSD in that both the constant speed drive unit and the generator are sealed in the same housing. [Figure 8-44]

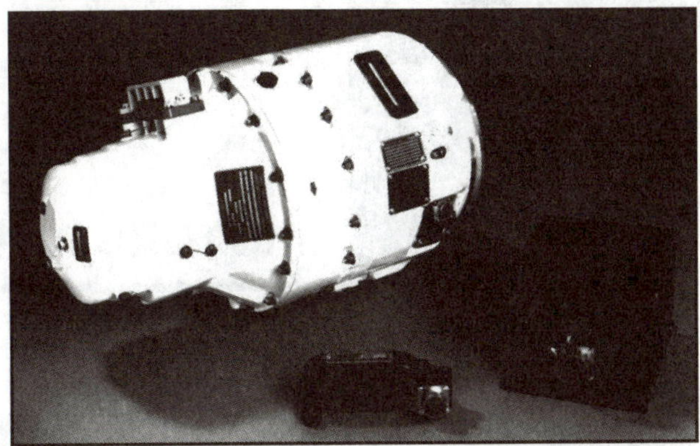

Figure 8-44. The constant speed drive unit is included in the housing with the Sunstrand Integrated Drive Generator above. Also shown is the generator's control unit and a current transformer assembly.

AC ALTERNATOR MAINTENANCE

Maintenance and inspection of alternator systems is similar to that of DC systems. The proper maintenance of an alternator requires the unit to be kept clean and all electrical connections tight and in good repair. Alternators and their drive systems differ in design and maintenance requirements; therefore, specific information is found in the manufacturer's service publications and in the maintenance program approved for a particular aircraft.

SECTION C

MOTORS AND STARTING SYSTEMS

Many aircraft functions require an application of force greater than a pilot can perform manually. For example, raising and lowering the landing gear by hand or extending and retracting the flaps would take a great deal of time and effort on larger, high performance aircraft. Electric motors can perform this and many other operations quickly and easily.

DC MOTORS

Many devices in an airplane, from the starter to the auto-pilot, depend upon the mechanical energy furnished by direct-current motors. A DC motor is a rotating machine that transforms direct-current electrical energy into mechanical energy.

MOTOR THEORY

As you know, the lines of flux between two magnets flow from the north pole to the south pole. At the same time, when current flows through a wire, lines of flux set up around the wire. The direction these flux lines encircle the wire depends on the direction of current flow. When the wire's flux lines and the magnet's flux lines are placed together, a reaction occurs. For example, when the flux lines between two magnetic poles are flowing from left to right and the lines of flux encircling a wire between the magnetic poles flow in a counterclockwise direction, the flux lines reinforce each other at the bottom of the wire. This happens because the lines of flux produced by the magnet and the flow of flux lines at the bottom of the wire are traveling in the same direction. However, at the top of the wire the flux lines oppose, or neutralize, each other. The resulting magnetic field under the wire is strong and the magnetic field above the wire is weak. Consequently, the wire is pushed away from the side where the field is the strongest. [Figure 8-45]

Using this same principle, if the current flow through the wire were reversed, the flux lines encircling the wire would flow in the opposite direction. The resulting combination of the magnetic flux lines and wire flux lines would create a strong magnetic field at the top of the wire and a weak magnetic field at the bottom. Consequently, the wire is pushed downward away from the stronger field.

PARALLEL CONDUCTORS

When two current-carrying wires are in the vicinity of one another they exert a force on each other. This force is the result of the magnetic fields set up around each wire. When the current flows in the same direction, the resulting magnetic fields

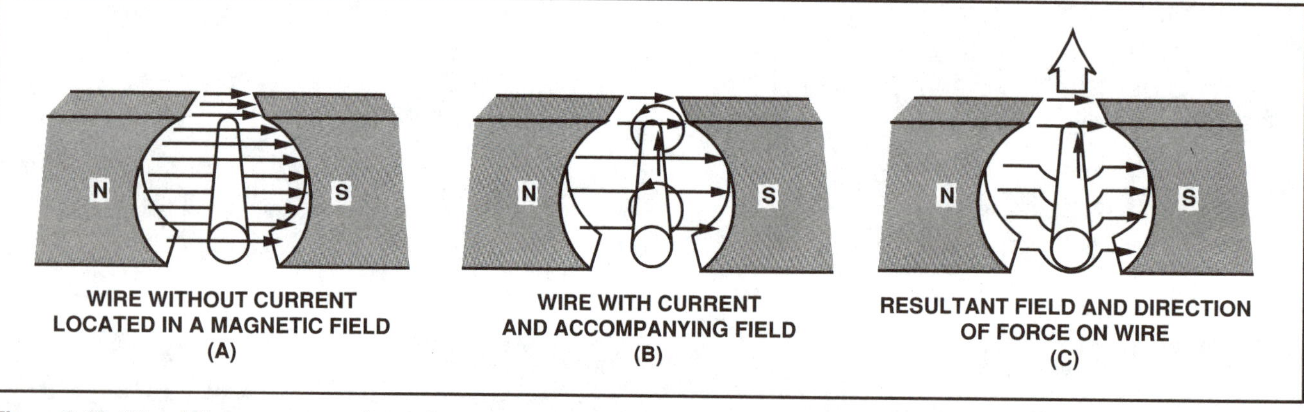

Figure 8-45. (A) — When no current flows through a wire that is between two magnets, the lines of flux flow from north to south without being disturbed. (B) — When current flows through the wire, magnetic flux lines encircle it. (C) — The flux lines from the magnet and the flux lines encircling the wire react with one another to produce a strong magnetic field under the wire and a weak magnetic field above it.

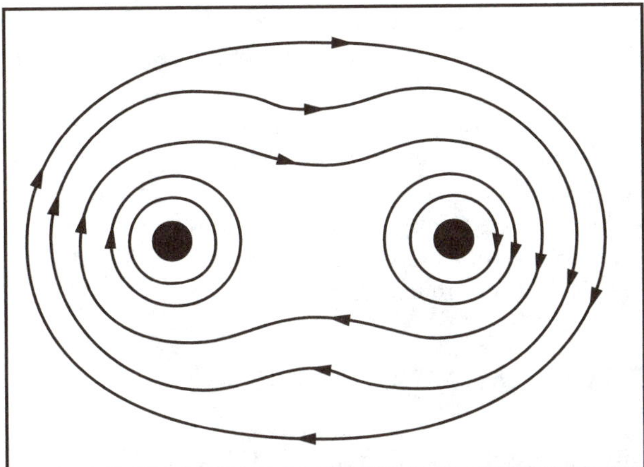

Figure 8-46. When two parallel wires have current flowing through them in the same direction they are forced in the direction of the weaker field, which is toward each other.

encompass both wires in a clockwise direction. These fields oppose each other and, therefore, cancel each other out. [Figure 8-46]

When the electron flow in the wires is opposite, the magnetic field around one wire radiates outward in a clockwise direction while the magnetic field around the second wire rotates counterclockwise. These fields combine, or reinforce each other between the wires. [Figure 8-47]

DEVELOPING TORQUE

When a current-carrying coil is placed in a magnetic field, the magnetic fields produced cause the coil to rotate. The force that produces rotation is called **torque**. [Figure 8-48]

The amount of torque developed in a coil depends on several factors including, the strength of the magnetic field, the number of turns in the coil, and the position of the coil in the field.

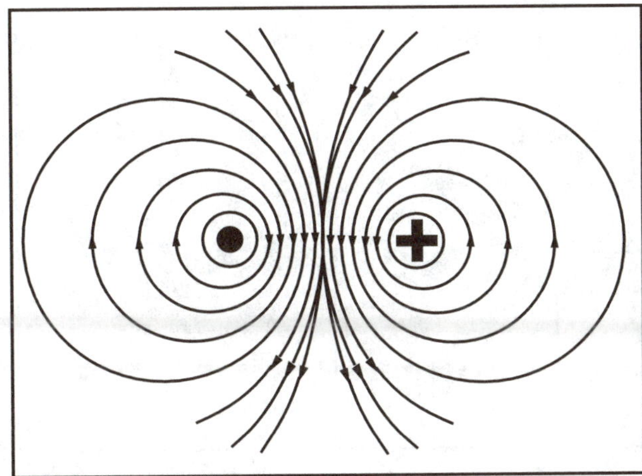

Figure 8-47. When the flow of electrons in two wires is opposite, the resulting magnetic fields force the wires apart.

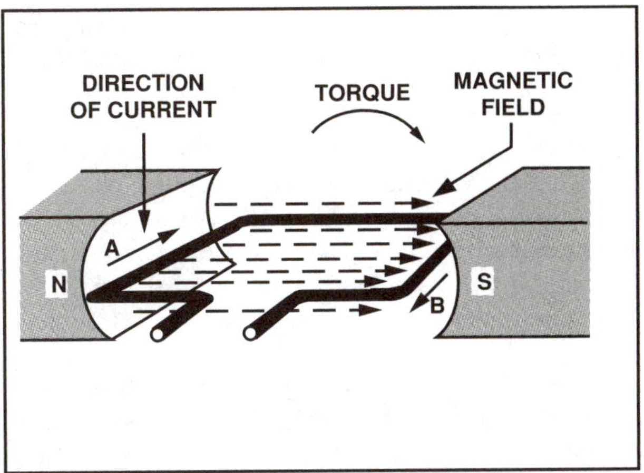

Figure 8-48. The coil above has current flowing inward on side A and outward on side B. Therefore, the magnetic field encircling wire A is counterclockwise while the magnetic field encircling wire B is clockwise. The resultant force pushes wire B downward, and wire A upward. This causes the coil to rotate until the wires are perpendicular to the magnetic flux lines. In other words, torque is created by the reacting magnetic fields around the coil.

The **right-hand motor rule** is used to determine the direction a current-carrying wire moves in a magnetic field. If you point your right index finger in the direction of the magnetic field and your second finger in the direction of current flow, your thumb indicates the direction the wire moves. [Figure 8-49]

BASIC DC MOTOR

Torque is the technical basis governing the construction of DC motors. Recall that a coil only rotates when it is at a 90 degree angle to the mag-

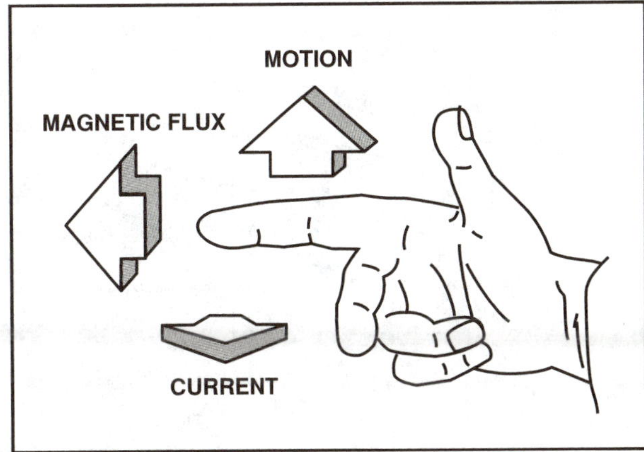

Figure 8-49. When using the right-hand motor rule, your right index finger indicates the direction the magnetic flux flows, while your second finger indicates the direction of current flow and your thumb the direction the coil rotates.

netic field produced by two magnets. Therefore, when a coil lines up with the magnetic field it does not rotate. This is because the torque at that point is zero.

The coil of a motor must rotate continuously in order for the motor to operate efficiently. Therefore, it is necessary for a device to reverse the coil current just as the coil becomes parallel with the magnet's flux lines. When the current is reversed, torque is again produced and the coil rotates. When a current-reversing device is set up to reverse the current each time the coil is about to stop, the coil rotates continuously.

One way to reverse the current in a coil is to attach a commutator similar to what is used on a generator. When this is done, the current flowing through the coil changes direction continuously as the coil rotates, thus preserving torque. [Figure 8-50]

A more effective method of ensuring continuous coil torque is to have a large number of coils wound on an armature. When this is done, the coils are spaced so that, for any position of the armature, a coil is near the magnet's poles. This makes torque both continuous and strong. However, it also means that the commutator must contain several segments.

To further increase the amount of torque generated, the armature is placed between the poles of an electromagnet instead of a permanent magnet. This provides a much stronger magnetic field. Furthermore, the core of an armature is usually made of soft iron that is strongly magnetized through induction.

DC MOTOR CONSTRUCTION

The major parts in a practical motor are the armature assembly, the field assembly, the brush assembly, and the end frames. This arrangement is very similar to a DC generator.

ARMATURE ASSEMBLY

The armature assembly contains a soft iron core, coils, and commutator mounted on a rotatable steel shaft. The core consists of laminated stacks of soft iron that are insulated from each other. Solid iron is not used because it generates excessive heat that uses energy needlessly. The armature windings are

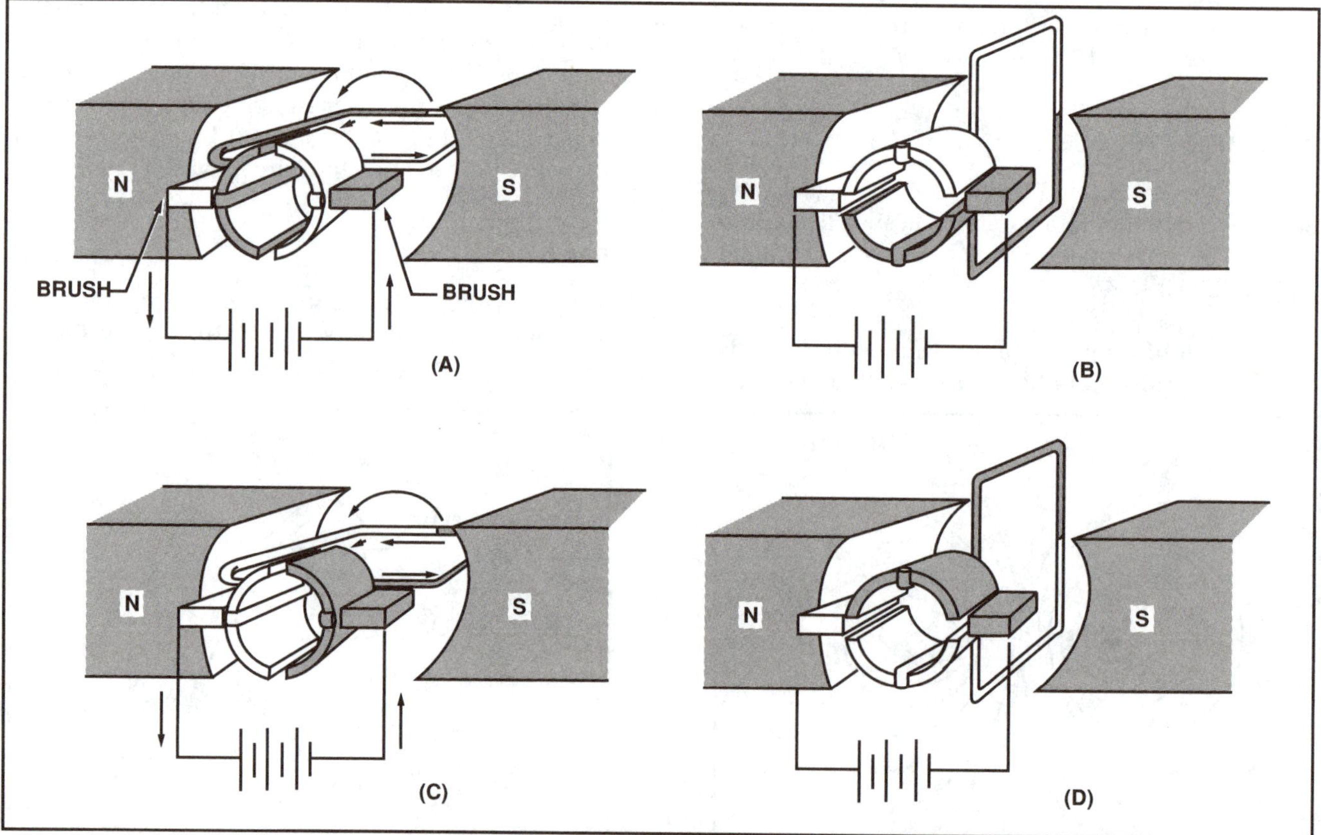

Figure 8-50. (A) — As current flows through the brushes to the commutator and coil, torque is produced and the coil rotates. (B) — As the coil becomes parallel with the magnetic lines of flux, each brush slides off one terminal and connects the opposite terminal to reverse the polarity. (C) — Once the current reverses, torque is again produced and the coil rotates. (D) — As the coil again becomes parallel with the flux lines, current is again reversed by the commutator and torque continues to rotate the coil.

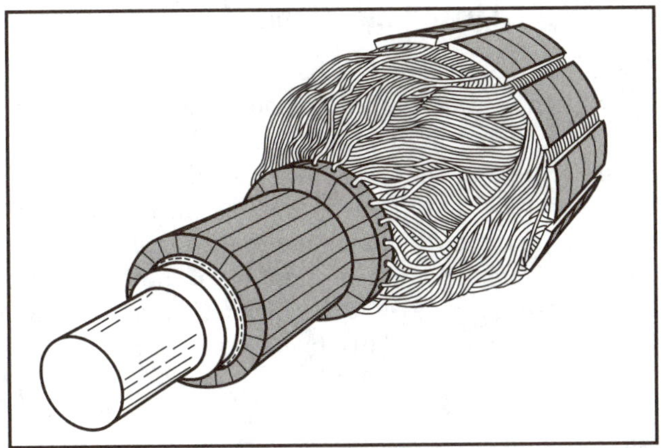

Figure 8-51. As you can see, the armature of a typical DC motor is similar to that of a DC generator.

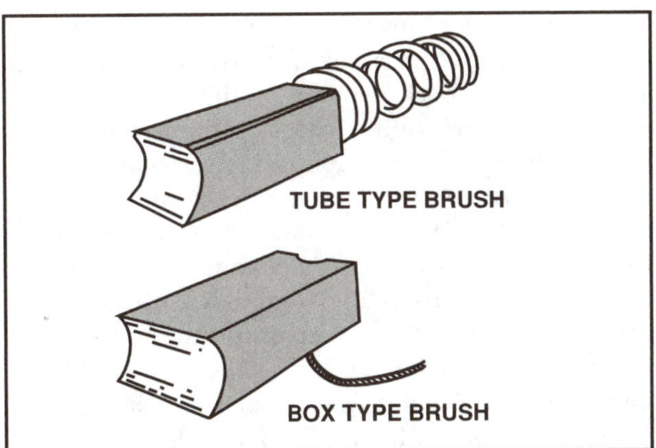

Figure 8-52. Two of the most common brushes used in DC motors are the tube type and box type.

made of insulated copper wire that is inserted into slots and protected by a fiber paper that is sometimes referred to as fish paper. The ends of the windings are physically connected to the commutator segments with wedges or steel bands. The commutator consists of several copper segments insulated from each other and the armature shaft by pieces of mica. Insulated wedge rings hold the segments in place. [Figure 8-51]

FIELD ASSEMBLY

The field assembly consists of the field frame, a set of pole pieces, and field coils. The field frame is located along the inner wall of the motor housing and contains the laminated steel pole pieces on which the field coils are wound. The field coils consist of several turns of insulated wire that fit over each pole piece. Some motors have as few as two poles, while others have as many as eight.

BRUSH ASSEMBLY

The brush assembly consists of brushes and their holders. The brushes are usually made of small blocks of graphitic carbon because of its long service life. The brush holders permit the brushes to move somewhat and utilize a spring to hold them against the commutator. [Figure 8-52]

END FRAME

The end frame is the part of the motor that the armature assembly rotates in. The armature shaft, which rides on bearings, extends through one end frame and is connected to the load. Sometimes the drive end frame is part of the unit driven by the motor.

MOTOR SPEED AND DIRECTION

Certain applications call for motors whose speed or direction are changeable. For example, a landing gear motor must be able to both retract and extend the gear while a windshield wiper motor must have variable speeds to suit changing weather conditions. Certain internal or external changes need to be made in the motor design to allow these operations.

CHANGING MOTOR SPEED

A motor in which the speed is controlled is called a **variable speed motor** and is either a shunt or series motor. Motor speed is controlled by varying the current in the field windings. For example, when the amount of current flowing through the field windings is increased, the field strength increases, causing the armature windings to produce a larger counter EMF which slows the motor. Conversely, when the field current is decreased, the field strength decreases, and the motor speeds up because the counter EMF is reduced. [Figure 8-53]

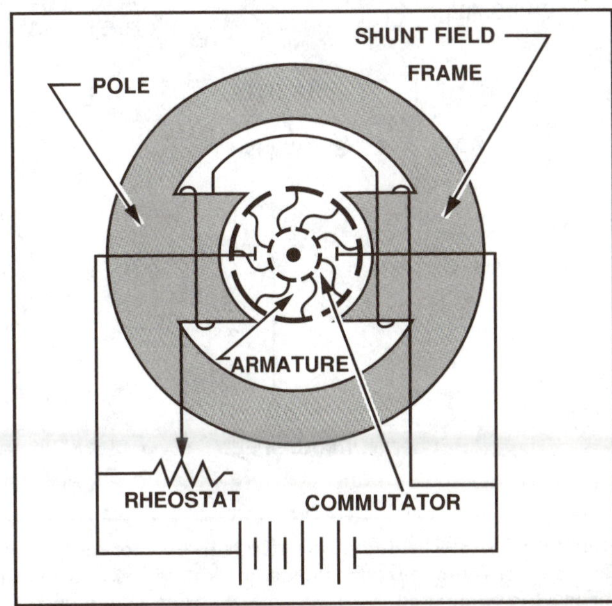

Figure 8-53. A shunt motor with variable speed control uses a rheostat to control the motor's speed.

In a shunt motor, speed is controlled by a rheostat that is connected in series with the field winding. Therefore, the speed depends on the amount of current flowing through the rheostat to the field windings. To increase motor speed, the resistance in the rheostat is increased. This decreases the field current which decreases the strength of the magnetic field and counter EMF. This momentarily increases the armature current and torque which, in turn, causes the motor to speed up until the counter EMF increases and causes the armature current to decrease to its former value. Once this occurs, the motor operates at a higher fixed speed.

To decrease motor speed, resistance in the rheostat is decreased. This action increases the current flow through the field windings and increases the field strength. The higher field strength causes a momentary increase in the counter EMF which decreases the armature current. As a result, torque decreases and the motor slows until the counter EMF decreases to its former value. Once the counter EMF and armature current are balanced, the motor operates at a lower fixed speed than before.

In a series motor, the rheostat speed control is connected in one of three ways. The rheostat is either connected in parallel or in series with the motor field, or in parallel with the motor armature. Each method of connection allows for operation in a specified speed range. [Figure 8-54]

REVERSING MOTOR DIRECTION

The direction of a DC motor's rotation is reversed by reversing the direction of current flow in either the armature or the field windings. In both cases, this reverses the magnetism of either the armature or the magnetic field the armature rotates in. If the wires connecting the motor to an external source are interchanged, the direction of rotation is not reversed since these wires reverse the magnetism of both the field and armature. This leaves the torque in the same direction.

One method for reversing the direction of rotation employs two field windings wound in opposite directions on the same pole. This type of motor is called a **split field motor**. A single-pole, double-throw switch makes it possible to direct current to either of the two windings. [Figure 8-55]

Some split field motors are built with two separate field windings wound on alternate poles. An example of this is the armature in a four-pole reversible motor. In this configuration, the armature rotates in one direction when current flows through one set of windings and in the opposite direction when current flows through the other set of windings.

Another method of reversal is called the **switch method**. This type of motor reversal employs a double-pole, double-throw switch that changes the

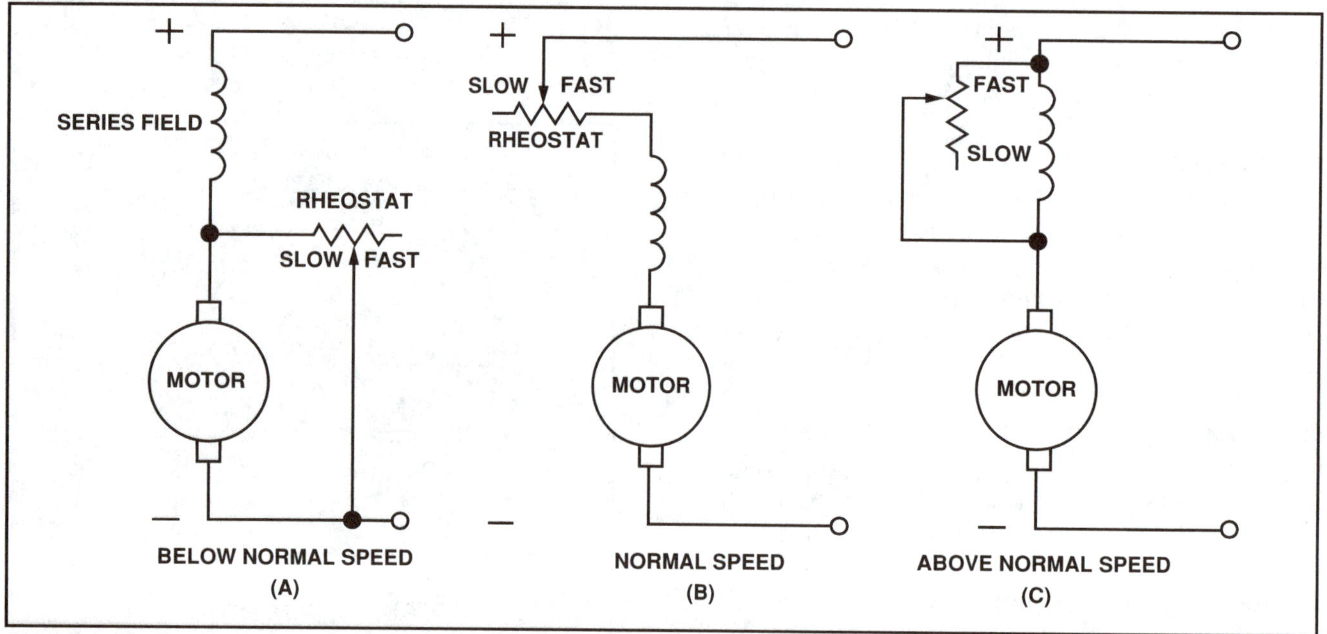

Figure 8-54. (A) — With a motor that is to be operated below normal speed, the rheostat is connected in parallel with the armature and the motor speed is increased by decreasing the current. (B) — When a motor is operated in the normal speed range, the rheostat is connected in series with the motor field. In this configuration, motor speed is increased by increasing the voltage across the motor. (C) — For above normal speed operation, the rheostat is connected in parallel with the series field. In this configuration, part of the voltage bypasses the series field causing the motor to speed up.

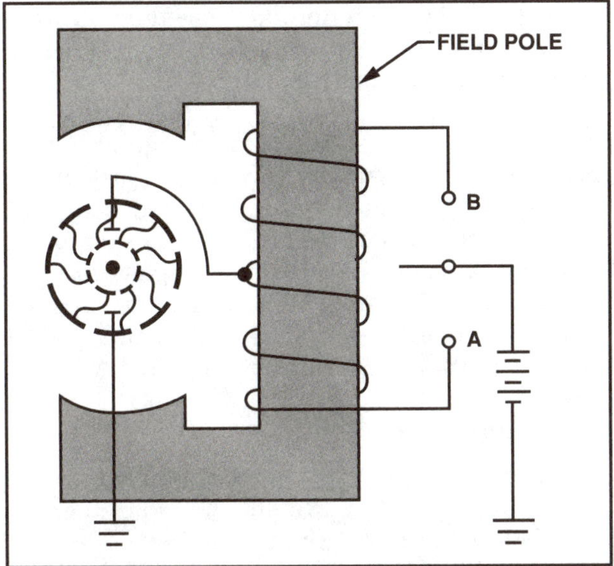

Figure 8-55. When the switch is in the lower position, current flows through the lower field winding creating a north pole at the lower field winding and at the lower pole piece. However, when the switch is placed in the up position, current flows through the upper field winding. This reverses the field magnetism and causes the armature to rotate in the opposite direction.

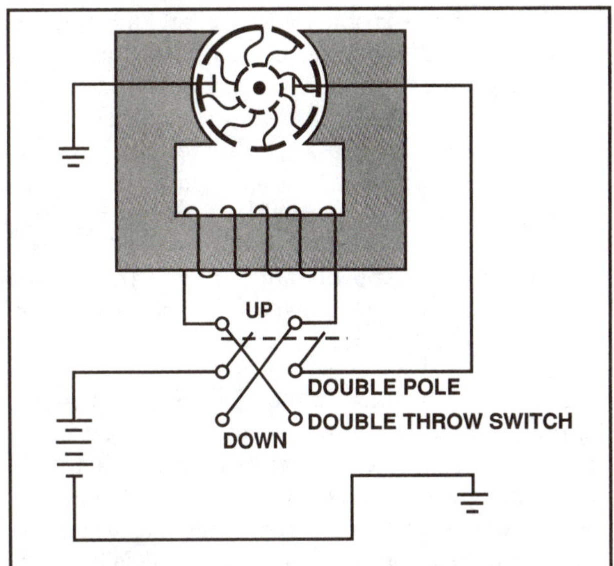

Figure 8-56. In the illustration above, a double-pole, double-throw switch is used to reverse the current through the field. When the switch is in the "up" position, current flows through the field windings. This establishes a north pole on the right side of the motor. When the switch is moved to the "down" position, polarity is reversed and the armature rotates in the opposite direction.

direction of current flow in either the armature or the field. [Figure 8-56]

TYPES OF DC MOTORS

DC motors are classified by the type of field-armature connection used and by the type of duty they are designed for. For example, there are three basic types of DC field-armature connections. They are the series, shunt, and compound.

SERIES DC MOTOR

In a series motor, the field windings consist of heavy wire with relatively few turns that are connected in series with the armature winding. This means the same amount of current flows through the field windings and the armature windings. In this configuration, an increase in current causes a corresponding increase in the magnetism of both the field and armature. [Figure 8-57]

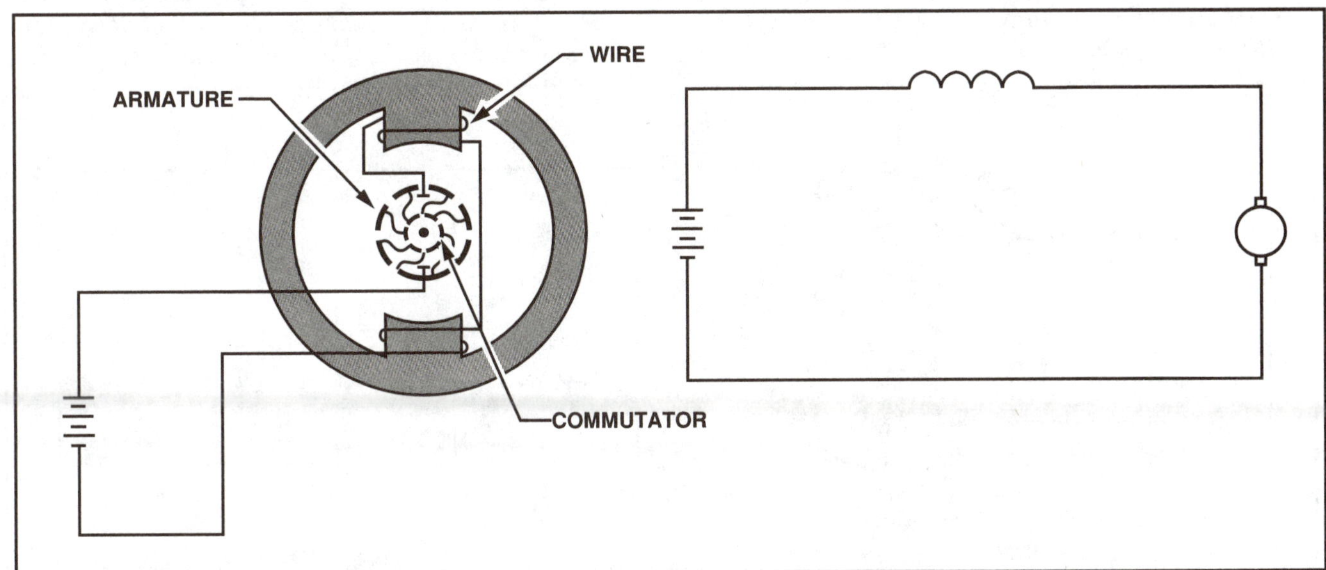

Figure 8-57. Since the field windings and armature in a series motor are connected in series, an increase of current through the field windings results in an increase of current in the armature.

The series motor is able to draw a large starting current because of the winding's low resistance. This starting current passes through both the field and armature windings and, therefore, produces a high starting torque. For this reason, series motors are often used in aircraft as starters and for raising and lowering landing gear, cowl flaps, and wing flaps. However, as the speed of a series motor increases, the counter EMF builds and opposes the applied EMF. This, in turn, reduces the current flow through the armature which reduces the current draw.

The speed of a series motor depends on the load applied. Therefore, any change in load is accompanied by a substantial change in speed. In fact, if the load is removed entirely, a series motor will operate at an excessively high speed and the armature could fly apart. In other words, a series motor needs mechanical resistance to stay within a safe operating range.

SHUNT DC MOTOR

In a shunt motor, the field winding is connected in parallel with the armature winding. To limit the amount of current that passes through the field, the resistance is high in the field winding. In addition, because the field is connected directly across the power supply, the amount of current that passes through the field is constant. In this configuration, when a shunt motor begins to rotate, most of the current flows through the armature, while relatively little current flows to the field. Because of this, shunt motors develop little torque when they are first started. [Figure 8-58]

As a shunt-wound motor picks up speed, the counter EMF in the armature increases causing a decrease in the amount of current draw in the armature. At the same time, the field current increases slightly which causes an increase in torque. Once torque and the resulting EMF balance each other, the motor will be operating at its normal, or rated, speed.

Since the amount of current flowing through the field windings remains relatively constant, the speed of a shunt motor varies little with changes in load. In fact, when no load is present, a shunt motor assumes a speed only slightly higher than the loaded speed. Because of this, a shunt motor is well suited for operations where a constant speed is desired and a high starting torque is not.

COMPOUND DC MOTOR

The compound motor is a combination of the series and shunt motors. In a compound motor there are two field windings: a shunt winding and a series winding. The shunt winding is composed of many turns of fine wire and is connected in parallel with the armature winding. On the other hand, the series winding consists of a few turns of large wire and is connected in series with the armature winding. The starting torque is higher in a compound motor than in a shunt motor and lower than in the series motor. Furthermore, variation of speed with load is less than in a series-wound motor but greater than in a shunt motor. The compound motor is used whenever the combined characteristics of the series and shunt motors are desired. [Figure 8-59]

TYPE OF DUTY

Electric motors must operate under various conditions. For example, some motors are used for intermittent operations while others operate continuously. In most cases, motors built for intermittent duty may only be operated for short periods of time before they must be allowed to cool. On the other

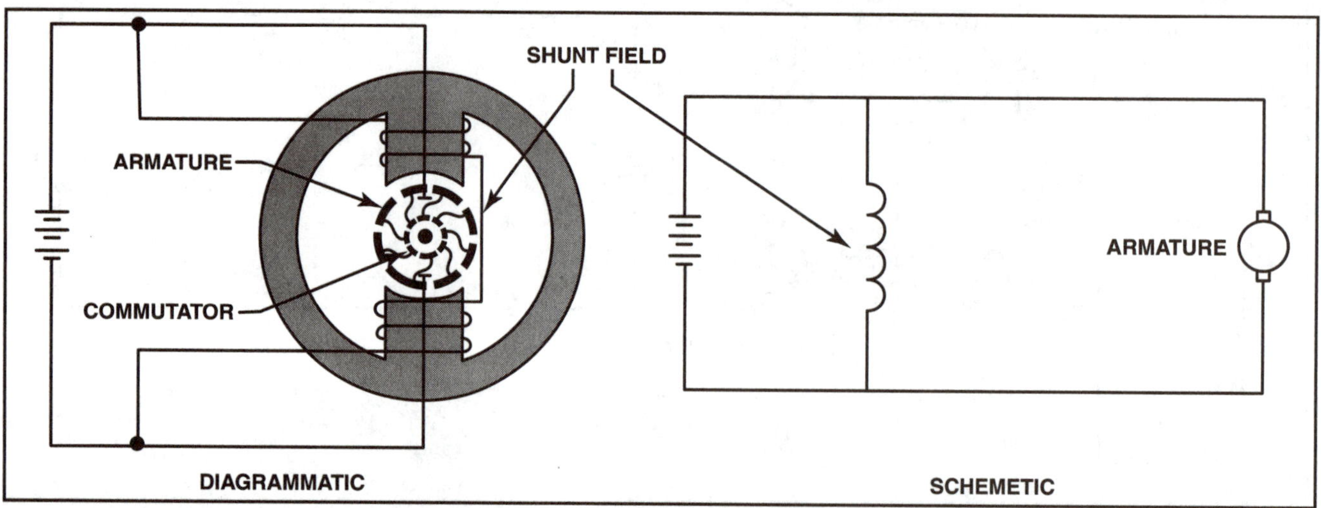

Figure 8-58. In a shunt-wound motor, the field winding is connected in parallel with the armature winding. Because of this, the amount of current that flows to the field when the motor is started is limited, and the resulting torque is low.

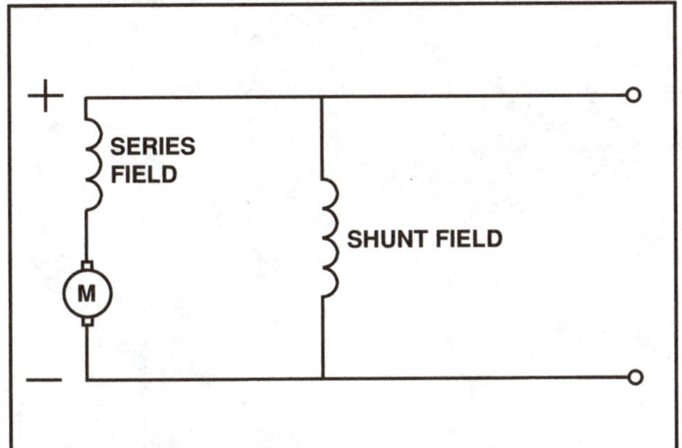

Figure 8-59. In a compound motor, one field winding is connected to the armature winding in series while the other is connected in parallel.

hand, motors built for continuous duty are operable at their rated power for long periods.

ENERGY LOSSES IN MOTORS

When electrical energy is converted to mechanical energy in a motor, some losses do occur. By the same token, losses also occur when mechanical energy is converted to electrical energy. Therefore, in order for machines to be efficient, both electrical and mechanical losses must be kept to a minimum. **Electrical losses** are classified as either copper losses or iron losses, while **mechanical losses** originate from the friction of various moving parts.

Copper losses occur when electrons are forced through the copper armature and field windings. These losses occur because some power is dissipated in the form of heat due to the inherent resistance possessed by copper windings. The amount of loss is proportional to the square of the current and is calculated with the formula:

$$\text{Copper Loss} = I^2R$$

Iron losses are divided into hysteresis and eddy current losses. **Hysteresis losses** result from the armature revolving in an alternating magnetic field and becoming magnetized in two directions. Since some residual magnetism remains in the armature after its direction is changed, some energy loss does occur. However, since the field magnets are always magnetized in one direction by DC current, they produce no hysteresis losses. **Eddy current losses** occur because the armature's iron core acts as a conductor revolving in a magnetic field. This sets up an EMF across portions of the core causing currents to flow within the core. These currents heat the core and, when excessive, can damage the windings. To keep eddy current losses to a minimum, a laminated core made of thin, insulated sheets of iron is used. The thinner the laminations, the greater the reduction in eddy current losses.

INSPECTION AND MAINTENANCE OF DC MOTORS

The inspection and maintenance of DC motors should be in accordance with the guidelines established by the manufacturer. The following is indicative of the types of maintenance checks typically called for:

1. Check the unit driven by the motor in accordance with the specific installation instructions.
2. Check all wiring, connections, terminals, fuses, and switches for general condition and security.
3. Keep motors clean and mounting bolts tight.
4. Check the brushes for condition, length, and spring tension. Procedures for replacing brushes, along with their minimum lengths, and correct spring tensions are given in the applicable manufacturer's instructions. If the spring tension is too weak, the brush could begin to bounce and arc causing commutator burning.
5. Inspect the commutator for cleanliness, pitting, scoring, roughness, corrosion, or burning. Check the mica between each of the commutator segments. If a copper segment wears down below the mica, the mica will insulate the brushes from the commutator. Clean dirty commutators with the recommended cleaning solvent and a cloth. Polish rough or corroded commutators with fine sandpaper (000 or finer) and blow out with compressed air. Never use emery paper because it contains metal particles which can cause shorts. Replace the motor if the commutator is burned, badly pitted, grooved, or worn to the extent that the mica insulation is flush with the commutator surface.
6. Inspect all exposed wiring for evidence of overheating. Replace the motor if the insulation on the leads or windings is burned, cracked, or brittle.
7. Lubricate only if called for by the manufacturer's instructions. Most motors used today do not require lubrication between overhauls.
8. Adjust and lubricate the gearbox or drive unit in accordance with the applicable manufacturer's instructions.

Troubleshoot any problems and replace the motor only when the trouble is due to a defect in the motor itself. In most cases, motor failure is caused by a defect in the external electrical circuit or by mechanical failure in the mechanism driven by the motor.

AC MOTORS

AC motors have several advantages over DC motors. For example, in many instances AC motors do not use brushes or commutators and, therefore, cannot spark like a DC motor. Furthermore, AC motors are well suited for constant-speed applications although some are manufactured with variable speed characteristics. Other advantages some AC motors have include their ability to operate on single or multiple phase lines as well as at several voltages. In addition, AC motors are generally less expensive than comparable DC motors. Because of these advantages, many aircraft are designed to use AC motors.

Because the subject of AC motors is very extensive, this text does not attempt to cover everything. However, those types of AC motors common to aircraft systems are covered in detail.

Because aircraft electrical systems typically operate at 400 hertz AC, an electric AC motor operates at about seven times the speed of a 60-hertz commercial motor with the same number of poles. In fact, a 400-hertz induction type motor typically operates at speeds ranging from 6,000 rpm to 24,000 rpm. This high rotation speed makes AC motors suitable for operating small high-speed rotors. Furthermore, through the use of reduction gears, AC motors are made to lift and move heavy loads such as wing flaps and retractable landing gear, as well as produce enough torque to start an engine.

TYPES OF AC MOTORS

There are three basic types of AC motors. They are the universal motor, the induction motor, and the synchronous motor. Each type represents a variation on basic motor operating principles.

UNIVERSAL MOTORS

Fractional horsepower AC series motors are called universal motors. A unique characteristic of universal motors is that they can operate on either alternating or direct current. In fact, universal motors resemble DC motors in that they have brushes and a commutator. Universal motors are used extensively to operate fans and portable tools like drills, grinders, and saws. [Figure 8-60]

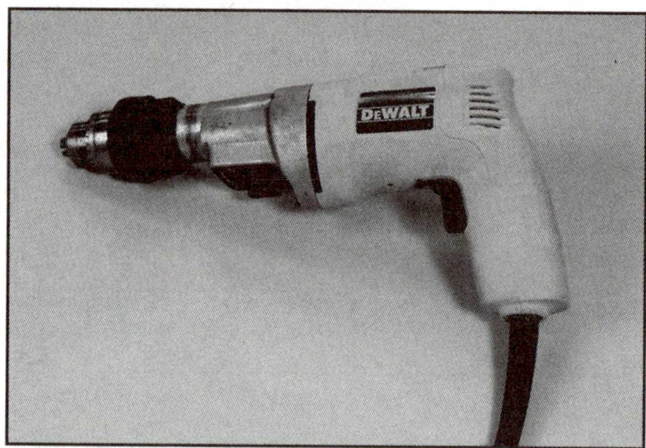

Figure 8-60. An electric drill uses a universal motor which is similar in construction to a series-wound DC motor.

INDUCTION MOTORS

The most popular type of AC motor is the induction motor. In an induction motor there is no need for an electrical connection between the motor housing and the rotating elements. Therefore, there are no brushes, commutators, or slip rings to contend with. Induction motors operate at a fixed rpm that is determined by their design and the frequency of AC applied. In addition, an induction motor can be operated on either single-phase or three-phase alternating current.

A single-phase induction motor is used to operate devices like surface locks, intercooler shutters, oil shutoff valves, and places where the power requirements are low. Single-phase induction motors require some form of starting circuit that automatically disconnects after the motor is running. Single-phase induction motors operate well in either rotational direction, with the direction determined by the starting circuit.

Unlike single-phase induction motors, three-phase induction motors are self-starting and are commonly used when high power is needed. Common applications for three-phase induction motors include engine starting, operating flaps and landing gear, and powering hydraulic pumps.

Construction

The two primary parts of an induction motor are the stator and the rotor. The stator is unique in the fact that instead of having field poles that extend outward, windings are placed in slots around the stator's periphery. These windings comprise a series of electromagnets that produce a magnetic field.

The rotor of an induction motor consists of an iron core made of thin circular laminations of soft steel that are keyed in to a shaft. Longitudinal slots are cut into the rotor's circumference and heavy copper or aluminum bars are embedded in them. These bars are welded to a heavy ring of high conductivity on either end. [Figure 8-61]

When AC is applied to the stator, the strength and polarity of the electromagnets changes with the excitation current. Furthermore, to give the effect of a rotating magnetic field, each group of poles is attached to a separate phase of voltage.

When the rotor of an induction motor is subjected to the revolving magnetic field produced by the stator windings, a voltage is induced in the longitudinal bars. This induced voltage causes current to flow through the bars and produce its own magnetic field which combines with the stator's revolving field. As a result, the rotor revolves at nearly a synchronous speed with the stator field. The only difference in the rotational speed between the stator field and the rotor is that necessary to induce the proper current into the rotor to overcome mechanical and electrical losses.

If a rotor were to turn at the same speed as the rotating field, a resonance would set up. When this happens, the rotor conductors are not cut by any magnetic lines of flux and no EMF is induced into them. Thus, no current flows in the rotor, resulting in no torque and little rotor rotation. For this reason, there must always be a difference in speed between the rotor and the stator's rotating field.

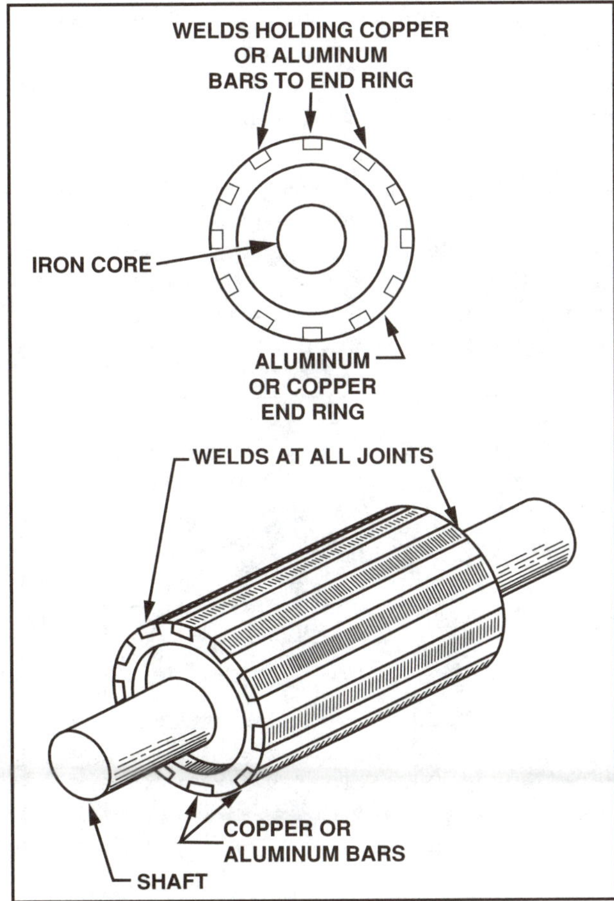

Figure 8-61. The complete rotor in an induction motor is sometimes called a squirrel cage and, therefore, motors containing this type of rotor are often called squirrel cage induction motors.

The difference in rotational speed is called **motor slip** and is expressed as a percentage of the synchronous speed. For example, if the rotor turns at 1,750 rpm and the synchronous speed is 1,800 rpm, the difference in speed is 50 rpm. The slip is therefore equal to 50/1,800 or 2.78 percent.

Single-Phase Induction Motor

A single-phase motor differs from a multi-phase motor in that the single-phase motor has only one stator winding. In this configuration, the stator winding generates a field that pulsates. This generates an expanding and collapsing stator field that induces currents into the rotor. These currents generate a rotor field opposite in polarity to that of the stator. The opposition of the field exerts a turning force on the upper and lower parts of the rotor which try to turn it 180 degrees from its position. Since these forces are exerted in the center of the rotor, the turning force is equal in each direction. As a result, the rotor will not begin turning from a standing stop. However, if the rotor starts turning, it continues to rotate. Furthermore, since the turning force is aided by the rotor momentum, there is no opposing force.

Shaded-Pole Induction Motor

The first effort in the development of a self-starting, single-phase motor was the shaded-pole induction motor. Like the generator, the shaded-pole motor has field poles that extend outward from the motor housing. In addition, a portion of each pole is encircled with a heavy copper ring. [Figure 8-62]

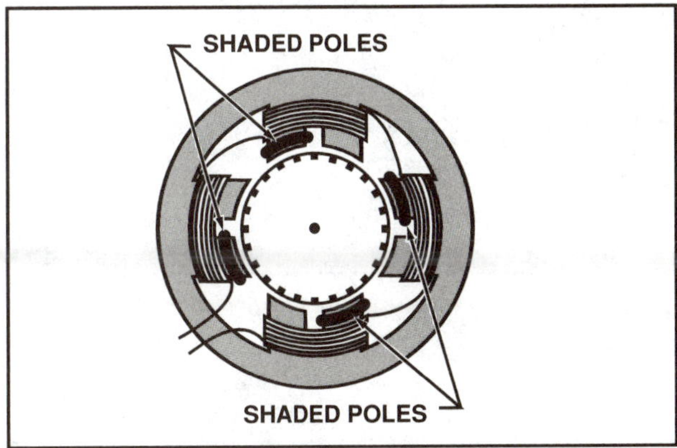

Figure 8-62. In a shaded-pole induction motor, a portion of each salient pole is encircled by a copper ring.

The presence of the copper ring causes the magnetic field through the ringed portion of the pole face to lag appreciably behind that of the other half of the pole. This results in a slight component of rotation in the field that is strong enough to cause rotation. Although the torque created by this field is small, it is enough to accelerate the rotor to its rated speed. [Figure 8-63]

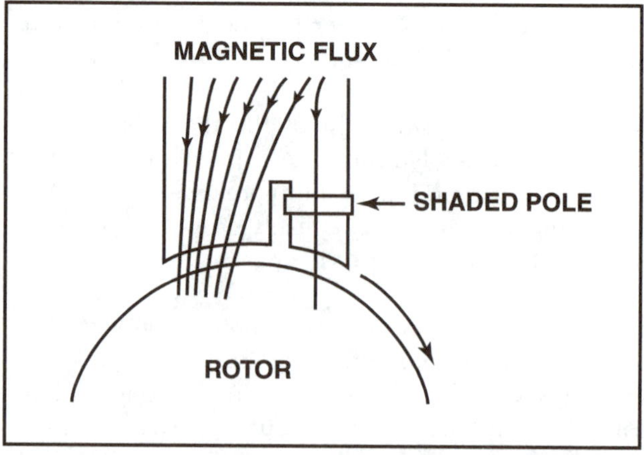

Figure 8-63. The portion of magnetic flux lines that pass through the shaded pole lag behind the opposite pole, thereby creating a slight component of rotation.

Split-Phase Motor

There are various types of self-starting motors, one type is known as split-phase motor. Split-phase motors have a winding that is dedicated to starting the rotor. This "start" winding is displaced 90 degrees from the main, or run, winding and has a fairly high resistance that causes the current to be out of phase with the current in the run winding. The out of phase condition produces a rotating field that makes the rotor revolve. Once the rotor attains approximately 25 percent of its rated speed, a centrifugal switch disconnects the start winding automatically.

Capacitor-Start Motor

With the development of high-capacity electrolytic capacitors, a variation of the split-phase motor was made. Motors that use high-capacity electrolytic capacitors are known as capacitor-start motors. Nearly all fractional horsepower motors in use today on refrigerators, oil burners, and other similar appliances are of this type.

In a capacitor-start motor, the start and run windings are the same size and have identical resistance values. The phase shift between the two windings is obtained by using capacitors connected in series with the start winding. [Figure 8-64]

Capacitor-start motors have a starting torque comparable to their rated speed torque and are used in applications where the initial load is heavy. Again, a centrifugal switch is required for disconnecting the start winding when the rotor speed is approximately 25 percent of the rated speed.

Although some single-phase induction motors are rated as high as 2 horsepower, most produce 1 horsepower or less. A voltage rating of 115 volts for the smaller sized motors and 110 to 220 volts for one-fourth horsepower and up is normally sufficient. Poly-phase motors are used for higher power

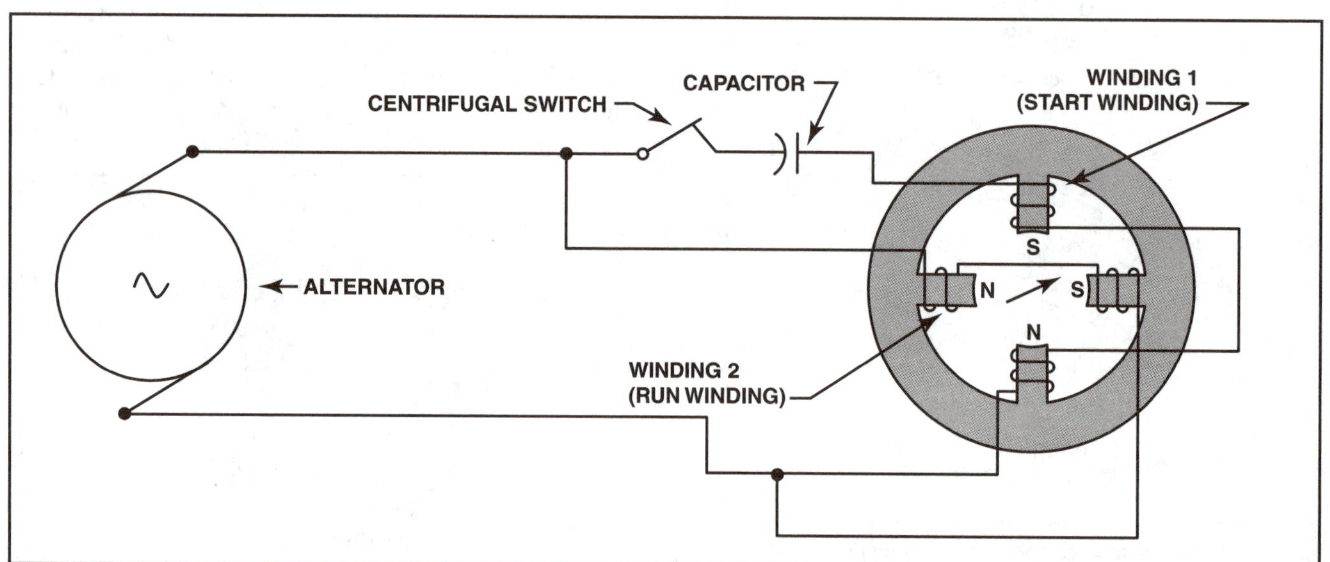

Figure 8-64. A single-phase motor with capacitor start windings has a capacitor connected in series with an alternator and the start winding.

ratings since they have much better starting torque characteristics.

Direction of Rotation

The direction of rotation for a three-phase induction motor is changed by reversing two of the motor leads. The same effect is obtained in a two-phase motor by reversing the connections on one phase. In a single-phase motor, reversing the connections to the start winding reverses the direction of rotation. Most single-phase motors designed for general application are built so you can readily reverse the connections to the start winding. On the other hand, a shaded-pole motor cannot be reversed because its rotational direction is determined by the physical location of the copper shaded ring.

After starting, if one phase of a three-phase motor is rendered useless, the motor will continue to run. However, it delivers only one-third of its rated power. On the other hand, a two-phase motor that loses one phase delivers only one-half its rated power. One thing to keep in mind is that neither motor will start if a wire connection to a phase is broken.

SYNCHRONOUS MOTORS

Like the induction motor, a synchronous motor uses a rotating magnetic field. However, the torque developed by a synchronous motor does not depend on the induction of currents in the rotor. Instead, the principle of operation of the synchronous motor begins with a multi-phase source of AC applied to a series of stator windings. When this is done, a rotating magnetic field is produced. At the same time, DC current is applied to the rotor winding producing a second magnetic field. A synchronous motor is designed so that the rotor is pulled by the stator's rotating magnetic field. The rotor turns at approximately the same speed as the stator's magnetic field. In other words, they are synchronized.

To understand the operation of a synchronous motor, use the following example. Assume that poles A and B in figure 8-65 are physically rotated clockwise in order to produce a rotating magnetic field. These poles induce the opposite polarity in the soft-iron rotor between them thereby creating an attraction between the rotating poles and the rotor. This attraction allows the rotating poles to drag the rotor at the same speed. [Figure 8-65]

When a load is applied to the rotor shaft, its axis momentarily falls behind that of the rotating field.

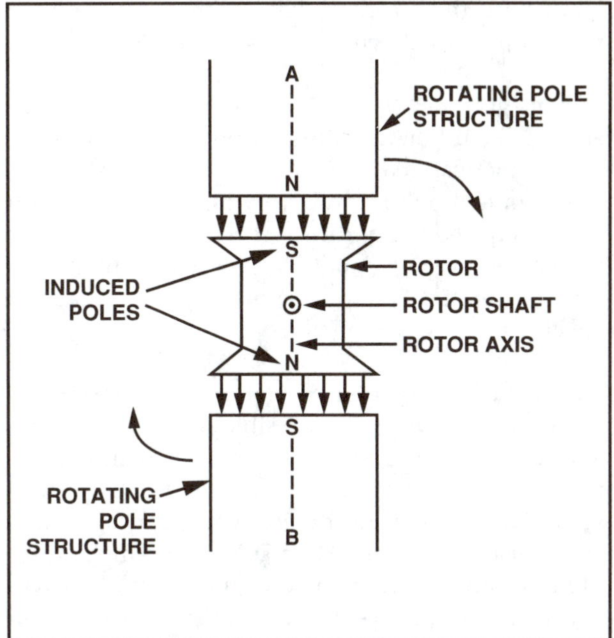

Figure 8-65. In a synchronous motor, a rotating magnet induces opposite magnetic fields in a soft iron rotor. The rotor then turns at the same speed as the magnet.

However, the rotor catches up and again rotates with the field at the same speed, as long as the load remains constant. If the load is too large, the rotor pulls out of sync with the rotating poles and is unable to rotate at the same speed. In this situation the motor is said to be overloaded.

The idea of using a mechanical means to rotate the poles is impractical because another motor would be required to do this. Therefore, a rotating magnetic field is produced electrically by using phased AC voltages. In this respect, a synchronous motor is similar to the induction motor.

The synchronous motor consists of a stator field winding that produces a rotating magnetic field. The rotor is either a permanent magnet or an electromagnet. If permanent magnets are used, the rotor's magnetism is stored within the magnet. On the other hand, if electromagnets are used, the magnets receive power from a DC power source through slip rings.

Since a synchronous motor has little starting torque, it requires assistance to bring it up to synchronous speed. The most common method of doing this is to start the motor with no load, allow it to reach full speed, and then energize the magnetic field. The magnetic field of the rotor then locks with the magnetic field of the stator and the motor operates at synchronous speed. [Figure 8-66]

The magnitude of the induced rotor poles is so small that sufficient torque cannot be developed for most practical loads. To avoid the limitation on motor operation, a winding is placed on the rotor and energized with direct current. To adjust the motor for varying loads, a rheostat is placed in series with the DC source to provide a means of varying the pole's strength.

A synchronous motor is not self-starting. Since rotors are heavy, it is impossible to bring a stationary rotor into magnetic lock with a rotating magnetic field. As a result, all synchronous motors have some kind of starting device. One type of simple starter used is another AC or DC motor which brings the rotor up to approximately 90 percent of its synchronous speed. The starting motor is then disconnected and the rotor locks in with the rotating field. Another method utilizes a second squirrel-cage type winding on the rotor. This induction winding brings the rotor almost to synchronous speed before the direct current is disconnected from the rotor windings and the rotor is pulled into sync with the field.

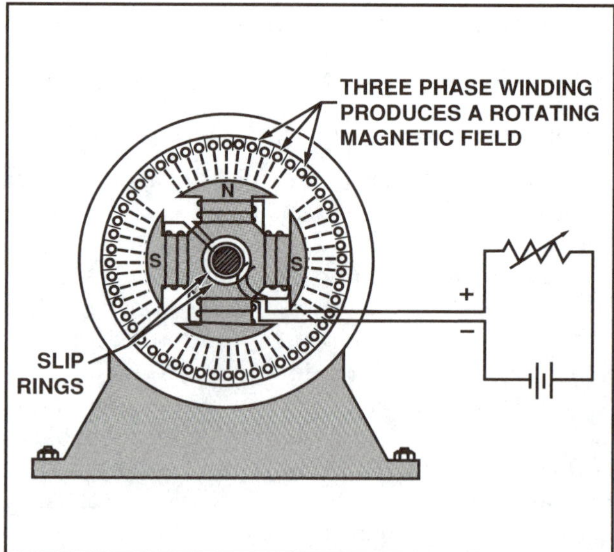

Figure 8-66. The weak field induced in the rotor poles limits the poles ability to produce torque. This problem is overcome by applying DC current through a rheostat to vary the pole's field strength.

RECIPROCATING ENGINE STARTING SYSTEMS

During the early days of aviation, aircraft engines were started by a procedure known as "hand propping." In other words, the propeller was pulled through the compression strokes by hand with the ignition on until the engine started. Although hand propping is still used today on some aircraft, it does have some definite drawbacks. For example, in cold weather, thick oil can make hand propping extremely difficult. In addition, as engines got larger, hand propping became more difficult and much more dangerous. Therefore, several methods were devised to replace hand propping with safer, more reliable starting procedures.

INERTIA STARTER

The inertia starter was one of the first types of mechanical engine starting devices used in aviation. With this type of starter, a hand crank is used to spin up a flywheel through a step-up gear drive assembly. Once the flywheel is spinning at a high speed, the hand crank is removed and the starter engage handle is pulled to extend a ratchet-type jaw that meshes with a mating ratchet on the crankshaft. The kinetic energy in the mass of the spinning flywheel is then converted to mechanical energy to drive the engine crankshaft. A torque-overload clutch located between the flywheel and ratchet jaws prevents damage to the engine or starter when the starter is first engaged.

As an improvement to the inertia starter, an electric motor was mounted on the starter and used to spin the flywheel for easier engine starts. However, the hand cranking feature was left intact to address the possible problem of insufficient battery power to drive the motor. The combination electric inertia starter with a manual backup was the standard for large engines through World War II.

DIRECT-CRANKING STARTERS

Today, the most widely used starting system on all types of reciprocating engines is the direct-cranking starter. A direct-cranking starter differs from the inertia starter in that it provides instant and continual cranking when energized. This eliminates the need to store preliminary energy in a flywheel.

Series-wound DC motors are the most common direct-cranking starter motors because they are capable of producing a high starting torque. Starter motor characteristics provide a relatively constant voltage throughout a starting cycle while drawing a very high current at the start of motor rotation. The high current draw provides the starting torque needed to crank an engine. However, as engine and starter speed increase, counter electromotive forces build and limit the amount of current the starter can draw. Typically, starter circuits do not contain fuses or circuit breakers. The reason for this is that initial starter motor current would create the nuisance of a tripped circuit breaker or blown fuse each time the engine is started.

SMALL ENGINE STARTERS

Some small horizontally opposed engines use a direct-cranking starter that utilizes a small series-wound electric motor with a small gear. The small gear meshes with a large gear that is part of an over-running clutch that drives a pinion, or drive gear. This type of starter is typically engaged by either a hand-pulled cable or a solenoid that engages a shift lever. [Figure 8-67]

Typically, the shift lever is attached by a cable or rod to a tee-handle or electrical switch that activates a solenoid. When the tee-handle is pulled or the switch is closed, the shift lever compresses the meshing spring and forces the pinion gear outward to mesh with the starter gear inside the engine accessory case. When the pinion and the starter gear are fully meshed, further movement of the shift lever closes the starter motor switch, and the starter cranks the engine. When the engine starts, the over-

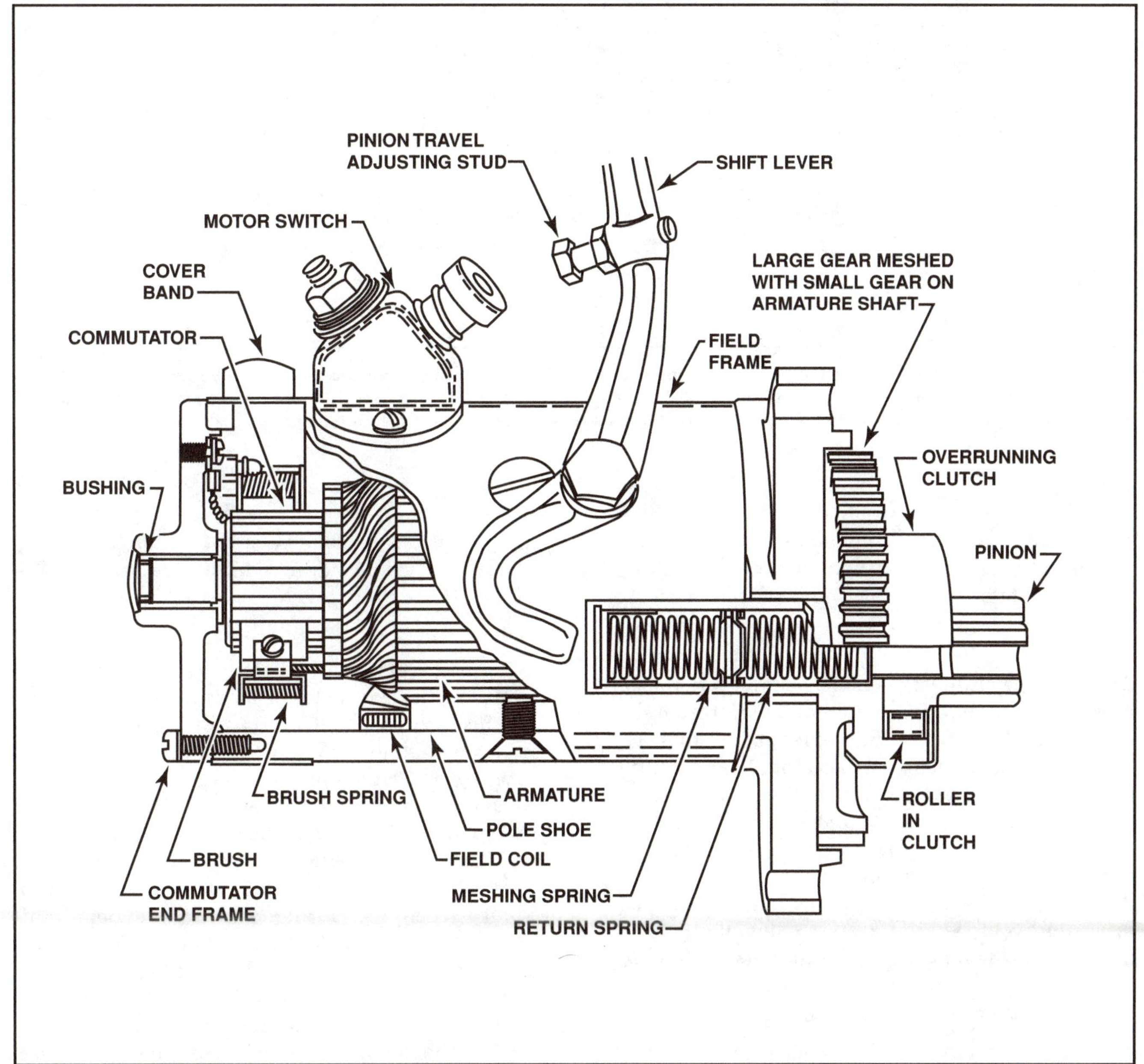

Figure 8-67. Some small horizontally opposed aircraft engines use a direct-cranking starter that utilizes a small DC motor to drive an over-running clutch. The over-running clutch drives a pinion, or drive gear that turns the engine.

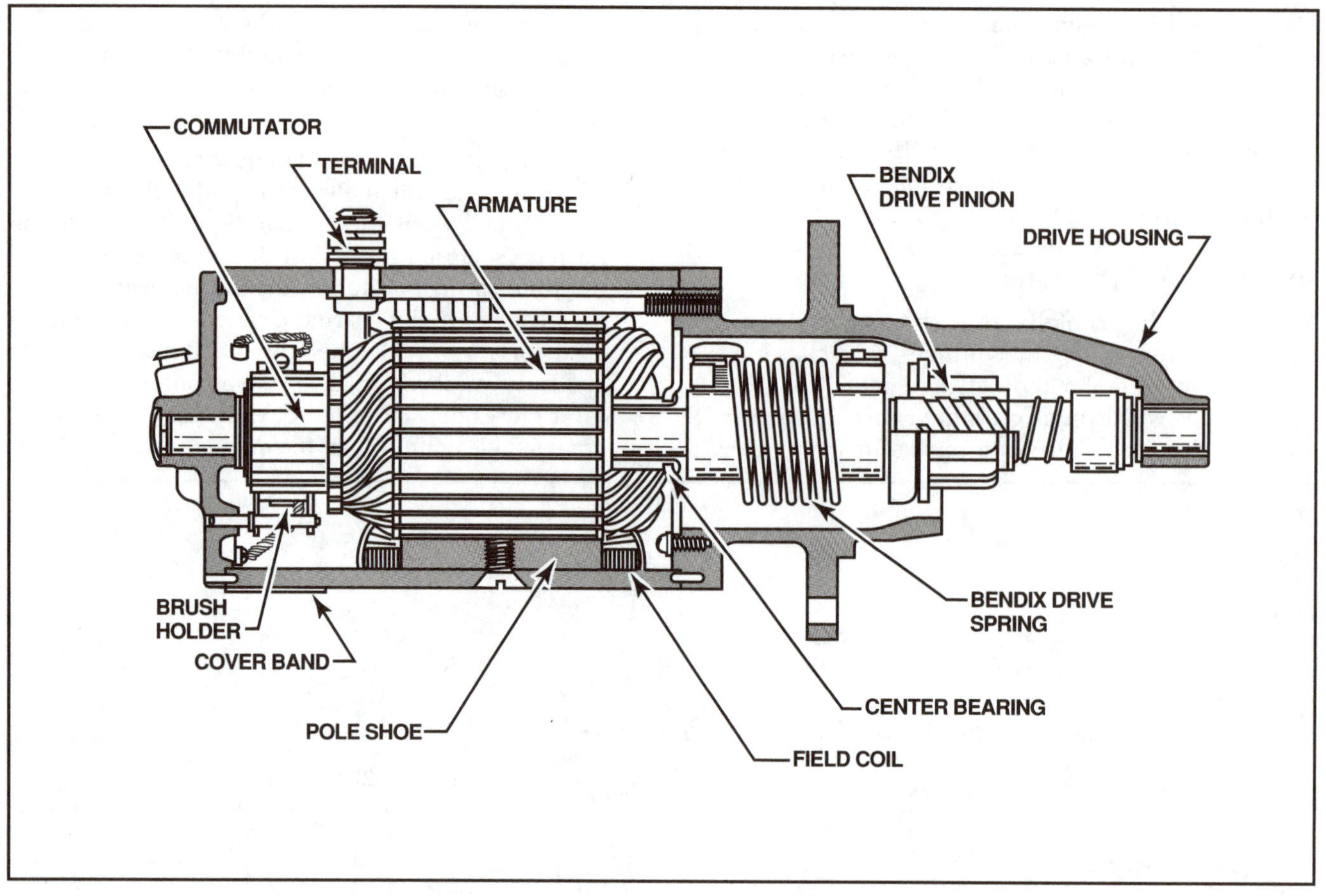

Figure 8-68. A direct-cranking starter similar to the type widely used in automotive applications utilizes a Bendix drive to turn the flywheel on an engine. Once the engine starts, the inertia created by the spinning flywheel spins the Bendix pinion gear backward until it disengages from the flywheel. This type of starter is used with many Avco-Lycoming engines.

running clutch allows the pinion to spin freely with the engine until the tee-handle or starter switch is released and the return spring pulls the pinion away from the starter gear.

Another type of direct-cranking electric starter also uses a series-wound DC motor but the over-running clutch is replaced by a Bendix drive similar to what is found on automobile engines. The **Bendix drive**, developed by the Bendix Corporation, consists of a drive spring, drive pinion, and drive shaft with helical splines. When the starter switch is closed, the starter motor spins the pinion through the Bendix drive spring. The drive pinion fits loosely over the drive shaft and, as the armature spins, the pinion moves forward on the helical splines. As the pinion moves forward, it engages the teeth on the engine's flywheel and the engine turns.

When the engine starts, the spinning flywheel gear begins to spin the Bendix drive pinion faster than the starter motor. This forces the pinion back along the helical splines until it disengages from the flywheel. [Figure 8-68]

Some new generation Teledyne-Continental aircraft engines use a starter mounted on the side of the accessory case. This type of starter utilizes a series-wound electric motor that drives the starter worm gear. The worm gear is permanently meshed with a worm wheel in the engine's accessory case. A clutch spring is attached to the worm wheel and, as the worm wheel turns, the spring tightens around a knurled drum on the engine's starter shaft. When the spring gets tight enough, the starter shaft begins to rotate at approximately the same speed as the worm wheel and starter motor. Attached to the starter shaft is a starter shaft gear that is permanently meshed with the crankshaft gear in the engine accessory case. Therefore, once the starter shaft is spun by the starter motor, the starter shaft gear turns the crankshaft. Upon

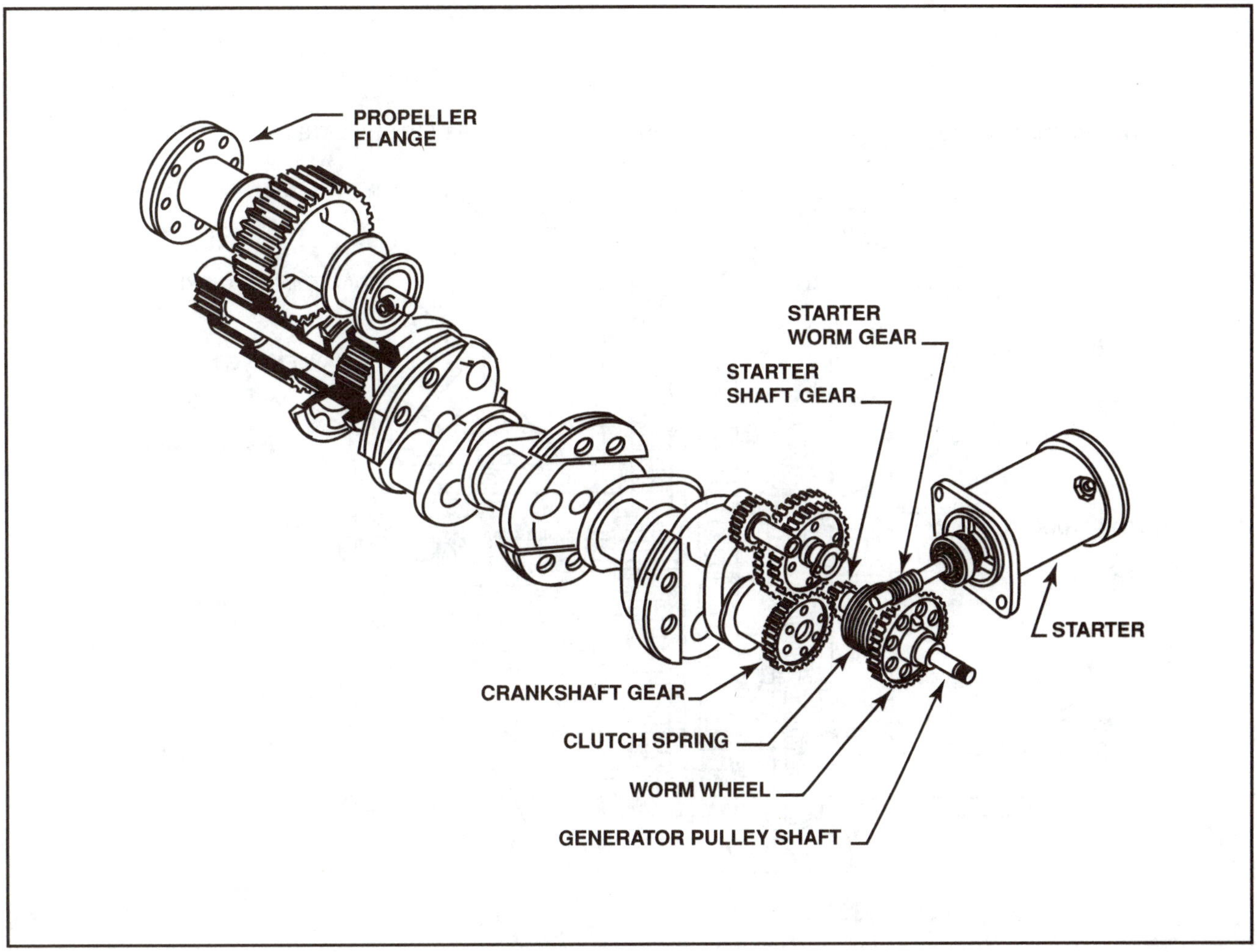

Figure 8-69. Commonly used on Teledyne-Continental aircraft engines, a side mounted starter equipped with a worm-gear drive assembly engages a worm wheel and spring clutch assembly to turn the engine over for starting.

Figure 8-70. High horsepower engines typically utilize a starter unit that contains a starter motor reduction gear assembly, and an engaging and disengaging mechanism.

engine start, the crankshaft will spin faster than the starter gear shaft causing the clutch spring to release the knurled drum on the starter shaft. This allows the engine to accelerate to idle speed without causing damage to the starter or the worm wheel mechanism before the starter is disengaged. The generator drive pulley is mounted on the end of the starter gear shaft and, with the clutch spring disengaged, serves as the generator drive shaft. [Figure 8-69]

LARGE ENGINE STARTERS

Because of the increased force required to turn over a high horsepower engine, a typical direct-cranking electric starter for large, reciprocating engines must employ some sort of reduction gear assembly. The reduction gear assembly, along with the motor assembly and an automatic engaging and disengaging mechanism, are contained in a single starter unit. [Figure 8-70]

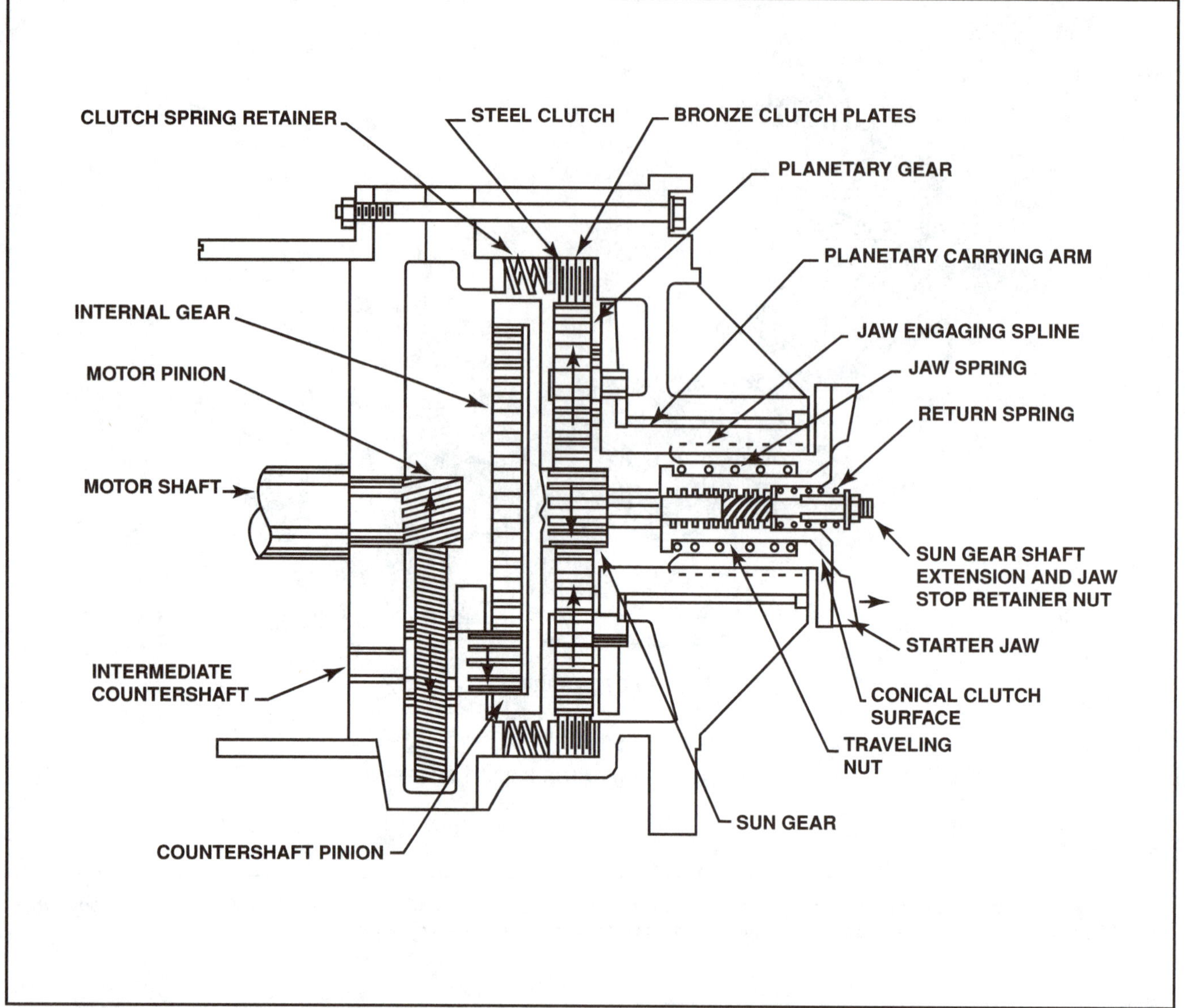

Figure 8-71. The reduction gear train on a starting motor used on a large reciprocating engine converts the motor's high speed low torque to the low speed high torque needed to crank an engine. To do this, the motor's pinion gear drives an intermediate countershaft assembly that, in turn, rotates the sun gear of a planetary reduction gear assembly. As the sun gear rotates, the planetary gears rotate around the sun gear and cause the starter jaw to engage the engine.

The motor section consists of all the components found in a typical motor as well as a motor pinion assembly. The starter motor used is typically a non-reversible series interpole motor whose speed varies directly with the applied voltage and inversely with the load.

The starter reduction gear assembly consists of a housing with an integral mounting flange, an integral gear assembly, a planetary gear reduction, a torque-limiting clutch, and a jaw and cone assembly. In this type of assembly, starter motor torque is transmitted to the starter jaw through an internal gear assembly and reduction gear assembly. [Figure 8-71]

TURBINE ENGINE STARTING SYSTEMS

Gas turbine engines are generally started by a starter that connects to the main gearbox. In this configuration, the starter rotates the compressor through the gearbox. On engines that utilize a dual axial compressor, the starter rotates the high speed compressor and N_1 turbine system only. Likewise, on turboprop and turboshaft engines utilizing a free-turbine, only the compressor and its associated turbine assembly is rotated by the starter.

Compressor rotation by a starter provides the engine with sufficient air for combustion and also aids the engine in self-accelerating to idle speed once combustion occurs. Neither the starter nor the turbine wheel have sufficient power on their own to bring an engine from rest to idle rpm. However, when used in combination, the process takes place smoothly in approximately 30 seconds on a typical engine.

Many starting systems have a speed sensor device which automatically disengages the starter after self-accelerating speed is reached. At this point, turbine power is sufficient to accelerate the engine to idle rpm. If an engine is not assisted to the correct speed, a hung start may occur. A hung start occurs whenever an engine lights up but does not accelerate to idle rpm. If a hung start occurs, the engine must be shut down and the cause for insufficient starting speed corrected before another attempt is made. Any attempt to accelerate an engine that is hung can often lead to a hot start, because the engine is operating with insufficient airflow to combust more fuel.

Starting systems for turboprop and turboshaft engines are designed according to whether the engine is a fixed shaft or free-turbine design. For example, with a fixed shaft turbiprop engine, the starter must rotate the engine and propeller. Therefore, starters used on fixed shaft turboprops engines typically develop more torque. In addition, to help reduce drag, fixed shaft turboprop engines are started with the propeller in low pitch allowing more speed and airflow. Free-turbine engines, on the other hand, present very little drag on turbine acceleration because only the gas generator portion of the engine is being turned by the starter. This factor allows the use of less powerfull, lighter weight starters. In addition, since since the propeller is not turned by the starter, the engne can be started with thepropeller blades in any position.

ELECTRIC STARTERS

Like reciprocating engines, several gas turbine engines utilize an electric starting motor. The two most common types of electric starter motors include the starter-generator and direct-cranking starter.

Figure 8-72. Units such as this starter-generator are frequently used on light gas turbine engines. To save weight and reduce complexity, a starter-generator turns the engine during the starting process and then becomes a generator to supply electrical power once the engine is running.

STARTER-GENERATORS

Starter-generators provide an efficient means of accomplishing both starting and power generation functions. In addition, since a starter-generator performs the functions of both a starter and generator, it provides an inherent weight-savings. Because of the efficiency and weight-saving features, starter-generators are widely utilized on both turboprop and corporate jet aircraft. [Figure 8-72]

There are several different types of starter-generators in use today. Most contain two field coils and a common armature winding. One field coil is connected in series with the armature and has a low resistance, while the second shut winding has a comparatively high resistance. When used as a starter, current flows through both the series field winding and the armature to produce the torque needed to rotate the engine. However, in the generator mode, the shut field receives current while the series field receives no current.

To properly control a starter-generator during the start sequence, there are several components that must be used in a starter-generator circuit. For example, in addition to needing a battery and/or master switch, many starter-generator circuits use an under-

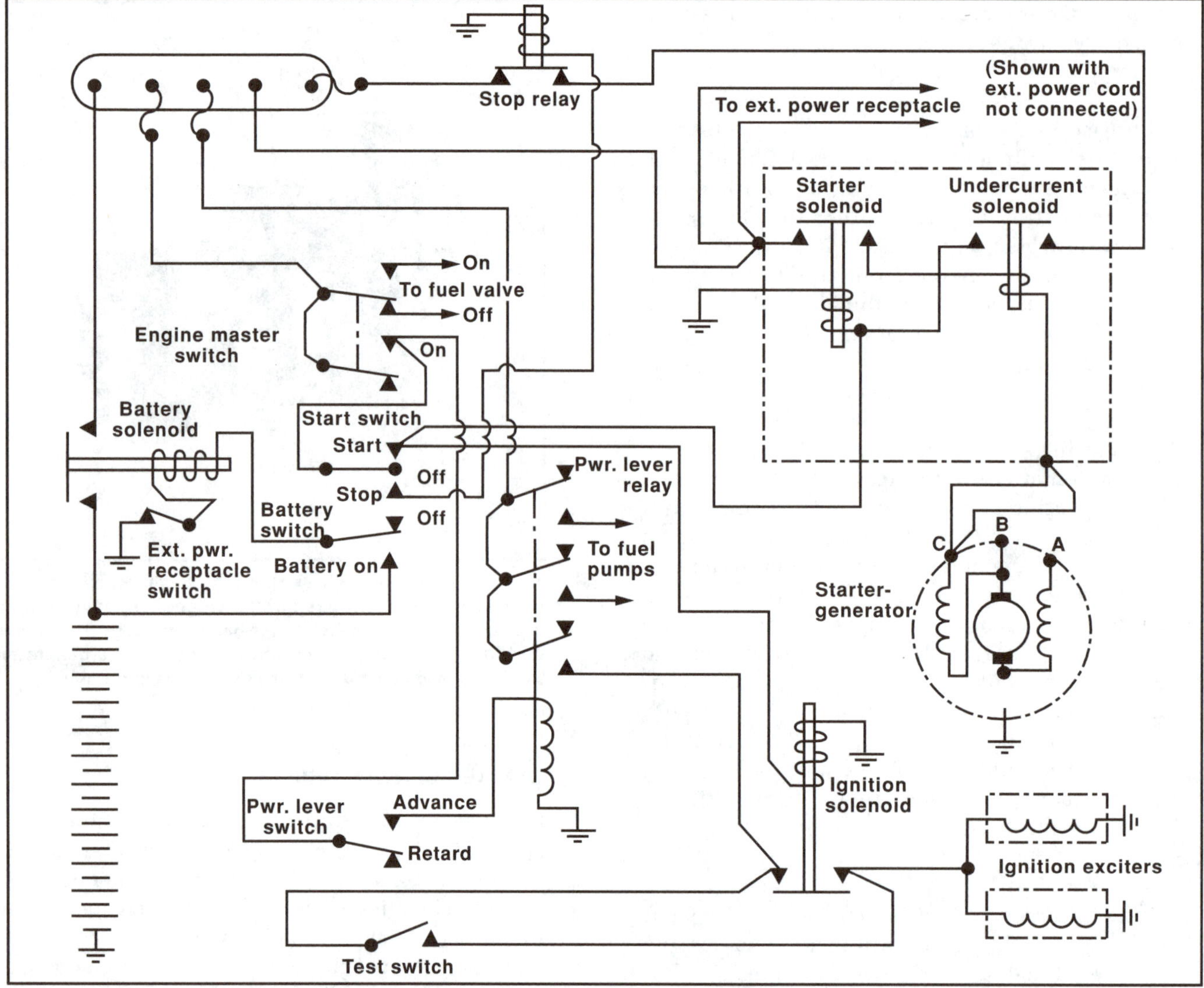

Figure 8-73. A typical aircraft turbine engine starter-generator circuit contains several switches, relays, and solenoids. This circuit can be used to track the sequence of the engine start, fuel flow, ignition, and electrical power generation events.

current controller, a start switch, some sort of power lever relay, and an ignition solenoid. [Figure 8-73]

The purpose of an undercurrent controller is to ensure positive action of the starter and to keep it operating until the engine is rotating fast enough to sustain combustion. A typical undercurrent controller contains two solenoids; a starter solenoid and an undercurrent solenoid. The starter solenoid controls the input to the starter, while the undercurrent solenoid controls the starter solenoid.

To start an engine equipped with an undercurrent solenoid, you must first close the battery and engine master switches. This completes the circuit from the aircraft's bus to the start switch, fuel valves, and power lever relay. Energizing the power lever relay starts the fuel pumps which provides the necessary fuel pressure for starting the engine.

As the start switch is turned on, two solenoids close, the starter solenoid and the ignition solenoid. The starter solenoid closes the circuit from the power source to the starter motor while the ignition solenoid closes the circuit to the ignition units. As soon as current begins flowing to the motor through the starter solenoid, the undercurrent solenoid closes. Once closed, the undercurrent relay completes a circuit from the bus to the starter solenoid coil and ignition solenoid coil, allowing the start switch to be returned to its neutral position while the start sequence continues.

As the motor builds up speed, the current draw of the motor begins to decrease. Once the current draw falls below approximately 200 amps, the undercurrent solenoid opens. This action breaks the circuit from the bus to the coil of the starter and ignition solenoid. This, in turn, stops current flow to the starter motor and ignition exciters.

Once the start sequence is complete, the engine should be operating efficiently and ignition should be self-sustaining. If, however, the engine hangs, or fails to reach sufficient speed to halt the starter operation, the start switch should be moved to the stop position to break the circuit from the positive bus to the main contacts of the undercurrent relay.

If there is not enough battery power to accelerate the engine to starting speed, most starter-generator circuits allow the use of an external power source. However, when external power is used, there must be a switch in the circuit that prevents the battery from being connected to the bus.

As an added feature in most starter-generator circuits, a means of testing the ignition exciters is typically provided. In the example used earlier, the ignition exciters are tested by means of a test switch that bypasses the ignition solenoid. To get current to the test switch, the battery switch and engine master switch must be turned on, while the power lever(s) must be advanced to close the power lever switch and relay.

STARTER-GENERATOR TROUBLESHOOTING

The need for troubleshooting is dictated by unsatisfactory starter-generator performance. Efficient troubleshooting is based on a systematic analysis of what is happening so you will be able to determine the cause of a malfunction. There is no magic in successful troubleshooting, but rather an application of logic and a thorough knowledge of the basics of engine operation. For example, if you are faced with a problem of deteriorating starter-generator performance, the first thing you should do is get all of the facts. Take nothing for granted, and ask the pilot questions. For example, find out if the trouble comes about suddenly or was it a gradual decrease in performance? Under what conditions does this performance loss show up?

After getting all of the facts, perform a ground check to see if the problem can be duplicated. The next step is to eliminate all of the areas that are not likely to cause the trouble. To assist in the troubleshooting process, some manufacturers provide troubleshooting charts. [Figure 8-74]

PROBABLE CAUSE	ISOLATION PROCEDURE	REMEDY
Engine Does Not Rotate:		
Low supply voltage to the starter.	Check voltage of the battery or external power source.	Adjust voltage of the external power.
Power switch is defective.	Check switch for continuity.	Replace switch.
Ignition switch in throttle quadrant.	Check switch for continuity.	Replace switch.
Start-lockout relay energized.	Check position of generator switch	Place switch in "OFF" position.
Battery series solenoid is defective.	With start circuit energized, check for 48 volts DC across battery series solenoid coil.	Replace solenoid if no voltage is present.
Starter solenoid is defective.	With start circuit energized, check for 48 volts DC across starter solenoid coil.	Replace solenoid if no voltage is present.
Defective starter	With starter circuit energized, check for proper voltage at the starter.	Replace solenoid if voltage is not present.
Start lock-in solenoid defective.	With starter circuit energized, check for 28 volts DC across the solenoid coil.	Replace solenoid if voltage is not present.
Start drive shaft in component drive gearbox is sheared.	Listen for sounds of starter rotation during an attempted start. If the starter rotates but the engine does not, the drive shaft is sheared.	Replace the engine.
Engine Starts But Does Not Accelerate To Idle:		
Insufficient starter voltage.	Check starter terminal voltage.	Use larger capacity ground power unit or charge batteries.

Figure 8-74. A typical starter-generator system troubleshooting guide facilitates the process of correcting starter-generator system faults.

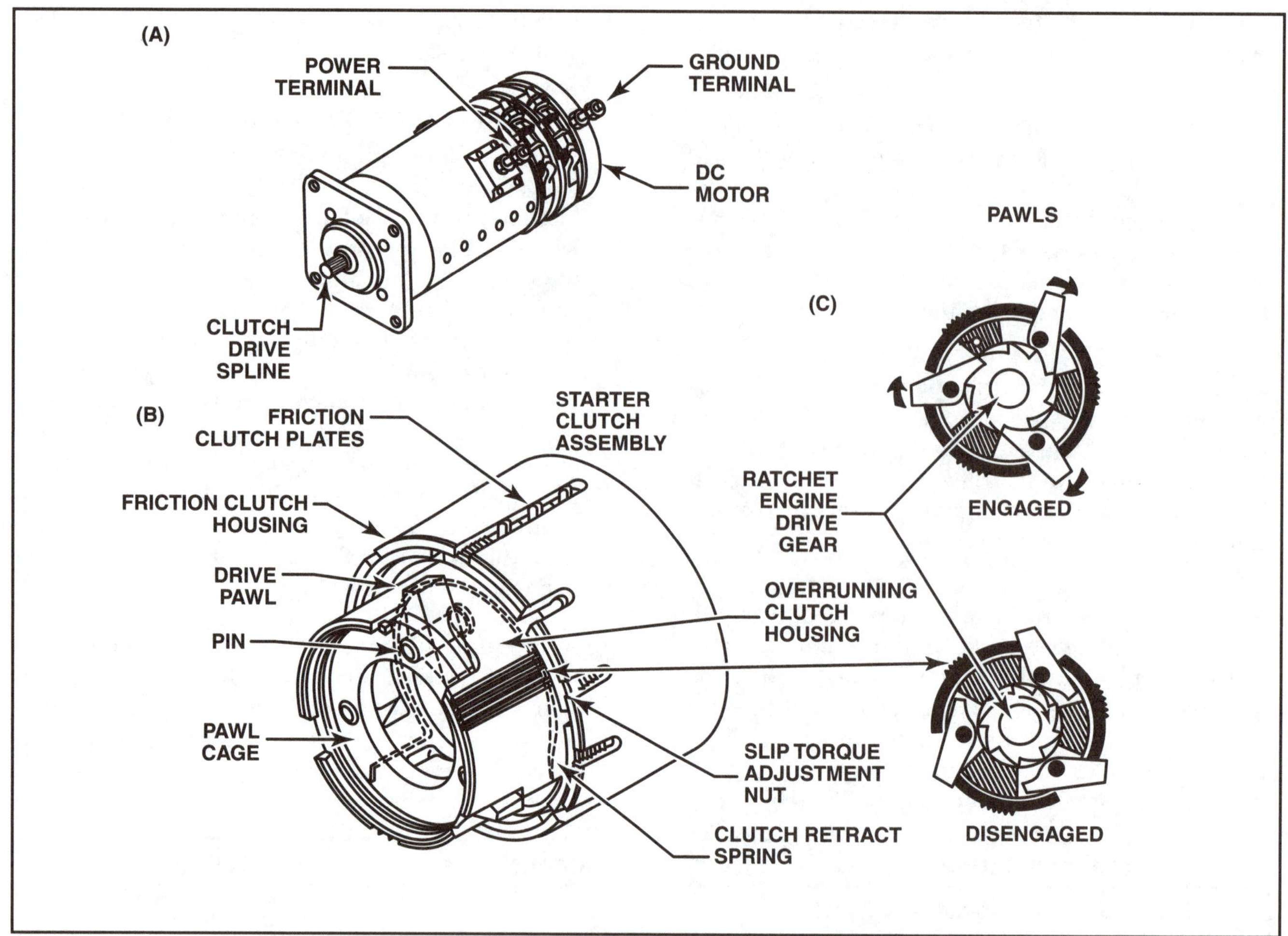

Figure 8-75. (A) — The electric motor used in a typical direct-cranking starter for a turbine engine is similar to the motors used with other starters. (B) — A typical direct-cranking starter for a turbine engine incorporates a clutch assembly. (C) — When engaged, the pawls in the clutch assembly engage the engine drive gear to rotate the engine. Once the engine starts, the engine drive gear accelerates and the pawls disengage.

DIRECT-CRANKING STARTERS

Direct-cranking starters are seldom used on large turbine engines; however, they are used frequently for starting auxiliary and ground power units. A typical direct-cranking electric starter used on a small turbine engine consists of an electric motor, a set of reduction gears, and an automatic engaging and disengaging clutch mechanism. [Figure 8-75]

The automatic clutch assembly performs two main functions. First, the clutch assembly prevents the starter from applying excessive torque to the engine accessory drive gearbox. To do this, an adjustable torque setting within the clutch assembly is set at approximately 130 inch-pounds of torque. Whenever the starter applies more than 130 inch-pounds of torque to the engine drive gear, small clutch plates within the clutch housing slip, thereby reducing the chance of damaging the drive gear. During starting, the friction clutch is designed to slip until the differential torque between the engine and starter falls below the slip torque setting.

The second function of the clutch assembly is to act as an over-run clutch. When the starter is rotated, centrifugal force causes the pawls to move inward against spring tension to engage the engine drive gear. As the armature drives the clutch housing, the housing bumps the pawls inward until they catch the engine drive gear. This occurs because the pawl cage assembly floats within the pawl clutch housing. Once the engine begins to exceed starter speed, the pawls slip out of the tapered slots of the engine drive gear and are disengaged by the retracting springs. This over-running feature prevents the engine from driving the starter to burst speed.

AIR TURBINE STARTERS

As an alternative to either of the electric starters just discussed, the air turbine, or pneumatic starter was

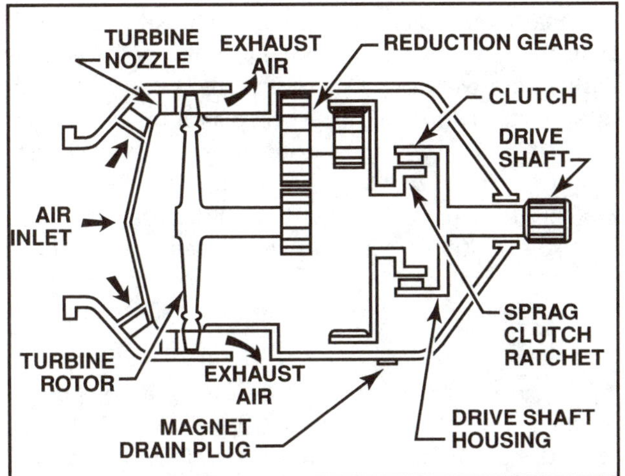

Figure 8-76. A typical air turbine starter consists of small turbine assembly, reduction gearing, and a clutch assembly.

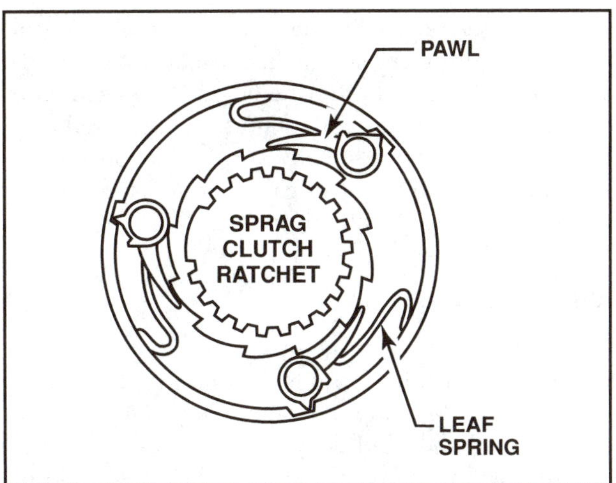

Figure 8-77. In the sprag clutch assembly used with pneumatic starters, the pawls are forced inward by leaf springs to engage the clutch ratchet. However, once the engine starts and the drive shaft housing accelerates beyond the speed of the starter, centrifugal force pulls the pawls away from the clutch ratchet.

developed. As its name implies, an air turbine starter utilizes a small turbine wheel to convert the velocity energy of a moving airstream into mechanical energy to turn an engine. A typical air turbine starter consists of a small turbine assembly, reduction gear assembly, and clutch assembly. Because there are so few parts in an air turbine starter, they typically weigh about one-fifth the weight of a comparable electric starter. This gives air turbine starters a high power-to-weight ratio. Because of this, pneumatic starters are used almost exclusively on commercial jet aircraft. [Figure 8-76]

To activate a pneumatic starter, a high volume air source of approximately 40 psig at 50 to 100 pounds per minute is required. The air source may be an onboard auxiliary power unit, ground power unit, or an operating engine bleed air source. Air is supplied to the starter inlet where it enters the air turbine assembly.

Two common types of turbine assemblies used on pneumatic starters are the radial inward flow turbine and the axial-flow turbine. As soon as air enters a pneumatic starter, the air passes through a set of turbine nozzle vanes. The vanes convert the low pressure, high volume air to a high velocity airstream that spins the turbine blades at high kinetic energy levels.

In a typical pneumatic starter, the turbine rotates at 60 to 80 thousand rpm. This rotational speed is reduced 20 to 30 times through a reduction gear assembly that is lubricated by an integral oil supply. The output end of the reduction gearing connects to a sprag clutch assembly which is located inside the drive shaft housing. A typical sprag clutch assembly consists of a set of pawls and a clutch ratchet. When standing still, the pawls are forced inward by small leaf springs to engage the sprag clutch ratchet. In this configuration, when the sprag clutch ratchet is turned by the starter, the drive shaft and housing also turn. Once the engine starts and accelerates to idle speed, centrifugal force pulls the pawls outward, disengaging the starter from the drive shaft housing. Once the start sequence is complete, the air supply is shut off automatically by a centrifugal cutout switch that closes the inlet air supply valve. This allows the sprag clutch ratchet and starter gear to coast to a halt while the drive shaft housing and pawls continue rotating at engine gearbox speed. [Figure 8-77]

To prevent a pneumatic starter from being damaged in the event the clutch does not release from the engine drive shaft housing during the start sequence, a drive shaft shear point is typically incorporated. In other words, if the engine starts to drive the starter, the drive shaft will shear once the engine induces a predetermined amount of torque on the starter.

As discussed earlier, when the engine begins accelerating to idle speed, the air supply powering the starter should shut off automatically. However, if this does not happen, most pneumatic starters have an air inlet design that chokes off the airflow so the starter turbine stabilizes at a maximum speed. If this feature were not incorporated, the airflow would accelerate the turbine assembly until it fails at its burst speed.

On some engines that use a pneumatic starter equipped with a sprag clutch, a clicking sound can sometimes be heard after the engine has been shut down and is coasting. This sound is considered normal and is the result of the spring tension on the pawls overcoming centrifugal force and forcing the pawls to ride on the clutch ratchet.

AIR SUPPLY VALVE

On aircraft that use a pneumatic starter, an air supply valve is installed in the air inlet line leading to the starter. A typical air supply valve consists of a control head and a butterfly valve. In most cases, the control head is actuated by a switch in the cockpit, while the butterfly valve is actuated pneumatically or manually. [Figure 8-78]

The following discussion describes how the components in the control head of an air supply valve regulate the amount of air supplied to the starter. To aid in understanding how the components work together, you should refer to the previous figure. As mentioned previously, the control head is actuated electrically by a switch in the cockpit. Once activated, the control crank rotates and pushes the control rod to extend the bellows fully. In addition, the control crank applies pressure to seat the pilot valve rod and displace the pilot valve cap. With the pilot valve cap off its seat, filtered air is allowed to flow to the servo piston. As air pressure compresses the servo piston, the butterfly valve opens and allows air to flow to the starter.

As pressure builds in the air supply line downstream from the butterfly valve, the control rod bellows partially compresses. As this occurs, the pilot valve rod lifts off its seat, allowing servo piston air to vent to the atmosphere. When downstream air pressure reaches a preset valve, the amount of air flowing to the servo piston will equal the amount of air being bled to the atmosphere and the system will be in a state of equilibrium. At this point, the control head is allowing maximum air pressure to the starter.

When a predetermined starter drive speed is reached, a centrifugal cutout flyweight switch de-energizes a solenoid which forces the control crank to release the pilot valve cap. Once the pilot valve cap seats, all air pressure vents to the atmosphere and the butterfly valve closes.

When the starter air valve cannot be controlled electrically due to a malfunction, a manual override handle can be used to position the butterfly valve. However, when attempting to start an engine using the manual override, make sure you follow the manufacturers procedures.

INSPECTION AND MAINTENANCE

Air turbine starters are pneumatic accessories designed to operate at high rpm in a high temperature environment. Because of this, adequate lubrication is crucial. Routine inspections of pneumatic

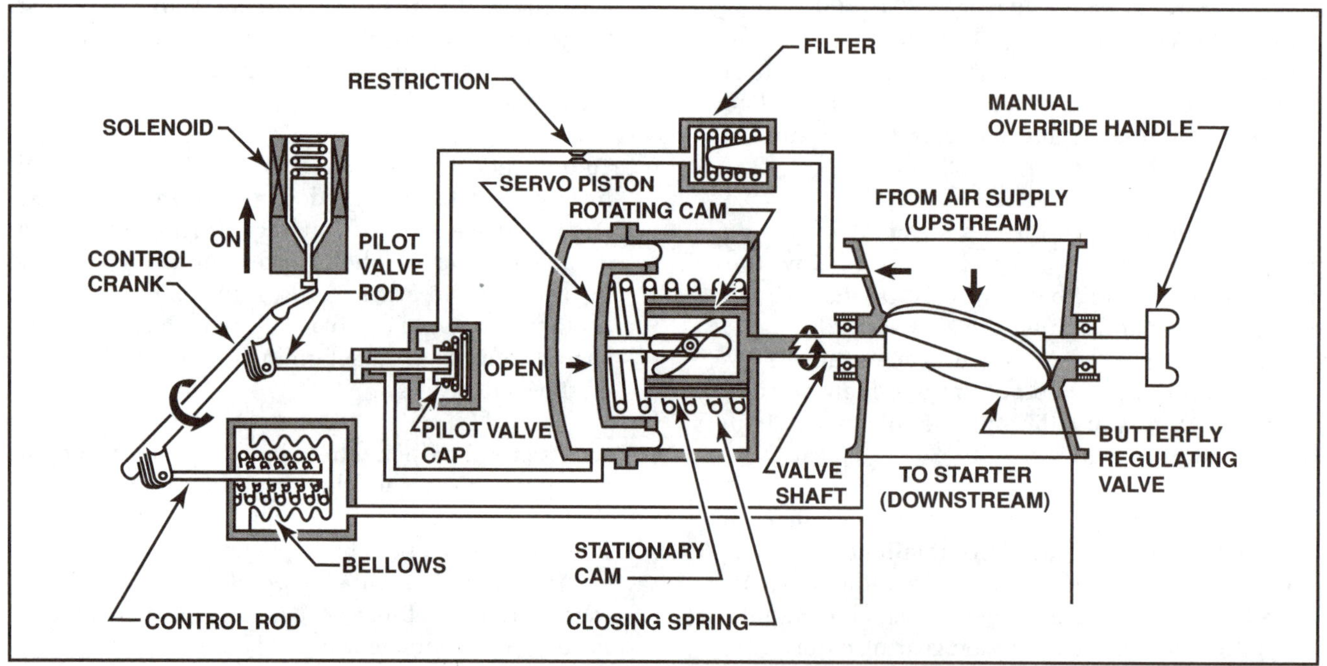

Figure 8-78. The air supply valve used with a pneumatic starter controls the amount of air that flows to the starter turbine.

pneumatic starters should include a check of the starter's oil level and examination of the magnetic drain plug. It is normal for small particles to be present on the drain plug, but particles that feel sandy or gritty are evidence of some sort of internal failure.

In addition to normal maintenance practices, there may be times when you have to troubleshoot a malfunction. To facilitate the troubleshooting process, some manufacturers provide a chart listing several common malfunctions as well as the probable cause and remedy. [Figure 8-79]

TROUBLE	PROBABLE CAUSE	REMEDY
Starter does not operate (no rotation)	No air supply	Check air supply.
	Electrical open in cutout switch	Check switch continuity. If no continuity, remove starter and adjust or replace switch.
	Skeared starter drive coupling	Remove starter and replace drive coupling.
	Internal starter discrepancy	Remove and replace starter.
Starter will not accelerate to normal cutoff speed	Low starter air supply	Check air source pressure.
	Starter cutout switch set improperly	Adjust rotor switch actuator.
	Valve pressure regulated too low	Replace valve.
	Internal starter malfunction	Remove and replace starter.
Starter will not cutoff	Low air supply	Check air supply.
	Rotor switch actuator set to high	Adjust switch actuator assembly.
	Starter cutout switch shorted	Replace switch and bracket assembly.
External oil leakage	Oil level too high	Drain oil and reservice properly.
	Loose vent, oil filler, or magnetic plugs	Tighten magnetic plug to proper torque. Tighten vent and oil filler plugs as necessary and lockwire.
	Loose clamp band assebly	Tighten clamp bandassembly to higher torque.
Starter runs, but engine does not turn over	Sheared drive coupling	Remove starter and replace the drive coupling. If couplings persist in breaking in unusually short periods of time, remove and replace starter.
Starter inlet will not line up with supply ducting	Improper installation of starter on engine, or improper indexing of turbine housing on starter	Check installation and/or indexing for conformance with manufacturer's installation instructions and the proper index position of the turbine housing specifed for the aircraft.
Metallic particles on magnetic drain plug	Small fuzzy particles indicate noemal wear	No remedial action required.
	Partcles coarser than fuzzy, such as chips, slivers, etc., indicate interal difficulty	Remove and replace starter.
Broken nozzle vanes	Large foreign particles in air supply	Remove and replace starter and check air supply filler.
Oil leakage from vent plug assembly	Improper starter instalation position	Check installed position for levelness of oil plugs and correct as required in accordance with manufacturer's installation instructions.
Oil leakage at drive coupling	Leaking rear seal assembly	Remove and replace starter.

Figure 8-79. To aid in troubleshooting a pneumatic starter, some manufacturers include a troubleshooting guide in their service manuals that indicate probable causes and remedies for specific malfunctions.

COMBUSTION STARTER

A combustion starter is a completely self-contained starter consisting of the same components found in a typical free turbine engine. In other words, a combustion starter has a compressor, combustion, turbine, and exhaust section; as well as its own fuel and oil supply, ignition system, and starting system. The compressor section typically consists of a small centrifugal compressor while the combustion section generally consists of a reverse flow combustion chamber. The air supply needed to operate a combustion starter is either drawn from the surrounding air, or supplied by another high pressure source.

Operation of a combustion starter is typically automatic. In other words, once a single start switch is actuated in the cockpit, the starter ignites and begins turning the free turbine. As soon as the free turbine begins rotating, the main engine is also rotated through a series of reduction gears. Once the main engine starts and reaches its self-sustaining speed, a cutout switch shuts down the combustion starter. [Figure 8-80

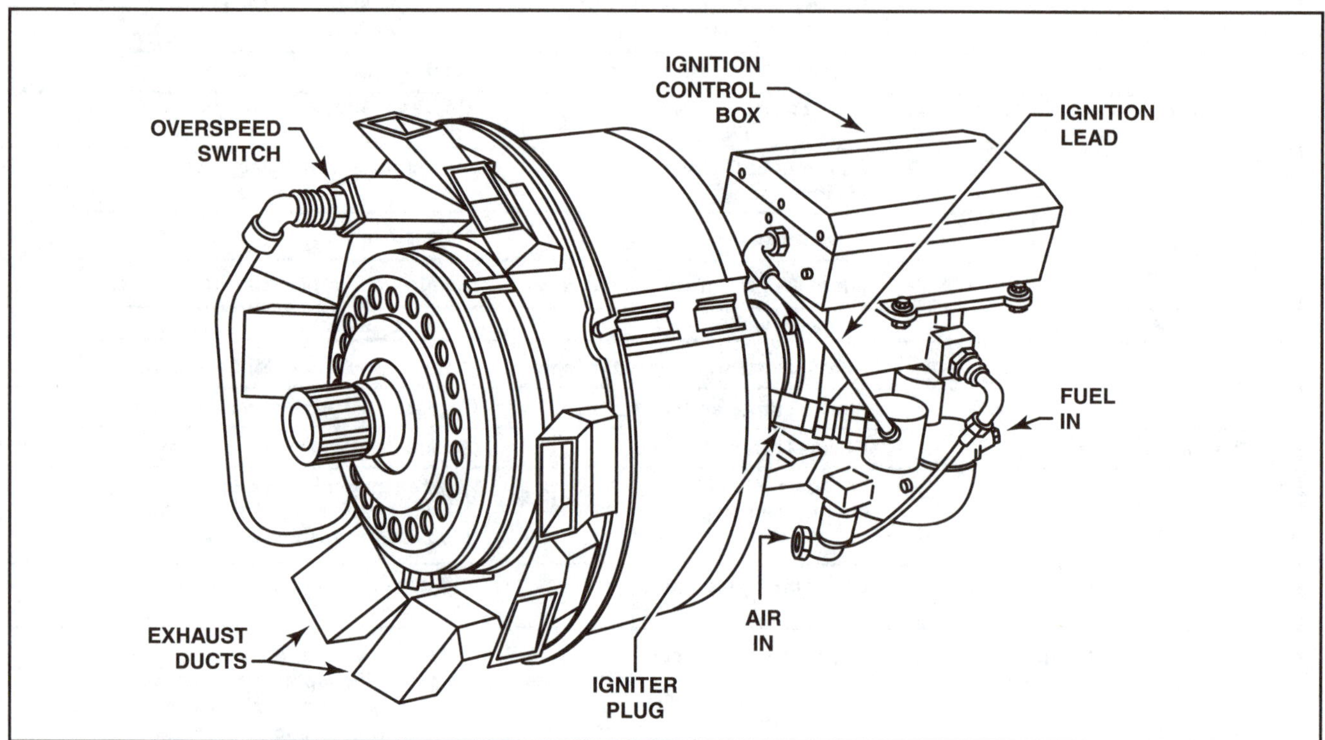

Figure 8-80. A combustion starter consists of a gas turbine engine that delivers engine starting power through a high-ratio reduction gear system. Operation of a typical combustion starter consists of actuating a single switch in the cockpit.

ELECTRICAL SYSTEM COMPONENTS

The satisfactory performance of any modern aircraft depends on the continuing reliability of electrical systems and subsystems. Improperly or carelessly installed or maintained wiring can be a source of both immediate and potential danger. Because of this, this section will look at the installation of wiring and circuit components that are primarily used in powerplant electrical systems.

The electrical installation in an aircraft consists of a source of electrical energy and an electrical load. Between the source and the load, there must be conductors of sufficient size to carry the required current without overheating or producing an excessive voltage drop. There must also be adequate circuit protection to ensure that excessive current cannot flow in the circuit. Excessive current can damage electrical equipment and produce enough heat to create a fire hazard.

WIRE

When choosing the wire for an electrical system, there are several factors that must be considered. For example, the wire selected must be large enough to accommodate the required current without producing excessive heat or causing an excessive voltage drop. In addition, the insulation must insulate enough to prevent electrical leakage as well as be strong enough to resist damage caused by abrasion.

WIRE TYPES

The majority of wiring in aircraft is done with stranded copper wire. In most cases, the wiring is coated with tin, silver, or nickel to help prevent oxidation. Prior to the mid 1990's, the wire used most often was stranded copper wire manufactured to MIL-W-5086 standards. This wire is made of strands of annealed copper covered with a very thin coating of tin. For insulation purposes, a variety of materials are used, including polyvinyl chloride (PVC), nylon, and glass cloth braid. Most of these insulators are rated to 600 volts. [Figure 8-81]

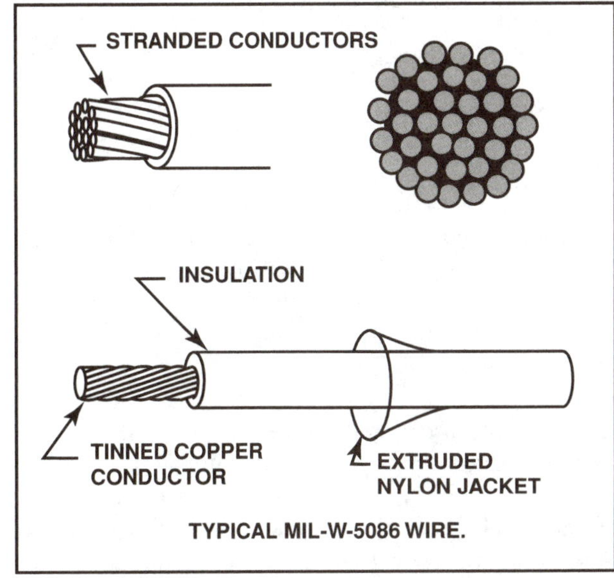

Figure 8-81. MIL-W-5086 wire consists of stranded copper conductors that are cabled with tin and wrapped in a PVC insulation. For added protection, most of this type of wiring is also covered in a nylon jacket.

In the mid 1990's it was discovered that polyvinyl chloride insulation emits toxic fumes when it burns. Therefore, a new group of mil spec wires, MIL-W-22759, was introduced which consists of stranded copper wire with Teflon™ insulation. Today, MIL-W-22759 is used in lieu of MIL-W-5086 in new wiring installations and should be used when replacing original aircraft wiring. However, prior to replacing any aircraft wiring, you should consult the manufacturer's service manual and service bulletins for specific instructions and information regarding both wire type and size.

Where large amounts of current must be carried for long distances, MIL-W-7072 aluminum wire is often used. This wire is insulated with either fluorinated ethylene propylene (FEP Fluorocarbon), nylon, or with a fiberglass braid. While aluminum wire does save weight, it does have a few disadvantages. For example, aluminum wire can only carry about two-thirds as much current as the same size copper wire. In addition, when exposed to vibration, aluminum wire can crystallize and break. In fact, aluminum wire smaller than six-gauge is not recommended because it is so easily broken by vibration.

In situations where you are going to replace a length of copper wire with aluminum wire, a handy rule of thumb is to always use an aluminum wire that is two wire gauge numbers larger than the copper wire it is replacing. Therefore, if you want to replace a piece of four-gauge copper wire with aluminum, you should use at least a two-gauge wire.

WIRE SIZE

Aircraft wire is measured by the **American Wire Gage (AWG)** system, with the larger numbers representing the smaller wires. The smallest size wire normally used in aircraft is 22-gauge wire, which has a diameter of about 0.025 inch. However, conductors carrying large amounts of current are typically of the 0000, or four aught size, and have a diameter of about 0.52 inch.

The amount of current a wire is capable of carrying is determined by its cross-sectional area. In most cases, a wire's cross-sectional area is expressed in circular mil sizes. A **circular mil** is the standard measurement of a round conductor's cross-sectional area. One mil is equivalent to .001 inches. Thus, a wire that has a diameter of .125 is expressed as 125 mils. To find the cross-sectional area of a conductor in circular mils, square the conductor's diameter. For example, if a round wire has a diameter of 3/8 inch, or 375 mils, its circular area is 140,625 circular mils (375 × 375 = 140,625).

The **square mil** is the unit of measure for square or rectangular conductors such as bus bars. To determine the cross-sectional area of a conductor in square mils, multiply the conductor's length by its width. For example, the cross-sectional area of a strip of copper that is 400 mils thick and 500 mils wide is 200,000 square mils.

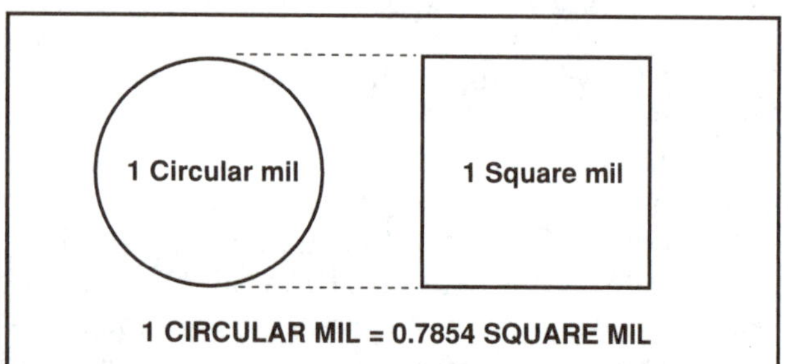

Figure 8-82. Relationship between circular mils and square mils.

NOMINAL SYSTEM VOLTAGE	ALLOWABLE VOLTAGE DROP VOLTS	
	CONTINUOUS OPERATION	INTERMITTENT OPERATION
14	0.5	1.0
28	1.0	2.0
115	4.0	8.0
200	7.0	14.0

Figure 8-83. When wiring a new component in an aircraft, you must know the system voltage, the allowable voltage drop, and the components duty cycle. As you can see in this figure, all of these factors are interrelated.

It should be noted that one circular mil is .7854 of one square mil. Therefore, to convert a circular mil area to a square mil area, multiply the area in circular mils by .7854 mil. Conversely, to convert a square mil area to a circular mil area, divide the area in square mils by .7854. [Figure 8-82]

When replacing wire to make a repair, all you typically have to do is replace damaged wire with the same size and type of wire. However, in new installations, several factors must be considered in selecting the proper wire. For example, one of the first things you must know is the system operating voltage. You also must know the allowable voltage drop and whether your wiring operates on a continuous or intermittent basis. [Figure 8-83]

To see why these factors are important, let's assume that you are going to install a cowl flap motor in a 28-volt system. Since cowl flaps are moved infrequently during a flight, a cowl flap motor is considered to operate on an intermittent basis. By looking at the chart in the previous figure, you can see the allowable voltage drop for a component installed in a 28-volt system that is operated intermittently is 2 volts. Once these three factors are known, an electric wire chart is used to determine the wire size needed for installation. [Figure 8-84]

Notice that the three curves extend diagonally across the chart from the lower left corner to the right side. These curves represent the ability of a wire to carry the current without overheating. Curve 1 represents the continuous rating of a wire when routed in bundles or conduit. If the intersection of the current and wire length lines are above this curve, the wire can carry the current without generating excessive heat.

If the intersection of the current and wire length lines falls between curve 1 and 2, the wire can

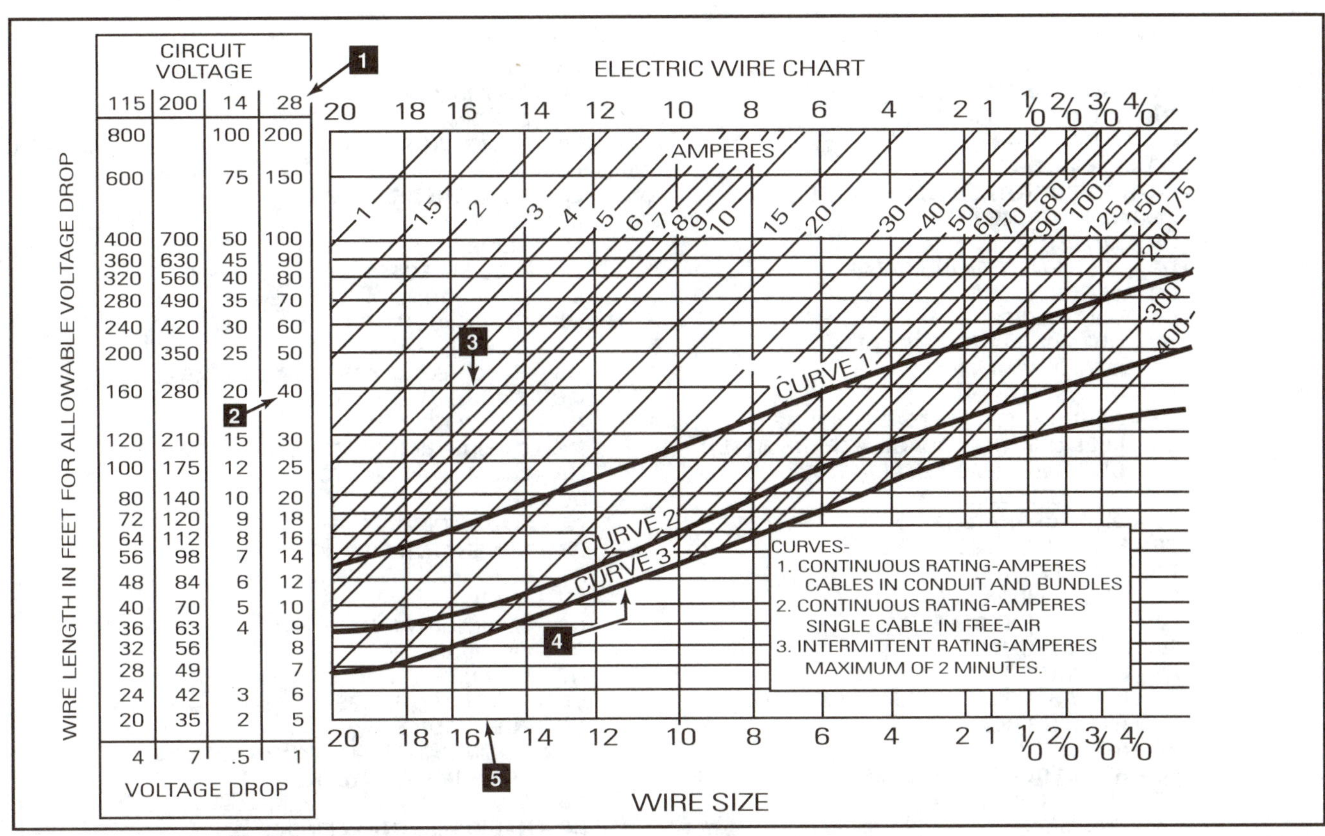

Figure 8-84. In this example, assume a 28-volt cowl flap motor draws six amps continuously and 40 feet of wire must be used for the installation. To determine the correct wire size, locate the column on the left size of the chart representing a 28-volt system (item 1). Move down in this column until you find the horizontal line representing a wire length of 40 feet (item 2). Follow this line to the right until it intersects the diagonal line for 6 amps (item 3). Because the wire carries an intermittent current, you must be at or above curve 3 on the chart (item 4). In this case, the intersection is above curve 3 and all you have to do is drop down vertically to the bottom of the chart. The line falls between wire sizes 14 and 16 (item 5). Whenever the chart indicates a wire size between two sizes, you must select the larger wire. In this case, a 14 wire is required.

only be used to carry current continuously in free air. If the intersection falls between curves 2 and 3, the wire can only be used to carry current intermittently.

WIRE MARKING

There is no standard system for wire identification among the manufacturers of general aviation aircraft. However, most manufacturers do put some form of identification mark about every 12 to 15 inches along a wire. The identification marking should identify the wire with regard to the type of circuit, location within the circuit, and wire size. Each manufacturer will have a code letter to indicate the type of circuit. For example, wire in flight instrumentation circuits are often identified with the letter "F" while the letter "N" is sometimes used to identify the circuit ground. Easy identification of each wire greatly facilitates troubleshooting procedures and saves time. [Figure 8-85]

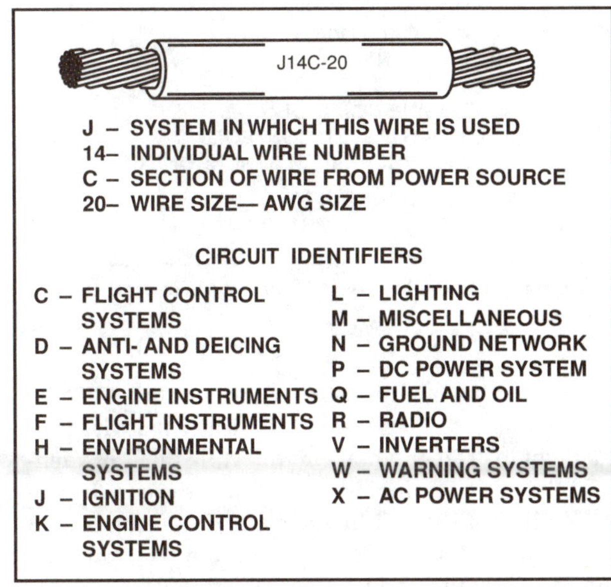

Figure 8-85.The marking J14C-20 indicates that this wire is part of an ignition circuit (J) and is the 14th wire in chat circuit (14). In addition, it is the third individual segment of wire number 14 (C) and it is a 20-gauge wire.

A – ARMAMENT
B – PHOTOGRAPHIC
C – CONTROL SURFACE
  CA – AUTOMATIC PILOT
  CC – WING FLAPS
  CD – ELEVATOR TRIM
D – INSTRUMENT (OTHER THAN FLIGHT OR ENGINE INSTRUMENT)
  DA – AMMETER
  DB – FLAP POSITION INDICATOR
  DC – CLOCK
  DD – VOLTMETER
  DE – OUTSIDE AIR TEMPERATURE
  DF – FLIGHT HOUR METER
E – ENGINE INSTRUMENT
  EA – CARBURETOR AIR TEMPERATURE
  EB – FUEL QUANTITY GUAGE & TRANSMITTER
  EC – CYLINDER HEAD TEMPERATURE
  ED – OIL PRESSURE
  EE – OIL TEMPERATURE
  EF – FUEL PRESSURE
  EG – TACHOMETER
  EH – TORQUE INDICATOR
  EJ – INSTRUMENT CLUSTER
F – FLIGHT INSTRUMENT
  FA – BANK AND TURN
  FB – PITOT STATIC TUBE HEATER & STALL WARNING HEATER
  FC – STALL WARNING
  FD – SPEED CONTROL SYSTEM
  FE – INDICATOR LIGHTS
G – LANDING GEAR
  GA – ACTUATOR
  GB – RETRACTION
  GC – WARNING DEVICE (HORN)
  GD – LIGHT SWITCHES
  GE – INDICATOR LIGHTS
H – HEATING, VENTILATING & DEICING
  HA – ANTI-ICING
  HB – CABIN HEATER
  HC – CIGAR LIGHTER
  HD – DEICING
  HE – AIR CONDITIONERS
  HF – CABIN VENTILATION
J – IGNITION
  JA – MAGNETO
K – ENGINE CONTROL
  KA – STARTER CONTROL
  KB – PROPELLER SYNCHRONIZER
L – LIGHTING
  LA – CABIN
  LB – INSTRUMENT
  LC – LANDING
  LD – NAVIGATION
  LE – TAXI
  LF – ROTATING BEACON
  LG – RADIO
  LH – DEICE
  LJ – FUEL SELECTOR
  LK – TAIL FLOODLIGHT
M – MISCELLANEOUS
  MA – COWL FLAPS
  MB – ELECTRICALLY OPERATED SEATS
  MC – SMOKE GENERATOR
  MD – SPRAY EQUIPMENT
  ME – CABIN PRESSURIZATION EQUIPMENT
  MF – CHEM O_2 – INDICATOR
P – DC POWER
  PA – POWER CIRCUIT
  PB – GENERATOR CIRCUITS
  PC – EXTERNAL POWER SOURCE
Q – FUEL & OIL
  QA – AUXILLIARY FUEL PUMP
  QB – OIL DILUTION
  QC – ENGINE PRIMER
  QD – MAIN FUEL PUMPS
  QE – FUEL VALVES
R – RADIO (NAVIGATION & COMMUNICATIONS)
  RA – INSTRUMENT LANDING
  RB – COMMAND
  RC – RADIO DIRECTION FINDER
  RD – VHF
  RE – HOMING
  RF – MARKER BEACON
  RG – NAVIGATION
  RH – HIGH FREQUENCY
  RJ – INTERPHONE
  RK – UHF
  RL – LOW FREQUENCY
  RM – FREQUENCY MODLUATION
  RP – AUDIO SYSTEM & AUDIO AMPLIFIER
  RR – DISTANCE MEASURING EQUIPMENT (DME)
  RS – AIRBORNE PUBLIC ADDRESS SYSTEM
S – RADAR
U – MISCELLANEOUS ELECTRONIC
  UA – IDENTIFICATION – FRIEND OR FOE
W – WARNING AND EMERGENCY
  WA – FLARE RELEASE
  WB – CHIP DETECTOR
  WC – FIRE DETECTION SYSTEM
X – AC POWER

Figure 8-86. A two-letter identification code is used in some wire marking systems to provide more detail on a wire's function and location.

A typical wire identification code would be F26D-22N. In this case, the letter "F" indicates the wire is in the flight instrumentation circuit, while the "26" identifies the wire as being the 26th wire in the circuit. The "D" indicates the fourth segment of the number 26 wire. The "22" is the gauge size of the wire, and the "N" indicates that the wire goes to ground.

Another wire marking system that is sometimes used employs a two-letter identification code. This marking system provides much more detail about the location of a given wire making it especially helpful in large aircraft having many systems. [Figure 8-86]

In addition to marking individual wires, wire bundles may have a specific identification number. In this case, pressure-sensitive tape or flexible sleeves are stamped with identification codes and wrapped around a wire bundle. Individual wires within each

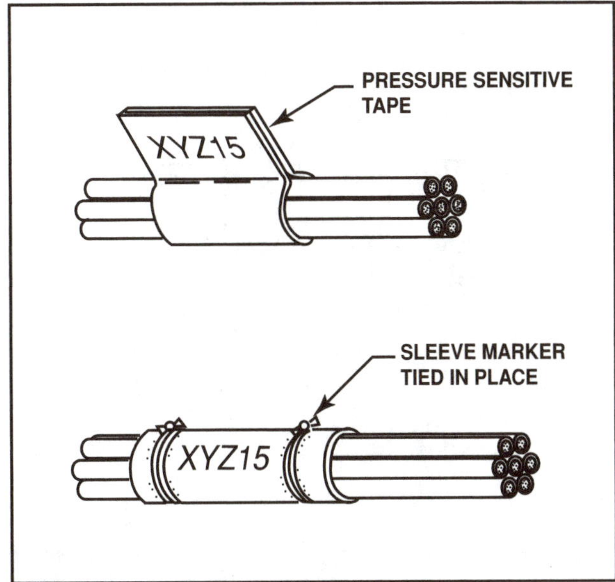

Figure 8-87. Several methods of identifying wire bundles include pressure-sensitive tape and sleeve markers tied in place.

bundle are usually hot-stamped for easy identification. Typically, wire bundles are marked near the points at which they enter and leave a compartment. [Figure 8-87]

WIRING INSTALLATION

As a general rule, electrical wiring is installed in aircraft either as open wiring or in conduit. With open wiring, individual wires or wire bundles are routed inside the aircraft structure without protective covering. On the other hand, when installed in conduit, electrical wiring is put inside either a rigid or flexible tubing that provides a great deal of protection.

OPEN WIRING

The quickest and easiest way to install wiring is to install it as open wiring. In addition, open wiring allows easy access when troubleshooting or servicing individual circuits.

To help provide a more organized installation, electrical wiring is often installed in bundles. Several methods of assembling wires into bundles may be utilized, depending on where a bundle is fabricated. For example, in the shop, wires stamped with identification markings may be lined up parallel to one another on a bench and tied together. However, inside an aircraft, wires may be secured to an existing bundle, or laid out to form a new bundle and tied together. In some cases, it may be helpful to connect one end of the wires to their destination terminal strip or connector before securing them together in a bundle. Wiring harnesses fabricated at a factory are typically made on a jig board prior to installation in an aircraft. This method allows the manufacturer to preform the wire bundles with the bends needed to fit the bundle in an aircraft. Regardless of the method of bundle assembly, a plastic comb can be used to keep individual wires straight and parallel in a bundle. [Figure 8-88]

Where possible, limit the number of wires in a single bundle. This helps prevent the possibility of a single wire faulting and ultimately damaging an entire bundle. In addition, no single bundle should include wires for both a main and back-up system. This helps prevent the possibility of neutralizing a system if a bundle were damaged. Another thing to keep in mind is that it is better to keep ignition wires, shielded wires, and wires not protected by a fuse or circuit breaker separate from all other wiring.

Once all the wires in a bundle are assembled, the bundle should be tied together every three to four inches. Typically, wire bundles that are assembled

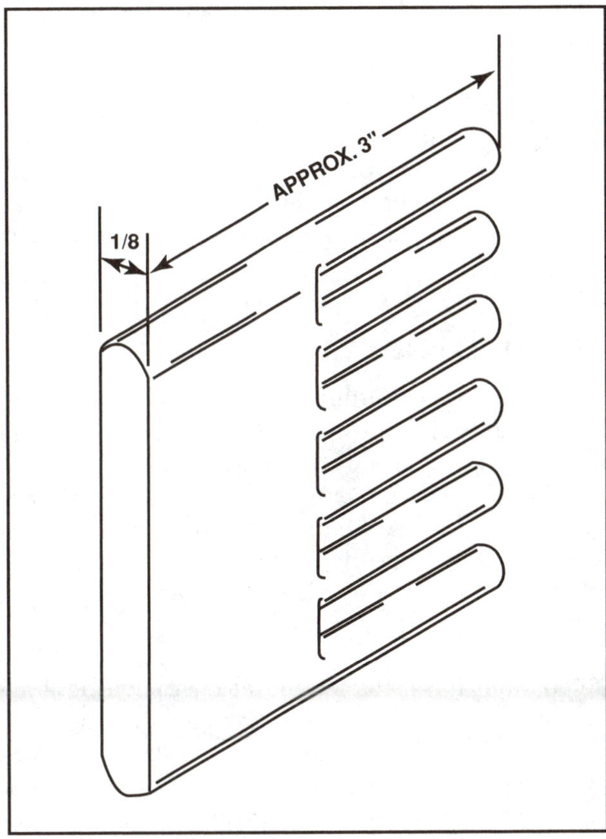

Figure 8-88. A plastic comb is a helpful tool used to keep wires straight and parallel when making up new wire bundles.

Figure 8-89. When tieing a wire bundle together with either linen or nylon cord, it is best to use a clove hitch that is secured by a square knot.

on a jig are tied together with waxed linen or nylon cord using a clove hitch secured with a square knot. [Figure 8-89]

In the field a patented nylon strap called a TYRAP™ is often used to hold wire bundles together. This small nylon strap is wrapped around the wire bundle and one end is passed through a slot in the other end and pulled tight. Once tight, the excess strapping is cut off.

Another method that is used to hold wire bundles together is with either single- or double-lacing. However, lacing should not be used with wire bundles installed around an engine because a break anywhere in the lacing cord loosens an entire section of the bundle.

Once tied, some wire bundles are covered with a heat-shrinkable tubing, a coiled "spaghetti" tubing or various other types of coverings made of Teflon, nylon, or fiberglass. However, when these coverings are used, a wire bundle is still considered to be open wiring.

ROUTING AND CLAMPING

All of the wire bundles installed in aircraft should be routed so they are at least three inches away from any control cable and so they will not interfere with any moving components. If there is any possibility that a wire or wire bundle could touch a control cable, some form of mechanical guard must be installed to keep the wire bundle and cable separated.

If possible, it is better to route electrical wiring along the overhead or the side walls of an aircraft rather than in the bottom of the fuselage. This helps prevent the wires from being damaged by fluids that may leak into low areas. In addition, electrical wiring must be routed where it cannot be damaged by persons entering or leaving the aircraft or by any baggage or cargo.

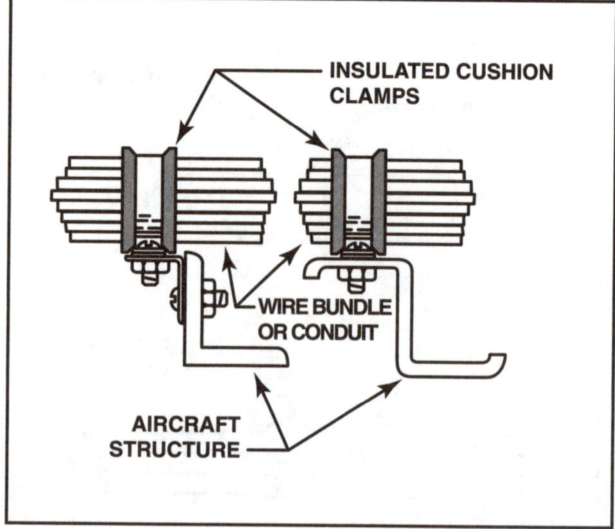

Figure 8-90. Cushion clamps, or Adel clamps, are used to support and secure wire bundles to the aircraft structure.

When electrical wires are routed parallel to oxygen or any type of fluid line, the wiring should be least six inches above the fluid line. However, the distance can be reduced to two inches as long as the wiring is not supported in any way by the fluid line and the proper mechanical protection is provided. Acceptable "secondary" protection typically includes additional clamps, approved sleeving, and the use of conduits.

Wire bundles must be securely clamped to the aircraft structure using clamps lined with a non-metallic cushion. In addition, the clamps should be spaced close enough together so the wiring bundle does not sag (maximum 1/2") or vibrate excessively. [Figure 8-90]

Another thing to keep in mind when securing wire bundles is that, once installed, you should be able to deflect a bundle about a half inch with normal hand pressure applied between any two supports. In addition, the last support should allow enough slack that a connector can be easily disconnected and reconnected for servicing. In some cases, a service loop in the wiring is the preferred method for providing adequate slack to enable equipment removal and replacement.

Any bundle that passes through a bulkhead should be clamped to a bracket which centers the bundle in the hole. In addition, if there is less than one-quarter inch clearance between the bundle and the hole, a protective rubber grommet must be installed. The grommet prevents wiring from being cut by the sharp edges of the metal hole should the centering bracket break or become bent. [Figure 8-91]

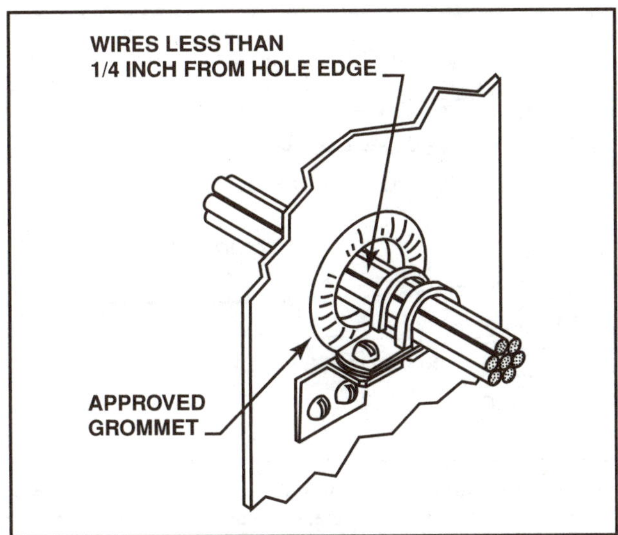

Figure 8-91. When a wire bundle must pass through a bulkhead or frame, a supporting bracket is required. If less than one-quarter inch clearance exists, a rubber grommet is installed to prevent possible wiring damage.

Where bundles must make a bend, use a bend radius that does not cause the wires on the inside of the bend to bunch up. Using a bend radius of approximately ten times the diameter of the wire bundle is a good practice.

CONDUIT

The method of installation that provides the best protection for electrical wiring is to enclose the wiring in either a rigid or flexible metal conduit. This is the preferred method of installation in areas such as wheel wells and engine nacelles where wire bundles are likely to be chafed or crushed.

The inside diameter of the conduit must be 25 percent larger than the maximum diameter of the wire bundle. When figuring the conduit size needed, bear in mind that the nominal diameter of a conduit represents the conduit's outside diameter. Therefore, you must subtract twice the wall thickness from the conduit's outside diameter to determine the inside diameter.

When installing a wire bundle inside a conduit, keep in mind that, if you find it difficult to slide a wire bundle through a conduit, blow some soapstone talc through the tubing first. The talc will act as a lubricant between the wiring and conduit wall. Another installation tip is to attach a long piece of lacing cord to the bundle and blow it through the tubing with compressed air. Once through the tubing, the lacing cord can be used to help pull the wire bundle through.

Like open wiring, conduit must be supported by clamps from the aircraft structure. In addition, a one-eighth inch drain hole must be made at the lowest point in each run of the conduit. This is done to provide a means of draining any moisture that condenses inside the conduit.

Fabricating conduit for electrical wiring requires you to remove all burrs and sharp edges from the conduit. In addition, bends must be made using a radius that will not cause the conduit tube to kink, wrinkle, or flatten excessively.

SHIELDING

Anytime a wire carries electrical current, a magnetic field surrounds the wire. If strong enough, this magnetic field could interfere with some of the aircraft instrumentation. For example, even though the tiny light that illuminates the card of a magnetic compass is powered with low-voltage direct current, the magnetic field produced by the current flow is enough to deflect the compass. To minimize this field, a two-conductor twisted wire is used to carry the current to and from this light. By using a twisted wire, the fields cancel each other.

Alternating current or pulsating direct current has an especially bad effect on electronic equipment. To help prevent interference, wires that carry AC or pulsating DC are often shielded. Shielding is a method of intercepting electrical energy and shunting it to electrical ground.

Most shielding consists of a braid of tin-plated or cadmium-plated copper wire that surrounds the insulation of a wire. Typically, the braid is connected to aircraft ground through a crimped-on ring terminal. When a wire is shielded, the radiated energy from the conductor is received by the braided shielding and passed to the aircraft's ground where it cannot cause interference.

Shielding in the powerplant electrical system is typically grounded at both ends of the wiring run. However, shielding in electronic circuit wiring is usually grounded at one end to prevent setting up a loop which could cause electromagnetic interference.

WIRING TERMINALS

Electrical wiring used in aircraft is generally terminated with solderless terminals that are staked, or crimped, on to the wire. **Crimping** is a term used to describe the squeezing of a terminal around a wire

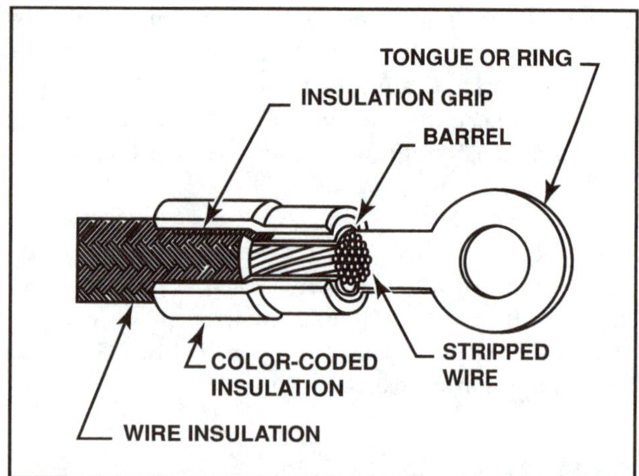

Figure 8-92. Wire gauge sizes 10 through 22 are typically terminated with preinsulated solderless terminals that are color-coded to identify various sizes.

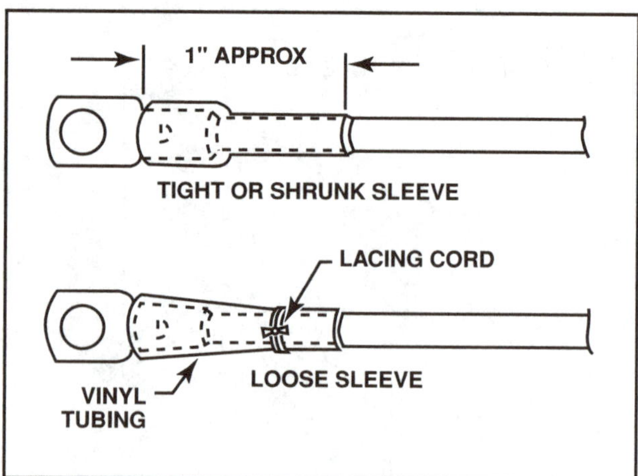

Figure 8-93. Solderless terminals installed on wire larger than 10-gauge require a separate piece of insulation. Heat-shrink tubing may be used or vinyl tubing may be secured over the terminal's barrel with lacing cord.

to secure the wire and provide a high quality electrical connection. There are several different types of terminals used in aircraft including the ring terminal, slotted terminal, and hook type terminal. However, the ring terminal is used most often because it virtually eliminates the possibility of circuit failure due to terminal disconnection.

Typically, solderless terminals used on 10-gauge and smaller wire use colored insulation to preinsulate the terminals. For example, terminals with red insulation are used on wire gauge sizes 22 through 18, while blue insulation identifies a terminal used on 16- and 14-gauge wires. If a terminal has yellow insulation, it is used for 12- and 10-gauge wires. [Figure 8-92]

Wires larger than 10-gauge typically use uninsulated terminals. In this case, a piece of vinyl tubing or heat-shrinkable tubing is used to insulate the terminal. However, the insulating material must be slipped over the wire prior to crimping. Then, after the crimping operation, the tubing is pulled over the terminal barrel and secured. [Figure 8-93]

When choosing a solderless terminal, it is important that the materials of the terminal and wire are compatible. This helps eliminate the possibility of dissimilar metal corrosion.

Before you can attach a wire to a terminal, the protective insulation must be removed. This is typically done by cutting the insulation and gently pulling it from the end of the wire. This process is known as **stripping** the wire. Whenever you are stripping a wire, you should expose as little of the conductor as necessary to make the connection. In addition, you must be careful not to damage the conductor beyond allowable limits. [Figure 8-94]

The FAA specifies limits for the number of nicked or broken strands on any conductor. For example, a 20-gauge copper wire with 19 strands may have 2 nicks and no broken strands. In general, the larger the number of strands or the larger the conductor, the greater the acceptable number of broken or nicked strands.

Special crimping tools are needed to crimp a terminal onto a wire. A properly crimped terminal provides a joint between the wire and the terminal as strong as the wire itself. The preferred crimping tool is a ratchet-type crimper that is periodically cali-

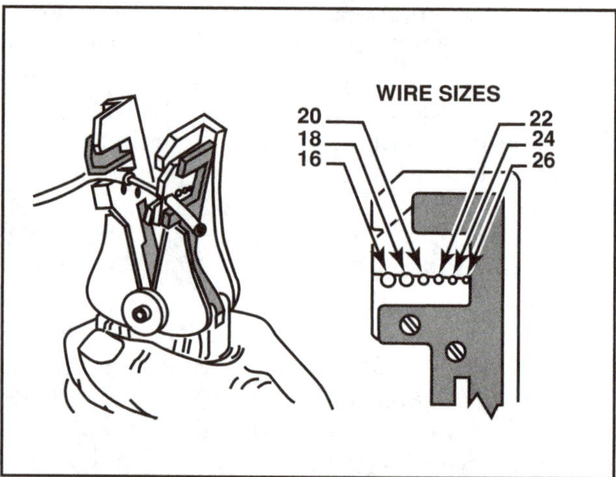

Figure 8-94. When stripping electrical wire, it is best to use a quality stripper that is designed for a specific size of wire.

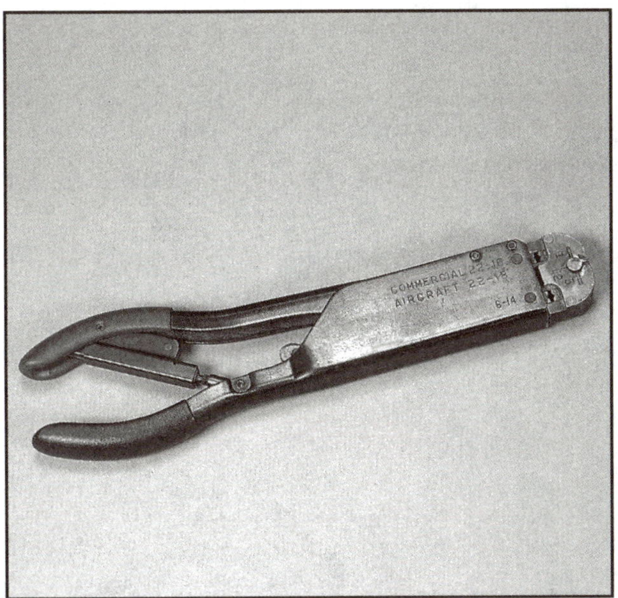

Figure 8-95. Ratchet-type crimping tools are periodically calibrated to provide a quality crimp on every terminal.

brated to ensure a consistent and proper crimp. When using a ratchet-type crimping tool, the handles of the tool will not release until the jaws have moved close enough together to properly compress the terminal barrel. [Figure 8-95]

Pneumatic crimping tools are often used on wire gauge sizes 0 through 0000 because of the force required to properly crimp the wire. Like the ratchet-type crimper, a pneumatic crimper must be calibrated periodically.

Aluminum wire presents some special problems when installing terminals. Aluminum wire oxidizes when exposed to air and the oxides formed become an electrical insulator. Therefore, to ensure a good quality electrical connection between an aluminum wire and terminal, the inside of a typical aluminum terminal is partially filled with a compound of petroleum jelly and zinc dust. This compound mechanically grinds the oxide film off the wire strands when the terminal is compressed and then seals the wire from the air, preventing the formation of new oxides. [Figure 8-96]

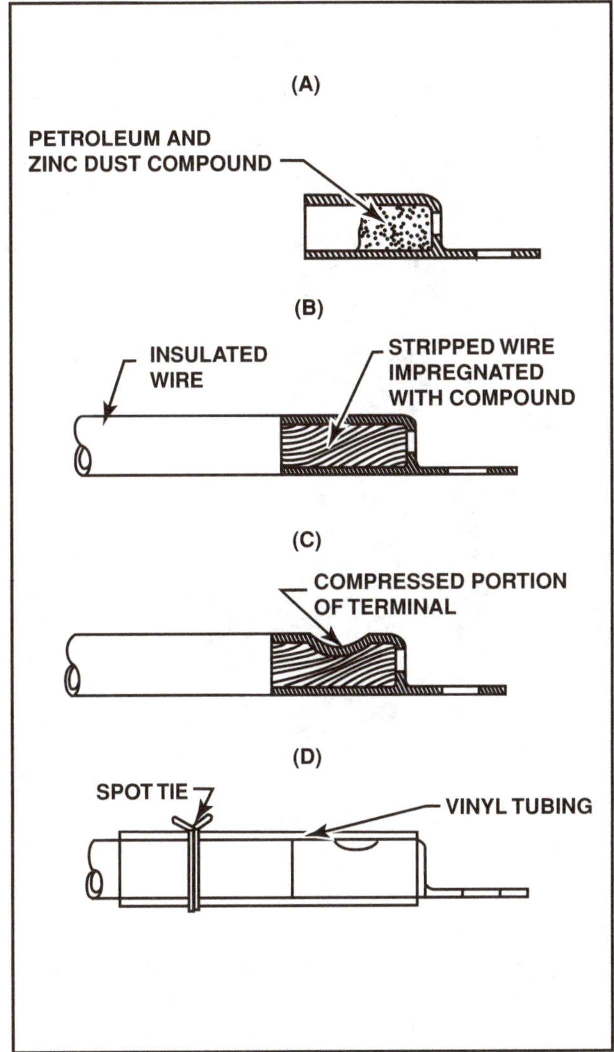

Figure 8-96. (A) — To help prevent oxidation, special terminals filled with a compound of petroleum jelly and zinc dust are required for terminating aluminum wiring. (B) — When a stripped wire is inserted into this type of terminal, the wire strands become impregnated with the petroleum jelly and zinc compound. (C) — As the terminal is crimped, the zinc dust cleans the wire while the petroleum jelly creates an airtight seal. (D) — Once crimped, a piece of vinyl tubing is tied over the terminal end to protect it from moisture.

CONNECTORS

Connectors are usually installed on wiring that is frequently disconnected. As an example, the wiring that is used to supply power to avionic components typically utilize multi-pin connectors that can be easily removed to perform maintenance. AN and MS connectors are the most common connectors used in aircraft electrical circuits and are available in a variety of sizes and types. Mating connectors consist of one connector with female contacts, or sockets, and another connector with male contacts, or pins. The ground side of an electrical power conductor is typically connected to a male connector while the power side of the conductor is attached to the female connector. This is done to reduce the chance of an accidental short between

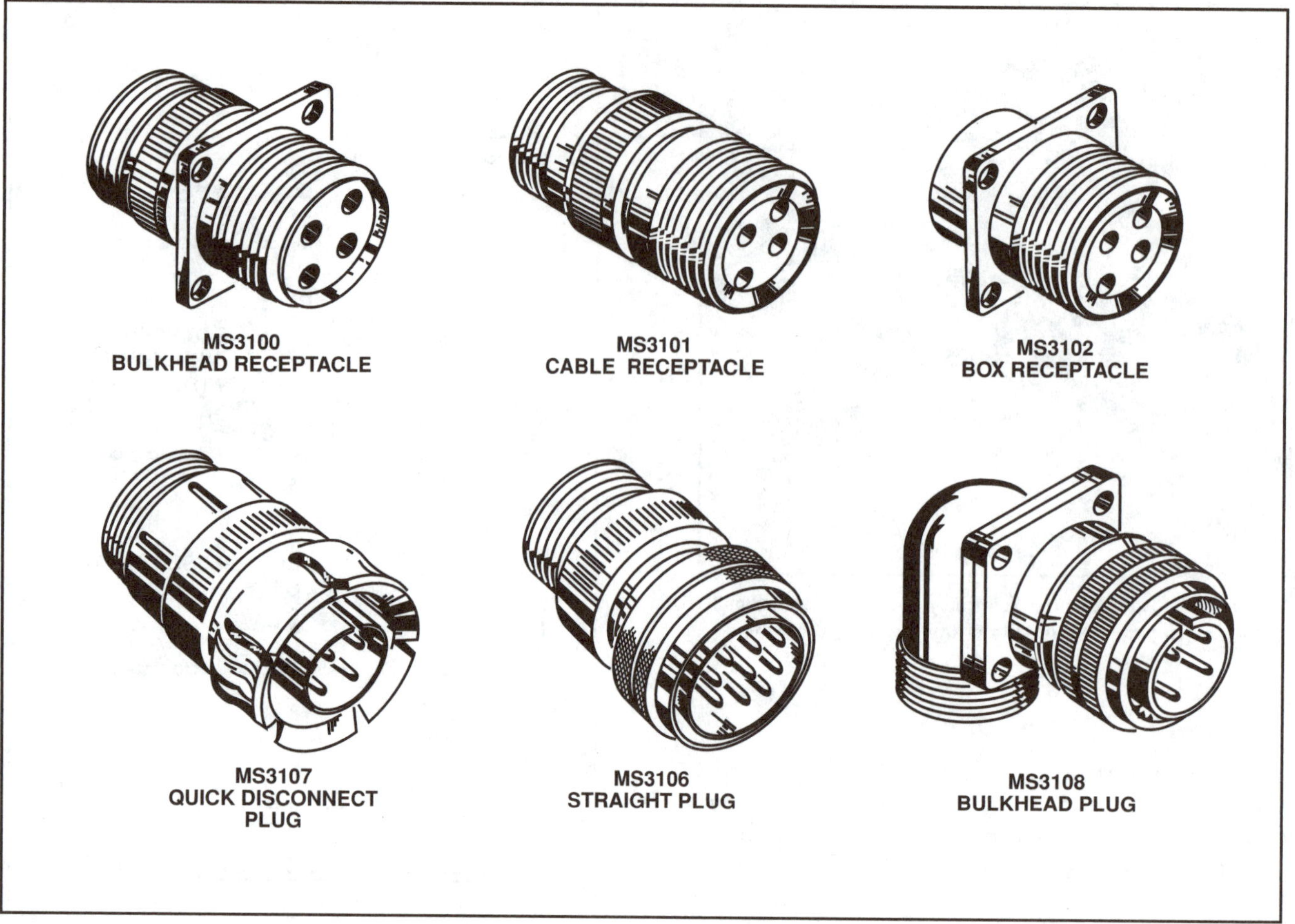

Figure 8-97. As you can see, electrical connectors come in many types and sizes. This provides a great deal of flexibility when attaching electrical wiring to various components.

the power side of a circuit and any conductive surface when the mating connectors are separated. [Figure 8-97]

There are two ways the wires are typically connected to the contacts in a connector. Newer plugs use tapered pins that are crimped onto the wire end. The pin is then slipped into a tapered hole in the pin or socket end of a connector. A special tool is used to remove or replace the pin if it is ever necessary.

Another type of connector plug requires the wires to be soldered into each end of a connector. To install a typical soldered connector, begin by stripping enough insulation from the end of each wire to provide approximately $^1/_{32}$ inch of bare wire between the end of the insulation and the end of a pin when inserted. Next, slip a specified length of insulated tubing over the end of each wire. Using an appropriate soldering iron, solder, and flux, apply a small amount of solder to the stripped portion of each wire. This is a process known as **tinning** the wires and greatly facilitates their insertion into the connector pins. Once the wires are tinned, fill the end of each pin, or solder pot, with solder. While keeping the solder in a solder pot molten, insert the appropriate wire. Once inserted, remove the soldering iron and hold the wire as still as possible until the solder solidifies. If the wire is moved before the solder solidifies, the solder will take on a granular appearance and cause excessive electrical resistance. Repeat this process until all pins and wires have been soldered in place. After all of the wires are in place, clean any remaining flux residue from the connector with an approved cleaner. [Figure 8-98]

Inspect the soldered connector before final assembly. If excess solder is bridging two pins or if some pins do not have enough solder, re-solder the connection. The solder in a properly soldered connection should completely fill each pot and have a slightly rounded top. However, the solder must not wick up into the strands of each wire or the wire may become brittle and break when bent. When you are satisfied with all of the soldered joints, slip the insulation tubing on each wire over its respective

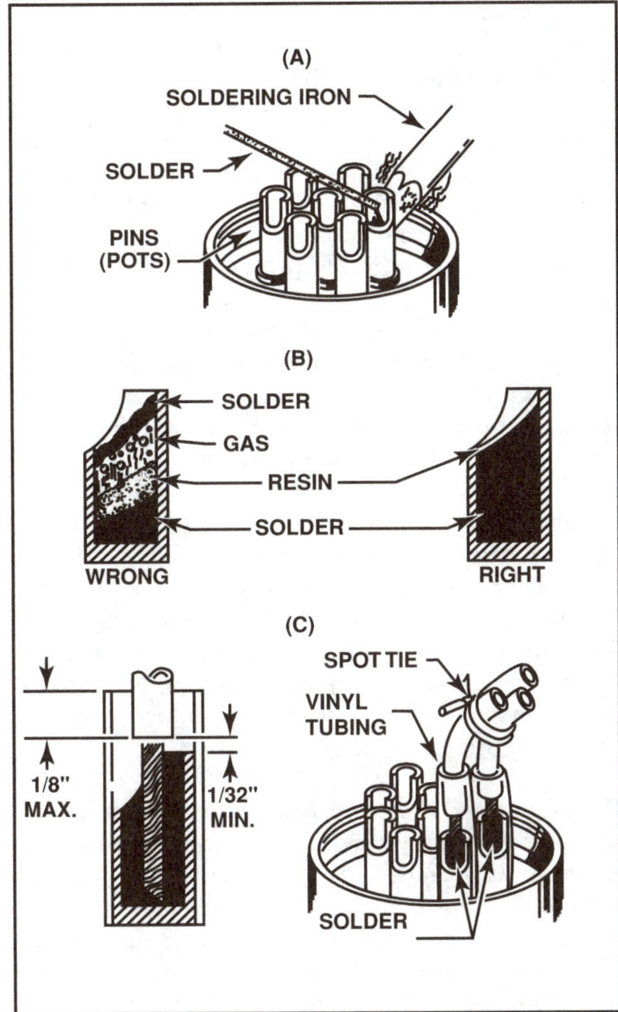

Figure 8-98. (A) — After the wires have been timed, fill a solder pot with solder. (B) — When doing this, make sure you allow enough time for the pot to heat up sufficiently. If this is not done, resin could become trapped in the solder producing a weak connection. (C) — Once installed, there should be a minimum of $^{1}/_{32}$ of an inch clearance between the wire insulation and the top of the solder joint. In addition, a piece of vinyl tubing should be slipped over each connection and the wires tied off.

solder pot. Once all solder pots are covered, spot tie the bundle just above the insulation tubing to keep it in place.

TERMINAL STRIPS

A terminal strip consists of a series of threaded studs that are mounted on a strip of insulating material. A typical terminal strip is made of a plastic or a paper-based phenolic compound that provides a high mechanical strength as well as good electrical insulation properties. In addition, most terminal strips have barriers between adjacent studs to keep the wires properly separated. [Figure 8-99]

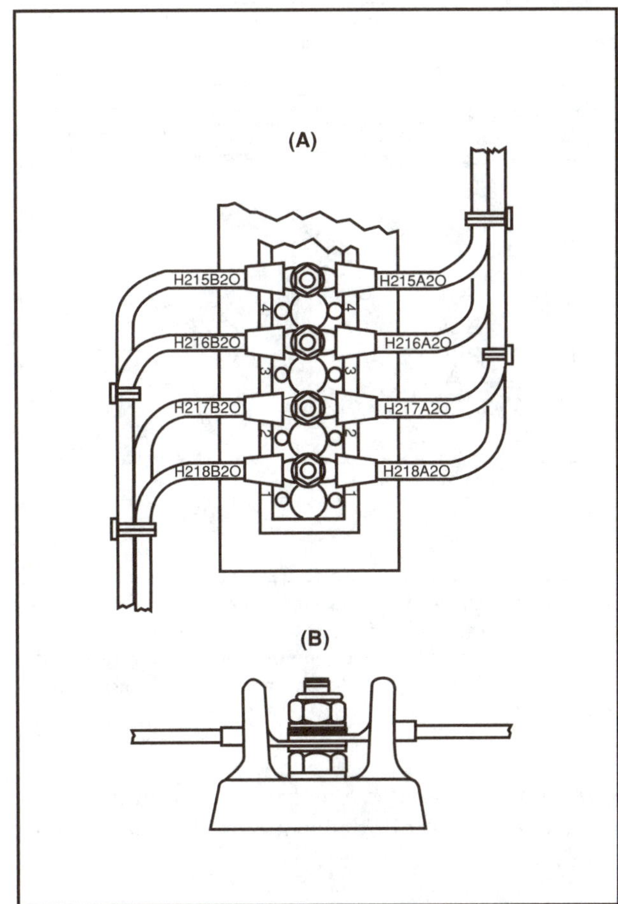

Figure 8-99. (A) — A common terminal strip used in aircraft consists of several studs set in a nonconductive base. (B) — To help prevent shorting between terminal connectors, most terminal strips have some sort of barrier between each stud.

The size of the studs on a terminal strip range from size 6 up to about 1/4-inch in diameter, with the smaller sizes suitable only for low current control circuits. The smallest terminal stud allowed for electrical power systems is a number 10. Terminal studs smaller than number 10 are seldom used in the powerplant portion of an electrical system since many of the circuits are electrical power circuits.

When attaching the terminal ends of a wire bundle to a terminal strip, fan the wires out from the bundle so the wires align with the terminal studs. A typical installation centers the wires and arranges them at right angles to the terminal strip. A short distance from the terminal strip, the wires are then turned 90 degrees to form a wire bundle.

Ideally, there should be only two wires attached to any one stud. However, the FAA allows up to four terminals to be stacked on any single stud. When attaching multiple terminals to one stud, or lug, the

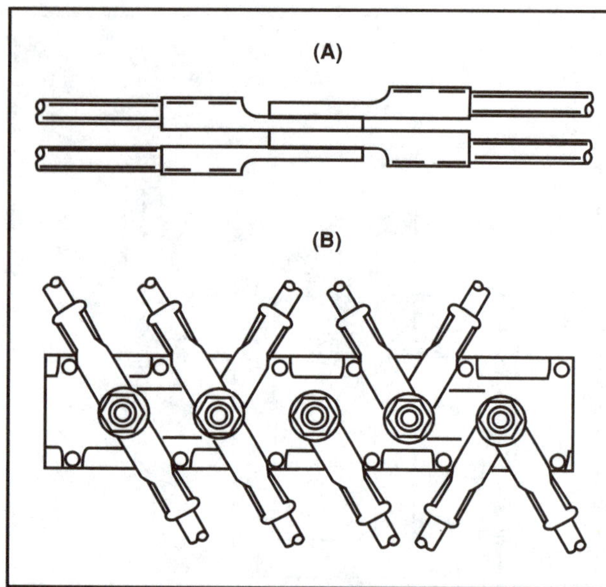

Figure 8-100. (A) — A typical method of attaching multiple wires to a terminal stud stacks and angles the wires out from each stud. (B) — Proper stacking of four terminals requires terminal tongues to be alternately placed up and down.

wires must be angled out from the terminal stud and stacked to avoid damaging the tongue of each terminal. [Figure 8-100]

JUNCTION BOXES

Junction boxes installed in aircraft powerplant compartments are typically made of an aluminum alloy or stainless steel. In addition, they are mounted in a way that minimizes the possibility of water getting into the box and causing electrical shorts or corrosion. Most junction boxes in powerplant compartments are mounted vertically to help prevent small hardware from becoming lodged between terminals and causing a short circuit or electrical fire.

Junction boxes should be isolated from electrical power whenever you are working in them. On occasions where it is necessary to apply power to circuits in a junction box for performing maintenance, be very cautious. A metal tool carelessly placed across several terminals could cause severe damage to the aircraft electrical system and components. In addition, remove any rings or a watch that you are wearing to avoid accidental shocks or burns.

BONDING

Bonding is a process that grounds all components in an aircraft together electrically. This prevents a difference in potential from building to the point that sparks jump from one component to another. For example, all the control surfaces on an aircraft are electrically grounded to the main aircraft structure with braided bonding straps. This helps prevent the inherent resistance in a control surface's hinge from insulating the control surface from the main structure. In the powerplant compartment, shock-mounted components are also bonded to the main structure with bonding straps.

Any electrical component which uses the aircraft structure as the return path for its current must be bonded to the structure. When selecting a bonding strap, it must be large enough to handle all the return current flow without producing an unacceptable voltage drop. An adequately bonded structure requires bonding straps that hold resistance readings to a negligible amount. For example, the resistance between any component and the aircraft structure must be three milliohms or less. In addition, a bonding strap must be long enough to allow free movement of a component as well as be made from a material which does not produce galvanic corrosion. [Figure 8-101]

The large flow of current from an electrical engine starter requires a heavy bonding strap between the engine and airframe. This is especially necessary on engines that are mounted in rubber shock mounts which have high electrical insulation properties. If a bonding strap is not installed between the engine and airframe, or if a break or extensive corrosion exists in an installed bonding strap, the risk of fire is greatly increased because much of the starter return current will be forced to pass through metal fuel and primer lines to reach ground.

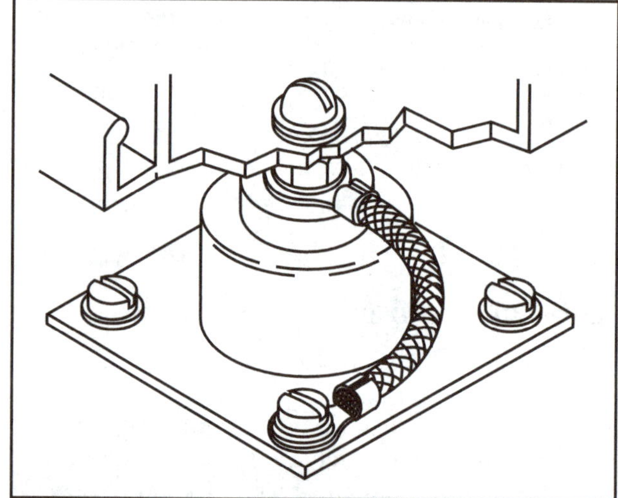

Figure 8-101. A braided bonding strap of adequate length and electrical capacity provides protection to shock-mounted components.

CIRCUIT PROTECTION

Electrical circuit protection devices are installed primarily to protect the wiring. To do this adequately, circuit protection devices should be located as close as possible to the electrical power source bus. The two types of circuit protection devices that are used on aircraft include circuit breakers and fuses. The exact type and size of circuit protection device required in a given electrical circuit is usually specified by the electrical equipment or aircraft manufacturer.

Since it is easier to reset a circuit breaker than replace a fuse, **circuit breakers** are used more than fuses as circuit protection devices in aircraft. The three basic types of circuit breakers used in aircraft electrical systems are the push-to-reset, push/pull, and toggle types. [Figure 8-102]

All aircraft circuit breakers are of the trip-free type which means that, once the breaker opens, the circuit remains open until the circuit cools regardless of the position of the operating control. With this type of breaker, it is impossible to hold the circuit closed if an actual fault exists.

Automatic reset circuit breakers automatically reset themselves after a cool-down period. However,

Figure 8-102. Most circuit protection for modern aircraft is provided by circuit breakers that can be reset in flight. The push/pull type is shown in the upper panel with the push-to-reset type in the lower panel.

FAR Part 23 requires manual reset of a tripped circuit breaker and prohibits the use of automatic reset types.

Although it is rare, some aircraft electrical circuits are protected with fuses. A **fuse** is made of a low-melting-point alloy enclosed in a glass tube. The fuse is installed in a circuit and, when current flow becomes excessive, the metal alloy melts and opens the circuit. Some fuses are designed to withstand a momentary surge of current, but create an open if the current is sustained. These slow-blow fuses have a small spring attached to a link so when the sustained current softens the link, the spring pulls the link apart and opens the circuit.

FAR Part 91 requires the operator of an aircraft using fuses as protective devices to carry a spare set. The spare set may consist of a complete replacement set of fuses or a quantity of three replacement fuses for each kind required.

A circuit breaker or fuse should open an electrical circuit before its conductors become hot enough to emit smoke. In order to achieve this, a circuit breaker or fuse is selected with time/current characteristics which fall below that of the associated conductor. Circuit protection should be matched to obtain maximum utilization of the equipment operated by the circuit. [Figure 8-103]

WIRE AND GAUGE COPPER	CIRCUIT BREAKER AMPERAGE	FUSE AMP
22	5	5
20	7.5	5
18	10	10
16	15	10
14	20	15
12	30	20
10	40	30
8	50	50
6	80	70
4	100	70
2	125	100
1		150
0		150

Figure 8-103. This chart is an example of the type used to select circuit breaker and fuse protection for copper conductors. Such charts are usually applicable to a specific set of ambient temperatures and wire bundle sizes.

NOMINAL SYSTEM VOLTAGE	TYPE OF LOAD	DERATING FACTOR
24 V.D.C.	LAMP	8
24 V.D.C.	INDUCTIVE (RELAY-SOLENOID)	4
24 V.D.C.	RESISTIVE (HEATER)	2
24 V.D.C.	MOTOR	3
12 V.D.C.	LAMP	5
12 V.D.C.	INDUCTIVE (RELAY-SOLENOID)	2
12 V.D.C.	RESISTIVE (HEATER)	1
12 V.D.C.	MOTOR	2

Figure 8-104. This sample switch derating chart is typical of the type used for selecting the proper nominal switch rating when the continuous load current is known.

SWITCHES

The purpose of a switch is to interrupt the flow of current to the component it controls. Switches are rated with regard to the voltage they can withstand and the current they can carry continuously. In most cases, a switch's rating is stamped on the switch housing.

When installing a switch in a circuit, the continuous current is not typically the limiting factor. For example, in circuit's having inductive loads, the continuous circuit is much less than the "rush-in" current required to initially power up the circuit. Therefore, any switch that is installed in an inductive circuit must be derated to prevent switch failure. [Figure 8-104]

SWITCH ORIENTATION

Hazardous errors in switch operation can be avoided by logical and consistent installation. For example, two position "on-off" switches should be mounted so that the "on" position is reached by an upward or forward movement of the toggle. In addition, switches that control movable aircraft components such as landing gear or flaps should be installed so the switch moves in the same direction as the desired motion.

Certain circuits must be operated only in an emergency. For these circuits, the switch is normally enclosed in a cover that must be lifted before the switch can be actuated. These switches are said to be guarded. If the circuit is one that could endanger a system if it were operated inadvertently, the cover may be safety-wired shut with a very light safety wire that can be broken if it becomes necessary to actuate the switch.

Specifically designed switches should be used in circuits where switch malfunctions or inadvertent activation would be hazardous. Such switches should be rugged and have sufficient contact capability to break, make, and carry the connected load current continuously.

RELAYS AND SOLENOIDS

Relays and solenoids allow electrical components to be controlled remotely. For example, with a solenoid, a very small switch can be used to control the high current needed to operate an aircraft engine starter. Relays and solenoids are quite similar, with only a mechanical difference. Normally a relay has a fixed soft iron core around which an electromagnetic coil is wound. Movable contacts are closed by the magnetic pull exerted by the core when the coil is energized, and are opened by a spring when the coil is de-energized. A solenoid, on the other hand, has a movable core that is pulled into the center of an electromagnetic coil when the coil is energized. Due to the movable core, solenoids typically respond quicker and are stronger than relays. Both relays and solenoids are used for electrical controls. Solenoids are typically used for high current applications and also find important use as mechanical control devices such as moving locking pins into and out of mechanically actuated devices. To eliminate the confusion between relays and solenoids, many aircraft manufacturers often refer to magnetically activated switches as contactors.

RECIPROCATING ENGINE IGNITION SYSTEMS

A typical ignition system must be capable of delivering a high voltage spark to each cylinder under all operating conditions. In addition, the spark must be created and delivered at the correct moment during the operating cycle. For example, if a particular engine fires 24 degrees before top dead center on the compression stroke, the ignition system must be able to deliver a spark at that specific time.

For obvious reasons, aircraft ignition systems must have a high degree of reliability. For this reason, FAR Part 33 states that "Each spark ignition engine must have a dual ignition system with at least two spark plugs for each cylinder and two separate electrical circuits with separate sources of electric energy, or have an ignition system of equivalent in-flight reliability." Several advantages are realized using two magneto systems; first, one magneto system serves as a backup if the other system fails, and second, it allows the use of two spark plugs in each cylinder which increases combustion efficiency and engine power output. Traditionally, the requirement for two separate sources of electric energy has been met using either a battery ignition system, a magneto ignition system, or a combination of the two.

BATTERY IGNITION SYSTEM

Some early aircraft engines utilized a battery as the source of electrical energy for one or both of the required ignition systems. This type of system is similar to that used in many automobiles. A typical battery ignition system consists of a battery, ignition coil, a set of breaker points, a cam, a capacitor, a distributor, and spark plugs. [Figure 8-105]

In a battery ignition system, the battery supplies current to the primary winding of an ignition coil. The **ignition coil** then steps up the voltage to the level necessary to create a spark in each cylinder. However, if you recall from your studies of coils, in order for a coil to step up voltage, the current flowing through the primary winding of the coil must pulsate. To convert the pure DC provided by a battery to pulsating DC, a set of **breaker points**, or **contacts**, are connected in series with the primary winding. Breaker points are a mechanical device consisting of two electrical contacts that are opened and closed at regular intervals to control when current flows through the primary winding. When the contacts are closed, the electrical circuit is complete

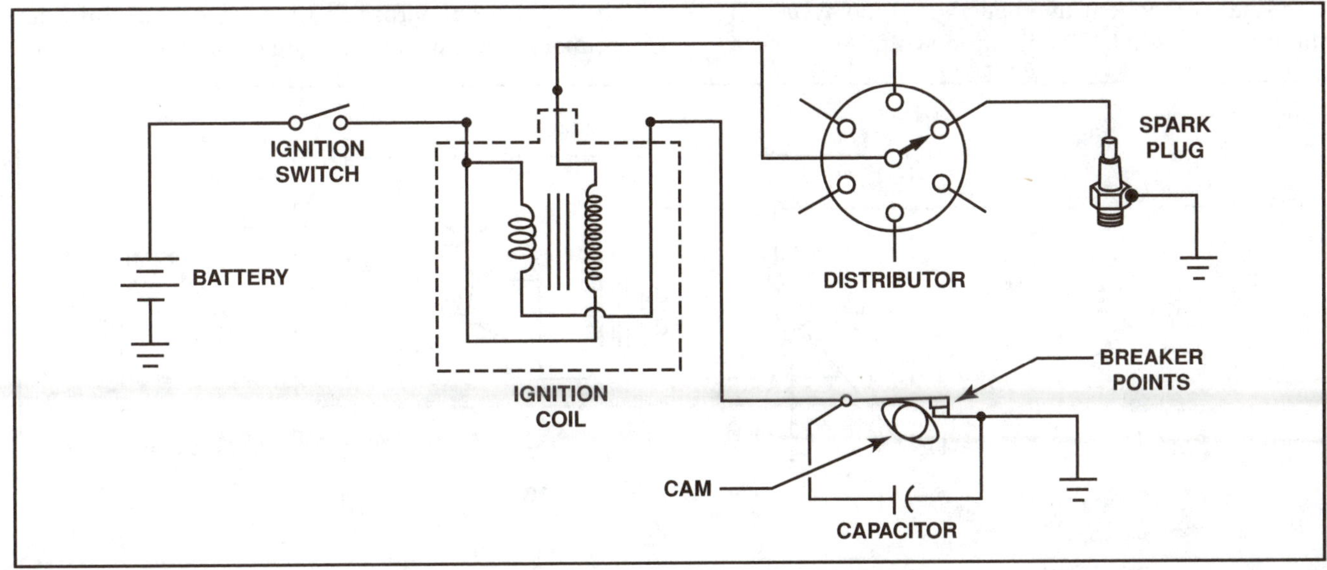

Figure 8-105. The major components in a battery ignition system include a battery, ignition coil, a set of breaker points, a cam, a capacitor, a distributor, and spark plugs.

and current flows through the primary winding. However, when the contacts are opened, the circuit is interrupted, and the magnetic field surrounding the primary winding collapses. As the magnetic field collapses, current is induced into the ignition coil's secondary winding.

In order to prevent arcing across the points when they open and increase the rate the magnetic field in the primary winding collapses, a capacitor, or **condenser**, is placed across the breaker points. If you recall from your studies on basic electricity, the faster a magnetic field collapses, the more current it can induce.

The device that opens and closes the points is called a **cam** and consists of a metal disc with two or more raised lobes. As the cam rotates, the lobes force the points apart to interrupt current flow in the primary winding. However, once the cam rotates to its low cam position, spring pressure forces the points closed again to complete the primary circuit and permit current to flow through the primary winding.

As current is induced into the secondary winding of the ignition coil, its voltage is stepped up and sent to the distributor. The **distributor** distributes the high voltage produced by the ignition coil to the spark plugs. A distributor consists of two components; a rotating finger and a distributor block. The rotating finger rotates within the distributor block and distributes the voltage produced by the ignition coil to the contacts mounted in the distributor block. From here, the voltage passes through individual ignition leads to the spark plugs.

The final component in a battery ignition system is the ignition switch. The ignition switch provides a means of controlling when an ignition system is active. For example, in a battery ignition system, when the ignition switch is "on" and the breaker points are closed, battery current flows through the ignition coil's primary circuit. However, when the ignition switch is "off," the primary circuit is opened, disabling the system.

MAGNETO IGNITION SYSTEMS

Today, nearly all aircraft reciprocating engines utilize a magneto ignition system. A **magneto** is basically a permanent-magnet AC generator that uses electromagnetic and induced current principles to develop high voltage energy to fire a set of spark plugs. All magneto systems are designated as either high-tension or low-tension systems.

HIGH-TENSION SYSTEMS

The basic components of a high-tension magneto system include a single high-tension magneto, a wiring harness, and a set of spark plugs. Unlike the battery ignition system, the magneto in a high-tension system utilizes a rotating magnet instead of a battery to induce voltage into an ignition, or **magneto coil**. The coil steps up the voltage just before it reaches the distributor and is distributed to the spark plugs. This results in a constant voltage from the magneto to the spark plugs. [Figure 8-106]

Currently, high-tension magnetos are available in either a single magneto or dual magneto configuration. A **single magneto** consists of a permanent magnet having two, four, or eight poles that are fixed to a single rotating shaft. The flux lines produced by the magnet cut across and induce current into the primary winding of the magneto coil. Once induced,

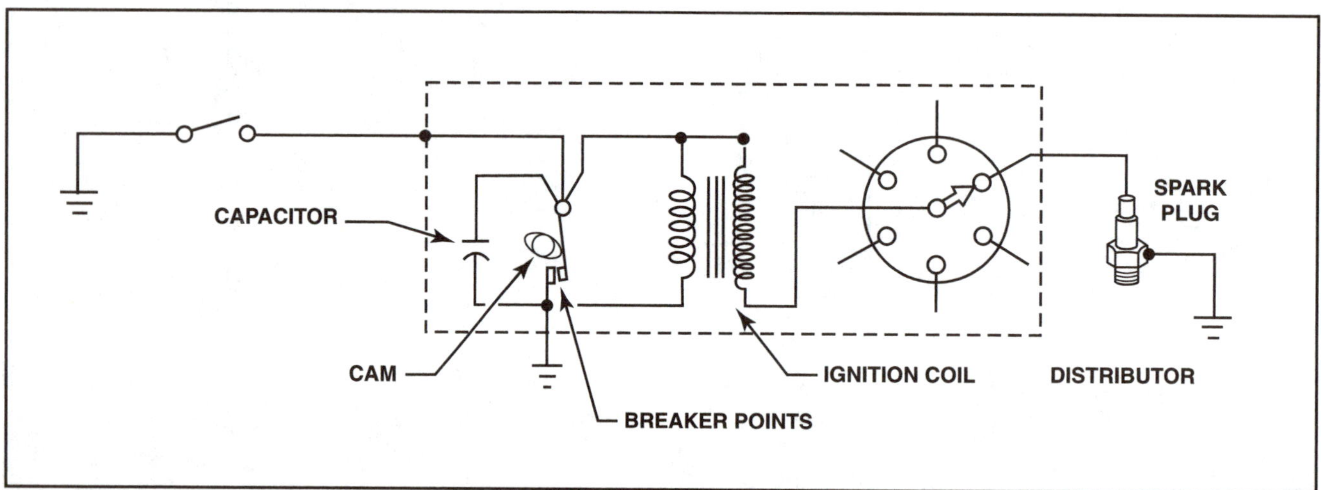

Figure 8-106. High-tension magneto systems generate high voltage energy using a magneto coil within the magneto housing. The high voltage pulses are then routed to the spark plugs through a distributor block and ignition leads.

Figure 8-107. A single magneto consists of a multi-pole magnet that induces current into a magneto coil. Once induced, the current is stepped up and distributed to the spark plugs.

the current is stepped up and distributed to the spark plugs. To comply with the requirement for a dual system, two single magnetos must be installed on a single engine. [Figure 8-107]

A **dual magneto** differs from a single magneto in that one housing contains two independent ignition systems that share a common rotating magnet. In other words, a dual magneto contains two of everything except the rotating magnet and cam. [Figure 8-108.]

Early high-tension magneto systems had problems associated with the production and distribution of high voltage pulses to the spark plugs. One of the main problems was known as flashover. **Flashover** is a term used to describe an occurrence inside a high-tension magneto where a spark jumps to the wrong electrode in the distributor block. High altitude operations increase the likelihood of flashover due to lower air density. The less dense the air, the less dielectric, or insulating strength the air has. Flashover can lead to **carbon tracking** which appears as a fine pencil-like carbon trail inside the distributor. Over time, carbon tracks can form a conductive path to ground, increasing the possibility of flashover.

Over the years, several design changes were made to prevent flashover inside a high-tension magneto. For example, some magneto manufacturers made their distributors larger to increase the distance a spark would have to jump. Others relied on a low-

Figure 8-108. The Bendix D-3000 dual magneto contains two separate and independent ignition systems that share a common four pole rotating magnet.

tension magneto system that distributed a relatively low voltage to a high-tension transformer near each spark plug. However, these measures were only partially effective. The most success in overcoming flashover came with the invention and use of improved ignition component materials with better insulation properties. In addition, the practice of pressurizing magnetos greatly improved ignition system performance at high altitudes. With a pressurized magneto, a regulated air source pumps air into the magneto housing to maintain a pressure above ambient. This made it more difficult for a spark to jump.

LOW-TENSION SYSTEMS

The low-tension magneto system was originally designed as a means of overcoming the problem of flashover experienced in early high-tension magnetos. A low-tension magneto differs from a high-tension magneto in that the magneto coil has only one winding. As a result, relatively low voltage is produced by the magneto and flashover is kept to a minimum.

To boost the voltage enough to create a spark, all low-tension systems utilize several high-tension transformers mounted on the cylinders near each

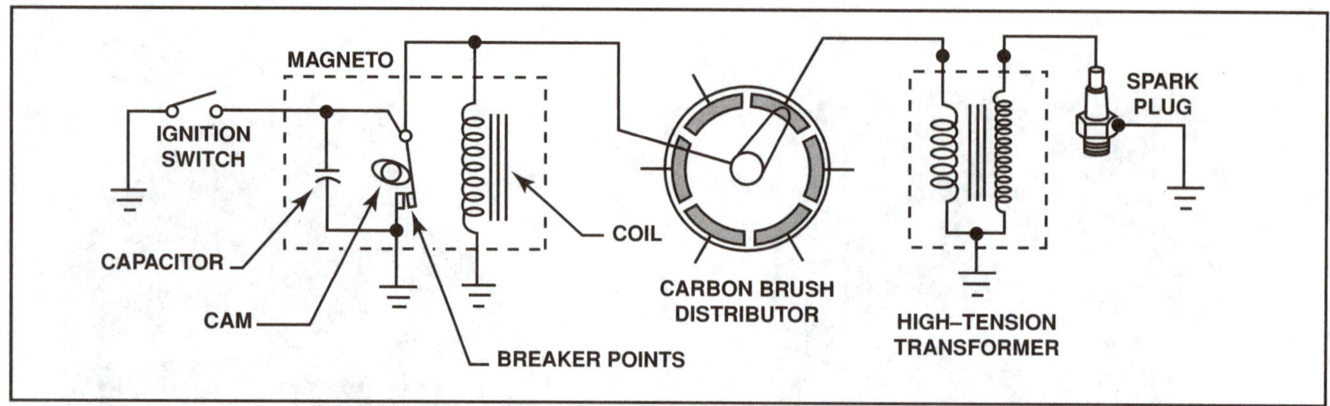

Figure 8-109. A low-tension magneto utilizes a magneto coil that has only one winding. As a result, the magneto produces and distributes a relatively low voltage that is stepped up by a high-tension transformer just before it reaches the spark plugs.

spark plug. Each transformer contains a primary coil and a secondary coil which boosts the magneto voltage enough to create a spark. [Figure 8-109]

Although low-tension magneto circuits overcame some of the problems intrinsic to older high-tension systems, they still had some limitations. For example, there are more components in a low-tension system. This is especially true on large radial engines where each cylinder requires one transformer for each spark plug.

Low-tension ignition systems were originally built for large 18 and 24 cylinder radial engines and, therefore, the demand for low-tension systems has largely disappeared. In addition, new construction materials and techniques have all but eliminated the need for a low-tension system.

MAGNETO OPERATING PRINCIPLES

High- and low-tension magneto systems operate on the same principle for generating electrical energy. However, since low-tension systems are not used in modern aircraft, the following discussion on operating principles focuses on a typical high-tension magneto.

A high-tension magneto consists of a mechanical system and three distinct circuits; a magnetic circuit, a primary electrical circuit, and a secondary electrical circuit. The operation of these circuits is controlled with a cockpit mounted ignition switch.

THE MECHANICAL SYSTEM

The mechanical system of a magneto includes the housing, the magneto drive shaft, and all of the non-electrical portions of the magneto. Most magnetos are encased in an aluminum alloy housing that mounts to an engine. Housings are made from an aluminum alloy because they will not interfere with the magnetic circuit. In addition, aluminum provides mechanical strength and rigidity for the mounting and is relatively light weight.

Magneto housings are designed with two different types of mounting provisions; base mount and flange mount. **Base-mounted** magnetos are bolted rigidly to a bracket on the engine accessory case. This type of mount is typically found on early radial engines. **Flange-mounted** magnetos, on the other hand, are more common and are used on horizontally opposed engines. The mounting flange on this type of magneto is cast as an integral part of the magneto housing. One type of flange-mount attaches to an engine with mounting bolts that pass through banana shaped slots. Another type of mount uses two L-shaped lockdown tabs to clamp the flange to the engine. Bolts pass through the tabs into threaded holes in the engine accessory case. [Figure 8-110]

Protruding from one end of a magneto's housing is a single hardened steel shaft that runs the length of the magneto. Mounted to this shaft inside the magneto are the rotating magnet, a gear that drives the distributor finger, and a cam. The shaft itself is typically supported by either ball or needle bearings.

There are two types of cams used in high-tension magnetos: uncompensated and compensated. An **uncompensated cam** is used for most modern reciprocating engines. This cam has a uniform distance between cam lobes because the number of degrees of crankshaft rotation between the firing of each

Figure 8-110. Both types of flange mounts used on magnetos allow the magneto to be rotated slightly so you can time the magneto to the engine.

spark plug is uniform. The number of lobes on an uncompensated cam is equal to the number of poles on the rotating magnet. This type of cam is normally mounted to the end of the rotating magneto shaft drive.

A **compensated cam** is used in magnetos installed on radial engines. With this type of cam, a separate cam lobe is provided for each cylinder. This is necessary because the number of degrees between spark plug firing events is not uniform. Unlike other reciprocating engines, the number of degrees of crankshaft rotation between cylinders reaching top dead center on a radial engine varies. This is caused by the elliptical path that link rods must follow. Therefore, compensation is provided by varying the distance between the cam lobes so each spark plug can fire at the proper time. The spacing between each lobe is tailored to a particular cylinder of a particular engine.

Since a compensated cam has one lobe for each cylinder, the cam must complete one revolution for every two revolutions of the crankshaft. Because of this, compensated cams are usually driven by a gear assembly.

THE MAGNETIC CIRCUIT

The magnetic circuit consists of a rotating permanent magnet, pole shoes, pole shoe extensions, and a coil core. A rotating magnet may have two, four, or eight magnetic poles. Magnets with more than two poles are arranged with alternating north and south poles that are spaced evenly around the magneto drive shaft. For example, on a four-pole magnet, all the poles are 90 degrees apart with both the two north and two south poles opposite each other. On an eight-pole magnet all the poles are 45 degrees apart.

Rotating magnets are often made from **Alnico**, an alloy of aluminum, iron, nickel, and cobalt. Due to its excellent magnetic properties, Alnico retains magnetism for an indefinite length of time. **Permalloy** is another alloy with similar qualities commonly used for rotating magnet construction.

The rotating magnet in a magneto is geared to the engine and rotates between two pole shoes. To complete the circuit, the pole shoes are joined at one end by the magneto coil core. Both the pole shoes and the coil core are constructed of several laminated layers of high-grade soft iron. The laminate architecture reduces eddy currents, keeping the magneto cooler and boosting efficiency. In addition, soft iron has a high permeability which allows flux lines to pass through it easily. [Figure 8-111]

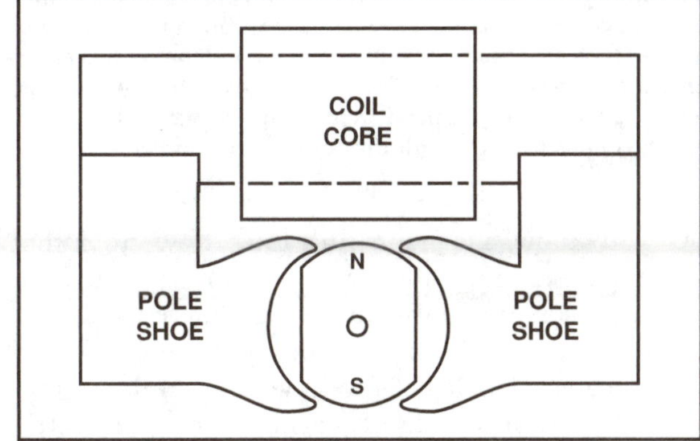

Figure 8-111. The components in a magnetic circuit include a rotating magnet, a set of pole shoes, and a coil core.

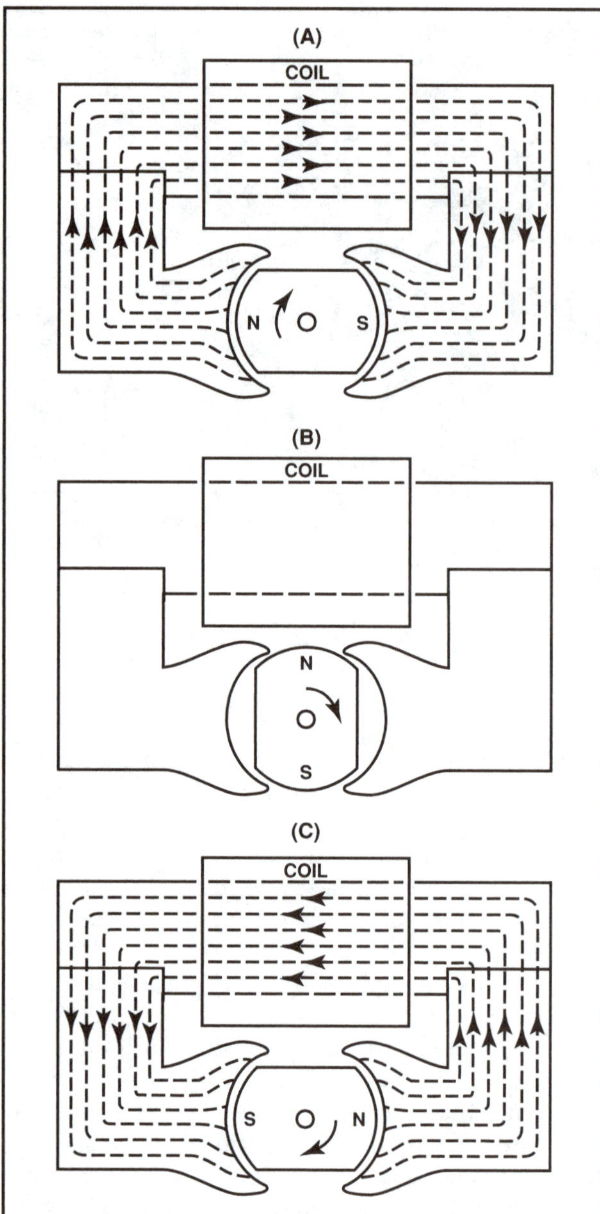

Figure 8-112. (A) — When the magnetic poles are aligned with the pole shoes, the magnet is in the full register position and the maximum number of flux lines flow through the coil core. (B) — However, when the magnetic poles are in the neutral position, no lines of flux pass through the coil core. (C) — Once past the neutral position, the number of flux lines passing through the coil's core increases until the magnet reaches the full register position again. However, this time the flux lines pass through the coil core the opposite way.

As you know, magnetic flux lines flow from the north pole to the south pole. Therefore, each time a pair of magnetic poles line up with the pole shoes, magnetic lines of flux flow through the coil core. The greatest density of flux lines flow through the coil core when a pair of magnetic poles are fully aligned with the pole shoes. This position is known as the **full register position** and it is at this position that the magnetic field is the strongest. As a magnet rotates beyond full register, the magnetic field slowly collapses until no lines of flux pass through the coil core. This position is the **neutral position** and represents the point where the magnetic field flowing through the coil is at its weakest point. Continued rotation of the magnet again aligns the magnetic poles with the pole shoes in the full register position. However, the orientation of the poles is opposite and, therefore, the flux lines flow in the opposite direction. [Figure 8-112]

One revolution of a two pole magnet produces two positions of maximum flux line concentration and two positions of zero flux flow in the coil core. In addition, the direction of flux travel reverses twice. Therefore, as a magnet rotates in a magneto, it produces a magnetic field that is continuously expanding and collapsing. This pulsating magnetic field induces current into the primary winding.

If you recall, when current flows through a conductor, a magnetic field is produced. This magnetic field resists changes in current flow. Therefore, as the rotating magnet induces current flow into the primary winding, the magnetic field produced by the initial current flow opposes additional current flow. However, once the flux density reaches its highest point and the magnetic field produced by the rotating magnet starts to collapse, the electromagnetic field produced by current flow attempts to sustain the collapsing field. In other words, primary current attempts to hold the flux in the core at a high value until the rotating magnet reaches the neutral position. [Figure 8-113]

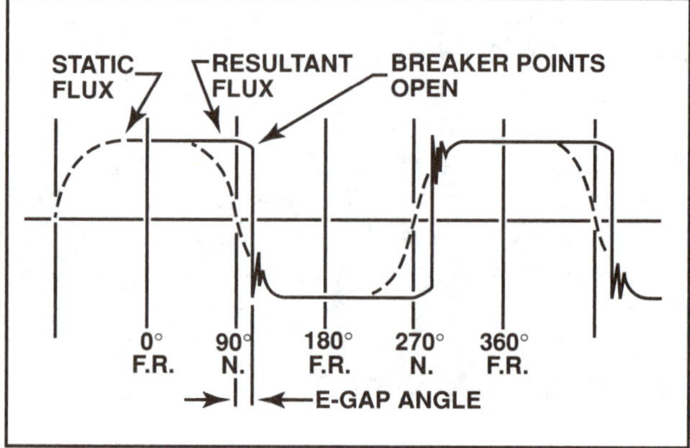

Figure 8-113. The static flux curve represents changes in flux concentration caused by magnet rotation with no current flow in the primary winding. When the primary circuit is completed and current flows, the combined effects of magnet rotation and current flow flatten the curve. The flux from the magnetic field produced by current flow combines with the flux produced by the rotating magnet to delay the collapse of the magnetic field.

Once a magnet rotates beyond magnetic neutral, a magnetic field of opposite polarity starts to build. At this point, the greatest magnetic field stress exists. The specific number of degrees beyond the neutral position where this occurs is known as the **efficiency gap**, or **E-gap angle**.

THE PRIMARY CIRCUIT

The primary electrical circuit in a magneto consists of the primary winding of an insulated magneto coil, a set of breaker points, and a capacitor. The primary winding in a typical magneto coil consists of 180 to 200 turns of 18 gauge copper wire. The wire is coated with an enamel insulation and is wound directly over the laminated core in the magnetic circuit. One end of the primary winding is attached to a ground lead while the other end connects to one end of the secondary winding and the ungrounded, or insulated, side of the breaker points. [Figure 8-114]

The breaker points are normally mounted to the magneto housing and held closed by a leaf-type spring. To open the points, a cam mounted on the end of the rotating magnet shaft is used to force one contact away from the other.

To allow the magnet to induce the maximum amount of current into the primary winding, the points are forced open when the greatest magnetic field stress exists. If you recall, the point where the greatest stress exists is the E-gap position. Opening the breaker points at this time interrupts the current flow in the primary circuit and allows current to be induced into the secondary coil. In addition, once the points close, the magnet is near the full register position so there is a quick reversal of the magnetic field in the coil core. The sudden flux reversal causes a high rate of flux change in the core.

Any time moving contact points interrupt a flow of current, an arc is produced between the points. As the points begin to separate, the electrical resistance of the points increases and the current flowing through the resistance produces heat. This heat becomes so intense that it ionizes the air allowing current to flow through it in the form of an arc. When arcing occurs, it delays the collapse of the magnetic field in the primary winding and causes metal to transfer from one breaker point to the other. If arcing is severe enough, it could weld the points together.

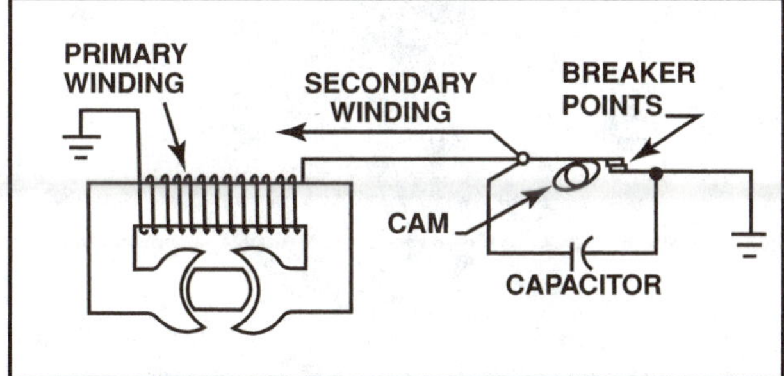

Figure 8-114. The primary circuit in a magneto consists of the primary winding of a magneto coil, a set of breaker points, and a capacitor.

To reduce arcing, a capacitor is installed in parallel with the points. With a capacitor installed, electrons flow into the capacitor when the points begin to open. By the time the capacitor is charged up enough to stop the flow of electrons, the points have opened far enough that no arcing can occur. With the flow of electrons in the primary winding stopped, the magnetic field collapses rapidly and induces a high voltage pulse into the secondary circuit.

In addition to accelerating field collapse and preventing arcing, the capacitor in some magnetos helps to reduce electromagnetic radiation from the primary lead. To do this, the capacitor is installed in parallel with the breaker points and in series with the ignition switch. Typically, this type of capacitor has a pigtail lead that connects to the insulated breaker point and a threaded terminal that connects to the ignition switch lead. When installed in a magneto, the capacitor's metal case grounds to the magneto housing. With this type of capacitor, any radio frequency energy that is induced into the primary lead when the points open is carried to ground before it leaves the magneto. This type of capacitor is known as a feed-through or filter capacitor. [Figure 8-115]

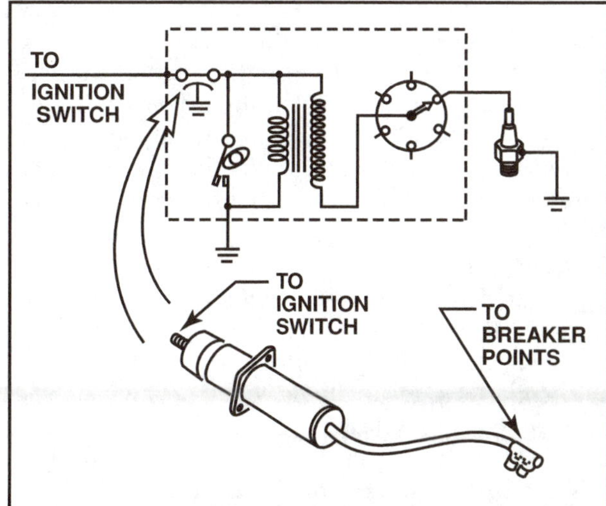

Figure 8-115. Some magnetos utilize a special feed-through capacitor to help reduce electrical noise generated by the breaker points. This helps to protect electronic equipment from voltage spikes.

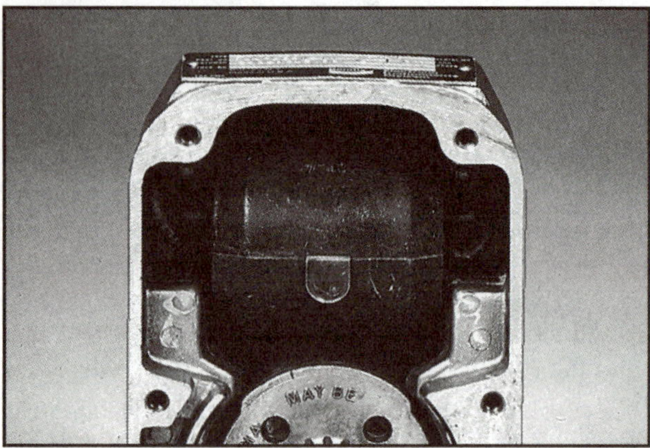

Figure 8-116. The high-tension terminal that is connected to the secondary winding appears as a tab that protrudes from the magneto coil. To insulate the primary and secondary winding, the entire magneto coil is typically encased in Bakelite™, varnished cambric, or some type of thermosetting plastic.

THE SECONDARY CIRCUIT

The secondary circuit of a magneto is the circuit which produces the high voltage energy required to cause a spark. The circuit components within the magneto that make up the secondary circuit include the secondary winding in the magneto coil and the distributor.

The amount of current induced into the secondary winding of a magneto coil is directly related to two factors; the rate at which the magnetic field around the primary winding collapses and the ratio of windings between the primary and secondary. Therefore, the secondary winding in a magneto coil is made from approximately 13,000 turns of very fine wire. This produces a turn ratio between the primary and secondary windings that is capable of producing a 20,000 volt pulse. One end of the secondary winding is attached to the primary winding to provide a path to ground while the opposite end is attached to a high voltage contact that protrudes from the magneto coil body. [Figure 8-116]

To allow current to flow from the secondary winding to the distributor, a spring loaded carbon brush mounted in the center of the distributor rotor presses against the high voltage contact on the magneto coil. As a result, high voltage energy passes through the carbon brush into the distributor rotor. The distributor rotor in a typical magneto consists of a conductive arm, or finger that carries the high voltage current to the electrodes for each spark plug in the distributor block. The rotor is driven by a gear that is mounted to the magneto drive shaft. [Figure 8-117]

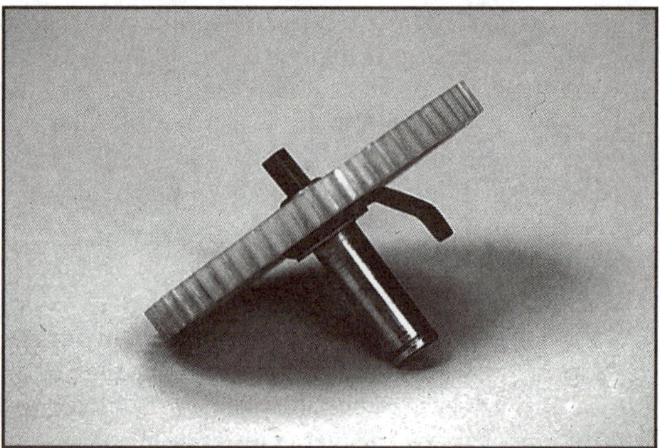

Figure 8-117. In a typical magneto, current is routed to the distributor rotor through a small carbon brush. From the distributor rotor, current is passed to the distributor block through a distributor finger.

The distributor rotor is geared to provide a high voltage path to the distributor block at definite points in its rotation. In fact, to allow an aircraft engine to operate, the distributor rotor must complete one revolution for every two revolutions of the crankshaft. With this 2:1 ratio, a magneto can fire all the spark plugs once for each 720 degrees of crankshaft rotation.

A typical distributor block is constructed of a lightweight insulating material and is mounted in one half of the magneto housing. One side of the distributor has a set of electrodes while the other side has a corresponding set of receptacles for receiving the spark plug leads. The electrodes and receptacles are arranged circumferentially around the distributor block. Each time the rotating magnet is in the E-gap position, the distributor finger lines up with an electrode on the distributor and delivers a high voltage pulse. [Figure 8-118]

Figure 8-118. The distributor block on a typical magneto is made of insulating material with electrodes on one side and spark plug wire receptacles on the other.

Once current reaches the distributor block, it is immediately routed through the spark plug leads to the spark plugs. At each spark plug, the current jumps the air gap between the center and ground electrodes thereby completing the electrical circuit from the spark plug back to the magneto.

SAFETY GAP

To help protect the secondary winding in a magneto coil, some magnetos provide an alternate path for current if there is an open in the secondary circuit. This backup ground path is called a **safety gap** and is connected in series with the secondary winding by two electrodes. One electrode is connected to a high-tension brush holder, while the other is connected to a ground plate. In this configuration, if the path to the spark plug gap becomes interrupted, the excessive voltage induced into the secondary winding jumps the safety gap to ground. This helps ensure that the voltage in the secondary winding does not rise high enough to damage the magneto coil.

MAGNETO SPEED

As mentioned earlier, the distributor rotor in a magneto always rotates at one-half the engine crankshaft speed. This is necessary because the engine crankshaft must complete two revolutions in order to fire each spark plug once. Although the rotational speed of the distributor is set, the speed of the rotating magnet shaft varies with the number of cylinders on the engine and number of poles on the rotating magnet. To determine the relationship between magneto speed and engine crankshaft speed, use the following formula:

$$\frac{\text{Number of cylinders}}{\text{2 x number of poles}}$$

For example, assume a six-cylinder engine uses a magneto with a two-pole magnet. Using the formula above, the magneto speed is determined to be $1^1/_2$ times the crankshaft speed.

$$\frac{6}{2 \times 2} = \frac{6}{4}$$

$$= \frac{3}{2}$$

$$= 1\frac{1}{2}$$

Based on this, when the engine is turning at 2,000 rpm, the magneto shaft is rotating at 3,000 rpm.

AUXILIARY IGNITION SYSTEMS

One of the primary limitations of magnetos is that, when the magnet inside a magneto turns at a slow speed, the magneto produces relatively little voltage. However, as magneto speed increases, the amount of current induced into the primary circuit increases and the magneto produces a higher voltage spark.

In most cases, the voltage generated at low magneto speeds is insufficient to fire a spark plug. The speed at which a magneto must rotate to produce enough voltage to fire a spark plug is known as a magneto's **coming-in speed**. Although the coming-in speed of different magnetos varies, a typical speed is between 100 and 200 rpm.

When attempting to start an engine, the starter motor cannot crank the engine fast enough for a magneto to reach its coming-in speed. In addition, since the spark event normally occurs prior to top dead center on the compression stroke, normal ignition timing can cause an engine to kick back when it is started. To help prevent engine kick back, some magnetos use a second set of **retard breaker points** to retard the spark during engine starting. The term **retard** indicates that the spark is delayed until later in the combustion cycle. In most cases, the spark is retarded until after the piston reaches top dead center on the compression stroke.

Although retarded ignition promotes easier starting, it does nothing to increase the voltage a magneto generates at slow rotational speeds. To do this, almost all magnetos incorporate some form of **ignition booster** or **auxiliary ignition unit**. Some of the more common ignition boosters include the impulse coupling, induction vibrator, shower of sparks ignition system, and booster magneto.

IMPULSE COUPLINGS

Impulse couplings are one of the most widely used auxiliary ignition devices found on magnetos. An impulse coupling is a small spring-loaded device that provides a magneto with a momentary high rotational speed and a retarded spark. To do this, an impulse coupling uses a spring loaded mechanical linkage that is wound up by the magneto drive gear and then released to momentarily increase the magneto's rotational speed. The components that make up an impulse coupling include the impulse coupling

Figure 8-119. The basic components of an impulse coupling include a body, or housing, a set of flyweights mounted to a cam, and a spring.

body, a set of flyweights mounted to a cam, and a coiled spring. [Figure 8-119]

The cam assembly of an impulse coupling is keyed to the magneto shaft while the impulse coupling body rotates with the engine. When assembled, the coiled spring inside an impulse coupling links the cam assembly and body together. When an engine is being turned by a starter, the flyweights on the impulse coupling contact stop pins on the magneto housing. The stop pins stop magneto shaft rotation while the engine continues to rotate and wind up the impulse coupling spring. At the same time that engine rotation brings a piston to top dead center, a projection on the impulse coupling body contacts a **trigger ramp** on the flyweights, forcing the flyweights off the stop pins. This releases the stored spring force and accelerates the magneto shaft fast enough to produce a high voltage, retarded spark. [Figure 8-120]

An impulse coupling produces a high voltage spark for every spark plug during the starting process. However, once an engine starts and the magneto begins spinning fast enough to provide a high voltage spark on its own, centrifugal force pulls the heel of the flyweights outward so they can no longer contact the stop pins. At this point, the impulse coupling is disabled and the sparks produced by the magneto revert back to their normal advanced timing.

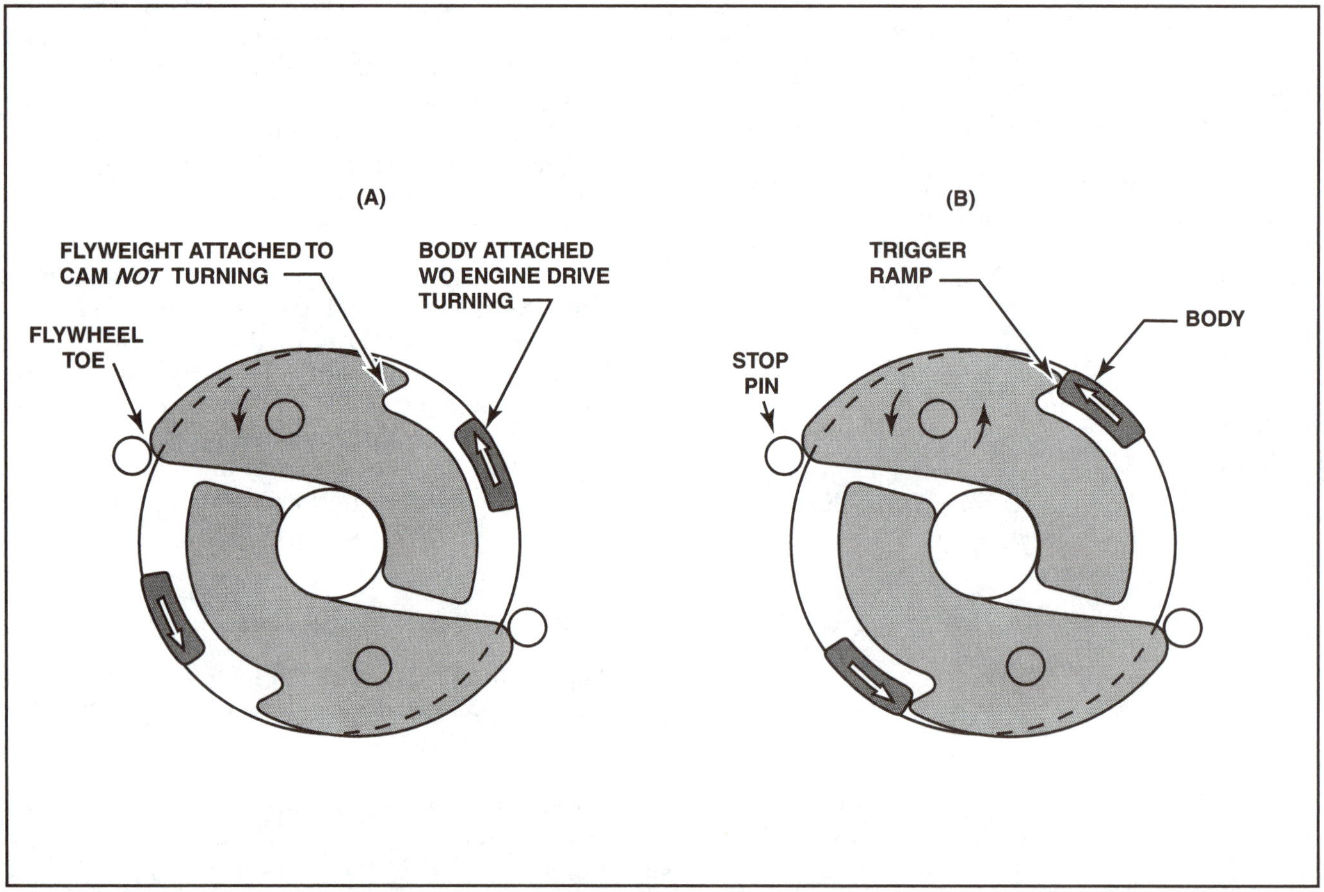

(A)

FLYWEIGHT ATTACHED TO CAM *NOT* TURNING

BODY ATTACHED WO ENGINE DRIVE TURNING

FLYWHEEL TOE

(B)

TRIGGER RAMP

BODY

STOP PIN

Figure 8-120. (A) — When the flyweights contact the stop pins, the magneto stops spinning while the engine continues to rotate the impulse coupling body. (B) — Once the body extensions contact the trigger ramp on each flyweight, the flyweights pivot off the stop pins and spring tension rotates the magnet inside the magneto at a high speed.

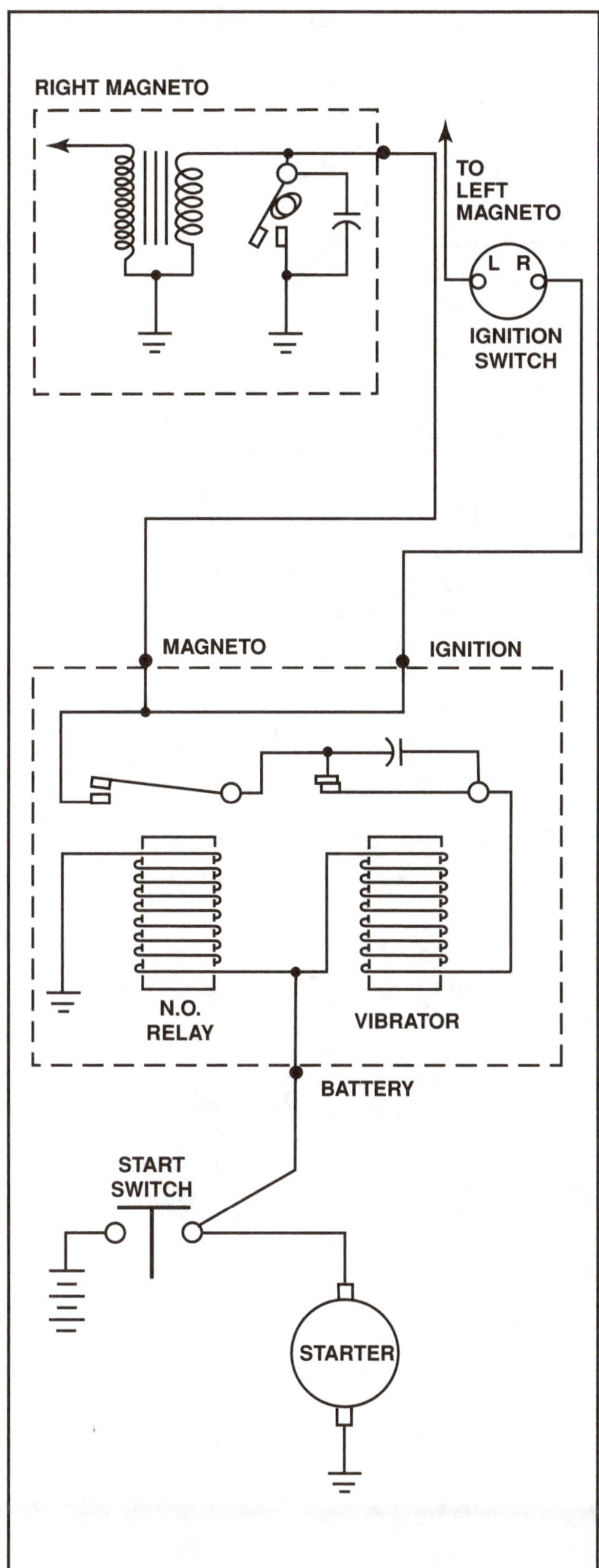

Figure 8-121. In an ignition system equipped with an induction vibrator, when the starter switch is closed, battery current flows into the induction vibrator. This closes a normally open relay and allows the vibrator coil to start producing pulsating DC that flows to the primary winding of the magneto coil.

INDUCTION VIBRATOR

Another type of auxiliary ignition unit is known as an **induction vibrator**. An induction vibrator supplies pulsating direct current to the primary winding of a magneto coil. As you know, any time pulsating current flows through the primary winding, current is induced into the secondary winding. The faster the pulsating DC, the greater the current induced into the secondary winding for starting. The frequency of the pulsating direct current is determined by the induction vibrator.

A typical induction vibrator operates whenever the engine starter switch is held in the "start," or "engage" position. With the switch in this position, battery current flows into the induction vibrator and pulsating current is produced. [Figure 8-121]

When the magneto breaker points are closed, the current produced by the vibrator coil flows to ground through the points. However, when the breaker points open, the pulsating DC flows through the primary winding. This allows the magneto to produce high voltage pulses that are sent to the distributor block for distribution to a spark plug. The frequency of the pulses produced by the vibrator coil allow multiple sparks to be produced at a spark plug as long as the points remain open. As soon as the points close, the pulsating current produced by the vibrator coil is again routed to ground. This process is repeated each time the breaker points open and pulsating current flows to the primary winding. Once the engine starts and the starter switch is disengaged, current stops flowing to the induction vibrator.

SHOWER OF SPARKS

A more modern version of the induction vibrator is know as the shower of sparks ignition system. This system works the same as the induction vibrator system except that, with the shower of sparks system, a set of retard breaker points are provided to retard the spark while the engine is being cranked. In most cases, the retard breaker points are located in the left magneto with the advance points. With this type of system, when the magneto switch is in the "start" position, a relay in the starting vibrator grounds the right magneto and provides pulsating current to the left magneto. However, since both the retard and advance points provide a path to ground for the starting vibrator current, both sets of points must be open before pulsating current flows to the primary winding. [Figure 8-122]

After the engine starts and the ignition switch is turned to the "both" position, battery power is removed from the starting vibrator. In addition, the right magneto is ungrounded and the retard points in the left magneto are electrically disconnected. At this point, both magnetos operate normally and produce advanced spark ignition.

In most cases, the starting vibrator used in a shower of sparks system is mounted to the aircraft firewall.

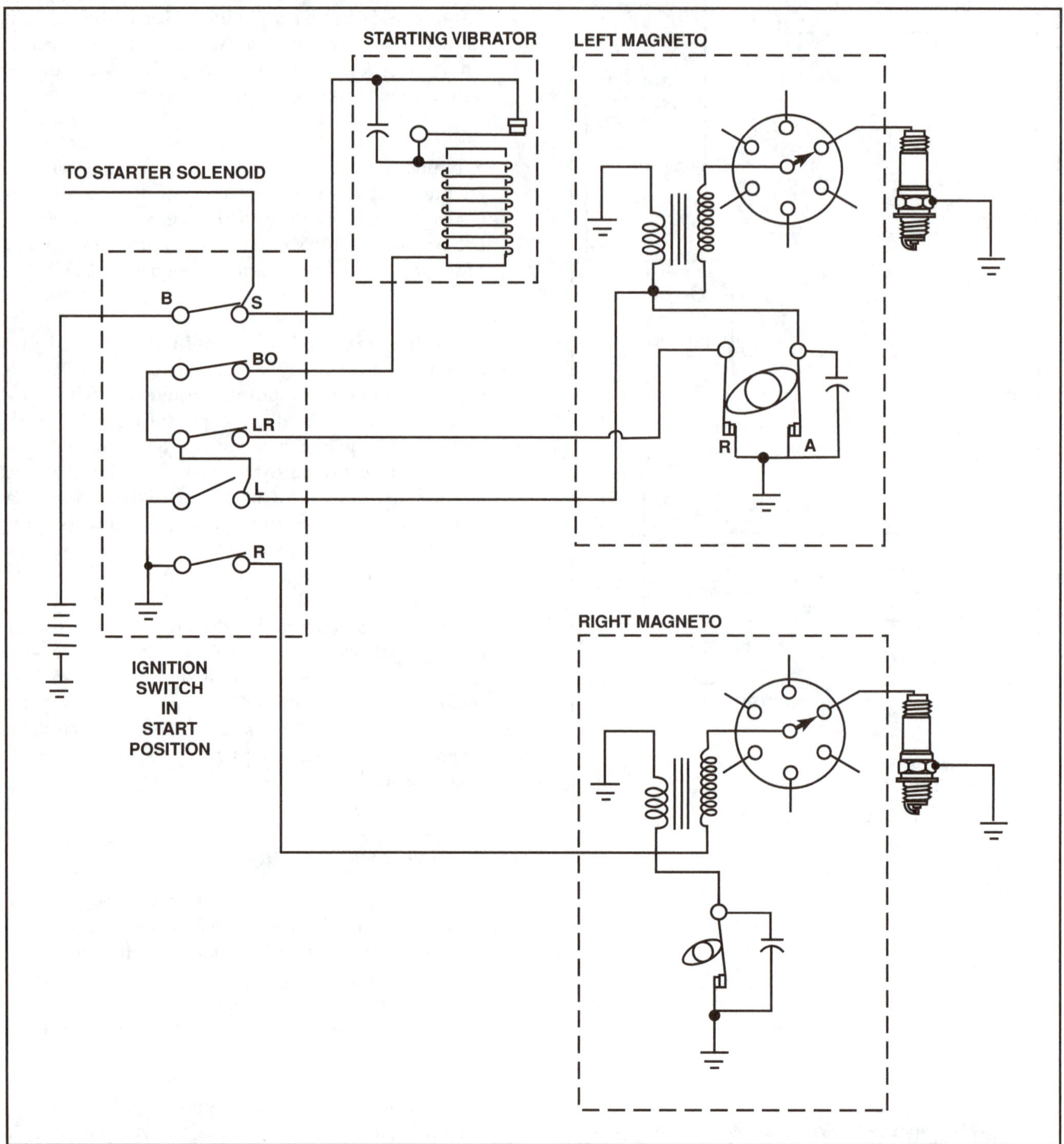

Figure 8-122. In the "start" position, battery power is applied to the starting vibrator and the right magneto is grounded. Once pulsating current is produced in the vibrator, it flows to the left magneto. Once both sets of points open, vibrator current flows to the primary winding and high voltage pulses are created. The distributor sends the high voltage pulses to the proper spark plug where a "shower of sparks" are produced.

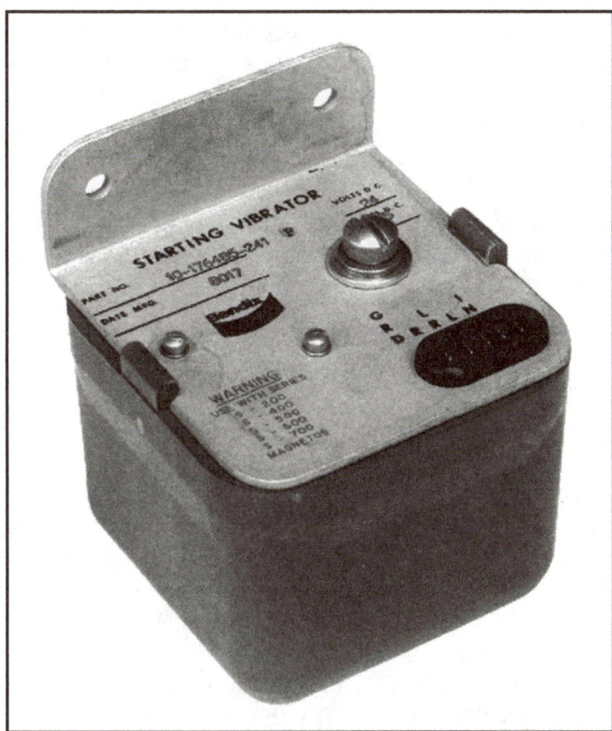

Figure 8-123. A typical vibrator unit consists of several solid state components that are sealed in a case and mounted to the aircraft's firewall.

In addition, several of the components used are solid state so there is little you can do for maintenance. Typically, if a component fails, the entire unit must be removed and replaced. [Figure 8-123]

BOOSTER MAGNETOS

Although booster magnetos are not used much today, they were widely used until the end of World War II. A typical booster magneto consisted of a separate magneto that was mounted inside the cockpit and turned by hand. Once adequate voltage was generated by a booster magneto, the output was sent to a special distributor that directed a spark to the cylinder just behind the one that was normally fired by the engine driven magneto. For example, consider a nine-cylinder radial engine with a firing order of 1-3-5-7-9-2-4-6-8. In this example, a booster magneto sends a spark to cylinder number 1 when the engine driven magneto is positioned to fire cylinder number 3. This retards the spark so that ignition occurs when a piston is already on the power stroke. [Figure 8-124]

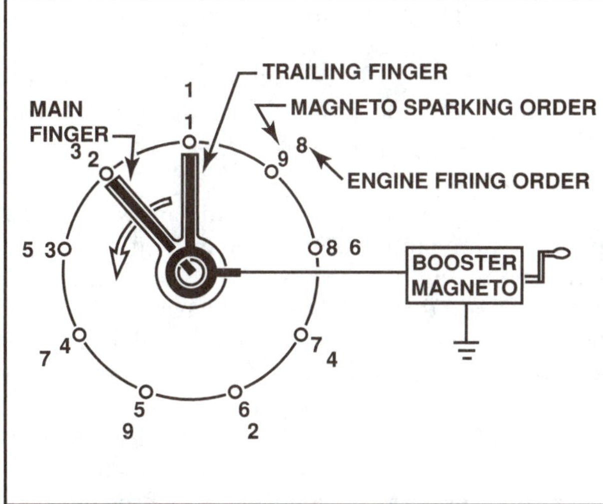

Figure 8-124. Booster magnetos utilize a trailing finger in the distributor rotor. The trailing finger delivered a hot retarded spark to each cylinder to promote engine starting.

IGNITION SWITCH

To provide a means of controlling when an ignition system is on and operating, an ignition switch is installed in all ignition systems. A typical ignition switch is located in the cockpit so a pilot has direct control over the ignition system. A magneto ignition switch operates differently from most other switches in that, when the switch is in the "OFF" position, the switch contacts are closed and the switch circuit is completed to ground. On the other hand, when placed in the "ON" position, the switch contacts are open and the switch circuit is open.

An ignition switch is wired in parallel with the breaker points; therefore, switching to "OFF" shorts the breaker points and grounds the primary coil. This prevents the magnetic field in the primary winding from collapsing and inducing current into the secondary winding. Conversely, when an ignition switch is in the "ON" position, its contacts are open and the breaker points interrupt primary current flow to produce the pulsating current necessary to generate a high energy spark. In other words, an ignition switch in the "ON" position has no effect on the primary circuit other than allowing the circuit to perform its function.

The ignition switch lead which connects the switch and the primary circuit is commonly referred to as the **P-lead**. A typical P-lead consists of several strands of copper wire that are shielded to help reduce radio interference.

A typical ignition switch controls both magnetos on an engine and has four positions: "OFF," "LEFT," "RIGHT," and "BOTH." When in the "OFF" position, the P-leads on both magnetos are grounded. In the "LEFT" position, the left magneto operates while the right magneto is grounded; however, in the "RIGHT" position, the right magneto operates while the left magneto is grounded. When switched to "BOTH," the left and right magnetos operate simultaneously to produce spark.

As an aviation maintenance technician, you should perform an operational check of an ignition switch any time maintenance is performed on an ignition system. To do this, start the engine using the manufacturers checklist. Once started, the engine is accelerated to between 1,500 and 1,700 rpm. When the engine rpm stabilizes, the ignition switch is moved from the "BOTH" to the "LEFT" position. At this point, the right magneto is grounded and, as a result, the engine rpm should drop slightly. If this is the case, the ignition switch should be moved back to the "BOTH" position and engine rpm should increase to its original value. Once it does, the ignition switch is moved from the "BOTH" to the "RIGHT" position. This grounds the left magneto causing a slight rpm drop. If this is the case, the ignition switch should be returned to the "BOTH" position. If, while operating on either the left or right magneto, engine rpm drops to zero, a short exists between the magneto and the ignition switch.

To complete the operational check, allow the engine rpm to stabilize at idle. Once stabilized, turn the magneto switch to the "OFF" position momentarily and then back to the "BOTH" position. When doing this, the engine should quit running while the ignition switch is in the "OFF" position. This verifies that the magnetos are grounded and that the ignition switch is operating properly. Failure of an engine to cease firing after turning the magneto switch to "OFF" is an indication of an open P-lead or faulty ignition switch. When conducting this check, the ignition switch must be moved as quickly as possible with the engine running at the slowest possible rpm. The reason for this is, when the ignition switch is turned off, fuel is still being drawn into the cylinders and, if excessive amounts of fuel accumulate before the switch is returned to "BOTH," the mixture could spontaneously ignite and cause the engine to backfire.

MAGNETO OVERHAUL

Most magnetos provide reliable operation and remain relatively trouble-free during the service life of an engine. In fact, most magnetos remain on an engine until the engine is overhauled. This is possible because the component materials used to build a magneto are extremely durable.

Since the tools and test equipment needed to overhaul a magneto are relatively expensive, magnetos are often sent to the manufacturer or a certified repair station for overhaul or exchange for rebuilt magnetos. However, as an aviation maintenance technician, you may overhaul a magneto; therefore, the following discussion looks at some of the general procedures for overhauling and testing a magneto.

DISASSEMBLY AND CLEANING

As with any accessory, whenever you disassemble and clean a magneto, you must follow the procedures outlined in the manufacturer's maintenance manual. In addition, all components should be handled carefully to avoid accidental damage. In the case of a rotating magnet, soft iron **keepers** should be placed across the poles of the magnet whenever it is removed. A keeper links the poles of a magnet and provides a highly permeable path for the lines of flux to flow. This helps the magnet to retain its magnetism.

Cleaning magneto components must be done only with approved solvents and cleaning methods. A list of the approved cleaning solvents is typically contained in the overhaul manual. For example, most manufacturers specify that acetone be used for cleaning grease and carbon tracks from capacitors and coils. Use of an unapproved cleaning solvent could damage the enamel insulation on the coil windings or the finish on the distributor block or rotor.

INSPECTION

When a magneto is overhauled, manufacturers typically require the replacement of several components. However, before discarding these components, it is a good idea to inspect them for evidence of a malfunction and excessive wear. Components that are typically replaced during an overhaul include the breaker point assembly, capacitor, all bearings, and the distributor block and rotor. In addition, hardware such as lock washers, gaskets, cotter pins, self-locking nuts or screws, and oil seals are always replaced.

The remaining components should be inspected as described in the manufacturers overhaul manual. This typically requires the use of some precision measuring equipment and specialized electrical testing equipment.

MAGNETO CASE

During an overhaul, a magneto case should be carefully inspected for cracks. Areas that are prone to cracking include the mounting flange, bearing surfaces, areas around threaded holes, and near mating surfaces. If cracking exists, the case must be replaced.

In addition to cracking, the bearing races and case interior should be inspected for signs of pitting or corrosion. If light corrosion exists, remove it using a method approved by the manufacturer. However, if excessive corrosion exists, the case must be replaced.

To help prevent corrosion, most magneto cases have one or more drains and at least one vent. The drain helps prevent condensation moisture from pooling inside the magneto case while the vent allows the corrosive gases produced by normal arcing to escape. In addition, good magneto ventilation helps to cool a magneto and evaporate light condensation.

ROTATING MAGNET

Both the magnet and magneto shaft should be visually inspected for physical damage and wear. In addition, most manufacturers require you to dimensionally inspect the magneto shaft to determine if it is within serviceable limits.

To determine if a magnet has sufficient strength, its field strength should be checked. This requires the use of a **magnetometer**, or **gauss meter**. In cases where the magnet has lost too much of its magnetism, it may be remagnetized by special equipment.

GEAR ASSEMBLIES AND BEARINGS

Distributor drive gear assemblies must be cleaned and inspected for excessive wear, cracks, and broken teeth. Excessive backlash or play in a distributor drive gear is cause for rejection of the gear assembly.

In most cases, all magneto shaft bearings and races must be replaced when a magneto is overhauled. However, some manufacturers permit you to reuse a bearing and its associated race. If this is the case, you must inspect and service the bearing as prescribed by the manufacturer.

MAGNETO COIL

When inspecting a magneto coil, carefully check the insulating material for cracks and burn marks. In addition, you should check the coil leads for general condition and security. Most manufacturers require you to check for continuity and resistance in each winding. Both of these checks can be done with either an ohmmeter or multimeter.

BREAKER ASSEMBLY

The breaker point assembly is subjected to the most intense wear of any component in a magneto. Because of this, a new set of points must be installed whenever a magneto is overhauled. However, before discarding the old points, you should inspect them for clues to other ignition system problems. For example, if a set of points are badly pitted, it may indicate that the capacitor is not working properly.

DISTRIBUTOR

If a manufacturer permits the reuse of a distributor assembly, you must inspect the distributor block and rotor for cracks, carbon tracks, soot, and other signs of arcing. In addition, the gear teeth on the distributor rotor should be checked for excessive play. To do this, most manufacturers instruct you to insert a specific size drill between each of the gear teeth. If the drill fits snugly, the gear is within tolerances. [Figure 8-125]

Another thing that must be checked on a distributor rotor is the distance between the rotor shaft and the end of the rotor finger. This provides an indirect indication of the distance between the rotor finger

Figure 8-125. To check for excessive wear between the teeth on a distributor gear, a specific sized drill is placed between the teeth. If the drill fits snugly, the gear is within specifications.

and the contacts in the distributor block. For example, if the distance between the rotor shaft and finger is too small, the gap between the rotor finger and distributor block will be too large.

If there are no signs of cracking or arcing on a distributor block, the distributor block should be tested. To check a distributor block for shorts or electrical leakage, a high-tension harness tester is typically used.

If replacement is not required and the distributor components are serviceable, you should prepare them for reassembly. In some cases, the rotor and distributor may have to be coated with wax to help prevent arcing. However, before doing this, you should refer to the manufacturer's instructions.

CAM

Magnetos traditionally use cams that are made of either a solid piece of metal or a phenolic compound. If the cam is made of metal and the manufacturer permits it to be reused, the cam must be dimensionally checked. However, if a phenolic cam is used, the old cam must be discarded and replaced.

ASSEMBLY AND INTERNAL TIMING

Once the magneto components are cleaned, inspected, and replaced as necessary, the magneto may be reassembled in accodance with the manufacturer's instructions. In most cases, reassembly begins with pressing new bearing races into the case halves and new bearings onto the magneto shaft. If the bearings are not sealed, they should be lubricated as prescribed.

Once the bearings and races are installed, you can install the magneto coil. Magneto coils are typically held in place by a set of retaining clamps or by two wedges that are driven in between the coil ends and the magneto case. Additional components that must be installed before the case halves are joined include the distributor block and rotor, breaker points, and capacitor.

Once all the components are installed in a magneto, you can join the case halves. However, when doing this, the magneto drive gear must be properly lined up with the distributor rotor gear. This step is part of the **internal timing** process and is necessary so that voltage is delivered to the proper contact in the distributor block at the correct time. Since internal timing procedures vary between magnetos, you should always follow the manufacturer's timing instructions.

When aligning the drive and distributor gears in a Bendix magneto, the rotating magnet should be placed in a neutral position. To do this, rotate the magnet shaft with your hand until you feel the magnet grab, or pull into alignment. In some cases, it will feel like the magnet has slipped into a detent. When this occurs, the magnet is in the neutral position and resists movement in both directions.

With the magnet in the neutral position, align the timing marks on the distributor gear and drive gear and mesh them together. In most cases, the distributor gear is marked so it can be used in both clockwise and counterclockwise rotating magnetos. A typical distributor gear has directional markings and two timing marks for each direction. To help you identify which marks you should use, distributor gears are typically marked with a "CW" and "CCW" indicating clockwise and counterclockwise, or "RH" and "LH" indicating right hand and left hand rotation. Additional marks are also included so a distributor gear mark can be seen through an inspection port in the magneto case. [Figure 8-126]

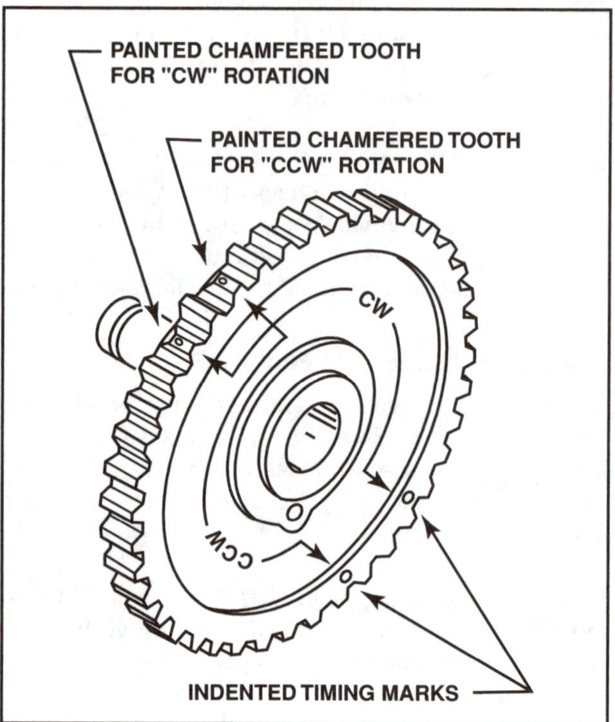

Figure 8-126. In most magnetos, the same distributor gear can be used for a clockwise rotating magneto or a counterclockwise rotating magneto. This distributor gear has an indented timing mark that aligns with the drive gear mark for rotation in either direction. Each indented timing mark has a corresponding chamfered tooth that is painted so it can be seen through an inspection port.

With the drive and distributor gears properly aligned, carefully slide the magneto case halves together. When doing this, it is important that you do not use excessive pressure or you could damage the distributor gear. In addition, you should avoid turning the case halves so you do not damage the carbon brush on the high-voltage tab protruding from the magneto coil. The case halves must contact each other all the way around their mating surfaces before they are screwed together.

Once the case halves are assembled, you must complete the internal timing procedure by adjusting the points to open when the magnet reaches the E-gap position. To do this, verify that the magnet is in the neutral position. In addition, verify that the distributor is ready to fire on the number 1 cylinder by observing the painted gear tooth offset to one side of the inspection port. Now, attach a timing scale to the magneto housing and a pointer to the screw attaching the cam to the magneto drive shaft. Set the pointer to zero on the scale and then rotate the magneto shaft in the normal direction of rotation until the pointer is aligned with the correct E-gap angle. [Figure 8-127]

Once you have the magnet in the E-gap position, there are two different tools you can use to hold the magnet in that position. One type of tool threads into the inspection port and locks the distributor gear so the magnet cannot turn. The other tool clamps directly to the magneto shaft and locks to the magneto flange by adjustable friction. [Figure 8-128]

Figure 8-127. To adjust the points in a Bendix magneto, you will need a Bendix timing kit containing a scale marked in degrees and a pointer. These items are used so you can identify when the magnet is in the E-gap position.

Once the magnet is locked in position, connect a magneto timing light across the breaker points. Now, adjust the breaker points so they just begin to open and the timing light comes on. Most timing light units are designed to illuminate when the breaker points begin to open. Once the points are set, lock them down and remove the holding tool. With your hand, rotate the magnet back to the neutral position so the indicator needle again reads zero. Now, slowly rotate the magnet to the E-gap angle. The points should just begin to open and the timing light come on just as the pointer reaches the E-gap angle. If this does not occur, adjust the points again using the procedures just discussed.

In some Bendix magnetos, a timing, or **index mark** is cast into the case while a second mark is stamped onto the cam. In this case, when the timing mark on the case and the mark on the cam are aligned, the magnet is in the E-gap position.

On magnetos equipped with a set of retard points, the retard points must be adjusted to open after the main points. The exact number of degrees the points are retarded is typically stamped on the casing inside the breaker housing. To set the retard points using an indicator needle, you must add the degrees of retard to the E-gap angle reading. For example, if the main breaker points open at 10 degrees, and the retard is supposed to be at 35 degrees, then the magnet must be rotated until the timing needle indicates 45 degrees. With the timing needle indicating 45

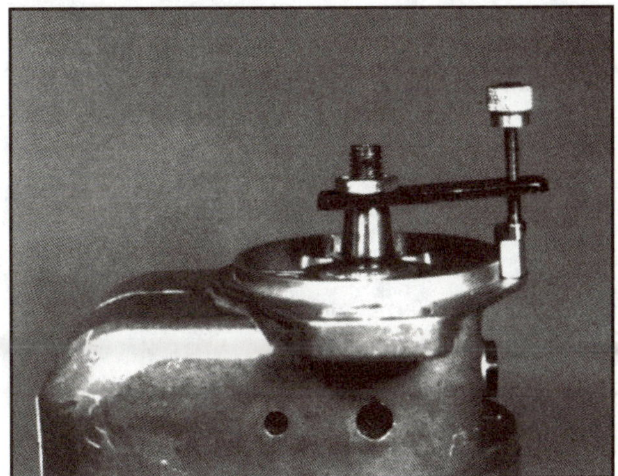

Figure 8-128. A magneto holding tool is provided in a Bendix timing kit for holding the magnet at the correct E-gap angle.

degrees, the magnet should be locked into position using a holding tool and the retard points adjusted so they just begin to open.

Once the points are adjusted, rotate the magneto drive shaft until the cam is in the high cam position. Using a thickness gauge, measure the point gap and compare it to the clearance specified in the maintenance manual. If the gap is not within specifications, readjust the points and recheck the timing with the timing light.

The internal timing procedures of a typical Slick magneto differ from those of a Bendix magneto in that the breaker points must be adjusted and set before the case halves are joined. To do this, the magnet is either locked in the E-gap position by a timing pin or by a special tool that is placed inside the magneto temporarily. Once the magnet is in the E-gap position, the points can be set using the process described earlier. [Figure 8-129]

Once a Slick magneto has been internally timed, the case halves may be joined. To do this, you must align the timing marks on the drive and distributor gears and then gently slide the case halves together. As discussed earlier, you must not force the case halves together or you could damage the distributor rotor.

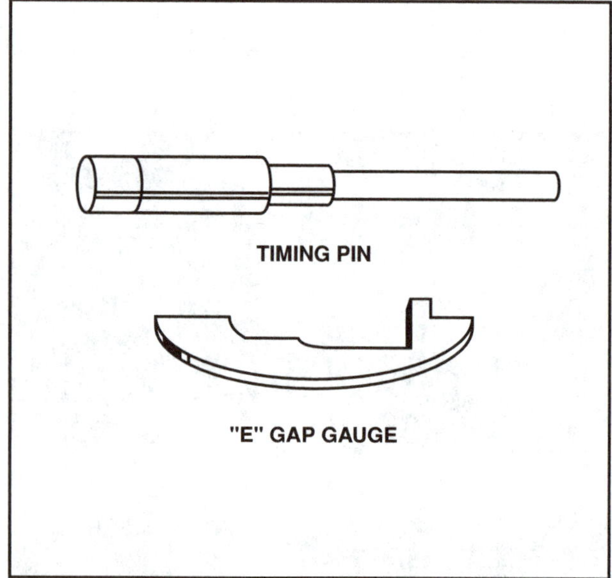

Figure 8-129. To set the magnet in a Slick magneto to the E-gap position, a special E-gap tool or a timing pin is used. Once the magnet is in the E-gap position, the breaker points are adjusted.

BENCH TESTING

After a magneto has been reassembled and internally timed, it must be tested. To do this, you must have access to a magneto test stand. There are several different types of magneto test stands manufactured. A typical test stand includes a variable-speed drive motor, a tachometer, and a spark rack.

To use a test stand, begin by mounting a magneto on the stand. Once mounted, verify that the gap between the points on the spark rack are set properly. This is crucial because, if the gap is too wide, excessive voltage could build in the magneto's secondary circuit causing a spark to discharge internally. If this happens, the magneto coil or distributor could be damaged. Bear in mind that the gap on the spark rack must be greater than the gap between spark plug electrodes because a spark will jump farther in free air than in a pressurized cylinder.

Once the gap on the spark rack is properly adjusted, connect the high-tension leads coming off the magneto to the spark rack. Since the motors used on most test stands can drive a magneto in either direction, you should verify the direction of rotation before engaging the motor. Once verified, slowly bring the magneto up to operating speed. As the magneto's coming-in speed is approached, you should begin to see sparking on the spark rack. After running the magneto at its maximum design speed and checking its performance, slowly decrease the rpm until the unit is stopped. Remove the magneto and record the test results. If the actual coming-in speed is higher than the specified speed, stop the test and troubleshoot the cause of the poor performance. Possible causes include improper internal timing, a weak capacitor, or a weak magnet.

In addition to verifying that a magneto fires properly, you can also check the strength of the rotating magnet. To do this, hold the breaker points open and check the ouput of the primary coil with an AC ammeter as the magneto is rotated at a specified speed. Compare the readings with values specified in the overhaul manual.

MAGNETO-TO-ENGINE TIMING

If a magneto performs accordingly on a test stand, it may be installed on an engine. When doing this, you must time the magneto to the engine. A variety of methods are used to time magnetos to engines, therefore, it is imperative that you follow the engine manufacturers instructions.

When timing two magnetos to an engine, the engine manufacturer can specify either synchronized or staggered ignition timing. **Synchronized ignition timing** requires both magnetos be timed to fire both spark plugs in each cylinder at the same time. **Staggered ignition timing**, on the other hand, requires the two spark plugs in each cylinder to be fired at slightly different times. When this is done, the spark plug located nearest a cylinder's exhaust port is typically fired first. The reason for this is that the fuel/air mixture near the exhaust port becomes diluted by exhaust gases and tends to burn more slowly than the mixture in the rest of the cylinder. Therefore, it is desirable to ignite the mixture in this area slightly ahead of the mixture in the rest of the cylinder.

Different procedures are used for timing flange- and base-mounted magnetos. Of the two, flange-mounted magnetos are more common and, therefore, the focus of the following discussion is timing a typical flange-mounted magneto to an engine.

FLANGE -MOUNTED MAGNETO

Before installing a magneto on an engine, the number one piston must be in its firing position. If you recall, this will be between 15 and 30 degrees before top dead center of the compression stroke. The exact position is indicated on the engine data tag, in the engine type certificate data sheet, and the engine maintenance manual. To position the piston, begin by removing the top spark plug from each cylinder. Next, place your finger over the number one spark plug hole and turn the prop in the normal direction of rotation until the number piston is on the compression stroke. The piston will be on the compression stroke when air is forced past your finger. Once on the compression stroke, continue rotating the engine until the number one piston is at top dead center between the compression and power strokes. Now, locate the engine **timing reference marks**. On Lycoming engines, these marks are typically on the front side of the flywheel. On Continental engines, the reference marks are usually on the propeller mounting flange. The exact location will be specified in the engine maintenance manual.

If the number one piston is at top dead center between the compression and power strokes, a "TC" reference mark will be aligned with a fixed index mark on the engine case or starter. A series of degree markings will also be visible. These markings represent the number of degrees before top dead center a piston is located. At this point, you need to rotate the engine opposite the direction of rotation until the degree mark representing the point where ignition is supposed to occur is a few degrees beyond the index mark. Now, rotate the engine in the normal direction of rotation until the ignition timing mark is aligned with the index mark. The exercise of moving the piston beyond the ignition timing mark and then back helps remove any play in the accessory drive gears. The engine is now positioned so the number one cylinder is ready to fire.

As an alternative to using the timing reference marks on the engine, there are more accurate instruments built that will indicate the position of the number one piston. One such device is the Time-Rite™ indicator. A Time-Rite indicator is considered more accurate because, once it is calibrated, it measures the actual number of degrees a piston is from top dead center. [Figure 8-130]

Once the engine is properly set, you may install the magnetos. When installing a magneto with an impulse coupling, be sure the impulse coupling is disengaged before mounting the magneto to the

Figure 8-130. With a Time-Rite indicator, you can accurately measure the position of a piston within a cylinder.

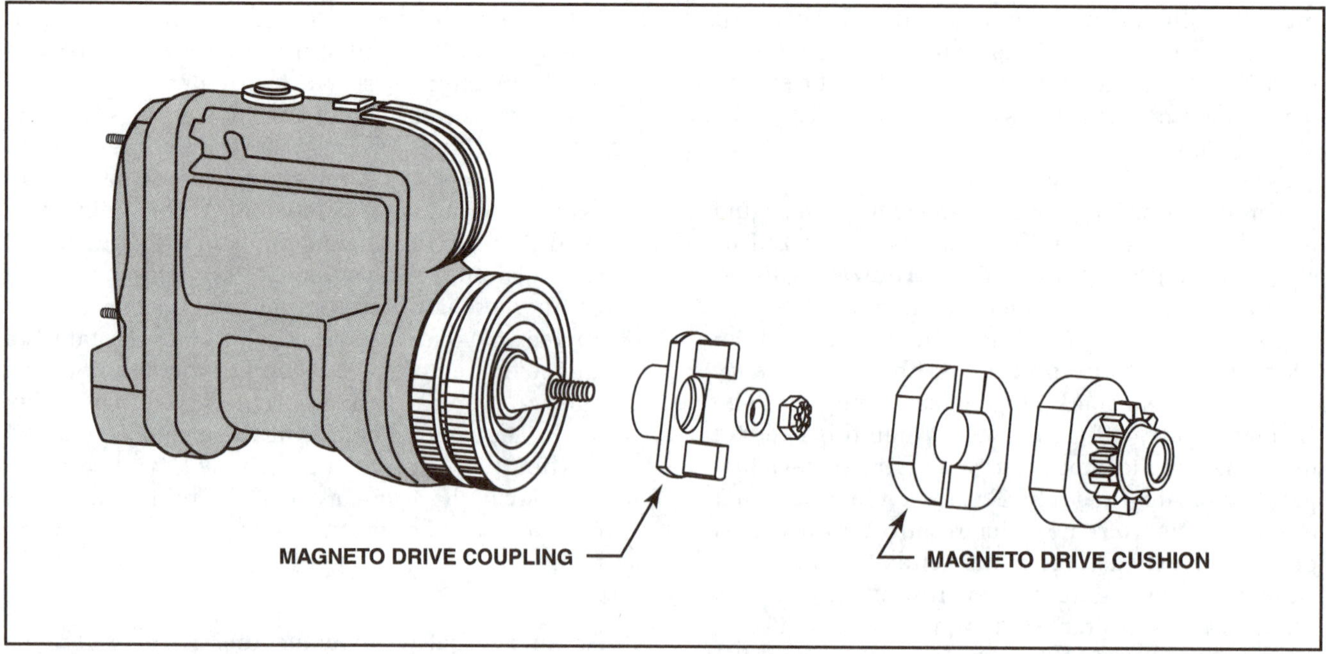

Figure 8-131. Some magnetos are mounted to an engine with an anti-vibration coupling. The engine drives the magneto through a rubber cushion held in a pressed steel retainer set into the magneto drive gear. The cushion reduces the amount of vibration that is transferred to the magneto.

engine. Other magnetos may utilize a rubber anti-vibration coupling that is installed between the accessory drive gear and the magneto. [Figure 8-131]

With the magneto locked in position to fire the number one spark plug and number one piston properly positioned, mount the magneto to the engine. As you slip the magneto drive gear into the accessory case, you may have to rotate the magneto somewhat to get the accessory gear and magneto drive gear to mesh. If the two gears do not mesh right away, do not try to force the magneto into the accessory case.

Once the magneto is in place, insert the mounting bolts and tighten them enough to support the magneto. However, make sure you leave the bolts loose enough so you can rotate the magneto. With the magneto installed, remove the magneto locking device. Forgetting to do so could result in substantial damage if the propeller is moved.

With the magneto mounted on the engine, attach a timing light to each magneto. Now, rotate each magneto until its respective timing light just comes on and tighten the magneto mounting bolts. If the propeller was not moved while you were installing the magneto, the magneto should be timed correctly. To verify the timing, rotate the propeller opposite the direction of normal rotation until both timing lights extinguish. Then, rotate the propeller forward until the timing lights just illuminate again. Now, check the timing reference marks on the engine. If the correct degree setting is opposite the index mark, the magneto is properly timed to the engine.

BASE-MOUNT MAGNETOS

On rare occasions, you may have to adjust the magneto-to-engine timing of a base-mounted magneto. These magnetos are typically found on radial engines and are coupled to the engine accessory drive with a vernier coupling. A vernier coupling is a special toothed coupling with a slotted rubber disk sandwiched between two gears with different numbers of teeth. The rubber disk is slotted to fit between the two gears in an almost infinite number of positions. Magneto-to-engine timing is adjusted by disconnecting the coupling and rotating the rubber disk the necessary number of slots.

OPERATIONAL CHECK

After reinstalling a magneto on an engine, a thorough operational check must be done. However, before doing this, you must verify the P-leads are correctly hooked up and that each of the spark plug leads are properly installed. When installing the spark plug leads, bear in mind that the numbers on the distributor represent the firing order of the magneto, not the engine cylinders. Therefore, you must match the firing order of the magneto to the firing order of the engine. For example, if a four cylinder engine has a firing order of 1-3-2-4, you must attach cylinder number 1 plug wire to distributor electrode number 1. Cylinder number 3 plug wire must be attached to distributor electrode number 2. Cylinder number 2 plug wire attaches to distributor electrode number 3 and the number 4 plug wire attaches to distributor electrode number 4.

Once you have verified that the entire ignition system is properly installed, you may proceed with the operational check. The first step in conducting an operational check is to start the engine using the manufacturers starting procedures. Once the engine is started and the rpm stabilizes at idle, listen for smooth engine operation. If engine operation is normal, advance the throttle to increase engine speed to the rpm specified in the checklist. Once engine rpm stabilizes, turn the magneto switch from "BOTH" to "LEFT" and allow the engine to stabilize. Note the drop in engine rpm, then return the magneto switch to "BOTH." The engine rpm should return to the original rpm setting. Now, move the magneto switch from "BOTH" to "RIGHT" and allow the engine rpm to stabilize. Note the drop in engine rpm, then return the magneto switch to "BOTH." Proper operation of the magnetos will result in a slight drop in rpm when the ignition switch is in the "RIGHT" and "LEFT" positions.

If, while operating on either the left or right magneto, an excessive rpm drop results, or, if the difference between the rpm drops on each magneto exceed allowable limits, you must troubleshoot the ignition system. The likely cause of a rapid rpm drop when switching to a single magneto is faulty or fouled spark plugs. On the other hand, a slow rpm drop could indicate incorrect ignition timing or improperly adjusted valves.

To complete the operational check, allow the engine rpm to stabilize at idle. Once stabilized, turn the magneto switch to the "OFF" position momentarily and then back to the "BOTH" position. When doing this, the engine should quit running while the ignition switch is in the "OFF" position. This verifies that the magnetos are grounded and that the ignition switch is operating properly. When conducting this check, the ignition switch must be moved as quickly as possible with the engine running at the slowest possible rpm. The reason for this is, when the ignition switch is turned off, fuel is still being drawn into the cylinders and, if excessive amounts of fuel accumulate before the switch is returned to both, the mixture could spontaneously ignite and cause the engine to backfire.

MAGNETO MAINTENANCE

As an aviation maintenance technician, you are sometimes limited in what you can do to a magneto. For example, if you are working on an aircraft that is using an older magneto, the only maintenance you may be able to do is time the magneto to the engine. However, in other cases, you may be able to inspect and perform corrective maintenance as necessary. The following discussion will examine some of the common maintenance items that you, as a maintenance technician, can perform.

When conducting a typical 100-hour or annual inspection, the magnetos should be thoroughly examined. However, in most cases, the magnetos can be inspected while they are still installed on the engine. Some of the things that should be inspected on a magneto include the integrity and security of the magneto case, the condition of the points, capacitor, and distributor, and the magneto-to-engine timing. In addition, you should perform an operational check to verify magneto performance.

CASE

The two most common types of damage that are found on a magneto case include cracking and corrosion. Areas where cracking is likely to occur include around the mounting flange and near screw holes. If a magneto case is cracked, the case must be replaced.

Although not as common as cracking, magnetos that are exposed to a salt-air environment can corrode. This is especially true for magneto cases that are made from an alloy containing magnesium. If minor corrosion is found, it can typically by removed and the magneto case painted to help prevent further corrosion. However, if corrosion resulting in severe pitting exists, the magneto case should be replaced.

In addition to salt air, clogged vents in a magneto case or a plugged orifice in a pressurized magneto case can lead to corrosion. Unvented moisture and gases from arcing form a corrosive atmosphere inside the magneto case. If these gases are not vented to the atmosphere, the nitric acid in the gases will corrode the internal parts of a magneto.

BREAKER ASSEMBLY

If a magneto's breaker assembly is accessible, it should be inspected. However, to do this, the P-lead typically must be disconnected. If this is the case, bear in mind that the magneto will be on regardless of the ignition switch position.

The points of a new breaker assembly have a smooth, flat surface with a dull gray, sandblasted, or frosted appearance. However, after a few hours of operation, points typically take on a wavy appearance. This is caused by metal transfer between the two points. Some metal transfer is normal; however, if excessive metal transfer takes place and the points become pitted or coarse-grained, the points must be replaced. Severe pitting shows up as a substantial protrusion on one contact with a corresponding pit on the other contact. [Figure 8-132]

Excessive wear on a breaker assembly can shift the internal timing of a magneto. For example, if a set of breaker points are worn, they will open early and advance the spark. In addition, the points will be open for a longer period of time resulting in a decrease in spark intensity.

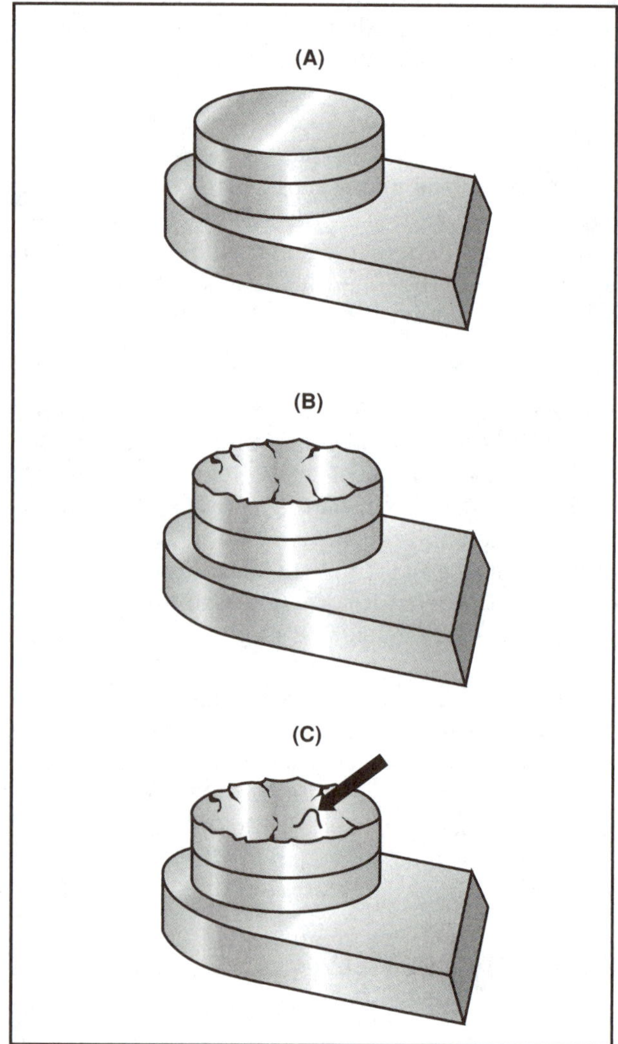

Figure 8-132. (A) — A new set of points are usually smooth and have a frosty appearance. (B) — After a few hours of operation, some metal transfers between the points and they take on a slightly wavy appearance. (C) — The mound extending above the surrounding surface on this contact indicates excessive wear requiring replacement of the breaker assembly.

In cases where the breaker points are serviceable, no attempt should be made to file or resurface them. Reworking breaker points will never produce a satisfactory surface. The presence of oil on the breaker surface will not necessarily keep the magneto from working. It will, however, attract contaminating metal and dirt particles that can lead to burning or pitting over time. To remove oil from the breaker point surface, open the points and insert a piece of clean hard cardboard, such as a business card, between the two contacts. Now, close the points to blot any oil from the surface. Re-open the points and remove the card. Never slide the cardboard between the closed points or particles could be left behind that will contaminate the points.

In addition to inspecting the breaker points, you should check the spring tension exerted on the points. This is done by attaching a small spring scale to the movable arm of the breaker assembly and carefully pulling the contact points apart. Open the points no more than one-sixteenth inch to prevent damage to the breaker spring. If spring tension readings are below acceptable levels, the points could float, or bounce at high speeds causing a loss of spark energy.

The breaker cam is visually checked for wear limits and damage such as pitting or distortion. Unless the cam surface is smooth and wear on the cam lobes are within limits, it must be replaced. Excessive wear may be traced to a dry lubrication pad on the breaker assembly. Excessive wear on a cam results in the points opening late and retarding the spark. In addition, a worn cam holds the points open for a shorter time which decreases the spark intensity.

CAPACITOR

Excessive point wear is typically caused by a defective capacitor. A capacitor is checked with a capacitance test device, sometimes called a **condenser tester**. These testers use AC voltage to check a capacitor's capacity and DC voltage to check for electrical leakage. If a capacitor's capacitance value is too low, the breaker points will likely become burned and pitted.

DISTRIBUTOR

The distributor block and rotor should be visually inspected for cracks, carbon tracks, soot, and other signs of arcing. A cracked distributor block or rotor typically provides a low resistance path to ground for secondary voltage; therefore, even a small crack requires component replacement.

SEALS

The presence of engine oil in a magneto generally indicates that an oil seal has failed. Since oil conducts electricity, anytime oil is found in a magneto, the magneto must be removed from the engine, disassembled, cleaned, and inspected.

TIMING

As part of a 100-hour and annual inspection, magneto-to-engine timing should be checked. To do this, attach a timing light to each magneto and rotate the engine until the number one piston is in the firing position. Now, rotate the engine opposite the direction of rotation until the timing lights go out. Once the lights extinguish, continue rotating the engine opposite the normal direction of rotation an additional 5 to 10 degrees. Now, rotate the engine in the normal direction until the timing lights just come on. Once on, check the engine timing marks to verify that the magnetos are firing at the appropriate time.

If a magneto performs unsatisfactorily during an operational check and the magneto-to-engine timing is correct, the magneto's internal timing may have to be adjusted. The only way to adjust a magneto's internal timing is to remove the magneto from the engine. Once removed, adjust the internal timing using the manufacturer's procedures. It is important to note that, anytime the breaker assembly in a magneto is removed for cleaning or replacement, the internal timing must be readjusted. Furthermore, anytime you time a magneto internally, you must also retime the magneto to the engine.

ENGINE ANALYZER

To aid in diagnosing engine problems, some older reciprocating engine aircraft were equipped with an analyzer that monitored engine performance. Aircraft, such as the Lockheed Constellation had large complex radial engines which benefitted from a continuous engine monitoring system. These monitoring systems tracked ignition system performance and engine vibration and displayed them on an adaptation of a laboratory oscilloscope. While some units were portable, most of these older monitoring systems were permanently installed and weighed approximately 45 pounds. [Figure 8-133]

Today, cylinder head temperature gauges and exhaust gas temperature gauges are primarily used

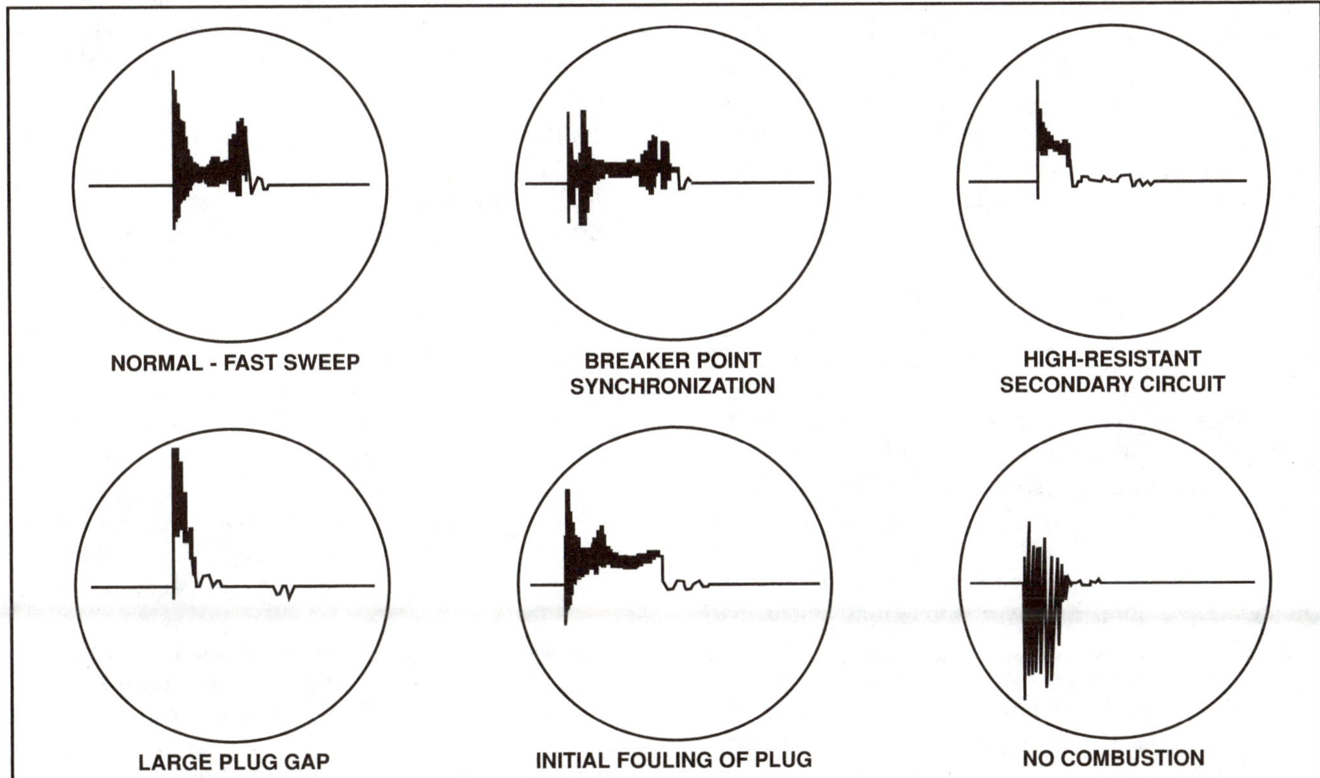

Figure 8-133. Multi-engine aircraft with large complex radial engines often used engine analyzers to monitor ignition system performance and engine vibrations. Some of the more basic indications of ignition system problems are indicated in this figure.

as indirect indicators of ignition system efficiency. Along with proper fuel/air mixture ratios, ignition timing greatly effects the amount of heat generated during the combustion process. This can easily be seen on digital cylinder head temperature gauges that monitor the temperature of each cylinder.

IGNITION HARNESS

In order for any ignition system to be efficient, the high energy voltage produced by a magneto must be delivered to the spark plugs with minimal loss. Therefore, the purpose of an ignition harness is to deliver high energy voltage from a magneto to the spark plugs through a low resistance electrical path that keeps electrical leakage to a minimum.

A typical ignition harness consists of 4, 6, or 8 individual **ignition leads.** One end of each ignition lead attaches to a receptacle on a magneto distributor block while the other end attaches to a spark plug.

CONSTRUCTION

The conductor used in a modern spark plug lead is made of either stranded wire or a single coiled conductor. The conductor is typically encased in one or two layers of rubber or silicone insulation which is covered with a braided metal shield. The insulation prevents current leakage while the shielding collects and channels the high frequency electromagnetic waves emanating from an ignition lead to ground to reduce radio interference. To help protect the shielding from chaffing and moisture, the shielding is typically impregnated with a silicone material. [Figure 8-134]

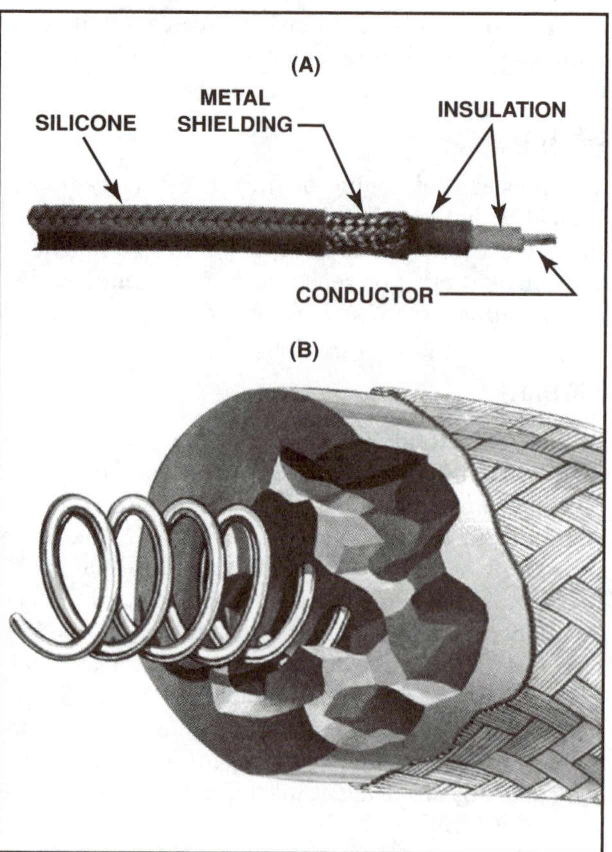

Figure 8-134. (A) — A typical ignition lead consists of a center conductor, one or more layers of insulation, and a layer of metal shielding that is impregnated with a silicone material. (B) — In addition to using stranded wire, some ignition leads use a single wire that is shaped into a continuous spiral.

There are two different size ignition leads used in aircraft ignition harnesses; 5 millimeter and 7 millimeter. The 5 millimeter is the size most commonly used today while 7 millimeter was used on some older ignition systems. In addition, most modern ignition leads are available with terminal ends to fit either a 5/8-24 shielded spark plug or the 3/4-20 all-weather spark plug.

Ignition leads are terminated with straight terminals whenever possible, however, some ignition leads may have to be bent to facilitate installation. If this is the case, sharp bends must be avoided. The reason for this is that, over time, the stress imposed by sharp bends causes weak points in the insulation which could allow high-tension current to leak. The 7 millimeter ignition leads require a large bend radius and, therefore, angled lead terminals are often used when a bend is required. Angled terminals are available with 70°, 90°, 110°, and 135° elbows. In addition, 5 millimeter straight terminal ends can be bent if a bracket is installed to hold the lead at a safe bend radius.[Figure 8-135]

The terminal ends used on modern ignition leads consist of a silicone rubber nose and coiled wire that slip into a spark plug body. This type of terminal is often referred to as an **all-weather** terminal because the silicone rubber forms a water tight seal at the top of the spark plug body. These terminals are crimped onto an ignition lead and the coiled wire screws over the end of the terminal so they can be replaced if they become damaged. [Figure 8-136]

Some older terminals are designed with a phenolic or ceramic insulator tube commonly referred to as a **cigarette**. This type of terminal contains a coiled spring that extends beyond the end of the insulator tube and provides positive electrical contact between the ignition lead and spark plug. [Figure 8-137]

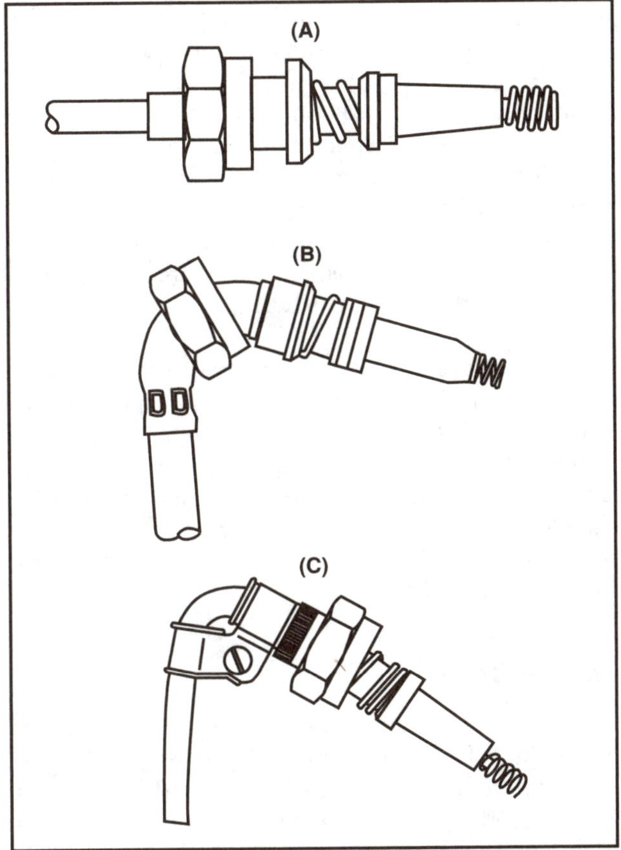

Figure 8-135. (A) — Ignition wiring is terminated with straight terminals whenever possible. (B) — However, if an installation requires a lead to be bent, angled terminals are available. (C) — In some situations, a bracket can be used with a straight terminal to hold the lead at an angle.

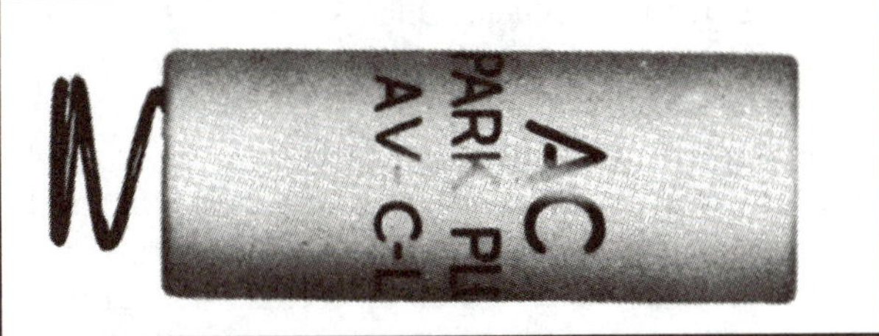

Figure 8-137. A phenolic or ceramic insulator tube is used in the ignition lead terminal of some older-style ignition harnesses.

When installing a cigarette-type terminal, the ignition lead insulation is cut away enough to allow the conductor wire to protrude through a hole in the back of the cigarette. The stranded wire conductor is then fanned out to secure the wire to the cigarette and provide good electrical contact.

Like the spark plug end of an ignition lead, the magneto end of modern leads also utilize crimp on type connectors. However, the exact type of connector used varies depending on the type of magneto installed. [Figure 8-138]

Another method that was used to connect ignition leads to a distributor block was with cable piercing screws. With this type of installation, the conductor of an ignition lead is cut so that it is even with the insulation. The lead is then inserted into a distributor block where a cable piercing screw is used to

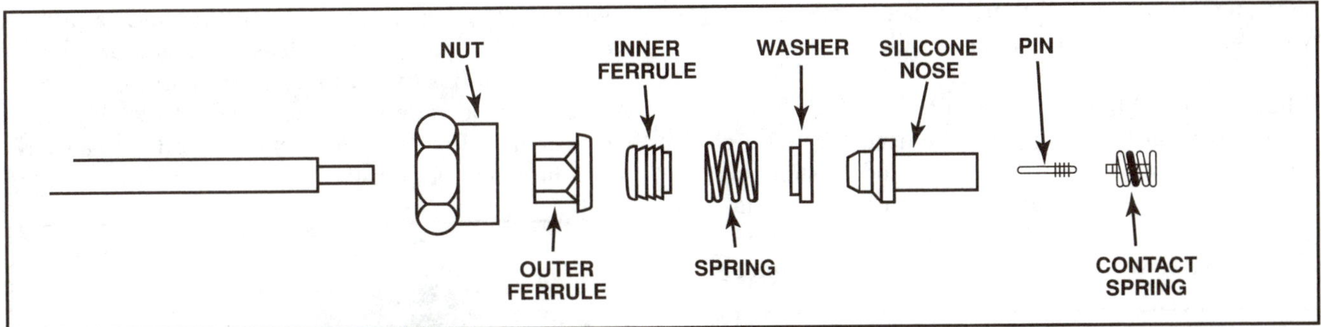

Figure 8-136. With an all-weather terminal, the terminal is crimped onto an ignition lead. In addition, the ignition shielding is held tightly between an inner and outer ferrule providing a durable ground connection.

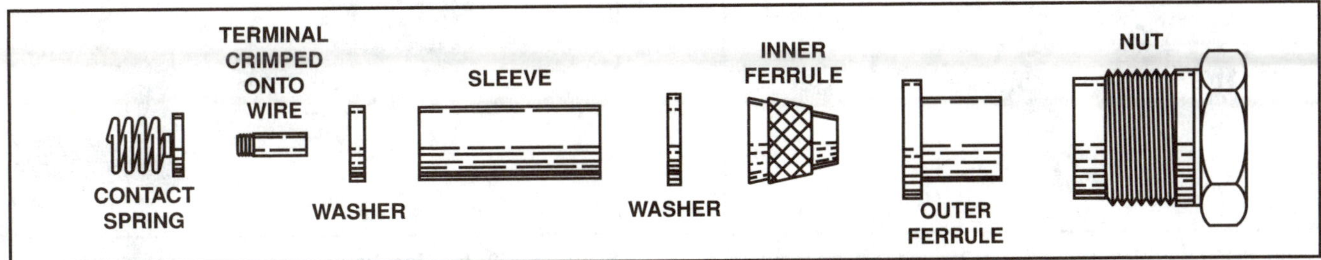

Figure 8-138. A typical magneto end of an ignition lead is crimped onto the lead using ferrules.

hold the lead in place. Once inserted, the screw forms threads in the lead's conductor.

When installing either the spark plug or magneto terminals on an ignition lead, the braided shield must be secured at both ends. If it is not, radio interference could occur when the engine is running. With terminals that are crimped on, the shielding is grounded through the attachment nut.

MAINTENANCE

Ignition harnesses typically provide hours of trouble free operation; however, at times, periodic maintenance may be required. Typical maintenance consists of repairing or replacing terminal ends or replacing a chaffed lead. In most cases, a single damaged ignition lead can be replaced without resorting to replacement of the entire harness. When ignition harness manufacturers supply individual replacement components, they also provide detailed information on replacement procedures. The approved methods and tools prescribed by the manufacturer for installing a new lead on a spark plug terminal or magneto terminal must be followed precisely. [Figure 8-139]

If an entire ignition harness must be replaced, you can typically purchase a harness kit for a specific engine make and model. The ignition harness kits usually make the assembly and installation of a complete harness fairly simple. In most cases, the ignition wires are precut to the proper length and all necessary terminal hardware is provided.

When removing the old ignition harness, retain the serviceable hardware and clamps used for routing the leads. If not already preassembled, install the terminals on the leads. Pay close attention to wire markings that indicate the distributor terminal-to-spark plug destinations for each lead. A typical marking such as 1T indicates a lead cut to length for the top spark plug in cylinder number one.

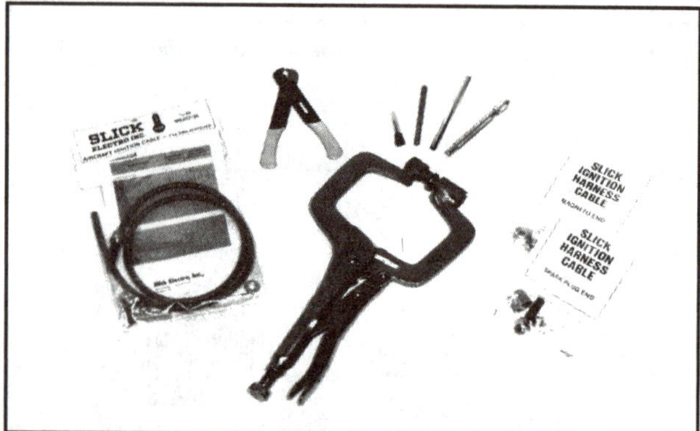

Figure 8-139. Special terminal installation tools are required when making an ignition harness repair.

Install the new harness on the magneto and route the leads to their respective cylinders. Ensure that the leads are routed around hot exhaust components and will not interfere with movement of the engine controls. Once properly routed, secure the harness with the clamps and hardware provided in the kit or with the old hardware.

In circumstances where an ignition lead system is causing radio interference, carefully inspect all the leads to verify that the shielding is properly grounded. If all leads are properly grounded and the interference persists, the existing shielding may be unable to carry all the electromagnetic interference to ground. In this case, a second layer of shielding may be installed.

TESTING

Any time a conductor carries high voltage energy and is installed near a conductive mass, the insulation around the conductor is exposed to what is known as **high voltage corona**. Repeated exposure to high voltage corona can cause the dielectric strength of the insulation to breakdown and increase the possibility of arcing. To help you detect a breakdown in the insulating strength of an ignition lead several different types of high-tension harness testers have been developed. One type of tester applies 15,000 volts DC to an ignition lead and then uses a microammeter to detect current leakage. Another type of detector applies high voltage to an ignition lead and insulation breakdown is indicated by the illumination of an indicator light or by the inability of a spark to jump an air gap in the tester. [Figure 8-140]

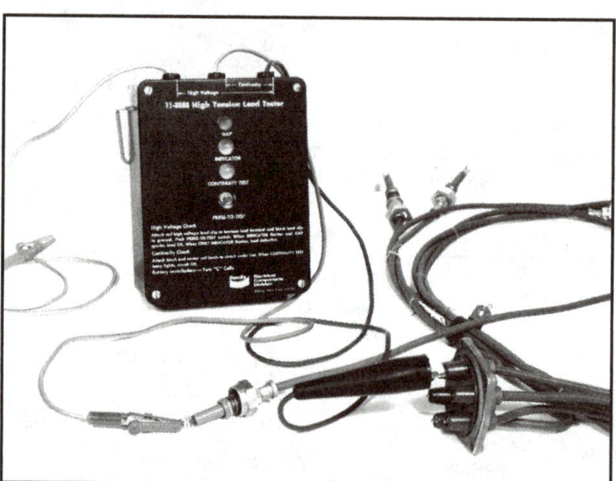

Figure 8-140. Ignition harness testers are useful for the detection of intermittent ignition harness problems.

SPARK PLUGS

The end result of the activity in an ignition system is the production of a spark that ignites the fuel/air mixture in a cylinder. Spark plugs transmit the short impulses of high voltage current from the ignition harness into the combustion chambers. The construction and operation of a spark plug is simple in concept but the demands placed on this part of an ignition system are high. To put the demands placed on a spark plug in perspective, consider the following, in an engine operating at 2,100 rpm, approximately 17 separate ignition events occur per second in each cylinder. Each ignition event begins with a 20,000 volt spark that jumps the air gap between a spark plug's electrodes. Furthermore, a spark plug must be able to operate in temperatures of 3,000°F or higher with gas pressures as high as 2,000 psi.

CONSTRUCTION

Although most spark plugs are similar in appearance, differences do exist among different spark plug types. Because of this, engine manufacturers specify the type of spark plugs that must be used in their engines. A typical spark plug consists of three major parts: a durable metal shell, a ceramic insulator, and an electrode assembly. [Figure 8-141]

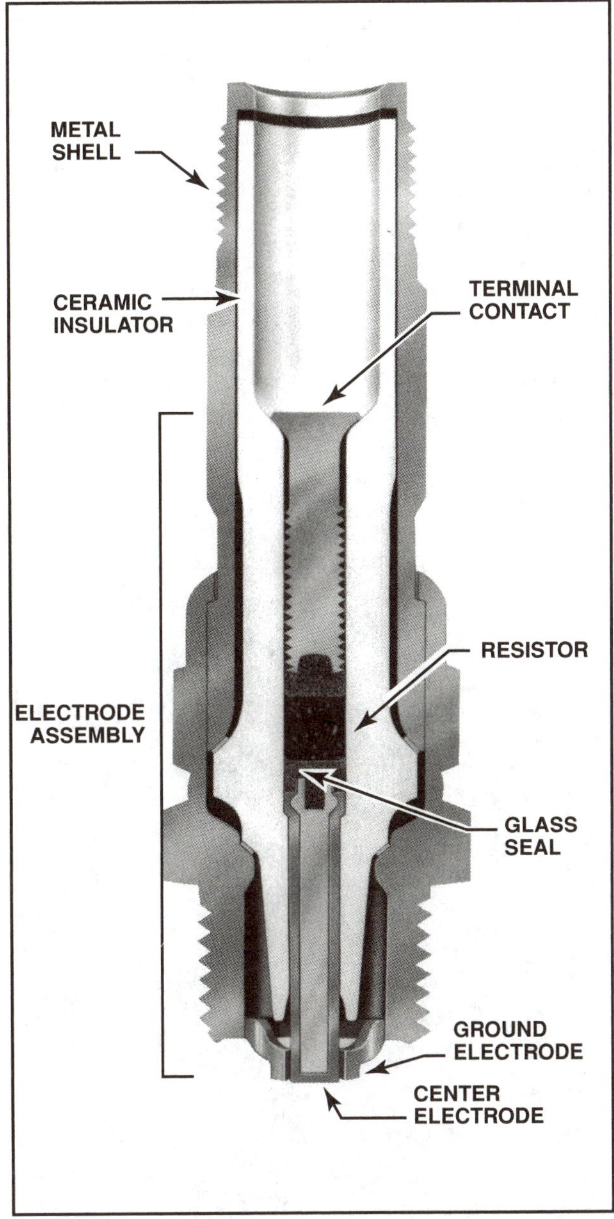

Figure 8-141. The three basic components of every spark plug include the metal shell, a ceramic insulator, and an electrode assembly.

The metal shell provides support for the internal components and provides an electrical path to ground for the braided shield of the ignition lead. All shielded spark plug shells are threaded at both ends. The threads on one end allow an ignition lead to be attached to the spark plug and are referred to as **terminal**, or **shield threads**. The threads on the opposite end permit the spark plug to be screwed into a cylinder. To facilitate the installation and removal of a spark plug, a hex, or six-sided nut is cast as part of the metal shell.

A spark plug's ceramic insulator prevents the high voltage current flowing through a plug from arcing to ground. In most cases, the insulator consists of two sections. One section extends from near the tip of the center electrode up to the terminal contact. The other section begins near the top of the spark plug barrel and extends downward to overlap with the first insulator section. Nickel gaskets between the spark plug shell and insulator prevent the escape of high-pressure gases from the cylinder.

The electrode assembly consists of a terminal contact, resistor, glass seal, a center electrode, and a set of outer electrodes. The terminal contact is where the terminal end of an ignition lead makes contact with the spark plug. At the opposite end of the terminal contact is a small resistor. The purpose of a resistor is to prevent capacitance afterfiring. **Capacitance afterfiring** describes the process by which electrical energy is induced into the ignition shielding when current flows through an ignition lead. Once the electrical potential in the shielding builds, the stored energy is released as a surge of current across the air gap of the spark plug. This lengthens the spark duration and accelerates wear of the spark plug electrodes. By inserting a resistor in a spark plug, the stored voltage in the shielding is dissipated so it can not jump the spark plug's air gap. The resistor typically has a value of 1,500 ohms.

The material used to construct the center and outer electrodes varies depending on the type of electrodes used. For example, with a **massive-electrode** spark plug, the outer, or ground electrodes are typically made of a nickel alloy while the center electrode is made of nickel-clad copper. On the other hand, with a **fine-wire electrode** spark plug the ground electrode is made of platinum or iridium and the center electrode is made of silver. [Figure 8-142]

The ground and center electrodes on all spark plugs are separated by an air gap of a specified width. The size of the air gap determines the amount of resistance a spark must overcome before it can jump the gap. Therefore, if the size of an air gap is not adjusted properly, the intensity of the spark produced will also be incorrect.

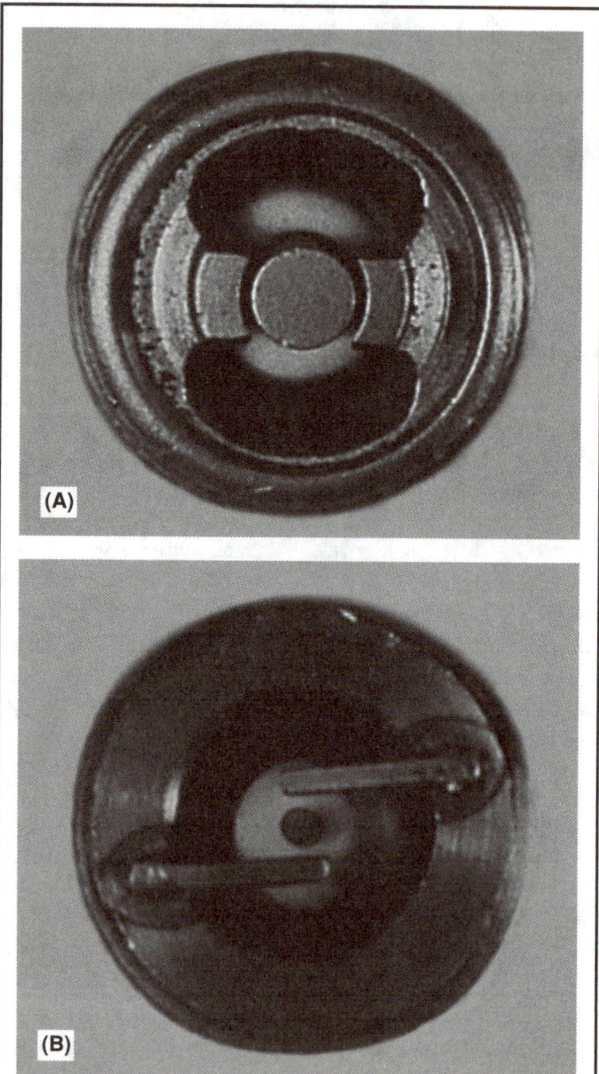

Figure 8-142. (A) — With a massive-electrode spark plug, 2, 3, or 4 ground electrodes surround a single center electrode. (B) — A fine-wire electrode spark plug has two square ground electrodes and one round center electrode.

SHELL THREAD CLASSIFICATION

Spark plugs are often classified according to the size of the shell threads that screw into the cylinder. In aviation, spark plug threads are either 14 millimeter or 18 millimeter. With the exception of the Fanklin engine, all modern aircraft engines use 18-mm spark plugs.

The terminal threads also come in two sizes; either $^5/_8$ inch — 24 thread or $^3/_4$ inch — 20 thread. Both sizes are still used in aircraft; however, the $^3/_4$ inch — 20 thread is becoming the size of choice. One of the reasons for this is because the $^3/_4$ inch — 20 thread is referred to as an all-weather spark plug. An **all-weather** type spark plug differs from other plugs in that the ceramic insulator inside the spark plug does not extend to the top of the plug shell. This leaves room for the silicone grommet on an all-weather terminal to form a watertight seal. [Figure 8-143]

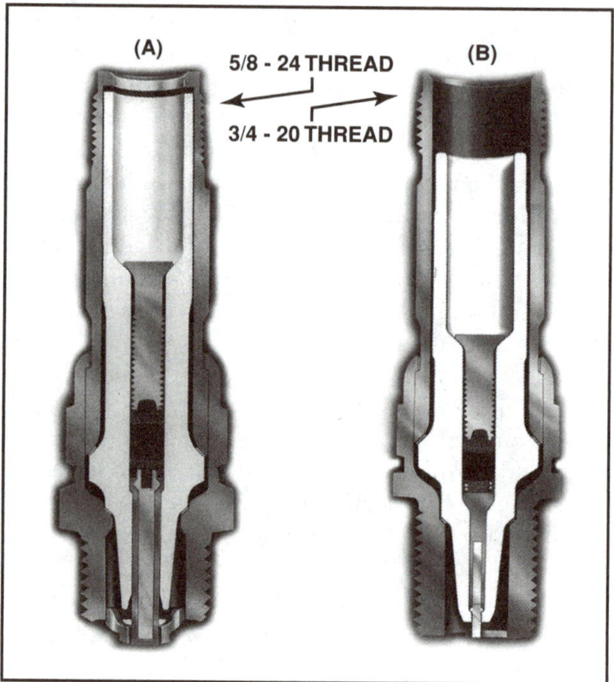

Figure 8-143. (A) — The $^5/_8$ inch — 24 thread is often used on older massive-electrode spark plugs. (B) — On the other hand, the $^3/_4$ inch — 20 thread is most often used with fine-wire electrode, all-weather spark plugs. With all-weather spark plugs, the ceramic insulator does not extend to the top of the shell so there is room for a resilient grommet on the ignition lead to form a watertight seal.

SPARK PLUG REACH

A spark plug's reach is defined as the linear distance from the shell gasket seat to the end of the shell threads, or shell skirt. Spark plugs are available in either **long reach** or **short reach** sizes to account for differences in cylinder head construction from engine to engine. On 14 millimeter plugs, the long reach dimension is 12.7 millimeter, or $^1/_2$ inch. while the short reach dimension is 9.53 millimeter, or $^3/_8$ inch. On 18 millimeter plugs, the long reach is 20.64 millimeter, or $^{13}/_{16}$ inch while the short reach dimension is 12.7 millimeter, or $^1/_2$ inch.

When the recommended spark plug is installed in an engine, the end of the threads should be flush with the cylinder head's inside wall. Therefore, if you install a spark plug with the wrong reach, the spark plug will either extend beyond or be recessed in the cylinder head. For example, if a long reach spark plug is installed where a short reach plug is required, the end threads of the plug will be directly exposed to the heat of combustion. In addition, the exposed threads will be susceptible to carbon buildup which could make it difficult to remove the plug for service. On the other hand, if a short reach plug is used in place of a long reach plug, the threads in the cylinder head will be exposed to combustion gases and possible damage. [Figure 8-144]

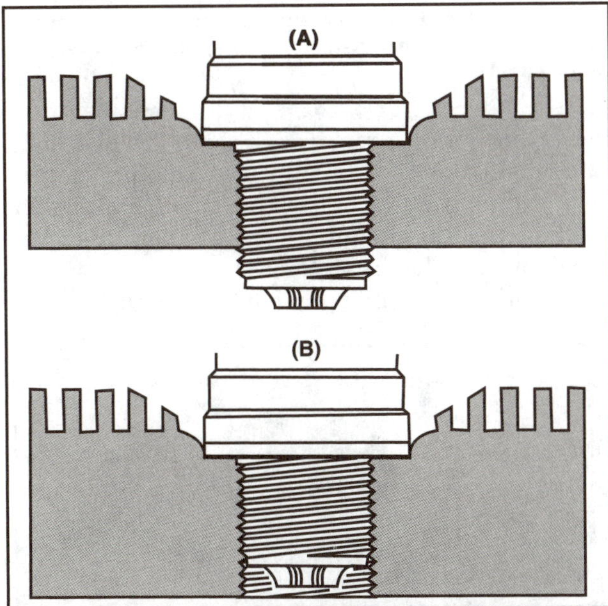

Figure 8-144. (A) — If a long reach plug is installed in a cylinder head requiring a short reach plug, the plug will extend into the cylinder head. This exposes the spark plug threads to the heat and corrosive gases produced during the combustion process. (B) — If a short reach plug is installed in place of a long reach plug, the spark plug will be recessed in the cylinder head. This can cause a decrease in combustion efficiency and will expose the threads in the cylinder head to carbon buildup.

HEAT RANGE

The heat range of a spark plug refers to the ability of a spark plug to conduct heat away from its firing tip to the cylinder head. Spark plugs are generally classified as "hot," "normal," or "cold" plugs depending how well they transfer heat. The primary factor in determining a plug's heat range is the length of the nose core. For example, cold plugs have a relatively short nose core that provides a rather large contact area between the ceramic insulator and plug shell. This large contact area allows heat to conduct readily to the cylinder head. On the other hand, hot plugs have a relatively long nose core that provides little contact area for heat to dissipate. [Figure 8-145]

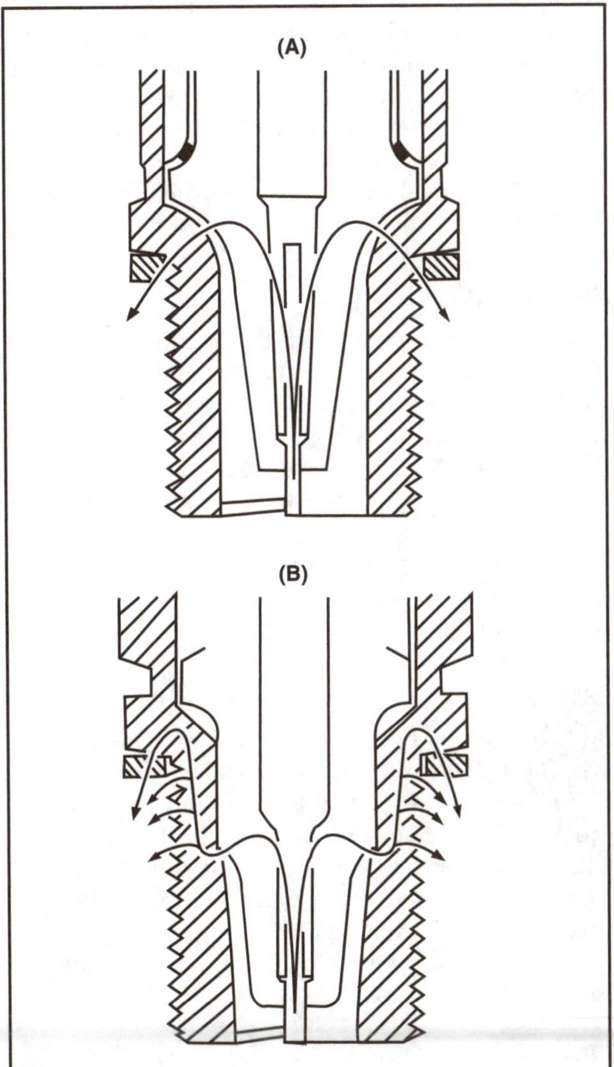

Figure 8-145. (A) — Hot spark plugs have long nose cores that provide relatively little contact area between the insulator and shell. The small amount of contact area slows the rate at which heat can be conducted away from the plug tip. (B) — Cold plugs, on the other hand, have a shorter nose core that permits a large contact area for dissipating heat.

All aircraft engines are certified to use spark plugs with a specific heat range. However, as a general rule, a high-compression engine operates at rather high temperatures and, therefore, uses cold spark plugs. On the other hand, lower compression engines typically operate at relatively low temperatures and use hot spark plugs. If a hot spark plug is installed in an engine requiring a cold spark plug the hotter operating temperature of the plug could lead to preignition or engine run-on. On the other hand, if a cold spark plug is installed in a cold-running engine, the plug could become fouled with unburned carbon and lead deposits.

Some circumstances require you to use a spark plug that may not be in the recommended heat range. For example, on small horizontally opposed engines that were originally designed to run on 80-octane avgas, a hotter spark plug may have to be used when 100LL avgas is used. The reason for this is that 100LL contains four to eight times as much tetraethyl lead as the 80-octane avgas and the higher levels of lead could cause lead fouling in the cooler spark plugs.

SERVICING

Manufacturers recommend the removal of spark plugs for inspection and servicing at regular intervals. In addition, removal, inspection, and cleaning of spark plugs is a 100-hour inspection item. However, engine problems such as intermittent missing at all engine speeds may indicate a defective or badly fouled spark plug requiring service. Anytime a spark plug becomes badly fouled, the spark flows through the electrodes directly to ground and ignition does not occur.

REMOVAL

Before you can remove a set of spark plugs, you must first remove the ignition leads. When removing an ignition lead it is best to hold the ignition lead with one hand and loosen the terminal nut with an open end wrench. Once the terminal nut is completely backed off, pull the terminal end straight out of the spark plug. Tilting a lead terminal to one side while removing it can crack the plug's core insulator. [Figure 8-146]

Once an ignition lead is removed, loosen the spark plug from the cylinder with a six-point deep socket. Be sure to place the socket squarely over the spark plug hex and keep it square while applying pressure. Tilting the socket increases the possibility of inflicting damage to the spark plug's ceramic insulator.

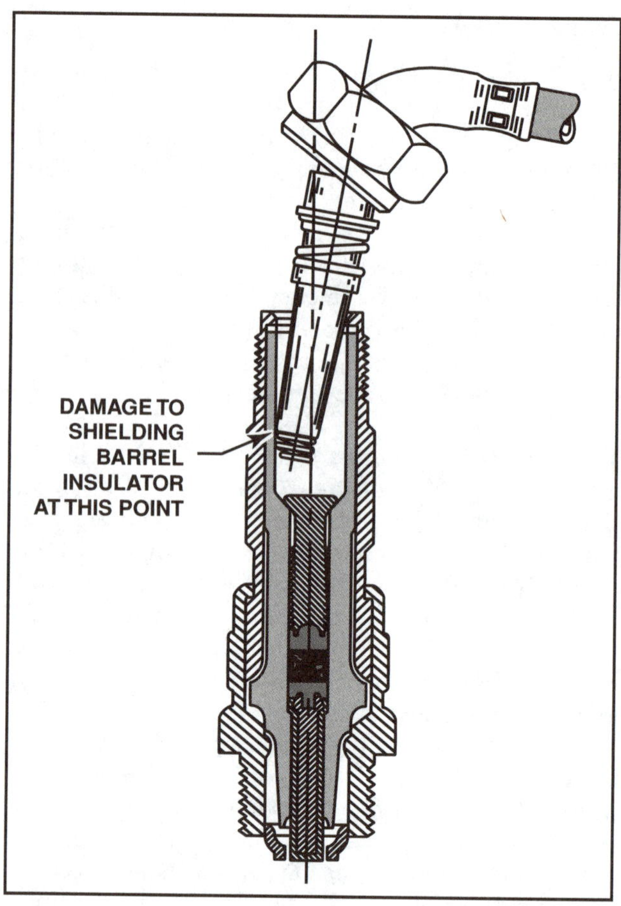

Figure 8-146. When removing an ignition lead from a spark plug, pull the terminal end straight out of the plug. If this is not done, the ceramic insulator in a spark plug could be damaged.

Once a spark plug is removed, it should be placed in a tray that holds each plug securely and prevents it from rolling around or striking another plug. In addition, the tray should provide a means of identifying where a plug came from in regard to cylinder number and position (top or bottom). [Figure 8-147]

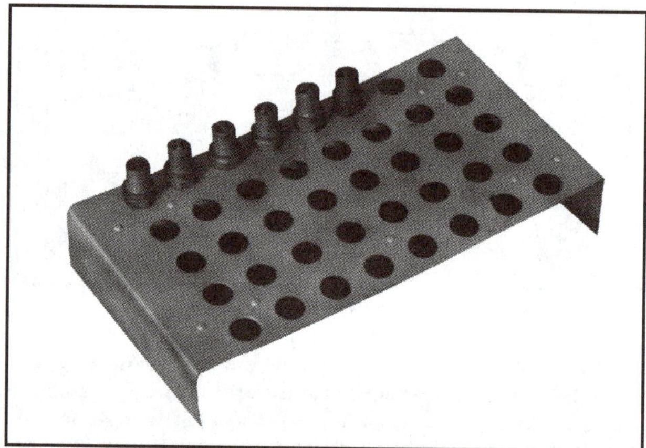

Figure 8-147. Spark plug trays hold plugs securely and provide an easy way of identifying what cylinder and position a specific plug came from.

Figure 8-148. A light deposit of dull brown material on a spark plug insulator indicates a normal combustion process.

VISUAL INSPECTION

Visual inspection of spark plugs reveals a great deal about the efficiency of an engine's combustion process. For example, if a spark plug insulator is covered with a dull brown deposit and there is little buildup in the firing cavity, normal combustion is occurring in the cylinder. [Figure 8-148]

When the firing cavity of a spark plug is filled with hard, bead-like deposits, excessive lead fouling is occurring. In this case, the cause of the fouling must be investigated and corrected. Typical causes of lead fouling include improper fuel vaporization, low cylinder head temperatures, or the use of spark plugs with an improper heat range. If all spark plugs in an engine show signs of severe lead fouling, you should consider installing spark plugs with a hotter heat range. [Figure 8-149]

Figure 8-149. Excessive lead deposits show up as hard bead-like deposits in the firing cavity of a spark plug.

Figure 8-150. Soft, black, sooty deposits indicate severe carbon fouling that can usually be traced to operating the engine with an excessively rich mixture.

Spark plugs that are covered with a soft, black, sooty deposit on all surfaces indicate a problem with carbon fouling. This condition has several causes including operation with an excessively rich mixture or a leaking primer. Black, sooty deposits on the engine's exhaust stack also confirm operation with an excessively rich mixture. [Figure 8-150]

Oil fouling is another type of contamination sometimes found on spark plugs. Oil fouling typically appears as a blackened, slippery coating on a spark plug's electrodes. Causes of oil fouling include broken or worn piston rings and worn valve guides. If oil fouling is severe enough an engine may have to be removed from service until repairs are completed.

The existence of a hard glaze on the insulator nose of a spark plug typically indicates that sand was ingested into the engine. Once in a combustion chamber, some of the silicates in sand melt with the heat of combustion. As the molten silicates cool, they form a glass-like coating on the surfaces of the spark plug. This silicon glaze is non-conductive at

Figure 8-151. If either the center or ground electrodes are worn to half their original size or severely distorted, the spark plug should be replaced.

low temperatures; however, at high temperatures, the glaze becomes conductive and can lead to spark plug misfiring. Sand ingestion is typically the result of an induction system leak or a worn air filter.

If the electrodes on a spark plug are worn to approximately half their original size, the spark plug should be replaced. In some cases, excessive wear can distort the shape of both the center and ground electrodes. [Figure 8-151]

Abnormal wear on both electrodes of a spark plug may be indicative of fuel metering problems. For example, if an excessively lean mixture exists, combustion temperatures can increase to a point that promotes electrode wear. An induction air leak can cause a lean mixture in carbureted engines while a partially clogged fuel nozzle can cause a lean mixture in fuel-injected engines.

In addition to inspecting a spark plug for excessive wear, you should examine the ceramic insulator at both ends for cracking. If any sign of cracking exists, the spark plug must be discarded and replaced. In addition, any spark plugs that have been dropped on a hard surface should automatically be discarded because the ceramic insulator may be cracked in an area that is not visible.

CLEANING

The first step in cleaning a set of spark plugs is to degrease them with an approved safety solvent. This should remove oil, grease, and other soft deposits from a plug's exterior and firing cavity. Once degreased, a spark plug may be dried with compressed air.

Lead and carbon deposits are typically removed with a vibrating cleaning tool. When using this type of tool, it is important that you use the proper cutting blade and hold the spark plug directly over the blades. If this is not done, you could damage the ceramic insulator and/or the electrodes. When properly used, a slight back and forth motion over the vibrating blades will chip away the lead deposits. [Figure 8-152]

After chipping away all lead deposits, an abrasive grit blasting cleaner unit may be used to complete the cleaning job. However, you must adhere to the manufacturer's instructions concerning grit type and air pressure settings. In most cases, a silica abrasive is not recommended because it can contribute to silica fouling.

When using a grit blast cleaner, begin by installing the proper size rubber adapter and then press the firing end of the spark plug into the adapter hole. To help prevent excessive erosion, move the plug in a circular motion while blasting and limit the blast to a few seconds. If this is not done, you could erode the electrodes of a fine-wire spark plug and reduce its operating life by as much as 200 to 300 hours.

After abrasive blasting, blow out all traces of the grit with clean air. If you used a wet-blast method, dry the plugs in an oven to avoid rusting. When the spark plugs are clean and dry, inspect them with a light and a magnifying glass. This should be done to verify that the insulator and electrodes are within serviceable limits and that all traces of the grit have been removed.

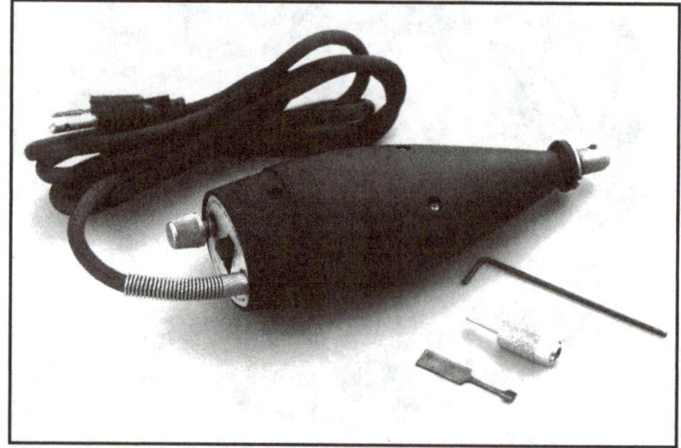

Figure 8-152. To remove lead deposits, a hand-held or stationary vibrating tool is often used.

If needed, clean the terminal end of a spark plug with an appropriate cleaning tool and approved cleaning compound. In addition, remove any remaining carbon or corrosion from the threads at both ends of the spark plug with a steel brush or wire wheel with soft bristles.

GAPPING

If a plug is determined to be in a serviceable condition, the gap between the center and ground electrodes must be checked and adjusted as necessary. To check the gap in a spark plug, a round wire gauge is used. In most cases, these gauges have two wires to measure both the minimum and maximum gap. For example, if a plug is supposed to have a gap of .016, an appropriate wire gauge will have a .015 and a .019 inch wire. In this case, the smaller wire must pass through the gap while the larger wire should be too big to pass through the gap.

If a spark plug gap is too large, the ground electrode may be forced inward to reduce the gap. However, to do this, you must have the proper tools and the manufacturer's instructions must be followed carefully. This is important because the use of improper gapping procedures increases the chances of damaging the nose ceramic and/or electrodes.

When adjusting the gap on a massive-electrode spark plug, the ground electrodes must remain parallel to the center electrode. The only way you can do this is if you use a special gapping tool. With most massive-electrode gapping tools, the spark plug must be clamped into the tool. Once this is done, the ground electrode is moved inward using a movable arm or threaded adjusting ram. When closing a gap, slowly move the ground electrode, being careful to avoid inadvertently closing the gap too much. This is important because any attempt to enlarge a gap on a massive-electrode plug usually results in electrode or insulator damage. [Figure 8-153]

When gapping a massive-electrode spark plug, it is important that you do not leave the wire gauge between the center and ground electrodes when the ground electrode is being moved. The reason this is not done is because if the wire gauge were left in position, an excessive side load would be placed on the center electrode that could crack the ceramic insulator.

Since the ground electrodes on a fine-wire spark plug are smaller than those on a massive-electrode

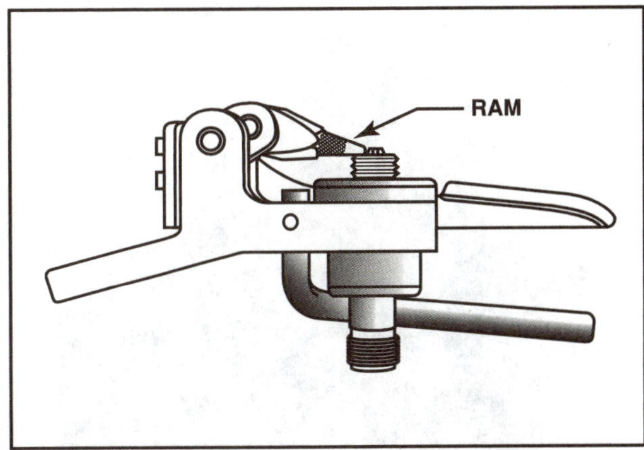

Figure 8-153. A special gapping tool similar to this is required for adjusting the gap of a massive-electrode spark plug.

plug, gapping a fine-wire spark plug is easier. However, the platinum and iridium electrodes are extremely brittle and can be broken easily; therefore, all fine-wire spark plugs must be handled with care. Using a special gapping tool, move the ground electrodes toward the center electrode until the specified gap exists. Again, avoid closing the gap too much because attempts to widen the gap risk damage to the ground electrodes. [Figure 8-154]

TESTING

Once a spark plug has been cleaned and gapped, it should be tested. To do this, you must have access to special testing equipment. The testing equipment

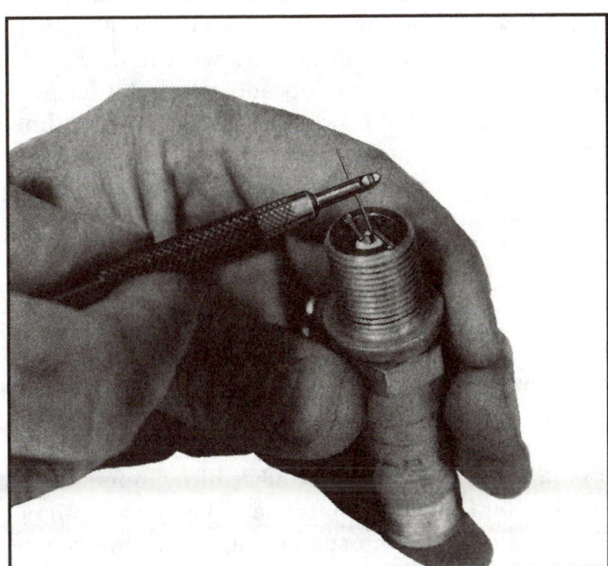

Figure 8-154. The gapping tool used with fine-wire spark plugs allows you the best possible chance of moving the ground electrodes without breaking them. In some cases, this type of tool may have a wire gauge that permits you to measure the gap once a plug has been gapped.

Figure 8-155. This unit is a combination spark plug cleaner and tester. It is widely used in maintenance shops to clean and test spark plugs.

places the firing end of a spark plug under pressure and provides the voltage necessary to fire the plug in rapid succession. [Figure 8-155]

INSTALLATION

When reinstalling a set of spark plugs you should rotate where the plugs were originally installed. This promotes even spark plug wear and extends plug service life. To understand why rotation provides this benefit, consider the fact that, every time a spark occurs, metal is transferred from one electrode to another. This same process of metal transfer can be seen when arc welding.

Polarity

If you recall, each time a rotating magnet in a magneto passes the neutral position, the polarity of the current changes. As a result, the sparks produced by a magneto alternate in polarity. This means that in an engine with an even number of cylinders, each spark plug fires with the same polarity every time. For example, assume sparks jump from the center electrode to the ground electrode on the spark plugs in the number one cylinder. If the number four cylinder is next in the firing order, sparks will jump from the ground electrode to the center electrode of those spark plugs. When the polarity of sparks on a spark plug do not change, one electrode looses metal relative to the other electrode. When a plug fires positively, the ground electrode looses more than the center electrode. On the other hand, when a plug fires negatively, the center electrode wears more than the ground electrode

Spark plug rotation after servicing allows each plug to fire with a polarity opposite to what it was previously firing. This balances electrode wear and increases the service life of a spark plug.

In addition to changing the firing polarity of a set of spark plugs, it is a good idea to swap the plugs in a cylinder from top to bottom. The reason for this is that lead and other impurities produced during the combustion process tend to precipitate to the lower plugs, causing them to wear. Therefore, to help equalize plug wear, the spark plugs for a given cylinder shold be switched from top to bottom. [Figure 8-156]

Before installing a spark plug, a small amount of anti-seize compound should be applied to the shell threads. Anti-seize compound of the correct type is

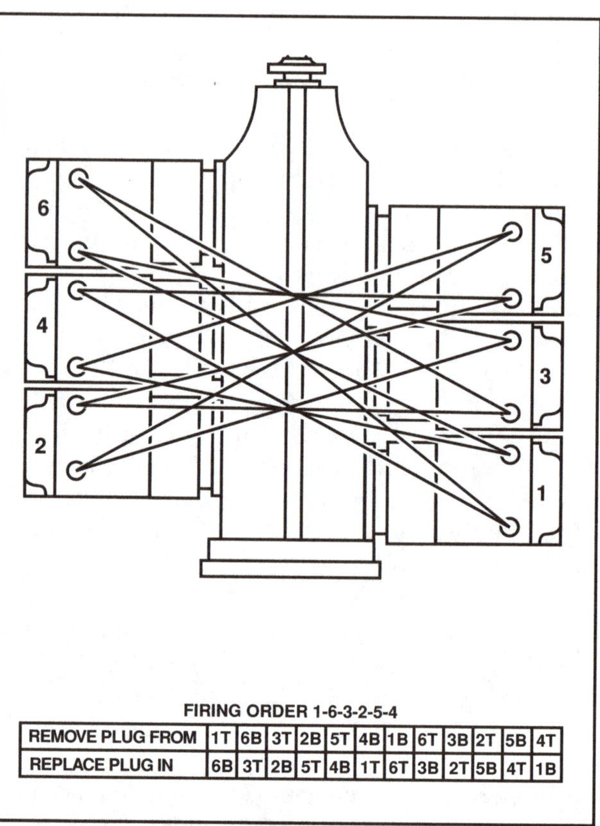

FIRING ORDER 1-6-3-2-5-4

REMOVE PLUG FROM	1T	6B	3T	2B	5T	4B	1B	6T	3B	2T	5B	4T
REPLACE PLUG IN	6B	3T	2B	5T	4B	1T	6T	3B	2T	5B	4T	1B

Figure 8-156. Spark plug rotation is an important practice which extends the service life of a set of spark plugs. A general rule you should follow when rotating a set of plugs is to rotate a plug to the cylinder next in the firing order and switch it from top to bottom.

usually supplied by spark plug manufacturers. Apply the compound sparingly to the second thread from the firing end of each spark plug. Never apply the compound to the firing end where it could run down over the electrodes. [Figure 8-157]

Most manufacturers recommend that the solid copper gasket used between a spark plug and cylinder be replaced whenever you reinstall a spark plug. The reason for this is that these gaskets tend to work harden over time. Once hardened, the gasket loses its ability to create a seal.

Some cylinder head temperature gauges use a gasket-type thermocouple pickup under one of the spark plugs. When gasket-type thermocouple pickups are used, they should be installed on the hottest operating cylinder. If a gasket-type pickup is used, no additional gasket is needed between the spark plug and cylinder head.

If a spark plug does not screw all the way down onto the cylinder head with finger pressure, carbon buildups may be present in the threads of the spark plug boss. If this is the case, use the appropriate spark plug thread cleaning tool or a suitable thread chaser to clear the buildups. In addition, inspect the threads with an inspection light to be certain they are clear and serviceable before reinstalling the spark plug.

Once all spark plugs have been installed and tightened by hand, a calibrated torque wrench and socket are used for final tightening. Snug down the spark plugs to the recommended torque value with one smooth pull. Next, wipe each lead terminal sleeve with a clean lint-free cloth moistened with acetone or other approved solvent. Slip the terminal sleeve straight into the spark plug barrel and tighten the terminal retainer nut finger-tight. Once all lead terminals are installed, tighten the terminal nuts approximately one-eighth inch with an open-end wrench.

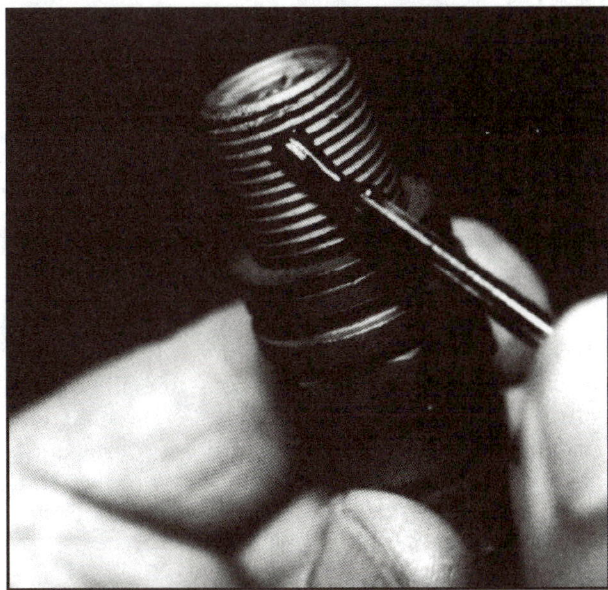

Figure 8-157. Apply anti-seize compound sparingly to the second thread from the firing end of each spark plug before installation.

SECTION F

TURBINE ENGINE IGNITION SYSTEMS

The primary function of a turbine engine ignition system is to ignite the fuel in the combustion chamber during engine starts. Once ignited, combustion becomes self-sustained and an ignition source is no longer required. Therefore, most turbine engine ignition systems are normally operated only for brief periods.

A secondary function of the ignition system is to provide standby protection against an in-flight flameout. To do this, most turbine engine ignition systems have continuous or automatic relight settings that can be selected in flight. Engines equipped with a continuous setting incorporate a separate low tension continuous duty circuit. With this type of system, a pilot can select continuous ignition with one or both igniter plugs. On engines equipped with an automatic relight setting, the ignition system monitors one or more parameters and provides ignition only when a monitored parameter falls below a specified operational value. One popular method of activating this type of system is to use pressure sensors installed at the compressor discharge. When used this way, a drop in discharge pressure automatically activates the ignition system.

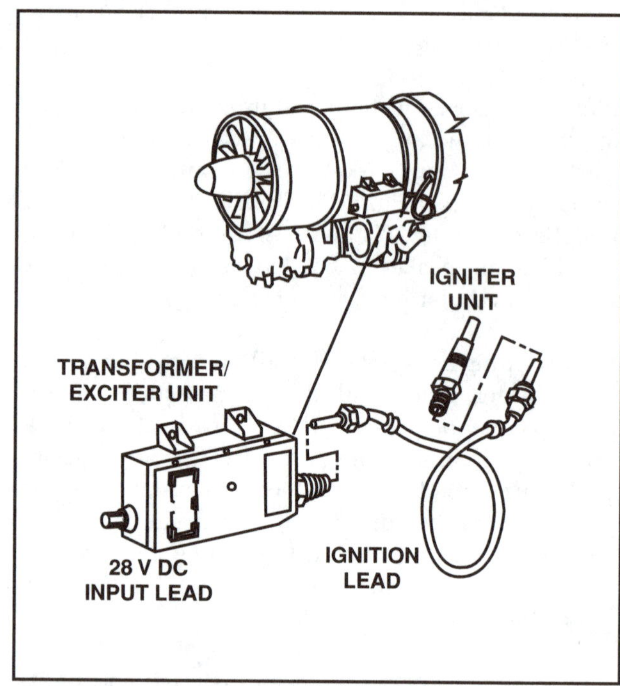

Figure 8-158. A turbine engine ignition system typically consists of two separate ignition circuits, each with a transformer, or exciter, ignition lead, and igniter unit.

CAPACITOR-DISCHARGE

Almost all turbine engines utilize a **capacitor-discharge** ignition system. Unlike the ignition systems used on reciprocating engines that produce a high voltage, low amperage spark, a capacitor-discharge ignition system delivers a high voltage, high amperage spark that has a high heat intensity. This high-energy spark is needed to ignite the fuel/air mixture in low temperatures and at high altitudes. To give you an idea as to the intensity of the spark produced by a capacitor-discharge system most turbine engine ignition systems are assigned a joule rating based on the amount of power they produce. One joule represents the number of watts in a spark times the duration of the spark. A typical spark lasts a few millionths of a second and, therefore, for one joule to be produced, the number of watts in the spark must be high. A typical capacitor-discharge ignition system produces a spark that may be as high as 20 joules and 2,000 amps.

The two common types of capacitor-discharge systems are the high-tension and low-tension systems. Both systems consist of two identical independent systems containing two transformers, or exciter units, two high-tension leads, and two igniter units. Each exciter unit, sometimes called an exciter box, generates electrical energy for operating the igniters. [Figure 8-158]

Most exciters are sealed units containing electronic circuitry that is potted in an epoxy resin. In some cases, both exciters are housed together as a single unit. In this case, the two exciter circuits are often considered to be one unit.

LOW-TENSION SYSTEM

In a low-tension system, 28 volts DC is supplied to each exciter unit. Each unit then steps up the 28 volts DC to produce the high voltage pulses necessary to fire one igniter unit. In order for an exciter unit to step up the input voltage, a coil must be used. In addition, the DC input current must be converted so it pulsates in the coil's primary winding. To do this, many low-tension systems use a vibrator type circuit. [Figure 8-159]

When a low-tension system is de-energized, a permanent magnet holds the points in the vibrator circuit closed. However, once the cockpit switch is closed, current flows from ground, up through the primary winding, across the points, and to the battery's positive terminal. As electromagnetic forces in the primary winding build and become stronger than the permanent magnet, the points are pulled open, and current flow stops. This action is repeated approximately 200 times per second and produces pulsating DC voltage. To prevent arcing at the points, a capacitor is installed in parallel with the points.

When current initially flows through the primary winding, a relatively small pulse is produced in the secondary winding. This pulse attempts to flow from the secondary winding to ground, up through the storage capacitor, and to the top side of the secondary winding. To stop current flow in this direction, a diode rectifier is installed between the top side of the secondary winding and the storage capacitor. To prevent this initial pulse from flowing to the igniter, a discharge tube is installed between the capacitor and igniter.

When the points open, the electromagnetic field surrounding the primary winding collapses, and a strong pulse is induced into the secondary winding. Secondary current now flows from the top of the secondary winding, through the rectifier, and into the storage capacitor. As electrons pile up on the top plate of the storage capacitor a negative charge accumulates and free electrons are repelled from the bottom plate of the capacitor to ground.

After repeated cycles, the storage capacitor builds a charge that is capable of jumping the gap in the discharge tube. The initial current surge ionizes the air gap, which makes it conductive and allows the capacitor to discharge fully to the igniter.

The igniter in a low-tension system is referred to as a **self-ionizing** or **shunted-gap-type** igniter. The firing end of the igniter contains a semi-conductor material which bridges the gap between the center and ground electrodes. When current initially flows to the igniter, it flows through the center electrode, the semi-conductor, the outer casing, and back to the capacitor. As soon as current flows through the semi-conductor, the semi-conductor heats up and its resistance increases. At the same time, the air gap heats up sufficiently to ionize and decrease resistance. Once the resistance across the air gap becomes less than the resistance across the semi-conductor, the capacitor fully discharges across the air gap to create a high energy capacitive discharge spark.

As a safety precaution, many ignition systems have a bleed resistor. The purpose of the bleed resistor is to allow the capacitor to slowly discharge when the system is de-energized. It also protects the circuit from overheating if the ignition system is energized with no igniter plugs installed.

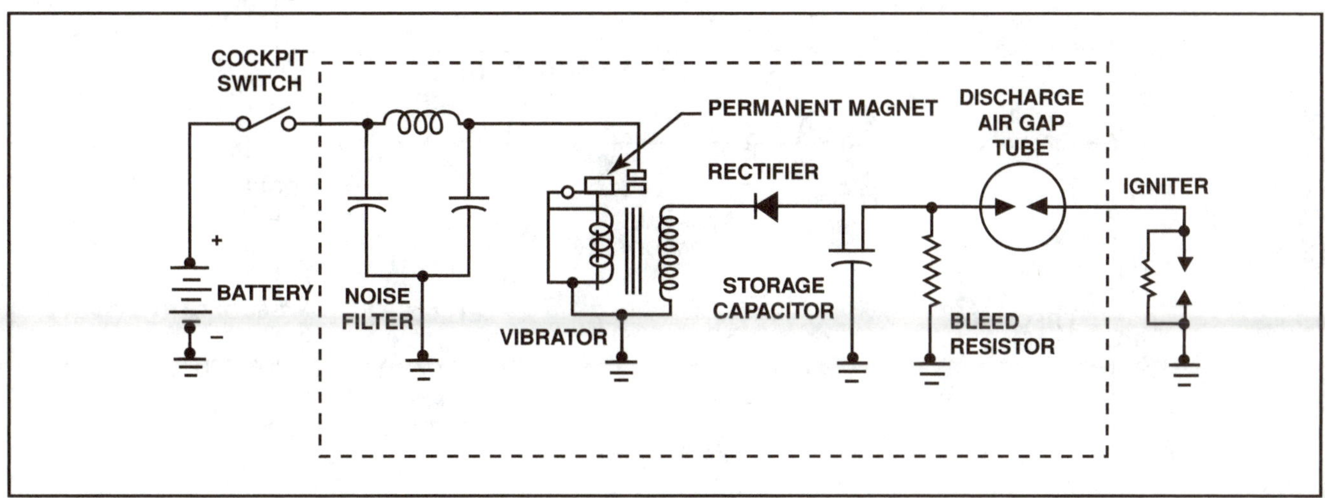

Figure 8-159. A low-tension DC system utilizes a 24 to 28 volt DC input and vibrator circuit to produce pulsating DC current that can be stepped up.

HIGH-TENSION SYSTEM

In a high-tension ignition system, 115 volt, 400 Hz alternating current is applied to the transformer/exciter unit. The use of alternating current eliminates the need for a vibrator circuit which, in turn, eliminates the problems associated with vibrating contacts. [Figure 8-160]

When 115 volts AC is applied to a high-tension circuit, the primary winding of the power transformer induces approximately 2,000 volts into the secondary winding during the first half cycle. Once induced into the secondary, current flows from the negative side of the winding and out to ground. Current then flows up from ground at rectifier tube A, through resistor R_1 and the doubler capacitor, and back to the positive side of the secondary winding. This charges the left side of the doubler capacitor to 2,000 volts. Rectifier tube B blocks any other current path during this half cycle.

During the second half cycle, the primary winding induces another 2,000 volts into the secondary winding. Once induced, the current flows from the positive side of the coil and charges the right side of the doubler capacitor to 2,000 volts. The doubler capacitor now has a total charge of 4,000 volts and current flows through resistor R_2, rectifier tube B, and the storage capacitor to ground. The circuit is completed when current passes through ground and back to the negative side of the secondary coil. During this half cycle, rectifier tube A blocks current flow from the doubler capacitor and R_1 to ground ensuring current flow to the storage capacitor.

Repeated pulses charge the storage capacitor to a point where the air gap in the discharge tube ionizes. When this occurs, current flows across the air gap and to the trigger transformer. Once at the trigger transformer, current flows through the primary winding and trigger capacitor to ground. The storage capacitor discharge through the primary winding of the trigger transformer induces a 20,000 volt pulse in the secondary winding. This 20,000 volt pulse ionizes the igniter plug air gap creating a low resistance path that allows both the trigger capacitor and storage capacitor to fully discharge at the igniter plug. The high-tension spark vaporizes and ignites fuel globules around the igniter electrodes.

IGNITERS

Igniters for gas turbine engines differ considerably from the spark plugs used on reciprocating engines. For example, the air gap on an igniter is much wider than that of a conventional spark plug and the electrode is designed to withstand a much more intense spark. An igniter plug is also less susceptible to fouling because the high energy spark

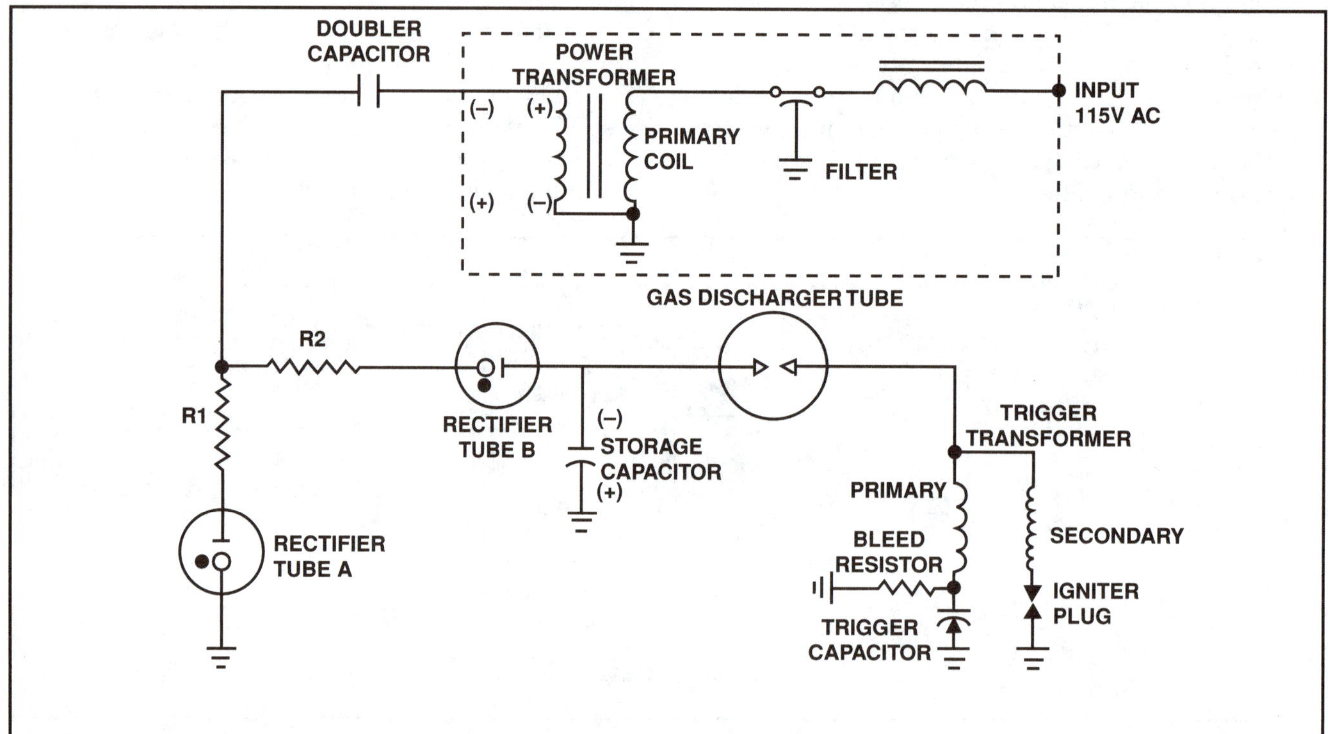

Figure 8-160. A high-tension AC input system utilizes 115 volt, 400 Hz alternating current.

removes carbon and other deposits each time the igniter fires. In addition, igniters generally have a long service life because they do not require continuous operation.

The construction of igniters is different from spark plugs. For example, the outer shell of most turbine engine igniters is made of a very high quality, nickel-chromium alloy. The reason for this is that nickel-chromium is corrosion resistant and has a low coefficient of heat expansion.

TYPES OF IGNITERS

Many varieties of igniter plugs are available and, therefore, procedures regarding the service and maintenance of igniters varies. Because of this, engine manufacturers specify the approved igniters for a given engine as well as the servicing instructions. [Figure 8-161]

When installed in an engine, the igniter tip must protrude the proper length into the combustor. In

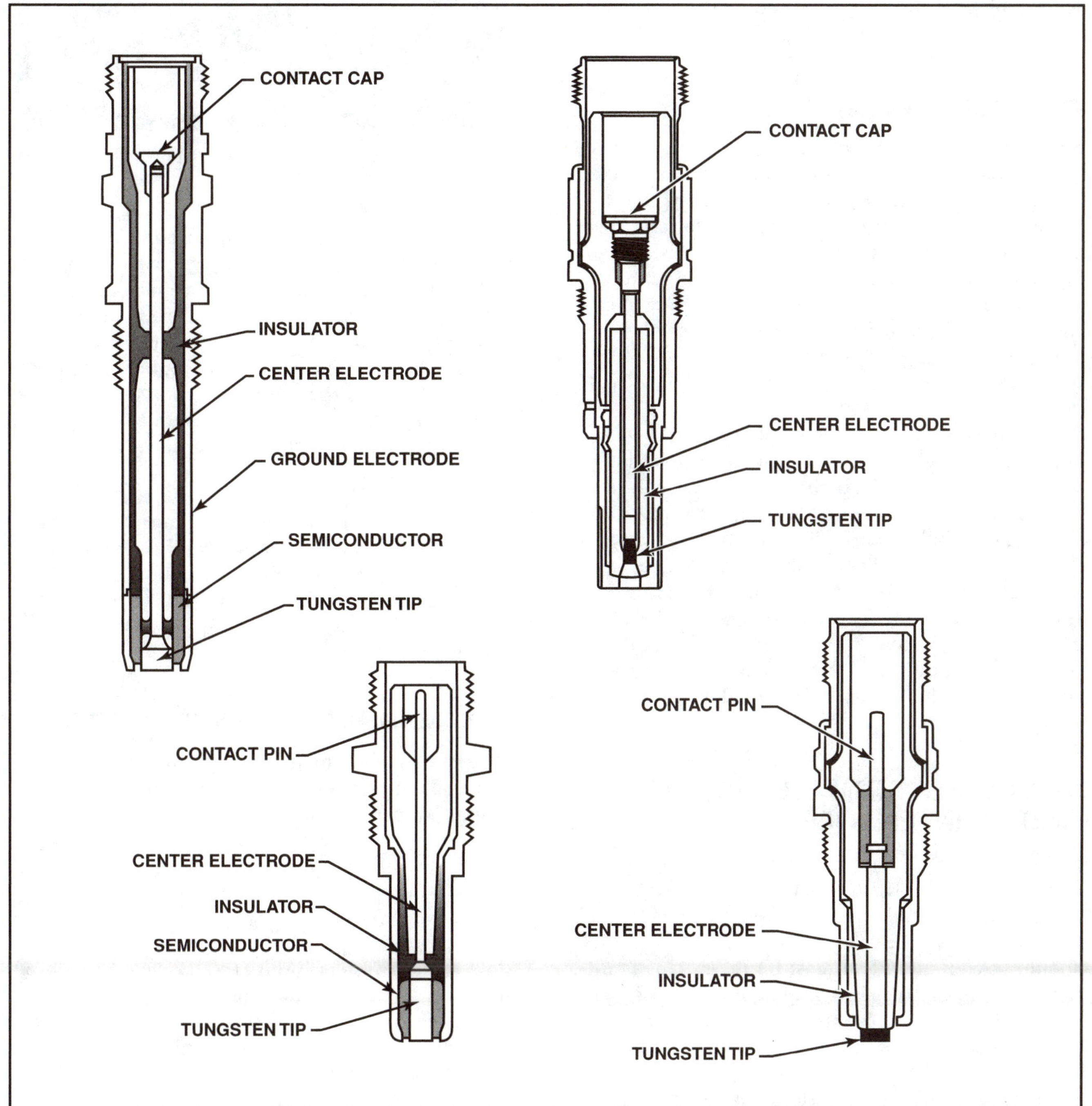

Figure 8-161. There are a number of different types of igniters used in turbine engines. The two igniters on the left are typical of a low voltage system while the two igniters on the right are typical of a high voltage system.

most cases, the igniter tip extends approximately 0.1 inch into the combustion chamber. However, in the case of a **constrained-gap igniter**, the igniter does not have to project into the combustion chamber. The reason for this is the center electrode of a constrained-gap igniter plug is recessed in the body of the plug. Therefore, in order for the high intensity spark to get from the center electrode to ground, it must jump out away from the plug's tip. This allows the tip of a constrained-gap igniter to remain partially recessed in the combustion chamber liner which, in turn, allows it to operate at cooler temperatures.

GLOW PLUGS

Some small turbine and turboprop engines incorporate a glow plug type igniter rather than a spark igniter. Although glow plugs are not considered to be an igniter in the strictest sense, they do serve the same purpose. A glow plug consists of a resistance coil that is very similar in appearance to an automobile cigarette lighter. However, with a glow plug, the coil generates a very high heat value that is capable of igniting a fuel/air mixture in extremely low temperatures.

In a typical glow plug ignition system, 24 to 28 volts is supplied to each glow plug causing it to become yellow hot. Once hot, air directed up through the glow plug coil mixes with fuel dripping from the main fuel nozzle. This is designed to occur when the main nozzle is not completely atomizing its discharge during engine start. The influence of the airflow on the dripping fuel acts to create a hot streak or torch-like ignition. After engine start, fuel flow through the glow plug is terminated and the air source keeps the igniter coil cool during normal engine operation. [Figure 8-162]

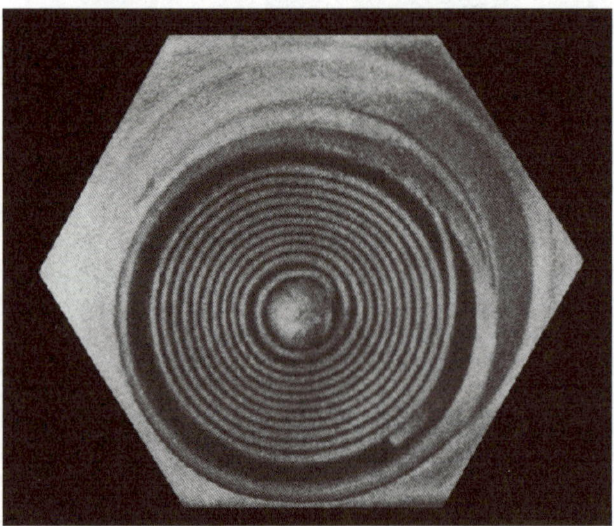

Figure 8-162. Glow plugs are similar in appearance to an automobile cigarette lighter.

IGNITION SYSTEM INSPECTION AND MAINTENANCE

Maintenance of a typical turbine engine ignition system consists primarily of inspecting, testing, troubleshooting, and replacing various components. However, when performing these operations, you should bear in mind that most turbine engine ignition systems produce lethal amounts of electrical current. Therefore, it is imperative that you follow the manufacturers recommended safety procedures.

For example, before you perform any maintenance on an ignition system ensure that the ignition switch is off. As a safety precaution, manufacturers typically recommend a waiting period after the ignition system is turned off before you begin disassembling any connections. To remove an igniter plug, disconnect the transformer input lead and wait the time prescribed by the manufacturer. Once the recommended time has passed, disconnect the igniter lead and ground the center electrode to the engine. Following these steps helps ensure that no lethal electrical charges are discharged during the removal process.

In situations where a transformer must be removed, you should exercise caution. The reason for this is that some older transformers contain amounts of radioactive material. The radioactive material is used to calibrate the discharge point to a preset voltage.

CLEANING AND SERVICING IGNITERS

The outer case of high voltage igniter plugs may be cleaned with a soft brush and approved solvent. Typically, ceramic insulators and electrode tips are cleaned with solvent and a felt swab. After cleaning, blow off the remaining solvent with dry compressed air.

The self-ionizing, or shunted-gap igniters used with low-tension systems are generally cleaned only on their outer casing. The semiconductor material at the firing end is easily damaged and manufacturers seldom permit any type of cleaning, regardless of the amount of carbon buildup.

If glow plug heater coils have carbon buildup which appears to fuse the coils together, the coil end can be immersed in carbon remover to soften the deposit. Once softened, a soft nylon or fiber brush is used to remove any remaining carbon. Finally, the coil is rinsed in warm water and blown dry with compressed air.

Inspection of a high voltage igniter plug or glow plug generally consists of a visual inspection and a dimensional check. Use of a technician's scale or suitable depth micrometer is recommended. Visually inspect self-ionizing igniters used in low-tension systems in the same manner but do not make dimensional checks. The delicate nature of the semiconductor material makes contact with any tool risky. The semiconductor material often consists of only a very thin coating over a ceramic base material.

If an igniter is determined to be faulty, follow the proper disposal procedures outlined by the manufacturer. The materials used in some igniters may require special handling.

After you have completed a visual and dimensional inspection, reinstall the serviceable igniters, or glow plugs and prepare the engine for an operational check. However, before an operational check is performed, ensure that no fuel is in any of the combustors. A fuel-wetted combustor may erupt in fire when the igniters are tested. The operational check should follow the guidelines established by the engine manufacturer and the aircraft ground runup checklist.

When operated, all igniters produce a snapping sound when they are fired. The sound emanates from the high intensity spark that jumps the air gap between the igniter electrodes. As a general rule, the more intense the spark, the louder the snapping noise. Therefore, to conduct an operational test, one person stands near the engine and listens for the snapping noise produced by each igniter while someone in the cockpit activates the ignition switch.

TROUBLESHOOTING

Logical troubleshooting procedures should be used when investigating an ignition system problem. To aid in this process, many engine manufacturers produce troubleshooting charts to help in the diagnosis and repair of commonly encountered problems. [Figure 8-163]

As a safety precaution, you should never energize a turbine engine ignition system for troubleshooting with the igniter plugs removed. If this is done, serious overheating or damage to the exciter box may result.

1. NO IGNITER SPARK WITH THE SYSTEM TURNED ON		
Possible Cause	**Check For**	**Remedy**
A. Ignition Relay	Correct Power Input to Transformer Unit	Correct Relay Problems, Refer to Starter-Generator Circuit
B. Transformer Unit	Correct Power Output, Observing Ignition System Cautions	Replace Transformer
C. High Tension Lead	Continuity or High Resistance Shorts With Ohmmeter and Megger-Check Unit	Replace Lead
D. Igniter Plug	1. Cracked Insulator or Damaged Semiconductor	Replace Plug
	2. Hot Electrode Erosion	Replace Plug
2. LONG INTERVAL BETWEEN SPARKS		
Possible Cause	**Check For**	**Remedy**
Power Supply	Weak Battery	Recharge Battery
3. WEAK SPARK		
Possible Cause	**Check For**	**Remedy**
Igniter Plug	Cracked ceramic Insulation	Replace Plug

Figure 8-163. This chart outlines the procedures to use when an ignition system produces a weak spark, no spark, or improper intervals between sparks.

CHAPTER 9

LUBRICATION SYSTEMS

INTRODUCTION

The primary purpose of a lubricant is to reduce friction between moving parts and, to a lesser degree, help in engine cooling. It is also used to seal and cushion moving parts, clean the engine interior, and protect against corrosion. Since engines require a lubricant which can circulate freely, liquid lubricants such as oils are the most widely used in aircraft engines.

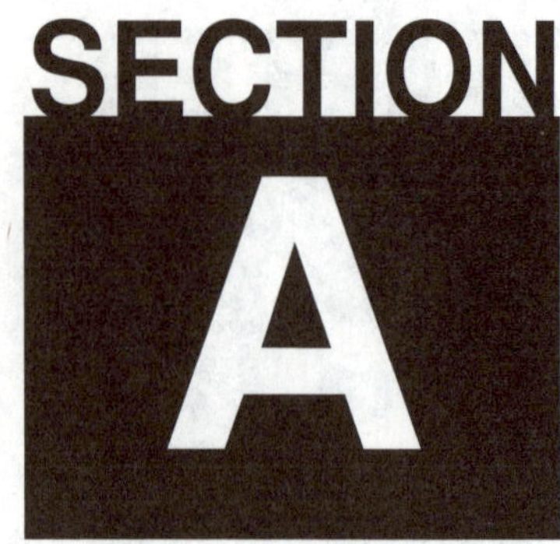

SECTION A ENGINE LUBRICATING OILS

Properties and characteristics of lubricating oils vary with the oil type. An oil with the correct specifications must always be used in each engine because use of the wrong oil could lead to damaged or failed engine components. With that caution in mind, consider the following discussion on oil properties and the various oil types. Typical applications of the different oil types are discussed, as well as the methods used to grade aircraft engine oils.

FUNCTIONS OF LUBRICATING OIL

Lubricating oil is often considered to be the life blood of an engine. Without it, the friction and wear produced between moving parts would cause an engine to wear at a very rapid rate. In addition to reducing friction, lubricating oil is responsible for removing a great deal of engine heat. If fact, without an ample supply of oil, most reciprocating engines will overheat. Additional functions of lubricating oils include creating a seal between moving parts, cushioning impact forces created by combustion, cleaning the engine, and protecting against corrosion.

REDUCE FRICTION

Many of the metal parts inside an aircraft engine have surfaces which appear smooth to the naked eye. However, if you were to microscopically examine those same parts, you would see a rather rough surface consisting of several peaks and valleys. When those engine parts rub against one another, the resulting friction soon wears away the metal. In order to reduce this friction, a film of lubrication oil is placed between the moving parts. Oil wets the surfaces, fills in the valleys, and holds the metal surfaces apart as long as the oil film remains unbroken. The engine parts then slide over each other on a film of oil rather than grind together. Therefore, friction is reduced and part wear is minimized. [Figure 9-1]

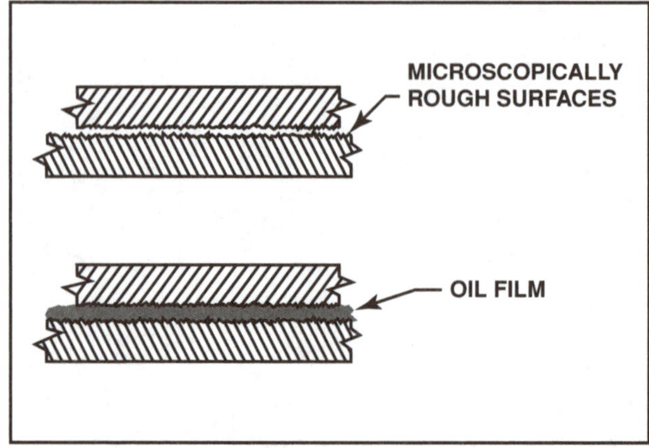

Figure 9-1. Engine parts that appear smooth to the naked eye reveal rough surfaces under a microscope. Lubricating oil separates these surfaces and minimizes wear.

The amount of clearance between moving parts is a determining factor when choosing the proper type and grade of oil. An oil must adhere to a part sufficiently and be thick enough to provide an adequate protective film that will not break down and allow metal-to-metal contact.

ABSORBS HEAT

In addition to reducing friction and wear, oil absorbs some of the heat produced by combustion as it circulates through the engine. The pistons and cylinder walls are especially dependent on lubricating oil for cooling. However, once the oil heats up, a means of cooling the oil must be provided. Therefore, several engine lubrication systems contain an oil cooler. An **oil cooler** is basically a heat exchanger that transfers the heat contained in the oil to the outside air.

SEALS

Oil also exhibits excellent wetting characteristics because the oil film has an ability to evenly coat metal surfaces. This characteristic of oil makes it a good sealing agent between moving parts. For example, the oil film on cylinder walls forms an effective seal with the piston rings in a cylinder. This helps prevent gas leakage during the combustion process.

CUSHIONS

The same characteristic of oil that makes it a good sealing agent also provides a cushioning effect between metal parts. For example, the thin film of oil between a rocker arm and its bushing absorbs some of the hammering shock from the valve action. The cushioning action also helps reduce some of the impact force between a crankshaft and its connecting rods.

CLEANS

The oil in a lubrication system also reduces engine wear by serving as a cleaning agent. As the oil circulates, it picks up foreign particles such as dirt, dust, carbon, and small amounts of water. These particles are held in suspension by the oil and carried to a filter where they are trapped and removed.

PROTECTS AGAINST CORROSION

Metal engine parts which are exposed to moist air and various chemicals have a tendency to rust or form other types of surface corrosion. This is especially true for cylinder walls and crankshafts which have been hardened by nitriding. The oil film which coats internal engine parts acts as a barrier, preventing oxygen and moisture from reaching the metal surface and causing it to corrode.

OIL CONSUMPTION

In the performance of all the previously mentioned functions, a portion of the lubrication oil is consumed. The amount of oil consumed depends on several factors such as engine rpm, engine temperature, operating clearances, and lubricant characteristics. Generally, higher rpm and temperatures, larger clearances and less viscosity correspond to higher consumption rates. Larger clearances are one reason why reciprocating engines typically consume more oil than turbine engines.

OIL PROPERTIES

Theoretically, the perfect engine oil is thin enough to circulate freely, yet heavy enough to stay in place and maintain a reasonable film strength. However, in practice, a compromise must be made and several factors must be considered in determining the proper grade of oil to use in a particular engine. Some of these factors include engine operating loads, rotational speeds of bearings, and operating temperatures. When determining the proper grade of oil to use there are several properties which must be considered.

VISCOSITY

One of the most important properties of an oil is viscosity, which is a measure of an oil's resistance to flow. An oil that flows slowly is viscous, or has a high viscosity. On the other hand, oil that flows freely has a low viscosity.

Oil viscosity is measured using an instrument known as the **Saybolt Universal Viscosimeter**. To measure an oil's viscosity, a specific quantity of oil must be heated to an exact temperature. Then, the number of seconds required for 60 cubic centimeters of the heated oil to flow through a calibrated orifice is recorded as a measure of the oil's viscosity. The recorded time is known as the **Saybolt Seconds Universal** viscosity or **S.S.U.** Typical aviation oils have an S.S.U. of 80, 100, or 120 when heated to 210°F.

Of all the factors that impact the viscosity of lubricating oil, temperature has the greatest effect. In fact, it is not uncommon for some high viscosity oils to become almost semi-solid in cold weather. When this happens, engine component drag increases and oil circulation dramatically decreases. On the other hand, low viscosity oils can become so thin at high temperatures that the oil can no longer maintain a solid film. When this happens, rapid wear and lower than normal oil pressure results. For these reasons, lower viscosity oils are typically used in cold climates and higher viscosity oils are usesd in warm climates.

Oils used in reciprocating engines usually have a relatively high viscosity for several reasons. One reason is that most reciprocating engines have large operational clearances and high operating temperatures. Therefore, a high viscosity oil is required to ensure an adequate oil film between the moving parts. In addition, most reciprocating engines operate at relatively high temperatures and, therefore, a high viscosity oil is needed to keep the oil from getting too thin at operating temperatures. Furthermore, high bearing pressures in reciprocating engines require the cushion that higher viscosity oils provide.

VISCOSITY INDEX

In addition to having a viscosity rating, many oils are assigned a **viscosity index**, or **VI** number. The viscosity index is a standard used to identify an oil's rate of change in viscosity for a given change in temperature. The index itself is based on a comparative analysis of the temperature-induced viscosity changes of two reference oils, arbitrarily chosen by the **American Society of Testing and Materials**, or **ASTM**. One oil is assigned a viscosity index rating of 100, and the other is rated at zero. The smaller the change in the viscosity for a given temperature change, the higher the viscosity index.

SPECIFIC GRAVITY

An oil's specific gravity is a comparison of the weight of an oil to the weight of an equal volume of distilled water at a specified temperature. For example, water weighs approximately 8 pounds per gallon. Therefore, an oil with a specific gravity of 0.9 weighs 7.2 pounds per gallon ($0.9 \times 8 = 7.2$).

The **American Petroleum Institute** or **API** has formulated a measurement for the specific gravity of oils which is an expansion of the regular specific gravity scale. The API scale is considered to be a more accurate measure of an oil's gravity because it provides more detail on that portion of the specific gravity where lubricating oils fall. However, in most cases, an oil's API number can be converted to a specific gravity number using a conversion chart.

COLOR

Oil color is determined by the amount of light that passes through an oil sample in a glass container when placed in front of a light of known intensity. The color test is conducted with a device known as an **ASTM union colorimeter**. The color is then compared to an ASTM color chart. A color reference number of 1.00 on the chart is pure white, and a reference number of 8.00 is darker than claret red.

With oils that are darker than number 8.00, the oil is diluted with kerosene to form a mixture which is 85 percent kerosene and 15 percent oil by volume. The mixture is then given a color rating in the same manner as other oils. If indirect, or reflected light is used to perform a color test, the oil color is referred to as a **bloom** and can be used to determine the origin of the oil.

CLOUD POINT

Another property of lubricating oil is known as cloud point. A particular oil's cloud point is the temperature at which paraffin wax and other solids normally held in a solution of oil begin to solidify and separate into tiny crystals. At this temperature, the oil begins to lose clarity and appears cloudy or hazy.

POUR POINT

An oil's pour point represents the lowest temperature at which the oil can flow or be poured. Pour point is an oil property which determines a given oil's ability to lubricate at low operating temperatures. As a general rule, the pour point of an oil should be within five degrees Fahrenheit of the average ambient starting temperature to ensure oil circulation.

FLASH POINT AND FIRE POINT

An oil's flash point is the temperature at which it begins to emit ignitable vapors. As temperature increases beyond the flash point, the oil's fire point is reached and sufficient vapors are emitted to support a flame. A typical lubricating oil has a fire point approximately 50 to 60°F higher than the flash point. An oil must be able to withstand the high temperatures encountered in an operating engine without creating a fire hazard. Therefore, these two temperature ratings are important when selecting the proper oil for an engine.

CARBON RESIDUE TEST

In the carbon residue test, a given amount of oil is placed in a stainless steel receptacle and heated to a controlled temperature until it evaporates. The container is weighed before and after the test. The difference in weight is then divided by the weight of the original oil sample to obtain the percertage of carbon, by weight, in the oil.

ASH TEST

An ash test is an extension of a carbon residue test in that it requires the carbon residue to be burned until only ash remains. The amount of ash remaining is then expressed as a percentage by weight of the carbon residue. New oil which leaves almost no ash is considered to be pure. On the other hand, the ash left by used oil can be analyzed for iron and lead content. The amount of iron and lead found provide clues to the amount of internal engine wear.

ENGINE OIL GRADING SYSTEM

Most commercial aviation oils are assigned numerical designations such as 80, 100, or 120 that approximate an oil's viscosity. This practice has proven to be much more workable than using actual Saybolt values to designate viscosity. The reason for this is that oil viscosity varies enough among commonly

SAE No.	COMMERCIAL AVIATION No.	AN SPECIFICATION (MILITARY)
SAE 30	GRADE 65	AN 1065
SAE 40	GRADE 80	AN 1080
SAE 50	GRADE 100	AN 1100
SAE 60	GRADE 120	AN 1120
SAE 70	GRADE 140	

Figure 9-2. This chart illustrates how a similar oil can have an SAE rating, a commercial aviation rating, and a Military rating.

used oils to produce several hundred grades when using Saybolt values.

To further simplify the oil grading process, a system designed by the **Society of Automotive Engineers (SAE)** was designed. The SAE system scale divides all oils into seven groups, ranging from SAE 10 to SAE 70. The groupings are based on an oil's viscosity at either 130°F or 210°F. In addition, an SAE rating with the letter "W," such as 20W indicates the oil is acceptable for use in cold, or winter, climates.

Although SAE ratings are used with most oils, there are still some oils that carry commercial aviation or military designations. It is important to note that SAE ratings are purely arbitrary and bear no direct relationship to other ratings. [Figure 9-2]

Use of the SAE system scale has eliminated much of the confusion in the designation of lubricating oils. However, it must not be assumed that an SAE designation covers all the important viscosity requirements. An SAE number indicates only the relative viscosity of an oil and does not indicate quality or other essential characteristics. There are good oils and inferior oils which have the same viscosities at a given temperature and, therefore, are classified as the same grade. Always bear in mind that an SAE rating on an oil container is not an endorsement or recommendation of that particular oil by the Society of Automotive Engineers. The only way to be sure that an oil meets the requirements of a particular engine is to be familiar with the individual characteristics of a given oil. [Figure 9-3]

TYPES OF OIL

Oils from a variety of sources have been used in aircraft. For example, the earliest aircraft engines used castor oil as a lubricant, which is a pure vegetable oil derived from castor beans. However, vegetable based lubricants have poor chemical stability and tend to oxidize when used in reciprocating engines. Because of this, vegetable based oils were soon replaced with mineral based oils. Mineral based oils tend to be much more chemically stable than vegetable based lubricants and are still the most widely used oils in reciprocating engines. A final type of oil that is used in aircraft engines is synthetic oil. Although synthetic oils are mostly used in turbine engines, a few synthetic lubricants are approved for use in reciprocating engines.

STRAIGHT MINERAL OIL

MIL-L-6082E is a straight mineral oil that has no additives and, for many years, the principle type of

	SAE 30 AVIATION 65 AN 1065	SAE 40 AVIATION 80 AN 1080	SAE 50 AVIATION 100 AN 1100	SAE 60 AVIATION 120 AN 1120
VISCOSITY				
S.S.U. @ 100°F	443.0	676.0	1,124.0	1,530.0
S.S.U. @ 130°F	215.0	310.0	480.0	630.0
S.S.U. @ 210°F	65.4	79.2	103.0	123.2
VISCOSITY INDEX	116.0	112.0	108.0	107.0
GRAVITY API	29.0	27.5	27.4	27.1
COLOR ASTM	1.5	4.5	4.5	5.5
POUR POINT °F	–20.0	–15.0	–10.0	–10.0
POUR POINT DILUTED °F	–70.0	–70.0	–70.0	–50.0
FLASH POINT °F	450.0	465.0	515.0	520.0
CARBON RESIDUE % W	0.11	0.23	0.23	0.40

Figure 9-3. This chart illustrates the characteristics of various oils. However, it is important to note that a given SAE rating only indicates a specific viscosity and does not guarantee any other characteristic.

oil used in aircraft. Although straight mineral oil is an effective lubricant, it does have some limitations. For example, when exposed to elevated temperatures in an aerated condition, straight mineral oil has a tendency to oxidize. In addition, if straight mineral oil becomes overly contaminated, a sludge can form that may clog filters and passages as well as score engine components. Because of this, the use of straight mineral oil has been limited to new or newly overhauled engines during their break-in period.

ASHLESS-DISPERSANT OILS

The most commonly used oil in reciprocating engines is ashless-dispersant, or **AD** oil that conforms to MIL-L-22851D. It does not have the carbon forming restrictions of straight mineral oil nor does it form ash deposits like detergent oils. In addition, all ashless-dispersant oils contain a **dispersant** that causes sludge-forming materials to repel each other and stay in suspension until they can be trapped by the oil filter. This provides several advantages in that oil passages and ring grooves remain free of harmful deposits.

In addition to a dispersant, several ashless-dispersant oils contain an anti-wear, anti-foam additive. However, these additives are unique in that they do not leave metallic ash deposits in an engine. Ash deposits are bad because they can lead to preignition and spark plug fouling.

Since ashless-dispersant oils are such an effective lubricant, most engine manufacturers do not recommend their use during an engine's break-in period. The reason for this is that, when an engine is first broken-in, some component wear must occur. For example, before a set of piston rings can effectively seal against a cylinder wall, the two surfaces must wear against each other to produce a sealable junction. If sufficient wear does not occur, the engine will consume excessive amounts of oil throughout its operating life. Therefore, to promote some degree of wear, most manufacturers recommend that new and newly overhauled engines be operated on straight mineral oil for the first 10 to 50 hours of operation or until oil consumption stabilizes. After this, the straight mineral oil should be drained and replaced by a quality ashless-dispersant oil for the remaining engine life.

MULTI-VISCOSITY OILS

Multi-viscosity oils were developed to help address some of the drawbacks of single viscosity oils. For example, if an SAE 10 oil is used in a warm climate, it will get too hot and lose its ability to maintain an adequate film on moving parts. On the other hand, if an SAE 30 oil is used in a cold climate, the oil will not circulate properly, especially when an engine is first started.

Multi-viscosity oils differ from single viscosity oils in that they provide adequate lubrication over a wider temperature range. This allows multi-viscosity oils to flow more quickly in cold weather and keep from thinning in hot weather. A typical multi-viscosity oil, such as SAE 15W50, can generally be safely used over the combined temperature range of an SAE 15 and SAE 50 oil.

SYNTHETIC OILS

Synthetic oils have multi-viscosity properties due to their chemical composition and are similar to automotive grades SAE-5 to SAE-20. They are a blend of chemical additives and certain **diesters**, which are synthesized extracts of mineral, vegetable, and animal oils. Stated in another way, synthetic oils are made by synthesizing raw materials to form a base stock rather than refining base stock from crude oil.

Because of their chemical make up, synthetic oils have an extremely low internal friction. In addition, they have a high resistance to thermal breakdown and oxidation. Because of this, synthetic oils are ideal for use in turbine engines and can typically go longer between oil changes. In addition, the wear characteristics of synthetic oil appears to be about the same as ashless-dispersant oil and superior to straight mineral oil.

One problem with synthetic oils is that they do not disperse and suspend contaminants as well as ashless-dispersant oils. Therefore, synthetic oils have a tendency to cause sludge build-up in reciprocating engines, especially in engines that are not operated frequently. Another problem with synthetic oil is that, in some cases, it can soften rubber products and resins. In fact, because of this, one manufacturer requires more frequent replacement of the intercylinder drain lines when synthetic oil is used. In addition, pleated paper oil filters must be examined more closely to be sure that the oil does not dissolve the resins and allow the filter to collapse.

As a general rule, synthetic oils are not compatible with, and cannot be mixed with, mineral based oils. In addition, most manufacturers recommend against mixing different brands or types of synthetic oils. If any mixing is allowed, it should follow strict guidelines of same-type and certain compatible brands.

Another negative characteristic of synthetic oil is its tendency to blister or remove paint wherever it is spilled. If a spill occurs, wipe it up immediately with a petroleum solvent. When servicing an engine filled with synthetic oil, you must avoid excessive or prolonged exposure to your skin. Synthetic lubricants contain additives which are readily absorbed through the skin and are considered highly toxic.

Synthetic oils are given a **Kinematic Viscosity Rating** in **centistokes (cSt)** rather than an SAE rating. Some synthetic lubricant container labels are marked with the centistoke value, or metric viscosity measurement. For example, a synthetic oil with a 3 centistoke rating is roughly equivalent to an SAE-5 oil rating. On the other hand, synthetic oil with a 5 centistoke rating has a viscosity approximately equal to an SAE 5W10 multi-viscosity mineral-based oil. Likewise, a 7 centistoke oil has a viscosity approximately equal to an SAE 5W20 multi-viscosity oil rating.

EXTREME PRESSURE LUBRICANTS

Extreme pressure (EP) lubricants, also known as **hypoid lubricants**, are specially formulated to provide protection under high loads. A hypoid lubricant contains additives that bond to metal surfaces to reduce friction under high pressures or high rubbing velocities. A typical hypoid lubricant consists of a mineral-based oil containing loosely held molecules of sulfur or chlorine. A propeller reduction case is one example where a hypoid lubricant is needed. The spur-type gears in propeller reduction cases operate under high tooth pressures and often require EP lubricants to prevent gear failure.

RECIPROCATING ENGINES

OIL DISTRIBUTION

As discussed in the previous section, the primary purpose of a lubrication system is to lubricate the internal engine components. To do this, lubricating oil must be distributed throughout an engine. Common ways of distributing oil include using pressure, splash, and spray lubrication techniques.

PRESSURE LUBRICATION

Pressure lubrication is the primary type of lubrication used in reciprocating engines. All pressure lubrication systems rely on a pump to supply pressurized oil to critical engine parts. In most cases, the pump used in a pressure system is a positive displacement, engine driven pump. The term **positive displacement** indicates that the pump moves a specific amount of fluid for each revolution of the pump. Once oil passes through an oil pump, it passes through several passages within the crankcase where it is distributed to various engine components. Typical components within an engine that are lubricated by pressurized oil include all plain bearings, crankshaft and camshaft main bearings, lower connecting rod bearings, and valve assemblies.

SPLASH LUBRICATION

In addition to pressure lubrication, many reciprocating engines depend on some splash lubrication. Splash lubrication is produced by the movement of internal components which splash oil around. This method of lubrication is very effective in engines where oil is stored in the crankcase. In this configuration, as a piston reaches the bottom of a stroke, its associated crank throw partially submerges in oil and splashes it onto other components. Components that are often lubricated by splashed oil include cylinder walls, camshaft lobes, upper bearings of connecting rods, piston pins, and accessory gears.

SPRAY LUBRICATION

Some large reciprocating engines are physically too big for splash lubrication to be effective. In this case, some form of spray lubrication is typically used. Spray lubrication uses the same pressurized oil in a pressure lubrication system; however, instead of routing the oil to a component through an oil passage, the oil is sprayed on to a component through a nozzle. Engine components that are lubricated by sprayed engine oil include some cylinder walls and camshaft lobes.

COMBINATION SYSTEM

In order to ensure adequate lubrication, all reciprocating engines rely on a combination of pressure and splash lubrication. However, on larger engines, adequate oil circulation can only be accomplished through the use of pressure, splash, and spray lubrication. [Figure 9-4]

SYSTEM CLASSIFICATION

Reciprocating engine lubrication systems are generally classified as either a wet-sump or dry-sump system. With a **wet-sump** system, all the oil is carried in the engine crankcase, much the way it is in a car. With this type of system, the oil is picked up by a pump and distributed throughout the engine. Once the oil has circulated, it drains down into the sump where it is picked up and recirculated. Some advantages of wet-sump systems include their relative simplicity and light weight. However, wet-sump systems do have some disadvantages in that their oil capacity is limited by the sump size and it is more difficult to cool the oil since it is contained within the engine which is a source of heat.

Dry-sump systems differ from wet-sump systems in that the oil is stored in a separate oil tank. This typically allows a larger quantity of oil to be carried. This makes dry-sump systems well suited to large radial engines. In this type of system, an oil pump

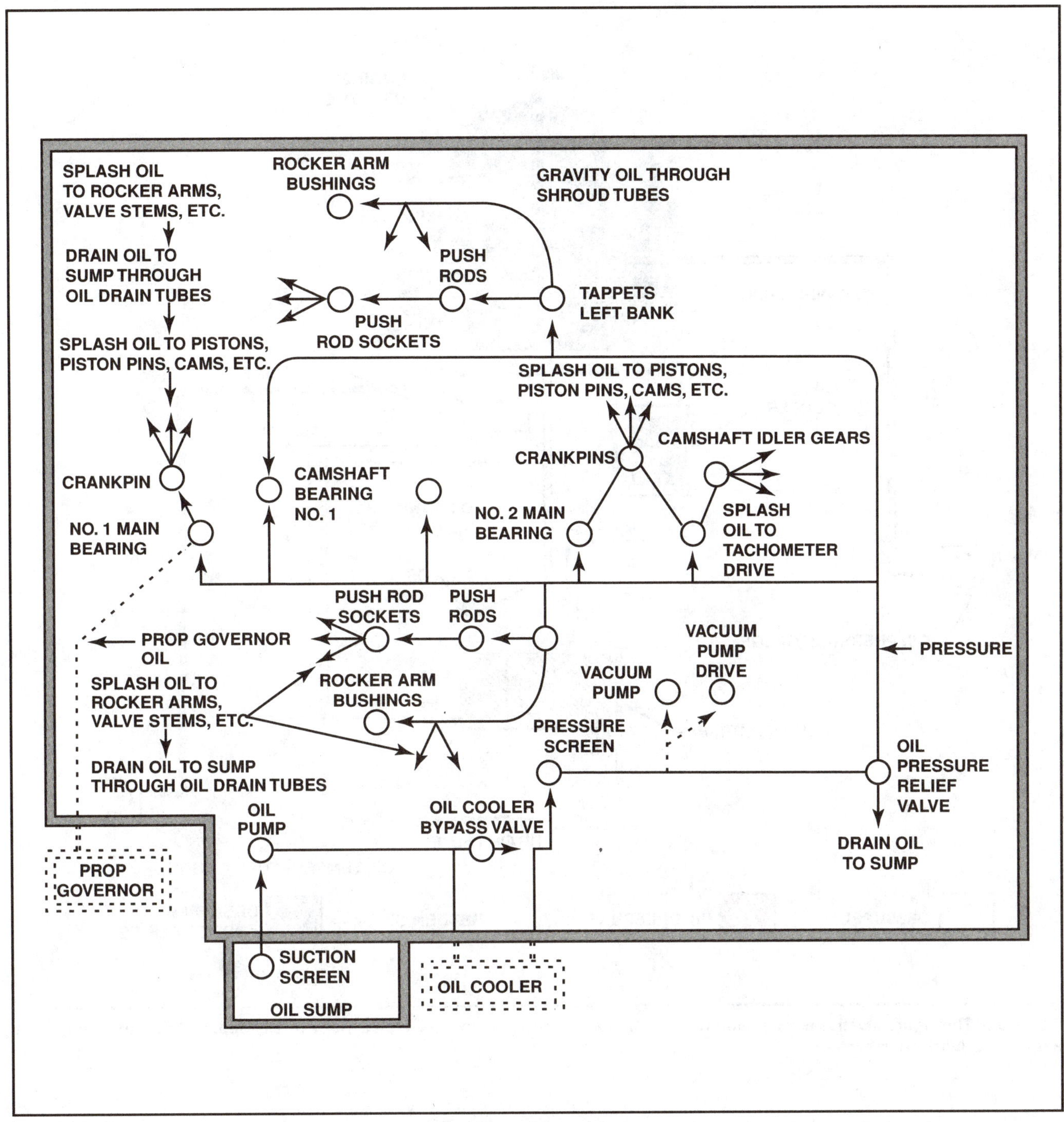

Figure 9-4. As you can see in the diagram above, a combination of lubrication methods are used in a typical wet-sump system.

pulls the oil from the oil tank and circulates it throughout the engine. Once circulated, the oil accumulates in the bottom of the crankcase where a **scavenge pump** picks up the oil and pumps it back to the tank. If the oil tank is installed so that it is higher than the engine oil inlet, check valves must be installed to prevent oil from draining back into the engine crankcase.

LUBRICATING SYSTEM COMPONENTS

A typical pressure lubrication system consists of an oil reservoir, oil pump, oil pressure relief valve, oil filter, oil cooler, vent lines, and all the necessary piping and connections. In addition, on engines that incorporate a dry-sump system, a scavenge

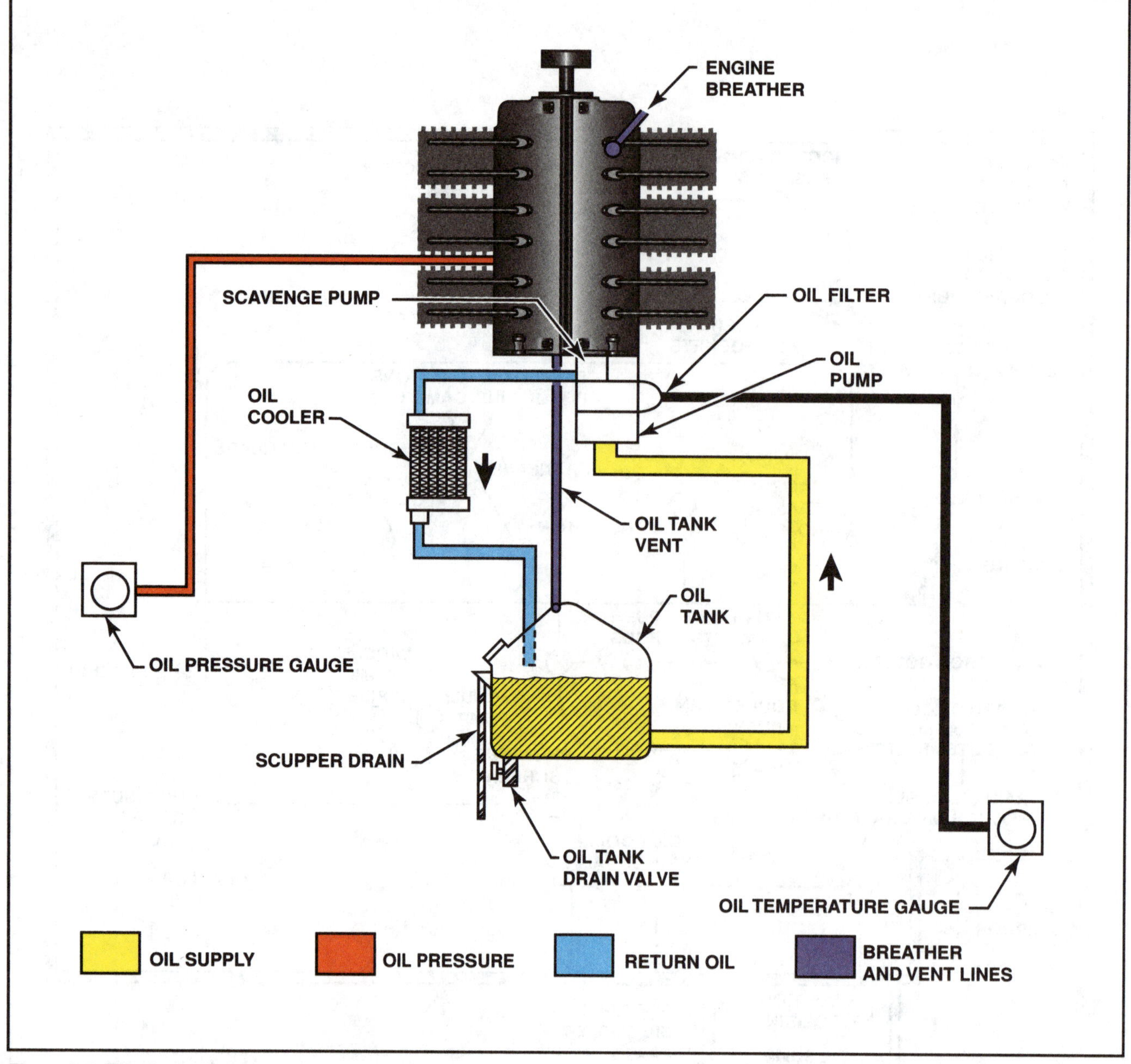

Figure 9-5. This figure illustrates the relationship of the various components in a typical horizontally opposed aircraft engine with a dry-sump lubrication system.

pump is required to move the oil back to the oil reservoir. To allow an operator to monitor the operation of a given lubrication system, most systems also include an oil temperature and oil pressure gauge. [Figure 9-5]

OIL RESERVOIR

An oil reservoir must be large enough to hold an adequate supply of oil to lubricate an engine. The amount of oil that is considered adequate is based on the maximum endurance of the airplane and the maximum acceptable oil consumption rate plus a margin to ensure adequate circulation, lubrication, and cooling. In the absence of a valid determination of aircraft range, several ratios of fuel-to-oil quantity may be used. for example, an aircraft without an oil reserve or transfer system must have a fuel-to-oil ratio of at least 30:1. However, if an aircraft has a transfer system, the ratio is reduced to 40:1.

As discussed earlier, the oil reservoir on a wet-sump engine is part of the engine crankcase. Therefore, a wet-sump oil reservoir is typically constructed of

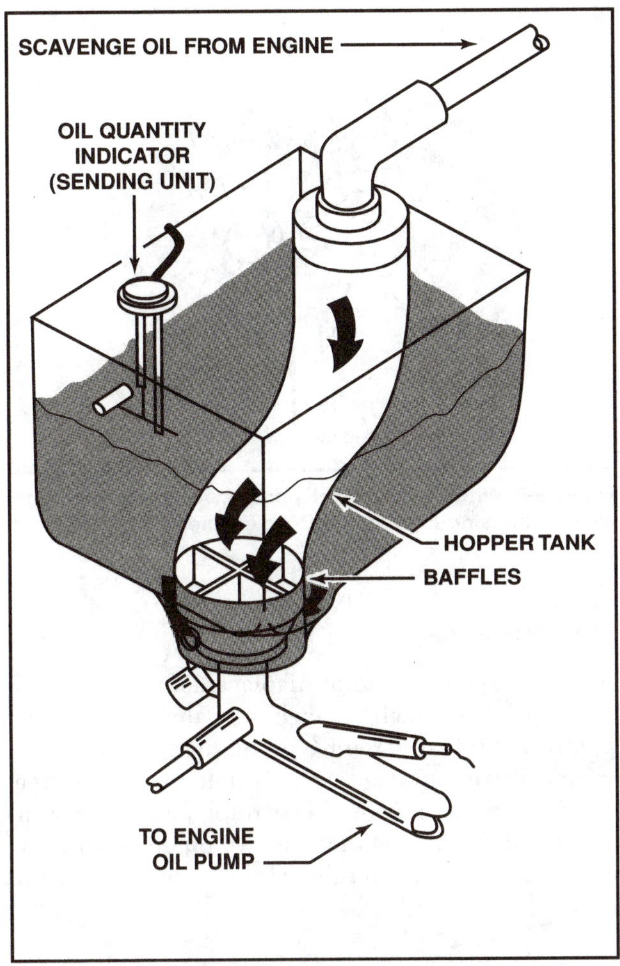

Figure 9-6. The hopper in an oil reservoir separates circulating oil from the surrounding oil in the tank. This cuts down on the amount of oil that is circulated and hastens the engine's warm-up time.

cast aluminum alloy. On the other hand, oil reservoirs used in dry-sump systems are typically constructed of an aluminum alloy. In addition, the reservoir in a dry-sump system is typically placed close enough to the engine and high enough above the oil pump inlet to ensure reliable gravity feed.

According to FAR Part 23, all oil reservoirs must have an expansion space at least 10 percent greater than the tank capacity, or 0.5 gallon, whichever is greater. The expansion space provides sufficient room for oil to expand as it heats and allows room for the collection of foam. Another FAR requirement is that all oil filler caps or covers must be marked with the word "OIL" and the permissible oil designations, or reference to the Airplane Flight Manual for permissible oil designations. As an added feature, the oil reservoirs installed in some dry-sump systems include a scupper drain. A **scupper drain** is basically a drain that is built into the filler cap well that catches overflow oil and drains it overboard when servicing the tank.

Most aircraft oil systems are equipped with a dipstick-type quantity gauge, sometimes referred to as a **bayonet gauge**. However, some large aircraft may be equipped with an oil quantity indicating system that shows the quantity of oil during flight. One such system consists of a float mechanism that rides on the surface of the oil and actuates an electric transmitter on top of the tank. The transmitter sends a signal to a cockpit gauge, which indicates oil quantity in gallons.

To prevent pressure buildup and ensure proper ventilation in all flight attitudes, an oil reservoir must be vented to the atmosphere. With a wet-sump system, the vent consists of a crankcase breather. However, on a dry-sump system, a vent line is typically run from the reservoir to the engine crankcase to prevent oil loss through the vent. This way, the vent line indirectly vents the reservoir to the atmosphere through the crankcase breather.

Some oil reservoirs, primarily those used with large radial engines, have a built-in **hopper**, or **temperature accelerating well**. The purpose of a hopper is to partially isolate a portion of the oil within the reservoir during start-up. By doing this, a smaller portion of the oil is circulated through the engine during start-up allowing the engine to warm up faster. A typical hopper extends from the oil return fitting on top of the oil reservoir to the outlet fitting in the bottom of the reservoir. To allow oil into the hopper from the main oil supply, the hopper tank is open at the lower end in some systems. However, in other systems, a series of flapper-type valves are used that allow oil into the hopper as oil is consumed. [Figure 9-6]

The oil within an oil reservoir in a wet-sump system is typically drawn up to an oil pump through a pipe that sticks down into the reservoir. However, in many dry-sump systems, an oil outlet is typically located at the lowest point of the reservoir. An exception to this is aircraft that are equipped with Hamilton-Standard Hydromatic feathering propellers. In this case, the oil reservoir feeds the pressure pump through a standpipe which extends into the oil tank while the supply line for propeller feathering is installed at the bottom of the reservoir. This arrangement ensures that enough oil will remain in the reservoir to feather the propeller if an

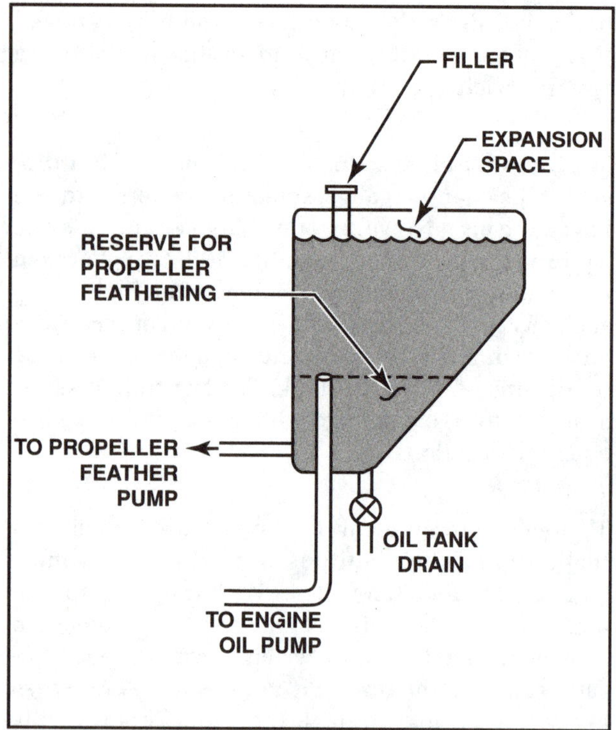

Figure 9-7. The oil reservoir used with a Hamilton-Standard Hydromatic feathering propeller utilizes two oil outlets. Engine oil is supplied through a standpipe while propeller feathering oil is drawn from the bottom of the tank. This way, there is always a reserve of oil available for propeller feathering.

oil line breaks and all of the engine oil is pumped overboard. [Figure 9-7]

OIL PUMPS

As mentioned earlier, all lubrication systems utilize constant displacement pumps. If you recall, a constant displacement pump moves a fixed volume of fluid per pump revolution. The two types of constant displacement pumps that are used in reciprocating engine lubrication systems include the gear and gerotor pump.

GEAR PUMP

The gear-type oil pump is the most common type of oil pump used in reciprocating engines. A typical gear-type pump consists of two meshed gears that rotate inside a housing. The gears and housing are precisely machined to keep clearances between them as small as possible. Oil is picked up by the gears at the pump inlet and then becomes trapped between the teeth and the housing. As the gears rotate, the trapped oil is released at the pump outlet. [Figure 9-8]

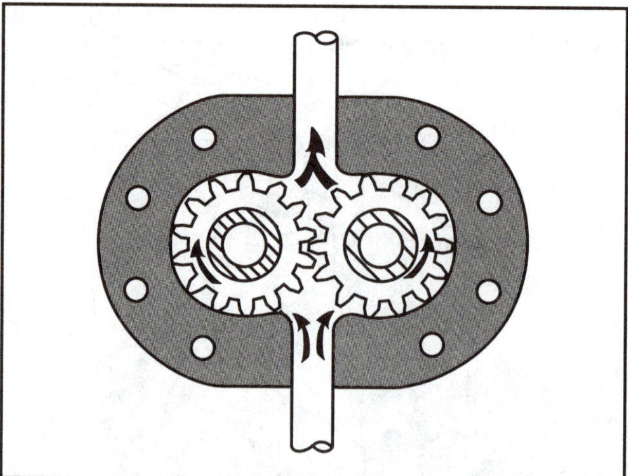

Figure 9-8. With a gear-type oil pump, two spur gears rotate inside a housing to pump oil to an engine.

GEROTOR PUMP

Another type of constant-displacement pump used to move oil through an engine is the gerotor-type pump. A typical gerotor-type pump consists of an engine driven spur gear that rotates within a free spinning rotor housing. The rotor and drive gear ride inside a housing that has two oblong openings. One opening is the oil inlet while the other is the oil outlet. [Figure 9-9]

SCAVENGE PUMP

In addition to a pressure pump, most dry-sump systems must utilize a scavenge pump to return oil to the oil reservoir. A scavenge pump may be either a gear- or gerotor-type pump that is driven by the engine. As a rule, scavenge pumps have a capacity that is greater than the pressure pump. The reason for this is that, after oil flows through an engine it typically has a greater volume due to foaming and thermal expansion. Therefore, in order to ensure that oil does not collect in the engine sump, the scavenge pump must be capable of pumping a greater volume of oil than the pressure pump.

PRESSURE RELIEF VALVE

In order to ensure adequate engine lubrication, an appropriate oil pressure must be maintained at all times. Therefore, in order for an engine driven oil pump to maintain system pressure at low engine speeds, it must produce excessive pressure at high engine speeds. To prevent excessive pressure from damaging an engine, a pressure relief valve must be installed in the oil system. A typical pressure relief valve consists of a spring loaded valve that is held

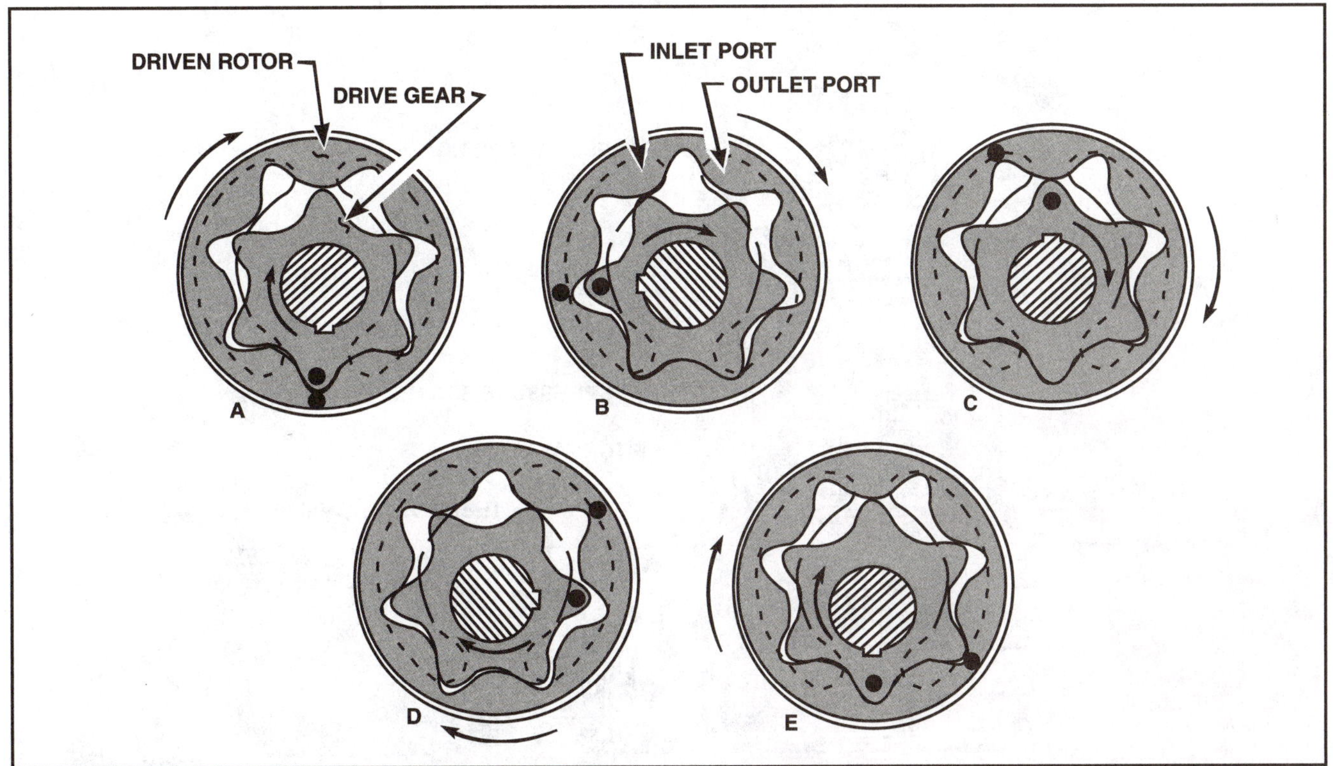

Figure 9-9. As a gerotor-type pump rotates, the space between the drive gear teeth and rotor housing alternately increase then decrease. As the space between the two increases at the oil inlet (A, B, and C), oil is drawn into the pump. However, as the space closes up at the outlet (D and E), oil is forced out of the pump.

in the closed position. With this type of valve, when oil pressure rises above a preset value, the valve off seats and returns excess oil to the reservoir or oil pump inlet. In a typical system, the relief valve is installed between the main supply pump and the internal oil system. [Figure 9-10]

Relief valves are typically set at a pressure that is lower than the output pressure of the pressure pump. Therefore, a small amount of oil constantly flows through the relief valve at cruise rpm. The exact amount of oil that is bypassed depends, in part, on the clearances between an engine's moving

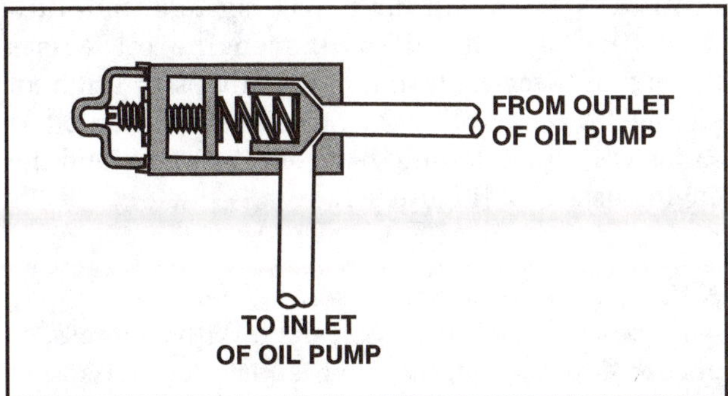

Figure 9-10. On all pressure lubrication systems, a pressure relief valve is needed to maintain the proper system pressure.

parts. For example, as the clearances between engine parts increase through normal wear, the pump continues to supply a constant volume of oil but the relief valve bypasses less oil back to the sump.

Most relief valves can be adjusted by turning a screw that increases or decreases spring pressure. The greater the spring pressure, the higher the resulting oil pressure. On some simple relief valves, spring tension is adjusted by either changing the spring or inserting one or more washers behind the spring. However, it is important to note that, if an oil pressure reading is low, you should not immediately increase the spring tension on the relief valve. Instead, it is best to determine why the pressure is low in the first place. For example, if too light an oil is used or if a piece of foreign material gets stuck between the relief valve and its seat, the oil pressure will indicate lower then normal. If this is the case, the reason for the low pressure reading should be corrected instead of making adjustments to the relief valve.

To help ensure adequate circulation during start up when the oil is cold, some engines utilize a compensated oil pressure relief valve. A **compensated oil**

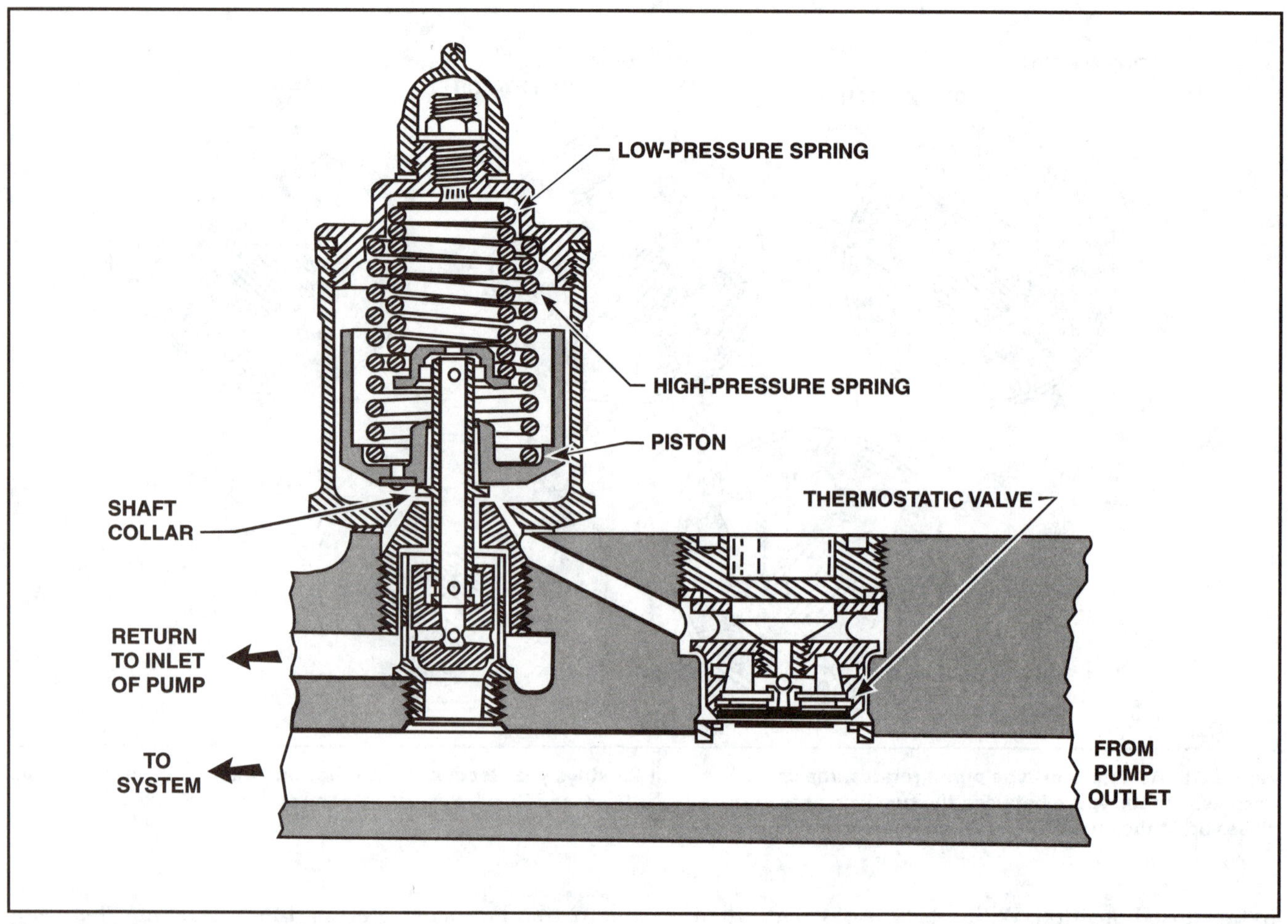

Figure 9-11. In a compensated oil pressure relief valve, when the oil is cold, a high- and low-pressure spring hold the relief valve closed to maintain an elevated system pressure. However, once the oil has warmed, the thermostatic valve allows pressurized oil to enter the relief valve and remove the high-pressure spring pressure from the relief valve.

pressure relief valve maintains a higher system pressure when the oil is cold then, once the oil warms up, it automatically lowers pressure to the normal operating range. This is accomplished through the use of two springs and a thermostatic valve. When the oil is cold, both springs hold the valve on its seat which, in turn, permits a higher oil pressure. However, once the oil warms up, the thermostatic valve opens a passage and allows oil to flow beneath a piston in the pressure relief valve. As the piston is forced upward, it removes the spring pressure exerted by the high-pressure spring. Normal operating pressure is then maintained by the force of the low-pressure spring alone. [Figure 9-11]

OIL FILTERS

Once oil is discharged from an oil pressure pump, it flows to an oil filter. The purpose of the filter is to remove solid particles that are suspended in the oil. This filtration is required to protect the engine's moving parts from solid contaminants.

At the present time, the two types of filtration systems that may be installed in aircraft engines are the full-flow system and the bypass system. In a **full-flow** filter system, all of the engine oil passes through a filter each time it circulates through an engine. To accomplish this, the filter is installed in series with the oil pump between the pump and the engine bearings. [Figure 9-12]

Although not as common, some older engines may still use a bypass filtration system. With a **bypass**, or **partial flow system**, the filter is installed in parallel with the engine bearings. In this type of system, only about 10 percent of the oil is filtered each time the oil circulates through the system. However, over

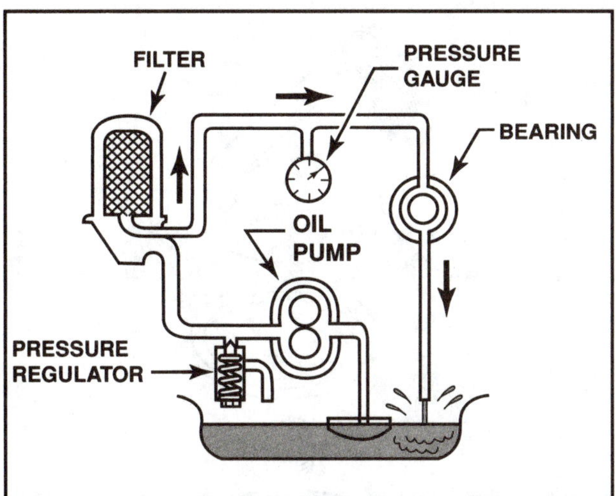

Figure 9-12. In a full-flow filtration system, all of the engine oil is filtered each time it circulates in an engine.

time, the entire oil supply will pass through the filter. [Figure 9-13]

FAR requirements dictate that all oil filters be constructed and installed in a way that permits full oil flow even if the filter becomes completely blocked. On a bypass oil filter system this is not a big deal since most of the oil bypasses the filter anyway. However, on a full-flow filter system some means of bypassing the filter must be provided. One way to meet this requirement is to incorporate an **oil bypass valve** that automatically lets oil bypass the filter entirely once it becomes plugged. Another way this is accomplished is to use a filter that is constructed with a spring loaded bypass valve inside the filter, or

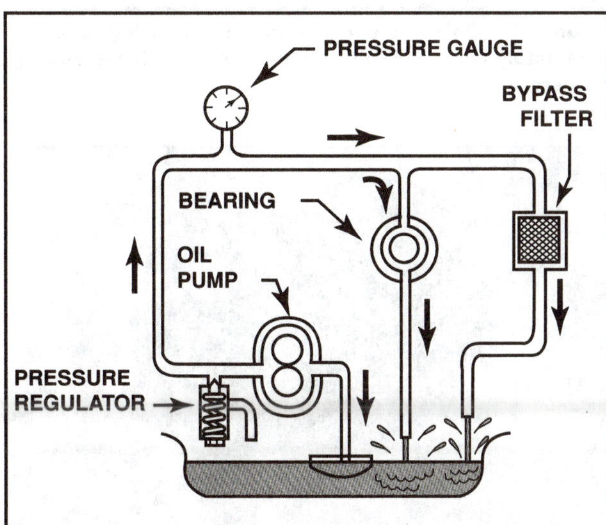

Figure 9-13. With a bypass filtration system, only about 10 percent of the oil passes through the filter each time the oil circulates through the engine. This type of system is primarily installed on older engines.

incorporate filter elements that are designed to collapse if pressure become excessive.

FILTER ELEMENTS

There are several different types of filters used in aircraft engines. However, there are only four methods of filtration that are approved for aviation use. The approved filtration methods include depth filtration, semi-depth filtration, surface filtration, and edge filtration.

Depth Filtration

Depth filters consist of a matrix of fibers that are closely packed to a depth of about one inch. Oil flows through this mat and contaminants are trapped in the fibers. Depth-type filters are very effective because the large number of filters used have the capacity to trap a large quantity of contaminants. However, one disadvantage of depth filters is that high pressure oil may occasionally form a channel through the filter element. If this ever occurs, the filter will lose a great deal of its effectiveness. [Figure 9-14]

Semi-Depth Filtration

The type of filter used most often in today's general aviation aircraft is a disposable, semi-depth filter made of resin-impregnated fibers. These fibers are formed into a long sheet, folded into pleats, and assembled around a perforated sheet steel core. The pleats increase the surface area of the filter element and allow greater filtering capacity in a smaller unit. Furthermore, the uniformity of the filter surface greatly reduces the ability of the oil to form a channel through the element. The filter element is

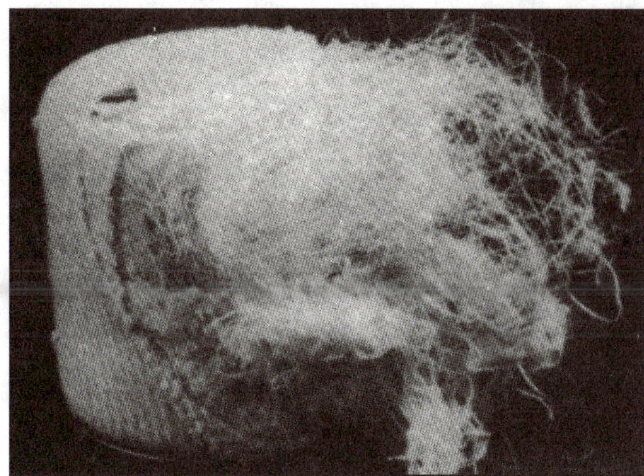

Figure 9-14. A depth filter consists of a closely-packed fiber matrix-type element.

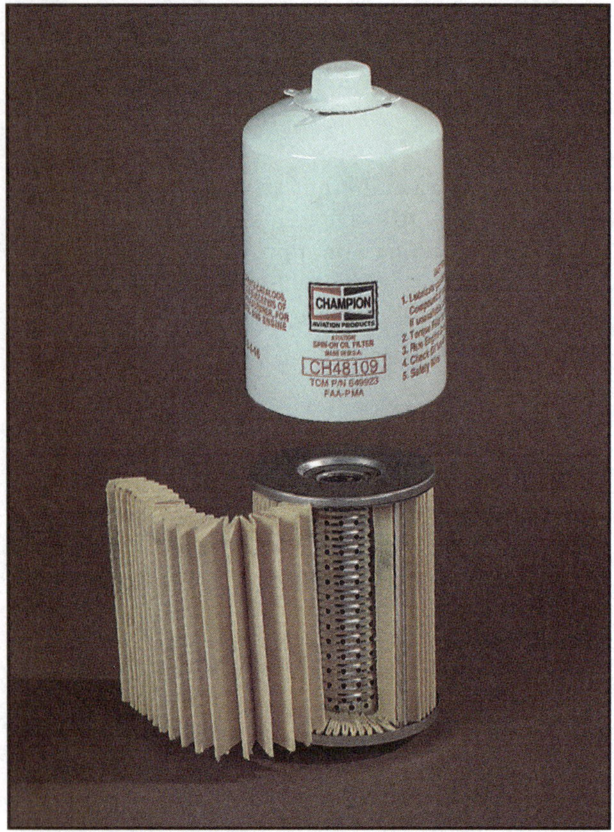

Figure 9-15. A typical spin-on type semi-depth filter consists of a pleated sheet of resin impregnated fibers that are assembled around a perforated sheet steel core. The entire element is contained in a thin metal housing.

mounted in a cylindrical steel casing which forms an integral part of the filter. A typical semi-depth filter mounts to the engine with a threaded fitting and, therefore, is often referred to as a **spin-on** filter. [Figure 9-15]

On some engines, the semi-depth filter element is installed in a removable can. In this case, the disposable center element is removed and replaced as needed while the can is used indefinitely. [Figure 9-16]

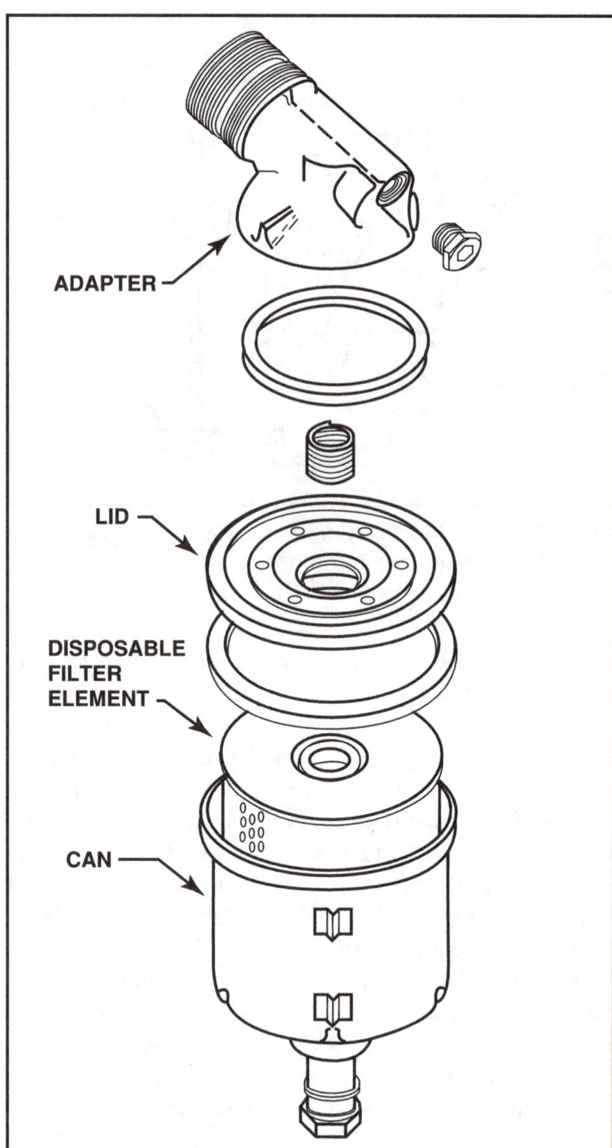

Figure 9-16. On some engines, the filter housing is reused indefinitely while a disposable filter element is replaced as necessary.

Surface Filtration

Several aircraft engines are equipped with a standard woven wire-mesh **oil screen**, or **strainer**. This screen filter is useful for trapping some of the larger contaminants that flow through the engine; however, it does little to catch the small contaminants. Because of this, some engines that use an oil screen also rely on a second, fine filter to catch any remaining contaminants. Decreasing the size of the wire mesh for better filtration is not a reasonable option because cleaning would be required too often to be practical. [Figure 9-17]

Figure 9-17. Many aircraft engines are provided with a screen-type surface filtration oil strainer. An oil strainer filters out large particles and helps prevent other filtering elements from becoming clogged.

Edge Filtration

Edge filters may be either the spiral-wound or Cuno type. A **spiral-wound element** consists of a long strip of wedge-shaped metal that is wound into a tight spiral. Ridges along the entire length of the strip separate the turns of the spiral a uniform amount. With this type of filter, the size of the particles filtered out of the oil depends on the thickness of the ridges. The thick side of the wedge is on the outside circumference of the spiral and contaminants collect on this edge as oil flows from the outside of the element to the inside. [Figure 9-18]

The **Cuno filter** consists of a large number of thin metal disks that are stacked on a center shaft. Thin spacers, which are attached to the filter housing, separate the disks so oil can pass between the disks. As with the spiral-wound edge filter, oil flows from the outside of the filter to the inside, leaving contaminants on the outside edge. The spacer thickness determines the size of the particle contaminants which are filtered out of the oil. Periodically, contaminants must be scraped from the outside edge of the disks. To do this, a handle is attached to the center shaft and used to rotate the disks. Since the spacers are fixed rigidly to the filter housing, they remain stationary and act as scrapers. Contaminants scraped from the disks accumulate in the bottom of the filter housing and are cleaned out during maintenance inspections. Cuno filters were commonly used on many large radial reciprocating engines but are seldom found on operational aircraft today.

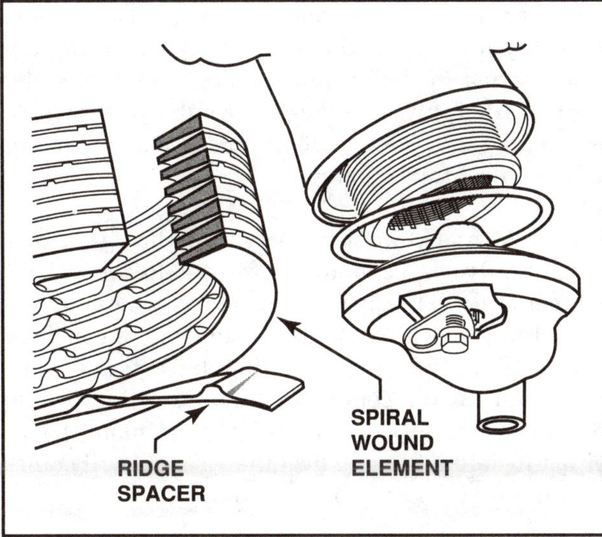

Figure 9-18. With a spiral-wound edge filter, a long piece of wedge-shaped metal is wound into a spiral. To permit oil to pass through the spiral, spacers are installed on every turn of the element. In this configuration, contaminants collect on the outside of the spiral as oil passes through the element.

OIL COOLER

If you recall, one of the functions of oil is to cool the engine; however, to do this, the heat absorbed by the oil must be removed. In most cases, excess heat is removed by an oil cooler, or **oil temperature regulator**. An oil cooler is an oil-to-air heat exchanger. When installed in a dry-sump system, the oil cooler is typically located between the scavenge pump outlet and storage reservoir. However, in a wet-sump system, the oil cooler may be located wherever the manufacturer deems it appropriate.

One type of oil cooler consists of a core with several copper or aluminum tubes enclosed in a double-walled **annular** shell, or **bypass jacket.** When the oil is cold, it flows through the bypass jacket and bypasses the core. However, once the oil heats up, it is routed through the core for cooling. The exact amount of oil that flows through the core is controlled by a **thermostatic control valve**, also referred to as a **bypass valve** or a **flow control valve.** When the oil is cold, the bypass valve is fully open and oil flows through the bypass jacket. However, as the oil warms up, the bypass valve slowly closes thereby forcing oil through the cooler core. [Figure 9-19]

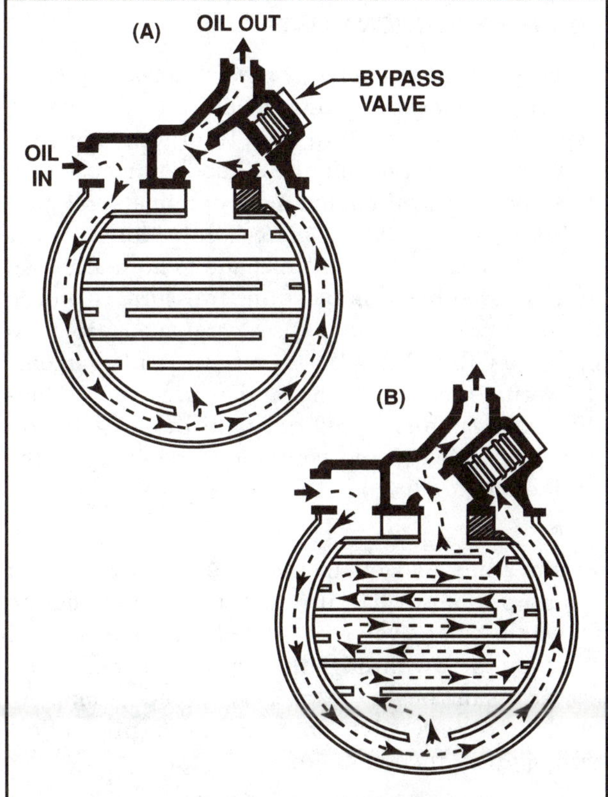

Figure 9-19. (A) — When the engine oil is cold, the bypass valve opens and allows the oil to bypass the oil cooler core. (B) — However, once the oil warms up, the bypass valve closes which, in turn, forces the oil to pass through the core where it transfers its heat to the passing airstream.

In the example just discussed, the bypass valve is part of the oil cooler. This is typical of oil coolers installed on radial engines. However, on horizontally opposed engines, the cooler and bypass valve are typically two separate units that are installed in parallel with each other. This eliminates the need for a bypass jacket around the oil cooler. With this type of system, when the oil is cold, it remains in the engine's lubrication passages and bypasses the cooler completely. On the other hand, once the oil heats up, the bypass valve forces some of the oil to flow through the cooler.

It is important to note that, if the bypass valve fails in either the open or closed position, oil will continue to circulate in the engine. However, if the oil cooler passages become partially clogged, oil flow could be reduced. For example, if an oil cooler passage becomes partially clogged, less oil will flow through the core and oil temperatures will rise. However, as the oil temperature rises, the bypass valve closes even further to direct more oil through the partially restricted core. This, in turn, can limit the amount of oil that circulates through the engine.

SURGE PROTECTION VALVE

When cold oil becomes congealed in a dry-sump system, the scavenge pump can build up a very high pressure in the oil return line. To prevent this high pressure from damaging the oil cooler or hose connections, some oil coolers incorporate a surge protection valve. A typical surge protection valve is installed at the oil cooler inlet and is normally held in the closed position by spring pressure. However, if the oil within the cooler is severely congealed, oil pressure will build at the cooler inlet and overcome the spring pressure acting on the surge valve. Once the surge valve is forced open, oil bypasses the oil cooler completely and continues circulating in the engine. [Figure 9-20]

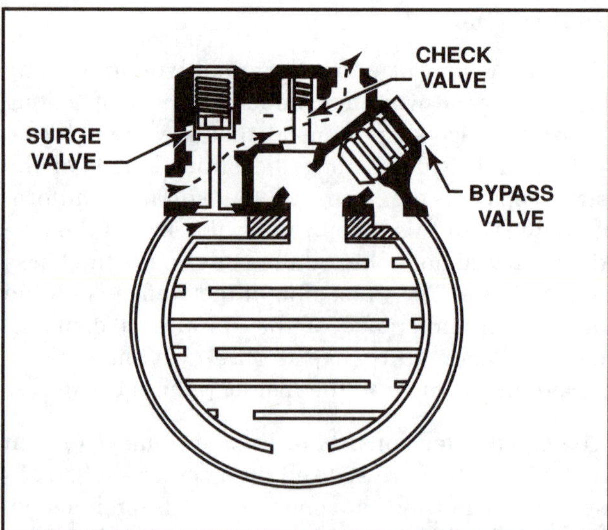

Figure 9-20. If the oil within an oil cooler becomes congealed and excessive oil pressure builds at the oil cooler inlet, the surge valve will open and allow the oil to bypass the oil cooler.

As the congealed oil in the engine and oil cooler heats up, the oil pressure will decrease enough to allow the surge valve to seat. This, in turn, will allow oil to flow through the bypass jacket of the oil cooler. As the engine reaches its operating temperature, the bypass valve closes and oil begins to flow through the oil cooler core.

AIRFLOW CONTROLS

By regulating airflow through the oil cooler, oil temperature can be controlled to meet various operating requirements. For example, the engine oil will reach its operating temperature more quickly if airflow to the oil cooler is cut off during engine warm-up. Airflow control to a radial engine oil cooler can be accomplished through the use of shutters installed on the rear of an oil cooler, or by a controllable flap on the air-exit duct.

An oil cooler air exit may be opened and closed manually by a control in the cockpit or automatically. To provide automatic control, a **floating control thermostat** that operates an electrical actuator is typically used. With this type of system, a thermostat inserted in the oil line leading from the cooler to the oil supply reservoir senses the oil temperature and sends electrical impulses that automatically control the actuator.

On horizontally opposed engines, the oil cooler bypass valve is generally sufficient to control oil temperatures. However, in instances where an aircraft flies in extremely cold climates, an airflow restrictor may be installed to limit the amount of airflow into an oil cooler. In this case, the airflow restrictor typically consists of a metal plate that is either installed directly over the face of an oil cooler or in front of a blast tube hole in the rear engine baffling.

OIL SEPARATOR

On engines that use a wet-type vacuum pump, engine oil is used to lubricate and seal the vacuum pump. However, as oil circulates through this type of pump, air bubbles become trapped in the oil. To eliminate this trapped air, an oil separator is installed on the outlet side of the vacuum pump. A typical oil separator consists of several baffle plates which cause the vacuum pump outlet air to swirl. As the air swirls, centrifugal force pulls the oil out of the air and deposits it on the baffle plates. From the baffles, the oil drains back to the engine through an oil outlet in the separator. By separating the air and oil, two things are accomplished. First, oil is prevented from flowing into the air system and damaging any rubber components such as de-icing boots; and second, excess air is not introduced into the oil system.

OIL DILUTION

On some large reciprocating engines that are operated in extremely cold temperatures, an oil dilution system may be installed. The purpose of such a system is to dilute the oil with fuel within the engine to help prevent the oil from congealing when it is cold. With a typical oil dilution system, fuel is injected into the oil pump before the engine is shut down. This distributes diluted oil throughout the lubrication system. This way, when the engine is started later, the diluted oil flows freely through the engine, ensuring adequate lubrication. Once the engine and oil warm up, the gasoline evaporates out of the oil and leaves the engine through the crankcase breather.

A typical oil dilution system consists of an oil dilution solenoid that is controlled from the cockpit, an oil dilution valve, and the necessary plumbing. As a general rule, the fuel line that injects fuel into the oil is never installed between the pressure pump and engine pressure system. The reason for this is that pressurized oil could flow into the fuel supply and contaminate the fuel.

On aircraft with an oil dilution system, engine oil pressure is an indirect indication of how the system is operating. For example, when starting an engine that has diluted oil, the oil pressure will be lower than normal. By the same token, if too much fuel is introduced into the oil or if the oil dilution valve is leaking, the oil pressure will be excessively low while oil temperature will be high.

OIL PRESSURE GAUGE

The engine lubrication system supplies oil under pressure to the moving parts of the engine. To allow a pilot to monitor the effectiveness of a given lubrication system, all aircraft engines are equipped with an oil pressure gauge that is calibrated in pounds per square inch. Since inadequate oil pressure can lead to oil starvation in engine bearings and excessive pressure can rupture gaskets and seals, the oil pressure in most reciprocating engines is typically regulated over a fairly narrow operating range.

Many oil pressure gauges utilize a Bourdon tube, because its design enables the gauge to measure relatively high fluid pressures. The gauge is connected by a metal tube directly to a point immediately downstream from the engine oil pump. Therefore, an oil pressure gauge measures the oil pressure being delivered to the engine. To protect the gauge from occasional pressure surges, most gauges have a small restriction at their inlet. In addition, most fittings that attach the oil line to the engine also have a small restriction to limit oil lost in the event the oil line breaks.

One disadvantage of this type of oil pressure indicating system is that it does not work well in cold weather because the oil in the line between the engine and cockpit gauge tends to congeal. The congealed oil then causes false readings of either low or no oil pressure. This error can be minimized by filling the oil line with a very light oil.

The trend in larger more modern aircraft is to replace Bourdon tube pressure instruments with electrical transmitters. This allows long oil filled lines between engines and instruments to be replaced with lightweight wire. In addition to saving weight, electrical transmitters also provide greater accuracy. With a typical electric transmitter, pressurized oil enters the inlet port of a transmitter and is then routed to a diaphragm assembly. As oil pressure increases or decreases, the diaphragm expands and contracts appropriately. The motion produced by the diaphragm's movement is amplified through a lever and gear arrangement that varies the electrical value of an indicating circuit by positioning a potentiometer. The position of the potentiometer is then reflected on the cockpit indicator.

Oil pressure instrument readings are a critical indicator of engine operation and should be monitored frequently, especially during engine starts. For example, some aircraft manuals caution you to shut down an engine after 30 seconds in warm weather or one minute in extremely cold weather if no sign of oil pressure is present. Engine shutdown in this case is a precaution taken to prevent possible damage to an engine until the reason for lack of oil pressure can be determined. On the other hand, excessive pointer oscillation typically indicates that air is trapped in the oil line leading to the instrument or that some unit in the oil system is functioning improperly. In addition, low oil pressure or fluctuations from zero to normal are often signs of low oil quantity.

OIL TEMPERATURE GAUGE

The oil temperature gauge allows you to monitor the temperature of the oil entering the engine. This is important because oil circulation cools the engine as it lubricates the moving parts. Most oil temperature gauges are calibrated in degrees Fahrenheit and sense oil temperature at the engine's oil inlet.

Most modern oil temperature systems are electrically operated and use either a Wheatstone bridge circuit or a ratiometer circuit. A **Wheatstone bridge** circuit consists of three fixed resistors and one variable resistor whose resistance varies with temperature. [Figure 9-21]

When power is applied to a Wheatstone bridge circuit and all four resistances are equal, no difference in potential exists between the bridge junctions. However, when the variable resistor is exposed to heat, its resistance increases, causing more current to flow through the fixed resistor R3 than the variable resistor. The disproportionate current flow produces a voltage differential between the bridge junctions, causing current to flow through the galvanometer indicator. The greater the voltage differential, the greater the current flow through the indicator and the greater the needle deflection. Since indicator current flow is directly proportional to the oil temperature, an indicator calibrated in degrees provides an accurate means of registering oil temperature.

A **ratiometer** circuit measures current ratios and is more reliable than a Wheatstone bridge, especially when the supply voltage varies. Typically, a simple ratiometer circuit consists of two parallel branches powered by the aircraft electrical system. One branch consists of a fixed resistor and coil, and the other branch consists of a variable resistor and coil. The two coils are wound on a rotor that pivots between the poles of a permanent magnet, forming a meter movement in the gauge. [Figure 9-22]

The shape of the permanent magnet provides a larger air gap between the magnet and coils at the bottom than at the top. Therefore, the flux density, or magnetic field, is progressively stronger from the bottom of the air gap to the top. Current flow through each coil creates an electromagnet that reacts with the polarity of the permanent magnet, creating torque that repositions the rotor until the magnetic forces are balanced. If the resistances of the temperature probe and fixed resistor are equal, current flow through each coil is the same and the indicator pointer remains in the center position. However, if the probe temperature increases, its resistance also increases, causing a decrease in current through the temperature sensing branch. Consequently, the electromagnetic force on the temperature sensing branch decreases, creating an

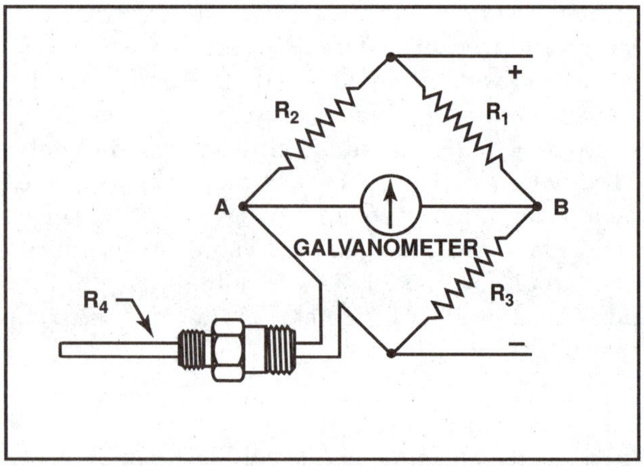

Figure 9-21. A typical Wheatstone bridge has three fixed resistors and one variable resistor. The temperature probe contains the variable resistor, whose resistance varies with the temperature of the oil flowing past the probe. The bridge in the circuit consists of a galvanometer that is calibrated in degrees to indicate temperature.

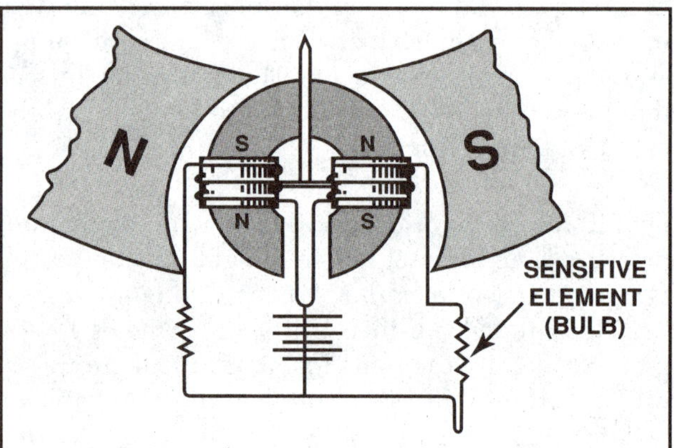

Figure 9-22. A ratiometer temperature measuring system operates with two circuit branches that balance electromagnetic forces. One branch contains a coil and fixed resistor while the other contains a coil and variable resistor, located in the temperature sensing probe. The coils are wound on a rotor which pivots in the center of a permanent magnet air gap.

imbalance that allows the rotor to rotate until each coil reaches a null, or balance. The pointer attached to the rotor then indicates the oil temperature.

Ratiometer temperature measuring systems are especially useful in applications where accuracy is critical or large variations of supply voltages are encountered. Therefore, a ratiometer circuit type oil temperature sensing system is generally preferred over Wheatstone bridge circuits by aircraft and engine manufacturers.

Some older oil temperature gauges used a **vapor pressure**, or Bourdon tube type instrument. With this type of instrument, a Bourdon tube is connected by a capillary tube to a liquid filled temperature sensing bulb. The bulb is installed in the engine's oil inlet line where the volatile liquid in the bulb is heated by the oil. As the liquid in the sensing bulb heats up, the capillary and Bourdon tubes also heat up. This causes the vapor pressure within the capillary and Bourdon tubes to increase, which, in turn, causes the Bourdon tube to straighten. The motion of the Bourdon tube is then transmitted to an indicator through a mechanical linkage.

SYSTEM MAINTENANCE

The maintenance practices discussed in this section are typical of those used on a horizontally opposed aircraft engine. However, the maintenance procedures discussed here are by no means all inclusive. Therefore, before conducting any maintenance on an aircraft's lubrication system you should consult the appropriate manufacturer's maintenance manuals and service bulletins. [Figure 9-23]

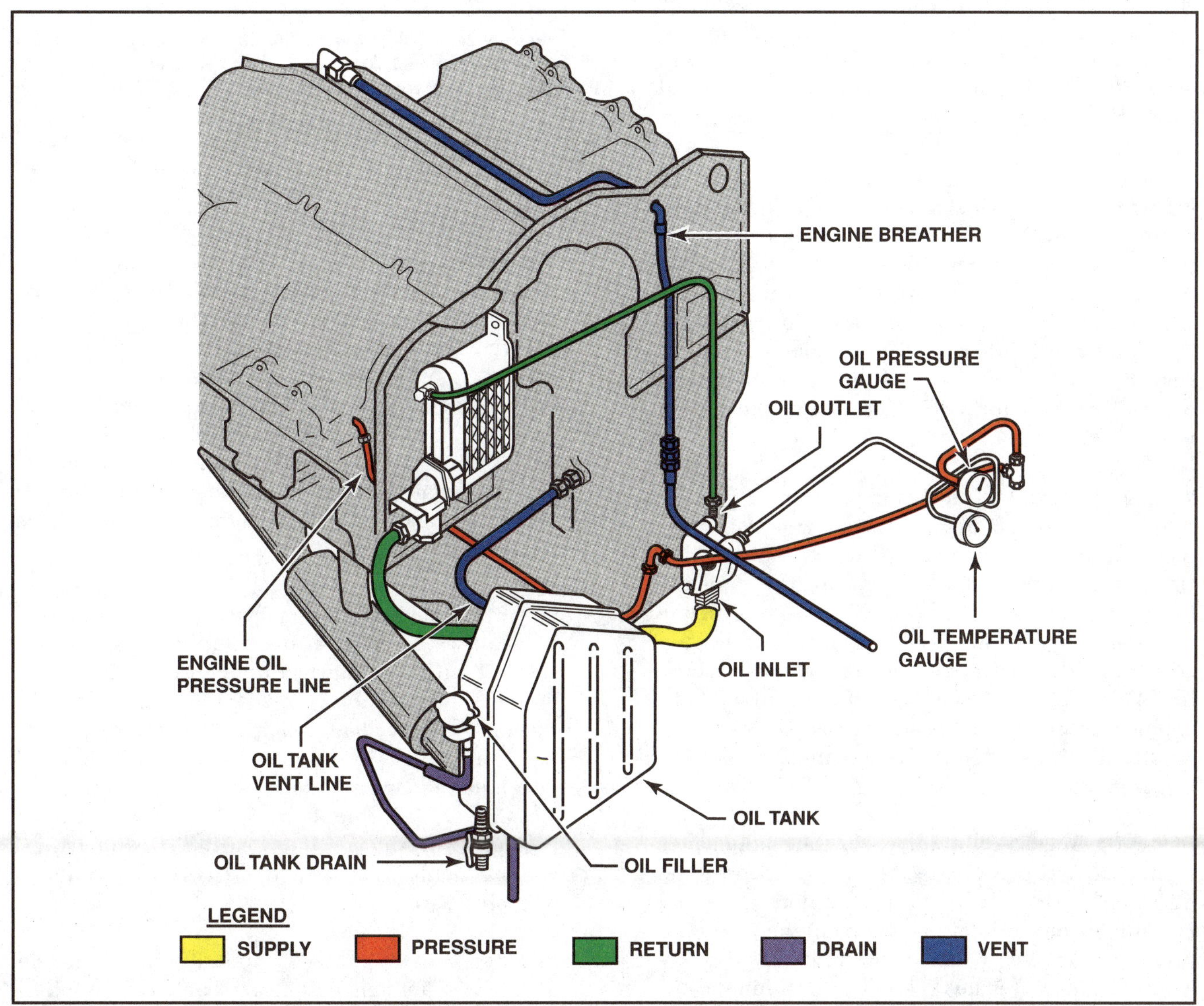

Figure 9-23. This figure illustrates the location of typical service items on a dry-sump system installed on a horizontally opposed engine.

OIL CHANGE AND SERVICING

In routine service, oil is constantly exposed to many substances that reduce its ability to protect moving parts. The primary source of oil contamination in a reciprocating engine is combustion byproducts that escape past the piston rings and oil carbonizing that occurs when oil becomes trapped in the pores of the cylinder walls and is burned. Additional contaminants that can become trapped in lubricating oils include gasoline, moisture, acids, dirt, carbon, and metal particles. If allowed to accumulate over a period of time, these contaminants can cause excessive wear on internal engine components. Certain clues that indicate internal engine wear include excessive oil consumption without evidence of any oil leaks. In this case, excessive oil consumption is typically caused by oil leaking past worn piston rings and being consumed in the combustion chambers. To prevent this type of engine damage, the entire lubrication system is drained at regular intervals and refilled with clean, fresh, oil. The recommended time interval between oil changes is typically based on the manufacturer's recommendations.

Prior to draining the engine oil, an engine should be run-up. In addition to warming the engine oil, a pre-inspection run-up allows you to verify that the oil temperature and pressure are within acceptable limits. Furthermore, a run-up agitates the oil supply so it holds the maximum amount of contaminants in suspension. This way, when the oil is drained, most of the contaminants will drain out of the engine with the oil.

Whenever possible, you should drain the engine oil into a clean container and place a large metal drip pan under the engine to catch any spills. Horizontally opposed wet-sump engines typically have oil drains located at the lowest point of the engine case. In many cases, the only way to gain access to an oil drain is to remove the lower cowling. However, with the large variety of aircraft-engine combinations, it is always best to consult the applicable aircraft maintenance manual for details. [Figure 9-24]

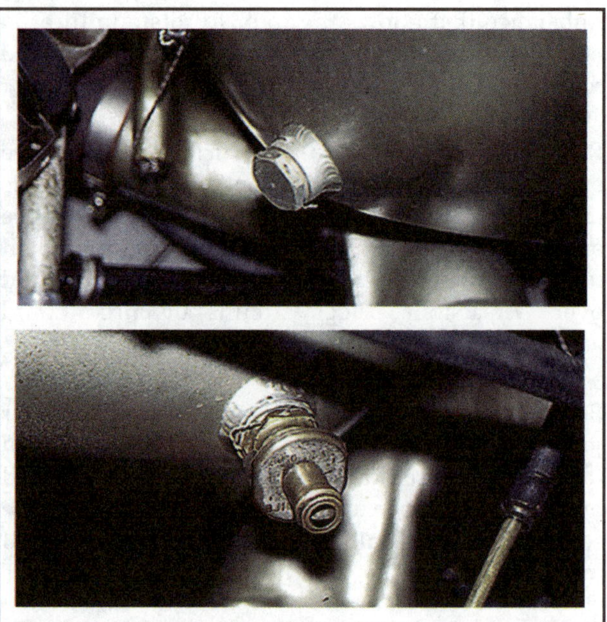

Figure 9-24. Most of the engine oil in a typical horizontally opposed engine is drained by removing one or more oil drain plugs or opening a drain valve.

Before opening an oil drain, check the maintenance manual for instructions regarding aircraft position. This step is important because the normal ground attitude of some aircraft may prevent the tank from draining completely. On engines that use a dry-sump engine, if it is not possible to position the aircraft as recommended and the amount of undrained oil is excessive, the oil reservoir can usually be sufficiently loosened and tilted to complete the oil drainage.

The presence of an excessive number of metal particles in the oil itself generally indicates an internal failure. However, due to the construction of aircraft oil systems, it is possible for metal particles to collect in the oil system sludge at the time of a previous engine failure. Furthermore, carbon buildup can break loose from an engine's interior and may be mistaken for metal particles. In any case, the source of any foreign particles in an engine's oil must be identified and corrected before the aircraft is released for flight.

One way to determine if a particle is metal or carbon is to place the material on a flat metal object and strike it with a hammer. If the particle is carbon, it will disintegrate, however, if it is metal, it will remain intact or change shape, depending upon its malleability. If you find some particles that are metal, use a magnet to determine whether the particles are ferrous or nonferrous. Ferrous particles are typically produced by wearing piston rings, whereas nonferrous particles are typically produced by main bearings.

Another way to correctly identify the type and quantity of foreign particles in an engine's oil is through regular participation in a **spectrometric oil analysis program**, or **S.O.A.P.**, which requires an oil

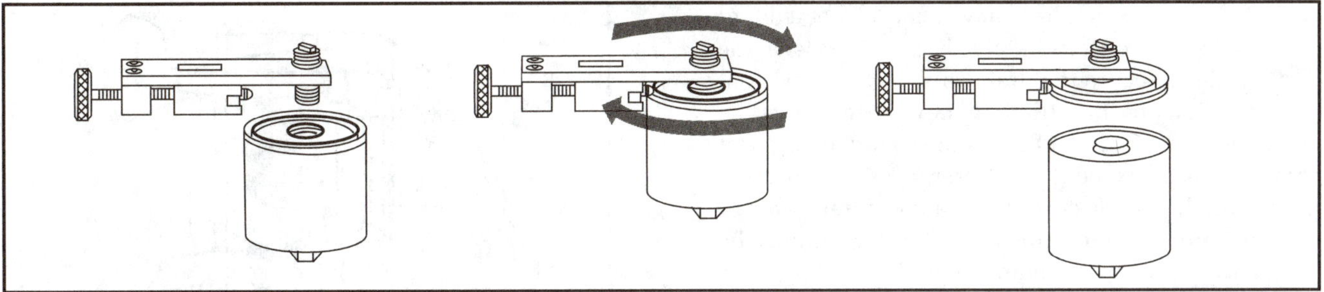

Figure 9-25. When replacing a disposable oil filter, it is a good practice to cut the filter open and inspect the filter element for metal particles. To do this, a special filter cutter is used.

sample to be sent to a laboratory for analysis. When this done, you are provided with a list of the type of particles found along with possible sources of the particles. In addition, if a laboratory observes a sudden increase in the amounts of metal that the test is designed to detect, they immediately contact the operator by telephone. When using spectrometric oil analysis, testing must occur on a regular basis to provide a baseline for comparison so accurate information can be obtained. A closely followed oil analysis program can detect problems before they become serious and prevent catastrophic engine failure.

OIL FILTER REPLACEMENT

Oil filter replacement and inspection is normally accomplished whenever the oil is changed. As discussed earlier, the two most common types of filter elements used in aircraft engines are disposable paper elements and a wire-mesh oil screen. When replacing a disposable filter, it is common practice to cut open the filter and inspect the element for the presence of any metal particles which might indicate an impending engine failure. Sealed, spin-on type filters are opened with a special roller-type can cutter. The cutter removes the top of the container without introducing metal particles that could provide false indications of impending engine problems. [Figure 9-25]

When servicing an engine equipped with an oil screen, the screen must be removed, inspected, and cleaned. When removing an oil screen, place a suitable container under the screen housing to collect the oil that will drain from the filter housing or cavity. The container must be clean to avoid contaminating the collected oil. Otherwise, contaminants already present in the container could falsely indicate imminent engine failure, possibly resulting in a premature engine removal.

Once an oil screen has been removed, inspect it for contamination and the presence of metal particles. Metal particles large enough to be trapped by the screen could indicate impending internal engine failure. After you have completed your inspection, the screen must be cleaned with an approved solvent prior to reinstallation in the engine. [Figure 9-26]

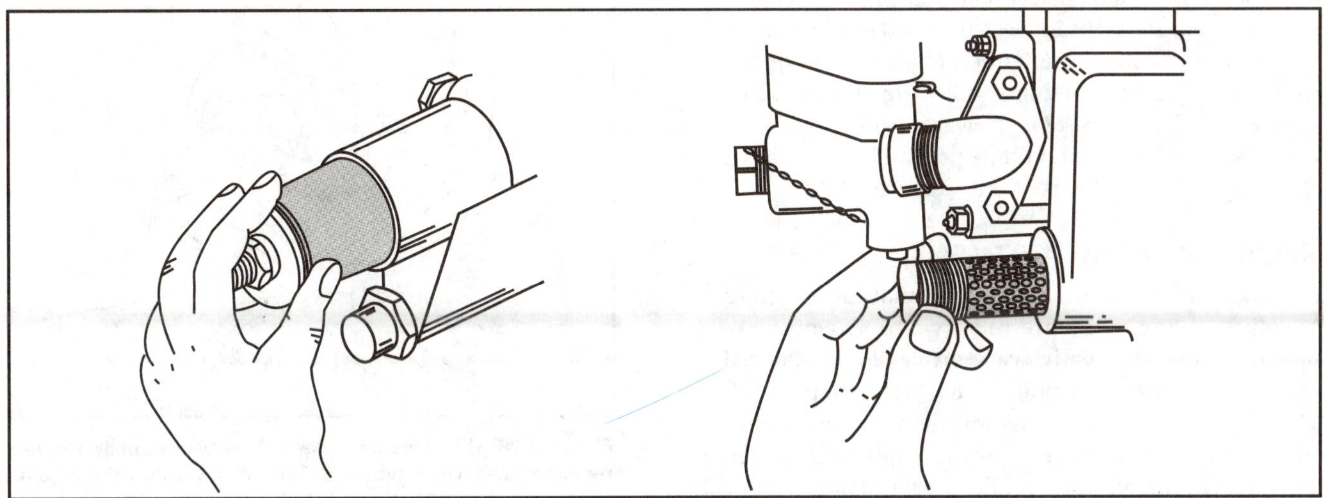

Figure 9-26. Some reciprocating engines employ reusable metal screens to trap sludge and large contaminants. If this is the case, there is usually a screen installed in the pressure system and the scavenge system.

Once the screens or filters have been inspected and the oil has been completely drained, replace the drain plug or secure the drain valve. On aircraft that utilize a disposable filter, a new filter must be installed and secured. On the other hand, on aircraft that use an oil screen, the screen must be cleaned, re-installed, and secured. Once all filters and/or screens are secured, the oil reservoir should be refilled with the recommended grade of oil.

Once the reservoir is filled, run up the engine long enough to warm the oil. After engine shutdown, allow a few minutes for the oil to settle, then check the oil level. If necessary, add oil to bring the level up to the prescribed quantity. In addition, inspect the areas around the oil drain plug, oil filter, and oil screen fitting for leaks.

OIL RESERVOIR

In some instances, the oil reservoir installed in a dry-sump system must be removed for cleaning or repair. To do this, begin by draining all the oil and disconnecting the oil inlet and vent lines. Once this is done, remove the scupper drain hose and bonding wire. Next, remove the safety wire and loosen the clamps of the securing straps which are fitted around the tank. While supporting the tank, remove the securing straps and lift the tank out of the aircraft. The tank is reinstalled by reversing the step sequence used in the tank removal.

OIL COOLER

Oil coolers are normally removed and cleaned during an engine overhaul. However, if an oil cooler loses a portion of its cooling effectiveness, there may be accumulations of sludge blocking portions of the cooler. If this is the case, the cooler must be removed and cleaned. Once the cooler is removed from the engine and cleaned, visually inspect it for cracks and other damage. Pay particular attention to all welded or soldered seams since they are subject to damage from excessive oil pressures. Once cleaning and repairs are complete, the cooler should be pressure tested as per the manufacturer's instructions. [Figure 9-27]

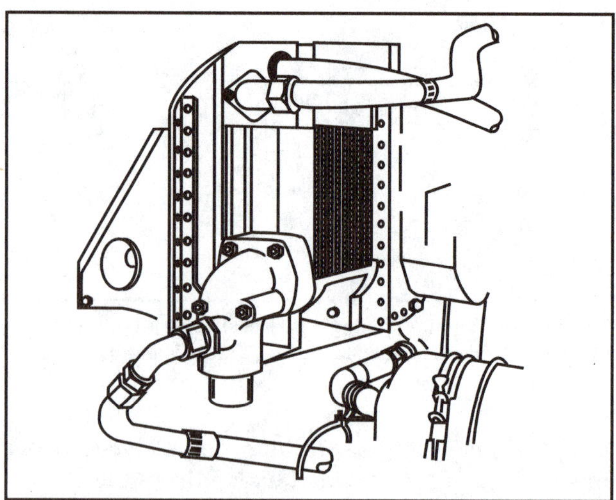

Figure 9-27. When inspecting an oil cooler, any sign of oil leakage may indicate a crack in the cooler's core. If this is the case, or if an oil cooler loses its effectiveness, the cooler should be removed, inspected, and pressure tested.

RELIEF VALVE ADJUSTMENT

During routine maintenance, you may be required to adjust the oil pressure relief valve. Oil pressure specifications typically vary from 35 to 90 psi depending on the engine model. The oil pressure must be high enough to ensure adequate lubrication of the engine and accessories at high speeds and powers. On the other hand, the pressure must not be excessive, since leakage and damage to the oil system may result.

Initial adjustment of an oil pressure relief valve is made by the overhaul shop on a newly overhauled engine prior to the initial test run. However, once an engine is installed on an aircraft and run, the relief valve pressure setting may require a slight readjustment. In addition, over time, the spring in a relief valve may weaken enough to require some adjustment.

To adjust an oil pressure relief valve, remove the cover nut, loosen the locknut, and turn the adjusting screw clockwise to increase the pressure, and counterclockwise to decrease the pressure. After each pressure adjustment, tighten the adjustment screw locknut and run-up the engine to check the oil pressure while the engine is running at an rpm specified by the manufacturer. [Figure 9-28]

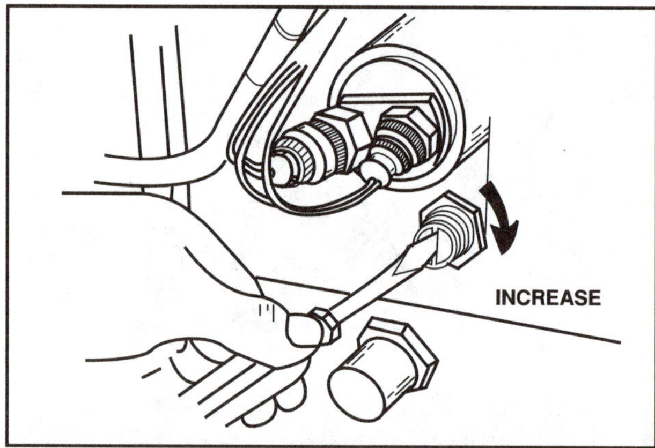

Figure 9-28. Oil pressure relief valves occasionally require readjustment. On a typical relief valve, turning the adjusting screw clockwise increases the maximum system pressure while turning the adjusting screw counterclockwise decreases system pressure.

TURBINE ENGINES

The lubrication system on a turbine engine supplies oil to moving parts within the engine which are subjected to friction and heating. In most cases, pressure lubrication is used to lubricate all the necessary components within a turbine engine. The reason for this is that, unlike reciprocating engines that have several moving parts that splash oil around the engine, a turbine engine has one or two rotating shafts that ride on bearings and an accessory gear box. Another difference is that turbine engines operate at much higher temperatures than reciprocating engines; therefore, the lubrication system must carry a greater amount of heat away from the components it lubricates. To do this, oil typically circulates through a turbine engine at a very high flow rate.

One of the most notable differences between reciprocating and turbine engine lubrication systems is that the oil in a turbine engine is completely sealed from combustion gases. As a result, very little oil is consumed by the engine. This allows a turbine engine oil reservoir to be smaller than that of a comparable size reciprocating engine. For example, the oil reservoir on a small turbine engine installed on a business jet typically holds only three to five quarts of oil. Another benefit of being sealed from the combustion gases is that the oil remains cleaner and can generally go longer between oil changes.

LUBRICATING OILS

The large operating tolerances and high bearing pressures in reciprocating engines require the use of a high viscosity oil. Turbine engines, on the other hand, are built with extremely tight tolerances and the ball and roller bearings used are subjected to relatively low pressures. Because of this, low viscosity oils are used in turbine engines.

In addition to having a low viscosity, the oil used in turbine engines must provide adequate lubrication over a wide temperature range, typically from –60°F to +400°F. Given these temperature extremes, a conventional mineral-based oil would congeal at the low temperature extremes and break down at the upper extremes. In addition, mineral-based oils tend to leave lacquer and carbon, or **coke** deposits when exposed to excessive temperatures. Because of this, synthetic oils are used almost exclusively in turbine engines.

In addition to its ability to lubricate over a wide temperature range, synthetic oils have a low volatility which helps prevent evaporation at high altitudes. In addition, most synthetic oils contain an anti-foaming additive which helps reduce foaming and ensures positive lubrication. Additional characteristics possessed by synthetic oils include having a high viscosity index, high flash point, low pour point, and excellent cohesion and adhesion properties. Cohesion is a characteristic of oil molecules that causes them to stick together under compression loads, while adhesion allows oil to adhere to surfaces under centrifugal loads.

Currently, there are two types of synthetic oils used in turbine engines: Type I, or MIL-L-7808 and Type II, or MIL-L-23699. Type I synthetic oil is an alkyl diester oil with a 3 centistoke rating. This type of synthetic oil has a very low viscosity and was used primarily in early turbine engines. On the other hand, Type II synthetic oil is a polyester lubricant that has a 5 centistoke rating and is used in most modern turbine engines.

As discussed in Section A, different types of synthetic oil should not be mixed. In addition, since some proprietary additives many not mix with others, some manufacturers recommend that different brands of synthetic oil not be mixed.

SYSTEM CLASSIFICATION

Like reciprocating engines, turbine engines may have either a wet-sump or dry-sump lubrication system. Currently, wet-sump lubrication systems are primarily used on some auxiliary power units; however, they were used extensively on early turbine engines. In a typical wet-sump system, oil is stored in an engine sump or accessory gearbox. From here, oil is pressurized and routed through

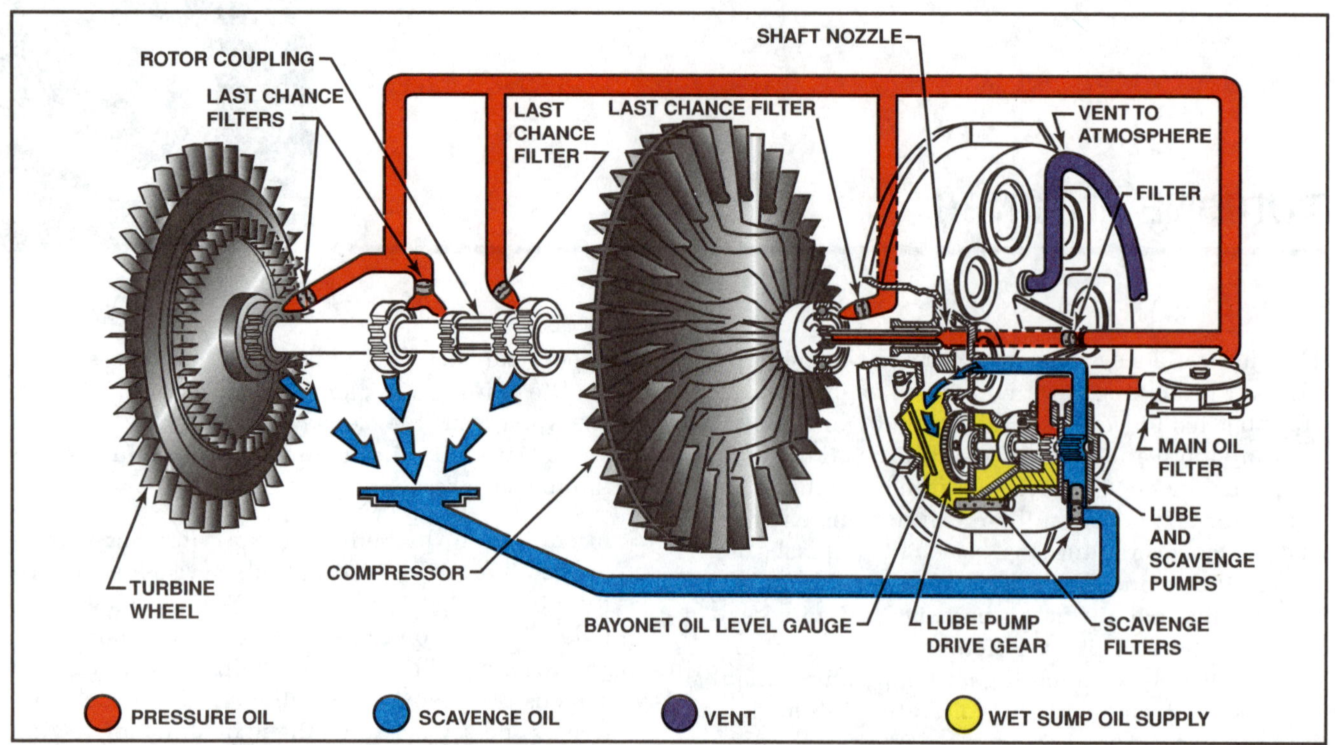

Figure 9-29. In this wet-sump lubrication system, pressurized oil flows from the oil pump through several filters before reaching the main rotor bearings and coupling. Once circulated through the bearings, one or more scavenge pumps return the oil to the accessory case.

multiple filters before reaching the main rotor bearings and couplings. Once the oil has lubricated the main bearings, it drains to low lying areas where scavenge pumps route the oil back to the sump or gearbox. Since the oil in a wet-sump system is generally stored in the accessory gearbox, the bearings and drive gears within the accessory gearbox receive oil through splash lubrication. [Figure 9-29]

Today, the majority of turbine engines utilize a dry-sump lubrication system consisting of pressure, scavenge, and breather subsystems. Dry-sump systems differ from wet-sump systems in that the oil is stored in a separate oil reservoir mounted either internally within the engine or externally on the engine or in the aircraft. In this type of system, an oil pump pulls oil from the oil tank and provides pressure and spray lubrication throughout the engine. Once circulated, the oil accumulates in low lying areas where scavenge pumps pick up the oil and pump it back to the reservoir.

A typical pressure lubrication system consists of an oil reservoir, pressure and scavenge pumps, pressure relief valve, several oil filters, oil jets, an oil cooler, and vent lines. In addition, to allow an operator to monitor the operation of a given lubrication system, most systems include an oil temperature and oil pressure gauge.

OIL RESERVOIR

The oil reservoir in a dry-sump system is usually constructed of sheet aluminum or stainless steel and is designed to furnish a constant supply of oil to the engine during all approved flight maneuvers. As mentioned earlier, in a dry-sump system, the oil reservoir may be mounted externally or internally. When mounted externally, the reservoir may be attached to the engine case or mounted inside the aircraft structure. On the other hand, when mounted internally, the oil reservoir is formed by an internal space, or cavity, within the engine structure. Common locations for internal oil reservoirs include cavities between major case sections and propeller reduction gear boxes.

The oil supply for a wet-sump system is typically located in the main gearbox at the lowest point within the engine. This position permits splash lubrication to be used on accessory gears and bearings.

To ensure a positive flow of oil to the oil pump inlet, most oil reservoirs are pressurized. Pressurizing the reservoir also helps to suppress oil foaming which, in turn, prevents pump cavitation. In most cases, pressurization is accomplished by installing an adjustable relief valve in the oil reservoir vent line. This way, reservoir pressure builds until the relief valve opens to relieve excess pressure. A typical relief valve is adjusted to maintain a reservoir pressure of approximately three to six psig.

If you recall from the previous section, FAR Part 23 requires that all oil reservoirs have an expansion space of at least 10 percent of the tank capacity, or 0.5 gallon, whichever is greater. The expansion space provides sufficient room for oil to expand as it heats and allows room for the collection of foam. In addition, all oil filler caps or covers must be marked with the word "OIL" and the permissible oil designations. As an added feature, most of the oil reservoirs installed in some dry-sump systems include a scupper drain.

As lubricating oil is agitated by an engine's moving parts, air typically becomes entrained in the oil. To remedy this problem, many oil tanks contain a some form of **deaerator**, or **air-oil separator**. In some engines, a separator may be installed in the accessory gearbox while other systems rely on a separator in the oil reservoir. One type of deaerator that may be installed in an oil reservoir swirls the air/oil mixture allowing centrifugal force to pull the oil from the air. Once separated, the oil drains into the reservoir while the air is vented overboard. Another type of deaerator consists of a tray in the top of the reservoir that the oil spreads out on when it is returned to the reservoir. As the oil spreads out into a thin layer, entrapped air separates from the oil. In oil reservoirs that are equipped with a dwell chamber, the oil/air mixture enters the **dwell chamber** at the bottom of the oil tank. Scavenge pump pressure then forces the oil upward through the dwell chamber and spreads it into a thin film facilitating the release of entrained air. [Figure 9-30]

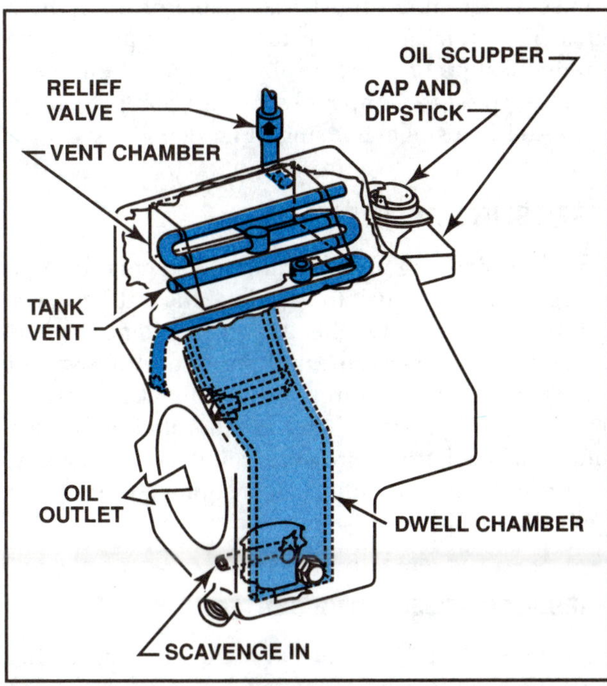

Figure 9-30. In oil reservoirs that are equipped with a dwell chamber, oil enters the bottom of the oil tank and passes through a dwell chamber. As this happens, the oil is spread into a thin film to facilitate the release of entrained air.

The most common method of checking the oil level in the tank is with a dipstick. In lieu of a dipstick, some oil tanks incorporate a sight gauge to satisfy the FAR requirements for a visual means of checking oil level. However, these glass indicators tend to cloud over after prolonged use and, therefore, many operators rely on the dipstick method. [Figure 9-31]

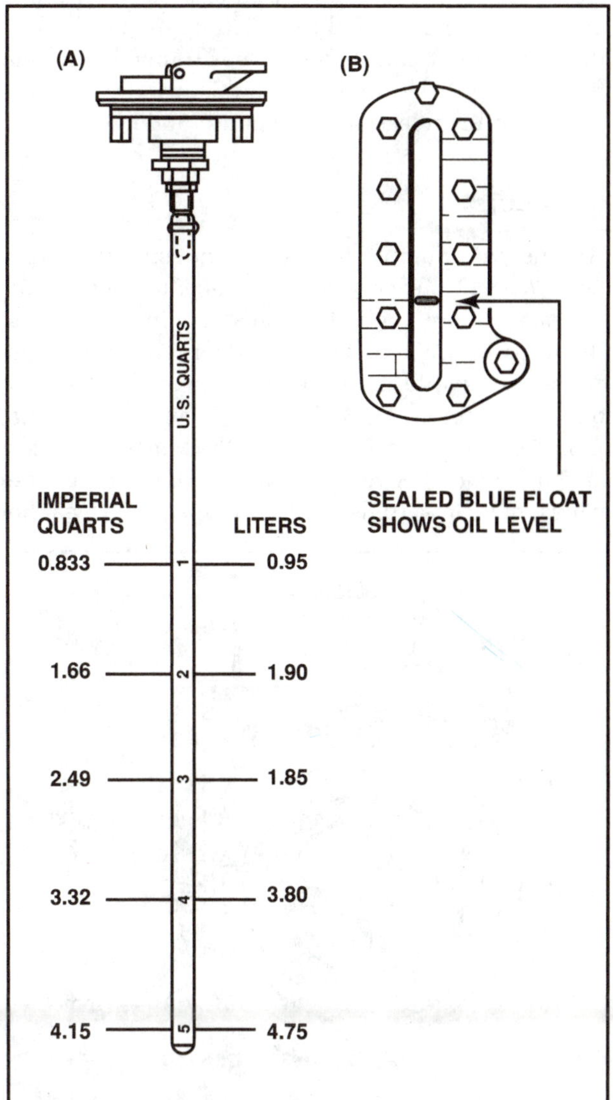

Figure 9-31. (A) — Many turbine engines utilize a conventional dipstick such as this to indicate the oil level in the main tank. (B) — Some tanks are equipped with a sight gauge on the side of the oil tank to provide a visual means of checking oil level.

OIL PUMPS

Like reciprocating engines, all turbine engine pressure lubrication systems utilize a constant displacement pump. If you recall, a constant displacement pump moves a fixed volume of fluid per revolution. The three types of constant displacement pumps that are used in turbine engines include the gear, vane, and gerotor.

GEAR PUMP

The gear-type pump is the most common type of oil pump used in turbine engines. A typical gear-type pump consists of two meshed gears that rotate inside a housing. The gears and housing are precisely machined to keep clearances between them as small as possible. Oil is picked up by the gears at the pump inlet and then becomes trapped between the teeth and the housing. As the gears rotate, the trapped oil is released at the pump outlet.

VANE PUMP

A vane-type pump consists of a housing that contains a steel sleeve with an off-center bore, four vanes, a hollow steel rotor, and a coupling that turns the rotor. In this type of pump, the rotor turns on its center axis while the vanes are free to slide in and out of the rotor. As each pair of vanes passes the pump inlet, the space between the vanes increases and oil floods between the vanes. However, as the vanes rotate toward the outlet, the space between the vanes decreases. This pressurizes the oil so that when the vanes reach the pump outlet, the oil is forced out of the pump. Of the pumps used in an oil system, the vane pump is considered to be more tolerant of debris. This makes the sliding vane pumps ideal for use in a scavenge system. [Figure 9-32]

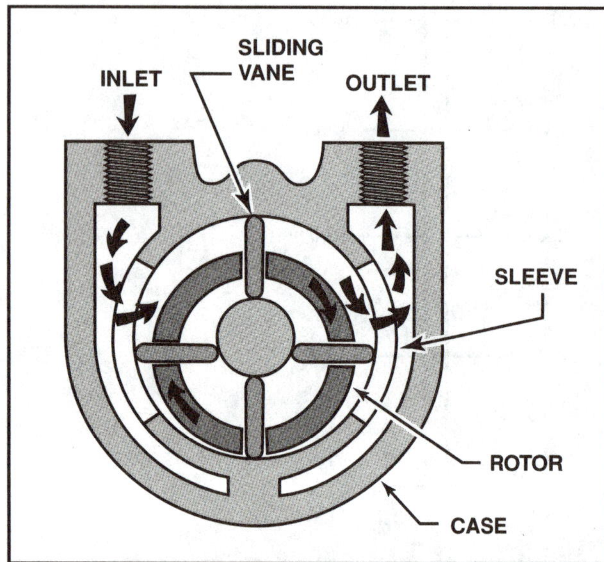

Figure 9-32. In a vane-type pump, a set of vanes slide in and out of the rotor as it rotates in the pump housing. Since the rotor is offset in the housing, the volume between each set of vanes alternatly increases and decreases allowing the pump to pull fluid in one side and force it out the other.

GEROTOR PUMP

Another type of constant-displacement pump used to move oil through a turbine engine is the gerotor-type pump. As discussed in the previous section, a typical gerotor-type pump consists of an engine-driven spur gear that rotates within a free spinning rotor housing. The rotor and drive gear ride inside a housing that has two oblong openings. One opening is the oil inlet while the other is the oil outlet.

SCAVENGE PUMP

In addition to a pressure pump, almost all turbine engine lubrication systems must utilize a scavenge pump to return oil to the oil reservoir. A scavenge pump may be a gear- vane-, or gerotor-type pump that is driven by the engine. As a rule, scavenge pumps have a capacity that is greater than a pressure pump. The reason for this is that after oil flows through an engine it typically has a greater volume due to foaming and thermal expansion. Therefore, to ensure that oil does not collect in the engine sump, the scavenge pump must be capable of pumping a greater volume of oil than the pressure pump. One unique feature of many turbine engine oil pumps is that the pressure pump and scavenge pump are often enclosed in a single housing. [Figure 9-33]

PRESSURE RELIEF VALVE

Some turbine engine lubrication systems rely on a pressure relief valve to regulate the oil pressure within the system. On the other hand, some systems do not use a pressure relief valve and allow full pump pressure to circulate within the system. Lubrication systems that have a relief valve are often referred to as pressure relief valve systems, while systems that do not incorporate a relief valve are called full-flow systems.

PRESSURE RELIEF VALVE SYSTEM

In a pressure relief valve system, oil flow to the bearing chambers is regulated by a spring-loaded relief valve that is held in the closed position. With this type of valve, when the oil pressure rises above a preset value, the valve off seats and returns excess

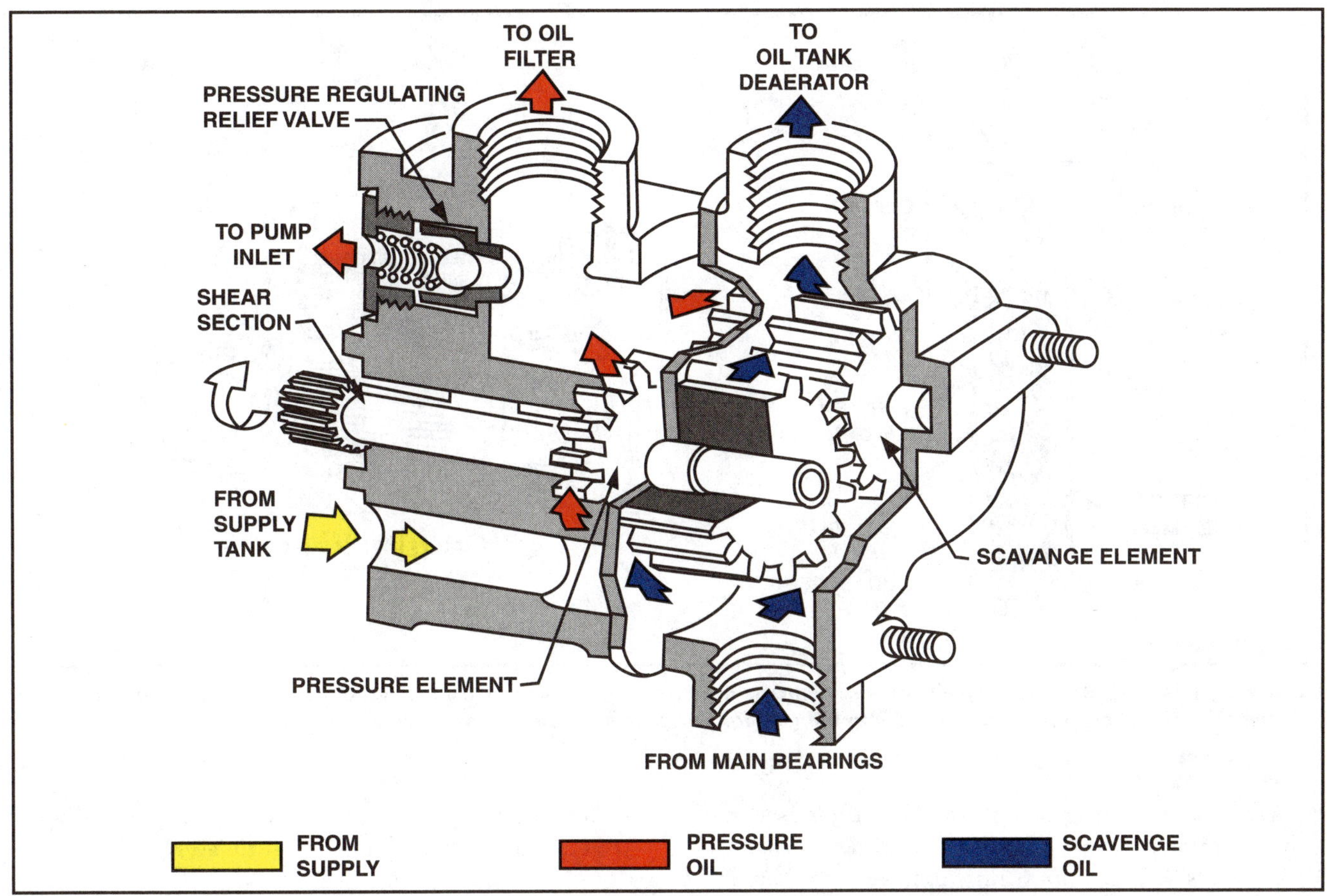

Figure 9-33. To help eliminate the added size and weight of a separate scavenge pump, many turbine engines utilize a single pump unit that houses both the pressure and scavenge pumps.

oil to the reservoir or oil pump inlet. The pressure required to open the valve typically corresponds to the oil pump's output capability when the engine is running at idle speed. This guarantees adequate oil pressure throughout the engine's operating range.

In a turbine engine, the pressure within the bearing chambers increases dramatically with increases in engine speed. As the pressure within the bearing chambers increases, the pressure differential between the bearing chambers and the lubrication system decreases. Therefore, as the pressure within the bearing chambers increases, less oil flows to the bearings. To prevent this from happening, some of the pressurized air within the bearing chambers is typically routed to the back side of the pressure relief valve to augment the spring pressure. This way, as the engine speed increases, the pressure within the lubrication system also increases.

FULL-FLOW SYSTEM

In a full-flow system, no pressure relief valve is used; therefore, the amount of oil that flows to the bearings is directly related to how fast the engine and oil pump are run. In this case, the size of the oil pump is determined by the oil flow required at the engine's maximum operating speed.

OIL FILTERS

Once oil is discharged from an oil pressure pump, it flows to an oil filter. The purpose of the filter is to remove solid particles that are suspended in the oil. The contaminants typically found in a turbine engine oil system include products of oil decomposition, metallic particles produced by engine wear, and corrosion. In addition, since large amounts of air move through a turbine engine, airborne contaminants can enter the oil system through the main bearing seals. Occasionally, dirt and other foreign matter may also be inadvertently introduced into the oil supply during servicing.

All turbine engines include an oil filter downstream from the oil pump. In addition, most engines force the oil to pass through another filter just prior to

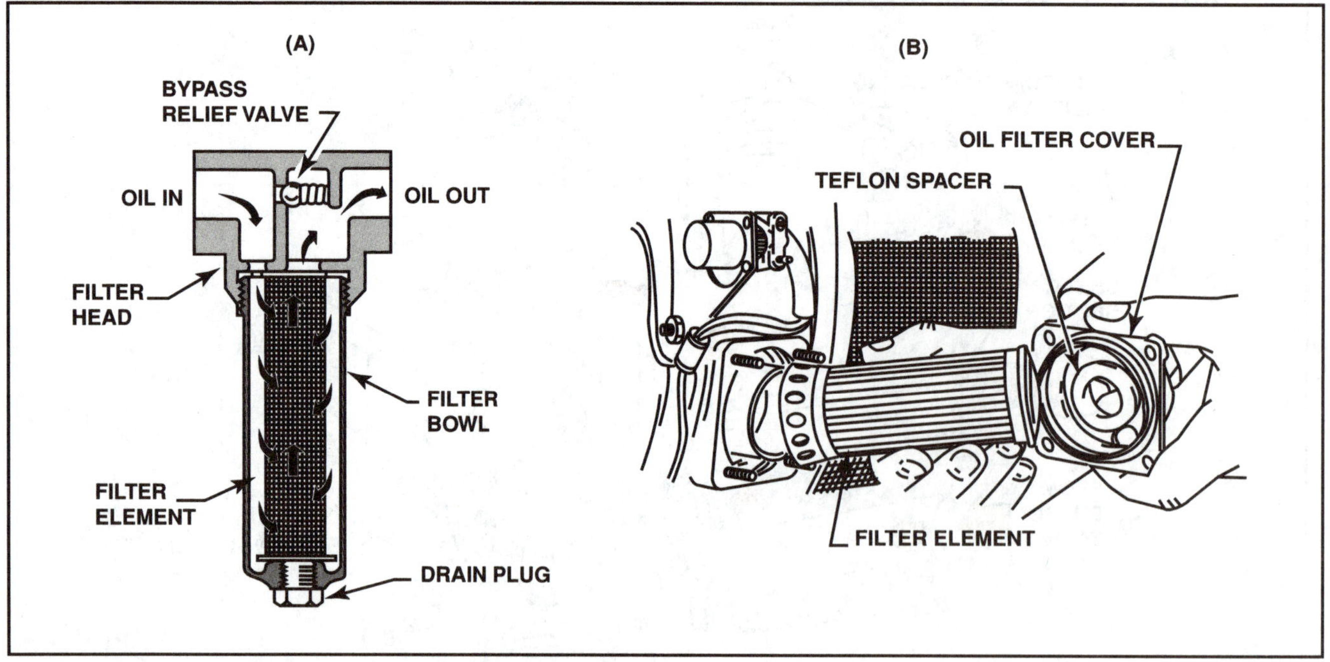

Figure 9-34. (A) — With a bowl-type filter, a screen-type filter element is inserted inside a removable filter bowl. (B) — In another installation, the filter element is inserted into the gearbox and then covered with a simple cover plate.

entering the bearing chambers. This filter is commonly referred to as a **last chance filter** because it represents the last opportunity to filter the oil before it enters the bearing chamber. Since last chance filters are placed deep within an engine, they are cleaned only when an engine is disassembled for overhaul.

On some engines, filtration is also provided in the scavenge subsystem. With this type of system, the oil is filtered prior to reaching the reservoir. This way, any contaminants that are flushed out of the bearing chambers do not make it back to the clean oil in the reservoir.

The effectiveness of a turbine engine oil filter is measured in microns. One **micron** represents a size or distance equal to one millionth of a meter, or approximately .000039 inch. To put micron measurements in perspective, consider that objects must be approximately 40 microns or larger to be distinguishable by the human eye.

Turbine engines utilize three types of filters; a wire-mesh oil screen, a screen disk, or a pleated-fiber filter. A typical wire-mesh filter is rated at 20 to 40 microns. In other words, particles larger than 40 microns in size are filtered from the oil supply. To create a larger surface area for filtration, many oil screens are pleated. Typically, installations that utilize screen-type filters include bowl-type in-line filters and gearbox filters. [Figure 9-34]

The screen-disk type filter is more common to Pratt & Whitney engines and consists of a series of wafer-thin screens that are separated by spacers. The screens are stacked on a perforated metal core and oil is filtered as it passes from the outer edge to the core. A typical rating on a screen disk filter is approximately 20 microns. In addition, its construction permits the filter to be disassembled and cleaned. This type of filter is often used in the pressurized portion of an oil system and fits into an annulus provided in the main accessory gearbox. [Figure 9-35]

Pleated-fiber filters are typically rated at about 15 microns and are similar to the filters used in reciprocating engines. A typical pleated-fiber filter element consists of millions of resin-impregnated fibers that are formed into a long sheet, folded into pleats, and assembled around a perforated steel core. Because of their construction, pleated-fiber filters are generally intended to be replaced at specific time intervals.

FAR requirements dictate that all oil filters be constructed and installed in a way that permits full oil flow even if the filter becomes completely blocked. Therefore, some means of bypassing the filter must

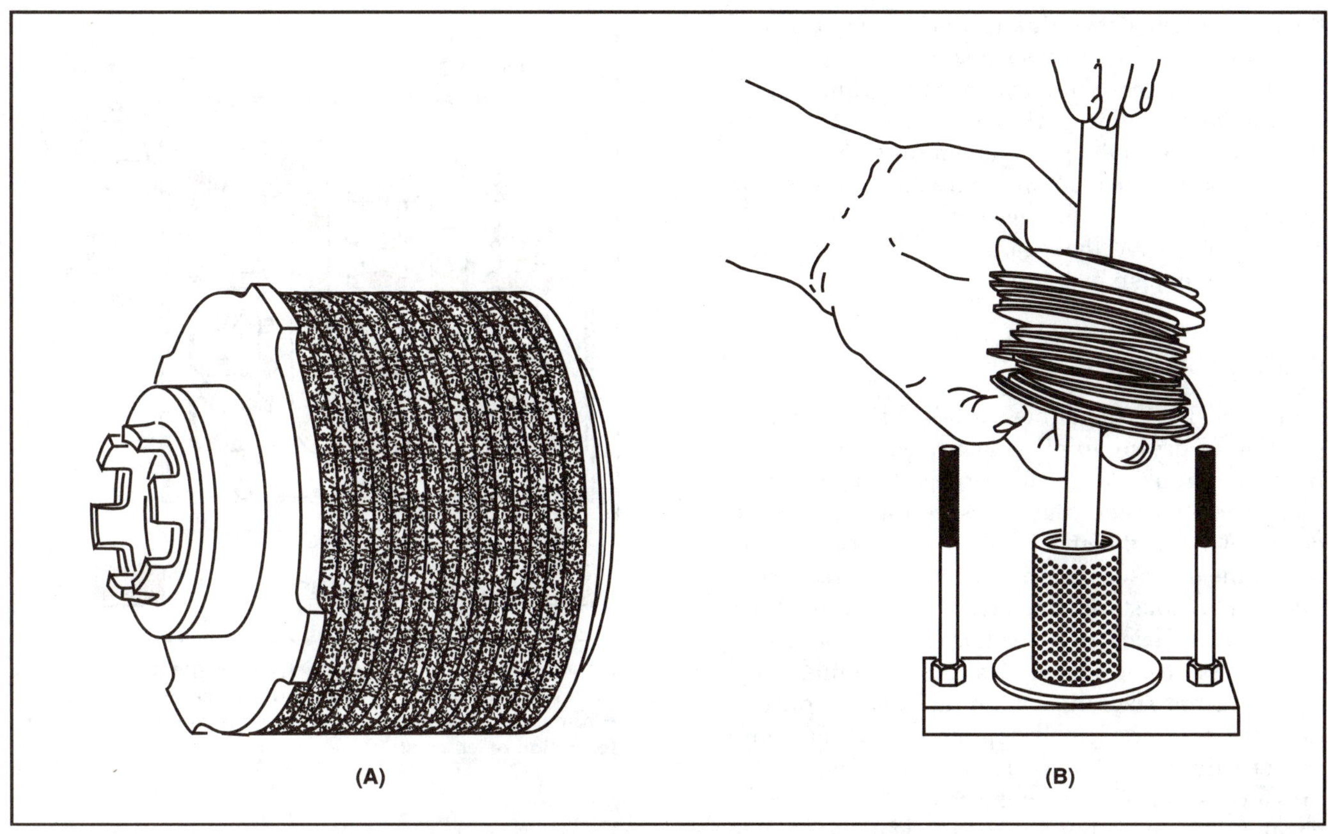

Figure 9-35. (A) — A typical screen-disk filter consists of several wafer-thin screens that are separated by spacers. (B) — This configuration allows the filter to be easily disassembled and cleaned.

be provided. The most common way of meeting this requirement is to incorporate an **oil bypass valve** that automatically lets oil bypass the filter entirely once it becomes plugged. Since the use of unfiltered oil to lubricate main bearings can cause extensive damage, most turbine powered aircraft incorporate a warning light in the cockpit to warn the operator when the filter is being bypassed.

OIL JETS

An oil jet is basically a fixed nozzle that provides a relatively constant oil flow to the main bearings at all engine speeds. Oil jets are located in the pressure lines adjacent to, or within, the bearing compartments and rotor shaft couplings. Due to the high rpm and high loading placed on main rotor bearings, constant oil flow to the bearings is vital. This is especially true for the turbine bearings since they are subjected to the most heat.

Oil jets can deliver lubrication oil in the form of a solid oil spray or an air-oil mist. While an air-oil mist is considered adequate for some types of bearings, a solid oil spray typically provides better lubrication. In fact, a solid oil spray is required in engines that utilize oil dampened bearings. This type of bearing relies on an oil film between the outer race and bearing housing to reduce rotor vibrations and compensate for slight rotor misalignments.

The small nozzle orifices in the tips of oil jets become clogged easily and, because they are located deep within an engine, they are not accessible for cleaning except during engine overhaul. Therefore, the oil must be free of particle contaminants. As discussed earlier, last chance filters are placed in the oil line upstream from the oil jets to help prevent nozzle clogs. However, bearing failure will inevitably result if the last chance filter becomes clogged.

VENT SYSTEM

In many turbine engines, the bearing chambers and accessory gearbox are vented to the oil reservoir. The primary purpose of a vent system is to vent excessive pressure in the bearing chambers so the pressure differential between the bearing chambers and the lubrication system is maintained and the oil jets maintain the proper spray pattern. In addition, the pressurized air within the bearing chambers and accessory gearbox provides a source of pressurization for the oil reservoir. If you recall, turbine engine oil reservoirs are pressurized to help ensure a positive flow of oil to the pump and minimize oil foaming. To control the amount of pressurization, the oil reservoir is vented to the atmosphere through a check relief valve that maintains a reservoir pressure of three to six psig.

CHECK VALVES

A check valve is sometimes installed in the oil supply line of dry-sump oil systems. The check valve prevents supply oil from seeping through the oil pump elements and high-pressure lines after shutdown. Without the check valve, oil could accumulate in the accessory gearbox, compressor rear housing, and combustion chamber. Such accumulations could cause excessive loading on the accessory drive gears during an engine start, contamination of the cabin pressurization air, or an internal oil fire. Check valves are usually spring-loaded, ball-and-socket valves constructed to allow the free flow of pressurized oil. The oil pressure required to open a check valve varies, but typically ranges from two to five psi.

OIL COOLER

As you know, one of the functions of oil is to cool the engine; however, to do this, the heat absorbed by the oil must be removed. In most cases, the excess heat is removed by an oil cooler. The oil cooler in a turbine engine may be located in either the pressure subsystem or the scavenge subsystem. When installed in the pressure subsystem, the lubrication system is sometimes referred to as a **hot tank system** because the scavenge oil is not cooled before it enters the reservoir. On the other hand, when the oil cooler is placed in the scavenge subsystem, the lubrication system is often referred to as a **cold tank system** because the oil is cooled just before it enters the reservoir.

The oil coolers used on some early turbine engines were simple oil-to-air heat exchangers similar to the oil coolers used on reciprocating engines. Although this type of oil cooler is effective, the cooler must be installed near the front of the engine so it is exposed to ram air. Modern oil coolers use fuel to cool the oil and, therefore, are termed oil-to-fuel heat exchangers. Using fuel to cool the oil is considered to be much more efficient than using air because two important functions are accomplished simultaneously. First, the oil is cooled to an acceptable operating temperature and second, the fuel is preheated which improves combustion. In addition, an oil-to-fuel oil cooler is typically easier to install since it does not have to be exposed to ram air.

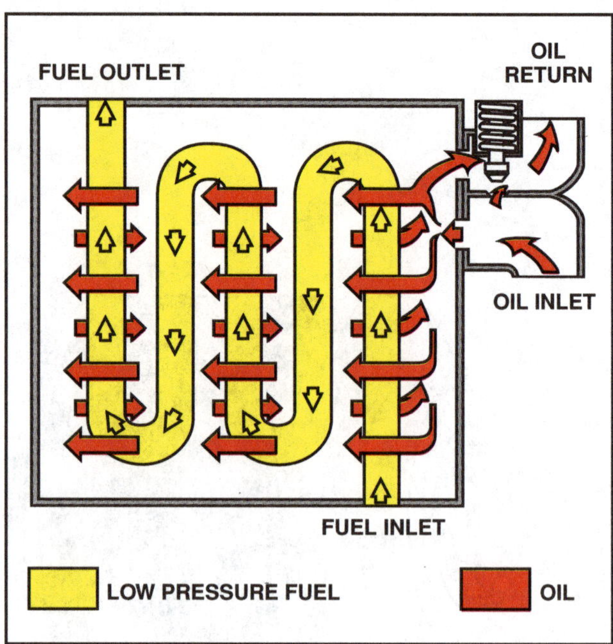

Figure 9-36. An oil-to-fuel heat exchanger transfers heat from the engine oil to the fuel. This cools the hot oil before it re-enters the engine and warms the fuel to prevent the formation of ice crystals.

A typical oil-to-fuel heat exchanger consists of a series of joined tubes with an inlet and outlet port. In a typical oil cooler, fuel flows through the cooler continuously while a thermostatic bypass valve controls the amount of oil that flows to the oil cooler. When the oil is cold, the bypass valve allows the oil to bypass the cooler. However, once the oil heats up, the bypass valve forces the oil to flow through the cooler. [Figure 9-36]

CHIP DETECTORS

Many scavenge subsystems contain permanent magnet chip detectors that attract and hold ferrous metal particles. These chip detectors are utilized for several reasons. First, any metal particles that are attracted to the detector are prevented from circulating in the engine and causing additional wear. Second, the collection of metal particles on a chip detector provide valuable information when troubleshooting engine problems.

As a general rule, the presence of small fuzzy particles or grey metallic paste is the result of normal

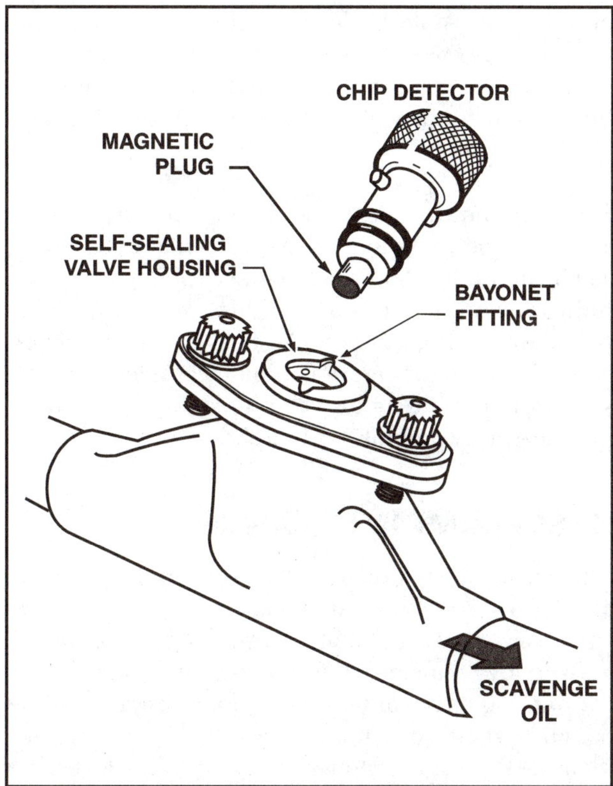

Figure 9-37. A magnetic chip detector is typically located in the oil return line where it collects ferrous particles suspended in the engine oil. During scheduled engine maintenance, the chip detector is removed and visually inspected.

engine wear and, therefore, is not a cause for concern. However, metallic chips or flakes are an indication of serious internal wear which must be investigated further. [Figure 9-37]

As an added feature, some chip detectors incorporate an electric circuit that operates an indicator light in the cockpit. With this type chip detector, sometimes called an **indicating chip detector**, a positive electrode is placed in the center of the detector while a negative, or ground electrode is placed on the detector shell. In this configuration, when metallic debris bridges the gap between the positive and ground electrodes, the indicator circuit is completed and the warning light illuminates. The flight crew must then respond to the warning and take the necessary precautions to prevent engine damage and ensure flight safety. Decisions on the proper response are usually based, in part, on the readings obtained from other engine instrument readings and whether or not the warning can be reset. [Figure 9-38]

A more modern type of chip detector is the **electric pulsed chip detector**. This type of detector is unique because it can discriminate between small wear-particles, which are considered non-failure related, and larger particles, which can be an indication of impending failure.

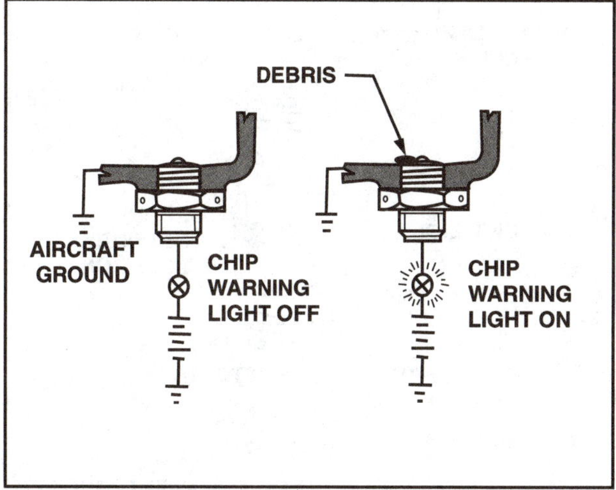

Figure 9-38. With a chip detector that incorporates a warning light, the indicating circuit is completed when a sufficient amount of ferrous debris collects on the magnet and bridges the gap between the positive and ground electrodes.

Pulsed detectors are designed to operate in a manual mode, or in a combination manual/automatic mode. In the manual mode, the warning light illuminates each time the gap is sufficiently bridged, regardless of the particle size. The engine operator may then fire an electrical pulse which discharges energy across the detector gap in an attempt to burn off insignificant debris. After doing this, if the warning light extinguishes and does not re-illuminate, the warning indication may be interpreted as a non-failure related cause. However, if the warning light remains illuminated, or repeatedly comes on after being cleared, maintenance should be scheduled to troubleshoot the cause.

In the automatic mode, a time delay relay is activated in the warning circuit. This relay prevents the warning light from illuminating immediately after the electrode gap is bridged. This way, if the gap is bridged by small debris, a pulse of electrical energy has time to automatically discharge across the gap before the warning light illuminates. If the resulting burn-off opens the gap the light remains extinguished. However, if the debris is large enough, it will remain in place after the burn-off cycle is completed and the warning light will illuminate when the time-delay relay closes. [Figure 9-39]

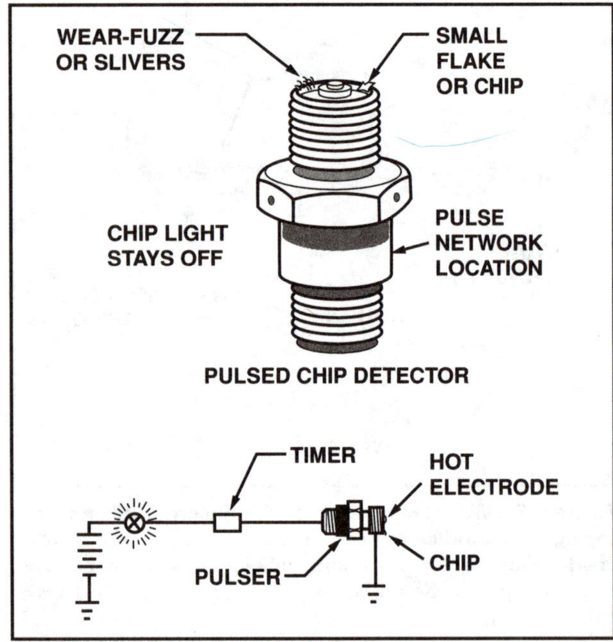

Figure 9-39. With an electric pulse chip detector, the engine operator can fire an electrical pulse across the gap of the detector to burn off insignificant debris. In addition, by incorporating a timer, the number of false warnings is greatly reduced.

OIL PRESSURE GAUGE

To allow you to monitor the effectiveness of a given lubrication system, all aircraft engines are equipped with an oil pressure gauge that is calibrated in pounds per square inch. A turbine engine pressure gauge is typically connected to the oil system downstream of the main oil filter. This location ensures an indication of the actual pressure being delivered to the engine. As an additional feature, some oil pressure systems incorporate a low-pressure warning light. When aircraft electrical power is turned on and the engine is not running, each engine's low oil pressure light illuminates. However, when starting the engine, the warning light should extinguish once oil pressure increases above the low limit marked on the oil pressure gauge.

OIL TEMPERATURE GAUGE

The oil temperature gauge allows you to monitor the temperature of the oil. This is important because oil circulation cools the engine as it lubricates the moving parts. The oil temperature sensor location in a turbine engine lubrication system is less critical than in a reciprocating engine. Therefore, engine manufacturers place the sensor in either the pressure subsystem or the scavenge subsystem. This option is possible because turbine engine lubrication systems have a flow rate of two to five times the oil tank capacity per minute. As a result, temperatures stabilize throughout the entire lubrication system very rapidly.

Some engine manufacturers prefer the temperature sensor to be installed in the scavenge subsystem. Their reason for this is it provides a slightly quicker indication of high friction buildup caused by failing parts, such as bearings and gears. However, of the two locations, it is more common to place the sensor in the pressure subsystem to sense the oil temperature at the engine's oil inlet.

SYSTEM MAINTENANCE

The maintenance practices discussed in this section are typical of those used on a turbine engine. However, the maintenance procedures discussed here are by no means all inclusive. Therefore, before conducting any maintenance on an aircraft's lubrication system you should consult the appropriate manufacturer's maintenance manuals and service bulletins.

Maintenance of turbine engine lubrication systems usually consists of adjusting, removing, cleaning, and replacing various components. For example, oil filters must be periodically cleaned or replaced and pressure relief valves may require occasional adjustments.

OIL CHANGE

In routine service, oil is constantly exposed to many substances that reduce its ability to protect moving parts. The primary source of oil contamination in turbine engines include gasoline, moisture, acids, dirt, carbon, and metal particles. If allowed to accumulate over a period of time, these contaminants can cause excessive wear on internal engine components.

The recommended time interval between oil changes is typically based on the manufacturer's recommendations. However, since the oil in turbine engines is sealed from the combustion gases, the time interval between oil changes is typically quite long. For example, a typical oil change interval on many business jets is 300 to 400 hours or 6 months, whichever comes first. On larger turbine engines that consume more than 0.2 quarts per hour, some operators rely on oil replenishment as an effective method of changing oil. The logic behind this is that normal replenishment will automatically change the oil at regular 50 to 100 hour intervals.

Whenever possible, you should drain the engine oil as soon as possible after the engine has been shut down. This helps ensure that the oil reservoir is as full as possible and that the maximum amount of contaminants are held in suspension. This way, when the oil is drained, most of the contaminants will drain out of the engine with the oil.

The oil in turbine engines is typically drained from the oil reservoir, the accessory gearbox sump, the main oil filter, and other low points in the system. In some cases, manufacturers recommend that the lubrication system be periodically flushed. Flushing procedures usually consist of filling the engine with the proper oil or cleaning agent and motoring the engine with the starter. Once this is done, the oil or cleaning agent is drained from the engine.

When draining the oil, inspect the oil closely for signs of contamination. For example, if the engine oil is observed to be dark brown or even blackish, but little or no contaminants are present, overheating is a likely cause. The discoloration is a chemical reaction that occurs when excessive heat causes oil decomposition. The cause of overheating could range from low oil quantity to engine malfunctions such as clogged oil jets or disintegrating bearings. Consult the engine logs for excessive oil consumption and thoroughly analyze other clues in accordance with the appropriate troubleshooting guides in the maintenance manual.

Given the high costs associated with turbine engine operation, the value of a spectrometric oil analysis program (S.O.A.P.) is unquestioned. As with reciprocating engines, a series of samples must be analyzed before an accurate trend forecast can be developed. On engines that do not receive regular oil changes, regular oil analysis is still recommended. To do this, samples must be drawn from the oil reservoir. In this case, oil samples should be drawn from the center of the oil tank within 15 minutes after engine shutdown to ensure that the sample retains wear materials and contaminants in suspension.

OIL FILTER REPLACEMENT

The oil filter should be removed at every regular inspection. The inspection, cleaning, and possible replacement is dictated by the type of filter element used. If the filter is the reusable type, the element should be disassembled, inspected, cleaned, and reinstalled. A disposable type filter must be inspected for metallic particles and replaced.

Contaminants which are large enough and heavy enough to be seen in filter bowls or on filter screens are always a matter of concern. In such cases, follow the manufacturer's recommended course of action to determine the source of the contaminants. If a spectrometric oil analysis program has been followed, a read-out of the various metals present in the latest oil sample can be compared to earlier test results. The results may affect the decision-making process of whether or not there is sufficient cause to dismantle the engine for closer inspection.

Traditional methods of hand cleaning reusuable filters in solvent are still commonly used and acceptable. However, several cleaning devices such as **ultrasonic cleaners** or **vibrator cleaners** are also available for filter and parts cleaning. With these types of cleaners, the filter is placed in a solvent bath and ultrasonic sound waves are pulsed through the solvent. The high frequency energy dislodges foreign materials and removes contaminants from a filter element. These units do a very thorough job of removing all contaminants from filtering elements. [Figure 9-40]

Once the screens or filters have been inspected and the oil has been completely drained, replace and secure the drain plug. On aircraft that utilize a disposable filter, a new filter must be installed and secured. On the other hand, on aircraft that use an oil screen, the screen must be cleaned, re-installed, and secured. Once all filters and/or screens are

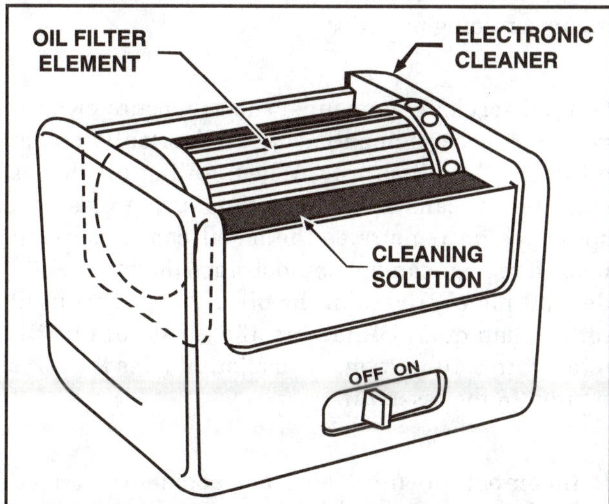

Figure 9-40. If approved by the engine manufacturer, reusable oil filter elements can be thoroughly cleaned by immersing them in a cleaning solution that is part of an ultrasonic cleaning device.

secured, the oil reservoir should be refilled with the recommended grade of oil. A sample list of typical synthetic lubricants you are likely to see include:

Type-1 (MIL-L-7808)	Type-2 (MIL-L-23699)
Aeroshell 300	Aeroshell 500 or 700
Mobil Jet I	Mobel Jet II
Stauffer I	Stauffer II
Castrol 3c	Castrol 205
Enco 15	Enco 2380
Exxon 15	Exxon 25
Exxon 2389	Exxon 2380
Caltex 15	Caltex2380
Shell 307	Texaco 7388, Starjet-5
Exxon 274	Caltex Starjet-5
	Chevron Jet-5
	Sinclair Type-2

As the sample list illustrates, no standard identification system is currently in use. In fact, you cannot depend on every oil product to include the type number or MIL Specification on the label. In some cases, you must refer to oil company literature for these specifications.

Synthetic oils for turbine engines are usually supplied in one quart containers to minimize the opportunities for contaminants to enter the lubrication system. However, many oil reservoirs are equipped with pressure remote filling capability. To utilize this feature, an oil pumping cart must be attached to the reservoir so you can manually pump oil into the reservoir. The oil filler cap is normally removed during this operation to prevent overservicing. Filling the oil tank by hand, however, is still practiced by many servicing facilities.

Ground servicing personnel should ensure cleanliness during servicing to avoid inadvertently contaminating the oil supply. When adding oil that is supplied in cans with metal tops, use a clean oil spout which penetrates the metal can top. Avoid using a regular can opener tool since doing so could deposit metal slivers in the oil. If bulk oil is used rather than quart containers, the oil should be filtered with a 10-micron, or smaller, filter as the oil is poured in the reservoir.

If incompatible lubricants are accidently mixed when filling an engine, many manufacturers require the oil system to be drained and flushed. Furthermore, when changing from one approved oil to another, the system typically must be drained and flushed if the oils are not compatible. Whenever an engine is filled with a new approved brand or type of oil, check the oil placard near the filler opening. If the new oil is not identified, change the placard or stencil accordingly.

Once the reservoir is filled, run up the engine long enough to warm the oil. After engine shutdown, allow a few minutes for the oil to settle, then check the oil level. If necessary, add oil to bring the level up to the prescribed quantity. In addition, inspect the areas around the oil drain plug, oil filter, and oil screen fitting for leaks.

OIL SERVICING

Turbine engines do use some oil; therefore, periodic oil servicing is required. When servicing the oil system, ensure that servicing is accomplished within a short time after shutdown. Manufacturers normally require this in order to prevent overservicing. **Overservicing** refers to filling the engine with too much oil. This can occur on engines when some of the oil in the storage tank seeps into lower portions of the engine after periods of inactivity. After engine runup, the oil supply is thoroughly agitated and areas of pooled oil are circulated in the system. This way, once the new oil is added, it is easier to establish the proper oil level in the oil reservoir.

Whenever you add oil to a turbine engine, you should make a note in the aircraft logbook as to the amount of oil added. A record of oil consumption provides a valuable trend analysis of engine wear at main bearing and seal locations.

When servicing the lubrication system, exercise care to avoid accidental oil contamination caused by silicone-based grease. Greases may be used at some point in the servicing process to hold O-rings in place during assembly; however, unapproved greases or excess grease can cause silicone contamination within a lubrication system. Silicone contamination can cause engine oil to foam, resulting in oil loss through oil tank vents. If severe enough, oil loss can cause oil pump cavitation and eventual engine damage.

OIL RESERVOIR

In some instances, the oil reservoir installed in a dry-sump must be removed for cleaning or repair. As you would expect, any repairs made to an oil reservoir must restore it to its original specifications. Therefore, after a repair is made, the reservoir must be pressure tested to its maximum operating pressure plus five psi. Only after a lubrication system component has successfully been tested can it be reinstalled on an engine.

OIL PRESSURE ADJUSTMENTS

Oil pressure is normally adjusted with a screwdriver at the oil pressure relief valve. The first step in adjusting a pressure relief valve is to remove the valve's adjusting screw acorn cap. Then, loosen the locknut and turn the adjusting screw clockwise to increase pressure, or counterclockwise to decrease pressure. Oil pressure adjustments must adhere to the specifications which are supplied by the engine manufacturer. The adjustment is usually made while the engine is idling, and the setting is then confirmed with the engine operating at approximately 75 percent of normal rated thrust. Several adjustments are typically required before the oil pressure stabilizes at the desired pressure. Once the correct pressure setting is achieved, the adjusting screw locknut is tightened and the acorn cap is installed and secured. [Figure 9-41]

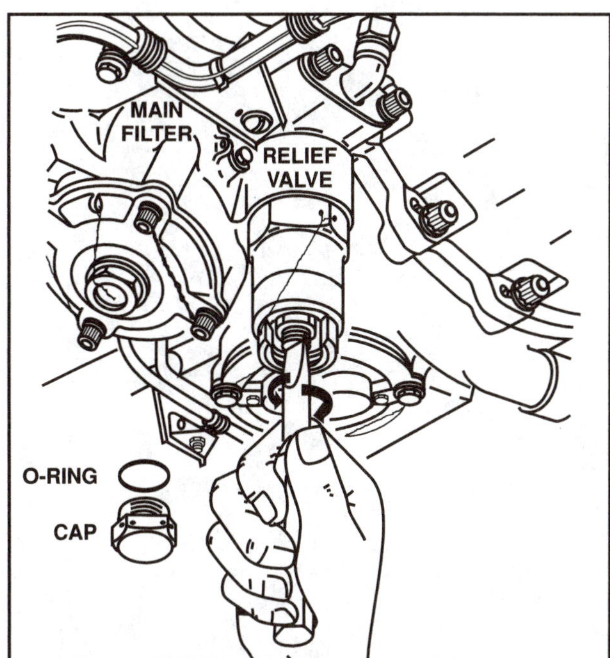

Figure 9-41. The oil pressure relief valve occasionally requires adjustment. With the engine operating at idle speed, turn the adjusting screw clockwise to increase oil pressure and counterclockwise to decrease oil pressure.

CHAPTER 10

COOLING SYSTEMS

INTRODUCTION

Aircraft engines are designed to convert heat energy into mechanical energy. However, in doing this, only about one-third of the heat produced is converted. The remaining two-thirds of the heat energy is wasted and must be removed from an engine. Therefore, cooling systems are designed to remove the unused heat energy produced by combustion and allow an engine to operate at its peak efficiency.

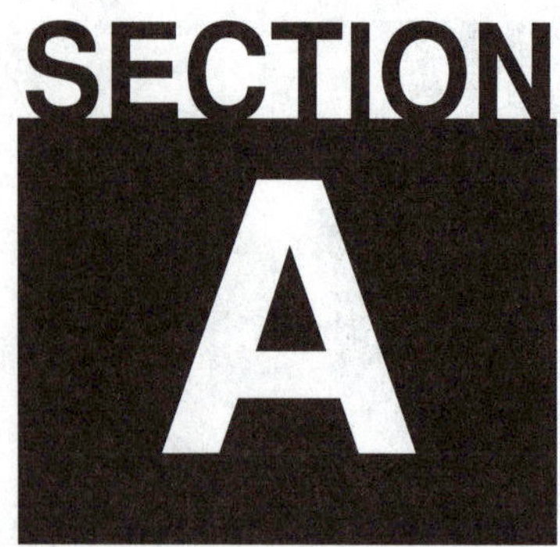

RECIPROCATING ENGINES

Of the heat that is generated by an internal combustion engine, approximately 30 percent is converted to useful work while 40 to 45 percent is expelled through the exhaust. The remaining 25 to 30 percent is absorbed by the oil and metal mass of the engine. It is this heat that is removed by an aircraft's cooling system. If not removed, engine performance suffers due to a decrease in volumetric efficiency and the adverse effect heat has on the fuel/air mixture. In addition, excessive heat shortens the life of engine parts and reduces the ability of the oil to lubricate. The two most commonly used methods of cooling an engine include direct air cooling and liquid cooling.

AIR COOLING

Almost all modern aircraft engines are air cooled. However, to be effective, an engine must have a great deal of surface area that readily gives up heat. To accomplish this, all air cooled engines utilize **cooling fins** that are either cast or machined into the exterior surfaces of the cylinder barrels and heads. The fins provide a very large surface area for transferring heat to the surrounding airflow. Additional cooling is sometimes provided by fins that are cast into the underside of pistons. When this is done, the additional surface area permits a greater amount of heat to be transferred to the engine oil.

The cylinder fins on early engines were relatively thick and shallow and provided little surface area for cooling. However, as engine design progressed and techniques of casting and machining improved, fin design evolved to produce deeper and thinner fins. Today, aircraft engines use steel cylinder barrels that have fins machined directly onto their surface. These barrels are screwed into aluminum cylinder heads with fins that are cast with the head. Since the exhaust valve region is typically the hottest part of a cylinder, more fin area is provided around the exhaust port. On the other hand, the intake portion of a cylinder head typically has few cooling fins because the fuel/air mixture cools this area sufficiently.

COWLINGS

An undesired side effect of air cooling is the penalty imposed by increased drag. Although early aircraft cruised at speeds where drag was of little concern, the drag problem became unacceptable once aircraft development achieved airspeeds over 120 miles per hour.

RADIAL ENGINE COWLING

To help reduce drag on aircraft equipped with radial engines, the **Townend ring**, or **speed ring** was developed. A Townend ring is an airfoil shaped ring that is installed around the circumference of a radial engine. The airfoil shape produces an aerodynamic force that smooths the airflow around the engine and improves the uniformity of air flowing around each cylinder. When installed properly, a Townend ring can reduce drag by as much as 11 percent on some aircraft. [Figure 10-1]

As new aircraft and engine designs produced higher cruising speeds, the need for a more efficient cooling system that provided less drag increased. In the early 1930's an engine cowling known as the **NACA cowling** was developed. This streamlined cowling completely covers all portions of a radial engine and extends all the way back to the fuselage. In addition,

Figure 10-1. To help reduce the drag caused by air flowing over the cylinders of radial engines, the Townend ring, or speed ring, is installed. In some cases, this ring reduces drag by as much as 11 percent.

Figure 10-2. Radial engines enclosed in NACA cowlings produce less drag and have improved engine cooling.

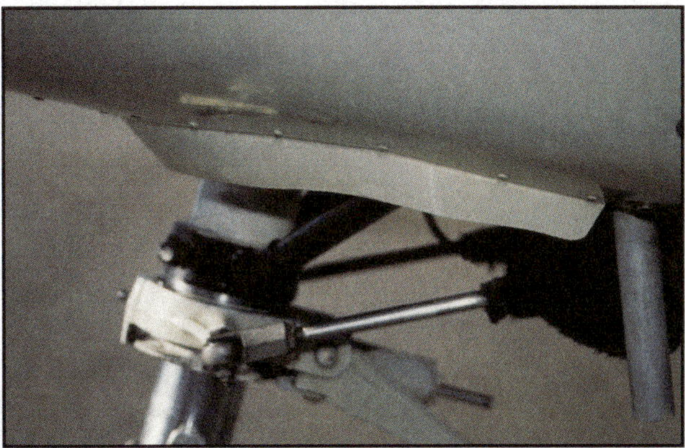

Figure 10-4. The flared portion of a lower cowl helps produce a low pressure area at the bottom of the cowling that draws inlet air down through the cylinders.

all NACA cowlings have an airfoil shape that actually produces thrust by converting the incoming air into a solid jet blast as it leaves the cowling. [Figure 10-2]

OPPOSED ENGINE COWLING

The cylinders on early horizontally opposed engines stuck out into the airstream to receive cooling air. However, since the cylinders were directly behind each other, a thin sheet metal hood had to be installed on each side of the engine to force air down between the cylinder fins. [Figure 10-3]

The cowling surrounding a modern reciprocating engine encloses the entire engine. With this type of cowling, cooling air enters through two forward facing openings and exits out one or more openings in the bottom rear of the cowl. The rest of the cowling is sealed with rubberized strips to prevent excessive air leakage. Because of the ram effect produced by forward motion and propwash, cooling air enters a cowling at a pressure above ambient. This produces what is know as **pressure cooling**.

Figure 10-3. The cowling on early horizontally opposed engines consisted of a thin sheet metal hood that forced cooling air down through the cylinder fins.

To facilitate the pressure cooling process, the outlet on most lower cowls is flared so that when outside air flows past the opening, an area of low pressure is created in the bottom of the cowling. This low pressure area draws inlet air down through the cylinders and into the lower cowl where it can exit the cowling. [Figure 10-4]

BAFFLES AND DEFLECTORS

Only 15 to 30 percent of the total ram airflow approaching an airborne engine cowling actually enters the cowling to provide engine cooling. Therefore, additional baffles and deflectors must be installed to maximize the effectiveness of the airflow. Baffles and deflectors are basically sheet metal panels which block and redirect airflow to provide effective cooling. Baffles and deflectors are installed between the cowling and engine, as well as between the engine cylinders. The baffles installed between the engine and cowling effectively divide the cowling into two separate compartments. This way, when air enters the upper cowl, it has no choice but to flow around the cylinders and into the lower cowl. On the other hand, the primary purpose of the baffles installed between the cylinders is to force cooling air into contact with all parts of a cylinder. These baffles are sometimes referred to as **inter-cylinder baffles** or **pressure baffles**. [Figure 10-5]

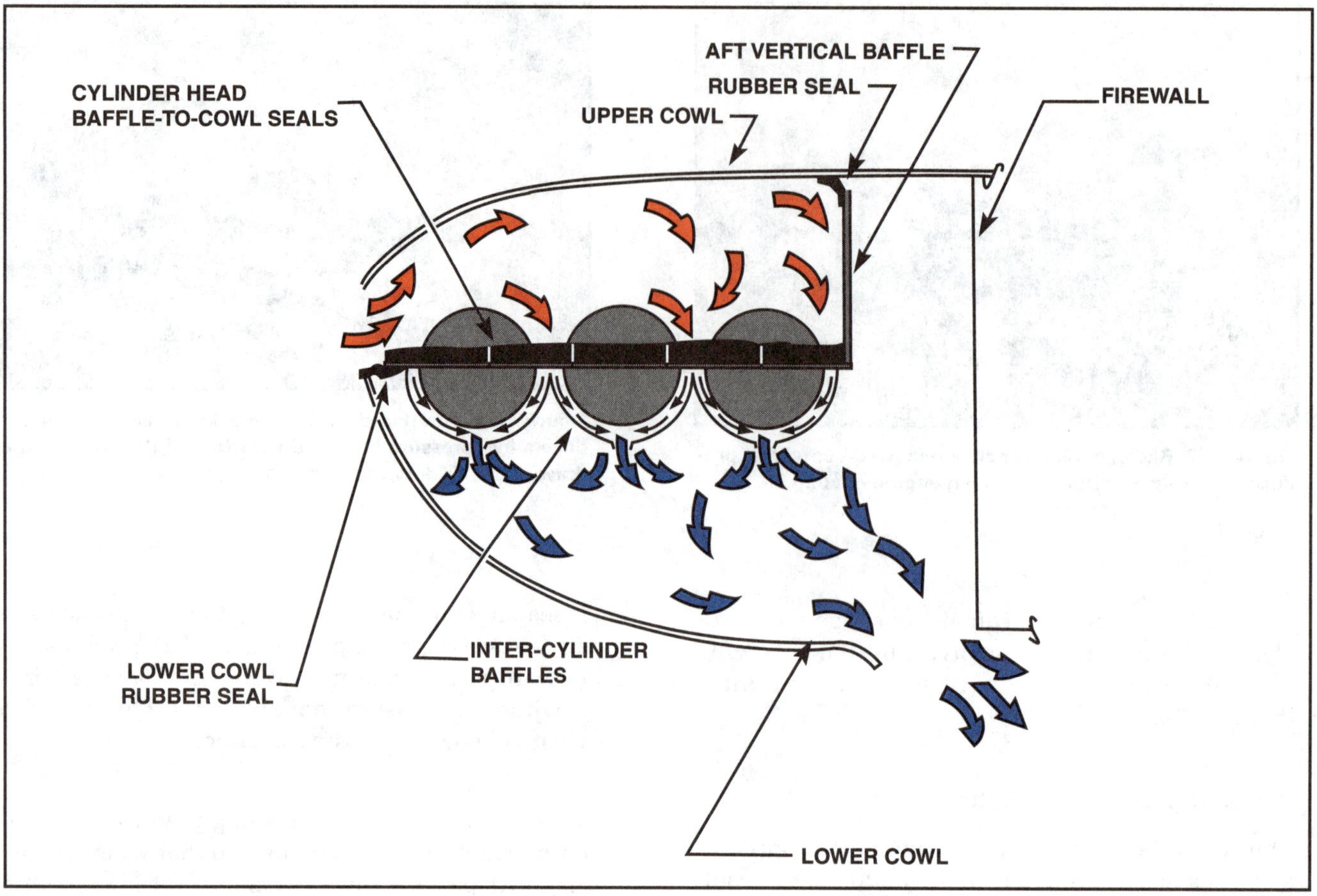

Figure 10-5. Cooling air is directed between the cylinders of a horizontally opposed aircraft engine by a series of baffles and seals.

COWL FLAPS

On some aircraft, the amount of cooling air that flows into the cowling is controlled through the use of cowl flaps. Cowl flaps are hinged doors that are installed at the bottom rear of the cowling where the cooling air exits. When the cowl flaps are open, a stronger low pressure area is created in the lower cowl and more air is pulled through the cylinders. On the other hand, when the cowl flaps are closed, the low pressure area becomes weaker and less cooling air is drawn between the cylinders. The position of the cowl flaps is controlled from the cockpit and are typically operated manually, electrically, or hydraulically. [Figure 10-6]

Cowl flaps are typically in the full open position during all ground operations. The reason for this is that, while operating on the ground, airflow through the cowling is greatly reduced. However, once an aircraft is established in level flight, more air is forced into the cowling. This allows the cowl flaps to be closed so that the drag produced by the cowl flaps can be eliminated.

AUGMENTOR SYSTEMS

Augmenter tubes may be used on some aircraft to augment, or increase, the airflow through the cylinders. Like cowl flaps, augmenter tubes create a low pressure area at the lower rear of the cowling in order to increase the airflow through the cylinder cooling fins. [Figure 10-7]

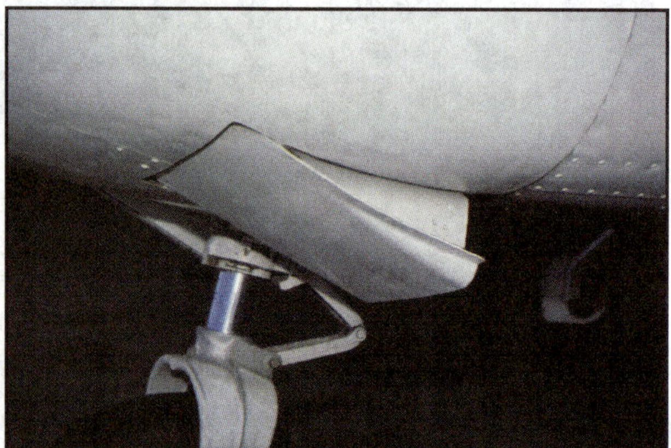

Figure 10-6. By installing cowl flaps on an aircraft, the operator can control the amount of air that flows into the cowling.

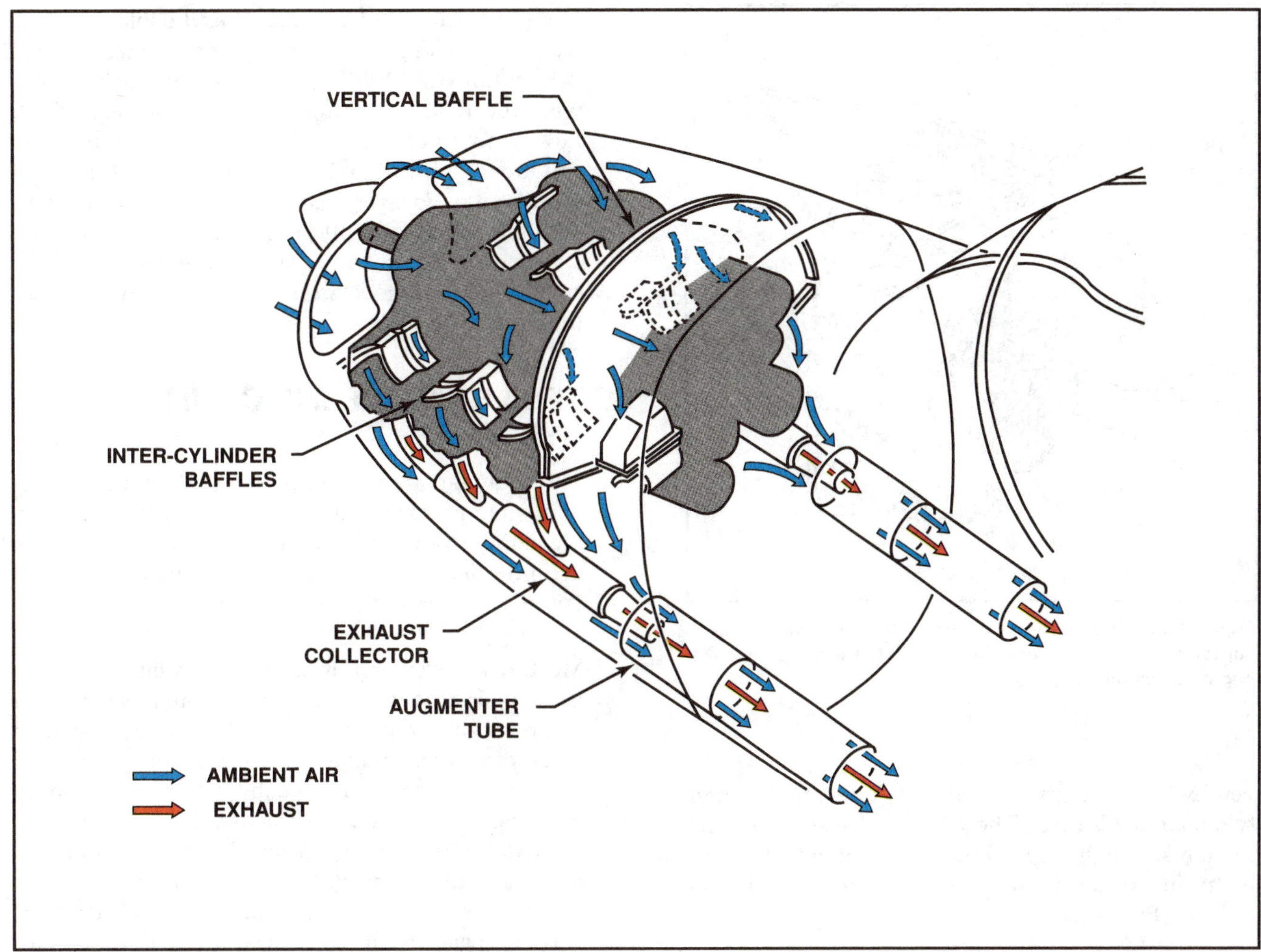

Figure 10-7. Some reciprocating engines use augmenter tubes to improve engine cooling. As exhaust gases flow from each exhaust collector into an augmenter tube, an area of low pressure is created which draws additional cooling air over the engine cylinders.

In an augmenter system, the exhaust gases from the engine are routed into a collector and discharged into the inlet of a stainless steel augmenter tube. The flow of high-velocity exhaust gases creates an area of low pressure at the inlet of the augmenter tube and draws air from above the engine through the cylinder fins. The combination of exhaust gases and cooling air exits at the rear of the augmenter tube.

BLAST TUBES

Many engine installations use blast tubes to direct cooling air into inaccessible areas of an engine compartment. A blast tube is basically a small pipe or duct that channels air from the main cooling airstream onto heat-sensitive components. Engine accessories such as magnetos, alternators, and generators are often cooled using blast tubes. Blast tubes, where used, are typically built into the baffles and are an integral part of the baffle structure.

HELICOPTER COOLING SYSTEMS

Helicopters present unique problems when it comes to cooling an engine. For example, helicopter engines generally operate at a high rpm for prolonged periods of time and, therefore, produce more heat. Furthermore, helicopters typically fly at much slower airspeeds than fixed-wing aircraft and do not benefit from ram airflow. Since the downwash from the main rotor is insufficient to cool an engine an alternate method of engine cooling is required. The most commonly used auxiliary engine cooling system in helicopters is a large belt-driven cooling fan.

As an example of a helicopter cooling fan assembly, consider the Bell 47 helicopter. The cooling fan is mounted on the front side of the engine and is dri-

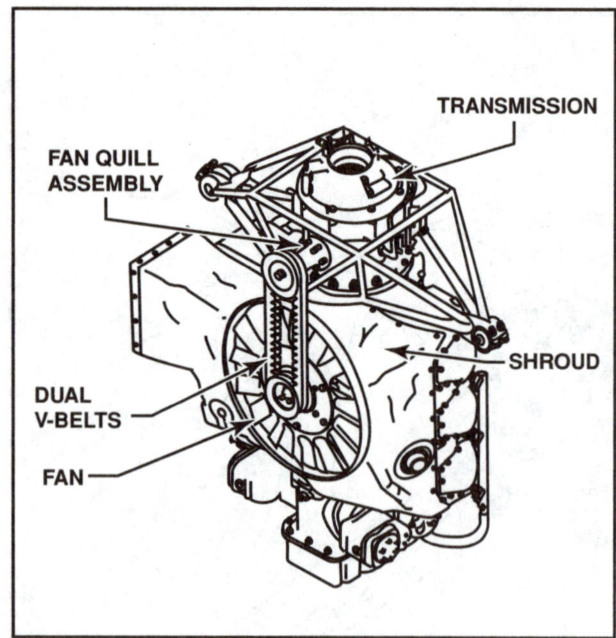

Figure 10-8. The cooling fan assembly on a Bell 47 helicopter is rotated by two V-belts that are driven by the engine transmission.

ven by the transmission fan quill assembly through two matched V-belts. The 1.2:1 quill gear ratio turns the fan at a higher speed than the engine in order to distribute an adequate supply of cooling air to the engine. [Figure 10-8]

LIQUID-COOLING

Liquid-cooled aircraft engines are constructed with a metal **water jacket** that surrounds the cylinders. As coolant circulates in the water jacket, heat passes from the cylinder walls and heads to the coolant. A coolant pump circulates the coolant in a pressurized loop from the water jacket to a radiator, where heat is transferred from the coolant to the air. To allow for higher engine temperatures and a smaller radiator, many liquid-cooled systems are pressurized.

Although liquid-cooled engines have been the standard for automotive and industrial engines for years, they have had limited success in aircraft. Early aircraft engine designs used liquid cooling; however, new air-cooled engine designs became the standard for several reasons. The primary reason for this is that the need for a radiator, water jacket, coolant, and other associated hoses and lines added a substantial amount of weight. In addition, air-cooled engines are not hampered by cold-weather operations as severely as liquid-cooled engines.

In spite of the disadvantages, liquid-cooled engines were used with great success in some American and British-built WWII fighter aircraft. Two such aircraft were the P-38 Lightning and P-51 Mustang which flew with liquid-cooled V-12 engines. A recently produced liquid-cooled engine, the Teledyne-Continental Voyager, uses a mixture of 60 percent ethylene glycol and 40 percent water as a coolant. The coolant is circulated at a high velocity and the small radiator is located in an area which produces the least amount of drag.

TEMPERATURE INDICATING SYSTEMS

The engine temperature can have a dramatic impact on engine performance. Therefore, most reciprocating engine powered aircraft are equipped with a cylinder head temperature (CHT) gauge that allows you to monitor engine temperatures.

Most cylinder head temperature gauges are galvanometer-type meters that display temperatures in degrees Fahrenheit. If you recall from your study of electricity, a galvanometer measures the amount of electrical current produced by a thermocouple. A **thermocouple** is a circuit consisting of two dissimilar metal wires connected together at two junctions to form a loop. Anytime a temperature difference exists between the two junctions, a small electrical current is generated that is proportional to the temperature difference and measurable by the galvanometer.

The two junctions of a thermocouple circuit are commonly referred to as a hot junction and a cold junction. The **hot junction** is installed in the cylinder head in one of two ways; the two dissimilar wires may be joined inside a bayonet probe which is then inserted into a special well in the top or rear of the hottest cylinder, or the wires may be imbedded in a special copper spark plug gasket. The **cold junction**, or **reference junction**, on the other hand, is typically located in the instrument case.

Thermocouple instrument systems are polarized and extremely sensitive to resistance changes within their electrical circuits. Therefore, several precautions must be observed when replacing or repairing them. First, be sure to observe all color-coding and polarity markings because accidentally reversing the wires causes the meter to move off-scale on the zero side. In addition, ensure that all electrical connections are clean and torqued to the correct value.

Thermocouple wiring leads are typically supplied in matched pairs and secured together by a common braid. Furthermore, the leads are a specified length, matched to the system to provide accurate temperature indications. The length of the leads cannot be altered because doing so changes their resistance. In some cases, the wiring leads are permanently attached to a thermocouple, necessitating the replacement of the entire wiring harness and thermocouple if a wire breaks or becomes damaged.

Simple CHT systems use a single indicator that monitors the hottest cylinder. With this type of system, overall engine temperature must be interpreted in a general way. There are, however, more complex systems which monitor each cylinder and can be set to warn you when a cylinder approaches its maximum temperature limit.

INSPECTION AND MAINTENANCE

All cooling system components should be inspected during a 100-hour or annual inspection. In addition, once a thorough visual inspection is complete, it should be followed up with all necessary repairs or replacements. Some of the components that are typically inspected include the cowling, cylinder fins, baffling, and cowl flaps.

COWLING

As you recall, only 15 to 30 percent of the total ram airflow enters the cowling. Therefore, the aerodynamic shape of a cowling must be clean and smooth to reduce drag and energy loss. This smoothness must be considered when accomplishing any repairs to a cowling or adjusting alignment of cowl panels and access doors.

Cowl panels must be visually inspected for dents, tears, and cracks. Such damage causes weakness in the panel structure and increases drag by disrupting the airflow. Furthermore, accumulations of dents and tears can lead to cracking and contribute to corrosion. Internal construction of cowl panels should be examined closely to ensure that the reinforcing ribs are not cracked and that the air seal is not damaged.

The cowl panel latches should be inspected for missing rivets and loose or damaged handles. In addition, you should check the safety locks for damaged rivets and the condition of the safety spring. Examine all support brackets carefully to verify the security of mounting and repair any cracks found in accordance with the manufacturer's instructions. Early detection of breaks and cracks provide an opportunity to limit the damage and extend the service life of a cowling.

CYLINDER COOLING FINS

The condition of the cooling fins plays a large role in their effectiveness and ability to provide adequate cylinder cooling. Therefore, cylinder cooling fins must be checked during each regular inspection.

The cooling fins on an engine are designed with a precise surface area to dissipate a certain amount of heat. Therefore, when cooling fins are broken off a cylinder, less fin area is available for cooling. An engine's **fin area** is the total area (both sides of the fin) exposed to the air. Anytime an excessive amount of fin area is missing, the formation of hot spots can occur on the cylinder.

The amount of fin damage permitted on a given cylinder is based on a percentage of the total fin area and is established by the manufacturer. Therefore, when performing repairs to a cylinder's cooling fins, the engine manufacturer's service or overhaul manual should be consulted to ensure the repair is within limits.

Generally, cracks in cooling fins which do not extend into the cylinder head may be repaired. A typical repair requires you to remove the damaged portion of the fin with a die grinder and rotary file. After removing the damage, finish file the sharp edges to a smooth contour. The percentage of total fin area that is removed must not exceed the limits established by the manufacturer. [Figure 10-9]

Cracks at the edge of a fin may be filed or stop drilled to prevent the crack from lengthening. In

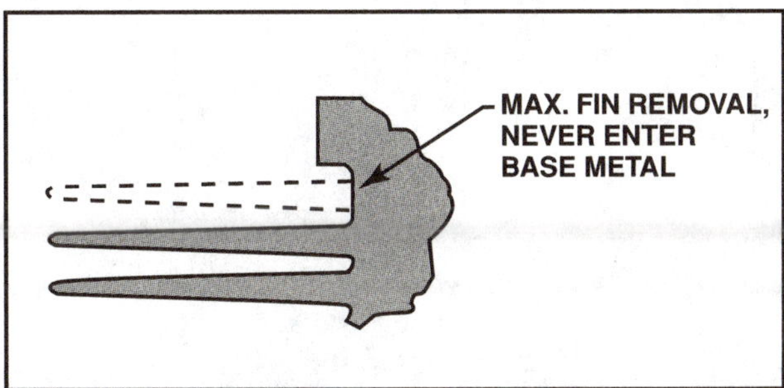

Figure 10-9. When repairing a damaged fin on a cylinder, you must not remove any of the primary cylinder casting. In addition, fin loss near spark plug openings or exhaust ports can cause dangerous local hot spots.

addition, any rough or sharp edges produced by broken fins may be filed to a smooth contour if damage and/or repair limits are not exceeded.

If a cooling fin is inadvertently bent on an aluminum cylinder head and no crack forms, the fin should be left alone. The reason for this is that aluminum cooling fins are very brittle and any attempt to straighten them could cause them to crack or break.

BAFFLES AND DEFLECTORS

Inspections which reveal defects in cylinder baffles and deflectors must be followed up with repairs to prevent loss of cooling efficiency. Since baffles are subject to constant vibration, work-hardening of the metal occurs considerably faster than on other components. Work-hardening can make engine baffles extremely brittle which increases the likelihood of fatigue cracking.

Using an inspection mirror and light, examine the baffles, deflectors, and shrouds for cracks, bent sections, dents, and loose attachment hardware. Small cracks that are just beginning can be stop-drilled and small dents can be straightened. These types of repairs extend the service life of baffles by slowing their deterioration.

When installing the cowling, take care to avoid damaging the air seals on the inter-cylinder baffles and the aft vertical baffle. These air seals are typically made from plastic, rubber, or leather strips and must be oriented to point in the direction shown in the manufacturer's service manual. Damaged air seals and improperly installed or loose baffles can cause cylinder hot spots to develop. If burned paint is found on a cylinder during the inspection, it could be evidence of a local hot spot.

COWL FLAPS

Inspect the cowl flaps visually for security of mounting and for signs of cracking. In addition, operate the cowl flaps to verify the condition of the hinges and operating mechanism.

If the cowl flaps were removed for maintenance, you must adjust them properly during reinstallation. Proper adjustment helps ensure the correct tolerances for the "open" and "closed" positions. Establishing the correct tolerance in both positions is of the utmost importance for maintaining correct cylinder head temperatures. For example, cowl flaps which open too far will allow too much cooling air to be drawn through the engine resulting in insufficient engine temperatures. On the other hand, cowl flaps which do not open far enough can cause cylinder head temperatures to exceed the specified limits for a given operating condition.

SECTION B

TURBINE ENGINES

Turbine engines, like reciprocating engines, are designed to convert heat energy into mechanical energy. However, like a turbine engine, the combustion process is continuous and, therefore, more heat is produced. Another difference is that, on turbine engines, most of the cooling air must pass through the inside of the engine. If only enough air were admitted into a turbine engine to support combustion, internal engine temperatures would rise to more than 4,000 degrees Fahrenheit. In practice, a typical turbine engine uses approximately 25 percent of the total inlet air flow to support combustion. This airflow is often referred to as the engine's **primary airflow**. The remaining 75 percent is used for cooling, and is referred to as **secondary airflow**.

When the proper amount of air flows through a turbine engine, the outer case will remain at a temperature between ambient and 1,000 degrees Fahrenheit depending on the section of the engine. For example, at the compressor inlet, the outer case temperature will remain at, or slightly above, the ambient air temperature. However, at the front of the turbine section where internal temperatures are greatest, outer case temperatures can easily reach 1,000 degrees Fahrenheit. [Figure 10-10]

COOLING REQUIREMENTS

To properly cool each section of an engine, all turbine engines must be constructed with a fairly intricate internal air system. This system must take ram and/or bleed air and route it to several internal components deep within the core of the engine. In most engines, the compressor, combustion, and turbine sections all utilize cooling air to some degree.

NACELLE AND COMPRESSOR

For the most part, an engine's nacelle and compressor are cooled by ram air as it enters the engine. To do this, cooling air is typically directed between the engine case and nacelle. To properly direct the cooling air, a typical engine compartment is divided into two sections; forward and aft. The forward section is constructed around the engine inlet duct while the aft section encircles the engine. A seal separates the two sections and forms a barrier that prevents combustible fumes that may be in the front section from passing into the aft section and igniting on the engine case.

In flight, ram air provides ample cooling for the two compartments. However, on the ground, airflow is

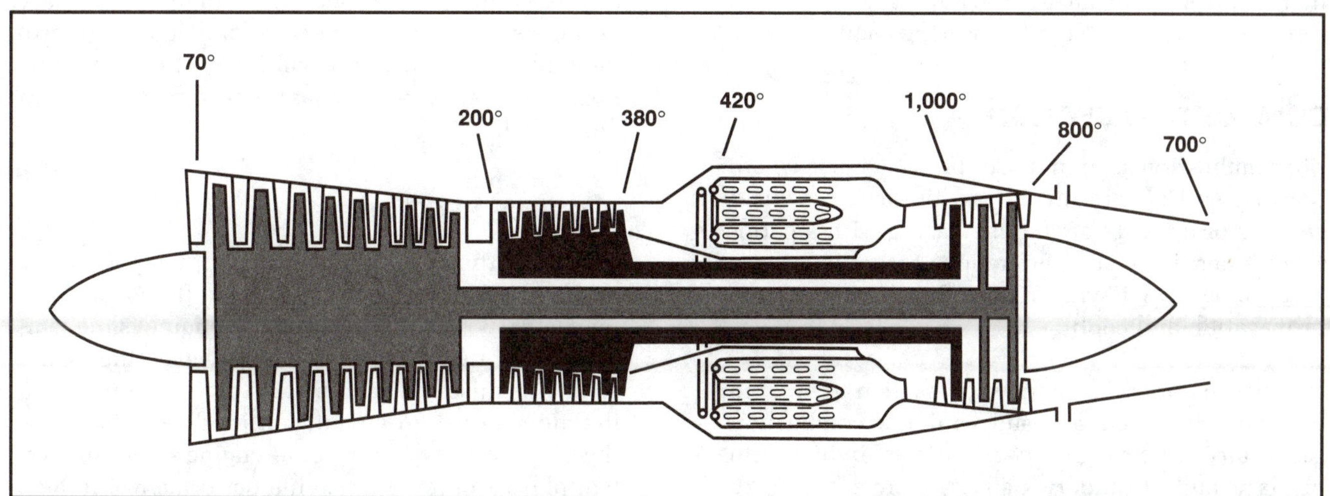

Figure 10-10. A properly cooled two-spool turbojet engine has outer-case temperatures which range from 70°F to 1000°F. Effective cooling airflow maintains these temperatures far below the internal engine temperatures.

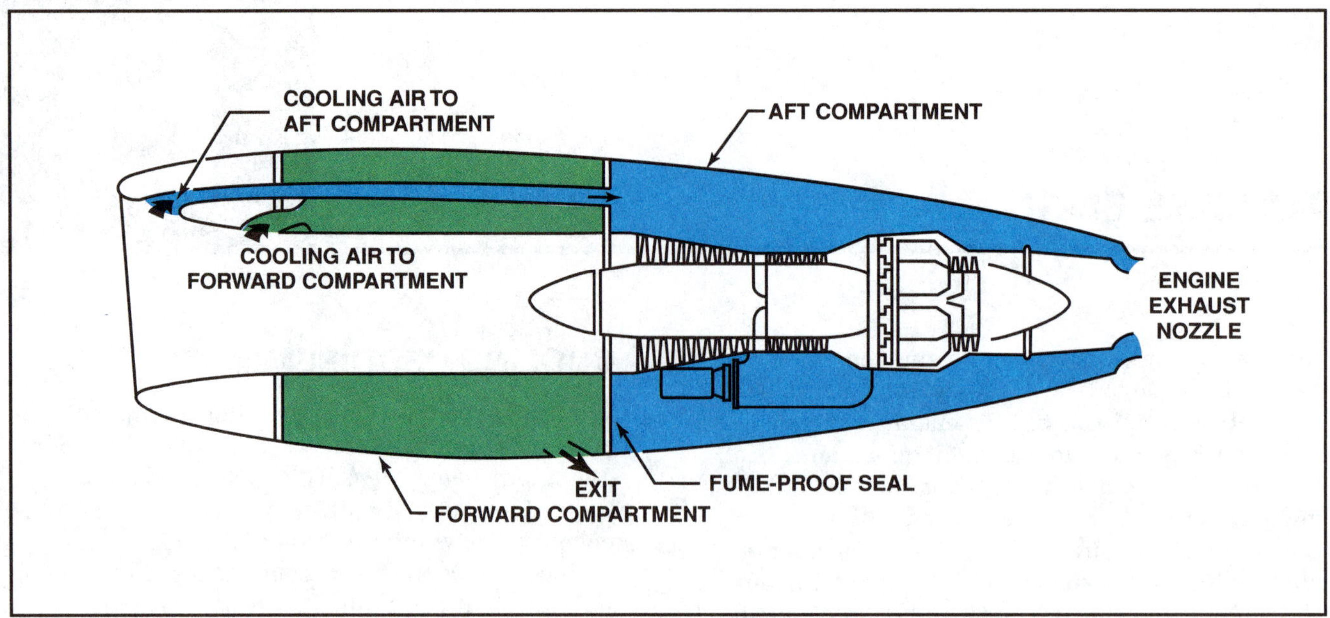

Figure 10-11. Nacelle cooling is typically accomplished by ram air that enters the nacelle at the inlet duct.

provided by the reduced pressure at the rear of the nacelle. The low pressure area is created by the exhaust gases as they exit the exhaust nozzle. The lower the pressure at the rear of the nozzle, the more air is drawn in through the forward section. [Figure 10-11]

As inlet air is compressed, its temperature increases. The heat produced by compression is, in turn, transferred to the components within the compressor section. This heat, along with the heat produced by mechanical friction, typically requires some cooling for the compressor main bearings. The cooling provided typically comes from bleed air that is taken from an early compressor stage and directed over, or through the bearing compartment.

COMBUSTION SECTION

The combustion section in a turbine engine is where the fuel and air are mixed and burned. A typical combustor consists of an outer casing with a perforated inner liner. The perforations are various sizes and shapes, all having a specific effect on flame propagation and cooling.

In order to allow the combustion section to mix the incoming fuel and air, and cool the combustion gases, airflow through a combustor is divided into primary and secondary paths. Approximately 25 percent of the incoming air is designated as primary while 75 percent becomes secondary. Primary, or **combustion air**, is directed inside the liner in the front end of a combustor. As this air enters the combustor, it passes through a set of **swirl vanes** which give the air a radial motion and slow down its axial velocity to about five or six feet per second.

The secondary airflow in the combustion section flows at a velocity of several hundred feet per second around the combustor's periphery. This flow of air forms a cooling air blanket on both sides of the liner and centers the combustion flames so they do not contact the liner. Some secondary air is slowed and metered into the combustor through the perforations in the liner where it ensures combustion of any remaining unburned fuel. Finally, secondary air mixes with the burned gases and cool air to provide an even distribution of energy to the turbine nozzle at a temperature that the turbine section can withstand.

TURBINE SECTION

When a turbine section is designed, temperature is an important consideration. In fact, the most limiting factor in running a gas turbine engine is the temperature of the turbine section. However, the higher an engine raises the temperature of the incoming air, the more thrust an engine can produce. Therefore, the effectiveness of a turbine engine's cooling system plays a big role in engine performance. In fact, many cooling systems allow the turbine vane and blade components to operate in a thermal environ-

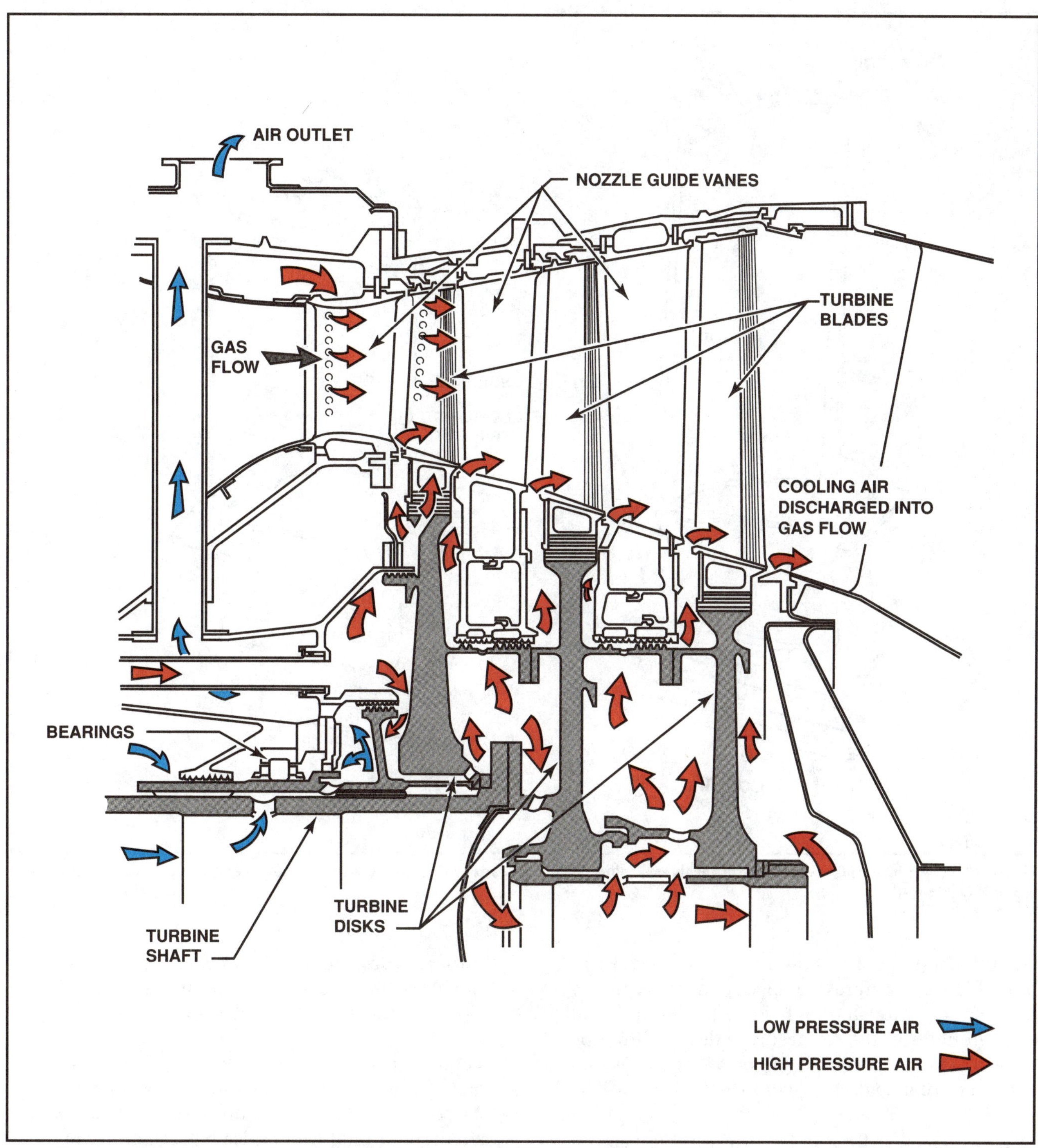

Figure 10-12. High pressure bleed air flows across the face of the turbine disks to remove heat. Low pressure bleed air flowing around the turbine bearings provides additional cooling.

ment 600 to 800 degrees Fahrenheit above the temperature limits of their metal alloys.

One of the most common ways of cooling the components in the turbine section is to use engine bleed air. For example, turbine disks absorb heat from hot gases passing near their rim and from the blades through conduction. Because of this, disk rim temperatures are normally well above the temperature of the disk portion nearest the shaft. To limit the effect of these temperature variations, cooling air is directed over each side of the disk. [Figure 10-12]

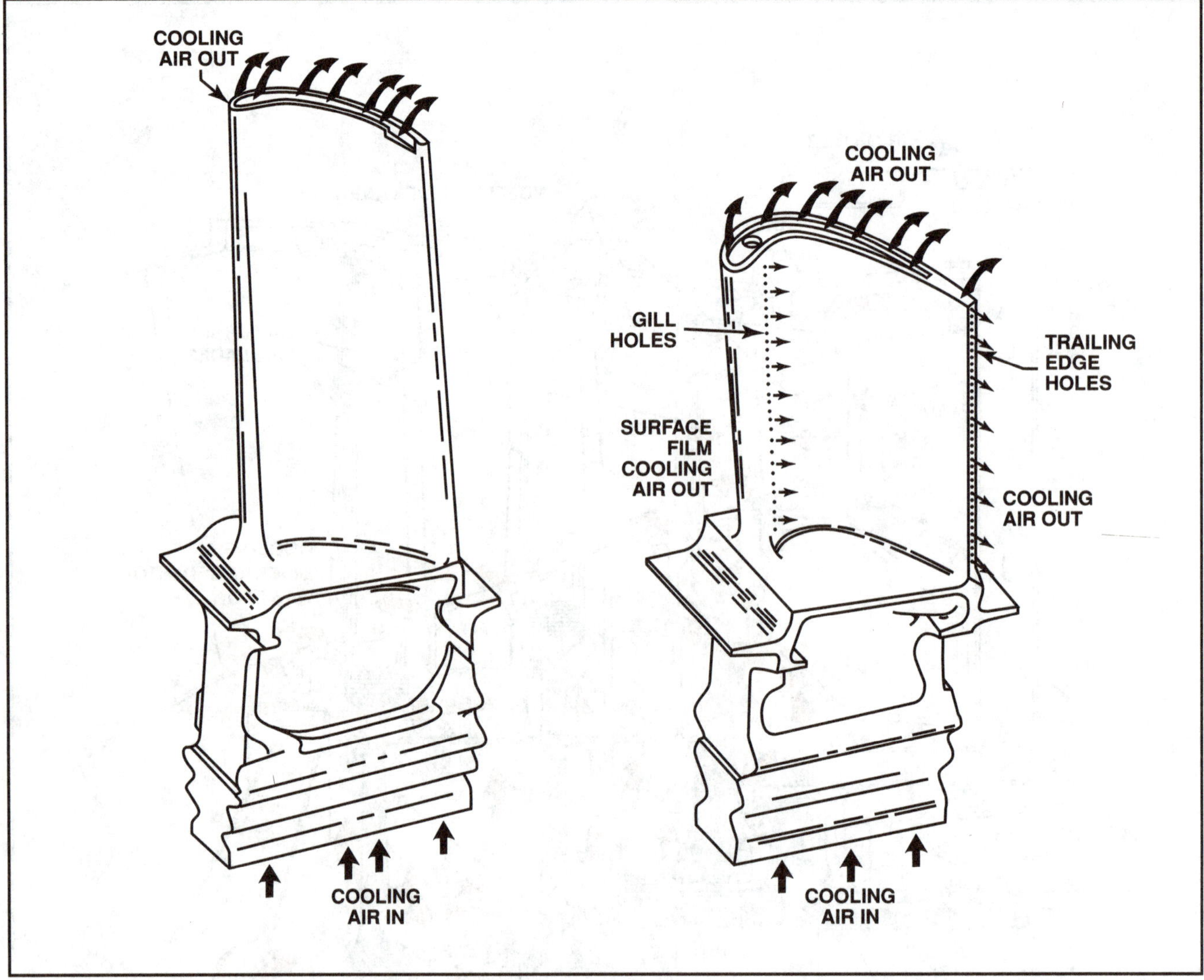

Figure 10-13. An internally cooled blade receives cooling air at the root and expels the air at the tip or through holes in the leading and trailing edges.

To sufficiently cool turbine nozzle vanes and turbine blades, compressor bleed air is typically directed in through the hollow blades and out through holes in the tip, leading edge, and trailing edge. This type of cooling is known as **convection cooling** or **film cooling.** [Figure 10-13]

In addition to drilling holes in a turbine vane or blade, some nozzle vanes are constructed of a porous, high-temperature material. In this case, bleed air is ducted into the vanes and exits through the porous material. This type of cooling is known as **transpiration cooling** and is only used on stationary nozzle vanes.

Modern engine designs incorporate many combinations of air cooling methods that use low and high pressure air for both internal and surface cooling of turbine vanes and blades. However, to provide additional cooling, the turbine vane shrouds may also be perforated with cooling holes.

Some high-bypass turbofan engines have electronic engine controls which feature **active tip clearance control** or **ACC.** ACC controls the thermal expansion rate of the turbine case by regulating the flow of cooling air around the turbine case. This provides optimum turbine blade tip clearance which increases an engine's efficiency.

ENGINE INSULATION BLANKETS

Engine insulation blankets are used to shield portions of an aircraft's structure from the intense heat radiated by the exhaust duct. In addition, the use of blankets reduce the possibility of leaking fuel or oil coming in contact with hot engine parts and accidentally igniting. Common places where insulation blankets may be used include the combustion, turbine, and exhaust sections.

Aluminum, glass fiber, and stainless steel are among the materials used in the manufacture of engine insulation blankets. Several layers of fiberglass, aluminum foil, and silver foil are covered with a stainless steel shroud to form a typical blanket. The fiberglass is a low-conductance material and the layers of metal foil act as radiation shields. Each blanket is manufactured with a suitable covering that prevents it from becoming oil-soaked. Although insulation blankets were used extensively on early engine installations, they are typically not required with modern turbofan engine installations. [Figure 10-14]

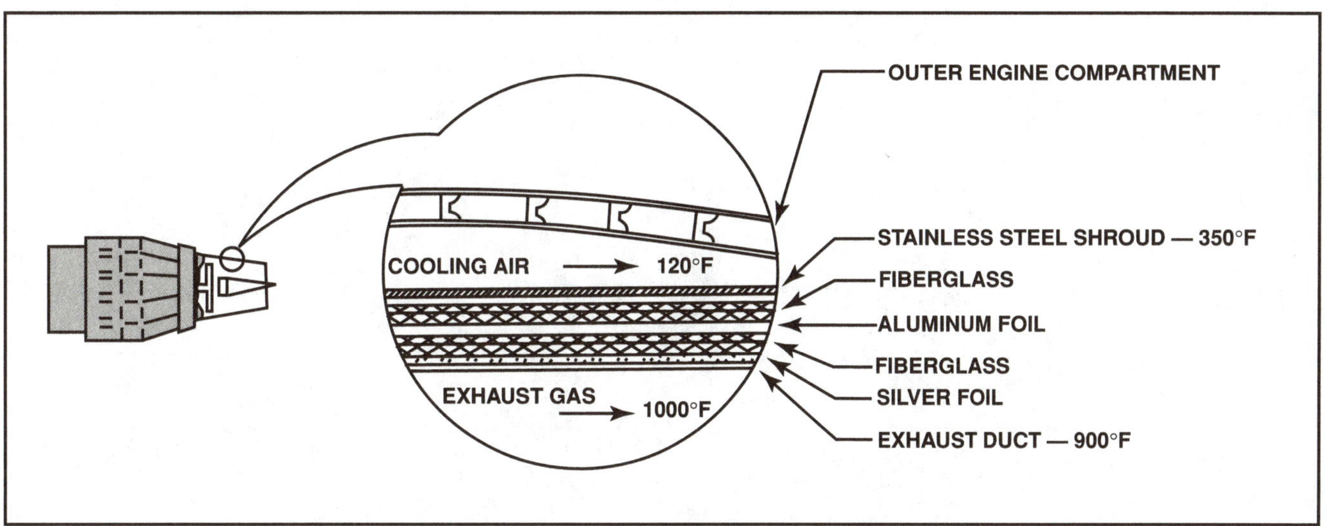

Figure 10-14. A blanket composed of metal foil, fiberglass, and a stainless steel shroud insulates the exterior of a turbine engine exhaust duct to reduce fire hazards and eliminate heat damage to adjacent structures.

CHAPTER 11

ENGINE FIRE PROTECTION

INTRODUCTION

An aircraft powerplant and its related systems constitute a natural fire hazard. For example, flammable materials such as fuel and oil are present in large quantities and are frequently pressurized. In addition, an engine's exhaust system encloses high-temperature gases and, in some cases, flames, that if allowed to escape through a defective component, could ignite fuel vapors. Because of these hazards, many aircraft are equipped with a fire protection system that can detect and extinguish fires in the engine compartment. Therefore, as an aircraft maintenance technician, you must be familiar with the operating principles, maintenance practices, and repair of fire protection systems.

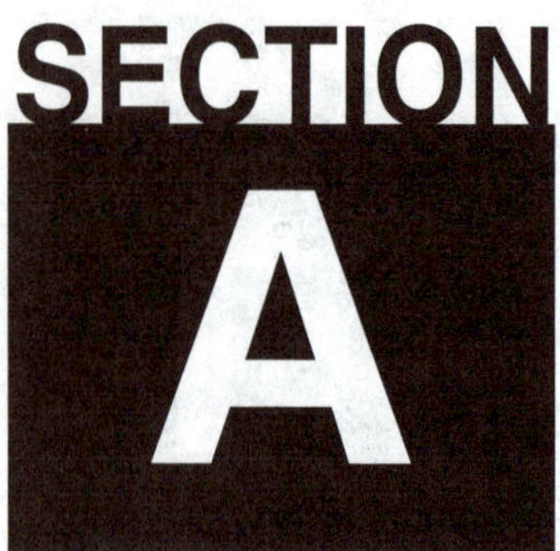

SECTION A

FIRE DETECTION SYSTEMS

Fire protection systems perform two separate functions: fire detection and fire extinguishing. The primary purpose of a **fire detection system** is to activate a warning device in the event of a fire. An ideal fire detection system should:

1. not cause false warning.
2. provide a rapid indication and accurate location of a fire.
3. provide a continuous indication when a fire exists.
4. provide an accurate indication that a fire is out.
5. provide an accurate indication that a fire has re-ignited.
6. provide a means for testing the system from the aircraft cockpit.
7. have detectors that resist exposure to oil, fuel, hydraulic fluid, water, vibration, extreme temperatures, and maintenance handling.
8. have detectors that are lightweight and easily mounted.
9. utilize detector circuitry that is powered by an aircraft's electrical system and does not require an inverter.
10. require minimal electrical current when armed.
11. allow each detector to activate both a cockpit light and an audible alarm.
12. have a seperate detection system for each engine.

There are a number of fire detection systems used in aviation today. Most of the systems used consist of one or more detectors that activate an alarm once the air surrounding the detector reaches a predetermined temperature. Because of this, fire detectors are sometimes referred to as **overheat detectors**.

ENGINE FIRE DETECTION SYSTEMS

Engine fire detection systems generally fall into two categories: spot-detection type systems and continuous-loop type systems. With a **spot-detection type system** individual fire detectors, or switches are used to detect a fire. However, with this type of system, a fire warning sounds only when a fire exists in the same location as the detector. Therefore, with a spot-detection system, fire detectors are placed in locations where a fire is likely to occur. The **continuous-loop type system** works on the same basic principle as the spot-type fire detectors except that a single switch in the form of a long tube is used instead of several individual switches. The small diameter tube is run completely around an engine nacelle or tail cone allowing for more complete coverage than any spot-type detection system.

The following paragraphs provide information on the most common types of fire detection systems found in modern aircraft. These systems include, the thermal switch, the thermocouple, the Fenwal, the Kidde, the Lindberg, and the Systron-Donner.

THERMOSWITCH DETECTOR

A thermoswitch fire detection system is a spot-type detection system that uses a number of thermally activated switches. Each switch, or sensor, consists of a **bimetallic thermoswitch** that closes when heated to a predetermined temperature. [Figure 11-1]

There are two basic types of thermoswitch systems, the single loop and the double loop. With a Fenwal

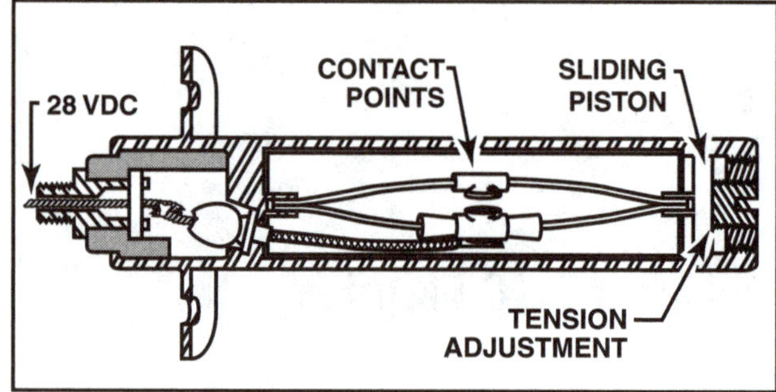

Figure 11-1. With a thermoswitch detector, the actual switch, or detector, is mounted inside a stainless steel housing. If a fire starts, the housing heats up and elongates causing the contact points to close. To adjust a thermoswitch, you must heat the housing to the required temperature and then turn the tension adjustment in or out until the contacts just close.

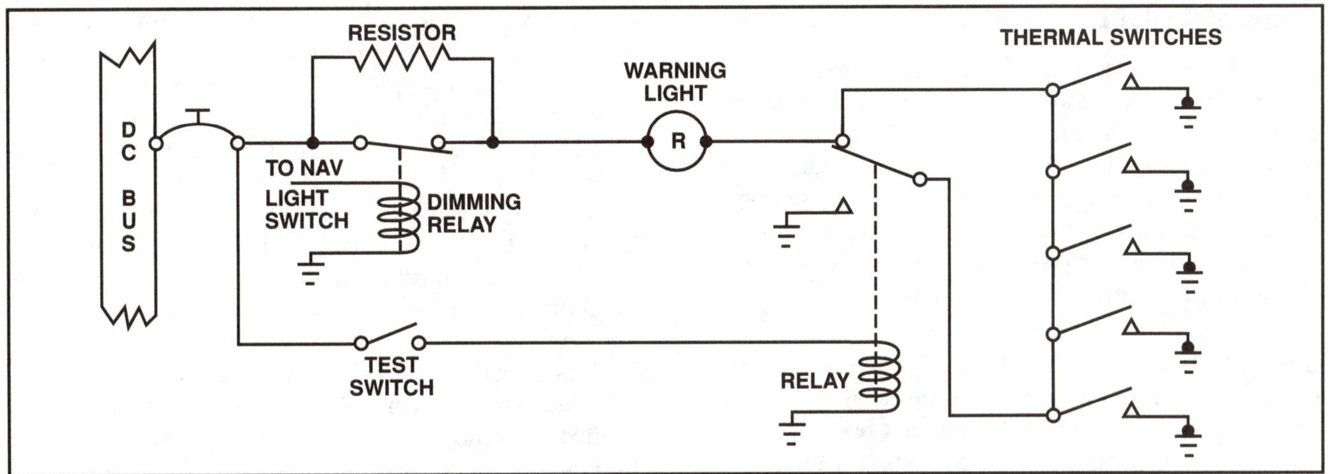

Figure 11-2. Fire detection systems using multiple thermal switches are wired so that the switches are in parallel with each other and the entire group of switches is in series with the indicator light. When one switch closes, a ground is provided for the circuit and the warning light illuminates.

single loop system, all of the thermoswitches are wired in parallel with each other, and the entire group of switches is connected in series with an indicator light. In this arrangement, once a thermoswitch closes, the circuit is completed and power flows to the warning light. [Figure 11-2]

To provide for circuit testing, a test switch is installed in the cockpit. Once the test switch is depressed, power flows to a relay that provides a ground to the warning light, simulating a closed thermoswitch. Once grounded, the warning light illuminates only if there is no break in the warning circuit. In addition to the test feature, most fire detection circuits include a dimming relay for night operations that, when activated, alters the warning circuit by increasing resistance. The increased resistance reduces the amount of current flowing to the light. In most airplanes, several circuits are wired through the dimming relay so all the warning lights may be dimmed at the same time.

In a **double loop** system all of the detectors are connected in parallel between two complete loops of wiring. The system is wired so that one leg of the circuit supplies current to the detectors while the other leg serves as a path to ground. With this double loop arrangement the detection circuit can withstand one fault, either an open or short circuit, without causing a false fire warning. For example, if the ground loop should develop a short, a false fire warning will not occur because the loop is already grounded. On the other hand, if the powered loop shorts, the rapid increase in current flow would trip a relay that causes the powered loop to become the ground and the grounded loop to become powered. [Figure 11-3]

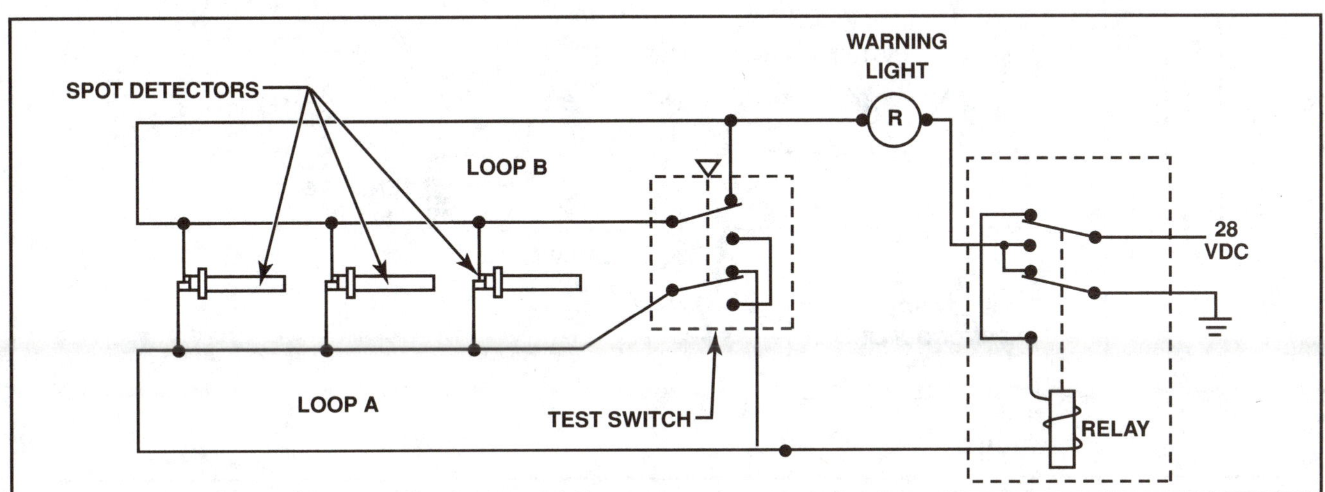

Figure 11-3. With the double loop thermoswitch system above, loop A is positive while loop B is negative. However, if an open or short develops in loop A, the sudden rush of current will activate a relay that causes the positive loop to become negative and the negative loop to become positive.

THERMOCOUPLE DETECTOR

A thermocouple-type, **Edison** fire detector system is similar to a thermoswitch system in that they are both spot-type detection systems. However, in a thermocouple system the detectors are triggered by the rate of temperature rise rather than a preset temperature. In other words, when the temperature of the surrounding air rises too rapidly, a thermocouple detector initiates a fire warning.

If you recall from your earlier studies, a thermocouple consists of a loop of two dissimilar metal wires such as chromel and constantan that are joined at each end to form two junctions. When a temperature difference exists between the two junctions, electrical current flows and a warning light is activated. In a typical thermocouple system, one or more thermocouples, called **active thermocouples** are placed in fire zones around an engine while a separate thermocouple, called the **reference thermocouple**, is placed in a dead air space between two insulated blocks. Under normal operations, the temperature of the air surrounding the reference thermocouple and the active thermocouples are relatively even and no current is produced to activate a warning light. However, when a fire occurs, the air temperature around the active thermocouples rises much faster than the air temperature around the reference thermocouple. The difference in temperature produces a current in the thermocouple circuit and activates a warning light and horn. [Figure 11-4]

In most thermocouple systems, the sensitive relay, slave relay, and a thermal test unit are contained in a **relay box**. A typical relay box can contain from one to eight identical circuits, depending on the number of potential fire zones. The thermocouples control the operation of the relays, while the relays control the warning lights. The test circuit includes a special **test thermocouple** that is wired into the detector circuit and a small electric heater. The test thermocouple and heater are mounted inside the relay housing and, when the test switch in the cockpit is closed, current flows through the heater which heats the test thermocouple. The temperature difference between the test thermocouple and the reference thermocouple produces a current flow that closes the sensitive relay and slave relay so the warning light can light. Approximately 4 milliamperes of current is all that is needed to close the sensitive relay and activate the alarm.

The total number of thermocouples used in a particular detector circuit depends on the size of the fire zone and the total circuit resistance. Typically, circuit resistance is less than five ohms. In addition, most thermocouple circuits contain a resistor connected across the slave relay terminals. This resistor absorbs the coil's self induced voltage when current ceases to flow through the coil and the magnetic field collapses. If this self induced voltage were not absorbed, arcing would occur across the sensitive relay contacts causing them to burn or weld.

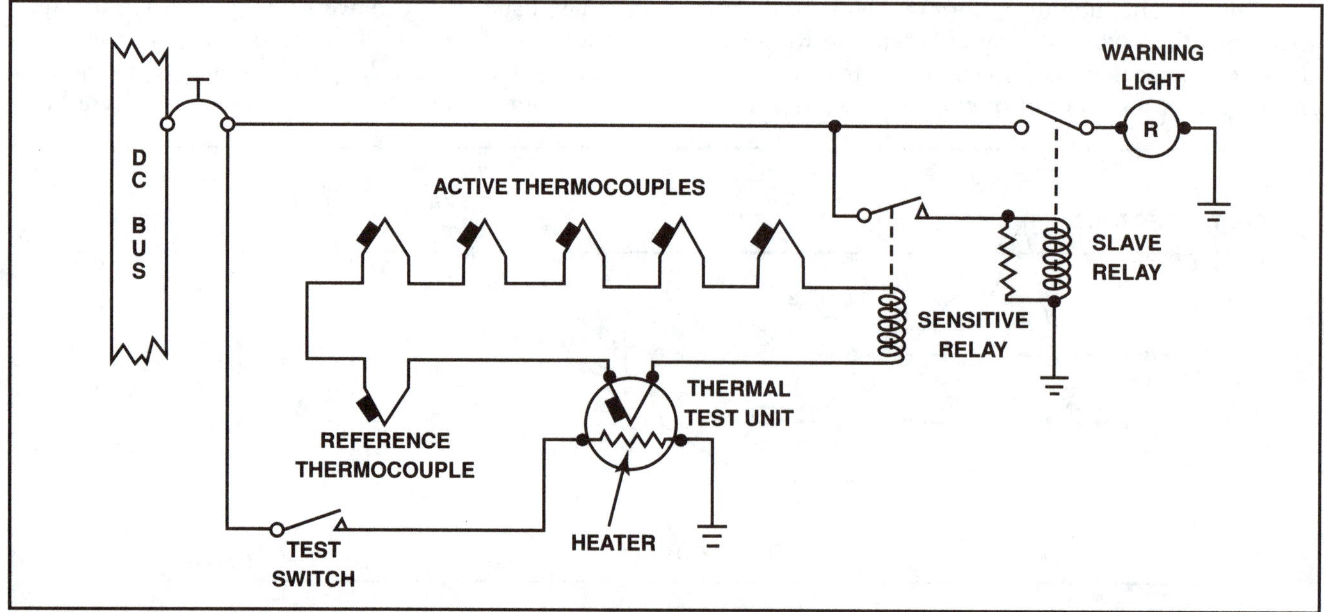

Figure 11-4. In a thermocouple fire detection circuit, the wiring system is typically divided into a detector circuit, an alarm circuit, and a test circuit. When a temperature difference exists between an active thermocouple and the reference thermocouple, current flows through the sensitive relay coil. When the sensitive relay closes it trips the slave relay which, in turn, allows current to flow to the warning light.

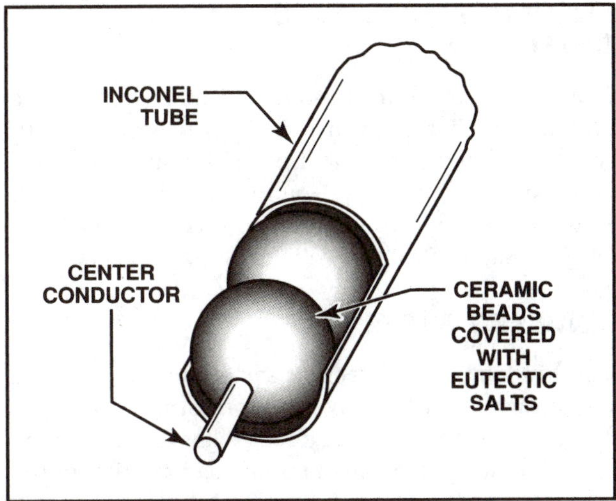

Figure 11-5. A Fenwal continuous loop sensing element consists of a sealed inconel tube containing a eutectic salt and a single, center conductor.

FENWAL SYSTEM

In addition to a thermoswitch detection system, Fenwal also produces a continuous-loop type system that consists of a single fire, or **overheat sensing element** that varies in length depending on the size of the fire zone. A typical sensing element can be anywhere from 1-foot to 15 feet long. As mentioned earlier, the sensing element used in a continuous-loop fire detection system consists of a flexible, small diameter inconel tube with a single wire electrode. The pure nickel electrode is surrounded by ceramic beads to prevent the electrode and conductor from touching each other. The beads in this system are wetted with a **eutectic salt** which has an electrical resistance that varies with temperature. [Figure 11-5]

The center conductor protrudes out each end of the inconel tube where an electric terminal is affixed to the electrode. Current is then applied to the conductor while the outer tube is grounded to the aircraft structure. At normal temperatures, the eutectic salt core material prevents electrical current from flowing between the center conductor and the tube. However, when a fire or overheat condition occurs, the core resistance drops and current flows between the center conductor and ground, energizing the alarm system.

The Fenwal system uses a magnetic amplifier control unit. This unit is a non-averaging controller that supplies power to the sensing element and sounds an alarm when the circuit to ground is completed through the inconel tube. [Figure 11-6]

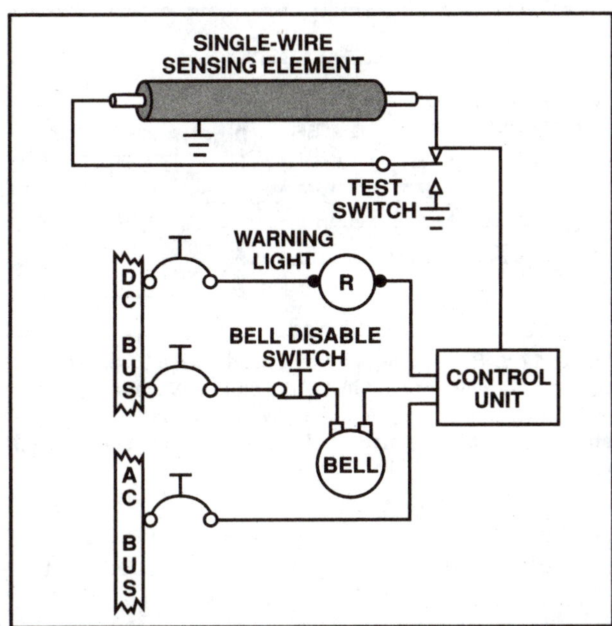

Figure 11-6. With a Fenwal continuous loop fire detection system, AC voltage is applied to the sensing element through the control unit. Once the air surrounding the sensing element reaches a predetermined temperature, the resistance of the eutectic salt within the element decreases enough to allow current to flow to ground. The control unit then senses the flow of AC current and closes a relay which grounds the warning circuit and illuminates the warning light.

KIDDE SYSTEM

The Kidde system is also a continuous-loop type system that consists of a single overheat sensing element that varies in length. The sensing element consists of a rigid, preshaped inconel tube with two wire conductors. The conductors are embedded in a **thermistor**, or **thermal resistor material** to prevent the two electrodes from touching each other and the exterior casing. Like the eutectic salt used in the Fenwal system, the thermistor material has an electrical resistance that decreases as the temperature increases. [Figure 11-7]

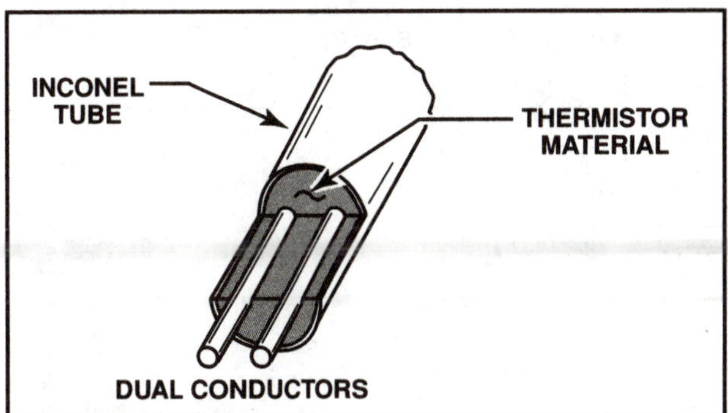

Figure 11-7. A Kidde sensing element consists of a sealed inconel tube containing two conductors that are embedded in a thermistor material.

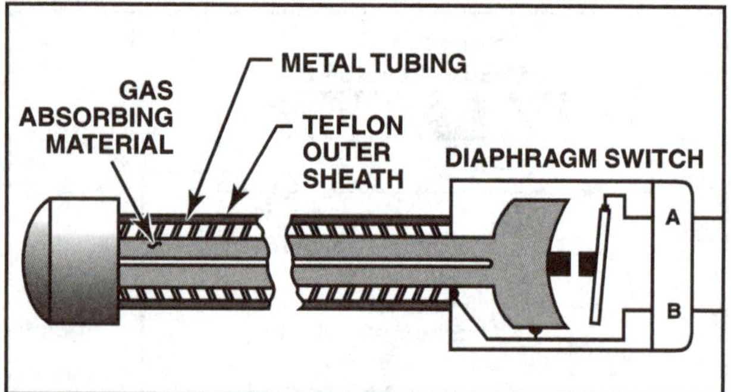

Figure 11-8. The sensing element used with a Lindberg continuous-loop system consists of a stainless steel tube that is filled with an inert gas and a gas absorbing material. One end of the tube is sealed while the other end is connected to a diaphragm switch.

One of the wires is electrically grounded to the outer tube at each end and acts as an internal ground, while the second wire is a positive lead. When a fire or overheat occurs, the resistance of the thermistor material drops, allowing current to flow between the two wires to activate an alarm.

Each conductor is connected to an **electronic control unit** mounted on separate circuit cards. In addition to constantly measuring the total resistance of the full sensing loop, the dual control unit provides for redundancy even if one side fails. In fact, both the Fenwal and Kidde systems will detect a fire when one sensing element is inoperative, even though the press-to-test circuit does not function.

PNEUMATIC CONTINUOUS-LOOP DETECTORS

Pneumatic continuous-loop detectors consist of a sealed tube that can warn of either overheat conditions or of specific spot fires. There are three primary systems presently found on todayís aircraft: Lindberg System, Systron-Donner System, and the Meggitt Safety System.

LINDBERG SYSTEM

The Lindberg fire detection system is a **pneumatic continuous-loop type system** consisting of a stainless steel tube filled with an inert gas and a discrete material that is capable of absorbing a portion of the gas. The amount of gas the material can absorb varies with temperature. One end of the tube is connected to a pneumatic pressure switch called a **responder** which consists of a diaphragm and a set of contacts. [Figure 11-8]

When the temperature surrounding the sensing element rises because of a fire or overheat condition, the discrete material within the tube also heats up and releases the absorbed gas. As the gas is released, the gas pressure within the tube increases and mechanically actuates the diaphragm switch in the responder unit. Once the diaphragm switch closes, the warning light illuminates and the alarm bell sounds. Because the Lindberg system works on the principle of gas pressure, it is sometimes referred to as a **pneumatic system**. [Figure 11-9]

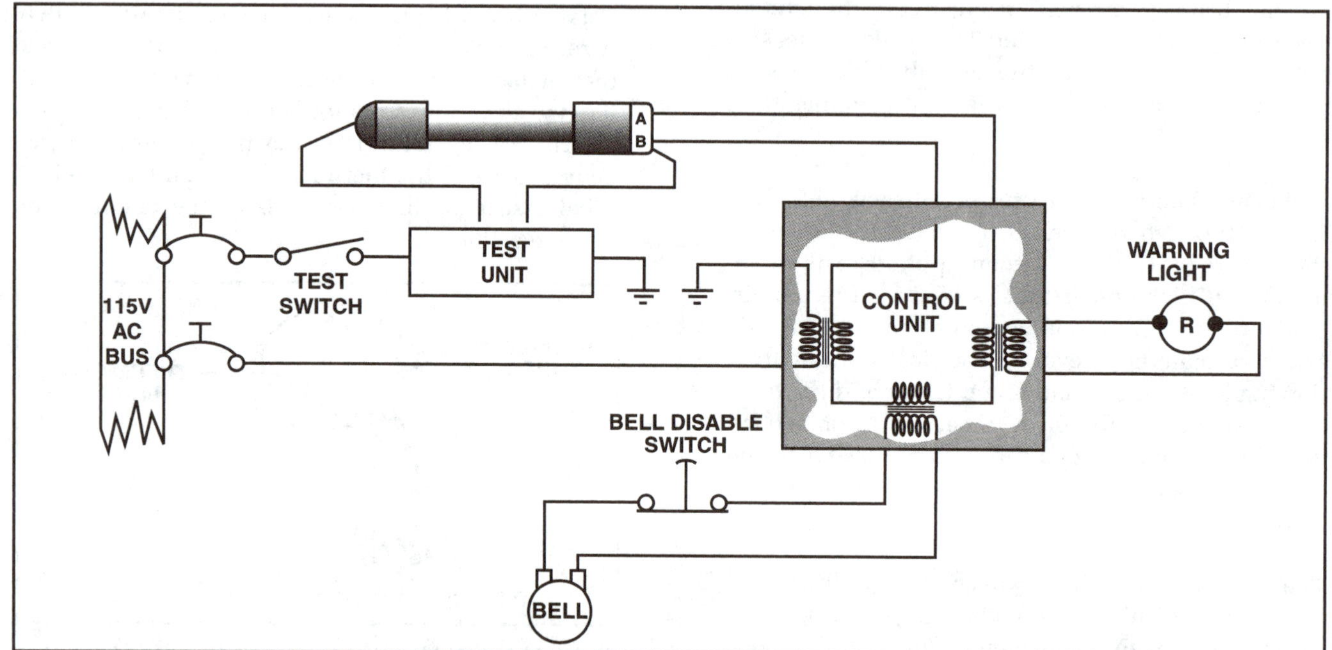

Figure 11-9. With a Lindberg fire detection system, power is supplied to both the control unit and test unit by the AC bus. When a fire or overheat condition exists, the diaphragm switch closes, completing the circuit for both the warning light and the bell.

To test a Lindberg system, low-voltage alternating current is sent through the element's outer casing. This current heats the casing until the discrete material releases enough gas to close the contacts in the diaphragm switch and initiate a fire warning. When the test switch is released, the sensing element cools allowing the discrete material to reabsorb the gas. Once absorbed, the contacts in the diaphragm switch open and the fire warning stops.

SYSTRON-DONNER SYSTEM

The Systron-Donner system is another pneumatic continuous-loop system that utilizes a gas filled tube with a titanium wire running through its center as a sensing element. The tube itself is made of stainless steel and is filled with helium gas. The titanium wire, on the other hand, acts as a gas absorption material that contains a quantity of hydrogen. For protection, the wire is either wrapped with an inert metal tape or inserted in an inert metal tube. One end of the sensor tube is connected to a responder assembly containing a diaphragm switch that provides a warning for both an overheat condition and a fire.

Like the Lindberg system, the Systron-Donner system's principle of operation is based on the gas laws. In other words, if the volume of a gas is held constant and the temperature increases, gas pressure also increases. The helium gas surrounding the titanium wire provides the systems **averaging** or **overheat** function. At normal temperatures, the helium pressure in the tube exerts an insufficient amount of force to close the overheat switch. However, when the average temperature along the length of the tube reaches an overheat level, the gas pressure increases enough to close the diaphragm switch which activates the alarm. Once the source of an overheat is removed, the helium gas pressure drops and the diaphragm switch opens.

The systems fire detection, or **discrete**, function is provided by the gas-charged titanium wire. When exposed to a localized high temperature, such as a fire or bleed air leak, the titanium wire releases hydrogen gas. This increases the sensor's total gas pressure which closes the diaphragm switch and trips the fire alarm. A typical Systron-Donner system sensor activates a fire alarm when exposed to a 2,000°F flame for five seconds. After a fire is extinguished, the sensor core material reabsorbs the hydrogen gas and the responder automatically resets the system. [Figure 11-10]

To check system integrity, the responder unit of a Systron-Donner system contains an **integrity switch** that is held closed by the normal gas pressure exerted by the helium. When the integrity switch is closed, depressing the test switch results in a fire warning. However, if the sensing element should become cut or severely chafed, the helium gas will

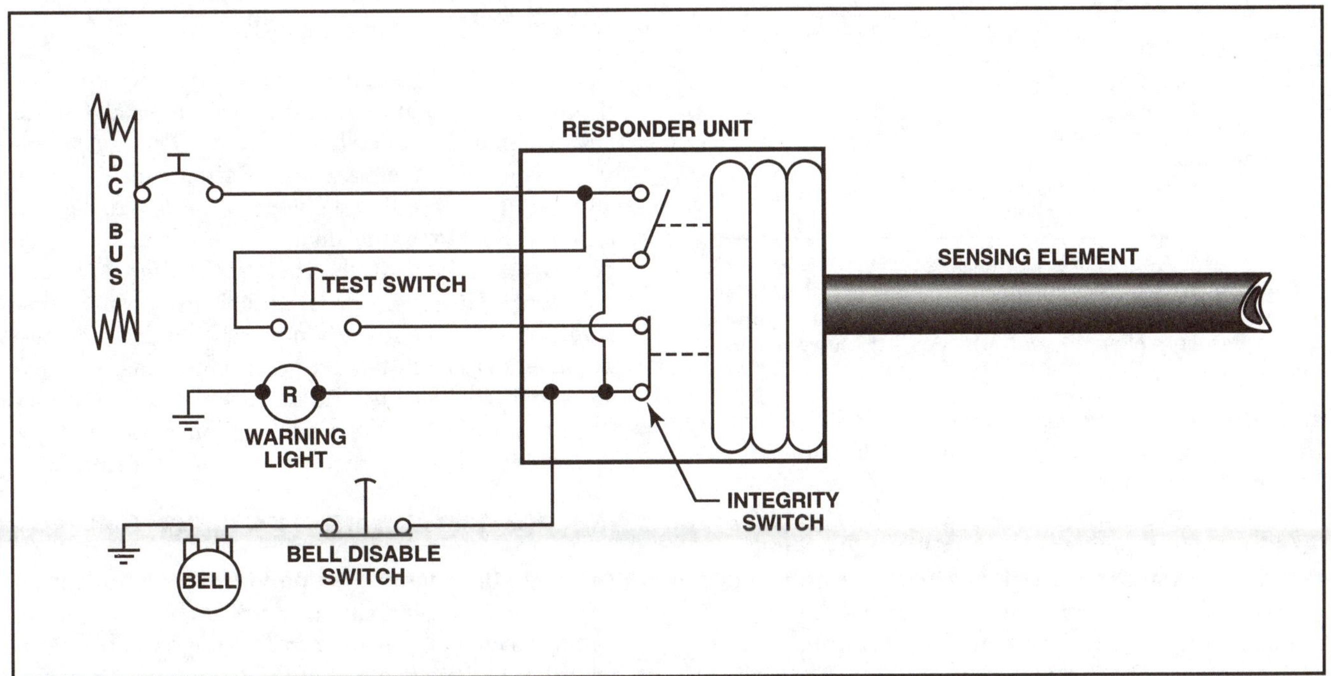

Figure 11-10. The Systron-Donner fire detection and overheat system consists of a helium-filled sensor tube surrounding a hydrogen-charged core. With this system, excessive temperatures increase the gas pressure which forces a diaphragm switch closed. Once closed, power flows to the warning light and bell.

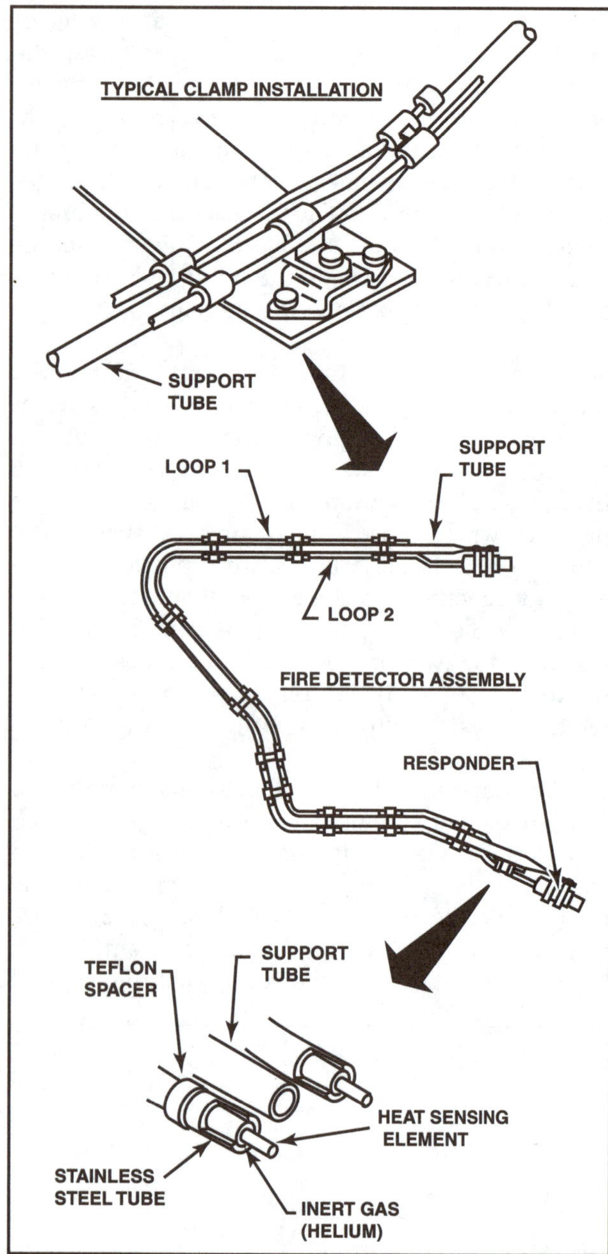

Figure 11-11. A typical installation of a Systron-Donner system consists of two independent loops attached to a support tube. The support tube establishes the routing of the detector element and provides attach points to the airplane.

escape and the integrity switch remains open. In this situation, depressing the test switch provides a "no test" indication.

Systron-Donner sensor elements are quite durable and can be flattened, twisted, kinked, and dented without losing their overheat and fire detection abilities. A typical sensing system consists of two separate sensing loops for redundancy. Both loops are required to sense a fire or overheat before an alarm will sound. However, if one loop fails, the system logic will isolate the defective loop and reconfigure to a single loop operation using the good loop. [Figure 11-11]

MEGGITT SAFETY SYSTEM

The Meggitt Safety System is the result of the merger of the Lindberg Company with the Systron-Donner Company. The present Meggitt pneumatic continuous-loop detector is very similar to the Systron-Donner System covered above. The primary difference is in the test circuit. The Meggitt system uses an integrity switch that is normally closed, but held open by the helium gas in the system. If the system is breached, the loss of gas allows the switch to close and illuminate a fault indication that the system is no longer functional.

FLAME DETECTORS

Another type of fire detection system you are likely to see on an aircraft is a flame detector system. Most flame detectors consist of a photoelectric sensor that measures the amount of visible light or infrared radiation in an enclosed area. The sensor is placed so it can see the surrounding area, and anytime there is an increase in the amount of light that strikes the cell, an electrical current is produced. Once enough current is produced and channeled through an amplifier, a fire warning is initiated.

SMOKE AND TOXIC GAS DETECTION SYSTEMS

In addition to the engine fire detection systems just discussed, there are a number of airframe detection systems you should be familiar with. The most common types of detectors used in aircraft cabin areas and cargo pits are flame detectors, smoke detectors, and carbon monoxide detectors. Each of these are discussed in detail in the *A&P Technician Airframe Textbook*. However, it is important to note that smoke detectors and carbon monoxide detectors are not used to detect fires in powerplant areas. The reason for this is because the air turbulence around an engine dissipates smoke and carbon monoxide gas too rapidly for the detector to recognize a fire.

INSPECTION AND TESTING

Although the engine cowl provides some protection for the sensing elements of a fire detection system, damage can still result from engine vibration and the removal and re-installation of cowl panels. This, combined with the relatively small size of the sensing elements, dictates the need for a regular inspec-

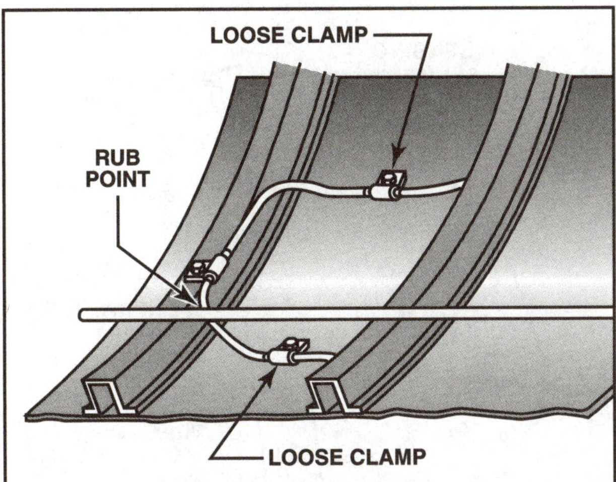

Figure 11-12. A loose clamp can result in interference between a cowl brace and a sensing element. This interference can cause the sensing element to wear which could create a short.

tion program. The following procedures are provided as examples of some general inspection practices that should be periodically accomplished on a typical fire detection system. However, these procedures should not be used in lieu of the manufacturer's approved maintenance directives or applicable instructions.

One of the first items that must be periodically checked is the routing and security of the sensing elements. Long, unsupported sections can vibrate excessively and cause damage to the element. The distance between clamps on straight runs is usually between 8 and 10 inches and is specified by each manufacturer. In addition, to ensure adequate support when a sensing element ends at a connector, a support clamp should be located about four to six inches from the connector fitting. On elements that are routed around certain components, a straight run of one inch is typically maintained from all connectors before a bend is started. Furthermore, the optimum bend radius for most continuous-loop type sensing elements is three inches. Common locations of cracked or broken elements are near inspection plates, cowl panels, engine components, or cowl supports. [Figure 11-12]

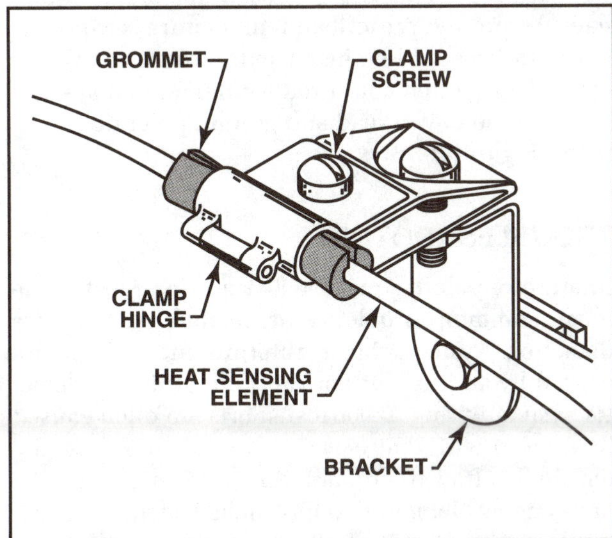

Figure 11-13. Grommets should be installed on the sensing element so both ends are centered on its clamp. The split end of the grommet should face the outside of the nearest bend. Clamps and grommets should fit the element snugly.

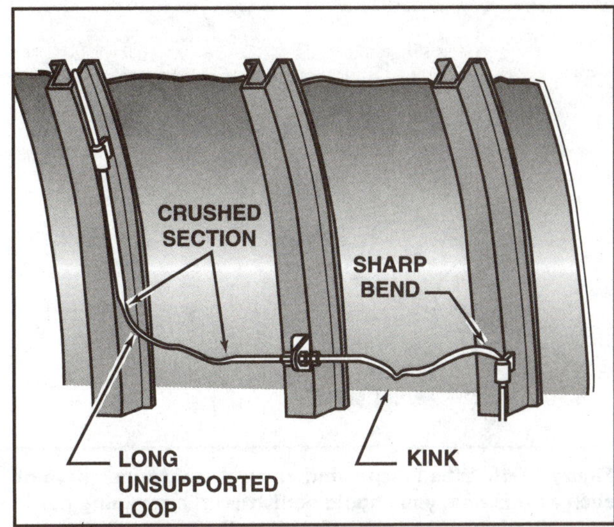

Figure 11-14. Fire sensing elements are located in exposed areas and, therefore, are subject to impact and abrasion. When inspecting fire elements, be alert for sharp bends, kinks, and crushed sections.

The clamps used to support most continuous-loop sensing elements consists of a small hinged piece of aluminum that is bolted or screwed to the aircraft structure. To help absorb some of the vibration produced by the engine, most support clamps use a rubber grommet that is wrapped around the sensing element. These grommets often become softened from exposure to oils and hydraulic fluid, or hardened from excessive heat. Therefore, the grommets should be inspected on a regular basis and replaced as necessary. [Figure 11-13]

In addition to checking for security, a continuous-loop sensing element should be checked for dents, kinks, or crushed areas. Each manufacturer establishes the limits for acceptable dents or kinks as well as the minimum acceptable diameter for a sensing element. It is important to note that if a dent or kink exists that is within the manufacturer's limits, no attempt should be made to straighten it. The reason for this is that by attempting to straighten a sensing element, stresses may be set up that could cause the tubing to fail. [Figure 11-14]

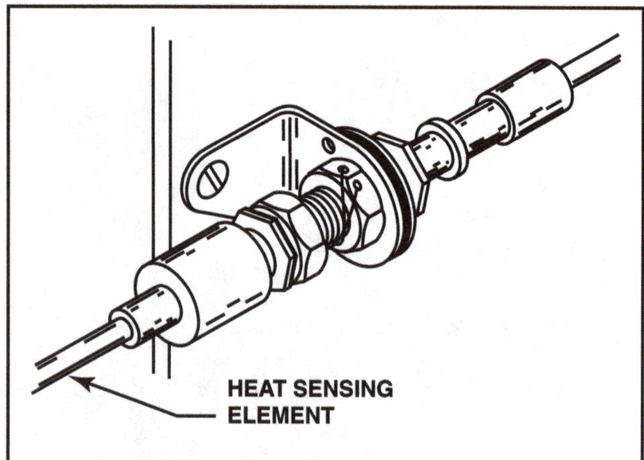

Figure 11-15. When inspecting an electrical connector joint such as this one, you should verify that the retaining nut is properly torqued and the safety wire is secure.

If shielded flexible leads are used, they should be inspected for fraying. The braided sheath is made up of many fine metal strands woven into a protective covering surrounding the inner insulated wire. Continuous bending or rough treatment can break the wire strands, especially those near the connectors, and cause a short circuit.

Nuts at the end of a sensing element should be inspected for tightness and proper safetying. Loose nuts should be retorqued to the value specified by the manufacturer. Some connection joints require the use of copper crush gaskets. If this type of gasket is present on a joint, it should be replaced anytime the connection is separated. Additional items to look for include pieces of safety wire or other metal particles that could short the sensing element. [Figure 11-15]

Thermocouple detector mounting brackets should be repaired or replaced when cracked, corroded, or damaged. When replacing a thermocouple detector, note which wire is connected to the plus (+) terminal of the defective unit and connect the replacement detector in the same way.

After the components of a fire detection system have been inspected, the system must be tested. To test a typical fire detection system, power is turned on in the cockpit and the fire detection test switch is placed in the "TEST" position. Once this is done, the red warning light should illuminate within the time period established for the system. On some aircraft an audible alarm will also sound.

On some continuous-loop fire detection systems a **Jetcal Analyzer** unit may be used to physically test the sensing element. A Jetcal Analyzer consists of a heating element that is used to apply a known heat value to a sensing element. The heat value displays on the potentiometer of the Jetcal control panel. When the alarm temperature is reached, the cockpit warning light will illuminate. If the light illuminates before the prescribed temperature setting, the entire loop should be inspected for dents, kinks, or other damage that could reduce the normal spacing between the power lead and ground potential of the loop. [Figure 11-16]

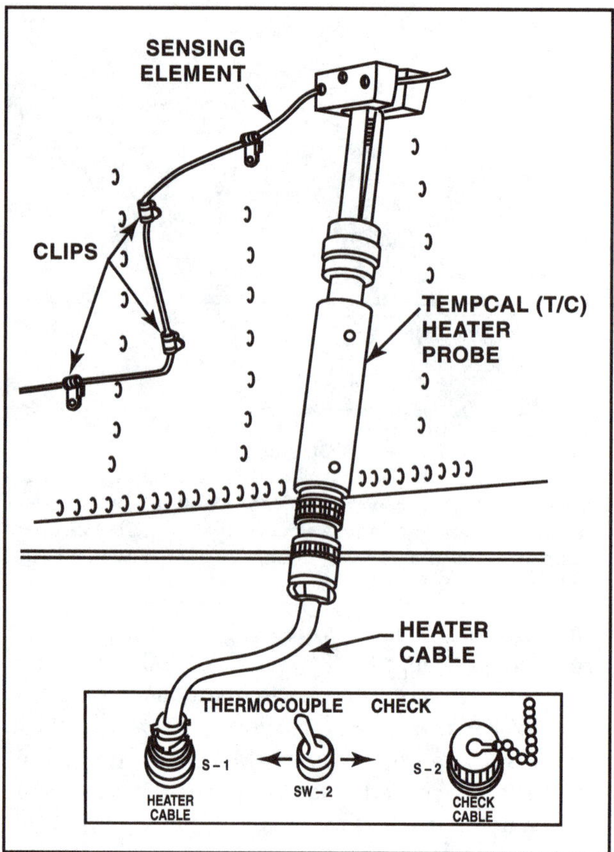

Figure 11-16. A Jetcal Analyzer heats the continuous-loop fire sensing element to test the fire warning system.

TROUBLESHOOTING

Intermittent alarms or false alarms are probably the most common problems associated with a fire detection system. Most intermittent alarms are caused by an intermittent short circuit in the detector system wiring. Electrical shorts are often caused by a loose wire that occasionally touches a nearby terminal, a frayed wire brushing against a structure, or a sensing element that has rubbed against a structural member long enough to wear through the insulation. Intermittent faults can often be located by applying power to the system and moving wires to recreate the short.

False alarms can typically be located by disconnecting the engine sensing loop from the aircraft wiring. If the false alarm continues, a short must exist between the loop connections and the control unit. However, if the false alarm ceases when the engine sensing loop is disconnected, the fault is in the disconnected sensing loop. The loop should be examined to verify that no portion of the sensing element is touching the hot engine. If there is no contact, the shorted section can be located by isolating and disconnecting elements consecutively around the entire loop. Kinks and sharp bends in the sensing element can cause an internal wire to short intermittently to the outer tubing. The fault can be located by checking the sensing element with a megohm meter, or megger, while tapping the element in the suspected area to produce the short.

Moisture in the detection system seldom causes a false fire alarm. However, if moisture does cause an alarm, the warning will persist until the contamination is removed or boils away and the resistance of the loop returns to its normal value.

Another problem you could encounter is the failure to obtain an alarm signal when the test switch is actuated. If this occurs, the problem could be caused by a defective test switch or control unit, the lack of electrical power, an inoperative indicator light, or an opening in the sensing element or connecting wiring. Kidde and Fenwal continuous-loop detectors will not test if a sensing element is shorted or broken; however, they will provide a fire warning if a real fire exists. When the test switch fails to provide an alarm, the continuity of a two-wire sensing loop can be determined by opening the loop and measuring the resistance of each wire. In a single-wire continuous-loop system, the center conductor should be grounded.

FIRE EXTINGUISHING SYSTEMS

Before you can fully understand how fires are extinguished, you must know what makes a fire burn. A fire is simply a chemical reaction that occurs when oxygen combines with a fuel to produce heat and, in most cases, light. Three elements must be present for a fire to occur, including: a combustible fuel, a supply of oxygen, and heat. If you remove any one of these three elements, combustion can not be sustained.

The easiest elements for a fire extinguishing agent to remove are the oxygen supply and the heat required to start combustion. Therefore, fire extinguishing systems are designed to dilute oxygen levels to a point that does not support combustion or to reduce the temperature below the ignition point.

CLASSIFICATION OF FIRES

All fires are classified by the National Fire Protection Association (NFPA) according to the type of combustible fuel involved. For example, a **Class A fire** is one in which solid combustible materials such as wood, paper, or cloth burn. An aircraft cabin fire is a good example of a Class A fire.

Class B fires, on the other hand, involve combustible liquids such as gasoline, oil, turbine fuel, hydraulic fluid, and many of the solvents used in aviation maintenance. Class B fires are the most common type of fire encountered in an engine nacelle.

Class C fires are those which involve energized electrical equipment. Special care must be exercised when trying to extinguish a Class C fire because of the dangers presented by both the electricity and the fire itself.

Class D fires involve a burning metal, such as magnesium, and burn extremely hot. Because Class D fires burn so hot, the use of water or other liquids on Class D fires causes the fire to burn more violently or explode.

ENGINE FIRE ZONES

The powerplant area is divided into fire zones based on the volume and smoothness of the airflow through the engine compartment. These classifications allow manufacturers to match the type of detection and extinguishing system to the fire conditions. Do not confuse these classifications with the NFPA fire classifications discussed earlier.

Class A fire zones have large quantities of air flowing past regular arrangements of similarly shaped obstructions. The power section of a reciprocating engine where the air flows over the cylinders is an example of a Class A fire zone.

Class B fire zones have large quantities of air flowing past aerodynamically clean obstructions. Heat exchanger ducts and exhaust manifold shrouds constitute Class B fire zones. Additional Class B fire zones include cowlings or tight enclosures that are smooth, free of pockets, and adequately drained so leaking flammables cannot puddle. Turbine engine surfaces sometimes fall within this class if the engine's surfaces are aerodynamically clean and all airframe structural formers are covered by a fireproof liner to produce a smooth enclosure.

Class C fire zones have relatively small quantities of air flowing through them. The compartment behind the firewall is considered to be a Class C fire zone.

Class D fire zones are areas that have little or no airflow. Wheel wells and the inside of a wing structure are typical Class D fire zones.

Class X fires zones have large volumes of air flowing through them at an irregular rate. Because of the sporadic airflow, Class X fire zones are the most difficult to protect from fire. In fact, the amount of extinguishing agent required to adequately protect a Class X fire zone is normally twice that required for other zones. Class X fire zones are common in engine nacelles.

FIRE EXTINGUISHING AGENTS

As mentioned previously, the three elements that are needed to support combustion are a combustible fuel, oxygen, and heat. If any one of these elements is removed, a fire will not burn. The fixed fire extinguisher systems used in most engine fire protection systems are designed to displace the oxygen with an inert agent that does not support combustion. The most common types of extinguishing agents used include carbon dioxide and halogenated hydrocarbons.

CARBON DIOXIDE

Carbon dioxide (CO_2) is a colorless, odorless gas that is about one and one-half times heavier than air. To be used as an extinguishing agent, carbon dioxide must be compressed and cooled until it becomes a liquid that can be stored in steel cylinders. When released into the atmosphere, carbon dioxide expands and cools to a temperature of about –110°F. Once cooled, it becomes a white solid that resembles snow and smothers a fire. After a fire is extinguished, the remaining carbon dioxide slowly changes from its solid state directly into a gas, leaving almost no residue.

Carbon dioxide is effective on both Class B and Class C fires. In addition, since carbon dioxide leaves almost no residue, it is well-suited for engine intake and carburetor fires. Furthermore, carbon dioxide is nontoxic and does not promote corrosion. However, if used improperly, carbon dioxide can cause physiological problems such as mental confusion and suffocation. Because of its variation in vapor pressure with temperature, it is necessary to store CO_2 in stronger containers than are required for most other extinguishing agents.

HALOGENATED HYDROCARBONS

A **halogen** element is one of the group that contains chlorine, fluorine, bromine, or iodine. Some hydrocarbons combine with halogens to produce very effective fire extinguishing agents that extinguish fires by excluding oxygen from the fire source and by chemically interfering with the combustion process. Halogenated hydrocarbon fire extinguishing agents are most effective on Class B and C fires, but can be used on Class A and D fires as well. However, their effectiveness on Class A and D fires is somewhat limited.

Halogenated hydrocarbons are numbered according to their chemical formulas with five-digit Halon numbers which identify the chemical makeup of the agent. The first digit represents the number of carbon atoms in the compound molecule; the second digit, the number of fluorine atoms; the third digit, the number of chlorine atoms; the fourth digit, the number of bromine atoms; and the fifth digit, the number of iodine atoms, if any. If there is no iodine present the fifth digit does not appear. For example, bromotrifluoromethane CF_3Br is referred to as Halon 1301, or sometimes by the trade name **Freon 13™**.

Figure 11-17. Halogenated hydrocarbon fire extinguishing agents provide effective fire suppression in aircraft engine compartments.

Halon 1301 is extremely effective for extinguishing fires in engine compartments of both piston and turbine powered aircraft. In engine compartment installations, the Halon 1301 container is pressurized by compressed nitrogen and is discharged through spray nozzles. [Figure 11-17]

A number of halogenated hydrocarbon agents have been used in the past, but are no longer in production. The reason for this is that some early Halon extinguishing agents produced toxic or corrosive gases when exposed to fire. For example, carbon tetrachloride (Halon 104) was the first generally accepted Halon extinguishing agent, and was very popular for electrical hazards. However, when exposed to heat, its vapors formed a deadly phosgene gas. Another once popular agent was methyl bromide (Halon 1001). However, methyl bromide is toxic to personnel and corrosive to aluminum alloys, magnesium, and zinc. Of all the halogenated hydrocarbon extinguishing agents, Halon 1301 is the safest to use from the standpoint of toxicity and corrosion hazards.

Because of changing regulations, and developing environmental impact data, you should keep abreast of current developments pertaining to the

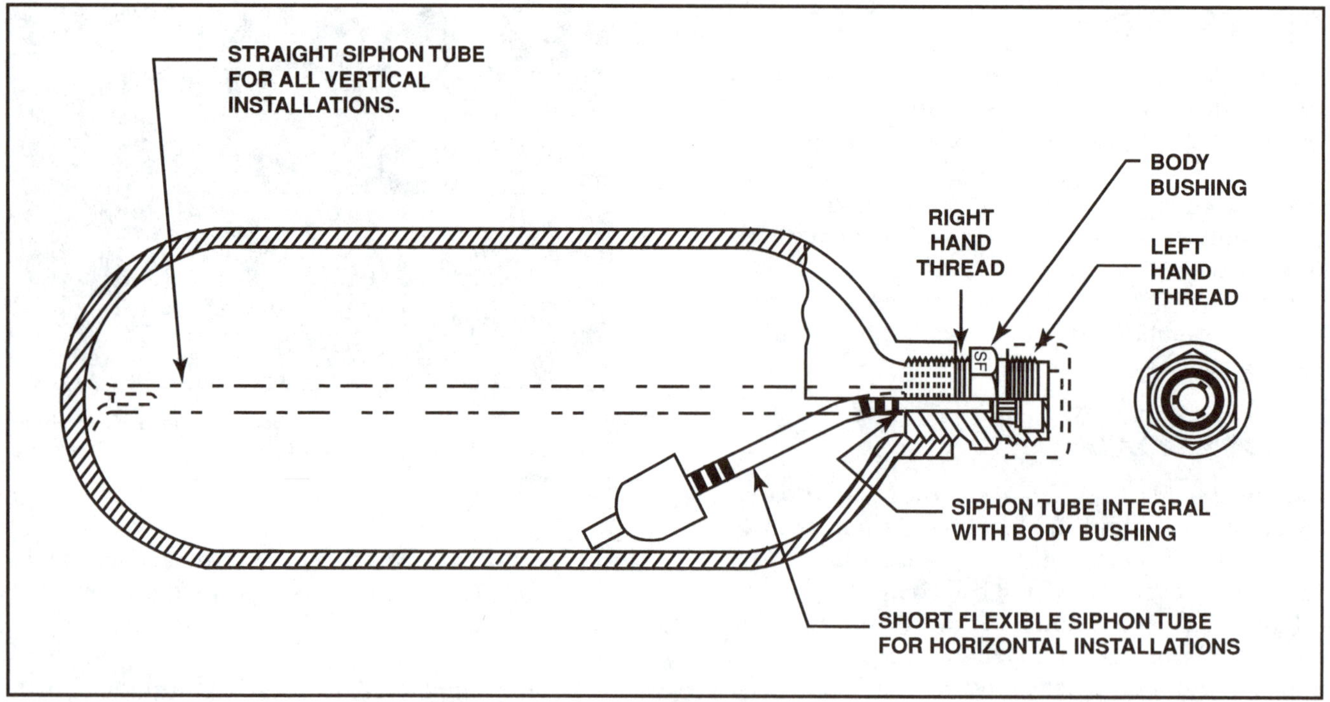

Figure 11-18. If a CO_2 cylinder is mounted vertically, a straight-siphon tube is used, however, if the cylinder is mounted horizontally, a short-flexible siphon tube must be used. The type of siphon tube installed is typically indicated by stamping a code on the body bushing. If an "SF" appears, a short-flexible siphon is installed. However, if an "S" appears, a straight siphon tube is installed. Other manufacturers stamp or stencil the type of siphon used on the cylinder body.

use of halogenated hydrocarbons as fire extinguishing agents. For example, several studies suggest that chloroflourocarbons (CFCs) such as Halon damage the ozone layer in the stratosphere, allowing higher levels of ultraviolet radiation to reach the earth. To reduce damage to the ozone layer, the Environmental Protection Agency banned the production of CFCs after December 31, 1995. However, existing stocks of CFCs were allowed to be used after this date. Several alternatives to CFCs have recently been developed and will most likely find applications as aviation fire extinguishing agents. For example, DuPont FE-25™ has proven to be an acceptable substitute for Halon 1301 as an extinguishing agent and has no harmful affect on the earth's ozone layer.

It is important for you, as an aviation maintenance technician, to be aware of EPA and FAA regulations governing the use and disposal of CFCs. Improper handling or disposal of halogenated hydrocarbons can lead to civil and criminal penalties.

FIRE EXTINGUISHING SYSTEMS

In an aircraft, it is important that the type of fire extinguishing system available be appropriate for the class of fire that is likely to occur. There are two basic categories of fire extinguishing systems: **conventional systems**, and **high-rate-of-discharge (HRD) systems**. Both systems utilize one or more containers of extinguishing agent and a distribution system that releases the extinguishing agent through perforated tubing or discharge nozzles. As a general rule, the type of system installed can be identified by the type of extinguishing agent used. For example, conventional systems usually employ carbon dioxide as the extinguishing agent while HRD systems typically utilize halogenated hydrocarbons.

CONVENTIONAL SYSTEMS

The fire extinguishing installations used in most older aircraft are referred to as conventional systems. Many of these systems are still used in some aircraft, and are satisfactory for their intended use. A conventional fire extinguisher system consists of a cylinder that stores carbon dioxide under pressure and a remotely controlled valve assembly that distributes the extinguishing agent to the engines.

Carbon dioxide cylinders come in various sizes, are made of stainless steel, and are typically wrapped with steel wire to make them shatterproof. In addition, the normal gas storage pressure ranges from

700 to 1,000 psi. Since the freezing point of carbon dioxide is so low, a storage cylinder does not have to be protected against cold weather; however, cylinders can discharge prematurely in hot climates. To prevent this, manufacturers sometimes charge a cylinder with about 200 psi of dry nitrogen before they fill the cylinder with carbon dioxide. When treated in this manner, most CO_2 cylinders are protected against premature discharge up to 160°F. The nitrogen also provides additional pressure during normal release of the agent.

Carbon dioxide cylinders are equipped internally with one of three types of **siphon tubes**. The cylinders used in aircraft typically utilize either a straight-rigid, or a short-flexible siphon tube. The type of siphon tube installed in the cylinder is determined by the cylinder's mounting position. [Figure 11-18]

The CO_2 within a cylinder is distributed through tubing from the CO_2 cylinder valve to the control valve assembly in the cockpit. Once past the control valve, the CO_2 proceeds to the engines via solid tubing installed in the fuselage and wing. Inside the engine compartment, the tubing is perforated so the carbon dioxide can be discharged. [Figure 11-19]

To operate a conventional fire extinguisher system, a selector valve in the cockpit must be manually set for the engine compartment that is on fire. Once this is done, a T-shaped control handle located next to the selector valve is pulled upward to actuate the release lever in the CO_2 cylinder valve. Once released, the compressed carbon dioxide flows in one rapid burst to the outlets in the distribution line of the affected engine compartment. Contact with the air converts the liquid CO_2 into a solid which smother the flames.

Some CO_2 systems have multiple bottles giving the system the capability of delivering extinguishing agent twice to any of the engine compartments. Each bank of CO_2 bottles is equipped with a red **thermo discharge indicator disk** and a yellow **system discharge indicator disk**. The red thermo discharge disc is set to rupture and discharge the carbon dioxide overboard if the cylinder pressure becomes excessively high (about 2,650 psi). On the other hand, the yellow system discharge disk ruptures whenever a bank of bottles has been emptied by a normal discharge. These disks are mounted so they are visible on the outside of the fuselage. This way, during a preflight inspection, the flight crew can identify the condition of the system.

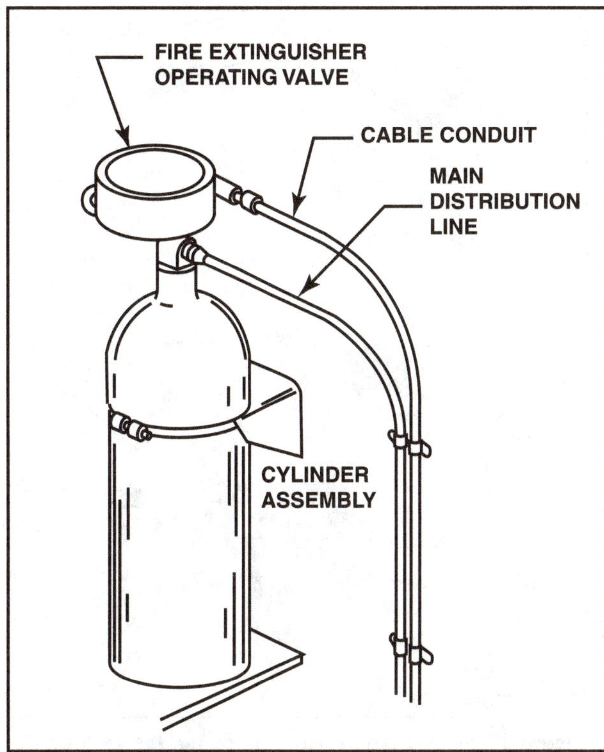

Figure 11-19. In a fire extinguishing system that utilizes carbon dioxide as an extinguishing agent, a sturdy cylinder assembly is mounted to the airframe and connected to a distribution line. In addition, an operating valve that is controlled from the cockpit is installed to hold the carbon dioxide in the cylinder until it's needed.

HIGH-RATE DISCHARGE SYSTEMS

High-rate-of-discharge (HRD) is the term applied to the fire extinguishing systems found in most modern turbine engine aircraft. A typical HRD system consists of a container to hold the extinguishing agent, at least one bonnet assembly, and a series of high-pressure feed lines.

The containers used in an HRD system are typically made of steel and spherically shaped. There are four sizes in common use today, ranging from 224 cubic inches to 945 cubic inches. The smaller containers generally have two openings, one for the **bonnet assembly** or **operating head**, and the other for a **fusible safety plug**. The larger containers are usually equipped with two bonnet assemblies.

Each container is partially filled with an extinguishing agent, such as Halon 1301, and sealed with a **frangible disk**. Once sealed, the container is pressurized with dry nitrogen. A container pressure gauge is provided so you can quickly reference the container pressure. The bonnet assembly contains

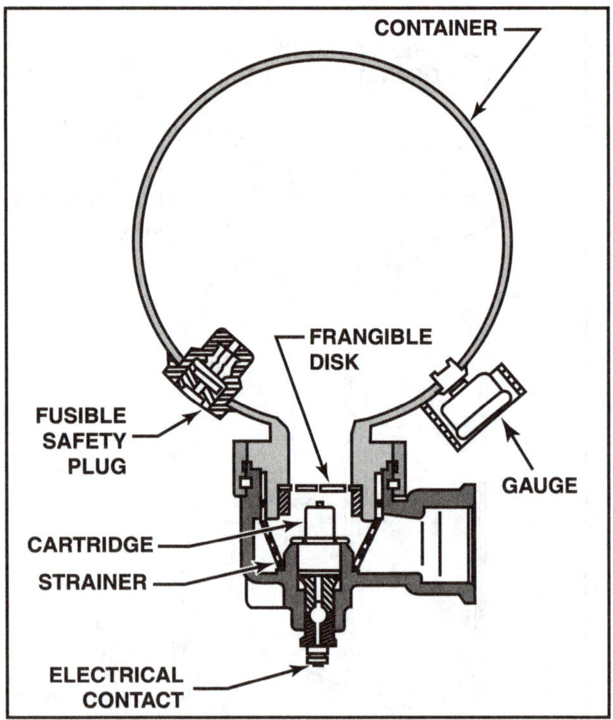

Figure 11-20. In a typical HRD container, the extinguishing agent is released within one to two seconds by an electrically actuated explosive that ruptures a frangible disk. Once broken, the disk fragments collect in a strainer while the extinguishing agent is directed to the engine nacelle.

an electrically ignited discharge cartridge, or **squib**, which fires a projectile into the frangible disk. Once the disk breaks, the pressurized nitrogen forces the extinguishing agent out of the sphere. To prevent the broken disk fragments from getting into the distribution lines, a strainer is also installed in the bonnet assembly. [Figure 11-20]

As a safety feature, each extinguishing container is equipped with a thermal fuse that melts and releases the extinguishing agent if the bottle is subjected to high temperatures. If a bottle is emptied in this way, the extinguishing agent will blowout a red indicator disk as it vents to the atmosphere. On the other hand, if the bottle is discharged normally, a yellow indicator disk blowns out. Like a conventional system, the indicator disks are visible from the outside of the fuselage for easy reference.

When installed on a multi-engine aircraft, the fire extinguishing agent containers are typically equipped with two firing bonnets. The two discharge ports allow one container to serve both engines. [Figure 11-21]

On large multi-engine aircraft, two extinguishing agent containers are generally installed, each with two firing bonnets. This allows twin-engine aircraft

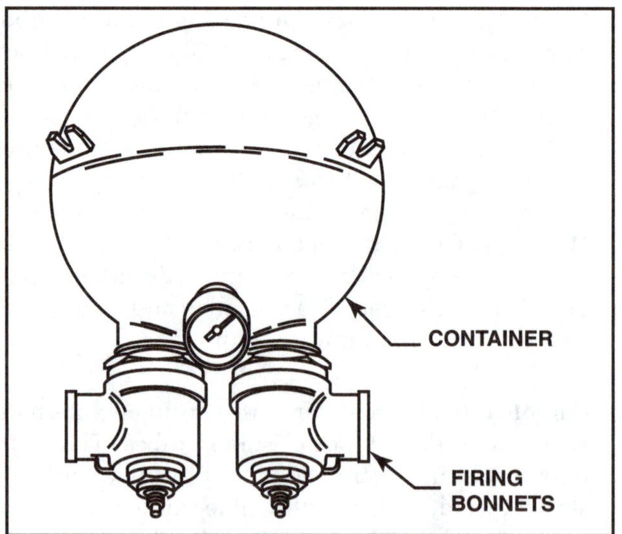

Figure 11-21. A typical extinguishing agent container on a multi-engine aircraft has two firing bonnets.

to have a dedicated container for each engine. In addition, the two discharge ports on each bottle provide a means of discharging both containers into one engine compartment. [Figure 11-22]

INSPECTION AND SERVICING

Regular maintenance of fire extinguishing systems includes inspecting and servicing the fire extinguisher bottles, removing and re-installing discharge cartridges, testing the discharge tubing for leaks, and testing electrical wiring for continuity. The following discussion looks at some of these common maintenance procedures to provide an understanding of the operations involved. However, as an aviation maintenance technician, you must understand that fire extinguishing system maintenance procedures vary substantially, depending on the design and construction of the particular unit being serviced. Therefore, the detailed procedures outlined by the airframe or system manufacturer should always be followed when performing maintenance.

CONTAINER PRESSURE CHECK

A pressure check of fire extinguisher containers is made periodically to determine that the pressure is between the minimum and maximum limits prescribed by the manufacturer. Aircraft service manuals contain pressure/temperature curves or charts that provide the permissible gauge readings corrected for temperature. If the pressure does not fall within the appropriate limits, the container must be removed and replaced with a properly charged container. [Figure 11-23]

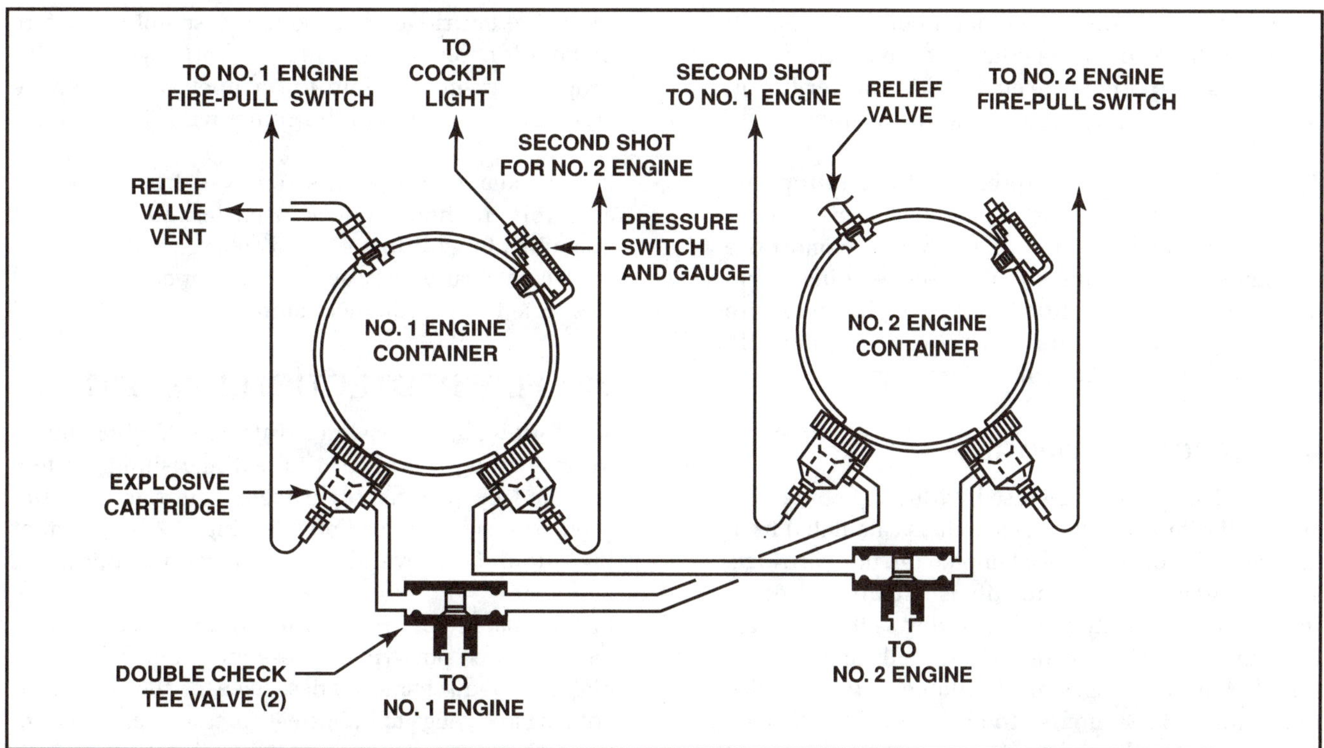

Figure 11-22. A typical high-rate-of-discharge extinguishing system installed on a large multi-engine aircraft utilizes two agent containers, each with two discharge ports. This permits two applications of extinguishing agent to any one engine.

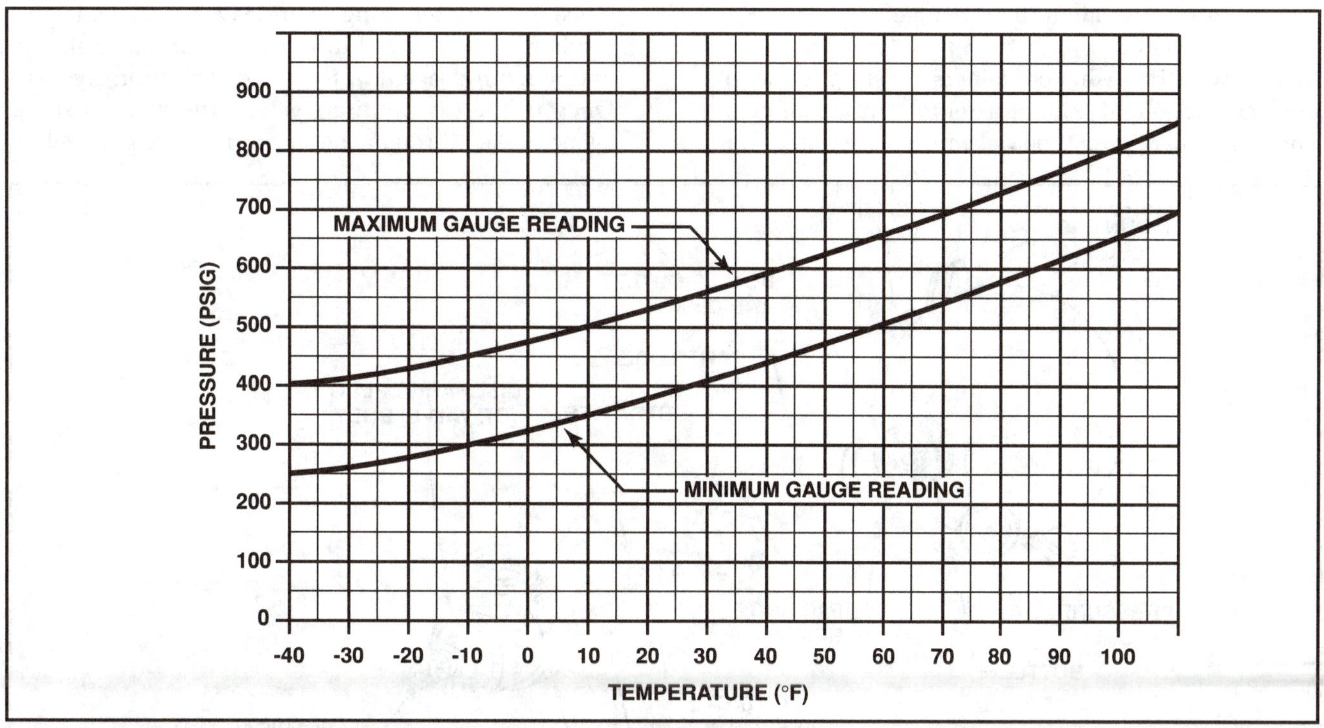

Figure 11-23. This pressure/temperature chart allows you to determine if a specific fire extinguishing bottle is properly charged. As an example, assume the ambient temperature is 70°F and you must check to see if a fire extinguishing container is properly charged. To do this, find 70 degrees at the bottom of the chart and follow the line up vertically until it intersects the minimum gauge reading curve. From here, move left horizontally to find a minimum pressure of about 540 psig. Next, go back to the 70° line and follow it up vertically until it intersects the maximum gauge reading curve. From this point, follow the horizontal line to the left to determine a maximum pressure of approximately 690 psig. As long as the pressure gauge on the container indicates between 540 psig and 690 psig, the container is properly charged.

Once you have determined that a bottle is properly charged, check to make certain that the glass on the pressure gauge is not broken. In addition, verify that the bottle is securely mounted to the airframe.

The only way to determine if the appropriate amount of extinguishing agent is in a given container is to weigh the container. Therefore, most fire extinguishing containers require re-weighing at frequent intervals. In addition to the weight check, fire extinguisher containers must be hydrostatically tested at five-year intervals.

DISCHARGE CARTRIDGES

The discharge cartridges used with HRD containers are life-limited and the service life is calculated from the manufacturer's date stamped on the cartridge. The manufacturer's service life is usually expressed in terms of hours and is valid as long as the cartridge has not exceeded a predetermined temperature limit. Many cartridges are available with a service life of up to 5,000 hours. To determine a cartridge's service life, it is necessary to remove the electrical leads and discharge hose from the bonnet assembly. Once this is done, the bonnet assembly can be removed from the extinguisher container so you can see the date stamped on the cartridge.

Most new extinguisher containers are supplied with their cartridge and bonnet assembly disassembled. Therefore, care must be taken in assembling or replacing cartridges and bonnet assemblies. Before installation on an aircraft, the cartridge must be properly assembled into the bonnet and the entire assembly connected to the container. [Figure 11-24]

If a discharge cartridge is removed from a bonnet assembly, it should not be used in another bonnet assembly. In addition, since discharge cartridges are fired electrically, they should be properly grounded or shorted to prevent accidental firing.

727 FIRE PROTECTION SYSTEM

The following discussion is intended to give you an overview of a typical fire extinguishing system installed on a transport category aircraft. The fire protection system used on a Boeing 727 is typical of those found on several aircraft in service today.

In the Boeing 727 powerplant fire extinguishing system, all three powerplant areas are protected by two high-rate-of-discharge bottles. Each of the two agent bottles has a gauge to indicate its pressure, and an electrical pressure switch is mounted on each bottle to activate a bottle discharge light on the instrument panel when the pressure on the agent bottle is below limits.

Once the extinguishing agent leaves a bottle, it proceeds to a two-way shuttle valve that channels the extinguishing agent into the distribution system. Once in the distribution system, the extinguishing agent passes through the appropriate engine selec-

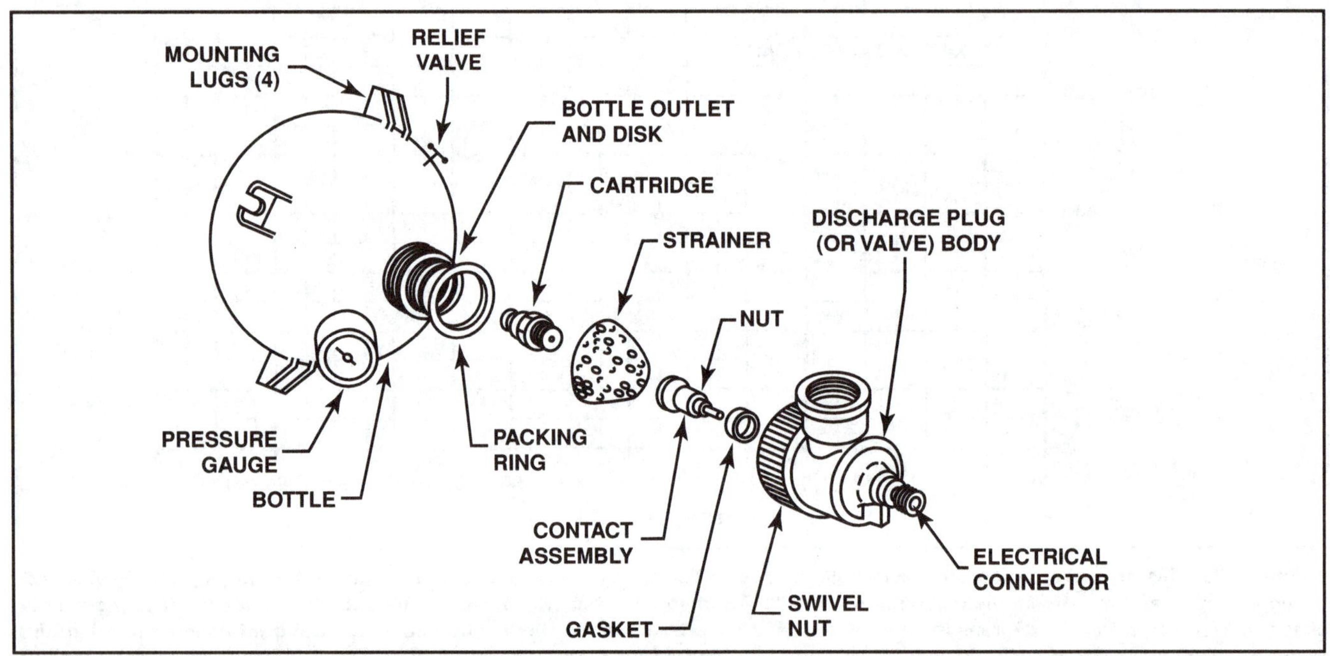

Figure 11-24. When assembling a discharge cartridge into a bonnet assembly, it is best to use an exploded view drawing like the one above. Once assembled, the entire bonnet assembly is attached to the container by means of a swivel nut that tightens against a packing ring gasket.

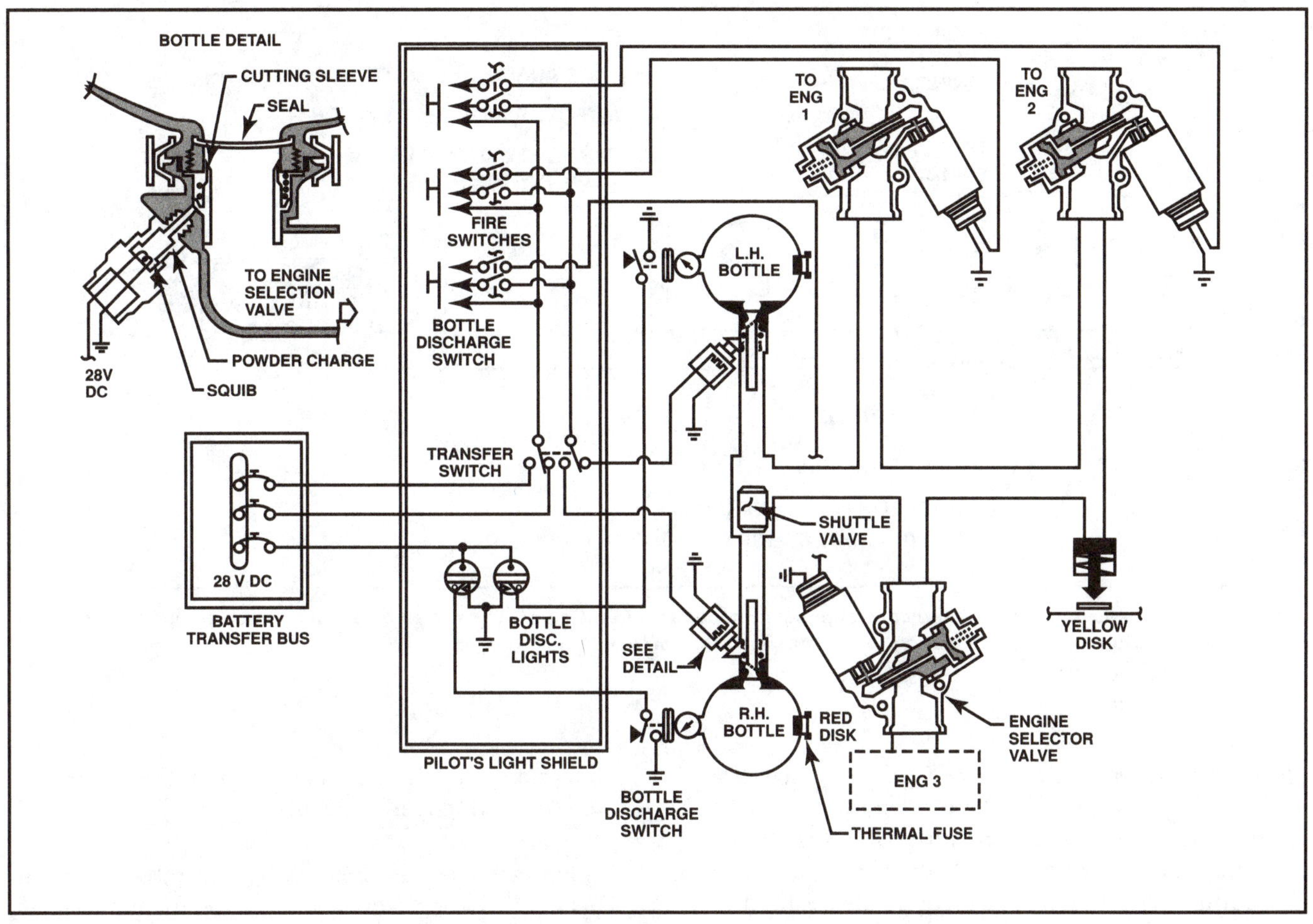

Figure 11-25. The Boeing 727 aircraft utilizes two fire bottles and three selector valves to provide fire suppression to all three engines. With this arrangement, the cockpit crew can discharge both bottles to a single engine.

tor valve to a series of discharge nozzles within the engine compartment. If the fire is not extinguished after discharging one bottle, the second bottle can be discharged and the extinguishing agent routed to the same engine. [Figure 11-25]

The controls for the 727 fire protection system consist of three engine fire warning lights, one wheel well fire warning light, a bottle transfer switch, a fire bell cutout switch, a fire detection system test switch, and a detector inoperative test switch. The fire warning lights are part of the fire detection system and illuminate whenever one of the fire detectors detects a fire. On the other hand, the bottle transfer switch allows the pilot to select which bottle of extinguishing agent is discharged. The fire bell disable switch silences the fire bell after it has been activated by a fire indication. The fire detection system test switch checks the continuity of the detectors and operation of the warning system. The detector inoperative test switch tests the circuits that activate the "Detector Inop" lights and, if the systems are functioning properly, momentarily illuminate the "Detector Inop" lights. [Figure 11-26]

When a fire is sensed, a red warning light inside the engine fire switch illuminates and the fire bell rings. When the warning light comes on, the pilot pulls the appropriate engine fire handle. This arms the fire extinguisher bottle discharge switch, disconnects the generator field relay, stops the flow of fuel and hydraulic fluid to the engine, and shuts off the engine bleed air. It also deactivates the engine-driven hydraulic pump low-pressure lights and uncovers the bottle discharge switch. If the pilot determines that a fire actually exists in the engine compartment, the extinguishing agent is released by depressing and holding the bottle discharge switch. When the discharge switch is depressed, electrical current causes the discharge cartridge to explode and shatter the frangible disk. With the frangible disk broken, the extinguishing agent is released into

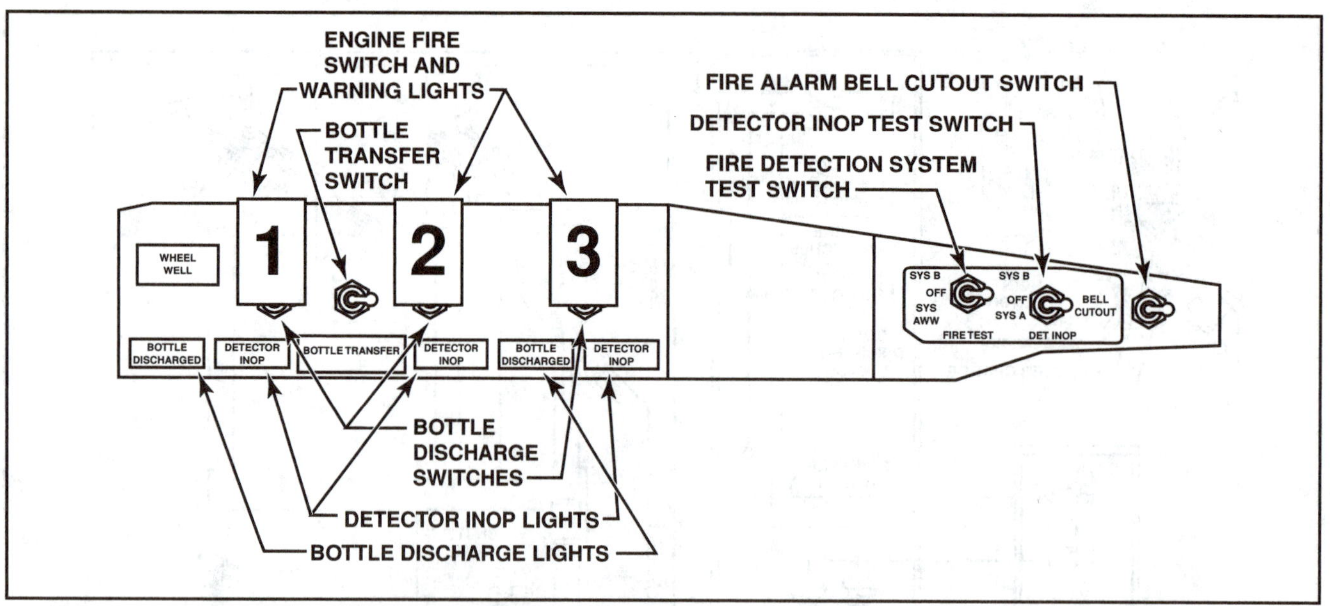

Figure 11-26. A typical Boeing 727 fire control panel provides an indication of wheel well or engine compartment fires, controls fire bottle discharge, and permits testing of the fire detector system.

the appropriate engine compartment. Once the extinguishing agent is discharged, the fire warning light should go out within thirty seconds. If the warning light does not go out, the pilot can move the bottle transfer switch to its opposite position to select the second bottle of extinguishing agent, and again push the bottle discharge switch. Once the fire extinguisher bottle has been discharged, or when its pressure is low, the appropriate bottle discharge light illuminates.

GROUND FIRE PROTECTION

Since the introduction of large turbine engine aircraft, the problem of ground fires has increased in seriousness. For this reason, a central ground connection to the aircraft's fire extinguishing system is incorporated on some aircraft. Such systems provide a more effective means of extinguishing ground fires and eliminate the necessity of removing and recharging the aircraft-installed fire extinguisher cylinders. These systems typically include a means for operating the entire system from one place on the ground, such as the cockpit or at the location of the fire extinguishing agent supply.

On aircraft not equipped with a central ground connection to the aircraft fire extinguishing system, means are usually provided for rapid access to the compressor, tailpipe, or burner compartments. The rapid access is typically by means of a spring-loaded or pop-out access door in the skin surrounding these compartments.

Internal engine tailpipe fires that take place during engine shutdown or false starts can be blown out by motoring the engine with the starter. If the engine is running, it can be accelerated to its rated speed to achieve the same result. However, if a tailpipe fire persists, a fire extinguishing agent can be directed into the tailpipe. However, keep in mind that excessive use of CO_2 or other agents that have a chilling effect can shrink the turbine housing onto the turbine and cause the engine to disintegrate. Therefore, exercise prudent judgment when directing fire extinguishing agents into a hot engine tailpipe.

CHAPTER 12

PROPELLERS

INTRODUCTION

Since the first powered flight, propellers have been used to convert aircraft engine power into thrust. Although many modern transport category aircraft are powered by turbojet or turbofan engines, most of the aircraft in use today are propelled by one or more propellers that are driven by either a turbine or reciprocating engine. Regardless of the engine type, the primary purpose of a propeller is to convert engine power to thrust. Therefore, as an aircraft maintenance technician, you must have a thorough understanding of the basic principles, maintenance, and repair of propeller systems.

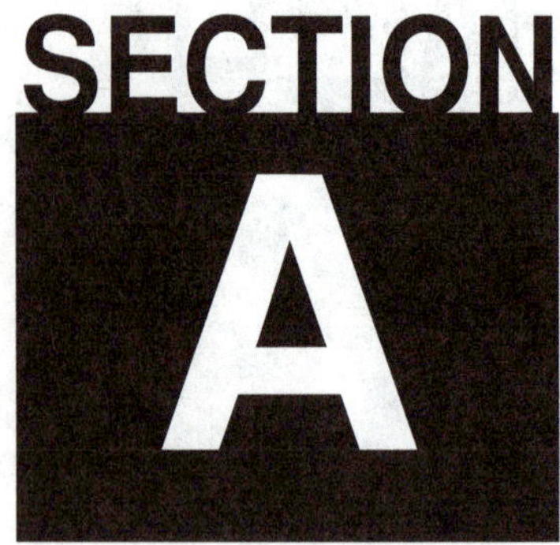

PROPELLER PRINCIPLES

With few exceptions, nearly all early aircraft designs used propellers to create thrust. During the latter part of the 19th century, many unusual and innovative propeller designs were tried on early flying machines. These early propeller designs ranged from simple fabric covered wooden paddles to elaborate multi-bladed wire-braced designs. As the science of aeronautics progressed, propeller designs evolved from flat boards which merely pushed air backward, to airfoils that produce lift to pull an aircraft forward. At the time the Wright brothers began their first powered flights, propeller design had evolved into the standard two-bladed style.

Development of propeller design with new materials has produced thinner airfoil sections and greater strength. Because of their structural strength, aluminum alloys are predominantly used as the structural material in modern aircraft propellers. However, you can still find several propellers that are constructed of wood.

Today, propeller designs continue to be improved through the use of new airfoil shapes, composite materials, and multi-blade configurations. Recent improvements include the use of composite materials to produce laminar flow symmetrical airfoils and gull wing propeller designs.

NOMENCLATURE

Before you can fully understand the principles of how a propeller produces thrust, you must be familiar with some basic terms and component names. All modern propellers consist of at least two blades that are connected to a central **hub**. The portion of a propeller blade that is nearest the hub is referred to as the **blade shank** whereas the portion furthest from the hub is called the **blade tip**. The propeller hub, or **hub assembly**, is bored out to create a **hub bore** which permits a propeller to be mounted on the engine crankshaft or to a reduction gear assembly. [Figure 12-1]

Each blade on a propeller acts as a rotating wing to produce lift and pull an aircraft through the air. Therefore, in addition to the basic nomenclature just discussed, propeller blades share much of the same nomenclature as aircraft wings. For example, all propeller blades have a **leading edge**, a **trailing edge**, and a **chord line**. If you recall from your study of airfoils, a chord line is an imaginary line drawn through an airfoil from the leading edge to the trailing edge. The curved, or cambered side of a propeller blade is called the **blade back** and the flat side is called the **blade face**. A propeller's **blade angle** is the acute angle formed by a propeller's plane of rotation and the blade's chord line. A propeller's plane of rotation is always perpendicular to the engine crankshaft. [Figure 12-2]

Propellers which allow changes in blade angle have removable blades that are secured to a hub assembly by a set of **clamping rings**. Each **blade root** has a flanged butt, or shoulder, which mates with grooves in the hub assembly. The blade shank on this type of blade is typically round and extends out to at least the end of the hub assembly; however, in some

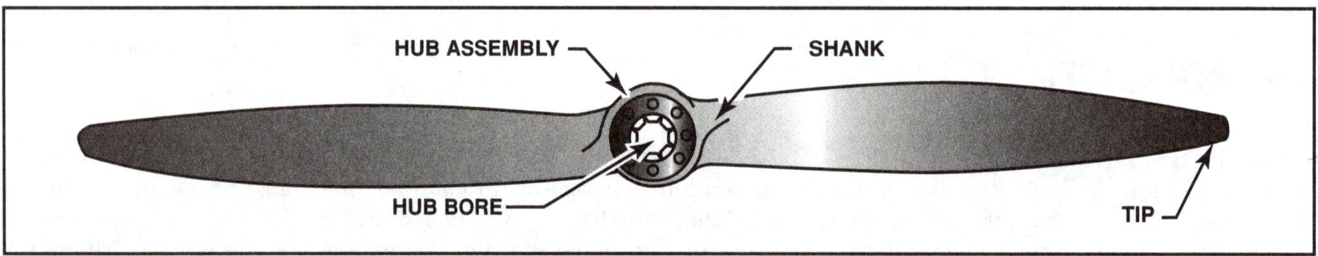

Figure 12-1. The blades of a single-piece propeller extend from the hub assembly. Blades have a shank and a tip, while the hub assembly has a hub bore and bolt holes that facilitate propeller mounting.

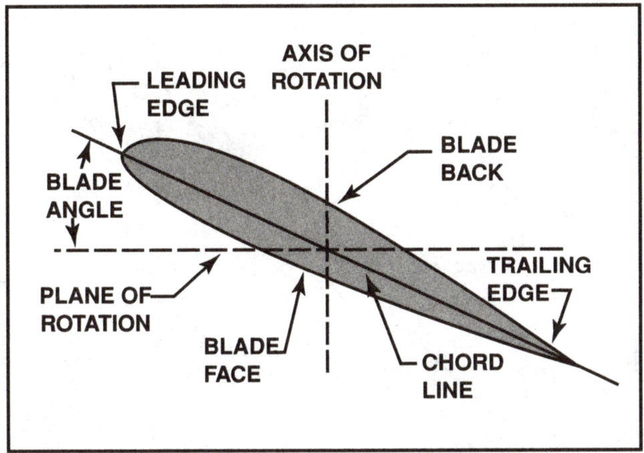

Figure 12-2. All propeller blades have a leading edge, a trailing edge, and a chord line. In addition, all propeller blades are set at a specific angle that is defined by the acute angle formed by the propeller's plane of rotation and the chord line.

cases, the shank may extend beyond the hub assembly and into the airstream. When this is the case, blade cuffs may be installed to improve air flow around the blade shank. A **blade cuff** is an airfoil-shaped attachment made of thin sheets of metal, plastic, or composite material. Blade cuffs mount on the blade shanks and are primarily used to increase the flow of cooling air to the engine nacelle. Mechanical clamping devices and bonding agents such as a rubber-base adhesive or epoxy adhesive are utilized to attach the cuffs to the blades. [Figure 12-3]

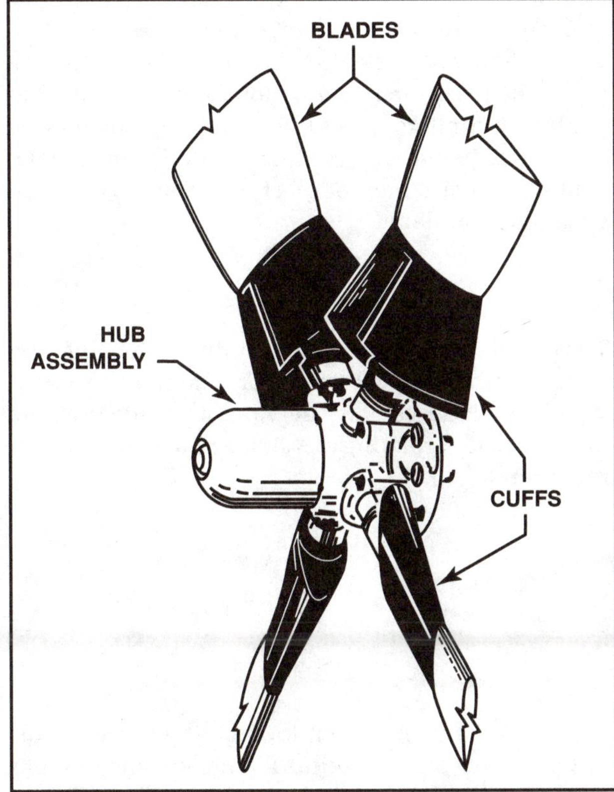

Figure 12-3. Some large turboprop propeller blades are fitted with blade cuffs to improve the airflow around the blade shanks.

To aid in identifying specific points along the length of a propeller blade, most blades have several defined **blade stations**. A blade station is simply a reference position on a propeller blade that is a specified distance from the center of the hub.

PROPELLER THEORY

When the propeller rotates through the air, a low pressure area is created in front of the blade, much like the wing's curvature creates a low pressure area above the wing. This low pressure area, combined with the constant, or high pressure area behind the blade allow a propeller to produce thrust. The amount of thrust produced depends on several factors including, the angle of attack of the propeller blades, the speed the blades move through the air, and the shape of the airfoil. The **angle of attack** of a propeller blade is the angle formed by the chord line of the blade and the relative wind. The direction of the **relative wind** is determined by the speed an aircraft moves through the air and the rotational motion of the propeller. For example, when a propeller rotates on a stationary aircraft, the direction of the relative wind is exactly opposite to the rotational movement of the propeller. Therefore, the propeller blade's angle of attack is the same as the propeller blade angle. [Figure 12-4]

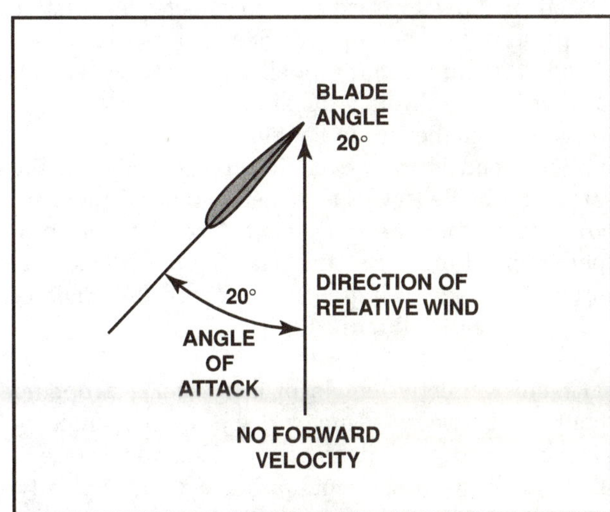

Figure 12-4. With no forward velocity, the relative wind is directly opposite the movement of the propeller blade. In this case, a propeller's angle of attack is the same as its blade angle.

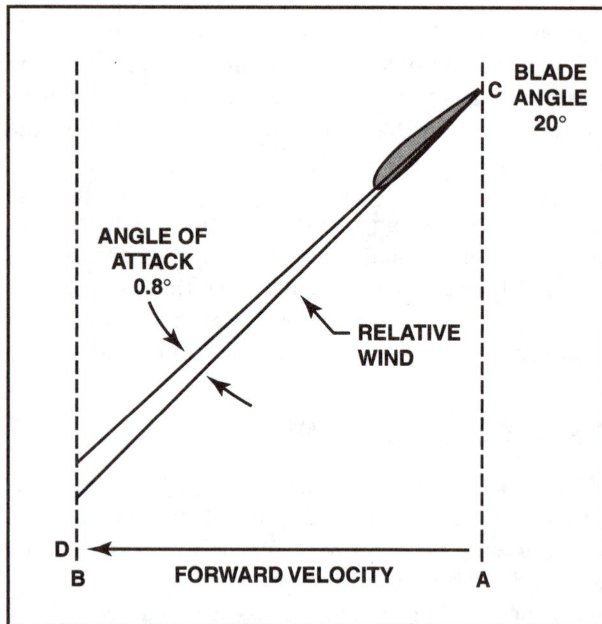

Figure 12-5. In forward flight, the airplane moves from point A to point B while the propeller moves from point C to point D. In this case, the propeller's trailing edge follows the path from C to D which represents the resultant relative wind. This results in an angle of attack that is less than the blade angle.

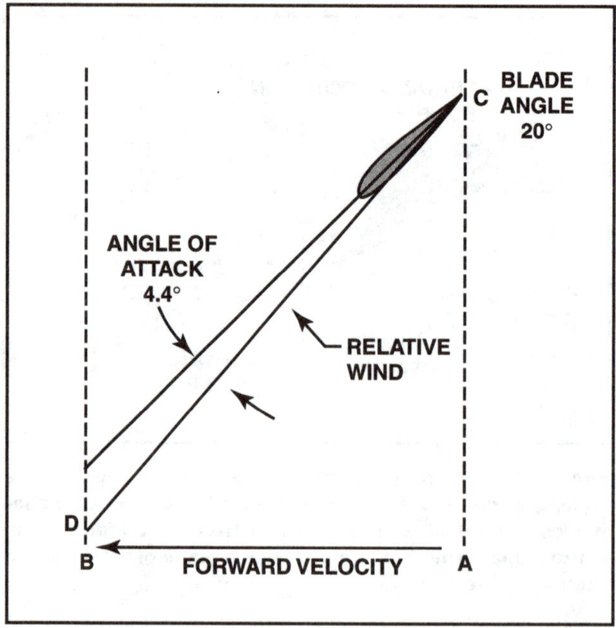

Figure 12-6. If the forward velocity of the aircraft remains constant, but a propeller's rotational speed increases, the propeller's trailing edge will move a greater distance for a given amount of forward movement. This increases the angle at which the relative wind strikes the propeller blade which, in turn, increases the angle of attack.

When the same aircraft begins moving forward, the relative wind changes direction. The reason for this is that, in addition to rotating, the propeller is also moving forward. The combination of the rotating and forward motion produce a resultant relative wind that is not directly opposite the movement of the propeller blade. In this case, the angle of attack will always be less than the blade angle. [Figure 12-5]

Based on how forward motion affects the relative wind acting on a propeller blade, it can be determined that for a given propeller speed, the faster an aircraft moves through the air, the smaller the angle of attack on the propeller blade. However, if propeller speed is increased, the trailing edge of the propeller blade travels a greater distance for a given amount of forward movement. Therefore, as propeller speed increases, the relative wind strikes the propeller blade at a greater angle and the angle of attack increases. [Figure 12-6]

The most effective angle of attack for a propeller blade is between 2 and 4 degrees. Any angle of attack exceeding 15 degrees is ineffective because of the possibility of a propeller blade stall. Typically, propellers with a fixed blade angle are designed to produce an angle of attack between 2 and 4 degrees at either a climb or cruise airspeed with a specific rpm setting.

Unlike a wing which moves through the air at a uniform rate, the propeller sections near the tip rotate at a much greater speed than those near the hub. The difference in rotational velocity along a propeller blade segment can be found by first calculating the circumference of the arc traveled by a point on that segment. If you recall from your general studies, the circumference of a circle is calculated with the formula:

$$2\pi r$$

The circumference is then multiplied by engine rpm to find rotational velocity. For example, to determine the blade velocity at a point 18 inches from the hub that is rotating at 1,800 rpm use the following formula:

$$\text{Velocity} = 2\pi r \times \text{rpm}$$

$$= 2 \times \pi \times 18 \times 1{,}800$$

$$= 203{,}575$$

At a point 18 inches from the hub the blade travels 203,575 inches per minute. To convert this to miles per hour, divide 203,575 by 63,360, the number of inches in one mile, and multiply the product by 60, the number of minutes in one hour.

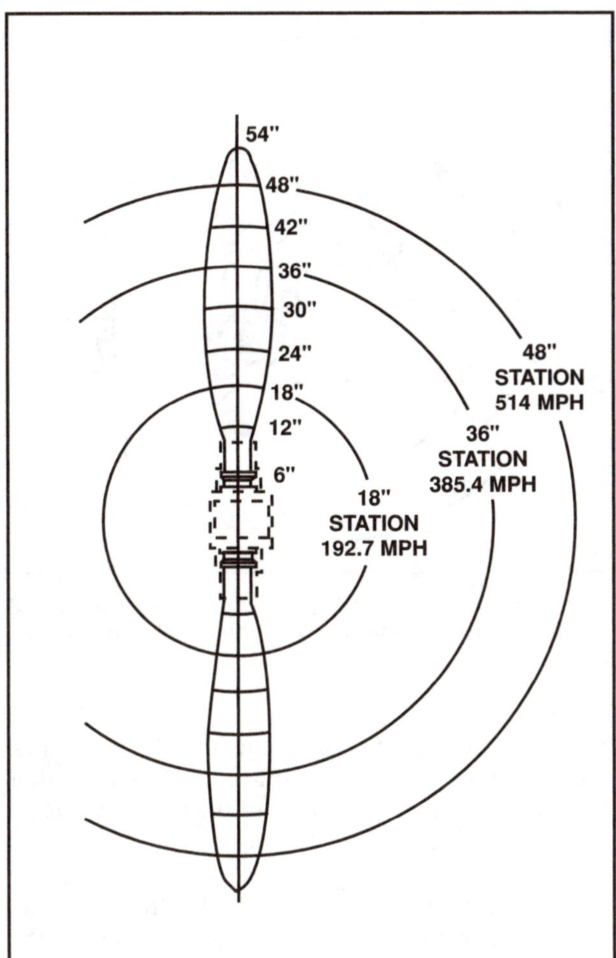

Figure 12-7. As a propeller blade rotates at a fixed rpm, each blade segment moves through the air at a different velocity.

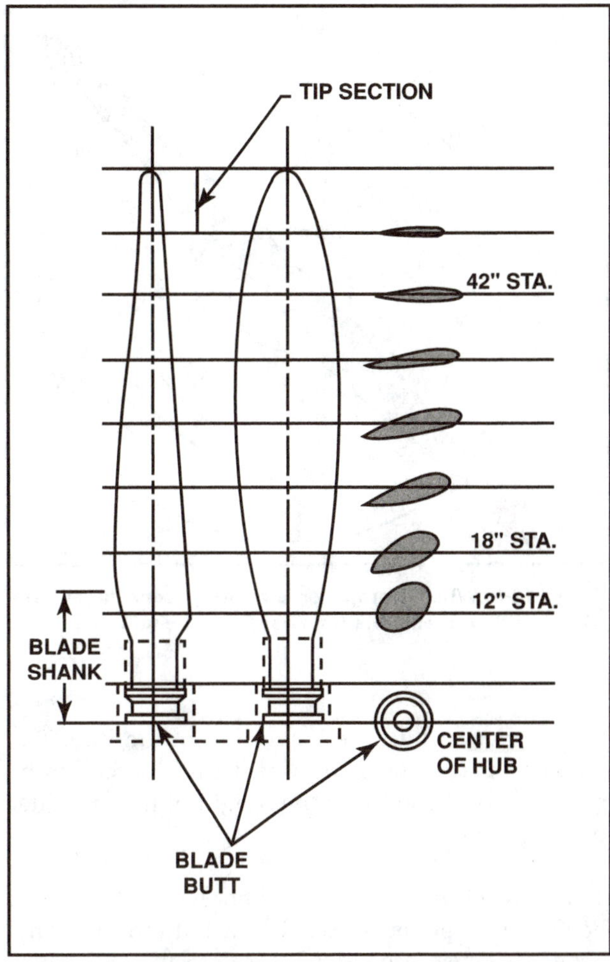

Figure 12-8. The variation in airfoil shape and blade angle along the length of a propeller blade compensates for differences in rotational speed and allows for a more even distribution of thrust along the blade.

$$\text{Velocity} = \frac{203{,}575}{63{,}360} \times 60$$

$$= 192.7 \text{ miles per hour}$$

The speed of the propeller at station 18 is 192.7 miles per hour. You can now compare this to the speed of the propeller at station 48. By applying the formulas just discussed, you can determine that, at station 48, the propeller is moving at a speed of 514 miles per hour. [Figure 12-7]

To compensate for the difference in velocity along a propeller blade, each small section of the propeller blade is set at a different angle. The gradual decrease in blade angle from the hub to the tip is called **pitch distribution**. This is what gives a propeller blade its twisted appearance. Blade twist allows the propeller to provide a fairly constant angle of attack along most of the length of the blade.

In addition to blade twist, most propellers are built with a thicker, low speed airfoil near the blade hub and a thinner, high speed airfoil near the tip. This, combined with blade twist, permits a propeller to produce a relatively constant amount of thrust along a propeller blade's entire length. [Figure 12-8]

FORCES ACTING ON A PROPELLER

A rotating propeller is subjected to many forces that cause tension, twisting, and bending stresses within the propeller. Of the forces that act on a propeller, **centrifugal force** causes the greatest stress. Centrifugal force can best be described as the force

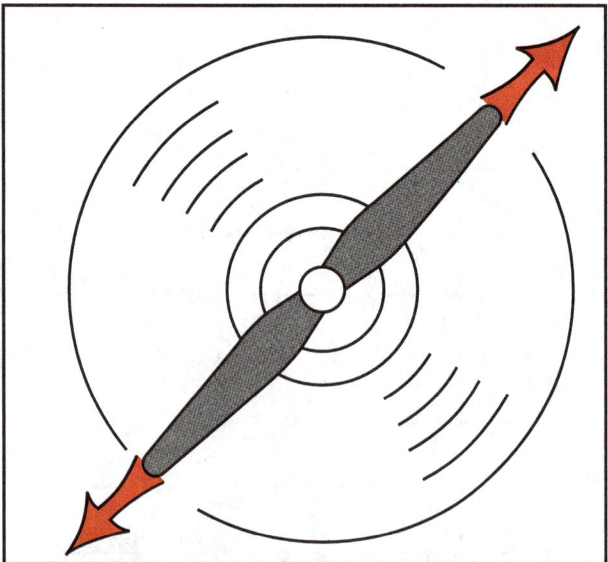

Figure 12-9. When a propeller is rotating, centrifugal force tries to pull propeller blades away from the hub.

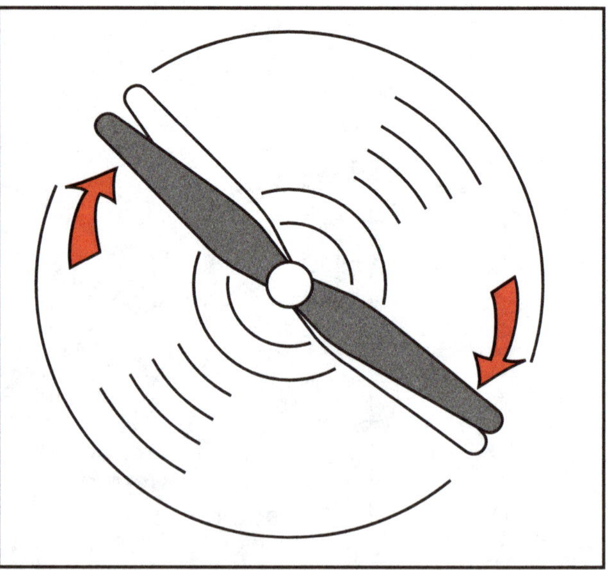

Figure 12-11. Torque bending forces exert a pressure that tends to bend the blades opposite the direction of rotation.

which tries to pull the blades out of the hub. The amount of stress created by centrifugal force can be greater than 7,500 times the weight of the propeller blade. [Figure 12-9]

Thrust bending force, on the other hand, attempts to bend the propeller blades forward at the tips. This occurs because propeller blades are typically thinner near the tip and this allows the thrust produced at the tip to flex the blade forward. Thrust bending force opposes centrifugal force to some degree. [Figure 12-10]

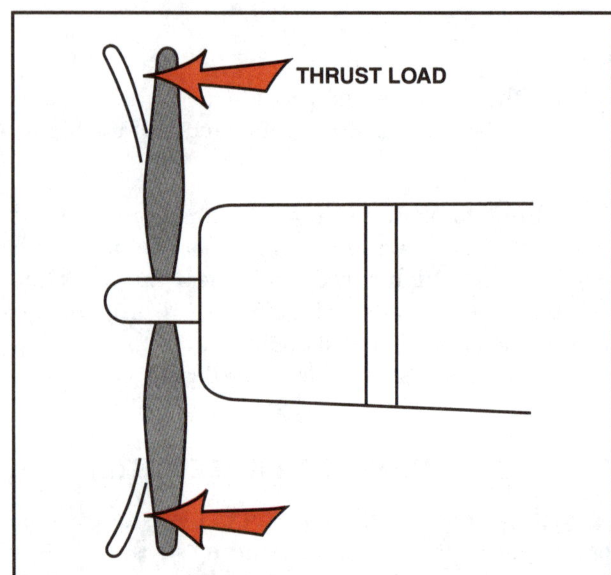

Figure 12-10. Thrust bending forces exert a pressure that tends to bend the propeller blade tips forward.

Torque bending forces occur as air resistance opposes the rotational motion of the propeller blades. This force tends to bend the blades opposite the direction of rotation. [Figure 12-11]

Aerodynamic twisting force results from the fact that, when a propeller blade produces thrust, the majority of the thrust produced is exerted ahead of the blade's axis of rotation. Therefore, aerodynamic twisting force tends to increase a propeller's blade angle. In some cases, aerodynamic twisting force is used to help change the blade angle on a propeller. [Figure 12-12]

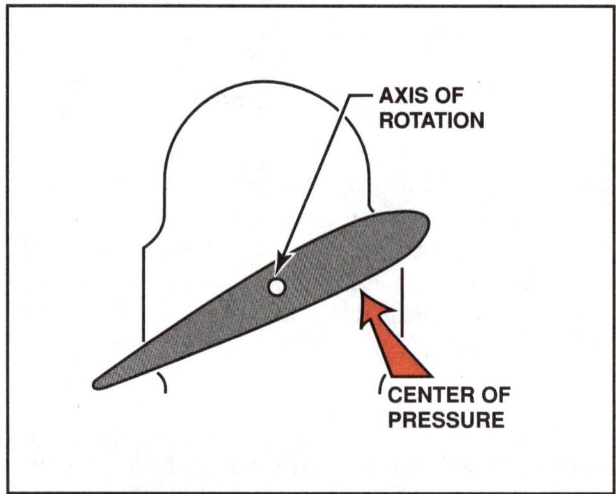

Figure 12-12. The majority of thrust produced by a propeller is exerted ahead of the blade's axis of rotation. This produces an aerodynamic twisting force that attempts to increase a propeller's blade angle.

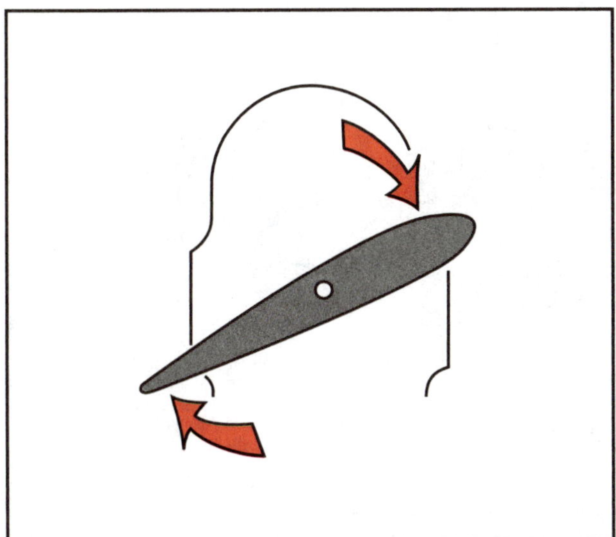

Figure 12-13. Centrifugal twisting force attempts to decrease blade angle by aligning a propeller's center of mass with its center of rotation.

Centrifugal twisting force opposes aerodynamic twisting force in that it attempts to decrease a propeller's blade angle. When a propeller rotates, centrifugal force tries to align the propeller's center of mass with its center of rotation. A propeller's center of mass is typically ahead of its center of rotation; therefore, when a propeller rotates, centrifugal force tries to decrease its blade angle. At operational speeds, centrifugal twisting force is greater than aerodynamic twisting force and is used in some propeller designs to decrease the blade angle. [Figure 12-13]

The final force that is exerted on a spinning propeller is **blade vibration**. When a propeller produces thrust, blade vibration occurs due to the aerodynamic and mechanical forces that are present. For example, aerodynamic forces tend to bend the propeller blades forward at the tips producing buffeting and vibration. On the other hand, mechanical vibrations are caused by the power pulses in a piston engine. Of the two, mechanical vibrations are considered to be more destructive than aerodynamic vibrations. The reason for this is that engine power pulses tend to create standing wave patterns in a propeller blade that can lead to metal fatigue and structural failure.

The location and number of stress points in a blade depend on the characteristics of the individual propeller/engine combination. While concentrations of vibrational stress are detrimental at any point on a blade, the most critical location is about six inches from the blade tips.

Most airframe-engine-propeller combinations have eliminated the detrimental effects of vibrational stresses by careful design. Nevertheless, some engine/propeller combinations do have a **critical range** where severe propeller vibration can occur. In this case, the critical range is indicated on the tachometer by a red arc. Engine operation in the critical range should be limited to a brief passage from one rpm setting to another. Engine operation in the critical range for extended periods can lead to structural failure of the propeller or aircraft.

Propeller design typically allows for some degree of vibrational stress. However, in situations where a propeller has been improperly altered, vibration may cause excessive flexing and work hardening of the metal to the extent that sections of the propeller blade could break off in flight.

PROPELLER PITCH

In the strictest sense, **propeller pitch** is the theoretical distance a propeller advances longitudinally in one revolution. Pitch and blade angle describe two different concepts, however, they are closely related and the two terms are often used interchangeably. For example, when a propeller is said to have a fixed pitch, what is actually meant is that the blades on the propeller are set at a fixed blade angle.

A propeller's **geometric pitch** is defined as the distance, in inches, that a propeller will move forward in one revolution if it were moving through a solid medium and did not encounter any loss of efficiency. Measurement of geometric pitch is based on the propeller blade angle at a point out from the propeller hub that is equal to 75 percent of the blade length.

When traveling through air, inefficiencies prevent a propeller from moving forward at a rate equal to its geometric pitch. Therefore, **effective pitch** is the actual amount a propeller moves forward in one revolution. Effective pitch varies from zero when the aircraft is stationary on the ground, to about 90 percent of the geometric pitch during the most efficient flight conditions. The difference between geometric pitch and effective pitch is called **slip**.

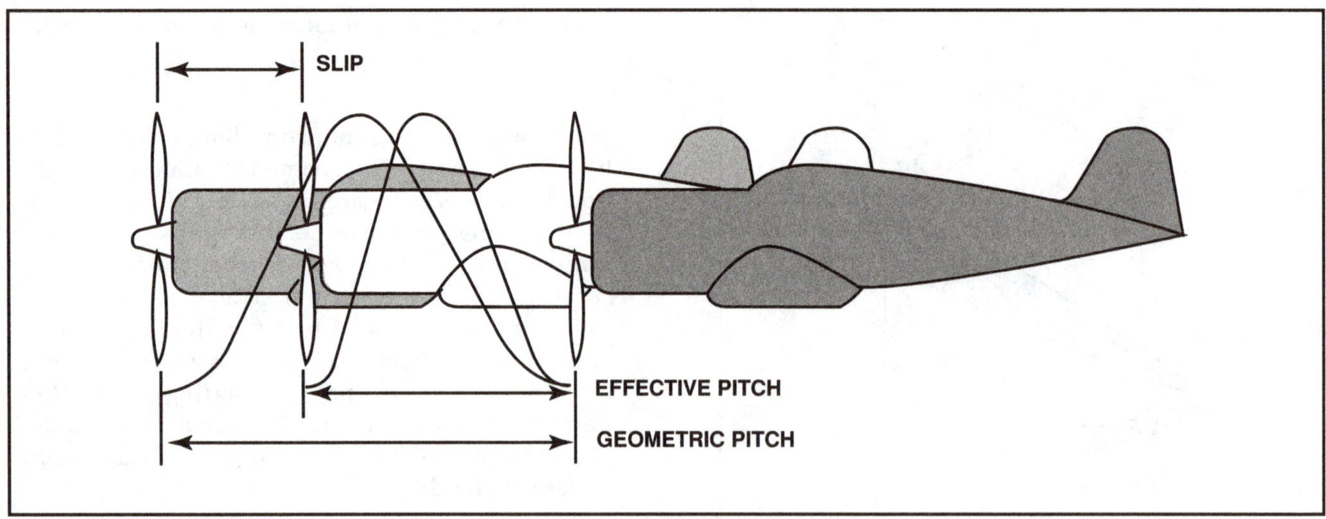

Figure 12-14. Geometric pitch is the theoretical distance a propeller would move forward if it were 100% efficient. Effective pitch, on the other hand, is the actual distance a propeller moves forward in one revolution. Slip is the difference between geometric and effective pitch.

Propeller slip represents the total losses caused by inefficiencies. [Figure 12-14]

If a propeller has a geometric pitch of 50 inches, in theory it should move forward 50 inches in one revolution. However, if the aircraft actually moves forward only 35 inches in one revolution, the effective pitch is 35 inches and the propeller is 70 percent efficient. In this case, slip represents 15 inches or a 30 percent loss of efficiency. In practice, most propellers are 75 to 85 percent efficient.

PROPELLER CLASSIFICATIONS

Propellers are typically classified according to their position on the aircraft. For example, **tractor propellers** are mounted on the front of an engine and pull an aircraft through the air. On the other hand, **pusher-type propellers** are mounted on the aft end of an aircraft and push an airplane through the air. Most aircraft are equipped with tractor-type propellers; however, there are several seaplanes and amphibious aircraft that are equipped with pusher propellers. A major advantage of the tractor-type propeller is that lower stresses are induced in the propeller as it rotates in relatively undisturbed air.

Both tractor- and pusher-type propellers effectively propel an aircraft through the air. However, in some instances one type of propeller may be better suited for a given airplane. For example, on land planes that have little propeller-to-ground clearance, pusher-type propellers are subject to more damage than tractor-type propellers. The reason for this is that rocks, gravel, and small objects that are dislodged by wheels are frequently thrown or drawn into a pusher-type propeller. On the other hand, it would be very difficult to install a tractor-type propeller on some amphibious aircraft.

Propellers also are classified by the method used to establish pitch. Typical classifications that are used here include fixed pitch, ground adjustable, controllable pitch, constant speed, reversible, and feathering.

The simplest type of propeller is a **fixed-pitch** propeller. Fixed-pitch propellers are designed for a particular aircraft to produce optimum efficiency at a specific rotational and forward speed. A fixed-pitch propeller with a low blade angle, often called a **climb propeller**, provides the best performance for takeoff and climb. On the other hand, a fixed-pitch propeller with a high blade angle, often called a **cruise propeller**, is more adapted to high speed cruise and high altitude flight. It is important to note that with this type of propeller, any change from the optimum rpm or airspeed reduces the efficiency of the propeller.

Ground-adjustable propellers are similar to fixed-pitch propellers in that their blade angles cannot be changed in flight. However, the propeller is constructed in a way that allows the blade angle to be changed on the ground. This type of propeller is found mostly on aircraft built between the 1920s and 1940s.

Controllable-pitch propellers have an advantage over ground adjustable propellers in that the blade angle may be changed while the propeller is rotating. This allows the propeller to assume a blade angle that provides the best performance for a particular flight condition. The number of pitch positions may be limited, as with a two-position controllable propeller; or the pitch may be adjusted to any angle between a minimum and maximum pitch setting.

Constant-speed propellers, sometimes referred to as **automatic propellers**, are unique in that once a pilot selects an operating rpm, the propeller blades automatically adjust to maintain the selected rpm. With this type of propeller, pitch control is provided by a controlling device known as a governor. A typical **governor** utilizes oil pressure to control blade pitch. Constant speed propeller systems provide maximum efficiency by allowing the pilot to control the propeller blade angle for most conditions encountered in flight.

Reversible-pitch propellers are a refinement of the constant-speed propeller. On aircraft equipped with a reversible propeller, the propeller blades can be rotated to a negative angle to produce reverse thrust. This forces air forward instead of backward and permits a shorter landing roll and improved ground maneuvering.

Most multi-engine aircraft are equipped with a **featherable** propeller. A feathering propeller is a type of constant-speed propeller that has the ability to rotate the propeller blades so that the leading edge of each blade is pointed straight forward into the wind. The only time a pilot selects the feather position is if an engine fails. Placing the blades in the feather position eliminates a great deal of the drag associated with a windmilling propeller.

PROPELLER CONSTRUCTION

Almost all propellers produced are made of wood, steel, aluminum, or some type of composite material. In the early years of aircraft development all propellers were made of wood. However, since wood is fairly susceptible to damage, steel propellers quickly found their way into aviation. Today, aluminum alloys are the predominant material used in the construction of both fixed- and adjustable-pitch propellers. In addition, some composite materials are now being utilized because of their light weight and flexibility.

WOOD

Wood was the most reliable material for fabrication of propellers for many years. Hardwoods such as birch, maple, and several others possess the flexibility and strength required for a propeller used on low horsepower engines of small aircraft. The molecular structure of wood allows it to absorb engine vibration to a large degree and does not support resonant vibrations. However, unless wood materials are coated with a tough protective layer of resin or other material, they are susceptible to damage from gravel and debris during ground operations.

ALUMINUM ALLOY

Today, the vast majority of propellers used are constructed of an aluminum alloy. Aluminum is more desirable than wood because it allows thinner, more efficient airfoils to be constructed without sacrificing structural strength. In addition, the airfoil sections on an aluminum propeller typically extend close to the hub providing better airflow for engine cooling. Furthermore, aluminum propellers require much less maintenance than wood propellers, thereby reducing the operating cost.

STEEL

Steel propellers and blades are found primarily on antique and older generation transport aircraft. Because steel is a heavy metal, steel blades are normally hollow consisting of steel sheets attached to a rib structure. The hollow area is then filled with a foam material to help absorb vibration and maintain a rigid structure.

COMPOSITE

Composite propeller blades are slowly gaining in popularity. Some advantages of composite propellers include the fact that they are lightweight and extremely durable. In addition, composites absorb vibration and are resilient, making them resistant to damage and corrosion.

SECTION B FIXED-PITCH PROPELLERS

The simplest type of propeller is a fixed-pitch propeller. As its name implies, the blade angle on a fixed-pitch propeller is fixed and cannot easily be changed. Because of this, fixed-pitch propellers achieve their optimum efficiency at a specific rotational and forward speed.

FIXED-PITCH CLASSIFICATIONS

A typical fixed-pitch propeller installed on a light aircraft has a diameter between 67 and 76 inches and a pitch between 53 and 68 inches. The exact diameter and pitch required for a specific airplane is specified by the aircraft manufacturer. In some cases, a manufacturer may authorize multiple propellers, each with a different pitch. In this case, a propeller with the lower blade angle provides the best performance for takeoff and climb and, therefore, is often called a **climb propeller**. The low blade angle allows the engine to develop its maximum rpm at the slower airspeeds associated with climbout. However, once the aircraft reaches its cruising altitude and begins to accelerate, the low blade angle becomes inefficient.

A fixed-pitch propeller with a slightly higher blade angle is called a **cruise propeller**. A cruise propeller is designed to be efficient at cruising speed and high altitude flight. However, because of the higher pitch, cruise propellers are very inefficient during takeoff and climbout.

A **standard propeller** is often referred to as a compromise between a climb propeller and cruise propeller. Each aircraft manufacturer usually designates a standard propeller which is designed to provide the best all-around performance under normal circumstances.

When an aircraft-engine combination is type certificated with a specified standard, climb, and cruise propeller, the aircraft operator may choose the type of fixed-pitch propeller which provides the best performance for the flight operations most often conducted. For example, an aircraft which frequently operates from short runways, or high field elevations generally perform better with a climb propeller. On the other hand, aircraft which are normally operated at sea level from airports with long runways may be equipped with a cruise propeller.

PROPELLER CONSTRUCTION

Almost all fixed-pitch propellers produced are made of either wood or aluminum. Of the two, aluminum is the most common, especially on production aircraft. However, there are still several classic and experimental aircraft that utilize wood propellers.

WOODEN PROPELLERS

A majority of fixed-pitch propellers were made from wood until World War II and wooden propellers are still in limited use on small utility aircraft. Hardwoods such as ash and birch are typically used to build a wooden propeller. However, other hardwoods that have been used include mahogany, maple, cherry, oak, and black walnut. Whatever type of wood is used, it must be free of grain irregularities, knots, pitch pockets, and insect damage.

A wooden propeller is constructed of a minimum of five layers of wood that are kiln-dried and laminated together with a waterproof resin glue. Each layer is normally the same thickness and type of wood; however, alternate layers of different wood types may be used. The reason laminated wood is used instead of a solid block of wood is that a laminated structure is less likely to warp. Once the layers of wood are laminated together, they form what is called a **propeller blank**.

During fabrication, the blank is rough-cut to shape and then allowed to season for a period of time. The waiting period allows the moisture in the wood to disperse equally through all of the layers. The rough-shaped blank, referred to as a **white**, is then finished to the exact airfoil and pitch dimensions required. In addition, the center bore and bolt holes

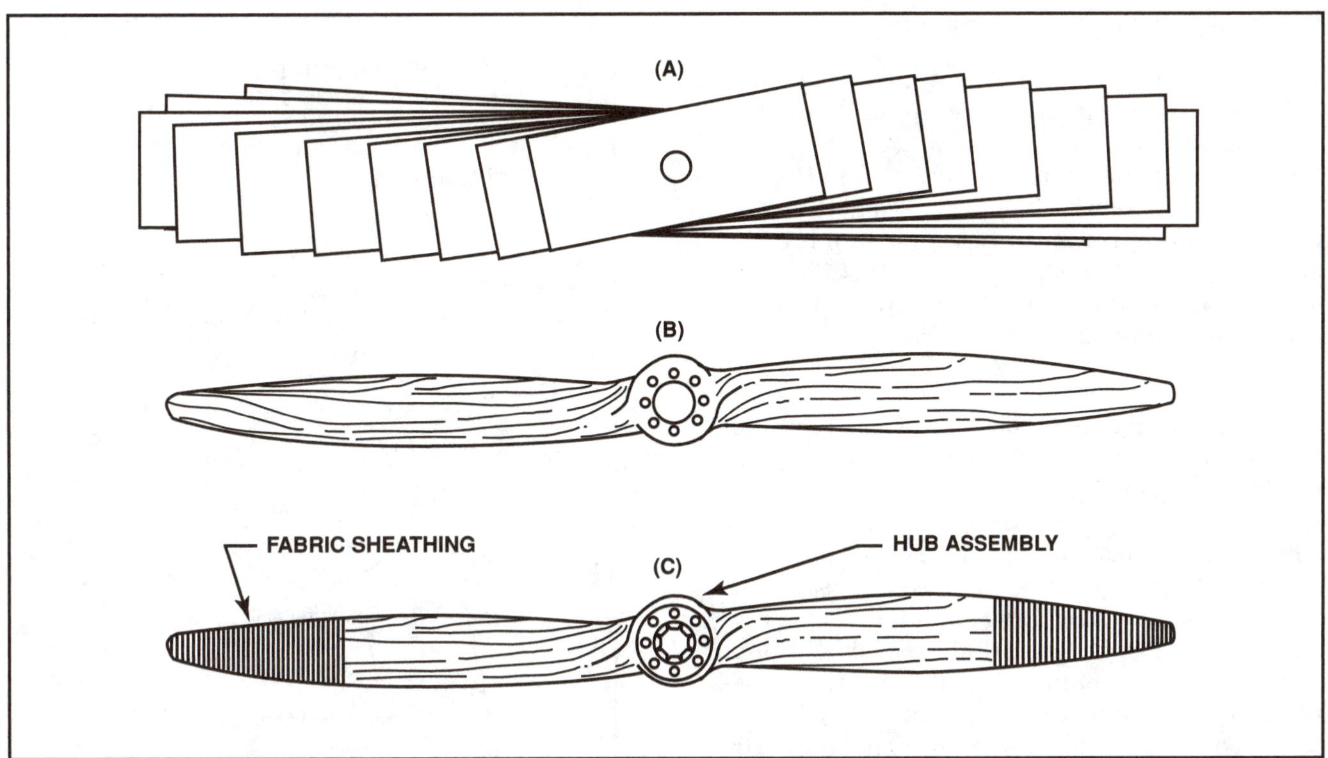

Figure 12-15. (A) — The first step in the manufacture of a wood propeller is to laminate planks together to form a propeller blank. (B) — The propeller blank is shaped and its hub is drilled to produce a "white." (C) — Once sanded smooth, a fabric sheathing and varnish coating are applied for reinforcement and protection.

are drilled and a metal hub assembly is inserted through the hub bore to accommodate the mounting bolts and face plate.

Once a propeller white is finished and sanded smooth, a cotton fabric is sometimes glued to the last 12 to 15 inches of the propeller blade. The fabric acts to reinforce the thin tip sections. Once applied, the fabric is doped to prevent deterioration caused by weather and the sun's rays. The entire propeller is then finished with clear varnish to protect the wood surface. In some cases, wood propellers may be finished with a black or gray plastic coating that provides additional protection against chipping. In this case, the propeller is said to be **armor coated**. [Figure 12-15]

Monel, brass, or stainless steel tipping is applied to the leading edge and tip of most wooden propellers to prevent damage from small stones. In order to permit the metal edging to conform to the contour of the leading edge, the metal must be notched. To attach the edging to the blade, countersunk screws are used in the thick blade sections while copper rivets are used in the thin sections near the tip. Once in place, the screws and rivets are secured with solder. Using a number 60 drill, three small holes are then drilled 3/16 inch deep into the tip of each blade. These holes allow moisture to drain from behind the metal tipping and allow the wood to breathe. [Figure 12-16]

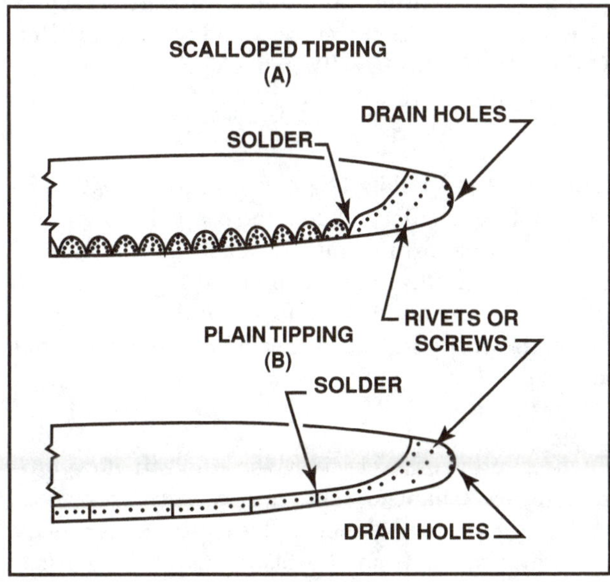

Figure 12-16. Metal tipping is applied to propeller blade tips and leading edges to help prevent erosion damage. Three small holes drilled in the tip of each blade release moisture and allow the wood to breathe.

ALUMINUM ALLOY PROPELLERS

Wood has given way to aluminum as the most often used material for fixed-pitch propeller fabrication. As mentioned earlier, propeller blades can be made thinner and more efficient without sacrificing structural strength when using aluminum instead of wood. In addition, aluminum has the strength and flexibility to accommodate the high horsepower engines available in today's small aircraft.

One of the biggest advantages of using aluminum is that aluminum alloy blades are less susceptible to damage from gravel and debris normally incurred during ground operations. Another advantage is that infrequent damage such as small nicks and upsets are easily dressed out with special files, making aluminum blades easier to repair than wooden blades. In addition, fixed-pitch aluminum propellers may be re-pitched to an approved blade angle by certified propeller repair stations when desired by the aircraft operator.

Although aluminum propellers offer several advantages over wood propellers, there are areas where aluminum propellers do not perform as well. For example, aluminum propellers are much more susceptible to damage caused by resonant vibrations. Because of this, aluminum propellers must be vibrationally tested during the certification process. In addition, aluminum propellers generally weigh more than a comparable wood propeller. On a light aircraft the difference can equate to several pounds.

Almost all propellers begin as a high strength aluminum forging. Once forged, the propeller is ground to the desired airfoil shape by machine and manual grinding. The final pitch is then set by twisting the blades to their desired angle. Once the blade angle is set, the propeller is heat treated to relieve internal stresses.

To help prevent excessive vibration, all new propellers are balanced both horizontally and vertically. Horizontal balance is typically achieved by removing metal from the blade tip while vertical balance is achieved by removing metal from a blade's leading and trailing edges. Some propeller models may be horizontally balanced by placing lead wool in balance holes near the boss while vertical balance is obtained by attaching balance weights to the side of the propeller hub. Once the propeller is balanced, the surfaces are finished by anodizing and painting.

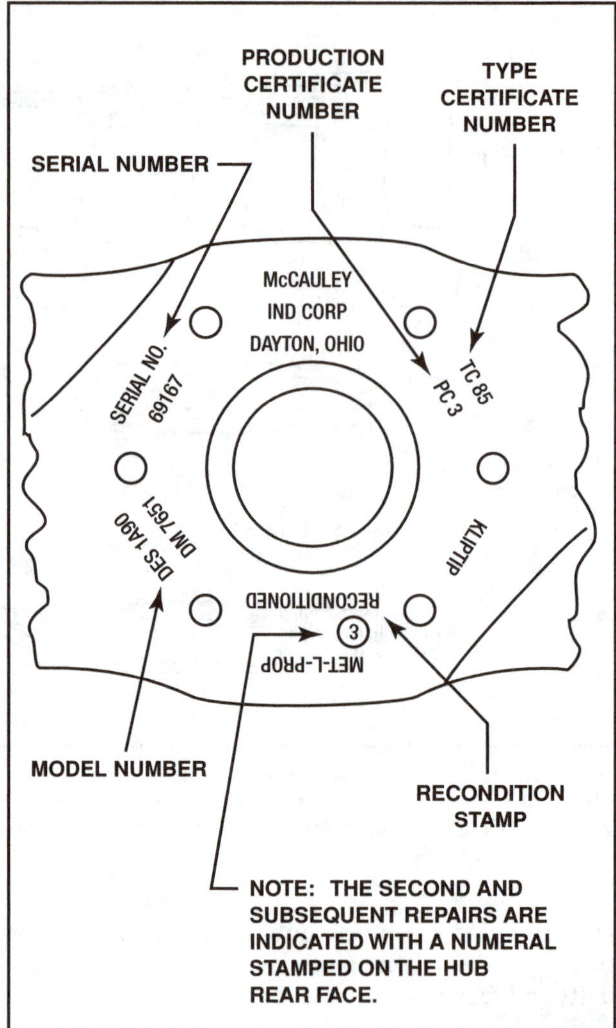

Figure 12-17. On McCauley fixed-pitch propellers, the builders name, model designation, serial number, type certificate number, and production certificate number are stamped around the propeller hub.

PROPELLER DESIGNATION

The Federal Aviation Regulations require that all propellers be identified with the builders name, model designation, serial number, type certificate number, and production certificate number if there is one. To comply with the FARs, most manufacturers of fixed-pitch propellers stamp all the required information on the propeller hub. [Figure 12-17]

Of the information presented on a propeller, the manufacturers model number provides the majority of the information you will need to be familiar with as a maintenance technician. For example, a McCauley propeller designated as 1A90/DM 7651 has a basic design designation of 1A90. The "DM" component of the designation indicates the type of crankshaft the propeller will fit, the blade tip contour, and other information pertaining to a specific aircraft installation. The "7651" indicates the propeller diameter is 76 inches, and the pitch of the propeller at the 75 percent station is 51 inches.

As another example, a Sensenich propeller designated as M74DM-61 has a designated diameter of 74 inches. The "D" component of the designation identifies the blade design, while the "M" identifies a specific hub design along with mounting information. The "61" designates the blade pitch in inches at the 75 percent station. [Figure 12-18

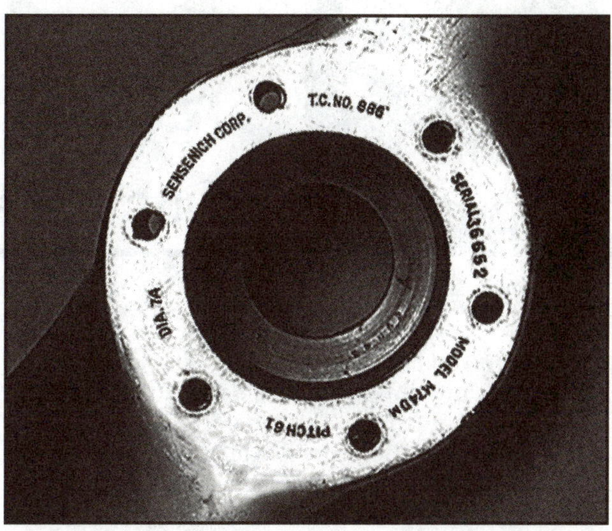

Figure 12-18. A Sensenich aluminum propeller has information stamped on the hub which identifies its hub design, blade design, blade length, and pitch. In addition, the number 1 stamped on one of the blade roots identifies that blade as blade number one.

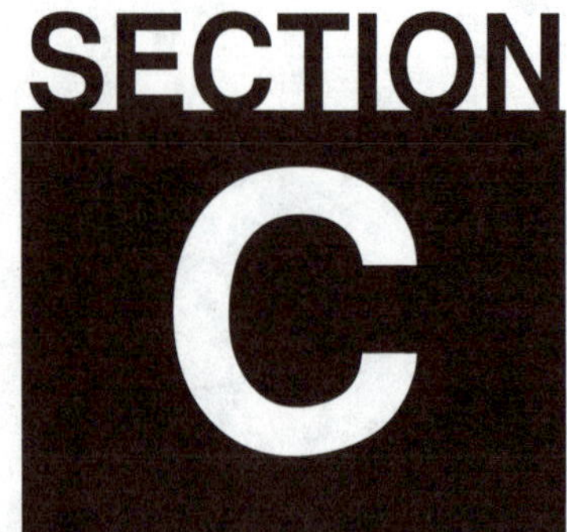

ADJUSTABLE-PITCH PROPELLERS

The design and construction of adjustable pitch propellers permit the aircraft operator to change the propeller blade angle. This offers the advantage of being able to set the propeller blade angle to obtain the maximum possible efficiency from a particular propeller/engine combination. While a few of the older adjustable pitch propellers could only be adjusted on the ground by a maintenance technician, most modern adjustable pitch propellers permit a pilot to change the propeller pitch in flight. The first adjustable pitch propeller systems developed offered two pitch settings; a low pitch setting and a high pitch setting. Today, however, nearly all adjustable pitch propeller systems are capable of a range of pitch settings.

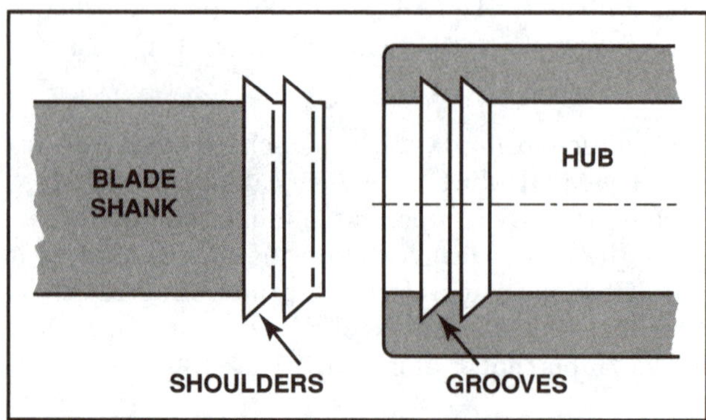

Figure 12-19. To help ensure that the propeller blades are not pulled out of the hub on a ground-adjustable propeller, shoulders are machined into the base of each blade shank. These shoulders fit into grooves that are machined into each hub half.

GROUND-ADJUSTABLE PROPELLERS

As mentioned in Section A, ground-adjustable propellers are constructed in a way that allows the blade angle to be changed when the aircraft is on the ground and the engine is shut down. This type of propeller is seldom used today and is usually found on older aircraft equipped with radial engines.

The hub of a ground adjustable propeller consists of two aluminum or steel halves that are machined to form a matched pair. The interior of each hub half is machined out so that the shank of two propeller blades can be held between the two hub halves. To prevent centrifugal force from pulling the blades out of the hub, the base, or butt, of each metal blade is machined with shoulders which fit into grooves that are machined into each hub half. If wooden blades are used, the shoulders are cast or machined into a metal sleeve that is fastened to the blade shank by lag screws. [Figure 12-19]

Once the blades are inserted between the two hub halves, bolts are normally used to secure the hub halves when steel blades are used. However, when wood or aluminum alloy blades are used, either bolts or clamp rings may be used to hold the hub halves together. [Figure 12-20]

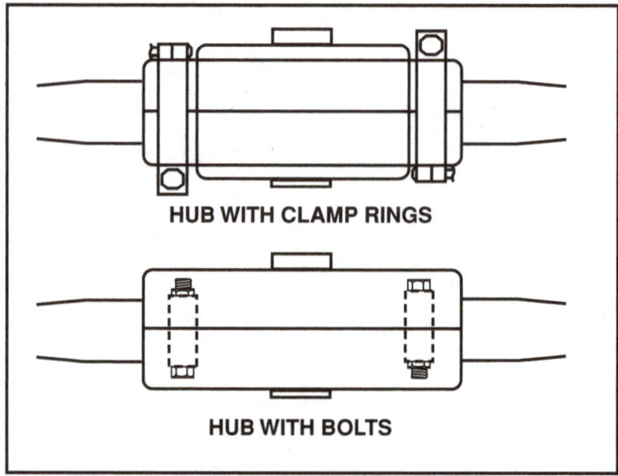

Figure 12-20. Ground adjustable propellers utilize either clamp rings or bolts to secure the hub halves and hold the blades tightly.

CONTROLLABLE-PITCH PROPELLERS

Controllable-pitch propellers have an advantage over ground adjustable propellers in that the blade angle may be changed while the propeller is rotating. This allows the propeller to assume a blade angle that provides the best performance for a particular flight condition. The number of pitch positions may be limited, as with a two-position controllable propeller; or the pitch may be adjusted to any angle between a minimum and maximum pitch setting.

TWO-POSITION PROPELLERS

One of the first controllable-pitch propellers that became popular was the Hamilton-Standard counterweight propeller. This propeller was developed in the 1930's and permitted the pilot to select one of two positions; low pitch or high pitch. The low pitch setting was used during takeoff and climb so the engine would turn at its maximum rpm and develop its full rated horsepower. On the other hand, the high pitch setting was used during the cruise phase of flight to permit more efficient high-speed flight while increasing fuel economy.

The primary components of a two-position propeller include the propeller hub, propeller blades, and a piston assembly. At the center of the Hamilton-Standard two-position propeller hub is the **spider**. A typical spider consists of two or three arms on which the blades are attached. The blades are made from an aluminum alloy and have hollow ends which fit over the arms of the spider. Once the blades are inserted on the hub, counterweight brackets are attached to the base of each blade.

Like the ground-adjustable propeller, the Hamilton-Standard propeller consists of a two piece hub that encloses the spider and holds the propeller blades in place. To allow the propeller blades to rotate between the low and high pitch stops, each blade rides on a set of roller bearings. In addition, a counterweight bracket is installed at the base of each propeller blade.

The blade angle on the Hamilton-Standard propeller is changed by using a combination of hydraulic and centrifugal forces. Hydraulic force is used to decrease blade angle while centrifugal force acting on a set of counterweights is used to increase blade angle. The hydraulic force used to decrease blade angle is derived from engine oil that flows out of the crankshaft and acts on a piston assembly that is mounted on the front of the propeller hub. The flow of engine oil into the piston assembly is controlled by a three-way selector valve that is mounted in the engine and controlled from the cockpit. When this valve is moved forward to decrease propeller blade angle, engine oil is routed into the piston assembly to force the piston outward. The piston assembly is linked to each counterweight bracket so that, as the piston moves out, it pulls the counterweights in and decreases the blade angle. Once the blades reach their low pitch stop in the counterweight assembly, oil pressure holds the blades in this position. [Figure 12-21]

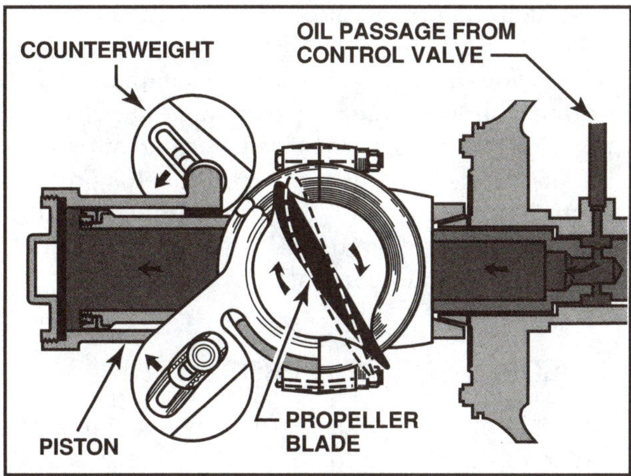

Figure 12-21. When low pitch is selected, engine oil pressure forces the cylinder forward. This motion moves the counterweights and blades to the low pitch position.

To move the blades to a high pitch position, the propeller control lever is moved aft, rotating the selector valve to release oil pressure in the propeller hub. With the oil pressure removed, the centrifugal force acting on the counterweights causes them to move outward, rotating the blades to their high pitch position. As the blades rotate, oil is forced out of the propeller cylinder and returned to the engine sump. The blades stop rotating when they contact their high pitch stops located in the counterweight assembly. [Figure 12-22]

In most cases, the pitch stops on a two-position propeller can be adjusted. To do this, a pitch stop adjusting nut is rotated until the desired blade angle is obtained.

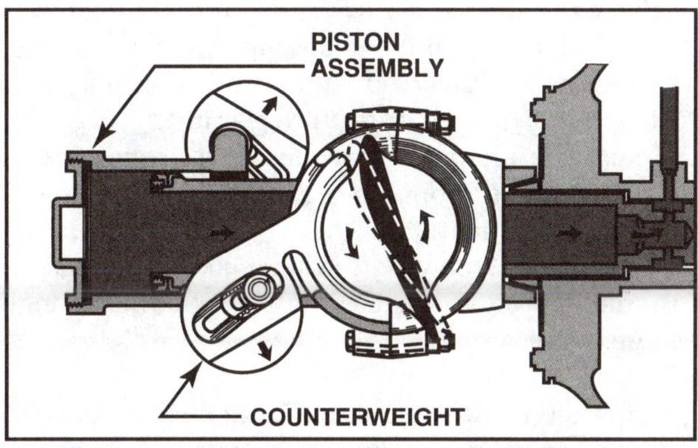

Figure 12-22. When high pitch is selected, engine oil pressure is removed from the piston assembly allowing centrifugal force to move the counterweights outward. This rotates the blades to the high pitch position.

Although the operation of a two-position propeller is fairly straight forward, there are some operational things you need to know. For example, prior to engine shutdown, the propeller should be placed in the high pitch position. If you recall, this retracts the piston assembly, which, in turn, helps protect it from corrosion and accumulations of dirt. Furthermore, most of the oil is forced from the piston where it could congeal in cold weather.

MULTIPLE-POSITION PROPELLERS

As technology advanced, the two-position propeller was improved to allow the operator to select any blade angle between the high and low pitch stops. This way, optimum engine/propeller efficiency can be maintained over a wider range of power settings and airspeeds. For example, during takeoff, the propeller blade angle is set at its lowest blade angle so the engine can generate its maximum power output. Then, once the aircraft is established in a climb, the blade angle can be increased slightly to provide the best climb performance. In cruise flight, the blade angle is further increased to obtain the best cruise performance.

CONSTANT-SPEED PROPELLERS

A constant-speed propeller, often called a variable-pitch or controllable-pitch propeller, is the most common type of adjustable-pitch propeller used on aircraft today. The main advantage of a constant-speed propeller is that it converts a high percentage of the engine's power into thrust over a wide range of rpm and airspeed combinations. The primary reason why a constant-speed propeller is more efficient than other propellers is because it allows the operator to select the most efficient engine rpm for the given conditions. Once a specific rpm is selected, a device called a governor automatically adjusts the propeller blade angle as necessary to maintain the selected rpm. For example, after selecting a desired rpm during cruising flight, an increase in airspeed or decrease in propeller load will cause the propeller blade angle to increase as necessary to maintain the selected rpm. On the other hand, a reduction in airspeed or increase in propeller load will cause the propeller blade angle to decrease.

The range of possible blade angles for a constant-speed propeller is called the propeller's **constant-speed range** and is defined by the high and low pitch stops. As long as the propeller blade angle is within the constant-speed range and not against either pitch stop, a constant engine rpm will be maintained. However, once the propeller blades contact a pitch stop, the engine rpm will increase or decrease as appropriate with changes in airspeed and propeller load. For example, once a specific rpm has been selected, and if aircraft speed decreases enough to rotate the propeller blades until they contact the low pitch stop, any further decrease in airspeed will cause engine rpm to decrease the same way as if a fixed pitch propeller were installed. The same holds true when an aircraft equipped with a constant-speed propeller accelerates to a faster airspeed. As the aircraft accelerates, the propeller blade angle increases to maintain the selected rpm until the high pitch stop is reached. Once this occurs, the blade angle cannot increase any further and engine rpm to increases.

On aircraft that are equipped with a constant-speed propeller, engine power output is controlled by the throttle and indicated by a manifold pressure gauge. The propeller blade angle, on the other hand, is controlled by a propeller control lever and the resulting change in engine rpm caused by a change in blade angle is indicated on the tachometer. By providing the operator a means of controlling both engine power output and propeller angle, the most efficient combination of blade angle and engine power output can be maintained for a variety of flight conditions. For example, during takeoff you want the engine to develop its maximum power; therefore, the throttle and the propeller control are advanced full forward so the engine can turn at its maximum rpm on takeoff. On the other hand, after the aircraft is established in cruise flight, the throttle can be retarded so the engine runs at a more economical speed and the propeller blade angle can be increased to increase propeller efficiency for higher speed flight.

One thing you must keep in mind when operating a constant-speed propeller is that, for a given rpm setting, there is a maximum allowable manifold pressure. Operating above this level may cause internal engine stress. Therefore, as a general rule, you should avoid high manifold pressures with low rpm settings.

OPERATING PRINCIPLES

Most constant-speed, non-feathering propellers rely on a combination of hydraulic and centrifugal forces to change the propeller blade angle. They use high-pressure oil to increase the propeller blade angle and the centrifugal twisting force inherent in all spinning propellers is utilized to decrease the blade angle. On the other hand, most feathering propellers utilize counterweights and centrifugal force to pull the blades to high pitch and oil pressure to force the blades to low pitch. To help prevent confusion between the operation of feathering and non-feathering propellers, the following discussion will focus on a typical non-feathering, non-counterweighted propeller assembly.

The device that is responsible for regulating the flow of high-pressure oil to the propeller is called the governor. A typical governor does three things; it boosts the engine oil pressure before it enters the propeller hub, it controls the amount of oil that flows to the propeller, and it senses the rotational speed of the engine.

A propeller governor is typically mounted either on the front of an engine near the propeller shaft or on the engine accessory case. In addition, all governors consist of three basic components; a gear-type boost pump, a pilot valve, and a speed sensitive flyweight assembly. [Figure 12-23]

A typical governor boost pump is installed in the base of a governor and boosts the oil pressure to between 180 and 300 psi depending on the system requirements. The force needed to drive the boost pump is provided by a drive shaft that extends into the engine where it mates with an engine drive gear. In some cases, the drive shaft may be hollow to provide a passage for return oil to flow back to the engine. Since most boost pumps are constant displacement pumps, excessive oil pressure is produced at high engine speeds; therefore, a spring-loaded relief valve is provided to prevent damage to seals and other components. This way, when the oil pressure increases enough to overcome the spring pressure acting on the relief valve, the valve opens and routes the excess oil back to the inlet side of the boost pump.

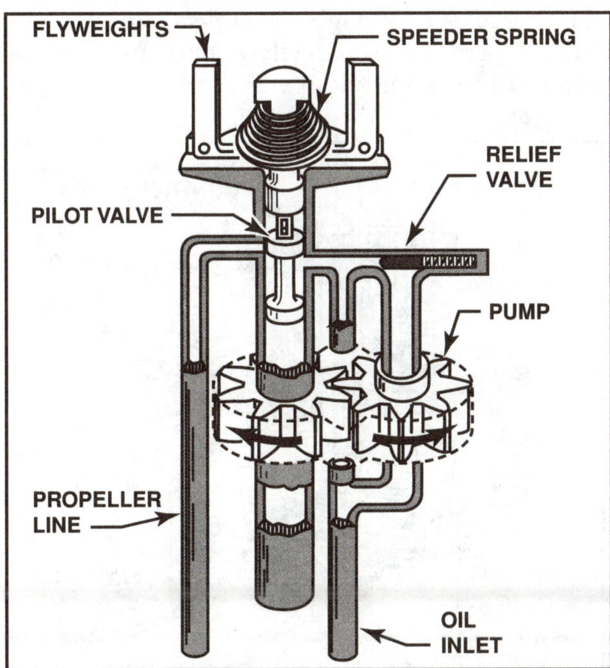

Figure 12-23. A typical propeller governor consists of a gear-type boost pump that increases the pressure of the oil before it enters the propeller hub, a pilot valve that controls the amount of oil flowing into and out of the propeller hub, and a flyweight assembly that senses engine speed and positions the pilot valve as needed to maintain a constant rpm.

The valve that is responsible for routing oil into and out of the propeller hub is called a **pilot valve**. Although the design of a pilot valve varies between manufacturers, they all perform the same basic function; they direct oil into and out of the propeller hub. A typical pilot valve is a shuttle-type valve that alternately covers and uncovers oil passages allowing oil to flow into or out of the propeller hub.

In order for a governor to adjust the propeller blade angle to maintain a constant rpm, it must be able to sense engine speed. The portion of a governor that senses engine speed is referred to as the **flyweight assembly**. A typical flyweight assembly consists of a set of **flyweights** mounted on a **flyweight head** that is driven by the same drive shaft that drives the boost pump. The pilot valve is located inside the drive shaft and extends into the flyweight assembly where it rests on the toe of each flyweight. This way, as the flyweights tilt in and out, the pilot valve is moved up or down. To allow the operator to select, or set, a desired blade angle, a **speeder spring** is provided to adjust the amount of pressure acting on the flyweights and pilot valve. [Figure 12-24]

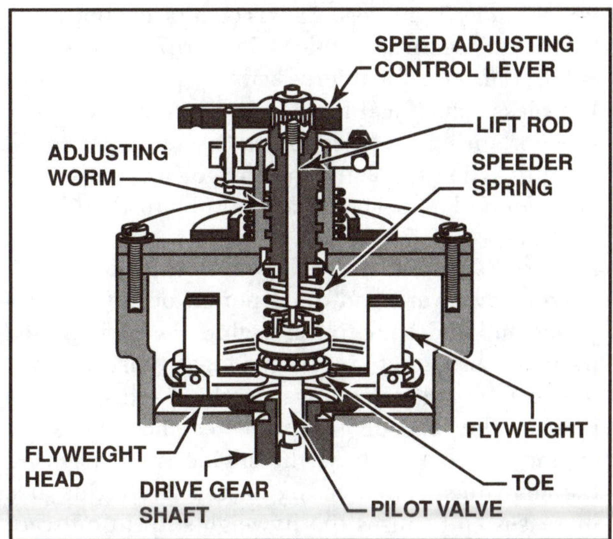

Figure 12-24. The flyweight assembly in a typical governor consists of a set of flyweights that are mounted to a flyweight head that is driven by the governor drive shaft. The pilot valve extends up through the drive shaft and rests on the toe of each flyweight so that, as the flyweights move, the pilot valve also moves. In addition, to allow the operator to select a blade angle, a speeder spring is provided so the amount of force acting on the flyweights and pilot valve can be adjusted.

When the engine is operating, the governor boost pump and flyweight assembly are driven by the governor drive shaft. When the propeller control in the cockpit is in the full forward, low pitch position, the speeder spring is fully compressed so that it holds the pilot valve down and allows no oil into the propeller hub. With no oil pressure acting on the pitch change mechanism in the propeller hub, centrifugal twisting force holds the blades in their low pitch position. This propeller setting is typically used during takeoff when the engine's maximum power output is needed.

When the propeller control in the cockpit is moved aft, speeder spring pressure is decreased and centrifugal force begins to tilt the flyweights outward. As the flyweights move outward, the pilot valve is pulled up and governor oil is directed to the propeller hub to increase the propeller blade angle. As the blade angle increases, engine rpm decreases causing a reduction in the amount of centrifugal force acting on the flyweights. This allows the flyweights to tilt inward and lower the pilot valve until the flow of oil to the propeller hub is cut off. At this point, speeder spring pressure and the centrifugal force acting on the flyweights are in balance and the governor is said to be on-speed.

Once a given rpm is selected, the governor automatically adjusts the propeller pitch to maintain the selected rpm. Therefore, any change in airspeed or load on the propeller results in a change in blade pitch. For example, if a climb is initiated from level flight, aircraft speed decreases and load on the propeller blades increases. As this occurs, engine speed begins to decrease which, in turn, reduces the amount of centrifugal force acting on the flyweights. With less centrifugal force acting on the flyweights, speeder spring pressure forces the flyweight to tilt inward. When this happens, the governor is said to be in an under-speed condition. [Figure 12-25]

As the flyweights move inward, the pilot valve moves downward and oil is ported out of the propeller hub and back to the engine. As oil is ported from the propeller hub, centrifugal twisting force moves the blades to a lower pitch. The lower pitch reduces the load on the propeller and allows the engine to accelerate. As the engine rpm increases, the centrifugal force acting on the flyweights also increases and causes the flyweights to tilt outward and return the governor to an on-speed condition.

This same process can be applied when airspeed increases or the load on the propeller decreases. However, in either of these situations, engine rpm increases causing the centrifugal force acting on the flyweights to increase. When this occurs, the flyweights tilt outward creating an over-speed condition. [Figure 12-26]

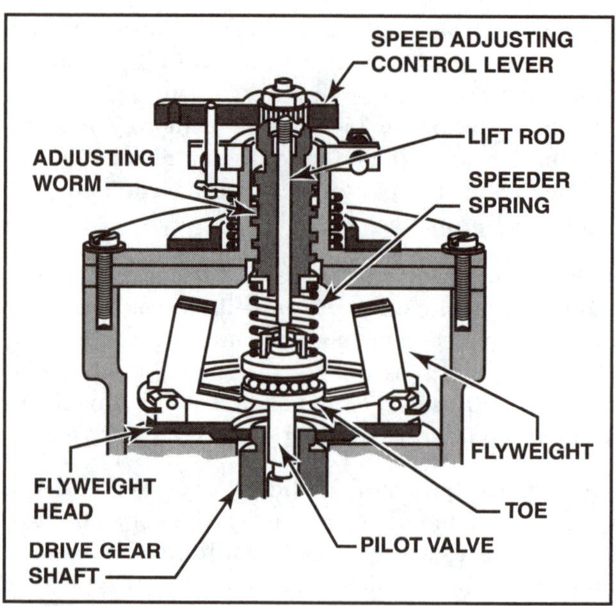

Figure 12-25. When a governor is in an under-speed condition, speeder spring pressure is greater than the centrifugal force and the flyweights tilt inward.

As the flyweights move outward, the pilot valve moves up and boost pump oil is directed to the propeller hub to increase blade pitch. The increased pitch increases the load on the propeller and slows the engine. As the engine rpm decreases, the centrifugal force acting on the flyweights also decreases and causes them to tilt in ward and return the governor to an on-speed condition.

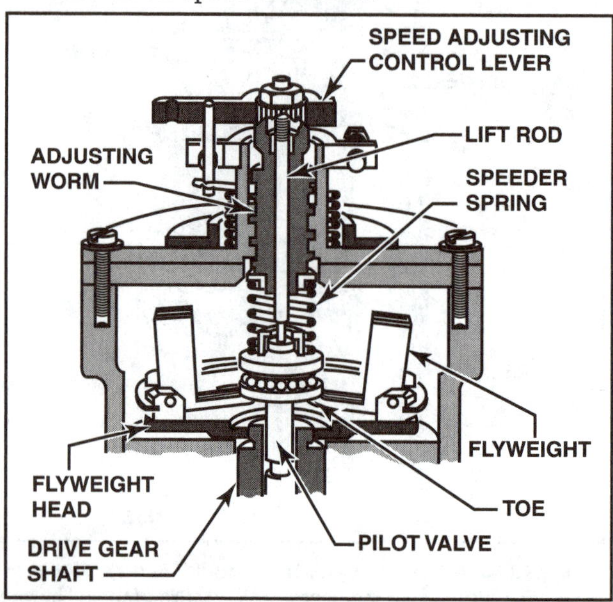

Figure 12-26. When a governor is in an over-speed condition, the centrifugal force acting on the flyweights overcomes the force of the speeder spring to tilt the flyweights outward.

Changes in throttle settings have the same effect on the governor as changes in airspeed and/or changes in propeller load. For example, advancing the throttle increases power output which, in turn, increases engine rpm. Therefore, to maintain the selected rpm, the governor must increase the propeller blade. By the same token, pulling the throttle back decreases power output and causes engine rpm to decrease. Therefore, in an attempt to maintain the original rpm setting, the governor must decrease the blade angle to unload the engine and propeller. One thing to keep in mind though is that, once the propeller blades reach the low pitch stop, the engine rpm will decrease with further power decreases.

As a safety feature to help protect the engine from over-speeding, all governors incorporate an adjustable stop screw that limits how low the blade pitch on a given constant-speed propeller can go. In addition, some governors incorporate a balance spring above the speeder spring that automatically sets the governor to produce a cruise rpm should the propeller control cable break.

McCAULEY CONSTANT-SPEED PROPELLERS

The McCauley constant-speed propeller system is one of the more popular systems used on light and medium size general aviation aircraft. For example, most Cessna aircraft that use a constant-speed propeller utilize a McCauley propeller system.

Currently, there are two types of constant-speed propellers that are installed on aircraft; the threaded series and the threadless series. Both use the same pitch change mechanism in the propeller hub; however, the method used to attach the propeller blades to the hub does differ. For example, a threaded series propeller uses a retention nut which screws into the propeller hub and holds the blades in the hub. This differs from the threadless-type blades which employ a split retainer ring to hold each blade in the hub. [Figure 12-27]

Both series of McCauley propellers are non-feathering and non-counterweighted. Therefore, oil

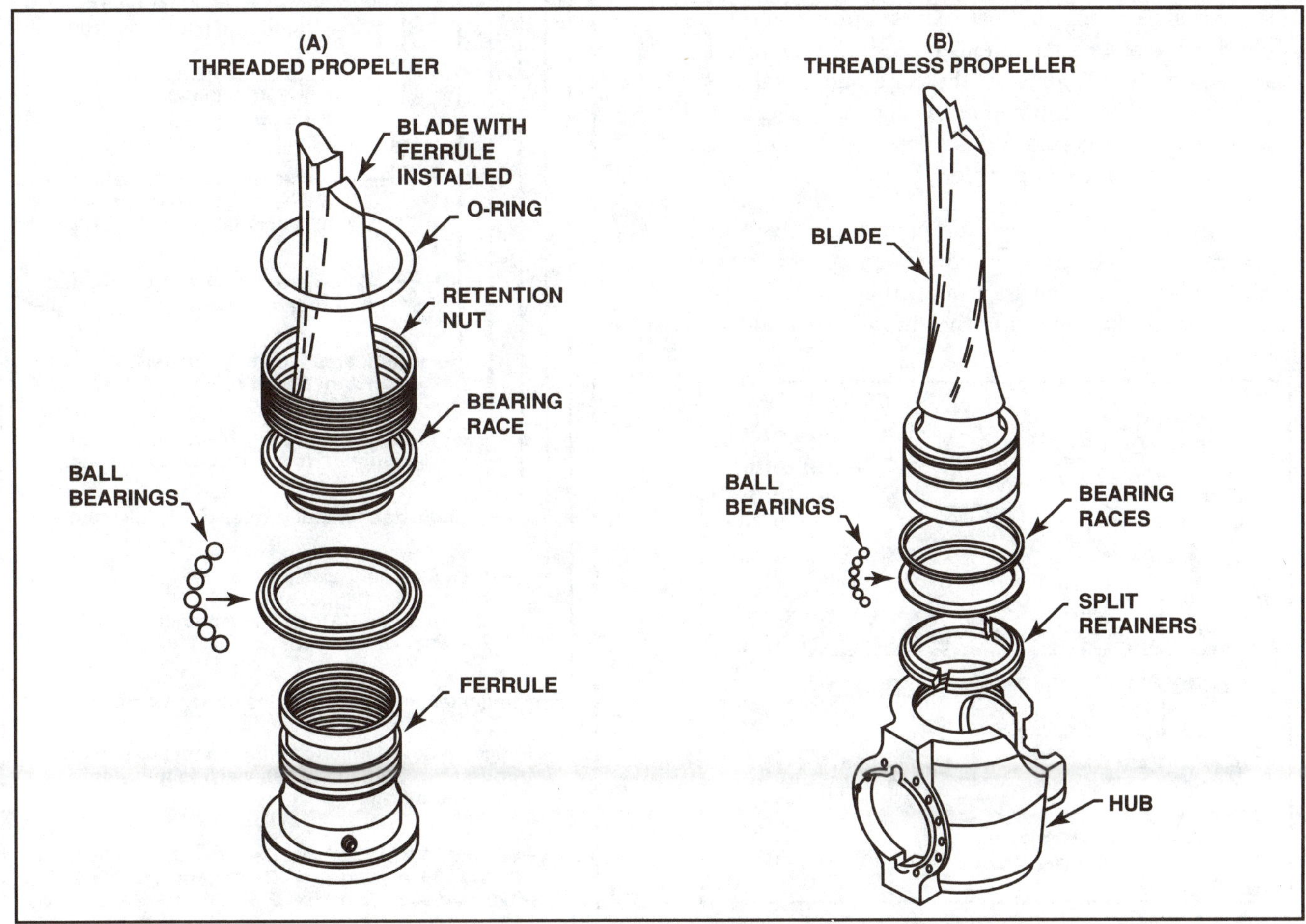

Figure 12-27. (A) — McCauley threaded blades use retention nuts and threaded ferrules to secure the propeller blades to the hub. (B) — The threadless design is the more modern of the two types of propeller blades and incorporates a split retainer ring to hold each propeller blade in place.

pressure is used to increase the propeller's blade angle while centrifugal twisting force and an internal spring are used to rotate the blades to low pitch. With this type of system, when a higher blade pitch is selected, high pressure oil is routed to the propeller hub where it pushes against a piston. Once the pressure builds enough to oppose the spring inside the hub and the centrifugal force exerted on the blades, the piston slides back toward the hub. This movement is transmitted to the propeller blades through blade actuating links to actuating pins located on each blade butt. [Figure 12-28]

The propeller blades, hub, and piston are made from an aluminum alloy. On the other hand, the propeller cylinder, blade actuating pins, piston rod, and spring are manufactured from either chrome or cadmium plated steel. To help prevent metal particles from wearing off the blade actuating links and becoming trapped inside the propeller hub, most actuating links are made of a phenolic material.

To prevent pitch change oil from leaking into the center of the propeller hub and down the propeller blade, O-ring seals are installed between the piston and the cylinder, the piston and the piston rod, and the piston rod and the hub. This way, the components making up the propeller's pitch-change mechanism can be lubricated with a grease and not depend on engine oil for lubrication during operation.

Some models of McCauley propellers use dyed oil permanently sealed in the hub. If red appears on the hub or blades, it is an indication that the hub may have a crack. In such case the propeller should be removed for repair.

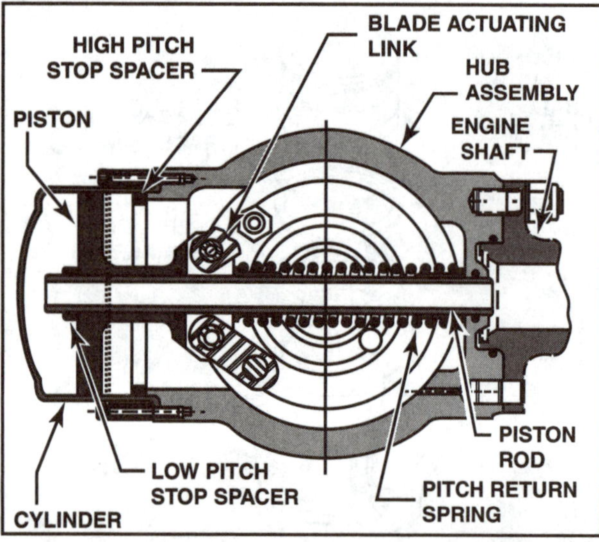

Figure 12-28. McCauley constant-speed propellers use oil pressure to increase the blade angle and a combination of centrifugal twisting force and spring pressure to decrease the blade angle.

Like other constant-speed propellers, the model designation codes of McCauley constant-speed propellers are longer to provide additional information. Important parts of the designation that you should be familiar with include the dowel pin location, the C-number, and the modification, or change letter, after the C-number. The modification or change designation indicates that a propeller complies with a required or recommended alteration. [Figure 12-29]

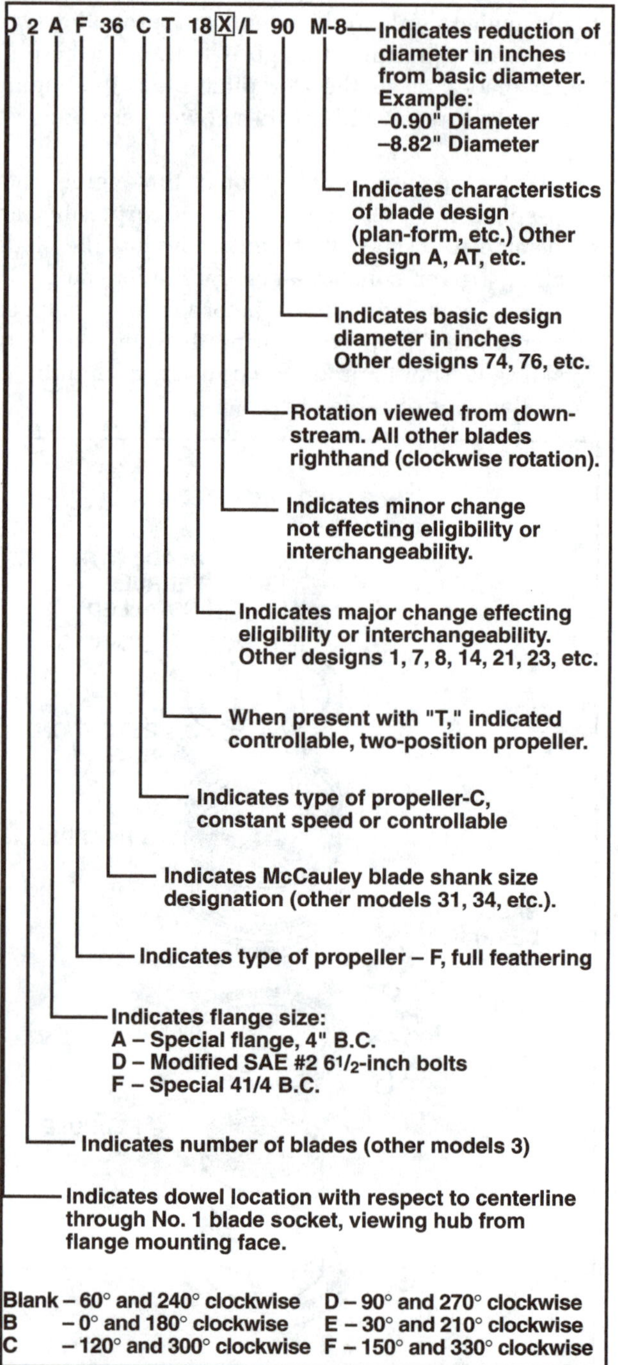

Figure 12-29. The McCauley designation system provides important information that must be known when determining which propeller will fit a specific aircraft.

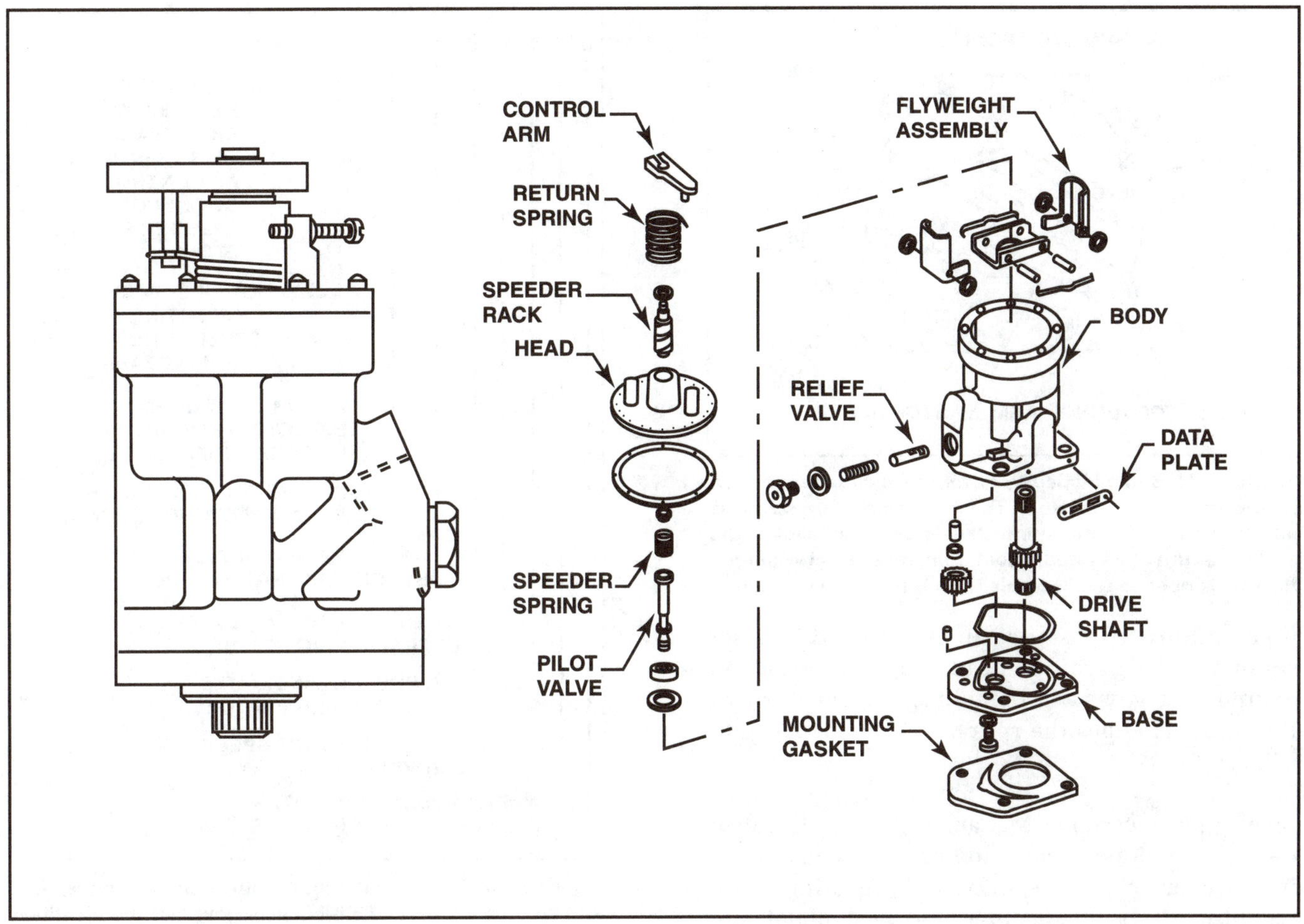

Figure 12-30. A McCauley non-feathering governor ports high pressure oil to the propeller hub to increase blade angle and releases oil pressure to decrease blade angle.

In addition to the designation code found on the propeller blades, several McCauley propeller hubs have a designation code of their own. In most cases, the code consists of two groupings of numbers that indicate the year the hub was manufactured and the number of hubs that were made in any one year. For example, a designation code of 72 1126 indicates that the hub was manufactured in 1972 and there were a total of 1,126 hubs made in that year.

McCAULEY GOVERNORS

McCauley governors use the same basic operating principles as the generic governors discussed earlier. That is, the governor directs high pressure oil to the propeller hub to increase the propeller blade angle. If you recall, this is directly opposite from the way the Hamilton-Standard system works. Another difference between the McCauley and Hamilton-Standard systems is that the McCauley governor produces an oil pressure of approximately 290 psi instead of the 180 to 200 psi Hamilton-Standard. [Figure 12-30]

Most McCauley governors use a control arm instead of a pulley to adjust the speeder spring pressure acting on the flyweights and pilot valve. The end of the control arm typically has between one and four holes that permit either a rigid control shaft, a flexible control cable, or a combination of the two to be connected to the arm.

For safety purposes, the governor control lever is spring-loaded to the high rpm setting. This way, if the propeller control cable breaks, the propeller blades will automatically go to low pitch allowing the engine to develop its maximum power output. As another safety feature, all McCauley governors incorporate a high rpm stop to prevent the engine and propeller from over-speeding. In some cases, a McCauley may also have an adjustable low rpm stop. Both the

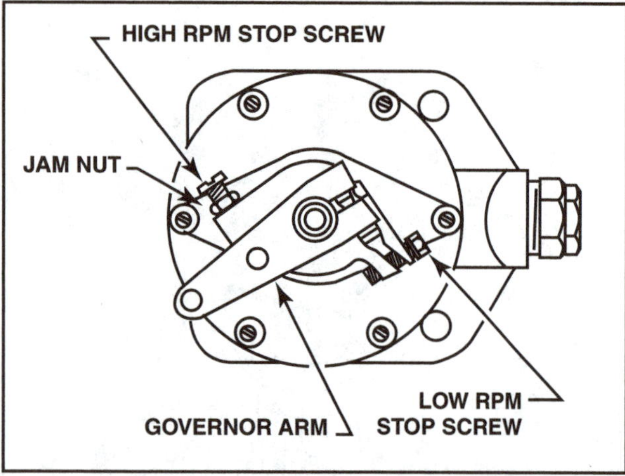

Figure 12-31. Some McCauley governors incorporate both a high and a low rpm stop. The high rpm screw is adjusted to set a minimum blade pitch that allows the engine to turn at its rated takeoff rpm at sea level when the throttle is opened to allowable takeoff manifold pressure.

high and low rpm stops can be adjusted by a set screw on the governor head. Depending on the engine and governor combination, one turn of the screw changes the rpm by 17, 20, or 25 rpm. [Figure 12-31]

Like other governors, McCauley governors utilize their own unique designation system. Some of the information provided in the designation code includes the specific features of a given model, any modifications that have been done, and ability to interchange the governor with another. For a full explanation of a given designation, it is best to consult a McCauley propeller maintenance manual. [Figure 12-32]

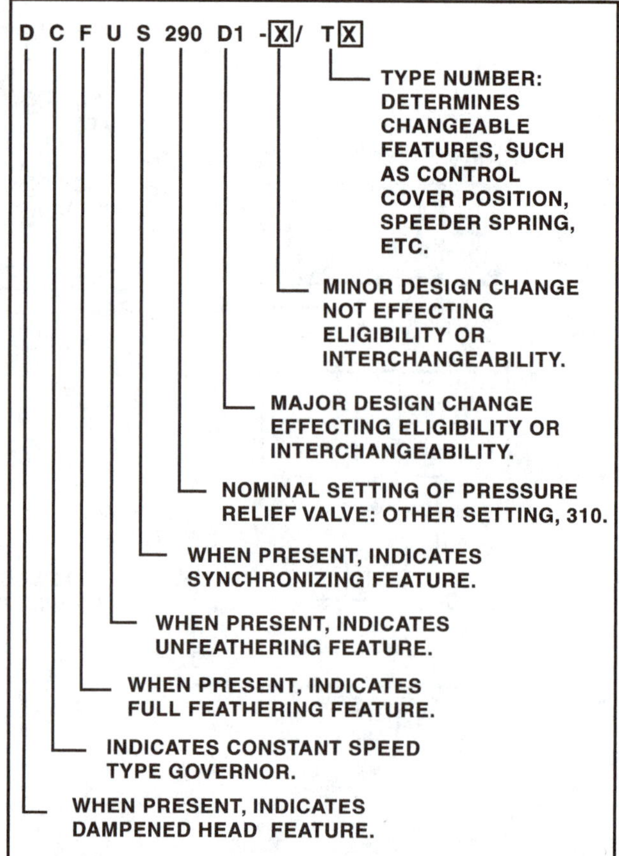

Figure 12-32. The model, modifications, interchangeability, and specific features of a McCauley governor are identified in the McCauley designation code.

HAMILTON-STANDARD CONSTANT-SPEED PROPELLERS

As propeller technology advanced, the two-position Hamilton-Standard counterweight propeller system was transformed into a constant-speed propeller system. To do this, a flyweight governor was developed and installed in place of a selector valve.

The propeller used with the Hamilton-Standard constant-speed system is essentially the same counterweight propeller used as the two-position propeller discussed earlier. However, since a counterweight propeller is used, oil pressure provides the force required to decrease blade angle while centrifugal force acting on the counterweights is used to increase the blade angle.

The governor used with a Hamilton-Standard constant-speed propeller is divided into three parts; the head, the body, and the base. The head contains the flyweights and flyweight assembly while the body and base house the pilot valve and boost pump.

In most cases, a Hamilton-Standard governor has a designation code that is stamped on the governor body. The designation system indicates the design of the head, body, and base. For example, a governor with a designation code of 1A3-B2H identifies a "1" head design, an "A" body design, and a "3" base. In addition, the "B2H" indicates the modifications made to the head, body, and base respectively.

HARTZELL CONSTANT-SPEED PROPELLERS

Hartzell constant-speed propeller systems are widely used in modern general aviation airplanes and share the market with McCauley. Currently, Hartzell produces two types of constant-speed propellers, a steel hub propeller and a Compact model. The Hartzell steel hub propeller is similar to the Hamilton-Standard constant-speed propeller in that the pitch change mechanism is exposed. On the

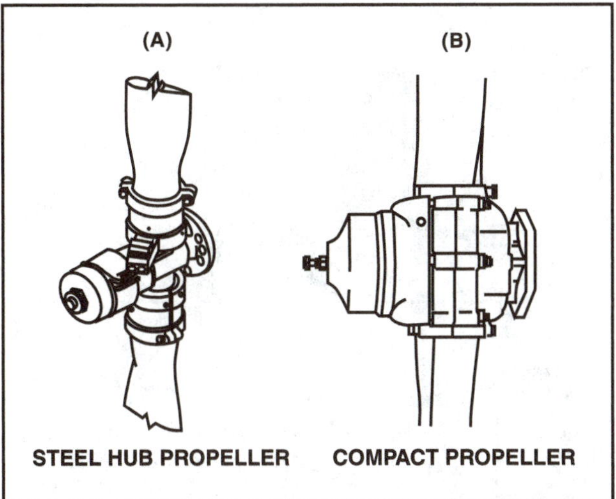

Figure 12-33. (A) — A Hartzell steel hub propeller has an exposed pitch-changing mechanism. (B) — On the other hand, the pitch changing mechanism on a Hartzell compact propeller is contained entirely within the hub.

other hand, the pitch change mechanism on a Hartzell compact propeller is housed inside the propeller head. [Figure 12-33]

Regardless of the type of hub used, Hartzell typically stamps a model designation code on both the propeller hub and the propeller blades. A typical designation system identifies the specific hub or blade model, any modifications that have been made, mounting type, and any specific features. [Figure 12-34]

STEEL HUB PROPELLERS

Hartzell steel hub propellers may or may not be counterweighed. If the propeller has counterweights, oil pressure is used to decrease blade angle while centrifugal force acting on the counterweights is used to increase blade angle. On the other hand, steel hub propellers that have no counterweights use oil pressure to increase blade angle and centrifugal twisting force to decrease the blade angle.

The central component of a Hartzell steel hub propeller is a steel spider. A typical spider consists of central hub and two arms. The two arms provide an attachment point for each propeller blade and house a bearing assembly that allows the blades to rotate. Once the blades are placed on the spider arms they are secured by two-piece steel clamps. to provide a means of changing pitch, a steel cylinder is threaded onto the front of the spider and an aluminum piston is placed over the cylinder. The piston is connected to the blade clamps on each

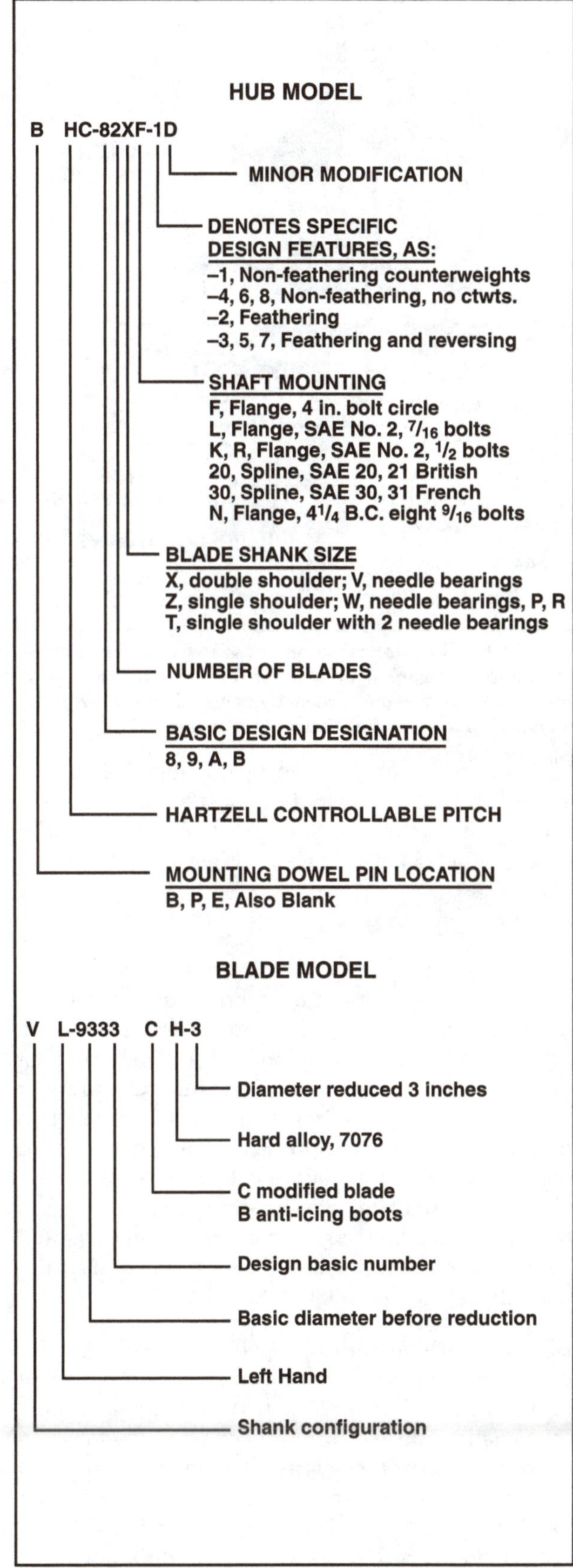

Figure 12-34. Hartzell constant-speed propellers carry two model designations numbers; one for the propeller hub and the other for the propeller blades.

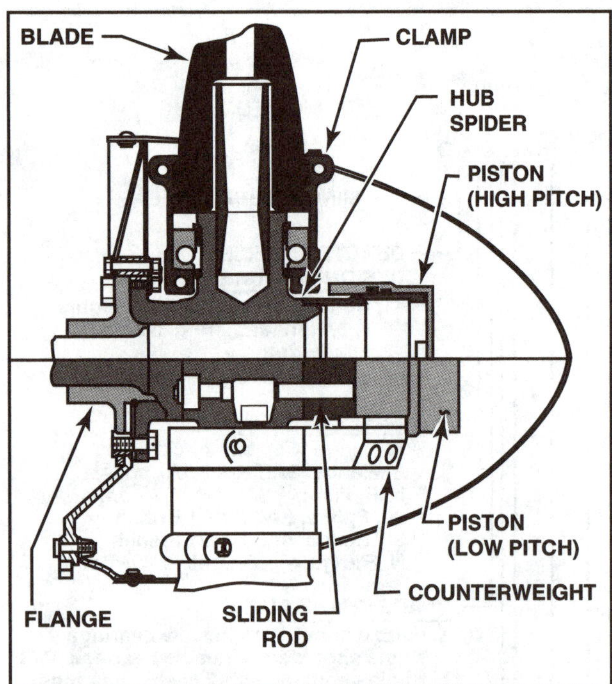

Figure 12-35. In a Hartzell constant-speed, counterweighted steel hub propeller, oil pressure forces an aluminum piston forward. This motion is then transmitted to the propeller blades through a sliding rod and fork system.

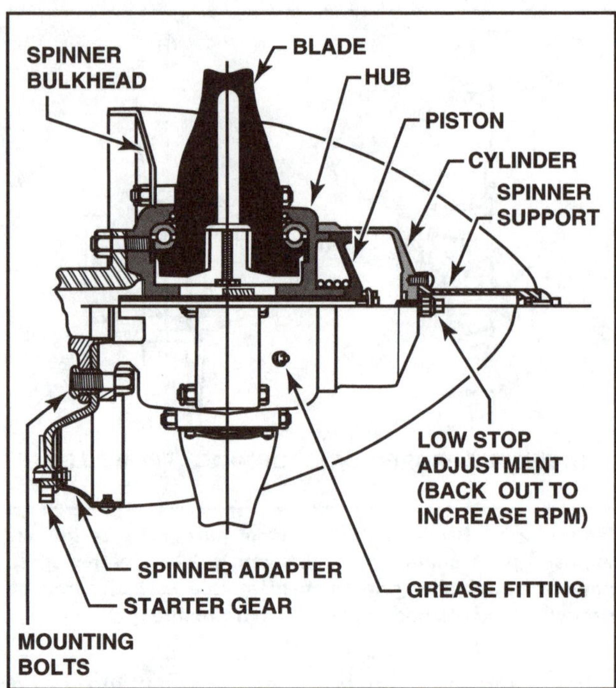

Figure 12-36. The aluminum hub of a compact propeller houses the entire pitch-change mechanism. Depending on the model, governor oil pressure may be used to increase or decrease blade angle.

blade by a sliding rod and fork system. This way, as oil is directed into and out of the propeller hub, the piston moves in and out and the propeller blades rotate as appropriate. [Figure 12-35]

COMPACT PROPELLERS

Hartzell compact propellers are more modern than steel hub propellers and incorporate several features that make the compact propeller hub smaller, lighter, and more dependable. A typical compact propeller hub is forged out of an aluminum alloy as two separate halves. Each half is machined out so that the shank of each propeller blade can be held between the two hub halves and so the entire pitch change mechanism can be contained. Once the blades and pitch changing mechanism are installed between the two hub halves, bolts are used to secure the halves together. [Figure 12-36]

Hartzell constant-speed propeller systems typically utilize either a Woodward governor or a modified Hamilton-Standard governor. Woodward governors are usually adjusted to produce approximately 275 psi of oil pressure when installed on an engine with a normal engine oil pressure of 60 psi. On the other hand, if a modified Hartzell governor is used, the output pressure does vary between different models. Therefore, to determine the pressure setting for a given Hartzell governor, you must refer to the appropriate Hartzell maintenance manual.

Like other governors, Hartzell propeller governors utilize their own unique designation systems. For example, a typical Hartzell designation code consists of a three-character code that designates the governors basic body style and major modifications, any major adjustments that were made to make it compatible with a specific system, and any minor adjustments that were made that do not affect eligibility. [Figure 12-37]

FEATHERING PROPELLERS

When an engine fails in flight, the propeller continues to **windmill**, or turn, slowly as air flows over the blades. This creates a considerable amount of drag that can adversely effect an aircraft's flight characteristics. To help eliminate the drag created by a windmilling propeller, design engineers developed a way to rotate the propeller blades to a 90 degree angle. This is known as feathering a propeller and eliminates the drag created by a windmilling propeller because it presents the smallest blade profile to the oncoming airstream. Today, all modern multi-engine, propeller-driven aircraft are equipped with feathering propellers. [Figure 12-38]

The operating principles discussed previously for constant-speed propellers also apply to feathering propeller systems. However, the propeller control

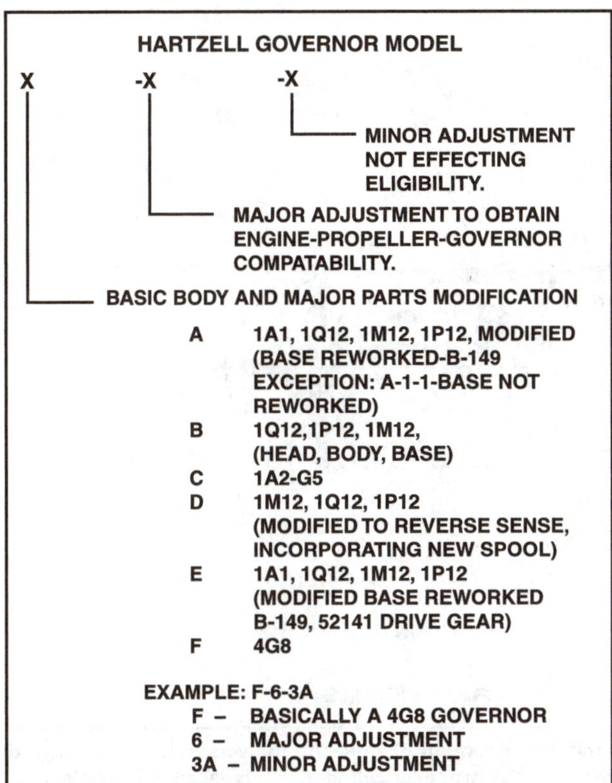

Figure 12-37. In the sample designation above, an F-6-3A propeller governor consists of a 4G8 governor with a major adjustment to obtain compatibility and a minor adjustment not effecting eligibility.

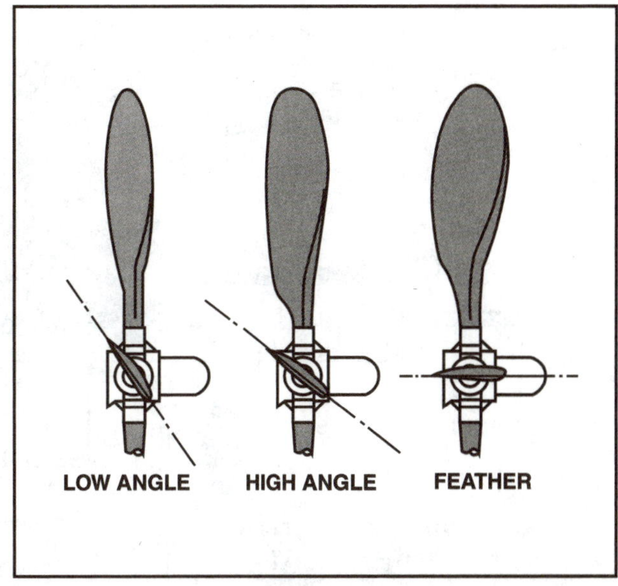

Figure 12-38. When a propeller is feathered, the blades are rotated beyond their normal high angle to an angle that is approximately 90 degrees to the plane of propeller rotation. This presents the smallest possible blade profile to the airstream and decreases aerodynamic drag.

lever in the cockpit typically incorporates an additional position that, when selected, rotates the propeller blades to their feathered position. In most cases, the propeller control is pulled all the way aft to feather the blades. If a propeller is feathered from a low blade angle, the blades will move from a low angle through a high angle before they reach their feathered position. On the other hand, if a propeller is feathered from a high blade angle, the blades will move from their high pitch setting directly into the feathered position.

On most aircraft, feathering functions are independent of constant-speed operation. In other words, the operator can override a constant-speed system to feather the propeller at any time. In fact, in some systems the propeller can be feathered without engine rotation.

Most manufacturers of constant-speed propellers also build feathering propellers. However, to help simplify this discussion only the Hartzell compact feathering propeller and the Hamilton-Standard hydromatic propeller will be discussed in detail.

HARTZELL COMPACT FEATHERING PROPELLERS

The constant-speed operation of a Hartzell compact feathering propeller is the same as the constant-speed model with one difference; the feathering propeller uses both governor oil pressure and centrifugal twisting force to rotate the blades to low pitch while some combination of a high-pressure nitrogen charge, an internal spring, or counterweights are used to increase blade angle. For example, one type of Hartzell compact feathering propeller utilizes a high-pressure nitrogen charge and a mechanical spring to increase blade angle and to feather the blades. The nitrogen charge is stored in the cylinder head and works in conjunction with a spring that is also contained within the propeller hub.

Another model of Hartzell compact propeller uses a combination of air pressure and centrifugal force acting on counterweights to feather and increase the angle of the propeller blades. With this type of propeller, the high-pressure nitrogen charge is again stored in the propeller hub while a counter-

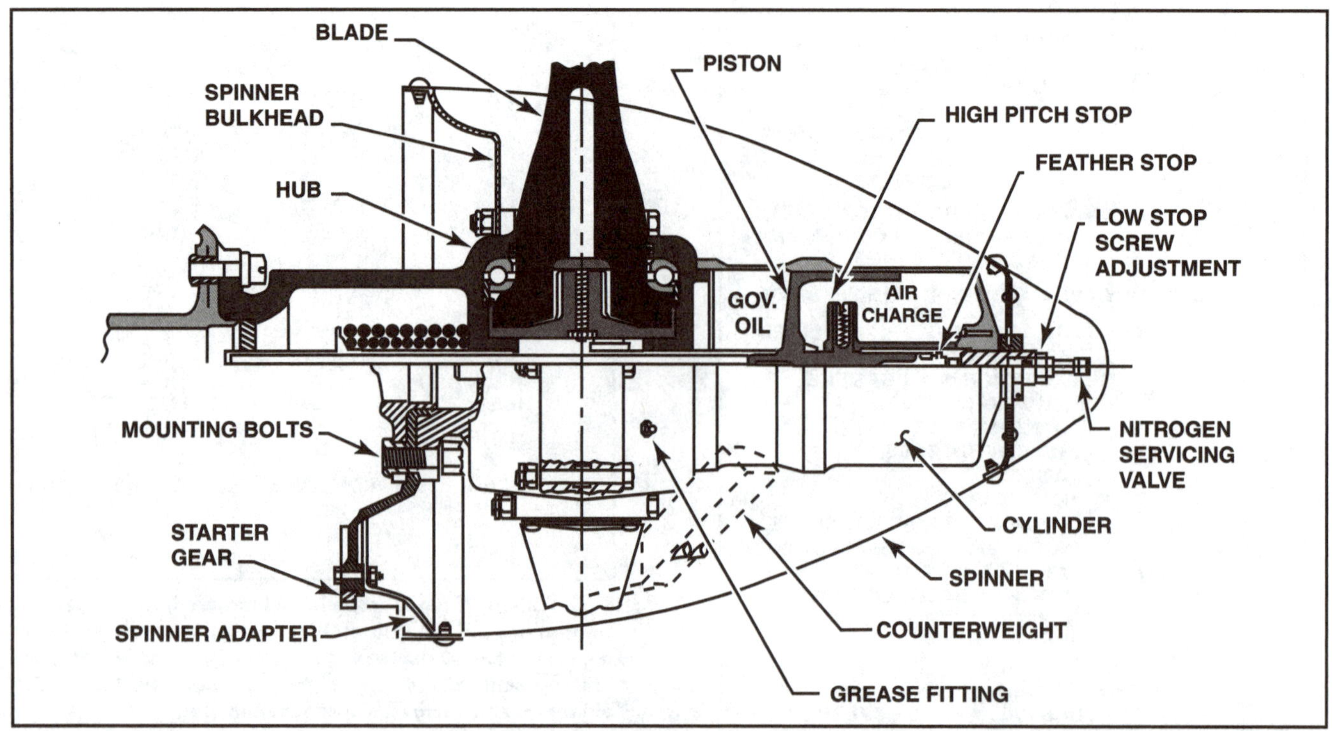

Figure 12-39. The Hartzell compact feathering propeller depicted above relies on governor oil pressure to decrease blade angle and a combination of blade mounted counterweights and compressed nitrogen in the propeller cylinder to increase blade angle.

weight is mounted to the base of each propeller blade. [Figure 12-39]

A safety feature inherent to both of these designs is that, if governor oil pressure drops to zero for any reason, the propeller automatically begins to move to the feathered position. This feature helps prevent further damage to the engine from a windmilling propeller and lowers aerodynamic drag on the aircraft.

To prevent the propeller from feathering when the engine is shut down on the ground, most Hartzell compact propellers utilize a latch stop called an **automatic high pitch stop**. The latch mechanism is comprised of spring-loaded latches fastened to the stationary hub which engage high-pitch stop-plates bolted to the movable blade clamps. As long as the propeller rotates faster than 800 rpm, centrifugal force allows the pins to overcome spring pressure and disengage the latches from the high-pitch stop-plates so that the propeller pitch may be increased to the feathering position. However, when the propeller is rotating below 800 rpm, the latch springs engage the latches with the high-pitch stops and prevent the propeller blade angle from increasing.

To feather a Hartzell compact feathering propeller, the propeller control is placed in the feather position. This action dumps all the oil pressure from the hub so the nitrogen charge and either spring pressure or centrifugal force can rotate the blades to the feather position. The speed at which the blades rotate to the feather position depends on how fast the oil drains from the propeller hub and the amount of force exerted by the nitrogen charge and either spring pressure or centrifugal force. Based on this, a typical Hartzell propeller takes between 3 and 10 seconds to feather.

Unfeathering is accomplished by repositioning the propeller control to the normal flight range and restarting the engine. As soon as the engine begins to turn over, the governor starts to unfeather the blades. Once partially unfeathered, the propeller will start windmilling and accelerate the unfeathering process. In order to facilitate engine cranking with the blades feathered, the feathering blade angle is set at 80 to 85 degrees at the 3/4 point on the blade. This allows the oncoming air to assist the engine starter. In general, restarting and unfeathering can be accomplished within a few seconds.

On aircraft where engine starting may be difficult, the propeller system may incorporate an accumulator in the governor to speed up the unfeathering process. The **accumulator** stores a quantity of oil under pressure until it is needed to unfeather the

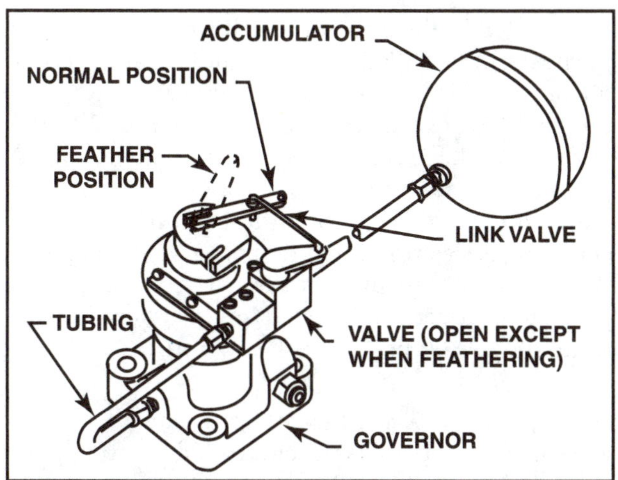

Figure 12-40. Some Hartzell and McCauley propellers use a hydraulic accumulator to unfeather the propeller in flight. The accumulator enables the governor to provide pressurized oil for unfeathering the propeller blades enough so the propeller can windmill.

propeller. In some cases, an accumulator allows the operator to unfeather the propeller prior to propeller rotation. [Figure 12-40]

A typical accumulator consists of a spherical container that is separated into two chambers by a diaphragm. One side of the accumulator is charged with nitrogen while the other is filled with oil. During normal engine and propeller operation, the oil side of the accumulator is open to the flow of pressurized oil and, therefore, the chamber fills with pressurized oil. When the propeller control is moved to the feather position, an accumulator valve closes and traps oil in the accumulator. This way, when the propeller control is moved out of the feather position, the accumulator valve is opened so the pressurized oil within the accumulator can flow to the propeller hub. Once the oil reaches the hub, it pushes on the piston enough to begin moving the propeller blades out of the feathered position.

HAMILTON-STANDARD HYDROMATIC PROPELLER

The second type of feathering propeller that will be discussed in detail is the Hamilton-Standard hydromatic propeller. This type of propeller is commonly found on medium and large radial engine transport aircraft built during the WWII era and, although they are not used much today, you should be familiar with its operating principles.

A typical non-reversing, full-feathering, Hamilton-Standard Hydromatic propeller is made up of three major assemblies, the hub, or barrel, assembly; the dome assembly; and the distributor valve. All three of these assemblies work as a single unit to permit constant-speed operation of the propeller. [Figure 12-41]

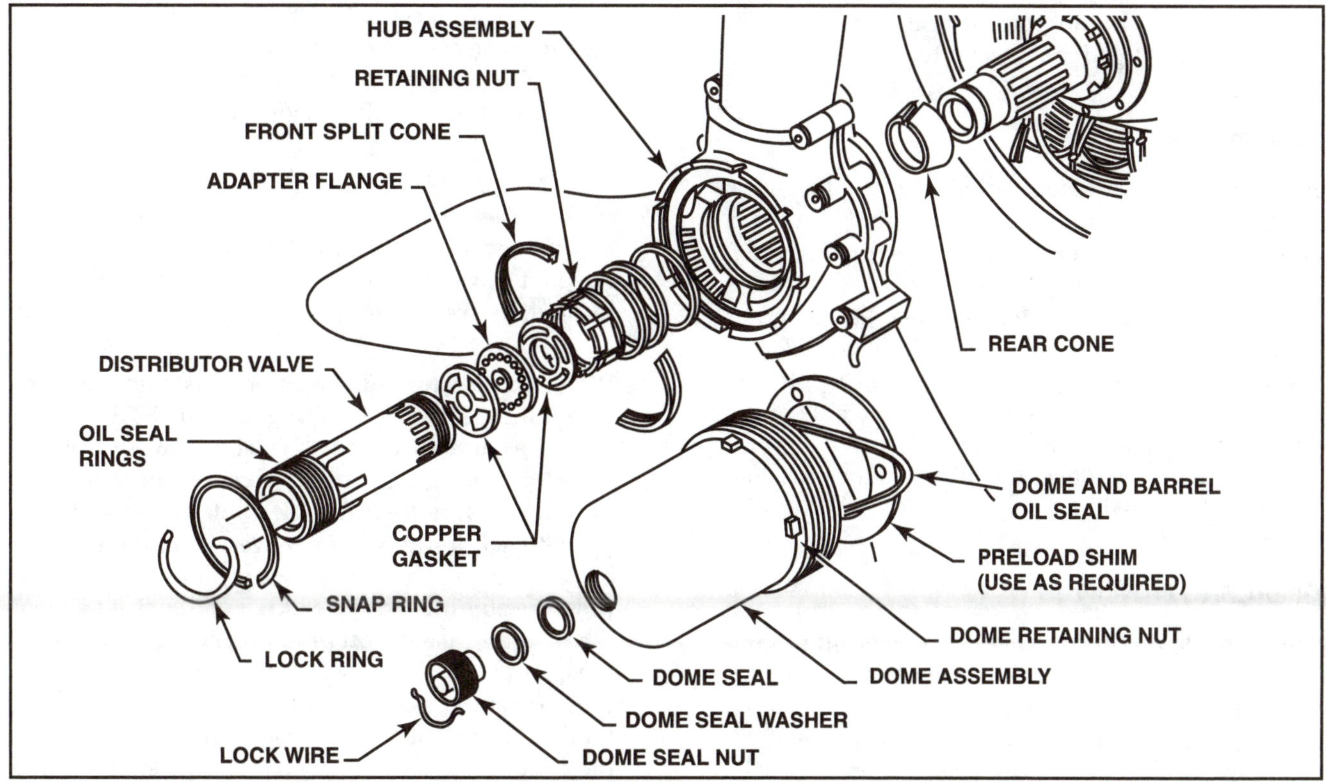

Figure 12-41. A Hamilton Standard Hydromatic propeller is made up of three major assemblies; the hub assembly, the dome assembly, and the distributor valve.

The hub assembly consists of two halves that house a spider and the propeller blades. The propeller blades used with a hydromatic propeller differ from those used in other constant-speed propellers in that the butt of each blade consists of a sector gear that meshes with pitch changing gear in the dome assembly. Each blade slips onto an arm on the spider and then the spider/blade assembly is placed between the two hub halves. To allow each blade to rotate freely within the hub, as well as hold the blades in place, a combination of bearings and spacers are installed between the blade butt and the hub.

The dome assembly houses the primary components of the pitch-change mechanism including a piston, a rotating cam, and a fixed cam. When the dome assembly is threaded into the propeller hub, oil pressure acts on the piston to move it fore and aft within the dome. As the piston moves, a set of cam rollers mounted to the piston engage the rotating cam causing it to turn within the fixed cam. Attached to the rear of the rotating cam is a beveled gear that engages each of the propeller blades so that, as the cam rotates, the blade angle of each propeller blade also changes.

The distributor valve acts as an extension to the engine's crankshaft and is installed in the center of the dome assembly. The purpose of the distributor valve is to direct both governor oil and engine oil into and out of the dome assembly.

GOVERNORS

A Hydromatic governor includes all of the basic governor components of the Hamilton-Standard constant-speed governor previously described. However, Hydromatic governors also contain a high pressure transfer valve that disables the governor constant-speed functions when the propeller is feathered or unfeathered. In addition, an electric pressure cutout switch is located on the side of the governor. The cutout switch automatically stops oil pressure delivery once the blades have reached their full-feathered position.

OPERATING PRINCIPLES

The hydromatic propeller differs from other constant-speed propellers in that no springs or counterweights are used to change blade angle. Instead, engine oil pressure acts on one side of the piston while governor oil pressure acts on the opposite side. Depending on the propeller model, governor oil pressure can be directed to either the inboard or outboard side of the piston. For the purposes of this discussion, assume that governor oil pressure is applied to the inboard side of the piston while engine oil pressure is applied to the outboard side. In this configuration, governor oil pressure is used to increase propeller blade angle while engine oil pressure in combination with centrifugal twisting force decrease blade angle. A typical engine oil pressure is between 60 and 90 psi while governor boosted oil pressure ranges from 200 to 300 psi.

During constant-speed operations, the routing of governor oil pressure is controlled by the pilot valve in the governor. For example, if the load on the propeller or aircraft speed increases, the propeller will begin to rotate faster creating an overspeed condition. When this occurs, centrifugal force tilts the flyweights outward, raising the pilot valve. With the pilot valve raised, governor boosted oil pressure is routed to the backside of the piston. At the same time, the oil in front of the piston is routed through the distributor valve and back to the inlet side of the governor. The difference in oil pressure between the front and back sides of the piston cause the piston to move forward. As the piston moves, it causes the cam rollers to move forward. Since the cam rollers engage a set of slots in the rotating cam, movement of the cam rollers causes the rotating cam to turn. As the rotating cam turns, the beveled gear on the back of the cam engage the gears affixed to the blades and rotate the blades to a higher pitch. [Figure 12-42]

As the blade angle increases, system rpm decreases and the flyweights begin to tilt back inward to lower the pilot valve. As this happens, the piston stops moving and the system returns to an on-speed condition.

When an underspeed condition exists, the amount of centrifugal force acting on the flyweights decreases and allows the flyweights to tilt inward. When this occurs, the pilot valve lowers and governor oil pressure from the back side of the piston is ported back to the governor were it is then routed back to the engine. At the same time, engine oil pressure continues to be exerted on the front side of the piston. Once the oil pressure on the back side of the piston decreases below that of the engine oil pressure and the centrifugal twisting force acting on the blades, the piston and cam rollers move aft. As the cam rollers move aft, the rotating cam is turned the opposite direction causing the propeller blade angle to decrease. [Figure 12-43]

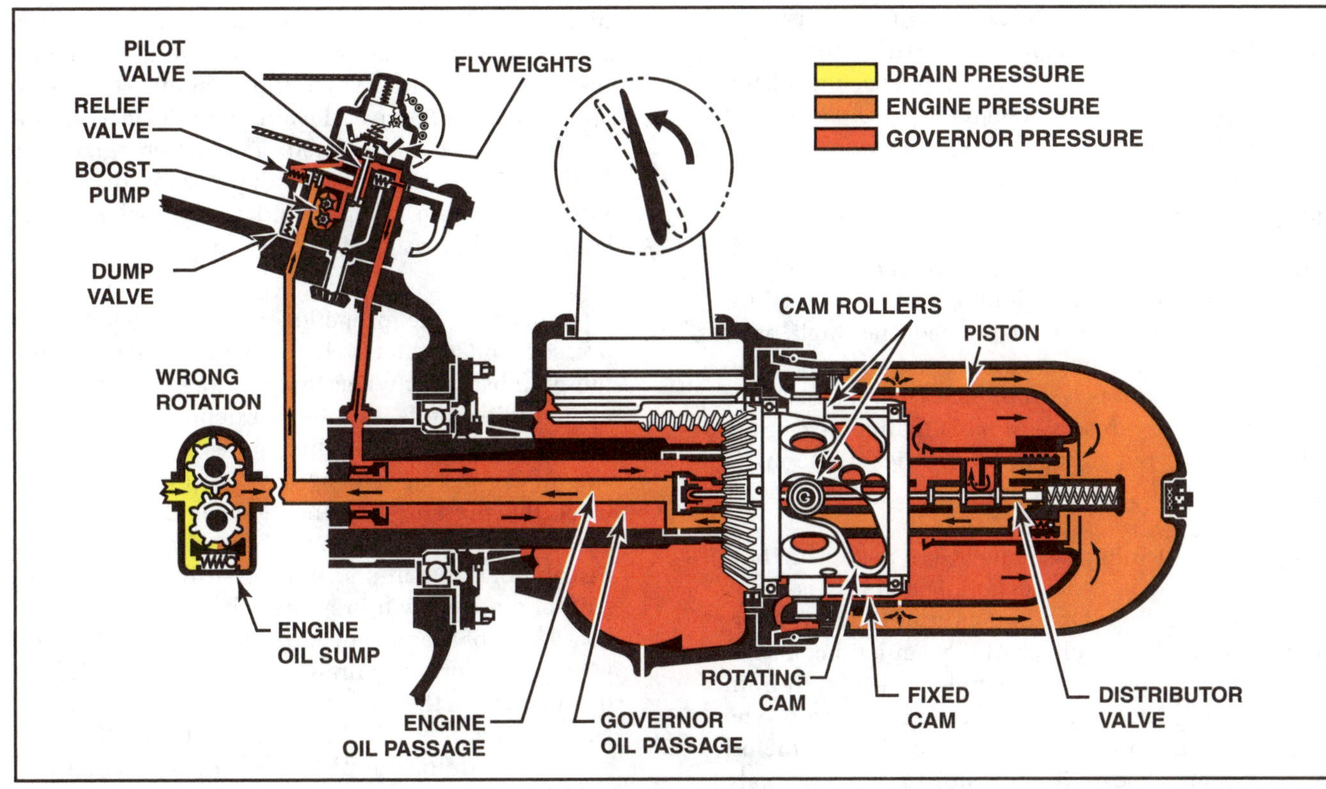

Figure 12-42. In an overspeed condition, governor oil pressure forces the piston in the dome assembly forward. When this happens, the cam rollers also move forward causing the rotating cam to turn. As the rotating cam turns, the beveled gear attached to the back of the cam engages the sector gears on the propeller blades and rotates the blades to a higher angle.

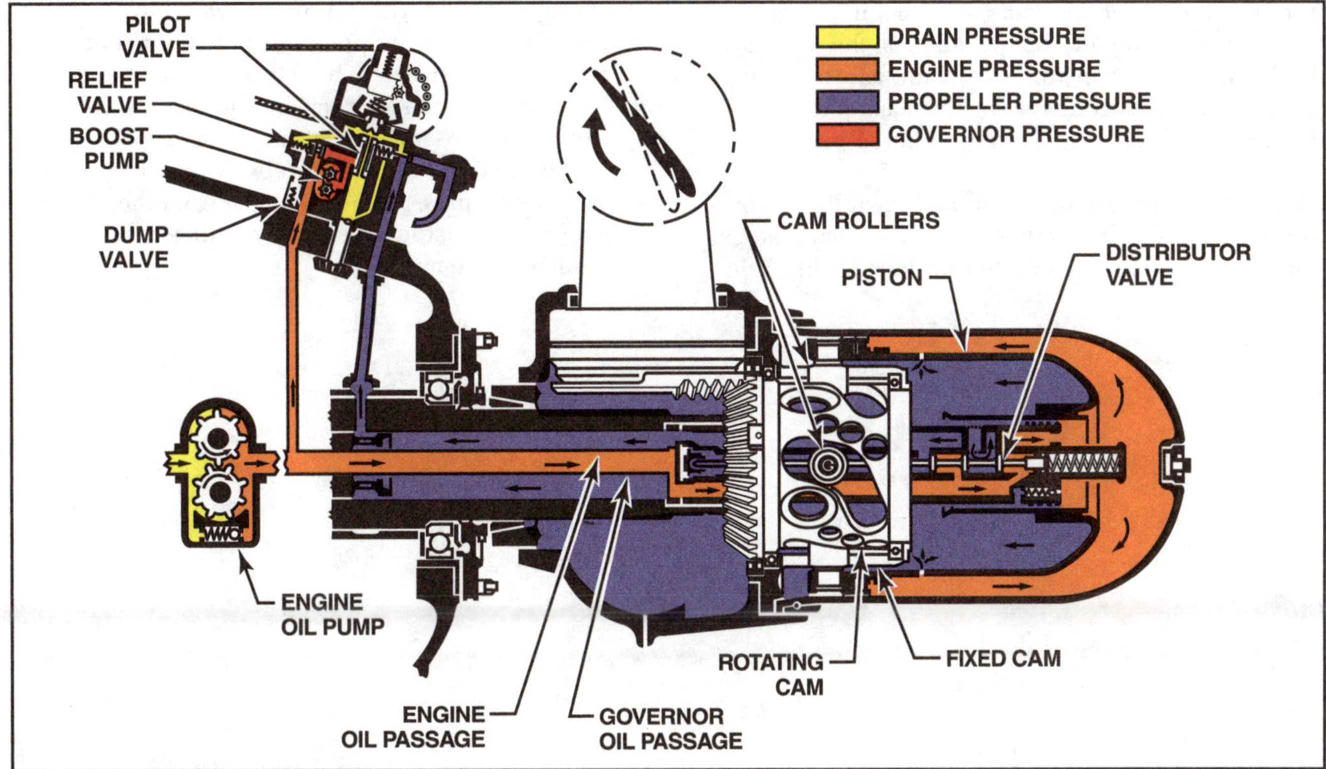

Figure 12-43. In an underspeed condition, governor oil pressure is ported back to the engine through the governor. Once the pressure behind the piston decreases below the engine oil pressure, the piston moves aft. As the piston moves aft, the rotating cam turns and drives the propeller blades to a lower blade angle.

As the blade angle decreases, system rpm increases and the flyweights begin to tilt back outward to raise the pilot valve. As this happens, the piston stops moving and the system returns to an on-speed condition.

FEATHERING

Unlike most other feathering propellers that rely on counterweights, springs, and/or compressed nitrogen, the hydromatic propeller requires high pressure oil to feather the blades. Therefore, in order to help ensure there is a supply of oil and a means of pressurizing it, a reserve of oil is maintained in the oil reservoir and a separate electric oil pump is installed in the propeller system.

To begin the feathering sequence, a feathering button is depressed in the cockpit. When this is done, a holding coil holds the button in until the feathering sequence is complete. At the same time, a solenoid relay is energized to complete the circuit from the aircraft battery to the feathering motor. The feathering pump draws the reserve oil from the oil reservoir and boosts its pressure to approximately 600 psi. From the pump, the oil is routed to the governor where it shifts a high-pressure transfer valve. Once the valve shifts, the governor is effectively disconnected from the system and auxiliary oil passes through the governor and governor oil passage to the inboard side of the piston. As the pressure builds behind the piston, the piston and cam rings move outward causing the rotating cam to turn until the propeller blades reach the feathered position.

When the rotating cam contacts the high pitch stop, the blades are fully feathered and the piston stops moving. At this point, the oil pressure behind the piston starts to build rapidly. The increasing pressure is sensed by the oil pressure cutout switch on the governor and, when the pressure builds to approximately 650 psi, the circuit to the feather button holding coil is opened. This de-energizes the feather relay and shuts off the electric oil pump. With the engine stopped and the propeller feathered, the oil pressure drops to zero.

To unfeather the propeller, the feather button is pressed and manually held in to prevent it from popping back out when the pressure cutout switch opens. With the feather button depressed, the electric oil pump starts pumping more oil to the inboard side of the piston causing the pressure to increase. Once the pressure becomes greater than the combined spring pressure and oil pressure holding the distributor valve in place, the distributor valve will shift and allow high pressure oil to flow to the outboard side of the piston. At the same time, a passage is provided for oil to drain from the inboard side of the piston to the governor inlet and back to the engine. The pressure differential between the front and back side of the piston moves the piston and cam rollers inboard causing the blades to rotate to a lower blade angle. [Figure 12-44]

Once the blade angle is decreased, the propeller starts to windmill, allowing the engine to be restarted. At this point, the feather button is released and the system returns to constant-speed operation. If the feather button is not released, excess oil pressure actuates a dome relief valve in the distributor valve. The relief valve off-seats and releases oil pressure over 750 psi from the outboard side of the piston when the rotating cam contacts the low blade angle stop.

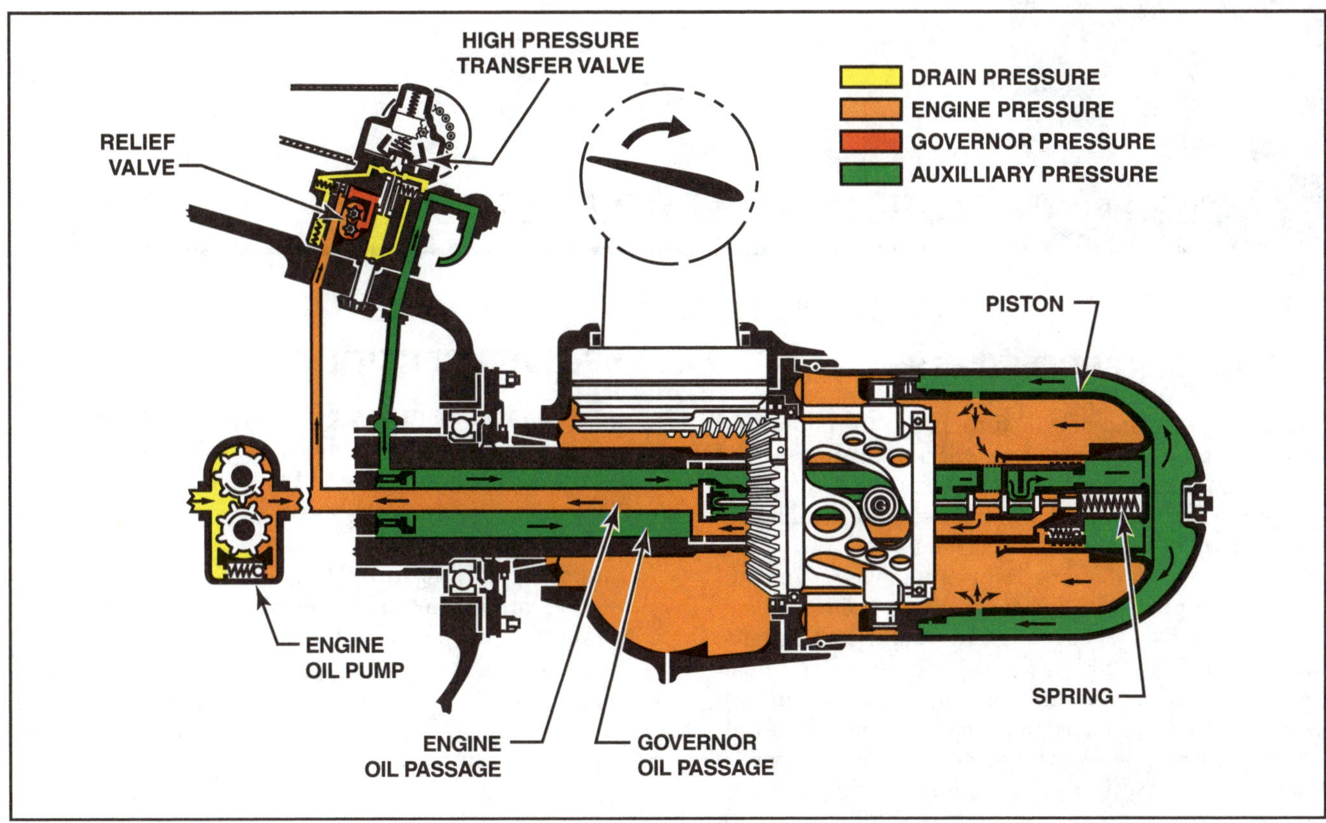

Figure 12-44. To unfeather a Hydromatic propeller, high pressure oil bypasses the governor and forces the distributor valve over so the oil is directed to the outboard side of the piston. At the same time, a passage is provided for oil to drain from the inboard side of the piston.

TURBOPROP PROPELLERS

OPERATING PRINCIPLES

Since the advent of the turboprop, propeller and engine manufacturer's have worked together to create new designs and manufacturing techniques to improve the reliability and efficiency in which propellers operate with turbine engines. Today, this effort has led to the creation of a wide assortment of turboprop propeller designs that are used on many aircraft ranging from relatively small, single-engine utility airplanes, to large multi-engine transport category airplanes. In this section, basic design and operational characteristics that are common to all turboprop engines will be discussed. Furthermore, a detailed description of a common turboprop propeller system as it is used on two different turboprop engines will be looked at in detail. By realizing the methods in which this propeller system operates, you will be able to understand the basic operating principles of most types of turboprop propeller systems.

PROPELLER SPEED REDUCTION

Although reciprocating and turboprop engine propeller systems share many similarities, there are distinct differences between the two. Most of these differences are the result of the operational differences between reciprocating and turboprop engines. For example, since turboprop engines operate at high rotational speeds, all turboprop designs must incorporate a reduction gear assembly that can convert the engine's high speed, low torque rotational speed to a more usable low speed and high torque. Although there are reduction gear assemblies used on some reciprocating engines, a turboprop reduction gear system must perform under more extreme operational conditions. For example, it is not uncommon for a turboprop to operate at rotational speeds in excess of 40,000 rpm. These speeds are far in excess of the 2,200 rpm that most turboprop propellers operate and, therefore, all turboprop engines must incorporate a reduction gear assembly.

POWER SECTIONS

The combination of a turboprop engine's reduction gear assembly and propeller is often referred to as the power section. Currently, there are two methods used to drive a turboprop's power section. In one design, the power section is driven directly by an integral turbine through a fixed shaft. In the other application, the power section is driven by a separate **free**, or **power turbine** that is not mechanically connected to the gas generator portion of the engine. In this case, the term power section generally refers to the power turbine, reduction gearbox, and the propeller. [Figure 12-45]

PROPELLER GOVERNING

All turboprop engines utilize constant-speed, feathering propellers. In addition, the propellers used are all controlled by one or more governors. As a general rule, turboprop engines use the same governing principles to control propeller pitch and maintain a constant rpm. However, propeller pitch changes are used more extensively with turboprop engines to produce changes in thrust. One reason this is necessary is because, unlike a reciprocating engine, a turboprop engine takes more time to react to fuel flow and power changes. With this delayed reaction time, turboprop aircraft cannot use varying engine rpm to effectively control the aircraft on the ground. Therefore, to facilitate ground handling characteristics, the gas generator speed is held relatively constant while propeller pitch is varied as necessary to produce the desired amount of thrust.

REVERSIBLE-PITCH PROPELLERS

In addition to providing constant-speed and feathering operations, most turboprop propellers are reversible. A reversing propeller is essentially a variable pitch, constant-speed propeller that is capable of operating with the propeller blades rotated beyond the normal low pitch limits. By allowing the propeller blades to rotate to a negative blade angle, the propeller's thrust is directed forward instead of

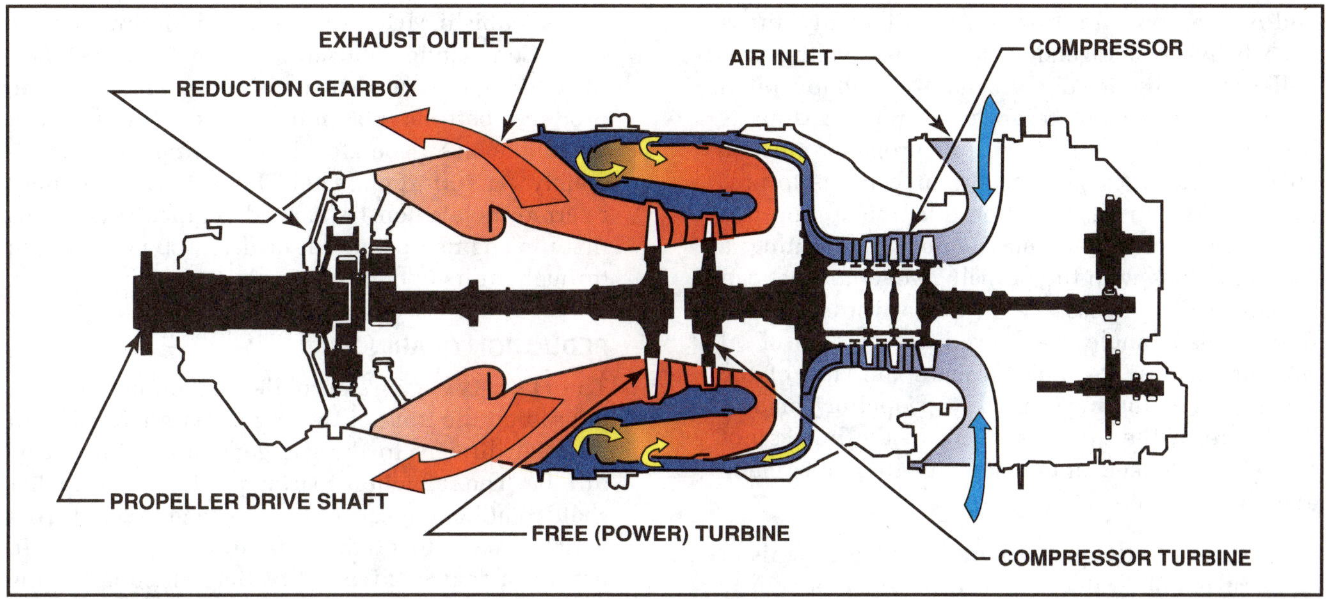

Figure 12-45. One of the most popular turboprop engines in use today is a free turbine design that houses the reduction gear assembly in the front section of the engine.

aft. This greatly reduces an aircraft's landing distance by producing reverse thrust similar to that of a thrust reverser installed on a turbojet or turbofan engine. As an added benefit, a reversing propeller also allows the aircraft operator to better control taxi speeds and back the aircraft up. These benefits ultimately improve an aircraft's landing performance as well as its maneuverability on the ground.

When a reversible propeller is operated in the standard, constant-speed mode, it is said to be operated in its **Alpha range**. On the other hand, when the blades are rotated so they produce zero or negative thrust, the propeller is being operated in its **Beta range**. On some aircraft, the Beta range may be divided into two ranges: a **Beta for taxi range** and a **Beta plus power range**. The Beta for taxi range includes the blade angles that fall between the bottom of the Alpha range to a blade angle that produces zero thrust. This range of blade angles is used primarily for taxiing and allows the gas generator to operate at a high rpm while limiting the amount of thrust being produced by the propellers. This allows the aircraft operator to better control the aircraft's speed on the ground without causing excessive wear to the braking system. On most engines with a Beta for taxi range, the power lever must be moved back past a detent below the flight idle position.

The Beta plus power range represents the range of blade angles that produce negative thrust. This range is primarily used when an aircraft must be landed in a short distance. When in the Beta plus power range, power lever movement also controls the amount of fuel that flows to the engine. In other words, the farther back you move the power lever, the greater the engine power output and the more reverse thrust produced. On most aircraft, the Beta plus power range is obtained by pulling the power lever back beyond the Beta for taxi range until the reversing range is reached. To help you identify the reversing range, the power lever quadrant is generally either striped or a placard is provided.

When operating an aircraft with reversible propellers, some cautions must be observed. For example, since a reversible propeller tends to stir up debris in front of the aircraft, it is possible for rocks or other foreign objects to be ingested into the engine or damage the propeller blades. Therefore, as a general rule, propeller reversing should only be accomplished on smooth, clean surfaces. In fact, some aircraft manufacturers may limit propeller reversing to a minimum forward speed. Another thing you should be aware of is that when reverse thrust is used to back an aircraft up, it is difficult to see what's behind the aircraft. In addition, if an aircraft is moving backward rapidly when the brakes are applied, it is possible for the aircraft's nose to rise off the ground, causing the tail to strike the ground.

From a mechanical standpoint, a reversible propeller is very similar to a typical constant-speed propeller. For example, depending on the make and model of propeller, oil pressure may be used to either increase or decrease blade angle. Opposing the oil pressure can be a combination of spring pressure, centrifugal force acting on counterweights, and/or compressed nitrogen. About the only difference between a reversing and non-reversing propeller is the absence of permanently fixed low pitch stops. The reason there are no low pitch stops is because the blades of a reversible propeller must be able to rotate through the low pitch limits to produce reverse thrust. Based on this, the appropriate blade angle must be maintained by creating a hydraulic lock with the propeller governor that can be changed as necessary. In other words, once a desired blade angle is achieved, the amount of oil pressure within the hub balances the sum of the other forces acting on the propeller blades. Therefore, if the quantity of oil in the hub is not changed, or locked, at this point, the propeller blade angle will remain set.

As a backup to the primary pitch lock mechanism, some reversible propellers incorporate a secondary method of locking the blade pitch. This way, if the primary pitch lock should fail, the secondary pitch lock will prevent the blades from rotating to reverse pitch.

TURBOPROP FUEL CONTROL

In most cases, the fuel control on a turboprop engine works in conjunction with the propeller governor to control the propeller blade angle. For example, at speeds above flight idle, both the fuel flow and propeller blade angle are controlled by the power lever position according to a predetermined schedule. This way, as more fuel is metered into the engine, the blade angle is automatically increased to maintain the most optimum efficiency. On the other hand, at speeds below flight idle, propeller blade angle is controlled almost exclusively by the power lever. The reason for this is that, when a turboprop engine is running below flight idle speed, governor control over propeller blade angle is incapable of handling the engine efficiently.

HARTZELL REVERSING PROPELLER SYSTEMS

The following discussion focuses on the Hartzell reversing propellers used with Allied-Signal TPE-331 and Pratt & Whitney PT6 engines. Many of the operational characteristics of Hartzell propellers are typical of propellers produced by other manufacturers for turboprop engines; therefore, a study of these propeller systems serves well as an overview of how most turboprop propeller systems operate.

ALLIED-SIGNAL TPE-331

Hartzell propeller systems are used on many aircraft equipped with TPE-331 model engines including the Mitsubishi MU-2, the Fairchild Merlin, and the Aero Commander 690 aircraft. The TPE-331 is a fixed shaft turbine that, depending on the model, produces between 665 and 1,100 shaft horsepower when the gas generator is operating at approximately 41,700 rpm. The TPE-331 is sometimes referred to as a constant-speed engine. This means that the engine operates at or near 100 percent rpm throughout its operational cycle.

REDUCTION GEARING

The TPE-331 engine's propeller reduction gearing is housed on the front of the engine with a fixed shaft coupled directly to the gas generator's third stage turbine. The reduction gearing produces a propeller shaft rotational speed of approximately 2,200 rpm which equates to a reduction ratio of about 14:1. To provide a degree of flexibility, the reduction gearing can be situated either above or below the engine's centerline to accommodate various airframe manufacturer's requirements. [Figure 12-46]

To prevent the propeller from driving the turbine and compressor sections of a fixed shaft turbine engine, the reduction gear portion of the engine incorporates a **negative-torque-sense (NTS) system** that automatically increases propeller pitch when negative torque exists. This condition can occur when the engine's power is rapidly decelerated and the propeller's pitch configuration causes the prop to windmill due to slipstreaming. In this situation, the NTS changes the propeller's pitch enough to prevent the propeller from driving the engine. Another benefit of the NTS is that, if the engine fails, the NTS will sense that loss of engine torque and automatically rotate the blades to their high-pitch position. Some engines may incorporate a separate **thrust sensitive signal (TSS)** that automatically feathers the propeller in the event of an engine failure.

PROPELLER

The propeller commonly used on a TPE-331 engine is a flange-mounted three- or four-bladed Hartzell steel hub, feathering and reversing propeller. With this type of propeller, the blades are moved to low pitch and reverse pitch with governor oil pressure. On the other hand, the blades are moved to high pitch and the feather position by a combination of spring pressure and centrifugal force acting on blade counterweights. However, to prevent the blades from rotating into the feather position during shutdown, a set of retractable pitch stops are incorporated. This is typical on fixed shaft turboprop engines so the air load on the propeller is minimized during subsequent engine starts. [Figure 12-47]

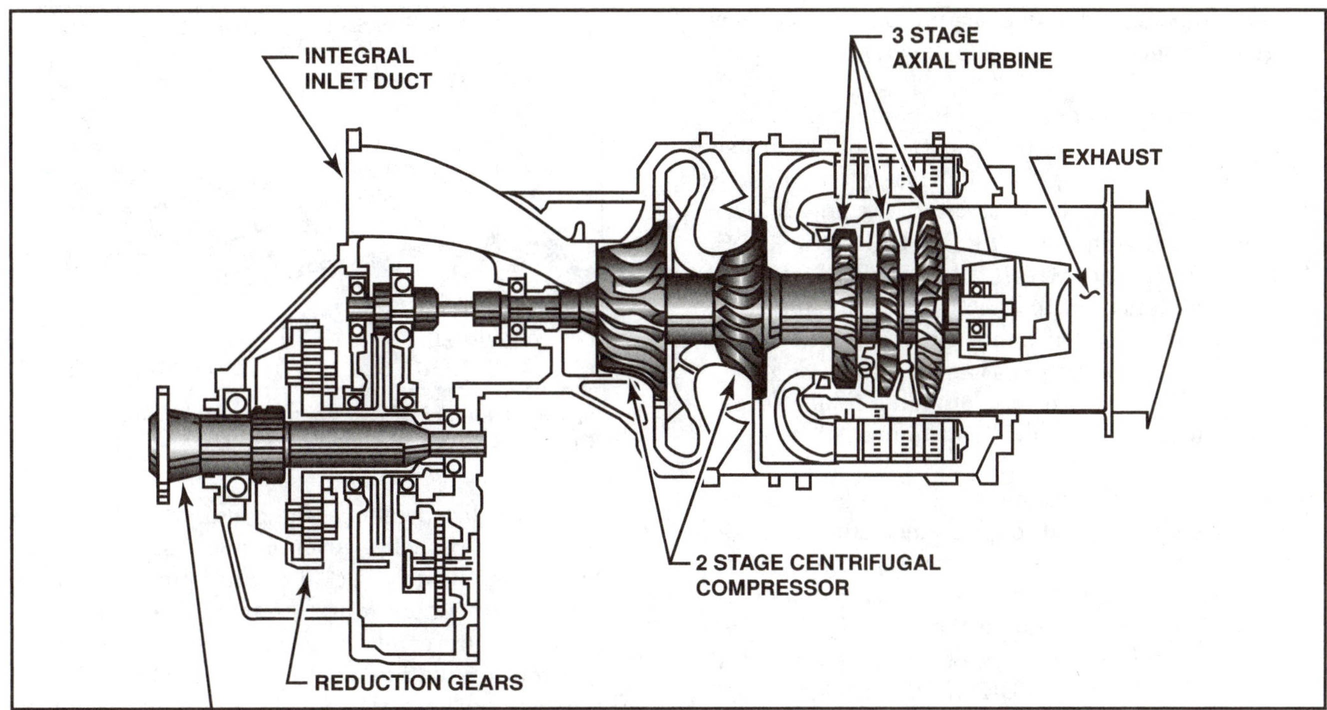

Figure 12-46. The Allied-Signal TPE-331 is a fixed shaft turbine engine with a two-stage centrifugal compressor and a three-stage axial turbine. Depending on the airframe/engine combination, the propeller reduction gearing may be installed either above or below the engine drive shaft.

The Hartzell propeller's construction is similar to that of the feathering steel hub design installed on reciprocating engines. However, installed in place of the low pitch stops is a **spacer** or **Beta tube**, which acts as a reverse pitch stop. The Beta tube also serves as an oil transfer tube between the propeller pitch control unit and propeller dome.

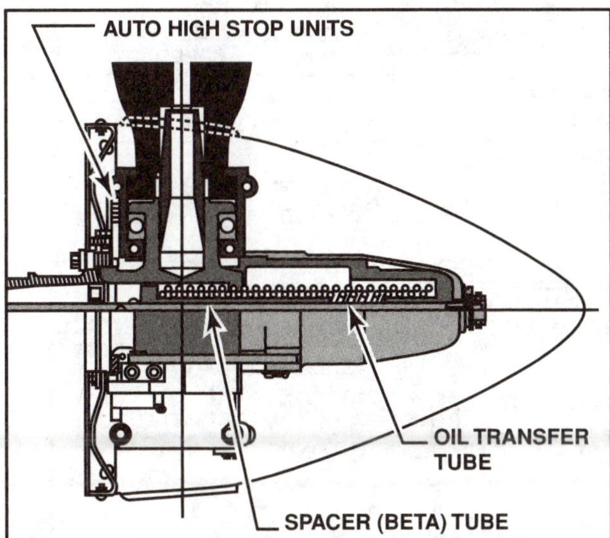

Figure 12-47. A Hartzell HC-B3TN-5 three-bladed propeller is often used on TPE-331 engines. This particular propeller relies on high pressure oil to move the blades to low and reverse pitch, while spring pressure and centrifugal force acting on counterweights increase propeller blade angle.

PROPELLER CONTROL

In flight, engine power output is controlled by the fuel control unit while propeller blade angle is controlled by a propeller governor similar to the governors used with other constant-speed propellers. The governor permits the operator to set a desired engine rpm and then directs oil into and out of the propeller hub to change the blade angle as engine load or power output changes.

During ground operations (Beta mode), a conventional fuel control and governor cannot properly regulate engine power output and propeller blade angle. Therefore, a separate **underspeed governor** controls fuel flow to the engine while a **propeller pitch control** mechanism is used to meter oil in and out of the propeller hub to control the blade angle. As a speed sensing device, the underspeed governor controls fuel flow to the engine to maintain a set power output. On the other hand, the propeller pitch control is needed because the governor does not have the ability to select a reverse blade angle.

COCKPIT CONTROLS

The controls for a typical TPE-331 turboprop installation are similar regardless of the aircraft. A typical installation consists of two engine controls; a **power lever** and a **speed**, or **condition**, **lever**. [Figure 12-48]

The power lever is mechanically connected to both the propeller pitch control and the fuel control so that fuel flow and propeller pitch can be coordinated for fuel scheduling. In most cases, the power lever has four positions: REVERSE, GROUND IDLE, FLIGHT IDLE, and MAXIMUM. During flight, the power lever functions to directly adjust the fuel control unit. On the other hand, during ground operations, the power lever bypasses the propeller governor and directly controls propeller blade angle through the propeller pitch control unit.

The condition lever is connected to the primary and underspeed governor through a mechanical linkage. The primary function of the condition lever is to control rpm and, in some installations, to manually shut off the fuel and feather the propeller. In most cases, the condition lever has three positions: CUT OFF, LOW RPM, and HIGH RPM. On installations where the feather valve is connected to the condition lever, propeller feathering is accomplished by moving the condition lever fully aft. However, if the condition lever is not mechanically linked to the feather valve, a separate feather handle is incorporated.

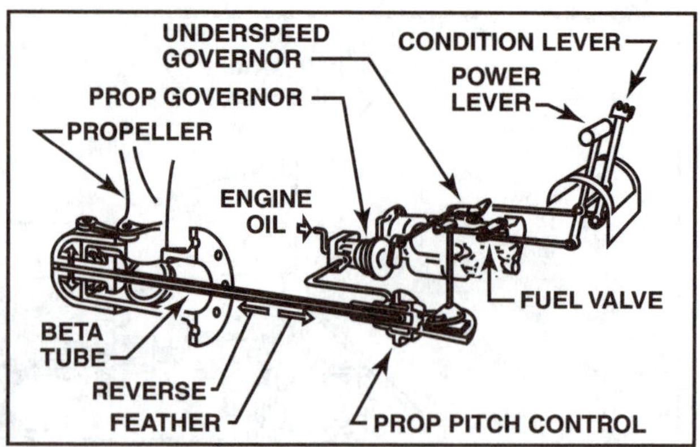

Figure 12-48. TPE-331 turboprop controls include a power lever and a speed, or condition, lever.

During flight operations, the condition lever sets the rpm on the propeller governor allowing the governor to vary the blade angle so engine rpm remains constant. Furthermore, during ground operation in the Beta range, the condition lever adjusts the underspeed governor on the fuel control unit. This action varies the fuel flow to maintain a fixed rpm in spite of blade angle changes caused by power lever adjustments.

In addition to the engine controls, most TPE-331 installations include an unfeathering switch, or button. As its name implies, this switch is used to

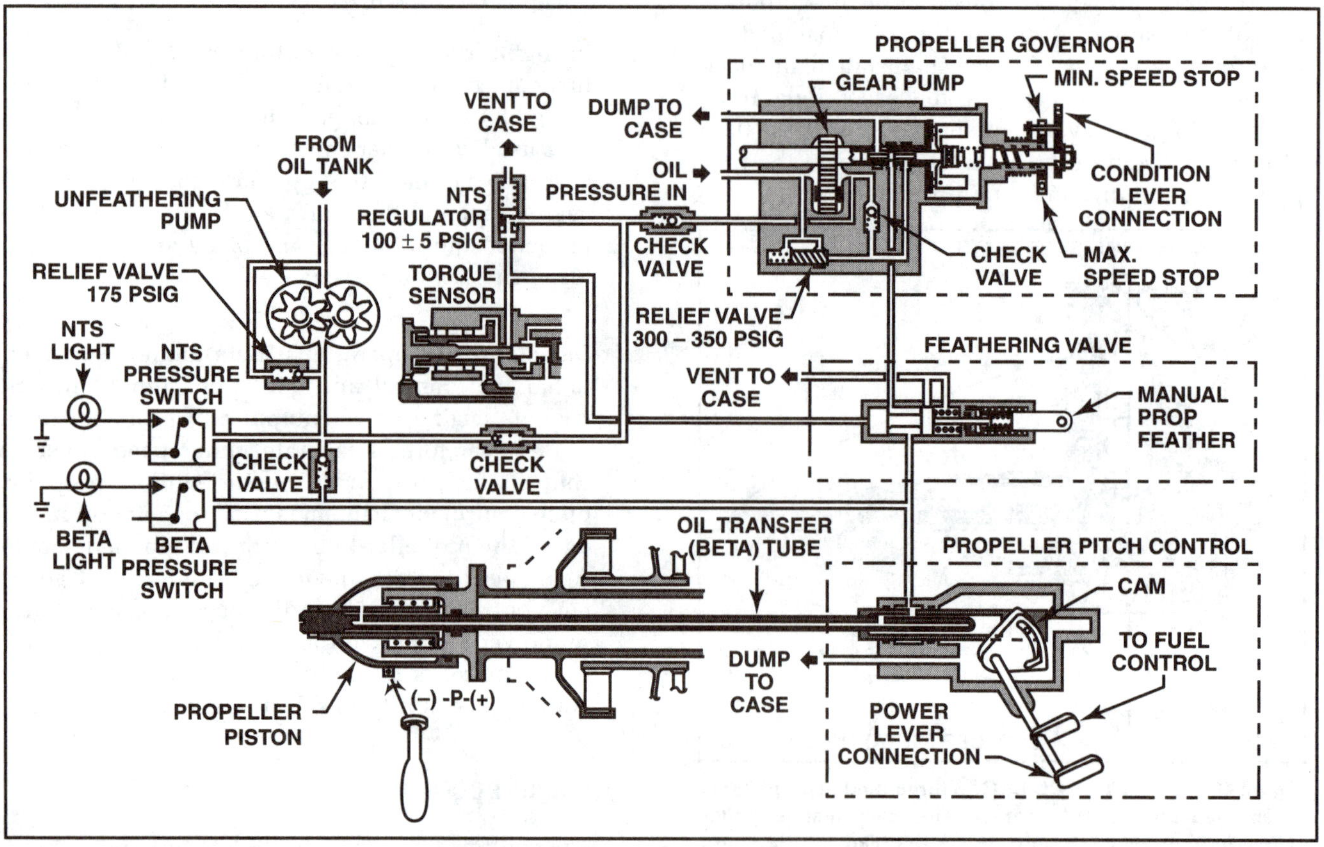

Figure 12-49. The schematic in this figure shows how each of the components in a TPE-331 turboprop propeller system operate to control the propeller.

unfeather the propeller when attempting to restart an engine. When the unfeathering switch is activated, current energizes an electric unfeathering pump that forces oil into the propeller dome to rotate the blades out of the feathered position. [Figure 12-49]

SYSTEM OPERATION

The two basic operating modes of the TPE-331 are the Beta mode and Alpha mode. If you recall, the Beta mode includes all ground operations including engine starting, taxi, and reverse thrust. In most cases, the Beta range includes all power settings from 65 to 95 percent N_1. On the other hand, the Alpha mode includes all operations from flight idle to full power or from 95 to 100 percent N_1. To better understand how each of the components within the TPE-331 operate to change the propeller blade angle, the following discussion will examine each component as an engine is started and operated in both the Beta and Alpha ranges.

To begin, assume that a TPE-331 is sitting idle on an aircraft with the propeller blades resting against the pitch stops. To start the engine, the power lever is placed in the GROUND IDLE position while the condition lever is placed in the LOW RPM position. Once the engine starts, the propeller latches are retracted by easing the power lever toward the reverse position. When this is done, the mechanical linkage connecting the power lever to the propeller pitch control (PPC) slides the follower sleeve in the PPC forward. This opens a port in the oil transfer, or Beta, tube allowing high pressure governor oil to be ported to the propeller hub. [Figure 12-50]

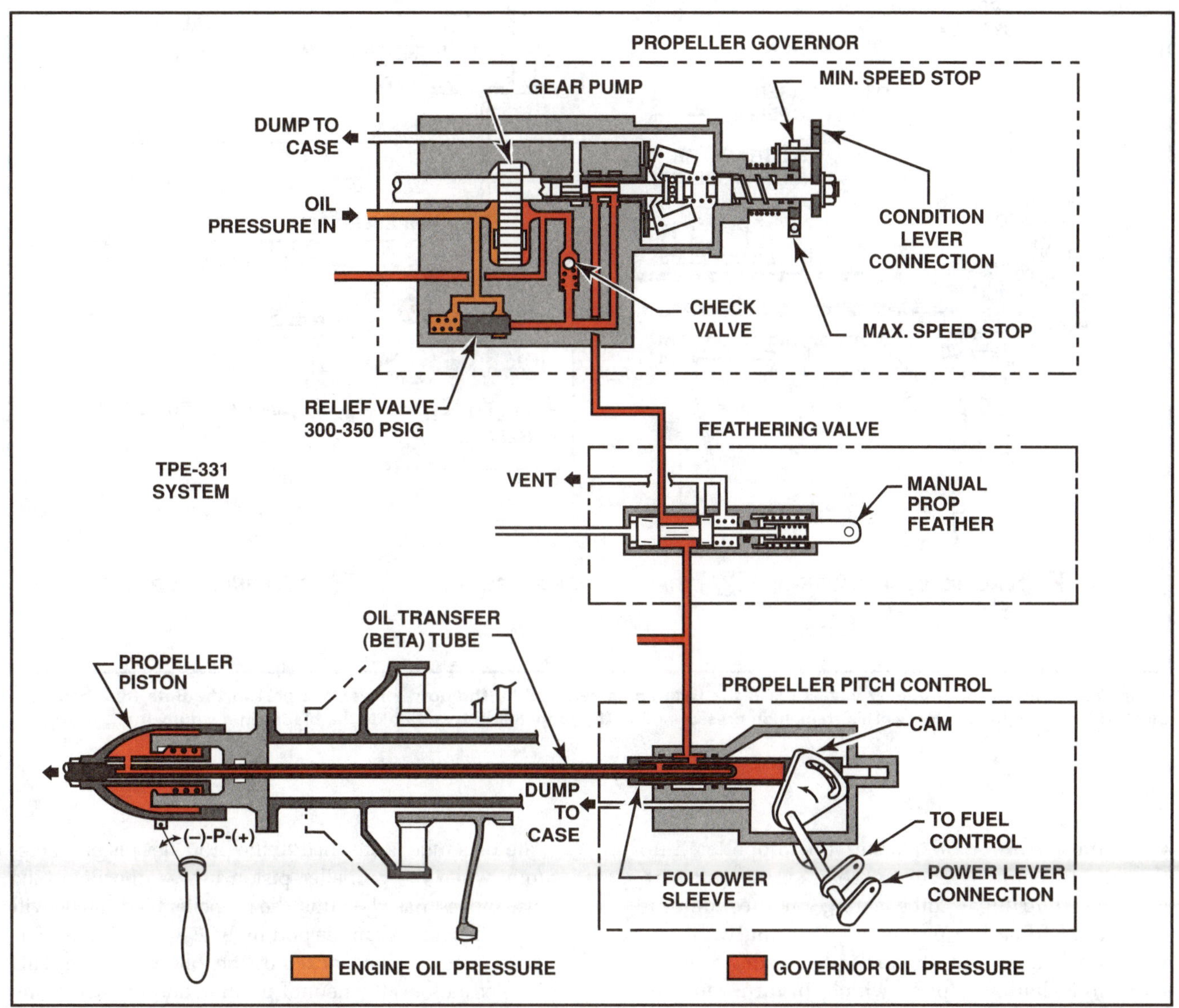

Figure 12-50. When the power lever is moved toward the REVERSE position, the follower sleeve in the propeller pitch control moves forward exposing an oil port in the oil transfer (Beta) tube. This allows high pressure governor oil to flow to the propeller hub and decrease the propeller blade angle.

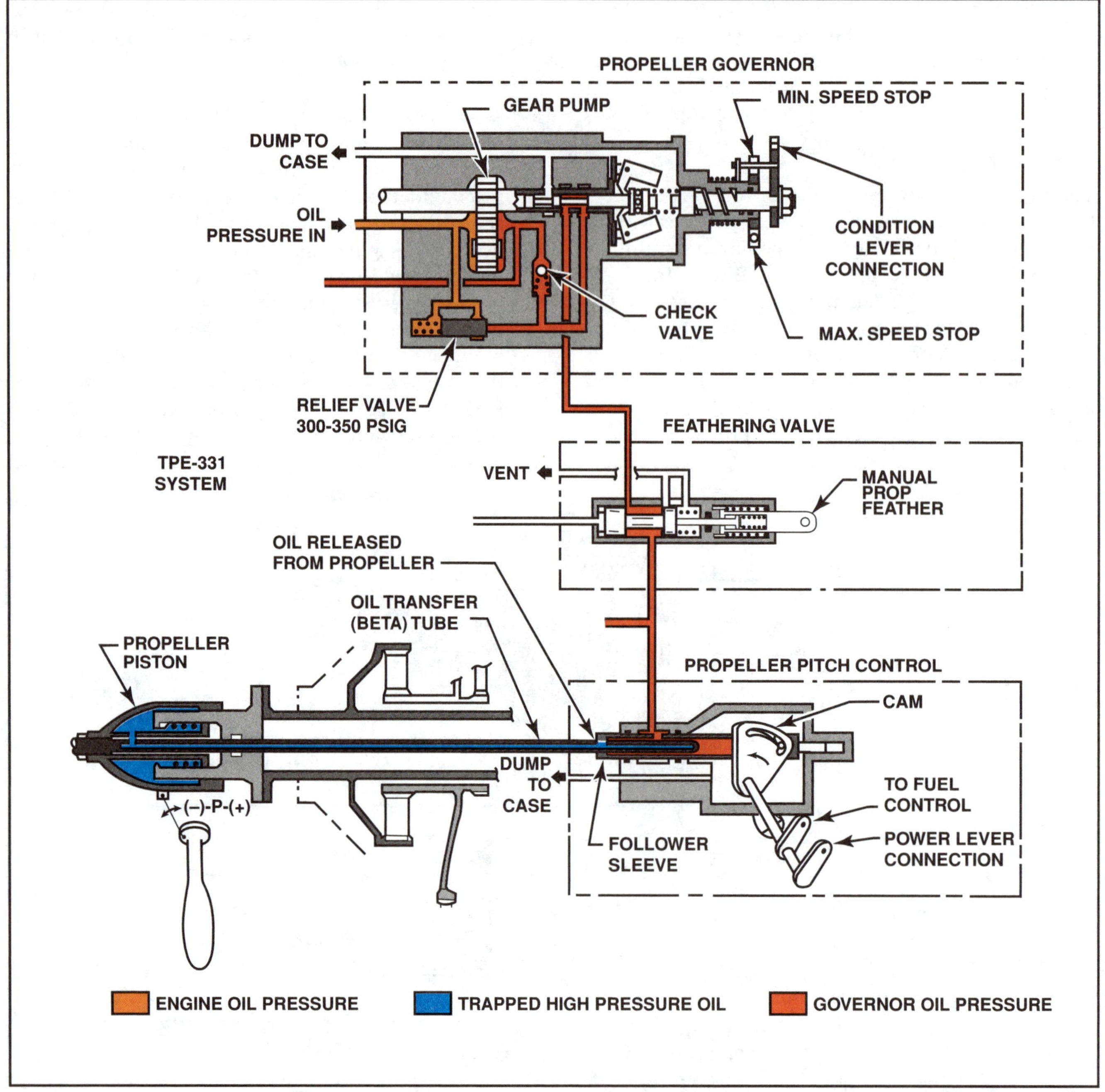

Figure 12-51. When the propeller blades reach the Beta angle selected by the power lever, the port in the Beta tube becomes blocked by the follower sleeve. This traps high pressure oil in the propeller hub and holds the blades in a set position.

Once the governor oil reaches the propeller hub, the oil pressure overcomes both spring pressure and the centrifugal force acting on the counterweights to force the propeller piston outward. As the piston moves out, the propeller blades begin to move to a shallower pitch which, in turn, removes the weight of the blades from the pitch stops. With the weight removed, centrifugal force retracts the pitch stops.

The Beta tube is attached to the propeller piston; therefore, when the propeller piston moves, the Beta tube also moves. Based on this, the propeller blade angle will stop changing when the port in the Beta tube moves forward enough to be blocked by the follower sleeve. This is referred to as the neutral position and represents the point where the oil pressure within the propeller hub balances both spring pressure and centrifugal force acting on the counterweights. [Figure 12-51]

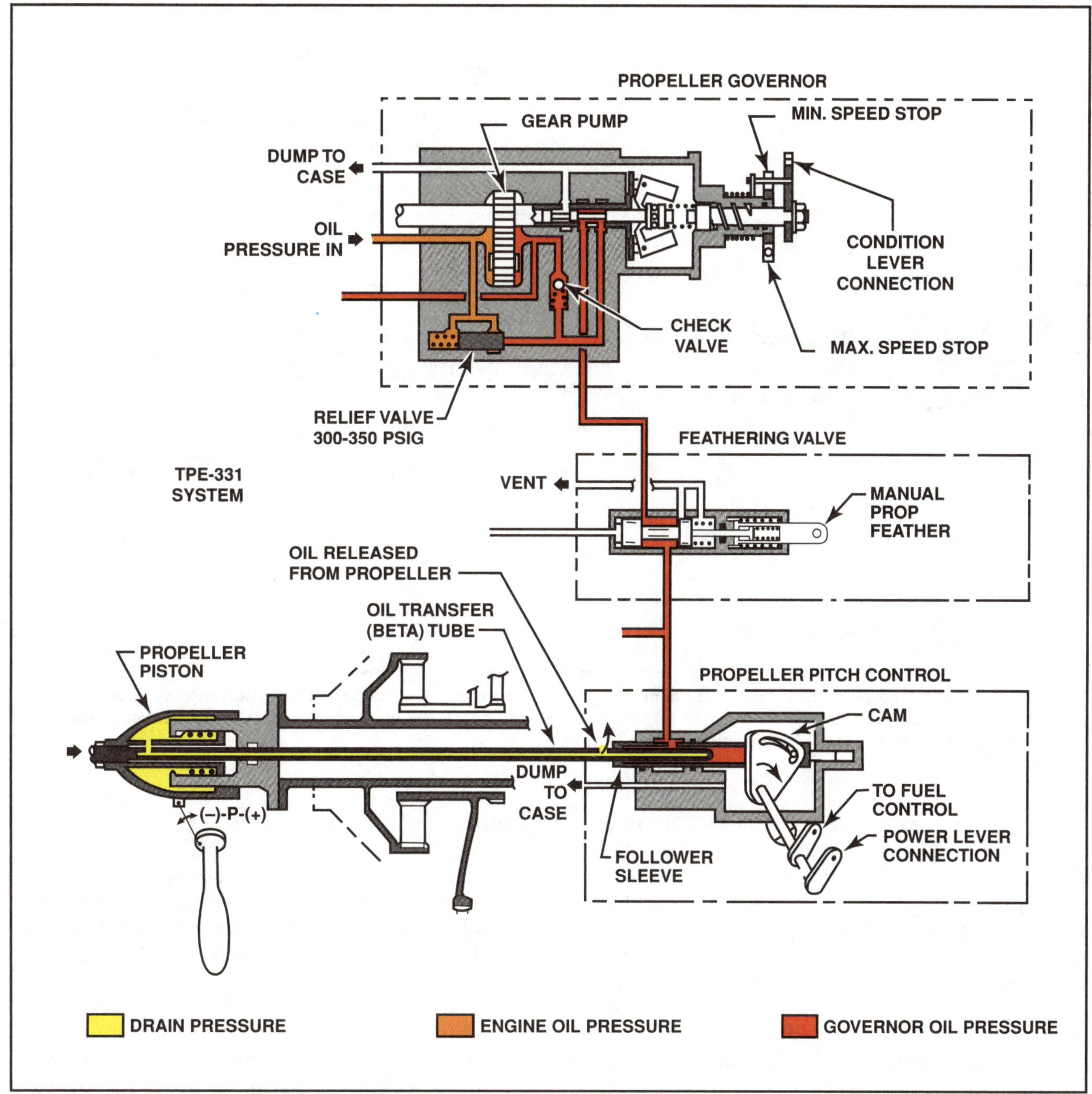

Figure 12-52. When the power lever is moved forward in the Beta mode, the follower sleeve in the propeller pitch control unports the Beta tube allowing oil to flow out of the propeller hub. This allows the combination of spring tension and centrifugal force acting on the counterweights to rotate the blades to a higher pitch.

Once the propeller moves to a lower pitch and the pitch stops retract, the power lever is moved forward to increase blade pitch. As the power lever moves, a mechanical linkage pulls the follower sleeve in the propeller pitch control aft, unporting the Beta tube. With the Beta tube oil port open, oil is free to flow into the gear reduction case. This allows the combination of spring tension and centrifugal force acting on the counterweights to force oil out of the propeller hub to increase the blade angle. As the blade angle increases, the propeller piston and Beta tube move aft until the Beta tube returns to its neutral position in the propeller pitch control unit. The result is a change in blade angle proportional to the degree of power lever movement. [Figure 12-52]

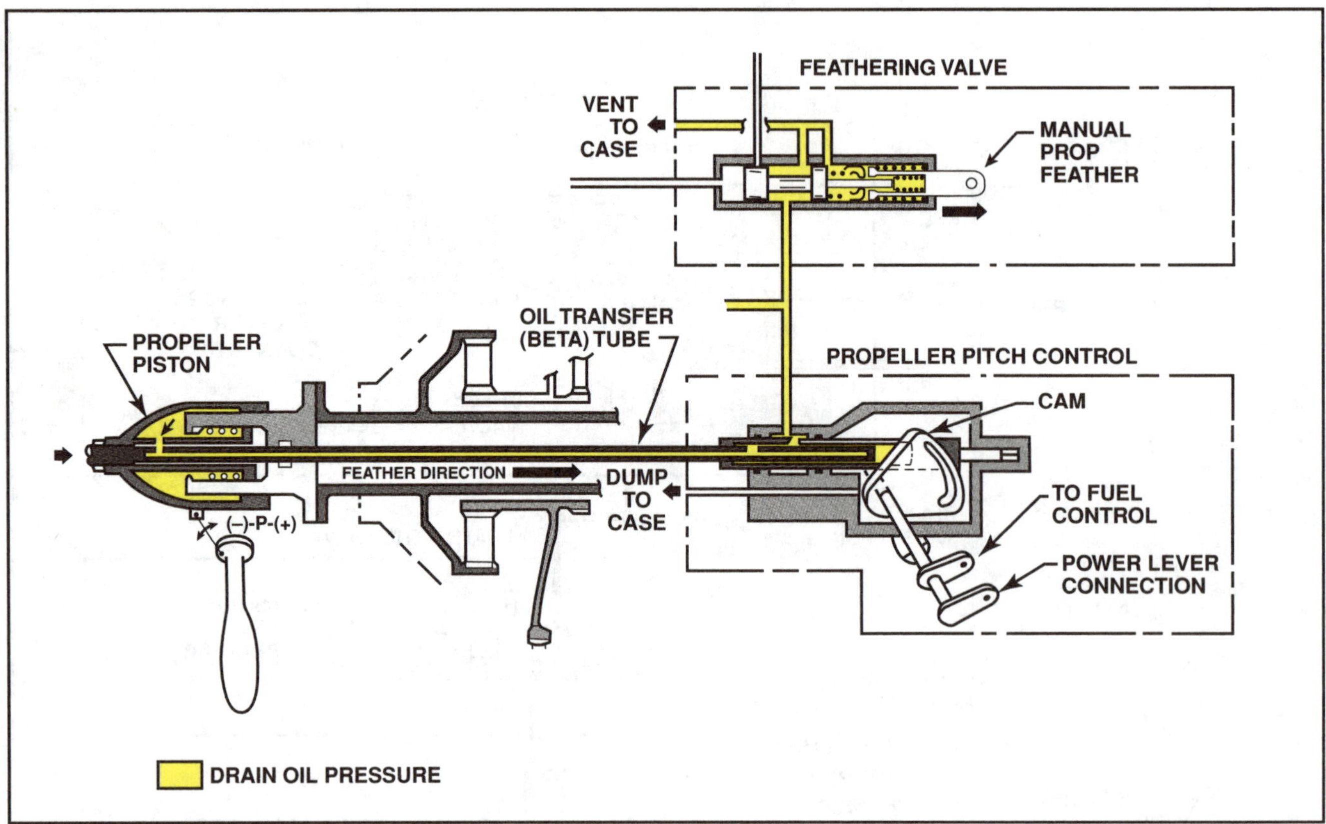

Figure 12-53. To feather a propeller on a TPE-331 engine, the feathering valve must be shifted so the oil within the propeller hub can drain back to the engine case. Once the oil pressure is relieved, spring tension and centrifugal force acting on the blade counterweights can rotate the blades to the feathered position.

Once the aircraft is in position for takeoff, the condition lever is moved to a high rpm setting and the power lever is moved to the FLIGHT IDLE position. With the condition lever in a high rpm position, the underspeed governor is fully opened and no longer controls fuel flow. In addition, when the power lever is moved forward to the FLIGHT IDLE position, the follower sleeve in the propeller pitch control is slid far enough forward that it can no longer cover the port in the Beta tube. This effectively eliminates the ability of the propeller pitch control to change the propeller pitch giving the propeller governor full control over the propeller blade angle. In this mode, the power lever is used to control fuel flow through the engine's fuel control unit and has no effect on propeller pitch changes.

In the Alpha, or flight, mode, the propeller governor is adjusted by the condition lever to set the system rpm in much the same manner as that used with a conventional constant-speed propeller system. When the condition lever setting is fixed, the power lever operates the fuel control unit to control the amount of fuel delivered to the engine. Moving the power lever forward increases fuel flow which, in turn, increases engine power. With the governor attempting to maintain a constant rpm, an increase in engine power causes the propeller governor to increase the propeller blade angle. On the other hand, a decrease in engine power causes the propeller governor to decrease the propeller angle.

To feather the propeller on a TPE-331 engine, the condition lever is moved full aft or the feather handle is pulled. This action causes the feather valve to shift and allow the oil in the propeller hub to return to the engine. With no oil pressure in the propeller hub, spring tension and centrifugal force acting on the counterweights can rotate the propeller blades to the feather position. [Figure 12-53]

To unfeather a propeller installed on a TPE-331 engine, an electric unfeathering pump is used. The pump is typically activated by a toggle switch that is located in the cockpit. Once the pump is turned on, it pumps oil to the propeller hub where it forces the propeller piston forward. As the piston moves outward, the blades rotate out of their feathered position and into high pitch. As soon as the blades unfeather, the propeller will begin to windmill and

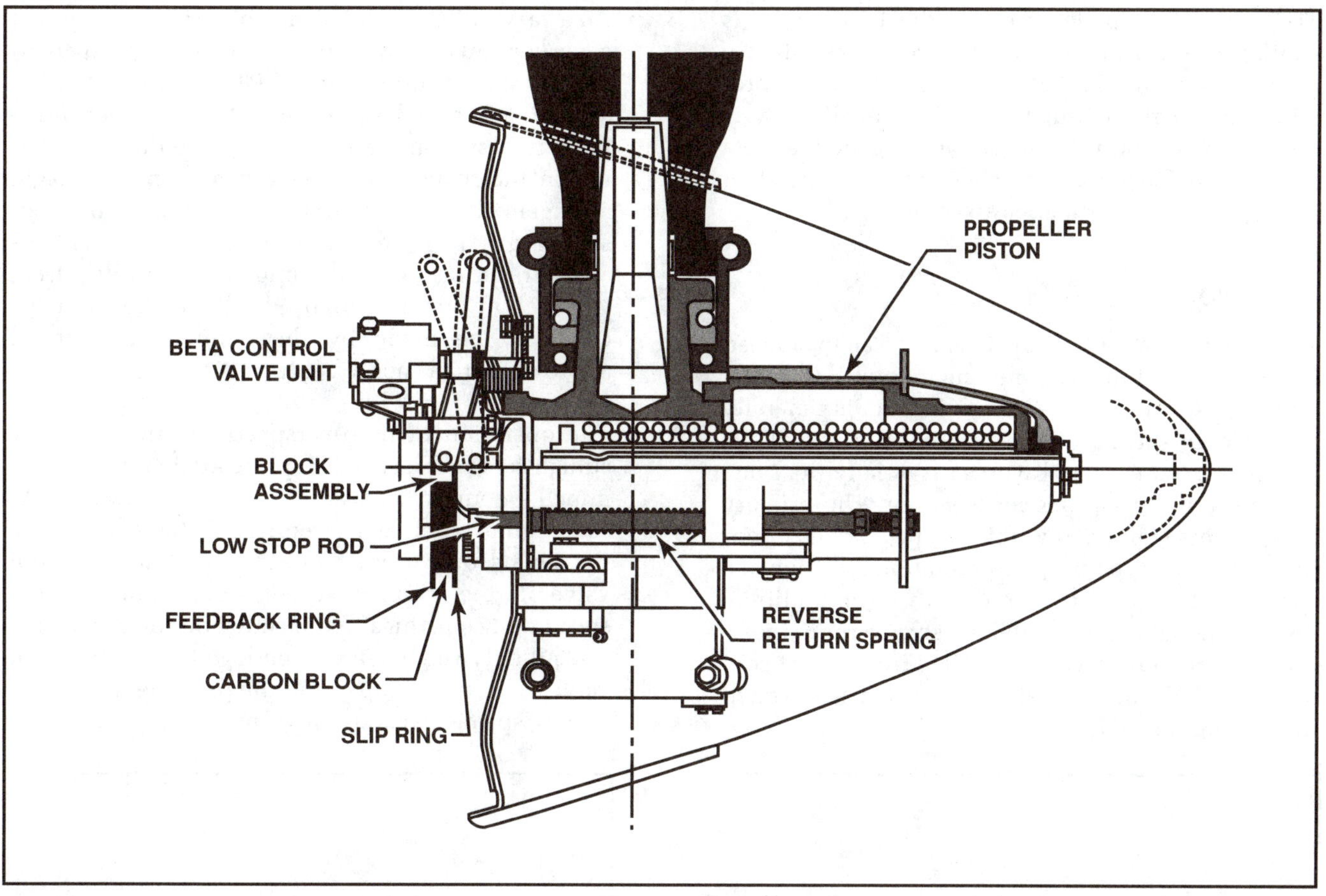

Figure 12-54. A propeller commonly used with the PT6 is a Hartzell three-bladed, steel hub, feathering and reversing propeller. Oil pressure moves the propeller's blades to low pitch, while the combined forces of a feathering spring and blade counterweights move the blades to high pitch and the feather position.

aid in an air start attempt. In some cases, the unfeathering pump can be used on the ground in the event the engine was shut down with a feathered propeller.

PRATT & WHITNEY PT6

The PT6 engine is a free-, or power, turbine engine that produces more than 600 horsepower at a gas generator speed of about 38,000 rpm. If you recall, in a free-turbine engine, there is no mechanical connection between the power turbine and the gas generator portion of the engine. Instead, the hot gasses produced by the gas generator section of the engine flow through the power turbine causing the power turbine to rotate. The rotational force of the power turbine is then transmitted by a shaft to a reduction gear assembly that rotates a propeller. In a typical PT6 turboprop engine, the reduction gear assembly produces a propeller rpm of 2,200 when the gas generator portion of the engine is operating at 100 percent output.

A key difference between a free-turbine engine and a fixed shaft engine is that, when a free-turbine engine is shut down, the propeller blades are placed in the feathered position. This can be done on a free-turbine engine because, during a normal engine start only, the compressor and its turbine are rotated by the starter while the power turbine initially remains motionless. This design greatly reduces the load on the starter motor and eliminates the need for a set of pitch stops.

PROPELLER

One type of propeller that is commonly used with the PT6 engine is the Hartzell HC-B3TN-3. This particular type of propeller is flange-mounted, has three-blades and a steel hub, and is reversible. With this type of propeller, governor oil pressure is used to rotate the propeller blades to a low or reverse pitch, while a feathering spring and counterweights attached to the blades are used to rotate the blades to high pitch and the feather position. [Figure 12-54]

The Hartzell propeller used on the PT6 engine is similar in construction to the Hartzell steel hub propeller used on the TPE-331 engine. However, to provide blade angle information to the propeller governor and fuel control when operating in the Beta range, a **feedback ring**, or **Beta slip ring**, is installed on the rear of the propeller assembly.

GOVERNOR

The PT6 engine utilizes a primary and an overspeed governor. In addition, some engines utilize a fuel topping governor. The primary governor is generally mounted in the 12 o'clock position on top of the gear reduction case and works essentially the same as a conventional propeller governor. The primary components contained within the primary governor include a gear-type oil pump, rotating flyweights, a speeder spring, and a pilot valve. In addition, depending on engine model, these governors incorporate either a **Beta valve** or a **Beta lift rod** that controls the blade angle when the propeller is operated in the Beta range. [Figure 12-55]

As a precaution in the event the primary propeller governor fails to limit the propeller's speed to its normal maximum rpm, many PT6 engines include a second **overspeed governor**. This governor functions in a similar manner as a conventional governor in that it uses a speeder spring and flyweight arrangement to prevent the propeller from overspeeding. The one major exception is that the speeder spring tension cannot be controlled from the cockpit nor is it field adjustable. Adjustments can only be made by the manufacturer or an approved repair facility. [Figure 12-56]

The operation of the overspeed governor is fairly straightforward; a speeder spring applies a predetermined amount of pressure to a set of flyweights. As the engine accelerates, centrifugal force pulls the flyweights outward which, in turn, raises a pilot valve. If the engine exceeds its maximum rated speed, the centrifugal force acting on the flyweights pulls the flyweights out far enough to raise the pilot valve so oil can escape from the propeller hub. This allows spring tension and centrifugal force acting

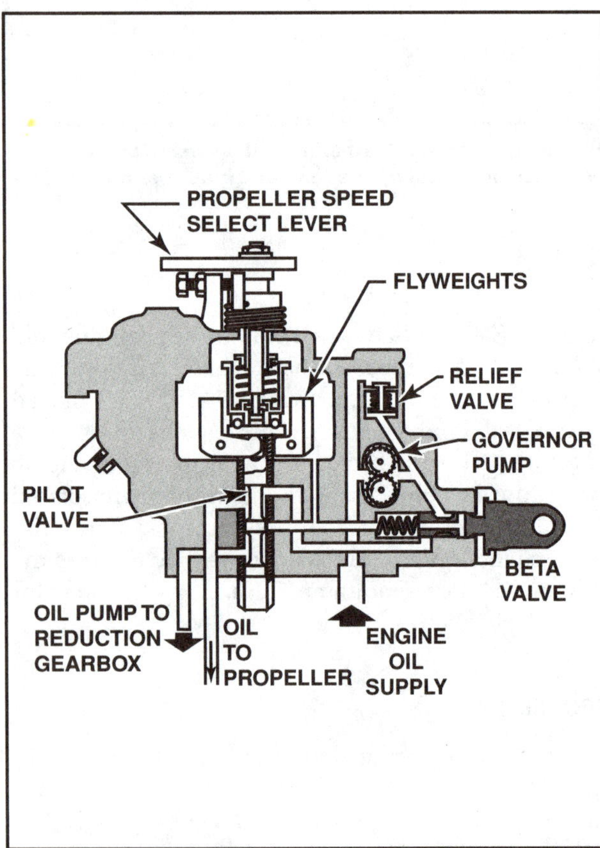

Figure 12-55. The primary governor used on a PT6 engine is similar to most governors in that a set of flyweights are used to sense engine speed and move a pilot valve as necessary to maintain a preset engine speed. However, to permit the governor to control the blade angle in the Beta range, a separate Beta valve is also incorporated.

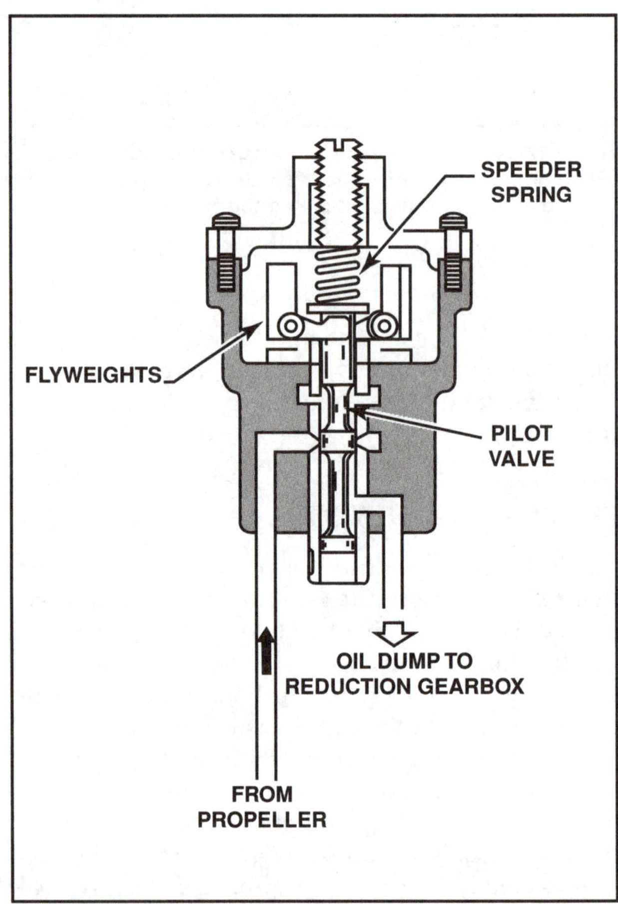

Figure 12-56. As a backup to the primary governor, many PT6 engines incorporate an overspeed governor that prevents the propeller and engine from exceeding their maximum rpm.

on the propeller blade counterweights to increase the blade angle and slow the engine.

To check the overspeed governor's operation, an electrical test solenoid is typically incorporated in the governor. This solenoid is activated by momentarily closing a toggle switch located in the cockpit. During a ground runup, this switch is depressed while the engine is run at a high rpm. If the overspeed governor is functioning properly, the propeller's maximum rpm will be somewhat less than the normal amount. Care should be taken, however, to make certain that this test switch is not released while the power lever is advanced or a real overspeed situation may occur.

As an additional safeguard to prevent propeller overspeed conditions, a fuel topping governor may also be installed on some PT6 engines. This governor also senses propeller rpm and, in the event the propeller rpm exceeds the maximum limits of the overspeed governor, the fuel topping governor dumps a portion of the bleed air that is used in the fuel control unit. In doing this, the fuel control is tricked into thinking that the gas generator is not developing as much power as it really is and the fuel control meters less fuel to the engine. Ultimately, the gas generator's rpm reduces which, in turn, reduces the propeller's rpm.

FUEL CONTROL UNIT

The fuel control unit is installed on the rear of the engine and is linked through a cam assembly to the Beta valve on the primary propeller governor and to the Beta slip ring on the propeller. The purpose for interconnecting the fuel control unit with the Beta valve and Beta slip ring is to provide input to the fuel control unit when operating in the Beta mode.

COCKPIT CONTROLS

The cockpit controls for the PT6 turboprop consist of a power lever, a propeller control lever, and, in most installations, a fuel cutoff, or condition, lever. The power lever is connected to a cam assembly on the side of the engine. From the cam assembly, mechanical linkages go to the fuel control unit, and the Beta valve on the primary governor. In the Alpha mode, the power lever controls engine power output by adjusting the fuel control to schedule the proper fuel flow for the desired gas generator performance. However, in the Beta range, the power lever controls both the fuel control unit and the propeller blade angle.

The propeller control lever is connected to the primary propeller governor and adjusts the tension applied to the governor's speeder spring in the same manner as a conventional constant speed governor arrangement. Full aft movement of the propeller control lever causes the oil pressure to be dumped from the propeller piston, thereby allowing the propeller to feather.

The fuel cutoff, or condition, lever is typically utilized only on reversing propeller installations and has two functions. First, it provides a positive fuel shutoff at the fuel control unit allowing the engine to be shut down. Secondly, the condition lever sets the gas generator's low and high idle rpm. The two positions for the condition lever are: LOW IDLE, which provides approximately 50 percent gas generator rpm, and HIGH IDLE, which allows the engine to obtain approximately 70 percent gas generator rpm. The low idle is used during ground operations, while the high idle is used during flight. [Figure 12-57 on page 12-44]

SYSTEM OPERATION

Like most turboprop engines, the PT6 engine operates in either an Alpha mode or a Beta mode. In most cases, the Beta range on a PT6 includes all power settings between 50 and 85 percent. On the other hand, the Alpha mode includes all operations from 95 to 100 percent. To better understand how each of the components within the PT6 operate to change the propeller blade angle, the following discussion will examine each component as an engine is started and operated in both the Beta and Alpha ranges.

To begin, assume that a PT6 engine is sitting idle on an aircraft with the propeller blades in the feathered position. To start the engine, the power lever is placed in the IDLE position while the propeller control lever and condition lever is placed in the FEATHER and FUEL CUTOFF positions respectively. Once the starter is engaged and the N_1 turbine reaches a specified speed, the condition lever is moved to the LOW IDLE position.

When the engine starts and you are ready to taxi, the propeller control lever is moved to a HIGH RPM setting and the power lever is adjusted as necessary to achieve a taxi speed. In situations where excessive taxi speeds result when the power lever is in the idle position, the lever can be moved past the detent into the Beta mode. When in the Beta mode, the primary

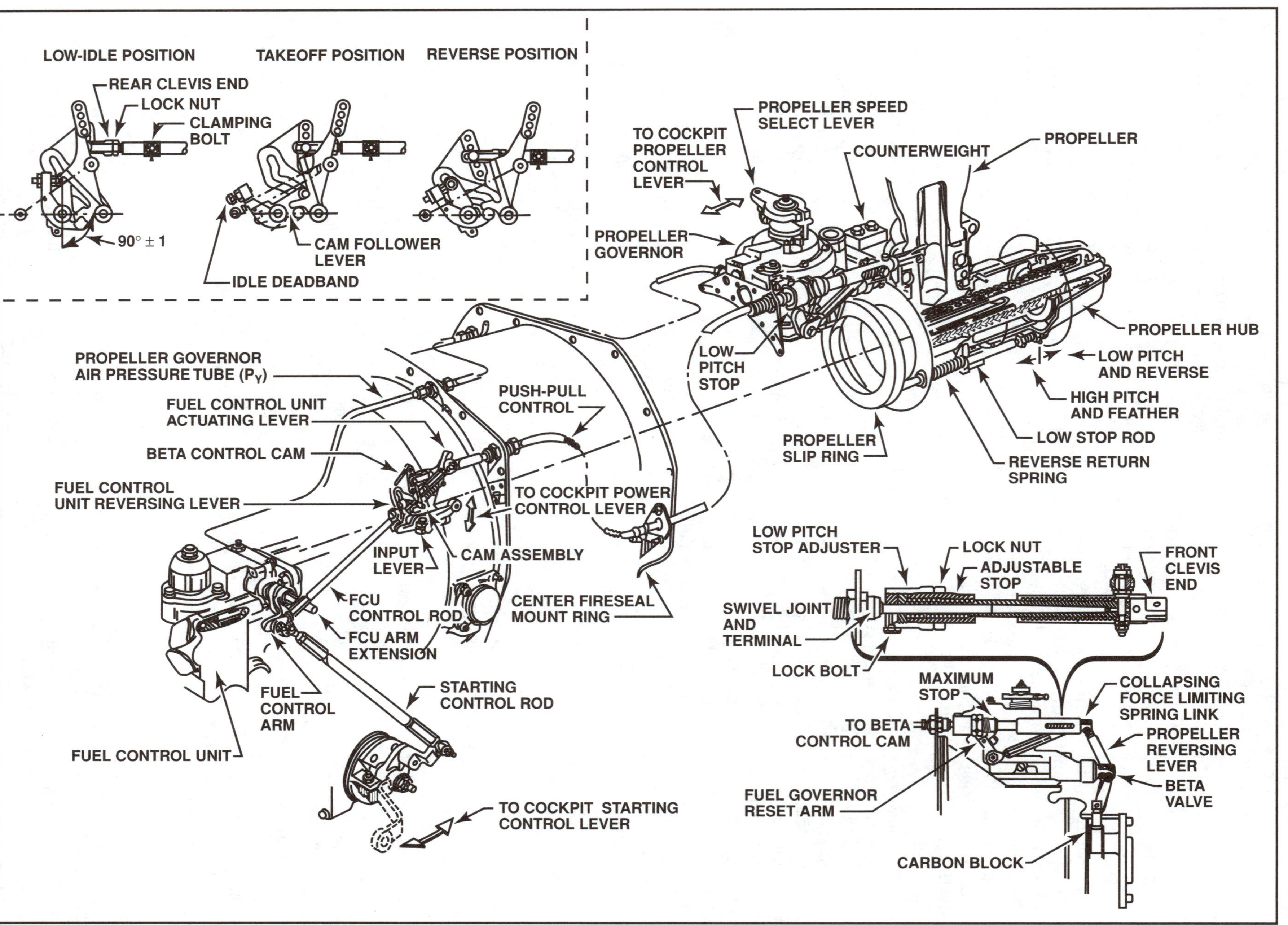

Figure 12-57. The figure above illustrates the location of the components on a PT6 engine that are used to control the engine speed and propeller pitch.

governor is in a underspeed condition with the pilot valve in its lowered position. This allows the power lever to control fuel flow and propeller blade angle.

As the power lever is moved aft into the Beta range, the Beta valve is pushed into the governor so that governor oil is ported to the propeller. As the pressurized oil flows into the propeller hub, the propeller piston moves outward to reduce the propeller blade angle. As the propeller piston moves outward, the feedback ring moves forward and the Beta valve is returned to the neutral position. [Figure 12- 58]

Once the propeller enters the reverse thrust portion of the Beta range, further movement of the power lever aft increases the fuel flow to the engine. This provides a means of varying the amount of reverse thrust produced during ground operations.

When the power lever is moved forward in the Beta range, the Beta valve is pulled out of the governor allowing oil to be released from the propeller piston. As oil leaves the hub, the propeller piston moves aft to increase the blade angle. At the same time, the feedback ring moves aft until the Beta valve is returned to the neutral position.

In the Alpha mode, the system rpm is high enough for the primary propeller governor to operate in its constant-speed mode. In other words, when the power lever is moved forward to increase engine output, the propeller governor increases the propeller blade angle to absorb the power increase and maintain the selected rpm. On the other hand, when the power lever is moved aft, the propeller blade angle is decreased by the governor to maintain the selected rpm.

To feather the propeller on a PT6 engine, the propeller control lever is moved full aft. This action causes the pilot valve in the primary governor to

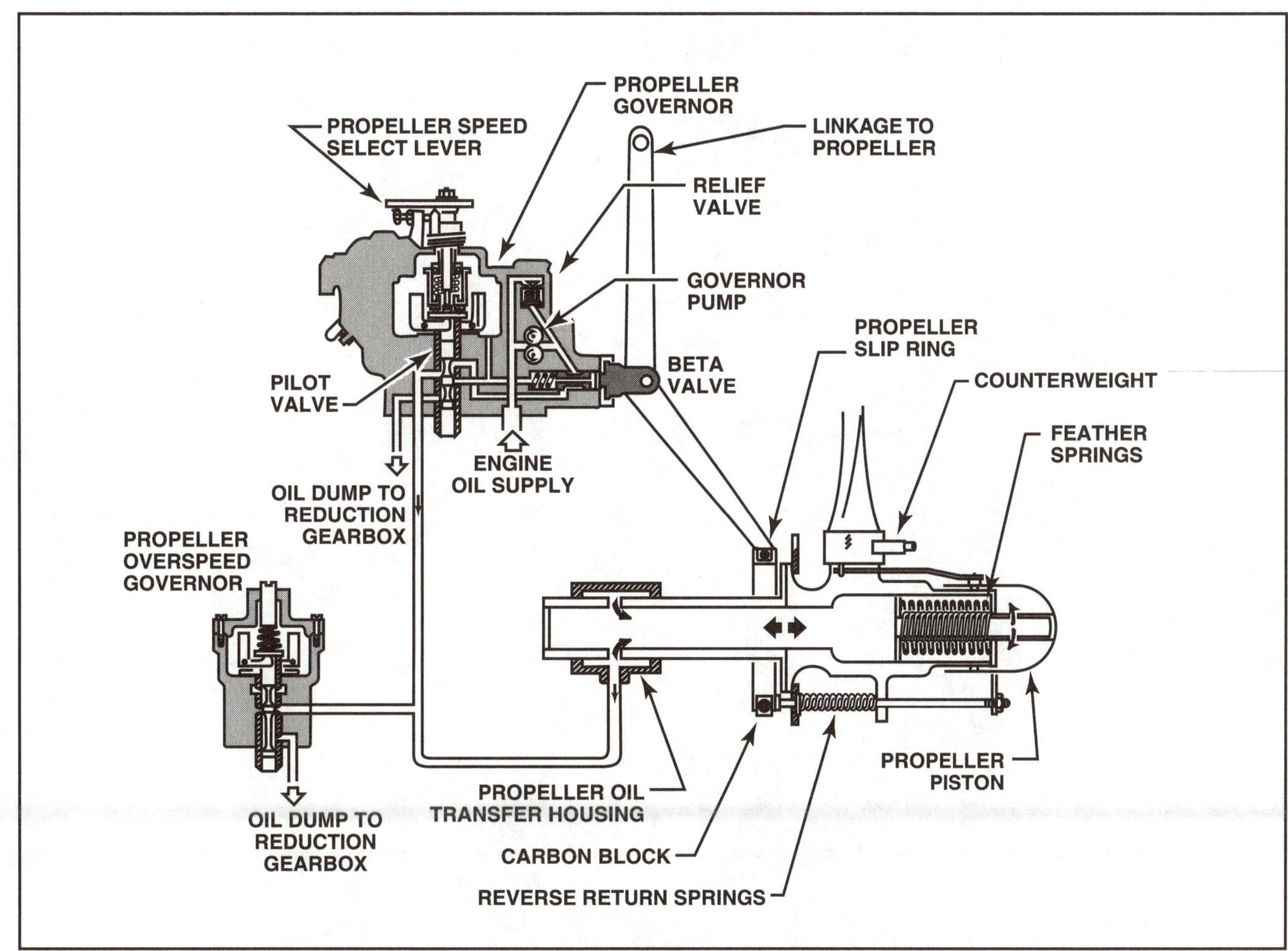

Figure 12-58. When the power lever is moved aft into the Beta range, the Beta valve is forced inward so that governor oil is directed to the propeller. As the propeller piston moves outward to decrease the propeller blade angle, the feedback ring moves forward and returns the Beta valve to its neutral position.

rise and allow the oil pressure in the propeller hub to return to the engine. With no oil pressure in the propeller hub, spring tension and centrifugal force acting on the counterweights attached to the base of each blade can rotate the propeller blades to the feather position.

To unfeather the propeller, the engine must first be started. Once the engine starts and the propeller is rotating, the propeller control lever is moved out of the feather position so pressurized oil can rotate the blades out of the feathered position to the selected blade angle or governor rpm setting.

AUXILIARY PROPELLER SYSTEMS

Several auxiliary systems are installed in aircraft to improve propeller performance and enhance the aircraft's all-weather capabilities. For example, some aircraft incorporate an auxiliary system that is designed to reduce propeller noise and vibration. Other auxiliary systems may be utilized to remove ice from propeller blades, thereby improving performance during flight in freezing precipitation.

SYNCHRONIZATION SYSTEMS

Anytime multiple engines and propellers are installed on an aircraft, the potential for excessive vibration and noise exists. A contributing factor to this problem is dissimilar rpm settings between the propellers. Based on this, one way to reduce the amount of noise and vibration produced is to match, or **synchronize**, the rpm settings on the engines. Currently, there are several synchronization systems used on multi-engine aircraft including the master motor synchronization system, the one engine master control system, and the synchrophasing system. Synchronizing systems control engine rpm and reduce vibration by setting all propellers at exactly the same rpm. Such a system can be used for all flight operations except takeoff and landing.

MASTER MOTOR SYNCHRONIZATION

An early type of synchronization system used on WWII four-engine aircraft consisted of a synchronizer master unit, four alternators, a master tachometer, a tachometer generator and contactor unit for each engine, an rpm master control lever, switches, and wiring. When activated, these components automatically control the speed of each engine and synchronize all engines at a selected rpm.

The **synchronizer master unit** incorporates a **master motor** which mechanically drives four **contactor units** that are electrically connected to an alternator. The alternator is a small three-phase, alternating current generator driven by an accessory drive of the engine. Therefore, the frequency of the voltage produced by the generator is directly proportional to the speed of the engine. When the system is activated, the desired engine rpm is selected by manually adjusting the rpm control lever until the master tachometer on the instrument panel indicates the desired rpm. Once set, any difference in rpm between an engine and the master motor will cause the corresponding contactor unit to operate the pitch-change mechanism of the propeller until the engine speeds match.

ONE ENGINE MASTER CONTROL SYSTEM

Today, many twin engine aircraft are equipped with a more modern propeller synchronizer system. These newer synchronizer systems typically consist of a control box that includes a comparative circuit, a special **master governor** on the left engine, a **slave governor** on the right engine, and an activator in the right engine nacelle. Both governors incorporate a frequency generator that produces a frequency proportional to the engine's rotational speed. [Figure 12-59]

With this type of system, the frequency generators built into the propeller governors generate a signal that is sent to the control box. A comparison circuit in the control box compares the rpm signal from the slave engine to the rpm signal from the master engine. If a difference in engine speed exists, the control box sends a correcting signal to the actuator to adjust the slave governor until the engine speeds match. In most installations, the comparator circuit has a limited range of operation. Therefore, the

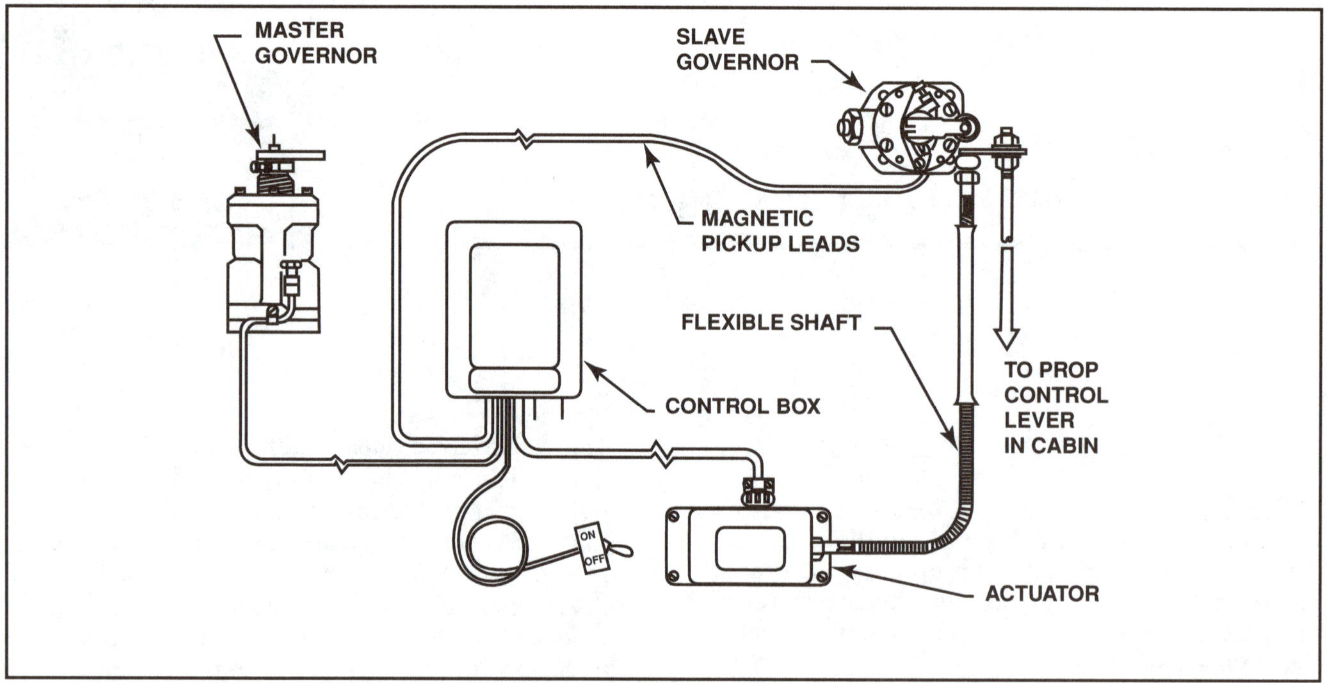

Figure 12-59. The basic units of a light twin propeller synchronization system are a control box, master governor, slave governor, and actuator.

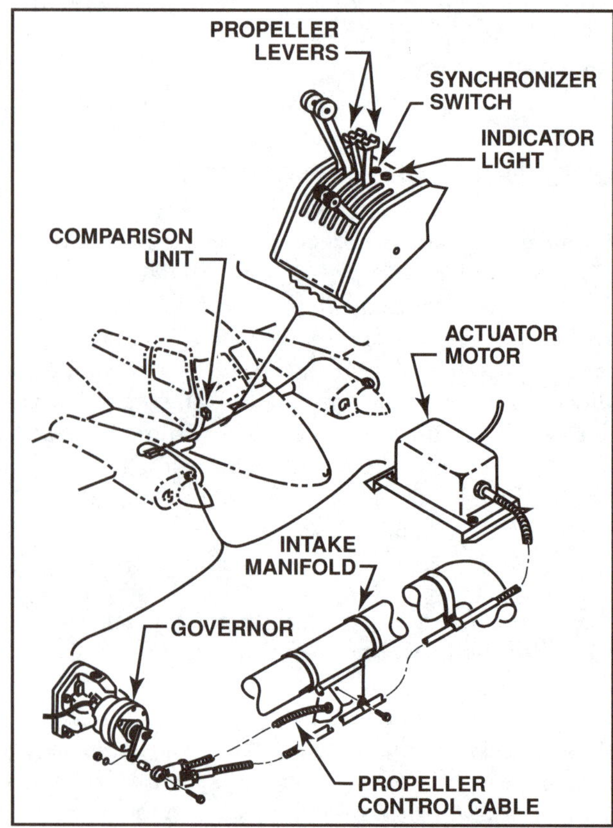

Figure 12-60. This view of a propeller synchronizer system shows the location of the various components when installed in a light twin-engine aircraft.

slave engine must be within approximately 100 rpm of the master engine for synchronization to occur. [Figure 12-60]

SYNCHROPHASING

Synchrophasing systems are a refinement of propeller synchronization systems in that they allow a pilot to control the angular difference in the plane of rotation between the propeller blades. This angular difference is known as the **phase angle** and can be adjusted by the pilot to achieve minimum noise and vibration levels. [Figure 12-61]

A typical synchrophasing system equips each engine with a magnetic pickup device known as a **pulse generator**. The pulse generator on each engine is keyed to the same blade of its respective propeller for comparison purposes. As the designated blade of each propeller passes the pulse generator, an electrical signal is sent to the phasing control unit. For example, consider a twin engine aircraft with pulse generators keyed to blade number one. Based on the electrical pulses from each pulse generator, the phasing control unit determines the relative position of

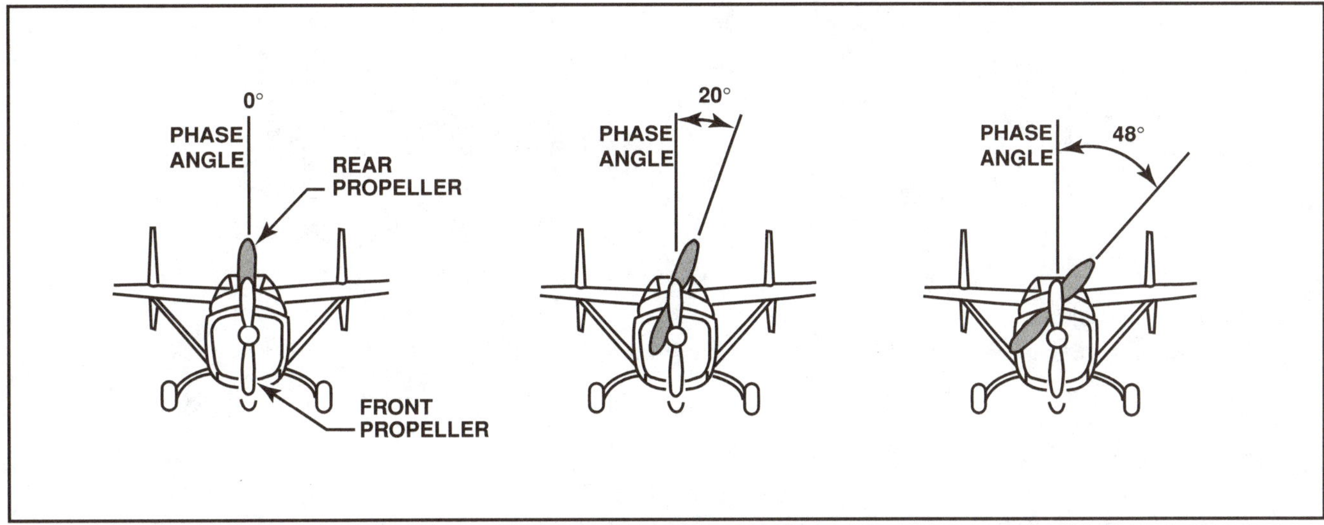

Figure 12-61. Synchrophasing allows a pilot to adjust the phase angle between the propellers for minimum noise and vibration levels.

each propeller's number one blade. A propeller manual phase control in the cockpit allows the pilot to manually select the phase angle which produces the minimum vibration and noise. The pulses from each engine are then compared and, if a difference exists, the phasing control unit electrically drives the slave governor to establish the selected phase angle between propellers. [Figure 12-62]

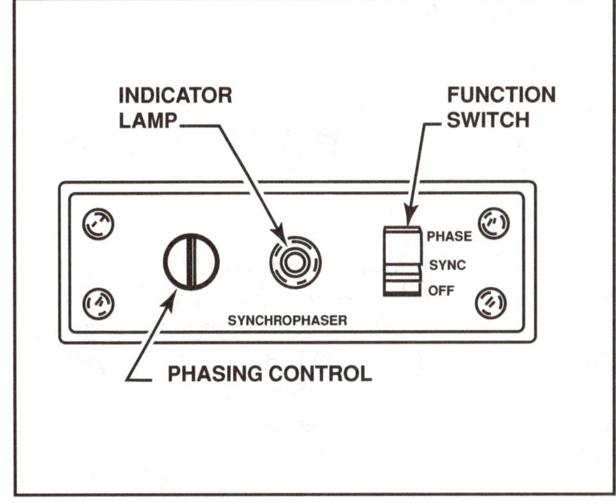

Figure 12-62. The synchrophasing control panel is mounted in the cockpit so cockpit crew members can adjust propeller blade phase angles in flight.

PROPELLER ICE CONTROL SYSTEMS

As aircraft use became more vital in the movement of cargo and passengers, the necessity to fly in nearly all weather conditions became more important. However, before flight in bad weather could be considered safe, auxiliary systems had to be devised that could either prevent or remove ice formations from an aircraft. Like the aircraft structure, propellers are susceptible to ice buildups and must be equipped with a system to remove ice accumulations. If allowed to accumulate, ice formations can distort a propeller blade's airfoil shape causing a loss in propeller efficiency and thrust. Furthermore, ice usually forms unevenly on a propeller blade and produces propeller unbalance and destructive vibration.

Currently, aircraft propellers may use either an anti-icing or a de-icing system. The difference between the two is that an **anti-icing** system prevents the formation of ice whereas a **de-icing** system removes ice after it has accumulated.

FLUID ANTI-ICING

A typical fluid anti-icing system consists of a control unit, a tank that holds a quantity of anti-icing fluid, a pump to deliver the fluid to the propeller, and nozzles. The control unit contains a **rheostat** which is adjusted to control the pump output. Fluid is pumped from the tank to a stationary nozzle

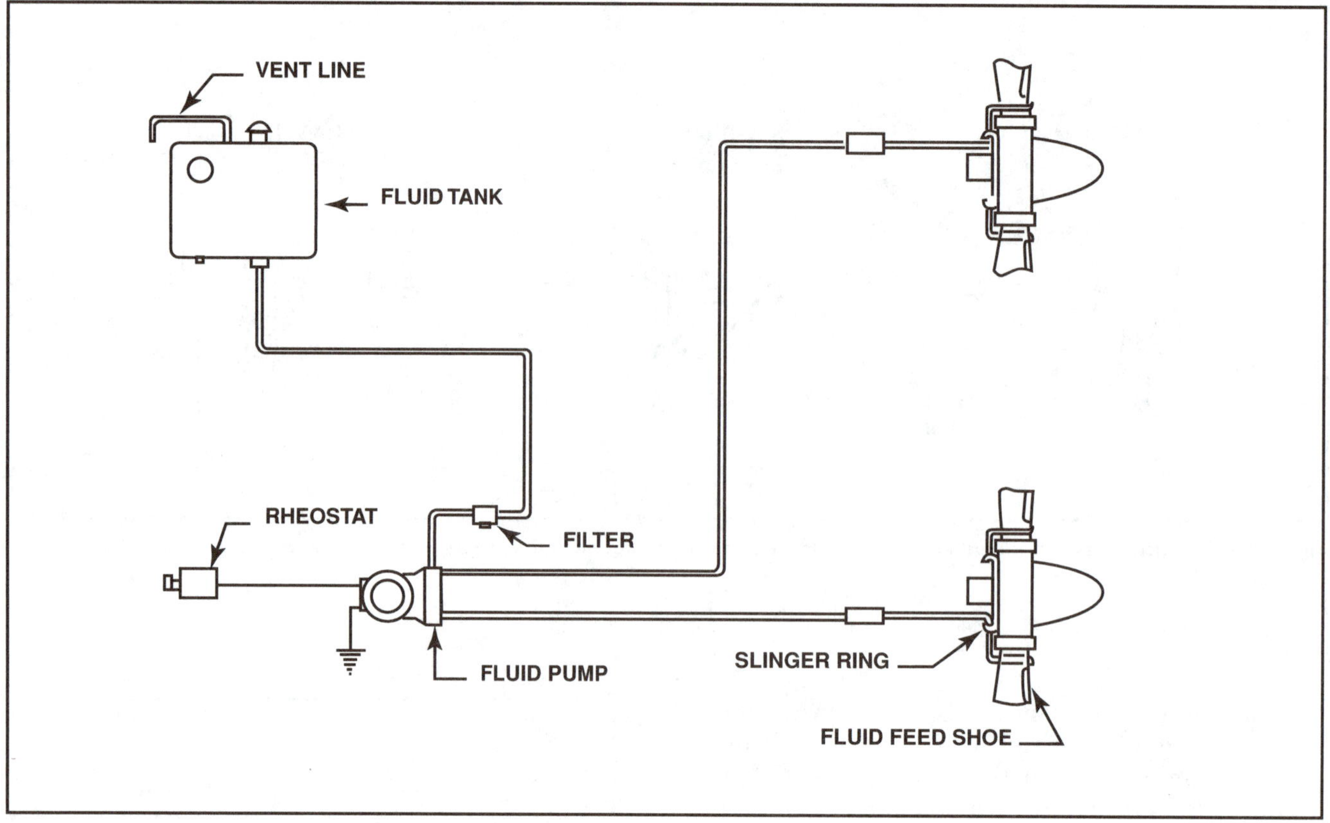

Figure 12-63. A typical propeller anti-icing system consists of a fluid tank, a rheostat control, a slinger ring for each propeller, and a fluid pump.

installed just behind the propeller on the engine nose case. As fluid passes through the nozzle, it enters a circular U-shaped channel called a **slinger ring**. A typical slinger ring is designed with a delivery tube for each propeller blade and is mounted on the rear of the propeller assembly. Once the fluid is in the slinger ring, centrifugal force sends the anti-icing fluid out through the delivery tubes to each blade shank. [Figure 12-63]

In order to disperse the fluid to areas which are more prone to ice buildups, feed shoes are typically installed on the leading edge of each propeller blade. Each **feed shoe** consists of a narrow strip of rubber that extends from the blade shank out to a blade station that is approximately 75 percent of the propeller radius. Feed shoes are molded with several parallel open channels that allow centrifugal force to direct fluid from the blade shank toward the blade tip. As anti-icing fluid flows along the channels, the relative wind also carries the fluid laterally from the channels over the leading edge of each blade.

The most commonly used anti-icing fluid is isopropyl alcohol because of its availability and low cost. Some other anti-icing fluids are made from phosphate compounds and are comparable to isopropyl alcohol in anti-icing performance. Anti-icing fluids made from phosphate compounds also have the advantage of reduced flammability, however, they are comparatively expensive.

ELECTRIC DE-ICE

A typical propeller de-icing system is electrically operated. An electrical propeller de-icing system consists of a power source, power relay, resistance heating elements, system controls, and a timer or cycling unit. The resistance heating elements may be mounted either internally or externally on each propeller blade. Externally mounted heating elements are known as de-icing boots and are attached to each blade with an approved bonding agent. System controls include an on/off switch, loadmeter, and protective devices such as current limiters or circuit breakers. The loadmeter is an ammeter which permits monitoring of individual circuit currents and visual verification of proper timer operation.

A typical electric propeller de-ice system supplies aircraft electrical system power to the propeller hub

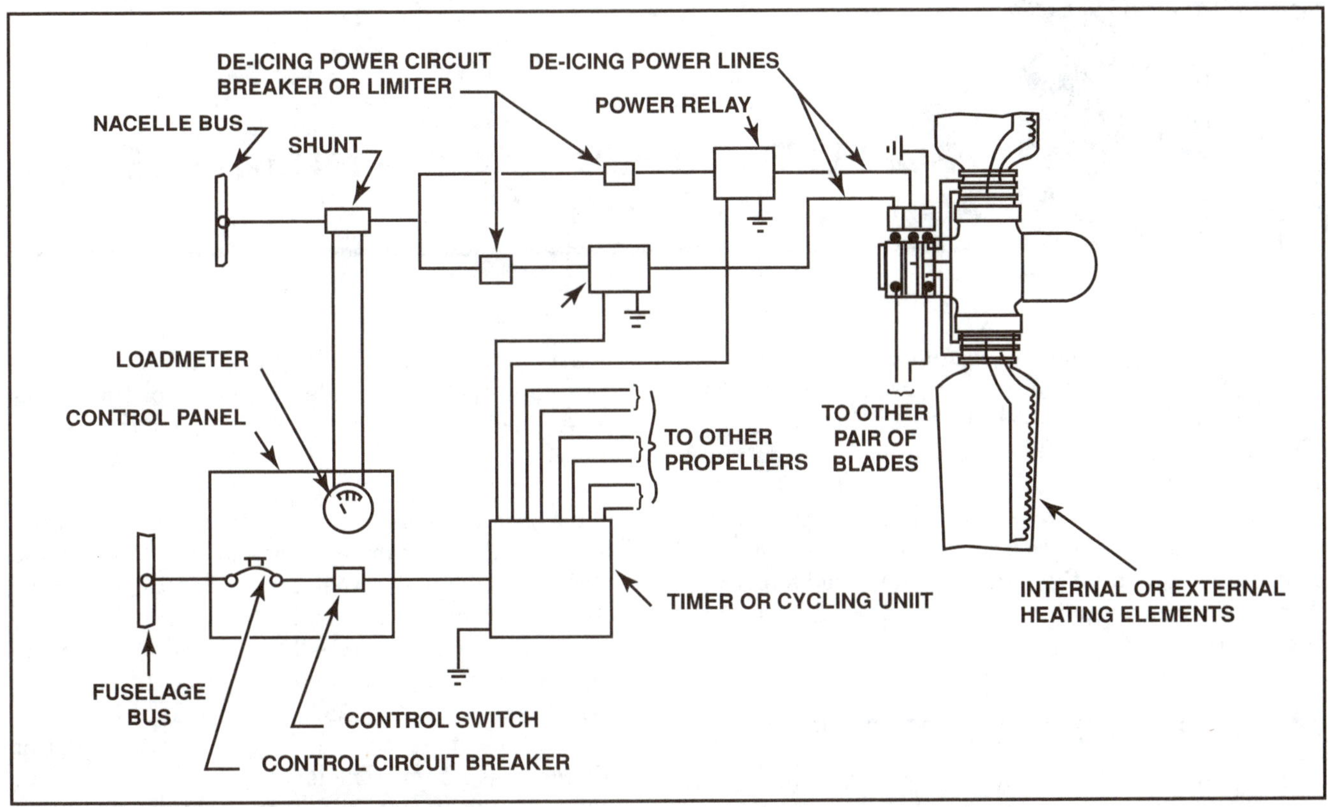

Figure 12-64. Aircraft electrical power is used to operate this propeller de-icing system. When the timer closes the relay, electrical current flows to the carbon brushes which, in turn, pass the current to the rotating slip rings on the propeller hub. Flexible connectors carry the current from the slip rings to each heating element.

through a set of brush blocks and slip rings. The **brush blocks** are mounted on the engine case just behind the propeller while the **slip rings** are mounted on the back of the propeller hub assembly. Flexible connectors on the propeller hub transfer power from the slip rings to each heating element. [Figure 12-64]

Electrical de-icing systems are usually designed for intermittent application of power to the heating elements for removal of small ice accumulations. De-icing effectiveness diminishes if ice accumulations are allowed to become excessive. Furthermore, proper control of heating intervals is critical in the prevention of runback. **Runback** refers to a condition where melted ice reforms behind a blade's leading edge. Heat should be applied just long enough to melt the ice face in contact with the blade. If the applied heat is more than that required to loosen the ice, but insufficient to evaporate all the resulting water, water can run back over the unheated blade surface and freeze again. Runback may result in a dangerous build-up of ice on blade areas which have no de-icing protection.

In addition to preventing runback, heating intervals are also carefully controlled to avoid excessive propeller vibrations. Ice accumulations must be removed from propeller blades evenly and in a balanced fashion from opposite blades to prevent excessive vibration. This is accomplished through the use of timing circuits that cycle power in a predetermined sequence to the blade heating elements. Cycling timers energize the heating elements for periods of 15 to 30 seconds with a complete cycle time of two minutes.

The de-icing boots may be checked for proper warming sequences during pre-flight inspections by turning the system on and feeling the boots. However, exercise caution and limit ground testing to prevent element overheating. Electric propeller de-icing systems are designed for use when the propellers are rotating, and for short periods of time during ground runup.

PROPELLER INSPECTION, MAINTENANCE, AND INSTALLATION

As an aviation maintenance technician, you will be required to inspect and perform routine maintenance on various types of propellers. Therefore, in addition to being familiar with propeller maintenance procedures, you must have a basic knowledge of maintenance regulations that relate to propellers. It is important to note that as a certified mechanic with a powerplant rating, you are authorized to perform only minor repairs and minor alternations to propellers.

MAINTENANCE REGULATIONS

FAR Part 43, Maintenance, Preventative Maintenance, Rebuilding, and Alteration, defines the different classes of maintenance for propeller systems. Appendix D lists the minimum requirements for 100-hour and annual inspections of propellers and their controls. For example, as a minimum during an annual or 100-hour inspection, propeller assemblies must be checked for cracks, nicks, and oil leakage. In addition, bolts must be inspected for proper torque and appropriate safetying. When equipped with anti-icing devices, those devices must be inspected for improper operations and obvious defects. Also, you are required to inspect propeller control mechanisms for improper operation, insecure mounting, and restricted travel.

Appendix A of FAR 43 lists propeller major alterations and repairs which must be performed by the manufacturer or a certified repair station. Propeller major alterations include changes in blade design, hub design, and governor or control design. Also included are installations of a propeller governors, feathering systems, de-icing systems, and parts not approved for the propeller. On the other hand, propeller major repairs include items such as retipping, replacement of fabric covering, and inlay work on wood propellers. Also included in fixed-pitch wood propeller major repairs are replacement of outer laminations and repair of elongated bolt holes in the hub. Any repairs to, or straightening of, steel propeller blades is considered to be a major repair. In addition, repairs to, or machining of, steel hubs is considered to be a major repair. Major repairs to aluminum propellers include shortening or straightening of blades and repairs to deep dents, cuts, scars, and nicks.

Other major repairs listed in Appendix A of Part 43 include the repair or replacement of internal blade elements such as internal de-icer heating elements. Also listed are controllable pitch propeller overhauls and repair of propeller governors. Given the number of items that are considered to be either major repairs or alterations to propellers, it may be difficult to differentiate whether a specific repair or alteration is minor or major. Therefore, if you are in doubt about the status of a contemplated alteration or repair, you should contact your local Flight Standards Office of the FAA.

AUTHORIZED MAINTENANCE PERSONNEL

Although you are restricted from performing major propeller alterations or repairs, you are responsible for minor repairs and alterations. In addition, you may install, adjust, and perform a 100-hour inspection of a propeller and its related components. Furthermore, an aviation maintenance technician holding an Inspection Authorization may perform an annual inspection on a propeller. However, that person may not approve for return to service major repairs and alterations to propellers or their related parts and appliances. Only an appropriately rated facility, such as a propeller repair station or the propeller manufacturer, may return a propeller or accessory to service after a major repair or alteration.

INSPECTION AND MAINTENANCE

Specific inspection items and minor maintenance tasks for which you are responsible depend on the type of propeller and its accessories. The following discussion provides generic information on typical inspection and maintenance procedures. However, the information provided here is only general in nature and, therefore, you should always consult the appropriate aircraft or propeller maintenance manuals and service bulletins for specific instructions and service limits.

WOOD PROPELLERS

A fixed-pitch wood propeller is simple in concept and operation; however, the fine details of its construction require close visual inspection. For example, both annual and 100-hour inspections require you to check for cracks, nicks, and properly torqued or safetied bolts. While required visual inspections are mostly conducted with the propeller mounted on the engine, there may be occasions when removal is necessary. For example, if excessive vibration exists, you may have to remove the propeller to check for elongated mounting bolt holes or proper balance.

To facilitate an inspection, a propeller should be cleaned. Wood propellers may be cleaned with warm water and a mild soap, using brushes or a cloth. If the aircraft operates near salt water, the propeller should be flushed with fresh water often. If a visual inspection after cleaning reveals defects which must be further examined or repaired, propeller removal may be necessary. Removal of a wood propeller is usually a simple matter of removing a spinner, safety devices such as cotter pins or wire, and the mounting bolts. In all instances, follow the recommended removal procedures outlined in the maintenance instructions for the aircraft and engine.

Common defects found in wood propellers include separation of the laminations and dents or bruises on the surface. Other possible damage includes cracks or scars across the blade back or face, broken sections, warping, and worn or oversize center bore and bolt holes. If a dent, bruise, or scar is found on a blade surface, inspect the damage with a magnifying glass while flexing the blade to help expose any cracks.

When inspecting metal tipping, look for looseness or slipping, loose screws or rivets, and cracks in the solder joints. If a crack is found in a solder joint near the blade tip, it may be an indication of wood deterioration. Therefore, the area near the crack should be inspected closely while flexing the blade tip. If no defects are found, the joint may be resoldered; however, the blade tip should be inspected at closer intervals for a recurrence of cracking. [Figure 12-65]

When inspecting the wooden blades installed on a ground-adjustable propeller, special attention should be given to the metal sleeve and shank area. The presence of cracks in these areas may indicate broken or loose lag screws.

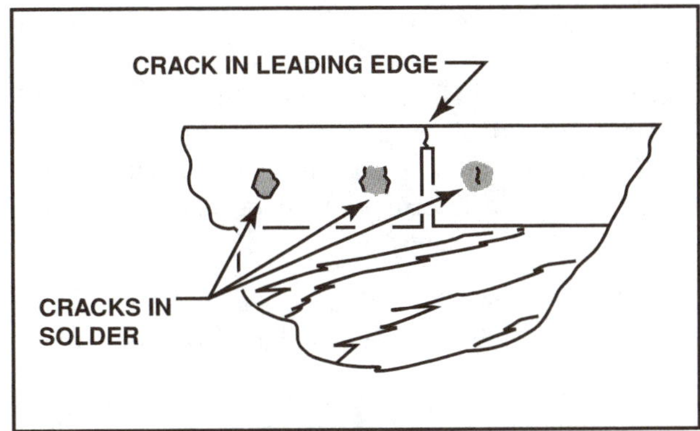

Figure 12-65. The metal tipping on a wood propeller should be inspected for cracks in the leading edge and in the solder covering the retaining screws. If a crack is found, a close inspection should be made of the entire area near the crack.

REPAIRS

Typically, small cracks parallel to the grain or small cuts on a wood propeller may be repaired by working resin glue into the crack. Once the glue is dry, the area is sanded with fine sandpaper and refinished with an approved varnish or other coating. Repairable tip fabric defects include cracks, bubbles, paint chipping, and wrinkles that appear when the tip is twisted or flexed. If the tip fabric has surface defects of 3/4 inch or less, and a breakdown in the wood structure is not suspected, the defect may be filled with several coats of lacquer. Once the lacquer has dried, the defect should blend in with the fabric surface. Defects larger than 3/4 inch should be referred to a repair station.

Typically, separated laminations are repairable when they occur in the outside lamination. However, the repair must be done by a certified propeller repair station or the manufacturer. Additional repairs that can be made by a propeller repair station and a propeller manufacturer include large cracks that require an inlay and restoration of elongated bolt holes with metal inserts. In addition, broken sections may be repairable, depending on the location and severity of the break. However, the determination of repairability and actual repairs must be done by a repair station or the manufacturer.

When repair work is done to a wooden propeller blade, a protective coating must be reapplied to the wood. However, restoration of the protective coating could change the propeller blade's balance. Therefore, the propeller's balance must be checked after the blade has been refinished. If an out-of-balance condition exists, it may be necessary to apply more protective coating on one blade than the other to achieve final balancing. More information on propeller balancing procedures is provided later in this section.

As with all propellers, there are some defects that cannot be repaired. For wooden propellers these include:

1. crack or deep cut across the grain
2. A split blade
3. Separated laminations, except for the outside laminations of a fixed-pitch propeller
4. Empty screw or rivet holes
5. Any appreciable warp
6. An appreciable portion of wood missing
7. An oversized crankshaft bore in a fixed-pitch propeller
8. Cracks between the crankshaft bore hole and bolt holes
9. Cracked internal laminations
10. Oversize or excessively elongated bolt holes

STORAGE

When a wood propeller is stored, it should be placed in a horizontal position to keep the moisture evenly distributed throughout the wood. In addition, the storage area should be cool, dark, dry, and well ventilated. Do not wrap the propeller in any material that seals it from the surrounding airflow. The reason for this is an airtight wrapping around wood propellers promotes wood decay.

ALUMINUM PROPELLERS

The properties of aluminum alloys make aluminum propellers durable and relatively inexpensive to maintain. However, some types of damage can be severe enough to cause blade failure. Therefore, aluminum propellers must be carefully inspected at regular intervals. In addition, if any damage is discovered that jeopardizes the integrity of a propeller, it must be repaired before further flight.

BLADE INSPECTION

A requirement for both annual and 100-hour inspections includes checking for cracks, nicks, and properly torqued or safetied bolts. As with a wood propeller, most inspections of a fixed-pitch aluminum propeller are conducted without removal. However, if operational problems such as vibrations occur, it may be necessary to remove the propeller for a detailed inspection of the hub area.

Removal procedures for a fixed-pitch aluminum propeller are the same as for a fixed-pitch wood propeller. However, the aluminum propeller may be heavier than a comparable sized wood propeller. If so, obtain help when necessary to support the propeller during removal and prevent damage to the propeller or personal injury.

Prior to an inspection, an aluminum propeller should be cleaned with a solution of mild soap and water using a soft brush or cloth to remove all dirt and grease. Acid or caustic cleaning materials should never be used on aluminum propellers because their use could lead to corrosion. Furthermore, avoid the use of power buffers, steel wool, steel brushes, or any other abrasive that may scratch or mar the blades. If a propeller has been subjected to salt water, it should be flushed with fresh water until all traces of salt have been removed. This should be accomplished as soon as possible after exposure to salt spray.

Once clean, aluminum blades are inspected for pitting, nicks, dents, cracks, and corrosion. Areas that are especially susceptible to damage include the leading edges and the blade face. To aid in the inspection process, you should inspect the entire propeller with a four-power magnifying glass. In addition, if a crack is suspected, a dye penetrant inspection should be performed. In many cases, a dye penetrant inspection will show whether visible lines and other marks are actually cracks or only scratches, saving the time and expense of unnecessary repairs.

Inspect the hub boss for damage and corrosion inside the center bore and on the surfaces which mount on the crankshaft. Also, inspect the bolt holes for cracks, excessive wear, and proper dimensions. Light corrosion can be cleaned from the hub boss with sandpaper. The affected area may then be painted or treated to help prevent further corrosion. Propellers with damage, dimensional wear, or heavy corrosion in the boss area should be referred to a repair station for appropriate repairs.

REPAIRS

When an inspection reveals surface damage such as nicks, scratches, or gouges on an aluminum alloy propeller blade, repairs should be made as soon as possible. By making prompt repairs, you help eliminate stress concentration points which, in turn, helps to prevent cracks and fatigue failure. Defects on a bladeís leading and trailing edges may be dressed out by using a combination of round and half round files. When a repair is complete, it should blend in smoothly with the edge and should not leave any sharp edges or angles. In all cases, the repair of surface defects on aluminum propeller blades must be made parallel to the length of the blade. In addition, the approximate maximum allowable size of a typical repair on a propeller edge is 1/8 inch deep by no more than 1 1/2 inches in length. [Figure 12-66]

Repairs to the face and back of a blade are performed with a spoon-like **riffle file** which is used to dish out the damaged area. The maximum allowable repair size of a typical surface defect on a blade face or back is 1/16 inch deep by 3/8 inch wide by 1 inch long. In addition, all repairs must be finished by polishing with very fine sandpaper, moving the paper in a direction parallel to the length of the blade. Once sanded, the surface should be treated with **Alodine**, paint, or other approved protective coating. [Figure 12-67]

Damage in the shank area of a propeller blade cannot be repaired in the field and should be referred to an overhaul facility for corrective action. Since all forces acting on the propeller are concentrated at the shank, any damage in this area is critical. Furthermore, transverse cracks of any size render an aluminum alloy blade unrepairable.

Contrary to popular belief, bent blades can often be repaired. To determine if a blade is repairable, begin by measuring the thickness of the blade where the bend is located. Once this is done, determine the blade station of the bend by measuring from the center of the hub to the center of the bend. With the center of the bend located, mark the blade one inch on each side of the bend and place a protractor tangent to the one inch marks to determine the bend angle. [Figure 12-68]

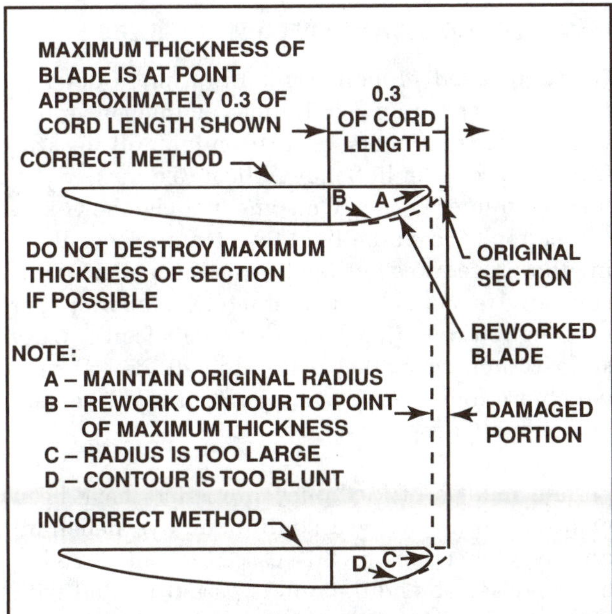

Figure 12-66. When making a repair to either the leading or trailing edge of a propeller, ensure that the repair will not exceed the propeller blade's minimum dimensions or change the profile of its leading edge.

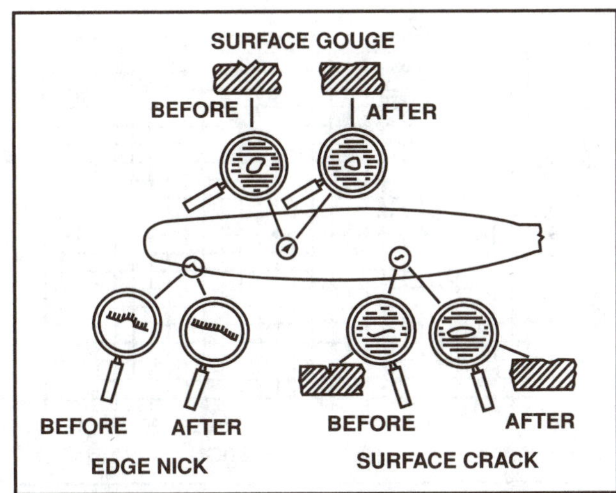

Figure 12-67. Repairs on the blade face and leading edge should blend into the blade profile to maintain smooth airflow over the propeller.

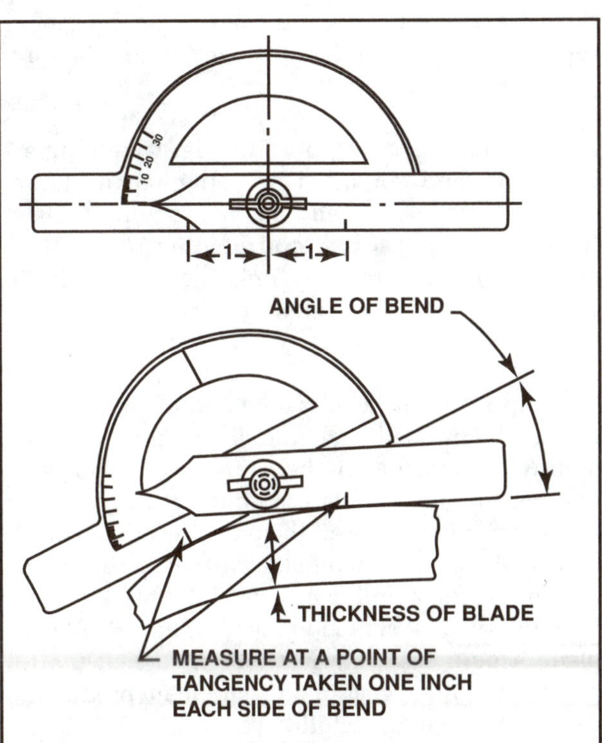

Figure 12-68. A protractor is used to determine the amount of bend in a propeller blade. Place the hinge over the center of the bend, set the protractor legs tangent to the blade one inch on each side of the bend centerline, and read the amount of bend in degrees on the protractor.

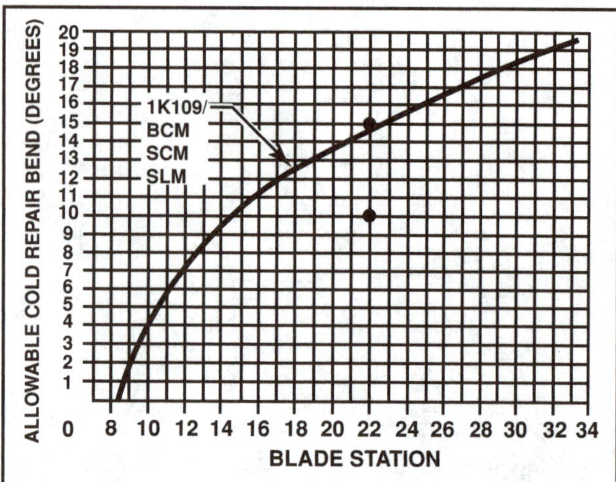

Figure 12-69. This chart shows the amount of bend damage at a given blade station that can be repaired by cold bending. Values that fall beneath the curve are repairable. For example, a 10 degree bend at blade station 22 can be repaired by cold bending. However, a 15 degree bend at station 22 cannot be repaired.

Many propeller manufacturers furnish charts that help a technician determine if a bend is repairable. In most cases, the chart consists of a graph with the blade station on one axis and the degree of bend on the opposite axis. When reading this type of chart, any bend below the graph line is repairable while any bend above the line is unrepairable. [Figure 12-69]

If the proper chart is not available, take the measurements and contact a propeller repair station for a decision before sending the propeller to them for straightening. Cold straightening repairs to a bent aluminum propeller must be accomplished by an appropriately rated repair station or the manufacturer.

Once a repair has been made to an aluminum propeller, the propeller should be cleaned with an approved solvent. This helps remove all traces of dye penetrant materials used during an inspection and subsequent repair. If the propeller was painted, repaint the face of each blade with one coat of zinc chromate primer and two coats of flat black lacquer from the six inch station to the tip. The back of each blade should have the last four inches of the tip painted with one coat of zinc chromate primer and two coats of a high visibility color.

If a high polish is desired, a number of good grades of commercial metal polish are available. However, after completing the polishing operation, all traces of polish should be removed.

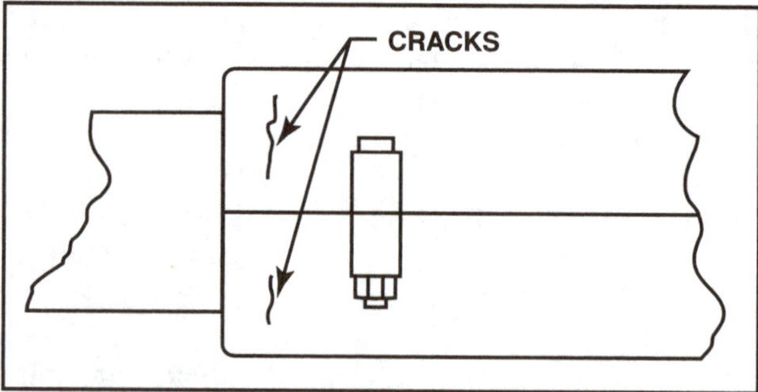

Figure 12-70. Cracks in the blade retention area of the hub of a ground-adjustable propeller are critical defects. Dye-penetrant inspection methods are used to detect such cracks.

GROUND-ADJUSTABLE PROPELLERS

When inspecting a ground-adjustable propeller, inspect the blades in the same manner as discussed earlier paying particular attention to the areas around the retention shoulders at the base of the blades. The corresponding blade retention areas of the hubs should also be closely inspected. A dye-penetrant inspection is recommended on the external surfaces in these areas during routine, 100-hour, and annual inspections. Unless complete disassembly of the propeller is necessary for other reasons, disassembly is not recommended at these inspection intervals. The reason for this is to reduce the wear and tear on the hub associated with disassembly and reassembly. [Figure 12-70]

McCAULEY CONSTANT-SPEED PROPELLERS

Constant-speed propellers require a more detailed inspection and, in general, more maintenance than fixed-pitch propellers. For example, oil leaking from the propeller hub may indicate a defective piston-to-cylinder O-ring. On some models, the O-ring can be replaced in the field by a technician following the procedures outlined in the propeller or aircraft service manual. On other models, the propeller must be returned to a propeller repair facility. Any seals, other than the piston-to-cylinder O-ring, which are found to be leaking require replacement by a propeller repair facility.

Certain models of McCauley propellers have been modified to allow for a continuous dye penetrant type of inspection. In this case, the hub breather holes are sealed and the hub is partially filled with oil that is dyed red. The red dye in the oil makes the location of developing cracks readily apparent, indicating that the propeller should be removed from service.

HARTZELL CONSTANT-SPEED PROPELLERS

Hartzell constant-speed propeller systems require the same types of inspection, maintenance, and repair as other constant-speed systems. However, an additional inspection is recommended to check a steel hub for cracks. Magnetic particle inspection is the preferred method of inspection when checking steel propeller hubs for cracks.

If grease leakage is detected on a Hartzell propeller, determine the cause and correct it as soon as possible. The most common causes of grease leakage are loose, missing, or defective grease fittings, or **zerks**. Other causes could be loose blade clamps, defective blade clamp seals, and overlubrication of the blade-to-hub joints.

If a zerk fitting is loose, missing or defective, it should be tightened or replaced as appropriate. Loose blade clamps should be torqued to the specified value for the particular model of propeller and resafetied. Check the blade angle to be certain that it does not change during retorquing.

When servicing a Hartzell constant-speed propeller, special care should be taken when lubricating the blade-to-hub joints to prevent damage to the blade seals. First, remove one of the two zerk fittings from the hub. Next, grease the blade-to-hub joint through the remaining zerk. Some propeller models should be serviced until grease comes out of the hole from which the zerk was removed. In contrast, other models require less grease. By following the recommended procedures, you prevent pressure from building up in the blade grease chamber and damaging the blade seals. After lubrication, reinstall the zerk fittings, replace the protective cap, and safety the cap to the zerk fitting.

HARTZELL FEATHERING COMPACT PROPELLERS

Inspection, maintenance, and repair procedures for a Hartzell feathering propeller system is the same as those for other Hartzell constant-speed systems. However, one additional check which should be accomplished at each 100-hour and annual inspection is the nitrogen charge within the propeller hub. If the charge is too low, it may not feather or respond properly to constant-speed operation and it may have a tendency to overspeed or surge. On the other hand, the propeller system may not reach full rpm and may feather upon engine shutdown if the nitrogen pressure is too high. When checking the nitrogen charge, ensure that the blades are latched in the low pitch position. If insufficient pressure exists, follow the manufacturer's instructions for servicing with nitrogen.

HAMILTON- STANDARD HYDROMATIC PROPELLERS

Hydromatic propellers are inspected, maintained, and repaired in accordance with the same procedures as other constant-speed systems. Inspections primarily involve a check for proper operation, looking for oil leaks, and inspecting external oil lines for signs of deterioration or abrasion.

Oil leaks in the propeller are normally caused by a defective gasket or loose hardware. If oil covers all of the propeller, the likely cause is a leaking dome plug. Oil leakage around the rear cone usually indicates a defective spider-shaft oil seal. If oil appears on the barrel immediately behind the dome, the dome gasket is leaking or the dome nut is loose. The dome plug seal and the dome-to-barrel gasket can be replaced in the field.

Signs of leaking oil around the blade shank area or between the barrel halves could indicate loose hub bolts or defective gaskets. Loose hub bolts can be retorqued, but leaking gaskets must be replaced by an overhaul facility. The propeller is lubricated by engine operating oil, therefore it needs no other lubrication.

PROPELLER LUBRICATION

All the adjustable pitch propeller systems just discussed require inspections and servicing at regular intervals. Lubrication is, in many cases, one of the required servicing procedures. The grease used to lubricate a propeller must have the proper anti-friction and plasticity characteristics. In other words, an approved grease reduces the frictional resistance of moving parts and molds easily into any form under pressure.

Propeller lubrication procedures are usually published in the manufacturerís instructions along with oil and grease specifications. Experience indicates that water sometimes seeps into the propeller blade bearing assemblies of some propeller models. For this reason the propeller manufacturer's greasing schedule and recommended oil and grease specifications must be followed to ensure proper lubrication of moving parts.

STEEL AND COMPOSITE PROPELLERS

Propellers made from steel or composite material may be cleaned and inspected in the same manner as wood or aluminum propellers. However, manufacturers of composite propellers may also include cleaning techniques and inspection items that are unique to composite materials. Manufacturer's instructions take precedence over general cleaning and inspection techniques.

With these propellers, you are restricted to inspections and cleaning. As you recall, any repairs made to correct defects in steel or composition propellers must be accomplished by an appropriately rated repair station or the manufacturer.

BLADE CUFF INSPECTION

If you recall, some propeller blades are fitted with blade cuffs to improve airflow over the blade shank and cooling airflow through the engine. When this is the case, the blade cuffs must also be inspected and checked for proper clearance. Longitudinal clearance of constant-speed propeller blades or cuffs must be at least 1/2 inch between propeller parts and stationary parts of the aircraft. This clearance must be measured with the propeller blades feathered or in the most critical pitch configuration.

GOVERNORS

As mentioned earlier, you, as an aviation maintenance technician, are somewhat limited as to what you can do with propeller systems. Nowhere is this more evident than with propeller governors. Inspection of governors is limited to checking for oil leaks and security of mounting. Maintenance consists of properly rigging the governor controls and verifying freedom of motion. Although you may remove and install propeller governors on an engine, inspections and repairs which require governor disassembly must be accomplished by a properly equipped and certified repair station.

BALANCING

Exact propeller balance is critical to proper engine and propeller performance. Any time maintenance is conducted or a repair is made that adds or removes weight from a propeller, you must check the propeller's balance. For example, if a wood propeller is refinished, the new varnish can create an imbalance if it is unevenly applied. In another example, a metal blade that is shortened because of tip damage requires shortening of the opposite blade to maintain balance.

Propellers are balanced both statically or dynamically. A propeller is **statically balanced** when the propeller's center of gravity coincides with its axis of rotation. On the other hand, a propeller is **dynamically balanced** when the centers of gravity of the blades rotate in the same plane of rotation.

STATIC BALANCE

Static balancing is accomplished by using either the knife-edge method or the suspension method. Of the two static balancing methods, the knife-edge method is simpler and more accurate.

To balance a propeller using the knife-edge method, a test stand consisting of two hardened steel edges must be used. In addition, the test stand must be located in a room or area that is free from any air motion or heavy vibration.

Before you check a propeller's balance, you should first verify that the blade angles are all the same. If the blade angles are correct you can check a propeller's balance by following the listed sequence of operations:

1. Insert a bushing in the propeller hub bore hole.
2. Insert a mandrel or arbor through the bushing to support the propeller on the balance knives.
3. Place the propeller assembly so that the ends of the arbor are supported on the test stand. The propeller must be free to rotate.

Once in the test stand, the propeller should be checked for horizontal and vertical balance. To check a two-bladed propeller assembly for vertical balance, position one blade in the vertical position. Next, repeat the vertical position check with the blade positions reversed from the first vertical check. If the propeller is balanced vertically, it will remain in a vertical position regardless of which blade is pointing up. On the other hand, if a vertical imbalance exists, the propeller will have a tendency to come to rest in a horizontal position. [Figure 12-71]

To check a two-bladed propeller assembly for horizontal balance, position the propeller in a horizontal position with both blades sticking straight out. If

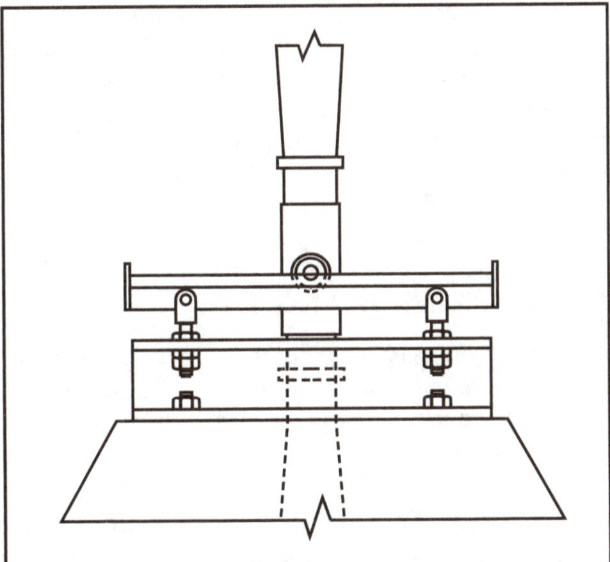

Figure 12-71. In a vertical balance check, the propeller blades are aligned vertically and an imbalance condition causes them to move to a horizontal position.

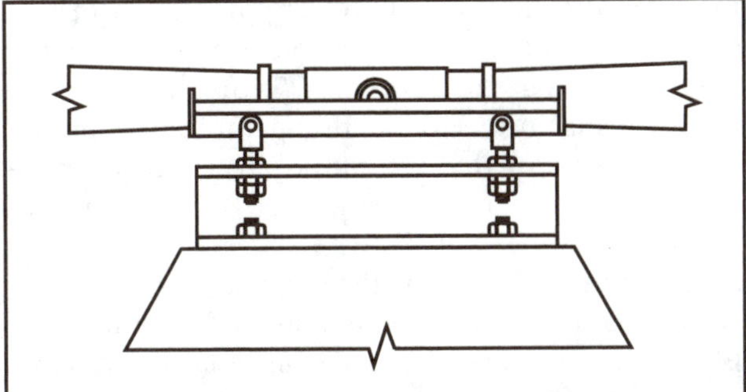

Figure 12-72. To check horizontal balance, the propeller is positioned horizontally. Any rotation from this position indicates a heavy blade.

the propeller is horizontally balanced, it will remain in a horizontal position. On the other hand, if a horizontal imbalance exists, one blade will tend to move downward causing the propeller to come to rest in a vertical position. [Figure 12-72]

A two-bladed propeller that is properly balanced will have no tendency to rotate in any of the test positions. If the propeller balances perfectly in all described positions, it should also balance perfectly in all intermediate positions. When necessary, check for balance in intermediate positions to verify the check in the originally described positions.

Static balancing of a three-bladed propeller requires placing the propeller in three basic test positions. First, rotate the propeller until blade number one is pointing downward. Similarly, place blade number two in the downward position, then blade number three. A properly balanced three-bladed propeller has no tendency to rotate from any of the three positions. [Figure 12-73]

In the suspension method for checking static balance, the propeller is hung by a cord. A disk is firmly attached to the cord and a cylinder is attached to the propeller. Any imbalance is determined by the eccentricity between the disk and the cylinder.

Out-of-Balance Repairs

When a propeller assembly exhibits a definite tendency to rotate, certain corrections to remove the imbalance are allowed. The addition of permanent fixed weights is permitted at acceptable locations when the total weight of the propeller assembly is under allowable limits. Likewise, the removal of weight is permitted from acceptable locations when the total weight of the propeller assembly is equal to the allowable limit.

The location for removal or addition of weight on a propeller is determined by the propeller manufac-

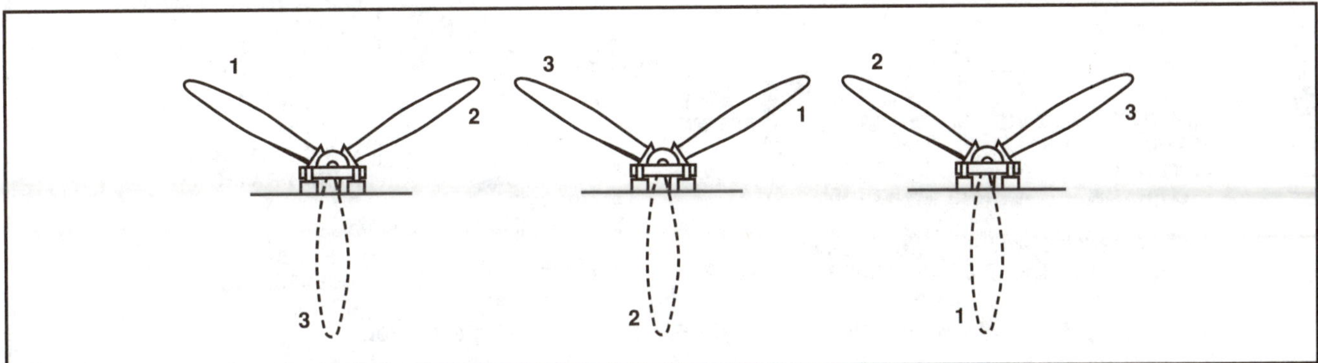

Figure 12-73. A three-bladed propeller is properly balanced when each blade can be placed in the six o'clock position with no tendency to rotate.

turer. The method and point of application of balance corrections must be in accordance with the manufacturer's instructions. Typically, vertical imbalance is corrected by adding a metal weight on the light side of the hub 90 degrees from the propeller's horizontal centerline. On a wooden propeller, horizontal imbalance is corrected by adding or removing solder at the propeller blade tips. Horizontal balance correction on an aluminum propeller often involves the removal of small amounts of metal by filing.

DYNAMIC BALANCE

A propeller exhibits dynamic balance when the centers of gravity of similar propeller elements, such as the propeller blades, rotate in the same plane of rotation. A dynamic imbalance resulting from improper mass distribution is usually negligible if the blades on a propeller track within limits. One reason for this is that the length of the propeller assembly along the engine crankshaft is very short compared to its diameter. Another reason is the fact that the blades track the same plane perpendicular to the axis of the crankshaft.

Modern methods of checking dynamic balance require the propeller, spinner, and related equipment to be installed on the aircraft. With the engine running, electronic equipment senses and pinpoints the location of an imbalance. In addition, the test equipment typically determines the amount of weight required to correct the condition.

CHECKING BLADE ANGLE

At times, you may be required to check the blade angle at a specific blade station. To do this, a **universal propeller protractor** is typically used. [Figure 12-74]

The frame of a typical protractor is made of aluminum alloy with three square sides at 90 degree angles. A bubble spirit level mounted on one corner of the front of the frame swings out to indicate when the protractor is level. A movable ring is located inside the frame and is used to set the zero reference angle for blade angle measurements. The ring is engraved with vernier index marks, which allow readings as small as one tenth

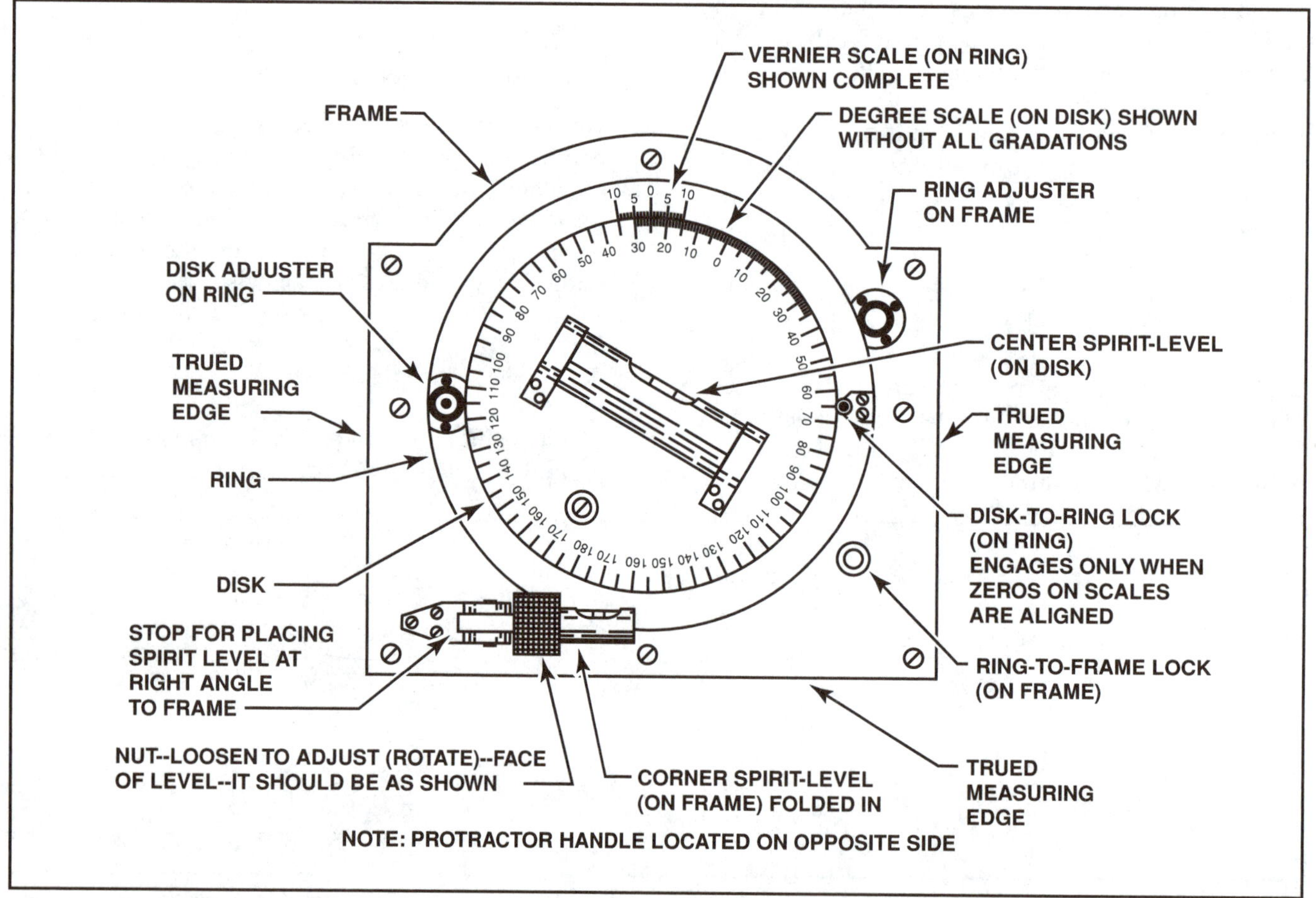

Figure 12-74. A universal propeller protractor such as this one is used to check propeller blade angle.

of a degree. A center disk is engraved with a degree scale from zero to 180 degrees, both positive and negative. In addition, the center disk contains a spirit level to indicate when the center disk is level.

Before measuring a propeller blade angle, determine the reference blade station from the aircraft manufacturer's maintenance manual. Mark this reference station on the blade with chalk or with a grease pencil. Next, establish the reference plane from the engine crankshaft centerline. Do not reference the airframe attitude because some engines are installed at an angle to help counter the effects of torque. To zero the protractor, loosen the ring-to-frame lock, align the zeros on the disk and the ring, and engage the disk-to-ring lock. Place the edge of the protractor on a flat surface of the propeller hub that is either parallel to, or perpendicular to, the crankshaft centerline. Now, turn the ring adjuster until the spirit level in the center of the disk is level. The corner level should also be leveled. Now, tighten the ring-to-frame lock, and release the disk-to-ring lock. The protractor is now aligned with the engine crankshaft. [Figure 12-75]

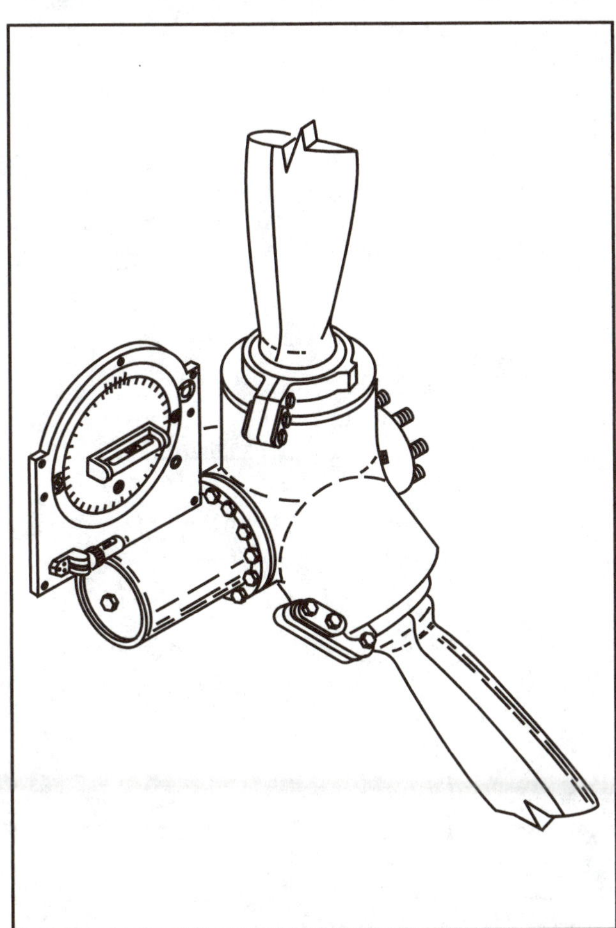

Figure 12-75. Before measuring propeller blade angle, the protractor must be "zeroed" or adjusted to a reference. A common reference is the propeller hub.

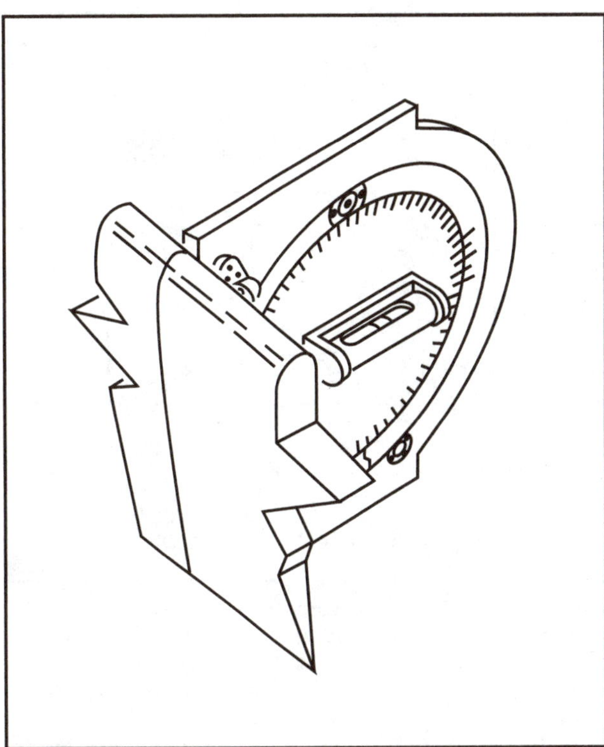

Figure 12-76. To measure the blade angle, the protractor is held against the blade face and the disk adjuster is rotated until the spirit level centers.

Once the protractor is zeroed, rotate the propeller until one blade is horizontal and place the protractor on the blade face at the reference station mark. Stand on the same side of the propeller facing in the same direction you were when zeroing the protractor. If you desire to measure from the other direction, you must zero the protractor from that side. With the protractor resting on the face of the blade, turn the disk adjuster until the spirit level centers. Now read the blade angle using the zero line on the ring as the index. Accuracy in tenths of degrees can be read from the vernier scale. To measure the angle of another blade, rotate the desired blade to the same horizontal position and repeat the process. [Figure 12-76]

If the face of the propeller blade is curved, use masking tape to attach a piece of 1/8 inch drill rod 1/2 inch from the leading and trailing edges. Once

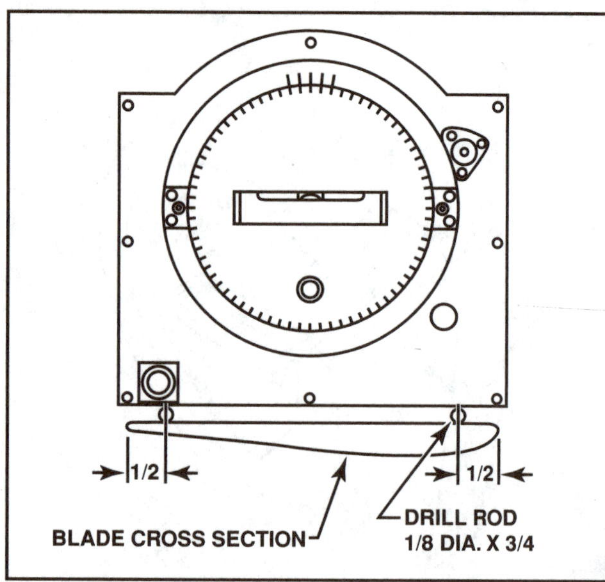

Figure 12-77. To compensate for blade curvature, small pieces of 1/4 inch drill rod are attached to the propeller blade to provide a level surface for the protractor.

the rods are secure, measure the angle with the protractor resting on the rods. [Figure 12-77]

If dissimilar blade angles exist on an aluminum fixed-pitch propeller, the blades can be repitched by a propeller repair station or the manufacturer. Consult the propeller repair facility and provide details on the amount of allowable pitch variation between blades.

BLADE ANGLE ADJUSTMENTS

All propeller systems other than fixed-pitch propellers require occasional blade angle adjustments. For example, ground-adjustable propellers are set to one blade angle while controllable pitch propellers require the setting of low and high blade angle limits. The method used to make blade angle adjustments depends on the propeller type. The following examples represent the more commonly used methods for adjusting blade angle.

GROUND-ADJUSTABLE PROPELLER

To adjust the propeller blade angle on a ground-adjustable propeller, you must first determine the reference blade station that must be used. This information is typically contained in the propeller or aircraft maintenance manual. Once the reference station is known, check the specifications for the blade angle range approved for the aircraft. A typical range for a ground-adjustable propeller is from 7 to 15 degrees.

In most cases, a blade angle adjustment to a ground-adjustable propeller can be made with the propeller on the aircraft or on a propeller bench. To make the actual adjustment, begin by placing a grease pencil mark across the hub and blade to mark their relative positions. The mark provides visual identification of the original blade angle setting and a reference mark for adjustment to the new blade angle. Once the blades are marked, loosen the hub bolts or clamps and rotate the propeller to a horizontal position.

To change the blade angle, the hub halves must be separated slightly once the clamps or bolts are loosened. The blades may then be rotated in the hub until the desired blade angle is set. To help you rotate a given propeller blade, a propeller blade paddle is typically used. If a blade binds, jiggle the blade as it is being rotated to the new angle. [Figure 12-78]

Using the universal propeller protractor, check the blade angle after tightening the hub clamps or bolts. While loose in the hub, the blades droop slightly and will move a small amount as the hub is tightened. Because of this, you may be required to repeat the procedure a few times until the blades are set properly. Typically, an acceptable blade angle tolerance between the desired angle and the actual angle is 0.1 degrees. Once the tolerance is met, the propeller hardware can be properly torqued and safetied.

COUNTERWEIGHT PROPELLER

On a counterweighted propeller, the propeller blade angles are adjusted by means of a set of stop

Figure 12-78. A propeller blade paddle makes the task of changing blade angles much easier.

nuts on an index pin located under each counterweight cap. To gain access to the index pin, remove the clevis pin which safeties the counterweight cap and remove the cap. Pull the index pin out of its recess in the counterweight or push it out from behind the counterweight bracket with a small tool. [Figure 12-79]

Alongside the recess which holds the index pin is a scale calibrated with half degree marks and a numerical scale from zero to ten. This scale is used to adjust and set the stop nuts on the index pin.

The propeller blade index number, also known as the base setting, should be stamped in a lead plug located near the index pin recess. This number indicates the maximum blade angle for which the propeller was adjusted during its last overhaul. The maximum blade angle is typically 25 degrees and is used to calculate where the stop nuts on the index pin should be positioned. For example, if the blade index is 25 degrees and the aircraft specifications specify a low blade angle of 17 and a high angle of 22 degrees, the stop nut positions are determined by subtracting the appropriate blade angle from the blade index. Therefore, to set the 17 degree low blade angle, the stop nut is positioned on the index pin so that the edge toward the center of the pin will align with the 8 degree (25 – 17 = 8) mark on the scale. On the other hand, to set the 22 degree high blade angle, the stop nut is positioned to line up its edge with the 3 degree (25 – 22 = 3) mark.

Once the stop nuts are set, the index pins are installed in the counterweights and the caps are replaced. With everything secured, the blades should be moved through their full range of travel. Once this is done, position the blades in their high blade angle and measure the blade angle at the specified reference station. A common reference station for a counterweighted propeller is the 42-inch station. Next, move the blades to their low blade angle stop and check these angles. Make small adjustments to the stop nut positions as necessary to bring the angles within acceptable limits.

HARTZELL CONSTANT-SPEED PROPELLERS

Hartzell steel hub propellers can be adjusted for the desired low blade angle by loosening the hub clamps and rotating the blades. However, you should realize that, anytime the low blade angle is changed, the high blade angle will also change. The reason for this is because the piston within the propeller hub can only travel a fixed amount. Once the desired blade angle is obtained, the clamps are retorqued and safetied.

The low pitch setting on a Hartzell compact propeller is adjusted with the adjusting screw on the hub cylinder. To make a blade adjustment, begin by loosening the jam nut on the adjusting screw and rotating the screw clockwise to increase the low blade angle, or counterclockwise to decrease the angle. When the desired angle is set, retighten the jam nut. When changing the blade angles, always refer to the aircraft specifications and the propeller manufacturer's manual for instructions about specific propeller models. [Figure 12-80]

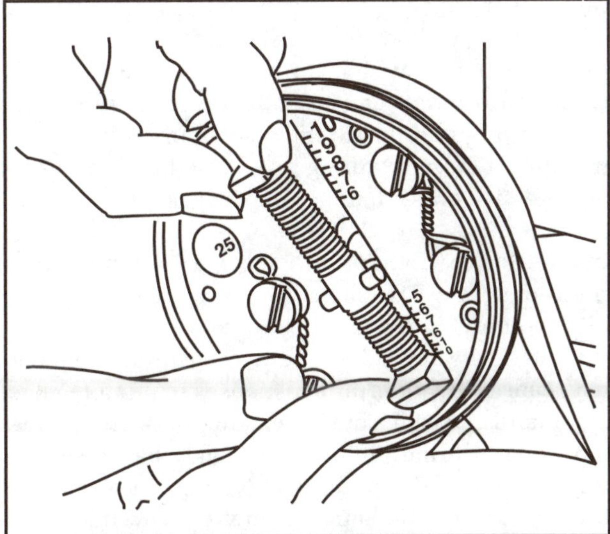

Figure 12-79. The propeller blade angle of a counterweight propeller is adjusted by positioning the stop nuts located on the index pins inside each of the counterweights.

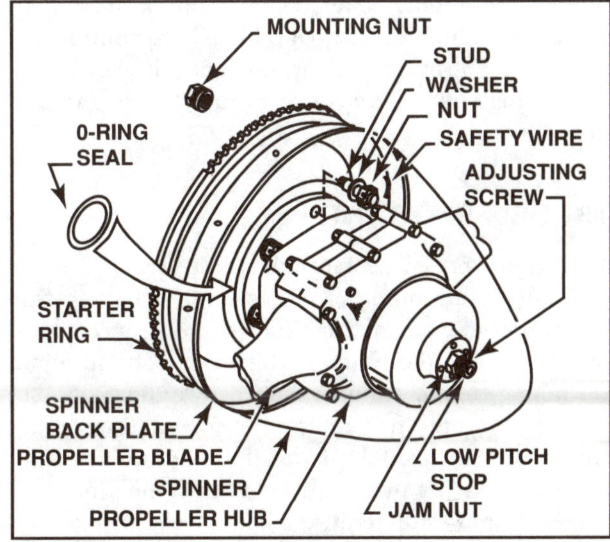

Figure 12-80. The low pitch setting for Hartzell compact propellers is adjusted with the adjusting screw on the hub cylinder.

BLADE TRACKING

Propeller blade tracking is a procedure which allows you to check the track of each propeller blade tip as it travels through its arc of rotation. In other words, by checking the tracking of a propeller, you compare the positions of the propeller blade tips relative to each other. This procedure is normally accomplished when troubleshooting a vibration problem or as a final check after balancing and reinstallating a propeller. Metal propellers up to six feet in diameter on light aircraft must track within 1/16 inch of each other. On the other hand, the track of a wood propeller should not be out more than 1/8 inch.

Before a propeller can be tracked, the aircraft must be locked in a stationary position. This is typically accomplished by chocking the wheels to prevent aircraft movement. Once this is done, place a fixed reference point on the ground that is within 1/4 inch of the propeller arc. This may be done by placing a board on blocks under the propeller arc and taping a piece of paper to the board. With the reference point in place, rotate the propeller blade and mark the track of each blade. The maximum difference in track for all of the blades should not exceed the limits mentioned above. [Figure 12-81]

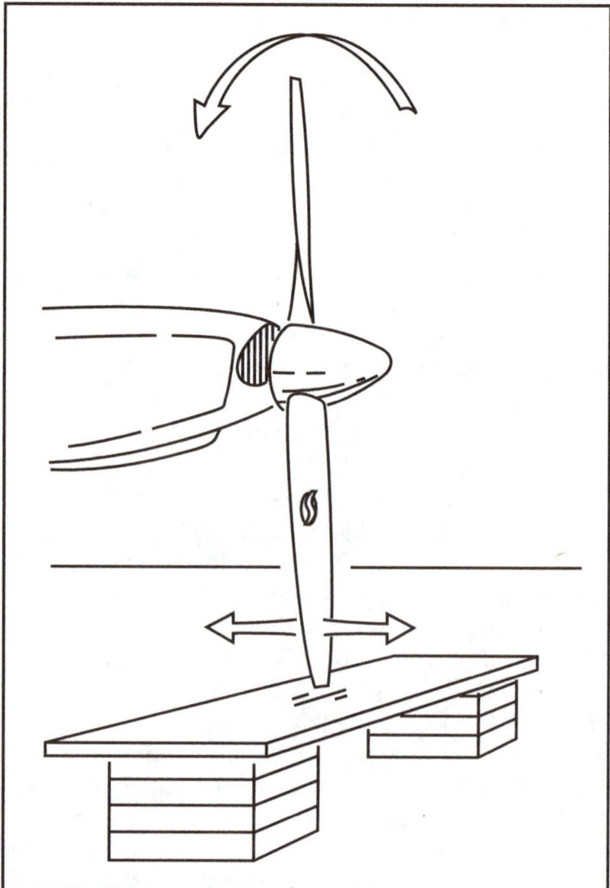

Figure 12-81. A propeller can be tracked by placing a board within 1/4 inch of the propeller arc. Rotate the propeller and mark the path each blade tip follows as it passes the board.

If the propeller track is off more than is allowed, the reason should be determined and the condition corrected. The easiest item to check is the torque of the propeller retaining bolts. If all bolts are properly torqued, the propeller should be removed to allow an inspection for the presence of debris or damage. In addition, it may be necessary to check the crankshaft for alignment. If no problems are found, the excessive out-of-track condition may be corrected by placing shims between the inner flange and the propeller.

TROUBLESHOOTING

The origins of powerplant vibrations are sometimes difficult to pinpoint. To determine whether the vibrations are emanating from the engine or propeller, observe the propeller hub, dome, or spinner. With the engine running between 1,200 to 1,500 rpm, observe the hub or spinner for rotation on an absolutely horizontal plane. If the propeller hub appears to swing in a slight orbit, or if the vibration becomes more apparent at higher rpms, the vibration is normally caused by the propeller. If the propeller hub oscillates, the difficulty is probably caused by engine vibration.

If excessive powerplant vibration is traced to the propeller, the problem could be one of several things. For example, dissimilar blade angle settings can lead to an uneven thrust distribution between propeller blades which, in turn, can lead to vibration. Additional causes of propeller vibration include propeller blade imbalance, improper blade tracking, a loose retaining nut, loose hub hardware, or excessive crankshaft spline wear.

In addition to vibration problems, a malfunctioning pitch-changing mechanism may require troubleshooting. For example, sludge in oil passages or the pitch selector valve of a two-position propeller may cause slow or erratic responses to pitch-change commands. Furthermore, erratic or jerky blade movement during pitch changes may be caused by trapped air in the cylinder. Cycling the propeller through its pitch-change operation several times usually purges air from the system. In addition, the linkage from the cockpit pitch control lever to the selector valve may become loose and fail to activate the selector valve. Operations in a marine environment can cause salt-water corrosion around the propeller cylinder and piston, leading to sporadic and unreliable pitch changes.

HAMILTON-STANDARD HYDROMATIC

Troubleshooting procedures and solutions discussed for other systems are generally applicable to the feathering hydromatic system. If the propeller fails to respond to the cockpit propeller control lever, but can be feathered and unfeathered, the cause is most likely a failure of the governor or governor control system. If the propeller fails to feather, check the system for electrical faults or for open wiring to the electrical components.

If the propeller fails to unfeather after feathering normally, the distributor valve is not shifting. On the other hand, if the propeller feathers and immediately unfeathers, the problem may be a short circuit in the holding coil wiring or an open circuit in the pressure cutout switch or its associated wiring. The same problem occurs if the feather button is short-circuited internally.

Sluggish movement of the propeller may be the result of a buildup of sludge in the propeller dome or a worn out piston-to-dome seal inside the dome. Sticking cam rollers may also interfere with smooth pitch-change movement and feathering operations.

Erratic or jerky operation of the propeller is an indication of the wrong preload shim being used between the dome and barrel assemblies. If this is the case, the dome will have to be removed so the proper shim can be installed.

PROPELLER INSTALLATION

The method used to attach a propeller to an engine crankshaft varies with the design of the crankshaft. Currently, there are three types of crankshafts used on aircraft engines, the flanged crankshaft, the tapered crankshaft, and the splined crankshaft. The general installation procedures for all three types are discussed in the following paragraphs. For specific instructions, you should refer to the aircraft and engine maintenance manuals.

FLANGED SHAFT

Flanged propeller shafts are used on most horizontally opposed reciprocating engines and some turboprop engines. The front of the crankshaft is formed into a flange four to eight inches across, perpendicular to the crankshaft centerline. Mounting bolt holes and dowel pin holes are machined into the flange. Some flanges have threaded inserts pressed into the bolt holes. [Figure 12-82]

Before installing a propeller on a flanged shaft, inspect the flange for corrosion, nicks, burrs, and other surface defects. In addition, the bolt holes and threaded inserts should be clean and in good condition. Any defects found should be repaired in accordance with the engine manufacturer's recommendations. Light corrosion can typically be removed with very fine sandpaper; however, if a bent flange is suspected, a run out inspection should be performed. If you do have to remove corrosion, clean the flange after sanding and check for smoothness. Once this is done, apply a light coat of engine oil or antiseize compound to the flange for corrosion prevention and ease of future propeller removal.

FIXED-PITCH PROPELLERS

Before installing a fixed-pitch propeller on a flanged shaft, inspect the mounting surface of the propeller to verify that it is clean and smooth. The attaching

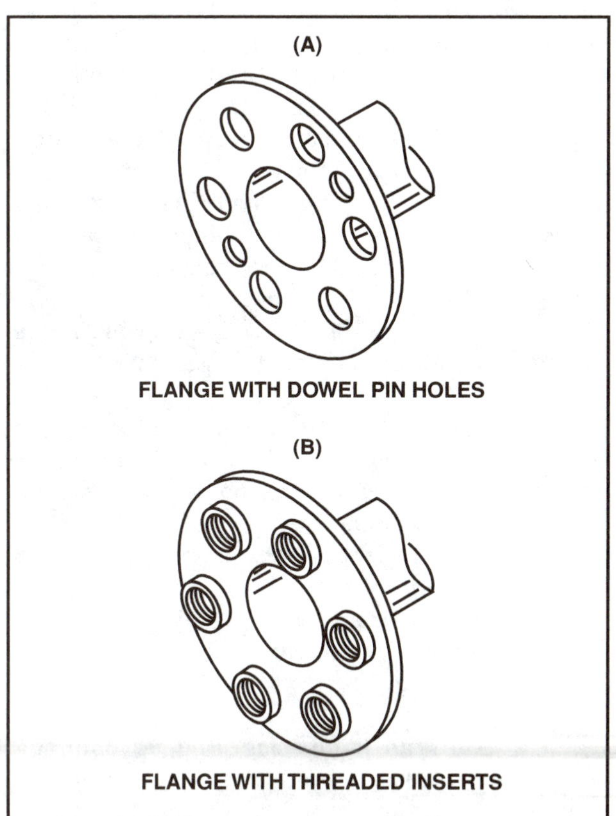

Figure 12-82. (A) — On a flanged crankshaft with dowel pin holes, the propeller is mounted to the crankshaft using bolts and nuts. The dowel pin holes are often arranged so the propeller can mount in only one position. (B) — Most installations utilize threaded inserts which are pressed into the crankshaft to eliminate the use of nuts.

Figure 12-83. When installing a propeller on a four-cylinder opposed engine, one of the blades should come to rest at the ten o'clock position to help reduce vibration and facilitate hand propping.

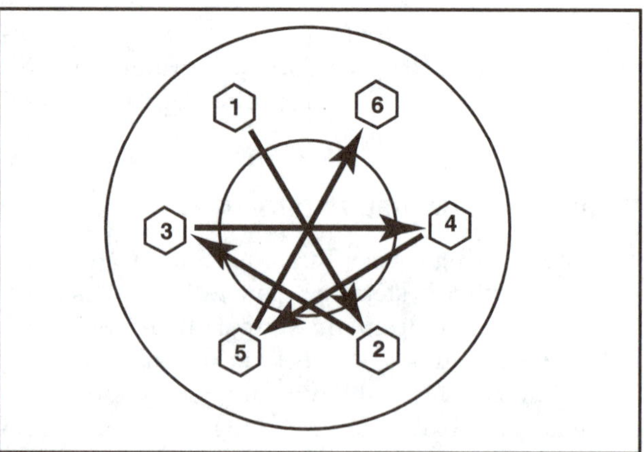

Figure 12-84. When installing a propeller on a flanged crankshaft, it is important to follow the propeller manufacturer's recommended sequence to avoid inducing stress in the propeller hub.

bolts should be in good condition and inspected for cracks with either a dye penetrant or magnetic particle inspection process. Washers and nuts should also be inspected, and new fiber lock nuts used if they are required in the installation.

Most flanges that use dowel pins allow the propeller to mount on the shaft in only one position. If there is no dowel, install the propeller in the position specified by the aircraft or engine maintenance manual. This is important because propeller position is critical for maximum engine life in some installations. If no position is specified on a four cylinder horizontally opposed engine, the propeller should be installed with the blades at the 10 o'clock and 4 o'clock positions when the engine is stopped. This reduces vibration in many instances and puts the propeller in the best position for hand propping. [Figure 12-83]

After attaching the bolts, washers, and nuts, tighten all of the bolts finger-tight. Then, use an approved torque wrench to tighten the bolts to a specified value in the recommended sequence. A typical torque value is 35 foot-pounds or higher for metal propellers and approximately 25 foot-pounds for wood propellers. In addition, a typical tightening sequence requires you to torque the bolts in a crossing pattern. [Figure 12-84]

When a **skull cap spinner** is used, a mounting bracket is installed behind two of the propeller mounting bolts. Once the mounting bracket is installed, the skull cap is attached to the bracket with a bolt and washer. [Figure 12-85]

If a full spinner is used, a rear bulkhead is slipped on the flange before the propeller is installed. After mounting the propeller, a front bulkhead is placed on the front of the hub boss before the bolts are inserted. After the bolts are tightened and safetied, the spinner is installed with machine screws. The machine screws are inserted through the spinner into nut plates on the bulkheads. If the spinner is indexed, line up the index marks during installation to avoid vibration. [Figure 12-86]

CONSTANT-SPEED PROPELLERS

Some Hartzell steel hub propellers and all Hartzell compact propellers are designed to mount on flanged crankshafts. However, before you mount a constant-speed propeller on the crankshaft, you should lubricate the O-ring in the rear of the hub with a light coat of engine oil. Once this is done, you can carefully mount the propeller on the flange. When doing this, pay particular attention to the O-ring to keep it from being damaged.

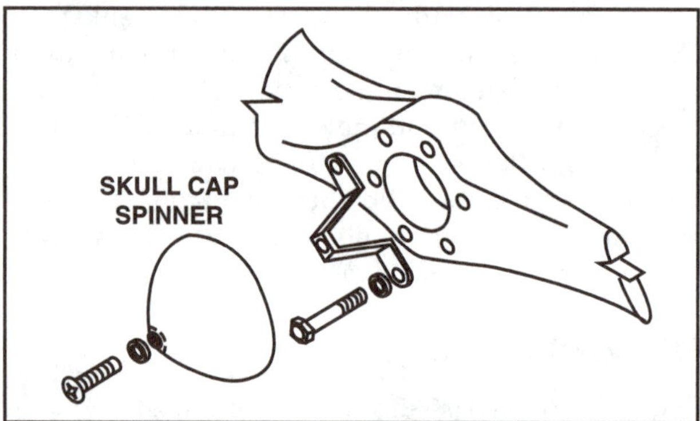

Figure 12-85. Some small training aircraft with flange mounted propellers utilize a skull cap spinner that requires a mounting bracket to be installed using two of the propeller mounting bolts.

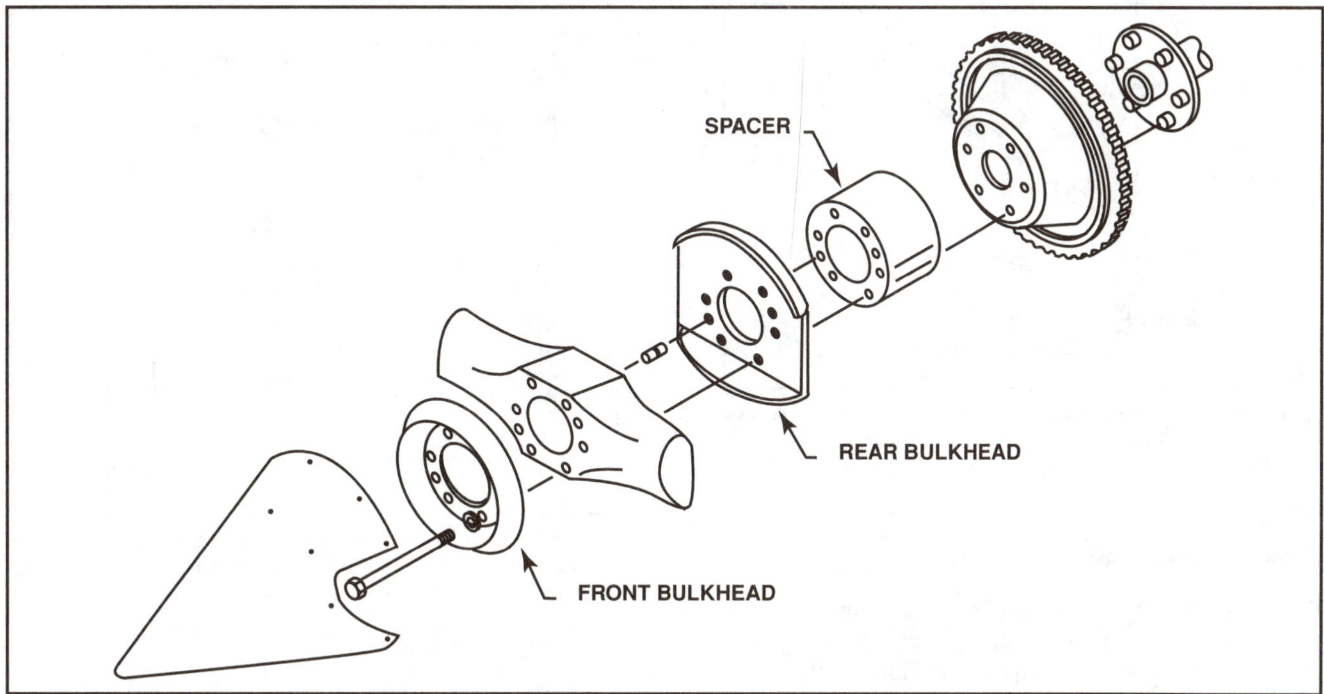

Figure 12-86. A full spinner mounts to forward and rear bulkheads with machine screws. On some smaller aircraft, the spinner may mount to only a rear bulkhead.

McCauley constant-speed propellers are also installed on flanged crankshafts. Like Hartzell propellers, an O-ring in the rear of the hub must be lubricated with a light coat of engine oil to allow its movement as the propeller is secured to the crankshaft flange. A dry O-ring can tear and become pinched during installation unless lubricated. [Figure 12-87]

When installing a constant-speed propeller that can be feathered, the installation and adjustment procedures are similar to that of other constant-speed models. However, if the blades are left in a feathered position, they should be rotated to their low pitch angle. For safety reasons, it is best to use a blade paddle on each blade.

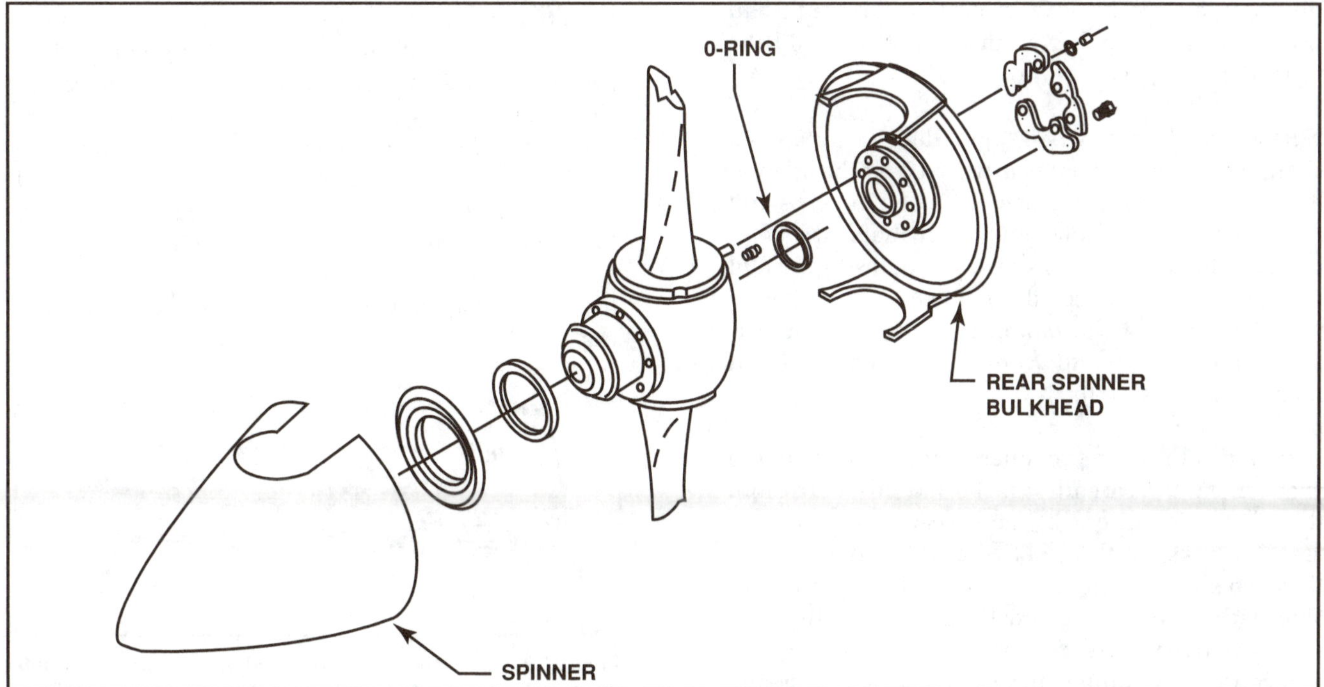

Figure 12-87. McCauley constant-speed propellers are installed on flanged crankshafts with an O-ring seal to prevent oil leakage.

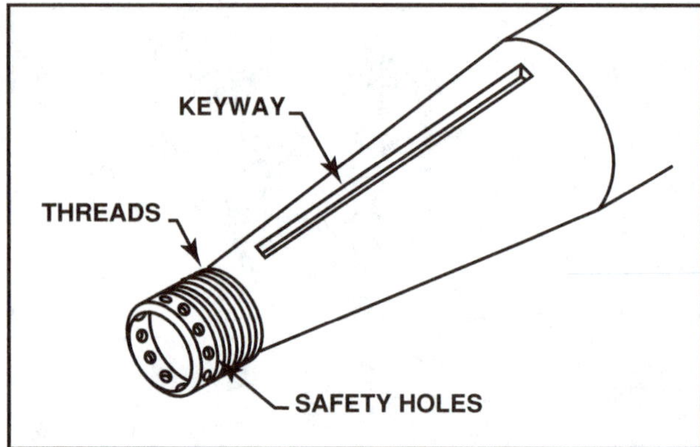

Figure 12-88. On some low horsepower engines, the crankshaft is tapered and is threaded on the end for propeller mounting.

TURBOPROPELLERS

When installing a constant-speed, reversing propeller, use the same basic procedures that are used for other flanged shaft propellers. One difference, however, is the addition of the Beta tube. The Beta tube is installed through the propeller piston after the propeller is installed, and is bolted to the forward part of the piston.

TAPERED SHAFT

Tapered shaft crankshafts are found on older engines that produce low horsepower. This type of crankshaft requires a hub to adapt the propeller to the shaft. To prevent the propeller from rotating on the shaft, a large keyway is cut into the crankshaft taper and the propeller so that a key can hold the propeller in place. [Figure 12-88]

When installing a wood propeller on a tapered shaft, the propeller boss is installed over the adapter hub and a faceplate is placed between the boss and mounting bolts. This faceplate distributes the compression load of the bolts over the entire surface of the boss. If a new fixed-pitch wood propeller is installed, inspect the mounting bolts for tightness after the first flight and again after the first 25 flight hours. [Figure 12-89]

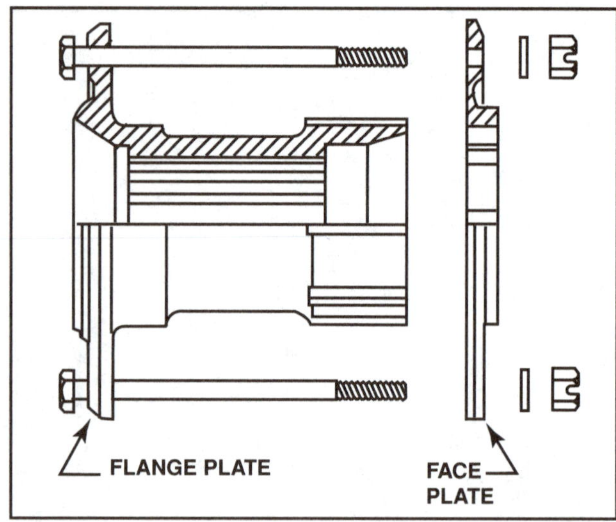

Figure 12-89. A typical mounting hub for a wood propeller uses a face plate to distribute the compression load evenly over the boss of the propeller hub.

Before installing the propeller on the crankshaft, the shaft must be carefully inspected for corrosion, thread condition, cracks, and wear in the keyway area. If cracks are allowed to develop in the keyway, they can spread rapidly and eventually cause crankshaft failure. It is good practice to inspect the keyway with dye penetrant at every 100-hour or annual inspection. Any minor surface defects found during the pre-installation inspection should be dressed or polished out in accordance with the engine manufacturer's maintenance manual. In addition, the propeller hub components and mounting hardware should be inspected for wear, cracks, and corrosion. Defective components must be replaced or repaired as necessary.

Before permanently installing the propeller, a trial fit of the hub on the crankshaft should be done using a liquid transfer ink such as Prussian Blue. **Prussian Blue** is a dark blue ink, or dye, which has the consistency of a light grease. This dye visibly reveals the amount of contact between two mating surfaces. To do a trial fit, begin by applying a thin, even coat of dye on the tapered section of the crankshaft. Once this is done, place the key in the keyway and install the hub on the crankshaft and torque the retaining nut. In practice, the hub, snap ring, and retaining nut are never disassembled. If, however, they were disassembled for inspection or repair, place the retaining nut against the hub and install the puller snap ring. Once assembled, the retaining nut may be torqued. [Figure 12-90]

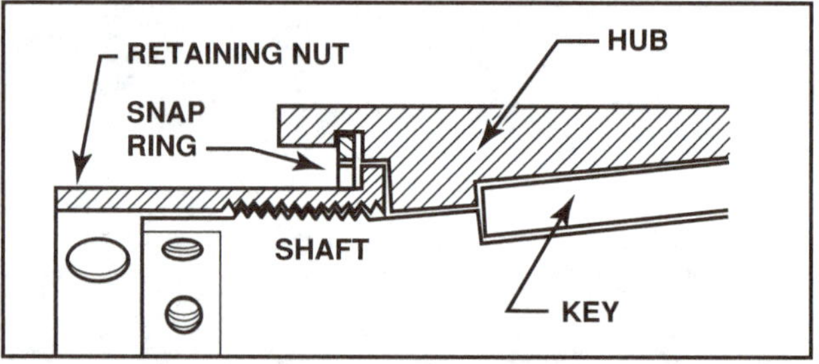

Figure 12-90. A snap ring is installed inside a propeller hub mounted on a tapered or splined shaft to aid in removing the propeller from the shaft.

The hub should then be removed from the crankshaft and inspected for the amount of ink transferred from the tapered shaft to the propeller. The ink transfer must indicate a minimum contact area of 70 percent. If insufficient contact is found, the crankshaft and hub should be inspected for the cause. The mating surfaces can be lapped with a polishing compound until a minimum of 70 percent contact area is achieved. After this is done, thoroughly clean the hub and crankshaft to remove all traces of Prussian Blue and polishing compound.

Once the minimum contact area is achieved, apply a very light coat of oil or antiseize compound to the crankshaft. Make sure that the key is installed properly, then place the hub assembly and propeller on the shaft. Be sure that the threads on the shaft and nut are clean and dry, then verify that the puller snap ring is in place before torquing the nut to the proper value. Failure to tighten the retaining nut to the proper torque results in play between the propeller, front cone and rear cone. Any space between the cones and the propeller produces galling and wear on their surfaces. Safety the retaining nut to complete the installation.

SPLINED SHAFT

Splined crankshafts are found on most radial engines, some horizontally opposed, and some inline engines. The splined shaft has grooves and splines of equal dimensions and a double width master spline to ensure that a hub will fit on the shaft in only one position. [Figure 12-91]

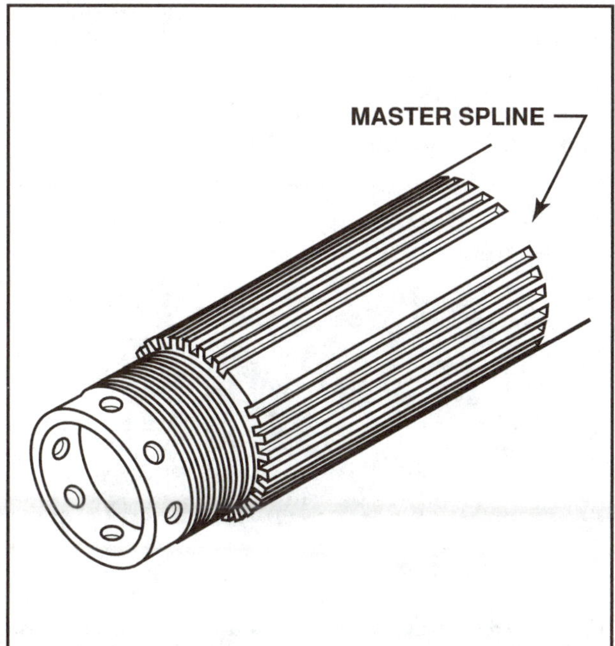

Figure 12-91. The master spline on a splined propeller shaft ensures that the propeller is correctly positioned when installed on the engine.

Before installing a propeller on a splined shaft, inspect the crankshaft for cracks, surface defects, and corrosion. If any defects exist, repair them in accordance with the engine manufacturer's instructions. Crankshaft and hub splines are inspected for wear with a go/no-go gauge which is 0.002 inch larger than the maximum space allowed between the splines. The splines are serviceable if the gauge cannot be inserted between the splines for more than 20 percent of the spline length. If the gauge goes in more than 20 percent of the way, the hub or the crankshaft is unairworthy and must be replaced.

To help ensure that the propeller hub is centered on the crankshaft, a front and rear cone are installed on each side of the propeller hub. The rear cone is typically made of bronze and is split to allow flexibility during installation and to ensure a tight fit. The front cone, on the other hand, is made in two pieces as a matched set. The two halves are marked with a serial number to identify them as mates in a set. [Figure 12-92]

In addition to the front and rear cones, a large retaining nut is used to tighten and hold the propeller in place. The retaining nut threads onto the end of the splined shaft and presses against the front

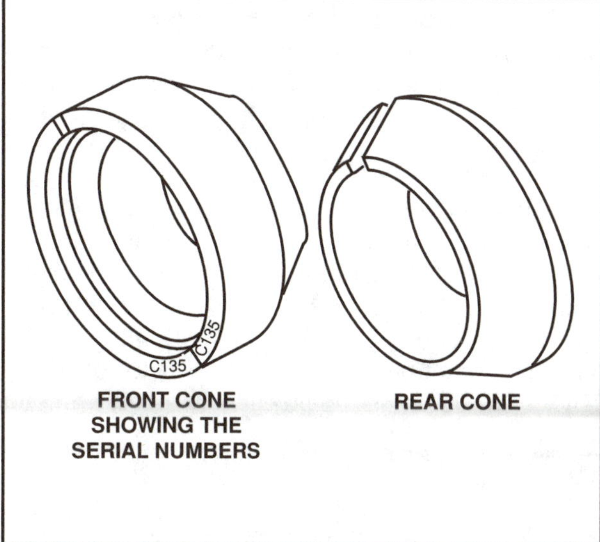

Figure 12-92. Splined propeller shafts require front and rear mounting cones to ensure that the propeller is properly aligned on the shaft.

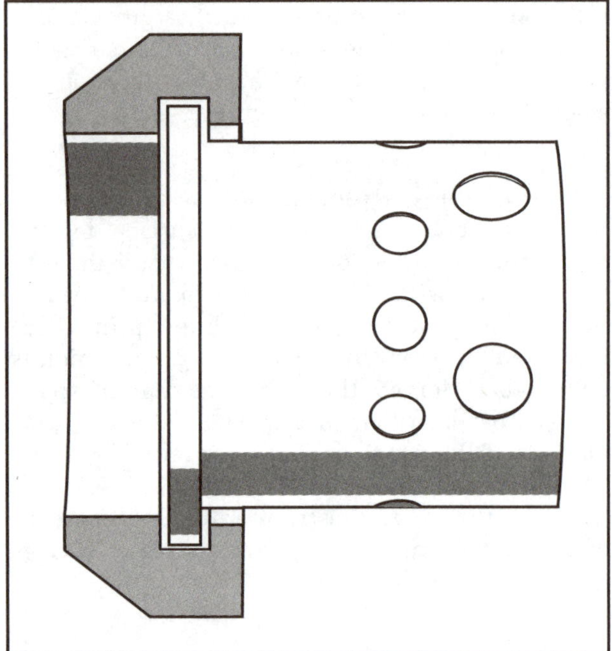

Figure 12-93. With a splined shaft installation, the propeller is held in place by a retaining nut that threads onto the end of the splined shaft and presses against the front cone.

cone to sandwich the propeller tightly between the front and rear cones. [Figure 12-93]

Like the tapered shaft, a trial installation of the propeller should be completed to ensure a proper fit. To do the trial installation, begin by applying a thin coat of Prussian Blue to the rear cone. Next, slip the rear cone and bronze spacer onto the crankshaft pushing them all the way back on the shaft. With the rear cone in place, align the hub on the master spline and push the hub back against the rear cone. Coat the front cone halves with Prussian Blue and place them around the lip of the retaining nut. Install the nut in the hub and tighten it to the proper torque.

After the retaining nut is torqued, immediately remove the retaining nut and front cone and note the amount of Prussian Blue transferred to the hub. A minimum of 70 percent contact is required. Then, remove the hub from the crankshaft and note the transfer of dye from the rear cone. As with the front cone, a minimum of 70 percent contact is required. If contact is insufficient, lap the hub to the cones using special lapping tools and fixtures.

If no dye is transferred from the rear cone during the transfer check, a condition known as **rear cone bottoming** may exist. This occurs when the apex, or point, of the rear cone contacts the land on the rear

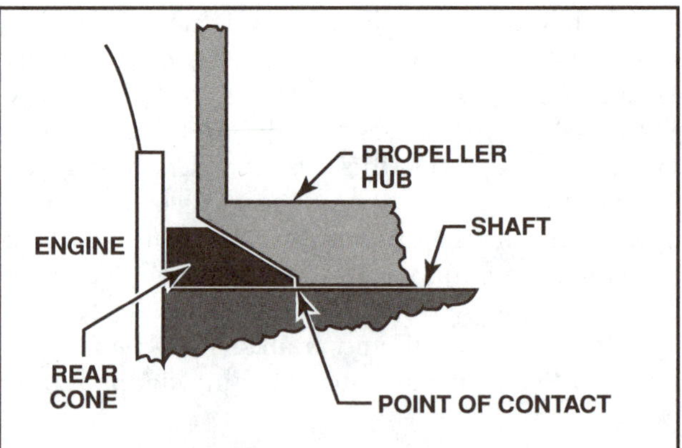

Figure 12-94. Rear cone bottoming occurs when the tip of the rear cone contacts the land on the rear seat of the hub before the hub seats on the cone. Removal of a specified amount of material from the cone's apex corrects this problem.

seat of the hub before the hub becomes seated on the rear cone. One way to correct rear cone bottoming is to remove up to 1/16 inch from the apex of the cone with sandpaper on a surface plate. [Figure 12-94]

Front cone bottoming occurs when the apex of the front cone bottoms on the crankshaft splines, before it has a chance to seat on the hub. Front cone bottoming is indicated by either the hub being loose on the shaft after the retaining nut has been torqued, or when there is no transfer of Prussian Blue to the front hub seat. Correct front cone bottoming by using a spacer of no more than 1/8 inch thickness behind the rear cone. This moves the hub forward, enabling the hub to properly seat on the front cone. [Figure 12-95]

Once a proper fit between the hub and splined shaft is ensured, reinstall the rear cone and permanently

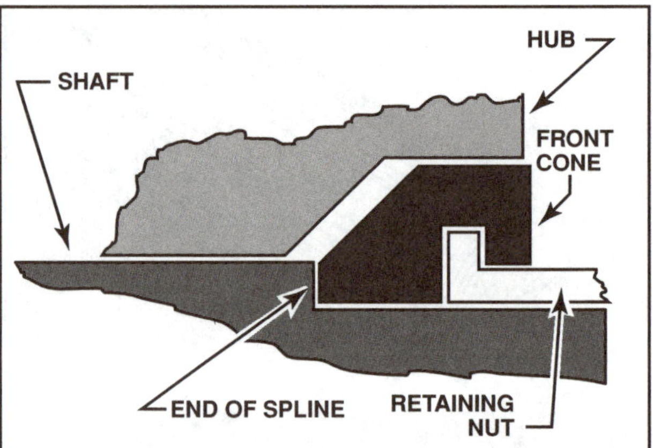

Figure 12-95. Front cone bottoming occurs when the apex of the front cone bottoms on the crankshaft splines. This prevents a good seat between the front cone and propeller hub. As a result, the propeller hub is loose, lacking a tight fit to the crankshaft.

mount the propeller on the shaft. As you recall, the position of the propeller on the hub in relation to the master spline is predetermined. Some installations require a certain blade to align with the master spline while other installations require the blades be perpendicular to the master spline position. Therefore, be sure to consult the engine maintenance manual for the requirements of a particular installation.

PROPELLER SAFETYING

Once a propeller is properly torqued, it must be safetied. There is no one correct way to safety a propeller installation because of the many different types of installations. For this reason, the discussion of safetying methods is limited to the types more commonly used.

A flanged shaft installation has the largest variety of safety methods because of its many variations. If the flange has threaded inserts installed, the propeller is held on by bolts screwed into the inserts. In this case, the bolt heads are drilled and safetied with 0.041 inch stainless steel safety wire, using standard safety wire procedures. [Figure 12-96]

If threaded inserts are not pressed into the flange, bolts and nuts are used to hold the propeller in place. Some installations use fiber lock nuts which require no safetying, but the nuts should be replaced each time the propeller is removed. For installations using castellated nuts and drilled

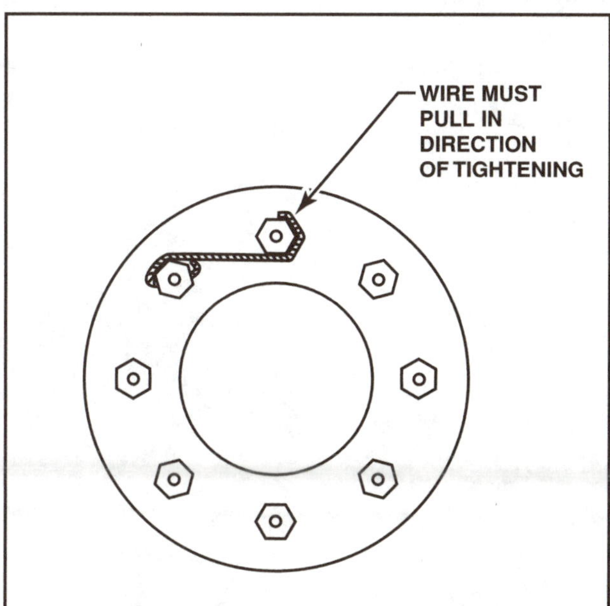

Figure 12-96. On propellers secured to a flanged hub with bolts, pairs of bolt heads are safety wired together to keep the bolts from loosening.

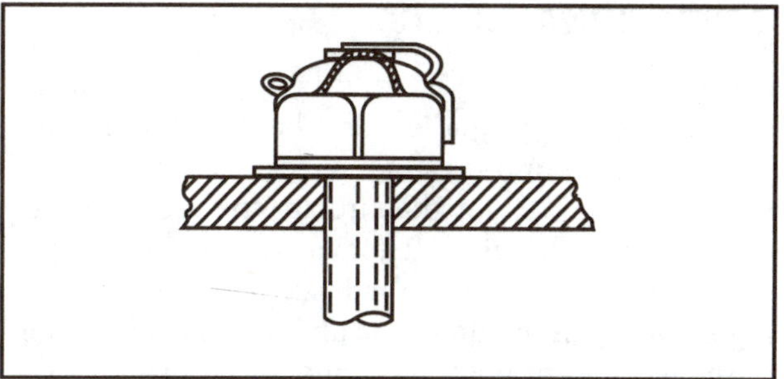

Figure 12-97. If the propeller installation uses castellated nuts with drilled bolts, safety the nuts with cotter pins.

bolts, the nuts are safetied to the bolts with cotter pins. [Figure 12-97]

The retaining nuts for tapered and splined shaft installations are safetied in the same way. In addition, a clevis pin is installed through the safety holes in the retaining nut and crankshaft. The clevis pin must be positioned with the head toward the center of the crankshaft. This allows centrifugal force to hold the clevis pin tightly in the hole against its flanged head. [Figure 12-98]

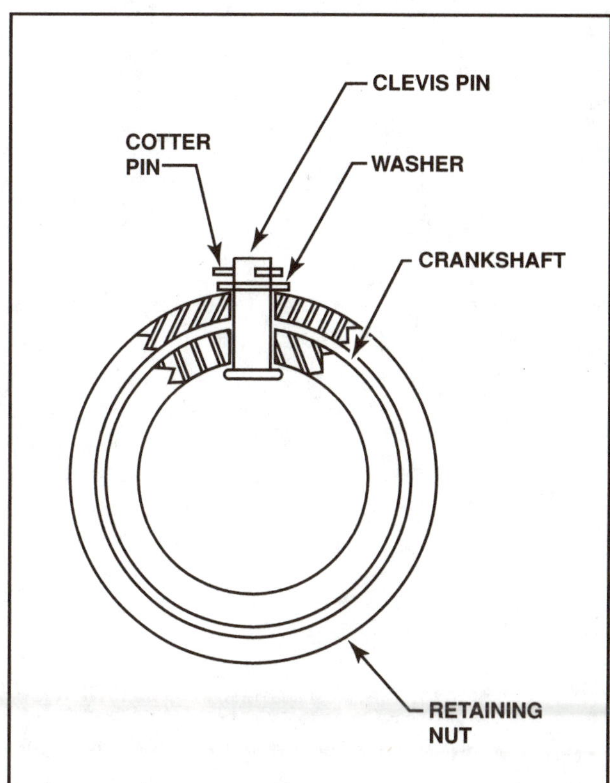

Figure 12-98. To safety the retaining nut on a tapered shaft propeller installation, a clevis pin is installed through the safety holes in the retaining nut and crankshaft. The clevis pin must be installed with its flanged head toward the center of the crankshaft.

OPERATIONAL CHECK

An operational check should be conducted once a constant-speed propeller has been installed and safetied. To conduct this check, follow ground runup procedures for the aircraft you are operating and position the aircraft for maximum safety. The first time a newly installed propeller operates at high rpm on an engine, it is always wise to be alert to the hazards of possible propeller failure.

All adjustable propeller systems share common features in regard to their control configuration. Propeller controls must be rigged so that an increase in rpm is obtained by moving the controls forward and a decrease in rpm is caused by moving the controls aft. Furthermore, engine throttles must be arranged so that forward thrust is increased by forward movement of the control, and decreased thrust is obtained by aft movement of the throttle.

When running-up an engine and testing a newly installed Hydromatic propeller, it is necessary to exercise the propeller several times. This is done by moving the governor control through its entire range of travel several times to free the dome of entrapped air.

Once all ground checks and adjustments are successfully completed, a test flight should be conducted. The test flight verifies the propeller system response to dynamic loads and determines if any other adjustments are necessary. After the test flight, check for oil leaks and component security.

INDEX

A

B

C

D

E

F

G

H

I

J

K

L

M

N

O

P

Q

R

U

V

Z